SANTA FE COLLEGE
HIGH SCHOOL DUAL ENROLLMENT PROGRAM
3000 NW 83RD STREET, R-05
GAINESVILLE, FLORIDA 32606
352-395-5490

D1540985

Florida

PRENTICE HALL

ECONOMICS

Arthur O'Sullivan
Steven M. Sheffrin
Grant Wiggins

PEARSON

Upper Saddle River, New Jersey   Boston, Massachusetts   Chandler, Arizona   Glenview, Illinois

The Wall Street Journal Classroom Edition is a supplemental educational program published since 1991 by Dow Jones and Company, publisher of *The Wall Street Journal*. The program is designed to improve the economic and business literacy of America's secondary-school students. The centerpiece of the program is a full-color student newspaper, published monthly from September to May. Regular features focus on business, economics, careers, entrepreneurship, technology, personal finance, and global interdependence. Articles are drawn directly from the pages of the daily *Wall Street Journal*.

Acknowledgments appear on pages R35–R37, which constitute an extension of this copyright page.

ISBN-13: 978-0-13-318971-1
ISBN-10: 0-13-318971-6
3 4 5 6 7 8 9 10 V011 13 12

About the Authors

Arthur O'Sullivan, Ph.D.

Arthur O'Sullivan is a professor of economics at Lewis and Clark College in Portland, Oregon. After receiving his B.S. degree in economics at the University of Oregon, he spent two years in the Peace Corps, working with city planners in the Philippines. He received his Ph.D. degree in economics from Princeton University in 1981 and has taught at the University of California, Davis, and Oregon State University. He recently accepted an endowed professorship at Lewis and Clark College, where he teaches microeconomics and urban economics.

Steven M. Sheffrin, Ph.D.

Steven M. Sheffrin is professor of economics and director of the Murphy Institute at Tulane University in New Orleans. Previously, he was dean of the division of social sciences and professor of economics at the University of California, Davis. He has been a visiting professor at Nuffield College, University of Oxford; the London School of Economics and Political Science; Princeton University; and Nanyang Technological University, Singapore. Professor Sheffrin is the author of numerous books and articles in the fields of macroeconomics, public finance, and international economics.

Consulting Author

Grant Wiggins

Grant Wiggins is the President of Authentic Education in Hopewell, New Jersey. He earned his Ed.D. from Harvard University and his B.A. from St. John's College in Annapolis. Wiggins consults with schools, districts, and state education departments on a variety of reform matters, organizes conferences and workshops, and develops print materials and Web resources on curricular change. He is the co-author of award-winning and highly successful materials on curriculum published by ASCD. His work has been supported by the Pew Charitable Trusts, the Geraldine R. Dodge Foundation, and the National Science Foundation.

Over the past twenty years, Wiggins has worked on some of the most influential reform initiatives in the country, including Vermont's portfolio system and Ted Sizer's Coalition of Essential Schools. He has established statewide consortia devoted to assessment reform for the states of North Carolina and New Jersey. Wiggins is the author of *Educative Assessment* and *Assessing Student Performance*, both published by Jossey-Bass. His many articles have appeared in such journals as *Educational Leadership* and *Phi Delta Kappan*.

FL Florida Academic Reviewers

Irene Flytzanis Ed.D.
Teacher/Dept. Chair Social Studies
Pinellas County Schools
Largo, FL

Dennis Dawson
Social Studies Teacher
St. Lucie County Schools
Ft. Pierce, FL

Kathleen Elliott
Teacher
Largo High, Pinellas County
Largo, FL

Paul Ryder
World History/AP Human Geography Teacher
Deland High School
Deland, FL

Justin Daniels
Teacher
Wilkinson Jr. High School
Middleburg, FL

Academic Reviewers

Klaus G. Becker
Department of Economics and Geography
Texas Tech University
Lubbock, TX

Bruce Coggins
Economics Department
Truman State University
Kirksville, MO

Antoinette Criss
College of Business
University of South Florida St. Petersburg
St. Petersburg, FL

Cory Koedel
Department of Economics
University of Missouri
Columbia, MO

Daniel E. Saros
Department of Economics
Valparaiso University
Valparaiso, IN

Understanding by Design Reviewer

Diane Van Ausdall
West Hartford, CT

Teacher Advisory Board

Elizabeth Brown
Jackson High School
Jackson, MI

Katherine Case
Parkville High School
Baltimore, MD

Michael J. Collazo
Brentwood High School
Brentwood, NY

Bruce Damasio
Towson University
Towson, MD

Lance Leach
Valparaiso High School
Valparaiso, IN

Len A. Lyberger
Palos Verdes Peninsula High School
Rolling Hills Estates, CA

Kenneth Mengani
Franklin K. Lane High School
Brooklyn, NY

Kurt Stiglbauer
Ridge View High School
Columbia, SC

Contents in Brief

INTRODUCTION

Go online with Unit 1
Find these interactive resources at PearsonSchool.com/PHecon

Visual Glossary online
- Opportunity Cost
- Incentives
- Free Enterprise

How the Economy Works online
- What does an entrepreneur do?
- How can innovation lead to economic growth?
- How are public goods created?

Video News Update Online
Powered by
The Wall Street Journal Classroom Edition
- Watch video clips of current economic issues in the news.

Economics on the go
- Action Graphs
- Content Review Audio
- Economic Dictionary Audio

WebQuest online
- The Economics WebQuest challenges students to use 21st-century skills to answer the Essential Question.

? Essential Question, Unit 1

How does economics affect everyone?

Chapter 1
How can we make the best economic choices?

Chapter 2
How does society decide who gets what goods and services?

Chapter 3
What role should government play in a free market economy?

Essential Question, Unit 2

Who benefits from the free market economy?

Chapter 4
How do we decide what to buy?

Chapter 5
How do suppliers decide what goods and services to offer?

Go online with Unit 2
Find these interactive resources at PearsonSchool.com/PHecon

Visual Glossary
online

- Law of Demand
- Law of Supply
- Equilibrium
- Perfect Competition

How the Economy Works
online

- How does elasticity affect consumer demand?
- What are production costs?
- How does a market react to a shortage?
- How is broadcasting regulated?

Video News Update Online
Powered by
The Wall Street Journal
Classroom Edition

- Watch video clips of current economic issues in the news.

Economics
on the go

- Action Graphs
- Content Review Audio
- Economic Dictionary Audio

WebQuest
online

- The Economics WebQuest challenges students to use 21st-century skills to answer the Essential Question.

Chapter 6
What is the right price?

Chapter 7
How does competition affect your choices?

MICROECONOMICS

Go online with Unit 3
Find these interactive resources at PearsonSchool.com/PHecon

Visual Glossary online

- Corporation
- Productivity of Labor

How the Economy Works online

- How can a small business grow?
- How can collective bargaining settle differences?

Video News Update Online
Powered by
The Wall Street Journal Classroom Edition

- Watch video clips of current economic issues in the news.

Economics on the go

- Action Graphs
- Content Review Audio
- Economic Dictionary Audio

WebQuest online

- The Economics WebQuest challenges students to use 21st-century skills to answer the Essential Question.

Essential Question, Unit 3

How can businesses and labor best achieve their goals?

Chapter 8
Why do some businesses succeed and others fail?

Chapter 9
How can workers best meet the challenges of a changing economy?

MACROECONOMICS

Go online with Unit 4
Find these interactive resources at PearsonSchool.com/PHecon

Visual Glossary online

• Money
• Capital Gains

How the Economy Works online

• How does the fractional reserve system work?
• What is the function of a municipal bond?

Video News Update Online
Powered by
The Wall Street Journal Classroom Edition

• Watch video clips of current economic issues in the news.

Economics *on the go*

• Action Graphs
• Content Review Audio
• Economic Dictionary Audio

WebQuest online

• The Economics WebQuest challenges students to use 21st-century skills to answer the Essential Question.

? **Essential Question, Unit 4**

How can you make the most of your money?

Chapter 10
How well do financial institutions serve our needs?

Chapter 11
How do your saving and investment choices affect your future?

MACROECONOMICS

Go online with Unit 5
Find these interactive resources at PearsonSchool.com/PHecon

Visual Glossary online

- Gross Domestic Product
- Inflation

How the Economy Works online

- What causes a recession?
- How do workers deal with structural unemployment?

Video News Update Online
Powered by
The Wall Street Journal Classroom Edition

- Watch video clips of current economic issues in the news.

Economics on the go

- Action Graphs
- Content Review Audio
- Economic Dictionary Audio

WebQuest online

- The Economics WebQuest challenges students to use 21st-century skills to answer the Essential Question.

Essential Question, Unit 5

Why does it matter how the economy is doing?

Chapter 12 How do we know if the economy is healthy?

Chapter 13 How much can we reduce unemployment, inflation, and poverty?

MACROECONOMICS

? Essential Question, Unit 6

What is the proper role of government in the economy?

Chapter 14
How can taxation meet the needs of government and the people?

Chapter 15
How effective is fiscal policy as an economic tool?

Chapter 16
How effective is monetary policy as an economic tool?

Go online with Unit 6
Find these interactive resources at PearsonSchool.com/PHecon

Visual Glossary online
• Progressive Taxes
• Fiscal Policy
• Monetary Policy

How the Economy Works online
• Where do your federal taxes go?
• What causes the national debt to spiral?
• How does the Fed make monetary policy?

Video News Update Online
Powered by
The Wall Street Journal
Classroom Edition

• Watch video clips of current economic issues in the news.

Economics on the go
• Action Graphs
• Content Review Audio
• Economic Dictionary Audio

WebQuest online
• The Economics WebQuest challenges students to use 21st-century skills to answer the Essential Question.

MACROECONOMICS

Go online with Unit 7

Find these interactive resources at
PearsonSchool.com/PHecon

Visual Glossary online

- Free Trade
- Globalization

How the Economy Works online

- How do specialization and trade benefit nations?
- What are the stages of economic development?

Video News Update Online

Powered by
The Wall Street Journal Classroom Edition

- Watch video clips of current economic issues in the news.

Economics on the go

- Action Graphs
- Content Review Audio
- Economic Dictionary Audio

WebQuest online

- The Economics WebQuest challenges students to use 21st-century skills to answer the Essential Question.

? Essential Question, Unit 7

How might scarcity divide our world or bring it together?

Chapter 17
Should free trade be encouraged?

Chapter 18
Do the benefits of economic development outweigh the costs?

FUTURE WATCH Personal Finance Handbook

Special Features

Action Graph
online

Graphs and charts labeled with the **Action Graph** icon have been specially enhanced online. To view these animated charts, visit **PearsonSchool.com/PHecon** The (online) label indicates an Action Graph.

▶ Graphs, Charts, and Tables

More than 250 graphs, charts, and tables to help you visualize key economic concepts.

Graphs, Charts, and Tables (continued)

▶ Economics & YOU

Read and view illustrations to understand how economic principles can affect high school students.

Economics & YOU
The Substitution Effect

When the price of one good increases, people have an incentive to buy substitutes. *Your decision to purchase a less expensive lunch is the substitution effect in action.*

| Roast Beef sandwich $4.50 $5.25 | Chili $1.99 |

REDUCED

The substitution effect also applies when a drop in price creates a cheaper alternative. *Your purchase of the reduced car is another example of the substitution effect.*

▲ A rise in the price of a good will cause consumers to buy more of a substitute good. **Has the substit**... been a factor in any of your recent purchase...

Complex and difficult content is visually displayed to explain how economic principles can affect you.

How the Economy Works

View the illustrated diagrams to understand the processes by which our economy operates.

Complex and difficult content is visually displayed to explain how our economy works.

Visual Glossary

Graphs, pictures, and cartoons help deepen your understanding of key economic terms.

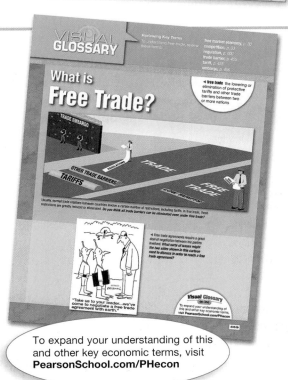

To expand your understanding of this and other key economic terms, visit **PearsonSchool.com/PHecon**

▶ Innovators

See how creative entrepreneurs and other individuals have affected our economy and daily life.

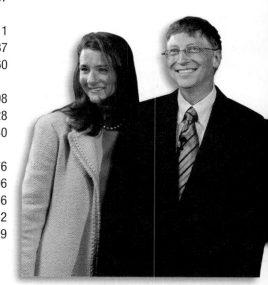

▲ Melinda and Bill Gates

▶ Career Center

Look into the future—explore your different career paths and opportunities.

Complex and difficult content is visually displayed to explain different career opportunities.

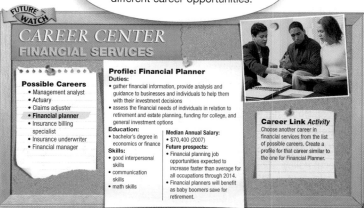

Case Study

Read articles by *The Wall Street Journal* to view real-life illustrations of economic principles.

Global Impact

Explore economic links between the United States and the world.

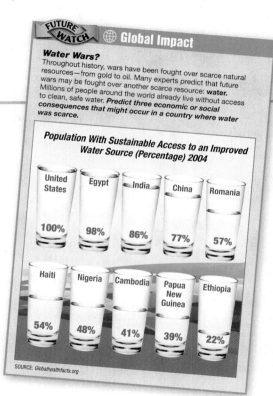

FUTURE WATCH 🌐 **Global Impact**

Water Wars?
Throughout history, wars have been fought over scarce natural resources—from gold to oil. Many experts predict that future wars may be fought over another scarce resource: **water.** Millions of people around the world already live without access to clean, safe water. *Predict three economic or social consequences that might occur in a country where water was scarce.*

Population With Sustainable Access to an Improved Water Source (Percentage) 2004

United States	Egypt	India	China	Romania
100%	98%	86%	77%	57%

Haiti	Nigeria	Cambodia	Papua New Guinea	Ethiopia
54%	48%	41%	39%	22%

SOURCE: Globalhealthfacts.org.

Economic Simulations

Your teacher may assign these hands-on, role-playing games to help you understand key economic concepts.

How to Use This Program

Economics is all around you.
Developing an understanding of the impact of economic principles on your day-to-day life will help you to make better economic choices. It will prepare you to live in a global economy. It is money in your pocket.

Economics is organized around Essential Questions. An Essential Question is a launching pad for exploring ideas. It doesn't have just one right answer. The answer to an Essential Question changes as you learn more or as circumstances change.

WebQuest online
To complete the Chapter Essential Question Webquest, visit **PearsonSchool.com/PHecon**

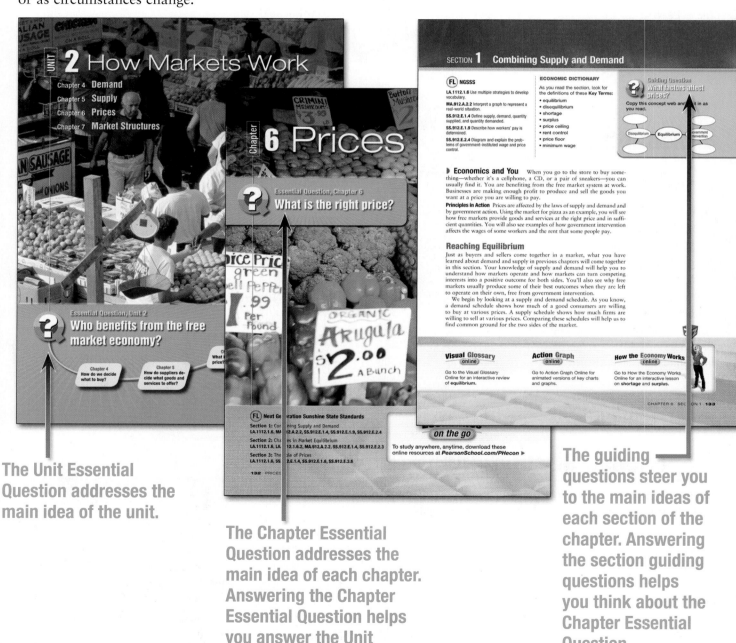

The Unit Essential Question addresses the main idea of the unit.

The Chapter Essential Question addresses the main idea of each chapter. Answering the Chapter Essential Question helps you answer the Unit Essential Question.

The guiding questions steer you to the main ideas of each section of the chapter. Answering the section guiding questions helps you think about the Chapter Essential Question.

"Once you have learned to question and to persist in your questioning, nothing can stop you. That's why a curriculum framed around Essential Questions is so important."

—From *Understanding by Design*, 2nd ed. by Wiggins & McTighe. © 2005 by Association for Supervision and Curriculum Development (ASCD).

Essential Questions Journal

Use your Essential Questions Journal to build answers to Essential Questions.

Also available online at PearsonSchool.com/PHecon

How to Use This Program

In your textbook

Every chapter has a How the Economy Works feature that helps you visualize economic principles in action.

1 Follow the numbered steps.

What does an **entrepreneur** do?

All entrepreneurs—whether they are starting a lawn-mowing service or founding a company that makes cars—have two things in common. First, they recognize a need or want. Then, they must assemble the factors of production to meet that need or want.

PEOPLE WANT A SNACK THAT IS BOTH TASTY AND HEALTHY.

WHAT IF I OPENED A SNACK BAR THAT SERVED FRUIT-AND-YOGURT SMOOTHIES?

1 A new business starts with an idea. Kelly recognizes something her town needs and does not have.

2 Kelly begins to pull together the factors of production she needs to turn her idea into reality.

Land: natural resources

HELP WANTED CASHIERS and SERVERS

Labor: people to do the work

Capital: human-made resources

Human Capital: acquired knowledge and skills

Physical Capital: objects used to create goods or to supply services

GRAND OPENING FROZEN YOGURT

3 Kelly took a financial risk by opening her own business. If the risk pays off, Kelly gets profits...her workers get wages...and her customers get a healthy snack.

Check Your Understanding
1. How will reading and other types of self-education help this entrepreneur succeed?
2. What impact does the concept of scarcity have on the decisions made by an entrepreneur?

How the Economy Works
online

For an animated, interactive version of this feature, visit PearsonSchool.com/PHecon

Recognize a Need or Want | **Assemble Factors of Production** | **Provide Goods or Services**

2 Match the stages with the colored band.

3 Check your understanding.

Go online at PearsonSchool.com/PHecon

Use an interactive version of How the Economy Works to help you learn. ▼

online

◀ Download the Visual Glossary or animated versions of How the Economy Works and Action Graphs to your MP3 player. Study anytime, anywhere.

VISUAL GLOSSARY

Use the Visual Glossary in your textbook and online to learn the meaning of key economic terms.

Find these related terms in the Economics Dictionary online, in English and in Spanish.

VISUAL GLOSSARY

Reviewing Key Terms
To understand free enterprise, review these terms:
entrepreneur, p. 5
profit, p. 25

free market economy, p. 30
incentive, p. 33
competition, p. 33
consumer sovereignty, p. 34

What is Free Enterprise?

◀ free enterprise an economic system in which decisions are made in a free market by private individuals and firms

The characteristics shown here form the foundation of the American free enterprise system. Choose two of the characteristics and explain how they protect your freedom of choice.

- Private Property
- Economic Freedom
- Competition
- Contracts
- Self-Interest
- Voluntary Exchange
- Legal Equality
- Profit Motive
- Consumer Sovereignty

American Free Enterprise

Visual Glossary online
To expand your understanding of this and other key economic terms, visit PearsonSchool.com/PHecon

50 PRICES

Action Graph online

Follow the references on the text page to the Action Graph. Action Graphs present economic principles in a graphic format.

GDP and the Business Cycle

One measure of a nation's economic well-being is **gross domestic product (GDP)**, the total value of all final goods and services produced in a country in a given year. In a period of macroeconomic expansion, or growth, a country produces more than it did before and GDP goes up. (See **Figure 3.2.**) In a period of contraction, or decline, the country produces less and GDP goes down. This pattern of a period of expansion, or growth, followed by a period of contraction, or decline, is called a **business cycle**.

Unlike the day-to-day ups and downs of the stock market, business cycles are major fluctuations. Each phase can last months or

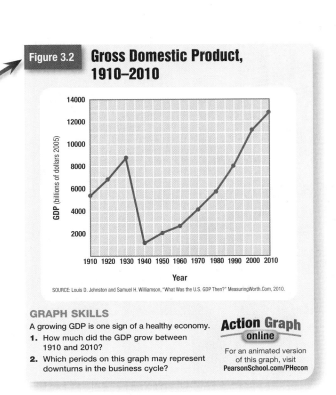

Figure 3.2 Gross Domestic Product, 1910–2010

SOURCE: Louis D. Johnston and Samuel H. Williamson, "What Was the U.S. GDP Then?" MeasuringWorth.Com, 2010.

GRAPH SKILLS

A growing GDP is one sign of a healthy economy.

1. How much did the GDP grow between 1910 and 2010?
2. Which periods on this graph may represent downturns in the business cycle?

Action Graph online
For an animated version of this graph, visit PearsonSchool.com/PHecon

Before long, you will be out on your own and managing your own house-hold. In order to be successful, you will have to manage your money, no matter how much or how little you have. The Personal Finance Handbook on pages PF1–PF49 gives you useful guidelines for making the most of your money and avoiding consumer errors.

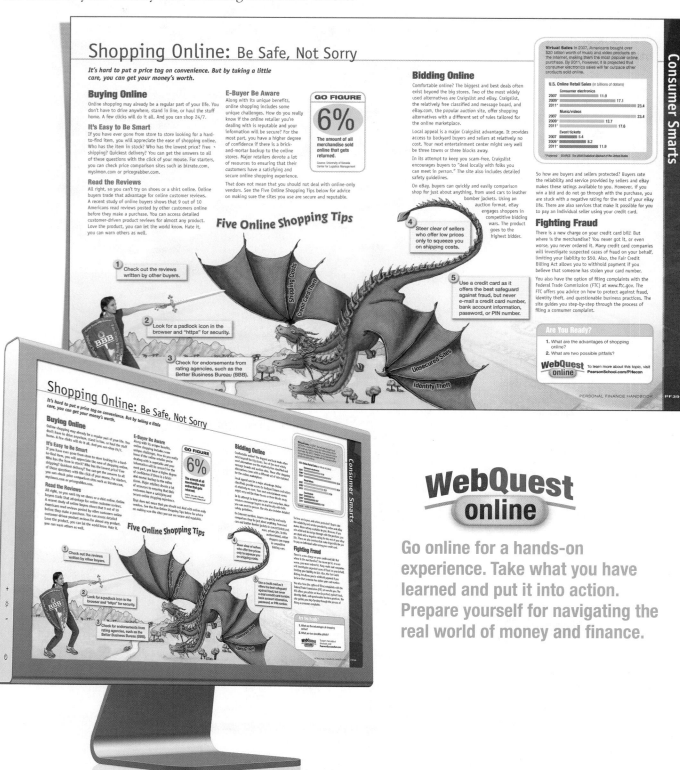

WebQuest online

Go online for a hands-on experience. Take what you have learned and put it into action. Prepare yourself for navigating the real world of money and finance.

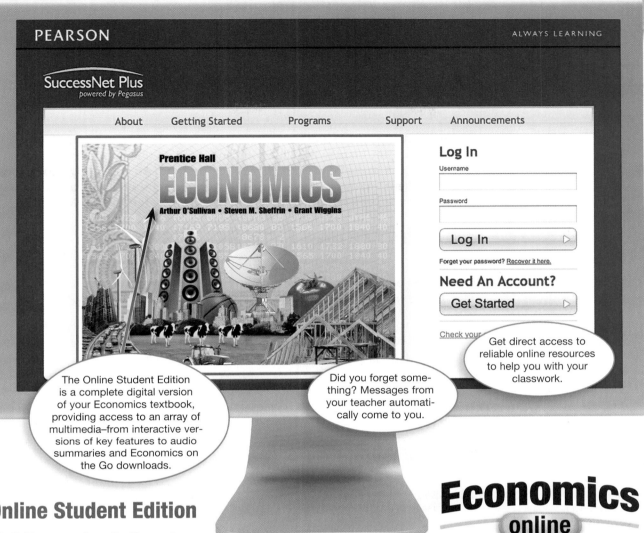

PEARSON
ALWAYS LEARNING

SuccessNet Plus
powered by Pegasus

About   Getting Started   Programs   Support   Announcements

Prentice Hall
ECONOMICS
Arthur O'Sullivan • Steven M. Sheffrin • Grant Wiggins

Log In
Username

Password

Log In ▷

Forget your password? Recover it here.

Need An Account?
Get Started ▷

Check your

The Online Student Edition is a complete digital version of your Economics textbook, providing access to an array of multimedia—from interactive versions of key features to audio summaries and Economics on the Go downloads.

Did you forget something? Messages from your teacher automatically come to you.

Get direct access to reliable online resources to help you with your classwork.

Online Student Edition

Visit Economics Online at
PearsonSchool.com/PHecon to access
your assignments, review key concepts,
and download Economics on the Go.

Economics
online

In Partnership

THE WALL STREET JOURNAL.
CLASSROOM EDITION

The Wall Street Journal Classroom Edition keeps you up-to-date on what is happening in your world.

Video News Update Online
Powered by
The Wall Street Journal
Classroom Edition

Go online for a current video related to the Essential Question topic.

In Partnership

THE WALL STREET JOURNAL.
CLASSROOM EDITION

SUPPLY SHOCK
Sawdust is just dust, right? Wrong. of it can ripple through the econom

By Joel Millman
The Wall Street Journal

Go online for a current article related to the Document-Based Assessment.

Graph Preview

Economists collect and evaluate data in order to develop and test their theories. They display their theories and the data that supports them in charts and graphs to make them easier to understand. As you study economics, you will see many graphs. Graphs that include the Action Graph logo have an animated version online that can be downloaded to your MP3 player.

▶ Interpreting Line Graphs

Economists track trends in the economy. Graphs are a useful way to present large amounts of data visually. Line graphs show changes over time. In order to interpret a graph, you have to identify the type of data that is being presented.

If you analyze the graph below, you can see a trend. In the span of time from 1994 to 2006, corporate bonds paid higher interest rates than 20-year treasury bonds. And both corporate bonds and 20-year treasury bonds had higher yields than municipal bonds.

The title of the graph tells you the topic of the graph.

The key identifies, by color, the three different kinds of bonds shown on the graph.

The label on the *y*-axis tells you what the numbers on the vertical axis represent.

On this graph, it is the rate of interest that the different kinds of bonds yield (or pay) each year.

Average Bond Yields, 1994–2006

Each point on the graph represents a value of the data. This chart shows that in the year 2000, corporate bonds were paying almost 8 percent interest, while 20-year treasury bonds were paying just above 6 percent interest, and municipal bonds were paying just below 6 percent interest.

SOURCE: *2008 Statistical Abstract of the United States*

The source line tells you where the data come from.

The label on the *x*-axis tells you what the numbers on the horizontal axis represent.

On this graph, it is the span of years over which the changes occurred.

Interpreting Bar Graphs

Bar graphs are often used to show the relationships between two or more sets of data and to illustrate trends. In the bar graph below, you can see the relationship between level of education and the mean, or average, income for men and women. You can use the data presented on this graph to make two generalizations about levels of income: on average, men make more money than women, and the more education that a person has, the more money they are likely to earn.

Follow the same steps used to interpret a line graph.

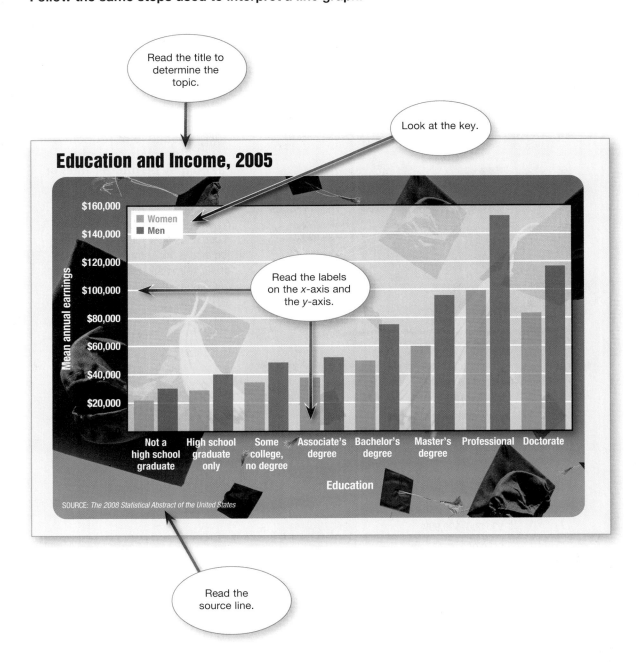

▶ Using Circle Graphs

Circle graphs show how individual parts relate to a whole. Also known as pie charts because they look like a pie cut in wedges, circle graphs represent 100 percent of a given field. The circle graph below shows income information about businesses run by a single proprietor. Use the key to identify what each segment represents.

If you match the blue color which occupies 67 percent of the circle with the information on the key, you see that 67 percent of businesses run by a single owner show income of less than $25,000 per year. Only one percent of businesses with a single owner earn $1,000,000 or more per year.

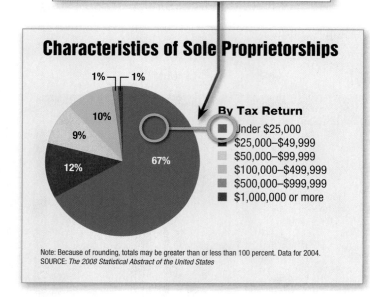

Characteristics of Sole Proprietorships

By Tax Return
- Under $25,000
- $25,000–$49,999
- $50,000–$99,999
- $100,000–$499,999
- $500,000–$999,999
- $1,000,000 or more

1% 1%
10%
9%
12%
67%

Note: Because of rounding, totals may be greater than or less than 100 percent. Data for 2004.
SOURCE: *The 2008 Statistical Abstract of the United States*

NOTE Because of rounding, the totals on a circle graph may be greater than or less than 100 percent.

For example: 5.8 rounds up to 6 percent, while 4.4 rounds down to 4 percent. When you add 5.8 and 4.4, the total is 10.2 percent. On a circle graph, this would display as 6 percent and 4 percent, adding up to a total of 10 percent.

Data can be transferred from a chart, or table, to a graph. The data in the chart below provide the same information as the circle graph above.

Income	Percentage
Under $25,000	67
$25,000–$49,999	12
$50,000–$99,999	9
$100,000–$499,999	10
$500,000–$999,999	1
$1,000,000 or more	1

▶ Understanding Population Pyramids

Population pyramids, or age structures, are graphical representations of the distribution of population by age and gender. They are called pyramids because in many instances they are wider at the bottom and narrower at the top.

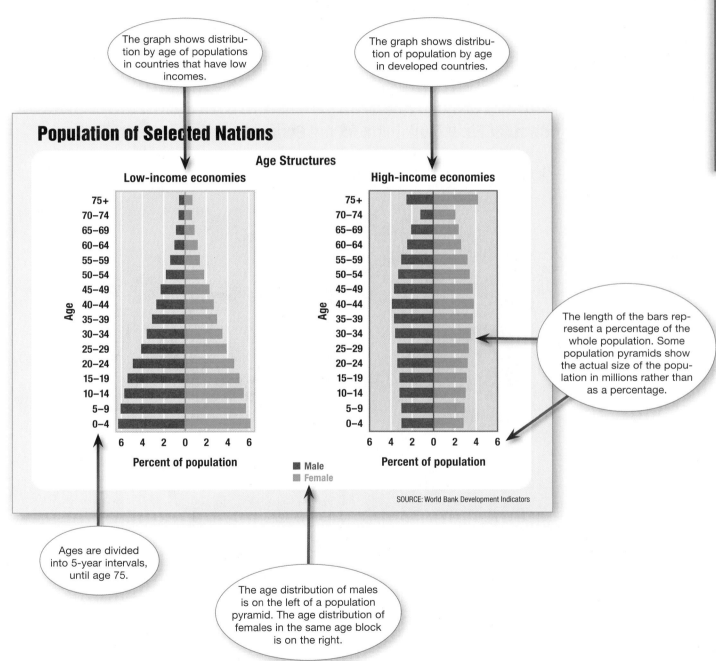

The graph shows distribution by age of populations in countries that have low incomes.

The graph shows distribution of population by age in developed countries.

Population of Selected Nations

Age Structures

Low-income economies

High-income economies

The length of the bars represent a percentage of the whole population. Some population pyramids show the actual size of the population in millions rather than as a percentage.

Percent of population

■ Male
■ Female

SOURCE: World Bank Development Indicators

Ages are divided into 5-year intervals, until age 75.

The age distribution of males is on the left of a population pyramid. The age distribution of females in the same age block is on the right.

▶ Reading Circular Flow Models

Some charts used in economics do not present data. They are used to illustrate an economic process. The circular flow model shows how three basic parts of the economy work together. In this illustration of the macroeconomy at work, the three elements are households or consumers, firms or businesses, and the government.

Everything on this simplified chart is happening at the same time. The movement of the economy never stops. Two other elements that would be included in a more complete circular flow diagram would be financial institutions and international trade.

Circular Flow Model of a Mixed Economy

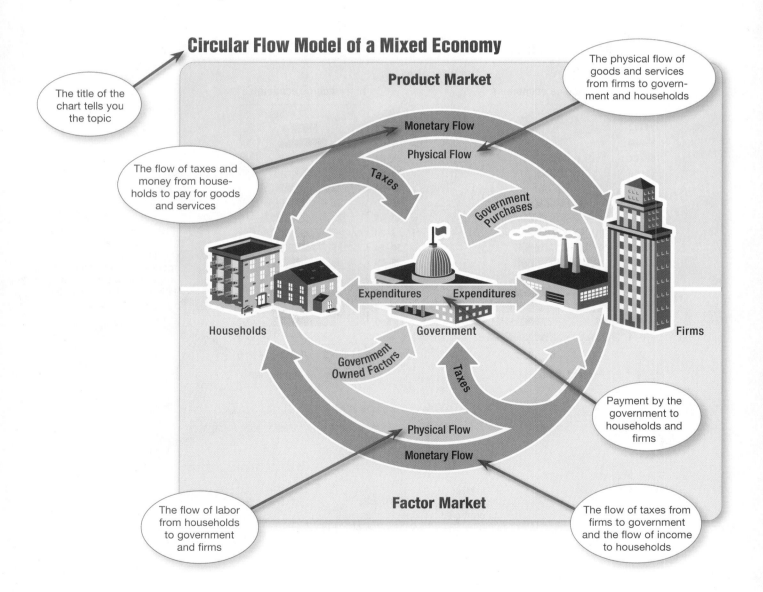

The title of the chart tells you the topic

The physical flow of goods and services from firms to government and households

The flow of taxes and money from households to pay for goods and services

Payment by the government to households and firms

The flow of labor from households to government and firms

The flow of taxes from firms to government and the flow of income to households

Product Market

Monetary Flow

Physical Flow

Taxes

Government Purchases

Expenditures   Expenditures

Households   Government   Firms

Government Owned Factors

Taxes

Physical Flow

Monetary Flow

Factor Market

Student Guide to NGSSS

Reading Florida's Next Generation Sunshine State Standards

Throughout this textbook, you will see a special coding system used to identify the Florida's **Next Generation Sunshine State Standards**. The example below will help you understand the codes.

SS.912.E.2.11

| SS: Social Studies | Grade Level: 9-12 | E: Economics | Benchmark: Economics: Assess the impact of negative and positive externalities on the local environment. |

Saturn V rocket at Kennedy Space Center, Cape Canaveral, FL.

Florida Next Generation Sunshine State Standards

Economics

	Florida Economics
LA.1112.1.6	Vocabulary Development-The student uses multiple strategies to develop grade appropriate vocabulary.
LA.1112.1.6.1	The student will use new vocabulary that is introduced and taught directly;
LA.1112.1.6.2	The student will listen to, read, and discuss familiar and conceptually challenging text;
LA.1112.1.6.3	The student will use context clues to determine meanings of unfamiliar words;
LA.1112.2.2	Nonfiction-The student identifies, analyzes, and applies knowledge of the elements of a variety of nonfiction, informational, and expository texts to demonstrate an understanding of the information presented.
LA.1112.2.2.2	The student will use information from the text to answer questions or to state the main idea or provide relevant details;
LA.1112.2.2.3	The student will organize information to show understanding or relationships among facts, ideas, and events (e.g., representing key points within text through charting, mapping, paraphrasing, summarizing, comparing, contrasting, outlining);
LA.1112.6.2	Research Process-The student uses a systematic process for the collection, processing, and presentation of information.
LA.1112.6.2.4	The student will understand the importance of legal and ethical practices, including laws regarding libel, slander, copyright, and plagiarism in the use of mass media and digital sources, know the associated consequences, and comply with the law.
LA.1112.6.3	Media Literacy-The student develops and demonstrates an understanding of media literacy as a life skill that is integral to informed decision making.
LA.1112.6.3.1	The student will distinguish between propaganda and ethical reasoning strategies in print and nonprint media;
MA.912.A.2	relations and functions-Draw and interpret graphs of relations. Understand the notation and concept of a function, find domains and ranges, and link equations to functions.
MA.912.A.2.1	Create a graph to represent a real-world situation.
MA.912.A.2.2	Interpret a graph representing a real-world situation.
MA.912.D.4	linear programming-Understand how to use linear programming and coordinate geometry to solve simple linear optimization problems.
MA.912.D.4.1	Solve maximal profit/minimal cost problems.
MA.912.F.3	Loans and Financing-Become familiar with and describe the advantages and disadvantages of short-term purchases, long-term purchases, and mortgages.
MA.912.F.3.1	Compare the advantages and disadvantages of using cash versus a credit card.
MA.912.F.3.2	Analyze credit scores and reports.
MA.912.F.3.3	Calculate the finance charges and total amount due on a credit card bill.
MA.912.F.3.6	Calculate total cost of purchasing consumer durables over time given different down payments, financing options, and fees.
SS.912.E.1	Understand the fundamental concepts relevant to the development of a market economy.
SS.912.E.1.1	Identify the factors of production and why they are necessary for the production of goods and services.

	Economics
SS.912.E.1.2	Analyze production possibilities curves to explain choice, scarcity, and opportunity costs.
SS.912.E.1.3	Compare how the various economic systems (traditional, market, command, mixed) answer the questions: (1) What to produce?; (2) How to produce?; and (3) For whom to produce?
SS.912.E.1.4	Define supply, demand, quantity supplied, and quantity demanded; graphically illustrate situations that would cause changes in each, and demonstrate how the equilibrium price of a product is determined by the interaction of supply and demand in the market place.
SS.912.E.1.5	Compare different forms of business organizations.
SS.912.E.1.6	Compare the basic characteristics of the four market structures (monopoly, oligopoly, monopolistic competition, pure competition).
SS.912.E.1.7	Graph and explain how firms determine price and output through marginal cost analysis.
SS.912.E.1.8	Explain ways firms engage in price and nonprice competition.
SS.912.E.1.9	Describe how the earnings of workers are determined.
SS.912.E.1.10	Explain the use of fiscal policy (taxation, spending) to promote price stability, full employment, and economic growth.
SS.912.E.1.11	Explain how the Federal Reserve uses the tools of monetary policy (discount rate, reserve requirement, open market operations) to promote price stability, full employment, and economic growth.
SS.912.E.1.12	Examine the four phases of the business cycle (peak, contraction-unemployment, trough, expansion-inflation).
SS.912.E.1.13	Explain the basic functions and characteristics of money, and describe the composition of the money supply in the United States.
SS.912.E.1.14	Compare credit, savings, and investment services available to the consumer from financial institutions.
SS.912.E.1.15	Describe the risk and return profiles of various investment vehicles and the importance of diversification.
SS.912.E.1.16	Construct a one-year budget plan for a specific career path including expenses and construction of a credit plan for purchasing a major item.
SS.912.E.2	Understand the fundamental concepts relevant to the institutions, structure, and functions of a national economy.
SS.912.E.2.1	Identify and explain broad economic goals.
SS.912.E.2.2	Use a decision-making model to analyze a public policy issue affecting the student's community that incorporates defining a problem, analyzing the potential consequences, and considering the alternatives.
SS.912.E.2.3	Research contributions of entrepreneurs, inventors, and other key individuals from various gender, social, and ethnic backgrounds in the development of the United States.
SS.912.E.2.4	Diagram and explain the problems that occur when government institutes wage and price controls, and explain the rationale for these controls.
SS.912.E.2.5	Analyze how capital investments may impact productivity and economic growth.
SS.912.E.2.6	Examine the benefits of natural monopolies and the purposes of government regulation of these monopolies.
SS.912.E.2.7	Identify the impact of inflation on society.
SS.912.E.2.8	Differentiate between direct and indirect taxes, and describe the progressivity of taxes (progressive, proportional, regressive).
SS.912.E.2.9	Analyze how changes in federal spending and taxation affect budget deficits and surpluses and the national debt.
SS.912.E.2.10	Describe the organization and functions of the Federal Reserve System.
SS.912.E.2.11	Assess the economic impact of negative and positive externalities on the local, state, and national environment.

	Economics
SS.912.E.2.12	Construct a circular flow diagram for an open-market economy including elements of households, firms, government, financial institutions, product and factor markets, and international trade.
SS.912.E.3	Understand the fundamental concepts and interrelationships of the United States economy in the international marketplace.
SS.912.E.3.1	Demonstrate the impact of inflation on world economies.
SS.912.E.3.2	Examine absolute and comparative advantage, and explain why most trade occurs because of comparative advantage.
SS.912.E.3.3	Discuss the effect of barriers to trade and why nations sometimes erect barriers to trade or establish free trade zones.
SS.912.E.3.4	Assess the economic impact of negative and positive externalities on the international environment.
SS.912.E.3.5	Compare the current United States economy with other developed and developing nations.
SS.912.E.3.6	Differentiate and draw conclusions about historical economic thought theorized by economists.
SS.912.G.2	Understand physical and cultural characteristics of places.
SS.912.G.2.2	Describe the factors and processes that contribute to the differences between developing and developed regions of the world.
SS.912.G.3	Understand the relationships between the Earth's ecosystems and the populations that dwell within them.
SS.912.G.3.3	Use geographic terms and tools to explain differing perspectives on the use of renewable and non-renewable resources in Florida, the United States, and the world.
SS.912.G.4	Understand the characteristics, distribution, and migration of human populations.
SS.912.G.4.4	Use geographic terms and tools to analyze case studies of issues in globalization.

This guide allows you to practice the skills you need to succeed in your Economics course. Using a variety of practice materials, it reviews key economic skills. On the following pages, review the sample questions and step-by-step instructions, which will help you answer each question.

Florida Standards Review Strategies		
Social Studies Skill	**What It Means To You**	**Page Reference**
Analyze Maps SS.912.G.3.3	Maps can illustrate how physical, political, and geographical regions relate to economics. Analyzing maps can help you to understand economic information about a region, such as its natural resources.	11, 77, 446, 447, 454, 501, 507, 508
Analyze Line Graphs MA.912.D.4.1	Relationships between different sets of information are important in economics. It is often useful to show these relationships on line graphs. By understanding how data sets relate, you can identify patterns that will give you an understanding of how the economy operates.	85, 116, 120, 121, 122, 195
Analyze Bar Graphs MA.912.A.2.2	Bar graphs are another way to display relationships between two or more sets of data. When you analyze graphs, including bar graphs, you often look for trends. This is a useful tool for economists.	16, 21, 76, 78, 79, 80, 81, 214, 220, 221, 225, 232, 472, 474, 476, 477, 478, PF12, PF15, PF17, PF27
Analyze Circle Graphs MA.912.A.2.1	Circle graphs, or pie charts, are another way to show economic data. They are particularly useful in helping to compare percentages of a whole.	242, 322, 398
Create Diagrams SS.912.E.2.12	Diagrams can help you visualize what is happening in a real economy. The circular flow diagram is an economic model that represents the flow, or movement, of goods, services, money, and the factors of production in a market or mixed economy.	31, 40, 44, 426, 428

Pensacola, Florida

Social Studies Skill	What It Means To You	Page Reference
Make Predictions SS.912.E.1.2	Making informed predictions is an essential skill for economists. When you do this, you look over sets of data and draw conclusions from them. Production possibility curves are one way to make predictions. These graphs show different ways to use an economy's productive resources.	13, 14, 17, 18, 164, 165
Analyze Cause and Effect SS.912.E.2.2	When you analyze cause and effect, you understand how actions lead to a particular result and look for solutions. In economics, a decision-making model can help you define a problem, analyze potential consequences, and consider alternatives.	8, 9, 10, 11, 12, 39, 234, 272, 329, 352, 388
Compare and Contrast Data SS.912.E.3.5	When you compare and contrast, you look for similarities and differences. Comparing and contrasting information can help you to draw conclusions or make economic choices.	38, 39, 44, 363, 367, 455, 463, 470, 480, 508
Evaluate Arguments LA.1112.6.3.1	In order to evaluate arguments effectively, you must be able to distinguish between propaganda and ethical reasoning. Propaganda is the promotion of specific ideas or views using persuasive techniques, usually with little or no factual evidence. Ethical reasoning presents an argument using facts to prove a case.	107, 174, 179

Pensacola, Florida

Analyze Maps

Maps can help illustrate how physical, political, and geographical regions relate to economics. Analyzing maps can help you to understand economic information about a region, such as its natural resources.

Answer Number 1. Base your answer on the map. Follow the steps to apply the skill.

Step 1 Read the map title.

Florida's Economic Activity and Resources

FLORIDA

P

P

P

Gulf of Mexico

- Farming
- Grazing
- Primarily forestland
- Limited agricultural activity
- Urban area
- Fishing

- Phosphates
- Uranium
- Lead
- Zinc
- Coal
- Petroleum

Step 2 Read the map key. The key uses symbols, colors, or patterns to represent economic information.

Step 3 Look at the map to get a general idea of what it shows. Look for places where symbols from the key appear on the map.

❶ **Since southern Florida has limited farmland, which other industries help to support Florida's economy there?**

A. Fishing

B. Lumber

C. Mining

D. Livestock

Step 5 Use the map to determine the best answer to the question.

Step 4 Read the question and all answer choices.

Analyze Line Graphs

Relationships between different sets of information are important in economics. It is useful to show these relationships on line graphs. By understanding how data sets relate, you can identify patterns that will give you an understanding of how the economy operates.

Answer Number 1. Base your answer on the graph. Follow the steps to apply the skill.

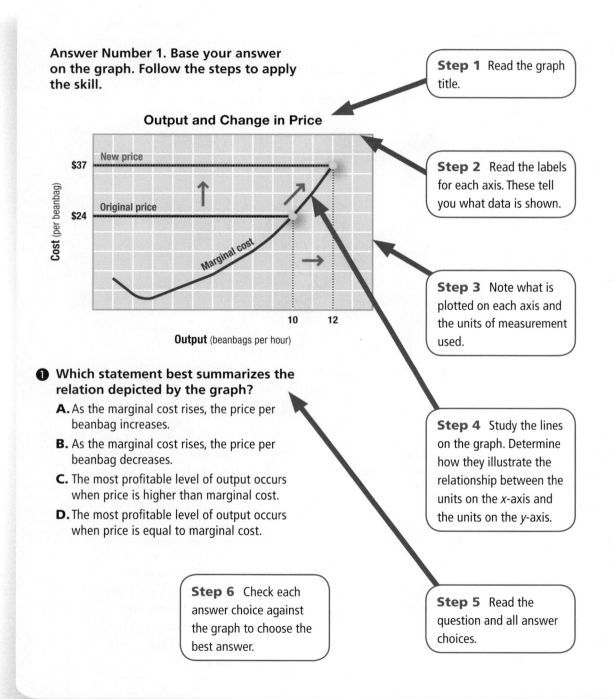

Step 1 Read the graph title.

Step 2 Read the labels for each axis. These tell you what data is shown.

Step 3 Note what is plotted on each axis and the units of measurement used.

Step 4 Study the lines on the graph. Determine how they illustrate the relationship between the units on the *x*-axis and the units on the *y*-axis.

Step 5 Read the question and all answer choices.

Step 6 Check each answer choice against the graph to choose the best answer.

❶ Which statement best summarizes the relation depicted by the graph?

A. As the marginal cost rises, the price per beanbag increases.

B. As the marginal cost rises, the price per beanbag decreases.

C. The most profitable level of output occurs when price is higher than marginal cost.

D. The most profitable level of output occurs when price is equal to marginal cost.

Analyze Bar Graphs

Bar graphs display the relationships between two or more sets of data. When you analyze graphs, including bar graphs, you often look for trends. This is a useful tool for economists.

Answer Number 1. Base your answer on the graph. Follow the steps to apply the skill.

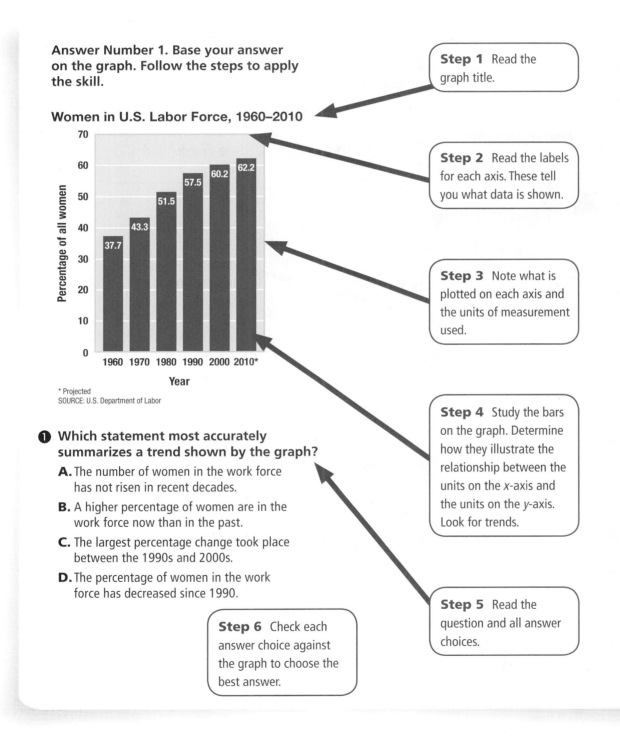

Women in U.S. Labor Force, 1960–2010

* Projected
SOURCE: U.S. Department of Labor

Step 1 Read the graph title.

Step 2 Read the labels for each axis. These tell you what data is shown.

Step 3 Note what is plotted on each axis and the units of measurement used.

Step 4 Study the bars on the graph. Determine how they illustrate the relationship between the units on the *x*-axis and the units on the *y*-axis. Look for trends.

❶ Which statement most accurately summarizes a trend shown by the graph?

  A. The number of women in the work force has not risen in recent decades.

  B. A higher percentage of women are in the work force now than in the past.

  C. The largest percentage change took place between the 1990s and 2000s.

  D. The percentage of women in the work force has decreased since 1990.

Step 5 Read the question and all answer choices.

Step 6 Check each answer choice against the graph to choose the best answer.

FL

Analyze Circle Graphs

Circle graphs, or pie charts, are another way to show relationships between different sets of economic data. They are particularly useful in helping to compare percentages of a whole.

Answer Number 1. Base your answer on the circle graph below. Follow the steps to apply the skill.

Federal Revenue

- 39%
- 32%
- 9%
- 13%
- 7%

■ Personal income taxes
■ Social Security, Medicare and unemployment, and other retirement taxes
■ Borrowing to cover deficit
■ Corporate Income taxes
■ Excise, customs, gift and miscellaneous taxes

SOURCE: The Internal Revenue Service, U.S. Department of Treasury

❶ What percentage of federal revenues do NOT come from personal income taxes and borrowing?

A. 52%

B. 53%

C. 54%

D. 55%

Step 1 Read the title to get an understanding of what the graph displays.

Step 2 Read the graph and its key. What information is being shown?

Step 3 Read the question and all answer choices.

Step 4 Use the information from the graph to add together the percentages from miscellaneous and personal taxes. Subtract this number from 100.

Step 5 Use your calculation to answer the question.

Create Diagrams

Diagrams can help you visualize what is happening in a real economy. The circular flow diagram is an economic model that represents the flow, or movement, of goods, services, money, and the factors of production in a market or mixed economy.

Answer Number 1. Base your answer on the circular flow diagram. Follow the steps to apply the skill.

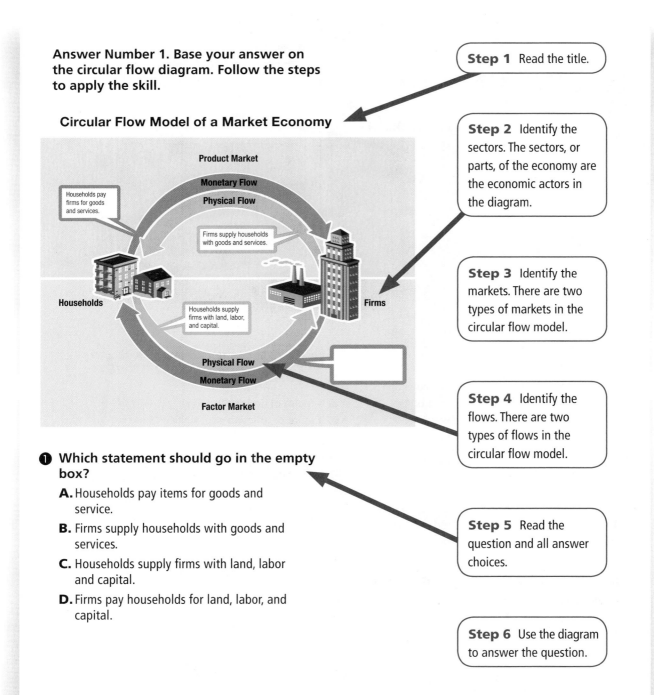

Step 1 Read the title.

Step 2 Identify the sectors. The sectors, or parts, of the economy are the economic actors in the diagram.

Step 3 Identify the markets. There are two types of markets in the circular flow model.

Step 4 Identify the flows. There are two types of flows in the circular flow model.

Step 5 Read the question and all answer choices.

Step 6 Use the diagram to answer the question.

❶ **Which statement should go in the empty box?**

A. Households pay items for goods and service.

B. Firms supply households with goods and services.

C. Households supply firms with land, labor and capital.

D. Firms pay households for land, labor, and capital.

Make Predictions

Making informed predictions is an essential skill for economists. When you do this, you look over sets of data and draw conclusions from them. Production possibility curves are one way to make predictions. These graphs show alternative ways to use an economy's productive resources.

Answer Number 1. Base your answer on the table and graph. Follow the steps to apply the skill.

Step 1 Read the title.

Step 2 Study the table. Identify the columns. Examine the list of possible combinations.

Capeland's Production Possibilities

Watermelons (millions of tons)	Shoes (millions of pairs)
0	15
8	14
14	12
18	9
20	5
21	0

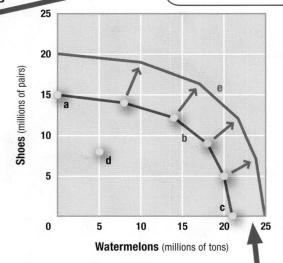

KEY
a. No watermelons, all possible shoes
b. A production possibilities frontier
c. No shoes, all possible watermelons

d. A point of underutilization
e. Future production possibilities frontier

Imagine that there is a country called Capeland. Capeland could use its resources to produce shoes or watermelons or could produce some of each. The production possibility curve shows how many of one good Capeland has to give up to produce more of the other good. For example, if Capeland produces 15 million pairs of shoes, it has no spare resources to produce watermelons.

Step 3 Read the graph key.

Step 4 Study the production possibilities curve. How does the information from the table translate to the graph?

❶ **If Capeland chose to produce 20 million tons of watermelons, what is the largest number of shoes the country produce?**
   A. 2 million pairs
   B. 5 million pairs
   C. 10 million pairs
   D. 20 million pairs

Step 5 Read the question and all answer choices.

Step 6 Use the table and graph to answer the question.

Analyze Cause and Effect

When you analyze cause and effect, you understand how actions lead to a particular result and look for solutions. In economics, a decision-making model can help you define a problem, analyze potential consequences, and consider alternatives.

Answer Number 1. Base your answer on the decision-making grid. Follow the steps to apply the skill.

Step 1 Read the title. The title identifies the issue.

Decision Making at the Margin

Causes	Effects	
Options	Benefit	Opportunity Cost
1st hour of extra study time	Grade of C on test	One hour of sleep
2nd hour of extra study time	Grade of B on test	2 hours of sleep
3rd hour of extra study time	Grade of B+ on test	3 hours of sleep

Step 2 Identify the options, or alternatives. Choosing different options will cause different outcomes.

Step 3 Identify the benefits and opportunity cost of each option. These are the effects that would result from each alternative chosen.

❶ **What are the two effects of studying for an extra two hours?**

A. Losing one hour of sleep and getting a C

B. Losing three hours of sleep and getting an A

C. Losing two hours of sleep and getting a B

D. Losing one hour of sleep and getting an A

Step 4 Read the question and all answer choices.

Step 5 Use the grid to answer the question.

Compare and Contrast Data

When you compare and contrast, you look for similarities and differences between sets of data. Comparing and contrasting information can help you to draw conclusions or make decisions about economic choices.

Answer Number 1. Base your answer on the chart. Follow the steps to apply the skill.

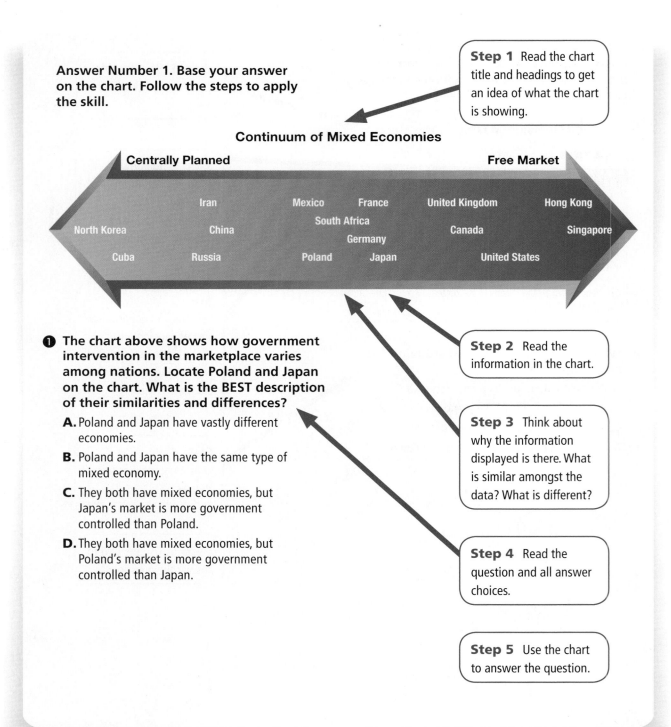

Step 1 Read the chart title and headings to get an idea of what the chart is showing.

Continuum of Mixed Economies

Centrally Planned → Free Market

Iran, Mexico, France, United Kingdom, Hong Kong
North Korea, China, South Africa, Canada, Singapore
Germany
Cuba, Russia, Poland, Japan, United States

① The chart above shows how government intervention in the marketplace varies among nations. Locate Poland and Japan on the chart. What is the BEST description of their similarities and differences?

A. Poland and Japan have vastly different economies.

B. Poland and Japan have the same type of mixed economy.

C. They both have mixed economies, but Japan's market is more government controlled than Poland.

D. They both have mixed economies, but Poland's market is more government controlled than Japan.

Step 2 Read the information in the chart.

Step 3 Think about why the information displayed is there. What is similar amongst the data? What is different?

Step 4 Read the question and all answer choices.

Step 5 Use the chart to answer the question.

Evaluate Arguments

In order to evaluate arguments effectively, you must be able to distinguish between propaganda and ethical reasoning. Propaganda is the promotion of specific ideas or views using persuasive techniques, usually with no factual evidence. Ethical reasoning presents an argument using facts to prove a case.

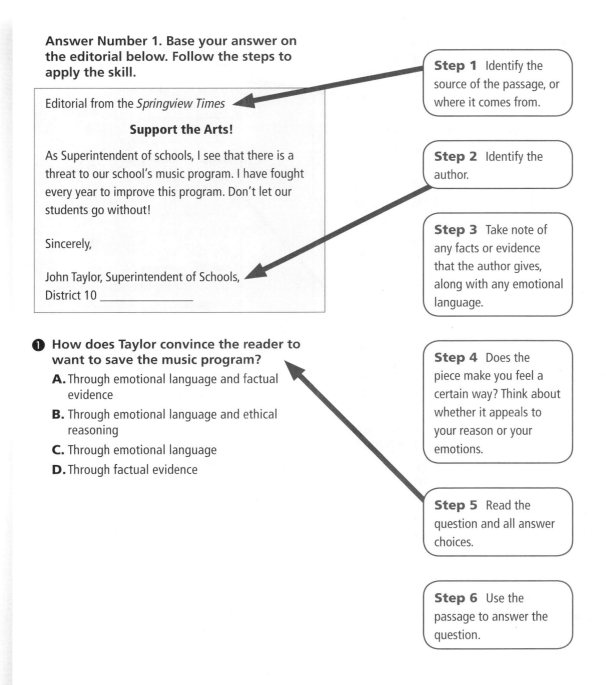

Answer Number 1. Base your answer on the editorial below. Follow the steps to apply the skill.

Editorial from the *Springview Times*

Support the Arts!

As Superintendent of schools, I see that there is a threat to our school's music program. I have fought every year to improve this program. Don't let our students go without!

Sincerely,

John Taylor, Superintendent of Schools, District 10 _____

Step 1 Identify the source of the passage, or where it comes from.

Step 2 Identify the author.

Step 3 Take note of any facts or evidence that the author gives, along with any emotional language.

❶ **How does Taylor convince the reader to want to save the music program?**

  A. Through emotional language and factual evidence

  B. Through emotional language and ethical reasoning

  C. Through emotional language

  D. Through factual evidence

Step 4 Does the piece make you feel a certain way? Think about whether it appeals to your reason or your emotions.

Step 5 Read the question and all answer choices.

Step 6 Use the passage to answer the question.

Evaluate Arguments (Continued)

In order to evaluate arguments effectively, you must be able to distinguish between propaganda and ethical reasoning. Propaganda is the promotion of specific ideas or views using persuasive techniques, usually with no factual evidence. Ethical reasoning presents an argument using facts to prove a case.

Answer Number 1. Base your answer on the editorials from the previous page and below. Follow the steps to apply the skill.

Editorial from the *Springview Times*

   John Taylor has added more money to the budget of the music program every year since he became superintendent. There is not a lot of money in the school system's budget, however. Taylor plans on ending the breakfast program in order to expand the music program. Hungry students are not able to focus on their school work. Research shows that students who don't eat breakfast get lower grades in school. Let's not lose an important program just to increase the budget of one department.

Sincerely,

Jane Smith, English teacher, Springview High School _____

Step 1 Identify the source of the passage, or where it comes from.

Step 2 Identify the author.

Step 3 Take note of any facts or evidence that the author gives, along with any emotional language.

Step 4 Does the piece make you feel a certain way? Think about whether it appeals to your reason or your emotions.

❶ **How does the information in this passage change your understanding of the issue?**

A. Increasing the music budget would directly cause students to get lower grades.

B. Increasing the music budget would deplete the school system's budget entirely.

C. No change. Smith uses emotional language, which muddles her argument.

D. Increasing the music budget would not be to the students' benefit.

Step 5 Read the question and all answer choices.

Step 6 Use the passage to answer the question.

1 Introduction to Economics

Essential Question, Unit 1

How does economics affect everyone?

Chapter 3
What role should government play in a free market economy?

Chapter 1
How can we make the best economic choices?

Chapter 2
How does a society decide who gets what goods and services?

? Essential Question, Chapter 1
How can we make the best economic choices?

FL **Next Generation Sunshine State Standards**

Section 1: Scarcity and the Factors of Production
LA.1112.1.6, SS.912.E.1.1, SS.912.E.2, SS.912.E.2.3

Section 2: Opportunity Cost
LA.1112.1.6, SS.912.E.1.1, SS.912.E.1.7, SS.912.E.3.6

Section 3: Production Possibilities Curves
LA.1112.1.6, MA.912.A.2, SS.912.E.1.2, SS.912.E.2.3

Economics
on the go

To study anywhere, anytime, download these
online resources at *PearsonSchool.com/PHecon* ▶

FL NGSSS

LA.1112.1.6 Use multiple strategies to develop vocabulary.

SS.912.E.1.1 Identify factors of production and their necessity to making goods and services.

SS.912.E.2 Understand the concepts relevant to the national economy.

SS.912.E.2.3 Research the contributions of key individuals of various backgrounds in the development of the U.S.

ECONOMIC DICTIONARY

As you read the section, look for the definitions of these **Key Terms:**

- need
- want
- goods
- services
- scarcity
- economics
- shortage
- entrepreneur
- factors of production
- land
- labor
- capital
- physical capital
- human capital

Guiding Question

How does scarcity force people to make economic choices?

Copy this cause-and-effect chart and fill it in as you read.

Needs and Wants	Resources
A. Definition:	A. Definition:
B. Unlimited	B.
C. Examples:	C. Examples:

Necessity of Making Choices

▶ Economics and You

There are so many ways you could spend your money. You really want that new video game. You also want to attend an upcoming concert. At the same time, you need to pay your car insurance. With limited funds, you can't have it all. How will you choose?

What's true for you is also true for your neighbors, your school, the gas station on the corner, a major television network, and the U.S. Congress. Economics is the study of how individuals, businesses, and governments make choices when faced with a limited supply of resources.

Principles in Action Scarcity forces us all to make choices by making us decide which options are most important to us. In this section, you will examine the problem of scarcity as it relates to such varied resources as water and the ingredients needed to make a plate of French fries.

Scarcity and Choice

The study of economics begins with the fact that people cannot have everything they need and want. A **need** is something essential for survival such as food or medical care. A **want** is something that we desire but that is not necessary for survival, such as video games or stylish haircuts.

People satisfy their needs and wants with goods and services. **Goods** are physical objects that someone produces, such as food, clothing, or video games. **Services** are actions or activities that one person performs for another. Medical care and haircuts are services.

need something essential for survival

want something that people desire but that is not necessary for survival

goods the physical objects that someone produces

services the actions or activities that one person performs for another

Visual Glossary
online

Go to the Visual Glossary Online for an interactive review of **opportunity cost.**

Action Graph
online

Go to Action Graph Online for animated versions of key charts and graphs.

How the Economy Works
online

Go to How the Economy Works Online for an interactive lesson on the role of the **entrepreneur.**

What does an **entrepreneur** do?

All entrepreneurs—whether they are starting a lawn-mowing service or founding a company that makes cars—have two things in common. First, they recognize a need or want. Then, they must assemble the factors of production to meet that need or want.

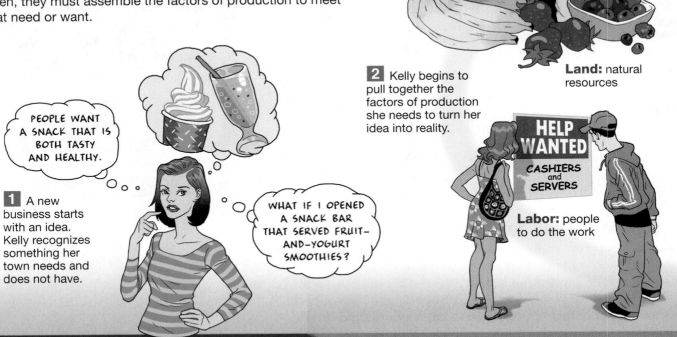

1 A new business starts with an idea. Kelly recognizes something her town needs and does not have.

PEOPLE WANT A SNACK THAT IS BOTH TASTY AND HEALTHY.

WHAT IF I OPENED A SNACK BAR THAT SERVED FRUIT-AND-YOGURT SMOOTHIES?

2 Kelly begins to pull together the factors of production she needs to turn her idea into reality.

Land: natural resources

HELP WANTED CASHIERS and SERVERS

Labor: people to do the work

Recognize a Need or Want

Assemble Factors of Production

The Problem of Limits

People's needs and wants are unlimited. When one want is satisfied, others arise. After eating lunch, you might want to go to a movie or buy some clothes. Goods and services, however, are limited. No one can have an endless supply of anything. Sooner or later, a limit is always reached. The fact that limited amounts of goods and services are available to meet unlimited wants is called **scarcity.**

At many different levels, scarcity forces people to make choices. You, for example, have to decide how to spend your time. If you decide to study for a test, you cannot go to the mall or do volunteer work at the same time. A store must choose between hiring ten new workers or paying for more advertising to attract new customers. A city council might debate whether to use its money to fix an aging school building or to hire more firefighters.

scarcity the principle that limited amounts of goods and services are available to meet unlimited wants

economics the study of how people seek to satisfy their needs and wants by making choices

shortage a situation in which consumers want more of a good or service than producers are willing to make available at a particular price

Economics is the study of how people seek to satisfy their needs and wants by making choices. Because people act individually, in groups (such as businesses), and through governments, economists study all three.

Scarcity Versus Shortage

Scarcity is not the same thing as shortage. A **shortage** occurs when consumers want more of a good or service than producers are willing to make available at a particular price. (You will learn how shortages are related to price in Chapter 6.) Shortages may be temporary or long-term.

Unlike shortages, scarcity always exists. There simply are not enough goods and services to supply all of society's needs and wants. This is because the resources that go into making those goods and services are themselves scarce.

✔ **CHECKPOINT** *What is the main focus of economics?*

Capital: human-made resources

Human Capital: acquired knowledge and skills

GRAND OPENING

FROZEN YOGURT

Physical Capital: objects used to create goods or to supply services

3 Kelly took a financial risk by opening her own business. If the risk pays off, Kelly gets profits...her workers get wages...and her customers get a healthy snack.

Check Your Understanding
1. How will reading and other types of self-education help this entrepreneur succeed?
2. What impact does the concept of scarcity have on the decisions made by an entrepreneur?

Provide Goods or Services

Entrepreneurs and the Factors of Production

How are scarce resources turned into goods and services? Entrepreneurs play a key role. **Entrepreneurs** are people who decide how to combine resources to create new goods and services. To make a profit, entrepreneurs are willing to take risks. They develop new ideas, start businesses, create industries, and fuel growth.

Anyone who opens a business, large or small, is an entrepreneur. Jean-Baptiste Say, an eighteenth-century French economist, thought the risk-taking entrepreneur so important that he should be considered a fourth factor of production.

The first task facing an entrepreneur is to assemble **factors of production**, or the resources used to make all goods and services. The three main factors of production are land, labor, and capital.

Land

Economists use the term **land** to refer to all natural resources used to produce goods and services. Natural resources are any materials found in nature that people use to make things or to provide services. These resources include fertile land for farming, as well as resources found in or on the land such as oil, iron, coal, water, and forests.

Labor

The second factor of production is labor. **Labor** is the effort people devote to tasks for which they are paid. Labor includes the medical care provided by a doctor, the classroom instruction provided by a teacher, and the tightening of a bolt by an assembly-line worker. Labor is also an artist's creation of a painting or a technician's repair of a television.

entrepreneur a person who decides how to combine resources to create goods and services

factors of production the resources that are used to make goods and services

land all natural resources used to produce goods and services

labor the effort people devote to tasks for which they are paid

capital any human-made resource that is used to produce other goods and services

physical capital the human-made objects used to create other goods and services

human capital the knowledge and skills a worker gains through education and experience

Capital

The term **capital** refers to any human-made resource that is used to produce other goods and services. Economists divide capital into two types—physical capital and human capital.

Human-made objects used to create other goods and services are **physical capital.** (Sometimes economists use the term capital goods for physical capital.) The buildings that house a computer manufacturing company are physical capital as are all the equipment and tools needed to make those computers.

In addition to producing physical capital, people can also invest in themselves. The

knowledge and skills a worker gains through education and experience is **human capital.** Computer designers go to college to study engineering, electronics, and computers. They build their human capital, making it possible for them to design and build faster and more powerful computers. Auto mechanics also increase their human capital through schooling and experience. This knowledge gives them the skills to diagnose and fix an engine that is not running properly.

An economy requires both physical and human capital to produce goods and services. Doctors need both stethoscopes and schooling to provide healthcare. Assembly-line workers use tools as well as their own skills acquired through training and practice.

Benefits of Capital

Capital is a key factor of production because people and companies can use it to save a great deal of time and money. Physical capital such as machines and tools help workers produce goods and services more easily and at less cost. As a result, they become more productive. Human capital such as technical knowledge has the same result. The more skills a worker gains, the more productive he or she becomes. Many businesses provide training for their employees for this reason.

To understand the benefit of investing in capital, consider the following example. A family of six people washes dishes by hand after every meal—breakfast, lunch, and dinner. That is a total of 21 meals per week. It takes 30 minutes per meal for two family members working together to scrape, stack, wash, rinse, dry, and put away the dishes. As a result, the family spends 21 hours a week cleaning dishes—time that could have been spent on other more productive activities.

Now, suppose that the family saves up and spends $400 on some physical capital—a dishwasher. Using the dishwasher, it takes only one family member 15 minutes after each meal to stack the dishwasher and another family member 15 minutes at the end of the day to put the

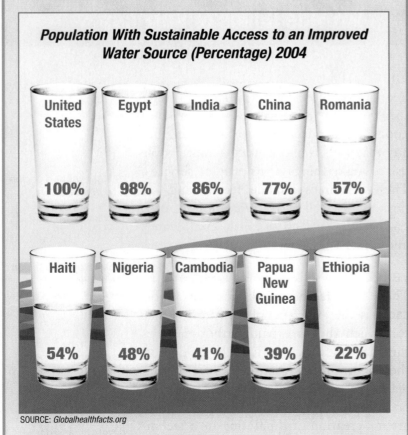

FUTURE WATCH 🌐 **Global Impact**

Water Wars?
Throughout history, wars have been fought over scarce natural resources—from gold to oil. Many experts predict that future wars may be fought over another scarce resource: *water*. Millions of people around the world already live without access to clean, safe water. *Predict three economic or social consequences that might occur in a country where water was scarce.*

Population With Sustainable Access to an Improved Water Source (Percentage) 2004

United States 100%
Egypt 98%
India 86%
China 77%
Romania 57%

Haiti 54%
Nigeria 48%
Cambodia 41%
Papua New Guinea 39%
Ethiopia 22%

SOURCE: *Globalhealthfacts.org*

dishes away. A chore that used to require 21 hours to complete now takes only 7 hours. This example shows the typical benefits of using capital:

1. *Extra time* The family saves 14 hours a week. This is time that can be used for other activities.
2. *More knowledge* By learning how to use the dishwasher, family members learn more about using household appliances in general. They can apply that knowledge to using washing machines, dryers, and other appliances.
3. *More productivity* With extra time and more knowledge, family members can use their resources and labor to do other chores, to learn other skills, or simply to enjoy themselves. Every member of the family benefits.

 CHECKPOINT *What are the factors of production?*

Scarce Resources

All goods and services are scarce because the resources used to produce them are scarce. Consider French fries. A typical portion of French fries might have started as potatoes in a field in Idaho. Ten gallons of water irrigated the half-foot plot where the potatoes grew. Nurtured with fertilizers and protected by pesticides, the potatoes grew until they were harvested, processed, frozen, and then transported to Seattle. There they were fried in corn oil from Nebraska, sprinkled with salt from Louisiana, and eaten in a restaurant.

All of the factors of production used to produce those French fries are scarce. First, the amount of land and water available for growing potatoes is limited. Second, the labor available to grow the crop and to harvest, process, transport, and cook the potatoes is limited by the size, time, age, and energy of the population. Finally, the amount of physical capital available to create the French fries, such as farm machines or cooking equipment, is also limited.

The same principles apply to a pair of blue jeans, an MP3 player, or a space shuttle. No matter what good or service we look at, the supplies of land, labor, and capital used to produce it are scarce. We would also notice another fact about those resources—each one has many alternative uses. Individuals, businesses, and governments have to choose which alternative they most want.

CHECKPOINT *Why are goods and services scarce?*

FL **LA.1112.2.2.2, LA.1112.1.6.1, SS.912.E.1.1, SS.912.E.2**

Essential Questions Journal
To continue to build a response to the Essential Question, go to your **Essential Questions Journal**.

SECTION 1 ASSESSMENT

Guiding Question

1. Use your completed cause-and-effect chart to answer this question: How does scarcity force people to make economic choices?
2. **Extension** Describe how scarcity of time, money, or resources affected a recent economic decision you made.

Key Terms and Main Ideas

3. What is the difference between **goods** and **services?**
4. How does **scarcity** differ from a **shortage?**
5. What does an **entrepreneur** do?
6. What is a benefit of using both **physical capital** and **human capital?**

Critical Thinking

7. **Classify** Identify the factor of production represented by each of the following: **(a)** fishing waters, **(b)** an office building, **(c)** clerks in a store, **(d)** a tractor, **(e)** a student in a cooking school. Explain.
8. **Infer** If companies can become more productive by increasing their physical capital, why would a company not buy up-to-date computers for all employees each year?
9. **Apply** Think of a good or service that you consumed today. List at least five factors of production used to produce that good or service. Include at least one example each of land, labor, and capital.

Quick Write

10. Look at the How the Economy Works feature in this section. Make a list of the risks an entrepreneur takes and the possible rewards he or she might gain. Then, write a brief paragraph explaining why entrepreneurs are important to the economy of a community or nation.

FL NGSSS

LA.1112.1.6 Use multiple strategies to develop vocabulary.

SS.912.E.1.1 Identify factors of production and their necessity to making goods and services.

SS.912.E.1.7 Graph and explain how price is determined through marginal cost analysis.

SS.912.E.3.6 Draw conclusions about historical economic theories of economists.

ECONOMIC DICTIONARY

As you read the section, look for the definitions of these **Key Terms:**

- trade-off
- "guns or butter"
- opportunity cost
- thinking at the margin
- cost/benefit analysis
- marginal cost
- marginal benefit

Guiding Question
How does opportunity cost affect decision making?

Copy this concept web and fill it in as you read. Add more ovals if necessary.

▶ **Economics and You** You are cleaning your bedroom. Boxes, clothes, and other items cover your bed, the floor, the entire room. Suddenly, your phone rings and a friend invites you to a party. You consider your options and quickly decide that going to the party will be more fun than cleaning your room.

Later, tired but happy, you enter your bedroom and realize that you now have to clear off your bed when all you want to do is sleep. Your decision to go to the party cost you the time you needed to clean up your room. Was the benefit of your choice worth the cost?

Principles in Action Every time we choose to do something, we give up the opportunity to do something else. As you will see, even such a simple decision as how late to sleep in the morning involves weighing costs and benefits. The Economics & You feature shows how scarcity and choice can affect the ways you spend your time and what services your community provides.

Trade-Offs

Economists point out that all individuals, businesses, and large groups of people—even governments—make decisions that involve trade-offs. A **trade-off** is the act of giving up one benefit in order to gain another, greater benefit. Trade-offs often involve things that can be easily measured, such as money, property, or time. But trade-offs may also involve values that are not so easy to measure. Such intangibles include enjoyment, job satisfaction, or the feeling of well-being that comes from helping somebody.

Individuals and Trade-Offs

At every stage of life, you have to make trade-offs. Taking a part in the school play prevents you from playing soccer or getting a part-time job. A few years from now, you might decide to turn down an exciting but low-paying job in favor of a less interesting job that pays better. Still later, you may choose to give up a vacation in order to put more money away for your retirement.

trade-off the act of giving up one benefit in order to gain another, greater benefit

Businesses and Trade-Offs

The decisions that businesses make about how to use their factor resources—land, labor, and capital—also involve trade-offs. A farmer who plants broccoli cannot at the same time use the same area of land to grow squash. A furniture company that decides to use all of its equipment to make chairs eliminates the possibility of using the same equipment to build tables or desks.

Governments and Trade-Offs

National, state, and local governments also make decisions that involve trade-offs. Economists and politicians use the term **"guns or butter"** to describe one of the common choices facing governments: the choice between spending money on military or domestic needs. A country that decides to produce more military goods ("guns") has fewer resources to devote to consumer goods ("butter") and vice versa. The steel needed to produce a tank cannot then be used to produce a tractor.

In November 2007, as U.S. troops fought in Iraq, one commentator described the tough choice facing American leaders and voters:

> ❝Like Santa with a wish list that cannot be satisfied, the country enters the New Year with a needs list that far exceeds our revenue sources. It appears once again that it is time to wage the debate of guns or butter. . . . Citizens are simultaneously confronted with funding a war abroad and dealing with rising health costs, increased fuel costs and declining human services at home.❞
>
> —Charles Bogue, "Guns or Butter," *Napa Valley Register*

In the end, the reason for the "guns or butter" trade-off is the same as the reason for any other trade-off: scarcity.

✔ **CHECKPOINT** *What are trade-offs?*

Determining Opportunity Cost

In most trade-offs, one of the rejected alternatives is more desirable than the rest. The most desirable alternative somebody gives up as the result of a decision is the **opportunity cost**. Take the farmer in the example above. If squash was the most profitable alternative to broccoli, then the opportunity cost of deciding to plant broccoli was the chance to plant squash.

Even simple decisions carry opportunity costs. Consider the following choices:

- Sleep late or wake up early to study for a test?
- Sleep late or wake up early to eat breakfast?
- Sleep late or wake up early to go on a ski trip?

Most likely, you did not choose "sleep late" for all three decisions. Your decision depended on the specific opportunity cost—the value to you of what you were willing to sacrifice.

"guns or butter" a phrase expressing the idea that a country that decides to produce more military goods ("guns") has fewer resources to produce consumer goods ("butter") and vice versa

opportunity cost the most desirable alternative given up as the result of a decision

 SS.912.E.3.6 Draw conclusions about historical economic theories of economists.

Economics & YOU
Trade-offs

You take a part-time job after school in order to save up money to buy a car. *Your trade-off is time for money and wheels.*

Your town can afford to fix local roads or keep the library open on mornings and Saturdays – but not both. *The town council trades off full library service for road improvements.*

CLOSED Due to staff cuts

Public Library

▲ Every decision we make involves trade-offs. That's why they can be difficult. *Describe one decision you made this week. Identify the trade-offs involved.*

VISUAL GLOSSARY

Reviewing Key Terms
To understand *opportunity cost,* review these terms:

need, *p. 3*
want, *p. 3*
scarcity, *p. 4*
trade-off, *p. 8*

What is
Opportunity Cost?

◀ **opportunity cost** the most desirable alternative given up as the result of a decision

KAREN'S DECISION-MAKING GRID

	Alternatives	
	Sleep late	**Wake up early to study**
Benefits	• Enjoy more sleep • Have more energy during the day	• Better grade on test • Teacher and parental approval • Personal satisfaction
Benefits forgone	• Better grade on test • Teacher and parental approval • Personal satisfaction	• Enjoy more sleep • Have more energy during the day
Opportunity cost	Extra study time	Extra sleep time

Opportunity cost is not just money, but *any* benefit you give up. To determine the opportunity cost of any alternative, you must first identify the benefits you will gain and the benefits you will give up. ***What is Karen's opportunity cost if she decides to sleep late?***

"*By pushing us halfway, we save money on gas. That way we'll have enough money to eat out.*"

◀ In this cartoon, scarcity of an important resource—money—has forced the family to make a strange decision. ***What decision has the family made? What is the opportunity cost of this decision?***

Visual Glossary
online
To expand your understanding of this and other key economic terms, visit **PearsonSchool.com/PHecon**

Using a Decision-Making Grid

At times, the opportunity cost of a decision may be unclear or complicated. Using a decision-making grid like the one in the Visual Glossary, opposite, can help you determine whether you are willing to accept the opportunity cost of a choice you are about to make.

In this particular example, a high school student named Karen is trying to decide whether to sleep late or get up early to study for a test. Because of the scarcity of time, she cannot do both.

To help her make her decision, Karen lists the benefits of each alternative on the grid. Waking up early to study will probably result in her receiving a better grade. She will also receive teacher and parental approval and experience a sense of personal satisfaction.

On the other hand, Karen enjoys sleeping. In addition, the extra sleep would give her more energy during the day. She would have to give up these benefits if she decided to get up earlier.

Making the Decision

Karen is a practical person. After considering the opportunity cost of each alternative, she decides that waking up early to study offers her the most desirable benefits. She knows that she is giving up the pleasure of more sleep and the extra energy it would provide. But she is willing to accept this opportunity cost.

If Karen faced other decisions with other opportunity costs, she might choose differently. What if the choice was between sleeping late and getting up early to have breakfast? What if her decision to sleep late or study was on a Saturday rather than on a school day? With each different set of alternatives, the possible benefits and opportunity costs change as well.

One thing does not change, though. We always face an opportunity cost. As economists say, "Choosing is refusing." When we select one alternative, we must sacrifice at least one other alternative and its benefits.

☑ **CHECKPOINT** *Why does every choice involve an opportunity cost?*

Thinking at the Margin

When economists look at decisions, they point out one more characteristic in addition to opportunity cost. Many decisions involve adding or subtracting one unit, such as one hour or one dollar. From an economist's point of view, when you decide how much more or less to do, you are **thinking at the margin.**

To understand what it means to think at the margin, think about folding a piece of paper with important notes on it to put in your pocket. If you fold the paper in half and then in half again, it can just squeeze into your pocket and will lay fairly flat. If you continued folding it in half two or three more times, it would fit more easily in your pocket. But the paper would also become more bulky with each additional fold. The question is, how many folds is the best number for fitting easily into your pocket and laying flat once inside?

Cost/Benefit Analysis

Deciding by thinking at the margin is just like making any other decision. Decision makers have to compare the opportunity costs and the benefits—what they will sacrifice and what they will gain. This decision-making process is sometimes called **cost/benefit analysis.**

To make rational, or sensible, decisions at the margin, you must weigh marginal costs against marginal benefits. The **marginal cost** is the extra cost of adding one unit, whether it be sleeping an extra hour or building one extra house. The **marginal benefit** is the extra benefit of adding the same unit. As long as the marginal benefits exceed the marginal costs, it pays to add more units.

Decision-Making at the Margin

Look again at the example of Karen's decision on how late to sleep. The decision-making grid in the Visual Glossary used an "all or nothing" approach. Either Karen was going to wake up early to study, or she was going to sleep late and not study at all that morning.

In reality, Karen could have decided from among several options rather than just two. She could have decided to get up

Personal Finance
To see how tradeoffs affect budgeting decisions, see your Personal Finance Handbook in the back of the book or visit PearsonSchool.com/PHecon

thinking at the margin
the process of deciding whether to do or use one additional unit of some resource

cost/benefit analysis
a decision-making process in which you compare what you will sacrifice and gain by a specific action

marginal cost the extra cost of adding one unit

marginal benefit the extra benefit of adding one unit

Figure 1.1

Decision Making at the Margin

Options	Benefit	Opportunity Cost
1st hour of extra study time	Grade of C on test	One hour of sleep
2nd hour of extra study time	Grade of B on test	2 hours of sleep
3rd hour of extra study time	Grade of B+ on test	3 hours of sleep

CHART SKILLS

Compare this chart to the one in the Visual Glossary. By comparing opportunity costs and benefits of each extra hour, Karen can decide how much sleep is the right amount.

1. What is the opportunity cost of one extra hour of sleep? What is the benefit?
2. At what point is Karen paying an added cost with little added benefit?

one, two, or three hours earlier. Making a decision about each extra hour would involve thinking at the margin.

To make a decision at the margin, Karen should look at the marginal cost of each extra hour of studying and compare it to the marginal benefit. In **Figure 1.1,** we can see that one hour of studying means an opportunity cost of an hour of sleep, while the probable benefit would be passing the test with a C. Two hours of studying means losing two hours of sleep and perhaps getting a B. When Karen gives up three hours of sleep, however, the probable benefit rises only slightly, to a grade of B+.

Karen concludes that the marginal cost of losing three hours of sleep is no longer worth the marginal benefit because her grade will improve only slightly. Based on her cost-benefit analysis, Karen decides to awaken two hours earlier.

Like opportunity cost, thinking at the margin applies not just to individuals, but to businesses and governments as well. Employers think at the margin when they decide how many extra workers to hire. Legislators think at the margin when deciding how much to increase spending on a government program.

✔ **CHECKPOINT** *How can a cost/benefit analysis help people make decisions?*

 LA.1112.1.6.1, LA.1112.2.2.2, SS.912.E.1.7, SS.912.E.2.2, SS.912.E.3.6

SECTION 2 ASSESSMENT

Essential Questions Journal	To continue to build a response to the Essential Question, go to your **Essential Questions Journal**.

❓ Guiding Question

1. Use your completed concept web to answer this question: How does opportunity cost affect decision making?
2. **Extension** Identify the opportunity cost of the most recent consumer purchase you made. Explain what you gave up and why you chose to purchase the item you did.

Key Terms and Main Ideas

3. Why do all economic decisions involve **trade-offs?**
4. How does the phrase **"guns or butter"** express the principle of trade-offs?
5. Why do many economic decisions involve **thinking at the margin?**
6. Why is it important to compare **marginal costs** to **marginal benefits?**

Critical Thinking

7. **Give Examples** Give two examples of a decision that your school or local government might have to make. Explain how each decision involves trade-offs.
8. **Analyze** Identify a possible opportunity cost for each of the following choices: **(a)** studying for a test on a Saturday afternoon, **(b)** using all the money you received for your birthday to pay for downloading songs, **(c)** spending four hours playing a video game on a Tuesday night, **(d)** having four slices of pizza for lunch.
9. **Make Decisions** What marginal costs and benefits might a business owner have to consider when trying to decide whether to hire one, two, or three additional workers?

Math Skills

10. You have a part-time job where you work 10 hours a week and earn $6 an hour. A friend tells you about another job, at a restaurant, where the pay is only $4 an hour, but in 10 hours of work you can earn as much as $25 in tips. Calculate the probable hourly pay rate for each job. What is the opportunity cost of taking the restaurant job? Would you change jobs? Why or why not?

Visit PearsonSchool.com/PHecon for additional math help.

NGSSS

LA.1112.1.6 Use multiple strategies to develop vocabulary.

MA.912.A.2 Draw and interpret graphs of relations.

SS.912.E.1.2 Analyze production possibilities curves to explain choice.

SS.912.E.2.3 Research the contributions of key individuals of various backgrounds in the development of the U.S.

ECONOMIC DICTIONARY

As you read the section, look for the definitions of these **Key Terms:**

• production possibilities curve
• production possibilities frontier
• efficiency
• underutilization
• law of increasing costs

Guiding Question
How does a nation decide what and how much to produce?

Copy this concept web and fill it in as you read. Add more ovals if necessary.

▶ **Economics and You**   Your class decides to sponsor a community breakfast as a fundraiser. Can you make more money by serving eggs or pancakes? Should you offer both? To decide, you'll have to look at the cost of ingredients, the number of workers you have, and the size of the kitchen. Also, does it take more time to scramble eggs or to flip pancakes? What you decide will affect how much money you make.

Nations face similar decisions about what to produce. For nations, however, the consequences of these decisions can be far more serious.

Principles in Action To decide what and how much to produce, economists use a tool known as a production possibilities curve. You will see how an imaginary country uses this tool to decide between producing two very different products: shoes and watermelons.

Production Possibilities

Economists often use graphs to analyze the choices and trade-offs that people make. Why? Because graphs help us see how one value relates to another value. A **production possibilities curve** is a graph that shows alternative ways to use an economy's productive resources. The axes of the graph can show categories of goods and services, such as farm goods and factory goods or capital goods and consumer goods. The axes can also display any pair of specific goods or services, such as hats on one axis and shoes on the other.

Drawing a Production Possibilities Curve

To draw a production possibilities curve, an economist begins by deciding which goods or services to examine. In this example, we will look at a fictional country called Capeland. Government economists in Capeland must decide whether to use the nation's scarce resources to manufacture shoes or to grow watermelons. The economists determine that, if Capeland used all of its resources to produce only shoes, it could produce 15 million pairs of shoes. At the other extreme, if Capeland used all of its resources to produce only watermelons, it could produce 21 million tons of watermelons.

production possibilities curve
a graph that shows alternative ways to use an economy's productive resources

Figure 1.2

Production Possibilities Curve

GRAPH SKILLS

The table shows six different combinations of watermelons and shoes that Capeland could produce using all of its factor resources. These figures have been used to create a production possibilities curve.

1. How much watermelon can Capeland produce if they are making 9 million pairs of shoes? What will the opportunity cost be if Capeland increases shoe production to 12 million?

2. Why would production at point d in the graph on the right represent an underutilization of resources?

Action Graph
online

For an animated version of this graph, visit
PearsonSchool.com/PHecon

Watermelons (millions of tons)	Shoes (millions of pairs)
0	15
8	14
14	12
18	9
20	5
21	0

KEY

a. No watermelons, all possible shoes
b. A production possibilities frontier
c. No shoes, all possible watermelons

d. A point of underutilization
e. Future production possibilities frontier

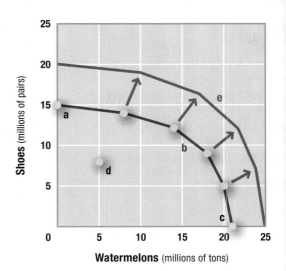

FL SS.912.E.1.2
Analyze production possibility curves to explain choice.

SS.912.E.1.15
Describe the risk and return profiles of various investment options.

production possibilities frontier
a line on a production possibilities curve that shows the maximum possible output an economy can produce

The Capeland economists use this information to create a production possibilities curve **(Figure 1.2)**. The vertical axis of the graph represents how many millions of pairs of shoes Capeland's factories can produce. The horizontal axis shows how many millions of tons of watermelons Capeland's farmers can grow. At Point **a**, Capeland is producing 15 million pairs of shoes but no watermelons. At Point **c**, Capeland is producing 21 million tons of watermelons but no shoes.

There is a third, more likely alternative. The citizens of Capeland can use their resources to produce *both* shoes and watermelons. The table shows four different ways that Capelanders could use their resources to produce both shoes and watermelons. Using the made-up data from the table, we can plot points on the graph. This line, is called the **production possibilities frontier,** shows combinations of the production of

both shoes and watermelons. Any spot on that line represents a point at which Capeland is using all of its resources to produce a maximum combination of those two products.

Trade-Offs

Each point on the production possibilities frontier reflects a trade-off. Near the top of the curve, factories produce more shoes, but farms grow fewer watermelons. Further down the curve, farms grow more watermelons, but factories make fewer pairs of shoes.

These trade-offs are necessary because factors of production are scarce. Using land, labor, and capital to make one product means that fewer resources are left to make something else.

 CHECKPOINT *How do production possibilities curves show alternative uses of resources?*

Efficiency, Growth, and Cost

Production possibilities curves give useful information. They can show how efficient an economy is, whether an economy is growing, and the opportunity cost of producing more of one good or service.

Efficiency

A production possibilities frontier represents an economy working at its most efficient level. **Efficiency** is the use of resources in such a way as to maximize the output of goods and services. However, sometimes economies operate inefficiently. For example, suppose some workers were laid off. The farms or factories where they worked would produce fewer goods.

Any point inside the production possibilities frontier indicates **underutilization,** or the use of fewer resources than the economy is capable of using. At Point **d** in **Figure 1.2,** Capeland is growing 5 million tons of watermelons and making 8 million pairs of shoes. This is inefficient because it is less than the maximum possible production.

Growth

A production possibilities curve is a snapshot. It reflects current production possibilities as if a country's resources were frozen in time. In the real world, however, available resources are constantly changing. If the quantity or quality of land, labor, or capital changes, then the curve will move. For example, a wave of immigration may increase a nation's labor supply. This rise in a factor of production increases the maximum amount of goods the nation can produce.

When an economy grows, economists say that the production possibilities curve has "shifted to the right." To see such a shift, look at line e in **Figure 1.2.** Notice that the possible output of both shoes and watermelons has increased at each point along the line.

However, when a country's production capacity decreases, the curve shifts to the left. A decrease could occur, for example, when a country goes to war and loses part of its land as a result.

efficiency the use of resources in such a way as to maximize the output of goods and services

underutilization the use of fewer resources than an economy is capable of using

SS.912.E.2.3
Research the contributions of key individuals of various backgrounds in the development of the U.S.

Innovators

Steven Levitt

"I just wander through life looking for anything that interests me,"

says economist Steve Levitt. "And every once in a while I stumble onto something that turns into a research idea." This wide curiosity has led him to publish books and articles on topics from illegal drug use to sumo wrestling. Levitt is one of a new generation of economists who are using economic principles such as scarcity and trade-offs to explore all human behavior.

When he was still barely in his early forties, Levitt was already a full professor at a major university. Brilliant but unorthodox, Levitt has shown a rare ability to observe human interactions and create mathematical models that predict future outcomes. He has done ground-breaking work on important "real world" issues, including:

• Does the prison system deter criminal behavior?
• Will adding more police lower the local crime rate?
• What strategies work best to combat drunk driving?

This innovative thinker has an ambition that may seem unusual for an economist. "I'd like to put together a set of tools that lets us catch terrorists," he says. For Levitt, catching terrorists is a matter of finding the right data.

Critical Thinking: *How can the concept of scarcity help explain a wide range of human behavior?*

Fast Facts

Steven Levitt
Born: May 29, 1967, in Minneapolis, MN
Education: B.A. in Economics from Harvard; Ph.D. in Economics from M.I.T.
Claim to Fame: Co-author of the best selling book *Freakonomics*

Gross Value of Manufacturing in Vietnam

Current prices (in trillions of dong)

SOURCE: International Monetary Fund, Vietnam Statistical Appendix, December 2007

The Vietnam Era?

PRODUCTION POSSIBILITIES

Many low-skill manufacturing jobs have migrated overseas. Now some higher-tech work is beginning to follow them out.

By Norihiko Shirouzu
The Wall Street Journal

 SS.912.G.4.4 Analyze case studies of globalization.

Vietnam is barely on the map of the global auto industry, but that is about to change. Nissan Motor sees the southeast Asian nation as a key piece in a strategy to dramatically reduce the cost of developing cars and to compete in the future with rising auto manufacturers from such countries as China and India.

For years, car makers have been slashing expenses by building assembly plants in low-cost countries such as Russia, Turkey and Mexico. Now, high-skill design and engineering operations, which have long remained in industrialized countries like the U.S., Germany and Japan, are starting to follow.

Honda Motor last year announced plans to create a development center in Guangzhou, China with one of its Chinese partners. General Motors has begun designing interiors in China for Buicks it will sell in the U.S.

Nissan has been aggressive among big car makers in moving engineering operations to the developing world. In downtown Hanoi, the capital of Vietnam, Nissan has assembled a team of 700 Vietnamese engineers who are designing basic auto parts such as fuel pipes and nozzles—at a fraction of the cost of doing the work in the auto maker's main engineering center in Japan. The Vietnamese engineers, many of whom have never driven a car before, earn about $200 a month—a 10th of what their counterparts bring home in Japan, according to Nissan.

Over time, Nissan is counting on shifts like these to save hundreds of millions, if not billions, of dollars and sees them as critical to surviving in a world where the cost of cars for consumers in developing markets is falling rapidly.

"If you have an engineer in Hanoi as compared to Japan, there is a lot of savings you can make," says Carlos Ghosn, CEO of Nissan.

But the auto makers like Nissan are still taking a risk. Among the big challenges Nissan faces is a lack of experience among the new college graduates it is recruiting in Vietnam and elsewhere.

Part of what makes it possible for Nissan to allow these engineers to design more of a car are continued advances in computer-aided design tools. But an over-reliance on "virtual engineering" tools at some auto makers' established design centers instead of working with actual components has bred quality problems in recent years.

Applying Economic Principles

Companies, like countries, can increase their productive capacity by shifting factors of production. Based on the above story, what changes did Nissan make in either land, labor, or capital?

Video News Update Online
Powered by
The Wall Street Journal
Classroom Edition

Use videos at **PearsonSchool.com/PHecon** as a springboard for a discussion on a current topic.

Cost

We can also use production possibilities graphs to determine the cost involved in a decision. Remember that cost does not necessarily mean money. To an economist, cost always means opportunity cost.

Looking at the table in **Figure 1.2**, we can see that the opportunity cost of moving from producing no watermelons to producing 8 million tons of watermelons is 1 million pairs of shoes. In other words, in order to produce 8 million tons of watermelons, Capeland had to sacrifice the opportunity to produce 1 million pairs of shoes. In the same way, if Capeland later decides to increase watermelon production from 8 million tons to 14 million tons—an increase of only 6 million tons—it costs 2 million pairs of shoes. In the first step, those 8 million tons of watermelons cost 1 million pairs of shoes. In the second step, an increase of only 6 million tons of watermelons cost an additional 2 million pairs of shoes. This amounts to 3 million pairs of shoes for 14 million tons of watermelons.

The switch from shoes to watermelons has increasing costs. Each time Capeland grows more watermelons, the sacrifice in terms of shoes increases. Eventually, it costs Capeland an additional 5 million pairs of shoes to increase watermelon production by only 1 million tons.

Economists explain these increasingly expensive trade-offs through the **law of increasing costs**. This principle states that as production shifts from making one item to another, more and more resources are necessary to increase production of the second item. Therefore, the opportunity cost increases.

Why does the cost increase? According to **Figure 1.3**, it is because some resources are better suited for use in farming while others are more appropriate for manufacturing. Moving resources from factory to farm production means that farmers must use resources that are not as suitable for farming. For example, when deciding to produce 8 million tons of watermelon, Capeland devoted its most fertile land to this crop. That shift used up the country's best land, so with each additional step, farmers had to use poorer land that produced less per acre than the fertile land could. To increase output on

law of increasing costs an economic principle which states that as production shifts from making one good or service to another, more and more resources are needed to increase production of the second good or service

Simulation *Activity*

Kitchen Challenge
You may be asked to take part in a role-playing game about increasing costs and efficient use of resources.

| Figure 1.3 | **Law of Increasing Costs** |

STEP 1
Initially, resources are used efficiently to make a balance of watermelons and shoes.

STEP 2
A decision is made to grow more watermelons. Less suitable resources are shifted to farm production. Farm production increases. Shoe production decreases.

STEP 3
A decision is made to grow even more watermelons, and more resources are shifted to farm production. Because the added land is less productive, a greater amount of it must be cultivated. Farm output increases. Shoe output decreases by an even greater amount.

Shoe factories

The most suitable land for farming is used to grow watermelons.

Land with rocky soil is now used to grow watermelons.

Land with rocky soil and poor drainage is now used to grow watermelons.

GRAPH SKILLS

This diagram illustrates the law of increasing costs. As production shifts from shoes to watermelons, more and more resources are needed.

1. Why would moving from Step 1 to Step 2 use up more resources than staying at Step 1?

2. Why do you think Capeland might decide to increase watermelon production in spite of the increasing costs?

"Things were done very differently on the farm when I was your age, Kenny."

▲ Technology has changed agriculture—but not quite in the way this cartoon shows. *What is one example of technology that really could help this dairy farmer increase production?*

the poorer land, farmers had to use more land and other resources. This left even fewer resources for producing shoes.

The law of increasing costs explains why production possibilities curve. As we move along the curve, we trade off more and more for less and less added output.

✔ **CHECKPOINT** *What information can a production possibilities curve reveal?*

FL LA.1112.1.6.1, LA.1112.2.2.2, MA.912.A.2, SS.912.E.1.2

Technology and Education

When economists collect data to create production possibility curves, they must first determine which goods and services a country can produce with its current resources. A country's resources include its land and natural resources, its workforce, and its physical and human capital.

Both human and physical capital reflect a vital ingredient of economic growth—technology. Technology is the process used to create goods and services. At any time, countries have used different forms of technology to produce shoes or watermelons or any of the thousands of products that are made. So economists must assess each country's level of technological know-how. Do workers in Capeland pick watermelons by hand? Do they use assembly lines to make shoes?

Technology is one of the factors that can increase a nation's efficiency. Therefore, many governments spend money investing in new technology. For the same reason, they may also invest in education and training so that its people can develop and use new technologies. Highly-skilled workers can increase efficiency and lead to economic growth.

✔ **CHECKPOINT** *How does technology increase production possibilities?*

Essential Questions Journal To continue to build a response to the Essential Question, go to your **Essential Questions Journal**.

SECTION 3 ASSESSMENT

🤔 Guiding Question

1. Use your completed concept web to answer this question: How does a nation decide what and how much to produce?

2. **Extension** Explain why a country might stop growing food and shift its resources to manufacturing clothing.

Key Terms and Main Ideas

3. What is a **production possibilities curve**?

4. What do economists mean by **efficiency**?

5. What do economists mean by growth? What factors can produce economic growth?

6. What is the impact of **underutilization** of resources?

Critical Thinking

7. **Judge** Suppose you were an economic adviser to the leader of Capeland. Based on the production possibilities curve in **Figure 1.2**, what combination of watermelons and shoes would you recommend? Why? What other information might help you make the best decision?

8. **Compare** How is the law of increasing costs similar to the concept of decision making at the margin?

9. **Apply** Explain how each of the following circumstances is likely to affect a nation's production possibilities frontier: the opening of a new college of engineering; an earthquake in the nation's chief farming region; a new type of chemical fertilizer; a shortage of oil.

Math Skills

10. Use the information in the table below to create a production possibilities curve. Then, identify which of the following points on the graph would represent the least efficient use of resources: 3 units of capital goods to 25 units of consumer goods; 9 units of capital goods to 20 units of consumer goods; 12 units of capital goods to 2 units of consumer goods.

Visit PearsonSchool.com/PHecon for additional math help.

Capital Goods (units)	Consumer Goods (units)
0	25
4	24
10	21
18	16
28	9
40	0

Chapter 1: What Is Economics?

Section 1 How does scarcity force people to make economic choices?

Section 2 How does opportunity cost affect decision making?

Section 3 How does a nation decide what and how much to produce?

Essential Question, Chapter 1
How can we make the best economic choices?

Impact of Scarcity

Needs and wants are unlimited.	Resources, goods, and services are scarce.

Need to make trade-offs and identify opportunity costs.

Impact on Individuals
- Make personal trade-offs (time, money)
- Make decisions at the margin

Impact on Businesses
- Balance factors of production: land, labor, capital
- Identify marginal costs and benefits

Impact on Nations
- Make budgetary trade-offs ("guns or butter")
- Determine production possibilities

Economic Dictionary

need, *p. 3*
want, *p. 3*
goods, *p. 3*
services, *p. 3*
scarcity, *p. 4*
economics, *p. 4*
shortage, *p. 4*
entrepreneur, *p. 5*
factors of production, *p. 5*
land, *p. 5*
labor, *p. 5*
capital, *p. 6*
physical capital, *p. 6*
human capital, *p. 6*
trade-off, *p. 8*
"guns or butter", *p. 9*
opportunity cost, *p. 9*
thinking at the margin, *p. 11*
cost/benefit analysis, *p. 11*
marginal cost, *p. 11*
marginal benefit, *p. 11*
production possibilities curve, *p. 13*
production possibilities frontier, *p. 14*
efficiency, *p. 15*
underutilization, *p. 15*
law of increasing costs, *p. 17*

Economics on the go

Study anytime, anywhere. Download these files today.

Economic Dictionary online
Vocabulary Support in English and Spanish

Audio Review online
Audio Study Guide in English and Spanish

Action Graph online
Animated Charts and Graphs

Visual Glossary online
Animated feature

How the Economy Works online
Animated feature

Download to your computer or mobile device at PearsonSchool.com/PHecon

Self-Test online To test your understanding of key terms and main ideas, visit PearsonSchool.com/PHecon

Key Terms and Main Ideas

To make sure you understand the key terms and main ideas of this chapter, review the Checkpoint and Section Assessment questions and look at the Quick Study Guide on the preceding page.

Critical Thinking

1. **Give Examples (a)** What are the three factors of production? **(b)** Choose a business in your community. Give two examples of each factor of production that would apply to that business.

2. **Apply (a)** What do entrepreneurs do? **(b)** Give two examples of people you consider to be successful entrepreneurs. **(c)** List three qualities you think an entrepreneur needs in order to succeed. Explain why each one would be important.

3. **Decide** Cars that weigh more tend to be safer than lightweight cars. At the same time, they use more gasoline because they are heavier. **(a)** Identify the trade-offs and opportunity cost involved in choosing either alternative. **(b)** Based on this information, which car would you choose to buy and why? **(c)** Would your answer change if the price of gasoline doubled? If you inherited a million dollars? If you had children? Explain how each factor would affect your cost/benefit analysis.

  LA.1112.6.3

4. **Predict (a)** If a drought struck a country, what would happen to the production possibilities curve of all farmers in the country? Why? **(b)** Would the production possibilities curve of other industries be affected by this drought? Why or why not?

Applying Your Math Skills

Interpreting Data From Graphs

Imagine that you are the chief economist of a country with the following production possibilities curve. Use your math skills to answer the following questions.
Visit PearsonSchool.com/PHecon for additional math help.

5. How do the maximum amounts of each product differ?

6. Assume this economy is producing at full efficiency. How many computers are being produced when there are 18 million televisions being produced?

7. What is the opportunity cost of producing 5 million computers?

8. What is the opportunity cost of producing 9 million computers?

9. What is the opportunity cost of each 1 million computers at point a compared to point b?

Graph: Televisions (in millions) on vertical axis (0–25), Computers (in millions) on horizontal axis (0–25), with points a, b, c, d, e, f.

Essential Questions Journal To respond to the chapter Essential Question, go to your **Essential Questions Journal**.

? Essential Question Activity

10. Complete this activity to answer the Essential Question **How can we make the best economic choices?** As you have learned, scarcity and opportunity cost lie at the heart of all economic decisions—including those you make. You have limited time and limited resources. Every time you choose one alternative, you give up something else. Using the worksheet in your Essential Questions Journal or the electronic worksheet available at **PearsonSchool.com/PHecon,** keep track of how you use your resources for the next three days.
    (a) In Column 1, record at least three items on which you spent your money and three activities on which you spent your time.
    (b) In Column 2, list the opportunity cost for each entry in Column 1. Remember that the opportunity cost is the next most desirable alternative—the thing you gave up when you made your choice.

After completing the chart, review your choices. Then, for each of the choices you made, answer the following questions: If you had it to do over again, would you make the same choice? Why or why not? Write your answers in Column 3.

11. **Modify** You have listed your choices and your trade-offs and evaluated your outcomes. Now, consider how your choices might have differed if your resources had differed. Write an answer to each of the following:
    (a) How would your choices change if you had 10 percent more money to spend?
    (b) What would you give up if you had five fewer hours of free time to use in those three days?
    (c) Pick one of the opportunity costs on your list. What conditions might have led you to make the opposite choice? Explain.

DOCUMENT-BASED ASSESSMENT

Should the federal government spend money on space exploration?

Since the 1950s, the federal government has spent billions of dollars on its space program. While many have applauded the achievements of astronauts and space scientists, some Americans think the money could have been better spent at home.

Document A

"The fundamental goal of this vision is to advance U.S. scientific, security, and economic interests through a robust space exploration program. In support of this goal, the United States will:

• Implement a sustained and affordable human and robotic program to explore the solar system and beyond;

• Extend human presence across the solar system, starting with a human return to the Moon before the year 2020, in preparation for human exploration of Mars and other destinations;

• Develop the innovative technologies, knowledge, and infrastructures both to explore and to support decisions about the destinations for human exploration; and

• Promote international and commercial participation in exploration to further U.S. scientific, security, and economic interests."

—President George W. Bush, "A Renewed Spirit of Discovery,"
January 14, 2004

Document B

We are 50 years into the space age, and yet space travel is just as expensive as it always was. . . .

One of the primary missions of NASA should have been to drive down the cost of space travel. Instead of spending half a billion dollars on each shuttle mission, it should have diverted some of the funds to make research and development a primary focus. New materials, new fuels and innovative concepts, which would make space exploration less expensive, should have been prioritized. The space station costs upward of $100 billion, yet its critics call it a "station to nowhere." It has no clearly defined scientific purpose.

—Michio Kaku, "The Cost of Space Exploration," Forbes.com
July 16, 2009

Document C

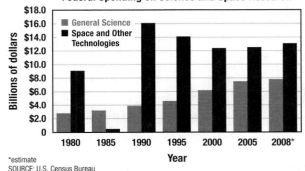

Federal Spending on Science and Space Research

*estimate
SOURCE: U.S. Census Bureau

 LA.1112.1.6.2, LA.1112.6.3, MA.912.A.2.2

ANALYZING DOCUMENTS

Use your knowledge of opportunity costs and Documents A, B, and C to answer questions 1–3.

1. **According to Document A, the primary goal of the American space program should be to**

   A. land humans on the moon.

   B. focus on unmanned, or robot, missions.

   C. prepare for human exploration of Mars.

   D. advance the interests of the United States.

2. **According to Document B, money for space exploration has been misspent because**

   A. shuttle missions have been unsuccessful.

   B. research has not been a primary focus.

   C. the space station has many critics.

   D. the space station remains in a fixed orbit.

3. **Document C shows that when spending on space and other technology has gone down, spending on general science research**

   A. has gone up.

   B. has gone down.

   C. has stayed the same.

   D. has surpassed it.

WRITING ABOUT ECONOMICS

Spending on programs like NASA's space exploration is an ongoing issue. Use the documents on this page and on the Web site below to answer the question: **Should the federal government spend money on space exploration?** Use the sources to support your opinion.

In Partnership

THE WALL STREET JOURNAL.
CLASSROOM EDITION

To read more about issues
related to this topic, visit
PearsonSchool.com/PHecon

2 Economic Systems

Essential Question, Chapter 2

How does a society decide who gets what goods and services?

Economics *on the go*

To study anywhere, anytime, download these online resources at *PearsonSchool.com/PHecon* ▶

NGSSS

LA.1112.1.6 Use multiple strategies to develop vocabulary.

LA.1112.6.2 Use a systematic process to collect, process, present information.

SS.912.E.1.3 Compare how various economic systems answer "What to produce"?

SS.912.E.2.1 Identify and explain broad economic goals.

ECONOMIC DICTIONARY

As you read the section, look for the definitions of these **Key Terms:**

- economic system
- factor payment
- profit
- safety net
- standard of living
- innovation
- traditional economy

Guiding Question

What goals and values affect how a society answers the key economic questions?

Copy this chart and fill it in as you read.

Economic Systems		
Answer Three Key Questions	**Based on Economic Goals**	**Types**
• What to produce	• Efficiency	•
•	•	•
•	•	•

▶ **Economics and You**   When you go to a supermarket, you see rows of shelves stacked with a wide variety of foods and household products. But imagine that the government limited your choice to just one brand of cereal and one brand of soap. Or imagine that the only goods available to you were what you and your neighbors could grow or make yourselves. All of these examples represent ways that different societies have dealt with the challenge of meeting people's needs and wants.

Principles in Action Each society faces three questions about the production and consumption of goods and services. As you'll see, these questions shape our freedom of choice—and also shape what we have to choose from.

Three Key Economic Questions

Resources are scarce everywhere. As a result, every society must answer three key economic questions:

- What goods and services should be produced?
- How should these goods and services be produced?
- Who consumes these goods and services?

The way a society answers these three questions defines its economic system. An **economic system** is the structure of methods and principles a society uses to produce and distribute goods and services.

economic system the structure of methods and principles that a society uses to produce and distribute goods and services

Visual Glossary
(online)

Go to the Visual Glossary Online for an interactive review of **incentives.**

Action Graph
(online)

Go to Action Graph Online for animated versions of key charts and graphs.

How the Economy Works
(online)

Go to How the Economy Works Online for an interactive lesson on **innovation and the economy.**

What Goods and Services Should Be Produced?

Each society must decide what to produce in order to satisfy the needs and wants of its people. While all people need food and shelter, societies face additional important considerations. Which consumer goods should we produce? How much of our resources should we devote to national defense, education, or consumer goods? Because resources are limited, each decision that a society makes about what to produce comes at an opportunity cost.

How Should Goods and Services Be Produced?

A society must also decide how to produce goods and services. What fuel should we use to generate electricity—oil, solar power, or nuclear power? Is education best delivered through public schools or private schools?

Although there are many ways to produce goods and services, all require land, labor, and capital. These factors of production can be combined in different ways. For example, look at **Figure 2.1**. Before the introduction of modern farming equipment, producing 15 bushels of wheat may have required 56 hours of labor, 1 acre of land, and simple hand tools. Today, mechanical equipment makes farming more efficient. Farmers can use just 2.9 hours of labor to produce 40 bushels of wheat on that same acre of land. While the amount of land used remains the same, labor has gone down, and the amount of capital needed has gone up.

These decisions involve trade-offs, too. What else could the society produce with those 56 hours of work in the time of hand tools? What could today's society make if the capital employed as mechanized farm equipment were used in some other way?

Who Consumes Goods and Services?

Societies also make decisions that determine how goods and services are consumed. How can people meet their

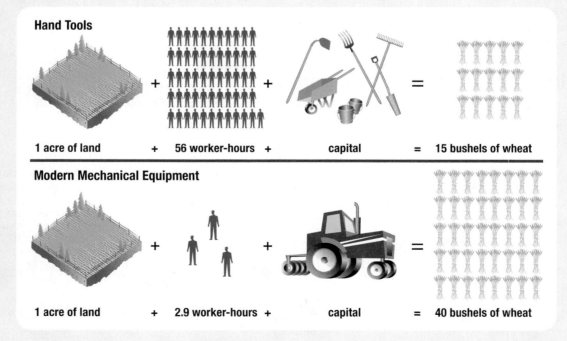

Figure 2.1 **Combining Factor Resources**

GRAPH SKILLS

Today, capital—not land—dominates the production of many goods, such as wheat.

1. Which method of production shown here is more efficient? Explain.

2. What factor of production would probably need to change in order for farmers using hand tools to produce as many bushels of wheat as farmers using machinery?

Hand Tools

1 acre of land + 56 worker-hours + capital = 15 bushels of wheat

Modern Mechanical Equipment

1 acre of land + 2.9 worker-hours + capital = 40 bushels of wheat

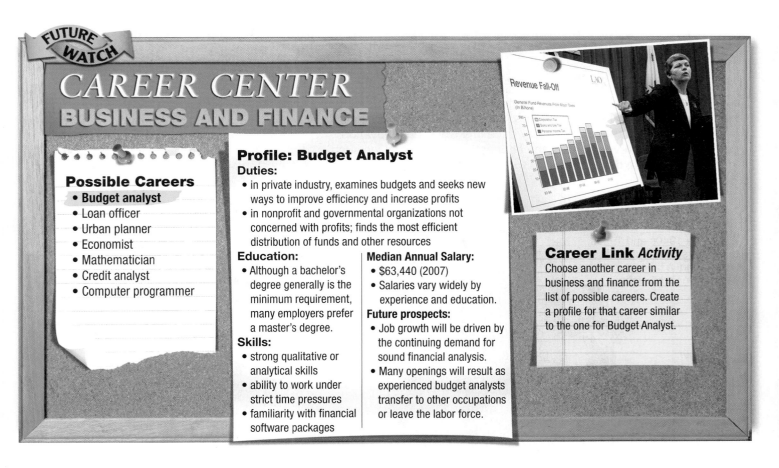

CAREER CENTER
BUSINESS AND FINANCE

Revenue Fall-Off

General Fund Revenues From Major Taxes
(in Billions)

☐ Corporation Tax
☐ Sales and Use Tax
■ Personal Income Tax

Possible Careers
- Budget analyst
- Loan officer
- Urban planner
- Economist
- Mathematician
- Credit analyst
- Computer programmer

Profile: Budget Analyst

Duties:
- in private industry, examines budgets and seeks new ways to improve efficiency and increase profits
- in nonprofit and governmental organizations not concerned with profits; finds the most efficient distribution of funds and other resources

Education:
- Although a bachelor's degree generally is the minimum requirement, many employers prefer a master's degree.

Skills:
- strong qualitative or analytical skills
- ability to work under strict time pressures
- familiarity with financial software packages

Median Annual Salary:
- $63,440 (2007)
- Salaries vary widely by experience and education.

Future prospects:
- Job growth will be driven by the continuing demand for sound financial analysis.
- Many openings will result as experienced budget analysts transfer to other occupations or leave the labor force.

Career Link *Activity*
Choose another career in business and finance from the list of possible careers. Create a profile for that career similar to the one for Budget Analyst.

---

needs for food and medical care? Who gets to drive a new luxury car and who can only afford bus fare? Who gets access to a college education?

The answer to such questions is largely determined by how societies distribute income. **Factor payments** are the income people receive in return for supplying factors of production—land, labor, or capital. Landowners collect rent, workers earn wages, and those who lend money receive payments called interest. Factor payments also include the profits that entrepreneurs earn if their enterprises succeed. **Profit** is the amount of money a business receives in excess of its expenses. Profits are the rewards entrepreneurs receive for taking the risk of starting a business.

How much should we pay the owners of the factors of production? How do we decide how much teachers should earn versus how much doctors should earn? The answers to such questions tell us a great deal about a society's values.

✔ **CHECKPOINT** *What are the three key economic questions?*

Economic Goals and Societal Values

Different societies answer the three economic questions based on the importance they attach to various economic goals. These goals include efficiency, freedom, security, equity, and growth. All societies pursue each of these goals to some degree.

Economic Efficiency

Because resources are always scarce, societies try to maximize what they can produce using the resources they have. If a society can accurately assess what its people need and want, it increases its economic efficiency. A manufacturer would be wasting resources producing desktop computers if people prefer laptops.

The goal of reducing waste also involves the second and third economic questions. Producers seek better ways to create goods and to make them available to consumers. An economy that cannot deliver the right goods in the right quantity to the right people at the right price is not efficient.

factor payment the income people receive in return for supplying factors of production

profit the amount of money a business receives in excess of its expenses

How can innovation lead to economic growth?

New resources, new inventions, new processes, new ways of doing business—all of them are innovations. Some innovations are small and limited in their effects. But every once in a while, an innovation comes along that revolutionizes the economy and society. One such innovation was the development of the microchip.

1 In the 1940s and 1950s, computers were huge. Most were found in military installations or university labs.

2 By the early 1960s, American scientists had developed the first microchips. Information could be stored in smaller and smaller spaces.

The Way Things Were

The Innovation

Personal Finance
For tips on achieving economic security through saving and retirement planning, see your Personal Finance Handbook in the back of the book or visit **PearsonSchool.com/PHecon**

safety net a set of government programs that protect people who face unfavorable economic conditions

Economic Freedom

Most people value the opportunity to make their own choices. Still, people all over the world face limitations on their economic freedom.

Americans face limitations as well. But in general, individual freedom is a key cultural value for Americans. We prize the freedom to buy what we can pay for, to seek work where we want, to own property, and to become entrepreneurs.

Economic Security

Most people do not like uncertainty. We want to know that we can get milk or bread every time we go to the grocery store. We want the security of knowing that we will get our paychecks every payday. Ideally, economic systems seek to reassure people that goods and services will be available when needed and that they can count on receiving expected payments on time.

We also want the security of knowing that help is available if we are in need. Many governments provide a **safety net,** or set of programs to protect people who face unfavorable economic conditions such as layoffs, injuries, or natural disasters. Most modern nations also provide some level of base income for retired persons to ensure that they can support themselves.

Economic Equity

Equity, or fairness, is another economic goal that is defined differently in different societies. Each society must decide how to divide its economic pie. Should everyone get the same share of the goods and services a nation produces? Or should one's consumption depend on how much one produces? How much should society provide for those who are unable or unwilling to produce?

3 By the 1980s, computers got smaller and cheaper to manufacture. The home computer had arrived...and ushered in a new period of economic growth.

New Markets: The home computer gave millions of buyers and sellers access to the Internet. Online marketing revolutionized the world economy.

New Goods: Hundreds of products on the market—from MP3 players to GPS systems—make use of microchip technology.

New Services: The home computer gave rise to related businesses, such as computer stores and computer repair services.

Check Your Understanding
1. Why was the microchip a turning point in the development of the Computer Age?
2. Describe another technological innovation that led to the creation of new goods or services.

Economic Growth

Economic Growth

A nation's economy must grow with its population so it can provide jobs for the new people joining the workforce. A nation's economy must grow if people are going to have more income. When that occurs, the nation improves its **standard of living,** or level of economic prosperity.

Innovation plays a huge role in economic growth. **Innovation** is the process of bringing new methods, products, or ideas into use. During the Industrial Revolution of the 1700s and 1800s, innovations in technology increased the efficiency of production and introduced new goods and services. Many problems arose, such as harsh conditions in factories and crowded cities, as well as increased pollution of air and water. Yet, the Industrial Revolution also sparked economic growth and led to an overall rise in standards of living. Today, innovations in computer and networking technology are changing how people work, do business, find information, and communicate.

Goals in Conflict

A society may value other goals than these. Environmental protection, full employment, or protecting national industries may be among a nation's chief economic goals.

Sometimes, economic goals conflict with one another. For example, when a society provides a safety net for all citizens, the added cost may slow economic growth. To protect the environment, a government may impose regulations on manufacturers which curb economic freedom. Thus, all nations must prioritize their economic goals, or arrange them in order of importance. Each choice comes with some kind of trade-off.

✔ **CHECKPOINT** *What are two examples of economic goals?*

standard of living level of economic prosperity

innovation the process of bringing new methods, products, or ideas into use

▲ Traditional economies exist in pockets of the modern world. Like earlier generations, this Peruvian woman makes a living producing fine textiles.

traditional economy
an economic system that relies on habit, custom, or ritual to decide the three key economic questions

 LA.1112.1.6.1, LA.1112.2.2.2, SS.912.E.1.3, SS.912.E.2.1

Traditional Economies

Societies have developed four different economic systems to address the three key economic questions. Each system reflects a different prioritization of economic goals. It also reflects the values of the societies in which these systems are found.

The oldest and simplest of economic systems is the traditional economy. A **traditional economy** relies on habit, custom, or ritual to answer the three key economic questions. There is little room for innovation or change.

The traditional economic system revolves around the family unit—often an extended family made up of several generations. Work tends to be divided along gender lines. Boys tend to take up the occupations of their fathers, while girls follow those of their mothers.

Traditional economies are usually found in communities that tend to stay relatively small and close. Often people in these societies work to support the entire community, rather than just themselves or their immediate families. In these societies, agricultural and hunting practices usually lie at the center of people's lives, laws, and religious beliefs.

Societies with traditional economies are economically successful if they meet their own needs. But they have few mechanisms to deal effectively with the effects of environmental disaster, such as a flood or drought. They also tend to be slow to adopt new ideas or technology. They may not have access to a wide range of goods. In most cases, these communities lack modern conveniences and have a relatively low standard of living.

In the next three sections, you will explore three economic systems that have dominated the modern world. They are the free market economy, the centrally planned economy, and the mixed economy.

✔ **CHECKPOINT** *What are the chief economic activities in a traditional economy?*

SECTION 1 ASSESSMENT

Essential Questions Journal To continue to build a response to the Essential Question, go to your **Essential Questions Journal**.

❓ Guiding Question

1. Use your completed chart to answer this question: What goals and values affect how a society answers the key economic questions?

2. **Extension** Describe how you think today's American society answers the three key economic questions.

Key Terms and Main Ideas

3. What is an **economic system**?

4. Why aren't all workers paid the same amount in **factor payments** for the resources they provide?

5. How does an entrepreneur make a **profit**?

6. Why does a government provide a **safety net** for its people?

7. What must happen for a nation's **standard of living** to improve?

8. What is likely to be the role of agriculture in a **traditional economy**?

Critical Thinking

9. **Illustrate** A clothing designer releases a new line of jeans. Show how the three economic questions are answered in the process.

10. **Analyze (a)** Why would it be inefficient for a manufacturer to produce audio cassettes instead of CDs today? **(b)** What resources would be wasted?

11. **Explain (a)** What types of investments on the part of manufacturers result in growth? **(b)** How does this help improve a nation's standard of living?

12. **Apply** Which basic economic goals can be achieved easily in a traditional economy? Which cannot? Explain.

Math Skills

13. It takes 14.5 hours to produce 200 bushels of wheat on five acres of land. **(a)** How many bushels could be produced on 23 acres? **(b)** Assuming the number of workers remains the same, how long would it take?

Visit PearsonSchool.com/PHecon for additional math help.

NGSSS

LA.1112.1.6 Use multiple strategies to develop vocabulary.

SS.912.E.1.3 Compare how various economic systems answer "What to produce"?

SS.912.E.2.1 Identify and explain broad economic goals.

SS.912.E.2.3 Research the contributions of key individuals of various backgrounds in the development of the U.S.

ECONOMIC DICTIONARY

As you read the section, look for the definitions of these **Key Terms:**

- market
- specialization
- free market economy
- household
- firm
- factor market
- product market
- self-interest
- incentive
- competition
- invisible hand
- consumer sovereignty

Guiding Question
What are the characteristics of a free market economy?

Copy this concept web and fill it in as you read. Add more ovals if necessary.

- Voluntary exchanges take place in markets
- **Free Market Economy**
- Needed because no one is self-sufficient

▶ **Economics and You**   Do you value freedom? If you thought about this question in terms of freedom of speech or freedom of religion, you probably said yes. What about the freedom to own property, get a job, or spend your money the way you want? To Americans, economic freedom is also highly valued. It has shaped the system under which we live.

Principles in Action Economic freedom is the chief characteristic of a free market economy. In this section, you will see how the free market affects every household and community, including yours. You will also see how one entrepreneur used the free market to make a fortune selling something many of us buy and use every day—cosmetics.

Why Markets Exist

What do a farmer's market, a sporting goods store, the New York Stock Exchange, and a community bulletin board where you posted a sign advertising baby-sitting services have in common? All are examples of markets. A **market** is any arrangement that allows buyers and sellers to exchange things. Markets eliminate the need for any one person to be self-sufficient. None of us produces all we require to satisfy our needs and wants. You probably did not grow cotton plants, process that cotton into cloth, or weave that cloth into the shirt you are wearing. Instead, you purchased your shirt at a store. Markets allow us to exchange the things we have for the things we want.

market any arrangement that allows buyers and sellers to exchange things

How do both of these pictures represent markets? ▼

Specialization

Instead of being self-sufficient, each of us specializes in a few products or services. **Specialization** is the concentration of the productive efforts of individuals and businesses on a limited number of activities. A baker specializes in making breads, cakes, and cookies. A nurse specializes in caring for the sick. An aircraft plant manufactures planes, not refrigerators.

Specialization leads to efficient use of capital, land, and labor. It is easier for people to learn one task or a few tasks very well than to learn them all. Because they concentrate on one or a few tasks, they can do their work more efficiently, saving resources by avoiding waste. For this reason, the top performers in most fields are specialists who have worked hard to sharpen their particular skills.

Specialization also benefits businesses. Focusing on a limited number of related products or services allows them to use capital and labor more efficiently.

Buying and Selling

Without specialization, markets would not be necessary. However, because each of us specializes in producing just a few goods or services, we need a mechanism that allows us to sell what we have produced and buy what we want.

In a modern market-based economy, people typically earn income by specializing in particular jobs. They then use this income to buy the products that they want to consume.

 CHECKPOINT *Why do markets exist?*

Free Market Economy

In a **free market economy,** answers to the three key economic questions are made by voluntary exchange in markets. The choices made by individuals determine what gets made, how it is made, and how much people can consume of the goods and services produced. Individuals and businesses make their own decisions about what to buy or sell. Market economies are also called capitalist economies because the capital that entrepreneurs invest in businesses is a vital part of the system.

In a free market system, individuals and privately owned businesses own the factors of production, make what they want, and

---

Innovators

Mary Kay Ash

"Pretend that every single person you meet has a sign around his or her neck that says, 'Make me feel important.'"

This philosophy helped Mary Kay Ash become one of the most successful American entrepreneurs.

In 1963, Ash used her life savings of $5000 to launch her "dream" company in Dallas. Her business plan for Mary Kay Cosmetics was simple but powerful. The firm trained women to sell quality cosmetics from their homes. Because sellers brought the product directly to busy homemakers, the firm was able to keep costs down. Ash motivated top achievers with incentives like diamond-studded bumblebee pins and pink luxury cars.

The dream became a hugely successful reality. Today, Mary Kay, Inc., boasts $2.5 billion in retail sales and 1.7 million sales reps in more than 30 countries. It is on *Fortune's* list of most admired companies.

At a time when males dominated the business world, Mary Kay Ash helped create wealth for hundreds of women, annually handing out over $50 million in sales commissions. And she made each of them feel important.

Critical Thinking *How did free market economics allow Mary Kay Ash to succeed?*

Fast Facts

Mary Kay Ash
Born: May 12, 1918, in Hot Wells, TX
Died: Nov. 22, 2001
Education: One year at the University of Houston
Claim to Fame: Founder of Mary Kay Cosmetics

Figure 2.2 Circular Flow Model of a Market Economy

Product Market

Monetary Flow

Physical Flow

Households pay firms for goods and services.

Firms supply households with goods and services.

Households

Households supply firms with land, labor, and capital.

Firms

Physical Flow

Monetary Flow

Firms pay households for land, labor, and capital.

Factor Market

GRAPH SKILLS
A circular flow model shows the interactions between households and firms in the free market.

1. What is the primary item that changes hands in the monetary flow?

2. Give one example from your own life of an exchange that takes place in the factor market.

Action Graph
online

For an animated version of this graph, visit
PearsonSchool.com/PHecon

buy what they want. In other words, individuals answer the three key economic questions of what to produce, how to produce it, and who consumes what is produced.

Households and Firms

The participants in a free market economy are households and firms. A **household** is a person or group of people living in a single residence. Households own the factors of production—land, labor, and capital. They are also consumers of goods and services.

A business, or **firm,** is an organization that uses resources to produce a product or service, which it then sells. Firms transform inputs, or factors of production, into outputs, or goods and services.

We can represent the exchanges that take place in a free market economy in a diagram called a circular flow model. Look at **Figure 2.2.** The diagram shows how households and firms exchange money, resources, and products in the marketplace. The inner ring of the diagram represents the flow of resources and products. The outer ring represents the flow of money.

Factor and Product Markets

As you can see from the lower half of the circular flow model, firms purchase factors of production from households. This arena of exchange is called the **factor market.** Firms purchase or rent land. They hire workers, paying them wages or salaries for their labor. They also borrow money from households to purchase capital, paying households interest or profits in return.

Now look at the top half of the circular flow model. The arena in which households buy the goods and services that firms produce is the **product market.**

If you follow the rings of the diagram, you will see that households purchase the products made by firms with the money they received from firms in the factor market. The flow between the factor market and the product market is truly circular.

✔ **CHECKPOINT** *What is the role of firms in the free market economy?*

household a person or group of people living in a single residence

firm an organization that uses resources to produce a product or service, which it then sells

factor market the arena of exchange in which firms purchase the factors of production from households

product market the arena of exchange in which households purchase goods and services from firms

Reviewing Key Terms
To understand *incentives,* review these terms:

entrepreneur, *p. 5*
labor, *p. 5*
profit, *p. 25*
free market economy, *p. 30*
self-interest, *p. 33*

What are Incentives?

◄ **incentive** the hope of reward or fear of penalty that encourages a person to behave in a certain way

The free market system is based on self-interest. Buyers want affordable goods and services, and entrepreneurs want profits. Employees want good pay, and employers want labor. Incentives influence people to behave in their own self-interest. *Choose one example from this chart and explain how positive and negative incentives lead to the same behavior.*

Positive Incentive
- Higher grades make it easier for Andre to get into a good college.
- Andre's parents promise him concert tickets if he improves his grades.

Negative Incentive
Andre's parents threaten to ground him if his grades continue to slump.

Response
Andre spends more time studying.

Positive Incentive
State government offers tax credit for commuters who use public transportation.

Negative Incentive
State raises gasoline taxes.

Response
Gas consumption drops as many workers take the bus rather than drive.

"WELL OF COURSE YOU OUTPERFORMED ME. THE INCENTIVES WERE STACKED IN YOUR FAVOR."

◄ The phrase 'carrot-and-stick' refers to the idea that a mule driver can make a donkey move forward either by dangling a carrot in front of him or by hitting him in the back with a stick. *How is the carrot in this cartoon an incentive?*

Visual Glossary
online
To expand your understanding of this and other key economic terms, visit **PearsonSchool.com/PHecon**

The Self-Regulating Nature of the Marketplace

How is it that firms and households cooperate to give each other what they want—factor resources, in the case of firms, and goods and services, in the case of households? After all, we live in a competitive society. According to Adam Smith, it is, in fact, competition and our own self-interest that keep the marketplace functioning.

Self-Interest

Adam Smith was a Scottish social philosopher who, in 1776, published a book titled *The Wealth of Nations*, in which he described how markets function. Smith observed that an economy is made up of countless individual transactions. In each of these exchanges, the buyer and seller consider only their **self-interest**, or an individual's own personal gain. Smith observed:

> ❝Give me that which I want, and you shall have this which you want.... it is in this manner that we obtain from one another the far greater part of those good [services] which we stand in need of. It is not from the benevolence of the butcher, the brewer, or the baker that we expect our dinner, but from their regard to their own interest.❞
>
> —Adam Smith, *The Wealth of Nations*

Self-interest, in other words, is the motivating force in the free market—the push that leads people to act.

Competition

Consumers, pursuing their self-interest, have the incentive to look for lower prices. An **incentive** is the hope of reward or fear of penalty that encourages a person to behave in a certain way. Many incentives are monetary, or based on money, such as the promise of higher wages or profits. Others are non-monetary, such as the prestige and personal satisfaction one gets from running a successful business.

Adam Smith observed that people respond in a predictable way to both positive and negative incentives. Consumers, for instance, will respond to the positive incentive of lower prices by buying more goods, because spending less money on a good lowers the opportunity cost of the purchase.

Firms, meanwhile, seek to make higher profits by increasing sales. Let's take, for example, a shirt manufacturer. The manufacturer finds that striped shirts are far outselling polka-dotted shirts. The manufacturer has the incentive—from more potential sales and profits—to produce more striped shirts. Other manufacturers, seeing consumers' desire for striped shirts, also have the incentive to make those shirts.

Now consumers can get all the striped shirts they want—but what will it cost them? What if all these producers charged high prices for those shirts so they could maximize their profits? The fact that there are so many producers prevents that. Suppose one manufacturer charges $30.00 for a striped shirt while the others sell them for $25.00. Consumers, pursuing their self-interest, will buy the lower-priced shirt. If the first manufacturer wants to sell any shirts, it will have to drop the price.

Economists call this struggle among producers for the dollars of consumers **competition**. While self-interest is the motivating force behind the free market, competition is the regulating force.

The Invisible Hand

Self-interest and competition work together to regulate the marketplace. Self-interest spurs consumers to purchase certain goods and services and firms to produce them. Competition causes firms to produce more and moderates their desire to raise prices. As a result, consumers get the products they want at prices that more closely reflect the cost of producing them.

All of this happens without any central planning or direction. No consumer or producer has made decisions based on what's good for the marketplace, yet the end result is a marketplace that operates efficiently. Adam Smith called this self-regulating mechanism the "invisible hand" of the marketplace.

✔ **CHECKPOINT** *Why is competition important in a free market?*

▲ Adam Smith's *The Wealth of Nations* was published the same year that the Continental Congress issued the Declaration of Independence. Both documents helped shape our way of life.

self-interest an individual's own personal gain

incentive the hope of reward or fear of penalty that encourages a person to behave in a certain way

competition the struggle among producers for the dollars of consumers

invisible hand a term coined by Adam Smith to describe the self-regulating nature of the marketplace

The Customer is King

▲ A customer is a consumer who does business with a particular firm. **What free market principle does this cartoon illustrate?**

consumer sovereignty
the power of consumers to decide what gets produced

FL SS.912.E.1.3, SS.912.E.3.6, SS.912.E.2.3, LA.1112.1.6.1, LA.1112.2.2.2, LA.1112.6.2

Advantages of the Free Market

As you saw, each society tries to achieve a variety of economic goals. Under ideal conditions, the free market meets many of these goals on its own.

1. *Economic efficiency* Because it is self-regulating, a free market economy responds efficiently to rapidly changing conditions. Producers provide only the goods and services that consumers want, and generally at prices consumers are willing to pay.

2. *Economic freedom* Free market economies have the highest degree of economic freedom of any system. Workers work where they want, firms produce what they want, and individuals consume what they want.

3. *Economic growth* Because competition encourages innovation, free markets encourage growth. Entrepreneurs are always seeking profitable opportunities, contributing new ideas and innovations.

4. *Additional goals* Free markets offer a wider variety of goods and services than any other system, because producers have incentives to meet consumers' desires. Consumers, in essence, have the power to decide what gets produced. This is called **consumer sovereignty.**

Despite the advantages of a free market economy, no country today operates under a pure, unregulated free market system. The same features that make free markets attractive also represent the weaknesses of the free market. The goals of economic equity and security are not always easy to achieve in a pure market system. In Section 4, you will read about how the free market system has been modified in order to better meet the entire array of economic goals.

✔ **CHECKPOINT** *Why does a free market economy result in the availability of a wider variety of goods and services?*

Essential Questions Journal
To continue to build a response to the Essential Question, go to your **Essential Questions Journal**.

SECTION 2 ASSESSMENT

🎯 Guiding Question

1. Use your completed concept web to answer this question: What are the characteristics of a free market economy?

2. **Extension** Give two examples of how an incentive influenced your behavior in your community, in school, or as a consumer.

Key Terms and Main Ideas

3. How does **specialization** make us more efficient?

4. What is the difference between a **household** and a **firm?**

5. How do **self-interest** and **competition** affect the free market?

6. Explain what Adam Smith meant by the "invisible hand" of the marketplace.

Critical Thinking

7. **Infer** How can specialization benefit both buyers and sellers in a free market economy?

8. **Connect** In a free market system, how are incentives related to the principle of consumer sovereignty?

9. **Explain** Why do you think no country has a pure free market economy?

Quick Write

10. Mary Kay Ash (see the Innovators feature) said that for a person to succeed in business they need to have enthusiasm, discipline, a willingness to work, determination, and an appreciation of others. Write a short essay in which you prioritize these qualities from most important to least important in terms of achieving success as an entrepreneur.

SECTION 3 Centrally Planned Economies

FL) NGSSS

LA.1112.1.6 Use multiple strategies to develop vocabulary.

SS.912.E.1.3 Compare how various economic systems answer "What to produce"?

SS.912.E.2.4 Diagram and explain the problems of government-instituted wage and price control.

SS.912.E.3.6 Draw conclusions about historical economic theories of economists.

ECONOMIC DICTIONARY

As you read the section, look for the definitions of these **Key Terms:**

- centrally planned economy
- command economy
- socialism
- communism
- authoritarian

Guiding Question

What are the characteristics of a centrally planned economy?

Copy this chart and fill it in as you read.

Features	Disadvantages
• Government owns all factors of production • •	• Results in poor quality goods, shortages, and falling production • •

Characteristics of Centrally Planned Economies

▶ **Economics and You**   Suppose you lived in Cuba. Each month, the government would give you cards entitling you to buy a set amount of food at low prices. However, this amount often will not last the entire month. To buy enough food for the rest of the month, you would need to pay much higher prices. If you are like most Cubans, this is difficult because your salary is low. Even if you had money, you might not be able to buy the food you want because shortages are common.

Why is the situation in Cuba so different from that in the United States? One reason is that the two countries have different economic systems. Cuba does not have a market economy, but a centrally planned one.

Principles in Action   The chief characteristic of an economy like Cuba's is the level of government control. In this section, you will see how the ideas of central planning were carried out in two powerful nations.

How Central Planning Works

In a **centrally planned economy,** the government, rather than individual producers and consumers, answers the key economic questions. A central bureaucracy decides what items to produce, how to produce them, and who gets them. The government owns both land and capital. In a sense it owns labor, too, because it controls where people work and what they are paid. The government directs workers to produce a certain number of trucks, so many yards of cotton fabric, and so on. Farmers are told what to plant and where to send their crops.

Centrally planned economies, also known as **command economies,** operate in direct contrast to free market systems. Command economies oppose private property, free market pricing, competition, and consumer choice. Free market forces of self-interest and competition are absent.

To see how such an economy works, we will follow the decision-making process for the production of uniforms for members of the military and the production of sweaters for consumers.

1. The top planners decide that more military uniforms than sweaters will be made. They send this decision to the materials committee.

centrally planned economy an economic system in which the government makes all decisions on the three key economic questions

command economy another name for a centrally planned economy

socialism a range of economic and political systems based on the belief that wealth should be distributed evenly throughout a society

communism a political system in which the government owns and controls all resources and means of production and makes all economic decisions

authoritarian describes a form of government that limits individual freedoms and requires strict obedience from its citizens

2. Knowing how much cotton is available, the materials committee decides how many uniforms and sweaters to produce. They send their decision to the makers of cotton, buttons, and elastic.

3. The cotton, the buttons, and the elastic arrive at factories, where they are used to make uniforms and sweaters.

Clearly, there is no consumer sovereignty under centrally planned economies. Many people might need new sweaters but be unable to buy them because the sweaters were not produced.

☑ **CHECKPOINT** *Who makes key decisions in a centrally planned economy?*

Socialism and Communism

The terms most often linked to central planning are socialism and communism. Though often used interchangeably, the terms actually describe different systems.

Socialism

Socialism is not a single economic system. Rather, the term describes a range of economic and political systems based on the belief that wealth should be evenly distributed throughout society. Economic equity, socialists argue, can exist only if the centers of economic power are controlled by the government or by the public as a whole, rather than by individuals or corporations.

In some nations, such as Sweden, socialism coexists with free market practices. Under this "market socialism," the government uses its powers of taxation to redistribute wealth and provide extensive services. Other socialists stress government ownership of the means of production. They consider socialism to be an intermediate stage between capitalism and communism.

Communism

In the 1800s, socialism gave rise to communism. Under **communism,** the central government owns and controls all resources and means of production and makes all economic decisions.

Communism derived largely from the writings of German philosopher Karl Marx. Unlike Adam Smith, who stressed the mutually beneficial relations between producers and consumers, Marx stressed the conflict between labor and capital. He believed that labor was the source of all value. But under capitalism, he said, all the profit created by the labor of workers ended up in the hands of capitalists, such as factory owners:

> **❝**Capitalist production...develops technology and the combining together of various processes...only by sapping the original sources of all wealth — the soil and the laborer.**❞**
> —Karl Marx, *The Communist Manifesto*

The inevitable result of capitalism, Marx argued, was the exploitation of workers and an unfair distribution of wealth.

Marx and later communists believed that a socialist society could only result from a violent revolution. While countries with socialist economies can be democratic, communist governments have always been authoritarian. **Authoritarian** governments limit individual freedoms and require strict obedience from their citizens. Every communist nation has been dominated by a single dictator or political party.

☑ **CHECKPOINT** *What beliefs did Karl Marx hold about capitalism?*

Shortages were a recurring problem in the Soviet Union. Consumers would often wait in long lines at stores, only to discover there was nothing to buy. ▼

Two Communist Economies

During the twentieth century, communist revolutions occurred in several countries. The histories of two of these nations, the Soviet Union and China, reveal key features of centrally planned economies.

The Soviet Union

In 1917, revolutionaries toppled the Russian government. This marked the beginning of what became the Soviet Union, the world's first communist state. In 1928, Soviet leader Joseph Stalin imposed the first in a series of strict five-year plans to boost industrial and agricultural production. Until it broke up in 1991, the Soviet Union continued to operate as a command economy.

Soviet economic planners sought to build national power and prestige. They allocated the best land, labor, and capital to the armed forces and to heavy industry. Heavy industry requires large capital investment and produces goods, such as chemicals or steel, used in other industries. The decision to favor heavy industry had a harsh effect on factories that made consumer goods. They were stuck with leftover, lower-quality resources. As a result, the goods available to consumers were few in number and poorly made. Severe shortages were common.

Agriculture faced similar problems. Farmers were forced to work on large, state-run farms. The government supplied all materials and set all wages. The results were often disastrous. While Russia had been a major exporter of wheat, the Soviet Union could not always produce enough grain to feed its own people.

Heavy industry and military might helped make the Soviet Union a world superpower, especially after World War II. But in time, economic weaknesses contributed to the fall of communism and the collapse of the state.

China

Like Russia, China adopted central planning as the result of a communist revolution. From 1949 to the late 1970s, government planners controlled every aspect of the Chinese economy.

▲ The communist government of China used posters like these to encourage laborers to work harder and produce more. *What kind of incentive might a poster like this offer workers?*

At first, the communist government allowed some farmland to remain in private hands while it focused on building industry. The government tried to build small factories to produce goods to be sold in nearby areas. But these goods were expensive to make and of very poor quality.

In the 1950s, the government forced many peasants onto farming communes. Within a few years, farm production dropped sharply. Facing shortages, the government eased its control over decisions made by workers on the communes. They also sent many factory workers to work on farms. The food crisis was solved, but China's economy continued to stumble.

Chinese leaders began to institute new economic policies in the 1970s. They gave farmers the chance to own more land and offered bonuses to factory managers for making better quality products. As a result, China's economy began to grow.

Today, the Chinese government still owns firms in major industries. Government planners control many key economic decisions. Still, China allows entrepreneurs far more economic freedom than in the past. Such changes have given a tremendous boost to China's economy.

✔ **CHECKPOINT** *What changes led to economic growth in China?*

Disadvantages of Centrally Planned Economies

Simulation *Activity*

Who Decides?
You may be asked to take part in a role-playing game about decision making in a traditional, free market, and command economy.

Despite the differences between centrally planned and free market economies, the two systems share many of the same basic goals. However, nations with centrally planned economies have often had trouble meeting these goals in practice.

1. *Economic efficiency* In a centrally planned economy, the government owns all production factors. Since the government fixes wages, workers lack the incentive to work faster or produce more. The large, complex bureaucracy needed to make thousands of economic decisions hurts efficiency as well. It is expensive to run and lacks the flexibility to adjust quickly to consumer demands and changing economic conditions.

2. *Economic freedom* Traditionally, command economies sacrifice individual freedoms in order to pursue societal goals. Sometimes, the results have been brutal: millions of peasants were killed in Stalin's drive to reform Soviet agriculture. But even in better circumstances, central planning discourages competition and takes most or all economic choices away from producers and consumers.

3. *Economic growth* Innovation is a key to economic growth. Command economies, however, do not tend to reward innovation—in fact, they discourage change. Managers must follow an approved government plan. There is no profit incentive to encourage entrepreneurship.

4. *Economic equity* In theory, a major goal of communism is to increase equity by distributing goods and services fairly. Such equity has proven rare, though. Government officials and people in favored careers enjoy higher incomes and access to a wider variety of higher quality goods. Ordinary people often suffer shortages and poorly made goods.

5. *Additional goals* Central planning has successfully met some goals. It can guarantee jobs and income. It can also be used to jump-start selected industries. For example, Stalin's five-year plans did increase output in heavy industries.

The disadvantages of central planning have caused leaders in many countries to move away from command economies and toward mixed economies. In the next section, you will read about today's mixed economies.

✔ **CHECKPOINT** *Why do centrally planned economies tend not to be efficient?*

FL SS.912.E.3.6, SS.912.E.3.5, LA.1112.1.6.1, LA.1112.2.2.2

SECTION 3 ASSESSMENT

Essential Questions Journal To continue to build a response to the Essential Question, go to your **Essential Questions Journal.**

Guiding Question

1. Use your completed chart to answer this question: What are the characteristics of a centrally planned economy?
2. **Extension** Suppose you were showing around a new arrival from Cuba or China. Where might you go in order to point out the differences between their economic system and ours?

Key Terms and Main Ideas

3. What does a **centrally planned economy** oppose that a market economy encourages?
4. How do **socialism** and **communism** differ?
5. What characterizes an **authoritarian** government?

6. Explain why each of the following goals is difficult to achieve in a centrally planned economy: **(a)** economic freedom, **(b)** economic growth.

Critical Thinking

7. **Infer** Which economic goal do you think was most important to Karl Marx: efficiency, growth, or equity? Explain.
8. **Explain (a)** What was the benefit of the Soviet Union's decision to concentrate on heavy industry? **(b)** What was the opportunity cost of this decision? Who paid it?
9. **Draw Conclusions** Who benefits and who suffers most from a centrally planned economy? How?

Math Skills

10. Look at the chart below. **(a)** What percentage of China's manufacturing employees live in urban units? In town/village units? **(b)** Compare the compensation of the two units. **(c)** What does this chart show you about China's economy?

Visit PearsonSchool.com/PHecon for additional math help.

Salary of Manufacturing Workers in China, 2002

Worker Category	Average Number of Workers	Annual Salary per Worker (in U.S. dollars)
All	100,610,000	1,252
Urban units	29,980,000	2,071
Town/village units	70,620,000	904

SOURCE: U.S. Bureau of Labor Statistics

NGSSS

LA.1112.1.6 Use multiple strategies to develop vocabulary.

SS.912.E.1.3 Compare how various economic systems answer "What to produce"?

SS.912.E.2.1 Identify and explain broad economic goals.

SS.912.E.2.2 Use a decision-making model to analyze public policy issues in the student's community.

SS.912.E.2.4 Explain the rationale of government-instituted price control.

SS.912.E.3.5 Compare the current U.S. economy with other developed nations.

ECONOMIC DICTIONARY

As you read the section, look for the definitions of these **Key Terms:**

- laissez faire
- private property
- mixed economy
- economic transition
- privatization
- free enterprise system

Guiding Question

What are the characteristics of a mixed economy?

Copy this chart and fill it in as you read.

Mixed Economies	
Elements of Market System	**Elements of Centrally Planned System**
• Private property • • • •	• Government involved in factor market • • •

▶ **Economics and You** As an American, you expect a high degree of economic freedom. But that does not mean you can walk into a convenience store after school and buy a pack of cigarettes. It doesn't mean that you, as a high school student, can get a part-time job operating a forklift in a factory. And it sure doesn't mean that you get to decide whether or not to pay taxes! Why not?

Principles in Action Most economies today—including ours—blend a market system with elements of central planning. You will see why governments step in to provide for your defense or fulfill other needs. In the Economics & You feature, you will see how government regulations prevent you from freely buying certain items in the marketplace.

The Rise of Mixed Economies

Every economic system has problems. Traditional economies have little potential for growth or change. Centrally planned economies stifle innovation, do not adequately meet consumer needs, and limit freedom. Even free market economies, with all their advantages, have drawbacks.

Reasons for Government Involvement

Early free market thinkers such as Adam Smith believed that, left alone, the free market would provide the greatest benefit for consumers and raise the standard of living. They favored **laissez faire,** the doctrine that government generally should not intervene in the marketplace. Yet even Smith acknowledged the need for a limited degree of government involvement.

Since Smith's time, government intervention has increased for several reasons. First, some needs of modern society would be difficult to meet in the marketplace. How well, for example, could a free market provide for national defense or highway systems? In addition, governments supply some needs in order to ensure that all members of society can benefit. For instance, a society could rely solely on private schools to educate its children. But then some families could not afford to send their children to school. To make sure that all members of society receive a basic education, the government provides public schools.

laissez faire
the doctrine that government generally should not intervene in the marketplace

▲ Defense is one type of service that a government can supply more effectively than the free market can.

private property
property that is owned by individuals or companies, not by the government or the people as a whole

mixed economy a market-based economic system in which the government is involved to some extent

Governments also play a role in the economy by protecting property rights. For instance, the Fifth and Fourteenth amendments to the Constitution declare that no person may be deprived of "life, liberty, or property, without due process of law." These amendments protect **private property,** or property owned by individuals or companies and not by the government or the people as a whole. As you will see in Chapter 3, private property is a fundamental element of the American economic system.

Finally, governments try to make sure that exchanges in the marketplace are fair. For instance, laws require businesses to give honest information to consumers or block firms from joining together to prevent competition and fix prices.

For all of these reasons, no nation today has a pure free market economy or a pure command economy. Instead, most modern economies are mixed. A **mixed economy** is a market-based economic system in which the government is involved to some extent. The degree of government involvement varies from nation to nation.

Balancing Needs and Freedom

As you have seen, every society must assess its values and prioritize its economic goals. Some goals are better met by the open market, while others may be better achieved through government action. In addition, societies must evaluate the opportunity cost of pursuing each goal.

What are you willing to give up? Are you willing to pay taxes to fund the army? To give money to people who lose their jobs? To give all people an education? In a mixed economy such as ours, questions like these can spark a heated debate.

✓ **CHECKPOINT** *What is one reason the government plays a role in the economy?*

Circular Flow Model of a Mixed Economy

To illustrate accurately how most modern economies work, we must add government to our circular flow diagram **(Figure 2.3)**. Government enters this flow in a variety of ways.

Figure 2.3   Circular Flow Model of a Mixed Economy

GRAPH SKILLS

This circular flow model shows how government typically interacts with households and firms in the marketplace.

1. According to this model, how does government affect the monetary flow in a mixed economy?

2. Give one real-life example of how government can interact with a firm in the product market.

Action Graph
online

For an animated version of this graph, visit
PearsonSchool.com/PHecon

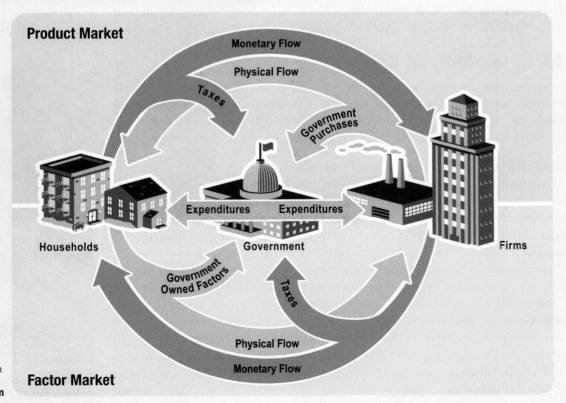

Figure 2.4 — Continuum of Mixed Economies

Centrally Planned → **Free Market**

North Korea · Iran · China · Cuba · Russia · Mexico · South Africa · Germany · Poland · France · Japan · United Kingdom · Canada · United States · Hong Kong · Singapore

GRAPH SKILLS

The degree of government intervention in the marketplace varies among nations.

1. Choose two nations on this continuum. Based on this diagram, write one sentence for each nation describing how its economic system differs from that of the United States.
2. Why is China a little bit farther to the right on this diagram than Cuba?

Government in the Factor Market

As you saw in **Figure 2.2,** firms purchase land, labor, and capital from households in the factor market. The same is true of governments. For example, the U.S. government pays 2.7 million employees $152.2 billion a year for their labor. State and local governments also employ large numbers of people. Every time a police officer gets a paycheck, a government is buying labor in the factor market.

Government in the Product Market

Like households, governments purchase goods and services from firms in the product market. Government offices need telephones and computers. Printing money requires many tons of paper and gallons of ink. The vast majority of these purchases are made from private firms.

Governments also provide certain goods and services by combining the factor resources they bought. The federal, state, and local governments for example, have used concrete, steel, and other products to build nearly 4 million miles of roads.

Transferring Money

As the outer ring of **Figure 2.3** shows, governments collect taxes from both households and businesses. Governments then transfer some of this money to businesses and individuals for a variety of reasons, such as providing funds to save a failing industry or making payments to disabled workers. The greatest such expenditure of the United States government is Social Security.

 CHECKPOINT *How are governments involved in the product market?*

Comparing Mixed Economies

As you read in Section 1, most modern economies are mixed economies. Governments are involved to some degree, but more in some cases than others. You can see these differences in **Figure 2.4,** which shows a continuum of mixed economies in today's world. A continuum is a range of possibilities with no clear divisions between them.

Mixed Economies Where Government Intervention Dominates

North Korea represents one extreme of the continuum. Like the former Soviet Union, communist North Korea has an

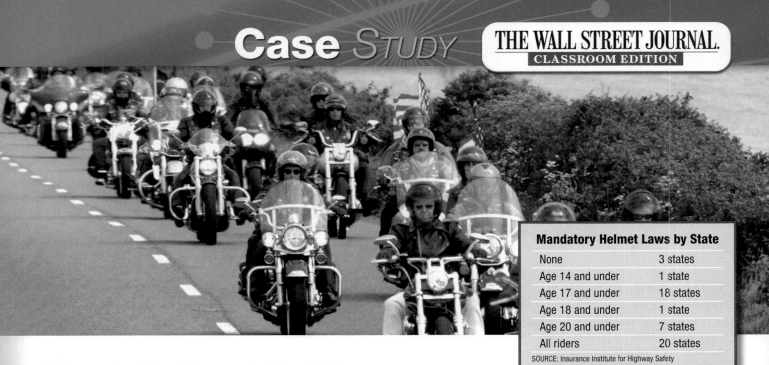

Mandatory Helmet Laws by State	
None	3 states
Age 14 and under	1 state
Age 17 and under	18 states
Age 18 and under	1 state
Age 20 and under	7 states
All riders	20 states

SOURCE: Insurance Institute for Highway Safety

Head-to-Head Battle

GOVERNMENT INTERVENTION

Policy makers are often called upon to weigh people's freedom of choice against concerns for their safety. Making such decisions requires a close examination of trade-offs—the basis of all economic analysis.

By Karen Lundegaard
The Wall Street Journal

 LA.1112.2.2 Use the text to answer questions.

His name is Sputnik. He wears his hair in a Mohawk. He has five earrings dangling from his left ear. And he's helping to write your state's safety laws.

Sputnik and other biker-lobbyists like him are fighting, state by state, for what they see as freedom on the road—the right to ride a motorcycle without a helmet. Others see it as an assault on safety and common sense.

Over nearly three decades, bikers have pushed successfully to weaken or eliminate helmet laws in 29 states. Since 1997, five states—Texas, Florida, Pennsylvania, Kentucky and Arkansas—have repealed laws requiring all motorcycle riders to wear helmets. Federal statistics show that, on average, in the years after the recent legislative changes, helmet use dropped, and motorcycle deaths increased.

That isn't slowing Sputnik, however. He has traveled to 39 states in recent years to motivate bikers with what he calls his "Five Steps to Freedom," a primer that begins with registering biker voters and aims ultimately at putting them in office.

Many bikers complain that helmets make it harder to see and hear and that they are too hot in the summer. Some motorcyclists also argue that researchers manipulate statistics to show that helmets save lives.

The statistical case for helmet laws seems solid, according to analysis of government figures. In each state that recently repealed its mandatory helmet law, motorcycle deaths have more than doubled, sometimes in as short a span as three years.

Nationally, motorcycle deaths rose 12% in 2003, to 3,661. That is the sixth straight year motorcycle deaths have risen, and the largest annual percentage increase since 1988. The national fatality rate increased 4.4%, to 6.82 deaths per 10,000 motorcycles, the highest such figure since 1990. That rate is four-and-a-half times as high as the auto-fatality rate.

Anti-helmet activists argue that the statistics can be manipulated and that a helmet's weight can actually make injuries worse, by bringing more force to bear on the rider's neck in a crash. Some surgeons and scientists reject that assertion as unsubstantiated.

Even so, Sputnik counters that "the government has no right to protect us from ourselves. They are to protect us from enemies, both domestic and foreign, and we are not our enemies."

Applying Economic Principles
How does the debate over helmet laws represent a conflict between different goals? Which goal do you think should be given a higher priority?

Video News Update Online
Powered by
The Wall Street Journal
Classroom Edition

Use videos at **PearsonSchool.com/PHecon** as a springboard for a discussion on a current topic.

economy almost totally dominated by the government. The government owns all the property and all economic output. State-owned industries produce 95 percent of North Korea's goods. Nearly all imports from other countries are banned, and production of goods and services by foreign companies is forbidden.

In China, the government long dominated the economy. But, as you read in Section 3, China's economy has been changing to allow more private ownership of farms and businesses. As a result, China's place on the continuum is closer to the center than that of North Korea.

Like many nations that have relied heavily on central planning in the past, China is now going through **economic transition,** a period of change in which a nation moves from one economic system to another. In China's case, the transition involves privatizing state-owned firms. **Privatization** is the process of selling businesses or services operated by the government to individual investors, and then allowing them to compete in the marketplace. As you will read in Chapter 18, economic transition is a difficult, and often painful, process.

Mixed Economies Where the Free Market System Dominates

At the other end of the continuum, with one of the world's freest markets, is Hong Kong. Hong Kong, once administered by Great Britain, is now a special administrative region of China. By agreement with the Chinese government, Hong Kong continues to operate largely under the free economic system it had while under British rule.

In Hong Kong, the private sector rules. The government protects private property and rarely interferes in the free market, aside from establishing wage and price controls on rent and some public services. The area is highly receptive to foreign investment and places virtually no barriers on foreign trade. Banks in Hong Kong operate independently of the government, and foreign-owned banks have nearly all the rights of domestic ones.

✔ **CHECKPOINT** *Why is China's economy more mixed than North Korea's?*

The United States Economy

While the American economy is a mixed system, the foundation of the United States economy is the free market. An economic system characterized by individual or corporate ownership of capital goods is called a **free enterprise system.** In a free enterprise system, investments in firms are made in a free market by private decision.

Government Intervention

The government of the United States plays a substantial role in the American economy. The American government keeps order, provides vital services, and promotes the general welfare. Federal and state laws protect private property. The marketplace operates with a limited degree of government regulation.

economic transition a period of change in which a nation moves from one economic system to another

privatization the process of selling businesses or services operated by the government to individual investors, and then allowing them to compete in the marketplace

free enterprise system an economic system characterized by private or corporate ownership of capital goods

Economics & YOU
Buying and Selling in a Mixed Economy

You walk into a store, put down your money, and walk away with an MP3 player. *In our free market, you can buy most goods without government interference.*

Pharmacy

A druggist can sell only medicines approved by the Food and Drug Administration. Regulations also determine what medicines can be bought only with a doctor's prescription. *In a mixed economy, the government restricts your ability to buy certain goods.*

▲ Government intervention is part of a mixed economy. *List two other goods or services that are affected by legal restrictions.*

The freedom to start a business is one of the most important features of the American free enterprise system. Magazines devoted to business topics are just one of many sources of information devoted to the needs of entrepreneurs—or people who want to be entrepreneurs. *How might a Web site or the Internet help an entrepreneur like this one?* ▶

Some Americans argue that there is a need for more government services and stricter regulation of business. Others, however, say that the government already intervenes too much in the economy. They call for relaxation of existing regulations.

Economic Freedom

Overall, the United States enjoys a high level of economic freedom. Foreign investment is encouraged. So, too, is free trade, although the government does protect some domestic industries and does retaliate against trade restrictions imposed by other nations. The banking industry operates under relatively few restrictions. Foreign-owned banks have few additional restrictions.

In the next chapter, you will read in detail about free enterprise and the economic roles of government in the United States.

✔ **CHECKPOINT** *Why is the United States said to have a free enterprise system?*

FL LA.1112.2.2.2, SS.912.E.1.3, SS.912.E.3.5, LA.1112.1.6.1, LA.1112.2.2.3, SS.912.E.2.8

Essential Questions Journal To continue to build a response to the Essential Question, go to your **Essential Questions Journal**.

SECTION 4 ASSESSMENT

🔎 Guiding Question

1. Use your completed chart to answer this question: What are the characteristics of a mixed economy?

2. **Extension** Look at **Figure 2.4** on page 41. List two reasons why the United States is where it is on the continuum.

Key Terms and Main Ideas

3. What is **laissez faire**?

4. How does the U.S. government protect **private property**?

5. Why have some nations begun an **economic transition** to a **free enterprise system**?

6. How is China carrying out **privatization**?

Critical Thinking

7. **Explain (a)** How does laissez faire differ from a centrally planned government? **(b)** Do you think a pure laissez faire system could work? Why or why not?

8. **Analyze** What benefits might citizens of a centrally planned economy derive from a move toward a market-based system? What risks might be involved?

9. **Describe (a)** Describe the type of market system in Hong Kong. **(b)** How does the system benefit entrepreneurs and investors?

10. **Contrast** Identify two ways that the American free enterprise system differs from North Korea's centrally planned system.

Quick Write

11. Sweden has a mixed economy that blends a free market with socialism. Around 56 percent of Sweden's gross domestic product is paid in taxes, compared to only 32 percent in the United States. In turn, Swedes pay very little for medical care and employers are required by law to provide a minimum of thirty days of vacation to employees. Write a brief essay comparing and contrasting the Swedish and American systems. Which do you think is more beneficial for workers?

QUICK STUDY GUIDE

Chapter 2: Economic Systems

Section 1 What goals and values affect how a society answers the key economic questions?

Section 2 What are the characteristics of a free market economy?

Section 3 What are the characteristics of a centrally planned economy?

Section 4 What are the characteristics of a mixed economy?

Essential Question, Chapter 2
How does a society decide who gets what goods and services?

Answering the Three Economic Questions

The Three Questions
- What goods and services should be produced?
- How should these goods and services be produced?
- Who consumes these goods and services?

Economic System	Three Questions Answered By:
Traditional	Habit, custom, ritual
Free market	Operation of market forces; invisible hand
Centrally planned	Government decision makers; bureaucracy
Mixed	Market forces with some government involvement

Economic Dictionary

economic system, *p. 23*

factor payment, *p. 25*

profit, *p. 25*

safety net, *p. 26*

standard of living, *p. 27*

innovation, *p. 27*

traditional economy, *p. 28*

market, *p. 29*

specialization, *p. 30*

free market economy, *p. 30*

household, *p. 31*

firm, *p. 31*

factor market, *p. 31*

product market, *p. 31*

self-interest, *p. 33*

incentive, *p. 33*

competition, *p. 33*

invisible hand, *p. 33*

consumer sovereignty, *p. 34*

centrally planned economy, *p. 35*

command economy, *p. 35*

socialism, *p. 36*

communism, *p. 36*

authoritarian, *p. 36*

laissez faire, *p. 39*

private property, *p. 40*

mixed economy, *p. 40*

economic transition, *p. 43*

privatization, *p. 43*

free enterprise system, *p. 43*

Economics on the go

Study anytime, anywhere. Download these files today.

Economic Dictionary online
Vocabulary Support in English and Spanish

Audio Review online
Audio Study Guide in English and Spanish

Action Graph online
Animated Charts and Graphs

Visual Glossary online
Animated feature

How the Economy Works online
Animated feature

Download to your computer or mobile device at PearsonSchool.com/PHecon

Self-Test To test your understanding of key terms and
online main ideas, visit **PearsonSchool.com/PHecon**

Key Terms and Main Ideas

To make sure you understand the key terms and main ideas
of this chapter, review the Checkpoint and Section Assessment questions and look at the Quick Study Guide on the
preceding page.

Critical Thinking

1. **Illustrate (a)** What are the
two ways that households
and firms interact in the
factor market? In the product
market? **(b)** Suppose you
were the owner of a music
store. Give three specific
illustrations of ways that your
business might interact with
households. **(c)** How might
the introduction of government into the circular flow
model affect your business?

2. **Explain (a)** Summarize Adam
Smith's attitude toward
government intervention in
the marketplace. **(b)** What are some reasons the government intervenes in a mixed economy? **(c)** Choose one
of these reasons and explain whether or not you think
Adam Smith would have approved.

3. **Evaluate (a)** List the major economic goals each
economic system tries to meet. **(b)** Choose two of the
following economic systems—traditional, free market, or
centrally planned—and explain which of the two systems
you think does the best job of achieving each goal.

4. **Predict (a)** Describe in one sentence the economic
system of the United States. **(b)** Look at **Figure 2.4.**
Describe three ways your life might change if the United

States moved either to the left or to the right on the
continuum of mixed economies.

Applying Your Math Skills

Making a Bar Graph

Per Capita Gross Domestic Product (GDP) is one statistic
economists use to measure the health of a nation's economy.
It is an estimate of the total value of goods and services
produced in a country per person. Look at the data below
and complete the activity that follows.

Visit PearsonSchool.com/PHecon for additional math help.

Per Capita GDP in U.S. Dollars, 2007

Canada	$38,200	Mexico	$12,500
China	$5,300	North Korea	$1,900
Cuba	$4,500	Poland	$16,200
France	$33,800	Russia	$14,600
Germany	$34,400	Singapore	$48,900
Hong Kong	$42,000	South Africa	$10,600
Iran	$12,300	United Kingdom	$35,300
Japan	$33,800	United States	$46,000

SOURCE: CIA World Factbook

5. Use the figures above to create a bar graph. Arrange
the countries in the order shown on the continuum in
Figure 2.4.

6. What is the per capita gross domestic product of Iran?
Of Hong Kong?

7. Which country has the highest per capita gross domestic
product? Which has the lowest?

8. How does the per capita gross domestic product of
the United States compare to those of Russia, France,
and Singapore? Express your answer as a fraction
or percentage.

9. Does this graph support the generalization that free-
market economies tend to be more efficient than
command economies? Explain.

Essential Question Activity

**Essential Questions
Journal** To respond to the chapter Essential Question,
go to your **Essential Questions Journal**.

10. Complete the activity to answer the Essential Question. **How does a society decide who gets what
goods and services?** Imagine that your class is
advising leaders of the newly formed nation, Ervola.
Many of the nation's new political leaders favor the use
of central planning, but business leaders favor a laissez
faire approach. Ervola must determine which economic
system will help it to meet the economic goals stated
in Section 1 of this chapter. Using the worksheet in
your Essential Questions Journal or the electronic
worksheet available at **PearsonSchool.com/PHecon,**
gather the following information: Before the debate,
participants should identify the economic goals and
determine how their team plans to meet each of them.

(a) For the affirmative, a student team will develop
arguments in favor of a strict command economy.

(b) For the negative, another student team will develop
arguments in favor of a totally free market economy.

11. **Modify**

(a) As a class, discuss and evaluate the arguments
given in the debate. Base your evaluation on the
logic of the arguments, the analysis the speakers
used, the evidence, the organization of the
speeches, and the persuasiveness of the arguments.

(b) Present an agreed-upon economic system to
recommend to the nation of Ervola. Include the
statements that most strongly support your
decision.

Does division of labor benefit or harm workers?

During the Industrial Revolution, factories began to increase the use of machinery and to divide production into many separate, specialized tasks. Free market thinker Adam Smith and communist thinker Karl Marx had very different views on this division of labor.

Document A

"[Take] the trade of the pin-maker. A workman not educated to this business...nor acquainted with the use of the machinery employed in it...could scarce, perhaps, with his utmost industry, make one pin in a day, and certainly could not make twenty. But in the way in which this business is now carried on...it is divided into a number of branches, of which the greater part are likewise peculiar trades. One man draws out the wire, another straights it, a third cuts it, a fourth points it.... Ten persons could make among them upwards of forty-eight thousand pins in a day."

—Adam Smith, *The Wealth of Nations*

Document B

"The greater division of labor enables one laborer to accomplish the work of five, 10, or 20 laborers; it therefore increases competition among the laborers fivefold, tenfold, or twentyfold.... The special skill of the laborer becomes worthless. He becomes transformed into a simple monotonous force of production, with neither physical nor mental elasticity.... The more the division of labor and the application of machinery extend, the more does competition extend among the workers, the more do their wages shrink together."

—Karl Marx, *Wage Labor and Capital*

Document C

▲ These food service workers are using an assembly line to prepare bowls of hot soup.

 FL LA.1112.1.6.2

ANALYZING DOCUMENTS

Use your knowledge of economic systems and Documents A, B, and C to answer questions 1–3.

1. **According to Document A, what does Adam Smith consider an important benefit to the division of labor?**
   A. It produces a more skilled workforce.
   B. It increases daily production.
   C. It improves the quality of products.
   D. It creates more jobs for workers.

2. **What is the main point of Document B?**
   A. Machines produce inferior goods.
   B. Competition is good for workers.
   C. Division of labor contributes to lower wages.
   D. Division of labor and use of machinery are in conflict.

3. **Which of the following views could Document C best be used to support?**
   A. Smith's views on economic efficiency
   B. Marx's views on economic equity
   C. Marx's views on capital
   D. Smith's views on the "invisible hand"

WRITING ABOUT ECONOMICS

Use the documents on this page and on the Web site below to answer the question: ***Does division of labor benefit or harm workers?*** Use the sources to support your opinion.

In Partnership

THE WALL STREET JOURNAL.
CLASSROOM EDITION

To read more about issues related to this topic, visit
PearsonSchool.com/PHecon

Chapter **3** American Free Enterprise

? **Essential Question, Chapter 3**

What role should government play in a free market economy?

FL **Next Generation Sunshine State Standards**

Section 1: Benefits of Free Enterprise
LA.1112.1.6, SS.912.E.2, SS.912.E.2.3, SS.912.E.2.4

Section 2: Promoting Growth and Stability
LA.1112.1.6, SS.912.E.1.10, SS.912.E.1.12, SS.912.E.2.1

Section 3: Providing Public Goods
LA.1112.1.6, LA.1112.1.6.2, SS.912.E.1, SS.912.E.2.11

Section 4: Providing a Safety Net
LA.1112.1.6, LA.1112.1.6.2, SS.912.E.1.9, SS.912.E.2.1, SS.912.E.2.4

Economics
on the go

To study anywhere, anytime, download these
online resources at **PearsonSchool.com/PHecon** ▶

NGSSS

LA.1112.1.6 Use multiple strategies to develop vocabulary.

SS.912.E.2 Understand the concepts relevant to the national economy.

SS.912.E.2.3 Research the contributions of key individuals of various backgrounds in the development of the U.S.

SS.912.E.2.4 Diagram and explain the problems of government-instituted wage and price control.

ECONOMIC DICTIONARY

As you read the section, look for the definitions of these **Key Terms:**

- profit motive
- open opportunity
- legal equality
- private property rights
- free contract
- voluntary exchange
- interest group
- patriotism
- eminent domain
- public interest
- public disclosure laws

Guiding Question

What are the benefits of free enterprise?

Copy this chart and fill it in as you read.

Free Enterprise System	
Characteristics	**Benefits**
• Profit motive	• Encourages innovation
•	•
•	•
•	

▶ **Economics and You**   Picture the dozens of services and products you use every week. Somebody had to think of each one and put it into action. Somebody figured out that people would rather rent DVDs from a Web site that offers tens of thousands of choices than go to a store that offers far fewer. Somebody invented a way to send photos as well as messages with cellphones.

Now, suppose *you* had one of these brilliant ideas—or just wanted to start your own neighborhood lawn care or baby-sitting service. Could you try to put your plan into action? Since you live in the United States, you can. Every day, American entrepreneurs begin new businesses that earn profits, create jobs, and offer new goods and services.

Principles in Action   The American free enterprise system makes it possible for people who have ideas and persistence to start businesses and make them successful. In this section, you will see how one Dominican immigrant built a successful business in the highly competitive U.S. fashion industry. You will also examine the vital role that you, as a consumer, play in the free enterprise system.

Basic Principles of Free Enterprise

For centuries, people have considered the United States to be a "land of opportunity," where anyone from any background might achieve success. Indeed, this country does offer special opportunities that have allowed business people the freedom to innovate and have contributed to our overall economic prosperity. Today, there are over 22 million unincorporated

Visual Glossary
online

Go to the Visual Glossary Online for an interactive review of **free enterprise.**

Action Graph
online

Go to Action Graph Online for animated versions of key charts and graphs.

How the Economy Works
online

Go to How the Economy Works Online for an interactive lesson on **providing public goods.**

VISUAL GLOSSARY

Reviewing Key Terms

To understand *free enterprise*, review these terms:

entrepreneur, *p. 5*
profit, *p. 25*

free market economy, *p. 30*
incentive, *p. 33*
competition, *p. 33*
consumer sovereignty, *p. 34*

What is Free Enterprise?

The characteristics shown here form the foundation of the American free enterprise system. ***Choose two of the characteristics and explain how they protect your freedom of choice.***

◀ **free enterprise** an economic system in which decisions are made in a free market by private individuals and firms

○ **Private Property**

○ **Economic Freedom**

○ **Competition**

○ **Contracts**

○ **Voluntary Exchange**

○ **Self-Interest**

○ **Profit Motive**

○ **Legal Equality**

○ **Consumer Sovereignty**

Visual Glossary
online

To expand your understanding of this and other key economic terms, visit PearsonSchool.com/PHecon businesses in America, including more than 3.5 million that are owned by members of minority groups. Many of these were started by a single entrepreneur or a small group of friends or family members.

Why has America been such an economic success? Certainly the United States enjoys many advantages in resources: open land, large reserves of natural resources, and a large, talented labor supply fueled by immigrants. But a key factor has also been the American tradition of free enterprise—the social and political commitment to giving people the freedom and flexibility to try out their business ideas and compete in the marketplace. This free enterprise system has several key characteristics.

Profit Motive

The American economy rests on recognition of the profit motive as a key incentive. The **profit motive** drives individuals and businesses to make decisions that improve their material well-being. As you have read, in a centrally planned economic system, the government decides what companies will be formed and how they will be run. In a free enterprise system, business owners and managers make such choices themselves based on what will increase their profits.

Reliance on the profit motive has several benefits. It forces business owners to exercise financial discipline because they are responsible for their own success or failure. It encourages entrepreneurs to take rational risks, and rewards innovation by letting creative companies grow. It also improves productivity by allowing more efficient companies to make more money.

Open Opportunity

The American economy also benefits from a tradition of **open opportunity**, the principle that anyone can compete in the marketplace. We accept that different people and firms will have different degrees of success. At the same time, we believe that anyone who wants to start a business should have a chance. This allows economic mobility up or down: no matter how much money you start out with, you can end up wealthier or poorer depending on how your business performs.

Legal Equality

We also have a commitment to **legal equality**—the principle that everyone has the same legal rights. Legal equality benefits the economy by maximizing a country's use of its human capital. Countries that restrict the legal rights of women or minorities lose the productive potential of a large portion of their society.

Private Property

In many ways, private property is the cornerstone of the free enterprise system. **Private property rights** give people the right to control their possessions and use them as they wish. The free enterprise system allows people to make their own decisions about their own property. Personal ownership provides an incentive for property owners to use their property wisely and conserve their resources.

Freedom to Buy and Sell

The right of **free contract** allows people to decide what agreements they want to enter into. A singer can sign an agreement with any sponsor or recording company. Consumers can choose to enter a credit card agreement with any of several banks.

The right of **voluntary exchange** allows people to decide what, when, and how they want to buy and sell. They are not forced to buy or sell particular goods at particular times or at specific prices. Voluntary exchange, in turn, encourages competition. As we have seen, competition provides consumers with the choice of a larger variety of goods, most of which are sold at reasonable prices.

✔ **CHECKPOINT** *What are three key economic rights that Americans enjoy?*

The Role of the Consumer

A basic principle of the free enterprise system is that consumers have the freedom to make their own economic choices. Through voluntary exchange, consumers send a signal to businesses, telling them what to produce and how much to make. Consumers also send a signal when they do not buy a good or service. They are telling the producer that the good or service is not desirable or is priced too high.

FUTURE WATCH

Personal Finance
For tips on buying or leasing a new vehicle, see your Personal Finance Handbook in the back of the book or visit **PearsonSchool.com/PHecon**

profit motive the incentive that drives individuals and business owners to improve their material well-being

open opportunity the principle that anyone can compete in the marketplace

legal equality the principle that everyone has the same legal rights

private property rights the principle that people have the right to control their possessions and use them as they wish

free contract the principle that people may decide what agreements they want to enter into

voluntary exchange the principle that people may decide what, when, and how they want to buy and sell

interest group a private organization that tries to persuade public officials to act in ways that benefit its members

patriotism love of one's country

eminent domain the right of a government to take private property for public use

Consumers can also make their wishes known by joining an **interest group**, a private organization that tries to persuade public officials to act in ways that benefit its members. One consumer interest group is the Consumers Union, which works to persuade political leaders to pass laws to protect consumers.

Businesses form interest groups as well. For instance, the National Retail Federation represents more than 1.6 million firms, from groceries to department stores. Interest groups have also formed around many economic issues, such as taxation, land use, and aid to farmers.

✔ **CHECKPOINT** *What role do consumers play in the free enterprise system?*

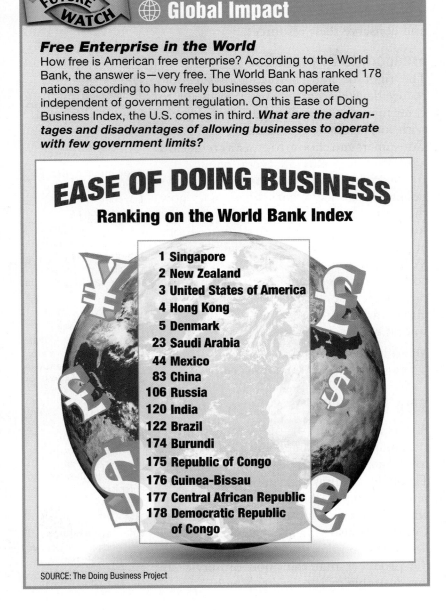

FUTURE WATCH 🌐 **Global Impact**

Free Enterprise in the World
How free is American free enterprise? According to the World Bank, the answer is—very free. The World Bank has ranked 178 nations according to how freely businesses can operate independent of government regulation. On this Ease of Doing Business Index, the U.S. comes in third. *What are the advantages and disadvantages of allowing businesses to operate with few government limits?*

EASE OF DOING BUSINESS
Ranking on the World Bank Index

1 Singapore
2 New Zealand
3 United States of America
4 Hong Kong
5 Denmark
23 Saudi Arabia
44 Mexico
83 China
106 Russia
120 India
122 Brazil
174 Burundi
175 Republic of Congo
176 Guinea-Bissau
177 Central African Republic
178 Democratic Republic of Congo

SOURCE: The Doing Business Project

Economic Freedom and the Constitution

The economic freedoms that Americans enjoy are an important source of **patriotism,** or love of one's country. The rights to own property or to become an entrepreneur are as basic to liberty as freedom of speech or the right to vote. According to a leading economist, these rights cannot be separated:

❝Economic freedom plays a dual role in the promotion of a free society. On the one hand, freedom in economic arrangements is … an end in itself. In the second place, economic freedom is also an indispensable means toward the achievement of political freedom.❞
— Milton Friedman, *Capitalism and Freedom*

Rights that allow people to engage in business activity are written into the framework of our nation: the Constitution. Perhaps the most important of these is the constitutional recognition of property rights.

Property Rights
In many countries, the government has the power to seize property for its own use. To prevent this, early American leaders protected private property under the Bill of Rights. The Fifth Amendment states that "no person shall be … deprived of life, liberty, or property, without due process of law; nor shall private property be taken for public use, without just compensation."

The Fifth Amendment was originally applied only to the federal government. The Fourteenth Amendment, ratified in 1868, extended the same limitations to the state governments.

These due process clauses prevent the government from taking property from its owner except when there is a public reason. For instance, when a state wants to add lanes to a highway, it may take land from people who own property along the route. This right of a government to take private property for public use is called **eminent domain.** Even then, the government must pay the person the fair value of the property that has been taken. This protection applies to businesses as well as to individuals.

Oscar de la Renta

Like many entrepreneurs, Oscar de la Renta had a vision—and was willing to take risks to pursue it. For this enterprising immigrant, America truly proved to be a land of opportunity.

Born in the Dominican Republic, de la Renta showed a talent for art. His parents sent him to Spain to study painting. But he became fascinated with fashion, and soon found work with a famous Spanish designer. His early career was spent designing for the rich.

In 1963, de la Renta moved to New York to work for another designer. "I came to America," he said, "because I felt the future was not [high fashion]. It was ready-to-wear." Two years later, he struck out on his own. His "off-the-rack" dresses quickly won awards. His clients have included three First Ladies and a long list of celebrities—but also thousands of middle income women.

Oscar de la Renta has never lost his interest in the arts, giving generously of his time as a board member of New York's Metropolitan Opera and Carnegie Hall. Nor has he forgotten his Latin roots. He served as chairman of the Spanish Institute, and helped build a school and day-care center for underprivileged Dominican children.

Critical Thinking: *How did the American economy provide an environment for Oscar de la Renta's success?*

Fast Facts

Oscar de la Renta

Born: July 22, 1932, in Santo Domingo, Dominican Republic

Education: Academy of San Fernando, Madrid, Spain

Claim to Fame: Successful fashion designer

Taxation

The Constitution also spells out how government can tax individuals and businesses. Congress has the power to tax only in the ways the Constitution allows.

Article I gives Congress the power to levy taxes. However, Section 9 requires that direct taxes be apportioned to states according to population. Thus, taxes collected from each state would be based on the number of people living in the state. This rule initially prevented Congress from passing an income tax, which would be a direct tax.

The Sixteenth Amendment, ratified in 1913, first gave Congress the right to set direct taxes based on income. Under current law, both individuals and corporations must pay federal income tax.

Contracts

Finally, the Constitution guarantees people and businesses the right to make contracts, which are legally binding agreements between people or businesses. Article I, Section 10 prohibits the states from passing any "Law impairing the Obligation of Contracts." This means that individuals or businesses cannot use the political process to get excused from their contracts. No legislature can pass a law changing the terms of someone's business agreement.

✔ **CHECKPOINT** *What constitutional protections make it possible for Americans to conduct business?*

The Role of Government in the Marketplace

The government's first role in the American free enterprise system is to carry out its constitutional responsibilities to protect property rights, contracts, and other business activities. Over time, Americans have come to expect the government to take other actions to promote the **public interest,** or the concerns of society as a whole. The government has passed laws to protect us from economic problems that affect us all, such as pollution or unsafe foods and medicines.

Information and Free Enterprise

In a free market system, consumer buying decisions determine what goods get produced. But consumers cannot make informed choices if they do not have

Simulation *Activity*

Whose Property Is It?
You may be asked to take part in a role-playing game about the incentives and responsibilities of owning property.

SS.912.E.2.3 Research the contributions of key individuals of various backgrounds in the development of the U.S.

public interest the concerns of society as a whole

Figure 3.1

Major Federal Regulatory Agencies

Agency and Date Created	Role
1906 Food and Drug Administration (FDA)	Sets and provides standards for food, drugs, and cosmetic products
1913 Federal Reserve System (FED)	Regulates banking and manages the money supply
1914 Federal Trade Commission (FTC)	Enacts and enforces antitrust laws to protect consumers
1933 Federal Deposit Insurance Corporation (FDIC)	Insures bank deposits, approves mergers, and audits banking practices
1934 Federal Communication Commission (FCC)	Regulates interstate and international communications by radio, television, wire, satellite, and cable
1934 Securities and Exchange Commission (SEC)	Administers federal laws concerning the buying and selling of securities
1935 National Labor Relations Board (NLRB)	Prevents or corrects unfair labor practices by either employers or unions
1958 Federal Aviation Administration (FAA)	Regulates civil aviation, air-traffic and piloting standards, and air commerce
1964 Equal Employment Opportunity Commission (EEOC)	Promotes equal job opportunity through enforcement of civil rights laws, education, and other programs
1970 Environmental Protection Agency (EPA)	Enacts policies to protect human health and the natural environment
1970 Occupational Safety and Health Administration (OSHA)	Enacts policies to save lives, prevent injuries, and protect the health of workers
1972 Consumer Product Safety Commission (CPSC)	Enacts policies for reducing risks of harm from consumer products
1974 Nuclear Regulatory Commission (NRC)	Regulates civilian use of nuclear products
1995 Surface Transportation Board (STB)	Resolves railroad rate and service disputes and reviews proposed mergers. Oversees certain trucking company, moving van, and shipping company rates

SOURCE: The White House and "Foundations of Business Administration," Professor Bauer-Ramazani

CHART SKILLS

All of these agencies represent ways the federal government intervenes in the marketplace.

1. Identify one agency meant to protect each of the following: **(a)** public safety, **(b)** fair competition, **(c)** equality.
2. How do you think the FCC promotes the public interest?

public disclosure laws laws requiring companies to provide information about their products or services

basic information about the products they are buying. In other words, educated consumers make the free market system work more efficiently. Because of this, one of the government's important roles in the economy is to make sure that producers provide consumers with information.

Toward this end, Congress has passed **public disclosure laws,** which require companies to give consumers important information about the products or services that they offer. Often this information is attached to the product when it is offered for sale. You may have seen energy efficiency tags on refrigerators, or heard car commercials in which the announcer reads off a long list of terms and conditions. Using this information, consumers can evaluate some important aspects of the products they are thinking about buying.

Other laws require businesses to make the information they supply honest and clear. The Federal Trade Commission Act says that advertisements cannot be deceptive. The Truth-in-Lending Act requires businesses offering loans to disclose certain information to consumers before they sign a loan agreement. Consumers use this information to protect themselves from false claims.

Protecting Public Health, Safety, and Well-Being

Although the government does not get directly involved in running private businesses, it does place some limits on their actions in the public interest. For example, the federal government and many states are actively involved in passing laws aimed at protecting consumers. The government sets manufacturing standards, requires that drugs be safe and effective, and supervises the conditions in which foods are produced to make sure they are sanitary. Labels on consumer packages must include information about safe operation of equipment or expiration dates for perishables.

A variety of federal and state agencies regulate industries whose goods and services affect the public interest. (See **Figure 3.1.**) For example, in response to growing public concern about the environment, the federal government formed the Environmental Protection Agency (EPA) in 1970. Businesses must follow certain rules set by the EPA or by state agencies to protect the environment. Gas stations, for example, must dispose of used motor oil properly and ensure that gas tanks cannot leak into surrounding soil.

Both individuals and businesses are subject to local zoning laws. Cities and towns often pass laws designating that certain areas can be used for residential or business purposes only. Zoning laws may forbid homeowners from running certain businesses out of their homes.

Negative Effects of Regulation

During the 1960s and 1970s, popular demand for government protection of consumers and of the environment resulted in the creation of several new governmental agencies and regulations. Government regulation, however, can have negative effects on both businesses and consumers. Businesses pointed out that the rules were costly to implement, cutting into profits and slowing growth. Highly regulated industries, such as the airlines and telephone companies, said that government rules and regulations stifled competition, resulting in prices that were unnecessarily high. The growth in government oversight of industry also raised government spending because the government had to hire workers to do the work.

In the 1980s and 1990s, public pressure for leaner, less costly government resulted in budget cuts that curtailed some government regulation of industry. Today, the

" IT LOOKS LIKE THEY'RE BRINGING IN THE NEW REGULATIONS MANUAL. "

government works to balance concerns raised by businesses with the need to protect the public.

☑ **CHECKPOINT** *Why does the government place some limits on the freedom of businesses?*

▲ Federal regulation requires the creation of complex rules and standards. *What is this cartoonist's view of federal regulation?*

(FL) LA.1112.2.2.2, SS.912.E.2, SS.912. E.2.4, LA.1112.2.2.3, LA.1112.1.6.1

Essential Questions Journal

To continue to build a response to the Essential Question, go to your **Essential Questions Journal.**

SECTION 1 ASSESSMENT

❓ Guiding Question

1. Use your completed chart to answer this question: What are the benefits of free enterprise?

2. **Extension** Identify which benefits of free enterprise you are enjoying if you **(a)** quit your job in order to take a different job at a higher salary, **(b)** buy a car from your neighbor, **(c)** sign a petition urging your county government to lower property taxes.

Key Terms and Main Ideas

3. How is the **profit motive** the driving force of the American economy?

4. How is the principle of **open opportunity** different from guaranteeing success to everyone in the marketplace?

5. How does the principle of **voluntary exchange** promote competition?

6. What is an **interest group?**

7. What kinds of information are required by **public disclosure laws?**

Critical Thinking

8. **Apply** How can inequality or discrimination hurt an economy's ability to maximize its human capital? Give two examples.

9. **Analyze** How do the decisions you make as a consumer affect the economy?

10. **Predict** What do you think might happen if the government passed a law saying it could overturn the terms of an existing contract between companies?

Quick Write

11. Create a two-column list. On one side, write the basic personal and political rights guaranteed to Americans. On the other side, list basic economic rights under the free enterprise system. Then, write a paragraph explaining in your own words how the two sets of rights are linked.

ECONOMIC DICTIONARY

As you read the section, look for the definitions of these **Key Terms**:

- macroeconomics
- microeconomics
- gross domestic product
- business cycle
- referendum
- obsolescence
- patent
- copyright
- work ethic

Guiding Question
How does the U.S. government encourage growth and stability?

Copy this flowchart and fill it in as you read. Add more boxes if necessary.

Promoting Economic Strength		
Employment	**Growth**	**Stability and Security**
• Goal: providing jobs for all able workers • Actions: steps to encourage job growth if needed	• Goal: • Actions:	• Goal: • Actions:

macroeconomics the study of economic behavior and decision-making in a nation's whole economy

microeconomics the study of the economic behavior and decision-making in small units, such as households and firms

The two major branches of economics are macroeconomics and microeconomics. **Which of these pictures represents macroeconomics? Explain.** ▼

▶ **Economics and You** Yesterday you bought a pack of gum ... or a new guitar ... or your first car. Your purchase was just one of millions of exchanges that took place across the country that day. These patterns of buying and selling are tracked by government economists who use the information to assess the state of the American economy.

Principles in Action Tracking economic data is one tool the government uses to promote economic growth and stability. As you will see, supporting education is another economic role taken by the government. You will also see how your participation in the electoral process can help to shape the economy.

Tracking Business Cycles

Even under our free enterprise system, the government intervenes to influence macroeconomic trends. **Macroeconomics** is the study of economic behavior and decision-making in a nation's whole economy. By contrast, **microeconomics** is the study of economic behavior and decision-making in small units, such as households and firms. (The prefix *macro-* means "large," while *micro-* means "small.")

GDP and the Business Cycle

One measure of a nation's economic well-being is **gross domestic product** (GDP), the total value of all final goods and services produced in a country in a given year. In a period of macroeconomic expansion, or growth, a country produces more than it did before and GDP goes up. (See **Figure 3.2.**) In a period of contraction, or decline, the country produces less and GDP goes down. This pattern of a period of expansion, or growth, followed by a period of contraction, or decline, is called a **business cycle.**

Unlike the day-to-day ups and downs of the stock market, business cycles are major fluctuations. Each phase can last months or even years. (You will learn more about GDP and the business cycle in Chapter 12.)

Making Predictions

Changes in the business cycles take place because individuals and businesses, acting in their own self-interest, make decisions about factors such as prices, production, and consumption. Business owners who think consumers are going to spend more in the future may increase production and hire more workers. If enough employers take these steps, the economy grows. On the other hand, concern about rising prices might lead consumers to buy fewer goods. If this decrease in consumer spending is widespread and lasts long enough, suppliers might be forced to cut production and lay off workers.

In Washington, armies of government economists track where the country is in the business cycle and try to predict what will happen in the future. They give this information to public officials so they can decide what actions to take—if any.

☑ **CHECKPOINT** *Why do government experts track the business cycle?*

Promoting Economic Strength

Because the market is vulnerable to business cycles, the government tries to create public policies that promote economic strength. Policymakers do so by pursuing three main goals: high employment, growth, and stability.

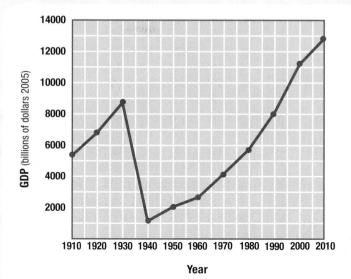

| Figure 3.2 | **Gross Domestic Product, 1910–2010** |

SOURCE: Louis D. Johnston and Samuel H. Williamson, "What Was the U.S. GDP Then?" MeasuringWorth.Com, 2010.

GRAPH SKILLS

A growing GDP is one sign of a healthy economy.

1. How much did the GDP grow between 1910 and 2010?
2. Which periods on this graph may represent downturns in the business cycle?

Action Graph *online*

For an animated version of this graph, visit **PearsonSchool.com/PHecon**

Employment

One aim of government economic policy is to ensure jobs for everyone who is able to work. In the United States, many economists consider an unemployment rate of between 4 percent and 6 percent to be evidence of a healthy economy. If the unemployment rate rises higher than that, government officials may take steps to encourage job growth.

Economic Growth

Part of the American Dream has always been for each generation to enjoy a higher standard of living than that of previous generations. For that to happen, the economy must grow to provide additional goods and services to succeeding generations. An increasing GDP is a sign of such growth. To help growth, the government may cut taxes or increase spending. Experts often disagree as to which approach stimulates economic growth more effectively.

FL SS.912.E.1.12 Examine the four phases of the business cycle.

gross domestic product the total value of all final goods and services produced in a country in a given year

business cycle a period of macroeconomic expansion, or growth, followed by one of contraction, or decline

referendum a proposed law submitted directly to the public

Stability and Security

The government also seeks to keep the economy stable. Consumers, producers, and investors need to feel confident that economic conditions will not fluctuate unpredictably. If this confidence wavers, economic growth may slow or even stop.

One indicator of economic stability is the general level of prices. A surge in overall prices puts a strain on consumers, especially poor people and those on fixed incomes. But if prices sink, producers feel the pain. For example, a jump in the price of milk hurts families with children, while a plunge in milk prices hurts dairy farmers. Either way, major fluctuations in price levels can send problems across the economy. The government thus seeks to prevent sudden, drastic shifts in prices.

Another sign of economic stability is the security of our financial institutions, such as banks or the stock market. Imagine going to the bank and finding it boarded up and empty. When we make a bank deposit or a stock purchase, we want to know that our money will be protected from fraud or mismanagement and shielded from the damaging effects of sudden economic downturns.

To provide such protections, the federal government monitors and regulates banks and other financial institutions. Some regulations protect bank deposits and retirees' pensions. Federal regulators also investigate fraud and manage interest rates and the flow of money through the economy. You will learn more about these functions in later chapters.

Economic Citizenship

Economic policy is made by elected officials and the workers they appoint. But it is the voters who put these officials in office. On a state and local level, voters have an even more direct say. Ballots often include **referendums,** proposed laws submitted directly to the public, on spending or other economic issues.

Voters, then, play a vital role in shaping government economic actions. Like others in a market economy, voters make choices based on self-interest. To fully determine what policies best serve their interests, Americans must understand the macroeconomic processes that shape our futures.

☑ **CHECKPOINT** *What three goals does the government try to meet when promoting economic strength?*

The people you elect will make vital decisions that affect your economic well-being. In addition, you may be asked to vote directly on important economic issues. *What will you need to know in order to make sensible choices?* ▼

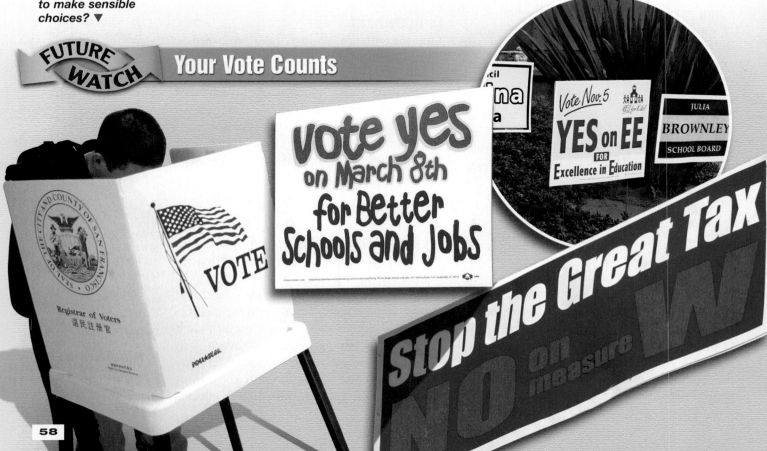

FUTURE WATCH **Your Vote Counts**

vote yes on March 8th for Better Schools and Jobs

Vote Nov. 5 YES on EE for Excellence in Education

JULIA BROWNLEY SCHOOL BOARD

Stop the Great Tax NO on measure W

CAREER CENTER
CONSTRUCTION AND MAINTENANCE

Possible Careers
- Brick mason and stonemason
- Carpenter
- Inspector
- **Electrician**
- Elevator installer and repairer
- Sheet metal worker
- Structural and reinforcing iron and metal worker

Profile: Electrician
Duties:
- install wiring systems in new homes and businesses
- maintain and upgrade existing electrical systems and repair electrical equipment

Education:
- Apprenticeship programs that combine on-the-job training with related classroom instruction.

Skills:
- good math and English skills
- manual dexterity and hand-eye coordination
- physical fitness
- good sense of balance

Median Annual Salary:
- $44,780 (2007)

Future prospects:
- Jobs are expected to increase as fast as average for all occupations through the year 2014.
- Demand will be driven by population growth and new technologies.

Career Link *Activity*
Choose another career in the construction and maintenance trades from the list of possible careers. Create a profile for that career similar to the one for Electrician.

Technology and Productivity

The American economy supports a far higher standard of living, in terms of GDP, than most economies of the world. As you read in Chapter 1, one way to preserve that high standard is by increasing productivity—producing more outputs from the same or a smaller quantity of inputs.

Technological Progress

Improved technology is a key factor in boosting productivity. Technological progress has long enabled the economy of the United States to operate more efficiently, increasing GDP and giving American businesses a competitive advantage in the world.

American history is full of innovations that improved productivity. Thomas Edison's invention of the light bulb made a longer workday possible. Henry Ford's use of the assembly line led to mass production of affordable cars. In recent times, computers have allowed workers to do more work in a shorter amount of time.

Innovation often leads to **obsolescence,** as older products and processes become out-of-date. Workers, too, may be subject to obsolescence. One example is telephone operators who lost their jobs due to computerized dialing systems. Still, these physical and human resources can be used in other ways. Old industrial buildings can be converted into stores or apartments. Workers can be retrained to do other jobs.

The Government's Role

To help maintain the country's technological advantage, the government promotes innovation and invention. Federal agencies fund scores of research and development projects at universities. The Morrill Acts of 1862 and 1890 created land-grant colleges that received federal land and money to pursue the study of "agriculture and the mechanical arts." Land-grant schools from the Massachusetts Institute of Technology to Texas A&M University have been powerhouses of innovation.

The government's own research institutions also produce a steady stream of new technologies. Probably the best-known of these federal institutions is the National Aeronautics and Space Administration (NASA). Technologies created by NASA, as part of the effort to send satellites and humans into space, have produced amazing spin-offs, or products with commercial uses. NASA

obsolescence situation in which older products and processes become out-of-date

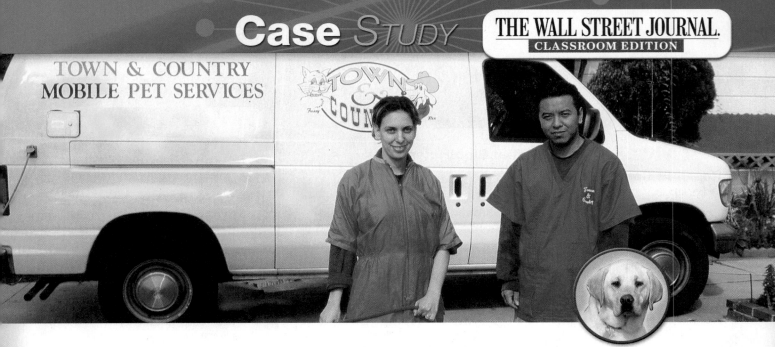

TOWN & COUNTRY
MOBILE PET SERVICES

Case STUDY

THE WALL STREET JOURNAL.
CLASSROOM EDITION

Business by the Bootstraps

ENTREPRENEURSHIP

Entrepreneurs spend a lot of their energy trying to raise capital. But there's another way.

By Kelly K. Spors
The Wall Street Journal

 SS.912.E.2.3 Research the contributions of key individuals of various backgrounds in the development of the U.S.

When Seth Riney started a hybrid-auto taxi service in Boston in 2003, he didn't pursue private investors. Instead, he found a more compatible financier: himself.

Mr. Riney traded in his 2002 Dodge Dakota pickup truck for a Toyota Prius. He kept a day job and worked early mornings and evenings ferrying around friends and family willing to pay for a lift. After a few months, he squirreled away enough money to hire his first employee and put a down payment on a second Prius. He kept adding more hybrids and more drivers as his cash stash grew.

Today, Mr. Riney's business, PlanetTran, has grown to a fleet of 35 hybrids and about 75 employees. He recently expanded his taxi service to San Francisco with the help of some inves-

tors. The company had $1.5 million in revenue in 2006, and Mr. Riney expects it will reach $4 million this year. "It was the kind of business that could grow organically without spending a lot of money in the early stages," he says.

Would-be entrepreneurs often think starting a successful business requires a large cash infusion to pay for an office, employees and professional marketing to make a cannonball splash in the market. But many are discovering the advantages of "bootstrapping"—or using little or no external capital and conserving as much cash as possible to grow the business.

Among the advantages: The fewer outside investors you take on, the less equity and control you forfeit to people who often have vastly different priorities than yours.

There are many methods that boot-strappers use to self-finance and save on cash. For starters, many tap into their own bank accounts, credit cards, and home-equity lines of credit. Of course, this is risky if the business fails. So one way to make sure you don't go broke early on is to keep a day job until the business is profitable enough to stand on its own.

Other bootstrappers do as much as possible to keep their costs low, whether it's buying used office equipment on eBay, using interns and freelancers instead of hired help or seeking out free advice. Many colleges and universities offer free and low-cost help to local entrepreneurs, such as legal or intellectual-property counseling by law students.

Video News Update Online
Powered by
The Wall Street Journal
Classroom Edition

Use videos at **PearsonSchool.com/PHecon** as a springboard for a discussion on a current topic.

Applying Economic Principles
Why would building a business through "bootstrapping" require a strong work ethic, or commitment to hard work? Give at least one example from this article or from your own knowledge.

spin-offs range from a muscle stimulator for people with paralysis to a scanner that allows firefighters to see "invisible flames" given off by alcohol or hydrogen fires.

The government also encourages innovation by granting patents and copyrights. A **patent** gives the inventor of a new product the exclusive right to produce and sell it for 20 years. A **copyright** grants an author exclusive rights to publish and sell his or her creative works. Patents and copyrights are an incentive to innovation because they protect people's right to profit from their creativity in the free market.

The American Work Ethic

While government incentives may encourage innovation, economic growth cannot occur without individual effort. When asked to account for his success in the movie and recording industries, Will Smith stated:

 I've never really viewed myself as particularly talented. I've viewed myself as slightly above average in talent. And where I excel is ridiculous, sickening work ethic. You know, while the other guy's sleeping? I'm working. While the other guy's eating? I'm working. 🙎

— Will Smith, *60 Minutes* interview

FL **SS.912.E.1.12, SS.912.E.1.10, SS.912.E.2.1, LA.1112.1.6.1, LA.1112.2.2.2**

◄ Americans patent thousands of inventions every year. These college entrepreneurs, Gavin McIntyre and Eben Bayer, created a new "green" insulation partly from mushrooms that they grew under their beds.

The **work ethic** Smith refers to is a commitment to the value of work. It not only means working hard, but also caring about the quality of one's work. The American work ethic has long been seen as a key ingredient in the nation's productivity and economic success.

✔ **CHECKPOINT** *How does improved technology help the economy?*

patent a government license that gives the inventor of a new product the exclusive right to produce and sell it

copyright a government license that grants an author exclusive rights to publish and sell creative works

work ethic a commitment to the value of work

Essential Questions Journal

To continue to build a response to the Essential Question, go to your **Essential Questions Journal**.

SECTION 2 ASSESSMENT

❓ Guiding Question

1. Use your completed flowchart to answer this question: How does the U.S. government encourage growth and stability?

2. **Extension** You are a member of Congress. Economic conditions in the country are excellent, and the economy is growing. Would you support a new spending plan aimed at providing jobs? Why or why not?

Key Terms and Main Ideas

3. Why is the government decision to increase or decrease spending a matter of **macroeconomic** policy?

4. How does **gross domestic product** provide a means to analyze economic growth?

5. Describe the **business cycle**.

6. How do **patents** act as an incentive to technological innovation?

7. How can technological innovation lead to **obsolescence?**

Critical Thinking

8. **Make Decisions** Suppose you had a job you did not like. If the economy was in the downward part of the business cycle, would you be more or less likely to quit your job to look for a better one? Why or why not?

9. **Predict** Suppose that Congress passed a bill funding research into alternative sources of energy. Which goals of governmental action in the economy would this funding meet?

10. **Analyze** Identify three individual qualities and actions that you think demonstrate a strong work ethic. Explain why you chose each one.

Math Skills

11. The chart below shows the length of periods of expansion and decline in the business cycle. Which expansion and which contraction lasted the longest? Based on this chart, how would you judge the health of the economy since 1958?

Visit PearsonSchool.com/PHecon for additional math help.

Periods of Expansion	Periods of Contraction
Apr. 1958–Apr. 1960	Apr. 1960–Feb.1961
Feb. 1961–Dec. 1969	Dec. 1969–Nov. 1970
Nov. 1970–Nov. 1973	Nov. 1973–Mar. 1975
Mar. 1975–Jan. 1980	Jan. 1980–July 1980
July 1980–July 1981	July 1981–Nov. 1982
Nov. 1982–July 1990	July 1990–Mar. 1991
Mar. 1991–Mar. 2001	Mar. 2001–Nov. 2001
Dec. 2001–Dec. 2007	Jan. 2008–June 2009
June 2009–Present	

SOURCE: National Bureau of Economic Research

FL NGSSS

LA.1112.1.6 Use multiple strategies to develop vocabulary.

LA.1112.1.6.2 Listen to, read, and discuss familiar and challenging texts.

SS.912.E.1 Understand concepts relevant to a market economy.

SS.912.E.2.11 Assess the impact of negative and positive externalities on the national environment.

ECONOMIC DICTIONARY

As you read the section, look for the definitions of these **Key Terms:**

- public good
- public sector
- private sector
- infrastructure
- free rider
- market failure
- externality

Guiding Question
Why does a society provide public goods?

Copy this chart and fill it in as you read.

Cause	Effect 1	Effect 2
• Market failure • Creating public goods	• •	• •

public good a shared good or service for which it would be inefficient or impractical to make consumers pay individually and to exclude those who did not pay

▶ **Economics and You**   You benefit from all kinds of services that federal, state, and local governments provide. You go to school, ride on roads, cross bridges, and use public parks. What would your life be like without these services? Or suppose that you could use a specific road or bridge only if your family had helped pay for it. How much would that complicate your life?

Principles in Action Even in a free market economy, the government must provide certain goods and services that the marketplace cannot. For example, you will see how the job of building a bridge would become almost impossible if it had to be done by the joint action of all the people and businesses that would benefit from it. Sometimes, the government has to step in.

Public Goods

Roads and bridges are a few of the many examples in which the government provides a public good. A **public good** is a shared good or service for which it would be inefficient or impractical (1) to make consumers pay individually and (2) to exclude those who did not pay.

Characteristics of Public Goods

Let us look at the first feature of public goods, making each consumer pay individually. How would you like to receive a bill for your share of launching a space shuttle, cleaning Mount Rushmore, or paying the salary of every soldier in the army? To simplify the funding of government projects in the public interest, the government collects taxes.

What about the second feature of a public good, excluding nonpayers? Imagine the arguments and traffic delays that would erupt if drivers who refused to pay to use a street were told they had to turn around and drive away. Also, as a society, we believe that certain facilities or services, such as libraries or protection from fire, should be available to all, rich or poor.

In the case of most public goods, it is simply not practical for a private business to provide the service, charge those who benefit, and exclude nonpayers from using the service. Take, for example, national parks like Yellowstone and Yosemite. If these parks were privately owned, the owner could charge a higher admission fee. Yet some benefits generated by the park, such as the preservation of wildlife, would be enjoyed by nonpayers

▲ Maintaining street signs and traffic lights is one economic role of the government.

as well as payers. The owner could neither charge people for that benefit nor exclude them from benefiting.

Public goods have another characteristic. Any number of consumers can use them without reducing the benefits to any single consumer. For the most part, increasing the number of consumers does not increase the cost of providing the public good. So if you are driving on a highway and eight other drivers enter it, they do not significantly reduce the road's benefits to you or increase the government's cost of providing the road.

Public goods are financed by the **public sector,** the part of the economy that involves the transactions of the government. The **private sector,** the part of the economy that involves transactions of individuals and businesses, would have little incentive to produce public goods.

Costs and Benefits

As you read in Section 1, governments step in to act in the public interest when they determine that the benefits of a policy outweigh the drawbacks, or the costs. In road construction, the benefits are obvious. Transportation is a vital part of the nation's **infrastructure,** the basic facilities that are necessary for a society to function and grow. American leaders have long regarded investment in infrastructure, not only as a means to provide needed public goods, but as a way to promote economic growth:

> ❝Whether we're talking about roads or bridges or mass transit, … sewage and water facilities, whether we're talking about broadband, or we're talking about the grid to transmit electricity, whether we're talking about schools … these infrastructure investments offer our nation job-creating opportunities to reinvigorate the American economy.❞
>
> — Nancy Pelosi, Speaker of the House, March 11, 2008

Transportation goes more smoothly when governments build roads. The drawback, though, is the economic freedom we give up. None of us individually gets to decide what roads will be built or where. In this case, the advantages clearly outweigh the drawback. In other cases, weighing benefits against costs is more complex.

Costs and benefits are critical in determining whether something gets produced as a public good. Two cost-benefit criteria must be present.

1. The benefit to each individual is less than the cost that each would have to pay if it were provided privately.
2. The total benefits to society are greater than the total cost.

If just one or a few people got together to fund the project, the cost to each of them would be much higher than the benefits each would gain. In such circumstances, the market would not provide the good.

But if you look at society as a whole, the picture changes. As long as the benefit all people gain exceeds the total cost, it makes sense for government to fund the project. From the individual's point of view, this situation is better too. The government can fund the project by collecting a small amount of money in taxes from a large number of people. That means the share paid by each person is much less than it would be if they had to fund the project alone or even through a small group.

public sector the part of the economy that involves the transactions of the government

private sector the part of the economy that involves the transactions of individuals and businesses

infrastructure the basic facilities that are necessary for a society to function and grow

These California firefighters are using expensive equipment to combat a raging forest fire. *What do you think might happen if individual consumers, rather than the government, had to pay for fire protection?* ▼

How are public goods created?

Some public goods are too costly for the free market to satisfy. In these cases, the government may intervene to provide public goods.

1 Farmers in Capp County have to drive an extra hundred miles to get their crops across the river. They want a new bridge built nearby.

Cost of new bridge: $10 million

Benefit of new bridge: $22 million

The 100 farmers would save $20,000 each.

An additional 1 million citizens would save $20 each.

Public Need

Costs and Benefits

Free-Rider Problem

A phenomenon associated with public goods is called the "free-rider problem." A **free rider** is someone who would not be willing to pay for a certain good or service, but would get the benefit of it anyway if it were provided as a public good. Unlike consumers in the free marketplace, free riders consume what they do not directly pay for.

You probably would not voluntarily contribute to build roads in a state you did not live in. Yet when the government builds and maintains a system of national roads, you share in the benefit. For example, the national road system makes it easier for trucking companies to bring goods to your state. And if you were traveling through the other state on vacation, you would certainly not refuse to drive on the road yourself. You receive the benefit whether you pay directly or not.

Try another example: Everyone on your street wants fire protection except one penny-pinching neighbor, who says it is not worth the money. Don't you want him to have fire protection anyway? If his house catches fire, yours could ignite as well. So local taxes pay for fire-fighting services for all property in an area, because all residents are better off if the government provides this service. Your free rider neighbor benefits from this service as well.

The free-rider problem suggests what would happen if the government stopped collecting taxes to fund public services. If it relied on voluntary contributions instead, many people would refuse to give money. Many public services would then have to be eliminated.

☑ **CHECKPOINT** *What two criteria must be present for a public good?*

free rider someone who would not be willing to pay for a certain good or service but who would get the benefits of it anyway if it were provided as a public good

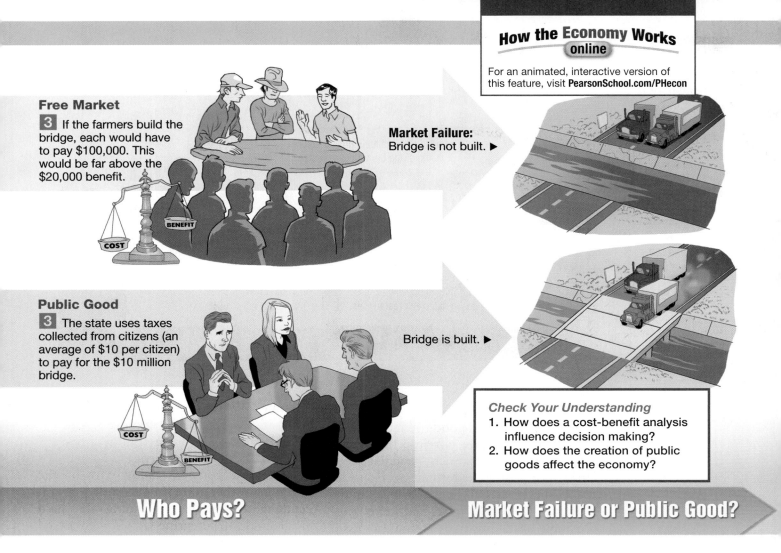

Free Market

3 If the farmers build the bridge, each would have to pay $100,000. This would be far above the $20,000 benefit.

COST / BENEFIT

Market Failure: Bridge is not built. ▶

Public Good

3 The state uses taxes collected from citizens (an average of $10 per citizen) to pay for the $10 million bridge.

COST / BENEFIT

Bridge is built. ▶

Check Your Understanding
1. How does a cost-benefit analysis influence decision making?
2. How does the creation of public goods affect the economy?

Who Pays?

Market Failure or Public Good?

Market Failures

Public goods are examples of what some economists call a market failure. The term **market failure** does not suggest that the free enterprise system does not work. Rather, it describes a specific situation in which the free market, operating on its own, does not distribute resources efficiently.

To understand market failure, recall how a successful free market operates: Choices made by individuals determine what goods get made, how they get made, and who consumes the goods. Profit incentives attract producers who, because of competition, provide goods and services that consumers need at prices they can afford.

In the road-building scenario, are these features present? No. If a company did build a road, it could charge a high price for tolls because it would have no competition. Also, companies would not choose to build roads in sparsely populated areas because they would see no chance to earn profits—a low population would mean too few drivers to charge.

As a result, the criteria for a properly functioning market system do not exist. For that reason, the road-building scenario is a market failure.

☑ **CHECKPOINT** *Why are public goods examples of market failure?*

Externalities

All of the examples above involve what economists call externalities. An **externality** is an economic side effect of a good or service that generates benefits or costs to someone other than the person deciding how much to produce or consume. Externalities may be either positive or negative.

market failure a situation in which the free market, operating on its own, does not distribute resources efficiently

externality an economic side effect of a good or service that generates benefits or costs to someone other than the person deciding how much to produce or consume

Figure 3.3 **Positive and Negative Externalities**

GRAPH SKILLS

Building a bridge creates dozens of externalities, both positive and negative, depending upon your point of view.

1. Why is use of the bridge by vacationers an externality?

2. Why would increased car traffic be considered a positive externality by some people and a negative externality by others?

In addition to its main goal of helping local farmers, the building of the Capp County Bridge creates externalities.

Positive externalities

• Bridge can be used by vacationers.
• Training local workers for bridge construction increases their job skills.
• Increased traffic improves business of local gas stations and restaurants.

Negative externalities

• Construction and traffic lowers air quality in the area.
• Local fishing industry suffers.
• Competition from bridge drives ferry company out of business.

SS.912.E.2.11 Assess the impact of negative and positive externalities on the environment.

Positive Externalities

As you read, public goods generate benefits to many people, not just those who pay for the goods. Such beneficial side effects are positive externalities. Consider the example of building a bridge in the How the Economy Works feature on page 64. Some of the positive externalities associated with the bridge are shown in **Figure 3.3**, above.

The private sector—both individuals and businesses—can create positive externalities, too. For instance:

• Walsh Computers hires underprivileged teenagers and trains them to be computer programmers. Walsh set up this training program to serve its own interests. However, the newly trained workers can be hired by other companies, who benefit from the workers' skills without having paid for them.

• Mrs. Ruiz buys an old house that is an eyesore in the neighborhood. She paints the house, cuts the grass, and plants flowers. Her neighbors were not involved in her decision, nor did they share the cost. Yet they receive benefits from it, such as higher property values and a better view.

In fact, many economists believe that the private sector generates positive externalities more efficiently than the public sector can, and at less cost to taxpayers.

Whether private or public, positive externalities allow someone who did not purchase a good to enjoy part of the benefits of that good. In the 1990s, several endangered species, including the bald eagle and the peregrine falcon, were saved from extinction. Protection of species critical to our ecosystem benefits us all.

Negative Externalities

Of course, as **Figure 3.3** shows, producing goods and services can also generate unintended costs, called negative externalities. Negative externalities cause part of the cost of producing a good or service to be paid for by someone other than the producer. For example:

• The Enchanted Forest Paper Mill dumps chemical wastes into a nearby river, making it unhealthy. The city of Tidyville, downstream from the mill, is forced to install special equipment at its water-treatment plant to clean up the chemicals. The community, not the polluter, is paying the cost of cleaning up the river.

• Your next-door neighbor, Mr. Fogler, takes up the accordion and holds Friday night polka parties in his backyard. Unfortunately, you hate polka music.

Government's Goals

Externalities are a sign of market failure because the costs or benefits of a good or service are not assigned properly. Understanding externalities helps us see another role that the government plays in the American economy.

First, the government may take action to create positive externalities. Education, for example, benefits students, yet society as a whole also benefits from an educated population. This is because educated workers are generally more productive.

Second, the government aims to limit negative externalities, such as pollution. Pollutants from coal-burning power plants and auto emissions can drift high into the atmosphere and come down in the form of acid rain, which causes ecological damage. Why is acid rain a negative externality? It is part of the cost of producing power and driving cars, but that cost was imposed upon people other than those who produce the pollution. The cost was damaged trees, lakes, and wildlife.

To address this negative externality, the federal government now requires new cars to have an expensive antipollution device called a catalytic converter. In addition, the Environmental Protection Agency offers incentives to power-plant operators to put "scrubbers" on their smokestacks to cut emissions. These actions transfer the costs of pollution back to its producers.

Government-Driven or Market-Driven Solutions?

As you saw, many economists think that the private sector produces more positive externalities than the government does. This belief has spurred debate over how to stop damage to the environment.

Since the 1970s, the government has often tried to halt pollution by creating strict regulations. Many economists say that this approach is inefficient because it increases costs. It also ties the hands of businesses by requiring specific solutions rather than encouraging innovation.

These economists want the government to allow market-driven solutions to environmental problems. In this approach, the government would still play a role by setting standards that industries would have to meet. Individual firms, though, would have more freedom to find ways to meet those goals.

✔ **CHECKPOINT** *What does the government do in response to negative externalities?*

▲ The Environmental Protection Agency tries to limit negative externalities not just by making regulations, but also by encouraging private action. *How does this poster deal with a negative externality of being a consumer?*

FL LA.1112.2.2.2, SS.912.E.1, SS.912.E.2.11, LA.1112.1.6.1, LA.1112.6.2

Essential Questions Journal — To continue to build a response to the Essential Question, go to your **Essential Questions Journal.**

SECTION 3 ASSESSMENT

? Guiding Question

1. Use your completed chart to answer this question: Why does a society provide public goods?

2. **Extension** Suppose people in your neighborhood want to have a community pool. Should the city government build the pool, or should it leave the matter up to the private sector? Explain your answer in economic terms.

Key Terms and Main Ideas

3. What are the two characteristics of **public good?**

4. What is an example of an action taken by the **public sector?** By the **private sector?**

5. Why are public goods examples of **market failure?**

6. Give an example of one positive and one negative **externality.**

Critical Thinking

7. **Analyze** Why is national defense an example of the free-rider problem?

8. **Connect** How do the concepts of limited resources and scarcity explain why the government does not try to meet all demands for providing public goods? What other factors might persuade government leaders to favor taking a more limited role in the economy?

9. **Apply** Because of the interstate highway system, transportation costs are lower. How is this an example of positive externalities?

Quick Write

10. Review the discussion about government-driven versus market-driven solutions for pollution. Write a position paper explaining which approach you favor. Make sure you take into account economic concepts such as property rights, economic freedom, economic growth, equity, efficiency, externalities, and the public good.

NGSSS

LA.1112.1.6 Use multiple strategies to develop vocabulary.

LA.1112.1.6.2 Listen to, read, and discuss familiar and challenging texts.

SS.912.E.1.9 Describe how workers' pay is determined.

SS.912.E.2.1 Identify and explain broad economic goals.

SS.912.E.2.4 Explain the rationale of government-instituted price control.

ECONOMIC DICTIONARY

As you read the section, look for the definitions of these **Key Terms**:

• poverty threshold
• welfare
• cash transfers
• in-kind benefits
• grant

Guiding Question
How does government help the poor?

Copy this chart and fill it in as you read.

Government Help for the Poor			
Cash Transfers	In-Kind Benefits	Medical Benefits	Education
• Temporary aid for needy families	•	•	•
	•	•	•
• Social Security	•	•	•
• Unemployment insurance	•	•	•
• Workers' compensation			

poverty threshold
an income level below that which is needed to support families or households

▶ **Economics and You**   You've seen it all around you: on TV shows, in the news, maybe even in your community. There are vast differences between people who have a lot of money, enough money, and very little money. On the average, Americans enjoy a high standard of living. Yet about 13 percent of Americans live in poverty. And for people under the age of 18, the number is even higher.

Principles in Action To help the poor, government programs take money from some people and redistribute it to others. Yet critics say such actions violate the economic principle of limited government intervention. The Economics & You feature shows how redistribution programs may both benefit and cost you. You will also see how the government encourages citizens like you to aid the needy.

The Poverty Problem

While the free market has proven better than any other economic system at generating wealth, that wealth is spread unevenly throughout society. This leaves some people below the **poverty threshold,** an income level below that which is needed to support families. The poverty threshold is determined by the federal government and adjusted periodically. In 2006, the poverty threshold for a single parent under age 65, with one child, was $13,896 per year. For a four-person family with two children, it was $20,444 per year.

The U.S. Bureau of the Census, part of the Department of Labor, sets the poverty threshold. It sets it at different levels, depending on the number of family members and their ages. Each year, the poverty threshold is adjusted based on the cost of the goods a family needs to buy. As prices rise, so does the poverty threshold.

Poverty conditions can exist anywhere, from city slums, to farming communities, to Indian reservations like this one. ▼

The Government's Role

As a society, we recognize some responsibilities to the very young, the very old, the sick, the poor, and the disabled. The government tries to provide a safety net for people in these groups, with help from various federal, state, and local government programs. These programs aim to raise people's standard of living, or their level of economic well-being as measured by the ability to purchase the goods and services they need and want.

The Welfare System

Since the 1930s, the main government effort to ease poverty has been to collect taxes from individuals and redistribute some of those funds in the form of welfare. **Welfare** is a general term that refers to government aid for the poor. It includes many types of programs that redistribute wealth from some people to others.

The nation's welfare system began under President Franklin Roosevelt during the Great Depression. Welfare spending greatly increased in the 1960s under President Lyndon Johnson's "War on Poverty."

Federal welfare programs came under increasing attack in the 1980s. Critics of welfare voiced increasing concern about people becoming dependent on welfare and being unable or unwilling to get off it. Some critics also claimed that income redistribution discourages productivity, thus actually aggravating poverty. In 1996, Congress responded by making sweeping changes in the welfare system. New reforms limited the amount of time people could receive welfare payments and gave states more freedom to experiment with antipoverty programs.

✔ **CHECKPOINT** *What is the goal of government welfare programs?*

Redistribution Programs

In Chapter 13, you will examine in greater detail the many causes of poverty as well as government attempts to solve the problem. Meanwhile, here is a brief overview of the major types of redistribution programs through which the federal government helps the poor, elderly, and disadvantaged.

Cash Transfers

State and federal governments provide **cash transfers**, direct payments of money to poor, disabled, or retired people. The following programs are cash transfers:

- *Temporary Assistance for Needy Families (TANF)* Launched in 1996, TANF does not provide direct federal welfare payments to the poor. Instead, federal money goes to the states, which design and run their own welfare programs. States must adhere to federal rules that create work incentives and establish a lifetime limit for benefits. TANF aims to move people from depending on welfare to joining the workforce.

welfare government aid to the poor

cash transfers direct payments of money by the government to poor, disabled, or retired people

Economics & YOU
Redistribution Programs

Campus East

Public colleges and universities often have lower tuition than private schools. *You can pay less to attend a public college, because states have redistributed tax money to support education.*

Pay Check / Social Security Tax

Social security taxes are taken out of your paycheck. *The money you pay to social security is redistributed to senior citizens so they can maintain a decent standard of living.*

▲ Redistribution of income is one way government meets people's needs. *Identify another way that the government may use your money to help somebody else.*

A Century of Federal Programs to Help Those in Need

1932 Franklin Roosevelt is elected President in the midst of the Great Depression

1950 Social Security extended to 3.5 million recipients; ADC becomes AFDC (Aid to Families with Dependent Children)

1933 Federal Emergency Relief Administration (FERA) founded

1910 1920 1930 1940 1950

1935 Congress creates Social Security, Aid to Dependent Children (ADC), and unemployment compensation

1948 Truman's Fair Deal begins

1916 Kern-McGillicuddy Act establishes workers' compensation for federal employees

SOCIAL SECURITY
000-00-0000
THIS NUMBER HAS BEEN ESTABLISHED FOR
SPECIMEN
SPECIMEN
SIGNATURE

▲ Throughout the 1990s, federal spending on social programs grew to include more and more people in need. **What are some of the trade-offs involved in spending on social programs?**

in-kind benefits goods and services provided for free or at greatly reduced prices

- *Social Security* The Social Security program was created in 1935, during the Great Depression. At the time, many elderly people lost their life savings and had no income. The program collects payroll taxes from current workers and then redistributes that money to current recipients. Those who receive Social Security include retired people, people unable to work because of a disability, and, in some cases, the widowed spouses or orphaned children of such individuals.

- *Unemployment insurance* Unemployment insurance is funded by taxes paid by employers. Compensation checks provide money to workers who have lost their jobs. Recipients must offer proof that they have made efforts to get work. As with TANF, states set the rules for this program. The program is supposed to supply only temporary help. As a result, most states pay benefits to workers for only 26 weeks.

In periods of high unemployment, however, the government may decide to pay the benefits longer.

- *Workers' compensation* This program is an insurance program for workers injured or disabled on the job. It is mandated by state law. Most employers pay workers' compensation insurance to cover future claims by employees.

In-Kind Benefits

The government also provides poor people with **in-kind benefits,** goods and services provided for free or at greatly reduced prices. One example is the food stamp program. People who qualify receive a card with a magnetic memory strip. It contains information about the value of food purchases the person is due that month. He or she can then use the card to help meet food expenses.

Another type of in-kind benefit is subsidized housing. Poor people are allowed to rent housing for less than the regular rent.

1965 Congress creates Medicare (for retirees and the disabled) and Medicaid (for the poor)

1996 AFDC changed to Temporary Assistance for Needy Families (TANF)

1974 Food Stamp program extended nationwide

1960　　1970　　1980　　1990　　2000

1964 Johnson's Great Society program expands welfare with new programs such as Head Start preschool education

2001 President Bush establishes White House Office of Faith-Based and Community Initiatives

The government pays the difference to the landlord.

Legal aid is legal advice given at no charge. This in-kind benefit covers contracts and other business matters. Poor people charged with a crime may be represented in court by public defenders, who are paid with tax dollars. (The right of an accused person to have legal counsel is guaranteed by the Sixth Amendment.)

Medical Benefits

Another social service that the U.S. government provides is health insurance for the elderly, the disabled, and the poor. Medicare covers Americans over age 65 and disabled people. Medicaid covers some poor people who are unemployed or not covered by their employer's insurance plans. Administered under the Social Security program, Medicare and Medicaid are enormously expensive programs. We will examine them further in Chapter 14.

A program called the Children's Health Insurance Program (CHIP) provides health insurance for children who are uninsured. CHIP is funded by both state and federal governments. States write the rules for the program within federal guidelines. The program covers more than 6.5 million children.

Education

Federal, state, and local governments all provide educational opportunities to those who need aid. The federal government funds programs from preschool to college. State and local programs aid students with learning disabilities.

Education programs add to the nation's human capital and labor productivity. As explained earlier in the chapter, improved education and technology can make an entire economy more productive.

✔ **CHECKPOINT** *Identify four programs that provide cash benefits to the poor.*

FUTURE WATCH

Personal Finance
For information on applying for financial aid for college, see your Personal Finance Handbook in the back of the book or visit **PearsonSchool.com/PHecon**

▲ Community programs like these help create a safety net by providing meals to senior citizens or children. *What are two ways that you can support such programs?*

grant a financial award given by a government agency to a private individual or group in order to carry out a specific task

Encouraging Private Action

In addition to providing direct assistance to the needy, federal and state governments also encourage private action. Federal tax law allows both individuals and corporations to take tax deductions for charitable donations. This policy provides an economic incentive to give money and property to relief organizations, as well as to other non-profit groups such as churches, hospitals, colleges, libraries, or museums. In 2006, American individuals and organizations gave $295 billion in deductible charitable contributions. As one tax expert noted:

> ❝It's always better to give than receive. The glory of charitable donations is that you give and receive at the same time.❞
> — Jeff Schnepper, "Give and Grow Rich With Charitable Deductions"

The government may also provide grants and other assistance to organizations that provide social services. A **grant** is a financial award given by a government agency to a private individual or group in order to carry out a specific task. Many people believe that private groups do a more effective job of helping people than the government can.

In 2001, President George W. Bush announced a controversial initiative, or new plan, that allowed religious organizations to compete for federal funds. The President believed that these groups provided a special compassion that made their programs particularly successful. Bush established an Office of Faith-Based and Neighborhood Partnerships to help religious groups work more effectively with the federal government. He also encouraged the states to create similar offices. Still, not everyone supported faith-based initiatives. Critics said that giving government money to religious organizations violated the First Amendment.

✔ **CHECKPOINT** *How does the tax law provide an incentive to help the needy?*

Essential Questions Journal To continue to build a response to the Essential Question, go to your **Essential Questions Journal**.

SECTION 4 ASSESSMENT

❓ Guiding Question

1. Use your completed chart to answer this question: How does government help the poor?

2. **Extension** Suppose you were a member of Congress during a time of economic contraction. Would you vote in favor of extending unemployment compensation payments beyond 26 weeks? Why or why not?

Key Terms and Main Ideas

3. What is the **poverty threshold?** Why does it vary according to how many people are in a household?

4. What are three examples of **cash transfers?**

5. How are unemployment insurance and workers' compensation alike?

6. What are **in-kind benefits?**

Critical Thinking

7. **Analyze** How does the TANF program seek to answer one of the common objections to the older welfare system?

8. **Make Decisions** Would it make economic sense for the government to spend money giving job training to people who receive TANF payments? Why or why not?

9. **Draw Conclusions** Do you think tax incentives are necessary to encourage charitable giving? Explain.

Math Skills

10. Assume that the poverty threshold is $13,896 per year for a family of one adult and one child. Based on a 40-hour work week, how much salary would a single parent with one child have to take home each week in order to be above the poverty threshold?

Visit PearsonSchool.com/PHecon for additional math help.

Chapter 3: American Free Enterprise

Section 1 What are the benefits of free enterprise?

Section 2 How does the U.S. government encourage growth and stability?

Section 3 Why does a society provide public goods?

Section 4 How does government help the poor?

Essential Question, Chapter 3
What role should government play in a free market economy?

Roles of the Government

Regulating Business

Examples	• Public disclosure
	• Environmental rules
	• Consumer safety

Promoting Growth

Examples	• Price stability
	• Regulation of banks
	• Patents and copyrights

Providing Public Goods

Examples	• Roads and bridges
	• Defense
	• Police and fire protection

Providing a Safety Net

Examples	• Social Security
	• Unemployment insurance
	• Medicare

Economic Dictionary

profit motive, *p. 51*

open opportunity, *p. 51*

legal equality, *p. 51*

private property rights, *p. 51*

free contract, *p. 51*

voluntary exchange, *p. 51*

interest group, *p. 52*

patriotism, *p. 52*

eminent domain, *p. 52*

public interest, *p. 53*

public disclosure laws, *p. 54*

macroeconomics, *p. 56*

microeconomics, *p. 56*

gross domestic product, *p. 57*

business cycle, *p. 57*

referendum, *p. 58*

obsolescence, *p. 59*

patent, *p. 61*

copyright, *p. 61*

work ethic, *p. 61*

public good, *p. 62*

public sector, *p. 63*

private sector, *p. 63*

infrastructure, *p. 63*

free rider, *p. 64*

market failure, *p. 65*

externality, *p. 65*

poverty threshold, *p. 68*

welfare, *p. 69*

cash transfers, *p. 69*

in-kind benefits, *p. 70*

grant, *p. 72*

Economics *on the go*

Study anytime, anywhere. Download these files today.

Economic Dictionary
online
Vocabulary Support in English and Spanish

Audio Review
online
Audio Study Guide in English and Spanish

Action Graph
online
Animated Charts and Graphs

Visual Glossary
online
Animated feature

How the Economy Works
online
Animated feature

Download to your computer or mobile device at PearsonSchool.com/PHecon

Self-Test online — To test your understanding of key terms and main ideas, visit **PearsonSchool.com/PHecon**

Key Terms and Main Ideas

To make sure you understand the key terms and main ideas of this chapter, review the Checkpoint and Section Assessment questions and look at the Quick Study Guide on the preceding page.

Critical Thinking

1. **Analyze (a)** What goals does the government hope to achieve by regulating banks? **(b)** What principles of free enterprise conflict with this regulation? **(c)** In this case, do you think the benefits of regulation outweigh the costs? Why or why not?

2. **Apply (a)** How do copyright laws protect property rights? **(b)** Some consumers download music or videos from Internet sites not authorized by the copyright holder. Do those actions violate copyright laws? **(c)** Do you think people who do this should be punishable under the law? Why or why not?

3. **Predict (a)** What are the two cost/benefit criteria that a public good must meet? **(b)** Identify which of the following you think meet this test: buying new computers for the library; building a shopping mall; building a cellphone tower. **(c)** Choose one of the above. Identify one positive and one negative externality that might result.

4. **Draw Conclusions (a)** What is the goal of government redistribution programs? **(b)** Do you think redistributing income is an appropriate role for the government to play in a free enterprise economy? Why or why not?

Applying Your Math Skills

Reading a Line Graph

Study the information in the graph below. Then, answer the questions that follow.

Visit PearsonSchool.com/PHecon for additional math help.

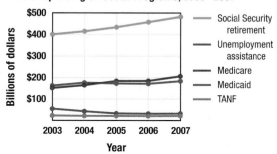

Federal Spending on Social Programs, 2003–2007

- Social Security retirement
- Unemployment assistance
- Medicare
- Medicaid
- TANF

SOURCE: U.S. Census Bureau, *Statistical Abstract of the United States*, 2008

5. Which is the most expensive of these programs? By how much does it exceed the next most expensive program in the final year shown?

6. Which two programs did not increase in cost between 2003 and 2007?

7. To find the percentage increase in spending from 2003 to 2007, you subtract the 2003 figure from the 2007 figure and then divide by the 2003 figure. The result, a decimal answer, is then converted to a percentage by multiplying by 100. Using that formula, what was the percentage increase of the three most expensive programs?

8. Which of these five programs is most likely to change with the business cycle? Why do you think so?

Essential Question Activity

Essential Questions Journal — To respond to the chapter Essential Question, go to your **Essential Questions Journal**.

9. As a citizen and a consumer, you will always be affected by the role of government in your economic life. Complete the following activity to answer the Essential Question **What role should government play in a free market economy?** For this activity, the class will be divided into four groups. Each group will look in depth at one of the following topics: government regulation; encouraging economic growth; providing public goods; providing an economic safety net. You will research your topic in print or use online news sources that illustrate the government's role. The worksheet in your Essential Questions Journal or the electronic worksheet available at **PearsonSchool.com/PHecon** lists some reliable sources and key words you can use in your search. After your group chooses a topic, prepare a brief presentation using the Summary Report form provided in your worksheet. Each group should report its findings and reactions to the whole class.

10. **Modify** After each group has completed the presentation of its findings, the entire class should evaluate the information and discuss the following questions:
    (a) Was the action taken by the government appropriate to the situation?
    (b) What other action might the government have taken?
    (c) What might have happened if the government had taken no action?
    (d) Based on this particular incident, do you think the government should have more or less influence on the economy?
    (e) Under what conditions might you feel differently?

DOCUMENT-BASED ASSESSMENT

When may a government take private property for public use?

According to the Fifth Amendment, a government may appropriate private property for public use (such as road building) as long as "just compensation" is given to the property owner. In a 2005 decision, the Supreme Court ruled that this principle of "eminent domain" also allowed a city to appropriate homes in a poor neighborhood so that developers could improve the area economically.

Document A

"The City has carefully formulated an economic development plan that it believes will provide appreciable benefits to the community, including—but by no means limited to—new jobs and increased tax revenue.... Because that plan unquestionably serves a public purpose, the takings challenged here satisfy the public use requirement of the Fifth Amendment.... Promoting economic development is a traditional and long accepted function of government."

—Justice John Paul Stevens, majority opinion, *Kelo* v. *New London*

[source: http://www.law.cornell.edu/supct/html/04-108.ZO.html]

Document B

"Under the banner of economic development, all private property is now vulnerable to being taken and transferred to another private owner, so long as it might be upgraded—i.e., given to an owner who will use it in a way that the legislature deems more beneficial to the public.... The beneficiaries are likely to be those citizens with disproportionate influence and power in the political process, including large corporations and development firms."

—Justice Sandra Day O'Connor, dissenting opinion, *Kelo* v. *New London*

Document C

RICHMOND TIMES-DISPATCH 6/05

FL LA.1112.1.6.2

ANALYZING DOCUMENTS

Use your knowledge of opportunity costs and Documents A, B, and C to answer questions 1–3.

1. **According to Document A, the majority of the Supreme Court in this case believed that**
   A. the principle of eminent domain was unconstitutional.
   B. economic development of a poor area was in the public interest.
   C. a government may take private property without offering compensation.
   D. the Fifth Amendment did not apply to this particular case.

2. **According to Document B, the use of eminent domain in this case was**
   A. justified because it would lead to improvements that were in the public interest.
   B. unjustified because it would not lead to improvements in the neighborhood.
   C. unfair because it would benefit some private citizens at the expense of others.
   D. fair because the people who lost their property would be paid for it.

3. **Which documents express similar viewpoints on the subject of eminent domain and private property?**
   A. A and B
   B. A and C
   C. B and C
   D. A, B, and C

WRITING ABOUT ECONOMICS

The Supreme Court decision in *Kelo* v. *New London* was highly controversial. Use the documents on this page and on the Web site below to answer the question: *When may a government take private property for public use?* Use the sources to support your opinion.

In Partnership

THE WALL STREET JOURNAL.
CLASSROOM EDITION

To read more about issues related to this topic, visit
PearsonSchool.com/PHecon

This databank gives you information about the economy of the United States, starting with its resources and producers. You will then take a closer look at American workers and consumers.

FL MA.912.A.2.2 Interpret a graph to represent a real-world situation.

U.S. Economy by Types of Business

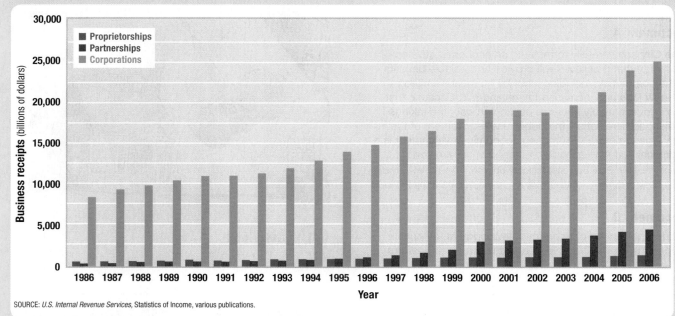

Legend:
- Proprietorships
- Partnerships
- Corporations

Y-axis: Business receipts (billions of dollars), 0 to 30,000
X-axis: Year, 1986 to 2006

SOURCE: *U.S. Internal Revenue Services*, Statistics of Income, various publications.

Number of Farms

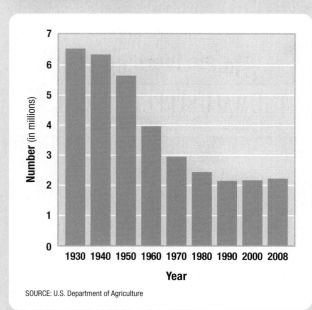

Y-axis: Number (in millions), 0 to 7
X-axis: Year, 1930, 1940, 1950, 1960, 1970, 1980, 1990, 2000, 2008

SOURCE: U.S. Department of Agriculture

Size of Farms

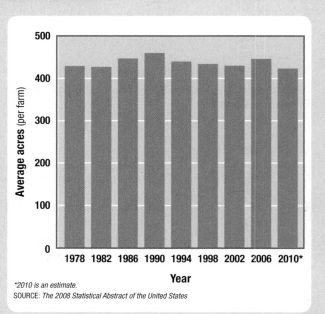

Y-axis: Average acres (per farm), 0 to 500
X-axis: Year, 1978, 1982, 1986, 1990, 1994, 1998, 2002, 2006, 2010*

*2010 is an estimate.
SOURCE: *The 2008 Statistical Abstract of the United States*

United States Economic Activity and Resources

Databank: The United States Economy

Characteristics of the United States Workforce, 2007

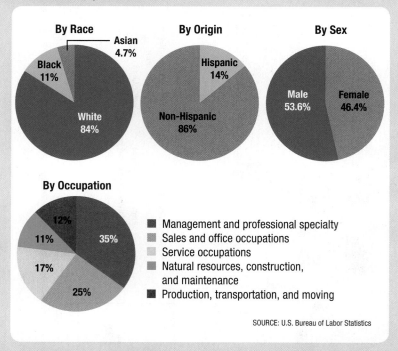

By Race
- Asian 4.7%
- Black 11%
- White 84%

By Origin
- Hispanic 14%
- Non-Hispanic 86%

By Sex
- Male 53.6%
- Female 46.4%

By Occupation
- 35% Management and professional specialty
- 25% Sales and office occupations
- 17% Service occupations
- 11% Natural resources, construction, and maintenance
- 12% Production, transportation, and moving

SOURCE: U.S. Bureau of Labor Statistics

Personal Income and Outlays

- Income
- Outlays

Dollars (in trillions) vs. Year (1990, 1993, 1996, 1999, 2001, 2004, 2007)

SOURCE: U.S. Bureau of Economic Analysis

Median Weekly Earnings, by Occupation and Sex, 2007

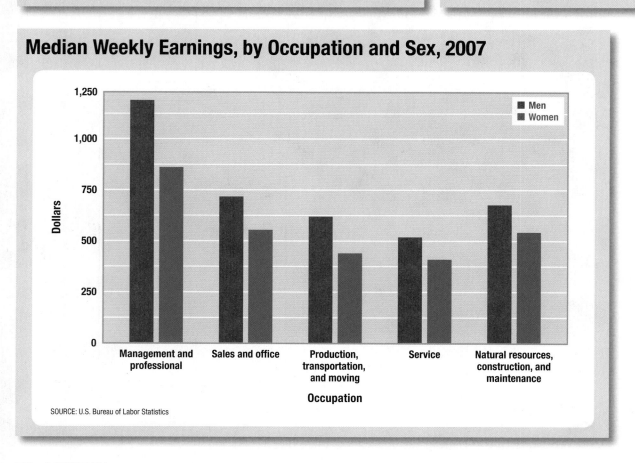

- Men
- Women

Dollars vs. Occupation (Management and professional, Sales and office, Production, transportation, and moving, Service, Natural resources, construction, and maintenance)

SOURCE: U.S. Bureau of Labor Statistics

MA.912.A.2.2 Interpret a graph to represent a real-world situation.
SS.912.E.2 Understand the concepts relevant to the national economy.

Fastest-Growing Occupations

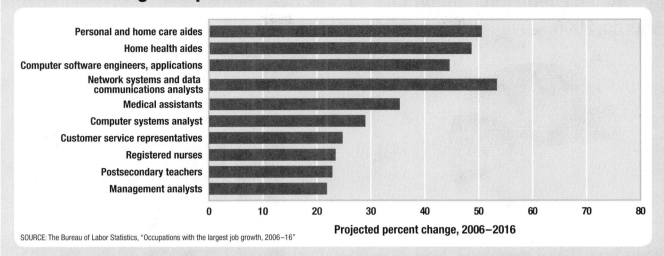

SOURCE: The Bureau of Labor Statistics, "Occupations with the largest job growth, 2006–16"

Unemployment Rates, 2007

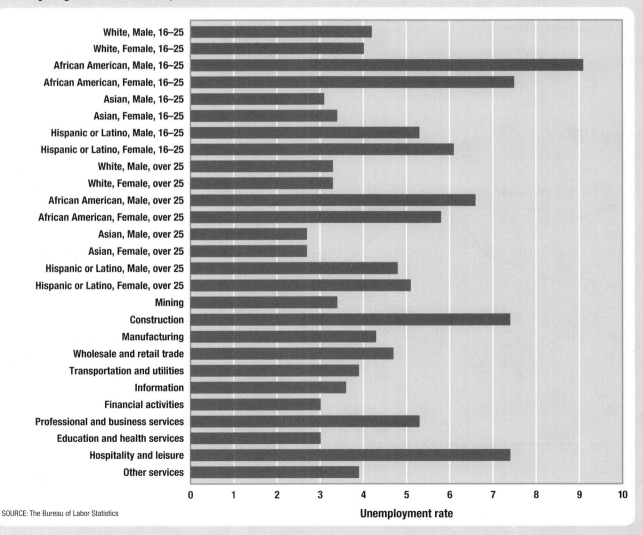

SOURCE: The Bureau of Labor Statistics

Databank: The United States Economy

United States Energy Production, by Source, 2008

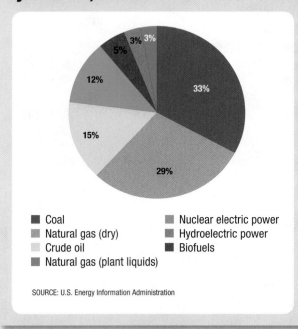

- ■ Coal
- ■ Natural gas (dry)
- ■ Crude oil
- ■ Natural gas (plant liquids)
- ■ Nuclear electric power
- ■ Hydroelectric power
- ■ Biofuels

SOURCE: U.S. Energy Information Administration

Home Ownership

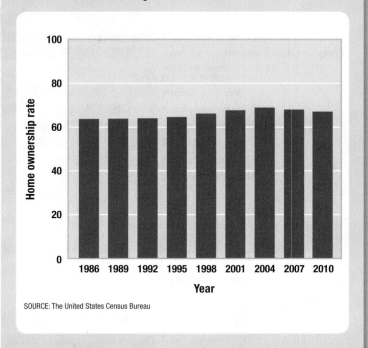

SOURCE: The United States Census Bureau

Housing Prices

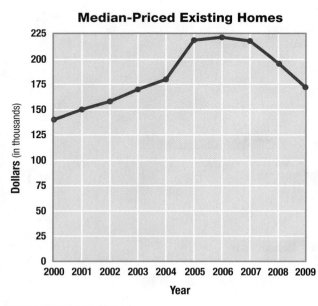

Median-Priced Existing Homes

Payment as Percentage of Median Income

SOURCE: National Association of Realtors®

FL **MA.912.A.2.2** Interpret a graph to represent a real-world situation.
SS.912.E.2 Understand the concepts relevant to the national economy.

Per Capita Retail Sales, by Type of Business, 2006

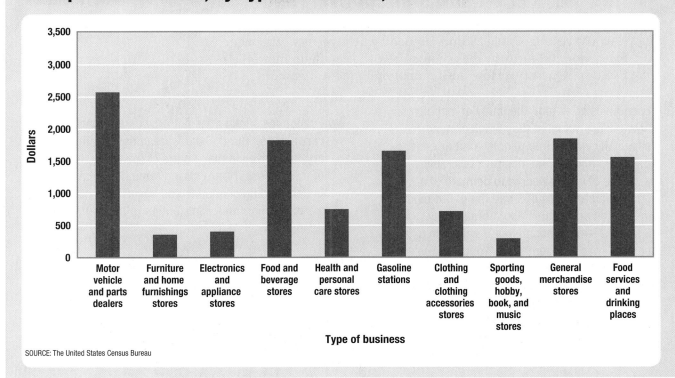

SOURCE: The United States Census Bureau

Selected Personal Consumption Expenditures, 2010

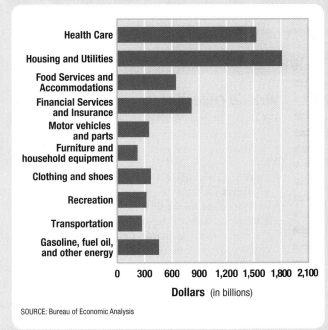

SOURCE: Bureau of Economic Analysis

Consumer Credit Debt

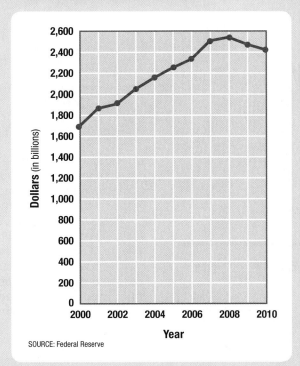

SOURCE: Federal Reserve

Unit 1 Challenge

 Essential Question, Unit 1
How does economics affect everyone?

VIDEO By Students For Students
For videos on Essential Questions,
go to *PearsonSchool.com/PHecon*

Some people think that economics does not affect them. In fact, it would be impossible to find anybody whose life is *not* touched by economics. Look at the opinions below, keeping in mind the Essential Question: How does economics affect everyone?

> Economics is, at root, the study of incentives: how people get what they want, or need, especially when other people want or need the same thing…. An incentive is simply a means of urging people to do more of a good thing and less of a bad thing. But most incentives don't come about organically. Someone—an economist or a politician or a parent—has to invent them. Your three-year-old eats all her vegetables for a week? She wins a trip to the toy store. A big steelmaker belches too much smoke into the air? The company is fined for each cubic foot of pollutants over the legal limit.
>
> —Steven D. Levitt and Stephen J. Dubner, *Freakonomics*

> Economics surely does not provide a romantic vision of life. But the widespread poverty, misery, and crises in many parts of the world, much of it unnecessary, are strong reminders that understanding economic and social laws can make an enormous contribution to the welfare of people.
>
> —Gary Becker, Nobel Prize acceptance speech, 1992

"The economy is slowing down. Last night the Tooth Fairy left me an IOU"

 Essential Question
Writing Activity

Consider the different views of economics expressed in the sources on this page. Review what you've learned in this unit and your own life experiences about the effects of economics. ***Then write a well-constructed essay expressing your view of how economics affects everyone.***

Writing Guidelines
- Address all aspects of the Essential Question Writing Activity.
- Support the theme with relevant facts, examples, and details.
- Use a logical and clear plan of organization.
- Introduce the theme by establishing a framework that is beyond a simple restatement of the question and conclude with a summation of the theme.

For help with Expository Writing, refer to the *Writer's Handbook* in the Reference section, page S-1.

Essential Questions Journal

To respond to the unit Essential Question, go to your **Essential Questions Journal**.

2 How Markets Work

Essential Question, Unit 2

Who benefits from the free market economy?

Chapter 7
How does competition affect your choices?

Chapter 6
What is the right price?

Chapter 4
How do we decide what to buy?

Chapter 5
How do suppliers decide what goods and services to offer?

4 Demand

Essential Question, Chapter 4

How do we decide what to buy?

FL **Next Generation Sunshine State Standards**

Section 1: Understanding Demand
LA.1112.1.6, LA.1112.1.6.2, MA.912.D.4.1, SS.912.E.1.4

Section 2: Shifts in the Demand Curve
LA.1112.1.6, LA.1112.6.3, MA.912.A.2.2, SS.912.E.1.4, SS.912.E.2.3

Section 3: Elasticity in Demand
LA.1112.1.6, LA.1112.6.2, MA.912.A.2.2, SS.912.E.1.4, SS.912.E.1.7

Economics
on the go

To study anywhere, anytime, download these
online resources at *PearsonSchool.com/PHecon* ▶

FL NGSSS

LA.1112.1.6 Use multiple strategies to develop vocabulary.

LA.1112.1.6.2 Listen to, read, and discuss familiar and challenging texts.

MA.912.D.4.1 Solve maximal profit/minimal cost problems.

SS.912.E.1.4 Define supply, demand, quantity supplied, and quantity demanded.

ECONOMIC DICTIONARY

As you read the section, look for the definitions of these **Key Terms:**

- demand
- law of demand
- substitution effect
- income effect
- demand schedule
- market demand schedule
- demand curve

Guiding Question

How does the law of demand affect the quantity demanded?

Copy this table and fill it in as you read.

Demand		
	As the price of a good goes down...	As the price of a good goes up...
Law of Demand		
Substitution Effect		
Income Effect		

▶ **Economics and You** Anyone who has ever shopped knows the difference between wanting to have something and being able to pay for it. Sometimes you can buy what you want, and other times, the price is just too high.

Principles in Action Price changes always affect the quantity demanded because people buy less of a good when its price goes up. By analyzing how the cost of pizza affects how much people are willing to buy, you will see how consumers react to a change in price. In the Economics & You feature, you will see how changes in price are an incentive.

Demand

Demand is the desire to own something and the ability to pay for it. To have demand for a good or service, *both* of these conditions must be present. We will look at the demand side of markets in this chapter. In the next chapter, we will look at the actions of sellers, which economists call the supply side. In Chapter 6, we will look at supply and demand together and study how they interact to establish the prices that we pay for most goods.

The Law of Demand

Anyone who has ever spent money will easily understand the law of demand. The **law of demand** says that when a good's price is lower, consumers will buy more of it. When the price is higher, consumers will buy less of it. All of us act out this law of demand in our everyday purchasing decisions. Whether your income is $10 or $10 million, the price of a good will strongly influence your decision to buy.

demand the desire to own something and the ability to pay for it

law of demand consumers will buy more of a good when its price is lower and less when its price is higher

Visual Glossary
(online)

Go to the Visual Glossary Online for an interactive review of **the law of demand.**

Action Graph
(online)

Go to Action Graph Online for animated versions of key charts and graphs.

How the Economy Works
(online)

Go to How the Economy Works Online for an interactive lesson on **elasticity of demand.**

VISUAL GLOSSARY

Reviewing Key Terms
To understand the *law of demand* review these terms:

free market economy, *p. 30*
consumer sovereignty, *p. 34*
demand, *p. 85*
substitution effect, *p. 87*
income effect, *p. 87*

What is the Law of Demand?

◄ **law of demand** consumers will buy more of a good when its price is lower and less when its price is higher.

LAW OF DEMAND

PRICE
As prices go down...

DEMAND
quantity demanded goes up.

PRICE
As prices go up...

DEMAND
quantity demanded goes down.

People will react to changes in price. *How do these two images reflect the law of demand in action?*

Visual Glossary
online

To expand your understanding of this and other key economic terms, visit **PearsonSchool.com/PHecon**

David Henderson, an economics professor who served as a senior economist with the President's Council of Economic Advisers, describes the importance of the law of demand:

> **The most famous law in economics, and the one that economists are most sure of, is the law of demand. On this law is built almost the whole edifice of economics.**
>
> —David Henderson, "Demand,"
> *The Concise Encyclopedia of Economics*

Now ask yourself a question: Would you buy a slice of pizza for lunch if it cost $2? Many of us would, and some of us might even buy more than one slice. But would you buy the same slice of pizza if it cost $4? Fewer of us would buy it at that price. Even real pizza lovers might reduce their consumption from 3 or 4 slices to just 1 or 2. How many of us would buy a slice for $10? Probably very few would pay that amount. As the price of pizza gets higher and higher, fewer of us are willing to buy it. That is the law of demand in action.

The law of demand is the result of not one pattern of behavior, but two separate patterns that overlap. These two behavior patterns are the substitution effect and the income effect. The substitution effect and the income effect describe two different ways that a consumer can change his or her spending patterns. Together, they explain why an increase in price decreases the amount purchased. As shown in **Figure 4.1,** the substitution effect and the income effect can change a consumer's buying habits.

The Substitution Effect

When the price of pizza rises, pizza becomes more expensive compared with other foods, such as tacos and salads. So, as the price of a slice of pizza rises, consumers have an incentive to buy one of those alternatives as a substitute for pizza. This causes a drop in the amount of pizza demanded. For example, instead of eating pizza for lunch on Mondays and Fridays, a student could eat pizza on Mondays and a bagel on Fridays. This change in consumption is known as the substitution effect. The **substitution effect** takes place when a consumer reacts to a rise in the price of

| | **Figure 4.1** | **The Law of Demand in Action** |

	Price of A Increases		Price of A Decreases	
	Consumption of A	Consumption of other goods	Consumption of A	Consumption of other goods
Income effect	↓	↓	↑	↑
Substitution effect	↓	↑	↑	↓
Combined effect	↓	↕	↑	↕

GRAPH SKILLS

Both the substitution effect and the income effect lead consumers to buy less of good A when it becomes more expensive. However, while the income effect leads consumers to spend less on other goods so they can afford good A, the substitution effect encourages consumers to replace expensive good A with other, less expensive substitutes.

1. How does an increase in the price of good A affect consumption of other goods?
2. How does a decline in the price of good A affect consumption of other goods?

one good by consuming less of that good and more of a substitute good.

The substitution effect can also apply to a drop in prices. If the price of pizza drops, pizza becomes cheaper compared to other alternatives. Consumers will now substitute pizza for tacos, salads, and other lunch choices, causing the quantity of pizza demanded to rise.

The Income Effect

Rising prices have another effect that we have all felt. They make us feel poorer. When the price of movie tickets, shoes, or pizza increases, your limited budget just won't buy as much as it did in the past. It feels as if you have less money. You can no longer afford to buy the same combination of goods, and you must cut back your purchases of some goods. If you buy fewer slices of pizza without increasing your purchases of other foods, that is the **income effect**.

One important fact to remember is that economists measure consumption in the amount of a good that is bought, not the amount of money spent to buy it. Although

substitution effect when consumers react to an increase in a good's price by consuming less of that good and more of a substitute good

income effect the change in consumption that results when a price increase causes real income to decline you are spending more on pizza, you are consuming fewer slices, so your consumption has gone down. If the price rises from $2 a slice to $4 a slice, you may decide to pay extra and order your usual lunch, but you certainly would not choose to buy more slices than before. When the price goes up, consumers spend more of their money on pizza, but they may demand less of it. Thus, the income effect has led to a decrease in the quantity demanded.

Remember, too, that the income effect also operates when the price is lowered. If the price of pizza falls, all of a sudden you feel wealthier. If you buy more pizza as a result of the lower price, that's the income effect.

✓ **CHECKPOINT** *What happens to demand for a good when the price increases?*

Economics & YOU

The Substitution Effect

When the price of one good increases, people have an incentive to buy substitutes. *Your decision to purchase a less expensive lunch is the substitution effect in action.*

Roast Beef sandwich $4.50 $5.25

Chili $1.99

REDUCED

The substitution effect also applies when a drop in price creates a cheaper alternative. *Your purchase of the reduced car is another example of the substitution effect.*

▲ A rise in the price of a good will cause consumers to buy more of a substitute good. *Has the substitution effect been a factor in any of your recent purchases?*

A Demand Schedule
The law of demand explains how the price of any item affects the quantity demanded of that item. Before we look at the relationship between price and the quantity demanded for a specific good, we need to look more closely at how economists use the word *demand*.

Understanding Demand
To have demand for a good, you must be willing and able to buy it at the specified price. Demand means that you want the good and can afford to buy it. You may desperately want a new car, a laptop computer, or a trip to Alaska, but if you can't truly afford any of these goods, then you do not demand them. You might demand digital music downloads, though, if at the current price you have enough money and want to buy some.

A **demand schedule** is a table that lists the quantity of a good that a person will purchase at various prices in a market. For example, the table on the left in **Figure 4.2** illustrates Ashley's individual "demand for pizza." The schedule shows specific quantities of pizza that a student named Ashley is willing and able to purchase at specific prices. For example, at a price of $4, Ashley's "quantity demanded" of pizza is two slices per day.

Market Demand Schedules
If you owned a store, knowing the demand schedule of one customer might not be as helpful as knowing how all of your customers would react to price changes. When you add up the demand schedules of every buyer in the market, you can create a market demand schedule. A **market demand schedule** shows the quantities demanded at various prices by all consumers in the market. A market demand schedule for pizza would allow a restaurant owner to predict the total sales of pizza at several different prices.

The owner of a pizzeria could create a market demand schedule for pizza slices by surveying his or her customers and then adding up the quantities demanded by all individual consumers at each price. The resulting market demand schedule will look

Figure 4.2
Demand Schedules

Individual Demand Schedule		Market Demand Schedule	
Price of a slice of pizza	Quantity demanded per day	Price of a slice of pizza	Quantity demanded per day
$1.00	5	$1.00	300
$2.00	4	$2.00	250
$3.00	3	$3.00	200
$4.00	2	$4.00	150
$5.00	1	$5.00	100
$6.00	0	$6.00	50

CHART SKILLS

Demand schedules show that the quantity demanded falls as the price rises.

1. How does market demand change when the price falls from $3 to $2 a slice?
2. What behaviors affect individual demand when pizza is $6 per slice?

like Ashley's demand schedule, but the quantities will be larger, as shown in **Figure 4.2.**

Note that the market demand schedule on the right in **Figure 4.2** contains the same prices as Ashley's individual demand schedule, since those are the possible prices that may be charged by the pizzeria. The schedule also exhibits the law of demand. At higher prices the quantity demanded is lower. The only difference between the two demand schedules is that the market schedule lists larger quantities demanded because the market demand schedule reflects the purchase decisions of all potential consumers in the market.

 CHECKPOINT *To have demand for a good, what two conditions must be met?*

The Demand Graph

What if you took the numbers in Ashley's demand schedule in **Figure 4.2** and plotted them on a graph? The result would be a demand curve. A **demand curve** is a graphic representation of a demand schedule.

How do economists create a demand curve? When they transfer numbers from a demand schedule to a graph, they always label the vertical axis with the lowest possible prices at the bottom and the highest price at the top. Likewise, they always label the quantities demanded on the horizontal axis with the lowest possible quantity at the left and the highest possible quantity at the right. All demand

graphs show that each pair of price and quantity-demanded numbers on the demand schedule is plotted as a point on the graph. Connecting the points on the graph creates a demand curve.

Reading a Demand Curve

Note two facts about Ashley's demand curve shown in **Figure 4.3** on page 90. First, the graph shows only the relationship between the price of this good and the quantity that Ashley will purchase. It assumes that all other factors that would affect Ashley's demand for pizza—like the price of other goods, her income, and the quality of the pizza—are held constant.

Second, the demand curve on the graph slopes downward to the right. If you follow the curve from the top left to the bottom right, you will notice that as price decreases, the quantity demanded increases. All demand schedules and demand curves reflect the law of demand, which states that higher prices will always lead to lower quantities demanded.

Ashley's demand curve in **Figure 4.3** shows her demand for slices of pizza. The market demand curve in **Figure 4.3** shows the quantities demanded by all consumers at the same prices. Thus, the prices listed on the vertical axis are identical to those in Ashley's demand curve. The quantities listed on the horizontal axis are much larger, corresponding to those in the market demand schedule in **Figure 4.2.**

demand curve a graphic representation of a demand schedule

▲ This 2006 magazine cover reflects the increased demand for luxury goods that began in 2003. But an economic downturn in late 2007 led to reduced demand for luxury items. *What other goods or services might consumers have less demand for during an economic downturn?*

Figure 4.3

Demand Curves

Ashley's demand curve shows the number of slices she is willing and able to buy at each price, while the market demand curve shows demand for pizza in an entire market.

1. How many slices does Ashley demand at is $4.00 per slice?

2. How are the demand curves similar?

For an animated version of this graph, visit **PearsonSchool.com/PHecon**

Ashley's Demand Curve

Price per slice (in dollars) / *Slices of pizza per day*

Market Demand Curve

Price per slice (in dollars) / *Slices of pizza per day*

Limits of a Demand Curve

The market demand curve in **Figure 4.3** can predict how people will change their buying habits when the price of a good rises or falls. For example, if the price of pizza is $3 a slice, the pizzeria will sell 200 slices a day.

This market demand curve is only accurate for one very specific set of market conditions. It cannot predict changing market conditions. In the next section, you will learn how demand curves can shift because of changes in factors other than price.

✔ **CHECKPOINT** *What is a market demand curve?*

FL MA.912.A.2.2, LA.1112.2.2.2, SS.912.E.1.4, LA.1112.2.2.3, MA.912.A.2, LA.1112.1.6.1

SECTION 1 ASSESSMENT

Essential Questions Journal To continue to build a response to the Essential Question, go to your **Essential Questions Journal**.

🤔 Guiding Question

1. Use your completed table to answer this question: How does the law of demand affect the quantity demanded?

2. **Extension** Can you think of a time when the price of something you wanted was raised or dropped? Briefly describe what happened to cause the price change, and how this affected your decision to buy or not buy the product.

Key Terms and Main Ideas

3. What two qualities make up **demand?**

4. According to the **law of demand,** what will happen when the price of a good increases?

5. Under the **substitution effect,** what will happen when the price of a good drops?

6. What does a **market demand schedule** show?

7. What is a **demand schedule** called when it is represented as a graph?

Critical Thinking

8. **Contrast** Describe the difference between the substitution effect and the income effect.

9. **Extend** Suppose you are a small business owner. How would a market demand schedule or a market demand curve be useful to you?

10. **Predict (a)** What can economists predict by creating a demand curve? **(b)** When would a demand curve not be useful?

Math Skills

11. Use the following market demand schedule to draw a demand curve for miniature golf.

Visit PearsonSchool.com/PHecon for additional math help.

Cost to Play a Game	Games Played per Month
$1.50	350
$2.00	250
$3.00	140
$4.00	80

NGSSS

LA.1112.1.6 Use multiple strategies to develop vocabulary.

LA.1112.6.3 Understand media literacy as a life skill.

MA.912.A.2.2 Interpret a graph to represent a real-world situation.

SS.912.E.1.4 Define supply, demand, quantity supplied, and quantity demanded.

SS.912.E.2.3 Research the contributions of key individuals of various backgrounds in the development of the U.S.

ECONOMIC DICTIONARY

As you read the section, look for the definitions of these **Key Terms:**

- *ceteris paribus*
- normal good
- inferior good
- demographics
- complements
- substitutes

Guiding Question

Why does the demand curve shift?

Copy this concept web and fill it in as you read.

▶ **Economics and You** The text message says it all: Raining 2 hrd! Your plans to go out to eat with your friends have suddenly been scuttled. No burger is worth the bother. Not only has your demand for burgers at any price dropped, your demand for home-delivered pizza at any price has risen.

Principles in Action Sometimes increases or decreases in demand are not connected to price. On a stormy night, the Burger Barn may be nearly empty while the phone is ringing off the hook at the Pizza Palace. As you will read, David Ogilvy, the Innovator featured on page 95, based his career on increasing consumers' demand.

ceteris paribus
a Latin phrase that means "all other things held constant"

Changes in Demand

When we counted the number of pizza slices that would sell as the price went up or down, we assumed that nothing besides the price of pizza would change. Economists refer to this assumption as ***ceteris paribus,*** the Latin phrase for "all other things held constant." The demand schedule took into account only changes in price. It did not consider the effects of news reports or any one of thousands of other factors that change from day to day.

A demand curve is accurate only as long as there are no changes other than price that could affect the consumer's decision. In other words, a demand curve is accurate only as long as the *ceteris paribus* assumption is true. When the price changes, we move along the curve to a different quantity demanded.

For example, in the graph of Ashley's demand for slices of pizza, an increase in the price from $2 per slice to $3 will make Ashley's quantity demanded fall from four slices to three slices per day. This movement along the demand curve

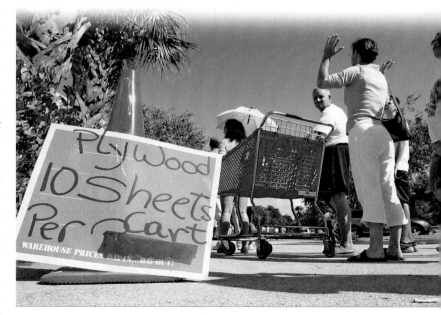

▲ Natural disasters such as hurricanes can create sudden demand for household goods. *Based on the image, how would the demand curve for plywood change?*

normal good a good that consumers demand more of when their incomes increase

is referred to as a *decrease in the quantity demanded*. By the same reasoning, a decrease in the price of pizza would lead to an *increase in the quantity demanded*.

When we drop the *ceteris paribus* rule and allow other factors to change, we no longer move along the demand curve. Instead, the entire demand curve shifts. A shift in the demand curve means that at every price, consumers buy a different quantity than before. This shift of the entire curve is what economists refer to as *a change in demand*.

Suppose, for example, that Ashley's town is hit by a heat wave, and Ashley no longer feels as hungry for pizza. She will demand fewer slices at every price. The graph on the left in **Figure 4.4** shows her original demand curve and her new demand curve, adjusted for hot weather.

✓ **CHECKPOINT** *What does a shift in the demand curve say about a particular good?*

FL MA.912.A.2.2 Interpret a graph to represent a real-world situation.

What Causes a Shift?

As you have read, a change in the price of a good does not cause the demand curve to shift. The effects of changes in price are already built into the demand curve. However, several other factors can cause demand for a good to change. These changes can lead to a change in demand rather than simply a change in the quantity demanded.

Income

A consumer's income affects his or her demand for most goods. Most items that we purchase are **normal goods,** goods that consumers demand more of when their incomes increase. In other words, an increase in Ashley's income from $50 per week to $75 per week will cause her to buy more of a normal good at every price level. If we were to draw a new demand schedule for Ashley, it would show a greater demand for slices of pizza at every price. Plotting the new schedule on a graph would produce a curve to the right of Ashley's original curve. For each of the prices on the vertical axis, the quantity demanded would be greater. This shift to the right of the curve is called *an increase in demand*. A fall in income would cause

---

| Figure 4.4 | **Graphing Changes in Demand** |

Decrease in Demand / Increase in Demand

GRAPH SKILLS

When factors other than price cause demand to fall, the demand curve shifts to the left. An increase in demand appears as a shift to the right.

1. If the price of a book rose by one dollar, how would you show the change on one of these graphs?
2. How does a change in the quantity demanded differ from a change in price?

 Action Graph online

For an animated version of this graph, visit PearsonSchool.com/PHecon

Who Needs to Eat?

ELECTRONICS

Americans are devoting more of their dollars to electronics—not enough to trigger a recovery, but enough to leave a mark on the economy.

By Emmeline Zhao
The Wall Street Journal

 SS.912.E.1.4 Define supply, demand, quantity supplied, and quantity demanded.

If Americans are cutting back on big purchases for the home, they're doing so while talking on their iPhones about their new flat-screen TVs.

Government data show that after pouring money into their homes during the previous decade, consumers are redirecting their purchases to eye-grabbing technology and socking away more of what's left over into savings.

David Wu, a Los Angeles high-school teacher, says he has spent about $4,000 on new technology over the past two years, including a high-tech mobile phone and a large-screen television. The 25-year-old says that because computers and other electronics are constantly evolving, he has an incentive to keep buying the latest items.

"With a toaster and microwave," he says, "as long as it works, I don't see myself buying a flashier one."

Over the course of a year, Spence Witten, 27, spent about $8,000 on new electronics, including a new smartphone, laptop, tablet computer and music player. He also bought a Blu-ray player and a $2,000 stereo system.

Mr. Witten says some home improvements fell down the list of priorities as a result of his electronics purchases. He could use a new toaster, microwave, professional wardrobe and hardwood floors for his Washington home, "but who needs to eat and buy more ties?"

The electronics boom alone isn't enough to sustain an economic recovery, says economist Chris Christopher; spending on technology accounts for only a sliver of the overall economy.

Still, the trend toward buying electronics at the expense of other goods is leaving its mark. Manufacturing, for example, has been especially strong in high-tech businesses.

Meanwhile, apparel marketers say the shift is eating into their sales. "Electronics has taken a huge chunk out of the average household spending budget," said Eric Wiseman, CEO of clothing maker VF. Apparel executives say the iPhone in particular has become an ornament in its own right.

Many hit by the weak economy cut spending on big-ticket items and services, including vacations. Sally Manesis, a 56-year-old from of New Canaan, Conn., recently installed a $5,000 home-entertainment system, equipped with a 64-inch flat-screen television, surround sound and a Blu-ray video player.

She says she thought about spending that money on a trip to Europe, but relaxing in the comforts of her home appealed to her more than long-distance travel.

Applying Economic Principles

Changes in the economy have affected demand for a variety of goods and services. Electronics sales have expanded as demand for household improvements and apparel has dropped. What are some of the factors that have caused this shift in demand?

Video News Update Online
Powered by
The Wall Street Journal
Classroom Edition

Use videos at **PearsonSchool.com/PHecon** as a springboard for a discussion on a current topic.

the demand curve to shift left. This shift is called a *decrease in demand*. For more information on normal goods, see **Figure 4.1** on page 87.

There are also other goods called inferior goods. They are called inferior goods because an increase in income causes demand for these goods to fall. **Inferior goods** are goods that you would buy in smaller quantities, or not at all, if your income were to rise and you could afford something better. Possible examples of inferior goods include macaroni and cheese, generic cereals, and used cars.

Consumer Expectations

Our expectations about the future can affect our demand for certain goods today. Suppose that you have had your eye on a new bicycle for several months. One day you walk into the store to look at the bike, and the salesperson mentions that the store will be raising the price in one week. Now that you expect a higher price in the near future, you are more likely to buy the bike today. In other words, the expectation of a higher price in the future has caused your immediate demand to increase.

If, on the other hand, the salesperson were to tell you that the bike will be on

sale next week, your immediate demand for the bicycle would fall to zero. You would rather wait until next week to buy the bike at a lower price.

The current demand for a good is positively related to its expected future price. If you expect the price to rise, your current demand will rise, which means you will buy the good sooner. If you expect the price to drop, your current demand will fall, and you will wait for the lower price.

Population

Changes in the size of the population will also affect the demand for most products. For example, a growing population needs to be housed and fed. Therefore, a rise in population will increase demand for houses, food, and many other goods and services.

Population trends can have a strong effect on certain goods. For example, when American soldiers returned from World War II in the mid- to late-1940s, record numbers of them married and started families. This trend led to the "baby boom," a jump in the birthrate from 1946 through 1964. Initially, the boom led to higher demand for baby clothes, baby food, and books on baby care. In the 1950s and 1960s, towns built thousands of new schools. Later, universities expanded and opened new campuses to make room for new students.

The baby boomers have now begun to retire. Over the next few decades the market will face rising demand for the goods and services that are desired by senior citizens, including medical care, recreational vehicles, and homes in the Sunbelt.

Demographics

Demographics are the statistical characteristics of populations, such as age, race, gender, occupation, and income level. Businesses use this data to identify who potential customers are, where they live, and how likely they are to purchase a specific product. Demographics also have a strong influence on the packaging, pricing, and advertising for a product.

Growing ethnic groups like Asians and Latin Americans can create shifts in demand for goods and services. In the United States, Hispanics accounted for about one half of the national population growth between

Hispanics, or Latinos, are now the largest minority group in the United States. Firms have responded to this shift by providing products and services for the growing Hispanic population. ▼

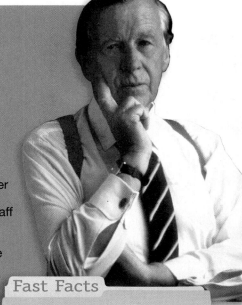

Innovators

David Ogilvy

"Unless your advertising contains a big idea, it will pass like a ship in the night."

Those words reflect the life experience of their author, David Ogilvy, a legendary ad man who brought a lot of big ideas to the advertising industry.

The son of a Scottish stockbroker, Ogilvy won a scholarship to Oxford. But he left Oxford in 1931, because he was, in his own words, a "dud." After working as a chef at the Hotel Majestic in Paris, he returned to England and sold stoves door-to-door. His brother got him his first advertising job with a London agency. "I loved advertising," Ogilvy later wrote. "I studied and read and took it desperately seriously."

He decided to seek his fortune in America. In 1938, Ogilvy joined the staff of George Gallup's National Research Institute. The experience convinced him that market research was the foundation of good advertising.

In 1948, Ogilvy founded his own ad agency in New York, which became known as Ogilvy & Mather. A series of stylish, successful ads for companies like Hathaway and Rolls Royce attracted blue-chip clients like Shell, General Foods, and American Express. Ogilvy's ads helped to generate demand and led to huge sales increases for his clients.

Ogilvy's lasting legacy is as a pioneer in the development of brand images. He recognized that branding is the key to a company's success: "Every advertisement should be thought of as a contribution to the complex symbol which is the brand image."

Critical Thinking: *List ways that advertising might affect demand.*

Fast Facts

David Ogilvy
Born: June 23, 1911
Died: July 21, 1999
Education: Oxford University
Claim to Fame: Founded the advertising agency Ogilvy & Mather

---

2003 and 2004. The Census Bureau estimates that by 2025, Hispanic Americans will make up 18.9 percent of the U.S. population. As their purchasing power grows, firms will devote more of their resources to producing goods and services demanded by Hispanic consumers.

Consumer Tastes and Advertising

Who can explain why bell-bottom blue jeans were everywhere one year and rarely seen the next? Is it the result of clever advertising campaigns, social trends, the influence of television shows, or some combination of these factors? Although economists cannot always explain why some fads begin, advertising and publicity often play an important role.

Changes in tastes and preferences cannot be explained by changes in income or population or worries about future price increases. Advertising is a factor that shifts demand curves because it plays an important role in many trends. Meanwhile, new media and new technology have led to new trends in advertising. Although broadcast television is still the biggest advertising medium, viewers can now watch television programs on the Internet, cellphones, or DVD players. Digital media makes it easier for consumers to avoid advertisements.

Marketers who want to reach these new media consumers are changing their traditional advertising strategies.

Spending for online ads continues to grow. Video is the fastest growing Internet ad format, topped only by search engine advertising. Ad spending on social network Web sites such as Facebook and MySpace, was estimated at $1.9 billion in 2008.

The popularity of social network Web sites has inspired companies to build their own sites. The goal is to connect with consumers on a personal level while promoting their products and brand names.

Companies spend money on advertising because they hope that it will increase the demand for the goods they sell. Considering the growing sums of money spent on advertising in the United States each year, companies must believe that this investment is paying off.

 CHECKPOINT *How will an anticipated rise in price affect current demand for a good?*

FL SS.912.E.2.3 Research the contributions of key individuals of various backgrounds in the development of the U.S.

Simulation *Activity*

Creating Demand
You may be asked to take part in a role-playing game about creating demand.

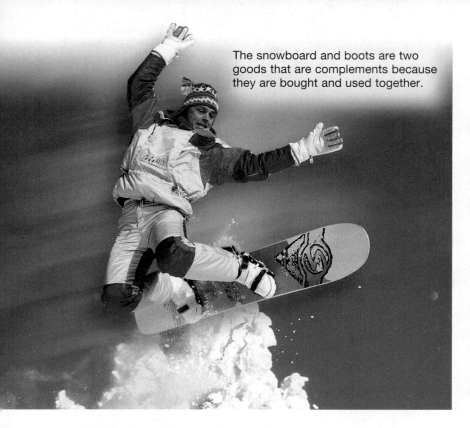
The snowboard and boots are two goods that are complements because they are bought and used together.

complements two goods that are bought and used together

substitutes goods that are used in place of one another

Prices of Related Goods

The demand curve for one good can also shift in response to a change in the demand for another good. There are two types of related goods that interact this way: complements and substitutes.

- **Complements** are two goods that are bought and used together.
- **Substitutes** are goods that are used in place of one another.

When we consider the demand for skis, ski boots are considered a complement. An increase in the price of ski boots will cause people to buy fewer boots. Because skis are useless without boots, the demand for skis will fall at all prices—after all, why buy new skis if you can't afford the ski boots you need?

Now consider the effect on the demand for skis when the price of snowboards rises. Snowboards are a substitute for skis, because consumers will often buy one or the other, but not both. A rise in the price of snowboards will cause people to buy fewer snowboards, and, therefore, people will buy more pairs of new skis at every price. Likewise, a fall in the price of snowboards will lead consumers to buy fewer skis at all price levels.

 CHECKPOINT *If the demand for a good increases, what will happen to the demand for its complement?*

 FL SS.912.E.1.4, LA.1112.2.2.3, LA.1112.1.6.3, LA.1112.1.6.1

Essential Questions Journal
To continue to build a response to the Essential Question, go to your **Essential Questions Journal**.

SECTION 2 ASSESSMENT

Guiding Question

1. Use your completed concept web to answer this question: Why does the demand curve shift?

2. **Extension** Suppose you are about to buy a new pair of shoes. Assume that the price of the shoes will not change. What other factors could affect your demand for the shoes?

Key Terms and Main Ideas

3. How is the *ceteris paribus* assumption related to demand curves?

4. How does consumers' income affect the demand for **normal goods?**

5. Name at least three goods that could be bought as **complements** to hamburgers.

6. List at least three goods that could be considered **substitutes** for movie tickets.

Critical Thinking

7. **Summarize (a)** Does a change in the price of a good cause the demand curve to shift? Why or why not? **(b)** What kinds of changes cause shifts in the demand curve?

8. **Contrast** How are normal goods and inferior goods different?

9. **Contrast (a)** If demand for a good increases, what will happen to the demand for its complement? **(b)** What will happen to the demand for its substitute? **(c)** Explain why the changes in demand for the complement and the substitute follow different patterns.

Quick Write

10. Based on what you have read in this section about shifts in the demand curve, write a short essay answering the following questions: How did your demand for a product change based on something other than price? What factors were responsible for this shift in demand? How might these factors have affected other people's demand for the product?

NGSSS

LA.1112.1.6 Use multiple strategies to develop vocabulary.

LA.1112.6.2 Use a systematic process to collect, process, present information.

MA.912.A.2.2 Interpret a graph to represent a real-world situation.

SS.912.E.1.4 Define supply, demand, quantity supplied, and quantity demanded.

SS.912.E.1.7 Graph and explain how price is determined through marginal cost analysis.

ECONOMIC DICTIONARY

As you read the section, look for the definitions of these **Key Terms:**

- elasticity of demand
- inelastic
- elastic
- unitary elastic
- total revenue

Guiding Question
What factors affect elasticity of demand?

Copy this chart and fill it in as you read.

Effect of a Price Change on Quantity Demanded		
Inelastic Demand	Elastic Demand	Unitary Elastic Demand

▶ **Economics and You**   Are there some products that you would continue to buy, even if the price were to rise dramatically? Are there other goods that you would cut back on, or stop buying altogether, if there was just a slight increase in price? How much is too much? No matter how you answer these questions, economists have a way to describe your behavior.

Principles in Action Economists have developed a way to calculate just how strongly people react to a change in price. Several factors—including the original price and how much you want or need a particular good—will determine your demand for that product. In this section, you will see how economists measure your behavior. This section's How the Economy Works shows how elasticity of demand affects your daily purchases.

Defining Elasticity

Economists describe the way that consumers respond to price changes as **elasticity of demand.** Elasticity of demand measures how drastically buyers will cut back or increase their demand for a good when the price rises or falls, respectively. If you buy the same amount or just a little less of a good after a large price increase, your demand is **inelastic,** or relatively unresponsive to price changes. If you buy much less of a good after a small price increase, your demand is **elastic.** A consumer with highly elastic demand for a good is very responsive to price changes.

Calculating Elasticity

In order to calculate elasticity of demand, take the percentage change in the quantity of the good demanded, and divide this number by the percentage change in the price of the good. The result is the elasticity of demand for the good.

The law of demand implies that the result will always be negative. That is because an increase in the price of a good will always decrease the quantity demanded, and a decrease in the price of a good will always increase the quantity demanded. For the sake of simplicity, economists drop the negative sign in the result. You can find the equation for elasticity in **Figure 4.5** on page 98.

elasticity of demand
a measure of how consumers respond to price changes

inelastic describes demand that is not very sensitive to price changes

elastic describes demand that is very sensitive to a change in price

unitary elastic
describes demand
whose elasticity is
exactly equal to 1

(FL) **SS.912.E.1.7**
Graph and explain
how price is
determined
through marginal
cost analysis.

Price Range

The elasticity of demand for a good varies at every price level. Demand for a good can be highly elastic at one price and inelastic at a different price. For example, demand for a glossy magazine will be inelastic when the price rises 50 percent, from 60 cents to 90 cents. The new price is still very low, and people will buy almost as many copies as they did before. However, when the price of a magazine increases 50 percent, from $4.00 to $6.00, demand will be much more elastic. Many readers will refuse to pay $2.00 more for the magazine. Yet in percentage terms, the change in the magazine's price is exactly the same as when the price rose from 60 cents to 90 cents.

Values of Elasticity

We have been using the terms *inelastic* and *elastic* to describe consumers' responses to price changes. These terms have precise mathematical definitions. If the elasticity of demand for a good at a certain price is *less* than 1, we describe demand as inelastic. If the elasticity is *greater* than one, demand is elastic. If elasticity is *exactly equal* to 1, we describe demand as **unitary elastic.**

When elasticity of demand is unitary, the percentage change in quantity demanded is

---

Figure 4.5	**Elasticity of Demand**

GRAPH SKILLS

Elasticity of demand describes how strongly consumers will react to a change in price.

1. What is the formula for computing elasticity of demand?

2. If a good's elasticity of demand is 0.2, how will consumers react to an increase in price?

Action Graph
online

For an animated version of this graph, visit
PearsonSchool.com/PHecon

To determine elasticity of demand, use the following formulas:

$$\text{Percentage change} = \frac{\text{Original number} - \text{New number}}{\text{Original number}} \times 100$$

$$\text{Elasticity} = \frac{\text{Percentage change in quantity demanded}}{\text{Percentage change in price}}$$

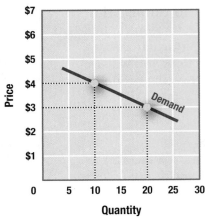

Example 1: Elastic Demand

The price decreases from $4 to $3, a decrease of 25 percent.

$$\frac{\$4 - \$3}{\$4} \times 100 = 25$$

The quantity demanded increases from 10 to 20. This is an increase of 100 percent.

$$\frac{10 - 20}{10} \times 100 = 100$$

Elasticity of demand is equal to 4.0. Elasticity is greater than 1 so demand is elastic. In this example, a small decrease in price caused a large increase in the quantity demanded.

$$\frac{100\%}{25\%} = 4.0$$

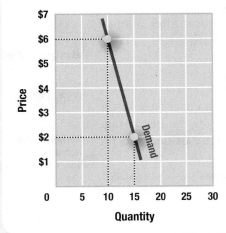

Example 2: Inelastic Demand

The price decreases from $6 to $2, a decrease of about 67 percent.

$$\frac{\$6 - \$2}{\$6} \times 100 = 67$$

The quantity demanded increases from 10 to 15, an increase of 50 percent.

$$\frac{10 - 15}{10} \times 100 = 50$$

Elasticity of demand is about 0.75. The elasticity is less than 1, so demand for this good is inelastic. The increase in quantity demanded is small compared to the decrease in price.

$$\frac{50\%}{67\%} = 0.75$$

◄ Grazing sheep are this homeowner's solution to the high price of gasoline. *How does this cartoon illustrate elasticity of demand?*

THEY WERE CHEAPER THAN BUYING GAS FOR THE MOWER.

exactly equal to the percentage change in the price. Suppose the elasticity of demand for a magazine at $2 is unitary. When the price of the magazine rises by 50 percent to $3, the newsstand will sell exactly half as many copies as before.

Think back to Ashley's demand schedule for pizza in Section 1. Ashley's demand schedule shows that if the price per slice were to rise from $2.00 to $3.00, her quantity demanded would fall from 4 slices to 3 slices per day. The change in price from $2.00 to $3.00 is a 50 percent increase. The change in quantity demanded from 4 slices to 3 is a 25 percent decrease. Dividing the 25 percent decrease in quantity demanded by the 50 percent increase in price gives us an elasticity of demand of 0.5.

Since Ashley's elasticity of demand at a price change from $2.00 to $3.00 is less than 1, we say that Ashley's demand for pizza is inelastic. In other words, price increase has a relatively small effect on the number of slices of pizza she buys.

Suppose we survey another customer and find that when the price of pizza rises by 40 percent, this person's quantity demanded falls by 60 percent. The change in the quantity demanded of 60 percent is divided by the change in price of 40 percent, equaling an elasticity of demand of 1.5 (60 percent/40 percent = 1.5). Since this result is greater than 1, this customer's demand is elastic. In other words, this customer is very sensitive to changes in the price of pizza.

CHECKPOINT *How do economists calculate elasticity?*

Factors Affecting Elasticity

Why is the demand for some goods so much less elastic than for other goods? Rephrase the question and ask yourself, "What is essential to me? What goods must I have, even if the price rises greatly?" The goods you list might have some traits that set them apart from other goods and make your demand for those goods less elastic. Several different factors can affect a person's elasticity of demand for a specific good.

Availability of Substitutes

If there are few substitutes for a good, then even when its price rises greatly, you might still buy it. You believe you have no good alternatives. For example, if your favorite musical group plans to give a concert that you want to attend, there really is no substitute for that ticket. You could go to a concert to hear some other band, but that would not be as good. You've got to have tickets for this concert, and nothing else will do. Under these circumstances, a moderate change in price is not going to change your mind. Your demand for that concert is inelastic.

How does **elasticity** affect **consumer demand**?

On any given day, the average consumer faces a series of spending decisions. Elasticity of demand describes how strongly buyers will react to a change in the price of a good. How does elasticity of demand affect your decision to buy or not to buy?

1 The price of your morning latte has increased from $3 to $4. Instead of the latte, you buy a regular coffee for $2. Because a substitute is available, your demand for the latte is **elastic.**

2 You notice that the price of gasoline has increased by twenty cents a gallon. Your car runs on gasoline and there are no substitutes. Despite the increase, your demand for gasoline is **inelastic.**

Availability of Substitutes

Similarly, demand for life-saving medicine is usually inelastic. For many prescription drugs, the only possible substitute is to try an unproven treatment. For this reason, people with an illness will continue to buy as much needed medicine as they can afford, even when the price goes up.

If the lack of substitutes can make demand inelastic, a wide choice of substitute goods can make demand elastic. The demand for a particular brand of apple juice is probably elastic because people can choose from several good substitutes if the price of their preferred brand rises.

Relative Importance

A second factor in determining a good's elasticity of demand is how much of your budget you spend on the good. If you already spend a large share of your income on a good, a price increase will force you to make some tough choices. Unless you want to cut back drastically on the other goods in your budget, you must reduce consumption of that particular good by a significant amount to keep your budget under control. The higher the jump in price, the more you will have to adjust your purchases.

If you currently spend half of your budget on clothes, even a modest increase in the cost of clothing will probably cause a large reduction in the quantity you purchase. In other words, your demand will be elastic.

However, if the price of shoelaces doubled, would you cut back on your shoelace purchases? Probably not. You may not even notice the difference. Even if you spend twice as much on shoelaces, they will still account for only a tiny part of your overall budget. Your demand for shoelaces is inelastic.

3 You need a new set of tires. The price for the same brand-name tire has increased by 20 percent. That price is too high, so you buy the cheaper tires. Your demand for the brand-name tire is **elastic.**

How the Economy Works
online
For an animated, interactive version of this feature, visit **PearsonSchool.com/PHecon**

5 **Elasticity of Demand** Your demand for a good is **inelastic** if you buy the same amount or just a little less after a price increase. Your demand for a good that has increased in price is **elastic** if the good has many substitutes, takes a big bite out of your budget, or is a luxury.

4 That new set of tires put a big dent in your budget. But you have a date, so takeout replaces dining out. Your demand for a restaurant dinner is **elastic.**

Check Your Understanding
1. How does knowing the elasticity of demand for a good help entrepreneurs?
2. What changes might make demand for gasoline more elastic over time?

Share of Budget   **Necessity Versus Luxury**

Necessities Versus Luxuries

The third factor in determining a good's elasticity varies a great deal from person to person, but it is nonetheless important. Whether a person considers a good to be a necessity or a luxury has a great impact on a person's elasticity of demand for that good. A necessity is a good people will always buy, even when the price increases. Parents often regard milk as a necessity. They will buy it at any reasonable price. If the price of a gallon of milk rises from $3.49 to $5.49, they will still buy as much milk as their children need to stay healthy. Their demand for milk is inelastic.

The same parents may regard steak as a luxury. When the price of steak increases slightly, say 20 percent, parents may cut their monthly purchases of steak by more than 20 percent, or skip steak altogether. Steak is a luxury, and consumers can easily

reduce the quantity they consume. Because it is easy to reduce the quantity of luxury goods demanded, demand is elastic.

Change Over Time

When a price changes, consumers often need time to change their spending habits. Consumers do not always react quickly to a price increase, because it takes time to find substitutes. Because they cannot respond quickly to price changes, their demand is inelastic in the short term. Demand sometimes becomes more elastic over time, however, because people can eventually find substitutes.

Consider the example of gasoline. A person might purchase a large vehicle that requires a greater volume of gasoline per mile to run. This person might work at a job many miles away from home and shop at a supermarket that is not local.

FUTURE WATCH
Personal Finance
For help with establishing a good credit rating, see your Personal Finance Handbook at the back of the book or visit **PearsonSchool.com/PHecon**

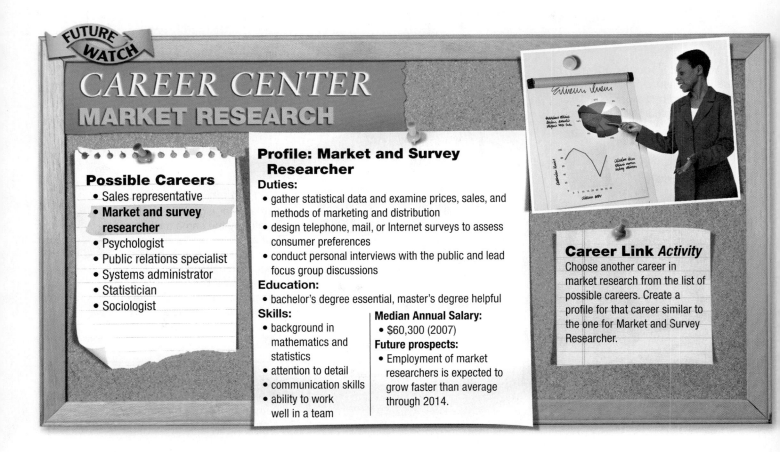

These factors determine how much gasoline this person demands, and none can be changed easily.

In the early 1970s, several oil-rich countries cut their oil exports to the United States. Gasoline prices rose quickly. In the short term, people could do little to reduce their consumption of gasoline. They still needed to drive to school and work. At first, drivers were more likely to pay the higher price for gasoline than they were to buy fuel-efficient cars or move closer to their workplaces.

However, because gas prices stayed high for a considerable period of time, some people eventually switched to more fuel-efficient cars, formed car pools, or used public transportation. In the long run, people reduced their consumption of gasoline by finding substitutes. Demand for gasoline, inelastic in the short term, is more elastic in the long term.

The story did not end there. In the early 1980s, the price of a gallon of gas began to fall. Gasoline prices, adjusted for inflation, stayed low for the next two decades. At first, people continued to buy fuel-efficient cars. But over time, many Americans switched to larger vehicles that got fewer miles to the gallon. Because the price of gas remained low, people gradually adjusted their habits and consumed more gasoline. Just as demand for gasoline responded slowly to an increase in price, it also responded slowly to a decrease in price.

In the early 2000s, gasoline prices shot up again. Once more, consumers were slow to change their car-buying habits and their demand for gasoline. If prices remain high over the long term, however, economists expect that demand for gasoline will again be more elastic.

✔ **CHECKPOINT** *What factors affect elasticity of demand?*

Elasticity and Revenue

Elasticity is important to the study of economics because elasticity helps us measure how consumers respond to price changes for different products. Elasticity is also an important tool for business planners like the pizzeria owner described in Sections 1 and 2. The elasticity of demand determines how a change in prices will affect a firm's total revenue, or income.

Computing a Firm's Total Revenue

A company's **total revenue** is defined as the amount of money the company receives by selling its goods. This is determined by two factors: the price of the goods and the quantity sold. If a pizzeria sells 150 slices of pizza per day at $4.00 per slice, total revenue would be $600 per day.

Total Revenue and Elastic Demand

The law of demand tells us that an increase in price will decrease the quantity demanded. When a good has an elastic demand, raising the price of each unit sold by 20 percent will decrease the quantity sold by a larger percentage, say 50 percent. The quantity sold will drop enough to actually *reduce* the firm's total revenue. The revenue table in **Figure 4.6**—drawn from the pizzeria's demand curve—shows how this can happen. An increase in price from $5 to $6, or 20 percent, decreases the quantity sold from 100 to 50, or 50 percent. As a result, total revenue drops from $500 to $300.

The same process can also work in reverse. If the firm were to reduce the price by a certain percentage, the quantity demanded could rise by an even greater percentage. In this case, total revenues could rise.

It may surprise you that a firm could lose revenue by raising the price of its goods. But if the pizzeria started selling pizza at $10 a slice, it would not stay in business very long. Remember that elastic demand comes from one or more of these factors:

- The availability of substitute goods
- A limited budget that does not allow for price changes
- The perception of the good as a luxury item

If these conditions are present, then the demand for the good is elastic, and a firm may find that a price increase reduces its total revenue.

Total Revenue and Inelastic Demand

Remember that if demand is inelastic, consumers' demand is not very responsive to price changes. When demand is inelastic, price and total revenue move in the same direction: An increase in price raises total revenue, and a decrease in price reduces total revenue. Thus, if a firm raises its price by 25 percent, the quantity demanded will fall, but not by enough to lower total revenue. As a result, the firm will have greater total revenues, because the higher price will make up for the lower quantity of sales. The firm brings in more money.

On the other hand, a decrease in price will lead to an increase in the quantity demanded even if demand is inelastic. However, the percentage of increase in the quantity demanded will be less than the percentage of increase in price, and the firm's total revenue will decrease. For example, if you lower the price of socks by 50 percent, you may sell only 20 percent more socks. The increase in the quantity sold does not compensate for the lost revenue.

✔ **CHECKPOINT** *How does elasticity affect revenue?*

total revenue the total amount of money a company receives by selling goods or services

| Figure 4.6 | Revenue Table |

Revenue Table

Price of a Slice of Pizza	Quantity Demanded (per day)	Total Revenue
$1.00	300	$300
$2.00	250	$500
$3.00	200	$600
$4.00	150	$600
$5.00	100	$500
$6.00	50	$300

CHART SKILLS

Setting prices too high or too low can hurt revenue.

1. What two factors determine total revenue?
2. When the price doubles from $2.00 to $4.00, is demand elastic, unitary elastic, or inelastic?

Figure 4.7 Elasticity and Revenue

Elastic Demand

As the price is lowered... Total revenue rises

As the price is raised... Total revenue falls

Inelastic Demand

As the price is lowered... Total revenue falls

As the price is raised... Total revenue rises

CHART SKILLS

Elasticity of demand determines the effect of a price change on total revenues.

1. Why will revenue fall if a firm raises the price of a good whose demand is elastic?
2. What happens to total revenue when price decreases, but demand is inelastic?

Elasticity and Pricing Policies

Because of these relationships, a firm needs to know whether the demand for its product is elastic or inelastic at a given price. The ways that elasticity of demand can affect a firm's total revenues are shown in **Figure 4.7**. This knowledge helps the firm make pricing decisions that lead to the greatest revenue. If a firm knows that the demand for its product is elastic at the current price, it knows that an increase in price would reduce total revenues. When the price of gasoline rose in 2008, demand for SUVs proved to be elastic. As a result, car manufacturers could not raise prices to compensate for lower sales.

On the other hand, if a firm knows that the demand for its product is inelastic at its current price, it knows that an increase in price will increase total revenue. In the next chapter, you will read more about the choices producers make to reach an ideal level of revenue.

 CHECKPOINT *Why does a firm need to know whether demand for its product is elastic or inelastic?*

(FL) **SS.912.E.1.4, SS.912.E.1.7, LA.1112.2.2.2, LA.1112.2.2.3, LA.1112.1.6.1**

Essential Questions Journal To continue to build a response to the Essential Question, go to your **Essential Questions Journal**.

SECTION 3 ASSESSMENT

 Guiding Question

1. Use your completed chart to answer this question: What factors affect elasticity of demand?
2. **Extension** Think about goods you buy regularly. Suppose the price of everything doubled. Which items would you continue to buy?

Key Terms and Main Ideas

3. What is **elasticity of demand?**
4. If demand for a good is **elastic,** what will happen when the price increases?
5. If demand for a good is **inelastic,** how will a drop in price affect demand for the good?
6. Name three factors that determine a good's elasticity.

7. Suppose demand for a product is elastic at a given price. What will happen to the company's **total revenue** if it raises the price of that product? Why?

Critical Thinking

8. **Analyze (a)** How does the percentage of your budget you spend on a good affect its elasticity? **(b)** Why is this the case?
9. **Summarize** Why does demand become more elastic over time?
10. **Interpret (a)** What factors determine a company's total revenue? **(b)** Do higher prices lead to increased revenues for a company? Explain your answer.

Math Skills

11. To find the elasticity of a good, divide the percentage change in the quantity demanded by the percentage change in price. Review this formula and the formula for finding the percentage changes for prices and for quantity demanded in **Figure 4.5** on page 98. Use the formulas to calculate the elasticity of demand in the following cases. Identify whether demand is elastic, inelastic, or unitary elastic. **(a)** When the price of a car wash rises from $10.00 to $11.00, the number of daily customers drops from 60 to 48. **(b)** A dentist with 80 patients cuts his fee for a cleaning from $60.00 to $54.00 and attracts two new patients.

Visit PearsonSchool.com/PHecon for additional math help.

Chapter 4: Demand

Section 2 Why does the demand curve shift?

Section 1 How does the law of demand affect the quantity demanded?

Section 3 What factors affect elasticity of demand?

Essential Question, Chapter 4
How do we decide what to buy?

Elasticity of Demand

Inelastic	Elastic	Unitary Elastic
• Not sensitive to price change	• Very sensitive to price change	• Percentage change in demand equals percentage change in price
• Price increase: demand is the same	• Price increase: demand is less	• Elasticity equals 1
• Elasticity less than 1	• Elasticity is greater than 1	

Economic Dictionary

demand, *p. 85*

law of demand, *p. 85*

substitution effect, *p. 87*

income effect, *p. 87*

demand schedule, *p. 88*

market demand schedule, *p. 88*

demand curve, *p. 89*

ceteris paribus, p. 91

normal good, *p. 92*

inferior good, *p. 94*

demographics, *p. 94*

complements, *p. 96*

substitutes, *p. 96*

elasticity of demand, *p. 97*

inelastic, *p. 97*

elastic, *p. 97*

unitary elastic, *p. 98*

total revenue, *p. 103*

Changes in Demand

Cause	Effect	Effect
Change in price	Change in the quantity demanded	Movement along a demand curve
More income	Increase in demand	Demand curve shifts to the right
Less income	Decrease in demand	Demand curve shifts to the left

Economics on the go

Study anytime, anywhere. Download these files today.

Economic Dictionary online
Vocabulary Support in English and Spanish

Audio Review online
Audio Study Guide in English and Spanish

Action Graph online
Animated Charts and Graphs

Visual Glossary online
Animated feature

How the Economy Works online
Animated feature

Download to your computer or mobile device at PearsonSchool.com/PHecon

Key Terms and Main Ideas

To make sure you understand the key terms and main ideas of this chapter, review the Checkpoint and Section Assessment questions and look at the Quick Study Guide on the preceding page.

Critical Thinking

1. **Infer (a)** According to the law of demand, what happens when the price of a good drops? **(b)** How is this change shown in a demand curve? **(c)** If a product gets bad publicity, how might that affect the demand curve?

2. **Draw Conclusions (a)** What is a right shift of the demand curve called? **(b)** What is a left shift of the demand curve called? **(c)** How would an increase in income affect the demand curve for a normal good?

3. **Calculate** Suppose that Susan mows lawns for six customers a week and charges $10.00 per lawn. **(a)** What is her total revenue? **(b)** Imagine that Susan raises her prices to $15.00 per lawn and loses two customers. What will happen to her total revenue? **(c)** Is the demand for Susan's lawn-mowing service at this price elastic or inelastic?

4. **Apply (a)** Suppose the price of a certain medicine rises by 50 percent. In the month following the change, sales decrease by 5 percent. Is the demand elastic or inelastic? **(b)** What factors might be responsible for the elasticity or inelasticity of this product? **(c)** After a year, sales of the medicine decrease by 50 percent. What might have happened?

Applying Your Math Skills

Making a Line Plot

Suppose a popular musician is selling a new song online. It costs $1.00 to buy the song from the musician's Web site. At that price, 200 people download the song every day. After the musician raises the price of the song to $1.50, only 100 people per day download the song. The musician then lowers the price to $0.75. At that price, 300 people per day download the song.

Use your math skills to determine and graph the elasticity of demand for the new song, and to answer the following questions:

Visit PearsonSchool.com/PHecon for additional math help.

Demand Curve for Song

5. Based on the original price of $1.00, would you describe demand for the song as inelastic, elastic, or unitary elastic?

6. **(a)** How many people would download the song per day if it cost $0.50? **(b)** How many people would download the song per day if it cost $1.75?

7. On the grid, create a demand curve for the new song. Show the demand for the song at each of the following prices: $0.50, $0.75, $1.00, $1.50, $1.75.

8. Describe how the slope of the graph would change if demand for the song became more elastic.

Essential Question Activity

9. We all make buying decisions on a daily basis. Complete this activity to answer the Essential Question **How do we decide what to buy?** Use the worksheet in your Essential Questions Journal or the electronic worksheet available at **PearsonSchool.com/PHecon** to record information about your recent purchases. Include items such as clothing, electronics, food, and entertainment. List the item, its cost, the quantity you purchased, the percentage of your budget that you spent on the item, and whether a substitute was available. You will be asked to share your list.

   After you have finished the worksheet, discuss demand as a class. Review the factors that affect demand and create a class list of all the factors that contributed to your decisions. For example, did you need the item, or did you just want it? Was it on sale? Did an advertisement influence you? Did you buy a substitute item?

10. **Modify** Students will use the list to analyze their buying decisions. Circle all of the items on the class list that were needs. Eliminate those items from the analysis. Now look at the remaining items. For each item, identify at least one factor that affected your demand. Go back to the Essential Question and write your own answers to these questions: How do I decide what to buy? Could I make better choices?

DOCUMENT-BASED ASSESSMENT

Should the government regulate advertising aimed at children?

Children in the United States are exposed to an onslaught of advertising—on television, in video games, and over the Internet. Critics say that the ads aimed at children are deceptive and create demand for unhealthy products. They want the government to regulate this advertising. Others believe that a self-regulating private sector is the answer.

Document A

"Children are bombarded by advertisements for junk food and for violent movies across the media they use—television, the Internet and video games. These aggressive marketing practices have negative effects on children's health and well-being by contributing to childhood obesity and aggressive behavior. As these media converge, we need rules to protect kids. We have been fighting to protect children from the harmful effects of advertising for many years...."

—childrennow.org, June 11, 2008

Document B

"Some in industry may criticize us for using our bully pulpit to encourage companies to do a better job of marketing healthier products to youth. Such criticism would be misguided. In many ways, industry self-regulation with encouragement from government is really a middle ground approach—somewhere between the government-mandated advertising restrictions adopted in some foreign nations (which might be subject to First Amendment challenge in this country) and the *laissez-faire* approach once urged by many in the business community. Indeed, especially here, a little government involvement—combined with a lot of private sector commitment—can go a long way toward the healthier future for our children that all of us want to see."

—Commissioner Jon Leibowitz, on the FTC Report: *Marketing Food to Children and Adolescents: A Review of Industry Expenditures, Activities, and Self-Regulation* July 29, 2008

Document C

"... No, he can't really fly... No, the bad guys don't really have a ray gun... No, this cereal really isn't the best food in the whole world... No, it won't make you as strong as a giant..."

 FL LA.1112.1.6.2, LA.1112.6.3.1

ANALYZING DOCUMENTS

Use your knowledge of advertising and Documents A, B, and C to answer questions 1–3.

1. **According to Document A, certain advertisements aimed at children can lead to**
   A. aggressive marketing practices.
   B. increased health and wellbeing.
   C. new multimedia rules.
   D. childhood obesity and aggressive behavior.

2. **Document B suggests that the best way to get companies to do a better job of marketing healthier products to children is**
   A. government-mandated advertising restrictions.
   B. a little government involvement and a lot of industry self-regulation.
   C. a First Amendment challenge to offending companies.
   D. a *laissez-faire* approach.

3. **In Document C, the father is teaching his young son**
   A. which products are the best ones to buy.
   B. that television is an interactive medium.
   C. the difference between advertising and reality.
   D. how to activate the closed caption feature.

WRITING ABOUT ECONOMICS

The influence of advertising on children is an ongoing issue. Use the documents on this page and resources on the Web site below to answer the question: *Should the government regulate advertising aimed at children?* Use the sources to support your opinion.

In Partnership

THE WALL STREET JOURNAL.
CLASSROOM EDITION

To read more about issues related to this topic, visit
PearsonSchool.com/PHecon

Chapter

5 Supply

Essential Question, Chapter 5

How do suppliers decide what goods and services to offer?

FL Next Generation Sunshine State Standards

Section 1: Understanding Supply
LA.1112.1.6, MA.912.A.2.2, SS.912.E.1.4, SS.912.E.2.3

Section 2: Costs of Production
LA.1112.1.6, MA.912.A.2.2, MA.912.D.4.1, SS.912.E.1.7

Section 3: Changes in Supply
LA.1112.1.6, MA.912.A.2.2, SS.912.E.1.4, SS.912.E.2.4, SS.912.E.2.7, SS.912.E.3

Economics
on the go

To study anywhere, anytime, download these online resources at *PearsonSchool.com/PHecon* ▶

NGSSS

LA.1112.1.6 Use multiple strategies to develop vocabulary.

MA.912.A.2.2 Interpret a graph to represent a real-world situation.

SS.912.E.1.4 Define supply, demand, quantity supplied, and quantity demanded.

SS.912.E.2.3 Research the contributions of key individuals of various backgrounds in the development of the U.S.

ECONOMIC DICTIONARY

As you read the section, look for the definitions of these **Key Terms:**

• supply
• law of supply
• quantity supplied
• supply schedule
• variable
• market supply schedule
• supply curve
• market supply curve
• elasticity of supply

Guiding Question
How does the law of supply affect the quantity supplied?

Copy this concept web and fill it in as you read.

▶ Economics and You

Suppose you were running a business. What would you do if you discovered that customers were still willing to buy your product if you raised the price 20 percent? Why not take an extra day off each week? You would still earn the same income with 20 percent less work. Or, like most entrepreneurs, would you react by producing more and increasing your revenue?

Principles in Action As prices rise, producers will offer more of a good, while new suppliers will enter the market to earn their share of the profits. The markets for music and pizza show how higher prices increase the quantity supplied, while the example of an orange grove helps to explain elasticity of supply over time.

The Law of Supply

Supply is the amount of goods available. How do producers decide how much to supply? According to the **law of supply,** producers offer more of a good as its price increases and less as its price falls. Economists use the term **quantity supplied** to describe how much of a good a producer is willing and able to sell at a specific price. A producer may also be called a supplier, a company, or an owner—whoever supplies a product to the market.

The law of supply develops from the choices of both current and new producers of a good. As the price of a good rises, existing firms will produce more in order to earn additional revenue. A price increase is

supply the amount of goods available

law of supply producers offer more of a good as its price increases and less as its price falls

quantity supplied the amount that a supplier is willing and able to supply at a specific price

Visual Glossary
online

Go to the Visual Glossary Online for an interactive review of the **law of supply.**

Action Graph
online

Go to Action Graph Online for animated versions of key charts and graphs.

How the Economy Works
online

Go to How the Economy Works Online for an interactive lesson on **production costs.**

VISUAL GLOSSARY

Reviewing Key Terms
To understand the *law of supply,*
review these terms:

demand, *p. 85*
law of demand, *p. 85*
supply, *p. 109*
law of supply, *p. 109*
quantity supplied, *p. 109*

What is the Law of Supply?

◄ **law of supply** producers offer more of a good as its price increases and less as its price falls

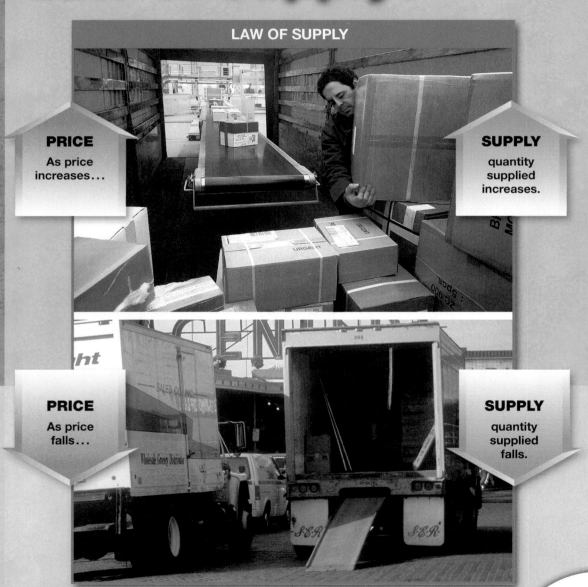

LAW OF SUPPLY

PRICE
As price increases...

SUPPLY
quantity supplied increases.

PRICE
As price falls...

SUPPLY
quantity supplied falls.

The price of a good determines how much of that good a supplier will provide. ***How is the law of supply different from the law of demand?***

Visual Glossary
online
To expand your understanding of this and other key economic terms, visit **PearsonSchool.com/PHecon**

also an incentive for new firms to enter the market to earn their own profits. If the price of a good falls, some firms will produce less, and others might drop out of the market. These two movements—individual firms changing their level of production and firms entering or exiting the market—combine to create the law of supply.

Higher Production

If a firm is already earning a profit by selling a good, then an increase in the price—*ceteris paribus*—will increase the firm's profits. The promise of higher revenues for each sale encourages the firm to produce more. The pizzeria you read about in Chapter 4 probably makes a reasonable profit by selling a certain number of slices a day at the market price. If the pizzeria wasn't making a profit, the owner would raise the price or switch from pizzas to something more profitable.

If the price of pizza rises, but the firm's cost of making pizza stays the same, the pizzeria will earn a higher profit on each slice. A sensible entrepreneur would produce and sell more pizza to take advantage of the higher prices.

Similarly, if the price of pizza goes down, the pizzeria will earn less profit per slice or even lose money. The owner will choose to sell less pizza and produce something else, such as calzones, which will yield more profit.

In both cases, the search for profit drives the supplier's decision. When the price goes up, the supplier recognizes the chance to make more money and works harder to produce more pizza. When the price falls, the same entrepreneur is discouraged from producing as much as before.

Market Entry

Profits appeal both to producers already in the market and people who may decide to join the market. As you have seen, when the price of pizza rises, a pizzeria provides a good opportunity to make money. If you were to open your own restaurant, a pizzeria would look like a safe bet. This is how rising prices draw new firms into a market and add to the quantity supplied of the good.

◀ Appliance makers try to profit from a trend. **Which trend are appliance makers trying to cash in on in this cartoon?**

Consider the market for music. In the late 1970s, disco music became popular. The music industry quickly recognized the popularity of disco, and soon, more and more groups released disco recordings. Groups that once recorded soul and rhythm and blues music chose to record disco albums. New entrants crowded the market to take advantage of the potential for profit. Disco, however, was a short-lived fad. By the early 1980s, stores couldn't sell disco albums.

This pattern of sharp increases and decreases in supply occurs again and again in the music industry. In the early 1990s, grunge music emerged from Seattle to become widely popular among high school and college students across the country. How did the market react? Record labels hired more grunge groups. Music stores devoted more space to grunge music. However, grunge soon lost its appeal, and many groups disbanded or moved on to new styles. Other styles of music, such as hip-hop and independent rock, achieved new popularity.

In each of these examples, many musicians joined the market to profit from a trend. Their actions reflected the law of supply, which says that the quantity supplied increases as the price of the good increases.

✓ **CHECKPOINT** *Why do firms increase production when the price of a good goes up?*

The Supply Schedule

Similar to a demand schedule, a **supply schedule** shows the relationship between price and quantity supplied for a specific good, or how much of a good a supplier will offer at various prices. The pizzeria discussed earlier might have a supply schedule that looks like the one in **Figure 5.1**. This table compares two **variables,** or factors that can change. These variables are the price of a slice and the number of slices supplied by a pizzeria. We could collect this information by asking the pizzeria owner how many slices she is willing and able to make at different prices, or we could look at records to see how the quantity supplied has varied as the price has changed. We will almost certainly find that at higher prices, the pizzeria owner is willing to make more pizza. At a lower price, she prefers to make less pizza and devote her limited resources to other, more profitable, items.

Like a demand schedule, a supply schedule lists supply for a very specific set of conditions. The schedule shows how the price of pizza, and only the price of pizza, affects the pizzeria's output. The other factors that could change the restaurant's output decisions, such as the costs of tomato sauce, labor, and rent, are assumed to remain constant.

A Change in the Quantity Supplied

Economists use the word *supply* to refer to the relationship between price and quantity supplied, as shown in the supply schedule. The pizzeria's supply of pizza includes all possible combinations of price and output. According to this supply schedule, the pizzeria's supply is 100 slices at $1.00 a slice, 150 slices at $2.00 a slice, 200 slices at $3.00 a slice, and so on. The number of slices that the pizzeria offers at a specific price is called the quantity supplied at that price. At $5.00 per slice, the pizzeria's quantity supplied is 300 slices per day.

A rise or fall in the price of pizza will cause the quantity supplied to change, but not the supply schedule. In other words, a change in a good's price moves the seller from one row to another in the same supply schedule, but does not change the supply schedule itself. When a factor other than the price of pizza affects output, we have to build a whole new supply schedule for the new market conditions.

Market Supply Schedule

All of the supply schedules of individual firms in a market can be added up to create a **market supply schedule.** A market supply schedule shows the relationship between prices and the total quantity supplied by *all* firms in a particular market. This information becomes important when we want to determine the total supply of pizza at a certain price in a large area, like a city.

Figure 5.1	Supply Schedule

Individual Supply Schedule

Price Per Slice of Pizza	Slices Supplied Per Day
$1.00	100
$2.00	150
$3.00	200
$4.00	250
$5.00	300
$6.00	350

Market Supply Schedule

Price Per Slice of Pizza	Slices Supplied Per Day
$1.00	1,000
$2.00	1,500
$3.00	2,000
$4.00	2,500
$5.00	3,000
$6.00	3,500

CHART SKILLS

The individual supply schedule lists how many slices of pizza one pizzeria will offer at different prices. The market supply schedule represents all suppliers in a market.

1. What does the individual supply schedule tell you about the pizzeria owner's decisions?
2. How does the market supply schedule compare to the individual supply schedule?

Figure 5.2

Supply Curves

Individual Supply Curve

Market Supply Curve

GRAPH SKILLS

Supply curves always rise from left to right. As price increases, so does the quantity supplied, as predicted by the law of supply.

1. How many slices will one pizzeria produce at $3.00 a slice?
2. How does a producer create a market supply schedule or curve?

Action Graph
online

For an animated version of this graph, visit
PearsonSchool.com/PHecon

The market supply schedule for pizza in **Figure 5.1** shows the supply of pizza for a hypothetical city. It resembles the supply schedule for a single pizzeria, but the quantities are much larger.

This market supply schedule lists the same prices as those in the supply schedule for the single pizzeria, since all restaurants will charge prices within the same range. The quantities supplied are much larger because there are many pizzerias in the community. Like the individual supply schedule, this market supply schedule reflects the law of supply. Pizzerias supply more pizza at higher prices.

The Supply Graph

When the data points in the supply schedule are graphed, they create a **supply curve**. A supply curve is a graphic representation of a supply schedule. A supply curve is very similar to a demand curve, except that the horizontal axis now measures the quantity of the good supplied, not the quantity demanded. The supply graph on the left in **Figure 5.2** shows a supply curve for one pizzeria. The graph on the right shows a **market supply curve** for all the pizzerias

in the city. The data used to draw the two curves are from the supply schedules in **Figure 5.1**. The prices shown along the vertical axes are the same in both graphs. However, the quantities of pizza supplied at each price are much larger in the market supply curve.

The key feature of the supply curve is that it always rises from left to right. As your finger traces the curve from left to right, it moves toward higher and higher output levels (on the horizontal axis) and higher and higher prices (on the vertical axis). This illustrates the law of supply, which says that a higher price leads to higher output.

 CHECKPOINT *What are the two variables represented in a supply schedule or a supply curve?*

Supply and Elasticity

In Chapter 4, you learned that elasticity of demand measures how consumers will react to price changes. Elasticity of supply is based on the same concept.

Elasticity of supply measures how firms will respond to changes in the price of a good. The labels *elastic, inelastic,* and

FL MA.912.A.2.2
Interpret a graph to represent a real-world situation.

supply curve a graph of the quantity supplied of a good at various prices

market supply curve a graph of the quantity supplied of a good by all suppliers at various prices

elasticity of supply a measure of the way quantity supplied reacts to a change in price

FL **SS.912.E.2.3** Research the contributions of key individuals of various backgrounds in the development of the U.S.

unitary elastic represent the same values of elasticity of supply as those of elasticity of demand. When elasticity is greater than one, supply is very sensitive to changes in price and is considered elastic. If supply is not very responsive to changes in price, and elasticity is less than one, supply is considered inelastic. When a percentage change in price is perfectly matched by an equal percentage change in quantity supplied, elasticity is exactly one, and supply is unitary elastic.

Elasticity of Supply and Time

What determines whether the supply of a good will be elastic or inelastic? The key factor is time. In the short run, a firm cannot easily change its output level, so supply is inelastic. In the long run, firms are more flexible, so supply is more elastic.

Elasticity of Supply in the Short Run

An orange grove is one example of a business that has difficulty adjusting to a change in price in the short term. Orange trees take several years to mature and grow fruit. If the price of oranges goes up,

an orange grower can buy and plant more trees, but he will have to wait several years for his investment to pay off. In the short term, the grower could take smaller steps to increase output. For example, he could use a more effective pesticide. While this step might increase his output somewhat, it would probably not increase the number of oranges by very much. Economists would say that his supply is inelastic, because he cannot easily change his output. The same factors that prevent the owner of the orange grove from expanding his supply will also prevent new growers from entering the market and supplying oranges in the short term.

In the short run, supply is inelastic whether the price increases or decreases. If the price of oranges falls, the grove owner has few ways to cut his supply. Years ago, he invested in land and trees, and his grove will provide oranges no matter what the price is. Even if the price drops drastically, the grove owner will probably pick and sell nearly as many oranges as before. His competitors have also invested heavily in land and trees and won't drop out of the market if they can survive. In this case, supply is inelastic whether prices rise or fall.

While orange groves illustrate a business in which supply is inelastic, other businesses have a more elastic supply. For example, a business that provides a service, such as a haircut, is highly elastic. Unlike oranges, the supply of haircuts is easily expanded or reduced. If the price rises, barbershops and salons can hire workers fairly quickly or extend their business hours.

In addition, new barbershops and salons will open. This means that a small increase in price will cause a large increase in quantity supplied, even in the short term.

If the price of a haircut drops, some shop owners will lay off workers or close earlier in the day. Others will leave the market. Quantity supplied will fall quickly. Because haircut suppliers can quickly change their operations, the supply of haircuts is elastic.

Elasticity in the Long Run

Like demand, supply can become more elastic over time. The orange grower could not increase his output much when the price of oranges rose, but he can plant more trees to increase his supply. This response becomes more effective over time, as the trees grow and bear fruit. After several years, he will be able to sell more oranges at the higher market price.

If the price drops and stays low for several years, orange growers who survived the first two or three years of losses might decide to grow something else. Given five years to respond instead of six weeks, the supply of oranges will be far more elastic. Just like demand, supply becomes more elastic if the supplier has a longer time to respond to a price change.

▲ Because the vines take three or four years to produce fruit, cranberries are another product for which supply is inelastic in the short term.

✔ CHECKPOINT *How does a business that is highly elastic respond to a fall in prices?*

FL SS.912.E.1.4, LA.1112.2.2.2, MA.912.A.2, LA.1112.2.2.3, LA.1112.1.6.1

SECTION 1 ASSESSMENT

Essential Questions Journal To continue to build a response to the Essential Question, go to your **Essential Questions Journal**.

❓ Guiding Question

1. Use your completed concept web to answer this question: How does the law of supply affect the quantity supplied?
2. **Extension** Describe how a recent change in supply has affected a product that you regularly purchase.

Key Terms and Main Ideas

3. What is the difference between **supply** and **quantity supplied?**
4. What does a **supply schedule** show?
5. What does a **market supply curve** show?

Critical Thinking

6. **Apply** Give an example of a variable other than price for each of these markets: **(a)** a rock band's concert tour, **(b)** an electronic equipment maker, **(c)** a bakery.
7. **Predict** When the price of gold rises, what will happen to the market for second-hand jewelry? Explain your answer.
8. **Analyze** State whether you think the supply of the following services is elastic or inelastic, and explain why: **(a)** a lawn-care service, **(b)** making movies, **(c)** professional baseball.

Math Skills

9. Use the following supply schedule for corn to create a supply curve.

Visit PearsonSchool.com/PHecon for additional math help.

Corn Supply Schedule

Price Per Ton	Quantity Supplied
100	50
150	75
200	100
250	125
300	150
350	175
400	200

NGSSS

LA.1112.1.6 Use multiple strategies to develop vocabulary.

MA.912.A.2.2 Interpret a graph to represent a real-world situation.

MA.912.D.4.1 Solve maximal profit/minimal cost problems.

SS.912.E.1.7 Graph and explain how price is determined through marginal cost analysis.

ECONOMIC DICTIONARY

As you read the section, look for the definitions of these **Key Terms:**

- marginal product of labor
- increasing marginal returns
- diminishing marginal returns
- fixed cost
- variable cost
- total cost
- marginal cost
- marginal revenue
- average cost
- operating cost

Guiding Question
How can a producer maximize profits?

Copy this table and fill it in as you read.

To Maximize Profit...	
Managing Labor	**Setting Output**
• Increase marginal returns	•
•	•

marginal product of labor the change in output from hiring one additional unit of labor

▶ **Economics and You**   You are making egg salad sandwiches for a picnic. The knife is the physical capital. Your labor, the bread, and the egg salad are the inputs. In a beanbag factory, the physical capital is one sewing machine and one pair of scissors. Its inputs are workers and materials, including cloth, thread, and beans. Each beanbag requires the same amount of materials. How does the company decide how many beanbags to produce? How many sandwiches should you make?

Principles in Action Producers think about the cost of making one more unit of a good when deciding how to maximize profits. You'll also see what happens when a factory's operating costs are greater than its revenue.

Labor and Output

One basic question that any business owner has to answer is how many workers to hire. Owners have to consider how the number of workers they hire will affect their total production. For example, at the beanbag factory, one worker can produce four beanbags per hour. Two workers can make a total of ten bags per hour, and three can make a total of seventeen beanbags per hour. As each new worker joins the company, total output increases. After the seventh worker is hired, production peaks at 32 beanbags per hour. When the firm hires the eighth worker, however, total output drops to 31 bags per hour. The relationship between labor, measured by the number of workers in the factory and the number of beanbags produced, is shown in **Figure 5.3**.

Marginal Product of Labor

The third column of **Figure 5.3** shows the **marginal product of labor,** or the change in output from hiring one more worker. This is called the marginal product because it measures the change in output at the margin, where the last worker has been hired or fired.

The first worker to be hired produces four bags an hour, so her marginal product is four bags. The second worker raises total output from four bags per hour to ten, so her marginal product of labor is six. Looking at this column, we see that the marginal product of labor increases for the first three workers, rising from four to seven.

▲ When workers specialize in specific tasks, output per worker increases and the firm enjoys increasing marginal returns.

Increasing Marginal Returns

The marginal product of labor increases for the first three workers because there are three tasks involved in making a beanbag. Workers cut cloth into the correct shape, stuff it with beans, and sew the bag closed. A single worker performing all these tasks can produce only four bags per hour. Adding a second worker allows each worker to specialize in one or two tasks. If each worker focuses on only one part of the process, she wastes less time switching between tasks and becomes more skillful at her assigned tasks. Because specialization increases output per worker, the second worker adds more to output than the first. The firm enjoys **increasing marginal returns.**

In our example, there are benefits from specialization, and the firm enjoys a rising marginal product of labor for the first three workers.

Diminishing Marginal Returns

When workers four through seven are hired, the marginal product of labor is still positive. Each new worker still adds to total output. However, the marginal product of labor shrinks as each worker joins the company. The fourth worker increases output by six bags, while the seventh increases output by only one bag. Why?

After the beanbag firm hires its first three workers, one for each task, the benefits of specialization end. At that point, adding more workers increases total output but at a decreasing rate. This situation is known as **diminishing marginal returns.** A firm with diminishing marginal returns of labor will produce less and less output from each additional unit of labor.

The firm suffers from diminishing marginal returns from labor because its workers have a limited amount of capital. Capital—any human-made resource used to produce other goods—is represented by the factory's single sewing machine and its pair of scissors. With three workers, only one needs to use the sewing machine, so this worker never has to wait to get to work. When there are more than three workers, the factory may assign more than one to work at the sewing machine.

So while one works, the other worker waits. She may cut fabric or stuff bags, but every bag must be sewn at some point, so she cannot greatly increase the speed of production.

The problem gets worse as more workers are hired and the amount of capital remains constant. Time wasted waiting for the sewing machine or scissors means that additional workers will add less and less to total output as shown in **Figure 5.4.**

Figure 5.3 | Marginal Product of Labor

Marginal Product of Labor

Labor (number of workers)	Output (beanbags per hour)	Marginal Product of Labor
0	0	—
1	4	4
2	10	6
3	17	7
4	23	6
5	28	5
6	31	3
7	32	1
8	31	–1

CHART SKILLS

The marginal product of labor is the increase in output added by the last unit of labor.

1. In this example, why does the marginal product of labor increase with the first three workers?
2. Why does the marginal product of labor decrease with more than four workers in this example?

increasing marginal returns a level of production in which the marginal product of labor increases as the number of workers increases

diminishing marginal returns a level of production at which the marginal product of labor decreases as the number of workers increases

Figure 5.4 | Marginal Returns

Labor (number of workers)

GRAPH SKILLS

Labor has increasing and then diminishing marginal returns.

1. What is the marginal product of labor when the factory employs five workers?
2. Why does the factory experience diminishing marginal returns with more than three workers?

What are production costs?

Production costs are the costs an entrepreneur must pay to run a business. Production costs are divided into two categories: fixed costs and variable costs.

1 Fixed Cost
Rent: Fixed costs are costs that do not change, no matter how much of a good is produced. The rent for the storefront is a fixed cost.

2 Fixed Cost
Manager: The new manager is essential to the operation of the store. The manager's salary is a fixed cost.

3 Variable Costs
Goods and electricity: Variable costs are costs that change as the level of production changes. The cost of all the merchandise the store sells is a variable cost. The cost of the electricity that the store uses during business hours is also a variable cost.

Fixed Cost

Negative Marginal Returns

As the table in **Figure 5.3** shows, adding an eighth worker actually decreases output by one bag. At this stage, workers get in each other's way and disrupt production, so overall output decreases. Of course, few companies ever hire so many workers that their marginal product of labor becomes negative.

✔ **CHECKPOINT** *How does capital affect marginal returns?*

Production Costs

Paying workers and purchasing capital are all costs of producing goods. Economists divide a producer's costs into two main categories: fixed costs and variable costs.

Fixed Costs

A **fixed cost** is a cost that does not change, no matter how much of a good is produced.

fixed cost a cost that does not change, no matter how much of a good is produced

variable cost a cost that rises or falls depending on the quantity produced

Most fixed costs involve the production facility—the cost of building and equipping a factory, office, store, or restaurant. Examples of fixed costs include rent, machinery repairs, property taxes, and the salaries of workers who run the business even when production temporarily stops.

Variable Costs

Variable costs are costs that rise or fall depending on the quantity produced. They include the costs of raw materials and some labor. For example, to produce more beanbags, the firm must purchase more beans and hire more workers. If the company wants to produce less and cut costs, it can buy fewer beans or reduce weekly hours for some workers. The cost of labor is a variable cost because it changes with the number of workers, which changes with the quantity produced. Electricity and heating bills are also variable costs,

4 Variable Cost

Part-time workers: Some companies hire part-time workers, whose hours are reduced when business is slow. The salaries for part-time workers are a variable cost.

5 Total Cost

When fixed costs and variable costs are added together, the result is a firm's total cost—the amount of money needed to operate a business.

Check Your Understanding
1. Would an advertisement for the store that runs every week in a local newspaper be a fixed cost or a variable cost?
2. Is the separate storage space the owner rents for two months a fixed cost or a variable cost?

Variable Cost

Total Cost

because the company only uses heat and electricity during business hours.

Total Cost

Costs for the firm that produces beanbags are shown in **Figure 5.5** on the next page. The firm's factory is fully equipped to produce beanbags. How does the cost of producing beanbags change as the output increases?

In our example, the fixed costs are the costs of the factory building and all the machinery and equipment. As shown in the second column in **Figure 5.5,** the fixed costs are $36.00 per hour.

Variable costs include the cost of beans, fabric, and most of the workers. As shown in the third column, variable costs rise with the number of beanbags produced. Fixed costs and variable costs are added together to find **total cost.** Total cost is shown in the fourth column.

Marginal Cost

If we know the total cost of production at several levels of output, we can determine the marginal cost of production at each level. **Marginal cost** is the additional cost of producing one more unit.

As shown in **Figure 5.5,** even if the firm is not producing a single beanbag, it still must pay $36.00 per hour for fixed costs. If the firm decides to produce just one beanbag per hour, its total cost rises by $8.00, from $36.00 to $44.00 per hour. The marginal cost of the first beanbag is $8.00.

For the first three beanbags, marginal cost falls as output increases. The marginal cost of the second beanbag is $4.00, and the marginal cost of the third beanbag is $3.00. Each additional beanbag is cheaper to make because of increasing marginal returns resulting from specialization.

At four beanbags per hour, the marginal cost starts to rise. The marginal cost of the

Personal Finance
For help with setting your own budget, see your Personal Finance Handbook in the back of the book or visit
PearsonSchool.com/PHecon

total cost the sum of fixed costs plus variable costs

marginal cost the cost of producing one more unit of a good

marginal revenue the additional income from selling one more unit of a good; sometimes equal to price

fifth beanbag per hour is $7.00, the sixth costs $9.00, and the seventh, $12.00. The rising marginal cost reflects diminishing returns of labor. The benefits of specialization are exhausted at three beanbags per hour. Diminishing returns set in as more workers share a fixed production facility.

☑ **CHECKPOINT** *Why does a closed factory still have production costs?*

Simulation *Activity*

How Is Output Set?
You may be asked to take part in a role-playing game about setting output.

 SS.912.E.1.7
Graph and explain how price is determined through marginal cost analysis.

MA.912.D.4.1
Solve maximal profit/minimal cost problems.

Setting Output

Behind all of the hiring decisions is the firm's basic goal: to maximize profits. Profit is defined as total revenue minus total cost. As you read in Chapter 4, a firm's total revenue is the money the firm gets by selling its product. Total revenue is equal to the price of each good multiplied by the number of goods sold. Total revenue when the price of a beanbag is $24.00 is shown in **Figure 5.5**. To find the level of output with the highest profit, we look for the biggest gap between total revenue and total cost. The gap is greatest and profit is highest when the firm makes 9 or 10 beanbags per hour. At this rate, the firm can expect to make a profit of $98.00 per hour.

Marginal Revenue and Marginal Cost

Another way to find the best level of output is to find the output level where marginal revenue is equal to marginal cost. **Marginal revenue** is the additional income from selling one more unit of a good. If the firm has no control over the market price, marginal revenue equals the market price. Each beanbag sold at $24.00 increases the firm's total revenue by $24.00, so marginal revenue is $24.00. According to the table, price equals marginal cost with ten beanbags, so that's the quantity that maximizes profit at $98 per hour.

To understand how an output of ten beanbags maximizes the firm's profits, suppose that the firm made only four beanbags per hour. Is it making as much money as it can?

From **Figure 5.5**, we know that the marginal cost of the fifth beanbag is $7.00. The market price for a beanbag is $24.00, so the marginal revenue from that beanbag is $24.00. The $17.00 difference between the marginal revenue and marginal cost represents pure profit for the company from the fifth beanbag. The company should increase production to five beanbags an hour to capture that profit on the fifth beanbag.

Figure 5.5 | **Production Costs**

CHART SKILLS

Firms consider a variety of costs when deciding how much to produce.

1. Why is the marginal revenue always equal to $24?

2. What is the average cost when output is seven beanbags per hour?

Beanbags (per hour)	Fixed Cost	Variable Cost	Total Cost (fixed cost + variable cost)	Marginal Cost	Marginal Revenue (market price)	Total Revenue	Profit (total revenue – total cost)
0	$36	$0	$36	—	$24	$0	$–36
1	36	8	44	$8	24	24	–20
2	36	12	48	4	24	48	0
3	36	15	51	3	24	72	21
4	36	20	56	5	24	96	40
5	36	27	63	7	24	120	57
6	36	36	72	9	24	144	72
7	36	48	84	12	24	168	84
8	36	63	99	15	24	192	93
9	36	82	118	19	24	216	98
10	36	106	142	24	24	240	98
11	36	136	172	30	24	264	92
12	36	173	209	37	24	288	79

The same calculations show that the company can capture a profit of $15.00 by producing a sixth beanbag per hour. The price of the seventh beanbag is $12.00 higher than its marginal cost, so that beanbag earns an additional $12.00 in profit for the company. The profit is available any time the company receives more for the last beanbag than the cost to produce it. Any rational entrepreneur would take this opportunity to increase profit.

Now suppose that the firm is producing so many beanbags per hour that marginal cost is *higher* than price. If the firm produces eleven beanbags per hour, it receives $24.00 for that eleventh beanbag, but the $30.00 cost of producing that beanbag wipes out the profit. The firm actually loses $6.00 on the sale of the eleventh beanbag. Because marginal cost is increasing, and price is constant in this example, the losses get worse at higher levels of output. The company would be better off producing less and keeping costs down.

The ideal level of output is where marginal revenue (price) is equal to marginal cost. Any other quantity of output would generate less profit. As **Figure 5.5** shows, profit per hour can be determined by subtracting total cost from total revenue. We can also determine profit by comparing price and average cost. **Average cost** is total cost divided by the quantity produced. At an output of 10 beanbags per hour, the average cost is $14.20 ($142—total cost—divided by 10). Profit is the difference between market price and average cost ($24 − 14.20 = $9.80) multiplied by the quantity ($9.80 × 10 = $98).

Responding to Price Changes

What happens if the price of a beanbag rises from $24.00 to $37.00? Thinking at the margin, the firm would probably increase production to twelve beanbags per hour. At that quantity, marginal cost is equal to the new, higher price. At the original price of $24.00, the firm would not produce more than ten beanbags, according to **Figure 5.6**. When the price rises to $37.00, marginal revenue soars above marginal cost at that output level. By raising production to 12 beanbags per

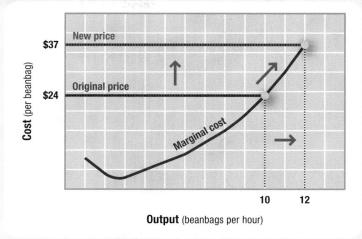

Figure 5.6 | Output and a Change in Price

GRAPH SKILLS
The most profitable level of output is where price (or marginal revenue) is equal to marginal cost.
1. What would happen to output if the market price fell to $20?
2. Why would the firm increase output if the price of a beanbag rose to $37?

Action Graph online
For an animated version of this graph, visit PearsonSchool.com/PHecon

hour, the firm earns profits on the eleventh and twelfth beanbags.

This example shows the law of supply in action. An increase in price from $24.00 to $37.00 causes the firm to increase the quantity supplied from ten to twelve beanbags per hour.

✔ **CHECKPOINT** *What is a firm's basic goal when it sets its level of output?*

The Shutdown Decision

Consider the problems faced by a factory that is losing money. The factory is producing at the most profitable level of output, where marginal revenue is equal to marginal cost. However, the market price is so low that the factory's total revenue is still less than its total cost, and the firm is losing money. Should this factory continue to produce goods and lose money, or should its owners shut the factory down?

In fact, there are times when keeping a money-losing factory open is the best choice. The firm should keep the factory open if the total revenue from the goods the factory produces is greater than the cost of keeping it open.

FL **SS.912.E.1.7** Graph and explain how price is determined through marginal cost analysis.

MA.912.A.2.2 Interpret a graph to represent a real-world situation.

average cost the total cost divided by the quantity produced

▲ When a factory is losing money, operating cost and revenue are the factors that determine whether or not the factory remains open.

operating cost the cost of operating a facility, such as a factory or a store

FL SS.912.E.1.7, LA.1112.1.6.1, LA.1112.2.2.2, LA.1112.2.2.3, MA.912.D.4.1

For example, if the price of beanbags drops to $7 and the factory produces at the profit-maximizing level of five beanbags per hour, the total revenue drops from $120 per hour to $35 per hour. Weigh this against the factory's **operating cost,** the cost of operating the facility. Operating cost includes the variable costs the owners must pay to keep the factory running, but not fixed costs, which the owners must pay whether the factory is open or closed.

According to **Figure 5.5,** if the factory produces five beanbags, the variable cost is $27 per hour. Therefore, the benefit of operating the facility (total revenue of $35) is greater than the variable cost ($27), so it makes sense to keep the facility running.

Consider the effects of the other choice. If the firm shuts down the factory, it would still have to pay all of its fixed costs. The factory's total revenue would be zero because it produces nothing for sale. Therefore, the firm would lose an amount of money equal to its fixed costs.

For this beanbag factory, the fixed costs equal $36 per hour, so the factory would lose $36 for each hour it is closed. If the factory produced five beanbags per hour, its total cost would be $63 ($36 in fixed costs plus $27 in variable costs) per hour, but it would lose only $28 ($63 in total cost minus $35 in revenue) for each hour it is open. The factory would lose less money while producing because the total revenue ($35) would exceed the variable costs ($27), leaving $8 to cover some of the fixed costs. Although the factory would lose money either way, it loses less money by continuing to produce and sell beanbags.

When will a business replace a factory that is operating at a loss? The firm will build a new factory and stay in the market only if the market price of beanbags is high enough to cover all the costs of production, including the cost of building a new factory.

✔ **CHECKPOINT** *When should a firm keep a money-losing factory open?*

SECTION 2 ASSESSMENT

Essential Questions Journal To continue to build a response to the Essential Question, go to your **Essential Questions Journal.**

❓ Guiding Question

1. Use your completed table to answer this question: How can a producer maximize profits?
2. **Extension** How would it help the company where you worked to maximize profits if you received advanced training?

Key Terms and Main Ideas

3. What does **marginal cost** refer to?
4. What are examples of **fixed costs** and **variable costs** for a farm?
5. What is **marginal revenue?**
6. Is **operating cost** a **fixed cost** or a **variable cost?** Why?

Critical Thinking

7. **Solve** Suppose you are advising a company that is seeing diminishing marginal returns. Other than reducing staff, what steps would you recommend to its managers to improve its performance?
8. **Decide** Suppose your company has two office spaces, one twice as large as the other. Would you add the same number of employees to each facility? Why or why not?
9. **Analyze (a)** Why would a company produce more units of a good if its marginal cost is less than its marginal revenue? **(b)** Why would the company not simply produce more and more units?

Math Skills

10. Using the table on page 120 as the base, change the Fixed Cost column to $20 and the Marginal Revenue column to $19. **(a)** Recalculate the Total Cost column, the Total Revenue column and the Profit column. **(b)** Based on the chart, what is the output that will maximize profit? **(c)** How much will the profit be? **(d)** Using the table you have created, make a graph that shows the most profitable level of output when the marginal revenue is $19.

Visit PearsonSchool.com/PHecon for additional math help.

SECTION 3 Changes in Supply

FL NGSSS

LA.1112.1.6 Use multiple strategies to develop vocabulary.

MA.912.A.2.2 Interpret a graph to represent a real-world situation.

SS.912.E.1.4 Graphically illustrate situations that cause economic change.

SS.912.E.2.4 Diagram and explain the problems of government-instituted wage and price control.

SS.912.E.2.7 Identify the societal impact of inflation.

SS.912.E.3 Understand the relationships of the U.S. economy and the international marketplace.

Guiding Question

Why does the supply curve shift?

Copy this table and fill it in as you read.

Supply	
Supply Increases	**Supply Decreases**
• Fall in the cost of an input	•
•	•
•	•

▶ **Economics and You**   You own a collection of original action figures from a popular movie. You notice that the price of these figures is increasing rapidly on Web auction sites. Should you sell the figures now, or wait? How would your decision affect the supply of these action figures?

Principles in Action Several factors, including the number of suppliers in a market, can lead to a shift in the supply curve. Government actions and global events also have an impact on supply. Input costs are the subject of the Economics & You feature.

Input Costs

Any change in the cost of an input used to produce a good—such as raw materials, machinery, or labor—will affect supply. A rise in the cost of an input will cause a fall in supply at all price levels because the good has become more expensive to produce. On the other hand, a fall in the cost of an input will cause an increase in supply at all price levels.

Effect of Rising Costs

Think of the effects of input costs on the relationship between marginal revenue (price) and marginal cost. A supplier sets output at the most profitable level, where price is equal to marginal cost. Marginal cost includes the cost of the inputs that go into production, so a rise in the cost of labor or raw materials will result in a higher marginal cost. If the cost of inputs increases enough, the marginal cost may become higher than the price, and the firm may not be as profitable.

If a firm has no control over the price, the only solution is to cut production and lower marginal cost until marginal cost equals the lower price. Supply falls at each price, and the supply curve shifts to the left, as illustrated in **Figure 5.7.**

Technology

Input costs can drop as well. Advances in technology can lower production costs in many industries. Automation, including the use of robotic tools, has spread throughout the manufacturing sector, saving on labor costs. Computers have simplified tasks and cut costs in many fields. Inexpensive e-mail allows

ECONOMIC DICTIONARY

As you read the section, look for the definitions of these **Key Terms:**

• subsidy
• excise tax
• regulation

The higher input costs that dairy farmers pay for feed, labor, and fuel result in higher prices for milk and other dairy products. ▼

subsidy a government payment that supports a business or market

excise tax a tax on the production or sale of a good

businesses to communicate in an instant. Future advances promise to decrease production costs even further.

Technology lowers costs and increases supply at all price levels. This effect is seen in a rightward shift in the supply curve in **Figure 5.7.**

✔ **CHECKPOINT** *How would a rise in the cost of inputs, such as raw materials, affect supply?*

Government's Influence on Supply

FL SS.912.E.2.7 Identify the societal impact of inflation.

The government has the power to affect the supplies of many types of goods. By raising or lowering the cost of producing goods, the government can encourage or discourage an entrepreneur or an industry within the country or abroad.

Subsidies

One method used by governments to affect supply is to give subsidies to the producers of a good, particularly for food. A **subsidy** is a government payment that supports a business or market. The government often pays a producer a set subsidy for each unit of a good produced. Subsidies generally lower costs, allowing a firm to produce more goods.

Governments have several reasons for subsidizing producers. During and after World War II, European countries faced food shortages. Today, European governments protect farms so that some will be available to grow food in case cheaper imports are ever restricted. In France, the government subsidizes small farms to protect the lifestyle and character of the French countryside.

Governments in developing countries often subsidize manufacturers to protect young, growing industries from strong foreign competition. Countries such as Indonesia and Malaysia have subsidized a national car company as a source of pride, even though imported cars were less expensive. In Western Europe, banks and national airlines were allowed to suffer huge losses with the assurance that the government would cover their debts. In many countries, governments have stopped providing industrial subsidies in the interest of free trade and fair competition.

In the United States, the federal government subsidizes producers in many industries. Farm subsidies are particularly controversial, especially when farmers are paid to take land out of cultivation to keep prices high. In these cases, more efficient farmers are penalized, and farmers use more herbicides and pesticides on lands they do cultivate to compensate for production lost on the acres the government pays them not to plant.

Taxes

A government can reduce the supply of some goods by placing an excise tax on them. An **excise tax** is a tax on the production or sale of a good. An excise tax increases production costs by adding an extra cost for each unit sold.

Economics & YOU

Input Costs

Rising costs for wheat, fertilizer, and fuel make this box of cereal more expensive to produce. *As a result of higher input costs, you pay more for your morning bowl of cereal.*

You receive special offers and discount coupons by e-mail. *Technology helps companies to reduce costs for advertising and postage.*

▲ Input costs affect the price you pay for a good or service. *Name two items that would become more expensive if sugar rose in price.*

Excise taxes are sometimes used to discourage the sale of goods that the government thinks are harmful to the public good, like cigarettes, alcohol, and high-pollutant gasoline. Excise taxes are indirect—they are built into the prices of these and other goods—so consumers may not realize that they are paying them. Like any increase in cost, an excise tax causes the supply of a good to decrease at all price levels. The supply curve shifts to the left.

Regulation

Subsidies and excise taxes represent ways that government directly affects supply by changing revenue or production costs. Government can also raise or lower supply through indirect means. Government regulation often has the effect of raising costs. **Regulation** is government intervention in a market that affects the price, quantity, or quality of a good.

Even members of government recognize the burden that regulation can place on business. In a 2006 speech to the Economic Club of New York, Treasury Secretary Henry M. Paulson Jr. described how over-regulation of business can affect economic progress:

> **❝**Excessive regulation slows innovation, imposes needless costs on investors, and stifles competitiveness and job creation.**❞**
>
> —Henry M. Paulson Jr., Secretary of the Treasury,
> washingtonpost.com, Nov. 11, 2006

For many years, pollution from automobiles harmed the environment. Starting in 1970, the federal government required car manufacturers to install technology to reduce pollution from auto exhaust. For example, new cars had to use lead-free fuel because scientists linked health problems to lead in gasoline. Regulations such as these increased the cost of manufacturing cars and reduced the supply. The supply curve shifted to the left.

 CHECKPOINT *How does an excise tax increase production costs?*

Other Influences on Supply

While government can have an important influence on the supply of goods, there are other important factors that influence supply.

 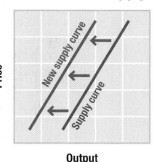

| Figure 5.7 | **Shifts in the Supply Curve** |

Increase in Supply   **Decrease in Supply**

Price / Output (Increase in Supply: Supply curve → New supply curve)

Price / Output (Decrease in Supply: New supply curve ← Supply curve)

GRAPH SKILLS

Factors that reduce supply shift the supply curve to the left, while factors that increase supply move the supply curve to the right.

1. Which graph best represents the effects of higher costs?

2. Which graph best represents advances in technology?

 Action Graph
online

For an animated version of this graph, visit **PearsonSchool.com/PHecon**

Changes in the Global Economy

As you read in earlier chapters, a large and rising share of goods and services are imported. The supplies of imported goods are affected by changes in other countries. Here are two examples of possible changes in the supply of products imported by the United States.

- The U.S. imports carpets from India. An increase in the wages of Indian workers would decrease the supply of carpets to the U.S. market, shifting the supply curve to the left.
- The United States imports oil from Russia. A new oil discovery in Russia could increase the supply of oil to the U.S. market and shift the supply curve to the right.

Import restrictions also affect supply. The total supply of a product equals the sum of imports and domestically produced products. An import ban on sugar would eliminate foreign sugar suppliers from the market, shifting the market supply curve to the left. At any price, a smaller quantity of sugar would be supplied. If the government restricted imports by establishing an import quota, the supply curve would shift to the

(FL) **SS.912.E.2.4** Diagram and explain the problems of government-instituted wage and price control. **MA.912.A.2.2** Interpret a graph to represent a real-world situation.

regulation government intervention in a market that affects the production of a good left, but the shift would be smaller than it would be for a total ban on sugar imports.

Future Expectations of Prices

If you were a soybean farmer, and you expected the price of soybeans to double next month, what would you do with the crop that you just harvested? Most farmers would store their soybeans until the price rose, cutting back supply in the short term.

If a seller expects the price of a good to rise in the future, the seller will store the goods now in order to sell more in the future. But if the price of the good is expected to drop in the near future, sellers will earn more money by placing goods on the market immediately, before the price falls. Expectations of higher prices will reduce supply now and increase supply later. Expectations of lower prices will have the opposite effect.

Inflation is a condition of rising prices. During periods of inflation, the value of cash in a person's pocket decreases from day to day as prices rise. Over many years, inflation has reduced the value of the dollar. However, a good will continue to hold its value, provided that it can be stored for a long period of time.

When faced with inflation, suppliers prefer to hold on to goods that will maintain their value rather than sell them for cash that loses its value rapidly. Inflation can affect supply by encouraging suppliers to hold on to goods as long as possible. In the short term, supply can fall dramatically.

During the Civil War, the South faced terrible inflation. There were shortages of food, and shopkeepers knew that prices on basic food items like flour, butter, and salt would rise each month. A few decided to hoard their food and wait for higher prices. They succeeded too well; the supply of food fell so much that prices rose out of the reach of many families. Riots broke out in Virginia and elsewhere when hungry people decided they weren't going to wait for the food to be released from the warehouses, and the shopkeepers lost their goods and their profits.

Number of Suppliers

Another factor to consider when looking at changes in supply is the number of suppliers in the market. If more suppliers enter a market to produce a certain good, the market supply of the good will rise and the supply curve will shift to the right. However, if suppliers stop producing the good and leave the market, the supply will decline. There is a positive relationship between the number of suppliers in a market and the market supply of the good.

✔ **CHECKPOINT** *What happens to supply if the price of a good is expected to rise in the future?*

Declining oil supplies have led to higher energy prices and the need to develop alternative energy sources. *Select three images and describe their connection to higher energy costs.* ▼

FUTURE WATCH **Impact of Rising Energy Costs**

Balloooning Problem

A SHIFT IN THE SUPPLY CURVE

Dwindling supplies and surging demand combine to inflate the price of helium.

By Ana Campoy
The Wall Street Journal

FL SS.912.E.1.4 Graphically illustrate situations that cause economic change.

Syracuse University physicist Gianfranco Vidali spends most of his time studying how molecules are made in outer space, but he has had to drop his interstellar research to address an earthly issue: the global shortage of helium.

The airy element best known for floating party balloons is also the lifeblood of a widening world of scientific research. Mr. Vidali uses the gas to recreate conditions similar to the cold of outer space. Without it, he can't work. So when his helium supplier informed him it was cutting deliveries to his lab, Mr. Vidali said, "it sent us into a panic mode."

Helium is found in varying concentrations in the world's natural-gas deposits, and is separated out in a special refining process. As with oil and natural gas, the easiest-to-get helium supplies have been tapped and are declining. Meanwhile, scientific research has rapidly multiplied the uses of helium in the past 50 years. It is needed to make computer microchips, flat-panel displays, fiber optics and to operate MRI scans and welding machines.

The technology explosion is sucking up helium supplies at dizzying rates. U.S. helium demand is up more than 80% in the past two decades, and is growing at more than 20% annually in developing regions such as Asia.

Meanwhile, supplies in the world's largest helium reserve near Amarillo, Texas, are expected to run out in eight years. Finding and developing new helium sources will take years and millions of dollars in investment.

"We're running on the edge of the supply-demand curve," says Jane Hoffman, global helium director for Praxair Inc.

Experts predict this situation will eventually price out many helium users, who will have to find substitutes or modify their technology. Some party balloon businesses are filling balloons with mixtures that contain less helium. Some welders are using argon.

Physicists are particularly affected by the helium shortage because their equipment requires more frequent helium refills. Myriam Sarachik, a physicist at City University of New York, might have to shut down her research, because helium now absorbs most of her lab's budget, leaving little extra for everything else.

"I'm going to retire. That's the handwriting on the wall," says Ms. Sarachik.

Applying Economic Principles

Advances in technology usually increase supply. But increased demand for helium used in new technologies has led to a helium shortage. Describe an event that might cause the supply curve for helium to shift to the right.

Video News Update Online
Powered by
The Wall Street Journal
Classroom Edition

Use videos at **PearsonSchool.com/PHecon** as a springboard for a discussion on a current topic.

Where Do Firms Produce?

So far, we have ignored the issue of where firms locate their production facilities. For many firms, the key factor is the cost of transportation—the cost of transporting inputs to a production facility and the cost of transporting the finished product to consumers. One firm will locate close to input suppliers when inputs, such as raw materials, are expensive to transport. Another firm will locate close to its consumers when output is more costly to transport.

Consider the example of a firm that processes tomatoes into tomato sauce. Suppose that the firm uses seven tons of tomatoes to produce one ton of sauce. The firm locates its plant close to the tomato fields—and far from its consumers—because it is much cheaper to ship one ton of sauce to consumers than to ship seven tons of tomatoes to a faraway plant. Tomato sauce producers cluster in places like California's Central Valley, where weather and soil conditions are favorable for the growing of tomatoes.

Now consider the example of a firm that bottles soft drinks. The firm combines concentrated syrup with local water, so the firm's output (bottled drinks) weighs more than its transportable input (syrup). As a result, the firm locates close to its consumers—and far from its syrup supplier—because the firm saves more on transporting soft drinks than it pays to transport its syrup. In general, if a firm's output is bulky or perishable, the firm will locate close to its consumers.

Other firms locate close to inputs that cannot be transported at all. Some firms are pulled toward concentrations of specialized workers such as artists, engineers, and computer programmers. Other firms are pulled toward locations with low energy costs. Many firms locate in cities because of the rich variety of workers and business services available in urban areas.

☑ **CHECKPOINT** *When is a firm likely to locate close to its consumers?*

 SS.912.E.1.4, SS.912.E.2.4, SS.912.E.3, LA.1112.1.6.1, LA.1112.2.2.2

SECTION 3 ASSESSMENT

Essential Questions Journal To continue to build a response to the Essential Question, go to your **Essential Questions Journal**.

❓ Guiding Question

1. Use your completed table to answer this question: Why does the supply curve shift?

2. **Extension** Give an example of how a change in the number of suppliers has changed the supply of a good or service.

Key Terms and Main Ideas

3. What is a **subsidy,** and how do subsidies affect the supply curve?

4. What is an **excise tax,** and how do excise taxes affect the supply curve?

5. What effect do **regulations** have on the supply curve? Why?

Critical Thinking

6. **Apply (a)** Suppose the United States buys most of its bananas from a particular country. If that country suffered a drought, what would happen to the supply curve for bananas? **(b)** What response by American companies would shift the curve in the opposite direction?

7. **Apply** Analyze and explain the impact on the supply curve for American-made computers from each of the following events: **(a)** The government places an excise tax on laptops, **(b)** An engineer invents a way to produce desktop cases more cheaply, **(c)** European countries end an import quota on American-made computers.

8. **Judge** If regulation increases price and decreases supply, why does the government issue regulations?

9. **Analyze (a)** Why would an auto-maker want to have manufacturing plants in several different regions? **(b)** Why would a software company not necessarily want facilities in several different regions?

Quick Write

10. In the past, animated movies were created by teams of artists drawing and coloring illustrations by hand. Now, many animation companies use computers to create these movies. Write a brief paragraph explaining what effect that change will have on the supply curve of animated movies.

Chapter 5: Supply

Section 1 How does the law of supply affect the quantity supplied?

Section 2 How can a producer maximize profits?

Section 3 Why does the supply curve shift?

Essential Question, Chapter 5
How do suppliers decide what goods and services to offer?

Economic Dictionary

supply, *p. 109*
law of supply, *p. 109*
quantity supplied, *p. 109*
supply schedule, *p. 112*
variable, *p. 112*
market supply schedule, *p. 112*
supply curve, *p. 113*
market supply curve, *p. 113*
elasticity of supply, *p. 113*
marginal product of labor, *p. 116*
increasing marginal returns, *p. 117*
diminishing marginal returns, *p. 117*
fixed cost, *p. 118*
variable cost, *p. 118*
total cost, *p. 119*
marginal cost, *p. 119*
marginal revenue, *p. 120*
average cost, *p. 121*
operating cost, *p. 122*
subsidy, *p. 124*
excise tax, *p. 124*
regulation, *p. 125*

Costs of Production

Marginal Product of Labor	Production Costs	Marginal Cost and Marginal Revenue
• Marginal product of labor: the change in output from hiring one more worker. • Increasing marginal returns: increased output per worker. • Diminishing marginal returns: additional workers produce less output.	• Fixed costs do not change, no matter how much of a good is produced. • Variable costs rise or fall depending on the quantity produced. • Fixed costs plus variable costs equal total cost.	• Marginal cost: the additional cost of producing one more unit. • Marginal revenue: the additional income from selling one more unit. • Most profitable level of output: marginal revenue equals marginal cost.

Changes in Supply

Cause	Effect	Effect
Change in price	Change in the quantity supplied	Supply curve: new price and quantity
Higher input costs	Supply falls at each price	Supply curve shifts to the left
Lower input costs	Supply increases at each price	Supply curve shifts to the right

Economics on the go

Study anytime, anywhere. Download these files today.

Economic Dictionary online — Vocabulary Support in English and Spanish

Audio Review online — Audio Study Guide in English and Spanish

Action Graph online — Animated Charts and Graphs

Visual Glossary online — Animated feature

How the Economy Works online — Animated feature

Download to your computer or mobile device at PearsonSchool.com/PHecon

Self-Test online   To test your understanding of key terms and main ideas, visit **PearsonSchool.com/PHecon**

Key Terms and Main Ideas

To make sure you understand the key terms and main ideas of this chapter, review the Checkpoint and Section Assessment questions and look at the Quick Study Guide on the preceding page.

Critical Thinking

1. **Give Examples (a)** Give two examples of industries that would draw new firms into the market if profits of existing businesses rose. **(b)** Give two examples of industries that would see fewer new firms enter the market, even if profits rose.

2. **Recognize (a)** What is the difference between an individual supply schedule and a market supply schedule? **(b)** How does a supply curve relate to a supply schedule? **(c)** How does a supply curve reflect the law of supply?

3. **Predict (a)** Suppose television networks raise the fees that cable television systems must pay to show their programs. How would that affect the supply of programs for cable television? **(b)** Do higher fees lead to a change in the quantity supplied or a change in supply? Explain.

4. **Apply (a)** Suppose you open a shoe repair shop. What fixed and variable costs would you have? **(b)** How would you calculate total revenue?

5. **Determine (a)** A company has the following total costs: 1 unit: $5, 2 units: $9, 3 units: $12, 4 units: $14, 5 units: $17. What is the marginal cost for each number of units? **(b)** At what point does the company see diminishing returns? Explain your answer.

Applying Your Math Skills

Calculating Production Costs

Study the information about Sal's Ice Cream Shop in the chart below. Note: Monthly supply costs apply to each month.

Visit PearsonSchool.com/PHecon for additional math help.

Monthly Costs	Expected Revenues
Rent: $2,000	April: $8,000
Manager's salary: $2,000	May: $8,000
Workers' wages: $3,000	June: $10,000
Supplies (April and May): $2,000	July: $12,000
Supplies (June and September): $3,000	August: $12,000
Supplies (July and August): $4,000	September: $10,000

6. The manager has a contract that requires Sal to pay his salary. **(a)** How much does Sal pay in fixed costs? **(b)** How much does he pay in variable costs? **(c)** What are Sal's total costs?

7. Should Sal close the ice cream shop in April or May? Why or why not?

8. In what months does Sal earn a profit? How much does he make?

9. Should Sal take steps to change the way he does business? Explain your answer.

? Essential Question Activity

Essential Questions Journal   To respond to the chapter Essential Question, go to your **Essential Questions Journal**.

10. Complete the activity to answer the Essential Question **How do suppliers decide what goods and services to offer?** For this activity, students will act as market researchers and conduct a poll to determine what one good or service their community needs most. Each student will poll three people in the community (family, friends, or other students) to have them identify the one good or service that best serves local needs. When the poll is completed, the class will separate poll results into five different categories: entertainment, food establishments, medical services, recreational facilities, and other. Use the worksheet in your Essential Questions Journal or the electronic worksheet available at **PearsonSchool.com/PHecon,** for instructions on how to conduct the poll.

11. **Modify** Students will form five marketing groups based on the poll categories. Each group will use poll results from one category to create a description of a business that supplies a good or service that satisfies the need of the *greater number* of people in the community. Note that two ideas could be combined to create one

business. Check listings in the telephone directory or Chamber of Commerce to determine if a similar business already exists in the community. Since a supplier needs an incentive, students should consider the necessity of the business turning a profit. Student groups will then present their business ideas to the class and ask students to vote for the one business plan from the five categories that is most likely to be successful. After students have made their selections, have them answer the following questions:

(a) Why do you think the business you chose would have a greater chance of success?

(b) Can you identify some fixed or variable costs for this business?

(c) How might the government regulate this good or service?

As a final exercise, present the choices from the original poll to a different class. Ask those students to vote on the product or service they think would benefit the majority of people in the community.

DOCUMENT-BASED ASSESSMENT

Should the government subsidize ethanol production?

The government pays subsidies to companies that produce ethanol, a fuel made from corn. In recent years, ethanol production has increased rapidly. Critics say that the subsidies are a waste of money, that corn-based ethanol cannot supply enough energy to reduce oil imports, and that using food crops for fuel causes other problems.

Document A

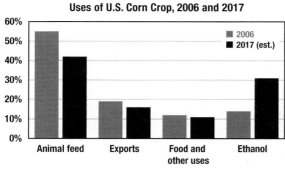

Uses of U.S. Corn Crop, 2006 and 2017

■ 2006
■ 2017 (est.)

SOURCE: USDA Agricultural Projections

Document B

With crude oil soaring to nearly $78 a barrel last year, the price of alternatives to gasoline soared as well. . . . The federal incentive for ethanol is a tax break of 51 cents a gallon. Last year, more than 5.3 billion gallons were produced. . . . President Bush is urging Congress and the nation's biofuels industry to accelerate the use of ethanol to curb gasoline consumption by 20 percent by 2017. . . . A big difference won't come about until refiners start turning corn stalks, wheat straw, wood chips and grasses into ethanol.

—*The Dallas Morning News*, January 30, 2007

Document C

In the United States, the explosive growth of the biofuels sector and its demand for raw stocks of plants has triggered run-ups in the prices not only of corn, other grains, and oilseeds, but also of [other] crops and products. . . . In Minnesota, land diverted to corn to feed the ethanol maw is reducing the acreage planted to a wide range of other crops, especially soybeans. Food processors with contracts with farmers to grow crops such as peas and sweet corn have been forced to pay higher prices to keep their supplies secure. Eventually, these costs will appear in the prices of frozen and canned vegetables. Rising feed prices are also hitting the livestock and poultry industries.

—*Issues in Science and Technology*, September 22, 2007

ANALYZING DOCUMENTS

Use your knowledge of subsidies and Documents A, B, and C to answer questions 1–3.

1. **Document A shows that as more corn is used for ethanol,**
   A. more will also be used for animal feed.
   B. exports of corn will increase.
   C. corn for food and other uses will drop slightly.
   D. the price of corn will rise.

2. **Document B explains that the subsidy for ethanol production**
   A. is $78 a barrel.
   B. is 51 cents a gallon.
   C. is going up by 20 percent.
   D. plays little role in ethanol production.

3. **Document C shows that the ethanol boom**
   A. results in higher food prices.
   B. drives farmers to grow soybeans.
   C. forces corn prices down.
   D. is likely to end by 2017.

WRITING ABOUT ECONOMICS

Whether to support ethanol production or not is an ongoing issue. Use the documents on this page and resources on the Web site below to answer the question: ***Should the government subsidize ethanol production?*** Use the sources to support your opinion.

6 Prices

Essential Question, Chapter 6

What is the right price?

FL **Next Generation Sunshine State Standards**

Section 1: Combining Supply and Demand
LA.1112.1.6, MA.912.A.2.2, SS.912.E.1.4, SS.912.E.1.9, SS.912.E.2.4

Section 2: Changes in Market Equilibrium
LA.1112.1.6, LA.1112.1.6.2, MA.912.A.2.2, SS.912.E.1.4, SS.912.E.2.3

Section 3: The Role of Prices
LA.1112.1.6, SS.912.E.1.4, SS.912.E.1.8, SS.912.E.3.6

Economics
on the go

To study anywhere, anytime, download these
online resources at *PearsonSchool.com/PHecon* ▶

NGSSS

LA.1112.1.6 Use multiple strategies to develop vocabulary.

MA.912.A.2.2 Interpret a graph to represent a real-world situation.

SS.912.E.1.4 Define supply, demand, quantity supplied, and quantity demanded.

SS.912.E.1.9 Describe how workers' pay is determined.

SS.912.E.2.4 Diagram and explain the problems of government-instituted wage and price control.

ECONOMIC DICTIONARY

As you read the section, look for the definitions of these **Key Terms:**

- equilibrium
- disequilibrium
- shortage
- surplus
- price ceiling
- rent control
- price floor
- minimum wage

Guiding Question
What factors affect prices?

Copy this concept web and fill it in as you read.

(concept web: Disequilibrium — Equilibrium — Government intervention)

▶ **Economics and You**   When you go to the store to buy something—whether it's a cellphone, a CD, or a pair of sneakers—you can usually find it. You are benefiting from the free market system at work. Businesses are making enough profit to produce and sell the goods you want at a price you are willing to pay.

Principles in Action   Prices are affected by the laws of supply and demand and by government action. Using the market for pizza as an example, you will see how free markets provide goods and services at the right price and in sufficient quantities. You will also see examples of how government intervention affects the wages of some workers and the rent that some people pay.

Reaching Equilibrium

Just as buyers and sellers come together in a market, what you have learned about demand and supply in previous chapters will come together in this section. Your knowledge of supply and demand will help you to understand how markets operate and how markets can turn competing interests into a positive outcome for both sides. You'll also see why free markets usually produce some of their best outcomes when they are left to operate on their own, free from government intervention.

We begin by looking at a supply and demand schedule. As you know, a demand schedule shows how much of a good consumers are willing to buy at various prices. A supply schedule shows how much firms are willing to sell at various prices. Comparing these schedules will help us to find common ground for the two sides of the market.

Visual Glossary
online

Go to the Visual Glossary Online for an interactive review of **equilibrium.**

Action Graph
online

Go to Action Graph Online for animated versions of key charts and graphs.

How the Economy Works
online

Go to How the Economy Works Online for an interactive lesson on **shortage** and **surplus.**

Figure 6.1 **Finding Equilibrium**

Combined Supply and Demand Schedule

Price of a Slice of Pizza	Quantity Demanded	Quantity Supplied	Result
$1.00	300	100	Shortage from excess demand
$2.00	250	150	
$3.00	200	200	Equilibrium
$4.00	150	250	Surplus from excess supply
$5.00	100	300	
$6.00	50	350	

CHART SKILLS

Market equilibrium will be found at the price at which the quantity demanded is equal to the quantity supplied.

1. How many slices are sold at $2.00 a slice?
2. How many slices are sold at equilibrium?

Supply and Demand Meet

The point where demand and supply come together is called the equilibrium. **Equilibrium** is the point of balance at which the quantity demanded equals the quantity supplied. At equilibrium, the market for a good is stable.

To find the equilibrium price and quantity, simply look for the price at which the quantity supplied equals the quantity demanded. In the combined supply and demand schedule for a pizza market in **Figure 6.1,** this occurs at a price of $3.00 per slice.

As you know, supply and demand schedules can be graphed. Look at the three graphs in the Visual Glossary on the next page. The first two graphs are the supply curve and the demand curve for pizza slices from the last two chapters. The third graph, Finding Equilibrium, combines the first two graphs. This graph shows both the number of slices that consumers in a market will buy at various prices and the number of slices that pizzerias will supply.

To find the equilibrium price and quantity on the graph, locate the point at which the supply curve and the demand curve

equilibrium the point at which the demand for a product or service is equal to the supply of that product or service

disequilibrium any price or quantity not at equilibrium; when quantity supplied is not equal to quantity demanded in a market

shortage when quantity demanded is more than quantity supplied

intersect. At that point, quantity supplied equals quantity demanded. As you can see, the supply and demand curves intersect at $3.00 per slice. At that price and only at that price, the quantity demanded and the quantity supplied are equal, at 200 slices per day. At that price, the market is in a state of equilibrium.

Market Benefits

In any market, supply and demand will be equal at only one price and one quantity. At this equilibrium price, buyers will purchase exactly as much of a good as firms are willing to sell.

Buyers who are willing to purchase goods at the equilibrium price will find ample supplies on store shelves. Firms that sell at the equilibrium price will find enough buyers for their goods. When a market is at equilibrium, both buyers and sellers benefit.

✔ **CHECKPOINT** *At what point on a combined supply and demand graph is the market at equilibrium?*

Disequilibrium

If the market price or quantity supplied is anywhere but at the equilibrium, the market is in a state of disequilibrium. **Disequilibrium** occurs when quantity supplied is not equal to quantity demanded in a market. In **Figure 6.1,** or in the Finding Equilibrium graph in the Visual Glossary, disequilibrium occurs at any price other than $3.00 per slice, or any quantity other than 200 slices. Disequilibrium can produce one of two outcomes: shortage or surplus.

Shortage

The problem of **shortage**—also known as excess demand—exists when the quantity demanded in a market is more than the quantity supplied. When the actual price in a market is below the equilibrium price, you have a shortage, because the low price encourages buyers and discourages sellers. For example, in **Figure 6.1,** a price of $2.00 per slice of pizza will lead to a quantity demanded of 250 slices per day but a quantity supplied of only 150 slices per day. At this price, there is a shortage of 100 slices per day.

VISUAL GLOSSARY

Reviewing Key Terms
To understand *equilibrium*, review these terms:

market, *p. 29*
law of demand, *p. 85*
demand curve, *p. 89*
law of supply, *p. 109*
supply curve, *p. 113*

What is Equilibrium?

◄ **equilibrium** the point at which the demand for a product or service is equal to the supply of that product or service

DEMAND CURVE

The **law of demand** says that buyers will purchase more of a certain product if the price is lower.

SUPPLY CURVE

The **law of supply** says that suppliers will offer more of a certain product if the price is higher.

FINDING EQUILIBRIUM

When supply equals demand, the market has reached **equilibrium**, or balance. *At the point of equilibrium, how many slices will the pizzeria supply at what price?*

◄ This cartoon shows the concept of equilibrium as it applies to the real estate market. *How does this cartoon show the relationship of supply and demand? What will happen to the market if supply becomes stronger than demand?*

Visual Glossary
online
To expand your understanding of this and other key economic terms, visit **PearsonSchool.com/PHecon**

Figure 6.2 — Shortage and Surplus

GRAPH SKILLS

Shortage and surplus both lead to a market with fewer sales than at equilibrium.

1. How much is the shortage when pizza is sold at $2.00 per slice?

2. Based on the second graph, how might the pizzeria solve the problem of excess supply?

Action Graph
online

For an animated version of this graph, visit PearsonSchool.com/PHecon

FL MA.912.A.2.2
Interpret a graph to represent a real-world situation.

When customers want to buy 100 more slices of pizza than restaurants are willing and able to sell, these customers will have to wait in long lines for their pizza, and some will have to do without. In the graph on the left in **Figure 6.2**, we have illustrated the shortage at $2.00 per slice by drawing a dotted line across the graph at that price.

If you were running the pizzeria, and you noticed long lines of customers waiting to buy your pizza at $2.00 per slice, what would you do? Assuming that you like to earn profits, you would probably raise the price. As the price increased, you would be willing to work harder and bake more pizzas, because you would know you could earn more money for each slice you sell.

From Shortage to Equilibrium

Of course, as the price rises, customers will buy less pizza, since it is becoming relatively more expensive. When the price reaches $3.00 per slice, you will find that you are earning more profit and can keep up with demand, but the lines are much shorter. Some days you may throw out a few leftover slices, and other days you may have to throw an extra pizza or two in the oven to keep up with customers, but

on the whole, you are meeting the needs of your customers. In other words, the market is now at equilibrium.

As long as there is a shortage and the quantity demanded exceeds the quantity supplied, suppliers will keep raising the price. When the price has risen enough to close the gap, suppliers will have found the highest price that the market will bear. They will continue to sell at that price until one of the factors described in Chapter 4 or Chapter 5 changes either the demand or the supply curve, and creates new pressures to raise or lower prices and, eventually, a new equilibrium.

Surplus

If the price is too high, the market will face the problem of surplus, also known as excess supply. A **surplus** exists when quantity supplied exceeds quantity demanded and the actual price of a good is higher than the equilibrium price. For example, at a price of $4.00 per slice of pizza, the quantity supplied of 250 slices per day is much greater than the quantity demanded of 150 slices per day. This means that pizzeria owners will be making 100 more slices of pizza each day than they can sell at that price.

surplus when quantity supplied is more than quantity demanded

The relatively high price encourages pizzeria owners to make more pizza, but it discourages customers from buying pizza, since it is relatively more expensive than other menu items. Some customers will buy one slice instead of two, while others will eat elsewhere. At the end of the day, it is likely that 100 slices will have to be thrown out.

From Surplus to Equilibrium

Before long, pizzeria owners will get tired of throwing out unsold pizza and will cut their prices. As the price falls, the quantity demanded will rise, and more customers will buy more pizza. At the same time, pizzeria owners will supply fewer pizzas. This process will continue until the price reaches the equilibrium price of $3.00 per slice. At that price, the amount of pizza that pizzeria owners are willing and able to sell is exactly equal to the amount that their customers are willing and able to buy.

Whenever the market is in disequilibrium and prices are flexible, market forces will push the market toward the equilibrium. Sellers do not like to waste their resources on a surplus, particularly when the goods cannot be stored for long, like pizza. And when there is a shortage, profit-seeking sellers realize that they can raise prices to earn more profits. For these reasons, market prices move toward the equilibrium level.

✔ **CHECKPOINT** *What market condition might cause a pizzeria owner to throw out many slices of pizza at the end of the day?*

Price Ceiling

Markets tend toward equilibrium, but in some cases the government intervenes to control prices. The government can impose a **price ceiling,** or a maximum price that can be legally charged for a good or service. The price ceiling is set below the equilibrium price.

Rent Control

A price ceiling is a maximum price, set by law, that sellers can charge for a good or service. The government places price ceilings on some goods that are considered "essential" and might become too expensive for some consumers. For example, in the early 1940s, New York City intro-

duced **rent control,** or price ceilings placed on apartment rents, to prevent inflation during a housing crisis. Later, other cities imposed rent control to help the poor cut their housing costs and enable them to live in neighborhoods that they could otherwise not afford. Let's examine how rent control affects the quantity and quality of housing available to consumers.

The housing market data for a hypothetical city is shown in **Figure 6.3** on the next page. Look at Graph A. The supply and demand curves for two-bedroom apartments meet at point *a*, where the rental price is $900 a month. At this equilibrium rent, consumers will demand 30,000 apartments and suppliers will offer 30,000 apartments for rent.

Suppose that the city government passes a law that limits the rent on two-bedroom apartments to $600 per month. This price ceiling is below the equilibrium price. The effect on the market is shown in Graph B in **Figure 6.3.** At a price of $600, the quantity of apartments demanded is 45,000 (point *c*), and the quantity supplied is 15,000 (point *b*). At such a low price, apartments seem inexpensive. Many people will try to rent apartments instead of living with their families or investing in their own houses.

However, some landlords will have difficulty earning profits or breaking even at these low rents. Fewer new apartment buildings will be built,

price ceiling a maximum price that can legally be charged for a good or service

rent control a price ceiling placed on apartment rent

Restaurants and other businesses often donate surplus food to charities. In New York City, an organization called City Harvest collects and distributes food to community programs throughout the city. *What other kinds of businesses might donate surplus food to charities?* ▼

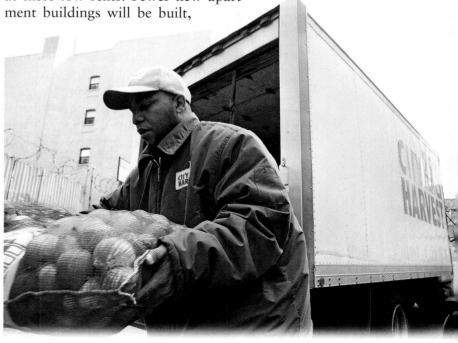

Figure 6.3 **The Effects of Rent Control**

GRAPH SKILLS

While rent control helps many tenants, it also creates disequilibrium in the housing market.

1. At what price is the market for apartments at equilibrium without rent control?

2. How does rent control lead to a shortage of desirable apartments?

Action Graph
online

For an animated version of this graph, visit
PearsonSchool.com/PHecon

A. Without Rent Control

B. With Rent Control

KEY

a. The supply and demand curves for two-bedroom apartments meet at the equilibrium rent of $900 per month.

b. With rent control keeping rents at $600 per month, landlords are willing to supply 15,000 two-bedroom apartments.

c. With rent control keeping rents at $600 per month, potential tenants are seeking 45,000 two-bedroom apartments.

  MA.912.A.2.2 Interpret a graph to represent a real-world situation.

and older ones might be converted into offices, stores, or condominiums. The result is a shortage of 30,000 apartments. The price ceiling increases the quantity demanded but decreases the quantity supplied. Since rents are not allowed to rise, this shortage will last as long as the price ceiling holds.

The Cost of Rent Control

When the price cannot rise to the equilibrium level, the market must determine which 15,000 of the 45,000 households will get an apartment, and which 30,000 will do without. Although governments usually pass rent control laws to help renters with the greatest need, few of these renters benefit from rent control. Methods besides prices—including long waiting lists, discrimination by landlords, a lottery system, and even bribery—may be used to allocate the scarce supply of apartments. Luck becomes an important factor, and sometimes the only way to get a rent-controlled apartment is to inherit it from a parent or grandparent.

In addition, since the rent controls limit landlords' profits, landlords may try to increase their income by cutting costs. Why should a landlord give a building a fresh coat of paint and a new garden if he or she can't earn the money back through higher rent? Besides, if there's a waiting list to get an apartment, the landlord has no incentive to work hard and attract renters. As a result, many rent-controlled apartment buildings become run-down, and renters may have to wait months to have routine problems fixed.

The Impact of Ending Rent Control

If rents were allowed to rise to the market equilibrium level, which is $900 per month, the quantity of apartments in the market would actually rise to 30,000 apartments. The market would be in equilibrium, and people who could afford $900 a month would have an easier time finding vacant apartments. Instead of spending time and money searching for apartments, and then having to accept an apartment in a poorly maintained building, many renters would be able to find a wider selection of apartments. Landlords would also have a greater incentive to properly maintain their buildings and invest in new construction.

On the other hand, once rent control is ended, people living in formerly rent-controlled apartments may no longer be able to afford the higher rents. As soon as the neighborhood improves, these renters may be priced out of their apartments, and replaced by people willing to pay the equilibrium price.

Certainly, the end of rent control benefits some people and hurts others. Nearly all economists agree that the benefits of ending rent control exceed the costs, and suggest that there are better ways to help poor households find affordable housing.

✓ **CHECKPOINT** *How does a price ceiling affect the quantity demanded and the quantity supplied?*

Price Floors

A **price floor** is a minimum price, set by the government, that must be paid for a good or service. Governments set price floors to ensure that certain sellers receive at least a minimum reward for their efforts. Sellers can include workers, who sell their labor.

The Minimum Wage

One price floor that is well-known is the **minimum wage,** which sets a minimum price that an employer can pay a worker for one hour of labor. The federal government sets a base level for the minimum wage, but states can make their own minimum wages even higher. A full-time worker being paid the federal minimum wage will earn less than the federal government says is necessary to support a couple with one child. Still, the minimum wage does ensure a lower limit for workers' earnings. But do the benefits to minimum-wage workers outweigh the loss of some jobs?

The supply curve of labor and the demand curve for labor are combined in **Figure 6.4.** This supply curve shows the number of workers available at various wage rates, and the demand curve shows the number of workers that employers will hire at various wages. (In this example, the worker is the supplier of labor that is bought by an employer.) If the minimum wage is set above the market equilibrium wage rate, the demand for workers will go down.

If the market equilibrium wage for low-skilled labor is $6.60 per hour, and the minimum wage is set at $7.25, the result is a surplus of labor. Firms will employ 2 million fewer low-skilled workers—including teenagers—than they would at the equilibrium wage rate, because the price floor on labor keeps the wage rate artificially high. If the minimum wage is below the equilibrium rate, it will have no effect, because employers would have to pay at least the equilibrium rate anyway to find workers in a free market.

We should note here that **Figure 6.4** is a theoretical model of the effects of a minimum wage. The real world is more complex, and some economists believe that the actual effect of the minimum wage on employment rates is not as severe as in this example.

Price Supports in Agriculture

Agricultural price supports are another example of price floors that are used for many farm products around the world. Like the minimum wage, price supports have both supporters and opponents.

During the Great Depression of the 1930s, the federal government began setting minimum prices for many commodities.

price floor a minimum price for a good or service

minimum wage a minimum price that an employer can pay a worker for one hour of labor

 MA.912.A.2.2 Interpret a graph to represent a real-world situation.

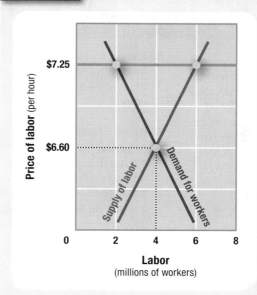

| Figure 6.4 | **Effects of Minimum Wage** |

GRAPH SKILLS

A minimum wage law can set the price of labor above the equilibrium price.

1. According to the graph, at what wage is the labor market at equilibrium?

2. What happens to the labor supply when the minimum wage is set at $7.25 per hour?

Action Graph
online

For an animated version of this graph, visit PearsonSchool.com/PHecon

NICKANDERSON©...

CONGRESS

FARM BILL

The Jolly Green Giant

This cartoon comments on federal programs that give financial aid to farmers. *Do you think this cartoonist probably favored or opposed price supports for farm products? Explain.*

Unlike the minimum wage, these price floors were not legal minimums set for buyers. Instead, whenever prices fell below a certain level, the government created demand by buying excess crops.

Supporters of price floors believed that they were necessary because American farms would not easily survive in a freely competitive agricultural market. If many American farms were to go out of business, the United States would have to depend on other nations for its vital food supply. Opponents of price supports argued that the regulations were a burden to farmers.

The government dictated what farmers should produce and in what quantities. Congress voted to phase out most of these programs in 1996, because they seemed to conflict with free market principles.

Some people worried that, without the government stepping in to buy up excess crops, farmers would begin to overproduce. One Minnesota farmer commented:

❝When you have bumper crops, if it truly is a supply-and-demand market, and you're supplying more than what the demand is, it's financial suicide.❞
—Brian Romsdahl, Minnesota Public Radio, 1998

Despite the effort to end price supports, many commodities, such as dairy products, remain relatively untouched by the new laws. For example, the Department of Agriculture has continued to buy tons of powdered milk in order to keep the price from dropping below the set minimum. This milk is stored in warehouses and even in caves across the country. In addition, the federal government often responds to low prices by providing emergency financial aid to farmers.

✔ **CHECKPOINT** *How does a minimum wage above the equilibrium rate affect the supply of labor?*

FL SS.912.E.1.4, SS.912.E.2.4, LA.1112.1.6.1, LA.1112.2.2.2, LA.1112.2.2.3

Essential Questions Journal To continue to build a response to the Essential Question, go to your **Essential Questions Journal**.

SECTION 1 ASSESSMENT

❓ Guiding Question

1. Use your completed concept web to answer this question: What factors affect prices?
2. **Extension** Consumers play a critical role in establishing prices. Describe how a specific buying decision that you might make could affect the price of an item.

Key Terms and Main Ideas

3. Under what conditions is a market at **equilibrium**?
4. Identify the two conditions that can lead to **disequilibrium** in a free market.
5. **(a)** When supply exceeds demand, what happens to prices? **(b)** How will the market return to equilibrium?

6. Identify two ways the government can intervene to control prices.
7. What is the purpose of the **minimum wage**?

Critical Thinking

8. **Contrast (a)** In a free market, what impact does a shortage have on consumers? **(b)** How does this differ from the effect on producers?
9. **Predict (a)** What action will a producer usually take when the price charged is higher than the equilibrium price? **(b)** Why might the producer choose to keep the price as it is?
10. **Summarize** Describe one argument for and one argument against rent control.

Math Skills

11. Look at the supply and demand schedule for cans of soda pop, below. **(a)** Use the information on the schedule to create a supply-and-demand curve. **(b)** Identify and label the equilibrium price. **(c)** What is the shortage when the price is $1.00 per can?

Visit PearsonSchool.com/PHecon for additional math help.

Combined Supply and Demand Schedule

Price of a can of soda pop	Quantity demanded	Quantity supplied
$.50	600	50
$1.00	500	200
$1.50	300	300
$2.00	200	500
$2.50	50	600

NGSSS

LA.1112.1.6 Use multiple strategies to develop vocabulary.

LA.1112.1.6.2 Listen to, read, and discuss familiar and challenging texts.

MA.912.A.2.2 Interpret a graph to represent a real-world situation.

SS.912.E.1.4 Graphically illustrate situations that cause economic change.

SS.912.E.2.3 Research the contributions of key individuals of various backgrounds in the development of the U.S.

ECONOMIC DICTIONARY

As you read the section, look for the definitions of these **Key Terms:**

• inventory
• fad
• search costs

Guiding Question

How do changes in supply and demand affect equilibrium?

Copy this flowchart and fill it in as you read.

Restoring Equilibrium			
Increase in supply	Decrease in supply	Increase in demand	Decrease in demand

▶ **Economics and You** Have you ever stood in a long line to buy concert tickets or the latest video game? Do you anxiously scan the signs at the pump to see if the price of gas is up or down? Have you ever seen ads trumpeting the words *"Great Bargains...Everything Must Go!"* These are all elements of the market system at work. And often, the one who gets the benefit—or pays the price—is you.

Principles in Action Changes in supply and demand upset market equilibrium and cause prices to change. Sometimes prices go up, sometimes prices go down. But either way, the principle of market equilibrium is at work. This section's How the Economy Works describes the events surrounding a market shortage. You will also see how changes in supply and demand affect a variety of products, from digital cameras to toys.

Moving Toward Equilibrium

Economists say that a market will tend toward equilibrium, which means that the price and quantity will gradually move toward their equilibrium levels. Why does this happen? Remember that a shortage will cause firms to raise prices. Higher prices cause the quantity supplied to rise and the quantity demanded to fall until the two values are equal. On the other hand, a surplus will force firms to cut prices. Falling prices cause quantity demanded to rise and quantity supplied to fall until, once again, they are equal. Through these relationships, the market price of a good and the quantity supplied will move toward their equilibrium values.

As you learned in Chapter 4 and Chapter 5, the changes in demand and supply described above are changes along a demand or supply curve. Assuming that a market starts at equilibrium, there are two factors that can push it into disequilibrium: a shift in the entire demand curve or a shift in the entire supply curve.

✔ **CHECKPOINT** *What changes can push a market into disequilibrium?*

The "sneaker blow-out" sign suggests that this store may be experiencing a surplus. ▼

Figure 6.5

Falling Prices and the Supply Curve

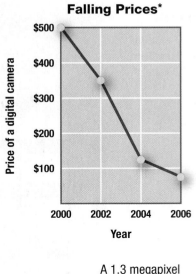

Falling Prices*

*Estimated data for a mid-priced digital camera

Shifting Supply Curve*

A 1.3 megapixel digital camera sold for $650 in 1998. ▶

An Increase in Supply

In Chapter 5, you read about the different factors that can shift a supply curve to the left or to the right. These factors include advances in technology, new government taxes and subsidies, and changes in the prices of the raw materials and labor used to produce the good.

Since market equilibrium occurs at the intersection of a demand curve and a supply curve, a shift of the entire supply curve will change the equilibrium price and quantity. A shift in the supply curve to the left or the right creates a new equilibrium. Markets tend toward equilibrium, so a change in supply will set into motion market forces that lead the market to a new equilibrium price and quantity sold.

To see what happens when the supply curve shifts to the right, we will look at a product that has undergone a radical market change in a relatively short period of time: the digital camera.

A Changing Market

Digital cameras were first introduced into the consumer market in 1994. These early digital cameras were far less sophisticated than the ones that people use today. They produced grainy pictures of lower quality than cameras that used film. The first digital cameras were also expensive, at a cost of $749 each.

Gradually, improved technology for producing digital cameras caused prices to fall. By 2000, a consumer could purchase a mid-priced digital camera for $500; just two years later, a similar camera cost about $350. Today, the same camera that cost $749 in 1994 sells for less than $100.

At the same time, the quality of digital cameras has improved. For the same price you paid in 2000, you can now get a digital camera that has more features and produces better quality photographs than the original $749 device.

Why has this happened? Advances in technology have lowered the cost of manufacturing digital cameras by reducing some of the input costs, such as computer chips. Advances in production have allowed manufacturers to produce digital cameras at lower costs. These lower costs have been passed on to consumers in the form of lower prices.

We can use the tools developed in Chapter 5 to graph the effect of these changes on the digital camera market's supply curve. As shown in **Figure 6.5,** the supply curve shifted to the right as manufacturers continued to offer a greater supply of digital cameras at lower prices. In 2000, no digital cameras were offered for $100. They were simply too expensive to develop and manufacture. Today, manufacturers can offer millions of cameras at this price and still make a profit.

Finding a New Equilibrium

Digital cameras evolved from an expensive luxury good to a mid-priced good when a new generation of computer chips reduced the cost of production. These lower costs shifted the supply curve to the right, where, at each price, producers are willing to supply a larger quantity.

This shift, shown in **Figure 6.6** using fictional quantities, has thrown the market into disequilibrium. At the old equilibrium price, suppliers are now willing to offer 4,000,000 digital cameras per year, up from 2,000,000.

In **Figure 6.6,** the increase in quantity supplied at the old equilibrium price is shown as the change from point *a* to point *b*. However, the quantity demanded at this price has not changed, and consumers will only buy 2,000,000 digital cameras. At this market price, unsold digital cameras— or **inventory,** the quantity of goods that a firm has on hand—will begin to pile up in the warehouse. When quantity supplied is greater than quantity demanded at a given price, there is a surplus. Something will have to change to bring the market to equilibrium.

As you know, suppliers will respond to a surplus by reducing prices. As the price falls from $900 to $450, more consumers buy digital cameras, and the quantity demanded rises. The combined movement of falling prices and increasing quantity demanded

can be seen in **Figure 6.6** as a change from point *a* to point *c*. Notice that this change is a movement along the demand curve, not a shift of the entire demand curve.

At point *c*, the price has fallen to a level where quantity supplied and quantity demanded is equal. Surplus is no longer a problem. This new equilibrium point marks a lower equilibrium price and a higher equilibrium quantity supplied than before the supply curve shifted. This is how equilibrium changes when supply increases, and the entire supply curve shifts to the right.

Changing Equilibrium

As improved technology caused the price of digital cameras to fall, sales increased. Market equilibrium then started moving gradually downward and to the right, where the quantities demanded and supplied are higher and prices are lower.

The supply curve for digital cameras has been moving to the right ever since the first cameras were sold. The curve continues to shift today as new technology drives down the production cost and market price of the most basic cameras.

inventory the quantity of goods that a firm has on hand

 MA.912.A.2.2 Interpret a graph to represent a real-world situation.

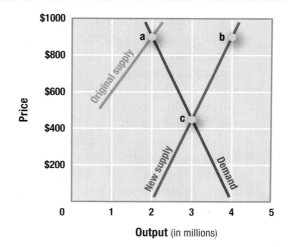

| Figure 6.6 | **A Change in Supply** |

GRAPH SKILLS
This graph shows how an increase in supply affects prices and demand.
1. What was the original equilibrium price?
2. What impact did the change in supply shown here have on the equilibrium price? Why?

Action Graph
online

For an animated version of this graph, visit PearsonSchool.com/PHecon

How does a market react to a shortage?

When supply and demand are balanced, a market is at equilibrium. But a sudden change in supply or demand can result in a shortage. How does the market react?

1 Disequilibrium The market can be thrown out of balance.
Demand increases Wants or needs may increase demand. For example:
• More people need warm coats during a cold winter.
• Advertising creates a new fad.

Supply decreases An interruption in production can affect supply. For example:
• A natural disaster disrupts the flow of raw materials.
• Problems at the factory slow down production.

2 Whether the cause is an increase in demand or a decrease in supply, the result is the same: **shortage!**

ZZ-CUBE
GET ONE NOW!
OR GET LEFT OUT

Shift in Supply or Demand

In real-life markets, equilibrium is usually not an unchanging, single point on a graph. The equilibrium in the digital camera market has always been in motion. The market equilibrium follows the intersection of the demand curve and the supply curve as that point moves downward along the demand curve.

Equilibrium is a "moving target" that changes as market conditions change. Manufacturers and retail sellers of digital cameras are constantly searching for a new equilibrium as technology and methods of production change. Consumers can easily recognize the impact of this search by the frequent price changes, sales, and rebates for digital cameras. Each of these tactics is designed to keep older cameras moving out of stores as fast as new cameras come in.

✔ **CHECKPOINT** *What happens to the equilibrium price when the supply curve shifts to the right?*

A Decrease in Supply

New technology or lower costs can shift the supply curve to the right. However, other factors that reduce supply can shift the supply curve to the left.

Consider the market for cars. If the price of steel or rubber rises, automobile manufacturers will produce fewer cars at all price levels, and the supply curve will shift to the left. If auto workers win higher wages, and the company must pay more for labor to build the same number of cars, supply will decrease. If the government imposes a new tax on car manufacturers, supply will decrease. In all of these cases, the supply curve will move to the left, because the quantity supplied is lower at all price levels.

When the supply curve shifts to the left, the equilibrium price and quantity sold will change as well. This process is the

3 The immediate effects of a shortage are obvious. People line up at stores or storm the Internet to buy the hard-to-find item . . . and the price goes up.

Z-CUBE
~~$149~~
$199

4 If the shortage continues, other suppliers will seek to enter the market. Demand is up, prices are up . . . and everybody wants a piece of the profit.

5 **A New Equilibrium** In time, supply and demand will balance out again. This may happen in two ways:

Quantity demanded decreases
• Fads end
• Higher prices drive buyers out of the market

Quantity supplied increases
• Problems in production are solved
• New suppliers fill in the gap

Whatever the cause, the hard-to-get item is no longer so hard to get . . . and the shortage ends.

Check Your Understanding
1. Why would a shortage of a product lead to a price increase?
2. What circumstances might lead to a shortage of bananas? Gasoline? Solar-powered cellphones?

The Market Reacts

A New Equilibrium

exact opposite of the change that results from an increase in supply. As the supply curve shifts to the left, suppliers raise their prices and the quantity demanded falls. The new equilibrium point will be at a spot along the demand curve above and to the left of the original equilibrium point. The market price is higher than before, and the quantity sold is lower.

✔ **CHECKPOINT** *What happens to price and quantity demanded when the supply curve shifts to the left?*

An Increase in Demand

Almost every year, we experience a new **fad**—a product that enjoys enormous popularity for a fairly short time. Around November, a new doll, toy, or video game emerges as the "must-buy" item of the season. Holiday shoppers across the country stand in long lines, waiting for stores to open, just to obtain that year's version of Tickle Me Elmo or Webkinz®.

As you read in Chapter 4, fads reflect the impact of consumer tastes and advertising on consumer behavior. Fads like these, in which demand rises quickly, are real-life examples of a rapid, rightward shift in a market demand curve. Let's see how a swift, unexpected increase in market demand can affect the equilibrium in a market for a hypothetical, trendy new toy.

The Shortage Problem

As **Figure 6.7** on page 147 shows, the fad causes a sudden increase in market demand, and the demand curve shifts to the right. This shift reflects a shortage at the original price of $24 (point *b*). Before the fad began, quantity demanded and quantity supplied were equal at 300,000 toys (point *a*). On the graph, the shortage appears as a gap at the $24 price level between the quantity

fad a product that is popular for a short period of time

Personal Finance
For more help in making wise online shopping decisions, see your Personal Finance Handbook in the back of the book.

SS.912.E.2.3 Research the contributions of key individuals of various backgrounds in the development of the U.S.

supplied of 300,000 toys and the new quantity demanded of 500,000 toys, shown at point *b*. The fad has caused the quantity demanded to increase by 200,000.

In the stores that carry the toy, the shortage appears as empty shelves or long lines. Shortage also appears in the form of **search costs**—the financial and opportunity costs that consumers pay in searching for a product or service. Driving to or calling different stores to find an available toy are examples of search costs. Today, the Internet has dramatically reduced search costs for many items, but finding the exact product you want can still be a costly and time-consuming process.

In the meantime, the available toys must be distributed in some other manner. In this case, long lines, limits on the quantities each customer may buy, and "first come, first serve" policies are used to distribute a limited number of toys among customers.

Return to Equilibrium

In time, firms will react to the signs of shortage by increasing their prices and the quantity supplied. Customers may

search costs the financial and opportunity costs that consumers pay when searching for a good or service

actually push prices up on their own if there is "bidding" in the market, as there is for real estate, antiques, fine art, and rare items. For example, if parents cannot find the toy they want at the store, they might offer the storekeeper an extra $10 to guarantee getting a toy from the next shipment. Through methods like this, the market price will rise until the quantity supplied equals the quantity demanded at 400,000 toys. All of these toys are sold at the new equilibrium price of $30, shown at point *c* in **Figure 6.7**.

When demand increases, both the equilibrium price and the equilibrium quantity also increase. The demand curve has shifted, and the equilibrium point has moved, setting in motion market forces that push the price and quantity toward their new equilibrium values.

✔ CHECKPOINT *How is equilibrium restored after a shortage?*

A Decrease in Demand

When a fad passes its peak, demand can fall as quickly as it rose. The shortage turns into a surplus for the once-popular toy, as parents look for new, trendier gifts for their children. Overflowing store shelves and silent cash registers, the symptoms of a surplus, replace long lines and policies that limit purchases.

As demand falls, the demand curve shifts to the left. Suppliers will respond to decreased demand for the once-fashionable toy by cutting prices on their inventory. Price and quantity supplied slide down to the equilibrium point shown at point *a* in **Figure 6.7**. The end of the fad has restored the original price and quantity supplied.

New technology can also lead to a decrease in consumer demand. Digital camera sales captured just 18 percent of the market in 2000. But in 2006, digital camera sales accounted for 92 percent of the market. Digital technology has led to a steep decline in film camera sales. Some firms have switched to digital camera production while others have left the market.

Digital technology has also changed the music industry. While sales of music CDs dropped by 20 percent in early 2007, digital sales of individual songs increased by 54 percent during the same period. New technology has caused the supply curve for CDs to shift to the left. However, in

FL SS.912.E.1.4, LA.1112.2.2.2, LA.1112.2.2.3, MA.912.A.2.2, LA.1112.1.6.1

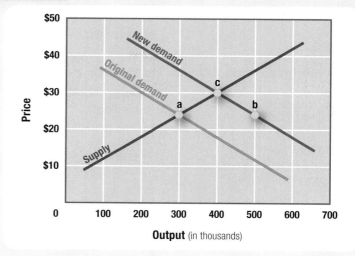

Figure 6.7   A Change in Demand

Price | Output (in thousands)

New demand
Original demand
Supply

GRAPH SKILLS

This graph shows how an increase in demand affects prices and supply.

1. What was the original equilibrium price?
2. What impact did the change in demand shown here have on the equilibrium price?

Action Graph online

For an animated version of this graph, visit **PearsonSchool.com/PHecon**

the future, new technology may lead to a change in demand for both digital cameras and digital music.

☑ **CHECKPOINT** *How does a demand curve reflect decreased demand?*

Essential Questions Journal

To continue to build a response to the Essential Question, go to your **Essential Questions Journal**.

SECTION 2 ASSESSMENT

❓ Guiding Question

1. Use your completed flowchart to answer this question: How do changes in supply and demand affect equilibrium?

2. **Extension** Shifts in either supply or demand can create a new equilibrium. Describe how increased supply of a good might benefit you as a consumer.

Key Terms and Main Ideas

3. What do **fads** reflect?

4. What kinds of goods require **search costs**?

5. What does a large **inventory** mean to a supplier?

Critical Thinking

6. **Explain** Why is equilibrium described as a "moving target"?

7. **Describe** What does a rapid increase in demand for a good mean for a consumer?

8. **Compare (a)** What are the signs of a shortage in a market? **(b)** What signs indicate that a market has a surplus?

9. **Review** The changing market for digital cameras was discussed in this section. **(a)** What factors caused the price of digital cameras to fall? **(b)** How did this affect the supply curve?

Math Skills

10. The graph shows the market for microwaves where an improvement in technology has shifted the supply

curve. **(a)** Use the letters to identify the following elements: original supply curve, new supply curve, demand curve, original equilibrium point, and new equilibrium point. **(b)** Has supply increased or decreased? Explain.

Visit PearsonSchool.com/PHecon for additional math help.

Microwaves

NGSSS

LA.1112.1.6 Use multiple strategies to develop vocabulary.

SS.912.E.1.4 Demonstrate how equilibrium of price is determined by supply and demand.

SS.912.E.1.8 Explain methods of price and nonprice competition.

SS.912.E.3.6 Draw conclusions about historical economic theories of economists.

ECONOMIC DICTIONARY

As you read the section, look for the definitions of these **Key Terms:**

• supply shock
• rationing
• black market

Guiding Question
What roles do prices play in a free market economy?

Copy this concept web and fill it in as you read.

Efficient resource allocation

Price System

▶ **Economics and You**   The price system is a delicate balance of supply and demand in which consumers, producers, and sellers all play a role. How does the price system affect you as a consumer? Consider the following example.

You want to buy a pair of athletic shoes, so you go to a local mall to compare prices. A discount shoe store offers low-end sneakers for $20. At other stores, you find that you can spend as little as $50 for brand-name sneakers, or more than $200 for a pair of designer basketball shoes. Basing your decision on the available supply, the price, and your demand, you buy the $50 sneakers.

Later, through online research, you find a pair of sneakers similar to the pair you bought, on sale for $5 less, including shipping. You buy the online sneakers with your credit card and return the sneakers you bought at the mall.

Principles in Action   In a free market economy, prices offer a number of advantages to both consumers and producers. Simple purchases would be much more complicated and inefficient without the price system to help us make informed decisions. In this section, you will see how prices affect consumer behavior and how producers respond. Economics & You shows how profits act as an incentive.

Prices in a Free Market

In Section 1, you read how supply and demand interact to determine the equilibrium price and quantity sold in a market. You also read about how prices change over time, based on shifts in the demand curve or supply curve. Prices are a key element of equilibrium. Price changes can move markets toward equilibrium and solve problems of shortage and surplus.

In a free market, prices are a tool for distributing goods and resources throughout the economy. Prices are nearly always the most efficient way to allocate, or distribute, resources. Prices help move land, labor, and capital into the hands of producers and finished goods into the hands of buyers. The alternative method for distributing goods and resources,

Giant Value/pharmacy®
where value is our middle name

48 RIVERSIDE SHPG CTR, YORK, CA
PHARMACY: 375-7883   STORE: 375-9986

REG#02 TRAN#2883 CSHR#88763 STR#1145

1 SUPER CLEAN DETRG 10.5		3.29F
F 2 OVAL PIC FRAME 2CT		6.69N
1 VALUE CLEAN FLR PL 24.5		1.79F
2 GV PROTEC RT BLOCK 7.7		2.25T
F 1 PROTEC RT LIP BALM .5Z		.99F
1 PEOPLE MAG SPC ED 0399		3.99T
1 TRIDENT WHITE 12CT		1.19B
F 2 EVERON AL BATTERIES 6CT		2.24T
1 GV PAIL/SHOVEL 1CT		.79T
3 GV SPRING WATER 16.9		2.99F
1 MILKY BAR W/NUTS .75Z		.59B

16 ITEMS	
SUBTOTAL	26.80
CA 5% TAX	1.34
TOTAL	28.14
CASH	28.14
CHANGE	.00

▲ Receipts are records of the prices we've paid. **How can receipts help you set a budget?**

FUTURE WATCH

CAREER CENTER
RETAIL

Possible Careers
- Procurement clerk
- Marketing
- Sales representative
- **Purchasing manager**
- Public relations director
- Order clerk
- Telemarketer

Profile: Purchasing Manager
Duties:
- buys the goods that a company resells to customers
- considers price, quality, availability, and technical support when choosing suppliers
- supervises a staff of purchasing agents

Education:
- bachelor's degree in business, engineering, or economics

Skills:
- mathematical and technological skills
- ability to conduct financial analysis
- knowledge of supply chain management
- good communication and negotiation skills

Median Annual Salary:
- $81,570 (2006)

Future prospects:
- Demand for purchasing managers in the service sector will outpace growth in the manufacturing sector.
- The Internet will continue to increase the productivity of purchasing managers.

Career Link *Activity*
Choose another career in retail from the list of possible careers. Create a profile for that career similar to the one for Purchasing Manager.

---

namely a centrally planned economy, is not nearly as efficient as a market system based on prices.

As you will see, prices play other vital roles in a free market economy. Prices serve as a language, as an incentive, and as a signal of economic conditions. The price system is flexible and free, and it allows for a wide diversity of goods and services.

✔ **CHECKPOINT** *List three roles that prices play in a free market system.*

The Advantages of Prices

Prices provide a common language for buyers and sellers. Could you conceive of a marketplace without prices? Without prices as a standard measure of value, a seller would have to barter for goods by trading shoes or apples for a sweater. A sweater might be worth two pairs of shoes to one customer, but another customer might be willing to trade three pairs of shoes for the same sweater. The supplier would have no consistent and accurate way to measure demand for a product. Such a system would be inconvenient, impractical, and inefficient.

Price as an Incentive

Buyers and sellers alike look at prices to find information on a good's demand and supply. The law of supply and the law of demand describe how people and firms respond to a change in prices. In these cases, prices are signals that tell producers or consumers how to adjust. Prices communicate to buyers and to sellers whether goods are in short supply or readily available.

In the example of the "fad" toy discussed in Section 2, the sudden increase in demand for the toy told suppliers that people wanted more of those toys, and soon! However, the signal that producers respond to is not simply the demand but also the high price consumers are willing to pay for the toy, well above the usual retail price. This higher price tells firms that people want more of the toys, but also that the firms can earn more profit by producing more toys, because they are in demand. Therefore, rising prices in a market will provide an incentive for existing firms to produce more of the goods that are in demand and will encourage new firms to enter a market.

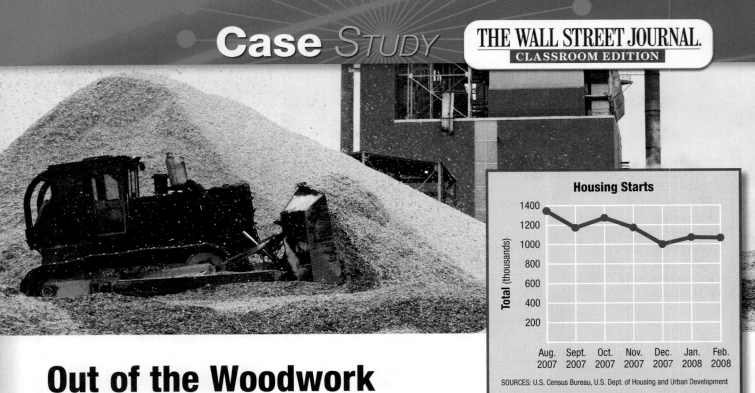

Housing Starts

SOURCES: U.S. Census Bureau, U.S. Dept. of Housing and Urban Development

Out of the Woodwork

SUPPLY SHOCK

Sawdust is just dust, right? Wrong. A shortage of it can ripple through the economy.

By Joel Millman
The Wall Street Journal

 SS.912.E.1.4 Demonstrate how equilibrium of price is determined by supply and demand.

Ernie Johnson figured $100-a-barrel oil was bound to happen someday. But he never thought he'd see sawdust at $100 a ton.

The price of sawdust has soared in recent years, up from about $25 a ton to more than $100 in some markets.

Blame the slump in housing construction: Fewer new homes mean fewer trees cut down for lumber, which leads to less sawdust and other wood waste, driving up the price.

"I've never seen sawdust so hard to find. We're having to go 400 miles to get it," says Mr. Johnson, the president of Johnson Bros. Contracting in Montana, which sells everything from chopped bark for landscapers to wood chips for pulp mills.

Sawdust may seem like a lowly commodity, but it is widely used in today's economy. Farms use sawdust and wood shavings as cozy and clean bedding for horses and chickens. Particle-board makers devour it by the boxcar to fashion a cheap building material. Auto-parts manufacturers blend a finely powdered sawdust called "wood flour" with plastic polymers to make a lightweight material to cover steering wheels and dashboards. Wineries use oak sawdust as a flavoring agent for some wines.

Perdue Farms, which raises broiler chickens, goes through seven million cubic feet of wood shavings a year. Oil-rig operators in Wyoming and Colorado pour sawdust into the caverns they find deep inside rock formations as they hunt for pools of petroleum. Sawdust gives drill bits something to grind through.

The shortage of sawdust and wood shavings has boosted the cost of boarding horses at the Lazy E Ranch in Guthrie, Okla. Two years ago, the Lazy E paid $950 per load of wood shavings for its horse stalls. Last month, Butch Wise, who manages the ranch, paid $2,650 a load. The ranch needs three loads a week.

"You'd think sawdust would be in plentiful and cheap supply, but it's not," he says.

As with every economic upheaval, there are winners as well as losers. With sawmill waste harder to find, opportunities for profit from scarcity are coming out of the woodwork. Boy Scout troops in Oregon fattened their coffers after the holidays by collecting discarded Christmas trees. Troop 618 in Beaverton made $3,000 hauling trees to a lumber recycler. Troop 728 made $10,000.

Applying Economic Principles

Bad loans and tight credit have led to a slowdown in housing construction. But home buyers aren't the only ones affected. Identify other ways that housing industry problems can ripple through the economy.

Video News Update Online
Powered by
The Wall Street Journal
Classroom Edition

Use videos at **PearsonSchool.com/PHecon** as a springboard for a discussion on a current topic.

Prices as Signals

Think of prices as a traffic light. A relatively high price is a green light that tells producers that a specific product is in demand and that they should use their resources to produce more. New suppliers will also join the market. But a low price is a red light to producers that a good is being overproduced. In this case, low prices tell a supplier that he or she might earn higher profits by using existing resources to produce a different product.

For consumers, a low price is a green light to buy more of a product. A low price indicates that the product carries a low opportunity cost for the consumer and offers a chance to get a good deal. By the same token, a high price is a red light that tells consumers to stop and think carefully before buying.

Flexibility

Another important aspect of prices is that they are flexible. When a supply shift or a demand shift changes the equilibrium in a market, price and quantity supplied need to change to solve problems of too much or too little demand. In many markets, prices are much more flexible than output levels. Prices can easily be increased to solve a problem of shortage, and they can just as easily be decreased to eliminate a problem of surplus.

For example, a **supply shock** is a sudden shortage of a good, such as gasoline or wheat. A supply shock creates a shortage because suppliers can no longer meet consumer demand. The immediate problem is how to divide up the available supply among consumers.

What are the options? Increasing supply can be a time-consuming and difficult process. For example, wheat takes time to plant, grow, and harvest. **Rationing,** a system of allocating goods and services using criteria other than price, is expensive and can take a long time to organize. Rationing is the basis of the economic system known as central planning, which you read about in Chapter 2.

Raising prices is the quickest way to resolve a shortage. A quick increase in prices can reduce quantity demanded to the same level as quantity supplied and avoid the problem of distribution. The people who have enough money and value the product most highly will pay the most for it. These consumers will be the only consumers still in the market at the higher price, and the market will settle at a new equilibrium.

Price System Is "Free"

A free market distribution system, based on prices, costs nothing to administer. Central planning, however, requires many administrators to collect information on production and decide how resources are to be distributed. In the former Soviet Union, the government employed thousands of bureaucrats in an enormous agency called GOSPLAN to organize the economy. During World War II, the United States government set up a similar agency, called the Office of Price Administration to prevent inflation and coordinate the rationing of important goods.

Unlike central planning, free market pricing distributes goods through millions of decisions made daily by consumers and suppliers. At the beginning of the section, looking at the prices of sneakers helped you decide what product to buy and which supplier to buy it from. A farmer looks at prices listed in crop reports and decides whether to grow corn instead of soybeans next year. Everyone is familiar with how prices work and knows how to use them. In short, prices help goods flow through the economy without a central plan.

✔ **CHECKPOINT** *How does the price system provide incentives for both producers and consumers?*

Choice and Efficiency

One benefit of a market-based economy is the diversity of goods and services that consumers can buy. Prices help consumers choose among similar products. You could have bought footwear along a wide range of prices, from the cheap $20 pair to the $200 designer basketball shoes. Based on your income, you decided on a pair of sneakers at the lower end of the price range. The prices provided an easy way for you to narrow your choices to

supply shock a sudden shortage of a good

rationing a system of allocating scarce goods and services using criteria other than price

During World War II, the federal government used rationing to control shortages. Each family was given tickets for such items as butter, sugar, or shoes. If you used up your allotment, you could not legally buy these items again until new tickets were issued. *How would you react if tomorrow the government passed a rationing law for gasoline, chocolate, or bottled water?* ▶

a certain price range. Prices also allow producers to target the audience they want with the products that will sell best to that audience.

In a command economy, however, one organization decides what goods are produced and how much stores will charge for those goods. To limit their costs, central planners restrict production to a few varieties of each product. As a result, consumers in the former Communist states of Eastern Europe and the Soviet Union had far fewer choices of goods than consumers in Western Europe and the United States. The government of the Soviet Union even built whole neighborhoods of identical apartment blocks and supermarkets with names such as "Supermarket No. 3."

Rationing and Shortages

Although goods in the Soviet Union were inexpensive, consumers could not always find them. When they did, they often had to wait hours for eggs or soap, and years for apartments or telephones. The United States experienced similar problems, although far less severe, when the federal government instituted temporary price controls during World War II.

The needs of the U.S. armed forces for food, metal, and rubber during World War II created tremendous shortages at home. In order to ensure that enough resources were available for military use, the government controlled the distribution of food and consumer goods.

Rationing in the United States was only a short-term hardship. Still, like rationing in the Soviet Union, it was expensive and inconvenient and left many consumers unhappy. Choices were limited, and consumers felt, rightly or wrongly, that some people fared better than others. However, rationing was chosen because a price-based system might have put food and housing out of the reach of some Americans, and the government wanted to guarantee every civilian a minimum standard of living during wartime.

The Black Market

Despite the World War II ration system, the federal government was unable to control the supply of all goods passing through the economy. A butcher could sell a steak without asking for ration points, or a landlord might be willing to rent an apartment at the rate fixed by the government only if the renter threw in a cash "bonus" or an extra two months' rent as a "deposit."

When people conduct business without regard for government controls on price or quantity, they are said to do business on the **black market**. Black markets allow consumers to pay more so they can buy a product when rationing makes it otherwise unavailable. Although black markets are a nearly inevitable consequence of rationing, such trade is illegal and strongly discouraged by governments.

Efficient Resource Allocation

All of the advantages of a free market allow prices to allocate, or distribute, resources efficiently. Efficient resource allocation means that economic resources—land, labor, and capital—will be used for their most valuable purposes. A market system, with its freely changing prices, ensures that resources go to the uses that consumers value most highly. A price-based system also ensures that resource use will adjust relatively quickly to the changing demands of consumers.

These changes take place without any central control, because the people who own resources—landowners, workers who sell their labor, and people who provide capital to firms—seek the largest possible returns. How do people earn the largest returns? They sell their resources to the highest bidder. The highest bidder will be that firm that produces goods that are in the highest demand. Therefore, the resources will flow to the uses that are most highly valued by consumers. This flow is the most efficient way to use our society's scarce resources in a way that benefits both producers and consumers.

☑ **CHECKPOINT** *What impact does rationing have on the availability of goods?*

Prices and the Profit Incentive

In a free market, efficient resource allocation goes hand in hand with the profit incentive. Suppose that scientists predicted extremely hot weather for the coming summer. In most parts of the country, consumers would buy up air conditioners and fans to prepare for the heat. Power companies would buy reserves of oil and natural gas to supply these appliances with enough power. Since demand would exceed supply, consumers would bid up the price of fans, and power plants would bid up the price of fuel.

Suppliers would recognize the possibility for profit in the higher prices charged for these goods, and they would produce more fans and air conditioners. Oil and natural gas fields would hire workers to pump more fuel for power plants. Eventually, more fans, air conditioners, and fuel would move into the market. The potential heat wave would have created a need among consumers for certain goods, and the rise in prices would have given producers an incentive to meet this need.

As we previously noted, efficient resource allocation occurs naturally in a market system as long as the system

black market a market in which goods are sold illegally, without regard for government controls on price or quantity

Economics & YOU
The Profit Incentive

SHREK 12

Movie producers are quick to create sequels of highly profitable films. *Your ticket purchase provides an incentive for the producer to make a sequel.*

As a high school athlete, you make an extra effort when you know a college scout is watching. *You profit by winning an athletic scholarship.*

▲ Financial rewards motivate people. *How have you provided or benefited from the profit incentive?*

works reasonably well. Landowners tend to use their scarce property in the most profitable manner. Workers usually move toward higher-paying jobs, and capital will be invested in the firms that pay the highest returns.

The Wealth of Nations

Adam Smith wrote about the profit incentive in his famous book *The Wealth of Nations*, published in 1776. Smith explained that it was not because of charity that the baker and the butcher provided people with their food. Rather, they provide people with bread and meat because prices are such that they will profit from doing so. In other words, businesses prosper by finding out what people want, and then providing it. This has proved to be a more efficient system than any other that has been tried in the modern era.

Market Problems

There are some exceptions to the general idea that markets lead to an efficient allocation of resources. The first problem, imperfect competition, can affect prices, and higher prices can affect consumer decisions. If only a few firms are selling a product, there might not be enough competition among sellers to lower the market price down to the cost of production. When only one producer sells a good, this producer will usually charge a higher price than we would see in a market with several competitive businesses. In the following chapter, you will read more about how markets behave under conditions of imperfect competition.

A second problem can involve negative externalities, which you learned about in Chapter 3. Negative externalities are side effects of production that can include unintended costs such as air and water pollution. They affect people who have no control over how much of a product is produced or consumed. Since producers do not have to pay these unintended costs, their total costs seem artificially low, and they will produce more than the equilibrium quantity of the good. The extra costs will be paid by consumers or, in some cases, by society at large.

Imperfect information is a third problem that can prevent a market from operating smoothly. If buyers and sellers do not have enough information to make informed choices about a product, they may not make the choice that is best for them.

✔ **CHECKPOINT** *Under what circumstances may the free market system fail to allocate resources efficiently?*

FL LA.1112.2.2.2, SS.912.E.1.4, SS.912.E.1.8, LA.1112.2.2.3, LA.1112.1.6.1

Essential Questions Journal — To continue to build a response to the Essential Question, go to your **Essential Questions Journal**.

SECTION 3 ASSESSMENT

Guiding Question

1. Use your completed concept web to answer this question: What roles do prices play in a free market economy?

2. **Extension** Prices often act as signals. Describe how prices acted as a signal or an incentive in the last two major purchases that you made.

Key Terms and Main Ideas

3. How does a **supply shock** affect equilibrium price?

4. How is **rationing** different from a price-based market system?

5. Why do buyers and sellers conduct business on the **black market?**

Critical Thinking

6. **Review (a)** What does a higher price for a good tell a producer? **(b)** What does a higher price for a good tell producers of other goods?

7. **Summarize (a)** What is the quickest way to solve a shortage? **(b)** What is the quickest way to eliminate a surplus?

8. **Explain (a)** What does efficient resource allocation mean? **(b)** Why is the price system an efficient way to allocate resources?

9. **Identify** Describe three market problems that prevent efficient allocation of resources.

Quick Write

10. Look at the illustrated Economics & You feature on the profit incentive in this section. List additional examples of how the desire for profit motivates people. Then write a short essay answering the following questions: Do you agree or disagree that incentives motivate people's actions? How do incentives affect your daily life?

Chapter 6: Prices

Section 1 What factors affect prices?

Section 2 How do changes in supply and demand affect equilibrium?

Section 3 What roles do prices play in a free market economy?

Essential Question, Chapter 6
What is the right price?

Economic Dictionary

equilibrium, *p. 134*

disequilibrium, *p. 134*

shortage, *p. 134*

surplus, *p. 136*

price ceiling, *p. 137*

rent control, *p. 137*

price floor, *p. 139*

minimum wage, *p. 139*

inventory, *p. 143*

fad, *p. 145*

search costs, *p. 146*

supply shock, *p. 151*

rationing, *p. 151*

black market, *p. 153*

Advantages of Price-Based System

	Free Market (price based)	Command Economy
Prices determined by	Supply and demand	Government bureaucracy
Use of rationing	Under emergency conditions	Normal
Response to changing conditions	Flexible	Rigid
Variety of goods available	Wide	Limited
Allocation of resources	Efficient (under ideal competitive conditions)	Less efficient

Shortage and Surplus

Shortage
- Demand greater than supply
- Prices go up
- Advantage to supplier: profits

- Disequilibrium
- Market forces tend toward new equilibrium

Surplus
- Supply greater than demand
- Prices go down
- Advantage to consumer: bargains

Economics on the go

Study anytime, anywhere. Download these files today.

Economic Dictionary online	**Audio Review** online	**Action Graph** online	**Visual Glossary** online	**How the Economy Works** online
Vocabulary Support in English and Spanish	Audio Study Guide in English and Spanish	Animated Charts and Graphs	Animated feature	Animated feature

Download to your computer or mobile device at PearsonSchool.com/PHecon

Self-Test online To test your understanding of key terms and main ideas, visit PearsonSchool.com/PHecon

Key Terms and Main Ideas

To make sure you understand the key terms and main ideas of this chapter, review the Checkpoint and Section Assessment questions and look at the Quick Study Guide on the preceding page.

Critical Thinking

1. **Predict (a)** What determines the equilibrium price of a product? **(b)** How do shortages and surpluses affect the equilibrium price? **(c)** Predict what would happen if a seller raised the price of an item at a time when there was a market surplus.

2. **Predict (a)** Why have some cities passed rent control laws? **(b)** Suppose that a city repealed its rent control laws. What effect do you think the repeal would have on landlords? On renters?

3. **Recognize Cause and Effect (a)** Identify the four basic causes for a shift in market equilibrium. **(b)** Describe how each of the following would affect equilibrium in the egg market: scientists breed a new chicken that lays twice as many eggs a week; an outbreak of food poisoning is traced to eggs; a popular talk show host convinces her viewers to eat an egg a day.

4. **Generalize (a)** What are search costs? **(b)** Under what market conditions are search costs important? **(c)** What impact has the Internet had on search costs? **(d)** Identify two other ways that the Internet has affected prices and markets. **(e)** In general, who do you think has benefited the most from the Internet: buyers or sellers? Explain your reasoning.

5. **Recommend** Suppose that a recent hurricane in the Caribbean has caused a supply shock in the market for sugar in the United States. **(a)** What are the usual effects of a supply shock on prices in a free market? **(b)** As a result of this change in supply, what choices do consumers and food producers face? **(c)** Suppose you were an adviser to the President. Would you recommend rationing sugar, setting a price ceiling on sugar, or taking no action? Explain your reasoning.

Applying Your Math Skills

Interpreting Data From Graphs

Imagine you own a bakery. The graph below shows supply and demand curves for whole-grain bagels. You now charge $3.00 for a bagel. Use your math skills to answer the following questions:

Visit PearsonSchool.com/PHecon for additional math help.

Equilibrium Graph for Bagels

6. At $3.00 per bagel, how many bagels do you sell on an average day?

7. How much money per day are you taking in from bagels?

8. How many bagels per day are you throwing away?

9. To reach the equilibrium price, how many more bagels could you expect to sell each day?

 Essential Question Activity

Essential Questions Journal To respond to the chapter Essential Question, go to your **Essential Questions Journal**.

10. Complete this activity to answer the Essential Question **What is the right price?** Imagine that your class is planning to sell T-shirts to raise funds for disaster relief in a nearby community. Using the worksheet in your Essential Questions Journal or the electronic worksheet available at **PearsonSchool.com/PHecon**, gather the following information:
    (a) What is the cost of buying 1,000 plain white T-shirts in bulk?
    (b) What is the cost of having a special design printed on the shirts?
    (c) What is the average price that stores in your area charge for a printed T-shirt?
    Using this information, decide what price you think people would be willing to pay for a T-shirt. You need to make enough money above your cost to make a donation. When you have made your decision, fill in your price on the worksheet. Write an explanation of how you arrived at the right price.

11. **Modify** You have set your price and begun selling your T-shirts. Now, choose two of the following situations. Describe how each of them might cause you to modify your plan:
    (a) Another school begins selling similar T-shirts for a dollar less than your price.
    (b) After a week, you have not sold enough T-shirts to cover what you spent to buy and print the shirts.
    (c) A local news broadcast raises questions about whether disaster relief funds are being spent wisely.

Does the minimum wage help or hurt the economy?

In the United States, the federal minimum wage sparks debate. Critics claim that the minimum wage creates unemployment through an unnatural price floor. Supporters say that a minimum wage is needed to help low-wage workers.

Document A

FL LA.1112.1.6.2, SS.912.E.1.9

Document B

"In the House debate last week, opponents again claimed that the small business community is vehemently opposed to an increase. They think small businesses will suffer or collapse even with our modest increase. That's preposterous. A recent Gallup poll found that 86% of small business owners don't think that the minimum wage affects their business—at all. In fact, small businesses have historically prospered after past increases. More than half the states have already acted to increase minimum wages above the federal level today, and these states are generating more small businesses than states with a minimum wage of $5.15 an hour."

—Sen. Edward M. Kennedy, TheHuffingtonPost.com, January 23, 2007

Document C

"Economic research has shown time and again that increasing the minimum wage destroys jobs for low-skilled workers while doing little to address poverty. . . . for every 10 percent increase in the minimum wage, employment for high school dropouts and young black adults and teenagers falls by 8.5 percent. . . . Most of the work still gets done, but customers may get stuck standing in longer lines, and teens suffer because they've been priced out of work. . . . increasing the minimum wage causes four times more job loss for employees without a high school diploma than it does for the general population."

—Kristen Lopez Eastlick, "Dude, where's my summer job?", examiner.com, June 9, 2008

ANALYZING DOCUMENTS

Use your knowledge of the minimum wage and Documents A, B, and C to answer questions 1–3.

1. **Document A shows that the minimum wage**
   A. is greeted enthusiastically by both workers and business.
   B. forces people to beg on the streets.
   C. is too low for workers, and too high for business.
   D. brings workers and businesses together.

2. **According to Document B, how does raising the minimum wage affect small businesses?**
   A. It forces small businesses to lay off workers.
   B. Small businesses prospered after previous minimum wage increases.
   C. Small businesses strongly oppose an increase.
   D. Without a minimum wage increase, small businesses will collapse.

3. **What is the main point of Document C?**
   A. Most minimum wage work gets done.
   B. Adults are not affected by an increase in the minimum wage.
   C. An increase in the minimum wage hurts low-skilled workers by causing many to lose their jobs.
   D. Increasing the minimum wage will not hurt the general population.

WRITING ABOUT ECONOMICS

Debate over the minimum wage is an ongoing issue. Use the documents on this page and resources on the Web site below to answer the question: *Does the minimum wage help or hurt the economy?* Use the sources to support your opinion.

In Partnership

THE WALL STREET JOURNAL.
CLASSROOM EDITION

To read more about issues related to this topic, visit
PearsonSchool.com/PHecon

Chapter 7

Market Structures

Essential Question, Chapter 7

How does competition affect your choices?

FL **Next Generation Sunshine State Standards**

Section 1: Perfect Competition
LA.1112.1.6, MA.912.A.2.2, SS.912.E.1.1, SS.912.E.1.6, SS.912.E.1.8

Section 2: Monopoly
LA.1112.1.6, SS.912.E.1.2, SS.912.E.1.6, SS.912.E.1.8, SS.912.E.2.3, SS.912.E.2.6

Section 3: Monopolistic Competition and Oligopoly
LA.1112.1.6, LA.1112.6.3, LA.1112.6.3.1, SS.912.E.1.6, SS.912.E.1.8

Section 4: Regulation and Deregulation
LA.1112.1.6, LA.1112.1.6.2, SS.912.E.1.8, SS.912.E.2.4, SS.912.E.2.6

Economics
on the go

To study anywhere, anytime, download these
online resources at *PearsonSchool.com/PHecon* ▶

NGSSS

LA.1112.1.6 Use multiple strategies to develop vocabulary.

MA.912.A.2.2 Interpret a graph to represent a real-world situation.

SS.912.E.1.1 Identify factors of production and their necessity to making goods and services.

SS.912.E.1.6 Compare the characteristics of the four market structures.

SS.912.E.1.8 Explain methods of price and nonprice competition.

ECONOMIC DICTIONARY

As you read the section, look for the definitions of these **Key Terms**:

• perfect competition
• commodity
• barrier to entry
• imperfect competition
• start-up costs

Guiding Question

What are the characteristics of perfect competition?

Copy this concept web and fill it in as you read.

▶ **Economics and You** You have decided to cook dinner. As you shop for produce at the local farmer's market, you see many fruits and vegetables being offered by several different suppliers. Yet each supplier charges the same price for fruits and vegetables. On the way home, you wonder why buying a leather jacket, a car, or a high-definition television isn't as simple as buying produce at the local farmer's market.

Principles in Action The farmer's market, with its identical goods and many buyers and sellers, is a rare, real-world example of a market in perfect competition. However, you will learn about factors that prevent perfect competition in most markets.

Four Conditions for Perfect Competition

Perfect competition, also called pure competition, is the simplest market structure. A perfectly competitive market is one with a large number of firms all producing essentially the same product. It assumes that the market is in equilibrium and that all firms sell the same product for the same price. However, each firm produces so little of the product compared with the total supply that no single firm can hope to influence prices. The only decision such producers can make is how much to produce, given their production costs and the market price.

While few industries meet all of the conditions for perfect competition, some come close. Examples include the markets for many farm

perfect competition
a market structure in which a large number of firms all produce the same product and no single seller controls supply or prices

Visual Glossary
(online)

Go to the Visual Glossary Online for an interactive review of **perfect competition.**

Action Graph
(online)

Go to Action Graph Online for animated versions of key charts and graphs.

How the Economy Works
(online)

Go to How the Economy Works Online for an interactive lesson on **regulation.**

products and the stocks traded on the New York Stock Exchange. These examples fulfill the four strict conditions for a perfectly competitive market:

1. Many buyers and sellers participate in the market.
2. Sellers offer identical products.
3. Buyers and sellers are well informed about products.
4. Sellers are able to enter and exit the market freely.

Many Buyers and Sellers

Perfectly competitive markets require many participants on both the buying and the selling sides. No individual can be powerful enough to buy or sell enough goods to influence the total market quantity or the market price. Everyone in the market must accept the market price as given.

As we saw in Chapter 6, supply and demand interact to determine both price and output. If a market has many independent buyers and sellers, it is not very likely that large enough groups of either buyers or sellers will work together to bargain for better prices. Instead, the market determines price without any influence from individual suppliers or consumers.

Identical Products

In a perfectly competitive market, there are no differences between the products sold by different suppliers. This is the second condition for perfect competition. If a rancher needs to buy corn to feed his cattle, he will not care which farmer grew the corn, as long as every farm is willing to deliver the corn he needs for the same price. If an investor buys a share of a company's stock, she will not care which particular share she is buying.

A product that is considered the same regardless of who makes or sells it is called a **commodity.** Examples of commodities include low-grade gasoline, notebook paper, sugar, and silicon chips. Identical products are a key to perfect competition for one reason: the buyer will not pay extra for one particular company's goods. The buyer will always choose the supplier with the lowest price.

commodity a product, such as petroleum or milk, that is considered the same no matter who produces or sells it

barrier to entry any factor that makes it difficult for a new firm to enter a market

imperfect competition a market structure that fails to meet the conditions of perfect competition

Informed Buyers and Sellers

The third condition for a perfectly competitive market is that buyers and sellers know enough about the market to find the best deal. Under conditions of perfect competition, the market provides the buyer with full information about the features of the product and its price. For the market to work effectively, both buyers and sellers have clear incentives to gather as much information as possible.

In most markets, a buyer's willingness to find information about prices and availability represents a trade-off. The time spent gathering information must be worth the amount of money that will be saved. For example, most buyers would not search the Internet or visit a dozen convenience stores to save five cents on a pack of chewing gum.

Free Market Entry and Exit

The final condition of perfectly competitive markets is that firms must be able to enter them when they can make money and leave them when they can't earn enough to stay in business. For example, when the first companies began earning a lot of money by selling frozen dinners, several competitors jumped into the market to seek profits with their own products. Later, when consumers didn't buy those dinners, the firms withdrew their products from the market.

Studies show that markets with more firms, and thus more competition, have lower prices. When one firm can keep others out of the market, it can sell its product at a higher price.

✅ **CHECKPOINT** *How does perfect competition ensure that prices aren't determined by individual suppliers or consumers?*

Barriers to Entry

Factors that make it difficult for new firms to enter a market are called **barriers to entry.** Barriers to entry can lead to **imperfect competition,** a market structure that fails to meet the conditions of perfect competition. Common barriers to entry include start-up costs and technology.

VISUAL GLOSSARY

Reviewing Key Terms
To understand *perfect competition*, review these terms:

market, *p. 29*
competition, *p. 33*
profit motive, *p. 51*
commodity, *p. 160*

What is Perfect Competition?

◄ **perfect competition** a market structure in which a large number of firms all produce the same product and no single seller controls supply or prices

A perfectly competitive market includes a large number of suppliers selling identical products called commodities. *Why isn't the market for automobiles a perfectly competitive market?*

PERFECT COMPETITION

Number of firms: Many

A B C D E F

Variety of goods: None

Brand A Brand B Brand C Brand D Brand E Brand F

Barriers to entry: None

ENTRY

Control over prices: None

No Control

SERIOUS COMPETITION
THINGYMAJIGS   WATCHAMACALLITS

◄ In a perfectly competitive market, both buyers and sellers are well informed about products. *What other condition of a perfectly competitive market does this cartoon represent?*

Visual Glossary online

To expand your understanding of this and other key economic terms, visit **PearsonSchool.com/PHecon**

Figure 7.1

Market Equilibrium in Perfect Competition

GRAPH SKILLS

In a perfectly competitive market, price and output reach their equilibrium levels.

1. What factors allow a perfectly competitive market to reach equilibrium?
2. What prevents any one firm from raising its prices?

Action Graph
online

For an animated version of this graph, visit PearsonSchool.com/PHecon

Quantity

  MA.912.A.2.2 Interpret a graph to represent a real-world situation.

Start-Up Costs

Entrepreneurs need to invest money in a new firm long before they can start earning income. Before a new sandwich shop can open, the owner needs to rent a store, buy a refrigerator, a freezer, and an oven, and print menus. The expenses that a new business must pay before it can begin to produce and sell goods are called **start-up costs.**

When the start-up costs in a market are high, entrepreneurs are less likely to enter that market. As a result, markets that involve high start-up costs are less likely to be perfectly competitive markets. For example, the start-up costs for a sandwich shop are much lower than the start-up costs for a lumber mill or a supermarket. An entrepreneur with a small income is much more likely to try her luck with a sandwich shop.

Use of the Internet reduced start-up costs in many markets, including books and music. However, many entrepreneurs discovered that a Web page did not attract and hold customers as easily as a shop window. The high costs of advertising, shipping, and discounting goods pushed many out of business. With a few exceptions, the Internet-based companies that have succeeded paid substantial start-up costs.

start-up costs the expenses a new business must pay before it can begin to produce and sell goods

Technology

When a school group needs to raise money, its members can sell goods like flowers, cookies, or candy. Some technically skilled students might offer to fix cars or bicycles. But very few student groups would be able to raise money by creating and selling a new computer word-processing program.

Some markets require a high degree of technological know-how—the knowledge and skills needed to create or repair something. A carpenter, pharmacist, or electrician can spend years in training before he or she has learned all the necessary skills. Computer software engineers need extensive training to develop, create, and customize computer software and manage computer network systems.

As a result, new entrepreneurs cannot easily enter these markets without a lot of preparation and study. These technological barriers to entry can keep a market from becoming perfectly competitive.

✔ **CHECKPOINT** *Which barrier to entry can be overcome by education or vocational training?*

Price and Output

One of the primary characteristics of perfectly competitive markets is that they are efficient. Competition within these markets keeps both prices and production costs low. Firms must use all inputs—land, labor, organizational skills, machinery and equipment—to their best advantage. As a result, the prices that consumers pay and the revenue that suppliers receive accurately reflect how much the market values the resources that have gone into the product. In a perfectly competitive market, prices correctly represent the opportunity costs of each product.

Prices in a perfectly competitive market are the lowest sustainable prices possible. Because many sellers compete to offer their commodities to buyers, intense competition forces prices down to the point where the prices just cover the most-efficient sellers' costs of doing business. As you read in Chapter 6, this equilibrium is usually the most efficient state a market can achieve. Equilibrium in a perfectly competitive market is shown in **Figure 7.1.**

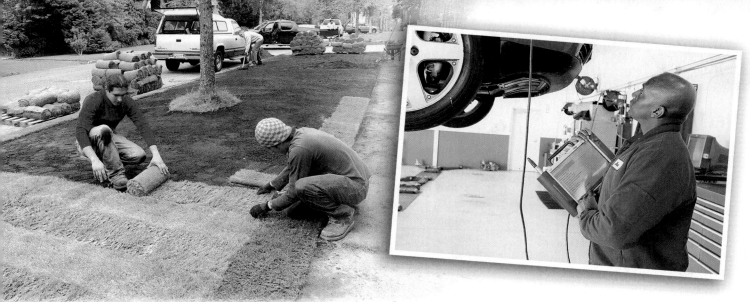

We saw in Chapter 5 that producers earn their highest profits when they produce enough that their cost to produce one more unit exactly equals the market price of the unit. Since no supplier can influence prices in perfectly competitive markets, producers will make their output decisions based on their most efficient use of available land, labor, capital, and management skills.

In the long run, output in a perfectly competitive market will reach the point where each supplying firm just covers all of its costs, including paying the firm's owners enough to make the business worthwhile.

✔ CHECKPOINT *How are output decisions made in a perfectly competitive market?*

▲ Landscaping presents no technical challenges and start-up costs are low. However, an auto-repair shop requires advanced technical skills. The equipment needed to run the shop makes start-up costs another significant barrier to entry.

FL SS.912.E.1.1, SS.912.E.1.6, SS.912.E.1.8, LA.1112.1.6.1, LA.1112.2.2.2

SECTION 1 ASSESSMENT

Essential Questions Journal
To continue to build a response to the Essential Question, go to your **Essential Questions Journal**.

Guiding Question

1. Use your completed concept web to answer this question: What are the characteristics of perfect competition?
2. **Extension** Imagine that you are baking a cake for a friend's birthday. You need flour, milk, and eggs. Three nearby stores sell the items you need. How will you decide where to buy your groceries?

Key Terms and Main Ideas

3. List the four conditions for **perfect competition.**
4. When does **imperfect competition** occur?
5. What are two examples of **barriers to entry** in the magazine market?
6. How do **start-up costs** discourage entrepreneurs from entering a market?
7. Why must firms use land, labor, and other resources efficiently in perfectly competitive markets?

Critical Thinking

8. **Apply** How many of these markets come close to perfect competition: **(a)** televisions, **(b)** bottled water, **(c)** pizza, **(d)** cars, **(e)** white socks, **(f)** baseballs, **(g)** paper clips? Explain your choices.
9. **Predict (a)** What are commodities? **(b)** Why must perfectly competitive markets always deal in commodities? **(c)** What would happen to a perfectly competitive market if it stopped dealing in commodities? Explain your answer.
10. **Recognize (a)** What are barriers to entry? **(b)** Other than technology and start-up costs, what are two specific examples of barriers that could prevent a company or individual from entering a market?

Quick Write

11. Reread Four Conditions for Perfect Competition in this section. Write a short essay answering the following questions: Why is perfect competition the simplest market structure? How well does the model of perfect competition fit the real world? Why do you think economists use this model?

ECONOMIC DICTIONARY

As you read the section, look for the definitions of these **Key Terms:**

• monopoly
• economies of scale
• natural monopoly
• government monopoly
• patent
• franchise
• license
• price discrimination
• market power

Copy this concept web and fill it in as you read.

monopoly a market in which a single seller dominates

▶ **Economics and You**   Unfortunately, you have been diagnosed with a rare and serious infection. The doctor prescribes a ten day supply of a new medication. At the pharmacy, you discover that the medicine costs $97.35—nearly ten dollars a pill! There are no substitutes, so you buy the medicine. Later, you learn that only one company has the right to produce that drug. The company says that revenue from the medicine pays for the research and development costs of producing it.

Principles in Action While there are different types of monopolies, all are characterized by a single seller that controls an entire market. This arrangement allows monopolies to control output and charge higher prices. This section's Innovators describes Andrew Carnegie's journey from ambitious monopolist to generous philanthropist.

Describing Monopoly

A **monopoly** forms when barriers prevent firms from entering a market that has a single supplier. While a perfectly competitive market has many buyers and sellers, monopoly markets have only one seller, but any number of buyers. In fact, barriers to entry are the principal condition that allows monopolies to exist.

Economists use a strict set of requirements to characterize a monopoly. Besides having a single seller and barriers to entry, a monopoly is also characterized by supplying a unique product. But suppliers may only appear to have a unique product, because if we take a broader view, we may uncover alternatives. For example, you might think that a convenience store on a highway in the middle of the desert has a monopoly. However, travelers can carry their own supplies in their car instead of paying high prices for items at the store. Or, if they have enough money, they can fly across the desert and bypass the store altogether. In other words, there are options. In a monopoly, the good or service provided has no close substitute.

▲ To prevent resources from being wasted, public water is a natural monopoly.

The problem with monopolies is that they can take advantage of their market power and charge high prices. Given the law of demand, this means that the quantity of goods sold is lower than in a market with more than one seller. For this reason, the United States has outlawed some monopolistic practices, as you will read in Section 4.

✔ **CHECKPOINT** *What are three characteristics of a monopoly?*

Forming a Monopoly

All monopolies have one trait in common: a single seller in a market. However, different market conditions can create different types of monopolies.

Economies of Scale

If a firm's start-up costs are high, and its average costs fall for each additional unit it produces, then it enjoys what economists call economies of scale. **Economies of scale** are characteristics that cause a producer's average cost to drop as production rises.

The graph on the left in **Figure 7.2** shows an average total cost curve for a firm without economies of scale. Follow the curve from left to right. As output increases from zero, the average cost of each good drops, and the curve initially slopes downward. This is because large, initial, fixed costs, like the cost of the factory and

machinery, can be spread out among more and more goods as production rises. If the factory cost $1,000 to build and each unit of output costs $10 to make, producing one unit will cost $1,010, but producing two units will cost $1,020, or only $510 each. However, if the industry has limited economies of scale, output will eventually rise to a level at which the limited scale economies are exhausted, and the cost of making each unit will rise. The average cost of producing each good increases as output increases, and the curve slopes upward to match the rising cost per unit.

A factory in an industry with economies of scale never reaches this second stage of rising costs per unit. As production increases, the firm becomes more efficient, even at a level of output high enough to supply the entire market. The graph on the right in **Figure 7.2** shows how cost and output are related in economies of scale. Follow the curve from left to right. As output increases, the cost per unit falls, and continues to fall.

A good example is a hydroelectric plant, which generates electricity from a dam on a river. A large dam is expensive to build. However, once the dam is built, the plant can produce energy at a very low additional cost simply by letting water flow through the dam. The average cost of the first unit of electricity produced is very high because the cost of the dam is so high. As output

economies of scale
factors that cause a producer's average cost per unit to fall as output rises

 SS.912.E.1.2
Analyze production possibilities curves to explain opportunity costs.

Figure 7.2 **Effect of Economies of Scale**

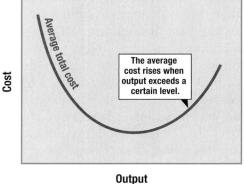

Average Total Cost Curve Without Economies of Scale

Cost

Average total cost

The average cost rises when output exceeds a certain level.

Output

Average Total Cost Curve With Economies of Scale

Cost

Average total cost

With economies of scale, the average cost of production falls when the firm produces more.

Output

GRAPH SKILLS

With economies of scale, production costs continue to fall as output increases.

1. Why do production costs fall as output increases?

2. Describe the cost curve for a firm without economies of scale.

natural monopoly a market that runs most efficiently when one large firm supplies all of the output

increases, the fixed costs of the dam can be spread over more units of electricity, so the average cost drops. In a market with economies of scale, bigger is better. An industry that enjoys economies of scale can easily become a natural monopoly.

However, new strategies are emerging. Some business leaders now favor sidestepping economies of scale:

> **❝Many business leaders are re-examining their assumptions about the benefits of scale. Scaling down, not up, and building "disposable factories" and even "disposable strategies" are becoming new keys to lowering costs and boosting performance. ❞**
>
> —George Stalk, *5 Future Strategies You Need Right Now,* Harvard Business School Press, 2008

Natural Monopolies

A **natural monopoly** is a market that runs most efficiently when one large firm provides all of the output. If a second firm enters the market, competition will drive down the market price charged to

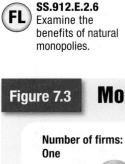

SS.912.E.2.6 Examine the benefits of natural monopolies.

customers and decrease the quantity each firm can sell. One or both of the firms will not be able to cover their costs and will go out of business.

Public water provides a good example of a natural monopoly. In a competitive market, different water companies would invest huge amounts of money to dig reservoirs and set up overlapping networks of pipes and pumping stations to deliver water to the same town. Companies would use more land and water than necessary. Each company would have to pay for all of the unneeded pipes and would serve customers no better than a single network.

In cases like this, the government often steps in to allow just one firm in each geographic area to provide these necessary services. The government action ensures that resources are not wasted by building additional plants when only one is needed. In return for monopoly status, a firm with a natural monopoly agrees to let government control the prices it can charge and what services it must provide.

Technology and Change

Sometimes the development of a new technology can destroy a natural monopoly. A new innovation can cut fixed costs and make small companies as efficient as one large firm.

When telephone calls were carried by thick copper wires, local telephone service was considered a natural monopoly. No one wanted to build more than one network of wires to connect thousands of homes and businesses. In the 1980s and 1990s, consumers began using cellular phones, which were portable and could carry phone calls via radio waves rather than through wires. Cellular technology reduced the barriers to entry in the local telephone market. Now that cellular phone companies can link to thousands or millions of customers with a few, well-placed towers, they don't need to invest in an expensive infrastructure of cables and telephone poles. Cellular phone companies are becoming as efficient as traditional wire-based phone services.

✔ **CHECKPOINT** *How can technology affect a monopoly?*

Figure 7.3 Monopoly

Number of firms: One

Variety of goods: None

Barriers to entry: Complete

Control over prices: Complete

ENTRY

Complete Control

CHART SKILLS

In a monopoly, one company controls the entire market.

1. How does the government regulate a natural monopoly?
2. Give examples of other natural monopolies.

Government Monopolies

In the case of a natural monopoly, the government allows the monopoly to form and then regulates it. In other cases, however, government actions themselves can create barriers to entry in markets and thereby create monopolies. A **government monopoly** is a monopoly created by the government.

Technological Monopolies

One way that the government can give a company monopoly power is by issuing a patent. A **patent** gives a company exclusive rights to sell a new good or service for a specific period of time. Suppose that Leland Pharmaceuticals developed a new, effective asthma medication called BreatheDeep that helped people with asthma to breathe more easily. If Leland's researchers could prove to the government that they had invented BreatheDeep, the government would grant Leland a patent. This patent would give Leland the exclusive right to sell BreatheDeep for 20 years.

Why would the government want to give a company monopoly power? Patents guarantee that companies can profit from their own research without competition. For this reason, patents encourage firms to research and develop new products that benefit society as a whole, even though the research and development costs may be very high. The patent allows firms to set prices that maximize their opportunity to make a profit.

Franchises and Licenses

A **franchise** is a contract issued by a local authority that gives a single firm the right to sell its goods within an exclusive market. National companies often grant franchises to entrepreneurs, who then sell that company's product in a local market.

A government entity can also grant a franchise. For example, the National Park Service picks a single firm to sell food and other goods at national parks, such as Yellowstone, Yosemite, and the Everglades. Your school may have contracted with one bottled-water company to install and stock vending machines. The franchise may include a condition that no other brand of water will be sold in the building. Governments,

 SS.912.E.2.3 Research the contributions of key individuals of various backgrounds in the development of the U.S.

government monopoly a monopoly created by the government

patent a license that gives the inventor of a new product the exclusive right to sell it for a specific period of time

franchise a contract that gives a single firm the right to sell its goods within an exclusive market

license a government-issued right to operate a business

parks, and schools use franchises to keep small markets under control.

On a larger scale, governments can issue a **license** granting firms the right to operate a business, especially where scarce resources are involved. Examples of scarce resources that require licensing include land and radio and television broadcast frequencies. The Federal Communications Commission issues licenses for individual radio and television stations. Local governments might license a single firm to manage all of their public parking lots.

Industrial Organizations

In rare cases, the government allows the companies in an industry to restrict the number of firms in a market. For example, the United States government lets Major League Baseball and other sports leagues restrict the number and location of their teams. The government allows team owners of the major professional sports leagues to choose new cities for their teams and does not charge them with violating the laws that prevent competitors from working together.

Major League Baseball has an exemption from these laws, which are known as antitrust laws, because they were originally passed to break up an illegal form of monopoly known as a trust. Other sports leagues do not have an official exemption, but the government treats them as it treats baseball. The restrictions that the leagues impose help keep team play orderly and stable by preventing other cities from starting their own major league teams and crowding the schedule.

The problem with this type of monopoly is that team owners may charge high prices for tickets. In addition, if you're a sports fan in a city without a major league team, you're out of luck.

✔ CHECKPOINT *What government actions can lead to the creation of monopolies?*

Output Decisions

If you had severe asthma, which can be fatal, what would BreatheDeep be worth to you? You would probably want the medicine no matter how much it cost. So Leland, the company that invented and patented the drug, could charge a very high price for its new medication. In fact, they could charge enough to earn well above what it cost to research and manufacture the drug. The resulting profits would give the company a reason, or incentive, for inventing the new medication in the first place. But could Leland sell as much medication as it wanted to at whatever price it chose?

Even a monopolist faces a limited choice—it can choose either output or price, but not both. The monopolist looks at the big picture and tries to maximize profits. This usually means that, compared to a perfectly competitive market for the same good, the monopolist produces fewer goods at a higher price.

The Monopolist's Dilemma

The law of demand states that buyers will demand more of a good at lower prices and less at higher prices. A possible demand curve for BreatheDeep is shown in **Figure 7.4**, on page 170 with prices in dollars on the vertical axis and doses on the horizontal axis. Many people with life-threatening asthma will pay whatever the medicine costs. But some people with milder asthma will choose a cheaper, weaker medicine if the price rises too high.

Trace the demand curve from left to right. At $12 per dose, consumers might demand 8,000 doses of BreatheDeep each week. But at $9 per dose, as many as 11,000 doses will sell. The law of demand means that when the monopolist increases the price, it will sell less, and when it lowers the price, it will sell more. Another way to interpret this graph is that if a monopolist produces more, the price of the good will fall, and if it produces less, the price will rise.

Falling Marginal Revenue

Remember from Chapter 5 that to maximize profits, a seller should set its marginal revenue, or the amount it earns from the last unit sold, equal to its marginal cost, or the extra cost from producing that unit. This same rule applies to a firm with a monopoly. The key difference is that in a perfectly competitive market, marginal revenue is always the same as price, and

Super Bowl Television Audience

A bar chart titled "Super Bowl Television Audience" showing Viewers (in millions) on the y-axis ranging from 80 to 92, for years 2001 through 2006.

SOURCE: Nielsen's Guide to the Super Bowl

The NFL's New Turf

MONOPOLY ON THE MOVE

A monopoly may be the sole player in its market. But it still has to compete.

By John Lyons
The Wall Street Journal

 SS.912.E.1.8 Explain methods of price and nonprice competition.

The National Football League is making a big marketing push to make soccer-mad Mexico a football haven, too.

In Mexico City, the NFL teamed with the Cinemex theater chains to show Monday night games live on big screens. The league sponsors youth flag-football tournaments to win young fans. By the time the Super Bowl rolls around, Mexicans will be drinking from cans emblazoned with team logos, and finding NFL team stickers in loaves of bread and bags of potato chips.

The NFL's efforts in Mexico have become a cornerstone in the league's strategy to win additional overseas fans, from Germany to China. Millions of Mexicans have spent some time in the U.S., making Mexico a natural expansion market. In 2005, the NFL chose Mexico City's giant Azteca soccer stadium for the first of its regular-season games ever to be played outside the U.S. More than 103,000 people showed up. The success of that game prompted the NFL to schedule up to two regular-season games a year in foreign sites such as Mexico City, Toronto, London, Frankfurt and Cologne, Germany.

The plan represents a big investment—and risk—for NFL team owners who forgo a home game, and all ticket sales that go with it, to send their players abroad. Owners are betting that the overseas games will produce more fans, who will buy team-licensed clothing and souvenirs. The NFL believes it can grab a bigger share of the $43 billion international sports market, where the football league is a relatively small player today.

Overseas marketing isn't new for the NFL: The league has played overseas exhibition games since 1986, and NFL Europa, a league of lesser pros that plays in the spring, has teams in five German cities and Amsterdam. But the league now believes its best marketing tool is exporting regular-season NFL games, with all the excitement of having the stars on the field and playing for keeps. The buzz created by these games should lead to increased merchandise sales and TV viewership—two sources of revenue that have long since outstripped ticket sales in financial importance.

"We're convinced we have the best game," says Mark Waller, who was hired last year to head an overseas push. "If we can be successful in the U.S., the world's most competitive market, there's no reason why we can't compete elsewhere."

Video News Update Online
Powered by
The Wall Street Journal
Classroom Edition

Use videos at **PearsonSchool.com/PHecon** as a springboard for a discussion on a current topic.

Applying Economic Principles
Why would the NFL want to influence the sports culture around the world? What advantages would the NFL have if it succeeds?

Figure 7.4 | Demand Schedule for BreatheDeep

Price	Weekly Demand	Total Revenue	Change in Revenue	Marginal Revenue (per dose)
$12	8,000	$96,000	—	—
$11	9,000	$99,000	$3,000	$3
$10	10,000	$100,000	$1,000	$1
$9	11,000	$99,000	−$1,000	−$1
$8	12,000	$96,000	−$3,000	−$3

When 8,000 doses are made, the market price is $12.

As production rises to 11,000 doses, the price falls to $9.

GRAPH SKILLS

By increasing output, a monopolist lowers the price of the good. Above a certain level of output, revenue also begins to decrease.

1. Why does revenue fall when production increases from 10,000 doses to 11,000 doses?
2. How does producing fewer goods benefit a monopolist?

each firm receives the same price no matter how much it produces. Neither assumption is true in a monopoly.

To understand how this happens, consider the demand schedule for Breathe-Deep in **Figure 7.4.** When BreatheDeep is sold at $12 per dose, consumers buy 8,000 doses per week, providing $96,000 in revenue. If Leland lowers the price of BreatheDeep to $11 per dose, 9,000 doses will be bought for a total revenue of $99,000. The sale of 1,000 more doses brought Leland $3,000 in new revenue.

In Chapter 5, you read that marginal revenue in most markets is equal to price. In this monopoly, the marginal revenue at a market price of $11 is roughly $3 per dose, far below the market price. This is because the lower market price affects both the 1,000 new doses sold and the 8,000 doses people buy for $11 each instead of $12.

Now suppose that Leland lowers the price of BreatheDeep from $11 to $10 per dose. Consumers will buy 10,000 doses, for a total revenue of $100,000. This time, the sale of 1,000 more doses brought only $1,000 in additional revenue. The $10,000 in revenue from 1,000 new sales barely

exceeds the $9,000 fall in revenue from selling the 9,000 doses for $10 each, not $11. The market price is $10 per dose, but the marginal revenue has fallen to a mere $1 for each dose of BreatheDeep sold.

As you've seen, when a firm has some control over price—and can cut the price to sell more—marginal revenue is less than price. In contrast, in a perfectly competitive market, the price would not drop at all as output increased, so marginal revenue would remain the same as price. The firm's total revenue would increase at a steady rate with production.

The table in **Figure 7.4** lists marginal revenues for several different prices. Note that marginal revenue actually becomes negative when the quantity demanded is greater than 10,000 doses per week.

Setting a Price

Leland will choose a level of output that yields the highest profits. As you read in Chapter 5, this is the point at which marginal revenue is equal to marginal cost.

In **Figure 7.4,** we have plotted the demand for BreatheDeep at market prices of $8, $9, $10, $11, and $12 per dose. According to **Figure 7.4,** output per week at these prices will be 12,000, 11,000, 10,000, 9,000, and 8,000 doses, respectively. These points form the market demand curve for BreatheDeep shown in red in **Figure 7.4.**

Then, based on this data, we plotted Leland's marginal revenue at these levels of output. These points form the marginal revenue curve shown in blue in **Figure 7.5.** The marginal revenue curve is at the bottom of the graph because a monopolist's marginal revenue is lower than the market price.

Marginal cost equals marginal revenue at point *a* in **Figure 7.5.** This is the most profitable level of output. The monopolist produces 9,000 units, the quantity at which marginal revenue and marginal cost are both $3. According to the market demand curve, the market price is $11 when 9,000 units are sold (point *b*). Therefore, the monopolist will set the price of each dose at $11 or set production at 9,000 units.

If dozens of firms sold BreatheDeep and the market were perfectly competitive, price and output would be different, as shown in **Figure 7.5.** In a perfectly competitive market, marginal revenue is always equal to market price, so the marginal revenue curve would be the same as the demand curve. Firms will set output where marginal revenue is equal to marginal cost, shown at point *c*. As you can see, a perfectly competitive market for BreatheDeep would have more units sold *and* a lower market price than a monopoly.

Profits

How much profit does the monopolist earn? As you recall from Chapter 5, profit can be determined by comparing price and average cost. For Leland, the company that makes BreatheDeep, the profit per dose is the difference between the market price and the average cost at that level of production. Suppose the average cost of producing 9,000 doses is $5, or slightly higher than the marginal cost. Each dose is sold for $11. The monopolist will earn a profit of $6 per dose ($11−$5), so the total profit is $54,000, or $6 per dose for 9,000 doses.

✔ **CHECKPOINT** *Where does a monopolist usually set output and price compared with a seller in a perfectly competitive market?*

Price Discrimination

The previous example assumed that the monopolist must charge the same price to all consumers. But in some cases, the monopolist may be able to divide consumers into two or more groups and charge a different price to each group. This practice is known as **price discrimination.**

Price discrimination is based on the idea that each customer has a maximum price that he or she will pay for a good. If a monopolist sets the good's price at the highest maximum price of all the buyers in the market, the monopolist will sell only to the one customer willing to pay that much. If the monopolist sets a low price, the monopolist will gain a lot of customers, but the monopolist will lose the profits it could have made from the customers who bought at the low price but were willing to pay more.

Although price discrimination is a feature of monopoly, it can be practiced by any company with market power. **Market power** is the ability to control prices and total market output. As you will read in the next section, many companies have some market power without having a true monopoly. Market power and price discrimination may be found in any market structure except for perfect competition.

price discrimination the division of consumers into groups based on how much they will pay for a good

market power the ability of a company to control prices and total market output

FUTURE WATCH
Personal Finance
For help with evaluating insurance needs, see your Personal Finance Handbook in the back of the book or visit **PearsonSchool.com/PHecon**

Figure 7.5 | Setting a Price in a Monopoly

GRAPH SKILLS

A monopolist sets output at a point (a) where marginal revenue is equal to marginal cost.

1. How does point *c* show the benefits to consumers in a perfectly competitive market?

2. Why is the marginal revenue curve at the bottom of the graph?

Action Graph
online

For an animated version of this graph, visit PearsonSchool.com/PHecon

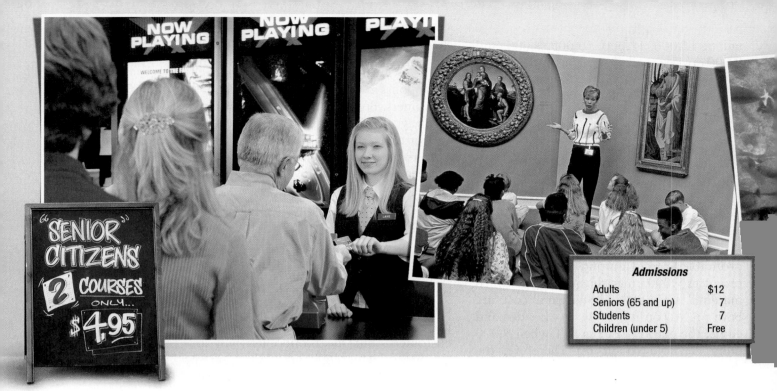

Admissions

Adults	$12
Seniors (65 and up)	7
Students	7
Children (under 5)	Free

▲ Discounts for senior citizens, children, and students are a popular form of price discrimination.

Targeted Discounts

In the monopolist's ideal world, the firm could charge each customer the maximum that he or she is willing to pay, and no less. However, this is impractical, so companies divide consumers into large groups and design pricing policies for each group. The different prices that firms charge each group for the same good or service are not related to production costs.

One common form of price discrimination identifies some customers who are not willing to pay the regular price and offers those customers a discount. Price discrimination can also mean that a company finds the customers who need the good the most, and charges them more for that good. Here are some examples of price discrimination.

- *Discounted airline fares* Airlines offer discounts to travelers who buy tickets several weeks in advance or are willing to spend a Saturday night at their destinations. Business travelers would prefer not to stay over on a Saturday night, but these tickets are appealing to vacationers who wouldn't otherwise pay to fly and don't mind the restrictions.
- *Manufacturers' rebate offers* At times, manufacturers of refrigerators, cars, televisions, and other items will refund a small part of the purchase price to buyers who fill out a rebate form and mail it back. People who take the time to fulfill the rebate requirements are likely more price-conscious than those who don't and may be unwilling to pay full price.
- *Senior citizen or student discounts* Many retirees and students have lower incomes than people who work full time. Zoos, theaters, museums and restaurants often offer discounts to people in these groups, because they are unlikely to be able to pay full price for what some consider luxuries.
- *Children fly or stay free promotions* Families with young children spend more of their income on food, clothing, and school expenses. As a result, they have less money to spend on vacations. Once again, firms would rather have their business and earn lower profits than earn no profits at all, so they offer discounts for families with children.

Limits of Price Discrimination

For price discrimination to work, a market must meet three conditions. Firms that use price discrimination must have some market power, customers must be divided into distinct groups, and buyers must not be in a position in which they can easily resell the good or service.

other words, monopolists must be able to guess the demand curves of different groups, one of which is more elastic, or price-sensitive, than the others. By grouping customers, firms can increase profits by charging each group a different price.

3. *Difficult resale* If one set of customers could buy the product at the lower price and then resell the product for a profit, the firm could not enforce its price discrimination. Because consumer goods like shoes, groceries, and clothes are easily resold, price discrimination works best in marketing services that are consumed on the spot. Examples include theme-park admissions and restaurant meals. Airlines can offer senior discounts because the company can ask for identification and proof of age before letting the customer board the plane.

Although most forms of price discrimination are perfectly legal, sometimes firms use price discrimination to drive other firms out of business. This illegal form of the practice is called predatory pricing, and you will read more about it in Section 4.

✔ **CHECKPOINT** *What three conditions must a market meet in order for price discrimination to work?*

1. *Some market power* For price discrimination to work, firms must have some control over prices. For this reason, price discrimination doesn't happen in perfectly competitive markets.

2. *Distinct customer groups* The price-discriminating firm must be able to divide customers into distinct groups based on their sensitivity to price. In

FL SS.912.E.1.6, SS.912.E.1.8, SS.912.E.2.6, LA.1112.1.6.1, LA.1112.2.2.2

SECTION 2 ASSESSMENT

Essential Questions Journal To continue to build a response to the Essential Question, go to your **Essential Questions Journal**.

🔁 Guiding Question

1. Use your completed concept web to answer this question: What are the characteristics of monopoly?

2. **Extension** Suppose your family wants to install a high-speed Internet connection at home. However, only one company offers the service in your area. How do you think this will affect the service? Do you think your family should still order the high-speed connection?

Key Terms and Main Ideas

3. Why must a **monopoly** supply a unique product?

4. What is the problem with monopolies?

5. Explain the rights that a **patent** gives a company.

6. What is **market power**?

7. Why must firms be able to divide customers into distinct groups in order for **price discrimination** to work?

Critical Thinking

8. **Compare (a)** What is a natural monopoly? **(b)** How are natural monopolies and government monopolies different? **(c)** How are they similar?

9. **Interpret (a)** List three different forms of price discrimination. **(b)** How does price discrimination benefit producers and consumers? **(c)** Do you think price discrimination is fair? Why or why not?

10. **Apply (a)** In your own words, define the term "economies of scale." **(b)** This section used the example of a hydroelectric power plant as an industry with economies of scale. Give two of your own examples of economies of scale.

Math Skills

11. Suppose that Abra Cadabra, Inc. sells 1,000 magic tricks per month for $5 each. Last month, Abra Cadabra launched a special promotion—magic tricks for only $4 each. Sales increased to 1,500 magic tricks for the month. **(a)** What is the company's marginal revenue for each extra magic trick? **(b)** Compare the marginal revenue with the price of the magic tricks. What does the difference tell you about competition in the magic trick market?

Visit PearsonSchool.com/PHecon for additional math help.

NGSSS

LA.1112.1.6 Use multiple strategies to develop vocabulary.

LA.1112.6.3 Understand media literacy as a life skill.

LA.1112.6.3.1 Distinguish between propaganda and ethical reasoning.

SS.912.E.1.6 Compare the characteristics of the four market structures.

SS.912.E.1.8 Explain methods of price and nonprice competition.

ECONOMIC DICTIONARY

As you read the section, look for the definitions of these **Key Terms:**

- **monopolistic competition**
- **differentiation**
- **nonprice competition**
- **oligopoly**
- **price war**
- **collusion**
- **price fixing**
- **cartel**

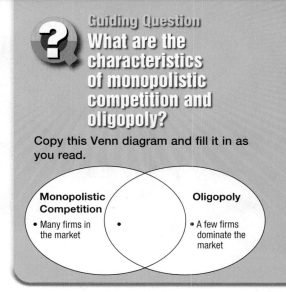

Guiding Question

What are the characteristics of monopolistic competition and oligopoly?

Copy this Venn diagram and fill it in as you read.

Monopolistic Competition
- Many firms in the market

Oligopoly
- A few firms dominate the market

---

monopolistic competition a market structure in which many companies sell products that are similar but not identical

▶ **Economics and You** At the supermarket, you roam through aisles filled with various brands of soap, toothpaste, and paper towels. Although they are produced by different companies, these everyday products are very similar. To compete, producers find ways to make their products unique to attract customers like you.

Principles in Action While monopolistic competition is similar to perfect competition, oligopoly describes a market with only a few large producers. These are the market structures most familiar to consumers. This section's Economics & You highlights competition outside of the price arena.

Monopolistic Competition

In **monopolistic competition,** many companies compete in an open market to sell products that are similar but not identical. Each firm is monopolistic—it holds a monopoly over its own particular product design. You can think of monopolistic competition as a modified version of perfect competition with minor differences in products.

The differences between perfect competition and monopolistic competition arise because monopolistically competitive firms sell goods that are similar enough to be substituted for one another but are not identical. Monopolistic competition does not involve identical commodities. An example of a monopolistically competitive market is the market for jeans. All jeans can be described as denim pants, but in stores, buyers can choose from a variety of brand names, styles, colors, and sizes.

Unlike perfect competition, monopolistic competition is a fact of everyday life. You and your friends probably buy from monopolistically competitive firms several times a week. Common examples include bagel shops, ice cream stands, gas stations, and retail stores.

▲ The market for jeans is monopolistically competitive because jeans can vary by size, color, style, and designer.

✓ **CHECKPOINT** *How does monopolistic competition differ from perfect competition?*

Four Conditions of Monopolistic Competition

Monopolistic competition develops from four conditions. As you read about the types of markets that favor monopolistic competition, note how similar they are to the rules that define perfect competition.

1. *Many firms* As a rule, monopolistically competitive markets are not marked by economies of scale. They do not have high start-up costs. Because firms can begin selling goods and earning money after a small initial investment, new firms spring up quickly to join the market.

2. *Few artificial barriers to entry* Firms in a monopolistically competitive market do not face the high barriers to entry discussed in Section 1. Patents do not protect anyone from competition, either because they have expired or because each firm sells a product that is distinct enough to fall outside the zone of patent protection. Just like a perfectly competitive market, a monopolistically competitive market includes so many competing firms that producers cannot work together to keep out new competitors.

3. *Little control over price* In a monopolistically competitive market structure, each firm's goods are a little different from everyone else's, and some people are willing to pay more for the difference. For this reason, firms have a bit of freedom to raise or lower their prices. However, unlike a monopoly, a monopolistically competitive firm has only limited control over price. If the price rises too high, consumers will buy a rival's product, because close substitutes are readily available. For example, many customers will choose a carton of brand-name orange juice over the store brand even if it costs $.50 more per carton. If the difference in price rose to $2 more per carton, however, most people would think seriously about buying the store brand of orange juice or some other drink altogether.

4. *Differentiated products* Firms have some control over their selling price

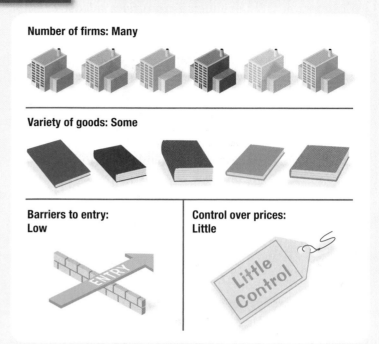

Figure 7.6 **Monopolistic Competition**

Number of firms: Many

Variety of goods: Some

Barriers to entry: Low

Control over prices: Little

CHART SKILLS
Many firms provide a variety of goods in a monopolistically competitive market.
1. Why do firms in monopolistic competition have limited control over prices?
2. What features of a monopolistically competitive market are similar to a perfectly competitive market?

because they can differentiate, or distinguish their goods from the other products in the market. The ability to differentiate goods is the main way that monopolistic competition differs from perfect competition. **Differentiation** enables a monopolistically competitive seller to profit from the differences between his or her products and competitors' products.

✔ **CHECKPOINT** *Why is it easy for firms to enter and leave a monopolistically competitive market?*

Nonprice Competition

The ability to differentiate products means that firms do not have to compete on price alone. The alternative is **nonprice competition,** or competition through ways other than lower prices. Nonprice competition takes several different forms.

differentiation making a product different from other, similar products

nonprice competition a way to attract customers through style, service, or location, but not a lower price

- *Physical characteristics* The simplest way for a firm to distinguish its products is to offer a new size, color, shape, texture, or taste. Running shoes, pens, cars, and toothpaste are good examples of products that can be easily differentiated by their physical characteristics. A pen is always a writing tool that uses ink, but many people will pay extra for a pen that looks or writes differently. Similarly, you can probably describe a "car" in only a few words, but factories around the world manufacture thousands of car models to fit a range of personalities, jobs, families, and incomes.
- *Location* Real estate agents say that the three most important factors when buying property are "location, location, location." Some goods can be differentiated by where they are sold. Gas stations, movie theaters, and grocery stores succeed or fail based on their locations. A convenience store in the middle of a desert differentiates its product simply by selling it hundreds of miles away from the nearest competitor. Such a location allows the seller to charge a lot more for a quart of water.
- *Service level* Some sellers can charge higher prices because they offer their customers a high level of service. Conventional restaurants and fast-food restaurants both offer meals to customers. However, conventional restaurants provide servers who bring the food to your table, whereas fast-food restaurants offer a more barebones, do-it-yourself atmosphere. Conventional restaurants and fast-food chains sell many of the same food items, but fast-food chains sell their meals for less. Customers at conventional restaurants pay more for the service and the relaxing atmosphere.
- *Advertising, image, or status* Firms often use advertising to point out differences between their own offerings and other products in the marketplace. These product differences are often more a matter of perception than reality. For example, a designer can apply his or her name to a plain white T-shirt and charge a higher price, even if the quality of fabric and stitching is no different than what generic T-shirts offer. Customers will pay extra for a designer or a brand-name T-shirt because the image and status that go with the name are worth the extra money to them.

✓ **CHECKPOINT** *What role does advertising play in monopolistically competitive firms?*

Prices, Output, and Profits

Economists study prices, output, and profits when comparing market structures. They find that under monopolistic competition, the market looks very much as it would under perfect competition.

Economics & YOU

Nonprice Competition

The designer athletic shoes are way more expensive than the sensible sneakers, but you buy them anyway. **The image and status associated with the designer shoe is a form of nonprice competition.**

The snacks would have cost less at the supermarket, but the Quick N Ez is so much closer to home. **The location of the convenience store is another example of nonprice competition.**

Quick N Ez

▲ Firms find ways other than price to distinguish their products. **Which recent purchase that you made was based on nonprice competition?**

Prices

Prices under monopolistic competition will be higher than they would be in perfect competition, because firms have some power to raise prices. However, the number of firms and ease of entry prevent companies from raising prices as high as they would if they were a true monopoly. As you have read, if a monopolistically competitive firm raised prices too high, most customers would buy the cheaper product. Because customers can choose among many substitutes, monopolistically competitive firms face more elastic demand curves than true monopolists do.

Output

The law of demand says that output and price are negatively related. As one rises, the other falls. Monopolistically competitive firms sell their products at higher prices than do perfectly competitive firms, but at lower prices than a monopoly. As a result, total output under monopolistic competition falls somewhere between that of monopoly and that of perfect competition.

Profits

Like perfectly competitive firms, monopolistically competitive firms earn just enough to cover all of their costs, including salaries for the workers. If a monopolistically competitive firm started to earn profits well above its costs, two market trends would work to take those profits away.

First, fierce competition would encourage rivals to find new ways to differentiate their products and lure customers back. If one company hires a basketball star to promote its soft drink, a rival might hire a popular singer. The rivalries among firms prevent any one firm from earning excessive profits for long.

Second, new firms will enter the market with slightly different products that cost less than the market leaders. If the original good costs too much, consumers will switch to these substitutes. You've seen this happen when a brand-name line of clothing or a video game becomes popular. Competitors quickly flood the market with cheap imitations to appeal to people who can't afford the original or don't care about the difference in quality.

Figure 7.7 Oligopoly

Number of firms: A few

Variety of goods: Some

Barriers to entry: High

Control over prices: Some

CHART SKILLS
In an oligopoly, a few large firms dominate a market.
1. Why are high barriers to entry an important part of oligopoly?
2. Why are there only a few firms in an oligopoly?

Although monopolistically competitive firms can earn profits in the short run, they have to work hard to keep their product distinct to stay ahead of their rivals. Often, they don't succeed.

Production Costs and Variety

Firms in monopolistic competition may not be able to produce their goods at the lowest possible average cost. Monopolistically competitive markets have many firms, each producing too little output to minimize costs and use resources efficiently. But consumers in these markets benefit from having a wide variety of goods to choose from.

✅ **CHECKPOINT** *What keeps monopolistically competitive firms from making high profits?*

Oligopoly

Oligopoly describes a market dominated by a few large, profitable firms. Oligopoly looks like an imperfect form of monopoly. Economists usually call an industry an oligopoly if the four largest firms produce at least 70 to 80 percent of the output.

oligopoly a market structure in which a few large firms dominate a market

Acting on their own or as a team, the biggest firms in an oligopoly may well set prices higher and output lower than in a perfectly competitive market. Examples of oligopolies in the United States include the markets for air travel, automobiles, breakfast cereals, and household appliances.

Barriers to Entry

An oligopoly can form when significant barriers to entry keep new companies from entering the market to compete with existing firms. These barriers can be technological or they can be created by a system of government licenses or patents.

In other cases, the economic realities of the market lead to an oligopoly. Take the soft-drink market, for example. The two big cola manufacturers have invested so much money to develop their brand names and sales networks over the last century that few companies think they can successfully challenge their grip on the market.

High start-up costs, such as expensive machinery, and large production facilities present additional barriers to entry. Many small airlines have had trouble competing with larger, better-financed rivals because airplanes are very expensive to buy and maintain. The biggest airlines compound the problem because they often own the most desirable gates at the airport, and already enjoy name recognition and the trust of the consumer.

Some oligopolies occur because of economies of scale. As you have read, when a firm experiences economies of scale, the average cost of production decreases as output increases. Greater economies of scale mean that there will be fewer firms in an industry. In a monopoly market, only one company can produce enough goods to earn a profit. In an oligopoly, perhaps three or four companies can reach a profitable level of output before the market becomes too crowded and revenue falls below costs.

Cooperation and Collusion

Oligopoly presents a big challenge to government, because oligopolistic firms often *seem* to work together as a monopoly, even when they are not actually doing so. Many government regulations try to make oligopolistic firms act more like competitive firms. When determined oligopolists work together illegally to set prices and bar competing firms from the market, they can become as damaging to the consumer as a monopoly.

The three practices that concern government the most are price leadership, collusion, and cartels. While these three practices represent ways that firms in an oligopoly can try to control a market, they don't always work. Each tactic includes an incentive for the firms to cheat and thereby undo any benefits.

FUTURE WATCH 🌐 Global Impact

The OPEC Cartel

The Organization of Petroleum Exporting Countries (OPEC) is an international cartel of major oil producers. OPEC members produce about 40 percent of the world's oil and control 75 percent of the world's oil reserves. Members meet regularly to set production quotas. Most experts agree that world oil supplies are not sufficient to meet increased demand. In 2008, the head of Libya's OPEC delegation made a prediction: *"The easy, cheap oil is over."*
How can OPEC affect world oil prices?

Share of Total Oil Reserves, 2006

7.2% — **European Union and OECD Members***
74.9% — **OPEC**
14.4% — **Non-OPEC**
10.6% — **Former Soviet Union**

* Organization for Economic Cooperation and Development   Note: Total may exceed 100 percent because of rounding.

SOURCE: *BP Statistical Review of World Energy, June 2007*

Sometimes the market leader in an oligopoly can start a round of price increases or price cuts by making its plans clear to other sellers. This firm becomes a price leader. Price leaders can set prices and output for entire industries as long as other member firms go along with the leader's policy. But disagreements among those companies can spark a **price war,** when competitors cut their prices very low to win business. A price war is harmful to producers but good for consumers because they will pay less for a good or service.

Collusion refers to an agreement among members of an oligopoly to illegally set prices and production levels. One outcome of collusion is called **price fixing,** an agreement among firms to sell at the same or very similar prices. Collusive agreements set prices and output at the levels that would be chosen by a monopolist. Collusion is illegal in the United States, but the lure of monopolistic profits can tempt businesses to make such agreements despite the illegality and risks.

Collusion is not, however, the only reason for nearly identical pricing in oligopolistic industries. Such pricing may actually result from intense competition, especially if advertising is vigorous and new lines of products are being introduced.

Cartels

Stronger than a collusive agreement, a **cartel** is an agreement by a formal organization of producers to coordinate prices and production. Although other countries and international organizations permit them, cartels are illegal in the United States. OPEC is perhaps the most familiar international cartel.

Cartels can survive only if every member keeps to its agreed output levels and no more. Otherwise, prices will fall, and firms will lose profits. However, each member has a strong incentive to cheat and produce more than its quota. If every cartel member cheats, too much product reaches the market, and prices fall. Cartels can also collapse if some producers are left out of the group and decide to lower their prices below the cartel's levels. Therefore, cartels usually do not last very long.

✔ **CHECKPOINT** *What role can market leaders play in an oligopoly?*

price war a series of competitive price cuts that lowers the market price below the cost of production

collusion an illegal agreement among firms to divide the market, set prices, or limit production

price fixing an agreement among firms to charge one price for the same good

cartel a formal organization of producers that agree to coordinate prices and production

FL SS.912.E.1.6, SS.912.E.1.8, LA.1112.1.6.1, LA.1112.2.2.2, LA.1112.6.3.1

SECTION 3 ASSESSMENT

Essential Questions Journal To continue to build a response to the Essential Question, go to your **Essential Questions Journal**.

❓ Guiding Question

1. Use your completed Venn diagram to answer this question: What are the characteristics of monopolistic competition and oligopoly?
2. **Extension** You want to buy a new pair of jeans. The store offers several brands and styles. Each one looks different. Prices and colors vary. How will you decide which jeans to buy?

Key Terms and Main Ideas

3. What four conditions define **monopolistic competition?**
4. How does **differentiation** help monopolistically competitive firms sell their products?
5. Explain what happens during a **price war.**
6. How do economists determine whether or not a market is an **oligopoly?**

7. How would **price fixing** and **collusion** help producers?

Critical Thinking

8. **Apply (a)** Name four kinds of non-price competition. **(b)** Which example would you use to promote the following products: a new brand of bottled water, in-home computer repair, and protein bars? Explain your reasoning.
9. **Extend (a)** What are the advantages of a monopolistically competitive market for consumers? **(b)** What are some of the disadvantages?
10. **Interpret (a)** In what ways does the government regulate oligopolies? **(b)** Why do you think the government has imposed these regulations?

Quick Write

11. Choose a product in a monopolistically competitive industry. Write an ad for your product. Your ad can be for television, radio, newspapers, or the Internet. Remember, there are many similar products on the market. How can you persuade consumers to buy your product? Then write a paragraph answering the following questions: Would you see an ad like this in a purely competitive market? Would you see this ad in a market with a monopoly? Why or why not?

FL NGSSS

LA.1112.1.6 Use multiple strategies to develop vocabulary.

LA.1112.1.6.2 Listen to, read, and discuss familiar and challenging texts.

SS.912.E.1.8 Explain methods of price and nonprice competition.

SS.912.E.2.4 Diagram and explain the problems of government-instituted wage and price control.

SS.912.E.2.6 Examine the purposes of government regulation of monopolies.

ECONOMIC DICTIONARY

As you read the section, look for the definitions of these **Key Terms:**

- predatory pricing
- antitrust laws
- trust
- merger
- deregulation

Guiding Question
When does the government regulate competition?

Copy this chart and fill it in as you read.

How Government Promotes Competition	
Regulation	**Deregulation**
•	•
•	•
•	

predatory pricing
selling a product below cost for a short period of time to drive competitors out of the market

▶ **Economics and You**   As a consumer, you have choices. You can choose from a variety of cellphone plans or Internet service providers. But you still have no choice when it comes to cable television service. Congress passed a law in 2007 that stated that no company could control more than 30 percent of the cable television market. A major cable company successfully argued in court that it had competition from other sources, such as satellite television.

Principles in Action   Sometimes the government takes steps to promote competition, but the limits of its actions can be tested in court. In this section, you will read about the tools the government uses to combat anticompetitive practices.

Market Power

Recall that market power is the ability of a firm to control prices and total market output. As you have read, monopoly and oligopoly can be bad for the consumer and for the economy as a whole. Markets dominated by one firm or a few large ones tend to have higher prices and lower output than markets with many sellers. Competition is reduced. Before we look at antitrust policies, let's look at ways in which a firm might try to increase its market power.

To control prices and output like a monopoly, the leading firms in a market can merge with one another, form a cartel, or set the market price below their costs for the short term to drive competitors out of business. The last practice is known as **predatory pricing.** Economists are skeptical about most claims of predatory pricing because the predator loses money each time it drives an endless series of rivals out of business.

✅ **CHECKPOINT** *How does a market with a few large firms act like a monopoly?*

Government and Competition

The federal government has a number of policies that keep firms from controlling the price and supply of important goods. If a firm controls

THE MONSTER MONOPOLY.

▲ Public outrage with powerful trusts in the late 1800s led Congress to pass antitrust legislation.

a large share of a market, the Federal Trade Commission and the Department of Justice's Antitrust Division will watch the firm closely to ensure that it does not unfairly force out its competitors. These government policies are known as **antitrust laws,** because a **trust** is a business combination similar to a cartel.

In 1890, Congress passed the Sherman Antitrust Act, which outlawed mergers and monopolies that limit trade between states. This and other laws gave the government the power to regulate industry, to stop firms from forming cartels or monopolies, and to break up existing monopolies. Over the years, Congress passed new laws to outlaw other anticompetitive practices.

Despite the antitrust laws, companies have used many strategies to gain control over their markets. Some firms require a customer who buys one product to buy other products from the same company, whether or not the customer wants them. For example, a tennis shoe manufacturer can demand that a chain also buy and resell its brand-name shirts, windbreakers, and watches if it wants to sell its shoes. Buying out competitors is another strategy used by many large firms.

Regulating Business Practices

The government has the power to regulate all of these practices if they give too much power to a company that already has few competitors. Microsoft is such a company. It sells operating systems, software that tells a computer how to run. In 1997, the Department of Justice accused Microsoft of using its near-monopoly over the operating-system market to try to take control of the browser market. A browser is a program that allows people to access Web sites.

Microsoft insisted that computer manufacturers selling its operating system must also include its browser. The government accused Microsoft of predatory pricing, because the company gave away its browser for free, a policy that could ruin the other browser company, Netscape. Microsoft's power in one market gave it a big—and possibly unfair—advantage in a related market.

Microsoft argued that the browser was part of its operating system and could not be sold separately. Microsoft's defenders said

Date	Event
1901	Theodore Roosevelt becomes President and begins enforcing the 1890 Sherman Antitrust Act, which outlaws mergers and monopolies that restrain trade between states
1911	Supreme Court breaks up John D. Rockefeller's Standard Oil Trust
1950	Celler-Kefauver Act allows government to stop mergers that could hurt competition
1982	AT&T agrees to break up its local phone service into several companies
2001	Department of Justice settles its lawsuit with Microsoft

Key Events in Federal Antitrust Policy

▲ Over the past century, the federal government has acted to promote competition in American industry.

that companies do compete with Microsoft, and people buy Microsoft software because they like it. In November 1999, a federal judge ruled against Microsoft. The company appealed, and in 2001, the Justice Department and Microsoft reached an agreement to settle the case. According to the settlement, Microsoft could link its browser to its operating system but could not force computer manufacturers to provide only Microsoft software on new computers.

Breaking Up Monopolies

In 1911, the government used the Sherman Antitrust Act to break up two monopolies, John D. Rockefeller's Standard Oil Trust and the American Tobacco Company. The Supreme Court ordered these powerful monopolies to split apart into competing firms. Antitrust laws have been put to use many times since then.

In 1982, the government broke American Telephone and Telegraph (AT&T) into seven regional phone companies, including BellSouth, USWest, and PacificBell. Because the government treated local telephone service as a natural monopoly, AT&T had legally controlled all the cables and networks that linked telephones in homes and businesses. The government stepped in only when AT&T used its legal monopoly in local phone

Simulation *Activity*

Is the Law Being Broken?
You may be asked to take part in a role-playing game about government regulation.

antitrust laws
laws that encourage competition in the marketplace

trust an illegal grouping of companies that discourages competition, similar to a cartel

How is broadcasting regulated?

The Federal Communications Commission (FCC) is a government agency that regulates the broadcasting industry. The FCC issues licenses to radio and television stations. Creating a new television station requires FCC approval.

1 A broadcaster who wants to start a new television station begins with a search for an unused frequency. If a frequency can be found, the broadcaster files a petition to add a new station with the FCC. An attorney can help with the complex process.

2 The FCC grants (or denies) the broadcaster permission to apply for the station. Applications are filed online. The broadcaster must announce his application in a Public Notice. The FCC will conduct an electronic auction of licenses for broadcast stations.

Applying for a New Television Station

service to take control of other markets for long-distance phone calls and communications equipment.

Today, the market for long-distance service has many firms and is more competitive. Although the break-up of AT&T cost thousands of workers their jobs, consumers have benefited from lower prices and improved technology.

Blocking Mergers

In addition to breaking up existing monopolies, the government has the power to prevent the rise of monopolies. The government does this by blocking mergers that might reduce competition and lead to higher prices. A **merger** occurs when a company joins with another company or companies to form a single firm. Government regulators also follow the effects of past mergers to check that they did not lead to unfair market control. You read in Section 1 that

merger when two or more companies join to form a single firm

prices often fall when the number of firms in a market increases. The reverse is also true. Prices often rise when the number of firms in a market falls.

When the government considers whether or not to approve a merger, it tries to predict the effects of the merger on prices and service. Sometimes it determines that the effects will be minimal. In 2000, the Federal Trade Commission (FTC) and the Federal Communications Commission both approved the merger of media giants America Online (AOL) and Time Warner. Approval came with several conditions designed to ensure consumer choice. Two years later, the government drew a different conclusion when the FTC blocked the merger of the glassware makers Libbey and Anchor Hocking. The FTC argued that the merger would create a monopoly. A federal court agreed, and the deal fell apart.

3 The FCC also sets broadcasting standards and monitors programs for indecent content. Stations that violate rules are subject to fines and penalties.

4 Broadcasting without a license is illegal. The FCC shuts down illegal broadcasters and takes their equipment. Illegal operation of an unlicensed station may result in criminal prosecution.

5 The FCC grants a construction permit for the new station to the highest bidder. The permit allows the station to broadcast before the FCC license has been issued.

Check Your Understanding
1. Who can apply for a license to broadcast?
2. What would happen if the FCC didn't limit the number of broadcasters?

Broadcasting Rules

FCC Approval

Preserving Incentives

While some mergers hurt consumers by reducing competition, others can actually benefit consumers. In these cases, corporate mergers will lower overall average costs and lead to lower prices, more reliable products or service, and a more efficient industry. The government must act carefully to make the right decision.

In 1997, the Justice Department and the FTC released new guidelines for proposed mergers. Companies now have the chance to prove that the merger would lower costs and prices or lead to a better product.

✔ **CHECKPOINT** *How does the government break up monopolies?*

Deregulation

In the late 1970s and 1980s, Congress decided that some government regulation was reducing competition. It passed laws to deregulate several industries. **Deregulation** means that the government no longer decides what role each company can play in a market and how much it can charge its customers.

Over several years, the government deregulated the airline, trucking, banking, railroad, natural gas, and television broadcasting industries. Depending on the degree of deregulation, the government's action allowed—or forced—firms in these industries to compete by eliminating many price controls and barriers to entry.

While deregulation weakens government control, antitrust laws strengthen it. Yet the government uses both deregulation and antitrust laws for the same purpose: to promote competition.

Many critics say that government efforts to regulate industries have created inefficiencies. In some cases, the economic facts that created the need for regulation in the

deregulation the removal of some government controls over a market first place have changed. In Section 2 you read how cellular phones challenged the natural monopoly of local phone service and opened the market to new companies. The trucking industry was also regulated as a natural monopoly from the early 1900s until 1978. By then, many had decided that the government was regulating industries that were not natural monopolies at all.

Judging Deregulation

Deregulation has met with mixed success. In most cases, many new firms entered the deregulated industries right away. Competition certainly increased in the airline, trucking, and banking industries. Typically, years of wild growth were followed by the disappearance of some firms. This weeding out of weaker players is considered healthy for the economy, but it can be hard on workers in the short term.

In the 1990s, several states deregulated their electricity markets to allow private, competing companies to produce and sell energy to homeowners. In some markets, energy prices fell, but elsewhere, customers paid more. California experienced a massive energy crisis in 2000 that forced the state to pay extraordinarily high rates for electricity.

Many attributed this crisis to companies like Enron that may have used deregulation rules to create an electricity shortage.

Airlines: A Complicated Deregulation

Many new airlines started operating after President Carter deregulated the industry in 1978, but some eventually failed or were acquired. Freed from regulatory restriction, many of the large airlines competed aggressively for the busiest routes. For most travelers, increased competition created lower prices. However, many busy airports now have one dominant airline. In some cases, fares are actually higher than before deregulation.

In the early 2000s, changing conditions transformed the airlines. Over-expansion and sharply rising labor costs squeezed profits. The terrorist hijackings of four commercial passenger jets on September 11, 2001, caused many people to stop flying. Revenues plunged while costs for security, insurance, and fuel rose. Several major airlines filed for bankruptcy. Due to market forces the future of the airline industry is still uncertain.

☑ **CHECKPOINT** *How does deregulation encourage competition in a market?*

FL SS.912.E.1.8, SS.912.E.2.4, SS.912.E.2.6, LA.1112.1.6.1, LA.1112.2.2.2

SECTION 4 ASSESSMENT

Essential Questions Journal To continue to build a response to the Essential Question, go to your **Essential Questions Journal**.

❓ Guiding Question

1. Use your completed chart to answer this question: When does the government regulate competition?
2. **Extension** Name a company that has a lot of market power today. Why do you think it has so much market power? Do you think this is fair? Why or why not?

Key Terms and Main Ideas

3. How does **predatory pricing** hurt competition?
4. What is the purpose of **antitrust laws?**
5. How did the Sherman Antitrust Act affect the monopolies of Standard Oil Trust and the American Tobacco Company?
6. Under what conditions will the government approve a **merger?**

7. How did **deregulation** change the air travel industry?

Critical Thinking

8. **Predict (a)** How does predatory pricing affect a company's market power? **(b)** Why might a firm not want to practice predatory pricing, even if it was legal? **(c)** When might a firm try to practice predatory pricing?
9. **Summarize (a)** Why did the government try to prevent Microsoft from including its browser when it sold its operating system? **(b)** What was the government's final decision? **(c)** Do you think the government achieved its goals? Why or why not?
10. **Examine (a)** Why does the government intervene in markets? **(b)** Is this consistent with the idea of laissez faire and free markets? Why or why not?

Quick Write

11. Reread Blocking Mergers in Section 4. Then write a short essay answering the following questions: Why does the government block mergers? What happens to prices when there are fewer firms in a market? Do you think the government should block the merger of the two largest American automobile manufacturers? Why or why not?

Chapter 7: Market Structures

Section 2 What are the characteristics of monopoly?

Section 3 What are the characteristics of monopolistic competition and oligopoly?

Section 1 What are the characteristics of perfect competition?

Section 4 When does the government regulate competition?

Essential Question, Chapter 7
How does competition affect your choices?

Comparison of Market Structures

	Perfect Competition	Monopolistic Competition	Oligopoly	Monopoly
Number of firms	Many	Many	A few dominate	One
Variety of goods	None	Some	Some	None
Control over prices	None	Little	Some	Complete
Barriers to entry	None	Low	High	Complete
Examples	Wheat, shares of stock	Jeans, books	Cars, movie studios	Public water

Regulation and Deregulation

Government passes antitrust laws

↓

Laws are used to regulate industry

↓

New laws limit unfair business practices

↓

Deregulation promotes competition

Economic Dictionary

perfect competition, *p. 159*

commodity, *p. 160*

barrier to entry, *p. 160*

imperfect competition, *p. 160*

start-up costs, *p. 162*

monopoly, *p. 164*

economies of scale, *p. 165*

natural monopoly, *p. 166*

government monopoly, *p. 167*

patent, *p. 167*

franchise, *p. 167*

license, *p. 168*

price discrimination, *p. 171*

market power, *p. 171*

monopolistic competition, *p. 174*

differentiation, *p. 175*

nonprice competition, *p. 175*

oligopoly, *p. 177*

price war, *p. 179*

collusion, *p. 179*

price fixing, *p. 179*

cartel, *p. 179*

predatory pricing, *p. 180*

antitrust laws, *p. 181*

trust, *p. 181*

merger, *p. 182*

deregulation, *p. 183*

Economics *on the go*

Study anytime, anywhere. Download these files today.

Economic Dictionary (online)
Vocabulary Support in English and Spanish

Audio Review (online)
Audio Study Guide in English and Spanish

Action Graph (online)
Animated Charts and Graphs

Visual Glossary (online)
Animated feature

How the Economy Works (online)
Animated feature

Download to your computer or mobile device at PearsonSchool.com/PHecon

Self-Test online — To test your understanding of key terms and main ideas, visit **PearsonSchool.com/PHecon**

Key Terms and Main Ideas

To make sure you understand the key terms and main ideas of this chapter, review the Checkpoint and Section Assessment questions and look at the Quick Study Guide on the preceding page.

Critical Thinking

1. **Apply** You are babysitting for children who want to start a lemonade stand. **(a)** List at least three items they will have to buy before they can start selling lemonade. How much do you think these start-up expenses will cost? **(b)** Would you recommend that the children set up a lemonade stand? Why or why not? **(c)** Suppose that another family down the street already has a lemonade stand. How would you recommend that the children compete?

2. **Draw Conclusions (a)** Why does government usually approve of natural monopolies? **(b)** Why does it regulate them? **(c)** Do you believe that public education is a natural monopoly? Why or why not?

3. **Make Judgments** Suppose that you are the mayor of your town. A local candy maker asks you to franchise his shop as the only approved chocolate shop in town. **(a)** What might be one benefit to the town in granting his request? **(b)** What would be a disadvantage? **(c)** Considering the benefit and disadvantage, would you agree to the candy maker's request?

4. **Compare and Contrast (a)** How do prices, output, and profits differ between monopolies and firms that engage in monopolistic competition? **(b)** How do they differ between monopolistically competitive and perfectly competitive firms? **(c)** Is monopolistic competition more similar to a monopoly or to perfect competition? Give specific reasons for your choice.

5. **Summarize (a)** Why did the government first pass antitrust laws? **(b)** What powers did these laws give the government? **(c)** Do you think the government should use these and similar laws to regulate companies? Why or why not?

Applying Your Math Skills

Making a Line Graph Create a line graph for an industry with economies of scale to show how much it costs to produce each given amount of a product. Suppose it costs $20,000 to set up and furnish a new restaurant. The cost for each meal the restaurant serves is $8. Use your math skills and the information above to answer the following questions:

Visit PearsonSchool.com/PHecon for additional math help.

6. How much does it cost to produce the first meal the restaurant serves?

7. How much does it cost per meal to produce two meals?

8. What is the cost per meal to produce ten meals? Fifty meals? One hundred meals? One thousand meals?

9. Based on your answers to questions 6, 7, and 8, create a line graph titled: Costs per Meal at the New Restaurant. If necessary, calculate additional points to put on your graph.

? Essential Question Activity

Essential Questions Journal — To respond to the chapter Essential Question, go to your **Essential Questions Journal**.

10. Complete this activity to answer the Essential Question **How does competition affect your choices?** To welcome a new student and inform them about the goods and services available in the community, the class will create a newcomer's kit. To create this kit, the class will generate a list of businesses that provide goods and services that would be helpful to a new student. The list will identify categories of goods and services such as fast food, clothing, sporting goods, entertainment, and automobile services. Use the worksheet in your Essential Questions Journal or the electronic worksheet available at **PearsonSchool.com/PHecon,** to gather information about the products or services. Then use the worksheet to answer the following questions:
    (a) Which categories have the greatest number of choices? Is there a wide range of prices?
    (b) Give one example of nonprice differentiation between products in a category.
    (c) Identify the market structure for each business.

11. **Modify** The class will use the information they have gathered to create a mini-business directory. Each business on the list will have an entry that provides basic information such as the name of the business, and its street or Web address. Entries for each business will highlight the type of goods or services that the business provides and their price range. Each entry should also include a rating. The rating could be in the form of a one to two sentence review. Or, students can create a rating system with a key that explains what the rating symbols mean. Students will also create a map for the directory that shows the locations of all the businesses. When the directory is finished, give it to the school guidance office so that it can be distributed to students who are new to the area.

When is government regulation necessary?

In 2007, some members of Congress introduced a bill that would ensure "net neutrality." The bill would prevent Internet service providers from charging fees to Web sites in order to run at higher speeds. Industry members and consumer interest groups clashed over the bill.

Document A

"Left free to create new business opportunities and services, broadband providers (including cable, DSL, satellite and wireless operators) have invested billions of dollars to bring high-speed Internet access to consumers nationwide. With bandwidth usage growing at a rapid pace, continued investment will be needed to keep broadband services robust.

If broadband providers are to continue to make these investments, and if consumers are going to be given the levels of services and innovative new products and features they desire, all at prices they can afford, broadband providers need to have continuing flexibility to develop new business models and pricing plans."

—National Cable & Telecommunications Association, January 2007

Document B

"[Without a net neutrality law,] Internet service providers would be free to block or impede any online content or services, for any reason. They could also charge websites or applications for 'priority service,' practically assuring that any site that couldn't or wouldn't pay their fees would no longer work as well or be as easy to find. That could spell the end of innovation, as small businesses, entrepreneurs, local governments, nonprofits and others would be locked out of a system controlled by the big telephone and cable companies. If network providers are allowed to control the flow of information, the open and freewheeling nature of the Internet could be lost."

—Common Cause, "Some Straight Talk on Net Neutrality"

Document C

 FL LA.1112.1.6.2, SS.912.E.2.6

ANALYZING DOCUMENTS

Use your knowledge of government regulation and Documents A, B, and C to answer questions 1–3.

1. **According to Document A, Internet service providers need the flexibility to charge additional fees so they can**

   A. increase corporate profits.
   B. expand broadband services.
   C. remain competitive with foreign companies.
   D. raise prices to consumers.

2. **According to Document B, a "net neutrality" bill is necessary to ensure**

   A. unlimited access to Web sites.
   B. low prices.
   C. expanded broadband service.
   D. consumer safety.

3. **The cartoon in Document C suggests that government regulation**

   A. is good for business.
   B. traps consumers.
   C. holds down innovation.
   D. raises prices.

WRITING ABOUT ECONOMICS

Whether to regulate Internet businesses is an ongoing issue. Use the documents on this page and resources on the Web site below to answer the question: *When is government regulation necessary?* Use the sources to support your opinion.

In Partnership

THE WALL STREET JOURNAL.
CLASSROOM EDITION

To read more about issues related to this topic, visit
PearsonSchool.com/PHecon

Essential Question, Unit 2

Who benefits from the free market economy?

VIDEO By Students For Students
For videos on Essential Questions, go to *PearsonSchool.com/PHecon*

People have different opinions about who benefits in the free marketplace. Look at the opinions below, keeping in mind the Essential Question: Who benefits from the free market economy?

> " I'm all for a free economy, but competitors need to play by some rules. Congress has the power to regulate this trade through the commerce clause of the Constitution and needs to begin to do so. "
>
> —Gatsby 999, msnbc.com

> " I suspect ignorance about economics leads many to believe that when two people exchange goods and money, one wins and the other loses. If rich capitalists profit, the poor and the weak suffer. That's a myth. How many times have you paid $1 for a cup of coffee and after the clerk said, "thank you," you responded, "thank you"? There's a wealth of economics wisdom in the weird double thank-you moment. Why does it happen? Because you want the coffee more than the buck, and the store wants the buck more than the coffee. Both of you win. "
>
> —John Stossel, Real Clear Politics.com, "The Double Thank-You Moment," May 30, 2007

NEWS — ECONOMIC DATA RELEASED

IT SAYS THE ECONOMY'S ON THE MOVE AGAIN.

LET'S BE CAREFUL IT DOESN'T RUN US DOWN THIS TIME!

E-mail: mail@frankandernest.com
©2006 Thaves / Dist. by NEA, Inc.
www.comics.com
11-13 THAVES

Essential Question Writing Activity

Consider the different views expressed in the sources on this page and what you have learned about the operation of the free market. ***Then write a well-constructed essay expressing your view of who benefits in a free market economy.***

Writing Guidelines

- Address all aspects of the Essential Question Writing Activity.
- Support the theme with relevant facts, examples, and details.
- Use a logical and clear plan of organization.
- Introduce the theme by establishing a framework that is beyond a simple restatement of the question and conclude with a summation of the theme.

For help in writing a Persuasive Essay, refer to the *Writer's Handbook* in the Reference section, page S-5.

Essential Questions Journal

To respond to the unit Essential Question, go to your **Essential Questions Journal**.

UNIT 3 Business and Labor

Essential Question, Unit 3

How can businesses and labor best achieve their goals?

Chapter 8
Why do some businesses succeed and others fail?

Chapter 9
How can workers best meet the challenges of a changing economy?

8 Business Organizations

Essential Question, Chapter 8

Why do some businesses succeed and others fail?

FL **Next Generation Sunshine State Standards**

Section 1: Sole Proprietorships
LA.1112.1.6, MA.912.A.2.2, SS.912.E.1.5, SS.912.E.2, SS.912.E.2.3

Section 2: Partnerships and Franchises
LA.1112.1.6, MA.912.A.2.2, SS.912.E.1.5, SS.912.E.2

Section 3: Corporations, Mergers, and Multinationals
LA.1112.1.6, MA.912.A.2.2, SS.912.E.1.5, SS.912.E.2

Section 4: Nonprofit Organizations
LA.1112.1.6, LA.1112.6.2.4, SS.912.E.1.5, SS.912.E.2, SS.912.E.2.3

Economics
on the go

To study anywhere, anytime, download these
online resources at *PearsonSchool.com/PHecon* ▶

FL **NGSSS**

LA.1112.1.6 Use multiple strategies to develop vocabulary.

MA.912.A.2.2 Interpret a graph to represent a real-world situation.

SS.912.E.1.5 Compare different forms of business.

SS.912.E.2 Understand the concepts relevant to the national economy.

SS.912.E.2.3 Research the contributions of key individuals of various backgrounds in the development of the U.S.

ECONOMIC DICTIONARY

As you read the section, look for the definitions of these **Key Terms:**

- sole proprietorship
- business organization
- business license
- zoning laws
- liability
- fringe benefits

Guiding Question

What are the risks and benefits of a sole proprietorship?

Copy this comparison chart and fill it in as you read.

Sole Proprietorships	
Advantages	**Disadvantages**
• Ease of start-up	• Unlimited personal liability
•	•
•	•
•	•
•	

▶ **Economics and You**   You may be one of the lucky people who is able to turn something you really like to do into a business. Imagine launching a web site that reviews video games or opening a baseball camp or a car detailing business. One of the many challenges you will face is finding the best way to organize your business.

Principles in Action The easiest business to set up is the one in which you are the only owner. In this section you will learn that being your own boss has its advantages as well as its disadvantages. In the Economics & You feature, you will see how doing business with a sole proprietorship might affect you.

The Role of Sole Proprietorships

A **sole proprietorship** is a business owned and managed by a single individual. In this type of **business organization,** which is the ownership structure of a company or firm, the lone entrepreneur earns all of the firm's profits and is responsible for all its debts. This type of company is by far the most popular in the United States. According to the Internal Revenue Service, more than 70 percent of all businesses are organized as sole proprietorships. Most sole proprietorships are small, however. All together they generate only about 4 percent of all United States sales.

Many types of businesses can flourish as sole proprietorships. Look around your neighborhood or town. It is more likely than not that your local bakery, your barber shop or hair salon, your bike-repair shop, and the corner grocery store are all sole proprietorships.

sole proprietorship
a business owned and managed by a single individual

business organization
the ownership structure of a company or firm

Visual Glossary
online

Go to the Visual Glossary Online for an interactive review of **corporation.**

Action Graph
online

Go to Action Graph Online for animated versions of key charts and graphs.

How the Economy Works
online

Go to How the Economy Works Online for an interactive lesson on how a small business grows.

Entrepreneurial Spirit

In some ways, the word *spirit* in the term *entrepreneurial spirit* says it all. There is a difference between people who expect to spend their lives working for someone else and those who want to work for themselves. Some people are driven by an idea or ambition to create their own jobs. But ambition is only a starting point. To be successful, sole proprietors have to be risk takers. They have to be willing to risk failure for greater satisfaction, and perhaps greater financial gain.

The profile of an entrepreneur includes other essential qualities. The person hoping to start a business has to be able to answer yes to a series of questions. Are you organized? Are you responsible? Are your energetic? Are you goal-oriented? Do you know how to run a business? You may be the best cook in the world, but if you know nothing about the business end of running a restaurant, you are likely to fail.

Steve Case, co-founder of America Online, is a model of the successful entrepreneur who believed in himself and had the vision that a company could thrive on the Internet.

> **❝**If you're doing something new, you've got to have a vision. You've got to have a perspective. You've got have some North Star you're aiming for, and you just believe somehow you'll get there.... You've got to stick with it, because these things are not overnight successes....**❞**
>
> —From an interview with Academy of Achievement,
> July 12, 2004

✓ CHECKPOINT *What is the most common form of business organization?*

Advantages of Sole Proprietorships

While you need to do more than just hang out a sign to start your own business, a sole proprietorship is simple to establish. It also offers the owner several advantages.

Simulation *Activity*

Be an Entrepreneur!
You may be asked to take part in a role-playing game that involves being an entrepreneur.

FL MA.912.A.2.2
Interpret a graph to represent a real-world situation.

| Figure 8.1 | **Characteristics of Sole Proprietorships** |

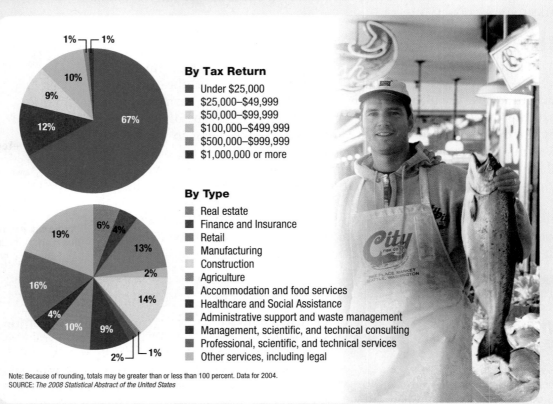

GRAPH SKILLS

Most sole proprietorships take in relatively small amounts of money, or receipts.

1. What percentage of sole proprietorships is engaged in retail trade?
2. Why might more sole proprietors be engaged in services than in manufacturing?

By Tax Return
- Under $25,000
- $25,000–$49,999
- $50,000–$99,999
- $100,000–$499,999
- $500,000–$999,999
- $1,000,000 or more

By Type
- Real estate
- Finance and Insurance
- Retail
- Manufacturing
- Construction
- Agriculture
- Accommodation and food services
- Healthcare and Social Assistance
- Administrative support and waste management
- Management, scientific, and technical consulting
- Professional, scientific, and technical services
- Other services, including legal

Action Graph
online

For an animated version of this graph, visit
PearsonSchool.com/PHecon

Note: Because of rounding, totals may be greater than or less than 100 percent. Data for 2004.
SOURCE: *The 2008 Statistical Abstract of the United States*

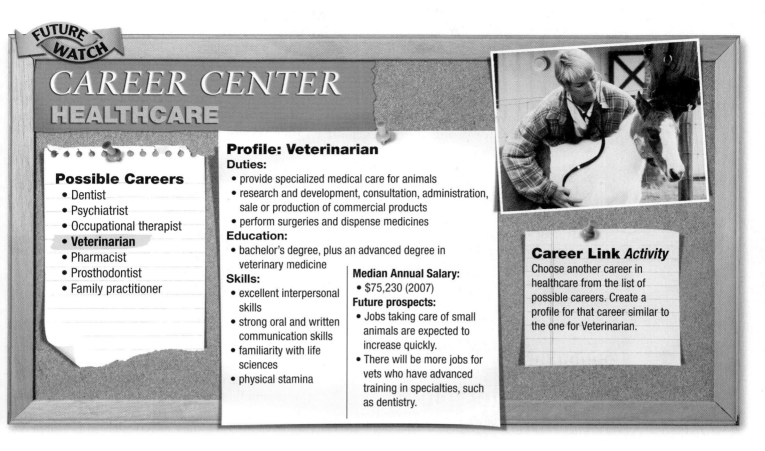

CAREER CENTER
HEALTHCARE

Possible Careers
- Dentist
- Psychiatrist
- Occupational therapist
- **Veterinarian**
- Pharmacist
- Prosthodontist
- Family practitioner

Profile: Veterinarian

Duties:
- provide specialized medical care for animals
- research and development, consultation, administration, sale or production of commercial products
- perform surgeries and dispense medicines

Education:
- bachelor's degree, plus an advanced degree in veterinary medicine

Skills:
- excellent interpersonal skills
- strong oral and written communication skills
- familiarity with life sciences
- physical stamina

Median Annual Salary:
- $75,230 (2007)

Future prospects:
- Jobs taking care of small animals are expected to increase quickly.
- There will be more jobs for vets who have advanced training in specialties, such as dentistry.

Career Link *Activity*
Choose another career in healthcare from the list of possible careers. Create a profile for that career similar to the one for Veterinarian.

Easy to Start and End

Easy start-up is the main advantage of the sole proprietorship. With just a small amount of paperwork and legal expense, just about anyone can start such a business. The exact requirements vary from city to city and state to state. Typically, though, sole proprietors must meet the following minimum requirements:

1. *Authorization* Many sole proprietors must obtain a **business license,** which is an authorization from the local government to operate a business. Certain professionals, such as doctors and day-care providers, may also need a special license from the state.

2. *Site permit* If not operating the business out of his or her home, a sole proprietor must obtain a certificate of occupancy to use another building for business. Some zoning laws prohibit doing business in a residential area.

3. *Name* If not using his or her own name as the name of the business, a sole proprietor must register a business name.

This paperwork often takes only a day or two to complete. Because they require little legal paperwork, sole proprietorships are usually the least expensive form of ownership to establish.

The federal government offers aid to entrepreneurs to help their businesses grow. Once a business has been started, the federal government's Small Business Administration provides a variety of loan programs and other support.

Relatively Few Regulations

A proprietorship is the least-regulated form of business organization. Even the smallest business, however, is subject to some regulation, especially industry-specific rules. For example, a soft pretzel stand would be subject to health codes, and a furniture refinishing business would have to follow laws about disposing of dangerous chemicals.

Sole proprietorships may also be subject to local **zoning laws.** Cities and towns often designate certain areas, or zones, for residential use and for business. Zoning laws may prohibit sole proprietors from operating businesses out of their homes.

business license authorization to operate a business issued by a local government

zoning laws laws in a city or town that designate certain areas, or zones, for residential and business use

liability the legal obligation to pay debts

Sole Receiver of Profit

A major advantage of the sole proprietorship is that the owner gets to keep all profits after paying income taxes. If the business succeeds, the owner does not have to share the success with anyone else. The desire for profits motivates many people to start their own businesses.

Full Control

Another advantage of sole proprietorship is that sole proprietors can run their businesses as they wish. This high degree of freedom appeals to entrepreneurs. Fast, flexible decision-making allows sole proprietorships to take full advantage of sudden opportunities. These entrepreneurs can respond quickly to changes in the marketplace. Finally, if sole proprietors decide to stop operations and do something else for a living, they can do so easily. They must, of course, pay all debts and other obligations, such as taxes, but they do not have to meet any other legal obligations to stop doing business.

✔ **CHECKPOINT** *Why are sole proprietorships easy to start and end?*

Disadvantages of Sole Proprietorships

As with everything else, there are trade-offs with sole proprietorships. The independence of this form of business organization comes with a high degree of responsibility.

Unlimited Personal Liability

The biggest disadvantage of sole proprietorship is unlimited personal liability. **Liability** is the legal obligation to pay debts. Sole proprietors are fully and personally responsible for all their business debts. If the business fails, the owner may have to sell personal property—such as a car or home—to cover any outstanding obligations. Business debts can ruin a sole proprietor's personal finances.

Limited Access to Resources

Suppose you start a landscaping business that grows quickly. You might need to expand your business by buying more equipment. But as a sole proprietor, you may have to pay for that equipment out of your own pocket. Banks are sometimes unwilling to offer loans to a business that has not been operating for very long. This makes it difficult or impossible for many sole proprietorships to expand quickly.

Physical capital may not be the only factor resource in short supply. Human capital may be lacking, too. A sole proprietor, no matter how ambitious, may lack some of the skills necessary to run a business successfully. For example, you may be great at sales, but not at accounting. You may love working outdoors landscaping, but hate to call on people to drum up business. Some aspects of the business suffer if the owner's skills do not match the needs of the business.

Economics & YOU

Sole Proprietorship

A clothing store owner takes pride in the quality of her customer service, wanting to make sure you get what you need. **You appreciate the personalized attention.**

The store owner is on vacation. **You are inconvenienced.**

SORRY we're **CLOSED** On Vacation Back August 1

▲ Every business has advantages and disadvantages. One advantage a sole proprietor has is the ability to set flexible business hours. **Why is this an advantage a sole proprietorship has over other types of businesses?**

Finally, as a sole proprietor, you may have to turn down work because you simply do not have enough hours in the day or enough workers to keep up with demand. A small business often presents its owner with too many demands, and that can be exhausting both personally and financially.

Lack of Permanence

A sole proprietorship has a limited life. If a sole proprietor dies or retires, the business simply ceases to exist if there is no one willing to buy it or run it. The same can happen if the owner suffers an extended illness or loses interest in the business.

Sole proprietorships often have trouble finding and keeping good employees. Small businesses generally cannot offer the security and advancement opportunities that many employees look for in a job. In addition, a sole proprietorship usually has limited access to capital, which means that most small business owners lack the resources to offer workers fringe benefits. **Fringe benefits** are payments to employees other than wages or salaries, such as

paid vacation, retirement pay, and health insurance. Lack of experienced employees can hurt a business. Once again, the other side of total control is total responsibility: a sole proprietor cannot count on anyone else to maintain the business.

 CHECKPOINT *What are the disadvantages of sole proprietorships?*

▲ The sole proprietor enjoys full control, and this includes a flexible work schedule. *How does this cartoon show a major disadvantage of a sole proprietorship?*

fringe benefits
payments to employees other than wages or salary

 SS.912.E.1.5, LA.1112.2.2.2, MA.912.D.4.1, SS.912.E.2, LA.1112.1.6.1

Essential Questions Journal
To continue to build a response to the Essential Question, go to your **Essential Questions Journal**.

SECTION 1 ASSESSMENT

⁇ Guiding Question

1. Use your completed comparison chart to answer this question: What are the risks and benefits of a sole proprietorship?
2. **Extension** Choose a business you are familiar with. Identify what resources you would need to start up a similar business.

Key Terms and Main Ideas

3. What is a **sole proprietorship?**
4. (a) What is **liability?** (b) Why is it the biggest disadvantage of a sole proprietorship?
5. What role do **business licenses** and **zoning laws** play in sole proprietorships?

6. How does the lack of fringe benefits affect the sole proprietor's ability to run a business?

Critical Thinking

7. **Analyze** Since sole proprietors cannot usually offer benefits to workers, why do some people work for sole proprietors rather than large companies?
8. **Identify (a)** In addition to a soft pretzel stand, name another sole proprietorship that would be subject to health codes. Explain. **(b)** Name a business other than furniture refinishing that would be subject to laws that regulate the disposal of dangerous chemicals. Explain.
9. **Infer** Why are some of the benefits of a sole proprietorship also its greatest disadvantages?

Math Skills

10. The table below shows data for the average homebased sole proprietorship (HBSP) and nonhomebased sole proprietorship. **(a)** Which type of business has the greatest expenditures and receipts? **(b)** Based on the total business expenses, which type has the most profitable ratio between receipts and expenses? **(c)** Why do you think that is so?

Visit PearsonSchool.com/PHecon for additional math help.

	HBSP	Non-HBSP
Receipts	$62,523	$178,194
Net income	$22,569	$38,243
Total business expenses	$39,958	$139,955
Cost of sales	$14,228	$64,334
Salaries and wages	$2,010	$17,315
Travel costs	$4,797	$4,948

SOURCE: Small Business Administration, Office of Advocacy

NGSSS

LA.1112.1.6 Use multiple strategies to develop vocabulary.

MA.912.A.2.2 Interpret a graph to represent a real-world situation.

SS.912.E.1.5 Compare different forms of business.

SS.912.E.2 Understand the concepts relevant to the national economy.

ECONOMIC DICTIONARY

As you read the section, look for the definitions of these **Key Terms:**

- partnership
- general partnership
- limited partnership
- limited liability partnership
- articles of partnership
- assets
- business franchise
- royalties

Guiding Question
What are the risks and benefits of partnerships and franchises?

Copy this chart and fill it in as you read. Add more boxes if necessary.

Advantages and Disadvantages	
Partnership	**Franchise**
• Easy, inexpensive to start up	• Owner sacrifices some freedom
•	•
•	•

▶ **Economics and You**   Would you ever consider setting up your own business? Suppose the idea is very appealing, but you aren't sure that you want to take on all the responsibilities needed to be successful. You may be great at doing the job, like repairing computers, but you may dread all the paperwork that goes along with being in business. Do you have to give up your dream?

Principles in Action Some business owners overcome their problems, whether it is a shortage of money or talent, by taking on a partner.

Types of Partnerships

A **partnership** is a business organization owned by two or more persons who agree on a specific division of responsibilities and profits. In the United States, partnerships account for nearly 9 percent of all businesses. They generate about 12 percent of all receipts and nearly a quarter of all the income earned by all businesses.

Partnerships are a good choice if owners are willing to share both the responsibility of running the business and the profits it earns. They can also be a good choice if the partners get along well and have skills that complement each other.

Partnerships fall into three categories: general partnerships, limited partnerships, and limited liability partnerships. Each divides responsibility and liability differently.

General Partnership

The most common type of partnership is the **general partnership.** In this type, all partners share equally in both responsibility and liability. Many of the same kinds of businesses that operate as sole proprietorships can operate as general partnerships. Doctors, lawyers, accountants, and other professionals often form partnerships. Small retail stores, farms, construction firms, and family businesses often form partnerships as well.

partnership a business organization owned by two or more persons who agree on a specific division of responsibilities and profits

general partnership a type of partnership in which all partners share equally in both responsibility and liability

Limited Partnership

In a **limited partnership,** only one partner is required to be a general partner. That is, only one partner has unlimited personal liability for the firm's actions. The remaining partner or partners contribute only money. If the business fails, they can lose only the amount of their initial investment. If the business succeeds, though, limited partners share in the profits. A limited partnership must have at least one general partner, but may have any number of limited partners.

Limited partners play no role in managing the business. The general partner runs the company. That control is the main advantage of being a general partner. The main drawback, of course, is the unlimited liability that the general partner has.

Limited Liability Partnerships

The **limited liability partnership** (LLP) is a newer type of partnership recognized by many states. In this type of partnership, all partners are limited partners.

An LLP functions like a general partnership, except that all partners have limited personal liability in certain situations, such as another partner's mistakes. Not all types of businesses are allowed to register as limited liability partnerships. Most states allow professionals such as attorneys, physicians, dentists, and accountants to register as LLPs.

✔ **CHECKPOINT** *What is a partnership?*

Advantages of Partnerships

Partnerships are easy to establish and are subject to few government regulations. They provide entrepreneurs with a number of advantages.

Ease of Start-Up

Like proprietorships, partnerships are easy and inexpensive to establish. The law does not require a written partnership agreement. Most experts, however, advise partners to work with an attorney to develop **articles of partnership,** or a partnership

---

limited partnership a type of partnership in which only one partner is required to be a general partner

limited liability partnership a type of partnership in which all partners are limited partners

articles of partnership a partnership agreement that spells out each partner's rights and responsibilities

FL **MA.912.A.2.2** Interpret a graph to represent a real-world situation.

| Figure 8.2 | **Characteristics of Partnerships** |

GRAPH SKILLS

Partnerships can range in size from a pair of house painters to an accounting firm with thousands of partners.

1. Using the data in these charts, describe partnerships in terms of industry and income.

2. Why do you think real estate businesses form the largest percentage of partnerships?

Action Graph
online

For an animated version of this graph, visit PearsonSchool.com/PHecon

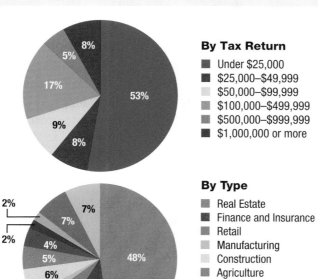

By Tax Return
- ■ Under $25,000
- ■ $25,000–$49,999
- ■ $50,000–$99,999
- ■ $100,000–$499,999
- ■ $500,000–$999,999
- ■ $1,000,000 or more

By Type
- ■ Real Estate
- ■ Finance and Insurance
- ■ Retail
- ■ Manufacturing
- ■ Construction
- ■ Agriculture
- ■ Accommodation and food services
- ■ Healthcare and Social Assistance
- ■ Management, scientific, and technical consulting
- ■ Professional, scientific, and technical services
- ■ Other services, including legal

Note: Because of rounding, totals may be greater than or less than 100 percent. Data is for 2004.
SOURCE: *The 2008 Statistical Abstract of the United States*

How can a **small business** grow?

All businesses begin with an idea to sell a product or service. Sole proprietors, working on their own, sometimes find that adding a partner will help them be more successful.

1 Calvin, an enterprising college student, has launched an online business, Hiyerminds.com. He creates and sells college survival kits to incoming freshmen. He keeps his costs down and makes a tidy profit. He is keeping up with a steady stream of orders and with his schoolwork.

2 Calvin finds that as his product becomes more popular, he can't manage the ordering and accounting part of the business. He decides to ask his friend Diego to join Hiyerminds.com as an equal partner. The partnership allows the business to expand.

Expansion

agreement. This legal document spells out each partner's rights and responsibilities. It outlines how partners will share profits or losses. It may also address other details, such as the ways new partners can join the firm, duration of the partnership, and tax responsibilities.

If partners do not develop their own articles of partnership, they will fall under the rules of the Uniform Partnership Act (UPA). The UPA is a law adopted by most states to establish rules for partnerships. The UPA requires common ownership interests, profit and loss sharing, and shared management responsibilities.

Like sole proprietorships, partnerships are subject to little government regulation. The government does not dictate how partnerships conduct business. Partners can distribute profits in whatever way they wish, as long as they abide by the partnership agreement or by the UPA.

Financial Impact
In a partnership, more than one person contributes **assets,** or money and other valuables. As a result, these businesses can raise more capital than a sole proprietorship. In addition, partnerships have improved ability to borrow funds for operations or expansion.

Partnerships offer advantages to employees as well. They can attract and keep talented employees more easily than sole proprietorships can. Graduates from top accounting schools, for example, often seek jobs with large and prestigious accounting LLPs, hoping to become partners themselves someday. Partnerships, like sole proprietorships, are not subject to any special taxes. Partners pay taxes on their share of the income that the partnership generates. The business itself does not have to pay taxes.

Personal Finance
For information about wages and the benefits businesses offer, see your Personal Finance Handbook in the back of the book or visit PearsonSchool.com/PHecon

assets the money and other valuables belonging to an individual or business

3 After a few months, Calvin and Diego begin having many disagreements about how to operate the business. Customer service suffers.

How the Economy Works
online

For an animated, interactive version of this feature, visit PearsonSchool.com/PHecon

5 As a result, Calvin and Diego hire employees to assemble the kits. Calvin focuses on finding new customers and Diego manages the business.

4 Calvin and Diego realize that their differences are bad for business and threaten their income. They revise the articles of partnership to set new rules about individual responsibilities and their business goals.

Check Your Understanding
1. What basic change did Calvin make in his small business to enable it to grow?
2. How did his solution create both advantages and disadvantages?

Conflict and Resolution　　　　　**Further Expansion**

Shared Decision Making

In a sole proprietorship, the owner has the burden of making all business decisions. In a partnership, the responsibility for the business may be shared. A sole proprietorship requires the owner to wear many hats, some of which might not fit very well. For example, the sole proprietor may have good managerial abilities but lack marketing skills and experience. In a successful partnership, however, each partner brings different strengths and skills to the business.

✔ **CHECKPOINT** *What are the advantages of partnerships?*

Disadvantages of Partnerships

Partnerships also present some disadvantages. Many of the disadvantages of sole proprietorships are present in partner-ships. Limited liability partnerships have fewer disadvantages than partnerships with general partners. All partnerships, however, have the potential for conflict.

Unlimited Liability

Unless the partnership is an LLP, at least one partner has unlimited liability. As in a sole proprietorship, any general partner could lose everything, including personal property, in paying the firm's debts. Since limited partners can lose only their invest-ment, they avoid this threat.

In a partnership, each general partner is bound by the acts of all other general partners. If one partner's actions cause the firm losses, then all of the general partners suffer. If one doctor in a partnership is sued for malpractice, all of the doctors in the partnership stand to lose. This problem is not present, of course, in limited liability partnerships.

business franchise
a semi-independent business that pays fees to a parent company in return for the exclusive right to sell a certain product or service in a given area

FL MA.912.A.2.2
Interpret a graph to represent a real-world situation.

Potential for Conflict

As in any close relationship, partnerships have the potential for conflict. If a business has more than one general partner, each one has only partial control over the firm. None of them enjoys as much freedom as sole proprietors do. Partnership agreements address technical aspects of the business, such as profit and loss. Many issues vital to the success of the business exist outside these guidelines, however. Partners need to ensure that they agree on matters such as work habits, management styles, ethics, and general business philosophies.

Still, friction between partners often arises and can be difficult to resolve. Many partnerships dissolve because of interpersonal conflicts. Partners must learn to communicate openly and find ways to resolve conflicts to ensure the survival of their business.

Lack of Permanence

Like a sole proprietorship, a partnership may not outlast the life of one of the general partners. If a partner dies or decides to leave, the partnership might cease to exist unless the articles of partnership state that the business can continue and the remaining partner, or partners, have the needed resources.

✓ **CHECKPOINT** *How do general partnerships differ from sole proprietorships in terms of control?*

Business Franchises

As you read in Section 1, sole proprietorships can suffer from a lack of resources or the lack of skills on the part of the owner. Some people solve these problems by forming partnerships. Others choose another form of business—a franchise.

What Is a Franchise?

In Chapter 7, you learned about franchises issued by government authorities. These franchises give one firm the sole right to sell its goods within a limited market, such as within a national park. In business, too, a franchise signals exclusive rights. A **business franchise** is a semi-independent business that pays fees to a parent company. In return, the business is granted the exclusive right to sell a certain product or service in a given area. Franchises offer a wide array of goods and services, from fast-food restaurants to stores that sell diamonds.

In this arrangement, the parent company is called a franchiser. The franchiser develops the products and systems to produce it efficiently and reliability. Franchisers then work with local franchise owners to help them produce and sell their products. Each owner is called a franchisee.

Franchising has become popular in recent years. This is because franchises allow each owner a degree of control. At the same time, the owners benefit from the support of the parent company. Of course, franchises offer both advantages and disadvantages.

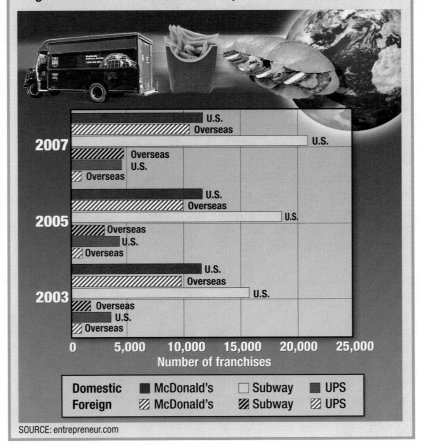

FUTURE WATCH ⊕ Global Impact

Global Business, Local Tastes

If you're like most Americans, you've probably visited a Subway or a McDonald's. But have you ever biggie-sized your chinese take-out? Or seen Subway's Halal menu? Americans traveling abroad will find the familiar face of U.S. business customized to meet local tastes. The graph below shows the global presence of three major U.S. companies. *What are some of the difficulties that businesses might encounter in their efforts to expand in other countries?*

Number of franchises (0, 5,000, 10,000, 15,000, 20,000, 25,000)

2007 — U.S. / Overseas (McDonald's), U.S. / Overseas (Subway), U.S. / Overseas (UPS)
2005 — U.S. / Overseas (McDonald's), U.S. / Overseas (Subway), U.S. / Overseas (UPS)
2003 — U.S. / Overseas (McDonald's), U.S. / Overseas (Subway), U.S. / Overseas (UPS)

| Domestic | ■ McDonald's | ☐ Subway | ■ UPS |
| Foreign | ▨ McDonald's | ▨ Subway | ▨ UPS |

SOURCE: entrepreneur.com

Advantages of Franchises

A franchise provides advantages a completely independent business cannot. First, a franchise comes with a built-in reputation. Consumers may already be familiar with the product and brand. Other benefits make running the business easier:

1. *Management training and support* Franchisers help owners gain the experience they need to succeed, with training and support programs.
2. *Standardized quality* Most parent companies require franchise owners to follow certain rules and processes to guarantee product quality. High-quality products attract customers.
3. *National advertising programs* Parent companies pay for advertising campaigns to establish their brand names. These ads can increase sales.
4. *Financial assistance* Some franchisers provide financing to help franchise owners start their businesses. This aid can help people with fewer resources become business owners.
5. *Centralized buying power* Franchisers buy materials in bulk for all of their franchise locations. They pass on the savings to their franchisees.

FL SS.912.E.1.5, SS.912.E.2, LA.1112.1.6.1, LA.1112.2.2.2, LA.1112.2.2.3

Disadvantages of Franchises

The biggest disadvantage of a franchise is that the owner must sacrifice some freedom in return for the parent company's guidance. Other disadvantages include:

1. *High franchising fees and royalties* Buying into a franchise is not cheap. Franchisers often charge high fees for the right to use the company name. They also charge franchise owners a share of the earnings, or **royalties.**
2. *Strict operating standards* Franchise owners must follow all of the rules laid out in the franchising agreement for such matters as hours of operation, employee dress codes, and operating procedures. If they do not, the owners may lose the franchise.
3. *Purchasing restrictions* Franchise owners must often buy their supplies from the parent company or from approved suppliers.
4. *Limited product line* Franchise agreements allow stores to offer only approved products. Franchisees usually cannot launch new product lines that might appeal more to local customers.

☑ **CHECKPOINT** *What are the advantages and disadvantages of franchises?*

royalties the share of earnings given by a franchisee as payment to the franchiser

---

Essential Questions Journal
To continue to build a response to the Essential Question, go to your **Essential Questions Journal**.

SECTION 2 ASSESSMENT

❓ Guiding Question

1. Use your completed chart to answer this question: What are the risks and benefits of partnerships and franchises?
2. **Extension** Your uncle is sole proprietor of a camera shop. You know much more about digital cameras than he does. He is looking for a partner. What questions would you ask him before you would consider going into business with him?

Key Terms and Main Ideas

3. List four reasons that make a **partnership** a good business choice.
4. How do **general partnerships, limited partnerships,** and **limited liability partnerships** differ?

5. What is the difference between the role of a franchiser and the role of a franchisee?

Critical Thinking

6. **Interpret** Why might physicians and lawyers find limited liability partnerships attractive?
7. **Compare** Think about the advantages and disadvantages of partnerships and franchises. From your point of view, which do you think would be a better way to be in business?
8. **Contrast (a)** Give an example of a business issue that partnership agreements address.
   (b) What is an example of issues outside legal guidelines that partners need to resolve themselves?

Quick Write

9. All articles of partnership spell out the rights and responsibilities of each partner. Some of the common sections found in articles of partnership include:

   Leadership This addresses the granting of one partner the rights to manage and administer the business.

   Misconduct expulsion This allows for the expelling of partners who commit gross misconduct that harms a business.

   Resolution of dispute This details how disagreements will be resolved.

   With a partner, draw up articles of partnership for a business.

NGSSS

LA.1112.1.6 Use multiple strategies to develop vocabulary.

MA.912.A.2.2 Interpret a graph to represent a real-world situation.

SS.912.E.1.5 Compare different forms of business.

SS.912.E.2 Understand the concepts relevant to the national economy.

ECONOMIC DICTIONARY

As you read the section, look for the definitions of these **Key Terms**:

- corporation
- stock
- closely held corporation
- publicly held corporation
- bond
- certificate of incorporation
- dividend
- limited liability corporation
- horizontal merger
- vertical merger
- conglomerate
- multinational corporation

Guiding Question
What are the risks and benefits of corporations?

Copy this Comparison Chart and fill it in as you read. Add more bullets if necessary.

Corporations	Sole Proprietorships/ Partnerships
Benefits: • limited liability for owners • • **Risks:** • •	**Benefits:** • owners have more control • **Risks:** • •

▶ **Economics and You**   Every day you use goods and services provided by a variety of businesses, both large and small. Did the bread you ate today come from a local bakery or a huge multinational food producer? Some goods can be provided by either. But what about the car or bus you took to school? Some products can be produced only by big businesses.

Principles in Action Goods and services that require huge amounts of capital to produce require a special kind of business organization, or ownership structure. Sole proprietorships and partnerships lack the resources to carry out expensive processes, such as making cars, or having operations that reach across the country or around the world. What form of business do these companies have? Most of these businesses are corporations.

Corporations

The most complex form of business organization is the corporation. A **corporation** is a legal entity, or being, owned by individual stockholders, each of whom has limited liability for the firm's debts. Stockholders own **stock,** a certificate of ownership in a corporation. Each person who owns stock is a part-owner of the corporation issuing it. If a corporation issues 1,000 shares of stock, and you purchase 1 share, you own 1/1000th of the corporation.

Sole proprietorships have no identity beyond that of the owners. A corporation, on the other hand, does have a legal identity separate from the identities of its owners. Legally, it is regarded much like an individual. A corporation may engage in business, make contracts, sue other parties or be sued by others, and pay taxes.

In the United States, corporations account for about 20 percent of all businesses but more than 80 percent of all sales. They generate nearly 60 percent of the net income earned in the nation. Because of the advantages of corporations, most large business firms do incorporate.

Types of Corporations

Some corporations issue stock to only a few people, often family members. These stockholders rarely trade their stock, but pass it on, typically within

corporation a legal entity, or being, owned by individual stockholders, each of whom has limited liability for the firm's debts

stock a certificate of ownership in a corporation

the family. Such corporations are called **closely held corporations.** They are also known as privately held corporations.

A **publicly held corporation,** however, has many shareholders who can buy or sell stock on the open market. Stocks are bought and sold in financial markets called stock exchanges, such as the New York Stock Exchange or the Tokyo Stock Exchange.

Corporate Structure

While the exact organization varies from firm to firm, all corporations have the same basic structure. The owners—the stockholders—elect a board of directors. The board of directors makes all the major decisions of the corporation. It appoints corporate officers, such as the chief executive officer or president. These officers run the corporation and oversee its operations. Corporate officers, in turn, hire managers and employees, who work in various departments such as finance, sales, research, marketing, and production.

✔ **CHECKPOINT** *What is the role of corporate officers?*

Advantages of Incorporation

Incorporation, or forming a corporation, offers advantages to both stockholders and the corporation itself. These advantages include limited liability for owners, transferable ownership, ability to attract capital, and long life.

Advantages for Stockholders

The primary reason that entrepreneurs choose to form a corporation is to gain the benefit of limited liability. Individual stockholders do not carry personal responsibility for the corporation's actions. They can lose only the amount of money they have invested in the business. If a corporation is sued and loses the case, it must pay the money award but the assets of individual stockholders cannot be touched.

Corporations usually also provide owners with more flexibility than other forms of ownership. Shares of stock are easily transferable. That is, stockholders can easily sell their stock to others and get money in return. That is not the case with other forms of business organization.

closely held corporation a type of corporation that issues stock to only a few people, who are often family members

publicly held corporation a type of corporation that sells stock on the open market

 MA.912.A.2.2 Interpret a graph to represent a real-world situation.

| Figure 8.3 | **Characteristics of Corporations** |

By Tax Return
- Under $25,000
- $25,000–$49,999
- $50,000–$99,999
- $100,000–$499,999
- $500,000–$999,999
- $1,000,000 or more

(Top pie chart values: 24%, 6%, 10%, 31%, 11%, 18%)

By Type
- Real Estate
- Finance and Insurance
- Retail
- Manufacturing
- Construction
- Agriculture
- Accommodation and food services
- Healthcare and Social Assistance
- Management, scientific, and technical consulting
- Professional, scientific, and technical services
- Other services, including legal

(Bottom pie chart values: 12%, 12%, 5%, 12%, 6%, 14%, 6%, 7%, 4%, 15%, 3%)

Note: Because of rounding, totals may be greater than or less than 100 percent. Data is for 2004.
SOURCE: *The 2008 Statistical Abstract of the United States*

GRAPH SKILLS
Approximately 44 percent of corporations are engaged in construction, manufacturing, real estate, and retail business.

1. What incentives to incorporate do businesses have in these industries?
2. Firms that sell services make up a large fraction of corporations. Given this fact, what can you conclude about the U.S. economy?

Action Graph
online

For an animated version of this graph, visit
PearsonSchool.com/PHecon

Reviewing Key Terms
To understand *corporation,* review these terms:

business organization, *p.191*
liability, *p. 194*
assets, *p. 198*
business franchise, *p. 200*
stock, *p.202*
publicly held corporation, *p. 203*

What is a Corporation?

◄ **corporation** a legal entity, or being, owned by individual stockholders, each of whom faces limited liability for the firm's debts

STOCKHOLDERS

BOARD OF DIRECTORS

CORPORATE OFFICERS

CORPORATE OFFICERS

MANAGERS

EMPLOYEES

"Whoever said 'The only thing we have to fear is fear itself' never had to face a room full of angry shareholders."

Five groups of people make up the organizational structure of a corporation. They are stockholders, board of directors, corporate officers, managers, and employees. *How does limited liability benefit each group?*

▲ The management of a corporation includes its officers and the board of directors. They make decisions that have a major impact on a corporation's earnings, which may result in profits or losses. In either case, the corporation's stockholders, or shareholders, will hold management accountable for the company's performance. *Under what circumstances might stockholders not be pleased with management?*

Visual Glossary
online

To expand your understanding of this and other key economic terms, visit **PearsonSchool.com/PHecon**

Advantages for the Corporation

The corporate structure also presents advantages for the firm itself. Corporations have more potential for growth than other business forms. By selling shares on the stock market, corporations can raise large amounts of capital.

Corporations can also raise money by borrowing it. They do this by selling bonds. A **bond** is a formal contract issued by a corporation or other entity that includes the promise to repay borrowed money with interest at fixed intervals.

Because ownership is separate from the running of the firm, corporate owners—that is, stockholders—do not need any special managerial skills. Instead, the corporation can hire various experts—the best financial analysts, the best engineers, and so forth.

Corporations also have the advantage of long life. Because stock is transferable, corporations are able to exist longer than simple proprietorships or even partnerships. Unless it has stated in advance a specific termination date, the corporation can do business indefinitely.

 CHECKPOINT *What are the four advantages of incorporating?*

Disadvantages of Incorporation

Corporations do have some disadvantages, including expense and difficulty of start-up, double taxation, potential loss of control by the founders, and more legal requirements and regulations.

Difficulty and Expense of Start-Up

Businesses that wish to incorporate must first file for a state license known as a **certificate of incorporation,** or corporate charter. The application includes crucial information, such as corporate name, statement of purpose, length of time that the business will run (usually "for perpetuity," or without limit), founders' names and addresses, where business is based, method of fundraising, and rules for management.

Once state officials review and approve the application, they grant the corporation its charter. Then the corporation organizes itself to produce and sell a good or service. Corporate charters can be difficult, expensive, and time consuming to create. Though most states allow people to

Business Goes Green
FUTURE WATCH

SolarCity

form corporations without legal help, few experts would recommend this shortcut.

Double Taxation

The law considers corporations legal entities separate from their owners. Corporations, therefore, must pay taxes on their income.

Corporate earnings are taxed a second time as well. When corporations determine their profits, they often choose to pay a share of those profits to stockholders in payments called **dividends.** These dividends count as income for the stockholder, and the stockholder must pay personal income tax on them. This double taxation keeps many firms from incorporating.

When stockholders sell shares, they must compare the selling price to how much they paid for them. If the selling price is higher, they earned what is called a capital gain. That gain is also taxed.

Some owners form **limited liability corporations** (LLCs). These businesses have the advantage of limited liability for owners, which all corporations enjoy. They also have tax advantages because the firm does not pay corporate income tax.

Loss of Control

The original owners of a corporation often lose control of the company. Corporate officers and boards of directors, not owners, manage corporations. These managers do not always act in the owners' best interests. They might be more interested in protecting their own jobs or salaries today than in making difficult decisions that would benefit the firm tomorrow.

▲ Corporations have a self interest in developing profitable products and services. Consumer concerns about global warming have spurred new companies—like SolarCity—to produce eco-friendly products and are driving other companies like 3M to respond with eco-conscious business lines.

bond a formal contract issued by a corporation or other entity that includes a promise to repay borrowed money with interest at fixed intervals

certificate of incorporation a license to form a corporation issued by a state government

dividend the portion of corporate profits paid out to stockholders

limited liability corporation a type of business with limited liability for the owners, with the advantage of not paying corporate income tax

Figure 8.4 | Horizontal Merger and Vertical Merger

Horizontal Merger

Independent oil refineries → Combined oil company

Vertical Merger

Coke fields
Iron ore deposits
Steel mills
Ships
Railroads
→ Combined steel company

Beginning in the 1880s, John D. Rockefeller's Standard Oil Company (left) combined horizontally with 40 other oil refineries. The power gained by Standard Oil and similar monopolies prompted passage of the Sherman Antitrust Act in 1890.

In 1899, Andrew Carnegie established the Carnegie Steel Company (right). He used the vertical merger to purchase companies that produced the raw materials needed to make steel, as well as companies that would move his products to market. Within a short time, Carnegie controlled the steel industry. Most vertical mergers, however, do not result in monopolies.

1. What are some modern examples of horizontal mergers and vertical mergers?
2. Explain the difference between horizontal mergers and vertical mergers.

More Regulation

Corporations face more regulations than other types of businesses. They must hold annual meetings for stockholders and keep records of all business transactions. Publicly held corporations are required to file quarterly and annual reports with the Securities and Exchange Commission (SEC). The SEC is a federal agency that regulates the stock market.

✔ **CHECKPOINT** *What are the disadvantages of incorporation?*

Corporate Combinations

horizontal merger the combination of two or more firms competing in the same market with the same good or service

vertical merger two or more firms involved in different stages of producing the same good or service

Corporations can grow very large. One way to grow is to raise money by selling stocks or bonds. Corporations may also grow by merging, or combining, with another corporation. The three kinds of mergers are horizontal mergers, vertical mergers, and conglomerates.

Horizontal Mergers

Horizontal mergers join two or more firms competing in the same market with the same good or service. In 2004, Cingular—a wireless telephone company—bought the wireless business of AT&T. This was a horizontal merger. Two firms might choose to merge if the newly established firm would result in economies of scale or would otherwise improve efficiency.

As you read in Chapter 7, the federal government watches horizontal mergers carefully. The resulting single firm might gain monopoly power in its market. If that is the case, the government might try to block the merger in court. Judges then listen to arguments and read evidence to decide whether to allow the merger.

Vertical Mergers

Vertical mergers join two or more firms involved in different stages of producing the same good or service. A vertical merger can allow a firm to operate more efficiently. A vertically combined firm can control all phases of production, rather than rely on the goods or services of outside suppliers. Sometimes firms take this step out of fear that they may otherwise lose crucial supplies. Antitrust regulators become concerned when firms in the same industry merge vertically, especially if supplying firms suffer. Most vertical mergers do not substantially lessen competition, however.

Conglomerates

Sometimes firms buy other companies that produce totally unrelated goods or services. When three or more unrelated businesses are involved, these combinations are called **conglomerates.** In a conglomerate, no one business earns the majority of the firm's profits. The government usually allows this kind of merger, because it does not result in decreased competition.

✅ **CHECKPOINT** *Why might the government block a horizontal merger?*

Multinational Corporations

The world's largest corporations produce and sell their goods and services in more than one country. They are called **multinational corporations** (MNCs). MNCs usually have headquarters in one country and branches in other countries. Multinationals must obey laws and pay taxes in each country where they operate.

FL SS.912.E.1.5, SS.912.E.2, LA.1112.1.6.1, LA.1112.2.2.2, MA.912.A.2.2

In the early 2000s, an estimated 64,000 multinational firms operated about 866,000 foreign branches. These foreign affiliates provided jobs for more than 53 million people. The United States, France, Germany, Britain, Japan, and China are home countries with the largest number of multinational corporations.

Advantages of Multinationals

Multinationals benefit consumers and workers by providing jobs and products around the world. Often the jobs they provide help people in poorer nations enjoy better living standards. MNCs also spread new technologies and production methods across the globe.

Disadvantages of Multinationals

On the downside, many people feel that multinational firms unduly influence the culture and politics in the countries in which they operate. While MNCs do provide jobs, critics say that in poorer countries those jobs are marked by low wages and poor working conditions.

✅ **CHECKPOINT** *How would you describe a multinational corporation?*

conglomerate a business combination merging more than three businesses that produce unrelated products or services

multinational corporation a large corporation that produces and sells its goods and services in more than one country

---

Essential Questions Journal	To continue to build a response to the Essential Question, go to your **Essential Questions Journal**.

SECTION 3 ASSESSMENT

🔍 Guiding Question

1. Use your completed Venn diagram to answer this question: What are the risks and benefits of corporations?
2. **Extension** As a stockholder, would you be more interested in the benefits or the risks of the corporation in which you held stock? Explain.

Key Terms and Main Ideas

3. **(a)** What is another name for a **closely held corporation? (b)** How does it differ from a **publicly held corporation?**
4. What is the financial impact on owners when a corporation is sued and loses its case?
5. **(a)** What is a **dividend? (b)** What kind of tax must be paid on dividends received by stockholders?
6. How do **horizontal mergers, vertical mergers,** and **conglomerates** differ?

Critical Thinking

7. **Explain (a)** Which business in a conglomerate earns the most profits? **(b)** Why is it that conglomerates do not tend to decrease competition?
8. **Analyze** Choose one corporation that does business in your community. What benefits do you think the community gains from this business being incorporated?
9. **Compare (a)** How does a multinational benefit consumers and workers? **(b)** How might a corporation benefit from becoming multinational?

Math Skills

10. The bar graph (right) shows the percentage of business types organized as partnerships and as corporations.
   (a) For which types of business is the partnership form of organization

most popular? **(b)** For which types of business is the corporation form of organization most popular? **(c)** Explain why you think this is so.

Visit PearsonSchool.com/PHecon for additional math help.

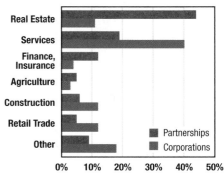

Percentage of Partnerships and Corporations by Type

- Real Estate
- Services
- Finance, Insurance
- Agriculture
- Construction
- Retail Trade
- Other

■ Partnerships
■ Corporations

0% 10% 20% 30% 40% 50%

SOURCE: *The 2008 Statistical Abstract of the United States*

ECONOMIC DICTIONARY

As you read the section, look for the definitions of these **Key Terms:**

- cooperative
- consumer cooperative
- service cooperative
- producer cooperative
- nonprofit organization
- professional organization
- business association
- trade association

Guiding Question
How are some businesses organized to help others?

Copy this chart and fill it in as you read. Add more bullets if necessary.

Cooperatives		
Consumer Cooperatives	**Service Cooperatives**	**Producer Cooperatives**
• Buy in large quantities to be able to sell at low prices • Members contribute work or membership fees	• •	• •

▶ **Economics and You**   Any time you go to a museum, the zoo, or a hospital, you are benefiting from a business organization whose main goal is to provide a service to you rather than to make a profit for itself. If you meet certain criteria, you may join a credit union whose main purpose is to benefit its members. Although these various institutions may appear like other businesses, they are not quite the same.

Principles in Action   Success in business is not measured only in dollars and cents. Some businesses are not organized to maximize profits. Instead their goals are to work for the good of all their members or to work for the good of society in general. In this section, you will learn about these other kinds of business organizations.

Cooperative Organizations

Ben Franklin, one of our nation's founders, was a remarkable innovator. In 1752, he organized a company that collected money from its members in order to make payments to any one of them who suffered losses from a fire. This group was America's first cooperative. Franklin explained the nature of this group in a letter to a Boston newspaper.

> **❝**I would leave this to the Consideration of all who are concern'd for their own or their Neighbour's Temporal Happiness; and I am humbly of Opinion, that the Country is ripe for many such *Friendly Societies*, whereby every Man might help another, without any Disservice to himself. **❞**
>
> —*The New-England Courant,* August 13, 1722

A **cooperative** is a business organization owned and operated by a group of individuals for their shared benefit. In other words, working together, the individuals help one another. Cooperatives are based on several principles, which include

- voluntary and open membership
- control of the organization by its members
- sharing of contributions and benefits by members

cooperative a business organization owned and operated by a group of individuals for their shared benefit

Cooperatives enjoy some tax benefits. Since they are not corporations, they do not pay income tax on their earnings as long as they handle those earnings in certain ways. At least 20 percent must be paid out to members. Members, of course, must then pay personal income taxes on that money. The cooperative invests as much as 80 percent of its earnings to expand its operations.

Cooperatives, or co-ops, are found in many industries, from farming and energy to healthcare and childcare. They fall into three main categories: consumer, or purchasing cooperatives; service cooperatives; and producer cooperatives. Any group of consumers or producers with common social or economic goals can band together to form a cooperative.

Consumer Cooperatives

Retail outlets owned and operated by consumers are called consumer cooperatives, or purchasing cooperatives. **Consumer cooperatives** sell merchandise to their members at reduced prices. By purchasing goods in large quantities, these cooperatives can obtain goods at a lower cost. They then pass the savings on to members by setting prices low. Examples of consumer cooperatives include discount price clubs, compact disc or book clubs, some health food stores, and housing cooperatives.

Some co-ops require members to work a small number of hours to maintain membership. For example, your health food store may require you to work 20 hours per month to remain in the cooperative. Consumer co-ops range in size from small buying clubs to Fortune 500 businesses.

Service Cooperatives

Cooperatives that provide a service, rather than goods, are called **service cooperatives.** Some service co-ops offer discounted insurance, banking services, healthcare, legal help, or baby-sitting services.

Credit unions, or financial cooperatives, are a special kind of service cooperative. People deposit money in these institutions. The credit unions then use those funds to lend money to members at reduced rates.

A farmers' co-op is an agriculture cooperative. Farmers pool resources to buy supplies at a discount, process their products, and then market and distribute those products. ▶

Producer Cooperatives

Producer cooperatives are agricultural marketing cooperatives that help members sell their products. These co-ops allow members to focus their attention on growing their crops or raising their livestock. The co-ops, meanwhile, market these goods for the highest prices possible. In a recent year, producer cooperatives sold more than $70 billion worth of crops and livestock. These groups are involved in marketing dairy products, grain, beef and chicken, and many other products. Some co-ops have more than a million members.

✔ CHECKPOINT *How do members benefit from cooperatives?*

Nonprofits

Some institutions function much like business organizations, but do not operate for the purpose of generating profit. For that reason, they are called **nonprofit organizations.** Nonprofit organizations are usually in the business of benefiting the public. Examples include museums, public schools, the American Red Cross, hospitals, adoption agencies, churches, synagogues, YMCAs, and many other

consumer cooperative
a retail outlet owned and operated by consumers that sells merchandise to members at reduced prices

service cooperative a type of cooperative that provides a service rather than a good

producer cooperative an agricultural marketing cooperative that helps members sell their products

nonprofit organization an institution that functions much like a business, but does not operate for the purpose of generating profit

CLICK
for a **CAUSE**

- World Hunger
- Politics
- Endangered Species
- Disabilities
- Peace
- Education
- Poverty
- Economy
- Health
- Global Warming
- Crime
- Justice

GO!

Charity 2.0

DoSomething.org
Nonprofit which seeks to get young people more involved in social action.

GiveMeaning.com
People can list projects to raise money, and visitors can contribute funds.

Kiva.org
Microfinance nonprofit allows visitors to make small loans to entrepreneurs in developing countries.

SOURCE: WSJ Research

Young Money

BUSINESS ORGANIZATIONS

Charitable giving used to be dominated by wealthy, middle-aged donors. Now, a new generation is using online tools to reinvent philanthropy.

By Rachel Emma Silverman
The Wall Street Journal

FL **SS.912.E.1.5** Compare different forms of business.

Joe Alamo didn't set out to become a do-gooder. But one day, while surfing on MySpace, he chanced onto the profile of Kiva.org, a nonprofit that allows people to make zero-interest "microfinance" loans over the Internet to needy entrepreneurs in developing countries.

Soon after, Mr. Alamo not only became a lender through Kiva, but also started a new Web site devoted to Kiva enthusiasts. "This is the first time I've ever gotten so involved with a charity," says Mr. Alamo, a 30-year-old Web designer.

He's among a rising tide of young donors and volunteers who are satisfying their philanthropic urges on the Internet. They're increasingly turning to blogs and social-networking Web sites, such as MySpace and Facebook,

to spread the word about—and raise funds for—their favorite nonprofits and causes. Some are turning to "viral fund-raising": sending appeals to their network of contacts that are forwarded on to others, to maximize the power of small donations.

Visitors to Change.org can join "virtual foundations" of peers dedicated to specific causes, such as fighting AIDS in Africa, and raise money for the charities or political candidates that support those issues. So far, its 30,000 members have raised nearly $50,000, says founder Ben Rattray, 27. Before launching the site, Mr. Rattray had never made a charitable donation, finding charities' traditional pitches to be "unengaging."

Established charities, to be sure, have long had programs targeted to

young donors, and many of them have used peer-to-peer fund-raising to help raise money. But many of these charities either tend to target wealthier donors or are focused on occasional events, rather than on ongoing operations.

Some of the newer Web-based nonprofits, such as DonorsChoose and Kiva, are attractive because contributors say they allow them to connect directly with their recipients. Donors or lenders can hand over money directly to, respectively, teachers and students in urban public schools or individual entrepreneurs in developing countries, rather than sending a check that ends up with an abstract recipient.

"You can donate money to a charity, but it seems like it just goes into a pile and you never know what really goes on there," says Mr. Alamo. "With Kiva, you just pick someone out and lend to them directly and watch what they do and how they succeed."

Applying Economic Principles

Why do you think social networking Web sites have proven to be so useful for nonprofit organizations? What might be other ways a nonprofit can make use of the Internet to further its goals?

Video News Update Online
Powered by
The Wall Street Journal
Classroom Edition

Use videos at **PearsonSchool.com/PHecon** as a springboard for a discussion on a current topic.

groups and charities. Almost all of them provide services rather than goods.

The government exempts nonprofit organizations from income taxes. The nonprofit must meet certain requirements to qualify for this tax-exempt status. Nonprofits cannot issue stock, so profits cannot be distributed to stockholders. The group must devote its activities exclusively to those that the Internal Revenue Service says will qualify. For instance, a charity must act only to help people, such as the poor or those disabled by illness or injury. An educational nonprofit must devote itself to the advancement of learning.

Nonprofits have some limits on their political activity. Charities and religious groups, for instance, can meet with members of Congress to try to influence laws being considered. They cannot devote too much of their resources to this lobbying activity, however.

Some nonprofit organizations provide support to particular occupations or geographical areas. These include professional organizations, business associations, trade associations, and labor unions.

Professional Organizations

Professional organizations work to improve the image, working conditions, and skill levels of people in particular occupations. The National Education Association for public school, college, and university workers, the American Veterinary Medical Association for veterinary professionals, the American Bar Association for lawyers, and the American Management Association for business professionals are examples.

Professional organizations keep their members up-to-date on industry trends. Many of these organizations provide members with employment-related services such as job boards, training workshops, and networking opportunities. They also set codes of conduct that members are expected to follow. For example, the American Medical Association sets guidelines for certain kinds of advertising. It wants doctors to present a professional, authoritative, and caring image as they seek new patients. The American Bar Association does not favor law firms that advertise their services for personal injury complaints.

professional organization a nonprofit organization that works to improve the image, working conditions, and skill levels of people in particular occupations

FL SS.912.E.2.3 Research the contributions of key individuals of various backgrounds in the development of the U.S.

Bill and Melinda Gates

"We believe that lives have equal value, no matter where they are being lived."

The well-known success story behind Bill and Melinda Gates begins with the Microsoft Corporation. As founder of the phenomenally successful high-tech firm, Gates built upon his vision that computer software could revolutionize business practices. In 1987, the software architect met his future wife, Melinda. Bill hired the then-recent Duke University graduate, who had earned degrees in computer science, economics, and business, to help him develop Microsoft into one of the world's premier technology companies.

Today Bill and Melinda Gates are investing much of their considerable wealth and resources to help the less fortunate. The couple has donated more than $24 billion to endow the Bill & Melinda Gates Foundation, the world's largest nonprofit corporation. Their foundation is fulfilling a unique mission to use financial and technological resources to improve the quality of life for people everywhere through extensive health, education, and agricultural programs. Some of these efforts include the funding of technology resources in U.S. public libraries, rice agricultural development in the Philippines, and global vaccination programs.

The Gateses are recognized for taking philanthropy to a new level, using their fortune to plant the seeds for a better life for all people.

Critical Thinking *How can a nonprofit organization such as the Bill & Melinda Gates Foundation help to create economic wealth worldwide?*

Fast Facts

Melinda French Gates (1965 -   )
Education: B.A. and M.B.A. at Duke University

Fast Facts

William (Bill) H. Gates, III (1955 -   )
Education: 2+ years at Harvard Univ.
Family Life: Married in 1994, three children
Claim to Fame: Founder of Microsoft Corporation, Co-founder of the Bill & Melinda Gates Foundation

An ethical and successful business will be clear about its return policies, because it is in its best interest to keep a good relationship with its customers. Much of its success depends on repeat business. ***What would you consider to be a good return policy?*** ▶

I NEVER PROMISED YOU HE COULD TALK... I SAID HE "CHATS."

RETURN POLICY

ATLANTIC FEATURE SYND. ©2002 MARK PARISI   offthemark.com

Business Associations

Business associations promote the collective business interests of a city, state, or other geographical area, or of a group of similar businesses. A city or state chamber of commerce, for instance, works with government officials to try to promote policies that will help businesses grow and thrive. Business associations may also address codes of conduct, just as professional associations do. Your local Better Business Bureau (BBB), sponsored by local businesses, is a nonprofit

business association
a group organized to promote the collective business interests of an area or group of similar businesses

trade association
nonprofit organizations that promote the interests of particular industries

FL SS.912.E.1.5, SS.912.E.2, LA.1112.1.6.1, LA.1112.2.2.2, LA.1112.6.2.4

group. It aims to protect consumers by promoting an ethical and fair marketplace. Consumers who have complaints about the actions of a local business can take them to the BBB. Workers there will contact the business and try to work out a solution that satisfies both parties.

Trade Associations

Nonprofit organizations that promote the interests of particular industries are called **trade associations.** The American Marketing Association, for example, aims to improve the image of companies that sell goods and services. All kinds of industries, from publishing to food processing, enjoy the support of trade associations. Many of these groups hire people, called lobbyists, to work with state legislatures and the U.S. Congress. They try to influence laws that affect an industry. These groups hold meetings that members can attend to improve their skills or learn about industry trends.

Labor Unions

A labor union is an organized group of workers whose aim is to improve working conditions, hours, wages, and fringe benefits for members. In the next chapter, you will read about their history and role.

✔ **CHECKPOINT** *How are nonprofit organizations similar to and different from corporations?*

Essential Questions Journal To continue to build a response to the Essential Question, go to your **Essential Questions Journal**.

SECTION 4 ASSESSMENT

❓ Guiding Question

1. Use your completed chart to answer this question: How are some businesses organized to help others?

2. **Extension** There are many nonprofit organizations that offer services in your community. Select one and explain how you would use your talents to help this organization help others.

Key Terms and Main Ideas

3. What is a **cooperative?**

4. How do **consumer cooperatives, service cooperatives,** and **producer cooperatives** differ?

5. **(a)** What is a **nonprofit organization? (b)** Give an example of one.

6. What is the purpose of **professional organizations, business associations,** and **trade associations?**

Critical Thinking

7. **Generalize** If cooperatives offer benefits to their members, why do you think everyone doesn't belong to them?

8. **Analyze (a)** Do you think professional organizations and business associations benefit consumers? **(b)** Explain your reasoning.

9. **Synthesize** What are the advantages and disadvantages of trade associations trying to influence legislation?

Quick Write

10. Think about a need, such as transportation, child care, or tutoring, that might be met through a cooperative. Write a brief proposal explaining how the cooperative would work to meet the need, including who could join, what would be the terms of membership, and what would be the benefits.

QUICK STUDY GUIDE

Chapter 8: Business Organizations

Section 1 What are the risks and benefits of a sole proprietorship?

Section 2 What are the risks and benefits of partnerships and franchises?

Section 3 What are the risks and benefits of corporations?

Section 4 How are some businesses organized to help others?

Essential Question, Chapter 8
Why do some businesses succeed and others fail?

Advantages and Disadvantages of Business Organizations

	Advantages	Disadvantages
Sole Proprietorship	• Ease of start-up • Fewer regulations • Sole receiver of profit • Full control • Easy to discontinue	• Unlimited personal liability • Limited access to resources • Lack of permanence
Partnership	• Ease of start-up • Shared decision making • More capital • Attractive to employees	• Unlimited liability • Lack of control • Potential for conflict • Lack of permanence
Business Franchise	• Built-in reputation • Management training/support • Paid national advertising • Financial assistance • Centralized buying power	• High fees/royalties • Strict operating standards • Purchasing restrictions • Limited product line
Corporation	• Potential for growth • Ability to raise capital/money • Long lifespan • Ability to hire specialists	• Difficult/expensive to start up • Double taxation • Loss of control • More regulation

Economic Dictionary

sole proprietorship, *p. 191*

business organization, *p. 191*

business license, *p. 193*

zoning laws, *p. 193*

liability, *p. 194*

fringe benefits, *p. 195*

partnership, *p. 196*

general partnership, *p. 196*

limited partnership, *p. 197*

limited liability partnership, *p. 197*

articles of partnership, *p. 197*

assets, *p. 198*

business franchise, *p. 200*

royalties, *p. 201*

corporation, *p. 202*

stock, *p. 202*

closely held corporation, *p. 203*

publicly held corporation, *p. 203*

bond, *p. 205*

certificate of incorporation, *p. 205*

dividend, *p. 205*

limited liability corporation, *p. 205*

horizontal merger, *p. 206*

vertical merger, *p. 206*

conglomerate, *p. 207*

multinational corporation, *p. 207*

cooperative, *p. 208*

nonprofit organization, *p. 209*

trade association, *p. 212*

Economics on the go

Study anytime, anywhere. Download these files today.

Economic Dictionary online	Audio Review online	Action Graph online	Visual Glossary online	How the Economy Works online
Vocabulary Support in English and Spanish	Audio Study Guide in English and Spanish	Animated Charts and Graphs	Animated feature	Animated feature

Download to your computer or mobile device at PearsonSchool.com/PHecon

Key Terms and Main Ideas

To make sure you understand the key terms and main ideas of this chapter, review the Checkpoint and Section Assessment questions and look at the Quick Study Guide on the preceding page.

Critical Thinking

1. **Predict (a)** What is the greatest disadvantage of sole proprietorships? **(b)** What personal financial problems could result? **(c)** How might that negatively affect future business ventures for that owner?
2. **Describe** How do rules and laws help determine the way partnerships are organized?
3. **Analyze (a)** What liability are stockholders subject to? **(b)** How can stockholders influence the actions of the corporation in which they have ownership?
4. **Explain (a)** How is a vertical merger formed? **(b)** Give examples of types of businesses that might be part of a vertical merger involving the canned food industry.
5. **Analyze (a)** Who benefits from the incorporation of a business? **(b)** Analyze the consequences of incorporating a landscaping business that is expanding.
6. **Drawing Conclusions (a)** What is the difference in government involvement in a sole proprietorship, partnership, and corporation? **(b)** Why do you think that the government is more involved in corporations?
7. **Evaluate (a)** Identify the qualities of a successful entrepreneur. **(b)** Choose the three that you think are most important and explain why.
8. **Analyze** A major meat producer decides to create a vertical merger that will advertise, "From the stable to your table."

(a) How could it achieve this goal? **(b)** What other business would it have to acquire?
9. **Solving Problems** A farmer has the choice of selling his milk to a multinational food conglomerate or to join with other farmers to form a cheese-making cooperative. **(a)** What is a cooperative? **(b)** What possible benefits does the cooperative provide individual farmers over selling their milk to a large corporation?

Applying Your Math Skills

Reading a Bar Graph

This bar graph shows the percentage of growth in franchises between 2000 and 2006. Look at the chart and answer the questions that follow.

Visit PearsonSchool.com/PHecon for additional math help.

Increase in Franchises, 2000–2006

Values: Fast food 20, Service 45, Maintenance 37, Retail stores 21, Business 38, Real estate 43, Restaurant 38, Baked goods 66, Child related 105, Travel 29, Sports 27

SOURCE: *Franchising World*, November 2007

10. Using the franchise graph, what would be the mean of those having positive growth? Give your answer to the nearest percent.
11. What would be the median percent of those having positive growth?
12. What would be the mode of the of those having positive growth?
13. Is any percent change actually equal to the group median? If so, which franchises grew median percentage?

Essential Question Activity

14. Complete either of the following activities to answer the Essential Question **Why do some businesses succeed and others fail?**

    Using the worksheet in your Essential Questions Journal or the electronic worksheet available at **PearsonSchool.com/PHecon,** gather the following information:
    • Conduct an interview with either a current or former sole proprietor, partner in a partnership, manager of a corporation, or a franchisee to uncover their personal view of the pros and cons of doing business. Focus on why he or she thought the business succeeded or failed.

    • Using information on the Internet or in a business magazine or newspaper, such as *The Wall Street Journal,* research why a specific entrepreneur or business succeeded or failed.
15. **Modify** In groups of three or four students, share the specific information that you gathered. Then, as a group, formulate a response to the Essential Question. Share your answer with the class. Together create a list of guidelines for business success.

DOCUMENT-BASED ASSESSMENT

Are corporate executives paid too much?

Some financial analysts think CEOs should be compensated for the risks they take. Others see unfair disparity between the amount of pay Chief Executive Officers (CEOs) and average workers receive.

Document A

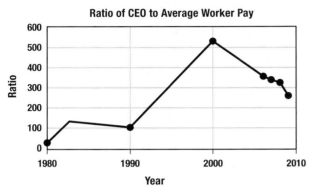

Ratio of CEO to Average Worker Pay

SOURCE: AFL-CIO and the Institute of Policy Studies.

Document B

Most CEOs . . . are highly intelligent, have advanced degrees—often from one of the top universities in this country or elsewhere in the world—and have worked 70 or more hours per week for most of their career. Even if they weren't CEO of a public company, people with a background like that get paid much more than the average person. . . .

I just read that U2 made . . . $3 million per show (about $1 million per hour). . . . I don't think most Americans want to impose an arbitrary cap on CEO pay any more than we want to impose a cap on U2's concert tour receipts because we know U2 would stop touring, and good CEOs would stop CEO-ing, and neither of those is to our benefit.

—*Fred Whittlesey, "The great overpaid CEO debate,"*
http://news.cnet.com

Document C

Nau, a retailer of outdoor clothing, has written new corporate ethics into its corporate bylaws. They stipulate that Nau will cap corporate officer salaries at 12 times the lowest salary paid at the company. Nau has generated tremendous buzz—and business—by making corporate social responsibility (CSR) integral to its business strategy. It clearly passes *The Economist's* test for generating long-term profits while serving the public good.

—*From "The New Corporate Ethics," by Mark Bain,* Direct Selling News, *January 2008*

 LA.1112.1.6.2, MA.912.A.2.2, SS.912.E.1.5

ANALYZING DOCUMENTS

Use your knowledge and Documents A, B, and C to answer questions 1–3.

1. **Document A shows that the ratio of CEO salaries to average worker pay**
   A. was greater in 1965 than in 2005.
   B. in 2000 meant that CEOs earned 500 times as much as workers.
   C. has not varied much since 1965.
   D. in 1965 meant that workers earned just as much CEOs.

2. **What is the main point of Document B?**
   A. Entertainers earn more than CEOs.
   B. CEOs are worth what they are paid.
   C. Caps on CEO pay would benefit public companies.
   D. CEOs have often gone to the best universities.

3. **According to Document C, what is Nau's goal?**
   A. to make news.
   B. to pay both CEOs and workers less.
   C. to ignore long-term profit issues.
   D. to integrate corporate and social responsibility.

WRITING ABOUT ECONOMICS

The disparity between CEO and average worker pay is both an economic and a social issue. Use the documents on this page and resources on the Web site below to answer this question: *Are corporate executives paid too much?* Use the sources to support your opinion.

In Partnership

THE WALL STREET JOURNAL.
CLASSROOM EDITION

To read more about issues related to this topic, visit
PearsonSchool.com/PHecon

9 Labor

Essential Question, Chapter 9

How can workers best meet the challenges of a changing economy?

FL **Next Generation Sunshine State Standards**

Section 1: Labor Market Trends
LA.1112.1.6, MA.912.A.2.2, SS.912.E.1.9, SS.912.E.3, SS.912.G.4.4

Section 2: Labor and Wages
LA.1112.1.6, MA.912.A.2.2, SS.912.E.1.9, SS.912.E.2.4

Section 3: Organized Labor
LA.1112.1.6, MA.912.A.2.2, SS.912.E.1.9, SS.912.E.2.3, SS.912.E.2.4

Economics
on the go

To study anywhere, anytime, download these
online resources at *PearsonSchool.com/PHecon* ▶

NGSSS

LA.1112.1.6 Use multiple strategies to develop vocabulary.

MA.912.A.2.2 Interpret a graph to represent a real-world situation.

SS.912.E.1.9 Describe how workers' pay is determined.

SS.912.E.3 Understand the relationships of the U.S. economy and the international marketplace.

SS.912.G.4.4 Analyze case studies of globalization.

ECONOMIC DICTIONARY

As you read the section, look for the definitions of these **Key Terms:**

- labor force
- outsourcing
- offshoring
- learning effect
- screening effect
- contingent employment
- guest workers

Guiding Question
How do economic trends affect workers?
Copy this chart and fill it in as you read.

How Economic Trends Affect Workers

Workforce Trends	Changing Labor Force	Trends in Wages and Benefits
• Growing importance of computers • More service workers, fewer goods workers • •	• Demand for workers with more education • •	• • •

▶ **Economics and You**   Have you considered how you want to earn a living when you get out of school? You may be one of those people who has been focused on a career goal for as long as you can remember or you may not have a clue. Is your goal to help others, make a lot of money, or travel? Whatever career you decide on, you will have to be prepared for change.

Principles in Action Economic trends affect workers in many ways. Over the past two decades, the U.S. economy has shifted from a manufacturing economy toward a service-producing economy. As jobs in industries such as technology and financial services have soared, the number of manufacturing jobs has dwindled.

Tracking the Labor Force

How do we know the direction of changes in the job market? Each month, the Bureau of Labor Statistics (BLS) of the United States Department of Labor surveys households to assemble information on the labor force. Economists define the **labor force** as all nonmilitary people who are employed or unemployed.

Employment and Unemployment

Economists consider people to be employed if they are 16 years or older and meet at least one of the following requirements:

- they worked at least one hour for pay in the past week;
- they worked 15 or more hours without pay in a family business, such as a farm or a family-owned store; and

labor force all nonmilitary people who are employed or unemployed

---

Visual Glossary
online

Go to the Visual Glossary Online for an interactive review of **productivity of labor.**

Action Graph
online

Go to Action Graph Online for animated versions of key charts and graphs.

How the Economy Works
online

Go to How the Economy Works Online for an interactive lesson on **collective bargaining.**

- they held jobs but did not work due to illnesses, vacations, labor disputes, or bad weather.

People who have more than one job are counted only once. In 2005, more than 7.5 million people had more than one job.

People who do not meet these criteria are counted as unemployed if they are either temporarily without work or are not working but have looked for jobs within the last four weeks. To be counted as unemployed, then, a person either must have work lined up for the future, or must be actively searching for a new job.

Some groups of people are considered to be outside the labor force. The BLS uses the term "discouraged workers" to describe people who once sought work but have given up looking for a job. They are not counted in employment statistics. In addition, full-time students, parents who stay at home to raise children, and retirees are not considered unemployed, and thus are not counted in employment statistics. **Figure 9.1** summarizes the groups that make up the U.S. labor force.

The Labor Market Today

The Bureau of Labor Statistics provides answers to two important economic questions. First, it says how many people are in the labor force. Second, it tells us how many are employed and unemployed at any given time. You can find BLS data in the Census Bureau's *Statistical Abstract of the United States*, available in print and on the Internet.

The BLS provides information about historical trends. For example, the percentage of the U.S. population in the labor force has increased from 59.2 percent in 1950 to 66.0 percent in 2005. The number of employed civilians in the U.S. in 2005 was about 141.7 million. Nearly 76 million of these workers were men. Almost 66 million were women.

The BLS also reports the unemployment rate each month. Economists studying the health of the economy monitor these monthly unemployment figures. In July 2007, the unemployment rate was 4.6 percent. The highest unemployment rate from 1997 to 2007 was 6.3 percent in June of 2003.

✔ **CHECKPOINT** *What important information can we learn from the Bureau of Labor Statistics?*

Occupational Trends

The job market does not stay the same all the time. It grows as the nation's economy and population grows. The jobs that make up the job market also change. New technologies or new industries bring new jobs to life—and cause others to fade. Shifts in the job market reflect major shifts in what our economy produces. You can better understand these changes by looking at them in a historical context.

A Changing Economy

At its founding, the United States was a nation of farmers. Most people had few job opportunities beyond the corn, wheat, cotton, and tobacco fields. In the 1800s in the North, however, this focus on agriculture gradually yielded to the Industrial Revolution. The coming of the machine age energized the economy and created

| Figure 9.1 | **Composition of U.S. Labor Force** |

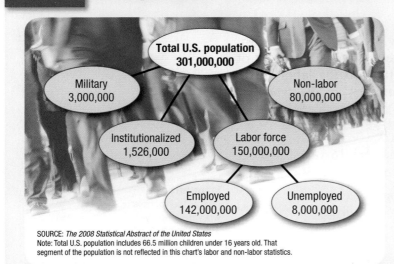

SOURCE: *The 2008 Statistical Abstract of the United States*
Note: Total U.S. population includes 66.5 million children under 16 years old. That segment of the population is not reflected in this chart's labor and non-labor statistics.

GRAPH SKILLS

This chart shows how the Bureau of Labor Statistics defines who is in the labor force and who is employed or unemployed.

1. What are the parts that form the total U.S. population?
2. How does being unemployed differ from not being part of the labor force?

new jobs in textile mills, shoe factories, and other new manufacturing enterprises.

By the early decades of the 1900s, heavy manufacturing had become the power-house of the U.S. economy. New corporate empires were born: John D. Rockefeller's Standard Oil in 1863; Andrew Carnegie's steelworks in the 1870s; Henry Ford's automobile company in 1903. These huge firms employed thousands of workers.

The mid-twentieth-century boom in electronics—led by radio and television—produced a new surge of factory jobs. Employment growth centered in the Northeast and Midwest, in companies such as General Electric, Westinghouse, Carrier, and Goodyear.

In the 1970s, the revolution in personal computers opened another new horizon for employment. As computer use continues to rise, the demand for computer-related occupations continues to grow. In this "Information Age," even some traditional jobs, from trucking to farming to car sales, now require some computer skills. By the early 2000s, over half of American workers reported using computers on the job. More than a quarter of all workers in the agriculture, forestry, fishing and construction industries used computers.

Fewer Goods, More Services

The spread of computers is not the only change that has transformed the American economy. In the past one hundred or so years, the United States has shifted from a manufacturing economy to a service economy. Our production of services is increasing faster than our production of goods. (See **Figure 9.2.**) In 2005, five workers produced services for every one who produced goods. The service sector includes financial services, banking, education, and online services.

Effects of International Competition

While the number of service jobs has increased, the United States has lost manufacturing jobs. In 1990, almost 17.7 million Americans worked in manufacturing industries. Fifteen years later, the number had fallen to 14.2 million. Many workers have been laid off due to plant closings or moves, too little work, or the replacement of jobs by new technology. These conditions can be the result of **outsourcing,** in which companies contract with another company to do a specific job that would otherwise be done by a company's own workers. Most companies will outsource work in some way.

In the past, limits on the mobility of capital and labor meant that most goods sold in the United States were made by American workers in American factories. Today, capital and labor can be easily moved from place to place—and even from country to country. The movement of some of a company's operations, or resources of production, to another country is known as **offshoring.** American firms can build factories and hire workers in countries where wages and other costs are lower. American stores can buy a wide range of goods made in foreign countries to sell in the United States.

As less-skilled manufacturing jobs moved overseas, the Americans who had filled these jobs had to find new work. Many went back to school or entered job-training programs to gain new skills.

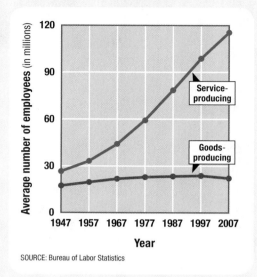

| Figure 9.2 | **Changes in Employment, by Industry** |

SOURCE: Bureau of Labor Statistics

GRAPH SKILLS
This chart shows the shift toward a service economy in the United States.

1. How many service-producing employees were added in the period shown?
2. Describe the changes in the U.S. economy since 1947.

Action Graph
online

For an animated version of this graph, visit
PearsonSchool.com/PHecon

 MA.912.A.2.2
Interpret a graph to represent a real-world situation.

SS.912.E.3
Understand the relationships of the U.S. economy and the international marketplace.

outsourcing the practice of contracting with another company to do a specific job that would otherwise be done by a company's own workers

offshoring the movement of some of a company's operations to another country

Figure 9.3 | Education and Income, 2005

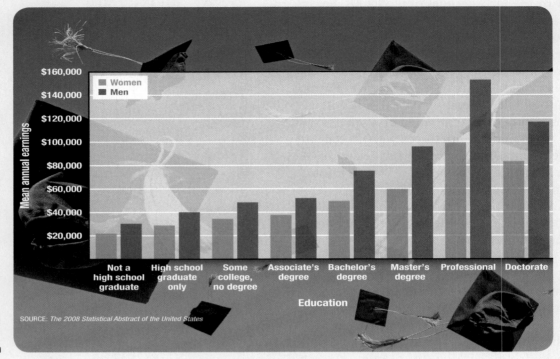

GRAPH SKILLS

This bar chart shows that higher levels of education correspond to higher income.

1. When are men and women likely to see the greatest potential increase in income?

2. What can be concluded about the opportunity costs for men and women of moving up to that higher-paying level?

Mean annual earnings

$160,000
$140,000
$120,000
$100,000
$80,000
$60,000
$40,000
$20,000

Women
Men

Not a high school graduate | High school graduate only | Some college, no degree | Associate's degree | Bachelor's degree | Master's degree | Professional | Doctorate

Education

SOURCE: *The 2008 Statistical Abstract of the United States*

Action Graph online

For an animated version of this graph, visit PearsonSchool.com/PHecon

---

FL MA.912.A.2.2 Interpret a graph to represent a real-world situation.

These shifts in demand for workers are another example of supply and demand in operation. Demand for skilled service workers is rising, so wages for skilled workers go up. These higher wages persuade more people to train for these jobs to meet the demand. Meanwhile, as demand for manufacturing workers drops off, there is a surplus of these workers who find that they must become more skilled in order to compete in the job market.

In recent years, businesses have looked abroad not just for factory workers but also for the labor of highly skilled workers. By the early 2000s, companies increasingly looked offshore for computer engineers, software programmers, and other high-skilled jobs. This trend has affected other fields, such as auto design and some medical services as well.

✓ **CHECKPOINT** *Why do companies engage in offshoring?*

The Changing Labor Force

Not only have jobs changed; workers have also changed. In the 1950s, a typical American worker was a white man who

had graduated from high school and had found a secure 40-hour-a-week job where he probably hoped to stay until retiring at age 65. Not anymore. Today, more women and members of minority groups are in the workforce. In addition, someone entering the workforce can expect to have four or five different jobs during his or her working life.

College Graduates

To get jobs, people must have human capital—the education, training, and experience that make them useful in the workplace. More and more, a high-school diploma alone is not enough to prepare a person for financial success. To get—and succeed in—a job, people need more education. Getting a good education, however, requires money, time, and effort. Higher earnings compensate these workers for their advanced-training costs.

Economists offer two explanations for the connection between educational advancement and higher wages. The theory that education increases efficiency of production and thus results in higher wages is called the **learning effect**. The statistics in **Figure 9.3** support this theory. They show that college-educated workers have

learning effect the theory that education increases efficiency of production and thus results in higher wages higher median income than high-school dropouts. Income continues to increase as people gain even more education. People with doctorates and professional degrees, such as doctors and lawyers, earn more than people with bachelor's degrees.

Another theory about the relationship of education to wages is called the **screening effect.** This theory suggests that the completion of college signals to employers that a job applicant is intelligent and hard-working. The skills and determination necessary to complete college may also be useful qualities for employees to have. According to this theory, a college degree does not increase productivity, but simply identifies people who may be good employees because of their perseverance and innate skills.

Women at Work

The changing face of the labor force can be seen at your local bank. A few decades ago, men greeted customers at the tellers' windows and served as loan officers. Today, most bank tellers and many loan officers are women. Women have also taken a greater role in national defense and in police and fire departments across the country.

Figure 9.4 shows that in 1960, almost 38 percent of women belonged to the labor force. By 2010, that rate was projected to be over 62 percent.

The increase may be due to several factors. One is that women were encouraged to pursue a higher education and add to their human capital. By increasing their human capital, they increased their potential earnings. With the expectation of earning more, more women entered the workforce. In addition, as more and more jobs become available in the service sector of the economy, fewer jobs call for physical strength. Instead, jobs require brainpower and personal skills, placing men and women on equal footing.

For women in their prime working years (**Figure 9.4** shows data for *all* women.), however, there appears to be a slight drop in employment. In 2008, the Bureau of Labor Statistics reported that 72.7 percent of women ages 25 to 54 were employed. This was down from 74.9 percent in 2000. Economists believe that women are being affected by the same economic problems as men, including layoffs and offshoring.

Temporary Workers

In another important trend, more and more businesses are replacing permanent, full-time workers with part-time and temporary workers. These temporary and part-time jobs are known as **contingent employment.**

Some temporary workers come from "temp" agencies. These are companies that have a pool of experienced workers who can be hired out to organizations on a short-term basis. The organization that needs the workers pays the temp agency. The agency, in turn, pays the worker a share of that fee, keeping the rest to cover expenses and profit.

Other temporary workers are hired directly by firms as contract workers, people hired for a specified time period or to complete a certain task.

Contingent employment is becoming more common even in occupations that had been very secure jobs. For example, some software engineers and attorneys are now hired as contract workers. When the workers complete their part of the project they were hired for, they are released. These highly skilled workers are generally well paid, with some earning as much as permanent workers.

screening effect the theory that the completion of college indicates to employers that a job applicant is intelligent and hard-working

contingent employment a temporary and part-time job

MA.912.A.2.2 Interpret a graph to represent a real-world situation.

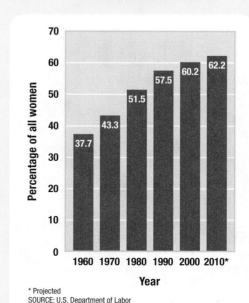

| Figure 9.4 | **Women in U.S. Labor Force, 1960–2010** |

* Projected
SOURCE: U.S. Department of Labor

GRAPH SKILLS

There has been a steady rise of women in the working world.

1. Which decade shows the largest increase in the percentage of women entering the labor force?
2. What might be the reasons why the increases are smaller in recent decades?

Action Graph
online

For an animated version of this graph, visit
PearsonSchool.com/PHecon

guest workers
members of the labor force from another country who are allowed to live and work in the United States only temporarily

Experts have identified several reasons for the increased use of temporary employees.

1. Flexible work arrangements allow firms to easily adjust their workforce to changing demand for their output. At times of reduced demand, they can easily lay off temporary workers or reduce workers' hours instead of paying employees who are idle. When business picks up, companies can rehire whatever workers they need.
2. Temporary workers in many industries are paid less and given fewer benefits (if any) than permanent, full-time workers. Thus, hiring more temporary workers cuts costs.

3. Discharging temporary workers is easier and less costly than discharging regular, permanent employees. Many employers give full-time employees severance pay of several weeks worth of wages or salary when they lay off workers. They do not have to make these payments to temporary workers.
4. Some workers actually prefer these flexible arrangements to traditional, permanent jobs. The market, then, reflects their preferences. On the other hand, BLS studies show that a majority of temporary workers would prefer permanent jobs.

The Impact of Foreign-Born Workers

One topic that has received much attention in recent years is the impact of foreign-born workers on the labor force. In 2005, foreign-born workers numbered about 22 million people, nearly 15 percent of all workers in the United States.

Many immigrant workers are able to become permanent residents. Some foreign-born workers are **guest workers.** They are allowed to live and work in the United States only temporarily. Companies that want to hire guest workers must show that they cannot meet their labor needs from native-born workers and that using guest workers will not lower the wages of native-born workers. If companies can prove this, the government gives them permission to bring in guest workers. Guest workers hold jobs in high-tech industries that demand highly skilled workers, and in lower-skilled work also, such as agricultural labor.

The impact of immigrants on the labor force is hotly debated. Some analysts say that immigrant workers hold down the wages of Americans. This effect shows supply and demand at work. As more immigrants enter the country, they increase the supply of workers. The demand of employers for workers does not necessarily increase, though. With greater quantity supplied than quantity demanded, employers can pay less for their workers as the market reaches a new equilibrium. The result, say critics of immigration, is that American-born workers see their wages drop. They also face stiffer competition for jobs.

FUTURE WATCH 🌐 **Global Impact**

Children in the Workforce

Throughout history, children have been exploited in the workforce. The goal of child labor laws in the United States is to protect the health, safety, and education of children. Although allowances are made for children as young as 12 to work on farms, as many as 500,000 children may work in America's fields. In other countries, although children may be protected to some extent, they remain a key factor in economic development. *Research the child labor laws in other countries and the United States. How do they compare?*

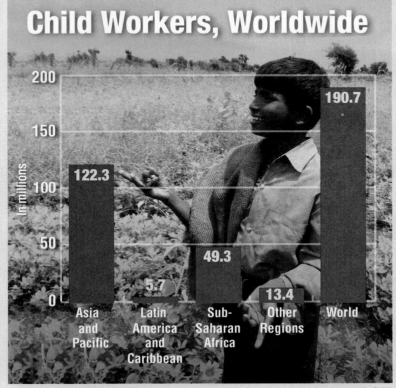

Child Workers, Worldwide

In millions

Region	Value
Asia and Pacific	122.3
Latin America and Caribbean	5.7
Sub-Saharan Africa	49.3
Other Regions	13.4
World	190.7

SOURCE: "The End of Child Labour: Within Reach," ILO, Geneva, 2006. Statistics on Child Labor is as per the Child Labor Coalition report "Children in the Fields: The Inequitable Treatment of Child Farmworkers," 2007

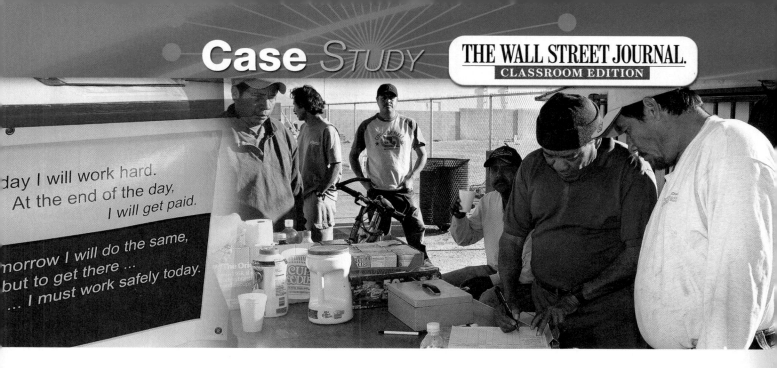

day I will work hard.
At the end of the day,
I will get paid.

morrow I will do the same,
but to get there ...
... I must work safely today.

Living Day to Day

DAY LABOR

Pinched by unemployment, more workers are taking up short-term manual labor to get by.

By Marie C. Baca
The Wall Street Journal

 SS.912.E.1.9 Describe how workers' pay is determined.

The face of day labor appears to be changing. Amid continued high joblessness, more women, non-Latinos and former white-collar workers are taking up manual labor. Employers say they are seeing more workers at curbside hiring sites or seeking work through less traditional routes such as Craigslist—people who at one time might have had full-time jobs.

Many lost desk jobs in the hard-hit auto, construction and financial industries. Some see manual labor such as housecleaning or hauling debris, where people are hired and paid for the day, as the only way to survive.

The new day laborers include single mother of two Debbie Helms, 34, of Akron, Ohio, a former bank teller who began cleaning homes a year ago. Her clients, who usually offer her $7 an hour, change on a day-to-day basis.

Juan Luis Ortega, 39, of Mountain View, Calif., who was laid off from his behind-the-counter job at a car dealership, now does yard work and other manual labor. College graduate Ryan Bherns in Wayzata, Minn., says he works whenever possible as a mover because his scaled-back hours as a substitute teacher aren't enough to pay his bills.

"It's a weird time for me and a lot of other people," says Mr. Bherns, 30.

Pablo Alvarado, executive director of the National Day Laborer Organizing Network, says the types of jobs available to day workers are also changing. The fall of the housing industry has left fewer jobs in construction, which provided steady wages; now most day-labor consists of moving and landscaping jobs that last only for a few hours, he says.

Day laborers often connect with employers at curbside hiring sites, with people congregating around large hardware stores and supermarkets, waiting for someone to pull up and offer a day's—or even a few hours'—work. At Chavez Supermarket in Redwood City, Calif., assistant manager Omar Flores says he sees more newcomers among the people seeking work outside the store.

Leah Lightfeldt, 21, of Fontana, Calif., began posting on Craigslist after she was let go as a furniture-store sales associate. In her post, she said she was willing to do house-cleaning and child care. Her typical day-labor job lasts a few hours and pays about $6 an hour, compared with $9 an hour at the furniture store. She says she's still looking for a long-term solution, explaining: "I've got to just keep trying."

Applying Economic Principles
Supply and demand play an important role in the labor market. Identify how the economic downturn has changed the nature of employment for many people.

Video News Update Online
Powered by
The Wall Street Journal
Classroom Edition

Use videos at **PearsonSchool.com/PHecon** as a springboard for a discussion on a current topic.

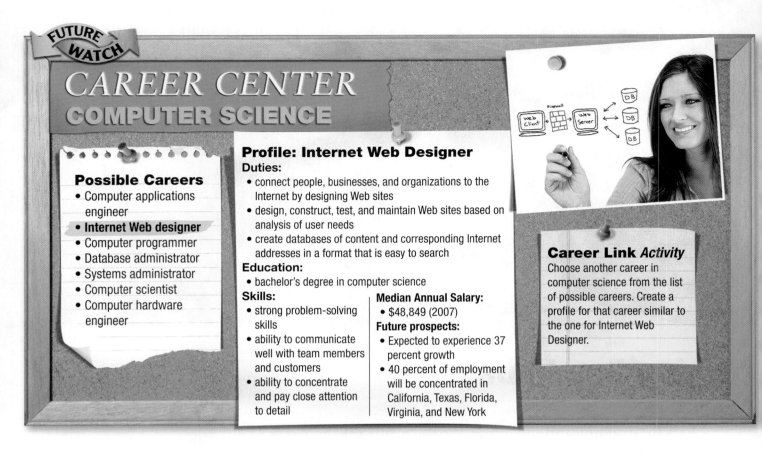

CAREER CENTER
COMPUTER SCIENCE

Possible Careers
- Computer applications engineer
- **Internet Web designer**
- Computer programmer
- Database administrator
- Systems administrator
- Computer scientist
- Computer hardware engineer

Profile: Internet Web Designer

Duties:
- connect people, businesses, and organizations to the Internet by designing Web sites
- design, construct, test, and maintain Web sites based on analysis of user needs
- create databases of content and corresponding Internet addresses in a format that is easy to search

Education:
- bachelor's degree in computer science

Skills:
- strong problem-solving skills
- ability to communicate well with team members and customers
- ability to concentrate and pay close attention to detail

Median Annual Salary:
- $48,849 (2007)

Future prospects:
- Expected to experience 37 percent growth
- 40 percent of employment will be concentrated in California, Texas, Florida, Virginia, and New York

Career Link *Activity*
Choose another career in computer science from the list of possible careers. Create a profile for that career similar to the one for Internet Web Designer.

Other analysts say that immigrant workers fill an important role in the economy. First, they say, lower-skilled immigrant workers do jobs that Americans are unwilling to do because the wages are low. As a result, important work gets done that would not be done otherwise. Second, because immigrants take those jobs, the companies that hire them can charge less for their goods or services, which benefits everyone.

✔ **CHECKPOINT** *How are education and income connected?*

Wages and Benefits Trends

Labor economists study not only who is in and out of the workforce, but how they are doing in terms of earnings and benefits. Today, the picture is mixed.

Real Wages Down

American workers enjoy higher wages than those in many other countries. In recent decades, though, the paychecks of American workers actually have been shrinking. The Bureau of Labor Statistics reports that average weekly earnings rose from $241 in 1980 to almost $590 in 2007. In reality, however, there has been no actual increase. To make a better comparison, economists make calculations to hold the value of the dollar constant. This takes away the effect of inflation—the rise of prices over time. In constant dollars, average wages actually declined to just about $222. In other words, real weekly wages have fallen about $19 in 27 years.

Why have average real wages decreased in the last couple of decades? One reason, as you have read, is that greater competition from foreign companies has decreased the demand for workers. Deregulation of many domestic industries, such as trucking, air travel, and telecommunications, may have forced firms to cut employees' wages as competition has intensified. The increased use of temporary work has also held down wages.

Cost of Benefits

For many workers, benefits such as pensions and health insurance are a significant share of total compensation. This share rose fairly steadily during the 1900s and early

2000s. By 2005, employer-provided benefits added $7.87 an hour to the cost of workers. Benefits now make up nearly 30 percent of workers' compensation. This adds up to a large cost for employers—especially since benefits like health insurance are becoming more expensive.

Social Security and Medicare taxes are included in these benefits, since they are used to pay benefits to retired and disabled workers. Most workers know that Social Security taxes are deducted from their paychecks each month. Did you know that employers pay a matching amount? Thus, workers and employers share this cost. In addition, Social Security and Medicare tax rates have risen substantially in recent decades, causing further increases in employers' benefits costs.

Employers are finding that these rising benefits costs increase the cost of doing business and thus cut into their profits. As a result some types of contingent employees, such as independent contractors, become an attractive labor resource for companies because these workers do not have to be paid benefits. Offshoring and outsourcing also help firms to cut their expenses. If benefits costs continue to rise, companies

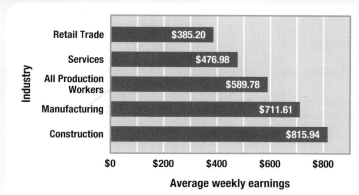

Figure 9.5 Earnings for U.S. Workers, 2005

Industry	Average weekly earnings
Retail Trade	$385.20
Services	$476.98
All Production Workers	$589.78
Manufacturing	$711.61
Construction	$815.94

SOURCE: Bureau of Labor Statistics

GRAPH SKILLS

This graph shows the differences in average weekly earnings among workers.
1. What is the average salary of a worker who is employed in a retail trade or services job?
2. Why might wages for workers in retail be lower than those for service workers?

Action Graph online

For an animated version of this graph, visit **PearsonSchool.com/PHecon**

will be pressured to pursue these steps to a greater extent. Those responses may prove unpopular with workers.

 CHECKPOINT *Why have real wages dropped in recent years?*

(FL) SS.912.E.1.9, SS.912.E.3, SS.912.G.4, LA.1112.1.6.1, LA.1112.2.2.2, MA.912.A.2.2

SECTION 1 ASSESSMENT

Essential Questions Journal
To continue to build a response to the Essential Question, go to your **Essential Questions Journal**.

Guiding Question
1. Use your completed chart to answer this question: How do economic trends affect workers?
2. **Extension** What kinds of jobs are available to high school students in your region? Which of these jobs might not exist 20 years from now? Why?

Key Terms and Main Ideas
3. Who does the **labor force** include?
4. **(a)** What is **offshoring?** **(b)** What economic changes have brought it about?
5. Historically, the United States economy changed from an economy based on agriculture, to manufacturing, and then to service. What brought about these changes?

Critical Thinking
6. **Conclude (a)** Who are "discouraged workers"? **(b)** Why do you think the government does not consider them unemployed?
7. **Predict** What do you think would happen in the U.S. economy, if the pool of immigrant labor was cut drastically?
8. **Identify** Provide an example of a time of high demand for temporary workers.
9. **Analyze Effects** What effect does increased benefits paid by employers have on workers' wages?

Math Skills
10. **Estimating Rates of Change** The graph at the right shows recent unemployment rates for women. **Figure 9.4**, on page 221 shows the

percentage of all women in the workforce over a selected period of time. Given that **Figure 9.4** projects data into 2010, what can be estimated about the unemployment rate for women in 2010? Why?

Visit PearsonSchool.com/PHecon for additional math help.

Annual Unemployment Rate for Women 20 Years and Over

*based on 10 months
SOURCE: Bureau of Labor Statistics

LA.1112.1.6 Use multiple strategies to develop vocabulary.

MA.912.A.2.2 Interpret a graph to represent a real-world situation.

SS.912.E.1.9 Describe how workers' pay is determined.

SS.912.E.2.4 Explain the rationale of government-instituted price control.

ECONOMIC DICTIONARY

As you read the section, look for the definitions of these **Key Terms**:

- derived demand
- productivity of labor
- equilibrium wage
- unskilled labor
- semi-skilled labor
- skilled labor
- professional labor
- glass ceiling
- labor union
- featherbedding

Guiding Question
Why do some people earn more than others?

Copy this concept web and fill it in as you read. Add more ovals if necessary.

▶ **Economics and You**   How important is it to you to make a lot of money? If it is very important, then you had better think carefully about what you want to do for a living. Some jobs and professions are very well paid. A top-notch surgeon can charge $150,000 for one operation. A lawyer might make $600 for an hour consultation, while the clerk at the local convenience store might make $8.00 an hour. What will determine the size of your paycheck?

Principles in Action   The law of supply and demand applies to the world of labor and wages. What people earn for what they do is largely a matter of how many people are willing and able to do the job and how much that job is in demand. Like eggs or airplanes or pet iguanas, labor is a commodity that is bought and sold. In a free market economy, the market finds its own equilibrium price for labor. In a mixed economy, the government also plays a role. In the Economics & You feature, you will see how government action affects the labor market for teen workers.

Supply and Demand for Labor

Employment or unemployment in a labor market depends on how closely the demand for workers—the number of available jobs—meets the supply of workers seeking jobs. Let's examine how supply and demand operate in labor markets.

Labor Demand

The demand for labor comes from private firms and government agencies that hire workers to produce goods and services. In most labor markets, dozens, or even hundreds, of firms compete with one another for workers.

derived demand a type of demand that is set by the demand for another good or service

Demand for labor is called a **derived demand** because it is derived, or set, by the demand for another good or service. In this case, that other demand is the demand for what a worker produces. For example, the demand for cooks in a market depends on the demand for restaurant meals.

In a competitive labor market, workers are usually paid according to the value of what they produce. For example, competition among restaurants results in a wage for cooks that reflects the cook's productivity.

productivity of labor the quantity of output produced by a unit of labor

Productivity of labor is the quantity of output produced by a unit of labor.

The productivity of a cook's labor, for example, can be measured as the cost of a meal. Suppose that most of the restaurants in a city pay $12 an hour for cooks and that each cook generates $20 an hour in revenue for the restaurants. The possibility of profit will attract other entrepreneurs to open restaurants. Competition will push up the wage for cooks. As a result, cooks will be paid close to the value of their productivity of labor. The flowchart in **Figure 9.6** shows the ripple effect that occurs when a new restaurant hires cooks at a higher wage.

Now look at the demand curve for labor, shown in the right-hand graph of **Figure 9.7** on page 229. Notice that it is negatively sloped, reflecting the law of demand. The higher the price of labor, the smaller the quantity of labor demanded by employers. Restaurants are more likely to hire more cooks at $12 an hour than at $16 an hour because the lower cost means they can earn more profits on each cook's labor.

Labor Supply

The supply of labor comes from people willing to work for wages. As the graph on the left in **Figure 9.7** shows, the supply curve is positively sloped, reflecting the law of supply. In other words, the higher the wage, the larger the quantity of labor supplied.

This is logical. It simply means that the higher the wage for a job, the greater the number of people who will be attracted to that job. A higher wage for cooks encourages people who would choose other occupations to acquire the training required to become a cook.

Equilibrium Wage

We know that at market equilibrium, the quantity of a good supplied will equal the quantity demanded. Economic factors— the supply of labor and the demand for it—combine to determine an equilibrium price. Because the equilibrium price makes the quantity that suppliers want to sell equal to the quantity that demanders want to buy, there is a tendency for the price or quantity not to change. That stability applies to the equilibrium price in one market, though. These factors may be different in different parts of the country, or at different times.

The **equilibrium wage** is the wage rate, or price of labor services, that is set when the supply of workers meets the demand for workers in the labor market. On a graph, the equilibrium wage is shown by the intersection of the supply and demand curves. (See **Figure 9.8** on page 230.) At equilibrium, there is no pressure to raise or lower wages.

How do these theories affect how much you should expect to earn working in a pet store or a grocery store next summer? It depends on supply and demand in your area. If stores do not hire many additional workers during the summer and a lot of teenagers wanted to work, the wage will be relatively low. On the other hand, if stores want to hire a lot of teenagers and few teens want to work, the wage will be higher.

✔ **CHECKPOINT** *What determines the equilibrium wage of labor?*

equilibrium wage the wage rate, or price of labor services, that is set when the supply of workers meets the demand for workers in the labor market

| Figure 9.6 | **Effects of Competition** |

Cooks are paid less than their productivity (the value of output).

↓

A new restaurant opens in town, offering higher wages for cooks.

↓

Other restaurants raise wages for cooks to compete for scarce labor.

↓

Cooks are paid closer to their productivity (the value of output).

GRAPH SKILLS

This flowchart shows how competition causes workers to be paid a wage close to their productivity.

1. Explain how the outcome of this scenario affects **(a)** the cooks, **(b)** the restaurants.
2. Describe the conditions in which a restaurant might not be motivated to raise its wages to compete for scarce labor.

VISUAL GLOSSARY

Reviewing Key Terms
To understand *productivity of labor*, review these terms:
production possibilities curve, *p. 13*
production possibilities frontier, *p. 14*
efficiency, *p.15*

law of increasing costs, *p. 17*
diminishing marginal returns, *p. 11?*
labor force, *p. 217*
derived demand, *p. 251*
learning effect, *p. 253*

What is Productivity of Labor?

◄ **productivity of labor** is the quantity of output produced by a unit of labor

The worker above is able to make 10 toys in an hour. The one on the right, however, has been trained to use new toy-making techniques. She is able to make 15 toys in an hour.

This worker uses a machine to make 300 toys in an hour.

Why are investments in training and technology important for a business? At what point would increased investment not result in increased productivity?

Visual Glossary
online

To expand your understanding of this and other key economic terms, visit **PearsonSchool.com/PHecon**

Figure 9.7 **Labor Supply and Demand**

GRAPH SKILLS

This graph shows (a) how the quantity of labor demanded varies depending on the price of labor, and (b) how the labor supply varies depending on the wage rate.

1. According to the demand curve, if each cook works a 40-hour work week, how many cooks will be hired at $12 an hour and $16 an hour?

2. Why is the supply curve positively sloped?

Action Graph
online

For an animated version
of this graph, visit
PearsonSchool.com/PHecon

Wages and Skill Levels

Why do lawyers earn more money than carpenters, and carpenters more than cashiers? Wages vary according to workers' skill levels and education, as well as according to supply and demand. Jobs are often categorized into four skill levels:

1. **Unskilled labor** requires no specialized skills, education, or training. Workers in these jobs usually earn an hourly wage. They include dishwashers, messengers, janitors, and many farm workers.

2. **Semi-skilled labor** requires minimal specialized skills and education, such as the operation of certain types of equipment. Semi-skilled workers usually earn an hourly wage. They include lifeguards, word processors, short-order cooks, and many construction and factory workers.

3. **Skilled labor** requires specialized abilities and training to do tasks such as operating complicated equipment. Skilled workers need little supervision, yet usually earn an hourly wage. They

include auto mechanics, bank tellers, plumbers, firefighters, chefs, and carpenters.

4. **Professional labor** demands advanced skills and education. Professionals are usually white-collar workers who receive a salary. Professionals include managers, teachers, bankers, doctors, actors, professional athletes, and computer programmers.

Labor supply and demand can create a significant difference in pay scales for workers with various skills. For example, the labor market for medical doctors is relatively high compared to construction workers. Because the supply of doctors is relatively low and the demand is relatively high, there is a high equilibrium wage.

By comparison, the supply of construction workers is high relative to the demand for them. Hence, the equilibrium wage for construction workers would be much lower than that for doctors.

Doctors and other highly educated workers—and those with extensive training and experience—enjoy demand for their services that is high relative to

 MA.912.A.2.2
Interpret a graph to represent a real-world situation.

unskilled labor
work that requires no specialized skills, education, or training

semi-skilled labor
work that requires minimal specialized skills and education

skilled labor work that requires specialized skills and training

professional labor
work that requires advanced skills and education

Figure 9.8

Equilibrium Wage

GRAPH SKILLS
This graph shows the wage at which the quantity demanded equals the quantity supplied.

1. Explain why a stable wage means stable restaurant prices.

2. Under what circumstances would the equilibrium wage be $8 an hour?

Action Graph
online

For an animated version of this graph, visit PearsonSchool.com/PHecon

FL SS.912.E.2.4
Explain the rationale of government-instituted price control.

MA.912.A.2.2
Interpret a graph to represent a real-world situation.

the supply, leading to higher earnings. The demand for workers with less education and training tends to be lower relative to the supply, so their earnings are lower. Experienced workers are desirable because they tend to be more productive than those newer to that job.

Another reason that earnings vary is differences in working conditions. The level of danger in doing a job, the physical or emotional stress involved, and the location of the work can all change the equilibrium wage.

Economic studies have shown that jobs with high accident and fatality rates pay relatively high wages. Workers who do dangerous jobs require compensation for the risks they take. Thus, there is a higher equilibrium wage rate for dangerous jobs, as shown in **Figure 9.9**.

✔ **CHECKPOINT** *How do education, training, and experience affect wages?*

Wage Discrimination

As we have seen, wages for a particular job should end up at the equilibrium price of labor for that job. However, some people are paid less because of the social group they belong to. For instance, in the past, women and members of minority groups often received lower wages than white male workers for the same work. This practice is wage discrimination.

Some employers defended wage discrimination against women by claiming that men needed the money to support families, while women were simply working to earn extra cash. Discrimination against minority workers reflected racial and ethnic prejudice in society. In recent decades, national or state legislators have tried to end these practices by passing laws prohibiting wage discrimination.

Laws Against Wage Discrimination
In the 1960s, the United States Congress passed several anti-discrimination laws that prevent companies from paying lower wages to some employees based on factors like gender or race that are not related to skill or productivity. The Equal Pay Act of 1963 required that male and female employees in the same workplace performing the same job receive the same pay. Title VII of the Civil Rights Act of 1964 prohibited job discrimination on the basis of race, sex, color, religion, or nationality. (Religious institutions and small businesses are exempt from the law.)

The Civil Rights Act also established the Equal Employment Opportunity Commission (EEOC) to enforce the provisions of the law. Workers who feel they have been discriminated against can complain to the EEOC, which will investigate the matter. If necessary, the commission can take companies to court to force them to comply with the law.

Pay Levels for Women
Despite protections, women still earn less than men. This earnings gap has closed somewhat, but not completely. Historically, this gap has been the result of three factors:

1. *"Women's work."* Women have historically been discouraged from entering certain high-paying occupations, such as doctors, lawyers, and corporate managers. Instead, they have been encouraged to pursue careers such as teaching, nursing, and clerical work. With so many women seeking work in these occupations,

Figure 9.9

Comparison: Wages for High-Risk, Low-Risk Jobs

Workers in high-risk jobs

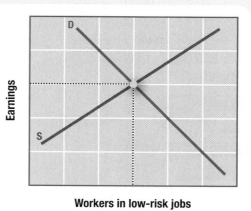

Workers in low-risk jobs

GRAPH SKILLS

These graphs show how wages compare for similar jobs with different degrees of risk.

1. Write a sentence that compares the demand curves on the two graphs.
2. Write a sentence that compares the two supply curves.

Action Graph
online

For an animated version of this graph, visit **PearsonSchool.com/PHecon**

---

the labor supply has been generally high. As you know, a large supply of labor tends to produce a relatively low equilibrium wage.

2. *Human capital.* Overall, women have had less education, training, and experience than men. This lack of human capital makes women's labor, in economic terms, less productive. As a result, fewer women are eligible for the higher-paying, traditionally male-dominated jobs in fields such as engineering.

3. *Women's career paths.* Even today, some employers assume that female employees are not interested in career advancement. This perception can be a roadblock for women in the workplace. The challenges many women face in trying to balance child-rearing and a career adds to this perception.

Much progress has been made in creating job opportunities for women. Yet some qualified women still find that they cannot receive promotions to top-level jobs. This unofficial barrier that sometimes prevents women and minorities from advancing to the top ranks of organizations that are dominated by white men is called a **glass ceiling.**

Pay Levels Across Society

On average, members of minority groups tend to receive lower pay than whites do. Part of the wage gap has been caused by a history of racial discrimination. On average, whites have had access to more education and work experience, enabling them to develop skills that are in demand. Non-discrimination laws, in part, are designed to give minority workers improved access to education and job opportunities so they can develop

glass ceiling an unofficial barrier that sometimes prevents women and minorities from advancing to the top ranks of organizations dominated by white men

 MA.912.A.2.2 Interpret a graph to represent a real-world situation.

◄ The term "corporate ladder" refers to the series of rungs, or steps, an employee climbs on the way to corporate leadership. Workers at the upper rungs of the corporate ladder have more responsibility, decision-making power, and income. *How does this cartoon symbolize a glass ceiling for women?*

Figure 9.10

Income for Full-Time Workers, by Gender and Ethnicity, 2005

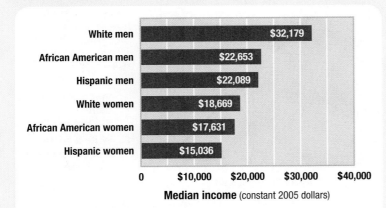

	Median income (constant 2005 dollars)
White men	$32,179
African American men	$22,653
Hispanic men	$22,089
White women	$18,669
African American women	$17,631
Hispanic women	$15,036

0   $10,000 $20,000 $30,000 $40,000

Median income (constant 2005 dollars)

SOURCE: *The 2008 Statistical Abstract of the United States*

GRAPH SKILLS

Despite the progress in efforts to end wage discrimination, significant differences exist between men and women and among workers of various minority groups.

1. According to the bar chart, which group has the lowest median income?
2. What factors might help explain why African American women earn more than Hispanic women?

Action Graph
online

For an animated version of this graph, visit
PearsonSchool.com/PHecon

MA.912.A.2.2
Interpret a graph to represent a real-world situation.

more human capital and lessen the wage gap. (See **Figure 9.10.**) The entire economy benefits when all workers have a higher level of skill and can be more productive.

 CHECKPOINT *What groups have been hurt by wage discrimination?*

Other Factors Affecting Wages

In addition to laws forbidding discrimination, several other factors can affect wages. These include minimum wage laws, workplace safety laws, employer actions, and labor unions.

Minimum Wage Laws

In 1938, Congress passed the Fair Labor Standards Act. This law created a minimum wage—the lowest amount employers could lawfully pay for most types of work—and required employers to pay overtime for work beyond 40 hours a week. Many states also have their own minimum wage

laws. Because of these laws, employers may be forced to pay more than the equilibrium wage for unskilled labor.

Supporters of the minimum wage argue that it helps the poorest American workers earn enough to support themselves. Opponents say that artificially increasing the price of labor actually causes a decrease in quantity demanded. In other words, individual employees will earn more, but companies will hire fewer of them. (See page 139 for more information on the debate over the minimum wage.)

Safety Laws

As you read in Chapter 3, the federal government created the Occupational Safety and Health Administration (OSHA) in 1970 to establish standards for safer working conditions. OSHA policies were issued in an effort to save lives, prevent injuries, and protect the health of workers in the private sector. All laws requiring certain minimum levels of safety also could have an impact on wages.

If a law or policy increases safety at work, it may also decrease wages because workers are willing to work for lower wages when jobs are safer. By holding down wages, the law lowers an employer's costs. Of course, the employer will usually have to spend money to comply with safety regulations, which may more than offset the employer's savings from any wage reduction.

Employers Respond to Wage Levels

Employers may also take actions to try to affect wage levels. For example, a company might try to cut labor costs by substituting machines for people. In other words, employers can replace human capital with physical capital.

Take furniture making, for example. In countries where labor is relatively cheap, furniture may be handmade by workers. In the United States, where labor is relatively expensive, manufacturers have substituted sophisticated machinery for more expensive human labor. Another increasingly common substitution involves customer service call centers, where automated answering services have replaced live telephone operators to direct incoming calls.

Other examples of substituting physical for human capital include automated teller machines (ATMs), which take the place of bank tellers, and mechanized assembly lines, which can eliminate the need for some manufacturing workers. These technological advances have greatly reduced the number of employees that banks and manufacturing companies hire.

Even if firms cannot use technology to replace labor, they may be able to reduce their labor costs in other ways. As you learned in Section 1, companies may outsource jobs to other parts of the world where labor is more plentiful, and therefore cheaper. They may also choose to hire temporary workers.

Unions

Workers who are unhappy with their wages also have several choices. In a competitive labor market, they might get higher-paying jobs from another employer. Some people change careers, either by choice or out of necessity. Although labor unions are becoming less of a force in the American economy, workers might decide to join a union and press for higher pay.

A **labor union** is an organization of workers that tries to improve working conditions, wages, and benefits for its members. One of the key goals of unions is to get wage increases for their members. As you will see in Section 3, unions allow workers to negotiate wage levels as a group rather than having to deal individually with employers. Their combined bargaining power is sometimes more effective at persuading employers to raise wages.

Nationally, union members do tend to earn higher wages than nonunion workers in similar jobs. In 2005, the average union wage was nearly $5 an hour higher than the average wage for nonunion wage earners. That amounts to a $200 difference in a 40-hour workweek.

Some economists argue that unions depress the wages of nonunion workers. They offer this reasoning:

1. Unions press employers to raise their members' wages.

2. When wages go up, the quantity of labor demanded goes down. Thus, the number of union jobs decreases.
3. As union jobs are cut, more workers are forced to seek nonunion jobs.
4. An increase in the supply of nonunion workers causes the wage rate for nonunion jobs to fall.

In addition, some unions have engaged in **featherbedding,** negotiating labor contracts that keep unnecessary workers on the company payroll. A notable example of this practice occurred in the railroad industry. In the early days of railroads, a "cabooseman" had to ride at the back of the train to operate a rear brake that stopped the train. Yet even after design

labor union an organization of workers that tries to improve working conditions, wages, and benefits for its members

featherbedding the practice of negotiating labor contracts that keep unnecessary workers on a company's payroll

Economics & YOU

Safety and Minimum Wage Laws

Many jobs teenagers hold are closely regulated by the federal government, which restricts hours and sets safety standards for workers under 18. *It is against the law for teens to operate a forklift because of the dangers.*

RESTRICTED AREA
NO ONE UNDER 18 ALLOWED TO OPERATE MACHINERY

PRODUCE

Oranges $1.69 lb

Some jobs, like stocking produce, are well-suited for young workers and pay the minimum wage.

▲ Explain the relationship between safety and wage levels. *Under what conditions might the teenager in the second picture not be allowed to work?*

▲ Sometimes when companies invest in technology, the work performed by human labor becomes automated, such as a welder's job in an auto factory. **What are some of the costs that are eliminated when a company replaces workers with machines?**

changes allowed the engineer at the front of the train to operate rear brakes, unions managed to keep caboosemen on the payroll. These workers received full wages and benefits for doing nothing.

People who support unions counter that without the ability to organize, workers have little power compared to that of employers. Unless workers join together, they say, employers can dictate

wage levels and working conditions. Since they can usually find replacement workers, their employees might have little real choice. The next section will trace the history of unions in the United States and further describe their advantages and disadvantages.

✓ **CHECKPOINT** *What three actions can employers take to reduce the cost of wages?*

 FL SS.912.E.1.9, SS.912.E.2.2, LA.1112.2.2.3, LA.1112.2.2.2, LA.1112.1.6.1

Essential Questions Journal To continue to build a response to the Essential Question, go to your **Essential Questions Journal**.

SECTION 2 ASSESSMENT

ⓠ Guiding Question

1. Use your completed concept web to answer this question: Why do some people earn more than others?

2. **Extension** Consider one of four job skill levels: unskilled, semi-skilled, skilled, or professional. Identify one job in that category. Describe the education or training you would need for that skill level. Would the job be in the higher or lower wage earning range?

Key Terms and Main Ideas

3. Why is the demand for labor called a **derived demand?**

4. If an advertising business buys new computers for its employees, how might its **productivity of labor** be affected?

5. What generally happens to the **equilibrium wage** when **(a)** demand for workers is low and supply is high, and **(b)** demand for workers is high and supply is low?

6. How does **skilled labor** differ from **professional labor?** Give an example of each.

Critical Thinking

7. **Compare** Choose two occupations, one that pays high wages and one that pays low wages. **(a)** Explain the reasons for the difference in wages in terms of supply and demand. **(b)** Are there any additional factors that could help explain the difference?

8. **Explain (a)** How do employers benefit from workplace safety laws? **(b)** How might such laws affect an employer with respect to employee lawsuits regarding safety?

Quick Write

9. Assume that a labor organizer is trying to get a union started in a local business and the local business is waging a campaign against unionization. Write a letter in support of the union or the business, in which you defend a pro- or anti-union position based on the principles of a free enterprise economy.

NGSSS

LA.1112.1.6 Use multiple strategies to develop vocabulary.

MA.912.A.2.2 Interpret a graph to represent a real-world situation.

SS.912.E.1.9 Describe how workers' pay is determined.

SS.912.E.2.3 Research the contributions of key individuals of various backgrounds in the development of the U.S.

SS.912.E.2.4 Explain the rationale of government-instituted price control.

ECONOMIC DICTIONARY

As you read the section, look for the definitions of these **Key Terms:**

- strike
- right-to-work law
- blue-collar worker
- white-collar worker
- collective bargaining
- mediation
- arbitration

Guiding Question

How do labor unions support the interests of workers?

Copy this chart and fill it in as you read.

How Unions Promote Workers' Interests	
Features of Union Contract	**Tools for Persuading Companies**
• Better wages and benefits • Better working conditions • •	• Collective bargaining • • •

▶ **Economics and You**   What comes to mind when you think of Labor Day? Do you think of the holiday as summer's last hurrah—a final weekend spent frolicking at the beach or enjoying a summer picnic at the park before school gets underway? The origins of the holiday can be traced to 1882, when labor leader Peter J. McGuire suggested a day celebrating the American worker. On September 5, 1882, some 10,000 workers marched in New York City in a parade sponsored by a labor group called the Knights of Labor. Twelve years later, Congress made Labor Day a federal holiday to be spent any way workers wished, including going to the beach or a picnic at the park.

Principles in Action Labor unions support the interests of workers with respect to wages, benefits, and working conditions. They provide workers with the power of collective bargaining, which has proven to be an effective tool to extract concessions from employers. Shifts in the U.S. economy, however, have had a major impact on unions. The loss of manufacturing-sector jobs and the increased number of women in the workplace have been major factors contributing to the steep decline in union membership over the past 50 years.

Labor and Labor Unions

As you read in Section 2, wages are determined by the forces of supply and demand. Competition among firms keeps a worker's wages close to his or her level of productivity. In general, workers who command the highest wages are those with specialized skills and who are in short supply.

What about employees who feel that they are paid too little, work too many hours, or labor in unsafe conditions? What can these employees do? One option is to seek better wages and working conditions with a different employer. Many economists, in fact, argue that a competitive labor market helps prevent low pay and dangerous working conditions because workers will leave companies with these characteristics to work elsewhere.

Figure 9.11 Key Events in the U.S. Labor Movement

Year	Event
1869	Knights of Labor founded
1886	11 dead, 50 injured in Haymarket Riot, fueling anti-union sentiment
1886	Samuel Gompers founds the American Federation of Labor (AFL)
1894	Courts halt Pullman Railroad Strike
1900	International Ladies' Garment Workers Union (ILGWU) founded
1910	Strike by ILGWU wins pay gains, shorter workdays
1911	Triangle Shirtwaist Company fire spurs action on workplace safety
1919	Strikes raise fear of revolution
1919	John L. Lewis becomes president of United Mine Workers by leading a successful strike
1932	Norris-La Guardia Act outlaws "yellow-dog" contracts, gives other protection to unions
1935	Wagner Act gives workers right to organize
1938	Congress of Industrial Organizations (CIO), headed by John L. Lewis, splits from AFL
1938	Fair Labor Standards Act creates minimum wage and bans child labor
1940s	Union membership peaks at 35 percent
1947	Taft-Hartley Act allows states to pass right-to-work laws
1955	AFL and CIO merge to create AFL-CIO
1960s	Government employees begin to organize
1962	César Chávez begins organizing the first farmworkers' union, which eventually establishes the first labor agreement with growers
1970s	Rise in anti-union measures by employers
2000s	Increase in public-sector unions; decline in overall union membership

CHART SKILLS

The American labor movement had its roots in the 1800s, when the rise of factories led to difficult and dangerous working conditions.

1. Why do you think the early years of the labor movement were marked by violence?
2. Describe the relationship shown here between labor laws and union membership in the 1900s.

Many American workers have tried to gain some control over their wages and working conditions by forming labor unions. They reason that an individual worker does not have the power to change how an employer acts but that by banding together, workers can win gains from employers. Today, only about one out of eight workers in the United States belongs to a labor union. In the past, though, unions had a strong influence on the nation's economy. In order to understand the role of labor unions today, we will look at how labor unions rose to power.

✔ **CHECKPOINT** *Why do workers join labor unions?*

The Labor Movement

The union movement took shape over the course of more than a century. It faced many obstacles along the way, including violence and legal challenges from companies. **Figure 9.11** highlights some of the key events in the U.S. labor movement.

Workers in the 1800s

Labor unions arose largely in response to changes in working conditions brought by the Industrial Revolution in the early and mid-1800s. The spread of manufacturing in this period introduced factory work to the United States.

By today's standards, this work was not enviable. In garment factories, iron plants, and gunpowder mills, laborers worked 12- to 16-hour days, 7 days a week, for meager wages. Working conditions were poor. Men, women, and children as young as five years old operated machines so dangerous that many people lost fingers and limbs. Injured workers often lost their jobs.

Today, many firms try to retain their most skilled workers by treating them well. In 1855, however, that was hardly the case. One factory boss bluntly summarized his attitude toward workers:

> ❝I regard people just as I regard my machinery. So long as they can do my work for what I choose to pay them, I keep them, getting out of them all I can.❞
>
> —Manager of a textile mill in Fall River, Massachusetts, 1855

Innovators

Walter Reuther

"There is no greater calling than to serve your fellow men. There is no greater contribution than to help the weak."

Measured by his own words, Walter Reuther was a natural leader. Born to poor immigrant parents, Reuther had little formal education. But his upbringing fostered in him a sense of courage and conviction, which helped him fight for worker rights and become one of the greatest leaders in the American labor movement.

As a local union boss in the United Auto Workers, Reuther used sit-down strikes to help organize manufacturing plants. On May 26, 1937, Reuther and three colleagues clashed with Ford Motor Company security forces outside a plant in Detroit, Michigan. News reporters witnessed a bloodbath as Reuther and his friends were badly beaten. The incident caused public outrage against Ford and was a key factor in helping the UAW gain public sympathy and support for worker rights. It was a strategic victory.

Reuther went on to make the UAW a major labor force, eventually becoming its president in 1947. He was a pioneer. He was one of the first American labor organizers to successfully negotiate for benefits that American workers take for granted today: decent hourly wages, paid vacations, health insurance, and employer-paid pensions.

Critical Thinking: *What impact did Reuther have on the costs of production (and the supply curve) of major American producers?*

Fast Facts

Walter Reuther

Born: September 1, 1907, in Wheeling, WV

Died: May 9, 1970

Education: Received H.S. diploma from Detroit City College at age 22

Claim to Fame: Early leader of the United Auto Workers union

Unions Take Hold

As early as the 1790s, whispers of worker discontent grew into organized protests. Skilled workers began to form unions to protect their interests. The chief tool of these early unions was the **strike,** an organized work stoppage intended to force an employer to address union demands. Employers responded by firing and replacing workers who tried to organize. Workers could not find help in the courts because the courts treated unions as illegal.

The man who started the United States labor movement was Samuel Gompers. The young cigarmaker rose within union ranks in New York City, focusing on three goals: higher wages, shorter hours, and safer work environments. In 1886, he founded the American Federation of Labor (AFL).

Employer Resistance

Attempts to unionize brought swift responses from employers. Viewing strikers as threats to free enterprise and social order, companies identified and fired union organizers. They forced workers to sign so-called yellow-dog contracts, in which workers promised not to join a union. (Yellow was slang for "coward.") Companies also used court orders called injunctions to force striking employees back to work. Some companies hired their own militias to harass union organizers or fight striking workers.

Congressional Protections

As the nation struggled through the Great Depression in the 1930s, Congress passed a number of measures that favored unions. The expansion of workers' rights in the 1930s contributed to a new rise in union strength. Membership grew, reaching about 35 percent of the nation's non-farm workforce in the 1940s.

Unions became a dominant force in many industries. They controlled the day-to-day operations of activities from shipbuilding to garbage collection to steel production. Unions amassed billions of dollars in union dues to cover the costs of union activities including organizing, making political donations, and providing aid to striking workers.

 CHECKPOINT *Why did union membership rise in the 1930s?*

FL **SS.912.E.2.3** Research the contributions of key individuals of various backgrounds in the development of the U.S.

SS.912.E.2.4 Explain the rationale of government-instituted price control.

strike an organized work stoppage intended to force an employer to address union demands

Decline of the Labor Movement

As they grew, some unions began to abuse their power. Some sought to preserve outdated and inefficient production methods in order to protect jobs. As you read in Section 2, some unions managed to preserve job positions that were unnecessary—called "featherbedding"—in order to keep more members employed. As a result, companies that badly needed to improve efficiency to stay competitive found that unions could be an obstacle.

The reputation of unions suffered further because of their links to organized crime. Corrupt crime bosses gained a foothold in many local unions and used union funds to finance illegal operations.

"Right-to-Work" Laws

In an effort to curb union power, Congress passed the Taft-Hartley Act in 1947. This act allowed states to pass **right-to-work laws,** measures that ban mandatory union membership. Today, most right-to-work states are in the South, which has a lower level of union membership than other regions.

Right-to-work laws may be one of several reasons for a decline in union membership in recent decades. By 2005, union membership had dropped to about 8 percent of the labor force. Today, unionism in the United States is far more limited than in many other countries.

Loss of Traditional Strongholds

One theory suggests that structural changes in the U.S. economy have caused union membership to decline. The charts in **Figure 9.12** illustrate these influential economic trends. For example:

1. Unions have traditionally been strongest among **blue-collar workers.**

Figure 9.12   U.S. Economic Changes That Have Affected Unions

CHART SKILLS
These charts show changes in industry and in the labor force.

1. What is the change indicated by each of these charts?
2. How have each of these changes affected union membership?

Action Graph
online

For an animated version of this graph, visit **PearsonSchool.com/PHecon**

U.S. Economic Activity as a Percent of GDP, 1959 and 2006

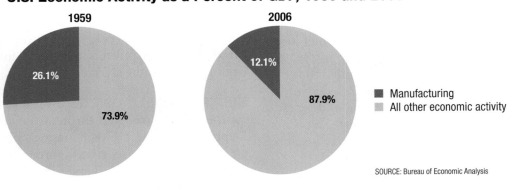

1959: 26.1%, 73.9%
2006: 12.1%, 87.9%

■ Manufacturing
■ All other economic activity

SOURCE: Bureau of Economic Analysis

Gender Makeup of the U.S. Labor Force, 1970 and 2005

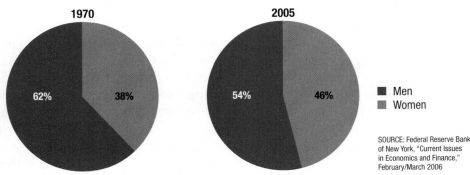

1970: 62%, 38%
2005: 54%, 46%

■ Men
■ Women

SOURCE: Federal Reserve Bank of New York, "Current Issues in Economics and Finance," February/March 2006

These workers perform manual labor, often in a manufacturing job, and earn an hourly wage. The decline of manufacturing activity, shown in the top chart in **Figure 9.12**, has caused union jobs to disappear.

Unions are weakest among white-collar employees. A **white-collar worker** is someone in a professional or clerical job who usually earns a weekly salary.

While white-collar workers generally do not belong to unions, workers in the public sector are an exception. Unionization among government workers has increased in recent decades. This growth of union membership has partially made up for losses in the private sector. Some people object when public sector workers like teachers go on strike. Members of these unions argue that, just as in the private sector, these unions are needed to promote the interests of their workers.

2. Certain manufacturing industries, such as automobiles, steel, and textiles, have traditionally employed large numbers of union workers. These industries have been hurt by foreign competition in recent years. As a result, many industries have laid off union workers, which has cut into union strength. The graphs in **Figure 9.13** show that despite the fact that there has been only a relatively modest decline in the number of production workers (also a traditional source of union membership), the percentage of workers belonging to unions has continued to fall sharply.

3. The rising proportion of women in the labor force (see bottom chart in **Figure 9.12**) also has affected union membership, since women have been less likely to join unions.

4. Seeking to reduce their production costs, some industries have relocated from the Northeast and Midwest to the South, which has historically been less friendly to unions.

Lessened Need for Unions

Another theory for union decline is that other institutions now provide many of

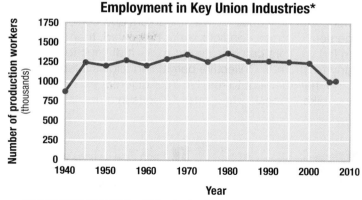

Figure 9.13 **Labor and Union Membership**

Employment in Key Union Industries*

*companies producing manufacturing-related goods and services
SOURCE: Bureau of Labor Statistics

Rates of Union Membership, 1940–2006

SOURCE: "Sluggish Institutions in a Dynamic World: Can Unions and Industrial Competition Coexist?," by Barry Hirsch and David MacPherson, *Journal of Economic Perspectives*, Fall 2007.

GRAPH SKILLS

These graphs show the rise and fall of union membership and the employment of production workers.

1. What was the peak of union membership?
2. What reasons might help explain why the rate of decline in union membership is greater than the rate of decline in production workers?

Action Graph
online

For an animated version of this graph, visit PearsonSchool.com/PHecon

the services that had been won in the past through union activity. For example, the government has passed laws setting workplace safety standards and a shorter workweek. It provides unemployment insurance and Social Security. More non-unionized employers offer benefits such as medical insurance.

✔ **CHECKPOINT** *What are three explanations for the decline in union membership?*

 MA.912.A.2.2 Interpret a graph to represent a real-world situation.

white-collar worker someone who works in a professional or clerical job and who usually earns a weekly salary

How can collective bargaining settle differences?

Conflicts commonly arise between workers and company management. If those conflicts are not resolved, then disgruntled workers can threaten to make it difficult for a company to operate. Collective bargaining allows a labor union and management to resolve their differences through a give-and-take process. This usually results in a new contract.

1 Each side defines an agenda before sitting down to negotiate. In the case of the local union, representatives meet to discuss strategy and concessions they wish to get from management. These contract disputes usually involve issues such as higher pay and better benefits. Management, on the other hand, will seek to win concessions from labor that will allow the company to increase efficiency and production, which could lead to higher profits.

2 Union leaders hold a series of negotiating sessions with management. Both sides list and explain their needs. To agree on a new contract, discussions revolve around strategies to satisfy those needs in ways that are beneficial for all.

Negotiations

Simulation *Activity*

How Do We Bargain?
You may be asked to take part in a role-playing game about compromise and negotiation in collective bargaining.

FUTURE WATCH

Personal Finance
For more information on wages and benefits, see your Personal Finance Handbook in the back of the book or visit PearsonSchool.com/PHecon

---

collective bargaining
the process in which union and company management meet to negotiate a new labor contract

Labor and Management

A union gains the right to represent workers at a company when a majority of workers in a particular work unit, such as a factory, vote to accept the union. After that, the company is required by law to bargain with the union in good faith to negotiate an employment contract.

Collective Bargaining

Picture a room and, on each side of a table, a team of lawyers and trained negotiators determined to get what they want—or at least part of it. This is **collective bargaining,** the process in which union and company management meet to negotiate a new labor contract.

Union contracts generally last two to five years and can cover hundreds of issues. The resulting contract spells out each side's rights and responsibilities for the length of the agreement.

Generally the union comes to the bargaining table with certain goals that set the agenda for collective bargaining talks. Let's examine those goals.

- *Wages and Benefits.* The union negotiates on behalf of all members for wage rates, overtime rates, planned raises, and benefits. In seeking higher wages, the union is aware that if wages go too high, the company may lay off workers to reduce costs.
- *Working Conditions.* Safety, comfort, worker responsibilities, and many other workplace issues are negotiated and written into the final contract.
- *Job Security.* One of the union's primary goals is to secure its members' jobs, so the contract spells out the conditions under which a worker may be fired. If a union member is discharged for reasons that the

3 Sometimes one side will decide
it can't budge on one or more of its
goals. For example, a union might
believe that workers' pay is too low.
Management decides it will compromise on job security and working
conditions but will not yield on pay,
because profits are down.

4 If neither side concedes,
negotiations break off. This can
lead to one of several possible
scenarios:
1. Both sides can agree to enter
into mediation, where a neutral third
party can help them settle their
differences.
2. Workers can vote to go on strike.
3. Management can lock
out workers.

5 Labor and management
generally don't benefit from a
prolonged work stoppage. Both
sides often come back to the
collective bargaining process to
reach a new contract.

Check Your Understanding
1. Identify two actions that can lead to a
work stoppage.
2. Why do you think both labor and
management reach a point where they
are willing to compromise?

Conflict Arises

Deal or No Deal

union believes to be in violation of
the contract, the union might file
a grievance, or formal complaint.
The union contract specifies how
such grievances are handled. The
procedure usually involves hearings by
a committee of union and company
representatives.

Strikes

When a contract is about to expire, or when
the union is negotiating its first agreement
with a company, the negotiators can wind
up in tough late-night bargaining sessions.
Most of the time, the parties manage to
reach an agreement. But when a deadlock
occurs, tensions escalate.

The union may ask its members to vote
to approve a strike. A strike is the union's
ultimate weapon. A strike, particularly a
lengthy one, can cripple a company. Some

firms can continue to function by using
managers to perform key tasks. They
may hire workers who do not belong to
the union, called "strikebreakers." If a
company can withstand a strike, it is in
a good bargaining position. Most firms,
however, cannot produce goods and services without their union workers.

A long strike can also be devastating to
workers, since they do not get paid while
they are not working. Many unions do
make some payments to their members
during a strike, funded by the dues the
union has collected. These payments can
help workers, but they are generally much
smaller than what the members would
have earned while working.

It may seem as though workers strike
frequently since strikes are often front-page
news when they do occur. In fact, the
collective bargaining process usually goes

For many striking workers, the rat is a symbol used to protest unfair work conditions and publicize that a business is using nonunion labor. **Why might this symbol be seen as an example of the historical relationship between unions and management?** ▶

mediation a settlement technique in which a neutral person, the mediator, meets with each side to try to find a solution that both sides will accept

arbitration a settlement technique in which a neutral third party listens to both sides and then imposes a decision that is legally binding for both the company and the union

(FL) SS.912.E.1.9, SS.912.G.4.4, LA.1112.2.2.2, LA.1112.1.6.1, MA.912.A.2.1

smoothly, with few strikes. In 2004, there were only 22 major strikes across the entire nation, involving about 100,000 workers. This number represents only a small fraction of the nation's workforce, however.

Outside Help Reaching Settlements

If a strike continues for a long time, the two sides sometimes call in a third party to help settle the dispute. They might agree to **mediation,** a settlement technique in which a neutral person, the mediator, meets with each side to try to find a solution that both sides will accept. A mediator often can help each side understand the other's concerns, leading to an agreement.

However, the decision reached by the mediator is nonbinding—that is, neither side is required to accept it. If either side rejects the mediator's decision, the dispute could continue indefinitely. Sometimes, the talks will end up in **arbitration.** In this settlement technique, a neutral third party listens to both sides and then imposes a decision. Since the company's management and the union had agreed to enter the arbitration stage, the decision is legally binding for both sides. It can be a risky step because the decision might be seen as more favorable to one side than the other.

✔ **CHECKPOINT** *What issues are addressed in collective bargaining?*

Essential Questions Journal To continue to build a response to the Essential Question, go to your **Essential Questions Journal.**

SECTION 3 ASSESSMENT

❓ Guiding Question

1. Use your completed chart to answer this question: How do labor unions support the interests of workers?

2. **Extension** Name two benefits workers take for granted now that did not exist before labor organized.

Key Terms and Main Ideas

3. What is the purpose of a **strike?**

4. How do **right-to-work laws** diminish union power?

5. How do **blue-collar workers** and **white-collar workers** differ in the types of work they perform? Give examples of each.

6. What is **collective bargaining?** Who usually sets the agenda for it?

7. In working toward a strike settlement, the two sides seek **mediation** and sometimes **arbitration.** How do the two techniques differ?

Critical Thinking

8. **Compare** What is the difference between the need for labor unions now and in the 1800s?

9. **Decide** Some manufacturing companies have been moving their factories to countries where nonunion labor is cheap. They say they do this to reduce costs and compete with foreign companies. United States unions have opposed the cuts in U.S. jobs, insisting that companies must care for their workers. Which side would you support if you were **(a)** a union worker, **(b)** a consumer, **(c)** an investor in the company? Explain your reasoning for each response.

10. **Reflect** Today, some white-collar professionals such as teachers and doctors belong to labor unions. **(a)** Do you think this is a good idea? Why or why not? **(b)** If you were to become a white-collar professional, would you want the support of a union? Explain.

Math Skills

11. **Drawing a Line Graph** The table below details the number of members in the United Auto Workers Union (UAW) in different years. **(a)** Construct a line graph from the data. Then, compare the graph to **Figure 9.13** on page 239. **(b)** What conclusions about the U.S. labor movement can you make from this comparison?

Visit PearsonSchool.com/PHecon for additional math help.

United Auto Workers

Years	Members
1979	1,527,858
1983	1,100,000
1987	1,000,000
1991	810,000
1995	780,000
1999	760,000
2003	638,722
2007	464,910

SOURCE: Department of Labor, Office of Labor Management Standards, LM Filings and "UAW membership hits post-WWII low" by David Shepardson, *Detroit News,* March 28, 2008.

QUICK STUDY GUIDE

QUICK STUDY GUIDE

Chapter 9: Labor

Section 1 How do economic trends affect workers?

Section 2 Why do some people earn more than others?

Section 3 How do labor unions support the interests of workers?

Essential Question, Chapter 9
How can workers best meet the challenges of a changing economy?

Trends in U.S. Labor

Occupational

- Overall shift from manufacturing to service sector jobs
- More women in the workplace
- More reliance on part-time and temporary workers
- Unskilled workers face competition from foreign workers
- Increased demand for educated workforce

Wages and Benefits

- General decline in wage levels
- Rise in benefits
- Minorities earning lower pay
- Increased regulation of wages
- Increase in safety laws

Decline of Unions

- Taft-Hartley Act spurs decline of labor unions
- Loss of manufacturing jobs erodes membership
- Public sector unions on the rise
- Government provides traditional union services
- More white-collar workers

Economic Dictionary

labor force, *p. 217*
outsourcing, *p. 219*
offshoring, *p. 219*
learning effect, *p. 221*
screening effect, *p. 221*
contingent employment, *p. 221*
guest workers, *p. 222*
derived demand, *p. 226*
productivity of labor, *p. 226*
equilibrium wage, *p. 227*
unskilled labor, *p. 229*
semi-skilled labor, *p. 229*
skilled labor, *p. 229*
professional labor, *p. 229*
glass ceiling, *p. 231*
labor union, *p. 233*
featherbedding, *p. 233*
strike, *p. 237*
right-to-work law, *p. 238*
blue-collar worker, *p. 238*
white-collar worker, *p. 239*
collective bargaining, *p. 240*
mediation, *p. 242*
arbitration, *p. 242*

Economics on the go

Study anytime, anywhere. Download these files today.

Economic Dictionary online — Vocabulary Support in English and Spanish

Audio Review online — Audio Study Guide in English and Spanish

Action Graph online — Animated Charts and Graphs

Visual Glossary online — Animated feature

How the Economy Works online — Animated feature

Download to your computer or mobile device at PearsonSchool.com/PHecon

Key Terms and Main Ideas

To make sure you understand the key terms and main ideas of this chapter, review the Checkpoint and Section Assessment questions and look at the Quick Study Guide on the preceding page.

Critical Thinking

1. **Decide (a)** Why do companies engage in offshoring? **(b)** How has offshoring led to the loss of factory jobs and jobs for highly skilled workers? **(c)** Suppose you are a worker and your job has been cut due to offshoring. What options would you have?

2. **Generalize (a)** Identify the negative impact some analysts say foreign-born workers have on the domestic work-force. **(b)** Identify the positive impact foreign-born workers have on the domestic workforce as noted by other analysts. **(c)** Why do you think that the U.S. Congress struggles with immigration reform?

3. **Predicting Consequences (a)** What does it mean for employers to replace human capital with physical capital? **(b)** Give examples of this trend. **(c)** How might this trend affect the workforce in the future?

4. **Describe (a)** Under what circumstances might it be in the best interest of workers to seek arbitration in order to settle contract negotiations? **(b)** Under what circumstances might management prefer that a contract dispute be settled in arbitration? **(c)** Under what circumstances might arbitration be favorable to both labor and management?

5. **Interpret** Why do you think that white-collar workers generally do not belong to unions?

6. **Discuss (a)** What are three explanations for the decline in union membership? **(b)** Choose one of these and describe how workers are affected. **(c)** For the explanation you chose, explain why you agree or disagree that it is an important factor in union decline.

Applying Your Math Skills

Finding the Percentage

Look at the chart showing full-time wages for union and nonunion members.

Visit PearsonSchool.com/PHecon for additional math help.

Weekly Wage for Full-Time Workers 16 Years and Older, 2006

Occupations	Union	Nonunion
Management, Professional	966	968
Service	638	404
Sales and Office	706	578
Construction, Maintenance, Natural Resources	934	608
Production, Transportation	741	519

SOURCE: Bureau of Labor Statistics

7. For which occupation do nonunion members have higher weekly wages? What percentage of change in wages is there for nonunion workers?

8. Express as a percentage the increase in wages for the remaining union members over those of nonunion members.

9. Which industry shows the greatest increase in wages for union members?

10. Why do you think that is so?

Essential Question Activity

Essential Questions Journal To respond to the chapter Essential Question, go to your **Essential Questions Journal**.

11. People who have successful careers know that their success depends on being able to plan ahead. Preparation helps to overcome setbacks, such as a job layoff, or if new technology makes skills obsolete. It also helps to be ready in case you start a family and need to have a job that helps meet your financial needs. Complete the activity to answer the Essential Question **How can workers best meet the challenges of a changing economy?** Think about the kind of careers that interest you the most. Identify your interests and potential careers using the worksheet in the Essential Questions Journal or the electronic worksheet available at **PearsonSchool.com/PHecon.**

12. **Modify** Review your completed career worksheet. Then research trends in the U.S. and global economy that will have an impact on your future career.

The trends listed below are seen by many economists as posing some of the greatest challenges for workers in the future.
- Climate Change
- Global Trade
- Speed of Technological Change
- Rise of Megacities
- Shifts in World Populations
- Genetic Engineering

Explain how your career choices will prepare you to meet those challenges.

DOCUMENT-BASED ASSESSMENT

(FL) LA.1112.1.6.2, SS.912.E.2.4

Should public sector employees have the right to strike?

Public sector workers in many nations have the right to form unions, engage in collective bargaining, and go on strike. The story, however, is much different in the United States. State and federal laws often place restrictions on the ability of public employees to form unions, negotiate contracts, and walk off the job. Government officials cite the need to protect the public interest. In turn, supporters of public workers cite the need to receive fair wages and benefits, and establish safe working conditions, just like workers in the private sector.

Document A

In 1990 the Louisiana Supreme Court ruled that "public sector employees are covered by the state's 'Little Norris LaGuardia Act' which protects 'all employees in the exercise of their right to engage in concerted activities.' The court rejected the ... argument that public employee strikes are illegal under common law (since Louisiana is not a common law state) and found that the state constitution gives public employees 'the same right to engage in collective bargaining as held by their counterparts in the private sector. Except for police strikes which by their nature endanger the public, public employee strikes are legal as long as they don't pose danger to public health and safety.'"

From "Public Employment in a Time of Transition"
By John Lund & Cheryl L. Maranto

Document B

"New York City Mayor Michael Bloomberg lashed out at union leaders for 'thuggishly' turning their backs on the city, vowing there would be no further contract negotiations until the strike (by the Metropolitan Transit Workers) ends. 'You can't break the law and use that as a negotiating tactic,' he said at an afternoon news conference. "This is unconscionable, he added.... The strike brought to a grinding halt all Metropolitan Transportation Authority buses and subways throughout the city.... City officials have said a transit strike could cost the city $440 million to $660 million a day.... Bloomberg said the strike affects everything from the restaurant and hotel industries to working-class New Yorkers who could lose their jobs as a result of the strike.... 'The economic consequences of the strike range from severe to devastating, depending on the business,' he said."

From CNN.com, December 20, 2005

Document C

Number of States with Strike Policies

	Police & Firefighters	State workers	Education workers	Municipal workers
Allowed without restriction	2	3	3	3
Allowed with minor restrictions	1	8	9	9
Prohibited, no penalty specified	10	6	4	7
Prohibited, penalties specified	22	14	19	14
Total states with strike policy	35	31	35	33

SOURCE: "Public Employment in a Time of Transition" by John Lund & Cheryl L. Maranto

ANALYZING DOCUMENTS

Use your knowledge of labor unions and Documents A, B, and C to answer questions 1–3.

1. **According to Document A, why did the Louisiana Supreme Court support public workers' right to strike?**
   A. Public workers, like police officers, are not essential to public safety.
   B. Public workers are covered under the state's "Little Norris LaGuardia Act."
   C. Public workers cannot engage in collective bargaining.
   D. The state's common laws allow it.

2. **What is the main point of Document B?**
   A. The transit workers' strike is illegal because union leaders are thugs.
   B. Mayor Bloomberg isn't going to negotiate with union leaders even if many New Yorkers end up losing their jobs.
   C. Mayor Bloomberg will not negotiate with workers because their strike is illegal.
   D. Transit workers are not suffering like other New Yorkers.

3. **Document C shows that**
   A. Only a few states allow strikes by public workers.
   B. Thirty-five states allow education employees to strike.

   C. Fourteen states allow municipal workers to strike without penalty.
   D. Most states do not allow strikes without some restrictions.

WRITING ABOUT ECONOMICS

The right of public employees to strike is of serious concern because of the necessity of their work. Use the documents on this page and resources on the Web site below to answer the question: **Should public sector employees have the right to strike?** Use the sources to support your opinion.

In Partnership

THE WALL STREET JOURNAL.
CLASSROOM EDITION

To read more about issues
related to this topic, visit
PearsonSchool.com/PHecon

Essential Question, Unit 3

How can businesses and labor best achieve their goals?

VIDEO By Students For Students
For videos on Essential Questions, go to *PearsonSchool.com/PHecon*

There are differing views on how business and labor can achieve their goals. Look at the opinions below, keeping in mind the Essential Question: How can businesses and labor best achieve their goals?

> Slower labor force growth will encourage employers to [encourage] greater labor force participation among women, the elderly, and people with disabilities.... Rapid technological change and increased international competition spotlight the need for the workforce to be able to adapt to changing technologies and shifting product demand. Shifts in the nature of business organizations and the growing importance of knowledge-based work also favor strong non-routine [thinking] skills, such as abstract reasoning, problem-solving, communication, and collaboration.
>
> —Lynn Karoly and Constantijn Panis, Rand Corporation

> I think the low road is where somebody thinks of only their immediate self-interest in solving their particular problem no matter what it costs to somebody else. Which means you'll have an owner of a company that'll make money...by destroying the community. I think you can have a labor union that...has a problem of protecting wages, jobs of its own members even at the expense of a regional development strategy.
>
> —Dan Swinney, Center for Labor and Community Research, Interview, 2005

"Gentlemen, nothing stands in the way of a final accord except that management wants profit maximization and the union wants moola."

 Essential Question
Writing Activity

Consider the different views of economics expressed in the sources on this page and what you have learned about the needs of business and labor. *Then write a well-constructed essay expressing your view of how business and labor can meet their goals.*

Essential Questions Journal

To respond to the unit Essential Question, go to your **Essential Questions Journal**.

Writing Guidelines

- Address all aspects of the Essential Question Writing Activity.
- Support the theme with relevant facts, examples, and details.
- Use a logical and clear plan of organization.
- Introduce the theme by establishing a framework that is beyond a simple restatement of the question and conclude with a summation of the theme.

For help in writing a Persuasive Essay, refer to the *Writer's Handbook* in the Reference section, page S-5.

4 Money, Banking, and Finance

Essential Question, Unit 4

How can you make the most of your money?

Chapter 10
How well do financial institutions serve our needs?

Chapter 11
How do your saving and investment choices affect your future?

Chapter 10 Money and Banking

Essential Question, Chapter 10

How well do financial institutions serve our needs?

FL **Next Generation Sunshine State Standards**

Section 1: Money
LA.1112.1.6, SS.912.E.1.13, SS.912.E.2, SS.912.E.2.7

Section 2: The History of American Banking
MA.912.A.2.2, MA.912.F.3, SS.912.E.2, SS.912.E.2.3, SS.912.E.2.10, SS.912.E.3.6

Section 3: Banking Today
LA.1112.1.6, MA.912.A.2.2, MA.912.F.3, SS.912.E.1.13, SS.912.E.1.14, SS.912.E.2

Economics
on the go

To study anywhere, anytime, download these
online resources at *PearsonSchool.com/PHecon* ▶

FL NGSSS

LA.1112.1.6 Use multiple strategies to develop vocabulary.

SS.912.E.1.13 Explain the functions and characteristics of money.

SS.912.E.2 Understand the concepts relevant to the national economy.

SS.912.E.2.7 Identify the societal impact of inflation.

ECONOMIC DICTIONARY

As you read the section, look for the definitions of these **Key Terms:**

- money
- medium of exchange
- barter
- unit of account
- store of value
- currency
- commodity money
- representative money
- specie
- fiat money

Guiding Question

How does money serve the needs of our society?

Copy this concept web and fill it in as you read.

▶ Economics and You

It's been a hot day, and you have just arrived at your neighborhood store after playing basketball. You grab a soda and search the pockets of your jeans for some money. You find a pen, keys, and a chewing gum wrapper, but, unfortunately, no money. Then you reach into your jacket pocket. Finally!—a crumpled dollar bill. You hand the money to the clerk and take a long, cold drink.

Principles in Action Money, like the dollar you used to buy the soda, serves the needs of individuals and society in many ways. It provides a means for comparing values of goods and services, and it serves as a store of value. Without it, we can't get the things we need and want. That's not the whole story of money, as you will see. In fact, money has functions and characteristics that you might never have thought about.

The Three Uses of Money

If you were asked to define money, you would probably think of the coins and bills in your wallet. Economists define money in terms of its three uses. To an economist, **money** is anything that serves as a medium of exchange, a unit of account, and a store of value.

Money as a Medium of Exchange

A **medium of exchange** is anything that is used to determine value during the exchange of goods and services. Without money, people acquire goods and services through **barter,** or the direct exchange of one set of

money anything that serves as a medium of exchange, a unit of account, and a store of value

medium of exchange anything that is used to determine value during the exchange of goods and services

barter the direct exchange of one set of goods or services for another

Visual Glossary
online

Go to the Visual Glossary Online for an interactive review of **money.**

Action Graph
online

Go to Action Graph Online for animated versions of key charts and graphs.

How the Economy Works
online

Go to How the Economy Works Online for an interactive lesson on **what happens when you put money in the bank.**

VISUAL GLOSSARY

Reviewing Key Terms
To understand *money,* review these terms:

goods, *p. 3*
services, *p. 3*
scarcity, *p. 4*
capital, *p. 6*

What is Money?

◄ **money** anything that serves as a medium of exchange, a unit of account, and a store of value

THE THREE FUNCTIONS OF MONEY

Medium of Exchange	Unit of Account	Store of Value

Money serves as a medium of exchange, a unit of account, and a store of value. *How does each illustration represent functions of money?*

◄ Money is essential to easy exchanges of property. This coil of feathers was used by people on the Santa Cruz Islands in the Pacific Ocean as payment at marriage ceremonies. *How does it represent one of the three functions of money?*

Visual Glossary
online
To expand your understanding of this and other key economic terms, visit **PearsonSchool.com/PHecon**

goods or services for another. Barter is still used in many parts of the world, especially in traditional economies in Asia, Africa, and Latin America. It is also sometimes used informally in the United States. For example, a person might agree to mow a neighbor's lawn in exchange for vegetables from the neighbor's garden. In general, however, as an economy becomes more specialized, it becomes too difficult to establish the relative value of items to be bartered.

To appreciate how much easier money makes exchanges, suppose that money did not exist, and that you wanted to trade your portable DVD player for a spanking new mountain bike. You probably would have a great deal of trouble making the exchange. First, you would need to find a person who wanted to both sell the model of mountain bike you want and buy your particular DVD player. Second, this person would need to agree that your DVD player is worth the same as his or her bike. As you might guess, people in barter economies spend a great deal of time and effort exchanging the goods they have for the goods they need and want. That's why barter generally works well only in small, traditional economies. In those small economies, people can devote much of their time to exchanging goods.

Now consider how much easier your transaction would be if you used money as a medium of exchange. All you would have to do is find someone who is willing to pay you $100 for your DVD player. Then you could use that money to buy a mountain bike from someone else. The person selling you the bike could use the $100 however he or she wished. By the same token, the person who pays $100 for your DVD player could raise that money however he or she wished. Because money makes exchanges so much easier, people have been using it for thousands of years.

Money as a Unit of Account

In addition to serving as a medium of exchange, money serves as a **unit of account.** That is, money provides a means for comparing the values of goods and services. For example, suppose you see a jacket

on sale for $30. You know this is a good price because you have checked the price of the same or similar jackets in other stores. You can compare the cost of the jacket in this store with the cost in other stores because the price is expressed in the same way in every store in the United States—in terms of dollars and cents. Similarly, you would expect seeing a movie in a theater to cost about $8.00, a new DVD rental about $3.50, and so forth.

Other countries have their own forms of money that serve as units of account. The Japanese quote prices in terms of yen, the Russians in terms of rubles, Mexicans in terms of pesos, and so forth.

Money as a Store of Value

Money also serves as a **store of value.** This means that money keeps its value if you decide to hold on to—or store—it instead of spending it. For example, when you sell your DVD player to purchase a mountain bike, you may not have a chance to purchase a bike right away. In the meantime, you can keep the money in your wallet or in a bank. The money will still be valuable and will be recognized as a medium of exchange weeks or months from now when you go to buy the bike.

Money serves as a good store of value with one important exception. Sometimes economies experience a period of rapid inflation, or a general increase in prices. For example, suppose the United States experienced 10-percent inflation during a particular year. If you sold your DVD player at the beginning of that year for $100, the money you received would have 10 percent less value, or buying power, at the end of the year. Inflation would have caused the price of the mountain bike to increase by 10 percent during the year, to $110. The $100 you received at the beginning of the year would no longer be enough to buy the bike.

In short, when an economy experiences inflation, money does not function as well as a store of value. You will read more about the causes and effects of inflation in Chapter 13.

✔ **CHECKPOINT** *Under what circumstance does money not serve as a good store of value?*

Simulation *Activity*

Use of Money
You may be asked to take part in a role-playing game about alternatives to printed money.

unit of account a means for comparing the values of goods and services

store of value something that keeps its value if it is stored rather than spent

▲ Without the portability, divisibility, and uniformity of our currency, sharing a restaurant bill would be very complicated. *What other characteristics are essential to a sound currency?*

The Six Characteristics of Money

The coins and paper bills used as money are called **currency.** In the past, societies have also used an astoundingly wide range of other objects as currency. Cattle, salt, dried fish, furs, precious stones, gold, and silver have all served as currency at various times in various places. So have porpoise teeth, rice, wheat, seashells, tulip bulbs, and olive oil.

These items all worked well in the societies in which they were used. None of them, however, would function very well in our economy today. Each lacks at least one of the six characteristics that economists use to judge how well an item serves as currency. These six characteristics are durability, portability, divisibility, uniformity, limited supply, and acceptability.

Durability

Objects used as money must withstand the physical wear and tear that comes with being used over and over again. If money wears out or is easily destroyed, it cannot be trusted to serve as a store of value.

Unlike wheat or olive oil, coins last for many years. In fact, some collectors have ancient Roman coins that are more than 2,000 years old. Although our paper money may not seem very durable, its rag (cloth) content helps $1 bills typically last at least a year in circulation. When paper bills wear out, the United States government can easily replace them.

Portability

People need to be able to take money with them as they go about their daily business. They also must be able to transfer money easily from one person to another when they use money for purchases. Paper money and coins are very portable, or easy to carry, because they are small and light.

Divisibility

To be useful, money must be easily divided into smaller denominations, or units of value. When money is divisible, people can use only as much of it as necessary for any exchange. In the sixteenth and seventeenth centuries, people actually used parts of coins to pay exact amounts for their purchases. Spanish dollars, widely circulated in the American colonies, were often cut into as many as eight "bits," or pieces. For this reason these coins came to be called "pieces of eight."

Today, of course, if you use a $20 bill to pay for a $5 lunch, the cashier will not rip your bill into four pieces in order to make change. That's because American currency, like currencies around the world, consists of various denominations—$5 bills, $10 bills, and so on.

Uniformity

Any two units of money must be uniform— that is, the same—in terms of what they will buy. In other words, people must be able to count and measure money accurately.

Suppose everything were priced in terms of dried fish. One small dried fish might buy an apple. One large dried fish might buy a sandwich. This method of pricing is not a very accurate way of establishing the standard value of products, because the size of a dried fish can vary. Picture the arguments people would have when trying to agree whether a fish was small or large. A dollar bill, however, always buys $1 worth of goods.

currency coins and paper bills used as money

Limited Supply

Suppose a society uses certain pebbles as money. These rare pebbles have been found only on one beach. One day, however, someone finds an enormous supply of similar pebbles on a different beach. Now anyone can scoop up these pebbles by the handful. Since these pebbles are no longer in limited supply, they are no longer useful as currency.

In the United States, the Federal Reserve System controls the supply of money in circulation. By its actions, the Federal Reserve is able to keep just the right amount of money available. You'll read more about how the Federal Reserve monitors and adjusts the money supply in Chapter 16.

Acceptability

Finally, everyone in an economy must be able to take the objects that serve as money and exchange them for goods and services. When you go to the store, why does the person behind the counter accept your money in exchange for a carton of milk or a box of pencils? After all, money is just pieces of metal or paper. Your money is accepted because the owner of the store can spend it elsewhere to buy something he or she needs or wants.

In the United States, we expect that other people in the country will continue to accept paper money and coins in exchange for our purchases. If people suddenly lost confidence in our currency's value, they would no longer be willing to sell goods and services in return for dollars.

✔ **CHECKPOINT** *Why would gold cease to be a good form of currency if scientists could create gold out of sand?*

Sources of Money's Value

Think about the bills and coins in your pocket. They are durable and portable. They are also easily divisible, uniform, in limited supply, and accepted throughout the country. As convenient and practical as they may be, however, bills and coins have very little value in and of themselves. What, then, makes money valuable? The answer is that there are actually several possible sources of money's value, depending on whether it is commodity money, representative money, or fiat money.

Americans used both commodity and representative money during the colonial period. Representative money was used until 1913, when the first Federal Reserve notes were issued. *What are some advantages of fiat money over commodity and representative money?* ▼

Sources of Money's Value

◄ **Commodity money**
Objects like this wheat once served as commodity money.

▲ **Representative money**
Representative money like this silver certificate could be exchanged for silver.

◄ **Fiat money**
Today, Federal Reserve notes are fiat money, decreed by the federal government to be an acceptable way to pay debts.

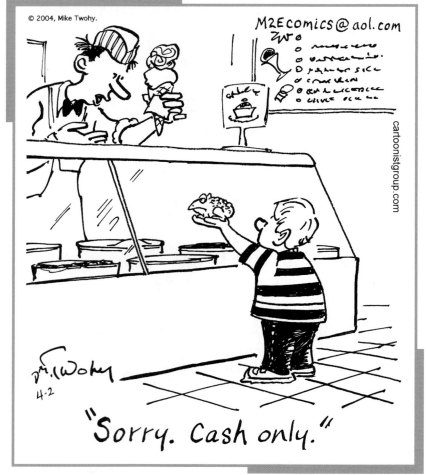

© 2004, Mike Twohy.

M2ECOMICS @ aol.com

"Sorry. Cash only."

▲ To be useful as commodity money, the commodity has to have some value. *Why are cattle more useful as commodity money than the frog?*

commodity money objects that have value in and of themselves and that are also used as money

representative money objects that have value because the holder can exchange them for something else of value

specie coined money, usually gold or silver, used to back paper money

Commodity Money

A commodity is an object. **Commodity money** consists of objects that have value in and of themselves and that are also used as money. For example, various societies have used salt, cattle, and precious stones as commodity money. The usefulness of objects is what gives them value. If not used as money, salt can preserve food and make it tastier. Cattle can be slaughtered for their meat, hides, and horns. Gems can be made into beautiful jewelry. Tobacco, corn, and cotton all served as commodity money in the American colonies.

As you can guess, commodity money tends to lack several of the characteristics that make objects good to use as money. Take cattle, for example. Cows and bulls are not all that portable, or even durable. A cow is not divisible, at least not if you want to keep it alive. That's why commodity money only works in simple economies. As the American colonies developed more complex economic systems, tobacco and

other objects were no longer universally accepted as money. The colonies needed a more convenient payment system. They turned to representative money to meet their needs.

Representative Money

Representative money makes use of objects that have value solely because the holder can exchange them for something else of value. For example, if your brother gives you an IOU for $20, the piece of paper itself is worth nothing. The promise that he will do all of your chores for a month may be worth quite a lot, however. The piece of paper simply represents his promise to you.

Early representative money took the form of paper receipts for gold and silver. Gold or silver money was heavy and thus inconvenient for customers and merchants to carry around. Each time someone made a transaction, the coins would have to be weighed and tested for purity. People therefore started to leave their gold in goldsmiths' safes. Customers would carry paper ownership receipts from the goldsmith to show how much gold they owned. After a while, merchants began to accept goldsmiths' receipts instead of the gold itself. In this way, the paper receipts became an early form of paper money.

Colonists in the Massachusetts Bay Colony first used representative money in the late 1600s when the colony's treasurer issued bills of credit to lenders to help finance King William's War. The bills of credit showed the exact amount that colonists had loaned to the Massachusetts government. Holders of these bills could redeem the paper for **specie,** or coins made of gold or silver.

Representative money was not without its problems. During the American Revolution, the Second Continental Congress issued representative money called Continentals to finance the war against England. Unfortunately, few people were able to redeem these early paper currencies for specie because the federal government had no power to collect taxes. Until the Constitution replaced the Articles of Confederation in 1789, the federal government depended on the states' voluntary contributions to fill the treasury. As a result, the federal treasury held very little gold or silver to back the Continentals. People even began to use the phrase "not worth a Continental" to refer to something of no value.

> **"** During the summer of 1780, this wretched "Continental" currency fell into contempt. As Washington said, it took a wagon-load of money to buy a wagon-load of provisions. At the end of the year 1778, the paper dollar was worth 16 cents in the northern states and twelve cents in the south. Early in 1789 its value had fallen to two cents and before the end of the year it took ten paper dollars to make a cent. A barber in Philadelphia papered his shop with bills. **"**
>
> —John Fiske, *The American Revolution*, 1896

Later, the United States government issued representative money in the form of silver and gold certificates. These certificates were "backed" by gold or silver. In other words, holders of such certificates could redeem them for gold or silver at a local bank. The United States government thus had to keep vast supplies of gold and silver on hand to be able to convert all paper dollars to gold if the demand arose. Some silver certificates circulated until 1968, but for the most part, the government stopped converting paper money into silver or gold in the 1930s.

Fiat Money

If you examine a dollar bill, you will see George Washington's picture on one side. To the left of the portrait are the words "This note is legal tender for all debts, public and private." In essence, these words mean that this Federal Reserve Note is valuable because our government says it is.

United States money today is fiat money. A fiat is an order or decree. **Fiat money,** also called "legal tender," has value because a government has decreed that it is an acceptable means to pay debts. Furthermore, citizens have confidence that the money will be accepted. It remains in limited supply, and therefore valuable, because the Federal Reserve controls its supply. This control of the money supply is essential for a fiat system to work. If the money supply grows too large, the currency may become worthless due to inflation.

fiat money objects that have value because a government has decreed that they are an acceptable means to pay debts

✔ **CHECKPOINT** *Why is commodity money impractical for use in our modern society?*

SS.912.E.1.13, SS.912.E.2, LA.1112.2.2.2, LA.1112.2.2.3, LA.1112.1.6.1

Essential Questions Journal To continue to build a response to the Essential Question, go to your **Essential Questions Journal.**

SECTION 1 ASSESSMENT

❓ Guiding Question

1. Use your completed concept web to answer this question: How does money serve the needs of our society?
2. **Extension** Money helps people and groups in a society meet their needs. Individuals, governments, and other groups use money to buy things they want and need. Describe a time when you used money to meet one of your needs.

Key Terms and Main Ideas

3. Identify the three uses of **money.**
4. Would a pair of sneakers be a good **store of value?** Explain why or why not.
5. Economists use six characteristics to judge how well an item serves as currency. List these six characteristics.

6. Describe how American dollars are divisible.
7. Salt has been used as money in some societies in the past. Is salt an example of **commodity money** or **representative money?** Explain.

Critical Thinking

8. **Contrast (a)** How does barter work? **(b)** How does this differ from the way money is used?
9. **Predict** What might happen if currency were not portable, or easy to carry?
10. **Summarize (a)** What was the problem with the Continentals issued during the American Revolution? **(b)** Describe a challenge facing governments that issue representative money in the form of silver and gold certificates.

Quick Write

11. Reread Sources of Money's Value in this section. Write a short essay answering the following questions: What are the advantages and disadvantages of each? Which kind of money do you think is the most practical? Consider how well each kind of money—commodity money, representative money, and fiat money—meets the six characteristics of currency.

CHAPTER 10 SECTION 1 **255**

NGSSS

MA.912.A.2.2 Interpret a graph to represent a real-world situation.

MA.912.F.3 Describe the advantages and disadvantages of short- and long-term purchases.

SS.912.E.2 Understand the concepts relevant to the national economy.

SS.912.E.2.3 Research the contributions of key individuals of various backgrounds in the development of the U.S.

SS.912.E.2.10 Describe the organization and functions of the Federal Reserve System.

SS.912.E.3.6 Draw conclusions about historical economic theories of economists.

ECONOMIC DICTIONARY

As you read the section, look for the definitions of these **Key Terms:**

- bank
- national bank
- bank run
- greenback
- gold standard
- central bank
- member bank
- foreclosure

Guiding Question

How has the American banking system changed to meet new challenges?

Copy this chart and fill it in as you read.

American Banking			
Pre-Civil War	**Later 1800s**	**Early 1900s**	**Modern Times**
•	•	•	•
•	•	•	•
•	•	•	•

bank an institution for receiving, keeping, and lending money

▶ **Economics and You** If you need a large sum of cash to make a purchase, do you get it from under your mattress, under a floorboard, or from a cookie jar? These options are unlikely in today's world. In the past, many Americans used to keep their savings hidden in similar places. However, times have changed. Today, almost all Americans prefer to entrust their savings to a **bank**—an institution for receiving, keeping, and lending money.

Principles in Action Over time, the American banking system has changed in order to meet new challenges. In earlier days, people distrusted banks because they sometimes distributed worthless money and caused financial panics. In this section, you will see how government regulations and the efforts of bankers such as the Innovator in this chapter, Amadeo Giannini, helped increase confidence in American banks. You will also see how American banking has developed over the years to meet the needs of a growing and changing population.

American Banking Before the Civil War

During the first part of our nation's history, local banks were informal businesses that merchants managed in addition to their regular trade. For example, a merchant who sold cloth, grain, or other goods might allow customers to deposit money. The merchant would then charge a small fee to keep the money safe. These informal banks were not completely safe, however. If a merchant went out of business or invested deposits in risky schemes, customers could lose all of their savings.

Two Views of Banking

After the American Revolution, the leaders of the new nation agreed on the need to establish a safe, stable banking system. Such a system was important for ensuring the economic growth of the new United States. The nation's leaders did not, however, agree on how that goal should be accomplished. The debate on banking between followers of Alexander Hamilton

▲ Alexander Hamilton, top, and Thomas Jefferson held very different views of how the new nation should satisfy its banking needs.

and followers of Thomas Jefferson was part of a larger political debate about the role of government in the young country.

As you may remember from your study of American history, the Federalists believed that the country needed a strong central government to establish order. The Antifederalists favored leaving most powers in the hands of the states. These two groups viewed the country's banking needs quite differently.

The Federalists, led by Alexander Hamilton, believed that a centralized banking system was a key to promoting industry and trade. After President Washington appointed Hamilton secretary of the treasury in 1789, Hamilton proposed a **national bank**—a bank chartered, or licensed, by the federal government. The bank would have the power to issue a national currency, manage the federal government's funds, and monitor other banks throughout the country.

The Antifederalists, led by Thomas Jefferson, opposed this plan. They feared that the wealthy would gain control of the bank and use its resources to increase their power. They supported a decentralized banking system. In this system, the states would establish and regulate all banks within their borders.

The First Bank of the United States

At first, the Federalists were successful in creating a strong central bank. In 1791, Congress set up the Bank of the United States, granting it a 20-year charter to operate. The United States Treasury used the Bank to hold the money that the government collected in taxes and to issue representative money in the form of bank notes, which were backed by gold and silver. The Bank also supervised state-chartered banks, making sure they held sufficient gold and silver to exchange for bank notes should the demand arise.

The Bank succeeded in bringing stability to American banking. However, opponents of the Bank charged that ordinary people who needed to borrow money to maintain or expand their farms and small businesses were being refused loans. In addition, the Antifederalists pointed out that the Constitution does not explicitly

GENERAL JACKSON SLAYING THE MANY HEADED MONSTER.

give Congress the power to create a national bank. Therefore, they argued, the Bank was unconstitutional. When Alexander Hamilton died in a famous duel with Vice President Aaron Burr in 1804, the Bank lost its main backer. The Bank functioned only until 1811, when its charter ran out.

Chaos in American Banking

Once the Bank's charter expired, state banks (banks chartered by state governments) began issuing bank notes that they could not back with specie—gold or silver coins. The states also chartered many banks without considering whether these banks would be stable and creditworthy.

Without any kind of regulation, financial confusion resulted. Prices rose rapidly. Neither merchants nor customers had confidence in the value of the paper money in circulation. Different banks issued different currencies, and bankers always faced the temptation to print more money than they had gold and silver to back.

The Second Bank of the United States

To eliminate this financial chaos, Congress chartered the Second Bank of the United States in 1816. Like the first Bank, the Second Bank was limited to a 20-year charter. The Second Bank slowly managed to rebuild the public's confidence in a national banking system.

▲ Andrew Jackson's opposition insured the downfall of the Second Bank of the United States, shown here as a many-headed monster. *Why did Jackson oppose the bank?*

national bank a bank chartered by the federal government

Figure 10.1

Developments in American Banking

The history of American banking shows a series of shifts between stability and instability.

1. What event reinforced the need for the creation of a central banking system in the United States?

2. What does the chart suggest about the role of government in banking during the twentieth century?

Date	Development
1780s	The Nation has no reliable medium of exchange. Federalists and Antifederalists disagree about a banking system.
1791	First Bank of the United States is established.
1811–1816	Period of instability follows expiration of First Bank's charter.
1816	Second Bank of the United States reestablishes stability.
1830s–1860s	President Jackson vetoes recharter of Second Bank in 1832, giving rise to the Free Banking Era.
1861–1863	Civil War makes clear the need for a better monetary and banking system.
1863–1864	National Banking Acts of 1863 and 1864 establish national banking system and uniform national currency.
1913	President Wilson signs the Federal Reserve Act.
1929	The Great Depression begins.
1933	President Roosevelt helps restore confidence in the nation's banks by establishing the FDIC.
1940s–1960s	Period of government regulation and long-term stability.
1980s	Period of deregulation; savings and loans face bankruptcies.
2000s	In 2007, a result of the subprime mortgage crisis is a sharp increase in the number of people who lose their homes because they can't pay their mortgage. This leads to the worst economic crisis since World War II.

Nicholas Biddle, who became president of the Second Bank in 1823, was responsible for restoring stability. If Biddle thought that a particular state bank was issuing bank notes without enough gold and silver reserves, he would surprise the bank with a great number of its notes all at once, asking for gold or silver in return. Some state banks, caught without the necessary reserves, went out of business. Others quickly learned to limit how many notes they issued.

Still, many Americans continued to be wary of the federal government's banking powers. They believed that the bank was a tool for the wealthy to further increase their wealth. Although the Supreme Court had ruled a national bank constitutional in 1819, President Andrew Jackson agreed with the bank's opponents. In 1832, Jackson vetoed its renewal.

The Free Banking Era

The fall of the Second Bank once again allowed state-chartered banks to flourish. For this reason, the period between 1837 and 1863 is known as the Free Banking, or "Wildcat," Era. Between 1830 and 1837 alone, the number of state-chartered banks nearly tripled. As you might expect, the sheer number of banks gave rise to a variety of problems.

1. *Bank runs and panics* State-chartered banks often did not keep enough gold and silver to back the paper money that they issued. This sometimes led to **bank runs**—widespread panics in which great numbers of people try to redeem their paper money at the same time. Many banks failed as a result, and public confidence plummeted.

2. *Wildcat banks* Some banks were located on the frontier. They were called wildcat banks because people joked that only wildcats lived in such remote places. Wildcat banks were inadequately financed and had a high rate of failure.

3. *Fraud* A few banks engaged in out-and-out fraud. They issued bank notes, collected gold and silver money from

bank run a widespread panic in which many people try to redeem their paper money at the same time people who bought the notes, and then disappeared. Customers who were left holding the notes lost their money.

4. *Many different currencies* State-chartered banks—as well as cities, private banks, railroads, stores, churches, and individuals—were allowed to issue currency. Notes of the same denomination often had different values, so that a dollar issued by the "City of Atlanta" was not necessarily worth the same as a dollar issued by the "City of New York." The profusion of currencies made it easier to create counterfeits, or worthless imitations of real notes.

CHECKPOINT *Why was a safe, stable banking system important to the young United States?*

Stability in the Later 1800s

By 1860, an estimated 8,000 different banks were circulating currency. To add to the confusion, the federal government played no role in providing paper currency or regulating reserves of gold or silver. The Civil War, which erupted in 1861, made existing problems worse.

Currency in the North and South

During the Civil War, both the Union and Confederacy needed to raise money to finance their military efforts. In 1861, the United States Treasury issued its first paper currency since the Continental. The official name of the currency was "demand notes," but people called them **greenbacks** because they were printed with green ink.

In the South, the Confederacy issued currency backed by cotton, hoping that a Confederate victory would ensure the currency's value. As the war weakened the Confederate economy, however, Confederate notes became worthless.

Unifying American Banks

With war raging, the federal government enacted reforms aimed at restoring confidence in paper currency. These reforms resulted in the National Banking Acts of 1863 and 1864. Together, these Acts gave the federal government the power to charter banks, the power to require that banks hold adequate gold and silver reserves to cover

their bank notes, and the power to issue a single national currency. The new national currency led to the elimination of the many different state currencies in use and helped stabilize the country's money supply.

The Gold Standard

Despite the reforms made during the Civil War, money and banking problems still plagued the country. In the 1870s, the nation adopted a **gold standard**—a monetary system in which paper money and coins had the value of certain amounts of gold. The gold standard set a definite value for the dollar, so that one ounce of gold equaled about $20. Since the value was set, people knew that they could redeem the full value of their paper money at any time.

Now, the government could issue currency only if it had enough gold in the treasury to back the notes. Because of the limited supply of gold, the government was prevented from printing an unlimited number of notes. The gold standard thus fulfilled an essential requirement of a banking system: a stable currency that inspires the confidence of the public.

CHECKPOINT *What powers did the National Banking Acts give to the federal government?*

Banking in the Early 1900s

Reforms such as creating a single national currency and adopting the gold standard helped stabilize American banking. They did not, however, provide for a central decision-making authority. Such an authority could help banks provide funds for growth and manage the money supply based on what the economy needed.

Continuing problems in the nation's banking system resulted in the Panic of 1907. Lacking adequate reserves, many banks had to stop exchanging gold for paper money. Several long-established New York banks failed, and many people lost their jobs because businesses could not borrow money to invest in future projects.

The Federal Reserve System

The Federal Reserve Act of 1913 established the Federal Reserve System. The Federal Reserve System, or Fed, served

greenback a paper currency issued during the Civil War

gold standard a monetary system in which paper money and coins had the value of certain amounts of gold

Amadeo P. Giannini

"Money itch is a bad thing. I never had that trouble."

Amadeo Giannini was determined to be a different kind of banker. Unlike other bankers of his time who catered to the rich, Giannini built his bank by providing services to everyday people.

Like many of his customers, Giannini was the son of Italian immigrants. At the age of 12, he went to work on the San Francisco docks. As a young man, he built a thriving business buying produce from local farmers. Although he had no previous training in banking, he opened a small bank in 1904. When a devastating earthquake hit the city in 1906, Giannini's bank was destroyed. However, he put a plank across two barrels in front of the ruined building and set up office. Here, he offered loans to people who had been devastated by the earthquake.

By the 1930s, he had merged with other banks and controlled the Bank of America, the world's largest commercial bank. Giannini provided banking services, such as home mortgages and small-business loans, to the average citizen. His generous lending helped local entrepreneurs, including those in the California wine and motion picture industries. He even loaned money to help the Walt Disney studio make *Snow White*, the first full length animated feature.

Giannini himself had little interest in personal wealth and he left a small estate at his death. He feared that great wealth would make him lose touch with the ordinary people he served.

Critical Thinking: *Why is a bank with a nationwide reach able to withstand regional economic downturns?*

Fast Facts

Amadeo P. Giannini
Born: May 6, 1870
Died: June 3, 1949
Education: No formal education beyond 8th grade
Claim to Fame: Founded the Bank of America, now the largest U.S.-owned bank

---

SS.912.E.2.10 Describe the organization and functions of the Federal Reserve System.

central bank a bank that can lend to other banks in time of need

member bank a bank that belongs to the Federal Reserve System

as the nation's first true **central bank,** or bank that can lend to other banks in time of need. It reorganized the federal banking system as follows:

- *Federal Reserve Banks* The system created as many as 12 regional Federal Reserve Banks throughout the country. All banks chartered by the national government were required to become members of the Fed. The Federal Reserve Banks are the central banks for their districts. **Member banks**—banks that belong to the Fed—store some of their cash reserves at the Federal Reserve Bank in their district.
- *Federal Reserve Board* All of the Federal Reserve Banks were supervised by a Federal Reserve Board appointed by the President of the United States.
- *Short-Term Loans* Each of the regional Federal Reserve Banks allowed member banks to borrow money to meet short-term demands. This helped prevent bank failures that occurred when large numbers of depositors withdrew funds during a panic.

- *Federal Reserve Notes* The system also created the national currency we use today in the United States—Federal Reserve notes. This allowed the Federal Reserve to increase or decrease the amount of money in circulation according to business needs.

You will read more about the role of the Federal Reserve and how the system works today in Chapter 16.

Banking and the Great Depression

The Fed helped restore confidence in the nation's banking system. It was unable, however, to prevent the terrifying Great Depression—the severe economic decline that began in 1929 and lasted more than a decade.

During the 1920s, banks loaned large sums of money to many high-risk businesses. Many of these businesses were unable to pay back their loans. Because of hard times on the nation's farms, many farmers also failed to repay bank loans. Then, the 1929 stock market crash led to widespread bank runs as depositors in all parts of the country rushed to withdraw their money. The combination of unpaid loans and bank runs resulted in the failure of thousands of banks across the country.

Banking Reforms

After becoming President in 1933, Franklin D. Roosevelt acted to restore public confidence in the nation's banking system. Only days after his inauguration, Roosevelt closed the nation's banks. This "bank holiday" was a desperate last resort to restore trust in the nation's financial system. Within a matter of days, sound banks began to reopen.

Later in 1933, Congress passed the act that established the Federal Deposit Insurance Corporation (FDIC). The FDIC insures customer deposits if a bank fails. By 2008, each depositor's basic accounts in one bank were insured up to $250,000.

In addition, federal legislation severely restricted individuals' ability to redeem dollars for gold. Eventually, currency became fiat money backed only by the government's decree that established its value. In this way, the Federal Reserve could maintain a money supply at adequate levels to support a growing economy.

✓ **CHECKPOINT** *How did the Federal Deposit Insurance Corporation (FDIC) help restore confidence in the banking industry?*

Two Crises for Banking

As a result of the many bank failures of the Great Depression, banks were closely regulated from 1933 through the 1960s. The government restricted the interest rates banks could pay depositors and the rates that banks could charge consumers for loans. By the 1970s, bankers were eager for relief from federal regulation.

The Savings and Loan Crisis

In the late 1970s and 1980s, Congress passed laws to deregulate, or remove some restrictions on, several industries. Unfortunately, this deregulation contributed to a crisis in a class of banks known as Savings and Loans (S&Ls). Government regulation had protected S&Ls from some of the stresses of the marketplace. Thus they were unpre-

pared for the intense competition they faced after deregulation.

There were other reasons for the crisis. During the 1970s, S&Ls had made long-term loans at low rates of interest. By the 1980s, interest rates had skyrocketed. This meant that S&Ls had to pay large amounts of interest to their depositors.

The S&L industry made many risky loans in the early 1980s. Losses on bad loans forced many banks out of business. A few S&L managers also used S&L funds for their own personal gain.

In 1989, Congress passed legislation that essentially abolished the independence of the savings and loan industry. This legislation expanded the insurance responsibilities of the FDIC.

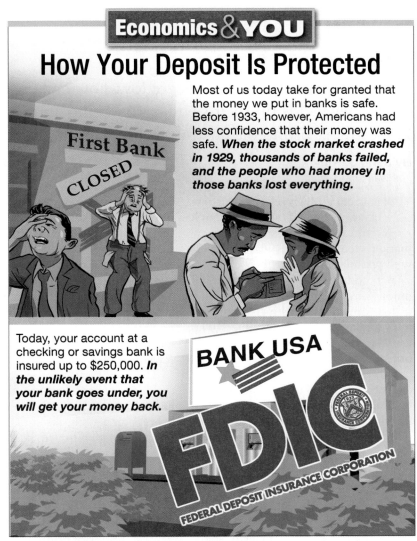

Economics & YOU

How Your Deposit Is Protected

Most of us today take for granted that the money we put in banks is safe. Before 1933, however, Americans had less confidence that their money was safe. *When the stock market crashed in 1929, thousands of banks failed, and the people who had money in those banks lost everything.*

First Bank
CLOSED

Today, your account at a checking or savings bank is insured up to $250,000. *In the unlikely event that your bank goes under, you will get your money back.*

BANK USA
FDIC
FEDERAL DEPOSIT INSURANCE CORPORATION

▲ The government has taken many steps to protect our savings and investments. *What other protections does the U.S. government provide?*

Interest Rates for 1 Month CDs

SOURCES: The Federal Reserve Statistical Release

Stirring Up Interest

BANKING SERVICES

At a time when interest rates are low, how can customers get higher yields on their savings? By being among the bank's most profitable customers.

By Jane J. Kim
The Wall Street Journal

 SS.912.E.1.14 Compare credit, savings, and investment services.

The Federal Reserve's interest-rate cuts are sending yields on bank certificates of deposit and money-market accounts lower, leaving savers with few places to park their cash.

But community banks and credit unions are pushing a new product called "reward checking accounts" with higher yields for customers who use their debit cards heavily and meet other requirements.

While some banks require customers to visit a branch to open an account or, in the case of credit unions, meet certain membership requirements, a handful of banks are offering the reward on checking accounts nationwide.

The accounts, which are insured by the Federal Deposit Insurance Corp. or its credit-union equivalent, come with a few strings. In order to earn the high yields, customers must get their bank statements delivered to them electronically, have at least one direct deposit or automatic debit in the account each month and use their debit cards at least 10 times a month. There are usually no monthly fees or minimum-balances requirements and many banks will also offer refunds of ATM fees charged by other banks.

The banks say they're able to pay the higher rates because they don't have to mail paper statements or process paper checks and also earn fees from debit-card transactions. BancVue, a company that provides reward checking accounts for roughly 400 banks and credit unions, says the accounts are on average twice as profitable to those financial institutions as a free checking account.

"It's sort of a game that banks are playing with their customers, but it's a pretty fair game overall," says Jim Bruene, publisher of Online Banking Report. "Most of what customers are being asked to do is relatively reasonable and can be good for tracking their finances."

So are these accounts right for you? If you're a frequent debit-card user, pay most of your bills online and rarely visit a bank branch, they are worth investigating.

There are catches. If you fail to meet one of the requirements, then you earn a paltry interest rate, typically less than 1%, on your entire balance (you'll get another chance to earn the higher yield the following month). Some banks also cap the amount of deposits that savers can earn the higher rates on, often at $25,000.

Applying Economic Principles
Low interest rates benefit people who want to borrow money. At the same time, they lower the return for bank depositors. Explain how depositors are getting higher yields on their savings.

Video News Update Online
Powered by
The Wall Street Journal
Classroom Edition
Use videos at **PearsonSchool.com/PHecon** as a springboard for a discussion on a current topic.

Financial "Meltdown" and Bailout

In late 2006, problems in the U.S. banking industry began to threaten the housing market. The episode quickly spiraled into a full-fledged crisis, the most serious threat to the U.S. economy since the Great Depression.

Beginning in the 1990s, U.S. banks decided to issue "subprime" loans to people seeking to purchase homes. The term "subprime" refers to loans that are made to borrowers with an unfavorable credit history. The higher interest rate banks charge because of the greater risk makes these loans more profitable.

Banks began to market these loans aggressively among people who did not qualify for standard loans. By 2005, subprime loans made up more than a quarter of all U.S. mortgages. Bankers also devised ways of packaging these mortgages in ways that they could be sold off to investors. The value of these bundled mortgages, of course, depended on the ability of individual homeowners to repay their loans.

The situation reached a crisis point when many homeowners had trouble repaying their loans. This led to a sharp rise in **foreclosures,** the seizure of property from borrowers who are unable to repay their loans. This hurt the lenders, as well as investors who had bought the mortgage bundles. A number of the nation's largest financial institutions that had invested heavily in subprime mortgages were forced into bankruptcy. The ripple effect was great, as hundreds of thousands of U.S. workers lost their jobs. Businesses and individuals found it difficult to get credit.

By late 2008, the U.S. economy was on the edge of a financial catastrophe. It was officially in a recession. Treasury Secretary Henry M. Paulson, President George Bush, and U.S. lawmakers organized a $700 billion bailout of banks, automakers, and Wall Street financial firms. The money was used to help them avoid bankruptcy and restart the flow of credit to businesses and individuals. In 2009 President Obama signed into law a $787 stimulus package, the largest in U.S. history. Approximately one-third of the package was devoted to tax cuts; the rest went to spending increases. These included infrastructure projects and support for state healthcare obligations. Despite this, recovery has been slow.

foreclosure the seizure of property from borrowers who are unable to repay their loans

☑ **CHECKPOINT** *How did the rash of subprime loans endanger the U.S. economy?*

FL SS.912.E.2, SS.912.E.2.10, SS.912.E.3.6, LA.1112.1.6.1, LA.1112.2.2.2

Essential Questions Journal To continue to build a response to the Essential Question, go to your **Essential Questions Journal**.

SECTION 2 ASSESSMENT

❓ Guiding Question

1. Use your completed chart to answer this question: How has the American banking system changed to meet new challenges?

2. **Extension** When would you feel safest keeping money in a bank: today, during the "Wildcat" Era, or during the early 1900s? Explain why.

Key Terms and Main Ideas

3. Identify the three functions of a **bank.**

4. List four banking problems that arose during the Free Banking, or "Wildcat," Era.

5. Under the **gold standard,** paper money and coins were equivalent to what?

6. As a **central bank,** what can the Federal Reserve System do for other banks?

7. Name one advantage of Federal Reserve notes, the national currency we use today.

Critical Thinking

8. **Contrast (a)** Explain the views of Alexander Hamilton and the Federalists about establishing a centralized banking system. **(b)** How did the Federalists' views differ from the views of Thomas Jefferson and the Antifederalists?

9. **Interpret (a)** When did the United States start issuing greenbacks? **(b)** What significant event happened at this time in history? **(c)** How are these two events related?

10. **Discuss** How did laws passed during the Great Depression change the type of money used in the United States?

Quick Write

11. Based on what you have read in this section about the history of the American banking system, write a short essay answering the following questions: What powers do you think the federal government should have to regulate banks? Why are these powers necessary?

NGSSS

LA.1112.1.6 Use multiple strategies to develop vocabulary.

MA.912.A.2.2 Interpret a graph to represent a real-world situation.

MA.912.F.3 Describe the advantages and disadvantages of short- and long-term purchases.

SS.912.E.1.13 Describe the composition of the money supply.

SS.912.E.1.14 Compare credit, savings, and investment services.

SS.912.E.2 Understand the concepts relevant to the national economy.

ECONOMIC DICTIONARY

As you read the section, look for the definitions of these **Key Terms:**

- money supply
- liquidity
- demand deposit
- money market mutual fund
- fractional reserve banking
- default
- mortgage
- credit card
- interest
- principal
- debit card
- creditor

Guiding Question

What banking services do financial institutions provide?

Copy this concept web and fill it in as you read.

Economics and You It's Friday. You just got your paycheck for the week. You take it to the bank, where you fill out a deposit slip and then stand in line and wait... and wait... and wait for the next available teller. Hold on a minute. That scenario is out-of-date! You don't have time for standing in line. You deposit your check quickly at an ATM. Or better yet, you have arranged to have your week's pay electronically deposited directly into your bank account.

Principles in Action Financial institutions provide these electronic services—and many others suited to the computer age. They issue credit cards, make loans to businesses, and provide mortgages to prospective home buyers. They also manage automated teller machines that enable a person to deposit or withdraw money in almost any place on the globe. In this section you'll learn more about electronic transactions, the fractional reserve system, and other aspects of banking today.

Measuring the Money Supply

You are familiar with paying for the items you need with currency—the bills and coins in your pocket. Currency is money. So are traveler's checks, checking account deposits, and a variety of other components. All of these components make up the United States **money supply**—all the money available in the United States economy. To more easily keep track of these different kinds of money, economists divide the money supply into several categories. The main categories are called M1 and M2.

M1

M1 represents money that people can gain access to easily and immediately to pay for goods and services. In other words, M1 consists of assets that have **liquidity,** or the ability to be used as, or directly converted into, cash.

As you can see from **Figure 10.2,** about 55 percent of M1 is made up of currency held by the public, that is, all currency held outside of bank vaults. Another large component of M1 is deposits in checking accounts. Funds in checking accounts are also called **demand deposits,** because checks can be paid "on demand," that is, at any time.

money supply all the money available in the United States economy

liquidity the ability to be used as, or directly converted into, cash

demand deposit money in a checking account that can be paid out "on demand," or at any time

Until the 1980s, checking accounts did not pay interest. When they began paying interest, the Fed introduced a new component to measure M1, called *other checkable deposits*, to describe those accounts. Today this category is not as meaningful as it once was, since many checking accounts pay interest if the balance is sufficiently high.

Traveler's checks make up a very small part of M1. Unlike personal checks, traveler's checks can be easily turned into cash.

M2

M2 consists of all the assets in M1 plus several additional assets. These additional M2 funds cannot be used as cash directly, but can be converted to cash fairly easily. M2 assets are also called *near money*.

For example, deposits in savings accounts are included in M2. They are not included in M1 because they cannot be used directly in financial exchanges. You cannot hand a sales clerk your savings account passbook to pay for a new backpack. You can, however, withdraw money from your savings account and then use that money to buy a backpack.

Deposits in **money market mutual funds** are also included as part of M2. These are funds that pool money from a large number of small savers to purchase short-term government and corporate securities. They earn interest and can be used to cover checks written over a certain minimum amount, such as $250. You will read more about money market mutual funds in Chapter 11.

☑ **CHECKPOINT** *Which category of the money supply includes deposits in money market mutual funds?*

Functions of Financial Institutions

Banks and other financial institutions are essential to managing the money supply. They also perform many functions and offer a wide range of services to consumers.

Storing Money

Banks provide a safe, convenient place for people to store money. Banks keep cash in fireproof vaults and are insured against the loss of money in the event of a robbery.

money market mutual fund a fund that pools money from small savers to purchase short-term government and corporate securities

 MA.912.A.2.2 Interpret a graph to represent a real-world situation.

FUTURE WATCH

Personal Finance
For more help in finding the right bank, see your Personal Finance Handbook in the back of the book or visit PearsonSchool.com/PHecon

---

Figure 10.2 **Major Components of the Money Supply**

M1 Components	Billions
Currency	$749.6
Demand deposits	$305.9
Other checkable deposits	$304.0
Traveler's checks	$6.7
Total M1	**$1,366.2**

M2 Components	Billions
Savings deposits	$2,902.1
Retail money market funds	$805.0
Small denomination time deposits	$398.7
Total M1	$1,366.2
Total M2	**$5,472.0**

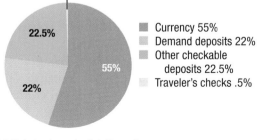

Currency 55%
Demand deposits 22%
Other checkable deposits 22.5%
Traveler's checks .5%

Savings deposits 53%
Retail money market funds 15%
Small denomination time deposits 7%
M1 25%

Individual categories may be affected by rounding.
SOURCE: Statistical Supplement to the *Federal Reserve Bulletin*, July 2007

GRAPH SKILLS
To keep track of the money supply in the United States, economists divide the money supply into two main categories, M1 and M2.

1. What is the largest component of M1? What is the largest component of M2?
2. What is the difference between M1 and M2?

Action Graph
online

For an animated version of this graph, visit PearsonSchool.com/PHecon

How does the **fractional reserve system** work?

In fractional reserve banking, banks keep a fraction of their funds on hand and lend the remainder to customers.

1 It's been a good week at Acme Products, so owner Don Hennessey is able to deposit **$10,000** in his account at the Friendly Bank.

2 Marco Gonzalez wants to buy a car. Friendly Bank can lend him 80 percent of the money Don deposited, or **$8,000.** The bank holds 20 percent, or **$2,000,** in reserve.

Original Deposit

Loans

As you read in Section 2, FDIC insurance protects people from losing their money if the bank is unable to repay funds.

Saving Money

Banks offer a variety of ways for people to save money. Four of the most common ways are savings accounts, checking accounts, money market accounts, and certificates of deposit (CDs).

Savings accounts and checking accounts are the most common types of bank accounts. They are especially useful for people who need to make frequent withdrawals. Savings accounts and most checking accounts pay interest at an annual rate.

Money market accounts and certificates of deposits (CDs) are special kinds of savings accounts that pay a higher rate of interest than savings and checking accounts. Money market accounts allow you to save and to write a limited number of checks. Interest rates are not fixed, but can move up or down. CDs, on the other hand, offer a guaranteed rate of interest. Funds placed in a CD, however, cannot be removed until the end of a certain time period, such as one or two years. Customers who remove their money before that time pay a penalty for early withdrawal.

Loans

Banks also perform the important service of providing loans. As you have read, the first banks started doing business when goldsmiths issued paper receipts. These receipts represented gold coins that the goldsmiths held in safe storage for their customers. They would charge a small fee for this service.

In early banks, those receipts were fully backed by gold—every customer who held

3 The car dealer who sold Marco the car puts the $8,000 in his bank account at the Even Friendlier Bank. The bank lends 80 percent, or **$6,400,** to Jack and Ginny Li, who are redecorating their living room. The bank holds the remaining **$1,600** in reserve.

5 From the original **$10,000,** three banks have lent out a total of **$19,520,** and placed **$4,880** in their reserves. The reserves protect the bank against demands for withdrawals.

4 The owner of the furniture store deposits the $6,400 in the Friendliest of All Bank. The bank then lends 80 percent of $6,400, or **$5,120,** to C.S. Perkins, to help him pay for college. The bank puts the remaining **$1,280** in reserve.

Check Your Understanding
1. By Step 3, how much of the original $10,000 is still being held in bank reserves?
2. What would happen if banks were required to keep all deposits in reserve?

Final Result

a receipt could be sure that the goldsmith kept the equivalent amount of gold in his safe. Gradually, however, goldsmiths realized that their customers seldom, if ever, asked for all of their gold on one day. Goldsmiths could thus lend out half or even three quarters of their gold at any one time and still have enough gold to handle customer demand. Why did goldsmiths want to lend gold? The answer is that they charged interest on their loans. By keeping just enough gold reserves to cover demand, goldsmiths could run a profitable business lending deposits to borrowers and earning interest.

A banking system that keeps only a fraction of its funds on hand and lends out the remainder is called **fractional reserve banking.** Like the early banks, today's banks also operate on this principle. They lend money to homeowners for home improvements, to families to pay for college tuition, and to businesses. The more money a bank lends out, and the higher the interest rate it charges borrowers, the more profit the bank is able to make.

By making loans, banks help new businesses get started, and they help established businesses grow. When a business gets a loan, that business can create new jobs by hiring new workers or investing in physical capital in order to increase production.

A business that gets a loan may also help other businesses grow. For example, suppose you and a friend want to start a window-washing business. Your business will need supplies like window cleaner and ladders, so the companies that make your supplies will also benefit. They may even hire workers to expand their businesses.

Bankers must, however, consider the security of the loans they make. Suppose

fractional reserve banking a banking system that keeps only a fraction of its funds on hand and lends out the remainder

Possible Careers
- Real estate agent
- **Real estate appraiser**
- Real estate manager
- Building inspector
- Surveyor
- Commercial industrial designer
- Grounds maintenance worker

Profile: Real Estate Appraiser

Duties:
- estimate the value of property for a variety of purposes, such as to assess property tax, to determine a sales price, or to determine the amount of a mortgage

Education:
- Must be licensed or certified, which requires advanced training and passing one or more examinations.

Skills:
- good analytical and mathematical skills
- ability to pay attention to detail and to work well with people or alone

Median Annual Salary:
- $46,130 (2007)

Future prospects:
- Employment of appraisers and assessors of real estate is expected to grow, depending on the market, faster than the average for all occupations.
- Employment of appraisers will grow with increases in the level of real estate activity.

Career Link *Activity*
Choose another career in real estate from the list of possible careers. Create a profile for that career similar to the one for Real Estate Appraiser.

---

default failing to pay back a loan

mortgage a specific type of loan that is used to buy real estate

credit card a card entitling its owner to buy goods and services based on the owner's promise to pay for those goods and services

interest the price paid for the use of borrowed money

principal the amount of money borrowed

Personal Finance
For more about simple and compound interest, see your Personal Finance Handbook in the back of the book or visit PearsonSchool.com/PHecon

borrowers **default,** or fail to pay back their loans. Then the bank may lose a large part, or even the entire amount, of the money it has loaned. Bankers therefore always face a trade-off between profits and safety. If they make too many bad loans—loans that are not repaid—they may go out of business altogether. (See your Personal Finance Handbook to learn more about banks and the services they offer.)

Mortgages

A **mortgage** is a specific type of loan that is used to buy real estate. Suppose the Lee family wants to buy a house for $250,000. They are unlikely to have the cash on hand to be able to pay for the house. Like almost all home buyers, they will need to take out a mortgage.

The Lees can afford to make a down payment of 20 percent of the price of the house, or $50,000. After investigating the Lees' creditworthiness, their bank agrees to lend them the remaining $200,000 so that they can purchase their new house. Mortgages usually last for 15, 25, or 30 years. According to the terms of their loan, the Lees are responsible for paying back the loan, plus whatever interest the bank charges, in regular monthly payments over a period of 25 years.

Credit Cards

Another service that banks provide is issuing **credit cards**—cards entitling their owners to buy goods and services based on the owners' promise to pay. How do credit cards work? Suppose you buy a sleeping bag and tent for $100 on May 3. Your credit-card bill may not arrive until June. You do not actually pay for the gear until you pay that bill. In the meantime, however, the credit-card issuer (often a bank) will have paid the sporting-goods store. Your payment repays the bank for the "loan" of $100. If you do not pay your credit-card bill in full when you receive it, you will end up paying a high rate of interest on that loan.

Simple and Compound Interest

As you have read, **interest** is the price paid for the use of borrowed money. The amount borrowed is called the **principal.** Simple interest is interest paid only on principal. For example, if you deposit

$100 in a savings account at 5 percent simple interest, you will make $5 in a year (assuming that interest is paid annually).

Suppose that you leave the $5 in interest in the bank, so that at the end of the year you have $105 in your account—$100 in principal and $5 in interest. Compound interest is interest paid on both principal and accumulated interest. That means that in the second year, as long as you leave both the principal and the interest in your account, interest will be paid on $105. In **Figure 10.3** you can see how an account paying compound interest grows over time.

Banks and Profit

The largest source of income for banks is the interest they receive from customers who have taken loans. Banks, of course, also pay out interest on customers' savings and most checking accounts. The amount of interest they pay out, however, is less than the amount of interest they charge on loans. The difference in the amounts is how banks cover their costs and make a profit.

✔ **CHECKPOINT** *Why are checking accounts more useful than CDs for people who must make frequent withdrawals?*

Types of Financial Institutions

Several kinds of financial institutions operate in the United States. These include commercial banks, savings and loan associations, mutual savings banks, and credit unions. During the 1990s, these financial institutions became more similar than dissimilar, although differences still remain.

Commercial Banks

Commercial banks, which traditionally served businesses, offer a wide range of services today. Commercial banks offer checking accounts, accept deposits, and make loans to businesses and to individuals. Some commercial banks are chartered by states and are regulated by state authorities and by the Federal Deposit Insurance Corporation (FDIC). About one third of all commercial banks are national banks and are part of the Federal Reserve System. Commercial banks provide the most services and play the largest role in the economy of any type of bank.

| Figure 10.3 | **Compound Interest** |

End of Year	Principal Amount	Interest Earned at 5%	Principal at End of Year
—	$100.00	$5.00	$105.00
1	$105.00	$5.25	$110.25
2	$110.25	$5.51	$115.76
5	$127.63	$6.38	$134.01
10	$162.90	$8.14	$171.04
15	$207.90	$10.39	$218.29

CHART SKILLS
The chart at left shows the money earned on a $100 deposit when interest is compounded yearly at 5 percent.

1. How many years does it take for the original deposit to double?
2. After five years, what is the total interest that the deposit-holder will have earned?

Figure 10.4 **How Banks Make a Profit**

CHART SKILLS

A bank uses the money customers have deposited to lend to businesses and other borrowers. The bank uses this income to cover its costs and make a profit.

1. What are the sources of a bank's income?

2. Why is the interest banks pay to depositors at a lower rate than the interest banks charge to lenders?

Money Enters Bank

- Deposits from customers
- Interest from borrowers
- Fees for services

BANK

Bank retains required reserves

Money Leaves Bank

- Interest and withdrawals to customers
- Loans to borrowers:
  - business loans
  - home mortgages
  - personal loans
- Bank's cost of doing business:
  - salaries
  - taxes
  - other costs

Savings and Loan Associations

Savings and Loan Associations (S&Ls), which you read about in Section 2, were originally chartered to lend money for building homes during the mid-1800s. Members of S&Ls deposited funds into a large general fund and then borrowed enough money to build their own houses. Savings and Loans are also called thrifts because they originally enabled "thrifty" working-class people—that is, people who were careful with their money—to save up and borrow enough to build or buy their own homes. Over time, S&Ls have taken on many of the same functions as commercial banks.

Savings Banks

Mutual savings banks (MSBs) originated in the early 1800s to serve people who made smaller deposits and transactions than commercial banks wished to handle. Mutual savings banks were owned by the depositors themselves, who shared in any profits. Later, many MSBs began to sell stock to raise additional capital. These institutions became simply savings banks because depositors no longer owned them.

Although savings banks were traditionally concentrated in the Northeast, they had an important influence on the national economy. In 1972, the Consumer's Savings Bank of Worcester, Massachusetts, introduced a Negotiable Order of Withdrawal (NOW) account, a type of checking account that pays interest. NOW accounts became available nationwide in 1980.

Credit Unions

Credit unions are cooperative lending associations usually established by and for particular groups, usually employees of a specific firm or government agency. Some are open to an entire community. Credit unions are commonly fairly small and specialize in consumer loans, usually at interest rates favorable to members. Some credit unions also provide checking account services.

Finance Companies

Finance companies make installment loans to consumers. These loans spread the cost of major purchases such as computers, cars, and large appliances over a number of months. Because people who borrow from finance companies more frequently fail to repay the loans, finance companies generally charge higher interest rates than banks do.

✔ **CHECKPOINT** *Which type of financial institution plays the largest role in the economy?*

Electronic Banking

Banks began to use computers in the early 1970s to keep track of transactions. As computers have become more common in the United States, their role in banking has also increased dramatically. In fact, computerized banking may revolutionize banking in much the same way that paper currency changed banking long ago.

Automated Teller Machines

If you use an Automated Teller Machine (ATM), you are already familiar with one of the most common types of electronic banking. ATMs are computers that customers can use to deposit money, withdraw cash, and obtain account information at their convenience. Instead of having to conduct banking business face-to-face with a teller during the bank's hours of operation, you can take care of your finances at an ATM.

ATMs are convenient for both banks and for customers, since they are available 24 hours a day and reduce banks' labor costs. Their popularity has made them a standard feature of modern banking.

Debit Cards

At an ATM, bank customers can use a **debit card** to withdraw money from an account. They can also use a debit card in stores equipped with special machines. When you "swipe" your debit card through one of those machines, the card sends a message to your bank to debit, or subtract money from, your checking account. The money goes directly into the store's bank account. For security, debit cards require

customers to use personal identification numbers, or PINs, to authorize financial transactions.

Home Banking

More and more people are using the Internet to conduct their financial business. Many banks, credit unions, and other financial institutions allow people to check account balances, transfer money to different accounts, automatically deposit their paychecks, and pay their bills via computer. Many Americans have also opened accounts with private online bill-paying services and money-transfer services that allow them to send money instantly over the Internet.

debit card a card used to withdraw money from a bank account

 MA.912.A.2.2 Interpret a graph to represent a real-world situation.

FUTURE WATCH

Personal Finance
For more help in beginning online banking, see your Personal Finance Handbook in the back of the book or visit **PearsonSchool.com/PHecon**

 Global Impact

Easy Access
The first electronic Automated Teller Machine network was unveiled in Dallas, Texas, in 1968. Today, there are more than 1.5 million ATMs throughout the world, in banks, stores, shopping centers, cruise ships, even on ships in the U.S. Navy. Every eight minutes a new ATM is installed somewhere in the world. ***Review the chart tracking the number of ATMs per 100,000 people in a number of countries. Do you think the wide gap in ATM access among nations will lessen over time? Why or Why not?***

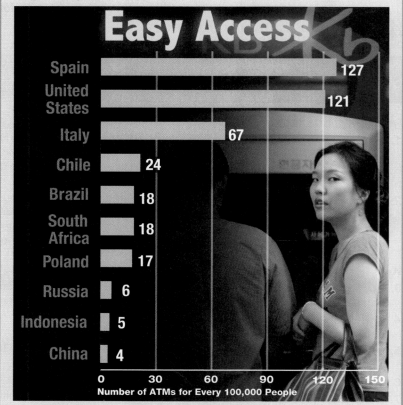

Easy Access

Country	Number of ATMs for Every 100,000 People
Spain	127
United States	121
Italy	67
Chile	24
Brazil	18
South Africa	18
Poland	17
Russia	6
Indonesia	5
China	4

SOURCE: Financial Sector Development Indicators, The World Bank

▲ Phone cards, gift cards, and mass transit cards are among the many useful types of stored-value, or smart, cards.

creditor a person or institution to whom money is owed

 FL SS.912.E.1.13, SS.912.E.1.14, SS.912.E.2.2, MA.912.F.3, MA.912.F.3.3

Automated Clearing Houses

Automated Clearing Houses (ACHs), located at Federal Reserve Banks and their branches, allow consumers to pay bills without writing checks. An ACH transfers funds automatically from customers' accounts to creditors' accounts. (A **creditor** is a person or institution to whom money is owed.) People can use ACHs to pay regular monthly bills such as mortgage payments, rent, utility bills, and insurance premiums. They save time and postage costs, and end any worries about forgetting to make a payment.

Stored-Value Cards

Stored-value cards, or smart cards, are similar to debit cards. These cards carry embedded magnetic strips or computer chips with account balance information. College students may be issued a smart card to pay for cafeteria food, computer time, or photocopying. Phone cards, with which customers prepay for a specified amount of long-distance calling, are also smart cards, as are gift cards. Some people even use a special kind of smart card in place of a bank account. They can make deposits, withdraw cash, or pay bills with the card.

Will stored-value smart cards someday replace cash altogether? No one can know for sure, but private companies and public facilities continue to explore new uses for smart card technology.

☑ **CHECKPOINT** *How does a debit card work?*

SECTION 3 ASSESSMENT

Essential Questions Journal	To continue to build a response to the Essential Question, go to your **Essential Questions Journal**.

❓ Guiding Question

1. Use your completed concept web to answer this question: What banking services do financial institutions provide?

2. **Extension** If you were opening a checking account at a local bank, what services would you expect your bank to provide?

Key Terms and Main Ideas

3. How does **fractional reserve banking** help banks earn a profit?

4. What happens when borrowers **default** on their loans?

5. Describe a situation in which a person would need a **mortgage** from a bank.

6. When would you pay **interest**?

7. List at least three services that are available through home banking over the Internet.

Critical Thinking

8. **Summarize (a)** What kinds of money are included in M1 and M2? **(b)** Why do economists use these different categories?

9. **Extend** If you are planning to leave money in a savings account for 10 years, would it be better to receive simple interest or compound interest? Explain.

10. **Contrast (a)** In what ways are debit cards and stored-value cards similar? **(b)** How are they different?

Math Skills

11. There is a simple formula for finding simple interest:

$$I = prt.$$

To find the interest (*I*), multiply your principal (*p*) times the interest rate (*r*) times the length of time (*t*). The interest rate must be expressed in the form of a decimal. For example, 1% interest would equal 0.01, and 10% interest would equal 0.10. The time is the number of years your deposit draws interest. Use this formula to answer the following questions:

(a) Suppose your bank pays an interest rate of 6% per year. What is the interest rate in decimal form? **(b)** Suppose you keep $500 in the bank for ten years, receiving 6% simple interest. Write the numbers into the formula to calculate simple interest. **(c)** How much interest will you receive at the end of the ten years?

Visit PearsonSchool.com/PHecon for additional math help.

Chapter 10: Money and Banking

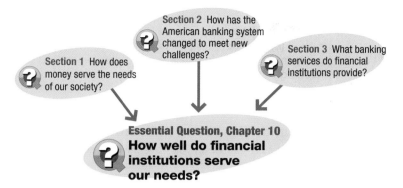

Section 2 How has the American banking system changed to meet new challenges?

Section 1 How does money serve the needs of our society?

Section 3 What banking services do financial institutions provide?

Essential Question, Chapter 10
How well do financial institutions serve our needs?

Developments in U.S. Banking

Problem	Problem Resolved by	Date
Many different currencies in the U.S.	National Banking Acts	1863, 1864
Gold did not support U.S. currency	U.S. adopts gold standard	1870s
No central decision-making authority to regulate banks	Federal Reserve System	1913
No central bank to monitor reserves	Federal Reserve System	1913
No insurance on savings deposits	FDIC	1933
No convenient way of getting bank credit for small purchases	First bank-issued credit card	1946
Difficult for people to get consumer credit	Development of credit unions	1909
Making deposits and withdrawals outside business hours	Automated teller machines	1968

Economic Dictionary

money, *p. 249*

medium of exchange, *p. 249*

barter, *p. 249*

unit of account, *p. 251*

store of value, *p. 251*

currency, *p. 252*

commodity money, *p. 254*

representative money, *p. 254*

specie, *p. 254*

fiat money, *p. 255*

bank, *p. 256*

national bank, *p. 257*

bank run, *p. 258*

greenback, *p. 259*

gold standard, *p. 259*

central bank, *p. 260*

member bank, *p. 260*

foreclosure, *p. 263*

money supply, *p. 264*

liquidity, *p. 264*

demand deposit, *p. 264*

money market mutual fund, *p. 265*

fractional reserve banking, *p. 267*

default, *p. 268*

mortgage, *p. 268*

credit card, *p. 268*

interest, *p. 268*

principal, *p. 268*

debit card, *p. 271*

creditor, *p. 272*

Economics on the go

Study anytime, anywhere. Download these files today.

Economic Dictionary online	**Audio Review** online	**Action Graph** online	**Visual Glossary** online	**How the Economy Works** online
Vocabulary Support in English and Spanish	Audio Study Guide in English and Spanish	Animated Charts and Graphs	Animated feature	Animated feature

Download to your computer or mobile device at PearsonSchool.com/PHecon

CHAPTER 10 ASSESSMENT

Key Terms and Main Ideas

To make sure you understand the key terms and main ideas of this chapter, review the Checkpoint and Section Assessment questions and look at the Quick Study Guide on the preceding page.

Critical Thinking

1. **Predict** Why is money acceptable to people in the United States? If American merchants stopped accepting dollars, predict how people might get the goods and services they needed.

2. **Evaluate (a)** Identify the powers the National Banking Acts of 1863 and 1864 gave to the federal government. **(b)** How did each of these powers help stabilize the American banking system? **(c)** Which of these reforms do you think contributed most to the stability of American money and banks? Why?

3. **Extend (a)** In what ways did the government regulate banks from the 1930s until the 1960s? **(b)** What factors contributed to the S&L crisis in the 1980s? **(c)** What regulations could help prevent another S&L crisis in the future?

4. **Select** Suppose you have $2,000 that you want to save in the bank for at least two years. **(a)** List four types of accounts where you could keep your money. **(b)** If interest rates were very high, which account would be best? Explain your choice.

5. **Summarize (a)** What are some reasons individuals need loans? **(b)** How do businesses benefit from being able to get loans? **(c)** How do banks profit from meeting these needs of individuals and businesses?

Applying Your Math Skills

Simple and Compound Interest

Interest works for you when you have savings and against you when you have debt. The formula for simple interest is principle × rate × time. To find a final balance with simple interest, add the interest and the principal. The formula will look like this:

$$B = prt + p$$

The formula to find a final balance using compound interest uses the same original values as the formula for simple interest: principal, interest rate expressed as a decimal, and time. Here is the formula for finding a balance using compound interest:

$$B = p(1 + r)^t$$

Visit PearsonSchool.com/PHecon for additional math help.

6. If you carried over a credit card balance of $400 on a credit card that charges 2% per month (24% per year), what would your balance be after one month?

7. If you missed the payment and incurred a $35 late fee, what would your balance be the second month if you made no additional charges?

8. If you made a $50 payment, what would your balance be the third month?

 Essential Question Activity

Essential Questions Journal — To respond to the chapter Essential Question, go to your **Essential Questions Journal**.

9. Complete this activity to answer the Essential Question **How well do financial institutions serve our needs?** Imagine that after many years of service, you become the manager of the bank that serves the neighborhood in which you grew up. Your responsibility to the bank is to increase its profits. However, you also want to do good works in your community. Using the worksheet in your Essential Questions Journal or the electronic worksheet available at **PearsonSchool.com/PHecon,** gather the following information:
   (a) In the first column, write the services you will offer your customers.
   (b) In the second column, write how these services will benefit your neighborhood. For example, how might giving people mortgages be good for the neighborhood?

Think about which services and benefits are most likely to attract customers to your bank. Based on your ideas, write one or more advertising slogans for your bank in the third column.

10. **Modify** Now suppose another bank opens down the block from your bank. Choose two of the following situations. Describe how each of them might cause you to modify the services you offer and how you choose to advertise.
   (a) The new bank offers free debit cards and electronic banking through the Internet.
   (b) The new bank offers low-interest mortgages—but only to borrowers who have an excellent history of paying back loans.
   (c) The new bank offers low interest mortgages to poor people who want to live in their own house but who may not be able to pay back their debt.

DOCUMENT-BASED ASSESSMENT

FL LA.1112.1.6.2, MA.912.A.2.2

Is the move toward a "cashless" economy good or bad?

In the United States, people are replacing cash and paper checks with credit cards, debit cards, and electronic banking in many situations. Some people argue that this development has negative consequences for individuals and the economy. Others believe that going "cashless" can benefit the economy.

Document A

Non-cash Payments, 2003

- Other electronic payments 12%
- Debit card 20%
- Credit card 23%
- Check 45%

Document B

"The less cash that flows through our hands, the more intangible it becomes and the more we lose our sense of its real value.... Technology is simply making it easy not to count every dollar....

"Before you apply for a new "smart card," consider the tradeoff for convenience. The next time you're making a major purchase, say for a new washing machine, go to the bank, take out $450 and count out that fistful of bills for the sales clerk. You'll have a fuller appreciation of the cost, the satisfaction of exchanging tangible earnings for your betterment — and a sense of just what we're losing."

—From "Cash: An Endangered Species," by Chris Plummer, CBS Marketwatch, June 8, 2004

Document C

"Debit cards are often more convenient for consumers than paper checks.... Banks offer debit cards both because consumers have come to expect them, and because debit card transactions can be less costly for banks to process than cash or check transactions. Finally, ... merchants find debit cards attractive because it is often faster and less costly to accept payments by debit card than by cash or check. Card payments have become increasingly important in situations where transaction speed is a priority for merchants, such as in check-out lines and at fast food restaurants."

—From "A Summary of the Atlanta Forum on Transforming U.S. Retail Payments," The Federal Reserve Board, February 6, 2007

ANALYZING DOCUMENTS

Use your knowledge of the "cashless" economy and Documents A, B, and C to answer questions 1–3.

1. **Document A shows that, of payments that were not made in cash, the largest number were made by**
   A. checks.
   B. credit cards.
   C. debit and credit cards combined.
   D. debit cards and other electronic payments.

2. **According to Document B, what is the problem with having fewer cash transactions?**
   A. Electronic transactions have serious security risks.
   B. People who do not use cash have a harder time keeping track of their money.
   C. There is no problem with having fewer cash transactions.
   D. People who use electronic transactions are often charged additional fees.

3. **The authors of Document B and Document C would probably agree that debit cards**
   A. are convenient for consumers.
   B. should be used in more places.
   C. benefit banks more than consumers.
   D. help consumers borrow money easily.

WRITING ABOUT ECONOMICS

Whether increasing electronic payments will help or harm the U.S. economy is an ongoing issue. Use the documents on this page and resources on the Web site below to answer the question: *Is the move toward a "cashless" economy good or bad?* Use the sources to support your opinion.

In Partnership

THE WALL STREET JOURNAL.
CLASSROOM EDITION

To read more about issues related to this topic, visit
PearsonSchool.com/PHecon

Chapter

11 Financial Markets

Essential Question, Chapter 11

?

How do your saving and investment choices affect your future?

FL **Next Generation Sunshine State Standards**

Section 1: Saving and Investing
LA.1112.1.6, LA.1112.6.2, SS.912.E.1.14, SS.912.E.1.15, SS.912.E.2.5

Section 2: Bonds and Other Financial Assets
LA.1112.1.6, MA.912.A.2.2, SS.912.E.1.14, SS.912.E.1.15

Section 3: The Stock Market
LA.1112.1.6, SS.912.E.1.14, SS.912.E.1.15, SS.912.E.2.3

Economics
on the go

To study anywhere, anytime, download these
online resources at *PearsonSchool.com/PHecon* ▶

NGSSS

LA.1112.1.6 Use multiple strategies to develop vocabulary.

LA.1112.6.2 Use a systematic process to collect, process, present information.

SS.912.E.1.14 Compare credit, savings, and investment services.

SS.912.E.1.15 Describe the risk and return profiles of various investment options.

SS.912.E.2.5 Analyze how capital investments impact productivity and economic growth.

ECONOMIC DICTIONARY

As you read the section, look for the definitions of these **Key Terms:**

- investment
- financial system
- financial asset
- financial intermediary
- mutual fund
- hedge fund
- diversification
- portfolio
- prospectus
- return

Guiding Question

What are the benefits and risks of saving and investing?

Copy this concept web and fill it in as you read.

Economics and You

Right now, you are making a huge investment. You are investing your time and energy in your education. This investment is likely to pay off later, in the form of a satisfying career. In the same way, businesses and governments look to the future. If a firm builds a new plant, it invests money today for the sake of earning more money later. If the government builds a new dam, it invests money today to ensure that people will have hydroelectric power in the future.

Principles in Action There are both benefits and risks to savings and investment. The savings you put in the bank will grow with almost no risk to the principle. However, as this section points out, a properly timed investment can bring a much greater reward than the same money put away in savings. On the other hand, if your investment is wrongly placed or ill-timed, you may wish you had never taken the money out of the bank.

Investing and Free Enterprise

In its most general sense, **investment** is the act of redirecting resources from being consumed today so that they may create benefits in the future. In more narrow, economic terms, investment is the use of assets to earn income or profit.

Investing, in fact, is an essential part of the free enterprise system. It promotes economic growth and contributes to a nation's wealth. When people deposit money in a savings account in a bank, for example, the bank may then lend the funds to businesses. The businesses, in turn,

FUTURE WATCH

Personal Finance
For more help in making wise investment decisions, see your Personal Finance Handbook in the back of the book or visit **PearsonSchool.com/PHecon**

investment the act of redirecting resources from being consumed today so that they may create benefits in the future; the use of assets to earn income or profit

Visual Glossary online

Go to the Visual Glossary Online for an interactive review of **capital gains.**

Action Graph online

Go to Action Graph Online for animated versions of key charts and graphs.

How the Economy Works online

Go to How the Economy Works Online for an interactive lesson on **the bond market.**

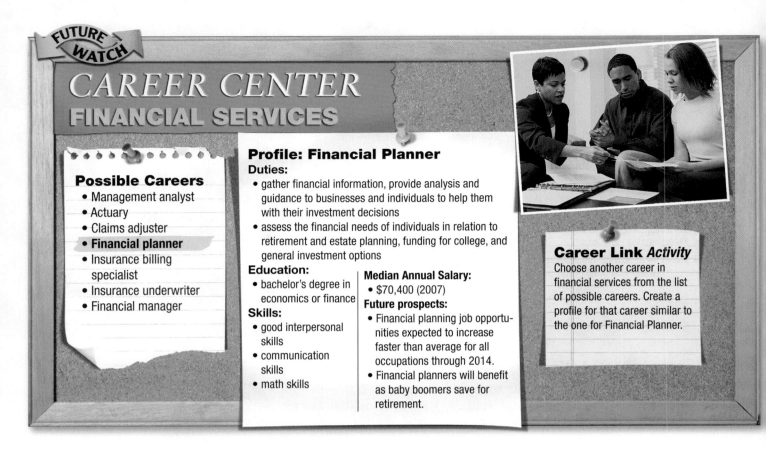

may invest that money in new plants and equipment to give them the resources to increase production. As these businesses use their investments to purchase new capital equipment for expansion and growth, they create new and better products and provide new jobs.

✔ **CHECKPOINT** *What role does investment play in the free enterprise system?*

The Financial System

In order for investment to take place, an economy must have a financial system. A **financial system** is the network of structures and mechanisms that allows the transfer of money between savers and borrowers.

Financial Assets

When people save, they are, in essence, lending funds to others. Whether they put cash in a savings account, purchase a certificate of deposit, or buy a government or corporate bond, savers obtain a document that confirms their purchase or deposit. These documents may be passbooks, monthly statements, bond certificates, or other records.

Such documents represent claims on the property or income of the borrower. These claims are called **financial assets,** or securities. If the borrower fails to pay back the loan, these documents can serve as proof in court that money was borrowed and that commitments were made that were not fulfilled.

The Flow of Savings and Investments

Figure 11.1 on the next page shows how the financial system brings together savers and borrowers, fueling investment and economic growth. On one side are savers—households, individuals, and businesses that lend out their savings in return for financial assets—for example, the promise of regular interest payments. On the other side are investors—governments and businesses—who invest the money they borrow to build roads, factories, and homes. Investors may also use these funds to develop new products, create new markets, or provide new services.

✔ **CHECKPOINT** *How does a bank serve as a way for savers and borrowers to transfer money between them?*

financial system the network of structures and mechanisms that allows the transfer of money between savers and borrowers

financial asset a claim on the property or income of a borrower

Financial Intermediaries

Savers and borrowers may be linked directly. As you examine **Figure 11.1**, you will notice that borrowers and savers may also be linked through a variety of institutions pictured as "in between" the two. These **financial intermediaries** are institutions that help channel funds from savers to borrowers. They include the following:

- *Banks, savings and loan associations, credit unions, and finance companies* As you read in Chapter 10, banks, S&Ls, and credit unions take in deposits from savers and then lend out some of these funds to businesses and individuals. Finance companies make loans to consumers and small businesses.

- *Mutual funds* A **mutual fund** pools the savings of many individuals and invests this money in a variety of stocks, bonds, and other financial assets. Mutual funds allow people to invest in a broad range of companies in the stock market. Investing in this way is less risky than purchasing the stock of only one or two companies that might do poorly.

- *Hedge funds* A **hedge fund** is a private investment organization that employs risky strategies that often made huge profits for investors. These investors are generally wealthy and often are knowledgeable about investing. Because hedge funds are private, they have not been regulated by the SEC and have not had to reveal information about themselves to the public.

- *Life insurance companies* The main function of life insurance is to provide financial protection for the family or other people named as beneficiaries of the insured. Working members of a family, for example, may buy life insurance policies so that, if they die, money will be paid to survivors to make up for lost income. Insurance companies collect payments called premiums from the people who buy insurance. They lend out to investors part of the premiums that they collect.

- *Pension funds* A pension is income that some retirees receive after working

financial intermediary an institution that helps channel funds from savers to borrowers

mutual fund an organization that pools the savings of many individuals and invests this money in a variety of stocks, bonds, and other financial assets

hedge fund a private investment organization that employs risky strategies that often made huge profits for investors

---

Figure 11.1	**Financial Intermediaries**

Savers make deposits to . . .   Financial Institutions that make loans to . . .   Investors

Commercial banks
Savings & loan associations
Savings banks
Mutual savings banks
Credit unions

Life insurance companies
Mutual funds
Pension funds
Finance companies

CHART SKILLS

Financial intermediaries, including banks and other financial institutions, accept funds from savers and make loans to investors. Investors include entrepreneurs, businesses, and other borrowers.

1. What advantages do financial intermediaries provide for savers?
2. What advantages do financial intermediaries provide for investors?

diversification
the strategy of spreading out investments to reduce risk

a certain number of years or reaching a certain age. In certain cases, injuries may qualify a working person for pension benefits. Employers may set up pension funds in a number of ways. They may contribute to the pension fund on behalf of their employees, they may withhold a percentage of workers' salaries to deposit in a pension fund, or they may do both. Employers set up pension funds to collect deposits and distribute payments. Pension fund managers invest those deposits in stocks, bonds, and other financial assets.

Now that you know something about the types of financial intermediaries, you may wonder why savers don't deal directly with investors. The answer is that, in general, dealing with financial intermediaries offers three advantages. Intermediaries share risks, provide information, and provide liquidity.

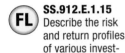
SS.912.E.1.15
Describe the risk and return profiles of various investment options.

Sharing Risk

As a saver, you may not want to invest your entire life savings in a single company or enterprise. For example, if you had

$500 to invest and your neighbor was opening a new restaurant, would you give her the entire $500? Since it is estimated that more than half of all new businesses fail, you would be wise not to risk all of your money in one investment. Instead, you would want to spread the money around to various businesses. This will reduce the chances of losing your entire investment.

This strategy of spreading out investments to reduce risk is called **diversification**. If you deposited $500 in the bank or bought shares of a mutual fund, those institutions could pool your money with other people's savings and put your money to work by making a variety of investments. In other words, financial intermediaries can diversify your investments and thus reduce the risk that you will lose all of your funds if a single investment fails.

Providing Information

Financial intermediaries are also good sources of information. Your local bank collects information about borrowers by monitoring their income and spending.

Figure 11.2 | **Types of Risk**

CHART SKILLS

Investors must always weigh the risks of investment against the potential rate of return on their investment.

1. How does diversification lessen the risks described in the chart?

2. What additional examples can you think of to illustrate each of the types of risk explained in this chart?

Name	Description	Example
Credit risk	Borrowers may not pay back the money they have borrowed, or they may be late in making payments.	You lend $20 to your cousin, who promises to pay you back in two weeks. When your cousin fails to pay you on time, you don't have money for the basketball tickets you had planned to buy.
Liquidity risk	You may not be able to convert the investment back into cash quickly enough for your needs.	Your MP3 player is worth $100. You need cash to buy concert tickets, so you decide to sell your MP3 player. To convert your MP3 player into cash on short notice, you have to discount the price to $75.
Inflation rate risk	Inflation rates erode the value of your assets.	Ricardo lends Jeff $1,000 for one year at 10 percent interest. If the inflation rate is 12 percent, Ricardo loses money.
Time risk	You may have to pass up better opportunities for investment.	Lili invests $100 in May's cleaning business, to be repaid at 5 percent interest one year later. Six months later, Lili is unable to invest in Sonia's pet-sitting business, which pays 10 percent interest, because she has already invested her savings.

---

280 FINANCIAL MARKETS

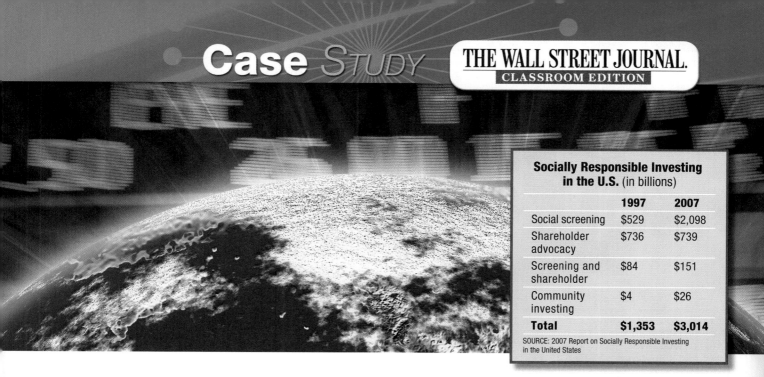

Socially Responsible Investing in the U.S. (in billions)		
	1997	**2007**
Social screening	$529	$2,098
Shareholder advocacy	$736	$739
Screening and shareholder	$84	$151
Community investing	$4	$26
Total	**$1,353**	**$3,014**

SOURCE: 2007 Report on Socially Responsible Investing in the United States

Principles and Principal

INVESTMENT

Socially responsible investing used to be about sacrificing choice and profits. Not anymore.

By Jilian Mincer
The Wall Street Journal

 SS.912.E.1.15 Describe the risk and return profiles of various investment options.

Socially responsible investing is growing up.

For many years, individuals who wanted to invest with their consciences had limited options, and many resigned themselves to making smaller returns in exchange for putting their money where their values were.

But in recent years, building a well-balanced, profitable portfolio using a socially responsible investing, or SRI, strategy has gotten easier. Greater awareness about the environment and growing demand for these kinds of investments have fueled the growth of high-quality options, meaning you can now build diversified SRI portfolios, including different types of mutual funds, bonds, exchange-traded funds and individual stocks.

Bruce M. Kahn, a vice president at Smith Barney, says that while socially

responsible investing traditionally was based on negative criteria—screening out investments connected to tobacco or guns, for example—the latest trend is to screen in companies with strong environmental and management records.

The theory behind this "sustainable" investing approach is that those are the types of companies that will be more profitable in the long term, he says.

There are now 173 different socially and environmentally screened mutual funds in 358 different share classes, the Social Investment Forum says. And a study last year by the consulting firm Mercer and the United Nations Environment Programme Finance Initiative found that SRI investments perform as well as or better than non-SRI investments over time.

Paul Hilton, a research director at Calvert Group, a top provider of

SRI funds, says there are three basic approaches to socially responsible investing: One of the most common is the use of screens to include or exclude certain securities, depending on social or environmental criteria such as strong records on community involvement or safe products, he says. A second part involves shareholder activism, whereby investors use their ownership to influence a company's behavior. The third is community investing, in which individuals invest in certificates of deposit and other vehicles that are federally insured but then lent to individuals in low-income communities.

Casey Neistat, New York filmmaker decided two years ago to move his assets into socially responsible investments. He favors funds that invest in companies with good environmental records and avoids funds with investments in China because of that nation's ties to the government in Sudan.

Still, Mr. Neistat says he can't afford to not make a profit. "I don't see this as charity," he says. "My gains have not dipped."

Applying Economic Principles
People who want to participate in socially responsible investing now have hundreds of mutual funds to choose from. Which of the three basic approaches to SRI cited by Paul Hilton do you think is the most effective? Explain your choice.

Video News Update Online
Powered by
The Wall Street Journal
Classroom Edition

Use videos at **PearsonSchool.com/PHecon** as a springboard for a discussion on a current topic.

"Forgive the mess. Warren just put everything into cash."

▲ Stocks are sometimes a good investment and sometimes they are not. *Is "Warren" optimistic or pessimistic about the prospects for stocks? How do you know?*

Finance companies collect information when borrowers fill out credit applications. Mutual fund managers know how the stocks in their **portfolios,** or collections of financial assets, are performing. As required by law, all intermediaries provide this and other information to potential investors in an investment report called a **prospectus.** The typical prospectus also warns potential investors that "past performance does not necessarily predict future results." An investment that looks great today may fizzle tomorrow. As economic conditions change, an investment once considered safe may look very risky.

By providing vital data about investment opportunities, financial intermediaries reduce the costs in time and money that lenders and borrowers would pay if they had to search out such information on their own. The information, however, is sometimes provided in lengthy documents with small type. So the careful investor must be knowledgeable and must study whatever information has been provided.

Providing Liquidity

Financial intermediaries also provide investors with liquidity. (Recall that liquidity is the ability to convert an asset into cash.) Suppose, for example, that you decide to invest in a mutual fund. Two years later, you need cash to pay your college tuition. You can get cash quickly by selling your shares in the mutual fund. Other investments are not so liquid. If you had purchased an investment-quality painting instead, you would need to find another investor who would buy the art from you. As you can see, financial intermediaries and the liquidity they provide are crucial to meeting borrowers' and lenders' needs in our increasingly complex financial system.

✔ **CHECKPOINT** *Why do savers and investors generally work through financial intermediaries?*

Liquidity, Return, and Risk

As you have read, most decisions involve trade-offs. For example, the trade-off for not going to a movie may be two additional hours of sleep. Saving and investing involve trade-offs as well.

Liquidity and Return

Suppose you save money in a savings account. Savings accounts are good ways to save when you need to be able to get to your cash for immediate use. On the other hand, savings accounts pay relatively low interest rates, about 2 to 3 percentage points below a certificate of deposit (CD). In other words, savings accounts are liquid, but they have a low return. **Return** is the money an investor receives above and beyond the sum of money that has been invested.

What if, however, you unexpectedly inherit $5,000? You do not need ready access to those funds, since your part-time job pays your day-to-day expenses. If you are willing to give up some degree of ready access to your money, you can earn a higher interest rate than you would earn if you put the money into a savings account. For example, you can invest your money in a CD that pays 4 percent interest. You would not be allowed to withdraw your money for, say, two years without paying a penalty. Therefore, before buying the CD, you would want to weigh the greater return on your investment against the loss of liquidity.

portfolio a collection of financial assets

prospectus an investment report that provides information to potential investors

return the money an investor receives above and beyond the sum of money initially invested

Return and Risk

Certificates of deposit (up to $250,000) are considered very safe investments because they are insured by the federal government. When you buy a CD valued at less than $250,000, you are giving up liquidity for a certain period of time, but you are not risking the loss of your money. What if, however, you decided to invest the money in a new company that your friends are starting? You must consider the risk you are now incurring. If the company succeeds, you could double your investment. However, it may take years before it is clear that the company is successful. If it fails, however, you could lose all or part of the money you invested. The government does not insure you against the risk of an investment gone bad. You may benefit from the rewards of a good investment, but you face the risks of a bad one.

To take another example, suppose your savings account is earning 2 percent interest. Would you be willing to lend money to your friend Emily for that same 2 percent interest rate, knowing that she rarely pays back loans on time? Probably not. For you to lend Emily the money, she would have to offer you a higher return than the bank could offer. This higher return would help offset the greater risk that Emily will not repay the loan on time—or that she does not repay the loan at all. Likewise, investors and lenders must consider the degree of risk involved in an investment they are considering and decide what return they would require to make up for the extra risk they may be taking on.

In general, the higher the potential return on an investment, the riskier the investment. Whenever individuals evaluate an investment, they must balance the risks involved with the rewards they expect to gain from the investment. Balancing this risk may be exceedingly tricky. As *Forbes* magazine has commented:

> "The risk/return tradeoff could easily be called the 'ability-to-sleep-at-night test.' While some people can handle the equivalent of financial skydiving without batting an eye, others are terrified to climb the financial ladder without a secure harness. Deciding what amount of risk you can take while remaining comfortable with your investments is very important...."
>
> *Forbes*, "The Risk-Return Tradeoff"

✔ **CHECKPOINT** *Which investment has greater liquidity, a savings account or a certificate of deposit?*

FL SS.912.E.1.14, SS.912.E.1.15, LA.1112.1.6.1, LA.1112.2.2.3, LA.1112.2.2.2

SECTION 1 ASSESSMENT

Essential Questions Journal To continue to build a response to the Essential Question, go to your **Essential Questions Journal.**

🔎 Guiding Question

1. Use your completed concept web to answer this question: What are the benefits and risks of saving and investing?
2. **Extension** Suppose you have $500 to invest. What questions and concerns would you have as you decide how to invest your money?

Key Terms and Main Ideas

3. What is **investment?**
4. Identify the three parts of the **financial system.**
5. Describe the main benefit of **diversification.**
6. What is the purpose of a **prospectus?**

7. List three examples of **returns** on an investment.

Critical Thinking

8. **Contrast (a)** How are mutual funds and hedge funds similar? **(b)** How are they different?
9. **Extend** What kinds of financial assets might you find in a portfolio?
10. **Infer (a)** Rank the following investments from the least risky to the most risky: a certificate of deposit, stock in one company, and a mutual fund. **(b)** Which has the greatest potential to have the highest possible return? Explain your answer.

Quick Write

11. Reread Investing and Free Enterprise and Liquidity, Return, and Risk in this section. Give two examples of a liquid investment and two examples of an investment that is not liquid. Then write a short essay answering the following question. Why would people invest money in an investment that is not liquid?

FL NGSSS

LA.1112.1.6 Use multiple strategies to develop vocabulary.

MA.912.A.2.2 Interpret a graph to represent a real-world situation.

SS.912.E.1.14 Compare credit, savings, and investment services.

SS.912.E.1.15 Describe the risk and return profiles of various investment options.

ECONOMIC DICTIONARY

As you read the section, look for the definitions of these **Key Terms:**

- coupon rate
- maturity
- par value
- yield
- savings bond
- inflation-indexed bond
- municipal bond
- corporate bond
- junk bond
- capital market
- money market
- primary market
- secondary market

Guiding Question

Why are bonds bought and sold?

Copy this chart and fill it in as you read.

Purpose of Bonds	
Issuer	**Investor**
• To finance war	• To support the government in times of need
•	•
•	•

coupon rate the interest rate that a bond issuer will pay to the bondholder

maturity the time at which payment to a bondholder is due

▶ **Economics and You**   It is 1942, and the world is at war. The United States has thrown all of its resources into the Allied effort to defeat the Axis powers. To keep the armed forces equipped, the government needs money. To raise that money, the Treasury Department begins selling savings bonds.

Americans from every walk of life support the war effort by buying these "war bonds." Even though money is tight, you manage to do your part by bringing a few nickels and dimes to school to buy war stamps. Added to the money that other students bring, the class collects enough stamps to buy a bond.

Principles in Action   Why are bonds bought and sold? Like the war bonds that helped finance our effort in World War II, bonds are sold by governments or corporations to finance projects. Using the example of a community that needs to construct a major road, you will see how municipal bonds offer the best method of financing expensive community projects. You will also learn another advantage of bonds. They usually offer a higher return than savings accounts, although they generally are riskier than savings accounts.

Bonds as Financial Assets

Bonds are basically loans, or IOUs, that represent debt that the seller, or issuer, must repay to an investor. Bonds typically pay the investor a fixed amount of interest at regular intervals for a specific amount of time. Bonds are generally lower-risk investments. As you might expect from your reading about the relationship between risk and return, the rate of return on bonds is usually also lower than for many other investments.

The Three Components of Bonds

Bonds have three basic components:

- *Coupon rate* The **coupon rate** is the interest rate that a bond issuer will pay to a bondholder.
- *Maturity* The time at which payment to a bondholder is due is called the bond's **maturity.** The length of time to maturity varies with different bonds. Bonds usually mature in 10, 20, or 30 years.

▲ Bonds generally pay a fixed amount of interest at regular intervals. *Are bonds usually lower or higher risk investments?*

- *Par value* A bond's **par value,** assigned by the issuer, is the amount to be paid to the bondholder at maturity. Par value is also called face value or principal.

Suppose that you buy a $1,000 bond from the corporation Jeans, Etc. The investor who buys the bond is called the holder. The seller of a bond is the issuer. You are, therefore, the holder of the bond, and Jeans, Etc. is the issuer. The components of this bond are as follows:

- *Coupon rate:* 5 percent, paid to the bondholder annually
- *Maturity:* 10 years
- *Par value:* $1,000

How much money will you earn from this bond, and over what period of time? The coupon rate is 5 percent of $1,000 per year. This means that you will receive a payment of $50 (0.05 × $1,000) each year for 10 years, or a total of $500 in interest. In 10 years, the bond will have reached maturity, and the company's debt to you will have ended. Jeans, Etc. will now pay you the par value of the bond, or $1,000. Thus, for your $1,000 investment, you will have received $1,500 over a period of 10 years.

Not all bonds are held to maturity. Over their lifetime they might be bought or sold, and their price may change. Because of these shifts in price, buyers and sellers are interested in a bond's yield, or yield to maturity. **Yield** is the annual rate of return on a bond if the bond is held to maturity (5 percent in the earlier example involving Jeans, Etc.).

Buying Bonds at a Discount

Investors earn money from interest on the bonds they buy. They can also earn money by buying bonds at a discount, called a discount from par. In other words, if Nate were buying a bond with a par value of $1,000, he may have to pay only $960 for it. When the bond matures, Nate will redeem the bond at par, or $1,000. He will thus have earned $40 on his investment, in addition to interest payments from the bond issuer.

Why would someone sell a bond for less than its par value? The answer lies in the

Figure 11.3   Discounts From Par

1. Sharon buys a bond with a par value of $1,000 at 5 percent interest.

Bond purchase without discount from par

2. Interest rates go up to 6 percent.

3. Sharon needs to sell her bond. Nate wants to buy it, but is unwilling to buy a bond at 5 percent interest when the current rate is 6 percent.

4. Sharon offers to discount the bond, taking $40 off the price and selling it for $960.

5. Nate accepts the offer. He now owns a $1,000 bond paying 5 percent interest, which he purchased at a discount from par.

Bond purchase with discount from par

CHART SKILLS

Investors can earn money by buying bonds at a discount, called a discount from par.

1. How do interest rates affect bond prices?
2. If Sharon buys the bond at $1,000 and sells it five years later at $960, would she necessarily have lost money on the purchase?

fact that interest rates continually change. For example, suppose that Sharon buys a $1,000 bond at 5 percent interest, the current market rate. A year later, she needs to sell the bond to help pay for a new car. By that time, however, interest rates have risen to 6 percent. No one will pay $1,000 for Sharon's bond at 5 percent interest when they could go elsewhere and buy a $1,000 bond at 6 percent interest. For Sharon to sell her bond at 5 percent, she will have to sell it at a discount. (See **Figure 11.3.**)

Bond Ratings

How does an investor decide which bonds to buy? Investors can check bond quality through independent firms that publish bond issuers' credit ratings. These firms include Standard & Poor's and Moody's. They rate bonds on a number of factors, focusing on the issuer's financial strength— its ability to make future interest payments and its ability to repay the principal when the bond matures.

Their rating systems rank bonds from the highest investment grade (AAA in Standard & Poor's system and Aaa in

Personal Finance
For more help in making wise investment decisions, see your Personal Finance Handbook in the back of the book or visit PearsonSchool.com/PHecon

par value a bond's stated value, to be paid to the bondholder at maturity

yield the annual rate of return on a bond if the bond is held to maturity

What is the function of a municipal bond?

Companies or governments sell bonds in order to finance projects. Most bonds are bought because the buyer expects to earn interest on the investment. Here's the story of one bond, known as a municipal bond: why it was issued and why it was bought.

1 The main state road connecting Mudville and Saltville is in terrible shape. People don't want to use it. The economies of both cities are suffering.

2 Mudville and Saltville and all the towns in between need a new road. But how can the citizens pay for it? The state steps in and proposes to repair the road and make it into a toll road. State voters approve the bond issue narrowly.

The Problem

Financing the Solution

Moody's) through the lower grades. An investment-grade bond is considered safe enough for banks to invest in. The lowest grade generally means that the bond is in default—that is, the issuer has not kept up with interest payments or has defaulted on paying principal.

The higher the bond rating, the lower the interest rate the company usually has to pay to get people to buy its bonds. For example, an AAA (or "triple A") bond may be issued at a 5 percent interest rate. A BBB bond, however, may be issued at a 7.5 percent interest rate. The buyer of the AAA bond trades off a lower interest rate for lower risk. The buyer of the BBB bond trades greater risk for a higher interest rate.

Similarly, the higher the bond rating, the higher the price at which the bond will sell. For example, a $1,000 bond with an AAA rating may sell at $1,100. A $1,000 bond with a BBB rating may sell for only

$950 because of the increased risk that the seller could default.

Holders of bonds with high ratings who keep their bonds until maturity face relatively little risk of losing their investment. Holders of bonds with lower ratings, however, take on more risk in return for potentially higher interest payments.

Advantages and Disadvantages to the Issuer

From the point of view of the investor, bonds are good investments because they are relatively safe. Bonds are desirable from the issuer's point of view as well, for two main reasons:

1. Once the bond is sold, the coupon rate for that bond will not go up or down. For example, when Jeans, Etc. sells bonds, it knows in advance that it will be making fixed payments for a specific length of time.

UNDER REPAIR

Drive Safely

CASH
↓
6

3 The bonds go on sale and sell well. The state's credit is good, and interest on the bond is tax exempt. There's enough money to begin construction on a new road.

4 With a new road, Mudville and Saltville prosper. Tolls from the road more than cover the interest that must be paid to bond holders.

CHECK

5 Investors are happy because they receive a nice check every three months. The citizens of Mudville and Saltville are happy because the repaired road makes travel between the two cities easier.

Check Your Understanding
1. What is the cost and benefit of buying a municipal bond?
2. Why do you think bond issues like this one must be approved by voters?

Problem Solved

2. Unlike stockholders, bondholders do not own a part of the company. Therefore, the company does not have to share profits with its bondholders if the company does particularly well.

On the other hand, bonds also pose two main disadvantages to the issuer:

1. The company must make fixed interest payments, even in bad years when it does not make money. In addition, it cannot change its interest payments even when interest rates have gone down.
2. If the firm does not maintain financial health, its bonds may be downgraded to a lower bond rating and, thus, may be harder to sell unless they are offered at a discount.

✓ **CHECKPOINT** *Why do some people invest in bonds with a low interest rate?*

Types of Bonds

Despite these risks to the issuer, when corporations or governments need to borrow funds for long periods, they often issue bonds. There are several different types of bonds.

Savings Bonds

You may already be familiar with savings bonds, which are sometimes given to young people as gifts. **Savings bonds** are low-denomination ($50 to $10,000) bonds issued by the United States government. The government uses funds from the sale of savings bonds to help pay for public works projects such as buildings, roads, and dams. Like other government bonds, savings bonds have virtually no risk of default, or failure to repay the loan.

The federal government pays interest on savings bonds. However, unlike most

savings bond a low-denomination bond issued by the United States government

inflation-indexed bond a bond that protects the investor against inflation by its linkage to an index of inflation

municipal bond a bond issued by a state or local government or a municipality to finance a public project

corporate bond a bond issued by a corporation to help raise money for expansion

other bond issuers, it does not send interest payments to bondholders on a regular schedule. Instead, the purchaser buys a savings bond for less than par value. For example, you can purchase a $50 savings bond for only $25. When the bond matures, you receive the $25 you paid for the bond plus $25 in interest.

Treasury Bonds, Bills, and Notes

The United States Treasury Department issues Treasury bonds, as well as Treasury bills and notes (T-bills and T-notes). These investments offer different lengths of maturity, as shown in **Figure 11.4**. Backed by the "full faith and credit" of the United States government, these securities are among the safest investments in terms of default risk.

One possible problem with bonds (and investments in general) is inflation. The purchase price and return on Treasury securities are governed by changing interest rates and market conditions. As a result, the value of Treasury securities as an investment must be carefully understood.

If a Treasury bond pays you 5 percent interest per year but the inflation rate is 3 percent, you are really getting just 2 percent interest on the bond. One type

of bond issued mainly by the government seeks to protect against inflation—a general rise in prices. The **inflation-indexed bond** links the principal and interest to an inflation index—a measure of how fast prices are rising. If the index rises by 3 percent, this bond's par value will also rise by 3 percent. As a result, you will receive the return on the bond that you expected when you bought it.

Municipal Bonds

State and local governments and municipalities (government units with corporate status) issue bonds to finance such projects as highways, state buildings, libraries, parks, and schools. These bonds are called **municipal bonds,** or "munis."

Because state and local governments have the power to tax, investors can assume that these governments will be able to keep up with interest payments and repay the principal at maturity. Standard & Poor's and Moody's therefore consider most municipal bonds to be safe investments. In addition, the interest paid on municipal bonds is not subject to income taxes at the federal level or in the issuing state. Because they are relatively safe and are tax-exempt, "munis" are very attractive to investors as a long-term investment. A high-quality municipal bond can pay a good return for quite a long time.

Corporate Bonds

As you read in Chapter 8, corporations issue bonds to help raise money to expand their businesses. These **corporate bonds** are generally issued in denominations of $1,000 or $5,000. The interest on corporate bonds is taxed as ordinary income.

Unlike governments, corporations have no tax base to help guarantee their ability to repay their loans. Thus, these bonds have moderate levels of risk. Investors in corporate bonds must depend on the success of the corporation's sales of goods and services to generate enough income to pay interest and principal.

Corporations that issue bonds are watched closely not only by the independent ratings firms, but also by the Securities and Exchange Commission (SEC). The SEC is

| Figure 11.4 | **Treasury Bonds, Notes, and Bills** |

	Treasury Bond	Treasury Note	Treasury Bill
Term	long-term	intermediate-term	short-term
Maturity	30 years	2, 5, or 10 years	4, 13, 26, or 52 weeks
Liquidity and safety	safe	safe	liquid and safe
Minimum purchase	$100	$100	$100
Denomination	$100	$100	$100

CHART SKILLS

Treasury bonds, notes, and bills represent debt that the government must repay the investor.

1. Which of these three types of government securities is the most liquid?

2. How do these three types of government securities differ?

an independent government agency that regulates financial markets and investment companies. It enforces laws prohibiting fraud and other dishonest investment practices.

Each bond is issued with an indenture agreement. It sets forth all the features associated with the bond. The interest rate is specified on the indenture agreement.

Junk Bonds

Bonds with a fairly high risk of default but a potentially high yield are known as **junk bonds.** These non-investment-grade securities became especially popular investments during the 1980s and 1990s, when large numbers of aggressive investors made—but also sometimes lost—large sums of money buying and selling them.

Junk bonds have been known to pay more than 12 percent interest at a time when government bonds were yielding only about 8 percent. On the other hand, the speculative nature of most junk bonds makes them very risky. Investors in junk bonds face a strong possibility that some of the issuing firms will default on their debt. Nevertheless, issuing junk bonds has enabled many companies to undertake activities that would otherwise have been impossible to complete. Junk bond funds, which pool large numbers of individual high-risk bonds, may reduce the risk somewhat for the average investor. Still, investment in junk bond funds can be hazardous.

✔ **CHECKPOINT** *Which type of bond might have been used to fund the construction of your school?*

Other Types of Financial Assets

In addition to bonds, investors may choose other financial assets. These include certificates of deposit and money market mutual funds, as well as stock. You will read more about stock in Section 3.

Certificates of Deposit

Certificates of deposit (CDs) are one of the most common forms of investment. As you read in Chapter 10, CDs are available through banks, which lend out the funds

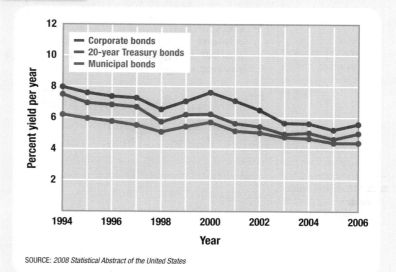

SOURCE: *2008 Statistical Abstract of the United States*

GRAPH SKILLS
From the early 1990s to the early 2000s, bond yields dipped slightly for all three types of bonds shown.
1. Which type of bond had the highest yield?
2. Which of the three types of bonds would you expect to carry the least risk? Explain your answer.

Action Graph
<u>online</u>

For an animated version of this graph, visit **PearsonSchool.com/PHecon**

deposited in CDs for a fixed amount of time, such as six months or two years.

CDs are attractive to small investors because they can deposit as little as $100. Investors can also choose among several terms of maturity. This means that if an investor foresees a future expenditure, he or she can buy a CD that matures just before the expenditure is due.

Money Market Mutual Funds

Money market mutual funds are special types of mutual funds. As you read in Section 1, financial intermediaries collect money from individual investors and then buy stocks, bonds, or other financial assets to form a mutual fund.

In the case of money market mutual funds, intermediaries buy short-term financial assets. Investors receive higher interest on a money market mutual fund than they would receive from a savings account. On the other hand, money market mutual funds are not covered by FDIC insurance. (As you read in Chapter 10, FDIC insurance protects

 MA.912.A.2.2 Interpret a graph to represent a real-world situation.

junk bond a bond with high risk and potentially high yield

capital market
a market in which money is lent for periods longer than a year

money market
a market in which money is lent for periods of one year or less

primary market
a market for selling financial assets that can be redeemed only by the original holder

secondary market
a market for reselling financial assets

bank deposits up to $250,000 per account.) This lack of insurance makes them slightly riskier than savings accounts.

CHECKPOINT *What is one advantage and one disadvantage of a money market mutual fund as compared with a savings account?*

Financial Asset Markets

Financial assets, including bonds, certificates of deposit, and money market mutual funds, are traded on financial asset markets. The various types of financial asset markets are classified in different ways.

Capital Markets and Money Markets

One way to classify financial asset markets is according to the length of time for which funds are lent. This type of classification includes both capital markets and money markets.

- *Capital markets* Markets in which money is lent for periods longer than a year are called **capital markets.** Financial assets that are traded in capital markets include long-term CDs and corporate and government bonds that require more than a year to mature.
- *Money markets* Markets in which money is lent for periods of one year or less are called **money markets.** Financial assets that are traded in money markets

include short-term CDs, Treasury bills, and money market mutual funds.

Primary and Secondary Markets

Markets may also be classified according to whether assets can be resold to other buyers. This type of classification includes primary and secondary markets.

- *Primary markets* Financial assets that can be redeemed only by the original holder are sold on **primary markets.** Examples include savings bonds, which cannot be sold by the original buyer to another buyer. Small certificates of deposit are also in the primary market because investors would most likely cash them in early rather than try to sell them to someone else.
- *Secondary markets* Financial assets that can be resold are sold on **secondary markets.** This option for resale provides liquidity to investors. If there is a strong secondary market for an asset, the investor knows that the asset can be resold fairly quickly without a penalty, thus providing the investor with ready cash. The secondary market also makes possible the lively trade in stock that is the subject of the next section.

CHECKPOINT *What are two ways of classifying financial asset markets?*

FL LA.1112.2.2.2, SS.912.E.1.14, SS.912.E.1.15, LA.1112.1.6.1, LA.1112.2.2.3

Essential Questions Journal To continue to build a response to the Essential Question, go to your **Essential Questions Journal**.

SECTION 2 ASSESSMENT

Guiding Question

1. Use your completed chart to answer this question: Why are bonds bought and sold?
2. **Extension** Would you prefer to buy a savings bond or a junk bond? Explain your preference.

Key Terms and Main Ideas

3. Identify the three components of bonds.
4. Why does the United States government issue **savings bonds?**
5. What is the advantage of an **inflation-indexed bond?**

6. Name two advantages of bonds for their issuers.
7. What kinds of financial assets are sold on **secondary markets?**

Critical Thinking

8. **Interpret** When would it be a good investment to sell bonds at a discount from par?
9. **Explain (a)** How are bonds rated? **(b)** How do you think these ratings are helpful to investors?
10. **Contrast (a)** What kinds of financial assets are traded in capital markets? **(b)** How are these different from the financial assets traded in money markets?

Math Skills

11. Suppose that you buy a municipal bond for $200 with an annual yield of 4 percent. How much money will you have earned when the bond reaches maturity in five years?

Visit PearsonSchool.com/PHecon for additional math help.

NGSSS

LA.1112.1.6 Use multiple strategies to develop vocabulary.

SS.912.E.1.14 Compare credit, savings, and investment services.

SS.912.E.1.15 Describe the risk and return profiles of various investment options.

SS.912.E.2.3 Research the contributions of key individuals of various backgrounds in the development of the U.S.

ECONOMIC DICTIONARY

As you read the section, look for the definitions of these **Key Terms:**

- share
- capital gain
- capital loss
- stock split
- stockbroker
- brokerage firm
- stock exchange
- futures
- options
- call option
- put option
- bull market
- bear market
- speculation

Guiding Question

How does the stock market work?

Copy this chart and fill it in as you read.

How the Stock Market Works	
Buying Stock	**Stock Trades**
• • •	• • •

▶ **Economics and You**   You hear it on the news every day. "Stock prices fell today in heavy trading" or "The bulls controlled Wall Street today as the Dow surged." Lots of long faces follow a drop in the stock market. A substantial rise prompts smiles and general enthusiasm. Lots of people—maybe even you—are interested in the stock market. But is the stock market a place where you should invest your precious resources?

Principles in Action If you want to know how the stock market works, you will not lack sources of information and advice. A section of your daily newspaper provides a list of stocks with the changes in price per share. Every television news broadcast highlights the latest price changes. You may even see stock prices crawling across the bottom of your TV screen. But just what is stock, exactly how is it traded, and when is it a good investment?

Buying Stock

Besides bonds, corporations can raise funds by issuing stock, which represents ownership in the corporation. Stock is issued in portions known as **shares.** By selling shares of stock, corporations raise money to start, run, and expand their businesses.

Benefits of Buying Stock

There are two ways for stockholders to make a profit:

- *Dividends* As you read in Chapter 8, many corporations pay out part of their profits as dividends to their stockholders. Dividends are usually paid four times per year (quarterly). The size of the dividend depends on the corporation's profit. The higher the profit, the larger the dividend per share of stock.
- *Capital gains* A second way an investor can earn a profit is to sell the stock for more than he or she paid for it. The

share a portion of stock

Stock certificates show the number of shares the holder owns. *What is the difference between a stock and a bond?* ▼

Reviewing Key Terms
To understand *capital gains*, review these terms.

capital *p. 6*
profit *p. 25*
stock *p. 202*
share *p. 291*

What are Capital Gains?

◀ **capital gain** the difference between the higher selling price and the lower purchase price of an investment

> **SELL SPLENDID TODAY!**

Bought: 300 shares of Splendid Widgets at $25
300 x 25 = $7,500.00

Sold: 300 shares of Splendid Widgets at $32.50
300 x $32.50 = $9,750

$9,750
-$7,500
———————
Profit (Capital Gain) $2,250.00

▲ Carey Williams seems to have a knack for the stock market. Two years ago, she bought 300 shares of Splendid Widgets at $25 a share. Since then, she has followed the market closely and happily watched the stock go up. Yesterday, when she checked the stock pages, she saw that it had reached $32.50 a share. Although she has done well with Widget, she will have to pay a capital gains tax on the profit, $2,250.

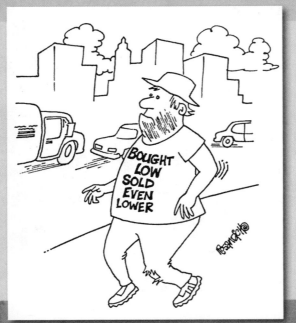

◀ Of course, not everyone does well in the stock market. If you sell a stock for less than you bought it, you incur a "capital loss." You do not have to pay a tax on a capital loss. In fact, you can usually deduct the loss from other capital gains that you may have.

Visual Glossary
online

To expand your understanding of this and other key economic terms, visit **PearsonSchool.com/PHecon**

difference between the higher selling price and the lower purchase price is called a **capital gain**. An investor who sells a stock at a price lower than the purchase price, however, suffers a **capital loss**.

Types of Stock

Stock may be classified in several ways, such as whether or not it pays dividends.

- *Income stock* By paying dividends, this stock provides investors with income.
- *Growth stock* This stock pays few or no dividends. Instead, the issuing company reinvests its earnings in its business. The business (and its stock) thus grows in value over time.

Stock may also be classified as to whether or not the stockholders have a vote in company policy.

- *Common stock* Investors who buy common stock are usually voting owners of the company. They usually receive one vote for each share of stock owned. They may use this vote, for example, to help elect the company's board of directors. In some cases, a relatively small group of people may own enough shares to give them control over the company.
- *Preferred stock* Investors who buy preferred stock are usually nonvoting owners of the company. Owners of preferred stock, however, receive dividends before the owners of common stock. If the company goes out of business, preferred stockholders get their investments back before common stockholders.

Stock Splits

Owners of common stock may sometimes vote on whether to initiate a stock split. A **stock split** means that each single share of stock splits into more than one share. A company may seek to split a stock when the price of stock becomes so high that it discourages potential investors from buying it.

For example, suppose you own 200 shares in a sporting goods company called Ultimate Sports. Each share is worth $100. After a 2-for-1 split, you own 400 shares of Ultimate Sports, or two shares of stock for every single share you owned before. Because the price is divided along with the stock, however, each share is now worth only $50. Thus a stock split does not immediately result in any financial gain. Shareholders like splits, however, because splits usually demonstrate that the company is doing well, and the lower stock price tends to attract more investors.

Risks of Buying Stock

Purchasing stock is risky because the firm selling the stock may earn lower profits than expected, or it may lose money. If so, the dividends will be smaller than expected or nothing at all, and the market price of the stock will probably decrease. If the price of the stock decreases, investors who choose to sell their stock will get less than they paid for it, experiencing a capital loss.

How do the risk and rate of return on stocks compare with the risk and rate of return on bonds? As you have read, investors expect higher rates of return when they take on greater risk. Because of the laws governing bankruptcy, stocks are more risky than bonds. When a firm goes bankrupt, it sells its assets (such as land and equipment) and then pays its creditors, including bondholders, first. Stockholders receive a share of the assets only if there is money left over after bondholders are paid. As you might expect, because stocks are riskier than bonds, the return on stocks is generally higher.

✓ **CHECKPOINT** *What are two ways that an investor can make a profit from buying stocks?*

How Stocks Are Traded

Suppose you decide that you want to buy stock. Do you call up the company and place an order? Probably not, because very few companies sell stock directly. Instead, you would contact a **stockbroker,** a person who links buyers and sellers of stock. Stockbrokers usually work with individual investors, advising them to buy or sell particular stocks.

Stockbrokers work for **brokerage firms,** or businesses that specialize in trading

capital gain the difference between the selling price and purchase price that results in a financial gain for the seller

capital loss the difference between the selling price and purchase price that results in a financial loss for the seller

stock split the division of each single share of a company's stock into more than one share

stockbroker a person who links buyers and sellers of stock

brokerage firm a business that specializes in trading stocks

Figure 11.6

Reading a Newspaper Stock Report

CHART SKILLS

Many newspapers publish daily reports of stock market transactions. The explanations of the abbreviations in this sample report will help you read stock market reports in your own daily paper.

1. Which of the companies listed pays the highest dividend?

2. How many of the companies listed reached their high price for the year on the day the chart was published? Which companies are they?

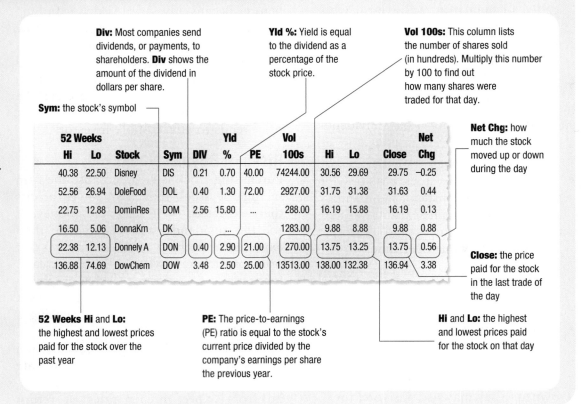

Div: Most companies send dividends, or payments, to shareholders. **Div** shows the amount of the dividend in dollars per share.

Yld %: Yield is equal to the dividend as a percentage of the stock price.

Vol 100s: This column lists the number of shares sold (in hundreds). Multiply this number by 100 to find out how many shares were traded for that day.

Sym: the stock's symbol

Net Chg: how much the stock moved up or down during the day

| 52 Weeks | | | | | Yld | | Vol | | | | Net |
Hi	Lo	Stock	Sym	DIV	%	PE	100s	Hi	Lo	Close	Chg
40.38	22.50	Disney	DIS	0.21	0.70	40.00	74244.00	30.56	29.69	29.75	–0.25
52.56	26.94	DoleFood	DOL	0.40	1.30	72.00	2927.00	31.75	31.38	31.63	0.44
22.75	12.88	DominRes	DOM	2.56	15.80	...	288.00	16.19	15.88	16.19	0.13
16.50	5.06	DonnaKrn	DK		...		1283.00	9.88	8.88	9.88	0.88
22.38	12.13	Donnely A	DON	0.40	2.90	21.00	270.00	13.75	13.25	13.75	0.56
136.88	74.69	DowChem	DOW	3.48	2.50	25.00	13513.00	138.00	132.38	136.94	3.38

52 Weeks Hi and Lo: the highest and lowest prices paid for the stock over the past year

PE: The price-to-earnings (PE) ratio is equal to the stock's current price divided by the company's earnings per share the previous year.

Close: the price paid for the stock in the last trade of the day

Hi and Lo: the highest and lowest prices paid for the stock on that day

stocks. Stockbrokers and brokerage firms cover their costs and earn a profit by charging a commission, or fee, on each stock transaction. Sometimes, they also act as dealers of stock, meaning that they buy shares at a lower price and sell them to investors at a slightly higher price, profiting from the difference, or "spread."

Stock Exchanges

A market for buying and selling stock is known as a **stock exchange.** Stock exchanges act as secondary markets for stocks and bonds. Most newspapers publish data on transactions in major stock exchanges. (See **Figure 11.6** to learn how to read a newspaper stock market report.)

Major United States stock markets include the New York Stock Exchange (NYSE) and Nasdaq. In addition, a large number of people trade stocks on the Internet, using online brokerage firms or special trading software. The ease of this approach also makes it very risky because snap judgments can often be wrong—and very costly.

stock exchange
a market for buying and selling stock

The New York Stock Exchange

The New York Stock Exchange (NYSE) is the country's largest and most powerful exchange. The NYSE began in 1792 as an informal, outdoor exchange in New York's financial district. Over time, as the financial market developed and the demand to buy and sell financial assets grew, the exchange moved indoors and became restricted to a limited number of members, who bought "seats" allowing them to trade on the exchange.

The NYSE handles stock and bond transactions for the top companies in the United States and in the world. The largest, most financially sound, and best-known firms listed on the NYSE are referred to as blue chip companies. Blue chip stocks are often in high demand, because investors expect the companies to continue to do business profitably for a long time.

Nasdaq

Despite the importance of organized markets like the New York Stock Exchange, many stocks, as well as bonds, are not traded on the floor of stock exchanges. Instead, they are traded directly, on the over-the-counter (OTC) market. Using a telephone or the Internet, investors may buy directly from a dealer or broker who will search other dealers or brokers on the OTC market for the best price.

The Nasdaq (National Association of Securities Dealers Automated Quotation) system was created in 1971 to help organize the OTC market through the use of automation. It grew rapidly in the 1990s in part by focusing on new-technology stocks. Today, the Nasdaq Stock Market (as it became known) is the second largest securities market in the country and the largest electronic market for stocks. It handles more trades on average than any other American market. True to its OTC roots, Nasdaq has no physical trading floor. Instead it has a telecommunications network through which it broadcasts trading information to computer terminals throughout the world.

Futures and Options

Futures are contracts to buy or sell commodities at a particular date in the future at a price specified today. For example, a buyer and seller might agree today on a price of $4.50 per bushel for soybeans that would not reach the market until six or nine months from now. The buyer would pay some portion of the money today, and the seller would deliver the goods in the future. Many of the markets in which futures are bought and sold are associated with grain and live-stock exchanges. These markets include the New York Mercantile Exchange and the Chicago Board of Trade.

Similarly, **options** are contracts that give investors the choice to buy or sell stock and other financial assets. Investors may buy or sell a particular stock at a particular price up until a certain time in the future—usually three to six months.

The option to buy shares of stock until a specified time in the future is known as a **call option.** For example, you may pay $10 per share today for a call option. The call option gives you the right, but not the obligation, to purchase a certain stock at a price of, say, $100 per share. If at the end of six months, the price has gone up to $115 per share, your option still allows you to purchase the stock for the agreed-upon $100 per share. You thus earn $5 per share ($15 minus the $10 you paid for the call option). If, on the other hand, the price has dropped to $80, you can throw away the option and buy the stock at the going rate.

The option to sell shares of stock at a specified time in the future is called a **put option.** Suppose that you, as the seller, pay $5 per share for the right to sell a particular stock that you do not yet own at $50 per share. If the price per share falls to $40, you can buy the share at that price and require the contracted buyer to pay the

futures contracts to buy or sell commodities at a particular date in the future at a price specified today

options contracts that give investors the right to buy or sell stock and other financial assets at a particular price until a specified future date

call option a contract for buying stock at a particular price until a specified future date

put option a contract for selling stock at a particular price until a specified future date

Economics & YOU

Risk *vs.* Return: Stocks and Bonds

Your grandmother, who does not like risk, gave you a savings bond when you were in grade school. *The rate of return is fixed, so you know exactly what the bond will be worth when you cash it in.*

You decide to take some money from your pay and buy a few shares of stock. *You can't predict how your stock will perform, so the possible risk and return are both greater than if you bought bonds.*

▲ Generally with investing in stocks and bonds, the greater the potential risk, the greater the potential return. *How do age and family circumstance affect the makeup of your investment choices?*

agreed-upon $50. You would then make $5 per share on the sale ($10 minus the $5 you paid for the put option). If the price rises to $60, however, you can throw away the option and sell the stock for $60.

Day Trading

Most people who buy stock hold their investment for a significant period of time—sometimes many years—with the expectation that it will grow in value. Day traders use a different strategy. They might make dozens of trades per day, sometimes holding a stock for just minutes or even seconds. The typical day trader, sitting in front of a computer, hopes to ride a rising stock's momentum for a short time and then sell the stock for a quick profit. Day trading is a bit like gambling—it is a very risky business in which traders can lose a great deal of money. As the United States Security and Exchange Commission has warned:

> **"** While day trading is neither illegal nor is it unethical, it can be highly risky. Most individual investors do not have the wealth, the time, or the temperament to make money and to sustain the devastating losses that day trading can bring. **"**
>
> —"Day Trading, Your Dollars at Risk," U.S. Securities and Exchange Commission

✅ **CHECKPOINT** *What two kinds of contracts allow investors to buy and sell commodities or financial assets at some later date?*

Measuring Stock Performance

You may have heard newscasters speak of a "bull" or "bear" market or of the market rising or falling. What do these terms mean and how are increases and decreases in the sale of stocks measured?

Bull and Bear Markets

When the stock market rises steadily over a period of time, a **bull market** exists. On the other hand, when the stock market falls or stagnates for a period of time, people call it a **bear market.** In a bull market, investors expect an increase in profits and, therefore, buy stock. During a bear market, investors sell stock in expectation of lower profits.

bull market a steady rise in the stock market over a period of time

bear market a steady drop or stagnation in the stock market over a period of time

The 1980s and 1990s brought the longest sustained bull market in the nation's history. Between 2000 and 2006, the market went through brief cycles of bear and bull markets. Then, the subprime mortgage crisis of 2008 gave the stock market a nasty jolt, and by the fall of the year, the nation entered a severe, and seemingly lengthy, bear market.

The Dow Jones Industrial Average

When people say "the stock market rose today," they are often referring to the Dow Jones Industrial Average, a measure of stock performance known simply as "the Dow." The Dow is the average value of a particular set of stocks, and it is reported as a certain number of points. For example, on a good day the Dow might rise 60 points.

The group of stocks listed on the Dow is intended to represent the market as a whole. To make sure it does, some of the stocks are periodically dropped and others added. Today, those stocks represent 30 large companies in various industries, such as food, entertainment, and technology.

S&P 500

The S&P 500 (Standard & Poor's 500) gives a broader picture of stock performance than the Dow. It tracks the price changes of 500 different stocks as a measure of overall stock market performance. The S&P 500 reports mainly on stocks listed on the NYSE, but some of its stocks are traded on the Nasdaq market.

✅ **CHECKPOINT** *What do investors tend to do during a bull market?*

The Great Crash and Beyond

Like the 1980s and 1990s, the 1920s saw a long-term bull market. Unfortunately, this period ended in a horrifying collapse of the stock market known as the Great Crash of 1929. The causes of this collapse contain important lessons for investors in the twenty-first century.

Investing During the 1920s

When President Herbert Hoover took office in 1929, the United States economy seemed to be in excellent shape. The booming economy had dramatically changed the lives of Americans. Factories produced a steady stream of consumer products, including refrigerators, washing machines, toasters, and automobiles. The stock market was soaring. In 1925, the market value of all stocks had been $27 billion. By early October 1929, combined stock values had hit $87 billion.

Despite widespread optimism about continuing prosperity, there were signs of trouble. A relatively small number of companies and families held much of the nation's wealth, while many farmers and workers were suffering financially. In addition, many ordinary people went into debt buying consumer goods such as refrigerators and radios—new and exciting inventions at the time—on credit. Finally, industries were producing more goods than consumers could buy. As a result, some industries, including the important automobile industry, developed large surpluses of goods, and prices began to slump.

FL MA.912.A.2.2
Interpret a graph to represent a real-world situation.

| Figure 11.7 | **The Dow, 1896–2010** |

January 1, 2009
After climbing to over **14,000** in October 2007, the Dow begins a slide caused by the global financial crisis. On January 20, 2009, the Dow slumps to **7,949** only to rise again.

October 9, 2002
DJIA closes at a five-year low, **7,286.27,** on worries of recession and war in Iraq.

September 17, 2001
The NYSE reopens after the September 11 terrorist attacks force a four-day closure. Biggest-ever point loss, **684.81** or **7.13%**

March 16, 2000
Biggest ever point gain, **499.19** or **4.93%** as technology boom peaks

May 3, 1999
DJIA reaches **11,014.69,** breaking the **11,000** points mark. It will attain an all-time high of **11,722.98** on January 14, 2000

November 21, 1995
DJIA first-ever close above **5,000** just nine months after **4,000**

October 19, 1987
Black Monday crash of record **22.61%,** or **508** points

August 12, 1982
Birth of long-term bull market, in some analysts' view

November 14, 1972
First close above **1,000,** called Wall Street's equivalent of breaking the sound barrier

February 8, 1971
NASDAQ Stock Market is born.

October 28–29, 1929
Stock market crashes of **12.82%** and **11.73%** back–to–back (**38.33** and **30.57** points) usher in Great Depression.

May 26, 1896
Index's launch by Charles Dow, at **40.94** points. Index then had only 12 stocks, not 30.

SOURCE: Dow Jones Indexes

CHART SKILLS

The Dow Jones Industrial Average (DJIA) has had some down years, but many more up years since it began measuring stock performance in 1896.

1. In which decade did the Dow first top 1,000? In which decade did it top 2,000? 3,000? 6,000? 8,000?

2. Which was the best decade for the Dow? Which was the lowest decade for the Dow?

Action Graph
online

For an animated version of this graph, visit
PearsonSchool.com/PHecon

Warren Buffett

BERKSHIRE HATHAWAY

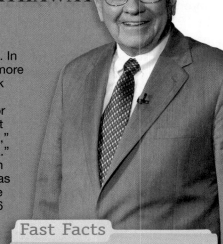

"Why should I buy real estate when the stock market is so easy?"

Warren Buffett believed he would be very rich someday, and he was right. In 2008, shares in his investment company, Berkshire Hathaway, traded at more than $125,000 for a single share. To many people, he is the ultimate stock market expert, nicknamed "the Oracle of Omaha."

Buffett learned how to invest at Columbia University, where a professor taught him to pick his investments by doing his own research. "You're not right or wrong because 1,000 people agree with you or disagree with you," the professor said. "You're right because your facts and reasons are right."

In 1965 Buffett purchased Berkshire Hathaway, a large manufacturer in the declining textile industry. Where others saw an aging dinosaur that was practically worthless, Buffett saw a business that could still produce large amounts of capital. Although the stock market valued Berkshire at $14.86 per share, Buffett knew the company had working capital (current assets minus liabilities) of more than $19 a share. Using the excess capital from Berkshire he went on to invest in a wide range of businesses, including insurance, utilities, and home furnishings. Like Berkshire Hathaway, the companies Buffett has bought are exceptional values.

Today Buffett focuses on a new venture—giving his money away. In 2006, he donated 80 percent of his fortune to charities.

Critical Thinking: *What do you think Warren Buffett meant when he said, "It's far better to buy a wonderful company at a fair price than a fair company at a wonderful price."*

Fast Facts

Warren Buffett
Born: August 30, 1930, in Omaha, NE
Education: B.A./B.S. University of Nebraska; M.S. Columbia University
Claim to Fame: Enormously successful stock market investor and philanthropist, with personal assets of more than $55 billion

---

FL SS.912.E.2.3
Research the contributions of key individuals of various backgrounds in the development of the U.S.

Another economic danger sign was the debt that investors were piling up by playing the stock market. The dizzying climb of stock prices encouraged widespread **speculation,** the practice of making high-risk investments with borrowed money in hopes of getting a big return. Before World War I, only the wealthy had bought and sold shares in the stock market. Now, however, the press was reporting stories of ordinary people making fortunes in the stock market. Small investors thus began speculating in stocks, often with their life savings.

The *Saturday Evening Post* printed a poem that captured the fever of the times:

**"Oh, hush thee, my babe, granny's bought some shares
Daddy's gone out to play with the bulls and the bears
Mother's buying on tips, and she simply can't lose,
And Baby shall have some expensive shoes"**

—Appeared in the *Saturday Evening Post,* 1929

To attract less-wealthy investors, stockbrokers encouraged a practice called buying on margin. Buying on margin allowed investors to purchase a stock for only a fraction of its price and borrow the rest from the brokerage firm. The Hoover administration did little to discourage such risky loans.

The Crash

By September 3, 1929, the Dow had reached an all-time high of 381 points. The rising stock prices dominated the news. Prices for many stocks soared far above their real values in terms of the company's earnings and assets.

After their peak in September, stock prices began to fall. Some brokers demanded repayment of loans. When the stock market closed on Wednesday, October 23, 1929, the Dow had dropped 21 points in an hour. The next day, worried investors began to sell, and stock prices fell further. Although business and political leaders told the public not to worry about their losses, widespread panic began.

By Monday, October 28, 1929, shares of stock were dropping in value to a fraction of what people had paid for them. Investors all over the country were racing

speculation the practice of making high-risk investments with borrowed money in hopes of getting a big return to get what was left of their money out of the stock market. On October 29, 1929, forever known as Black Tuesday, a record 16.4 million shares were sold, compared with the average 4 to 8 million shares per day earlier in the year. The Great Crash had begun.

The Aftermath of the Crash

During the bull market that led up to the Crash, about 4 million people had invested in the stock market. Although they were the first to feel the effects of the Crash, eventually the whole country was affected. The Crash was one cause of the Great Depression, in which millions of Americans lost their jobs, homes, and farms.

Massive unemployment became the most obvious sign of the deepening depression. By 1933, more than one quarter of the labor force was out of work.

Many Americans lost their homes as well as their jobs during the Great Depression. Desperate for shelter, they erected shacks of scrap wood, old tin, and other materials that they could scavenge. As more and more shacks sprang up, they formed shabby little villages. The residents, who

blamed their troubles on the policies of President Hoover, called these shanties "Hoovervilles."

Mistakes in monetary policy slowed the nation's recovery. In 1929, the Federal Reserve had begun limiting the money supply in order to discourage speculation. With too little money in circulation, individuals and businesses could not spend enough to help the economy improve.

Changing Attitudes Toward Stocks

After the Depression, many people saw stocks as risky investments to be avoided. As late as 1980, a relatively small percentage of American households held stock. Gradually, however, attitudes began to change. For one thing, the development of mutual funds made it easy to own a wide range of stocks. Americans became more comfortable with stock ownership.

After a period of very strong growth, stocks crashed again on "Black Monday," October 18, 1987. The Dow lost 22.6 percent of its value that day—nearly twice the one-day loss that began the Great Crash of 1929. However, this time the market rebounded on

Worried investors gather outside the New York Stock Exchange in October 1929. *Why was the man in the inset willing to sell his auto cheaply?* ▼

FINAL NEWS EDITION

World

Market in Panic as Stocks Are Dumped in 12,894,600 Share Day; Bankers Halt It

Outside J. P. Morgan & Co.'s

$100. WILL BUY THIS CAR. MUST HAVE CASH LOST ALL ON THE STOCK MARKET each of the next two days, and the impact on the economy was much less severe. The Fed moved quickly to add liquidity and reduce interest rates to stimulate economic growth. Within two years, the Dow had returned to pre-crash levels.

Starting in 1990, stock prices began to soar on the strength of a growing economy and a technology boom. Many people bought stock for the first time, investing heavily in Internet-based companies and other new, high-tech enterprises. A so-called dot.com boom raised stock prices of Internet-based securities to wildly unrealistic levels. At the end of the 1990s, almost half of American households owned mutual funds.

Scandals Rock the Stock Market

By that time, however, investors had begun worrying that many companies—especially the new ones—could not make enough money to justify their high stock prices. Those prices began dropping, and a lot of investors lost most or all of their prior gains. In 2001, an economic downturn and the September 11 terrorist attacks further battered the stock market.

That same year, the stock market took yet another hit. An enormous energy-trading company named Enron filed for bankruptcy in December after revealing that it had falsely reported profits for several years in order to cover up huge losses. The price of

its once high-flying stock fell from $90 per share to less than $1. Soon, several other large firms faced similar financial scandals.

In 2002, Congress responded to the scandals with the Sarbanes-Oxley Act. This legislation was aimed at reforming lax accounting practices. As a result of Sarbanes-Oxley, top corporate leaders now have to verify that financial reports are accurate or face criminal charges.

A Market in Turmoil

In time, the stock market recovered and reached new heights, boosted by a red-hot real estate market. In October 2006, the Dow passed the 11,700-point mark. It reached 14,000 in 2007. Then, as investors realized the full extent of the subprime mortgage crisis, the stock market again nosedived.

By the end of 2008, it had plunged back to the 8,000 range. Trillions of dollars worth of investments were lost and people saw their retirement savings lose much of their value. Safe investments, such as corporate and municipal bonds, also were badly hit. The financial crisis even caused the collapse of the renowned investment firm Lehman Brothers. Although the stock market has made a partial recovery, investors are still uneasy.

☑ **CHECKPOINT** *What was the Great Crash of 1929?*

 FL SS.912.E.1.14, SS.912.E.1.15, LA.1112.1.6.1, LA.1112.2.2.2, LA.1112.2.2.3

Essential Questions Journal — To continue to build a response to the Essential Question, go to your **Essential Questions Journal**.

SECTION 3 ASSESSMENT

❓ Guiding Question

1. Use your completed flowchart to answer this question: How does the stock market work?
2. **Extension** Suppose you had $1,000 to invest in the stock market. How would you go about investing your money?

Key Terms and Main Ideas

3. Describe the job of a **stockbroker.**
4. Identify two major United States **stock exchanges.**
5. What is a **capital gain?** A **capital loss?**

6. How did **speculation** contribute to the Great Crash of 1929?
7. What factors caused stock prices to rise in the 1990s and 2000s?

Critical Thinking

8. **Contrast (a)** In what ways are futures and options similar? **(b)** How are they different?
9. **Extend** Would you buy stock during a bear market? Why or why not?
10. **Infer (a)** Name the main causes of the Great Crash of 1929. **(b)** What lessons can investors learn from the Crash?

Quick Write

11. Reread The Great Crash and Beyond in this section. Suppose you were a newspaper reporter at the time of the Crash. Write a short article answering the following questions. What caused the Crash? What are the effects of the Crash on individuals? What are the effects on businesses? How do you think the stock market will perform in the future? Remember, you are writing from the point of view of someone in 1929!

Chapter 11: Financial Markets

Section 1 What are the benefits and risks of saving and investing?

Section 2 Why are bonds bought and sold?

Section 3 How does the stock market work?

Essential Question, Chapter 11
How do your savings and investment choices affect your future?

Risk, Liquidity, Return

	Risk	**Liquidity**	**Return**
Certificate of Deposit	Least risk	Least liquidity	Potentially, least return
Bonds	Minimal risk	Must be held to maturity; however, can be sold on bond market for current price	Greater return than CDs, but potentially less return than individual stocks and mutual funds.
Individual Stocks	Greatest risk	Can be sold at current price on stock market	Greatest potential return
Mutual Funds	Less risk than individual stocks; more than bonds	Can be sold at current price on stock market	Potentially, less return than stocks, more than bonds.

Economic Dictionary

investment, *p. 277*
financial system, *p. 278*
financial asset, *p. 278*
financial intermediary, *p. 279*
mutual fund, *p. 279*
hedge fund, *p. 279*
diversification, *p. 280*
portfolio, *p. 282*
prospectus, *p. 282*
return, *p. 282*
coupon rate, *p. 284*
maturity, *p. 284*
par value, *p. 285*
yield, *p. 285*
savings bond, *p. 287*
inflation-indexed bond, *p. 288*
municipal bond, *p. 288*
corporate bond, *p. 288*
junk bond, *p. 289*
capital market, *p. 290*
money market, *p. 290*
primary market, *p. 290*
secondary market, *p. 290*
share, *p. 291*
capital gain, *p. 293*
capital loss, *p. 293*
stock split, *p. 293*
stockbroker, *p. 293*
brokerage firm, *p. 293*
stock exchange, *p. 294*
futures, *p. 295*
options, *p. 295*
call option, *p. 295*
put option, *p. 295*
bull market, *p. 296*
bear market, *p. 296*
speculation, *p. 298*

Economics *on the go*

Study anytime, anywhere. Download these files today.

Economic Dictionary online
Vocabulary Support in English and Spanish

Audio Review online
Audio Study Guide in English and Spanish

Action Graph online
Animated Charts and Graphs

Visual Glossary online
Animated feature

How the Economy Works online
Animated feature

Download to your computer or mobile device at PearsonSchool.com/PHecon

Key Terms and Main Ideas

To make sure you understand the key terms and main ideas of this chapter, review the Checkpoint and Section Assessment questions and look at the Quick Study Guide on the preceding page.

Critical Thinking

1. **Discuss (a)** Which is a more liquid investment, a business or a bond? Explain your answer. **(b)** What risk do investors face if they keep their bonds until they reach maturity? **(c)** What risks do they face if they sell them before maturity?

2. **Infer (a)** What is the main advantage of mutual funds? **(b)** How did the development of mutual funds change the stock market? **(c)** How does the choice of whether to buy a particular stock or a mutual fund relate to the life situation of the purchaser?

3. **Compare and Contrast (a)** What are the advantages of bonds for investors? **(b)** What are the risks of investing in bonds? **(c)** How are these advantages and risks similar to and different from those of investing in stocks?

4. **Evaluate (a)** Describe the scandals that rocked the stock market in the early 2000s. **(b)** How did the United States government respond to these scandals? **(c)** Do you have faith in the stock market? Why or why not?

Applying Your Math Skills
Finding the Percent of a Number

You can find the percent of a number by multiplying the original number by the percent in decimal or fraction form. Remember, percentages represent hundredths of a quantity. As a fraction, percents are expressed as the percent over one hundred. As a decimal, single-digit percents are shown in the hundredths place. Double-digit percents are shown in the tenths and hundredths places. For example, four percent could be expressed as the fraction 4/100 (which can be reduced to 1/25), or as the decimal 0.04. Twenty-seven percent could be expressed either as the fraction 27/100 or as the decimal 0.27.

Suppose you bought $400 worth of stock two years ago. Since then, the stock's value has risen by 12 percent. You decide to sell your shares. Use your math skills, and the tips above, to answer the following questions.

Visit PearsonSchool.com/PHecon for additional math help.

5. **(a)** How much profit will you make on the sale? **(b)** Add the profit to the original price to find the total value of the stock you want to sell.

6. You are planning to sell the stock through a stockbroker, who charges a commission of 5 percent on the entire value of the sale. How much will you have to pay the stockbroker?

7. How much money will you receive from the sale after you pay this fee?

8. After you sell the stock and pay the stockbroker, you decide to reinvest your principal and profits in a different stock. After another year, the new stock's value has declined by 10 percent. How much is your stock worth now?

 Essential Question Activity

Essential Questions Journal — To respond to the chapter Essential Question, go to your **Essential Questions Journal**.

9. Complete this activity to answer the Essential Question: **How do your saving and investment choices affect your future?** Imagine that you have just turned 21 when you learn that a relative you have never met has died—and left you $5,000. According to the will, you must provide a plan for investing the money in the stock, mutual fund, and bond markets that will meet the financial needs you expect to have when you are 30 years old. Using the worksheet in your Essential Questions Journal or the electronic worksheet available at **PearsonSchool.com/PHecon,** gather the following information:
   (a) What career path do you expect to be following when you are 30? How much money do you expect to be making?
   (b) What financial responsibilities will you have when you are 30? Will you have student loans to pay? Will you have a family to support? Will you own a house? Will you have expensive interests such as travel or collecting?

   (c) Based on your income and your responsibilities, how much money will you need from your investments? Will you depend on that income, or can you risk losing some of it?

Use your answers to these questions about your financial needs to help you make your investment plan. Remember to diversify between relatively safe and relatively high-return investments, depending on your predicted needs.

10. **Modify** When you are 30, you decide to review your investment. Look at the situations below. Briefly describe how each of them might cause you to change your investment plan.
    (a) Interest rates are very high.
    (b) There is a bull market with low interest rates.
    (c) The stock market is doing well, but many economists are predicting a bleak future in the next year for stocks.
    (d) You are about to buy a house—and become the parent of twins!

Should financial markets be more strictly regulated?

In the early 2000s, investor confidence in the stock market was shaken by a series of scandals, such as the bankruptcy of Enron. To restore the faith of investors, Congress passed legislation to regulate corporate accounting. Today, some people support increased government regulation of financial markets. Others believe that government regulation is harmful to the financial markets.

Document A

"In an unregulated market, investors will not have enough information to guide their investments, which should not be based on rumor. Companies have incentives not to share information, such as bad news about themselves or information about others that is not commonly known. That's why regulators require companies to fully disclose information. That way, the entire market is better informed. This results in a greater willingness of firms or individuals to invest."

—Randall Dodd, director of the Financial Policy Forum, in *The Wall Street Journal Classroom Edition*

Document B

"The long-term impact of increasing strict rules and regulations can be just as damaging as the fraud and manipulation that occurs in an open system—probably more so. The increase of rules and regulation adds costs and administrative effort. In effect, companies face disincentives to engage in fair and honest activity. Thus, overregulation is also a destructive activity."

—U.S. Congressman Jeff Flake (Republican, Arizona), in *The Wall Street Journal Classroom Edition*

Document C

ANALYZING DOCUMENTS

Use your knowledge of the regulation of U.S. financial markets and Documents A, B, and C to answer Questions 1–3.

1. **Which document's author would be most likely to agree with the following idea: "In order to limit harm to others, better regulations are needed"?**
   A. Document A
   B. Document B
   C. Document C
   D. Documents A and C

2. **What does the cartoonist who drew Document C think of new government regulations on financial markets?**
   A. They are necessary to prevent widespread financial problems.
   B. They may cause problems, but they will give investors the information they need.
   C. They are unconstitutional.
   D. They are lengthy and overly complex.

3. **The authors of Document A and Document B disagree that**
   A. regulation makes companies behave honestly.
   B. company leaders who commit fraud should be punished.
   C. the government has the ability to regulate companies.
   D. investors need information.

Unit 4 Challenge

Essential Question, Unit 4
How can you make the most of your money?

There are many differing opinions about how individuals can make the most of their money. Look at the opinions below, keeping in mind the Essential Question: How can you make the most of your money?

VIDEO By Students For Students
For videos on Essential Questions, go to *PearsonSchool.com/PHecon*

> "Legend has it that Albert Einstein once called compound interest the most powerful force in the universe. Compound interest is the engine that can turn even meager savings into a nice nest egg over time. Inattention to debt puts you on the wrong side of that equation. You spend dollars that could be put to work making you wealthy. You want to be on the right side—the side that uses debt to make money but avoids debt when it hurts.... Stop watching your money go up in smoke."
>
> —Mary Dalrymple, "Habits for Wealth: Dump Your Debt Habit"

> "I don't know what the stock market will do tomorrow. (And, let me be equally clear, neither does anyone else.) Bad things may happen tomorrow. Certainly, bad things will happen on some days.... You get a great return [from stocks] by noticing that the day-to-day price of the market doesn't have much to do with the real long-term value of the best companies within that market. You get an even better return than the market averages by never mixing up three very important facts: Extreme stock market pessimism is great for buyers, extreme exuberance is great for sellers...and stocks are long-term investments."
>
> —John Casper, "Lessons Learned"

Essential Question
Writing Activity

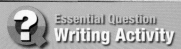

Consider the different views of economics expressed in the sources on this page and what you have learned about banking and financial institutions. ***Then write a well-constructed essay expressing your view of how you can make the most of your money.***

Writing Guidelines
- Address all aspects of the Essential Question Writing Activity.
- Support the theme with relevant facts, examples, and details.
- Use a logical and clear plan of organization.
- Introduce the theme by establishing a framework that is beyond a simple restatement of the question and conclude with a summation of the theme.

For help in writing a Persuasive Essay, refer to the *Writer's Handbook* in the Reference section, page S-5.

Essential Questions Journal

To respond to the unit Essential Question, go to your **Essential Questions Journal**.

5 Measuring Economic Performance

Essential Question, Unit 5

Why does it matter how the economy is doing?

Chapter 12
How do we know if the economy is healthy?

Chapter 13
How much can we reduce unemployment, inflation, and poverty?

Chapter

12 Gross Domestic Product and Growth

Essential Question, Chapter 12

How do we know if the economy is healthy?

FL Next Generation Sunshine State Standards

Section 1: Gross Domestic Product
LA.1112.1.6, MA.912.A.2.2, SS.912.E.2.1, SS.912.E.2.11, SS.912.E.3, SS.912.E.3.4, SS.912.G.2.2

Section 2: Business Cycles
LA.1112.1.6, MA.912.A.2.2, SS.912.E.1.12, SS.912.E.2.1, SS.912.E.2.5

Section 3: Economic Growth
LA.1112.1.6, SS.912.E.2.1, SS.912.E.2.3, SS.912.E.2.5

Economics
on the go

To study anywhere, anytime, download these online resources at *PearsonSchool.com/PHecon* ▶

NGSSS

LA.1112.1.6 Use multiple strategies to develop vocabulary.

MA.912.A.2.2 Interpret a graph to represent a real-world situation.

SS.912.E.2.1 Identify and explain broad economic goals.

SS.912.E.2.11 Assess the impact of negative and positive externalities on the national environment.

SS.912.E.3 Understand the relationships of the U.S. economy and the international marketplace.

SS.912.E.3.4 Assess the impact of negative and positive externalities on the international environment.

SS.912.G.2.2 Describe the factors that contribute to the differences between developing and developed regions.

ECONOMIC DICTIONARY

As you read the section, look for the definitions of these **Key Terms:**

- national income accounting
- gross domestic product
- intermediate goods
- durable goods
- nondurable goods
- nominal GDP
- real GDP
- gross national product
- depreciation
- price level
- aggregate supply
- aggregate demand

Guiding Question

What does the GDP show about the nation's economy?

Copy this chart and fill it in as you read to make four statements about GDP and list four drawbacks to this economic measure.

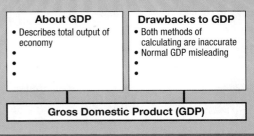

About GDP	Drawbacks to GDP
• Describes total output of economy	• Both methods of calculating are inaccurate
•	• Normal GDP misleading
•	•
•	

Gross Domestic Product (GDP)

▶ **Economics and You**   How much attention do you pay to the economic news? If you're like most people your age—or most Americans in general—your answer is probably, "Not much." After all, you'd have to be some kind of genius to keep track of the GDP, the GNP, the NNP, the NI, the DPI, and the rest of the economic alphabet soup. Who has the time? And who cares anyway?

But, whether you care or not, the GDP, the NI, and the rest do affect you. What's more, you affect them. Every time you buy a shirt or rent a movie or get a paycheck, you toss your bit into the alphabet soup.

Principles in Action Economists have developed many tools to monitor the nation's economic performance. They even have a way to measure how much money families like yours have to spend. You will learn what these measures tell us—and don't tell us—about the economy.

Gross Domestic Product

Economists use a system called **national income accounting** to monitor the U.S. economy. They collect and organize macroeconomic statistics on production, income, investment, and savings. The Department of Commerce then presents this data in the form of National Income and Product Accounts (NIPA). The government uses NIPA data to determine economic policies, as you will read about in Chapters 15 and 16.

national income accounting a system economists use to collect and organize macroeconomic statistics on production, income, investment, and savings

Visual Glossary
online

Go to the Visual Glossary Online for an interactive review of **Gross Domestic Product.**

Action Graph
online

Go to Action Graph Online for animated versions of key charts and graphs.

How the Economy Works
online

Go to How the Economy Works Online for an interactive lesson on what causes a **recession.**

What is Gross Domestic Product?

◄ **gross domestic product** the dollar value of all final goods and services produced within a country's borders in a given year

Dollar Value	Final Goods & Services	Within a Country's Borders
✓ **YES** Cash value of all goods and services sold	✓ **YES** Goods and services offered to consumers	✓ **YES** American or foreign companies producing in the United States
✗ **NO** Cost of producing goods and services	✗ **NO** Intermediate goods used to produce other goods and services	✗ **NO** American companies producing overseas

 Money paid by shoppers in New York for corn grown in Iowa — ✓ **YES**

 Money paid by buyers in Indiana for cars made by a Japanese company at a factory in Kentucky — ✓ **YES**

 Fees charged to patients by a dentist in Texas — ✓ **YES**

 Money paid by a computer factory in New Mexico for computer chips produced in California — ✗ **NO**

 Cost of processing wood pulp into paper at a factory in Maine — ✗ **NO**

 Money paid by shoppers in Florida for jeans manufactured in Mexico by a company headquartered in North Carolina — ✗ **NO**

GDP ADDING MACHINE

▲ Basically, gross domestic product tracks exchanges of money. To understand GDP, you need to understand which exchanges are included in the final calculation—and which ones are not. ***Look at the six examples shown here. Compare each one to the definition of gross domestic product and explain why it is or is not included in the GDP.***

Visual Glossary
online
To expand your understanding of this and other key economic terms, visit **PearsonSchool.com/PHecon**

Defining GDP

The most important measure in NIPA is **gross domestic product** (GDP), which is the dollar value of all final goods and services produced within a country's borders in a given year. To help you understand GDP, let us examine each part of this definition:

- *Dollar value* refers to the total cash value of the sales of all goods and services produced in a country's households, firms, and government in a calendar year. Since different quantities of goods such as oranges, computers, and movie tickets are sold at different prices, economists figure out the average prices of these items and the total number sold during the year. These cash figures are then used to calculate GDP.
- *Final goods and services* are products in the form sold to consumers. They differ from **intermediate goods,** which are products used in the production of final goods. The memory chips that a computer maker buys to put into its machines are intermediate goods; the computer is a final good.
- *Produced within a country's borders* is especially important to remember. Because we are trying to find the country's gross *domestic* product, we can look only at the goods and services produced within that country. For example, the GDP of the U.S. economy includes cars made in Ohio by a Japanese car company but not cars made in Brazil by an American automaker.
- *In a given year* takes into account when a good was produced. Suppose your neighbor sells you his used car. When the car was originally made, it was counted in the GDP of that year. Thus, it would be inaccurate to count it toward GDP again this year when it was resold.

Expenditure Approach

Government economists calculate GDP two ways. In one method, they use the expenditure approach, sometimes called the output-expenditure approach. First, economists estimate the annual expenditures, or amounts spent, on four categories of final goods and services:

1. consumer goods and services
2. business goods and services
3. government goods and services
4. net exports

Two of these categories need explanation. First, bear in mind that consumer goods include two kinds of goods. They are **durable goods**—those that last for a relatively long time, such as refrigerators and DVD players—and **nondurable goods**—those that last a short period of time, such as food, light bulbs, and sneakers.

Net exports are found by adding up exports—goods produced in the country but purchased in other countries—and then subtracting imports. Imports, of course, were produced in another country.

After finding the value of those four categories, economists add them together to arrive at the total expenditures on goods and services produced during the year. This total equals GDP. **Figure 12.1** provides a simplified example of calculating GDP with the expenditure approach.

Income Approach

The second method to calculate GDP, known as the income approach, calculates GDP by adding up all the incomes in the economy. The rationale for this approach is that when a firm sells a product or service, the selling price minus the dollar value of goods and services purchased

gross domestic product the dollar value of all final goods and services produced within a country's borders in a given year

intermediate goods products used in the production of final goods

durable goods those goods that last for a relatively long time, such as refrigerators, cars, and DVD players

nondurable goods those goods that last a short period of time, such as food, light bulbs, and sneakers

---

Figure 12.1	**Expenditure Approach**

❶ Suppose an economy's entire output is cars and trucks.

❷ This year the economy produces:

10 cars at $15,000 each = $150,000
+ 10 trucks at $20,000 each = $200,000
———————————————————
Total = $350,000

❸ The economy's GDP for this year is $350,000.

CHART SKILLS

The expenditure approach is a practical way of calculating GDP.

1. What would the economy's GDP be if the entire output was 15 cars at $15,000 each and 11 trucks at $20,000 each?
2. Using the expenditure approach, explain how a new housing complex would add to the GDP.

Figure 12.2 **Income Approach**

❶ Suppose an economy's entire output is cars and trucks.

❷ All employed citizens, therefore, would work in the car and truck industry, or for its suppliers.

❸ The combined selling price of all the cars and trucks reflects the money paid to all the people who helped build the vehicles.

❹ The economy's GDP for this year, then, is the sum of the income of all its working citizens, or $350,000.

Engineers   Designers   Planners   Assembly-line workers   Managers   Suppliers (metal, glass, etc.)

Combined income = $350,000

CHART SKILLS

The income approach is generally a more accurate way of calculating GDP than the expenditure approach.

1. What would the economy's GDP be if the auto company in the example also had to pay the $15,000 in fees to an advertising agency?
2. Using the income approach, explain how a new housing complex would add to the GDP.

from other firms represents income for the firm's owners and employees.

Suppose your neighbor bought a newly built house for $200,000. That $200,000 (minus what the builder spent on lumber, plaster, etc.) is income shared by all of the people who helped build and sell the house—including the contractor, the bricklayer, the roofers, and the real estate broker. Each of these people may get only a small share of the house's selling price. However, if we added up all those shares, we would arrive at $200,000 (minus what the builder spent on lumber, plaster, etc.) worth of income generated by the sale. In other words, the house's selling price is equal to the amount of income earned by all of the people who helped build and sell it.

This same logic holds for all goods and services. Thus, we may calculate GDP by adding up all income earned in the economy, as shown in **Figure 12.2.**

In theory, calculating GDP with the income approach and the expenditure approach should give us the same total. In

nominal GDP GDP measured in current prices

real GDP GDP expressed in constant, or unchanging, prices

fact, there are usually differences because of errors in the underlying data. Economists who work in the federal government take those differences into account. They first determine GDP using both approaches. Then they compare the two totals and make adjustments to offset the differences. This gives them a more accurate result.

✔ **CHECKPOINT** *Why are imports not included in gross domestic product?*

Nominal Versus Real GDP

Government officials use gross domestic product to find out how well the economy is performing. To help them understand what is really going on in the economy, economists distinguish between two measures of GDP, nominal and real.

Nominal GDP

In **Figures 12.1** and **12.2**, we calculated **nominal GDP**—that is, GDP measured in current prices. Because it is based on current prices, this type of GDP is also called "current GDP." To calculate nominal GDP, we simply use the current year's prices to calculate the value of the current year's output. **Figure 12.3** shows how the definition of nominal GDP applies to the small economy that produces only cars and trucks.

Real GDP

The data in **Figure 12.3** reveal a problem with nominal GDP. The GDP of Year 2 is higher than that of Year 1 even though the output of cars and trucks in the two years is the same. The difference is due to an increase in prices. As a result of these price increases, the higher GDP figure in the second year is misleading. To correct for this distortion, economists determine **real GDP,** which is GDP expressed in constant, or unchanging, prices.

Look at the third section of **Figure 12.3.** Notice that GDP in Year 2 is based on the prices from Year 1. By using real GDP, economists can discover whether an economy is actually producing more goods and services, regardless of changes in the prices of those items. In **Figure 12.3,** we can quickly see that output did not increase in Year 2.

✔ **CHECKPOINT** *What problem is solved by using real GDP?*

Limitations of GDP

Even though GDP is a valuable tool, it is still not a perfect yardstick. For instance, GDP does not take into account certain economic activities or aspects of life. These include nonmarket activities, the underground economy, negative externalities, and quality of life.

Nonmarket Activities

GDP does not measure goods and services that people make or do themselves, such as caring for children, mowing the lawn, cooking dinner, or washing the car. GDP does rise, however, when people pay someone else to do these things for them. When these nonmarket activities are shifted to the market, GDP goes up, even though production has not really increased.

The Underground Economy

A large amount of production and income is never recorded or reported to the government. For instance, transactions on the black market—the market for illegal goods—are not counted. Income from illegal gambling goes unreported. So do "under the table" wages that some companies pay workers to avoid paying business and income taxes.

Many legal, informal transactions are also not reported, for example, selling your bike to a friend or trading that bike for a stereo. If you earned money baby-sitting, mowing lawns, or shoveling snow, those payments are not included in the GDP either, even though goods and services were produced and income was earned.

Negative Externalities

Unintended economic side effects, or externalities, have a monetary value that often is not reflected in GDP. (See Chapter 3, Section 3, for a discussion of externalities.) For example, a power plant that emits smoke and dust is polluting the air. That negative result is not subtracted from GDP.

Quality of Life

Although some economists and politicians interpret rising GDP as a sign of rising well-being, we should remember that additional goods and services do not necessarily make people any happier. In fact, some things that are not counted in GDP contribute greatly to most people's quality

SS.912.E.2.11
Assess the impact of negative and positive externalities on the national environment.

Figure 12.3   Nominal and Real GDP

Year 1: Nominal GDP

❶ Suppose an economy's entire output is cars and trucks.

❷ This year the economy produces:

> 10 cars at
> $15,000 each = $150,000
> + 10 trucks at
> $20,000 each = $200,000
> _____
> Total = $350,000

❸ Since we have used the current year's prices to express the current year's output, the result is a nominal GDP of $350,000.

Year 2: Nominal GDP

❶ In the second year, the economy's output does not increase, but the prices of the cars and trucks do:

> 10 cars at
> $16,000 each = $160,000
> + 10 trucks at
> $21,000 each = $210,000
> _____
> Total = $370,000

❷ This new GDP figure of $370,000 is misleading. GDP rises because of an increase in prices. Economists prefer to have a measure of GDP that is not affected by changes in prices. So they calculate real GDP.

Year 2: Real GDP

❶ To correct for an increase in prices, economists establish a set of constant prices by choosing one year as a base year. When they calculate real GDP for other years, they use the prices from the base year. So we calculate the real GDP for Year 2 using the prices from Year 1:

> 10 cars at
> $15,000 each = $150,000
> + 10 trucks at
> $20,000 each = $200,000
> _____
> Total = $350,000

❷ Real GDP for Year 2, therefore, is $350,000.

CHART SKILLS

Real GDP reflects actual changes in output without the misleading effects of price increases.

1. How much did the real GDP increase by in the second year if output stayed the same but prices increased by $1,000 for each car and $1,500 for each truck?

2. Using the figures from Year 1 as your base, calculate the real GDP for Year 3 in which 15 cars and 14 trucks were sold.

Figure 12.4 Measurements of the Macroeconomy

These equations summarize the formulas for calculating some of the key macroeconomic measurements.

1. Using the information on the chart, define gross national product.
2. Why might economists track so many different indicators of the nation's economic health?

Action Graph
online

For an animated version of this graph, visit PearsonSchool.com/PHecon

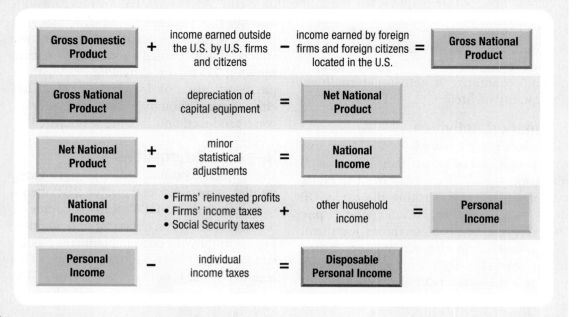

| Gross Domestic Product | + | income earned outside the U.S. by U.S. firms and citizens | − | income earned by foreign firms and foreign citizens located in the U.S. | = | Gross National Product |

| Gross National Product | − | depreciation of capital equipment | = | Net National Product |

| Net National Product | +− | minor statistical adjustments | = | National Income |

| National Income | − | • Firms' reinvested profits • Firms' income taxes • Social Security taxes | + | other household income | = | Personal Income |

| Personal Income | − | individual income taxes | = | Disposable Personal Income |

of life, such as pleasant surroundings, ample leisure time, and personal safety.

All of these limitations suggest that GDP is a somewhat flawed measure of output and income and a poor measure of people's well-being. Nevertheless, while the measure may be imperfect, when calculated consistently over a period of time, GDP helps reveal economic growth rates. For this reason, economists and policymakers closely watch the nation's GDP.

✔ **CHECKPOINT** *What are two economic activities that GDP does not include?*

Other Output and Income Measures

As you have read, our system of National Income and Product Accounts provides numerous measurements of the performance of the nation's economy. While gross domestic product is the primary measure of income and output, economists also look at other measures to focus on specific parts of the economy. Many of these other yardsticks are derived from GDP. **Figure 12.4** shows how GDP is used to determine five other economic measures.

The first is **gross national product** (GNP), the annual income earned by a nation's

gross national product the annual income earned by a nation's firms and citizens

depreciation the loss of the value of capital equipment that results from normal wear and tear

firms and citizens. GNP is a measure of the market value of all goods and services produced by Americans in one year. Study the chart above to see how GNP is related to GDP.

GNP does not account for **depreciation,** or the loss of the value of capital equipment that results from normal wear and tear. The cost of replacing this physical capital slightly reduces the value of what we produce. GNP minus the cost of depreciation of capital equipment is called net national product (NNP). NNP measures the net output for one year, or the output made after the adjustment for depreciation.

Once they have calculated NNP, government economists adjust their figures to account for minor discrepancies between different sources of data. After making these minor adjustments to NNP, they get another measure, called national income (NI).

From NI, we can find out how much pretax income businesses actually pay to U.S. households. This is found by subtracting profits that firms reinvest in the business and the income taxes and Social Security taxes they pay out. What remains is called personal income (PI).

Finally, we want to know how much money people actually have to spend after they pay *their* taxes, a figure called disposable personal income (DPI). To find DPI, we take personal income and subtract individual income and Social Security taxes.

See how far we have come. Beginning with GDP, the value of all goods and services produced in a year, we wind up knowing how much cash Americans have to spend or put in the bank.

 CHECKPOINT *What does disposable personal income show?*

Influences on GDP

So far, we have defined GDP, calculated it, and learned about its limitations. One important issue remains, however: What influences GDP? That is, in a real economy, what factors can make GDP go up or down? These questions go to the heart of macroeconomics.

Aggregate Supply

As you read earlier, market supply is the amount of a particular good or service available for purchase at all possible prices in an individual market. But how do we look at supply and prices on a macroeconomic level? Think of aggregate supply as a supply curve for the whole economy.

First, economists add up the total supply of goods and services produced for sale in the economy—in other words, GDP. Then they calculate the **price level,** the average of all prices in the economy. Now they can determine **aggregate supply,** the total amount of goods and services in the economy available at all possible price levels.

In a nation's economy, as the prices of most goods and services change, the price level changes. Firms respond by changing their output. For example, if the price level rises, which means that the prices of most goods and services are rising, firms have an incentive to increase their output. Similarly, as prices throughout the economy fall, companies' profits shrink. In response, they reduce output. You can see this effect in the aggregate supply (AS) curve in **Figure 12.5**. As the price level rises, real GDP, or aggregate supply, rises. As the price level falls, real GDP falls.

price level the average of all prices in the economy

aggregate supply the total amount of goods and services in the economy available at all possible price levels

 MA.912.A.2.2 Interpret a graph to represent a real-world situation.

Figure 12.5 **Aggregate Supply and Demand**

GRAPH SKILLS

Aggregate supply and demand represent supply and demand on a nationwide scale. The far right-hand chart shows what happens to GDP and price levels when aggregate demand shifts from AD$_1$ to AD$_2$.

1. What do the positive (upward to the right) and negative (downward to the right) slopes of these curves mean?
2. If a country goes to war, causing an increase in government demand for all kinds of goods, how might real GDP and price levels be affected?

Action Graph online

For an animated version of this graph, visit PearsonSchool.com/PHecon

Aggregate Demand

Aggregate demand is the amount of goods and services in the economy that will be purchased at all possible price levels. As price levels in the economy move up and down, individuals and businesses change how much they buy—in the opposite direction that aggregate supply changes.

For example, a lower price level translates into greater purchasing power for households, because the real value of money rises as price levels drop. The dollars that we hold are worth more at lower price levels than they are at higher price levels. Therefore, falling prices increase wealth and demand. This scenario is called the wealth effect.

On the other hand, as the price level rises, purchasing power declines, causing a reduction in the quantity of goods and services demanded. The aggregate demand (AD) curve shows this relationship between price and real GDP demanded. As you can see from **Figure 12.5**, this curve is negatively sloped; that is, it moves downward to the right. Consumers account for most of aggregate demand, but business spending on capital investment, government spending, and foreigners' demand for export goods all play roles, too.

Aggregate Supply/Aggregate Demand Equilibrium

When we put together the aggregate supply (AS) and aggregate demand (AD) curves, we can find the AS/AD equilibrium in the economy as a whole. Look at **Figure 12.5**. The intersection of the AS and AD_1 curves indicates an equilibrium price level of P_1 and an equilibrium real GDP of Q_1.

Now consider how GDP might change. Any shift in either the AS or AD curve will cause real GDP to change. For example, the graph shows aggregate demand falling from line AD_1 to line AD_2. As a result, the equilibrium GDP (Q_2) falls, and so does the equilibrium price level (P_2).

Any shift in aggregate supply or aggregate demand will have an impact on real GDP and on the price level. In the next section, we will discuss some factors that may cause such shifts.

✓ **CHECKPOINT** *What four types of demand are included in aggregate demand?*

 FL LA.1112.2.2.2, SS.912.E.2.1, SS.912.E.3, SS.912.G.2.2, LA.1112.1.6.1

SECTION 1 ASSESSMENT

Essential Questions Journal To continue to build a response to the Essential Question, go to your **Essential Questions Journal**.

❓ Guiding Question

1. Use your completed chart to answer this question: What does the GDP show about the nation's economy?

2. **Extension** Your purchasing choices help reflect economic trends. Suppose that you are among the many consumers who choose the same model of a new U.S.-made cellphone in a given year. How does that affect the GDP?

Key Terms and Main Ideas

3. **(a)** What is the difference between **intermediate goods** and final goods? **(b)** Why are intermediate goods not included in GDP?

4. How does **nominal GDP** differ from **real GDP**?

5. **(a)** If **aggregate demand** rises, what happens to real GDP? **(b)** What happens to the **price level?**

6. How does **gross domestic product** differ from **gross national product?**

Critical Thinking

7. **Describe (a)** List four factors that make up the GDP. **(b)** Describe how economists use this information to determine the GDP for a specific year.

8. **Analyze (a)** Why do economists calculate GDP by both the expenditure approach and the income approach? **(b)** Why is the expenditure approach sometimes called the "output-expenditure approach"?

9. **Interpret (a)** What incentive do rising prices give to firms? **(b)** What might prevent firms from earning increased profits during a time of rising prices?

10. **Identify** In addition to declining business investments, what other factors lead to negative changes in aggregate demand?

Math Skills

11. Suppose that a very small economy produces only televisions and computers. Determine nominal GDP and real GDP in Year 4, using the following chart:

Visit PearsonSchool.com/PHecon for additional math help.

Production	Year 1 (base)	Year 4
Computers	10 sold at $2,000 each	17 sold at $2,500 each
Televisions	15 sold at 500 each	20 sold at $550 each

SECTION 2 Business Cycles

 NGSSS

LA.1112.1.6 Use multiple strategies to develop vocabulary.

MA.912.A.2.2 Interpret a graph to represent a real-world situation.

SS.912.E.1.12 Examine the four phases of the business cycle.

SS.912.E.2.1 Identify and explain broad economic goals.

SS.912.E.2.5 Analyze how capital investments impact productivity and economic growth.

ECONOMIC DICTIONARY

As you read the section, look for the definitions of these **Key Terms:**

- business cycle
- expansion
- economic growth
- peak
- contraction
- trough
- recession
- depression
- stagflation
- leading indicators

Guiding Question

What factors affect the phases of a business cycle?

Copy this table and fill it in as you read to explain what economic factors influence the phases of a business cycle.

Business Investment	Interest Rates and Credit	Consumer Expectations	External Shocks
• Increased investment boosts aggregate demand, gross GDP • Decreased investment cuts AD, causing GDP decline	• •	• •	• •

▶ **Economics and You** Sometimes, you don't have to read the newspaper to tell how the economy is doing. You can see the signs all around you. They may be *Help Wanted* signs in front of local stores and factories—when the economy is doing well, businesses hire and it's easier for you to find a part-time job. Or they may be *Closed* or *Going Out of Business* signs in the windows of those same businesses. You might even get an idea by counting the number of *For Sale* or *Foreclosure* signs where you live. The ups and downs of the economy affect us all.

Principles in Action The national economy undergoes periodic cycles of good times, then bad times, and then good times again. Recognizing this pattern, economists try to predict what the economy will do in the future—what can be done to make the good times last longer and keep the bad times brief. In this section, you will learn what factors affect these ups and downs and how they have shaped the country's economy. You will also see how the actions of ordinary consumers and borrowers can affect the phases of the economy and how long these phases last.

Phases of a Business Cycle

As you read in Chapter 3, a **business cycle** is a period of macroeconomic expansion followed by a period of macroeconomic contraction. Economists also call these periods of change "economic fluctuations."

Business cycles are not minor, day-to-day ups and downs. They are major changes in real gross domestic product above or below normal levels. The typical business cycle consists of four phases: expansion, peak, contraction, and trough.

1. *Expansion* An **expansion** is a period of economic growth as measured by a rise in real GDP. To economists, **economic growth** is a steady, long-term increase in real GDP. In the expansion phase, jobs are plentiful, the unemployment rate falls, and businesses prosper.
2. *Peak* When real GDP stops rising, the economy has reached its **peak,** the height of an economic expansion.

business cycle a period of macroeconomic expansion followed by one of macroeconomic contraction

expansion a period of economic growth as measured by a rise in real GDP

economic growth a steady, long-term increase in real GDP

peak the height of an economic expansion, when real GDP stops rising

Figure 12.6

Tracking a Business Cycle

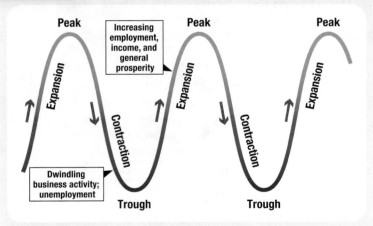

GRAPH SKILLS

A business cycle reaches a peak, then falls into a contraction. When the contraction reaches the low point, a new expansion begins.

1. What is the low point of the cycle called? What is the period of increasing business activity called?
2. In which part of a business cycle do you think the United States is right now? Give evidence to support your conclusion.

Action Graph
online

For an animated version of this graph, visit
PearsonSchool.com/PHecon

---

contraction a period of economic decline marked by falling real GDP

trough the lowest point of an economic contraction, when real GDP stops falling

recession a prolonged economic contraction

depression a recession that is especially long and severe

stagflation a decline in real GDP combined with a rise in the price level

3. *Contraction* After reaching its peak, the economy enters a period of **contraction,** an economic decline marked by falling real GDP. Falling output generally causes unemployment to rise.

4. *Trough* When the economy has "bottomed out," it has reached the **trough** (trawf), the lowest point in an economic contraction. At that point, real GDP stops falling and a new period of expansion begins.

During a contraction, GDP is always falling. But other economic conditions, such as price levels and the unemployment rate, may vary. Economists created terms to describe contractions with different characteristics and levels of severity. They include:

- *Recession* If real GDP falls for two consecutive quarters (at least six straight months), the economy is said to be in a recession. A **recession** is a prolonged economic contraction. Generally lasting from 6 to 18 months, recessions are typically marked by unemployment reaching the range of 6 percent to 10 percent.

- *Depression* If a recession is especially long and severe, it may be called a **depression.** The term has no precise definition but usually refers to a deep recession with features such as high unemployment and low economic output.

- *Stagflation* This term combines parts of *stagnant*—a word meaning unmoving or decayed—and *inflation*. **Stagflation** is a decline in real GDP (output) combined with a rise in the price level (inflation).

Although economists know much about business cycles, they cannot predict how long the phases in a particular cycle will last. The only certainty is that a growing economy will eventually experience a downturn, and that a contracting economy will eventually bounce back.

✓ **CHECKPOINT** *What are the four phases of a business cycle?*

What Keeps a Business Cycle Going?

The shifts that occur during a business cycle have many causes, some more predictable than others. Often, two or more factors will combine to push the economy into the next phase of a business cycle. Typically, a sharp rise or drop in some important economic variable will set off a series of events that bring about the next phase. Business cycles are affected by four main economic variables:

1. business investment
2. interest rates and credit
3. consumer expectations
4. external shocks

Business Investment

When the economy is expanding, businesses expect their sales and profits to keep rising. Therefore, they may invest heavily in building new plants and buying new equipment. Or they may invest in the expansion of old plants in order to increase the plants' productive capacity. All of this investment spending creates additional output and jobs, helping to increase GDP and maintain the expansion.

At some point, however, firms may decide that they have expanded enough or that demand for their products is dropping. They cut back on investment spending; as a result, aggregate demand falls. The result is a decline in GDP and also in the price level. The drop in business spending reduces output and income in other sectors of the economy.

When that occurs, industries that produce capital goods slow their own production and begin to lay off workers. Other industries might follow, causing overall unemployment to rise. Jobless workers cannot buy new cars, eat at restaurants, or perhaps even pay their rent. If the downward spiral picks up speed, a recession results.

Interest Rates and Credit

In the United States economy, consumers often use credit to purchase "big ticket" items—from new cars and houses to home electronics and vacations. The cost of credit is the interest rate that financial institutions charge their customers. If the interest rate rises, consumers are less likely to buy those new cars and appliances.

Businesses, too, look to interest rates in deciding whether or not to purchase new equipment, expand their facilities, or make many other large investments. When interest rates are low, companies are more willing to borrow money. When interest rates climb, business borrowing falls. One result of rising interest rates, then, is less output. Such a result may lead to a contraction phase.

Consider one example of the impact of interest rates on the business cycle. In the early 1980s, high consumer interest rates helped bring on the worst economic slump in the United States since the Great Depression. Some credit-card interest rates reached 21 percent. As a result, the cost of expensive items usually purchased using credit was too high for many Americans. With reduced consumer spending, the economy entered a recession that pushed unemployment rates over 9 percent—the highest since the Depression.

Consumer Expectations

Consumer spending is determined partly by consumers' expectations. If people expect the economy to begin contracting, they may reduce their spending because they expect layoffs and lower incomes.

This reduced spending can actually help bring on a contraction, as firms respond to reduced demand for their products. Thus consumer expectations often become self-fulfilling prophecies, creating the very outcome that consumers fear. In the summer of 2007, consumer confidence fell. By September, consumer confidence was the lowest it had been in two years. This low level of consumer confidence affected the holiday shopping season at the end of the year.

High consumer confidence has the opposite effect on the economy. If people expect a rapidly growing economy, they will also expect abundant job opportunities and rising incomes. Thus, they will buy more goods and services, pushing up gross domestic product.

External Shocks

Of all the factors that affect the business cycle, perhaps most difficult to predict are external shocks, which you read about in Chapter 6. External shocks can dramatically affect an economy's

Simulation *Activity*

Ups and Downs
You may be asked to take part in a role-playing game about the ups and downs of the business cycle.

CREDIT CARD SERVICE DESK

ACTUALLY, SIR, THE "GOLD" PART OF YOUR GOLD CARD REFERS TO THE INTEREST RATE, NOT THE CREDIT LIMIT.

7-31
THAVES

E-mail:BobThaves@aol.com
©2000 Thaves/Dist. by NEA, Inc.
www.comics.com

◄ High interest rates are one of the pitfalls of easy access to credit. *How do high interest rates affect businesses as well as individuals?*

What causes a recession?

Recessions are an inevitable part of the business cycle. A number of conditions and events may trigger a recession– or deepen a recession that has already begun.

1 The economy has enjoyed an extended period of growth. Businesses are expanding, spending is up, and unemployment and inflation are largely under control.

2 Despite the best efforts of government and business, recessions occur. Here are four possible reasons:

External shock War breaks out in a nation where U.S. banks and businesses have invested heavily. This nation is also an important supplier of goods to the U.S.

Business investment The war cuts into the assets of many U.S. firms. They lay off workers and cut back on plans to expand.

Peak

Contraction

aggregate supply. Examples of negative external shocks include disruptions of the oil supply, wars that interrupt trade, and droughts that severely reduce crop harvests.

Let's consider what might happen if a shock occurred. Suppose that the nation's supply of imported oil was suddenly cut off. Immediately, the price of any remaining oil would skyrocket. This rapid increase would have a powerful ripple effect on the economy. Oil is used to produce many goods, and petroleum products fuel the trucks, trains, and airplanes that transport goods from factories to stores. The oil shortage and high prices would force firms to reduce production and raise prices. In other words, GDP declines and the price level rises. This economic condition is particularly harmful to businesses and households and difficult for policymakers to fix.

Of course, an economy may also enjoy positive external shocks. The discovery of a large deposit of oil or minerals will contribute to a nation's wealth. A growing season with a perfect mix of sun and rain may create bountiful harvests that drive food prices down. Positive shocks tend to shift the AS curve to the right, lowering the price level and increasing real GDP.

External shocks usually come without much warning. The other key factors capable of pushing an economy from one phase of the business cycle to another are more predictable. So economists track business investment, interest rates, and consumer expectations in order to more accurately forecast new stages of the business cycle.

✔ **CHECKPOINT** *How are external shocks different from the other factors that affect the business cycle?*

Interest rates and credit
As the war and threat of recession continue, banks are slower to extend credit. Interest rates creep up.

Consumer expectations
Predictions about a long recession discourage people from spending.

3 As these factors feed into one another, unemployment rises and business activity dwindles. In time, though, the cycle will move into a new phase of expansion.

UNEMPLOYMENT DEPT.

Check Your Understanding
1. How can interest rates help bring on a recession?
2. Look at the four headings under #2. For each one, identify a condition that might lead to an economic expansion.

Trough

Business Cycle Forecasting

Predicting changes in a business cycle is difficult. For example, in the summer of 1929, John J. Raskob, Senior financial officer of General Motors, declared his firm belief that the United States was on the verge of the greatest industrial expansion in its history.

> **"** In my opinion the wealth of the country is bound to increase at a very rapid rate… Anyone who believes that opportunities are now closed and that from now on the country will get worse instead of better is welcome to the opinion—and whatever increment it will bring. I think that we have scarcely started… I am firm in my belief that anyone not only can be rich but ought to be rich. **"**
>
> —John Jakob Raskob, Interview in the *Ladies Home Journal*, August 1929

Less than two months later, the stock market crashed, setting off the worst depression in American history.

Economists today know a lot more about the workings of our economy than Raskob did in 1929. However, economic predictions are still tricky. To predict the next phase of a business cycle, forecasters must anticipate movements in real GDP before they occur. This is no easy task, given the large number of factors that influence the level of output in a modern economy.

Government and business decision makers need economic predictions to be accurate, however, so they can respond properly to changes in a business cycle. If businesses expect a contraction, they may postpone building new factories. If government policymakers expect a contraction, they may take steps to try to prevent a recession.

United States Real GDP, 1925–1945

GDP (in billions of 2000 dollars)

Stock market crashes

U.S. enters World War II

Year: 1925 1926 1927 1928 1929 1930 1931 1933 1935 1937 1939 1941 1943 1945

SOURCE: Louis D. Johnston and Samuel H. Williamson, "The Annual Real and Nominal GDP for the United States, 1790–Present." Economic History Services, October 2005, URL : http://www.eh.net/hmit/gdp/

▲ Declining GDP and high unemployment were two major signs of the Great Depression, the longest recession in U.S. history. *In what year did the Great Depression hit its trough? How long did it take for GDP to return to its pre-Depression peak?*

MA.912.A.2.2 Interpret a graph to represent a real-world situation.

Economists have many tools available for making these predictions. The **leading indicators** are a set of key economic variables that economists use to predict future trends in a business cycle.

The stock market is one leading indicator. Typically, the stock market turns sharply downward before a recession begins. For example, the crash of the Nasdaq exchange in 2000 preceded the recession of 2001. Interest rates are another indicator. As you have seen, interest rates have a strong effect on consumer and business spending.

The Conference Board, a private business research organization, maintains an index of ten leading economic indicators, including stock prices, interest rates, and manufacturers' new orders of capital goods. Economists and policymakers closely watch this index, which is updated monthly. However, like the other important tools used to forecast changes in the business cycle, it is not altogether reliable.

leading indicators a set of key economic variables that economists use to predict future trends in a business cycle

✔ **CHECKPOINT** *Why is it difficult to predict the future of a business cycle?*

Business Cycles in American History

Economic activity in the United States has indeed followed a cyclical pattern. Periods of GDP growth alternate with periods of GDP decline.

The Great Depression

As you read earlier, before the 1930s many economists believed that when an economy declined, it would quickly recover on its own. This explains why, when the U.S. stock market crashed in 1929, and the economy took a nosedive, President Herbert Hoover felt little need to change his economic policies.

However, the Great Depression did not rapidly cure itself. Rather, it was the most severe economic downturn in the history of industrial capitalism. Between 1929 and 1933, GDP fell by about a quarter, and unemployment rose sharply. In fact, one out of every four workers was jobless, and those who could find work often earned very low wages.

As the effects of the Great Depression spread throughout the world, it affected economists' beliefs about the macro-economy. The depression, along with the publication of John Maynard Keynes's *The General Theory of Employment, Interest, and Money*, pushed economists to consider the idea that modern market economies could fall into long-lasting contractions. In addition, many economists accepted Keynes's idea that government intervention might be needed to pull an economy out of a depression. You will read more about Keynes and his ideas in Chapter 15.

The depression also affected American politics. Rejecting Hoover, voters in 1932 elected the Democratic governor of New York, Franklin Delano Roosevelt, to the presidency. Roosevelt soon began a series of government programs, known as the New Deal, designed to get people back to work.

Programs such as the Works Progress Administration and the Civilian Conservation Corps got able-bodied workers back on the job and earning income, which they then spent supporting their families. In this way, spending increased throughout the economy.

Still, although the New Deal relieved some of the effects of hard times, it did not end the Great Depression. Not until the United States entered into World War II did the economy achieve full recovery. The sudden surge in government defense spending boosted real GDP well above pre-depression levels.

Some Later Recessions

Thankfully, no economic downturns since the 1930s have been nearly as severe as the Great Depression. We have had recessions, though.

In the 1970s, Arab members of the Organization of Petroleum Exporting Countries (OPEC) placed an embargo on oil shipped to the United States and quadrupled the price of its oil. These actions caused external shocks in the American oil market. As oil prices skyrocketed, raw material costs rose, and the economy quickly contracted into a period of stagflation.

Reeling from higher-than-ever prices for gasoline and heating fuel prices, Americans began looking for ways to conserve energy. They turned down their heat; bought smaller, more fuel-efficient cars; and began researching energy alternatives to petroleum. When the United States and other nations developed more of their own energy resources, OPEC finally lowered its oil prices.

As you read earlier, there was another recession in the early 1980s. High interest rates and other factors caused real GDP to fall and the unemployment rate to rise to over 9 percent in the early 1980s.

Following a brief recession in 1991, the U.S. economy grew steadily, with real GDP rising each year during the 1990s.

MA.912.A.2.2
Interpret a graph to represent a real-world situation.

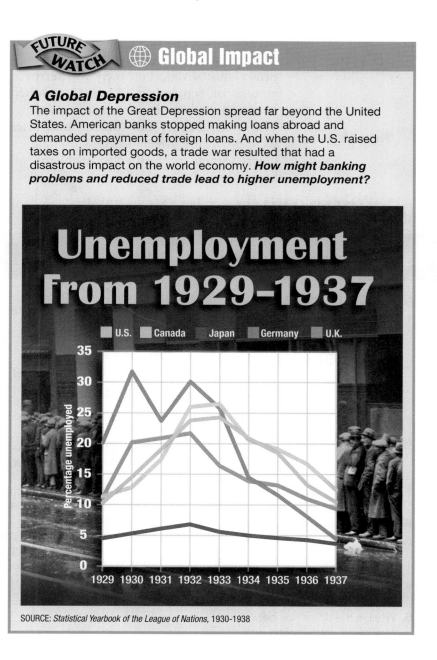

A Global Depression

The impact of the Great Depression spread far beyond the United States. American banks stopped making loans abroad and demanded repayment of foreign loans. And when the U.S. raised taxes on imported goods, a trade war resulted that had a disastrous impact on the world economy. *How might banking problems and reduced trade lead to higher unemployment?*

Unemployment From 1929-1937

■ U.S. ■ Canada ■ Japan ■ Germany ■ U.K.

Percentage unemployed

1929 1930 1931 1932 1933 1934 1935 1936 1937

SOURCE: *Statistical Yearbook of the League of Nations, 1930-1938*

The country enjoyed record growth, low unemployment, and low inflation. Some economists began to suggest that the nature of the business cycle had changed. Perhaps we had learned how to control recessions and promote long-term growth.

Much of this growth was fueled by the rise of Internet companies, called dot.coms, after part of their Internet address. As the dot.com boom of the 1990s ended, however, the U.S. growth slowed. Businesses and individuals invested billions of dollars in new technology that proved to be unprofitable and, in some cases, worthless. The negative effects of the technology crash spread throughout the economy to other industries. In March 2001, the country slipped into a recession.

Economists hoped this decline would prove short-lived, but then the terrorist attacks of September 11, 2001, resulted in a sharp drop in consumer spending. The hotel, airline, and tourism industries were especially affected. Many companies blamed their performance problems on September 11.

The Business Cycle Today

The recession ended in November 2001 when the economy began to grow slowly. Historically low interest rates prevented the economy from slipping back into a recession. However, unemployment continued to rise steadily over the following years as companies laid off more workers and kept spending low. Growth was not strong enough to dispel the feeling of bad times even though the recession had ended.

The economy did recover, though. By late 2003, it was surging, with GDP growing at a rate of 7.5 percent over three months. After that, growth slowed, though it did continue. High gasoline prices in 2006 caused the economy's growth to slow even further. Difficulties in the home mortgage market spiraled into a financial crisis and economic recession in 2008. In the following years the economy improved slowly, though the unemployment rate remained high.

✔ **CHECKPOINT** *What was a lasting effect of the Great Depression?*

 FL SS.912.E.1.12, LA.1112.1.6.1, LA.1112.2.2.2, LA.1112.6.2, MA.912.A.2.1

SECTION 2 ASSESSMENT

Essential Questions Journal To continue to build a response to the Essential Question, go to your **Essential Questions Journal.**

❓ Guiding Question

1. Use your completed table to answer this question: What factors affect the phases of a business cycle?

2. **Extension** High interest rates affect individuals as well as the business cycle itself. Suppose you wanted to purchase a new cellphone but did not have the money to pay for it. If someone offered you the money at 15 percent interest over a six-month period, would you be interested? What might you do instead of borrowing the money?

Key Terms and Main Ideas

3. **(a)** What is a **business cycle? (b)** In its **trough** phase, what has happened to the economy?

4. How can interest rates push a business cycle into a **contraction?**

5. What is the difference between a **recession, depression,** and **stagflation?**

6. Why is the stock market considered to be a **leading indicator** of economic change?

Critical Thinking

7. **Analyze** As a consumer, at which point in a business cycle would you prefer to be, the peak or the trough? Why? As a producer, at which point would you prefer to be?

8. **Research (a)** Select the recession of the 1970s, 1980s, or early 1990s. Explain what economic activity triggered it. **(b)** How did the economy recover? **(c)** Can such recessions be prevented?

9. **Identify (a)** What role did World War II play in ending the Great Depression? **(b)** Were the New Deal programs of Franklin Delano Roosevelt effective? Explain.

10. **Differentiate (a)** What factors other than declining business investments lead to changes in aggregate demand? **(b)** Is the price level a cause or an effect?

Math Skills

11. **(a)** Draw a line graph plotting four quarters of a year showing the real GDP. The first quarter reports 4.6 trillion, the second 4.3 trillion, the third 4.5 trillion, and the fourth 4.9 trillion. **(b)** On the graph, label the expansion, peak, contraction, and trough.

Visit PearsonSchool.com/PHecon for additional math help.

NGSSS

LA.1112.1.6 Use multiple strategies to develop vocabulary.

SS.912.E.2.1 Identify and explain broad economic goals.

SS.912.E.2.3 Research the contributions of key individuals of various backgrounds in the development of the U.S.

SS.912.E.2.5 Analyze how capital investments impact productivity and economic growth.

ECONOMIC DICTIONARY

As you read the section, look for the definitions of these **Key Terms:**

• real GDP per capita
• capital deepening
• saving
• savings rate
• technological progress

Guiding Question
How does the economy grow?

Copy this table and fill it in as you read to explain how an economy grows.

Changes in Real GDP	
Causes of Growth	**Causes of Decline**
• Capital deepening (more business investment) • Higher saving rate • Population growth with capital growth • •	• Less business investment • Lower saving rate • • •

▶ **Economics and You**   If you had lived in a typical American home 125 years ago, you would have owned a box filled with ice to preserve food, a wood-burning stove, and a horse or bicycle for transportation. For most of us today, those necessities of life have turned into a refrigerator-freezer; a furnace powered by gas, oil, or electricity; and a car. Clearly, as far as material possessions go, Americans of your generation are generally much better off today than they were 100 years ago. The biggest reason is economic growth.

Principles in Action   Economic growth, allows successive generations to have more and better goods and services than their parents had. In this section, we will describe how economic growth enables an entire society to make major improvements in its quality of life. Economics & You shows how you both benefit from and contribute to economic growth.

real GDP per capita
real GDP divided by the total population of a country

Measuring Economic Growth

The basic measure of a nation's economic growth rate is the percentage of change in real GDP over a period of time. For example, real GDP in 1996 was $8.3 trillion, and in 2006, it was $11.3 trillion. The economic growth rate for this decade was about 36 percent ($11.3 trillion − $8.3 trillion) ÷ $8.3 trillion × 100).

GDP and Population Growth

To satisfy the needs of a growing population, real GDP must grow at least as fast as the population does. This is one reason that economists prefer a measure that takes population growth into account. For this, they rely on **real GDP per capita**, which is real GDP divided by the total population of a country (*per capita* means "for each person"). **Figure 12.7** shows growth in real GDP per capita.

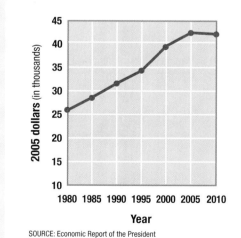

Figure 12.7   **Real GDP per Capita**

2005 dollars (in thousands)

Year

SOURCE: Economic Report of the President

GRAPH SKILLS

Americans have seen a fairly steady rise in their standard of living.

1. What has been the most recent trend in change in GDP?

2. Does this graph indicate that every American family improved its standard of living? Explain.

Action Graph
online

For an animated version of this graph, visit **PearsonSchool.com/PHecon**

capital deepening the process of increasing the amount of capital per worker

Real GDP per capita is considered the most accurate measure of a nation's standard of living. As long as real GDP is rising faster than the population, real GDP per capita will rise, and so will the standard of living. Economists can see how the standard of living has changed over time by comparing real GDP per capita from two different time periods. They can also examine the growth rates of real GDP per capita to compare the economic strength of two different nations.

GDP and Quality of Life

GDP measures standard of living, which relates to material goods. We cannot use it, however, to measure people's quality of life. As you read in Section 1, GDP excludes many factors that affect the quality of life, such as the state of the environment or the level of stress people feel in their daily lives.

In addition, while real GDP per capita represents the average output per person in an economy, it tells us nothing about how that output is distributed across the population. There are a number of ways that economists measure how income is distributed in the United States, such as "personal income distribution" and

"functional income distribution." These measures, while complicated, are important. If most of the income in a nation goes to relatively few people while the majority earn next to nothing, the typical person will not enjoy a very high standard of living even if the real GDP per capita figure is high.

Despite these facts, real GDP per capita is a good starting point for measuring a nation's quality of life. Nations with greater availability of goods and services usually enjoy better nutrition, safer and more comfortable housing, lower infant mortality, longer life spans, better education, greater job opportunities, and other indicators of a favorable quality of life.

Since economic growth has an enormous impact on quality of life, economists devote significant resources to figuring out what causes a nation's real GDP to rise. They focus on the roles of capital goods, technology, and a few related factors.

✔ **CHECKPOINT** *How is high GDP per capita linked to quality of life?*

Capital Deepening

Physical capital, the equipment used to produce goods and services, makes an important contribution to the output of an economy. With more physical capital, each worker can be more productive, producing more output per hour of work. Economists use the term *labor productivity* to describe the amount of output produced per worker.

Even if the size of the labor force does not change, more physical capital will lead to more output—in other words, to economic growth. This process of increasing the amount of capital per worker, called **capital deepening**, is one of the most important sources of growth in modern economies. (See **Figure 12.8.**)

Human capital, the productive knowledge and skills acquired by a worker through education and experience, also contributes to output. Firms, and employees themselves, can deepen human capital through training programs and on-the-job experience. Better-trained and more-experienced workers can produce more output per hour of work.

| Figure 12.8 | **Capital Deepening** |

GRAPH SKILLS

There are many benefits of capital deepening, as shown here.

1. What is capital deepening?

2. Suppose you own a small clothing shop. Why should buying a new line of clothes and providing special training for sales staff result in capital deepening?

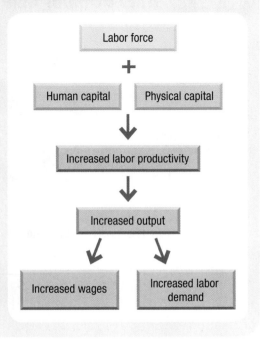

Along with increasing output per worker, capital deepening tends to increase job opportunities and workers' earnings. To understand why this happens, consider the effect of greater worker productivity on the demand for workers. As you read in Chapter 9, if workers can produce more output per hour, they become more valuable to their employers. As a result, employers will demand more workers. This increase in demand will increase the equilibrium wage rate in the labor market.

Therefore, with a labor force of a given size, capital deepening will increase output and workers' wages. How, then, does an economy increase its stock of capital per worker? It does so through saving and investment.

✔ **CHECKPOINT** *Why does capital deepening work with human capital?*

Saving and Investment

To see how saving and investment are related, consider an economy with no government sector and no foreign trade. In this simplified economy, consumers and business firms purchase all output. In other words, output can be used for consumption (by consumers) or investment (by firms). Income that is not used for consumption is called **saving.**

Since output can only be consumed or invested, whatever is not consumed must be invested. Therefore, in this simplified economy, saving is equal to investment. The proportion of disposable income that is saved is called the **savings rate.**

To see this another way, look at an individual's decision, as shown in **Figure 12.9.** Shawna had an after-tax income of $30,000 last year, but she spent only $25,000. That left her with $5,000 available for saving. She used some of her leftover income to purchase shares in a mutual fund, giving her ownership of some stocks and bonds. She put the rest of the money into a savings account at her bank.

Through her mutual-fund firm, her bank, and other intermediaries, Shawna's $5,000 was made available to businesses. The firms used the money to invest in new plants and equipment. So, when Shawna chose not to spend her entire income but

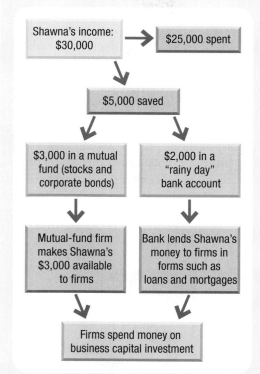

Figure 12.9 | **How Saving Leads to Capital Deepening**

Shawna's income: $30,000 → $25,000 spent

$5,000 saved

$3,000 in a mutual fund (stocks and corporate bonds)

$2,000 in a "rainy day" bank account

Mutual-fund firm makes Shawna's $3,000 available to firms

Bank lends Shawna's money to firms in forms such as loans and mortgages

Firms spend money on business capital investment

GRAPH SKILLS

Saving leads to capital deepening by providing funds for financial institutions to invest.

1. How much money has Shawna made available for investment in this example?

2. If people saved a high proportion of their incomes, how might the economy be affected?

to save a share, the amount that she saved became available for business investment.

If we consider the economy as a whole, the process works the same way. If total saving rises, more investment funds become available to businesses. Those firms will use most of these funds for capital investment. That is, they will expand the stock of capital in the business sector.

Higher saving, then, leads to higher investment, and thus to higher amounts of capital per worker. In other words, higher saving leads to capital deepening. Now we can understand why most nations promote saving. In the long run, more saving will lead to higher output and income for the population, raising GDP and the standard of living.

The United States has a low savings rate. To obtain the investment funds they need, businesses and the government borrow from other countries with higher savings rates.

✔ **CHECKPOINT** *How is saving linked to capital deepening?*

Personal Finance
For tips on savings and investment, see your Personal Finance Handbook in the back of the book or visit PearsonSchool.com/PHecon

saving income not used for consumption

savings rate the proportion of disposable income that is saved

Population, Government, and Foreign Trade

Now we will consider a slightly more realistic economy that has population growth, a government sector, and foreign trade. First, think about the effect of population growth on capital accumulation.

Population Growth

Population growth does not necessarily preclude economic growth. However, if the population grows while the supply of capital remains constant, the amount of capital per worker will shrink. This process, the opposite of capital deepening, leads to lower living standards. In fact, some relatively poor countries, such as Bangladesh, have large labor forces but small capital stocks.

The result is that output per worker—and earnings per worker—are relatively low. Conversely, a nation with low population growth and expanding capital stock will enjoy significant capital deepening.

Government

Government can affect capital deepening in several ways. If government raises tax rates to pay for additional services or to finance a war, households will have less money. People will reduce saving, thus reducing the money available to businesses for investment. In these cases, the government is taxing households in order to pay for its own consumption spending. The net effect is reduced investment.

On the other hand, a different result occurs if government invests the extra tax revenues in public goods, such as roads and telecommunications. These public goods are called infrastructure, the underlying necessities of modern life. Spending on infrastructure increases investment. To see why, consider what share of income the average household saves.

Suppose that, on average, households save 10 percent of their income. In this case, for every extra dollar in tax revenue the government collects, household saving (and investment) drops by 10 cents. However, government investment in infrastructure rises by $1. The net result is an increase in total investment of 90 cents. This kind of spending, then, is capital deepening, since the government is taxing its citizens to provide investment goods.

Foreign Trade

Foreign trade can result in a trade deficit, a situation in which the value of goods a country imports is higher than the value of goods it exports. (You will read more about trade deficits in Chapter 17.) Running a trade deficit may not seem like a wise practice, but if the imports consist of investment goods, the practice can foster capital deepening. Investment goods are the structures and equipment purchased by businesses.

Capital deepening can offset the negative effects of a trade deficit by helping generate economic growth, helping a

Economics & YOU

Economic Growth

When the economy is on the upswing, financial institutions are more likely to lend money. *A strong economy means you have greater access to loans that help pay for education.*

Student Loans!! *APPLY HERE*

Many economists see teen spending as a huge source of future economic growth. *When you spend money responsibly, you help the economy expand.*

▲ Economic growth has enabled our high standard of living. *How would you be affected if the economy stopped growing?*

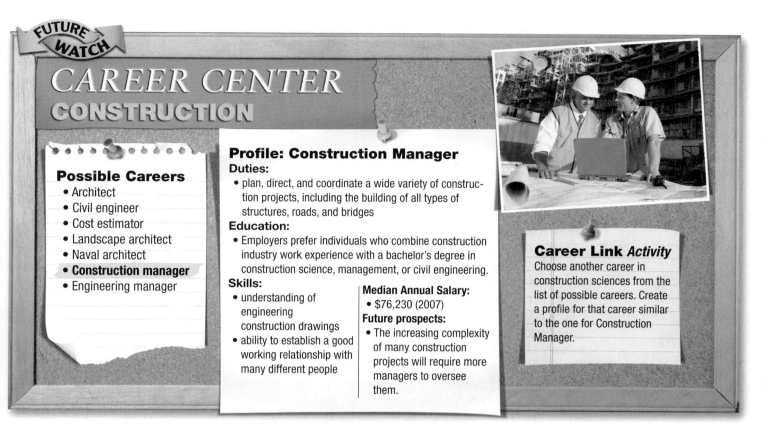

CAREER CENTER
CONSTRUCTION

Possible Careers
- Architect
- Civil engineer
- Cost estimator
- Landscape architect
- Naval architect
- **Construction manager**
- Engineering manager

Profile: Construction Manager

Duties:
- plan, direct, and coordinate a wide variety of construction projects, including the building of all types of structures, roads, and bridges

Education:
- Employers prefer individuals who combine construction industry work experience with a bachelor's degree in construction science, management, or civil engineering.

Skills:
- understanding of engineering construction drawings
- ability to establish a good working relationship with many different people

Median Annual Salary:
- $76,230 (2007)

Future prospects:
- The increasing complexity of many construction projects will require more managers to oversee them.

Career Link *Activity*
Choose another career in construction sciences from the list of possible careers. Create a profile for that career similar to the one for Construction Manager.

---

country pay back the money it borrowed in the first place. In the mid-1800s, for example, the United States financed the building of the transcontinental railroad in part by borrowing funds from investors in other countries. The borrowing created a trade deficit, but it also helped create a much higher rate of economic growth than would have occurred otherwise. The railroad promoted new industries and opened up vast areas to farming, leading to a huge increase in the nation's farm output.

Of course, not all trade deficits promote capital deepening. In this regard, trade deficits are similar to government taxation. Whether they encourage capital deepening and economic growth depends on how the funds are used. If they are used for short-term consumption, the economy will not grow any faster, and it will not have any additional GDP to pay back the debts. If the funds are used for long-term investment, however, they will foster capital deepening. The resulting economic growth will bring the country prosperity in the future.

✔ **CHECKPOINT** *Do higher tax rates increase or reduce investment?*

Technological Progress

Another key source of economic growth is technological progress. This term usually brings to mind new inventions or new ways of performing a task, but in economics, it has a more precise definition. **Technological progress** is an increase in efficiency gained by producing more output without using more inputs.

Technological progress occurs in many ways. It can result from new scientific knowledge—for example, nano-technology, making computer chips smaller and smaller—that has practical uses. It can be a new invention that allows workers to produce goods more efficiently. It could even be a new method for organizing production. All of these advances raise a nation's productivity. Increased productivity means producing more output with the same amounts of land, labor, and capital. With technological progress, a society enjoys higher real GDP per capita, which leads to a higher standard of living.

Measuring Technological Progress

In most modern economies, the amount of physical and human capital changes

technological progress an increase in efficiency gained by producing more output without using more inputs all the time. So does the quantity and quality of labor and the technology used to produce goods and services. These interconnected variables work together to produce economic growth. How then can we isolate and measure the effects of technological progress?

Robert Solow, a Nobel Prize-winning economist from the Massachusetts Institute of Technology, developed a method for doing so. Solow's method was to determine how much growth in output comes from increases in capital and how much comes from increases in labor. He concluded that any remaining growth in output must then come from technological progress.

Between 1929 and 1982, the average annual growth rate of real GDP was 2.92 percent. Using Solow's method, economist Edward Denison has estimated that technological progress boosted the real GDP 1.02 percent per year, on average. Denison determined that increases in capital and labor were responsible for 0.56 percent and

(FL) **SS.912.E.2.3**
Research the contributions of key individuals of various backgrounds in the development of the U.S.

1.34 percent of the average annual growth, respectively (2.92 − 0.56 − 1.34 = 1.02). Technological progress, then, was the second most important factor in promoting economic growth in that period.

Causes of Technological Progress

Since technological progress is such an important source of economic growth, economists have looked for its causes. They have found a variety of factors that influence technological progress.

1. *Scientific research* Scientific research can generate new or improved production techniques, improve physical capital, and result in better goods and services.

2. *Innovation* When new products and ideas are successfully brought to the market, output goes up, boosting GDP and business profits. Yet innovation often requires costly research. Companies willing to carry out that research need assurance that they will profit from the products they develop.

Innovators

Jerry Yang

YAHOO!

"On the outside, Yahoo is a fun and irreverent place, but on the inside we are extremely competitive."

It has become a familiar story. Two engineering students meet in college and turn their personal hobby into a technology-based start-up company. The company grows beyond all expectations and alters the lives of its founders, employees, users, and shareholders. And in this case the company, Yahoo! Inc., changes the face of business on a global scale.

Jerry Yang was born in Taiwan in 1968 and moved to the U.S. with his mother and brother at the age of 10. He co-founded Yahoo! with another Stanford student, David Filo, while studying for a doctoral degree at Stanford University in 1994. By 2008, Microsoft, the giant software company, had offered more than $45 billion to take it over.

Yang and Filo created Yahoo! to organize their own Internet searches. When they showed their new program to friends, Yang and Filo realized its huge business potential. Today Yahoo! is an Internet giant with more than 500 million users worldwide and a well-respected brand name. It is a starting point for many consumers as they search the Web. Yahoo! offers personalized home pages, e-mail, music, news, and more. In a global economy that requires many office workers to access, organize, and manage information on a daily basis, Yahoo! has proved its great value to society.

Critical Thinking: *How does technological progress, such as the development of Internet search engines like Yahoo!, affect the nation's GDP and overall economic growth?*

Fast Facts

Jerry Yang
Born: 1968, in Taipei, Taiwan
Education: Stanford University, B.S. and M.S. in Electrical Engineering
Claim to Fame: Founder of Internet search engine Yahoo.com

7 Most Networked Economies in 2007–2008 (ranked by Internet use and innovation)	
Ranking	**Country**
1	Denmark
2	Sweden
3	Switzerland
4	United States
5	Singapore
6	Finland
7	Netherlands

SOURCE: World Economic Forum, *Global Information Technology Report, 2007–2008*

Off the Beaten Superhighway

TECHNOLOGICAL PROGRESS

Some small cities, tired of waiting for faster Internet service, are beginning to build their own.

By Christopher Rhoads
The Wall Street Journal

 SS.912.E.2.2 Use a decision-making model to analyze public policy issues in the student's community.

Internet traffic is growing faster than at any time since the boom of the late-1990s. Places like Chattanooga, Tenn., are trying hard not to get stuck in the slow lane.

Some 60 towns and small cities, including Bristol, Va., Barnsville, Minn., and Sallisaw, Okla., have built state-of-the-art fiber networks, capable of speeds many times faster than most existing connections from cable and telecom companies. Many others, including Chattanooga, have launched or are considering similar initiatives.

The efforts highlight a battle over Internet policy in the U.S. Once the undisputed leader in the technological revolution, the U.S. now lags a growing number of countries in the speed, cost and availability of high-speed Internet.

While cable and telecom companies are spending billions to upgrade their service, they're focusing their efforts mostly on larger U.S. cities for now.

Smaller ones such as Chattanooga say they need to fill the vacuum themselves or risk falling further behind and losing better-paying jobs. Chattanooga's city-owned electric utility began offering ultrafast Internet service to downtown business customers five years ago. Now it plans to roll out a fiber network to deliver TV, high-speed Internet and phone service to some 170,000 residential customers. The city has no choice but to foot the bill itself for a high-speed network—expected to cost $230 million—if it wants to remain competitive in today's global economy, says Harold DePriest, the utility's CEO.

Mr. DePriest compares his agency's plan for high-speed Internet to the rollout of electricity, which came to many parts of Tennessee only in the 1930s as a result of the federal government's Tennessee Valley Authority project. That was three decades after many businesses and homes in major urban areas were first electrified.

It's a risky bet. Some municipal Internet efforts, including wireless projects known as Wi-Fi, have failed in recent months. And some private-sector Internet providers, like phone and cable companies, are raising opposition, saying the initiatives are a poor use of taxpayer money and create unfair competition.

Mr. DePriest remains undeterred. He expects to have most of the network completed within three years, serving 80% of the city. "The issue is, does our community control our own fate," says Mr. DePriest. "Or does someone else control it?"

Applying Economic Principles
What are the potential benefits and drawbacks of a small city investing in high-speed Internet? Would such an investment promote capital deepening?

Video News Update Online
Powered by
The Wall Street Journal
Classroom Edition
Use videos at **PearsonSchool.com/PHecon** as a springboard for a discussion on a current topic.

The government issues patents to provide that assurance. A patent is a set of exclusive rights to produce and sell a product for a particular period of time. It is given to people who can show that they have discovered or invented a new product or process. Currently, patents last 20 years. A patent helps companies recover the cost of research by earning profits before its competitors can copy its new products.

Government aids innovation in several other ways as well. Through organizations such as the National Science Foundation and the National Institutes of Health, the United States government sponsors *basic research*. This term describes theoretical research that is often expensive and might not bring a new product to market in a timely way.

3. *Scale of the market* Larger markets provide more incentives for innovation, since the potential profits are greater. For this reason, larger economies will come up with more technological advances.

4. *Education and experience* As you read earlier, firms increase their human capital by providing education and on-the-job experience for their employees. Human capital makes workers more productive, which accelerates economic growth. It can also stimulate growth in another way. A more educated and experienced workforce can more easily handle technological advances and may well create some new advances, too.

5. *Natural resource use* Increased use of natural resources can create a need for new technology. For example, new technology can turn previously useless raw materials into usable resources. It can also allow us to obtain and use resources more efficiently, develop substitute resources, and discover new resource reserves. Because price is based on the cost of obtaining a resource (and not necessarily on its scarcity), new technology can also lead to lower prices.

✔ **CHECKPOINT** *How is technological progress related to the economic growth of a nation?*

 LA.1112.2.2.2, SS.912.E.1.14, SS.912.E.2.1, SS.912.E.2.5, LA.1112.1.6.1

Essential Questions Journal To continue to build a response to the Essential Question, go to your **Essential Questions Journal**.

SECTION 3 ASSESSMENT

❓ Guiding Question

1. Use your completed table to answer this question: How does the economy grow?

2. **Extension** Suppose an uncle left you $500 and you had three choices to use the money. You could (1) save the $500 in a bank, (2) buy computer equipment, or (3) keep it in your closet. How would each of these actions affect the growth of the economy?

Key Terms and Main Ideas

3. **(a)** What is **real GDP per capita?** **(b)** Why do economists measure it?

4. **(a)** What is **capital deepening?** **(b)** How does it contribute to economic growth?

5. What role does **saving** play in the process of economic growth?

6. What is the effect of the United States having a low **savings rate?**

7. How do patents encourage **technological progress?**

Critical Thinking

8. **Examine (a)** What is real GDP per capita unable to measure? **(b)** How does that limit economists' knowledge of individuals' standard of living? **(c)** Why do economists use it anyway?

9. **Connect (a)** What is the connection between saving and capital deepening? **(b)** Is it possible for capital deepening to occur without saving? Explain.

10. **Explain (a)** How can foreign trade lead to a trade deficit? **(b)** Explain why a trade deficit caused by foreign trade may not necessarily be bad for the economy.

11. **Describe (a)** Identify five factors that influence technological progress. **(b)** Which of these factors is the most important? Explain your answer.

Quick Write

12. In the mid-1800s, railroad companies borrowed money from foreign investors to create a transcontinental rail line. The completed railroad made enough money to pay off the loans and return a profit. Identify a possible transportation or communications project that might benefit the country or your community. Write an outline for a proposal relating to this project. Explain what benefits the project would provide and whether you favor borrowing money in order to accomplish the project.

Chapter 12: Gross Domestic Product and Growth

Section 1 What does the GDP show about the nation's economy?

Section 2 What factors affect the phases of a business cycle?

Section 3 How does the economy grow?

Essential Question, Chapter 12
How do we know if the economy is healthy?

Important Measures of Economic Growth

	Definition	Does Not Include	How Compiled?
Gross Domestic Product (GDP)	Dollar value of all final goods and services produced within a country's borders in a year	Products made in another country by an American manufacturer	Expenditure Approach Income Approach **Variations:** Nominal GDP Real GDP
Gross National Product (GNP)	Annual income earned by U.S.-owned firms and U.S. citizens	Depreciation	GDP plus income earned outside U.S. by U.S. firms and citizens minus income earned by foreign firms and foreign citizens located in the U.S.
Net National Product (NNP)	GNP with the cost of replacing the physical capital	Taxes	GNP minus cost of depreciation
National Income (NI)	How much pretax income businesses actually pay to U.S. households		NNP minus taxes

Economic Dictionary

national income accounting, *p. 307*

gross domestic product, *p. 309*

intermediate goods, *p. 309*

durable goods, *p. 309*

nondurable goods, *p. 309*

nominal GDP, *p. 310*

real GDP, *p. 310*

gross national product, *p. 312*

depreciation, *p. 312*

price level, *p. 313*

aggregate supply, *p. 313*

aggregate demand, *p. 314*

business cycle, *p. 315*

expansion, *p. 315*

economic growth, *p. 315*

peak, *p. 315*

contraction, *p. 316*

trough, *p. 316*

recession, *p. 316*

depression, *p. 316*

stagflation, *p. 316*

leading indicators, *p. 320*

real GDP per capita, *p. 323*

capital deepening, *p. 324*

saving, *p. 325*

savings rate, *p. 325*

technological progress, *p. 327*

Economics on the go

Study anytime, anywhere. Download these files today.

Economic Dictionary online	**Audio Review** online	**Action Graph** online	**Visual Glossary** online	**How the Economy Works** online
Vocabulary Support in English and Spanish	Audio Study Guide in English and Spanish	Animated Charts and Graphs	Animated feature	Animated feature

Download to your computer or mobile device at PearsonSchool.com/PHecon

Key Terms and Main Ideas

To make sure you understand the key terms and main ideas of this chapter, review the Checkpoint and Section Assessment questions and look at the Quick Study Guide on the preceding page.

Critical Thinking

1. **Connect (a)** Why is it important for economists to determine the influences on a nation's real GDP? **(b)** Identify two of the factors on which they focus. **(c)** Select one and give an example of how it affects the nation's GDP.

2. **Compare (a)** Compare the factors that affect the phases of a business cycle in peak periods. **(b)** Which factor is the most difficult to predict? **(c)** How do economists attempt to understand the timing of a business cycle?

3. **Interpret (a)** What major event allowed the U.S. to recover from the Great Depression? **(b)** With regard to this event, what sector, government or private, saw the greater spending increase? Why? **(c)** Name goods and services that would have been a part of this increased spending.

4. **Infer (a)** Why did a 21 percent credit card interest rate in the 1980s create a problem within the business cycle? **(b)** What happened to the unemployment rate during this period? **(c)** Why might the government not lower interest rates to spur the economy when inflation is high?

5. **Infer (a)** Why is real GDP per capita used to measure economic growth? **(b)** In what ways is this measure more effective than other measures?

6. **Graph** Review the circular flow diagram on page 40. Redraw it to add the flow of personal savings from households to financial institutions and lending by financial institutions to firms.

Applying Your Math Skills

Interpreting Data From Graphs

How do you measure a nation's economic health? Use the chart below to answer the following questions.

Visit PearsonSchool.com/PHecon for additional math help.

Economic Health of Selected Countries

Country	GDP Per Capita (2007, in thousands)	Unemployment Rate (% of labor force, 2007)
Czech Rep.	$24.2	6.6
Germany	$34.2	9.1
U. K.	$35.1	5.4
U. S.	$45.8	4.6

SOURCE: World Bank

7. Which country has the lowest unemployment rate? Which country has the highest unemployment rate?

8. What information would you need to know in order to find out which country had the highest total GDP?

9. How does the economic health of the United States compare with that of the other countries shown? On what evidence do you base your answer?

Essential Question Activity

Essential Questions Journal — To respond to the chapter Essential Question, go to your **Essential Questions Journal**.

10. Complete the activity to answer the Essential Question **How do we know if the economy is healthy?** Work in groups to gather information to take the current pulse of the American economy. Track your data over a three-year period. Using the worksheet in your Essential Questions Journal or the electronic worksheet available at **PearsonSchool.com/PHecon,** gather the following information:
    (a) What trend does the real Gross Domestic Product of the United States reveal?
    (b) Was there a business cycle contraction phase? If so, how long did it last?
    (c) At what point during these three years did the rate of inflation peak?

11. **Modify** Once you have collected your information, provide a forecast for the next three months (quarter).
    (a) Select one of the economic indicators used.
    (b) In which phase of the business cycle does the graph end? Do you anticipate a change? If so, to which phase?
    (c) Determine the pattern that this indicator has followed over the past three years. Indicate what you think it might do within the next quarter.

How can economic growth be balanced with environmental concerns?

The economy of the United States depends heavily on foreign oil. Some American leaders want to limit this economic dependence by allowing greater domestic oil drilling, especially in the protected Arctic National Wildlife Refuge (ANWR) in Alaska.

Document A

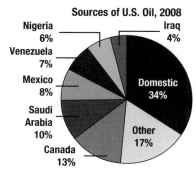

Sources of U.S. Oil, 2008

Nigeria 6%
Iraq 4%
Venezuela 7%
Mexico 8%
Saudi Arabia 10%
Canada 13%
Domestic 34%
Other 17%

SOURCE: U.S. Department of Energy

Document B

"REASONS TO SUPPORT ANWR DEVELOPMENT

• Only 8% of ANWR would be considered for exploration....

• Federal revenues would be enhanced by billions of dollars from bonus bids, lease rentals, royalties and taxes....

• Materials, services and infrastructure needed for oil production...will create hundreds of thousands of... jobs nationwide.

• Between 1977 and 2004 the Arctic oil industries spent over $50 billion within the nation's economy....

• Today the US imports 60% of our oil from abroad. That represents over $400 billion dollars a year being sent abroad. Oil imports are the single largest contributor to our national debt. Every barrel of ANWR oil would replace a barrel imported from abroad. With ANWR oil the jobs, the money, and the infrastructure stay at home."

—"Top ten reasons to support ANWR development," anwr.org

Document C

"What would America gain by allowing heavy industry into the refuge? Very little. Oil from the refuge would hardly make a dent in our dependence on foreign oil.... Oil produced from the Arctic Refuge would come at enormous, and irreversible, cost. The refuge is among the world's last true wildernesses, and it is one of the largest sanctuaries for Arctic animals.... Only by reducing American reliance on oil—foreign and domestic—and investing in cleaner, renewable forms of power will our country achieve true energy security.... If America made the transition to more efficient vehicles, far more oil would be saved than the Arctic Refuge is likely to produce."

—Natural Resources Defense Council, 2005

ANALYZING DOCUMENTS

Use your knowledge of economic concerns, the environmental effects of oil drilling, and Documents A, B, and C to answer questions 1–3.

1. **Document A best supports the conclusion that the United States**

   A. has limited reserves of oil.
   B. depends on foreign sources for most of its oil supply.
   C. has sufficient oil available for its immediate needs.
   D. should not use foreign sources of oil.

2. **According to Document B, oil drilling would support economic growth by**

   A. enabling the United States to sell oil to foreign countries.
   B. creating government and private revenue.
   C. leading to tax cuts.
   D. increasing U.S. oil imports.

3. **What is the main point of Document C?**

   A. Drilling in ANWR would increase dependence on foreign oil.
   B. Drilling in ANWR would be too expensive to be profitable.
   C. The environmental costs of drilling in ANWR would outweigh the benefits.
   D. U.S. dependence on foreign oil is not a major economic problem.

WRITING ABOUT ECONOMICS

Maintaining our energy supplies and natural resources is at the forefront of the news today. Use the documents on this page and other resources on the Web site below to answer the question: *How can economic growth be balanced with environmental concerns?*

In Partnership

THE WALL STREET JOURNAL.
CLASSROOM EDITION

To read more about issues related to this topic, visit
PearsonSchool.com/PHecon

(FL) MA.912.A.2.2, SS.912.E.2.1

13 Economic Challenges

Essential Question, Chapter 13

How much can we reduce unemployment, inflation, and poverty?

Skilled Trades

Food And Lodging

Transportation /

BANKING
AND
FINANCIAL

MAINTENANCE /
CLEANING /
JANITORIAL /
HOUSEKEEPING

OFFICE /
ADMINISTRATIVE
INCLUDES JOB LISTINGS FOR
CUSTOMER SERVICE REPS

CONSTRUCTION /
SKILLED TRADES

FOOD
AND
LODGING

TRANSPORTA
DRIVI

Management

Personal Care / C
Health

nction / Assembly

Sales and Marketing

Security / Law Enforcement

Technolo

MANAGEMENT
POSITIONS

P

DUCTION /
SSEMBLY

SALES
AND
MARKETING

SECURITY /
LAW
ENFORCEMENT

TECHNOL
JOBS

Job Opportunities

FL **Next Generation Sunshine State Standards**

Section 1: Unemployment
LA.1112.1.6, SS.912.E.1.12, SS.912.E.2.1, SS.912.E.2.3, SS.912.G.4.4

Section 2: Inflation
LA.1112.1.6, MA.912.A.2.2, SS.912.E.1.12, SS.912.E.2.7, SS.912.E.3.1, SS.912.E.3.6

Section 3: Poverty
LA.1112.1.6, MA.912.A.2.2, SS.912.E.1.9, SS.912.E.2.4, SS.912.G.4

Economics
on the go

To study anywhere, anytime, download these
online resources at *PearsonSchool.com/PHecon* ▶

NGSSS

LA.1112.1.6 Use multiple strategies to develop vocabulary.

SS.912.E.1.12 Examine the four phases of the business cycle.

SS.912.E.2.1 Identify and explain broad economic goals.

SS.912.E.2.3 Research the contributions of key individuals of various backgrounds in the development of the U.S.

SS.912.G.4.4 Analyze case studies of globalization.

ECONOMIC DICTIONARY

As you read the section, look for the definitions of these **Key Terms**:

- frictional unemployment
- structural unemployment
- globalization
- seasonal unemployment
- cyclical unemployment
- unemployment rate
- full employment
- underemployed
- discouraged worker

Guiding Question

What are the causes of unemployment?

Copy this concept web and fill it in as you read to identify the causes of unemployment.

Frictional: people between jobs for own reasons — Types of Unemployment — Seasonal: company or industry shuts down for a season

▶ **Economics and You** Many people face unemployment at some point in their lives. For the jobless worker it is a very personal issue. For the government, it is a national economic issue. Economists measure the health of the economy by tracking the number of people who are out of work. The government pays close attention to these statistics so that it can take actions that will spur economic recovery.

Principles in Action General economic conditions, lengthy job searches, and seasonal production schedules are some of the factors that cause unemployment. A woman who believes in "keeping the humanity in human resources" is profiled in this section's Innovators.

Types of Unemployment

Economists look at four categories of unemployment: frictional, seasonal, structural, and cyclical. Sometimes, factors outside the economy can cause unemployment. The various kinds of unemployment have different effects on the economy as well as on the people who are unemployed.

Frictional Unemployment

Unemployment always exists, even in a booming economy. **Frictional unemployment** occurs when people take time to find a job. For example, people might change jobs, be laid off from their current jobs, or need some time to find the right position after they finish their schooling. They might be returning to the workforce after a long period of time. In the following examples, all three people are considered frictionally unemployed.

frictional unemployment type of unemployment that occurs when people take time to find a job

Visual Glossary
(online)

Go to the Visual Glossary Online for an interactive review of **inflation.**

Action Graph
(online)

Go to Action Graph Online for animated versions of key charts and graphs.

How the Economy Works
(online)

Go to How the Economy Works Online for an interactive lesson on **structural unemployment.**

How do workers deal with structural unemployment?

The United States has shifted from a manufacturing economy to a service economy. Many workers do not have the skills needed for jobs in the new technology-based industries. Structural unemployment occurs when workers' skills don't match the jobs that are available.

1

Reginald's position as an accounting manager was eliminated after the company upgraded to a new computer software program.

Jennifer's job was outsourced when the furniture manufacturer she worked for moved to another country.

Matthew's job as a landscaper was eliminated when the Parks Department's budget was cut.

UNEMPLOYMENT BENEFITS

TRAINING CENTER

Jobhunt.com

2 **Reginald** contacts former associates and gets a couple of interviews.

Jennifer realizes that she needs to get training in another field.

Matthew searches online for a new job, but discovers that his high school education leaves him unqualified for many positions.

Structural Unemployment

- Hannah was not satisfied working as a nurse in a large hospital. Last month she left her job to look for a position at a small health clinic.
- Since Jorge graduated from law school three months ago, he has interviewed with various law firms to find the one that best suits his needs and interests.
- Liz left her sales job two years ago to care for an aging parent. Now she is trying to return to the workforce.

None of these three people found work immediately. While they look for work, they are frictionally unemployed. In the large, diverse U.S. economy, economists expect to find many people in this category.

Unemployment insurance, which provides income to laid-off workers seeking new jobs, may contribute slightly to frictional unemployment. A worker receiving unemployment insurance faces

structural unemployment type of unemployment that occurs when workers' skills do not match those needed for the jobs available

somewhat less financial pressure to find a new job immediately.

Structural Unemployment

As you read in Chapter 9, the structure of the American economy has changed over time. Two centuries ago, people needed basic farming skills to survive. As the country developed an industrial economy, farm workers moved to urban areas to work in factories. Today, service industries are rapidly replacing manufacturing industries, and information services are expanding at breakneck speed.

All these shifts lead to upheavals in the labor market. When the structure of the economy changes, the skills that workers need to succeed also change. Workers who lack the necessary skills lose their jobs. **Structural unemployment** occurs when workers' skills do not match those needed for the jobs that are now available.

How the Economy Works online

How the Economy Works
online

For an animated, interactive version of this feature, visit **PearsonSchool.com/PHecon**

3 **Reginald's** recent experience inspires him to earn a degree in business technology management.

Jennifer gets into a federal job training program for people who have lost their jobs due to globalization. She is studying to become a biomedical technician.

Matthew, who likes to work with his hands, takes a friend's advice and enrolls in a technical school. He is training to become a plumber.

4 **Reginald** continues his studies and his job search. Although he gets some temporary jobs, Reginald is underemployed.

Jennifer finds a good position as a technician at a pharmaceutical company.

Matthew will earn more money as a plumber than he did as a landscaper.

> *Check Your Understanding*
> 1. Identify three causes of structural unemployment.
> 2. How can the education system help reduce structural unemployment?

Retraining

Employment

There are five major causes of structural unemployment.

- *The development of new technology* New inventions and ideas often push out older ways of doing things. For example, downloading music has hurt the sales of compact discs. Firms making CDs have let workers go, and those workers must find jobs in another field.
- *The discovery of new resources* New resources replace old resources. The discovery of petroleum in Pennsylvania in 1859 severely hurt the whale-oil industry. Whaling ship crews lost their jobs and did not have the skills needed for the petroleum industry.
- *Changes in consumer demand* Consumers often stop buying one product in favor of another. Many people now favor athletic shoes over more traditional kinds of shoes. As a result, traditional shoemaking jobs have declined.
- *Globalization* The mobility of capital and labor has fueled a shift from local to international markets. Countries have become more open to foreign trade and investment in a trend called **globalization.** As a result, companies often relocate jobs or entire facilities to other countries where costs are lower. Celia, for example, spent many years working on an automobile assembly line in Michigan. When her company moved much of its auto assembly work to Mexico where labor is less expensive, Celia lost her job. Unfortunately, there were no local jobs that matched Celia's skills.
- *Lack of education* People who drop out of school or fail to acquire the minimum skills needed for today's

globalization the shift from local to global markets as countries seek foreign trade and investment

Personal Finance
For more about how to find a job, see your Personal Finance Handbook in the back of the book or visit PearsonSchool.com/PHecon

Migrant farm workers face seasonal unemployment once the harvest season is over. ▼

job market may find themselves unemployed, employed part-time, or stuck in low-wage jobs. For example, Martin barely managed to graduate from high school. When he was hired as a clerk by a local clothing store, he had trouble using the computerized checkout register. The store manager fired Martin after just two months because he lacked the skills needed for the job.

Policymakers in the 1990s and 2000s recognized that computer technology, globalization, and other structural changes threatened the futures of many workers. As a result, they developed job-training programs to help workers gain new skills, especially computer skills.

Retraining takes time, however, and the new skills do not ensure that the trainees will obtain high-wage jobs. Some companies offer their own training programs. In this way, they can teach trainees the specialized skills they need to become valued employees.

Seasonal Unemployment

Gregory is a brick mason for a small construction company in the northeastern United States. Every winter Gregory's employer lays off all seven of his employees when cold weather forces an end to outdoor work. In the spring, he hires them back again for the new

construction season. Gregory and his co-workers are examples of people who experience seasonal unemployment.

In general, **seasonal unemployment** occurs when industries slow or shut down for a season or make seasonal shifts in their production schedules. Seasonal unemployment can also occur as a result of harvest schedules or vacations. When this school year ends, you or your friends may need some time to find the perfect summer job. Until you do so, economists will count you as seasonally unemployed.

As with frictional unemployment, economists expect to see seasonal unemployment throughout the year. Government policymakers do not take steps to prevent this kind of unemployment, because it is a normal part of a healthy economy.

Still, the lives of seasonally unemployed workers can be extremely difficult. Migrant agricultural workers, for example, travel throughout the country to pick fruits and vegetables as various crops come into season. They know that their work will likely end when winter arrives. Migrant workers can also have periods of unemployment even during harvest season, depending on the weather. Heat, cold, rain, and drought can ruin harvest schedules by causing fruits and vegetables to ripen sooner or later than expected. Instead of moving smoothly from crop to crop, migrant workers might lose work time waiting for a crop to be ready for picking.

Cyclical Unemployment

Unemployment that rises during economic downturns and falls when the economy improves is called **cyclical unemployment**. During recessions, or downturns in the business cycle, the demand for goods and services drops. The resulting slowdown in production causes the demand for labor to drop as well, and companies begin to lay off employees. Many of these laid-off employees will be rehired when the recession ends and the business cycle resumes an upward trend. Although economists expect cyclical unemployment, it can severely strain the economy and greatly distress the unemployed.

The most damaging example of cyclical unemployment in the twentieth century was the Great Depression. During the Great Depression, one out of every four workers was unemployed. Many remained jobless for years. In 1935, President Franklin D. Roosevelt proposed, and Congress passed, the Social Security Act. In addition to providing monthly payments for retirees and people who could not support themselves, the Social Security Act established a program of unemployment insurance.

Today, unemployment insurance still provides weekly payments to workers who have lost their jobs. The payments usually provide about half of a worker's lost wages each week for a limited amount of time.

Factors Outside the Economy

Sometimes events outside the economy can cause unemployment. The September 11, 2001, terrorist attacks on the World Trade Center and the Pentagon cost the country an estimated 1.5 to 2 million jobs. Many of the lost jobs were in the travel and tourism industries. About 20 percent of the lost jobs were in the airline industry. In Manhattan, the area around the World Trade Center site was especially hard-hit, and New York City lost some 150,000 jobs.

Natural disasters also affect employment. In October 2005, Hurricane Katrina slammed into the Gulf Coast region. The powerful storm caused widespread destruction and thousands of people lost their jobs. Many families were relocated to other areas while their communities were being rebuilt. Months later, unemployment among people affected by Hurricane Katrina was still higher than the national average.

☑ **CHECKPOINT** *Why are policymakers less concerned about frictional and seasonal unemployment?*

Measuring Employment

The amount of unemployment in the nation is an important clue to the health of the economy. For this reason, the government keeps careful track of how many people are unemployed, and why.

To measure employment, the United States Bureau of the Census conducts a monthly household survey for the Bureau of Labor Statistics (BLS). For this survey, called the Current Population Survey, interviewers

---

Figure 13.1 **Calculating the Unemployment Rate**

To calculate the unemployment rate, use the following formula:

Number of people unemployed **divided by** number of people in the civilian labor force **multiplied by** 100

For example,
if the number of people unemployed = 7 million and the number of people in the civilian labor force = 151.4 million

then,
$$7 \div 151.4 = .046$$
$$.046 \times 100 = 4.6$$

Therefore,
the unemployment rate is 4.6%

SOURCE: Bureau of Labor Statistics

CHART SKILLS
To calculate the unemployment rate, follow the steps in the chart.

1. In May 2008, the civilian labor force was 154.5 million and 8.5 million were unemployed. What was the unemployment rate?

2. Does the unemployment rate accurately reflect the number of people who are unemployed? Why or why not?

---

poll 60,000 families about employment during that month. This sample is designed to represent the entire population of the United States. The BLS, a branch of the U.S. Department of Labor, analyzes the data from the survey to identify how many people are employed and how many are unemployed. Using these numbers, the BLS computes the **unemployment rate,** or the percentage of the nation's labor force that is unemployed.

Determining the Unemployment Rate

As you read in Chapter 9, the labor force is composed of civilians age 16 and older who have a job or are actively looking for a job. To determine the unemployment rate, BLS officials add up the number of employed and unemployed people. That figure equals the total labor force. Then they divide the number of unemployed people by the total labor force and multiply by 100. As **Figure 13.1** shows, the result is the percentage of people who are unemployed.

For example, in September 2007, the Current Population Survey showed that 146.3 million people were employed, and 7.2 million were unemployed. The total labor force, therefore, was 153.5 million. Dividing 7.2 million by 153.5 million, and then multiplying the result by 100, yields

unemployment rate
the percentage of the nation's labor force that is unemployed

SS.912.E.2.3 Research the contributions of key individuals of various backgrounds in the development of the U.S.

an unemployment rate of 4.7 percent for that month.

Adjusting the Unemployment Rate

When you see the unemployment rate for a particular month, it has usually been "seasonally adjusted." This means that the rate has been increased or decreased to take into account the level of seasonal unemployment. Taking this step allows economists to more accurately compare unemployment rates from month to month. This comparison helps them better detect changing economic conditions.

The unemployment rate is only an average for the nation. It does not reflect regional differences. Some areas, such as the coal-mining region of Appalachia in the southeastern United States, have long had a higher-than-average unemployment rate. The BLS and individual state agencies therefore establish unemployment rates for states and other geographic areas. These rates help pinpoint trouble areas on which policymakers can focus attention.

full employment the level of employment reached when there is no cyclical unemployment

underemployed working at a job for which one is over-qualified or working part-time when full-time work is desired

✔ **CHECKPOINT** *How is the unemployment rate calculated?*

Full Employment

Look at **Figure 13.2.** Notice the low levels of unemployment in the late 1990s and early 2000s. As you read earlier, zero unemployment is not an achievable goal in a market economy, even under the best of circumstances. Economists generally agree that in an economy that is working properly, an unemployment rate of around 4 to 6 percent is normal. Such an economy would still experience frictional, seasonal, and structural unemployment. In other words, **full employment** is the level of employment reached when no cyclical unemployment exists.

Underemployment

Full employment means that nearly everyone who wants a job has a job. But are all those people satisfied with their jobs? Not necessarily. Some people working at low-skill, low-wage jobs may be highly skilled or educated in a field with few opportunities. They are **underemployed**, that is, working at a job for which they are over-qualified, or working part-time when they desire full-time work.

For example, Jim, a philosophy major, earned a graduate degree in philosophy. When he left school, Jim found that although the economy was booming, he could not find jobs in which he could apply his knowledge of philosophy. Jim found a part-time job that did not pay well and did not challenge his mind. He was underemployed.

Underemployment also describes the situation of people who want a permanent, full-time job but have not been able to find one. Many part-time workers and seasonal workers fit into this category.

Discouraged Workers

Some people, especially during a long recession, give up hope of finding work. These **discouraged workers** have stopped searching for employment and may rely on other family members or savings to support them. Although they are without jobs, discouraged workers do not appear in the unemployment rate determined by the Bureau of Labor Statistics because they are not actively looking for work.

If underemployed and discouraged workers were included, the unemployment rate would be much higher than reported. Some

FL LA.1112.2.2.2, SS.912.E.1.12, SS.912.E.2.1, LA.1112.2.2.3, LA.1112.1.6.1

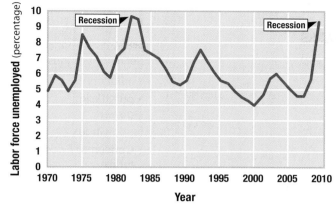

Figure 13.2 Unemployment Rate

SOURCE: Bureau of Labor Statistics

GRAPH SKILLS

The unemployment rate peaked in 1982 and 2009.

1. In what years was the unemployment rate between 4 and 6 percent, the rate considered normal for a healthy economy?
2. Why does a high unemployment rate correspond with a recession?

estimates are that the 2009 unemployment rate would have been above 17 percent.

✔ **CHECKPOINT** *What kinds of unemployment are present even in a healthy economy?*

discouraged worker
someone who wants a job but has given up looking

SECTION 1 ASSESSMENT

Essential Questions Journal
To continue to build a response to the Essential Question, go to your **Essential Questions Journal**.

🤔 Guiding Question

1. Use your completed concept web to answer this question: What are the causes of unemployment?
2. **Extension** Suppose that you are unemployed and looking for work. You are a good worker, but it is taking you longer than expected to find a job. What might be making your search so difficult?

Key Terms and Main Ideas

3. What are some factors that affect **seasonal unemployment?**
4. When does **cyclical unemployment** take place?
5. What is **globalization?**
6. How does the Bureau of Labor Statistics determine the **unemployment rate?**
7. Why isn't **full employment** the same as zero unemployment?

Critical Thinking

8. **Contrast (a)** What are frictional unemployment and structural unemployment? **(b)** Give an example of each. **(c)** In what ways are frictional unemployment and structural unemployment different?
9. **Apply** After a car accident, Santo needed six months to recover. Since his recovery, he has spent the last year trying to find work in his former occupation, medical technology. So far, he has not found a position, even though the economy is booming. Which of the four kinds of unemployment best describes Santo's situation? Explain.
10. **Calculate (a)** What is the formula for calculating the unemployment rate? **(b)** Determine the unemployment rate for a month in which 125.4 million people were employed and 7.3 million people were unemployed.

Quick Write

11. A recent magazine article listed the jobs of the future along with the jobs that won't exist in twenty years. One promising career is computer software engineer. However, there will be little need for film processors in the future. Write a paragraph on each occupation. Suggest reasons why there will be a greater need for computer software engineers and less need for film processors.

FL NGSSS

LA.1112.1.6 Use multiple strategies to develop vocabulary.

MA.912.A.2.2 Interpret a graph to represent a real-world situation.

SS.912.E.1.12 Examine the four phases of the business cycle.

SS.912.E.2.7 Identify the societal impact of inflation.

SS.912.E.3.1 Demonstrate the impact of inflation on world economies.

SS.912.E.3.6 Draw conclusions about historical economic theories of economists.

ECONOMIC DICTIONARY

As you read the section, look for the definitions of these **Key Terms**:

- inflation
- purchasing power
- price index
- Consumer Price Index
- market basket
- inflation rate
- core inflation rate
- hyperinflation
- quantity theory
- wage-price spiral
- fixed income
- deflation

Guiding Question
What are the causes and effects of inflation?

Copy this chart and fill it in as you read to explain the causes and effects of inflation.

Inflation	
Causes	**Effects**
• Growth of the money supply • Changes in aggregate demand, as during wartime •	• Decreases purchasing power • •

inflation a general increase in prices across an economy

purchasing power the ability to purchase goods and services

▶ **Economics and You**   At first, the changes are hardly noticeable. You pay more for lunch at your favorite eatery. Your personal grooming products are more expensive. Clothing prices are higher. A ticket for the movies costs two dollars more. You realize that as a result of these steady price increases, your money doesn't buy as much as it did just a few months ago.

Principles in Action As you will see, you cannot escape rising prices. Economists believe that the money supply, changes in demand, and increased production costs all contribute to a rise in prices throughout the economy. This section's Economics & You shows how higher prices can affect your life.

The Effects of Rising Prices

Josephine and Jack Barrow have owned the same house for 50 years. Recently, they had a real estate agent estimate their home's present market value. The Barrows were astounded. The house that they had bought for $12,000 was now worth nearly $150,000—a rise in value of more than 1,100 percent.

How could the value of a house, or anything else, increase so much? The main reason is inflation. **Inflation** is a general increase in prices across an economy. Over the years, prices generally go up. Since World War II, real estate prices have risen greatly.

The Barrows were pleased that they could get so much money for their house. Then they realized that inflation had raised the prices of all houses, just as it had also raised wages and the prices of most other goods and services. As a result, they could not buy a similar house in their area for $12,000 or even $120,000.

Another way to look at the Barrows' situation is that inflation had shrunk the value, or purchasing power, of the Barrows' money. **Purchasing power** is the ability to purchase goods and services. As prices rise, the purchasing power of money declines. That is why $12,000 buys much less now than it did 50 years ago.

Food Prices*

	March 1996	March 2008
Bread, white (per lb.)	0.85	1.35
Eggs, large (per dozen)	1.14	2.20
Milk, whole (per gallon)	2.54	3.78

* U.S. City average
Source: Bureau of Labor Statistics

▲ The effects of inflation over the years can be seen in this comparison of prices for basic food items.

✓ **CHECKPOINT** *Why does purchasing power decrease over time?*

Price Indexes

Housing costs are just one element that economists consider when they study inflation. The economy has thousands of goods and services, with millions of individual prices. How do economists compare the changes in all these prices in order to measure inflation? The answer is that they do not compare individual prices; instead, they compare price levels. As you read in Chapter 12, price level is the cost of goods and services in the entire economy at a given point in time.

To help them calculate price level, economists use a price index. A **price index** is a measurement that shows how the average price of a standard group of goods changes over time. A price index produces an average that economists compare to earlier averages to see how much prices have changed over time.

Using Price Indexes

Price indexes help consumers and businesspeople make economic decisions. For example, after Marina read in the newspaper that prices for consumer goods had been rising, she increased the amount of money she was saving for a new car. She wanted to be sure that when the time came to buy the car, she had saved enough money to pay for it.

The government also uses indexes in making policy decisions. A member of Congress, for example, might push for an increase in the minimum wage if she thinks inflation has reduced purchasing power.

The Consumer Price Index

Although there are several price indexes, the best-known index focuses on consumers. The **Consumer Price Index** (CPI) is computed each month by the Bureau of Labor Statistics (BLS). The CPI is determined by measuring the price of a standard group of goods meant to represent the "market basket" of a typical urban consumer. This **market basket** is a representative collection of goods and services. By looking at the CPI, consumers, businesses, and the government can compare the cost of a group of goods this month with what the same or a similar group cost months or even years ago.

Figure 13.3 **CPI Market Basket Items**

Category	Examples
Food and Drinks	cereals, coffee, chicken, milk, restaurant meals
Housing	rent, homeowners' costs, fuel oil
Apparel and upkeep	men's shirts, women's dresses, jewelry
Transportation	airfares, new and used cars, gasoline, auto insurance
Medical care	prescription medicines, eye care, physicians' services
Entertainment	newspapers, toys, musical instruments
Education and communication	tuition, postage, telephone services, computers
Other goods and services	haircuts, cosmetics, bank fees

SOURCE: Bureau of Labor Statistics

CHART SKILLS

The CPI market basket helps economists calculate the average inflation rate for the country.

1. Why might an individual family experience an inflation rate that is higher or lower than the national average?
2. Which categories of market basket items are currently experiencing sharp price increases?

As you can see from **Figure 13.3**, the CPI market basket is divided into eight categories of goods and services. These categories and a few examples of the many items in each group are shown above.

About every 10 years, the items in the market basket are updated to account for shifting consumer buying habits. The BLS determines how the market basket should change by conducting a Consumer Expenditure Survey. The BLS conducted one such survey from 2000 to 2001, collecting spending information from 10,000 families. Another 7,500 families kept diaries, noting everything they purchased during a two-week period for both years. This process resulted in the list of market basket items used today.

Price Indexes and the Inflation Rate

Economists also find it useful to calculate the **inflation rate**—the percentage rate of change in price level over time. (To learn how to calculate the inflation rate, go to page 358.) Since the CPI is the most familiar price index, we will focus on it. How does the BLS determine the CPI and use it to calculate the inflation rate?

price index a measurement that shows how the average price of a standard group of goods changes over time

Consumer Price Index a price index determined by measuring the price of a standard group of goods meant to represent the "market basket" of a typical urban consumer

market basket a representative collection of goods and services

inflation rate the percentage rate of change in price level over time

VISUAL GLOSSARY

Reviewing Key Terms
To understand *inflation*, review these terms:

business cycle, *p. 57*
inflation, *p. 342*
purchasing power, *p. 342*
price index, *p. 343*
inflation rate, *p. 343*

What is Inflation?

◀ **inflation** a general rise in prices across an economy

The Effects of Inflation on Entertainment

	1985	1995	2005
Average Price of a Ticket for a Major League Baseball Game	$10.14	$10.65	$21.17
Average Price of a Movie Theater Ticket	$3.55	$4.35	$6.41
Average Price for a Top 25 Concert Ticket	$15.31	$25.40	$56.88

SOURCE: EH. Net Encyclopedia; www.teammarketing.com; National Association of Theatre Owners; www.msnbc.msn.com

Inflation has driven up the price you pay for admission to different kinds of entertainment. ***What inputs may have contributed to higher ticket prices for these events?***

◀ In this cartoon, inflation has caused the cost of living to skyrocket while wages remain the same. ***How will consumers react to an increase in the cost of goods and services? How might an increase in wages affect prices?***

Visual Glossary online

To expand your understanding of this and other key economic terms, visit **PearsonSchool.com/PHecon**

Determining the CPI

To determine the CPI, the BLS establishes a base period to which it can compare current prices. Currently, the base period is 1982–1984. The cost of the market basket for that period is assigned the index number 100. Every month, BLS representatives update the cost of the same market basket of goods and services by rechecking all the prices. Each updated cost is compared with the base-period cost to determine the index for that month. As costs rise, the index rises.

The BLS determines the CPI for a given year using the following formula.

$$\text{CPI} = \frac{\text{updated cost}}{\text{base period cost}} \times 100$$

For example, suppose the market basket cost $200 during the base period and costs $360 today. The CPI for today would be:

$$\frac{\$360}{\$200} \times 100 = 180$$

In this example, the CPI rose from 100 in the base period to 180 today.

Types of Inflation

Inflation rates in the United States have changed greatly over time. When the inflation rate stays low—between 1 and 3 percent—it does not typically cause problems for the economy. In this environment, businesses and governments can make plans. When the inflation rate exceeds 5 percent, however, the inflation rate itself becomes unstable and unpredictable. This makes planning very difficult.

As you can see in **Figure 13.4**, the inflation rate sometimes spikes sharply, as in 1974 and 1980. These sharp increases in the inflation rate were due in part to increases in prices in world food and oil markets. In order to study long-term trends in the inflation rate, analysts need to set aside temporary spikes in food and fuel prices. To do this, economists have developed the concept of a core inflation rate. The **core inflation rate** is the rate of inflation excluding the effects of food and energy prices.

By far the worst kind of inflation is **hyperinflation,** or inflation that is out of control. During periods of hyperinflation, inflation rates can go as high as 100 or

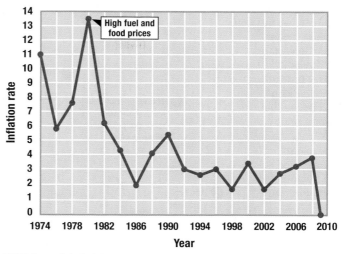

| Figure 13.4 | **Inflation Rate** |

SOURCE: Bureau of Labor Statistics

GRAPH SKILLS

Sharp inflation rate increases in 1974 and 1980 were due in part to increases in food and oil prices. An inflation rate of 1 to 3 percent does not typically cause economic problems.

1. In what two years was the inflation rate highest?
2. Why was the period from 1974 to 1982 a difficult time for people on fixed incomes?

even 500 percent per month, and money loses much of its value. This level of inflation is rare, but when it occurs it often leads to a total economic collapse.

 CHECKPOINT *How do economists calculate the CPI?*

Causes of Inflation

Where does inflation come from? Price levels can rise steeply when demand for goods and services exceeds the supply available at current prices, such as during wartime. They can also rise steeply when productivity is restricted, for example, when a long drought leads to poor harvests.

Nobody can explain every instance of rising price levels. However, economists have several theories about the causes of inflation. These include the growth of the money supply, changes in aggregate demand, and changes in aggregate supply. Economists look at all these elements when they try to understand the inflation process.

Simulation *Activity*

Creating a Teenage Consumer Price Index
You may be asked to create a Teenage Consumer Price Index as part of a role-playing game.

 MA.912.A.2.2 Interpret a graph to represent a real-world situation.

core inflation rate the rate of inflation excluding the effects of food and energy prices

hyperinflation inflation that is out of control

| Figure 13.5 | **The Wage-Price Spiral** |

CHART SKILLS

Inflation caused by the push of higher costs can lead to a wage-price spiral of increasing prices.

1. Why do rising food prices fuel a wage-price spiral?

2. How might globalization and outsourcing affect the wage-price spiral?

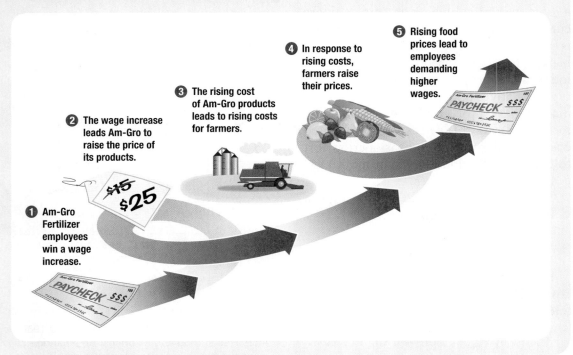

❶ Am-Gro Fertilizer employees win a wage increase.

❷ The wage increase leads Am-Gro to raise the price of its products.

❸ The rising cost of Am-Gro products leads to rising costs for farmers.

❹ In response to rising costs, farmers raise their prices.

❺ Rising food prices lead to employees demanding higher wages.

Growth of the Money Supply

The **quantity theory** of inflation states that too much money in the economy causes inflation. Therefore, the money supply should be carefully monitored to keep it in line with the nation's productivity as measured by real GDP.

Economists at the University of Chicago developed a popular version of this theory in the 1950s and 1960s. They maintained that the money supply could be used to control price levels in the long term. The key to stable prices, they said, was to increase the supply of money at the same rate as the economy was growing.

Changes in Aggregate Demand

As you learned in Chapter 12, aggregate demand is the amount of goods and services in the economy that will be purchased at all possible price levels. Inflation can occur when demand for goods and services exceeds existing supplies. During wartime, for example, the government's need for military supplies puts pressure on producers. The heavy demand for new equipment, supplies, and services increases the value of those items, pushing prices up. Wages also rise as the demand for labor increases along with the demand for goods.

Changes in Aggregate Supply

Finally, inflation occurs when producers raise prices in order to meet increased costs. Higher prices for raw materials can cause costs to increase. Wage increases, however, are most often the biggest reason, because wages are the largest single production cost for most companies.

One cause of wage increases is low unemployment. Employers must then offer higher wages to attract workers. Wage increases can also occur as a result of collective bargaining.

For example, Jen is a union laborer at Am-Gro Fertilizer. The union she belongs to recently won a large wage increase from the company. The increased cost for labor led Am-Gro to raise its prices in order to maintain its profits.

Such a situation can lead to a spiral of ever-higher prices, because one increase in costs leads to an increase in prices, which leads to another increase in costs, and on and on. The process by which rising wages cause higher prices, and higher prices cause

quantity theory the theory that too much money in the economy causes inflation higher wages, is known as the **wage-price spiral.** The effect of a wage-price spiral on Am-Gro Fertilizer is shown in **Figure 13.5.**

☑ **CHECKPOINT** *What are the three causes of inflation?*

Effects of Inflation

High inflation is a major economic problem, especially when inflation rates change greatly from year to year. Buyers and sellers find planning for the future difficult, if not impossible. The effects of inflation can be seen mainly in purchasing power, income, and interest rates.

Effects on Purchasing Power

You have seen, in the example of Jack and Josephine Barrow's house, how inflation can erode purchasing power. In an inflationary economy, a dollar will not buy the same number of goods that it did in years past. When there is no inflation, $1.00 buys the same amount of goods it did in the previous year. If the inflation rate is 10 percent this year, however, $1.00 will buy the equivalent of only $.90 worth of goods today. In this case, the purchasing power of a dollar has fallen.

Effects on Income

Inflation sometimes, but not always, erodes income. If wage increases match the inflation rate, a worker's real income stays the same. People who do not receive their income as wages, such as doctors, lawyers, and businesspeople, can often increase their incomes by raising the prices they charge in order to keep up with inflation.

Not all people are so fortunate. If workers' wages do not increase as much as inflation does, they are in a worse economic position than before. Since prices are higher, their income has less purchasing power.

People living on a fixed income are especially hard hit by inflation. A **fixed income** is income that does not increase even when prices go up. The Barrows, for example, who are retired, are hurt by high inflation. The portion of their income from Social Security payments rises with the price level, because the government raises Social Security benefits to keep up

with inflation. Much of their income, however, comes from a pension fund that pays them a fixed amount of money each month. Inflation steadily eats away at the real value of that pension check.

Effects on Interest Rates

People receive a given amount of interest on money in their savings accounts, but their true return depends on the rate of inflation. For example, Sonia had her savings in an account that paid 7 percent interest. At the same time, the annual inflation rate was 5 percent. As a result, the purchasing power of Sonia's savings increased that year by only 2 percent, because 5 percent of her interest was needed to keep up with inflation.

wage-price spiral the process by which rising wages cause higher prices, and higher prices cause higher wages

fixed income income that does not increase even when prices go up

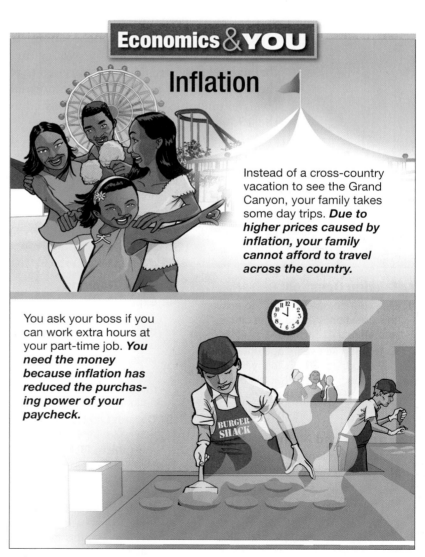

Instead of a cross-country vacation to see the Grand Canyon, your family takes some day trips. *Due to higher prices caused by inflation, your family cannot afford to travel across the country.*

You ask your boss if you can work extra hours at your part-time job. *You need the money because inflation has reduced the purchasing power of your paycheck.*

▲ As a consumer, you can feel the pinch of higher prices. *How has inflation changed your spending habits?*

deflation a sustained drop in the price level

When a bank's interest rate matches the inflation rate, savers break even. The amount they gain from interest is taken away by inflation. However, if the inflation rate is higher than the bank's interest rate, savers lose money.

✓ **CHECKPOINT** *What happens when income doesn't keep pace with inflation?*

Recent Trends in Inflation

Americans over age 30 have experienced fairly low inflation rates for most of their lifetimes. In the late 1990s, unemployment levels were low. Typically, low unemployment leads to higher inflation because companies compete for scarce workers by offering higher wages. Rising wages can push the inflation rate up, as you know from the discussion of the wage-price spiral. However, inflation crept along at less than 3 percent. Some economists suggested that the economy was going through a lucky streak. Others argued that the economy was returning to the normal levels of unemployment that had existed in the 1950s and 1960s.

As the economy entered a period of recession and slow growth in the 2000s, inflation fell to less than 2 percent. Rising unemployment and falling capital investment removed two factors that might have led to inflation due to increases in aggregate supply. Prices at times seemed to be falling. Some experts even predicted a period of **deflation,** or a sustained drop in the price level. However, the economy recovered.

Although inflation remained relatively low through 2007, by mid-2008, soaring energy costs had pushed the inflation rate past 4 percent. The CPI recorded its biggest monthly gain since 1982. Consumers, pressured by sharp price increases for food and gasoline, had less demand for big-ticket items such as household appliances and automobiles.

By the end of 2008, the economy was in crisis. A severe recession led to a slowdown in economic activity. Global demand for oil dropped and the price of gasoline plunged by 30 percent in one month. The CPI was 3 percent lower than it had been just three months earlier. The record decline in retail prices and sales put added pressure on the federal government to solve the economic crisis and avoid a deflationary spiral in prices.

✓ **CHECKPOINT** *How does low unemployment lead to higher inflation?*

FL SS.912.E.2.7, SS.912.E.3.1, LA.1112.2.2.2, SS.912.E.1.12, LA.1112.1.6.1

SECTION 2 ASSESSMENT

Essential Questions Journal To continue to build a response to the Essential Question, go to your **Essential Questions Journal**.

🤔 Guiding Question

1. Use your completed chart to answer this question: What are the causes and effects of inflation?

2. **Extension** Ten years ago you could buy a soda for $0.75. Today the same soda costs $1.25. What factors might have caused the price of the soda to rise?

Key Terms and Main Ideas

3. How does **inflation** influence **purchasing power**?

4. Why is the **Consumer Price Index** important?

5. What is **hyperinflation?**

6. What causes a **wage-price spiral,** and how does it affect the economy?

7. What are three possible effects of inflation? Explain or give an example of each.

Critical Thinking

8. **Explain (a)** What categories of goods and services are included in the CPI market basket? **(b)** What is the purpose of including these categories? **(c)** Why might an individual family experience an inflation rate that is higher or lower than the national average?

9. **Contrast (a)** How is the core inflation rate different from the inflation rate? **(b)** What is the purpose of calculating these two separate rates? **(c)** In what situation might the core inflation rate *not* be useful?

10. **Apply (a)** According to the quantity theory, what causes inflation? **(b)** Based on this theory, how can inflation be prevented? **(c)** What tools can the government use to achieve this goal? Give at least two examples.

Math Skills

11. Suppose the market basket cost $800 during the base period and $1,800 today. What is the CPI for today? (Remember, to calculate CPI, divide today's cost by the base period cost and multiply by 100.)

Visit PearsonSchool.com/PHecon for additional math help.

FL NGSSS

LA.1112.1.6 Use multiple strategies to develop vocabulary.

MA.912.A.2.2 Interpret a graph to represent a real-world situation.

SS.912.E.1.9 Describe how workers' pay is determined.

SS.912.E.2.4 Diagram and explain the problems of government-instituted wage and price control.

SS.912.G.4 Understand the characteristics of human populations.

ECONOMIC DICTIONARY

As you read the section, look for the definitions of these **Key Terms**:

- poverty threshold
- poverty rate
- income distribution
- food stamp program
- Lorenz Curve
- enterprise zone
- block grant
- workfare

Guiding Question

What factors affect the poverty rate?

Copy this table and fill it in as you read to explain the causes of poverty.

Causes of Poverty	
Lack of education	Less education equals lower wages
Location	

▶ **Economics and You**

The United States has millions of people living in poverty. It also has one of the highest per capita GDPs in the world. How can that be? Looking at poverty rates among different groups of Americans reveals some important reasons.

Principles in Action Statistically, you are at greater risk for living in poverty if you come from a single-parent home, live in the inner city, or do not have at least a high school education. Other factors, including the way that income is distributed, also affect the poverty rate.

poverty threshold
the income level below which income is insufficient to support a family or household

Limited job opportunities and lower levels of education are some of the factors that contribute to rural poverty. ▼

The Poor

As you have read, the United States Bureau of the Census conducts extensive surveys to gather data about the American people. Its economists then analyze the data and organize it to reveal important characteristics. One key feature they look at is how many families and households live in poverty. The Census Bureau defines a *family* as a group of two or more people related by birth, marriage, or adoption who live in the same housing unit. A *household* is all people who live in the same housing unit, regardless of how they are related.

The Poverty Threshold

According to the government, a poor family is one whose total income is less than the amount required to satisfy the family's minimum needs. The Census Bureau determines the income level, known as the poverty threshold, required to meet those minimum needs. The **poverty threshold** is the income level below which income is insufficient to support a family or household.

The poverty threshold, or poverty line, varies with the size of the family. For example, in 2006, the poverty threshold for a single parent under age 65 with one child was $13,896. For a family of four with two children, it was $20,444. If a family's total income is below the poverty threshold, everyone in the family is counted as poor.

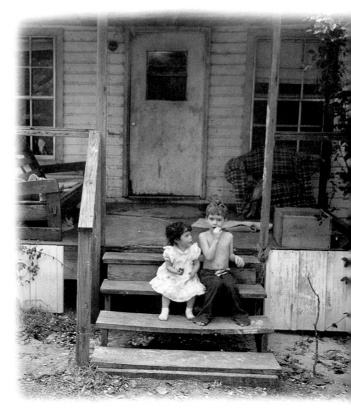

Figure 13.6

Poverty Rate

In 2008, 13.2 percent of the population equals 39.8 million people.

1. What happened to the poverty rate from 1994 to 2000?
2. Why do you think the government tracks the poverty rate?

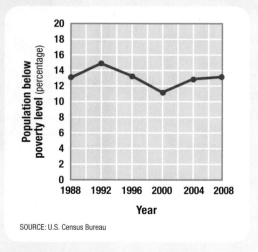

SOURCE: U.S. Census Bureau

The Poverty Rate

Trends in the national poverty rate are shown in **Figure 13.6.** The **poverty rate** is the percentage of people who live in households with income below the official poverty threshold.

Poverty rates for various groups are shown in **Figure 13.7.** We can use poverty rates to discover whom the government considers to be poor and what factors seem to contribute to poverty. Poverty rates differ sharply by groups, according to several different indicators:

- *Race and ethnic origin* The poverty rate among African Americans, Hispanics, and Native Americans is more than twice the rate for white Americans.
- *Type of Family* Families with a single mother have a poverty rate more than four times greater than that of two-parent families.
- *Age* The percentage of children living in poverty is significantly larger than that for any other age group. Adults over 65 are the next largest group.
- *Residence* Inner city residents have double the poverty rate of those who live outside the inner city. People who live in rural areas also have a higher poverty rate, especially in regions where job prospects are limited.

poverty rate the percentage of people who live in households with income below the official poverty threshold

✔ **CHECKPOINT** *What is one reason for the higher poverty rate in rural areas?*

Causes of Poverty

Put simply, a family is poor when the adults in the family fail to earn enough income to provide for its members' basic needs. This failure to earn adequate income is often the result of unemployment.

As you read in Section 1, millions of Americans are unemployed for a variety of reasons. While they are out of a job, their families might well fall below the poverty threshold. Many other poor adults are not even considered a part of the labor force. Some suffer from chronic health problems or disabilities that prevent them from working. Others are discouraged workers who are no longer looking for work.

Many poor adults do have jobs, however. In fact, more than half of poor households have someone who works at least part-time, and one in five have a full-time, year-round worker. For these "working poor," the problem is usually low wages or a limited work schedule, rather than the lack of a job. For example, Ray makes $9.00 an hour as a full-time clerk in a clothing store. While he is at work, his wife stays at home with their two young children. Although Ray works 40 hours per week, and his salary is well above the minimum wage, his annual earnings amount to just $18,720, which is below the poverty threshold for a family of four.

Economists agree that poverty and lack of income go hand in hand, but they have different ideas about the causes of poverty. Here are some of the most important explanations for why some people are poor.

Shifts in Family Structure

Single-parent families are more likely to live in poverty than two-parent families. That is especially the case when the lone parent is a single mother. The divorce rate has risen significantly since the 1960s, as has the number of children born to unmarried parents. These demographic shifts tend to result in more single-parent families and more children living in poverty.

Location

In most American cities, racial minorities are concentrated in the inner cities, far from the higher-wage jobs in suburban areas. Many of these inner-city residents do not own cars, and mass-transit systems are often not an efficient means of commuting from the inner city to the suburbs. As a result, people who live in the inner city earn less than people living outside the inner city. Similar obstacles exist for many people living in rural areas, where there is little business or industry.

Racial and Gender Discrimination

White workers generally earn higher salaries than minority workers, and men generally earn more than women. Much of this income inequality can be explained by differences in hours worked, education, and work experience. Part of the inequality, however, results from racial and gender discrimination. Even when all the workers in a group are equally productive, whites are often paid more than African Americans, and men are often paid more than women. Economists agree, however, that discrimination based on race or gender has been diminishing.

Growth of Low-Skill Service Jobs

In the past, less-educated people could earn good wages working in manufacturing jobs. Globalization, the decline in manufacturing, and the rise of the service economy has led to a decline in the number of higher-paying manufacturing jobs. More workers with less education now work in low-skill service jobs, where wages are often not as high as they are for factory jobs.

Lack of Education

The median income of high school dropouts in 2006 was $25,912, which was above the poverty threshold for a family of four in that year. High-school graduates earned about two-thirds more than the dropouts and college graduates earned more than three times as much.

✔ **CHECKPOINT** *What are three causes of poverty?*

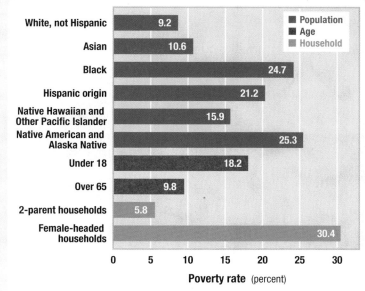

Figure 13.7   Poverty Rates by Group, 2008

SOURCE: U.S. Census Bureau

GRAPH SKILLS

Households headed by women, African Americans, Hispanics, and Native Americans are more likely than other groups to have incomes below the poverty threshold, as this recent data shows.

1. Which population group has the highest poverty rate?
2. Why do you think differences exist in poverty rates among groups?

Income Distribution

In 2006, the estimated median household income in the United States was $48,023, which means that half the households earned more than this amount and half earned less. This figure tells only part of the income story. To fully understand poverty in this country, you also need to understand **income distribution,** or how the nation's total income is distributed among its population.

Income Inequality

Income distribution in the United States is shown in **Figure 13.8** on page 353. These figures do not reflect the effects of taxes or non-cash government aid such as housing subsidies, healthcare, or food stamps. The **food stamp program** helps low-income people buy food. Benefits are provided on an electronic card that is accepted at most food stores.

 MA.912.A.2.2
Interpret a graph to represent a real-world situation.

income distribution
the way in which a nation's total income is distributed among its population

food stamp program
government program that helps low-income recipients to buy food

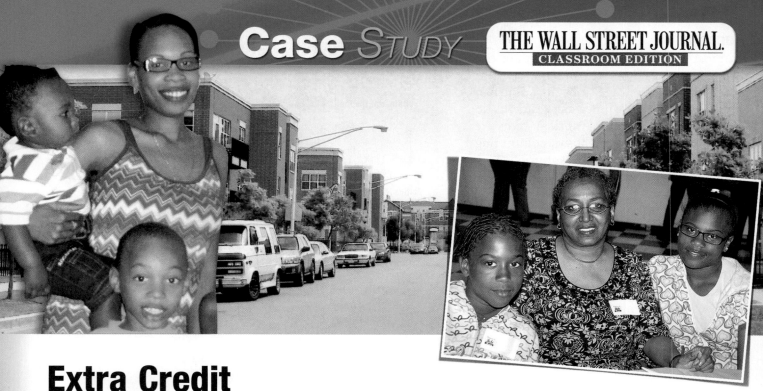

Extra Credit

ANTIPOVERTY PROGRAMS

Incentive programs for the poor offer an alternative to traditional welfare.

By Jonathan Eig
The Wall Street Journal

FL SS.912.E.2.2 Use a decision-making model to analyze public policy issues in the student's community.

Consumers earn rewards for flying, for using credit cards and for staying at hotels. In one low-income Chicago neighborhood, residents are earning rewards for paying their rent, getting their children to school every day and seeking work.

The "Pathways to Rewards" program has awarded about $19,000 in prizes to about 130 people since its inception. It is one of several small, local programs around the country attempting to use incentives to help the poor improve their lives.

At a recent rewards banquet, more than 150 people gathered in a church basement to celebrate and cash in points for prizes. Devant-e and Ireyonna Brown, 10 and 7, rode off on new bicycles with points earned for school attendance and volunteer work. Their

mother, Marilyn, walked away with a DVD player, thanks to points earned mostly for attending PTA meetings.

In the Pathways program, participants tell a counselor what they want to buy and how much it costs. Then the required number of points is set. Each point is worth one dollar. When the participant accumulates enough points, the counselor arranges either a gift certificate or a check made out to the store. Cash is never exchanged.

Incentive-based programs have sprung up in recent years because they are more politically palatable than traditional welfare benefits, and because advocates say such programs offer a better chance of changing the behaviors tied up with poverty. But incentives aren't safety nets. And it's not clear whether they are enough to

prompt meaningful long-term changes for those entrenched in poverty.

No one is saying this small experiment will be enough to transform a poor neighborhood. "It's a piece of the puzzle," says Crystal Palmer, a social worker with the nonprofit Near West Side Community Development Corp., a partner in the Pathways to Rewards program.

"The clients who are doing well [in Pathways] are the clients who are already motivated," says Vorricia Harvey, program director for the Near West Side CDC. "It's an incentive to say, 'You're doing well, keep it up.'"

Some social workers and area residents complain that Pathways is paying people to do things they ought to be doing anyway. Even some of the program's participants say there's truth to that. "But why not use it to my advantage?" asks Willie Wright. She used her points to help buy a computer.

Applying Economic Principles
Rewards programs are one approach to changing behaviors linked to poverty. But rewards programs do not provide basic necessities as traditional welfare programs do. Use the information in this section to give examples of other ways that people might be able to pull themselves out of poverty.

Video News Update Online
Powered by
The Wall Street Journal
Classroom Edition

Use videos at **PearsonSchool.com/PHecon** as a springboard for a discussion on a current topic.

Look at the table on the left side of **Figure 13.8.** To compute the numbers in the table, economists take four steps.

1. First, they rank the nation's households according to income.
2. Then, they divide the list into fifths, or quintiles, with equal numbers of households in each fifth. The lowest fifth, which appears at the top of the list, includes the poorest 20 percent of households. The highest fifth, shown at the bottom of the list, includes the richest 20 percent of households. The first column in **Figure 13.8** shows this division into quintiles.
3. Next, they compute each group's average income by adding up the incomes of all the households in the group, and then dividing by the number of households.
4. Finally, they compute each group's share, or percentage, of total income by dividing the group's total income by the total income of all the groups. The second column shows each group's share. The third column shows the cumulative total. (For example, the lowest two fifths of households earned 12 percent of total income.)

Compare the share of the poorest fifth with that of the richest fifth. If you divide richest by poorest, you will see that the richest fifth receives nearly 15 times the income of the poorest fifth.

Now look at the graph on the right side of **Figure 13.8.** It shows that the numbers for shares of total income, when they are plotted on a graph, form a curve. This graph, called the **Lorenz Curve,** illustrates the distribution of income in the economy.

Let's see what this Lorenz Curve tells you. First, read the label on each axis. Then look at the straight line running diagonally across the graph. This reference line represents complete equality. Under conditions of complete equality, each quintile would receive one fifth of total income. That means the lowest 20 percent of households would receive 20 percent of total income, as shown by the point (lowest, 20). Similarly, the lowest 40 percent (the first two quintiles) would receive 40 percent of total income, as shown by the point (second, 40), and so on.

Lorenz Curve the curve that illustrates income distribution

 MA.912.A.2.2 Interpret a graph to represent a real-world situation.

| Figure 13.8 | **Income Distribution** |

Percent of Total Income, 2006

Quintile	Percent of income for quintile	Cumulative: Percent of income for this and lower quintiles
Lowest fifth	3.4%	3.4%
Second fifth	8.6%	12.0%
Third fifth	14.5%	26.5%
Fourth fifth	22.9%	49.4%
Highest fifth	50.5%	100.0%

Note: Because of rounding, totals may be greater than or less than 100 percent.
SOURCE: U.S. Census Bureau

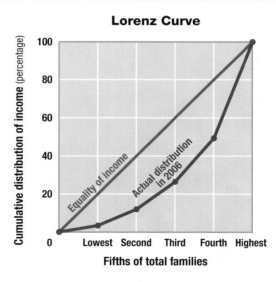

Lorenz Curve

GRAPH SKILLS

The table (left) shows family income ranked by category. When plotted on a Lorenz Curve (right), these data show the distribution of income in the United States.

1. What percent of total income did the lowest three fifths of households make in 2006?
2. How would taxes and government programs affect the Lorenz Curve?

Action Graph
online

For an animated version of this graph, visit
PearsonSchool.com/PHecon

In 2006, the distribution of income was not equal, as the Lorenz Curve indicates. For example, the point (lowest, 3.4) shows that the lowest 20 percent, or one fifth, of households received just 3.4 percent of the nation's total income. The point (second, 12) shows that the lowest 40 percent, or two fifths, of households received only 12 percent of the income. The area on the graph between the line of equality and the Lorenz Curve represents the amount of inequality in income distribution. The larger the area between the curves, the greater the income inequality.

Income Gap

As you can see from **Figure 13.8,** the wealthiest fifth of American households earned more income (50.5 percent) than the bottom four fifths combined. A study published in 1999 showed that after taxes are deducted, the richest 2.7 million Americans receive as much income as the poorest 100 million Americans. Why are there such differences in income among Americans? Here are some factors.

- *Differences in skills and education* Some people are more highly skilled than others, so they earn higher wages. Labor skills are determined by education, training, and by a worker's natural ability.

- *Inheritances* Some people inherit large sums of money and earn income by investing it. Others inherit businesses that produce income from profits.
- *Field of work* Wages are determined by the demand for labor. As you read in Chapter 9, labor demand is a "derived demand" because it is set by demand for what people produce. People who produce goods with a low market value usually earn lower wages.

James Webb, a former Secretary of the Navy who won election to the United States Senate in 2006, commented on the growing income gap:

“America's top tier has grown infinitely richer and more removed over the past 25 years…. The top 1 percent now takes in an astounding 16 percent of national income, up from 8 percent in 1980.”

—James Webb, Democratic Senator-elect from Virginia, *The Wall Street Journal,* Nov. 15, 2006

In fact, in the last two decades, the distribution of income has become less equal. Since 1977, the share of income earned by the lowest three fifths has decreased by 12 percent, while the share earned by the top 1 percent has more than doubled.

✓ **CHECKPOINT** *What does income distribution tell economists?*

The electronic benefits transfer card authorizes the transfer of government benefits, such as food stamps, for payment to retailers. Private charities run soup kitchens and food pantries to help the poor. ▶

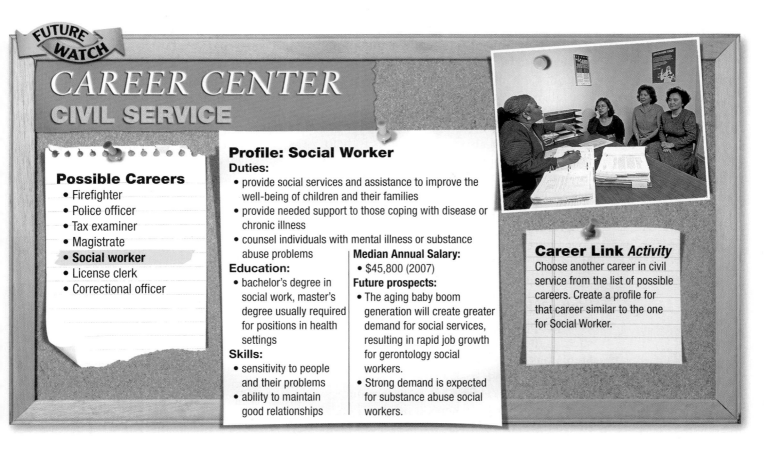

CAREER CENTER
CIVIL SERVICE

Possible Careers
- Firefighter
- Police officer
- Tax examiner
- Magistrate
- **Social worker**
- License clerk
- Correctional officer

Profile: Social Worker

Duties:
- provide social services and assistance to improve the well-being of children and their families
- provide needed support to those coping with disease or chronic illness
- counsel individuals with mental illness or substance abuse problems

Education:
- bachelor's degree in social work, master's degree usually required for positions in health settings

Skills:
- sensitivity to people and their problems
- ability to maintain good relationships

Median Annual Salary:
- $45,800 (2007)

Future prospects:
- The aging baby boom generation will create greater demand for social services, resulting in rapid job growth for gerontology social workers.
- Strong demand is expected for substance abuse social workers.

Career Link *Activity*
Choose another career in civil service from the list of possible careers. Create a profile for that career similar to the one for Social Worker.

Antipoverty Policies

As you read in Chapter 3, the government spends billions of dollars on programs designed to reduce poverty. This money is spent mainly on cash assistance, education, medical benefits, and non-cash benefits such as food stamps and subsidized housing.

Critics of antipoverty programs say that much of the money is wasted. Many argue that the programs themselves harm the very people they are intended to help. The criticisms have led to new policies. These include the Earned Income Tax Credit, the establishment of enterprise zones, job training and other employment assistance, housing assistance, and welfare reform.

The Earned Income Tax Credit

One of the government's most successful antipoverty programs is the Earned Income Tax Credit (EITC). The EITC is a refundable tax credit that low-income families with children receive when they file their federal income tax return. Eligibility is based on the taxpayer's earned income and the number of qualifying children. In 2010 for example, a married couple with an earned income of $40,363 and two children would receive a maximum credit of $5,036.

Established in 1975 to offset the impact of the Social Security payroll tax on low-income families, the EITC has been expanded over the years. A report by the Center on Budget and Policy Priorities said that in 2005, the EITC lifted more than four million people above the official poverty line and was "the nation's most effective antipoverty program for working families."

Enterprise Zones

Enterprise zones, which became popular in the 1980s, are areas where companies can locate and be free of certain state, local, and federal taxes and restrictions on business operations. Zones benefit businesses by lowering their costs. They help local people by making it easier for them to find work. By providing jobs, these zones can help revitalize rundown areas such as inner cities.

Employment Assistance

In recent decades, federal and state governments have designed job-training programs to help workers who lack the skills to

enterprise zone area where businesses can locate free of certain state, local, and federal taxes and restrictions

block grants federal funds given to the states in lump sums

workfare a program requiring work in exchange for temporary government assistance

earn an adequate income. In addition, the federal government has made a minimum wage mandatory since 1938. The minimum wage ensures that workers' hourly pay will not fall below a certain point.

Housing Assistance

The government also has programs to help poor people obtain affordable housing. In one approach, the government makes payments to landlords who then lower the rent they would otherwise charge. In another program, poor people receive vouchers that cover part of the rent they pay. The third approach is government-owned housing, which charges low rental fees.

Welfare Reform

Poor people often cannot afford basic needs, such as food and medical care. The United States has long had a welfare system that provides for those basic needs, especially for children and the elderly. That system underwent major reform when President Clinton signed the Personal Responsibility and Work Opportunity Reconciliation Act of 1996.

This welfare-reform plan responded to criticisms that welfare encouraged poor people to remain unemployed in order to keep receiving aid. It replaced the traditional antipoverty program for poor families (Aid to Families with Dependent Children, or AFDC) with a new program called Temporary Assistance for Needy Families (TANF). TANF eliminated cash assistance for poor families. Instead, the federal government provides **block grants,** or lump sums of money, to the states. The states are now responsible for designing and implementing programs to move most poor adults from welfare dependence to employment. TANF also set a 5-year limit on receipt of benefits.

The plan calls for a shift from welfare to **workfare**—a program requiring work in exchange for temporary assistance from the government. It was hoped that this reform would reduce poverty by providing poor Americans with labor skills and access to a steady, adequate income.

✓ **CHECKPOINT** *What was the goal of TANF?*

 FL SS.912.E.1.9, SS.912.E.2.4, SS.912.G.4, LA.1112.1.6.1, LA.1112.2.2.2

SECTION 3 ASSESSMENT

Essential Questions Journal To continue to build a response to the Essential Question, go to your **Essential Questions Journal**.

Guiding Question

1. Use your completed table to answer this question: What factors affect the poverty rate?
2. **Extension** Two candidates for your state legislature have outlined their plans to reduce poverty in the state. The candidates will debate next week, and the public is invited to submit suggestions. What one suggestion would you offer to reduce poverty?

Key Terms and Main Ideas

3. How is the **poverty threshold** related to the **poverty rate?**
4. Explain how a family can include working adults but still have an income below the poverty threshold.
5. How does lack of education contribute to poverty?
6. What is the **Lorenz Curve** and what does a current Lorenz Curve show about the distribution of income in the United States?

7. Describe at least three ways in which the government combats poverty.

Critical Thinking

8. **Extend (a)** What kinds of families are more likely to live in poverty? **(b)** Why do you think these families have a greater risk of being poor?
9. **Predict (a)** What are three reasons for differences in income among Americans? **(b)** Do you think these differences are a problem? Why or why not? **(c)** In what ways might the government help make these differences smaller?
10. **Explain (a)** How did the Personal Responsibility and Work Opportunity Reconciliation Act of 1996 change the assistance the government provides to poor families? **(b)** What are some benefits of these new programs? **(c)** What are some drawbacks? Explain your answers.

Quick Write

11. Reread the text under the Income Gap heading in this section. Then write two paragraphs on the income gap. In the first paragraph, describe how the income gap affects society, including economic growth and standard of living. In the second paragraph, predict what the long-term effects would be if the income gap increased, or what the long-term effects would be if the income gap decreased.

Chapter 13: Economic Challenges

Section 1 What are the causes of unemployment?

Section 2 What are the causes and effects of inflation?

Section 3 What factors affect the poverty rate?

Essential Question, Chapter 13

How much can we reduce unemployment, inflation, and poverty?

Economic Indicators

Unemployment rate	The percentage of the nation's labor force that is unemployed	To find the unemployment rate, divide the number of unemployed people by the total labor force and multiply by 100.
Inflation rate	The percentage rate of change in price level over time as measured by the Consumer Price Index	To calculate the inflation rate, subtract the base year CPI from the current CPI. Then divide the result by the base year CPI and multiply that result by 100.
Poverty rate	The percentage of people who live in households with income below the official poverty threshold	The government establishes a poverty threshold, an income level below which total income is insufficient to support a family or household.

Economic Dictionary

frictional unemployment, *p. 335*

structural unemployment, *p. 336*

globalization, *p. 337*

seasonal unemployment, *p. 338*

cyclical unemployment, *p. 338*

unemployment rate, *p. 339*

full employment, *p. 340*

underemployed, *p. 340*

discouraged worker, *p. 341*

inflation, *p. 342*

purchasing power, *p. 342*

price index, *p. 343*

Consumer Price Index, *p. 343*

market basket, *p. 343*

inflation rate, *p. 343*

core inflation rate, *p. 345*

hyperinflation, *p. 345*

quantity theory, *p. 346*

wage-price spiral, *p. 347*

fixed income, *p. 347*

deflation, *p. 348*

poverty threshold, *p. 349*

poverty rate, *p. 350*

income distribution, *p. 351*

food stamp program, *p. 351*

Lorenz Curve, *p. 353*

enterprise zone, *p. 355*

block grant, *p. 356*

workfare, *p. 356*

Economics on the go

Study anytime, anywhere. Download these files today.

Economic Dictionary online
Vocabulary Support in English and Spanish

Audio Review online
Audio Study Guide in English and Spanish

Action Graph online
Animated Charts and Graphs

Visual Glossary online
Animated feature

How the Economy Works online
Animated feature

Download to your computer or mobile device at PearsonSchool.com/PHecon

Self-Test online To test your understanding of key terms and main ideas, visit PearsonSchool.com/PHecon

Key Terms and Main Ideas

To make sure you understand the key terms and main ideas of this chapter, review the Checkpoint and Section Assessment questions and look at the Quick Study Guide on the preceding page.

Critical Thinking

1. **Predict (a)** What does the unemployment rate tell about a country's economy? **(b)** How is full employment related to the unemployment rate? **(c)** What issues might arise if the economy reached full employment?

2. **Apply (a)** What might cause inflation in food prices? **(b)** How would you react to higher food prices? **(c)** How could this type of inflation contribute to unemployment and poverty? Explain your answers.

3. **Draw Conclusions (a)** According to the quantity theory, how can the government limit inflation? **(b)** What other tools can the government use to control inflation? **(c)** Why would the government want to reduce inflation?

4. **Extend (a)** What are the most recognized causes of poverty? **(b)** What kinds of assistance might a poor family be able to get from the government? **(c)** What combination of personal action and good fortune could help a person rise out of poverty?

5. **Make Judgments (a)** On May 25, 2007, President George W. Bush signed a bill to increase the federal minimum wage in three steps: to $5.85 per hour starting in July 2007; to $6.55 per hour starting in July 2008; and to $7.25 per hour starting in July 2009. What are some possible results of raising the minimum wage? **(b)** Why

do you think the government chose to raise the minimum wage in stages, rather than all at once? **(c)** Do you think this is a good strategy? Why or why not?

Applying Your Math Skills

Calculate the Inflation Rate

Use your math skills and the formula below to answer the following questions. Suppose that the CPI for last year was 164 and that for this year it is 168.

Visit PearsonSchool.com/PHecon for additional math help.

Calculating the Inflation Rate
To calculate the inflation rate, use the following formula:
CPI for Year A **minus** CPI for Year B **divided by** CPI for Year B **multiplied by** 100
For example, If the CPI for 2004 (Year A) = 188.9 and the CPI for 2003 (Year B) = 184.0
then, **188.9 − 184.0 = 4.9** **4.9 ÷ 184.0 = .027** **.027 x 100 = 2.7**
Therefore, the inflation rate for 2004 was 2.7%.

6. Calculate the inflation rate from last year to this year.
7. Suppose the CPI for the year before last year was 160. What was the inflation rate from the previous year to last year?
8. If the inflation rate were 0%, what would the CPI be for next year?
9. If the inflation rate were 10%, what would the CPI be for next year?

 Essential Question Activity

Essential Questions Journal To respond to the chapter Essential Question, go to your **Essential Questions Journal**.

10. Complete this activity to answer the Essential Question **How much can we reduce unemployment, inflation, and poverty?** Your class should be divided into three groups. Each group is advising the President of the United States on ways that the federal government can help reduce unemployment, inflation, and poverty. Using the worksheet in your Essential Questions Journal or the electronic worksheet available at **PearsonSchool.com/PHecon,** gather the following information:
    (a) With globalization accelerating, and the loss of America's manufacturing base, what can we do to reduce unemployment? What is one benefit and one drawback of your plan?
    (b) What strategy or strategies would you recommend to reduce inflation? What is one benefit and one drawback of your plan?

    (c) What strategy or strategies would you recommend to reduce poverty? What is one benefit and one drawback of your plan?

11. **Modify** Present your group's ideas to the class. As a class, discuss the suggestions from all the groups.
    (a) What are the best ideas for reducing unemployment? What are the best ideas for controlling inflation? What are the best ideas for reducing poverty?
    (b) Do any of these ideas and goals conflict with each other? (For example, cutting taxes without reducing government spending could trigger inflation. Cutting taxes and cutting spending on entitlement programs could put more children below the poverty level.) How?
    (c) How can these conflicts best be resolved?
    (d) At the conclusion of your discussion, identify which steps you think would be most effective and most acceptable to the majority of the population.

Should the government help the poor?

In the United States, the federal government and local governments provide many kinds of welfare assistance to the poor. Some people argue that this aid is necessary to help reduce poverty. Others believe that providing welfare is not an appropriate role for government, and that private organizations can do a better job of helping the poor. Some also feel that government aid makes people less able and willing to earn a living independently.

Document A

"Voluntary charities and organizations, such as friendly societies that devoted themselves to helping those in need, flourished in the days before the welfare state turned charity into a government function…. Today, government welfare programs have supplemented the old-style private programs…. Releasing the charitable impulses of the American people by freeing them from the excessive tax burden so they can devote more of their resources to charity, is a moral and constitutional means of helping the needy."

—Representative Ron Paul (R-TX) in the U.S. House of Representatives, February 13, 2003

Document B

"What's most overwhelming about urban poverty is that it's so difficult to escape—it's isolating and it's every-where….When you're in these neighborhoods, you can see what a difference it makes to have a government that cares. You can see what a free lunch program does for a hungry child. You can see what a little extra money from an earned income tax credit does for a family that's struggling. You can see what prenatal care does for the health of a mother and a newborn. So don't tell me there's no role for government in lifting up our cities."

—Senator Barack Obama (D-IL) speech in Washington, DC, July 18, 2007

www.barackobama.com

Document C

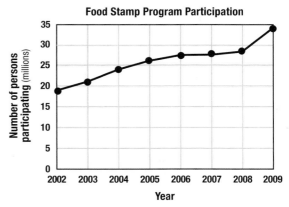

Food Stamp Program Participation

SOURCE: United States Department of Agriculture, Food and Nutrition Service

FL LA.1112.1.6.2, SS.912.E.2.4

ANALYZING DOCUMENTS

Use your knowledge of government aid to the poor and Documents A, B, and C to answer questions 1–3.

1. **According to Document A, what does Representative Ron Paul believe would be a better alternative to federal welfare payments to the poor?**
   - **A.** local government welfare programs
   - **B.** private charities
   - **C.** state government welfare programs
   - **D.** ignoring poverty

2. **The author of Document B believes**
   - **A.** that ending poverty is too costly.
   - **B.** that Americans hear too much about poverty.
   - **C.** that fighting poverty is a job for government.
   - **D.** that government is not accountable for poverty.

3. **What does Document C suggest?**
   - **A.** Food stamps are preventing poverty.
   - **B.** The food stamp program is unsuccessful.
   - **C.** Poverty is increasing, so more people need food stamps.
   - **D.** The food stamp program should be privatized.

WRITING ABOUT ECONOMICS

Whether government aid is the best way to reduce poverty is an ongoing question. Use the documents on this page and resources on the Web site below to answer the question: *Should the government help the poor?*

In Partnership

THE WALL STREET JOURNAL.
CLASSROOM EDITION

To read more about issues related to this topic, visit
PearsonSchool.com/PHecon

Essential Question, Unit 5

Why does it matter how the economy is doing?

Does economic news about GDP or inflation really matter to ordinary people? Plenty of people think that it does. Look at the opinions below, keeping in mind the Essential Question: Why does it matter how the economy is doing?

"Economists readily concede that GDP is not a one-number-fits-all view of what's going on. Some suggest changes to make it more useful and more accurate.... 'What we need to end up with is two separate accounts [of the economy]—a market price account and a quality of life account,' says Rob Atkinson, an economist in Washington.... 'It is an opportunity to think more accurately about our economic well-being.'"

—Mark Trumbull, "Does GDP Really Capture Economic Health?" Christian Science Monitor, March 12, 2008

"The U.S. economy is taking hits from all directions, or that's how it seems to many Americans.... Home foreclosures are multiplying. People with houses can't sell them. Home prices and sales dropped dramatically in January, and there's no sign of improvement soon. Banks no longer provide easy credit. Stock-market investments are on a roller-coaster ride. Pay checks don't buy as much today as yesterday.... Americans want to know what will turn the economy around. They want help and answers—from Congress and the president."

—Miami Herald, February 29, 2008

"I DON'T UNDERSTAND HOW HIGH INTEREST RATES AND THE NATIONAL DEFICIT AFFECT MY ALLOWANCE."

Essential Question Writing Activity

Consider the different views of economics expressed in the sources on this page and what you have learned about measuring economic performance. ***Then write a well-constructed essay expressing your view of why it is important to keep track of the economy.***

Writing Guidelines

- Address all aspects of the Essential Question Writing Activity.
- Support the theme with relevant facts, examples, and details.
- Use a logical and clear plan of organization.
- Introduce the theme by establishing a framework that is beyond a simple restatement of the question and conclude with a summation of the theme.

For help in writing a Persuasive Essay, refer to the *Writer's Handbook* in the Reference section, page S-5.

Essential Questions Journal

To respond to the unit Essential Question, go to your **Essential Questions Journal**.

UNIT 6 Government and the Economy

Essential Question, Unit 6

What is the proper role of government in the economy?

Chapter 16
How effective is monetary policy as an economic tool?

Chapter 14
How can taxation meet the needs of government and the people?

Chapter 15
How effective is fiscal policy as an economic tool?

14 Taxes and Government Spending

Essential Question, Chapter 14

?Q **How can taxation meet the needs of government and the people?**

Economics *on the go*

To study anywhere, anytime, download these
online resources at **PearsonSchool.com/PHecon** ▶

SECTION 1 What Are Taxes?

 NGSSS

LA.1112.1.6 Use multiple strategies to develop vocabulary.

MA.912.A.2.2 Interpret a graph to represent a real-world situation.

SS.912.E.2.8 Differentiate between direct and indirect taxes.

SS.912.E.3.5 Compare the current U.S. economy with other developed nations.

ECONOMIC DICTIONARY

As you read the section, look for the definitions of these **Key Terms:**

- tax
- revenue
- progressive tax
- proportional tax
- regressive tax
- tax base
- individual income tax
- corporate income tax
- property tax
- sales tax
- incidence of a tax

Guiding Question

What are the features of a tax system?

Copy this concept web and fill it in as you read.

▶ Economics and You

You're looking forward to getting your first paycheck. You figure that at $7 per hour, you should be getting $140 for the 20 hours you worked. When you open the envelope, you find that the check is for much less than $140. Where did the money go? The answer is ... taxes! The federal government and most state governments levy taxes on personal income. Is this fair?

Principles in Action Fairness is one of the main features of a tax system. But what is fair to one person may not be fair to another. For example, at first glance, it may seem fair that all Americans are taxed at the same rate. However, in this section, you will learn why most Americans believe that the person who earns more money should pay a higher percentage of income in taxes. This concept, known as progressive taxation, lies at the base of our income tax system.

The Government's Authority to Tax

Looking at all of the taxes taken from your paycheck can be discouraging. You worked hard for that money, and now it is being taken away. Similar feelings of frustration over taxes helped persuade American colonists to declare their independence from Britain. Unlike those colonists, however, an overwhelming majority of citizens today consent to having a portion of their earnings taken by the government. We authorize the federal government, through the Constitution and our elected representatives in Congress, to raise money in the form of taxes.

Visual Glossary
online

Go to the Visual Glossary Online for an interactive review of **progressive taxes.**

Action Graph
online

Go to Action Graph Online for animated versions of key charts and graphs.

How the Economy Works
online

Go to How the Economy Works Online for an interactive lesson on your **federal taxes.**

The Purpose of Taxation

A **tax** is a required payment to a local, state, or national government. Taxation is the primary way that the government collects money. Taxes give the government the money it needs to operate.

The income received by a government from taxes and other nontax sources is called **revenue.** Without revenue from taxes, the government would not be able to provide the goods and services that we not only benefit from, but that we expect the government to provide. For example, we authorize the government to provide national defense, highways, education, and law enforcement. We also ask the government to provide help to people in need. All of these goods and services cost money—in workers' salaries, in materials, in land and labor. All members of our society share these costs through the payment of taxes.

The Power to Tax

Taxation is a powerful tool. The founders of the United States thought long and hard before giving this tool to their new national government. The Constitution they created assigned each branch of the government certain powers and responsibilities. The first power granted to the legislative branch—Congress—is the power to tax. This clause is the basis for all federal tax laws.

Limits on the Power to Tax

The Constitution also spells out specific limits on the government's power to tax. Two of those limits are in the taxation clause. First, the purpose of a tax must be "for the common defense and general welfare." A tax cannot bring in money that goes to individual interests. Second, federal taxes must be the same in every state. The federal gas tax, for example, cannot be 4 cents per gallon in Maryland and 10 cents per gallon in South Dakota.

Other provisions of the Constitution also limit the kinds of taxes Congress can levy, or impose. For example, Congress cannot tax church services, because that would violate the freedom of religion promised by the First Amendment. Another clause of the Constitution prohibits taxing exports.

The government can collect taxes only on imports—goods brought into the United States. (Congress can restrict or prohibit the export of certain goods, however, such as technology or weapons.)

Yet another clause of the Constitution (Article 1, Section 9, Clause 4) prohibited Congress from levying direct taxes unless they were divided among the states according to population. The Sixteenth Amendment overturned this clause when it legalized a direct tax on citizens' personal income. This income-tax amendment was ratified in 1913.

✔ CHECKPOINT *For what purpose does the government collect taxes?*

Tax Structures and Tax Bases

Despite the constitutional limits on its power, the government actually collects a wide variety of taxes. Economists describe these taxes in different ways. First, they describe how the tax is structured. Economists describe three different tax structures: progressive, proportional, and regressive. Second, they describe a tax according to the object taxed—the tax base.

Progressive Taxes

A **progressive tax** is a tax for which the percentage of income paid in taxes increases as income increases. People with higher incomes pay a higher percentage of their income in taxes. People with very small incomes might pay no tax at all.

The federal income tax is the clearest example of a progressive tax in the United States. A sample progressive income tax system is shown in the Visual Glossary. Notice that the tax rate in this example rises from 15, to 25, and then to 30 percent as income rises. This is a progressive tax rate structure because as income rises, the percentage of income paid in taxes also rises.

Proportional Taxes

A **proportional tax** is a tax for which the percentage of income paid in taxes remains the same at all income levels. Leslie Wilson, a corporate executive, earns $350,000 per

tax a required payment to a local, state, or national government

revenue the income received by a government from taxes and other nontax sources

progressive tax a tax for which the percentage of income paid in taxes increases as income increases

proportional tax a tax for which the percentage of income paid in taxes remains the same at all income levels

VISUAL
GLOSSARY

Reviewing Key Terms
To understand *progressive taxes,* review these terms:

economic growth, *p. 315*
tax, *p. 364*
revenue, *p. 364*

What are Progressive Taxes?

◀ **Progressive Taxes** taxes for which the percentage of income paid in taxes increases as income increases.

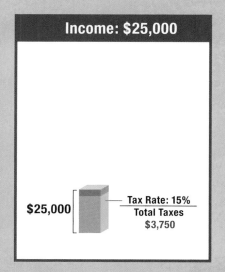

Income: $25,000

$25,000 — Tax Rate: 15%
Total Taxes
$3,750

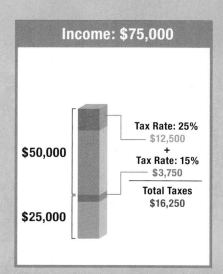

Income: $75,000

$50,000

Tax Rate: 25%
$12,500
+
Tax Rate: 15%
$3,750

Total Taxes
$16,250

$25,000

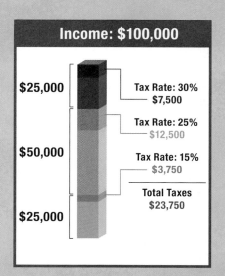

Income: $100,000

$25,000 — Tax Rate: 30%
$7,500

$50,000 — Tax Rate: 25%
$12,500

Tax Rate: 15%
$3,750

Total Taxes
$23,750

$25,000

In a progressive tax structure, the higher a taxpayer's income, the greater percentage he or she must pay in taxes. Above are three examples of how progressive taxes have an impact on people with different incomes. **What would be the total tax on taxable income of $65,000?**

▲ With a progressive tax system, some people pay a higher rate of taxes than others. *What is the complaint that the "millionaire" expresses?*

Visual Glossary
online

To expand your understanding of this and other key economic terms, visit **PearsonSchool.com/PHecon**

Figure 14.1

Elasticities of Demand and Tax Effects

Graph A

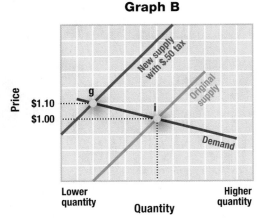

Graph B

GRAPH SKILLS

If demand for a good is relatively inelastic (Graph A), a new tax will increase the price by a relatively large amount, and consumers will pay a large share of the tax.

1. Under what conditions, elastic or inelastic demand, would price of the good increase from $1.00 to $1.10?

2. Who bears the burden of a tax if demand is relatively elastic?

Action Graph
online

For an animated version of this graph, visit
PearsonSchool.com/PHecon

MA.912.A.2.2
Interpret a graph to represent a real-world situation.

regressive tax a tax for which the percentage of income paid in taxes decreases as income increases

tax base the income, property, good, or service that is subject to a tax

individual income tax a tax based on a person's earnings

corporate income tax a tax based on a company's profits

property tax a tax based on real estate and other property

sales tax a tax based on goods or services that are sold

year. Tony Owens, a nurse, earns $50,000 per year. If a 6 percent proportional tax were levied on their incomes, Leslie would pay 6 percent of $350,000, or $21,000, in taxes. Tony would pay 6 percent of $50,000, or $3,000, in taxes. With a proportional income tax, whether income goes up or down, the percentage of income paid in taxes stays the same.

Regressive Taxes

A **regressive tax** is a tax for which the percentage of income paid in taxes decreases as income increases. For example, although the sales tax rate remains constant, a sales tax is regressive. This is because higher-income households spend a lower proportion of their incomes on taxable goods and services. As a result, although they may pay more actual dollars in sales taxes, the proportion of their income spent on sales taxes is lower than that of lower-income households.

Tax Bases

A **tax base** is the income, property, good, or service that is subject to a tax. Different taxes have different bases. The **individual income tax** is based on a person's earnings.

The **corporate income tax** uses a company's profits as its base. The **property tax** is based on real estate and other property. The tax base for the **sales tax** is goods or services that are sold. When government policymakers create a new tax, they first decide what the base will be for the tax: income, profits, property, sales, or some other category.

✓ **CHECKPOINT** *Is the federal income tax proportional, progressive, or regressive?*

Who Bears the Tax Burden?

Government tax policies affect individuals, businesses, and even whole regions. They may benefit some regions more than others. Thus, it is important to think about who actually bears the burden of the tax. Taxes affect more than just the people who send in the checks to pay them. Why? The answer lies in supply and demand analysis.

Suppose that the government imposes a gasoline tax of $.50 per gallon and collects the tax from service stations. You may think that the burden of the tax falls only on the service stations, because they mail the checks to the government. Graphs A and B in **Figure 14.1**, however, provide a different set of answers. Graph A represents the effect of a gasoline tax when demand is inelastic. Graph B reflects elastic demand.

Both graphs show two supply curves: an original supply line and a line showing the supply after the $.50 tax is imposed. When a tax is imposed on a good, the cost of supplying the good increases. The supply of the good then decreases at every price level.

Before the tax, the market was in equilibrium, and consumers bought gas at $1.00 per gallon. This is shown as point *i* on both graphs. If demand for gas is relatively inelastic (that is, if consumers buy about the same amount no matter what the price), the tax will increase the price of each gallon by a relatively large amount. Consumers will bear a large share of the tax. This is shown in Graph A. Demand is inelastic, so the demand curve is relatively steep, and a $.50 tax increases the equilibrium price by $.40 (from $1.00 to $1.40 from point *i* to point *f*). In other words, consumers pay about four fifths of the tax.

In contrast, if demand is relatively elastic, the demand curve will be relatively flat, as in Graph B. Consumers will pay a relatively small part of the tax. As Graph B shows, a $.50 tax increases the equilibrium price by only $.10 (from $1.00 to $1.10 from point *i* to point *g*). In this case, consumers pay only one fifth of the tax. The service stations pay the other four fifths.

This example shows the **incidence of a tax**—that is, the final burden of a tax. When policymakers consider a new tax, they examine who will actually bear the burden. As in the example above, producers can "pass on" a portion of the burden to consumers. Generally, the more inelastic the demand, the more easily the seller can shift the tax to consumers. The more elastic the demand, the more the seller bears the burden.

✔ **CHECKPOINT** *Who bears the greater burden of a tax when demand is inelastic?*

Characteristics of a Good Tax

Although it is sometimes difficult to decide whether a specific tax is proportional, progressive, or regressive, economists do generally agree on what makes a good tax. A good tax should have four characteristics: simplicity, efficiency, certainty, and equity, or fairness.

- *Simplicity* Tax laws should be simple and easily understood. Taxpayers and businesses should be able to keep the necessary records and pay the taxes on a predictable schedule.
- *Efficiency* Government administrators should be able to assess and collect taxes without spending too much time or money. Similarly, taxpayers should be able to pay taxes without giving up too much time or paying too much money in fees.

incidence of a tax the final burden of a tax

FL **SS.912.E.3.5** Compare the current U.S. economy with other developed nations.

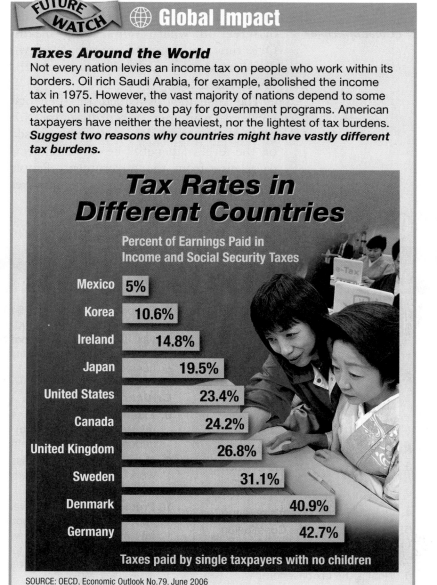

FUTURE WATCH 🌐 **Global Impact**

Taxes Around the World
Not every nation levies an income tax on people who work within its borders. Oil rich Saudi Arabia, for example, abolished the income tax in 1975. However, the vast majority of nations depend to some extent on income taxes to pay for government programs. American taxpayers have neither the heaviest, nor the lightest of tax burdens. *Suggest two reasons why countries might have vastly different tax burdens.*

Tax Rates in Different Countries

Percent of Earnings Paid in Income and Social Security Taxes

Country	Percent
Mexico	5%
Korea	10.6%
Ireland	14.8%
Japan	19.5%
United States	23.4%
Canada	24.2%
United Kingdom	26.8%
Sweden	31.1%
Denmark	40.9%
Germany	42.7%

Taxes paid by single taxpayers with no children

SOURCE: OECD, Economic Outlook No.79, June 2006

▲ The gasoline tax is an example of the benefits-received principle. **How does it fit that principle?**

- *Certainty*
  Certainty is also a characteristic of a good tax. It should be clear to the taxpayer when a tax is due, how much money is due, and how the tax should be paid.
- *Equity* The tax system should be fair, so that no one bears too much or too little of the tax burden.

Determining Fairness

Although everyone agrees that a tax system should be fair to taxpayers, people often disagree on what "fair" really means. Over time, economists have proposed two different ideas about how to measure the fairness of a tax.

The first idea is called the benefits-received principle. According to this principle, a person should pay taxes based on the level of benefits he or she expects to receive from the government. People who drive, for example, pay gasoline taxes that are used to build and maintain highways. In this way, the people who receive the most benefit from the roads also contribute the most to their upkeep.

The second idea about fairness is called the ability-to-pay principle. According to this principle, people should pay taxes according to their ability to pay. The ability-to-pay principle is the idea behind a progressive income tax: people who earn more income pay more taxes.

Balancing Tax Revenues and Tax Rates

How much revenue does a good tax generate? The answer is "enough, but not too much." That is, enough so that citizens' needs are met, but not so much that the tax discourages production. For example, if a company has to pay $100,000 in taxes, it will not be able to use that $100,000 to expand production. If tax rates are lower, however, the company can use more of its income to stimulate production rather than to pay taxes. Ultimately, many people argue, the economy benefits from lower, rather than higher, tax rates.

 CHECKPOINT *What are the four characteristics of a good tax?*

(FL) SS.912.E.2.8, LA.1112.1.6.1,
LA.1112.2.2.2, LA.1112.2.2.3

SECTION 1 ASSESSMENT

Essential Questions Journal To continue to build a response to the Essential Question, go to your **Essential Questions Journal**.

Guiding Question

1. Use your completed concept web to answer this question: What are the features of a tax system?
2. **Extension** Tax revenue helps governments provide citizens with goods and services. What kind of taxes do you pay to get these services?

Key Terms and Main Ideas

3. Where does the U.S. government get the power to impose **taxes** today?
4. What is a government's **revenue?**
5. Name two limits the Constitution places on the government's power to tax.
6. What is the tax base for the **sales tax?**

7. Suppose Michelle earns $40,000 per year and Rosa earns $100,000 per year. Under a **proportional tax,** who would pay a greater percentage of her income in taxes?

Critical Thinking

8. **Extend (a)** What does it mean if a tax system is efficient? **(b)** Why is it important that taxes be efficient?
9. **Contrast** How do progressive taxes work? How are they different from regressive taxes?
10. **Predict** Suppose the government imposed a new tax on toothpaste. **(a)** Who would probably end up bearing the incidence of the tax? **(b)** Give a reason for your answer.

Math Skills

11. **Finding Sales Tax** To find sales tax, start by converting the percent of the tax into a decimal. Multiply the decimal by the price of the item that is taxed. Your result is the amount of the sales tax. To find the total cost of the product, add the original price to the sales tax. Suppose Victor buys a pair of pants that cost $38. He has to pay 8 percent sales tax on the pants. What is the total amount Victor has to pay?

Visit PearsonSchool.com/PHecon for additional math help.

SECTION 2 Federal Taxes

NGSSS

SS.912.E.2.8 Differentiate between direct and indirect taxes.

SS.912.E.2.9 Analyze how changes in federal spending affect budget deficits, surpluses, and the national debt.

ECONOMIC DICTIONARY

As you read the section, look for the definitions of these **Key Terms:**

• withholding
• tax return
• taxable income
• personal exemption
• tax deduction
• tax credit
• estate tax
• gift tax
• tariff
• tax incentive

Guiding Question

What taxes does the federal government collect?

Copy this table and fill it in as you read.

Type of Tax	Description
Individual income	Taxes paid throughout year. Employers withhold taxes from pay. Individuals file taxes. Tax is progressive.
Corporate income	
Social insurance	
Excise	
Estate	
Gift	
Import	

▶ **Economics and You** The United States has a government "of the people, by the people, for the people." For that government to function, it needs the economic backing of the American people. If you work and pay income taxes, you are helping to support the work the government does.

Principles in Action The income tax is just one of the wide variety of taxes collected by the federal government. As you will read in this section, individual taxpayers like you are not the only source of federal revenues. Federal revenues come from corporate income taxes, social insurance taxes, excise taxes, estate and gift taxes, and taxes on imports.

Individual Income Taxes

The government's main source of revenues comes from the federal tax on individuals' taxable income. As **Figure 14.2** shows, about 39 percent of the federal government's revenues come from the payment of individual income taxes.

"Pay-As-You-Earn" Taxation

The amount of federal income tax a person owes is determined on an annual basis. In theory, the federal government could wait until the end of the tax year to collect individual income taxes. In reality, that would be a problem for both taxpayers and the government. Like other employers, the government has to pay regularly for rent, supplies, services, and employees' salaries. A single annual payment from all the nation's taxpayers at once would make meeting these expenses difficult.

Figure 14.2 Federal Revenue

- Personal income taxes
- Social Security, Medicare and unemployment, and other retirement taxes
- Borrowing to cover deficit
- Corporate Income taxes
- Excise, customs, gift and miscellaneous taxes

SOURCE: The Internal Revenue Service, U.S. Department of Treasury

GRAPH SKILLS

The main sources of government revenue are the taxes shown on this graph.

1. What are the largest sources of federal revenue shown on the graph?
2. What percentage of federal revenues do not come from individual and corporate income taxes?

CHAPTER 14 SECTION 2 **369**

Figure 14.3

Federal Income Tax Rates, 2008

Schedule	If your taxable income is over –	but not over –	the tax is	of the amount over –
Schedule X – use if your filing status is single	$0	$8,025	10%	$0
	$8,025	$32,550	$802.50 plus 15%	$8,025
	$32,550	$78,850	$4,481.25 plus 25%	$32,550
	$78,850	$164,550	$16,056.25 plus 28%	$78,850
	$164,550	$357,700	$40,052.25 plus 33%	$164,550
	$357,700	no limit	$103,791.00 plus 35%	$357,700
Schedule Y – use if your filing status is married filing jointly	$0	$16,050	10%	$0
	$16,050	$65,100	$1,605.00 plus 15%	$16,050
	$65,100	$131,450	$8,962.50 plus 25%	$65,100
	$131,450	$200,300	$25,550.00 plus 28%	$131,450
	$200,300	$357,700	$44,828.00 plus 33%	$200,300
	$357,700	no limit	$96,770.00 plus 35%	$357,700

SOURCE: Internal Revenue Service, Revenue Procedure 2007-66.

FUTURE WATCH

Personal Finance
For more help in understanding tax liabilities, see your Personal Finance Handbook in the back of the book or visit **PearsonSchool.com/PHecon**

withholding taking tax payments out of an employee's pay before he or she receives it

tax return a form used to file income taxes

Similarly, many people might have trouble paying their taxes in one large sum. For these reasons, federal income tax is collected in a "pay-as-you-earn" system. This means that individuals usually pay most of their income tax throughout the calendar year as they earn income. They have until mid-April of the following year to pay any additional income taxes they owe.

Tax Brackets

The federal income tax is a progressive tax. In other words, the tax rate rises with the amount of taxable income. The 2008 tax rate schedules shown in **Figure 14.3** both have six rates, defined in the column headed "the tax is." Each applies to a different range of income, or tax bracket. For example, married couples who filed a return together (a joint return) and had a taxable income of $16,050 or less paid 10 percent income tax. The highest rate—35 percent—was paid by high-income single people or married couples on the portion of their taxable incomes that exceeded $357,700. Each year, the IRS publishes new tax rate schedules that reflect any changes in the federal tax code.

Tax Withholding

Employers are responsible in part for carrying out the system of collecting federal income taxes. They do so by **withholding,** or taking payments out of your pay before you receive it. The amount they withhold is based on an estimate of how much you will owe in federal income taxes for the entire year. After withholding the money, the employer forwards it to the federal government as an "installment payment" on your upcoming annual income tax bill.

Filing a Tax Return

After the calendar year ends, employers give their employees a report stating how much income tax has already been withheld and sent to the government. The employee uses that information to complete a tax return. A **tax return** is a form used to file income taxes. On it, you declare your income to the government and figure out how much of that income is taxable.

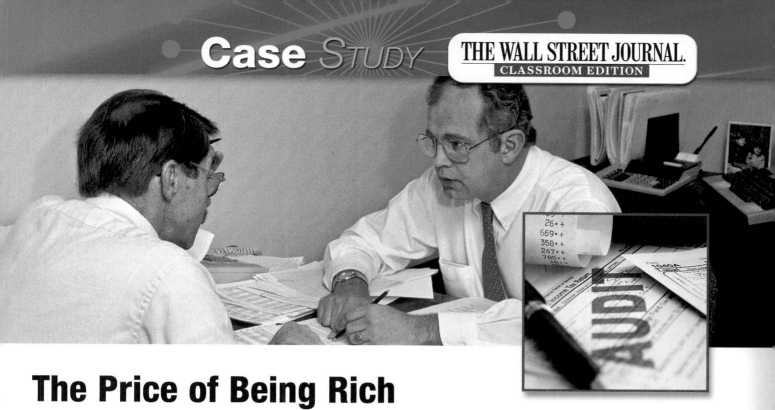

The Price of Being Rich

TAXATION

The IRS uses audits to crack down on people who may not be paying all the taxes they're supposed to. Now, a lot of high-income earners are feeling the heat.

By Tom Herman
The Wall Street Journal

 LA.1112.2.2 Use the text to answer questions.

The Internal Revenue Service is turning up the heat on high-income taxpayers, especially those who work for themselves.

Internal Revenue Service officials say audits of taxpayers making $100,000 or more rose 14% in 2007 from 2006. Recent IRS data also show a 29% increase in audits of people making $200,000 or more—and an 84% surge in audits of those with incomes of $1 million or more.

The push comes as the agency faces heavy pressure from Congress to raise additional revenue and shrink the nation's $290 billion "tax gap," or the difference between what's collected and what should be collected each year.

IRS research indicates much of the tax-noncompliance is committed by self-employed workers, such as consultants and small-business owners, whose taxes aren't withheld from their paychecks and whose income isn't reported separately to the government. By contrast, compliance is much higher among people whose pay is reported by their employers and whose taxes are withheld from their pay.

It's not just Americans who face the IRS's intensified crackdown. IRS officials say they have uncovered "significant noncompliance" among foreign athletes, such as golf and tennis stars, and foreign musicians who perform in the U.S., says Barry Shott, an IRS deputy commissioner.

IRS officials won't divulge any names of foreign athletes or entertainers under scrutiny. But Mr. Shott says the cases involve not only taxation of prize money won by athletes competing in U.S. events but also product-endorsement money.

The IRS relies on numerous techniques to choose which returns are audited. Many returns are selected on the basis of a secret computerized-scoring system. Computer programs assign each tax return a score that evaluates the potential for inaccuracies, based on the IRS's experience with similar returns.

Many returns are picked because of "mismatches"— something a taxpayer reported doesn't match what was reported separately to the IRS by employers, banks or other financial institutions. Some returns get selected because of a tip from confidential informants, such as former business partners, ex-spouses or an angry neighbor.

Applying Economic Principles

From the viewpoint of the federal government, describe two costs and two possible benefits of conducting tax audits.

Video News Update Online
Powered by
The Wall Street Journal
Classroom Edition

Use videos at **PearsonSchool.com/PHecon** as a springboard for a discussion on a current topic.

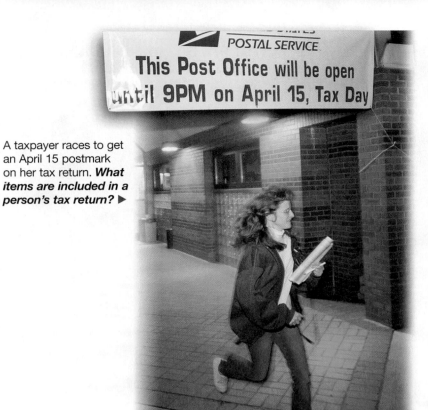

A taxpayer races to get an April 15 postmark on her tax return. *What items are included in a person's tax return?* ▶

taxable income the earnings on which tax must be paid; total income minus exemptions and deductions

personal exemption a set amount that taxpayers may subtract from their gross income for themselves, their spouse, and any dependents

tax deduction a variable amount that taxpayers may subtract from their gross income

tax credit a variable amount that taxpayers may subtract from the total amount of their income tax

Taxable income is a person's gross (or total) income minus exemptions and deductions. Gross income includes earned income—salaries, wages, tips, and commissions. It also includes income from investments such as interest on savings accounts and dividends from stock. **Personal exemptions** are set amounts that you subtract from your gross income for yourself, your spouse, and any dependents. **Tax deductions** are variable amounts that you can subtract, or deduct, from your gross income. Deductions include such items as interest on a mortgage, donations to charity, significant medical expenses, and state and local tax payments.

Once you determine how much tax you owe, you can apply any tax credits that you may be allowed. A **tax credit** is an amount that you can subtract from the total amount of your income tax. You can claim a credit for such things as a portion of the cost of child-care and higher education.

Completing a tax return allows you to determine whether the amount of income taxes you have already paid was higher or lower than the actual amount of tax you owe. If you have paid more than you owe, the government sends you a refund.

If you have paid less than you owe, you must pay the balance to the government. All federal income tax returns must be sent to the Internal Revenue Service, or IRS, by midnight on April 15 (or the next business day if April 15 falls on a weekend or holiday).

✔ **CHECKPOINT** *What is the difference between a personal exemption and a tax deduction?*

Corporate Income Taxes

Like individuals, corporations must pay federal income tax on their taxable income. Corporate taxes made up just over 10 percent of federal revenues in recent years.

Determining corporate taxable income can be a challenge, because businesses can take many deductions. That is, they can subtract many expenses from their income before they reach the amount of income that is subject to taxation. For example, companies deduct the cost of employees' health insurance. Many other costs of doing business can also be deducted.

Like individual income tax rates, corporate income tax rates are progressive. In 2007, rates began at 15 percent on the first $50,000 of taxable income. On the highest corporate income, above $18,333,333, the tax rate was 35 percent.

✔ **CHECKPOINT** *Why is it difficult to determine a corporation's taxable income?*

Social Security, Medicare, and Unemployment Taxes

In addition to withholding money for income taxes, employers withhold money for taxes authorized under the Federal Insurance Contributions Act, or FICA. FICA taxes fund two large government social-insurance programs, Social Security and Medicare. Employees and employers share FICA payments.

Social Security Taxes

Most of the FICA taxes you pay go to the Social Security Administration to fund Old-Age, Survivors, and Disability Insurance (OASDI), or Social Security. Social Security was established in 1935 to ease the hardships of the Great Depression.

From the start, Social Security provided old-age pensions and unemployment insurance to workers. Today, it also provides benefits to surviving family members of wage earners and to people whose disabilities keep them from working.

Each year the government establishes an income cap for Social Security taxes. In 2008, the cap was $102,000. No Social Security taxes could be withheld from a taxpayer's wages and salaries above that amount.

Medicare Taxes

FICA taxes also fund Medicare. The Medicare program is a national health insurance program that helps pay for healthcare for people over age 65. It also covers people with certain disabilities.

Both employees and self-employed people pay the Medicare tax on all their earnings. There is no ceiling as there is for Social Security payments.

Unemployment Taxes

The federal government also collects an unemployment tax, which is paid by employers. In effect, the tax pays for an insurance policy for workers. If workers are laid off from their jobs through no fault of their own, they can file an "unemployment compensation" claim and collect benefits for a fixed number of weeks. In order to collect unemployment benefits, an unemployed person usually must show that he or she is actively looking for another job. The unemployment program is financed by both state and federal unemployment taxes.

☑ **CHECKPOINT** *What is the Medicare program?*

Other Types of Taxes

What are the taxes on gasoline and cable television service called? If you inherit money from your great aunt, will you have to pay a tax? Why are some imported products so expensive? To answer these questions, you need to look at excise, estate, gift, and import taxes.

Excise Taxes

As you read in Chapter 5, an excise tax is a general revenue tax on the sale or manufacture of a good. Federal excise taxes apply to gasoline, cigarettes, alcoholic beverages, telephone services, cable television, and other items.

Estate Taxes

An **estate tax** is a tax on the estate, or total value of the money and property, of a person who has died. It is paid out of the person's estate before the heirs receive their share. A person's estate includes not only money, but also real estate, cars, furniture, investments, jewelry, paintings, and insurance.

As of 2008, if the total value of an estate is $2 million or less, there is no federal estate tax. Because an estate tax is a progressive tax, the rate rises with increasing value. That is, a $5 million estate will be taxed by the federal government at a higher rate than a $3 million estate.

Gift Taxes

The **gift tax** is a tax on the money or property that one living person gives to another. The goal of the gift tax, established in 1924, was to keep people from avoiding estate taxes by giving away their money before they died. The tax law sets limits on gifts, but still allows the tax-free transfer of fairly large amounts each year. Under current law, a person can give up to $12,000 a year tax-free to each of several different people.

Import Taxes

Taxes on imported goods (foreign goods brought into the country) are called

estate tax a tax on the total value of the money and property of a person who has died

gift tax a tax on the money or property that one living person gives to another

After Christmas, even Santas need the support of unemployment insurance. *How is the unemployment program financed?* ▼

In sunny climates, solar panels can help reduce energy consumption. *How does the government provide tax incentives to encourage solar panels?* ▶

tariff a tax on imported goods

tax incentive the use of taxation to discourage or encourage certain types of behavior

tariffs. Today, most tariffs are intended to protect American farmers and industries from foreign competitors rather than to generate revenue. Tariffs raise the price of foreign items, which helps keep the price of American products competitive. You will read more about tariffs in Chapter 17.

FL SS.912.E.2.9, LA.1112.1.6.1, LA.1112.2.2.2, LA.1112.2.2.3

Taxes That Affect Behavior

The basic goal of taxation is to create revenue. However, governments sometimes use tax policy to discourage the public from buying harmful products. They also use taxes to encourage constructive or helpful behavior. The use of taxation to discourage or encourage certain types of behavior is called a **tax incentive.**

Federal taxes on tobacco products and alcoholic beverages are examples of so-called sin taxes. Their main purpose is to discourage people from buying and using these products.

Incentives also come in the form of tax credits. Congress has tried to encourage energy conservation by offering a variety of credits to consumers and industry. To persuade people to purchase more fuel-efficient cars, buyers of hybrid vehicles received an income tax credit. Owners of homes and commercial buildings can also claim credits for improvements that decrease the use of oil and other fossil fuels, including insulation and replacement windows.

✅ **CHECKPOINT** *What are the taxes on gasoline and cable television service called?*

Essential Questions Journal To continue to build a response to the Essential Question, go to your **Essential Questions Journal**.

SECTION 2 ASSESSMENT

🎯 Guiding Question

1. Use your completed table to answer this question: What taxes does the federal government collect?

2. **Extension** How do federal taxes affect your life? For example, suppose the federal government announced a new tax credit for income from savings accounts. What if the government imposed a high tax on chocolate? How would you respond?

Key Terms and Main Ideas

3. What kind of form do taxpayers use to file income taxes?

4. Would a person earning $15,000 per year and a person earning $300,000 per year be in the same federal income tax bracket? Why or why not?

5. When would you have to pay a **gift tax?**

6. What is a **tax incentive?**

Critical Thinking

7. **Predict (a)** Explain how "pay-as-you-earn" taxation works. **(b)** Why is this system important? **(c)** What might happen if the government did not use this system to collect income taxes?

8. **Contrast (a)** How are the systems for collecting Social Security and Medicare taxes similar? **(b)** List one way they are different. **(c)** Which system of collecting do you think makes more sense?

9. **Extend** Contributions to charitable organizations such as the American Cancer Society are tax deductible. **(a)** What does this mean? **(b)** Explain the reason for this tax policy. **(c)** What is your opinion of this tax deduction?

Quick Write

10. Based on what you have read in this section about tax incentives, write a short essay answering the following question. What kind of behavior do you think the government should encourage or discourage in its tax policy? How can the government do this through its tax policy?

NGSSS

LA.1112.1.6 Use multiple strategies to develop vocabulary.

SS.912.E.1.10 Explain the use of fiscal policy to promote price stability.

SS.912.E.2.3 Research the contributions of key individuals of various backgrounds in the development of the U.S.

SS.912.E.2.9 Analyze how changes in taxation affect budget deficits, surpluses, and national debt.

ECONOMIC DICTIONARY

As you read the section, look for the definitions of these **Key Terms:**

• mandatory spending
• discretionary spending
• entitlement

Guiding Question

How does the federal government spend its income?

Copy this table and fill it in as you read.

Federal Spending	
Mandatory	**Discretionary**
• Social Security • •	• • •

▶ **Economics and You**   Suppose that each year you were given a million dollars to spend on serious expenses. So much money! So many choices! Where would you begin? In the same way, the federal government, with a budget of around $2.8 trillion, faces a similar "dilemma" every year.

Principles in Action Through the democratic process, the American public chooses between candidates who often have different ideas on how the federal government should spend its income. As you will read, government spending meets numerous needs. Our elected leaders have decided that much of the money should provide for our health and welfare.

mandatory spending spending that Congress is required by existing law to do

discretionary spending spending about which Congress is free to make choices

Mandatory and Discretionary Spending

In reality, when the government receives the $2.8 trillion in the form of taxes, most of it is already accounted for. After the government fulfills all its legal obligations, only about a third of the money remains to be spent.

The graph in **Figure 14.4** shows the major categories of federal spending. Some of these categories, such as Social Security and Medicare, are mandatory. **Mandatory spending** refers to money that Congress is mandated, or required, by existing law to spend on certain programs or to use for interest payments on the national debt. Other categories, such as defense and education, are discretionary. **Discretionary spending** is spending about which lawmakers are free to make choices.

Figure 14.4	**Federal Spending, 2006**

- Department of Defense, Military
- Medicare, and other retirement
- Homeland Security
- Social Security
- Other
- Net interest on the debt

SOURCE: The Internal Revenue Service, U.S. Department of Treasury
Note: Because of rounding, totals may be greater than or less than 100 percent.

GRAPH SKILLS

The federal government spends the funds it collects from taxes and other sources on a variety of programs.

1. Which are the three largest categories of expenditures in the federal budget?
2. On which area(s) does the federal government spend more: military and homeland security or dealing with the needs of elderly and retired citizens?

entitlement social welfare program that people are "entitled to" benefit from if they meet certain eligibility requirements

FL SS.912.E.2.3
Research the contributions of key individuals of various backgrounds in the development of the U.S.

In general, the percentage of federal spending that is mandatory has grown in recent years. The percentage of discretionary spending has decreased.

✓ **CHECKPOINT** *Is spending for Medicare mandatory or discretionary?*

Entitlement Programs

Except for interest on the national debt, most of the mandatory spending items in the federal budget are for entitlement programs. **Entitlements** are social welfare programs that people are "entitled to" benefit from if they meet certain eligibility requirements, such as being at a particular income level or age. The federal government guarantees assistance for all those who qualify. As the number of people who qualify rises, mandatory spending rises as well. As a result, managing costs has become a major concern.

Some, but not all, entitlements are "means-tested." In other words, people with higher incomes may receive lower benefits or no benefits at all. Medicaid, for instance, is means-tested. Social Security

is not. A retired person who has worked and paid Social Security taxes is entitled to certain benefits. Similarly, military veterans and retired federal employees are entitled to receive pensions from the government.

Entitlements are a largely unchanging part of government spending. Once Congress has set the requirements, it cannot control how many people become eligible for each kind of benefit. Congress can change the eligibility requirements or reduce the amount of the benefit in order to try to keep costs down. Such actions, however, require a change in the law.

Social Security

Social Security makes up a huge portion of all federal spending. About 50 million Americans receive monthly benefits from the Social Security Administration. Of those beneficiaries, some are disabled workers, but the great majority are retired workers. Many of those retirees rely solely on their Social Security checks to support themselves.

The Social Security system faces an uncertain future today. To understand the

---

Innovators

Frances Perkins

❝The large majority of our citizens need protection against the loss of income due to unemployment, old age, death of the breadwinners and disabling accident and illness, not only on humanitarian grounds, but in the interest of our national welfare.❞

With these words, delivered on national radio in 1935, Labor Secretary Frances Perkins unveiled an extraordinary plan for "social insurance"—the plan that became our Social Security program. Perkins helped write the Social Security Act, and later developed and administered the Social Security System and other key entitlement programs.

Frances Perkins fought for the rights of workers throughout her long career. In 1929, as Industrial Commissioner of New York State, she reduced the number of hours a woman was allowed to work in a factory to 48. Later, as the first female Cabinet member, she helped win workers the right to unionize and to earn a guaranteed minimum wage.

Her greatest achievement was the Social Security Act. "The real roots of the Social Security Act were in the Great Depression of 1929. Nothing else would have bumped the American people into a social security system except something so shocking, so terrifying, as that depression."

Critical Thinking: *Why did Perkins believe that Social Security was "in the interest of our national welfare"? Why is Social Security controversial today?*

Fast Facts

Frances Perkins
Born: April 10, 1880, in Boston, MA
Died: May 14, 1965, in New York, NY
Education: Columbia University, M.A. in economics and social history
Claim to Fame: Secretary of Labor, 1933–1945; drafted and promoted President Franklin D. Roosevelt's legislation for Social Security

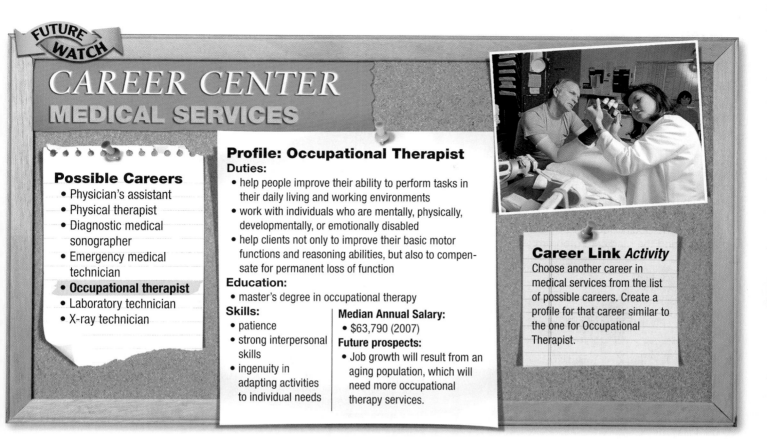

CAREER CENTER
MEDICAL SERVICES

Possible Careers
- Physician's assistant
- Physical therapist
- Diagnostic medical sonographer
- Emergency medical technician
- **Occupational therapist**
- Laboratory technician
- X-ray technician

Profile: Occupational Therapist

Duties:
- help people improve their ability to perform tasks in their daily living and working environments
- work with individuals who are mentally, physically, developmentally, or emotionally disabled
- help clients not only to improve their basic motor functions and reasoning abilities, but also to compensate for permanent loss of function

Education:
- master's degree in occupational therapy

Skills:
- patience
- strong interpersonal skills
- ingenuity in adapting activities to individual needs

Median Annual Salary:
- $63,790 (2007)

Future prospects:
- Job growth will result from an aging population, which will need more occupational therapy services.

Career Link *Activity*
Choose another career in medical services from the list of possible careers. Create a profile for that career similar to the one for Occupational Therapist.

---

uncertainty, you must understand how the Social Security system is set up. American workers pay into the system through taxes. Those taxes go toward benefits for people who are no longer working. That is, the money that you pay into Social Security today does not go into a fund for your own future retirement. It goes toward supporting people who have already retired.

For the system to function properly, there must be enough workers paying in to support all the retired workers receiving benefits. Although the system has worked well until now, the population increase known as the baby boom threatens to undermine it. As the millions of baby boomers—the generation born after World War II—start to retire, the ratio of existing workers to retirees will fall.

The system may not reach crisis levels for several decades. But unless something is done, today's high school students might receive only limited benefits from Social Security when they retire.

Medicare

Medicare serves about 42 million people, most of them over 65 years old. The program pays for hospital care and for the costs of physicians and medical services. It also pays healthcare bills for people who suffer from certain disabilities and diseases.

Like Social Security, Medicare is funded by taxes withheld from people's paychecks. Monthly payments paid by people who make certain levels of taxable income and receive Medicare benefits also help pay for the program.

Medicare costs have been growing rapidly, partly as a result of expensive technology, but also because people are living longer. The basic problem facing Medicare is the same as that facing Social Security. In 1995, there were four people paying Medicare taxes for every Medicare recipient. By 2050, there will only be two people paying taxes for every recipient.

Medicaid

Medicaid benefits low-income families, some people with disabilities, and elderly people in nursing homes. It is the largest source of funds for medical and health-related services for America's poorest people. The federal government shares the costs of Medicaid with state governments.

Where do your **federal taxes** go?

Not everybody is happy about all the taxes taken from their paychecks. However, taxes give the government the money it needs to operate.

1 Federal Spending: Deductions from your paycheck finance many federal programs, but among the largest of the expenses are defense spending, the Social Security program, and the Medicare program.

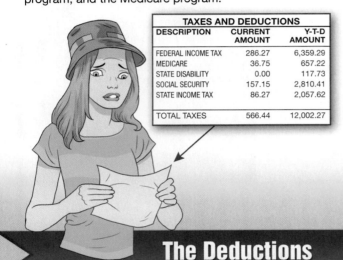

TAXES AND DEDUCTIONS		
DESCRIPTION	CURRENT AMOUNT	Y-T-D AMOUNT
FEDERAL INCOME TAX	286.27	6,359.29
MEDICARE	36.75	657.22
STATE DISABILITY	0.00	117.73
SOCIAL SECURITY	157.15	2,810.41
STATE INCOME TAX	86.27	2,057.62
TOTAL TAXES	566.44	12,002.27

2 Defense spending makes up about one fifth of the federal budget. It is a discretionary item and can be changed each year by government planners. However, since it pays for the salaries of everyone in the armed forces as well as weapons, planes, and ships, it has generally gone up each year.

The Deductions

Defense

Other Mandatory Spending Programs

Other means-tested entitlements benefit people and families whose incomes fall below a certain level. Requirements vary from program to program. Federal programs include food stamps and child nutrition. The federal government also pays retirement benefits and insurance for federal workers, as well as veterans' pensions and unemployment insurance.

Some members of Congress have pushed for additional government programs related to healthcare. One reason is that healthcare costs have increased at more than twice the rate of inflation over the last few decades. The average expenditure for healthcare rose from $891 per person in 1960 to $5,670 in 2003. To keep pace, health insurance costs have also skyrocketed. As a result, some 50 million Americans had no health insurance in 2009.

To resolve this problem, leaders have called for either a single-payer system organized by the government, or health-care tax credits. Others have insisted we rely on market forces. President Obama signed legislation in 2010 that would require uninsured Americans to purchase health insurance through competitive private exchanges in their state. Some low-income families would get government subsidies.

☑ CHECKPOINT *What entitlement program costs the federal government the most money?*

Discretionary Spending

Spending on defense accounts for about half of the federal government's discretionary spending. The remaining funds available for

3 **Social Security** is the largest category of federal spending. It is one of the government's most important and successful programs, providing more than $500 billion in benefits to Americans each year.

Social Security

4 **Medicare** provides benefits to people who are 65 years or older or who suffer from certain disabilities. Total Medicare spending reached $440 billion in 2007.

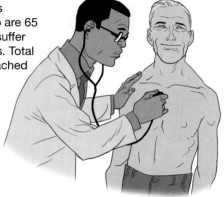

These deductions from paychecks can be unwelcome, but the programs they pay for are essential to the well-being of the United States.

Check Your Understanding
1. Why does the federal government take money from the paychecks of American workers?
2. List two areas where the money aids the safety and security of Americans. List two areas where the deductions improve the quality of life of Americans.

Medicare

discretionary spending are divided among a wide variety of programs.

Defense Spending

Defense spending has dropped somewhat since the end of the Cold War as a percentage of the total federal budget. As you can see from the graph in **Figure 14.4,** defense spending consumes about 19 percent of the federal budget.

The Department of Defense spends most of the defense budget. It pays the salaries of all the men and women in the army, navy, air force, and marines, as well as the department's civilian employees. Defense spending, of course, also buys weapons, missiles, battleships, tanks, airplanes, and ammunition equipment.

Other Discretionary Spending

You may be surprised at how small a portion of federal spending goes into the category that could be labeled "everything else." Here are some of the many programs that this category of federal spending pays for:

- education and training
- scientific research
- student loans
- law enforcement
- environmental cleanup
- disaster aid

This part of the federal budget also pays the salaries of the millions of people who work for the civilian branches of the federal government. They include park rangers, FBI agents, file clerks, senators and members of Congress, geologists, CIA agents, Cabinet secretaries, meat inspectors, and many others.

✔ **CHECKPOINT** *Approximately how much of the federal government's discretionary spending goes toward defense?*

▲ Many large local projects are funded with Federal government aid. **What point is the cartoon making about how states get funding?**

Federal Aid to State and Local Governments

Some federal tax dollars find their way to state and local governments. In total, about $404 billion a year in federal monies is divided among the states. This is an average of about $1,400 per person.

As you have read, state and federal governments share the costs of Medicaid and unemployment compensation. They also share in funding other social programs.

Additional federal money goes to the states for education, lower-income housing, highway construction, mass-transit, health-care, employment training, and dozens of other programs.

Federal grants-in-aid are grants of federal money for certain closely defined purposes. States must use the federal funds only for the purpose specified and obey the federal guidelines for which aid is given.

State and local governments rely on federal aid for a variety of needs. But nothing reveals that reliance as vividly as a disaster. For example, after Hurricane Katrina slammed into coastal Louisiana, Mississippi, and Alabama in 2005, those states did not have the resources to deal with the widespread destruction and human misery that the storm left behind. They looked to the federal government for help. Although critics denounced the federal relief agencies for their slow response, Congress appropriated $116 billion to help the states recover from the disaster.

☑ **CHECKPOINT** *Why did states call on the federal government for help after Hurricane Katrina?*

 SS.912.E.1.10, SS.912.E.2.4, SS.912.E.2.9, LA.1112.1.6.1, LA.1112.2.2.2

Essential Questions Journal To continue to build a response to the Essential Question, go to your **Essential Questions Journal.**

SECTION **3** ASSESSMENT

🔔 Guiding Question

1. Use your completed table to answer this question: How does the federal government spend its income?

2. **Extension** What federal government services do you use in your life? What services do you think you might use in the future?

Key Terms and Main Ideas

3. What are means-tested **entitlements?**

4. Name at least three examples of federal **discretionary spending.**

5. Whose retirements are funded by the money today's wage earners are now paying into Social Security?

6. What services does Medicaid provide, and who benefits from these services?

7. List at least three programs in which state governments and the federal government share funding.

Critical Thinking

8. **Extend (a)** How are mandatory spending and discretionary spending different? **(b)** How can a mandatory spending program be changed into a discretionary spending program?

9. **Discuss** What problems do entitlement programs cause? Why might it be difficult for lawmakers to make changes to entitlement programs?

10. **Select (a)** Why have some members of Congress pushed for additional government programs related to healthcare? **(b)** Describe the health-care legislation passed in 2010.

Quick Write

11. Reread the part of this section titled Entitlement Programs. Then suppose you are running for federal office. Write a short essay answering the following questions. What public needs should government move to fill immediately? Would you propose any new entitlement programs? If so, what would they be? Would you propose eliminating or modifying any existing entitlement programs? Explain your answers.

NGSSS

LA.1112.1.6 Use multiple strategies to develop vocabulary.

MA.912.A.2.2 Interpret a graph to represent a real-world situation.

SS.912.E.1.10 Explain the use of fiscal policy to promote price stability.

ECONOMIC DICTIONARY

As you read the section, look for the definitions of these **Key Terms:**

• budget
• operating budget
• capital budget
• balanced budget
• tax exempt
• real property
• personal property
• tax assessor

Guiding Question

How do local governments manage their money?

Copy this table and fill it in as you read.

Revenue Collection		Revenue Spending	
State		Local	
• Sales tax	•	• Education	•
•	•	•	• Police and fire protection
•	• Excise tax	•	
•	•	•	•

▶ **Economics and You**   You and your family are thinking about colleges. Which one offers the courses you want? How much does it cost? During your research, you find that colleges within your state's university system are far less expensive than private schools. The reason is that your state government pays part of the cost of running the state colleges. In fact, higher education is one of the largest areas of state government spending.

Principles in Action Because they are democracies, local governments manage their money in accordance with priorities set by elected local government officials. In this section, you will examine these priorities. For example, in the Economics & You feature, you will see that while school tax increases can be painful to the taxpayer, the programs they fund are sometimes essential to quality education and necessary to enriching the school experience.

State Budgets

Like families and individuals, governments must plan their spending ahead of time. That planning involves drawing up a budget. A **budget** is an estimate of future revenues and expenses. While the federal government has just one budget for planned revenue and expenses, states have two budgets: operating budgets and capital budgets.

Operating Budgets

A state puts together an **operating budget** to plan for its day-to-day spending needs. Those expenses include salaries of state employees, supplies such as computers and paper, and maintenance of state facilities, such as recreation areas and roadside parks.

Capital Budgets

A state also draws up a **capital budget** to plan for major capital, or investment, spending. If the state builds a new bridge, the money comes from this budget. Most of these expenses are met by long-term borrowing or the sale of bonds.

budget an estimate of future revenue and expenses

operating budget a budget for day-to-day spending needs

capital budget a budget for spending on major investments

Balancing State Budgets

In most states, the governor prepares the budget with the help of a budget agency. The legislature then discusses and eventually approves the budget. Unlike the federal government, 49 states require **balanced budgets**—budgets in which revenues are equal to spending. These laws, however, apply only to the operating budget, not the capital budget. That makes it easier to balance a state budget than to balance the federal budget.

✓ **CHECKPOINT** *Would the construction of a new courthouse come out of a state's operating budget or capital budget?*

Where Are State Taxes Spent?

Spending policies differ among the 50 states. You are probably most familiar with state spending on education, highways, police protection, and state recreation areas. You can see other significant spending categories in **Figure 14.5.**

Education

Every state spends taxpayer money to support at least one public state university. Some, such as California, have large systems with many campuses throughout the state. In many states, tax dollars also support agricultural and technical colleges, teacher's colleges, and two-year community colleges.

State governments also provide financial help to their local governments, which run public elementary, middle, and high schools. The total amount of money spent per student varies among the states. The national average is $8,701 per student per year.

Public Safety

State police are a familiar sight along the nation's highways. The state police enforce traffic laws and help motorists in emergencies. State police also maintain crime labs that can assist local law-enforcement agencies. State governments build and run corrections systems. These institutions house people convicted of state crimes.

Highways and Transportation

Building and maintaining highway systems is another major state expense. State crews resurface roads and repair bridges. Some money for roads comes from the federal government. In turn, states contribute money to federal and interstate highway systems.

States pay at least some of the costs of other kinds of transportation facilities, such as waterways and airports. Money for such projects may also come from federal and local government budgets.

Public Welfare

States look after the health and welfare of the public in various ways. State funds support some public hospitals and clinics. State regulators inspect water supplies and test for pollution.

As you have read, states also help pay for many of the federal programs that assist individuals, such as unemployment compensation benefits. Because states determine their own benefits, they can meet local needs better than the federal government can. For example, during a local recession, they may decide to extend the number of weeks that people can claim benefits.

Arts and Recreation

If you've hiked in a state forest or picnicked in a state park, you've enjoyed another benefit of state tax dollars. Nature reserves and parks preserve scenic and historic places for people to visit and enjoy. States also run museums and help fund music and art programs.

Administration

Besides providing services, state governments need to spend money just to keep running. Like the federal government, state governments have an executive branch (the governor's office), a legislative branch, and a court system. State tax revenues pay the salaries of all these and other state workers, including judges, maintenance crews in state parks, the governor, and professors in state universities.

✓ **CHECKPOINT** *Where does a state get the money to fund public schools, prisons, and highway construction?*

balanced budget a budget in which revenue and spending are equal

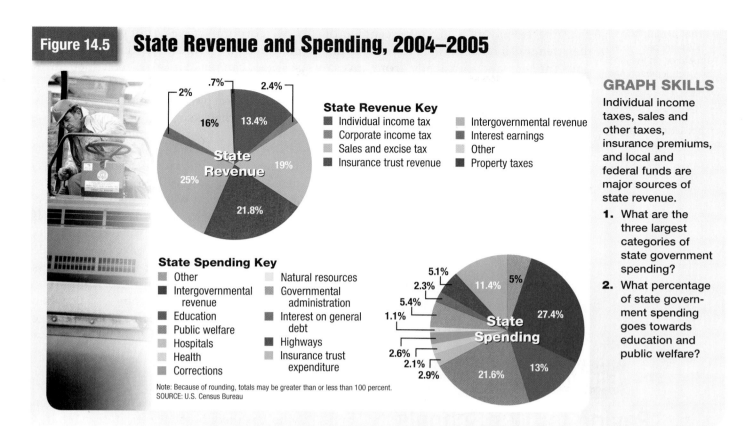

Figure 14.5 | State Revenue and Spending, 2004–2005

State Revenue

.7%
2%
2.4%
16%
13.4%
19%
25%
21.8%

State Revenue Key
- Individual income tax
- Corporate income tax
- Sales and excise tax
- Insurance trust revenue
- Intergovernmental revenue
- Interest earnings
- Other
- Property taxes

State Spending Key
- Other
- Intergovernmental revenue
- Education
- Public welfare
- Hospitals
- Health
- Corrections
- Natural resources
- Governmental administration
- Interest on general debt
- Highways
- Insurance trust expenditure

State Spending

5.1%
2.3%
5.4%
1.1%
2.6%
2.1%
2.9%
11.4%
5%
27.4%
13%
21.6%

Note: Because of rounding, totals may be greater than or less than 100 percent.
SOURCE: U.S. Census Bureau

GRAPH SKILLS

Individual income taxes, sales and other taxes, insurance premiums, and local and federal funds are major sources of state revenue.

1. What are the three largest categories of state government spending?
2. What percentage of state government spending goes towards education and public welfare?

State Tax Revenue.

For every dollar a state spends, it must take in a dollar in revenue. Otherwise, it cannot maintain a balanced budget. The 50 states now take in more than $500 billion a year from taxes. Where does this money come from? The pie chart on the left in **Figure 14.5** shows you the major sources of state revenue.

Just as the United States Constitution limits the federal government's power to tax, it also puts limits on the states. Because trade and commerce are considered national enterprises, states cannot tax imports or exports. They also cannot tax goods sent between states. Nonprofit organizations, religious groups, and charities are usually **tax exempt;** that is, they are not subject to taxes.

Sales Tax

Sales taxes are a main source of revenue for state governments. A sales tax is a tax on goods and services. The tax—a percentage of the purchase price—is added on at the cash register and paid by the purchaser.

All but a few of the 50 states collect sales taxes. Their sales tax rates range from 2.9

to 7.25 percent. Some local governments have their own, additional sales tax. In every state, some categories of products are exempt from sales tax. For example, many states do not charge sales tax on basic needs such as food and clothing.

Even states without a sales tax impose excise taxes that apply to specific products and activities. Some are sin taxes—taxes that are intended to discourage harmful behavior—on products like alcoholic beverages and tobacco. Other taxes apply to hotel and motel rooms, automobiles, rental cars, and insurance policies. Many states also tax gasoline. This state gasoline tax is in addition to the federal tax.

Individual Income Tax

Individual income taxes are another large contributor to many states' budgets. People pay this state income tax in addition to the federal income tax. **Figure 14.5** shows that state individual income taxes contribute about 13 percent of state revenue.

Some states tax incomes at a flat rate (that is, as a proportional tax). Others use a progressive tax—either by creating their own progressive rate structure, or by

 MA.912.A.2.2 Interpret a graph to represent a real-world situation.

tax exempt not subject to taxes

CHAPTER 14 SECTION 4 **383**

real property land and any permanent structures on the land to which a person has legal title

personal property movable possessions or assets

charging taxpayers a given percentage of their federal income tax. A few states tax only interest and dividends from investments, not wages and salaries.

Corporate Income Tax

Most states collect income taxes from corporations that do business in the state. Some states levy taxes at a fixed, flat rate on business profits. A few charge progressive rates—that is, higher tax rates for businesses with higher profits.

As you can see from **Figure 14.5**, corporate income taxes make up only a small portion of state tax revenues—about 2 percent. Nevertheless, corporate income taxes can influence a state's economy.

Low corporate taxes, along with a well-educated workforce and efficient public services, can make it easier to attract entrepreneurs and new businesses to a state. Politicians keep this fact in mind when they determine their state's taxing policies.

Other State Taxes

Besides the corporate income tax, businesses pay a variety of other state taxes and fees. Do you want to be a hairdresser, a carpenter, or a building contractor? If so, you will have to pay a licensing fee. A licensing fee is a kind of tax that people pay to carry on different kinds of business within a state.

Some states charge a transfer tax when documents such as stock certificates are transferred and recorded. Other states tax the value of the stock shares that corporations issue.

As you read in Section 2, the federal government taxes the estate of a person who has died. Some states, in turn, charge an inheritance tax on the value of the property that goes to each heir.

Some states also tax property. That includes real estate, or **real property**—land and any permanent structures on the land to which a person has legal title. It also includes **personal property**—movable possessions or assets—such as jewelry, furniture, and boats. Some states even tax property that is intangible ("not able to be touched"), such as bank accounts, stocks, and bonds. Today, however, most property taxes, especially on real estate, are levied by local governments.

✅ **CHECKPOINT** *What two categories of taxes provide the largest contribution to state revenues?*

Local Government Spending and Revenue

Your local government plays a part in many aspects of everyday life, including public elementary, middle, and high schools. Local governments hire police and firefighters. They build roads, libraries, hospitals, and jails. They pay teachers. Even though this is the level of government closest to you, it may be the one you know the least about.

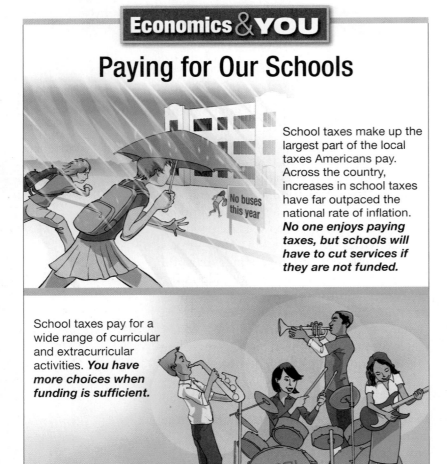

Economics & YOU

Paying for Our Schools

No buses this year

School taxes make up the largest part of the local taxes Americans pay. Across the country, increases in school taxes have far outpaced the national rate of inflation. *No one enjoys paying taxes, but schools will have to cut services if they are not funded.*

School taxes pay for a wide range of curricular and extracurricular activities. *You have more choices when funding is sufficient.*

SKOOL BAND

▲ In many communities, school taxes are subject to community vote. *In your community, do taxpayers vote on school tax proposals?*

Figure 14.6 **Local Revenue and Spending, 2004–2005**

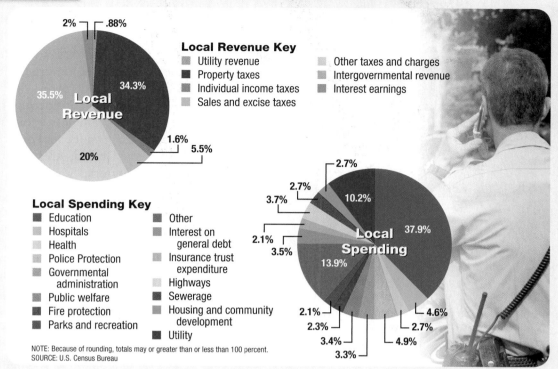

Local Revenue

2% — .88%
34.3%
35.5%
20%
1.6%
5.5%

Local Revenue Key
- Utility revenue
- Property taxes
- Individual income taxes
- Sales and excise taxes
- Other taxes and charges
- Intergovernmental revenue
- Interest earnings

Local Spending Key
- Education
- Hospitals
- Health
- Police Protection
- Governmental administration
- Public welfare
- Fire protection
- Parks and recreation
- Other
- Interest on general debt
- Insurance trust expenditure
- Highways
- Sewerage
- Housing and community development
- Utility

Local Spending

2.7%
2.7%
3.7%
10.2%
2.1%
3.5%
37.9%
13.9%
2.1%
2.3%
3.4%
3.3%
4.9%
2.7%
4.6%

NOTE: Because of rounding, totals may or greater than or less than 100 percent.
SOURCE: U.S. Census Bureau

CHART SKILLS

Property taxes and state and federal funds (intergovernmental revenue) are the major sources of local revenue.

1. What are the three largest categories of local government spending?

2. How do the sources of local revenue compare with state revenue sources shown on page 383?

Forms of Local Government

You probably think of "local government" as a town or city. There are other types as well, including townships, counties, and special districts, such as school districts. Today, there are more than 87,000 local government units in the United States. Together they collect about $484 billion in tax revenues.

The Jobs of Local Government

Local governments carry major responsibilities in many areas, such as public school systems, law enforcement (local police, county sheriff's departments, park police), and fire protection. They manage public facilities (libraries, airports, public hospitals) and parks and recreational facilities (beaches, swimming pools, zoos). They monitor public health (restaurant inspection, water treatment, sewer systems), public transportation, elections (voter registration, ballot preparation, election supervision, vote counting), record keeping (birth/death certificates, wills, marriage licenses) and social services (food stamps, child-care and welfare).

Many of these responsibilities are reflected in the Local Revenue and Spending pie charts in **Figure 14.6**. In some towns and cities, separate commissions or private corporations carry out some of these jobs. You can see, though, that local governments touch our lives every day.

Property Tax

Property taxes are levied on property owners in local communities to offset the expense of services such as street construction and maintenance. An official called a **tax assessor** determines the value of the property. Property taxes are usually figured as a fixed dollar amount per $1,000 of the assessed value. They are a main source of funding for public schools.

Other Local Taxes

Local taxes are similar to the types of taxes imposed by the states. Besides property taxes, local governments levy sales, excise, and income taxes. These taxes affect not only residents of a community but also visitors. In fact, many are designed specifically to raise revenue from nonresidents.

 MA.912.A.2.2
Interpret a graph to represent a real-world situation.

tax assessor an official who determines the value of property

▲ Wall-to-wall traffic jams are prompting a few large cities to consider a congestion tax. *What are the main arguments for or against such a tax?*

Suppose you've gone on a school trip to New York City. The room rate for your hotel is $200 a night. When you see the bill in the morning, however, it's $230.25! Three different taxes have been added—an 8.375 percent sales tax, a hotel room occupancy tax of $2 per room plus 5 percent of the room rate, and an additional fee of $1.50 per room. Many other cities have taxes aimed at tourists and business travelers. Besides hotel taxes, they include sales taxes on rental cars, airport taxes, and taxes on movie or theater tickets. Some large cities collect income taxes as payroll taxes.

A few large cities are also considering the idea of a congestion tax. The local government would charge drivers a fee for entering a congested, or overcrowded, area of the city between certain hours. Supporters of a congestion tax say many commuters would opt to use mass transit instead of automobiles. This would not only help clear clogged streets but would also decrease the emission of gases into the atmosphere that contribute to local air pollution. Critics counter that the city's businesses would be hurt, as many people would decide to stay out of the downtown area—and spend their money elsewhere.

✔ **CHECKPOINT** *What type of tax is a main source of funding for public schools?*

FL SS.912.E.1.10, SS.912.E.2.8, LA.1112.1.6.1, LA.1112.2.2.2, MA.912.A.2.2

Essential Questions Journal To continue to build a response to the Essential Question, go to your **Essential Questions Journal**.

SECTION 4 ASSESSMENT

🤔 Guiding Question

1. Use your completed table to answer this question: How do local governments manage their money?
2. **Extension** What local government services do you use in your everyday life?

Key Terms and Main Ideas

3. What is a **balanced budget**?
4. List at least four programs and services on which states spend their money.
5. What kinds of organizations are **tax exempt**? What does this mean?
6. Identify at least three kinds of state taxes and fees that businesses pay.
7. What is the job of a **tax assessor**?

Critical Thinking

8. **Predict** Suppose a state operating budget included more spending than revenue. **(a)** What action might lawmakers take to balance the budget? **(b)** Now suppose the operating budget includes more revenue than spending. How might lawmakers react?
9. **Contrast (a)** What are the main tax sources of state revenue? **(b)** How do they differ from the main tax sources of local revenue?
10. **Make Inferences (a)** Describe the differences between real property and personal property. **(b)** Which type of property is taxed more frequently?

Math Skills

11. **Reading a Bar Graph** Look at the double bar graph below. Use it to answer the following questions: **(a)** What do the blue bars represent? **(b)** Which source or sources of local government revenue increased as a percentage of total revenue between 1995 and 2009?

For added practice in reading a bar graph, see the Math Home Video Tutor.

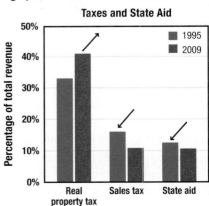

Taxes and State Aid

Legend: ■ 1995 ■ 2009

Y-axis: Percentage of total revenue (0% to 50%)

X-axis categories: Real property tax, Sales tax, State aid

SOURCE: 2009 Annual Report on Local Governments, Office of the New York State Controller, page 21

Chapter 14: Taxes and Government Spending

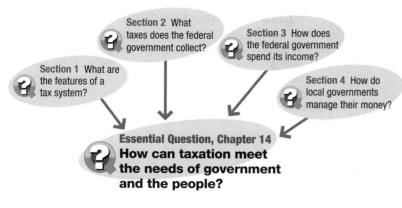

Section 2 What taxes does the federal government collect?

Section 1 What are the features of a tax system?

Section 3 How does the federal government spend its income?

Section 4 How do local governments manage their money?

Essential Question, Chapter 14
How can taxation meet the needs of government and the people?

Three Types of Tax Structures

Type of Tax	Description	Example	Ron's Taxes on a $50,000 Income	Mary's Taxes on a $150,000 Income
Proportional	A constant percentage of income is taken in taxes as income increases	Some state taxes	$7,500, or 15 percent of income	$22,500, or 15 percent of income
Progressive	A larger percentage of income is taken in taxes as income increases	Income tax	$5,000, or 10 percent of income	$45,000, or 30 percent of income
Regressive	A smaller percentage of income is taken in taxes as income increases	Sales tax	$2,000, or 5 percent of total purchases of $40,000; tax bill is 4 percent of income	$3,000, or 5 percent of total purchases of $60,000; tax bill is 2 percent of income

Two Types of Government Spending

Mandatory	Discretionary
• Interest on national debt • Medicare • Medicaid • Social Security	• Defense • Education • Law enforcement • Environmental cleanup

Economic Dictionary

tax, *p. 364*

revenue, *p. 364*

progressive tax, *p. 364*

proportional tax, *p. 364*

regressive tax, *p. 366*

tax base, *p. 366*

individual income tax, *p. 366*

corporate income tax, *p. 366*

property tax, *p. 366*

sales tax, *p. 366*

incidence of a tax, *p. 367*

withholding, *p. 370*

tax return, *p. 370*

taxable income, *p. 372*

personal exemption, *p. 372*

tax deduction, *p. 372*

tax credit, *p. 372*

estate tax, *p. 373*

gift tax, *p. 373*

tariff, *p. 374*

tax incentive, *p. 374*

mandatory spending, *p. 375*

discretionary spending, *p. 375*

entitlement, *p. 376*

budget, *p. 381*

operating budget, *p. 381*

capital budget, *p. 381*

balanced budget, *p. 382*

tax exempt, *p. 383*

real property, *p. 384*

personal property, *p. 384*

tax assessor, *p. 385*

Economics *on the go*

Study anytime, anywhere. Download these files today.

Economic Dictionary online
Vocabulary Support in English and Spanish

Audio Review online
Audio Study Guide in English and Spanish

Action Graph online
Animated Charts and Graphs

Visual Glossary online
Animated feature

How the Economy Works online
Animated feature

Download to your computer or mobile device at PearsonSchool.com/PHecon

Key Terms and Main Ideas

To make sure you understand the key terms and main ideas of this chapter, review the Checkpoint and Section Assessment questions and look at the Quick Study Guide on the preceding page.

Critical Thinking

1. **Select (a)** What are two principles that help determine the fairness of a tax? **(b)** How might these principles conflict with each other? **(c)** Which of these principles do you think is more important? Why?

2. **Compare and Contrast (a)** Suppose your state imposed a new tax on milk. How would this decision affect the owner of an ice cream store? **(b)** How would it affect wealthy consumers? **(c)** Would it affect poor consumers the same way? Why or why not?

3. **Evaluate (a)** If you get a part-time job, what taxes will you probably pay on your earnings? **(b)** Briefly explain how the government will collect these taxes. **(c)** Do you think it is fair that you must pay these taxes? Why or why not?

4. **Rank (a)** Imagine that you are a member of Congress. What are the three most important forms of discretionary spending that you support? **(b)** Why did you select these categories?

5. **Extend (a)** You have the chance to open a restaurant in a suburban area or in the center of the city. What financial considerations would help you make your decision? **(b)** Suppose the city announces that it will adopt congestion taxes. How will this affect your decision?

Applying Your Math Skills

FL SS.912.E.2.2

Using Pie Graphs to Understand Budgets

A pie graph is a useful way to present large amounts of information visually. The pie chart divides the information very much like a cherry pie into slices that represent the proportion of some whole number. In this case, the information being presented is federal spending in a particular year, 1970. Within each slice is a number that stands for the percent of each category of the total federal budget. By multiplying the total amount of spending in a year, in this case $195.6 billion, by the percentage of federal spending shown on the graph, you can find the amount of money actually spent for that category of spending in that year. Use your math skills and the pie graph to answer the questions below.

Visit PearsonSchool.com/PHecon for additional math help.

6. Which is greater: the amount spent on social security, health, and education in 1970 or the amount spent on defense?

7. About how much money was spent on social security in 1970? How much was spent on defense in 1970?

8. Compare this chart with the one on page 375. If federal spending in 2006 was estimated at $2,931 billion, how much was spent on social security in 2006? On defense?

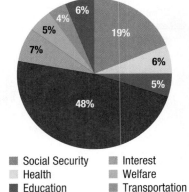

- ■ Social Security
- ■ Health
- ■ Education
- ■ Defense
- ■ Interest
- ■ Welfare
- ■ Transportation
- ■ Other

SOURCE: usgovernmentspending.com

? Essential Question Activity

9. Complete this activity to answer the Essential Question **How can taxation meet the needs of government and the people?** Suppose you are on the council of your local community. At current tax rates, the community will have $59 million in revenue in the coming year. You have collected the estimated spending needs for all budget categories—education, fire and police protection, maintenance, etc. Using the worksheet in your Essential Questions Journal or the electronic worksheet available at **PearsonSchool.com/PHecon**, gather the following information:
   (a) What is the difference between your spending needs and your revenue?
   (b) Can you best meet this shortage by raising taxes, cutting services, or some combination of the two? What are the advantages and disadvantages of each alternative?

   (c) Create a budget and tax proposal.

10. **Modify** Evaluate the impact of each of the following on your proposed budget.
   (a) Asbestos must be removed from two school buildings in your community. The cost of the cleanup is $3 million.
   (b) Your fire department wants to replace its outmoded pumper truck with a more up-to-date model. The cost is $500,000.
   (c) You are having trouble hiring road maintenance workers because neighboring communities pay higher wages. In order to compete, you have to raise wages and benefits a total of $750,000.

DOCUMENT-BASED ASSESSMENT

Should entitlements be cut to help balance the budget?

Almost two-thirds of federal expenditures are entitlements such as Social Security, Medicare, and Medicaid. As these social welfare programs continue to grow, people debate about whether to limit their benefits in order to reduce the budget deficit.

Document A

America's debt problem is mainly an entitlement spending problem.

Serious entitlement reform would involve concentrating limited resources on the poor, eliminating subsidies for the rich, and moving support for the middle class from a system of defined benefits to defined contributions. . . .

Properly understood, the budget battle is not between big spenders and budget hawks. It is between those who want to spend larger and larger portions of the budget on health care and transfers to the elderly, and those who want to use budget resources for *anything* else.

—"Federal Entitlements Will Crowd Out Other Spending in 25 Years," www.sacbee.com, August 1, 2010

 LA.1112.1.6.2

Document B

"I had another bad dream about Social Security."

Document C

The recent financial crisis has certainly deepened the fiscal challenge. But it has done something else too. It has driven home that Social Security is, and must remain, the bedrock of retirement income security. There is simply no alternative. Private income sources cannot do what social insurance does—only social insurance provides absolute inflation protection, spreads risks over generations and across the whole population, provides wage insurance, and is immune to fluctuations in asset values. Yes, changes in economic and demographic conditions can force changes in social insurance. But those changes are gradual, not abrupt.

—"Health Care, Entitlements, and the Federal Budget," www.brookings.edu, June 15, 2009

ANALYZING DOCUMENTS

Use your knowledge of entitlement programs and Documents A, B, and C to answer questions 1–3.

1. **What is one reason the authors of Document A want to cut entitlement benefits?**
   A. They use too much of the budget.
   B. The elderly do not deserve benefits.
   C. To free up funds for healthcare and the elderly
   D. The rich do not deserve benefits.

2. **What problem does Document B address?**
   A. Not everyone is entitled to Social Security.
   B. The government plans to replace Social Security.
   C. The future funding of Social Security is uncertain.
   D. Children benefit most from Social Security.

3. **According to Document C, why should Social Security not be cut?**
   A. It fluctuates easily when property values change.
   B. It is risky only to younger generations.
   C. It does not face changes when population figures change.
   D. It provides a steady supply of income security.

WRITING ABOUT ECONOMICS

To what extent entitlements can and should be limited is an ongoing issue. Use the documents on this page and resources on the Web site below to answer the question: *Should entitlements be cut to help balance the budget*

In Partnership

THE WALL STREET JOURNAL.
CLASSROOM EDITION

To read more about issues related to this topic, visit **PearsonSchool.com/PHecon**

15 Fiscal Policy

Essential Question, Chapter 15

How effective is fiscal policy as an economic tool?

BUDGET
OF THE U.S. GOVERNMENT

FISCAL YEAR 2008

OFFICE OF MANAGEMENT AND BUDGET

 Next Generation Sunshine State Standards

Section 1: Understanding Fiscal Policy
LA.1112.1.6, LA.1112.6.2, MA.912.A.2.2, SS.912.E.1.10, SS.912.E.2.9

Section 2: Fiscal Policy Options
LA.1112.1.6, MA.912.A.2.2, SS.912.E.1.10, SS.912.E.2.1, SS.912.E.2.3, SS.912.E.3.6

Section 3: Budget Deficits and the National Debt
LA.1112.1.6, MA.912.A.2.2, SS.912.E.1.10, SS.912.E.1.13, SS.912.E.2.9, SS.912.E.3.1

Economics
on the go

To study anywhere, anytime, download these
online resources at *PearsonSchool.com/PHecon* ▶

NGSSS

LA.1112.1.6 Use multiple strategies to develop vocabulary.

LA.1112.6.2 Use a systematic process to collect, process, present information.

MA.912.A.2.2 Interpret a graph to represent a real-world situation.

SS.912.E.1.10 Explain the use of fiscal policy to promote economic growth.

SS.912.E.2.9 Analyze how changes in federal spending affect budget deficits, surpluses, and the national debt.

ECONOMIC DICTIONARY

As you read the section, look for the definitions of these **Key Terms:**

- fiscal policy
- federal budget
- fiscal year
- appropriations bill
- expansionary policy
- contractionary policy

Guiding Question

What are the goals and limits of fiscal policy?

Copy this table and fill it in as you read.

Fiscal Policy	
Goals	**Limits**
• increase economic growth	• difficulty of changing spending levels
•	•
•	•
•	•

▶ **Economics and You** Does your family have a household budget? Or have you ever tried to budget your own money? Either way, you know that you have to take a close look at how much money you have coming in and how much you have to spend. Your goal is to get those two figures in line. But it's not easy. Sometimes it requires giving something up. Sometimes—although you try to avoid it—it may even require borrowing money. No matter what, making the plan takes time. Somebody has to sit down with a calculator and a stack of bills and a checkbook and a calendar and figure it all out.

Now, imagine how much more effort it would take if your expenses totaled $3.1 *trillion* a year. Suppose everyone in the house had to agree on every single item in the budget, and you had to send it to somebody else for a final okay. Now you have an idea what the U.S. federal government must do before it can spend your tax money.

Principles in Action Unlike a family, the federal government is not just interested in making income meet expenses. As you will see, the government may also use its taxing and spending policies to speed up economic growth—or even to slow it down.

FUTURE WATCH

Personal Finance
For tips on creating your own budget, see your Personal Finance Handbook in the back of the book or visit **PearsonSchool.com/PHecon**

Setting Fiscal Policy: The Federal Budget

As you saw in Chapter 14, the federal government takes in and spends huge amounts of money. In fact, it spends an average of $7.7 billion every day. This tremendous flow of cash into and out of the economy has a large impact on aggregate supply and aggregate demand.

Visual Glossary
online

Go to the Visual Glossary Online for an interactive review of **fiscal policy.**

Action Graph
online

Go to Action Graph Online for animated versions of key charts and graphs.

How the Economy Works
online

Go to How the Economy Works Online for an interactive lesson on the **national debt.**

fiscal policy the use of government spending and revenue collection to influence the economy

federal budget a written document estimating the federal government's revenue and authorizing its spending for the coming year

fiscal year any 12-month period used for budgeting purposes

The government's taxing and spending decisions are shaped both by budgetary needs and by fiscal policy.

Fiscal policy is the use of government spending and revenue collection to influence the economy. Fiscal policy is a tool used to expand or slow economic growth, achieve full employment, and maintain price stability. The federal government makes key fiscal policy decisions—how much to spend and how much to tax—each year when it establishes the federal budget.

Federal Budget Basics

The **federal budget** is a written document estimating the federal government's revenue and authorizing its spending for the coming year. Like any organization's budget, it lists expected income and shows exactly how the money will be spent.

The federal government prepares a new budget for each fiscal year. A **fiscal year** is a 12-month period used for budgeting purposes. It is not necessarily the same as the January-to-December calendar year. The federal government uses a fiscal year that runs from October 1 through September 30.

The federal budget takes about 18 months to prepare. During this time, citizens, Congress, and the President debate the government's spending priorities. There are four basic steps in the federal budget process.

Agencies Write Spending Proposals

The federal budget must fund many offices and agencies in the federal government, and Congress cannot know all of their needs. So, before the budget is put together, each federal agency writes a detailed estimate of how much it expects to spend in the coming fiscal year.

These spending proposals are sent to a special unit of the executive branch, the Office of Management and Budget (OMB). The OMB is part of the Executive Office of the President. As its name suggests, the OMB is responsible for managing the federal government's budget. Its most important job is to prepare that budget.

The Executive Branch Creates a Budget

The OMB reviews the federal agencies' spending proposals. Representatives from the agencies explain their spending proposals to the OMB and try to persuade the OMB to give them as much money as they have requested. Usually, the OMB gives each agency less than it requests.

The OMB then works with the President's staff to combine all of the individual agency budgets into a single budget document. This document reveals the President's overall spending plan for the coming fiscal year. The President presents the budget to Congress in January or February.

Congress Debates and Compromises

The President's budget is only a starting point. The number of changes Congress makes to the President's budget depends on the relationship between the President and Congress. Congress carefully considers, debates, and modifies the President's proposed budget. For help, members of Congress rely on the assistance of the Congressional Budget

| Figure 15.1 | **Creating the Federal Budget** |

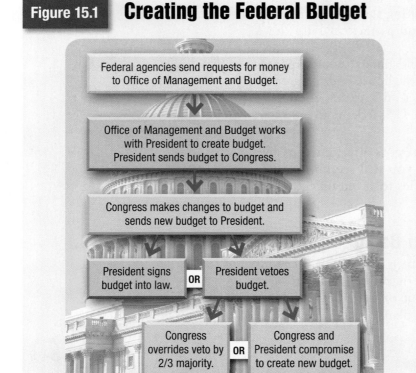

CHART SKILLS

Congress and the White House work together over the course of the year to put together a federal budget.

1. Who takes the first step in the budget process?
2. What happens to the proposed budget if it is vetoed by the President?

VISUAL GLOSSARY

Reviewing Key Terms
To understand *fiscal policy*, review these terms.

gross domestic product, *p. 309*
aggregate demand, *p. 314*
depression, *p. 316*
revenue, *p. 364*
balanced budget, *p. 382*

What is Fiscal Policy?

Fiscal policy has been described as the economic toolbox of the federal government. *Choose one of the tools shown in the toolbox here and explain how it might be used to influence the nation's economy.*

◀ **fiscal policy** the use of government spending and revenue collection to influence the economy

Increase Government Spending

Cut Taxes

Decrease Government Spending

Raise Taxes

Federal Government

HERE WE GO.. HOLD ON..ANY MINUTE NOW.. GET READY.

TAX CUT

TAX CUT

TAX CUT

TAX

ECONOMY

grimmy.com

TRIBUNE MEDIA SERVICES 2001 DAYTON DAILY NEWS

MIKE PETERS

◀ This cartoon appeared at a time when the national economy was in a downturn. The man in the balloon is then-President George W. Bush, who believed that tax cuts would lead to economic growth by giving people more money to spend. *How is Bush's action an example of using fiscal policy? Does the cartoonist believe the plan will work?*

Visual Glossary
online

To expand your understanding of this and other key economic terms, visit **PearsonSchool.com/PHecon**

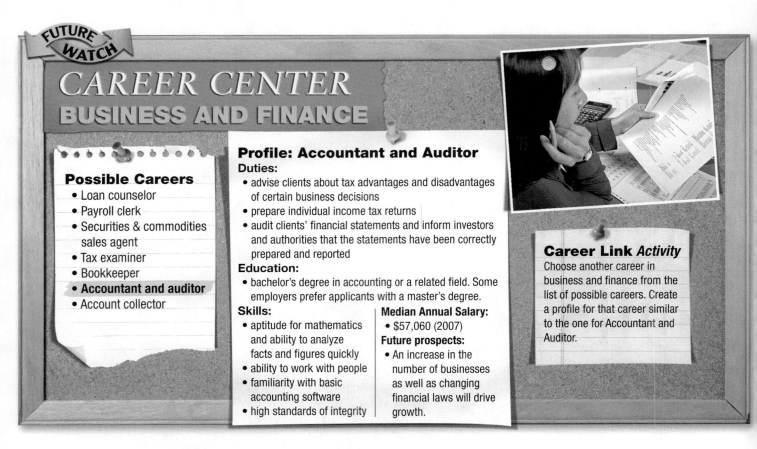

Office (CBO). Created in 1974, the CBO gives Congress independent economic data to help with its decisions.

Much of the work done by Congress is done in small committees. Working at the same time, committees in the House of Representatives and the Senate analyze the budget and hold hearings at which agency officials and others can speak out about the budget. The House Budget Committee and Senate Budget Committee combine their work to propose one initial budget resolution, which must be adopted by May 15, before the beginning of the fiscal year. This resolution is not intended to be final. It gives initial estimates for revenue and spending to guide the legislators as they continue working on the budget.

Then, in early September, the budget committees propose a second budget resolution that sets binding spending limits. Congress must pass this resolution by September 15, after which Congress cannot pass any new bills that would spend more money than the budget resolution allows.

Finally, the Appropriations Committee of each house submits bills to authorize specific spending, based on the decisions Congress has made. By this time, the new fiscal year is about to start and Congress faces pressure to get these **appropriations bills** adopted and submitted to the President quickly before the previous year's funding ends on September 30. If Congress cannot finish in time, it must pass short-term emergency spending legislation known as "stopgap funding" to keep the government running. If Congress and the President cannot even agree on temporary funding, the government "shuts down" and all but the most essential federal offices close.

In the White House

Once Congress approves the appropriations bills, they are sent to the President, who can sign the bills into law. If the President vetoes any of the bills, Congress has two options. It can vote to override the President's veto—a difficult task, because an override requires a 2/3 majority vote. More often, Congress works with the President to write an appropriations bill on which both sides can agree. Once that is completed, the President signs the new budget into law.

✔ **CHECKPOINT** *What two offices help the President and the Congress make budget decisions?*

appropriations bill
a bill that authorizes a specific amount of spending by the government

Fiscal Policy and the Economy

Government officials who take part in the budget process debate how much should be spent on specific programs such as defense or education. They also consider how much should be spent in all. The total government spending can be raised or lowered to help increase or decrease the output of the economy. Similarly, taxes can be raised or lowered to help reduce or boost output.

Fiscal policy that tries to increase output is known as **expansionary policy.** Fiscal policy intended to decrease output is called **contractionary policy.** By carefully choosing to follow expansionary or contractionary fiscal policy, the federal government tries to make the economy run as smoothly as possible.

Expansionary Fiscal Policy

Governments use an expansionary fiscal policy to raise the level of output in the economy. That is, they use expansionary policy to encourage growth, either to try to prevent a recession or to move the economy out of a recession. Recall from Chapter 12 that a recession is the part of the business cycle that occurs when output declines for two quarters, or three-month

periods, in a row. Expansionary fiscal policy involves either increasing government spending or cutting taxes, or both.

If the federal government increases its spending, or buys more goods and services, it triggers a chain of events that raises output and creates jobs. Government spending increases aggregate demand, which causes prices to rise, as shown in **Figure 15.2.** According to the law of supply, higher prices encourage suppliers of goods and services to produce more. To do this, firms will hire more workers. In short, an increase in demand will lead to lower unemployment and to an increase in output. The economy will expand.

Tax cuts work much like higher government spending to encourage economic expansion. If the federal government cuts taxes, individuals have more money to spend, and businesses keep more of their profits. Consumers have more money to spend on goods and services, and firms have more money to spend on land, labor, and capital. This spending will increase demand, prices, and output.

Contractionary Fiscal Policy

At some stages in the business cycle, the government may follow contractionary fiscal policy. Contractionary fiscal policy

expansionary policy
a fiscal policy used to encourage economic growth, often through increased spending or tax cuts

contractionary policy
a fiscal policy used to reduce economic growth, often through decreased spending or higher taxes

 MA.912.A.2.2 Interpret a graph to represent a real-world situation. **SS.912.E.1.10** Explain the use of fiscal policy to promote economic growth.

Figure 15.2 — Effects of Expansionary Fiscal Policy

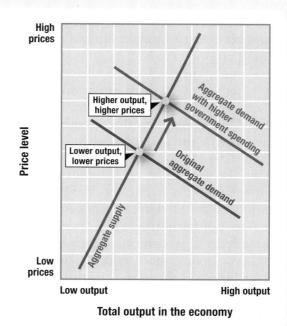

- To expand the economy, the government buys more goods and services.
- Companies that sell goods to the government earn profits, which they use to pay more to their workers and investors, and to hire new workers.
- Workers and investors have more money and spend more in shops and restaurants.
- Shops and restaurants buy more goods and hire more workers to meet their needs.
- In the short term, government spending leads to more jobs and more output.

High prices / Low prices
Price level
Low output / High output
Total output in the economy

Aggregate supply
Higher output, higher prices
Lower output, lower prices
Aggregate demand with higher government spending
Original aggregate demand

GRAPH SKILLS

Expansionary fiscal policy helps the economy by increasing aggregate demand and output.

1. How do increases in government spending affect aggregate supply?
2. How do increases in aggregate supply affect prices?

Action Graph
online

For an animated version of this graph, visit **PearsonSchool.com/PHecon**

Figure 15.3 **Effects of Contractionary Fiscal Policy**

GRAPH SKILLS

By cutting spending, the government can slow economic growth.

1. Why would the government want to slow economic growth?

2. How does lower government spending affect equilibrium?

Action Graph
online

For an animated version of this graph, visit
PearsonSchool.com/PHecon

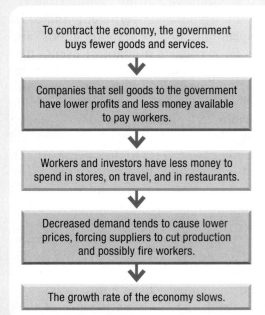

To contract the economy, the government buys fewer goods and services.

↓

Companies that sell goods to the government have lower profits and less money available to pay workers.

↓

Workers and investors have less money to spend in stores, on travel, and in restaurants.

↓

Decreased demand tends to cause lower prices, forcing suppliers to cut production and possibly fire workers.

↓

The growth rate of the economy slows.

MA.912.A.2.2 Interpret a graph to represent a real-world situation.

Simulation *Activity*

Expand or Contract?

You may be asked to take part in a role-playing game about the use of expansionary and contractionary fiscal policy.

tries to decrease aggregate demand, and by decreasing demand, reduce the growth of economic output. If contractionary fiscal policy is strong enough, it may slow the growth of output to zero, or even lead to a fall in gross domestic product (GDP).

Why would the government institute policies intended to decrease economic output? The government sometimes tries to slow down the economy because fast-growing demand can exceed supply. When demand exceeds supply, producers must choose between raising output and raising prices. If producers cannot expand production enough, they will raise their prices, which can lead to high inflation. Left unchecked, inflation cuts into consumers' purchasing power and discourages economic growth and stability.

Contractionary fiscal policy aimed at slowing the growth of total output generally involves two alternatives. The Federal government could decrease spending, or raise taxes, or both.

If the federal government spends less, or buys fewer goods and services, it triggers a chain of events that may lead to slower GDP growth. A decrease in government spending leads to a decrease in aggregate demand, because the government is buying less than before. Decreased demand tends

to lower prices. According to the law of supply, lower prices encourage suppliers to cut their production and possibly lay off workers. Lower production lowers the growth rate of the economy and may even reduce GDP. This chain of events is the exact opposite of what happens when the government increases spending. The government uses the same tools to try to influence the economy in both cases, but in different ways, and with very different goals.

When the federal government raises taxes, individuals have less money to spend on goods and services or to save for the future. Firms keep less of their profits and decrease their spending on land, labor, and capital. As a result of these decreases in demand, prices tend to fall. Producers of goods and suppliers of services tend to cut production. This slows the growth of GDP.

✔ **CHECKPOINT** *What are the two categories of contractionary fiscal policy and two categories of expansionary fiscal policy?*

Limits of Fiscal Policy

On paper, fiscal policy looks like a powerful tool that can keep the economy in perfect balance. In reality, fiscal policy can be clumsy and difficult to put into practice.

Difficulty of Changing Spending Levels

Increasing or decreasing the amount of federal spending is not an easy task. As you read in Chapter 14, many of the spending categories in the federal budget are entitlements that are fixed by law. More than half of the federal budget is set aside for programs such as Medicaid, Social Security, and veterans benefits before Congress even begins the budget process. The government cannot change spending for entitlements under current law. Also, it must continue to pay the interest on the national debt. As a result, significant changes in federal spending generally must come from the smaller, discretionary spending part of the federal budget. This gives the government less leeway for raising or lowering spending.

Predicting the Future

Governments use fiscal policy to prevent big changes in the level of GDP. Despite the statistics, however, it is difficult to know the current state of the economy. As you read in Chapter 12, no one can predict how quickly the business cycle will move from one stage to the next, nor can anyone identify exactly where in the cycle the economy is at any particular time.

Predicting future economic performance is even more difficult.

> **"**If economists forecast well, then the lag would not matter. They could tell Congress in advance what the appropriate fiscal policy is. But economists do not forecast well. Most economists, for example, badly under predicted both the rise in unemployment in 1981 and the strength of the recovery that began in late 1982. Absent accurate forecasts, attempts to use discretionary fiscal policy to counteract business cycle fluctuations are as likely to do harm as good.**"**
>
> —David N. Weil, professor of economics at Brown University

Delayed Results

Although changes in fiscal policy affect the economy, changes take time. Once government officials decide when and how to change fiscal policy, they have to put these changes into effect within the federal budget, which itself takes more than a year to develop. Finally, they have to wait for the change in spending or taxing to affect the economy.

By the time the policy takes effect, the economy might be moving in the opposite direction. The government could propose massive public spending on highways in the middle of a recession, only to have the economy recover before construction begins. In cases like this, fiscal policy would only strengthen the new trend, instead of correcting the original problem. If the government continued to spend money freely on highways in the middle of a recovery, it could lead to high inflation and a labor shortage.

Political Pressures

The President and members of Congress, who develop the federal budget and the federal government's fiscal policy, are elected officials. If they wish to be reelected, they must make decisions that please the people who elect them, not necessarily decisions that are good for the overall economy.

For example, government officials have an incentive to practice expansionary fiscal policy by boosting government spending and lowering taxes. These actions are usually popular with voters. Government spending benefits the firms that receive government contracts and the individuals who receive direct payments from the government. Lower taxes leave more disposable income in people's pockets.

On the other hand, contractionary fiscal policy, which decreases government spending or raises taxes, is often unpopular. Firms and individuals who expect income from the government are not happy when the income is reduced or cut off. No one likes to pay higher taxes, unless the tax revenue is spent on a specific, highly valued good or service.

Coordinating Fiscal Policy

For fiscal policy to be effective, various branches and levels of government must plan and work together. This is very difficult to do. For example, if the federal government is pursuing contractionary policy, state and local governments should, ideally, pursue a similar fiscal policy. Yet, state and local governments may be pursuing different fiscal policies than the federal government.

For example, after the federal government cut income taxes in 2001 and 2003, many state and local governments raised income and property taxes to close budget deficits and avoid deep spending cuts. The federal government was willing to cut taxes and run a deficit in poor economic times, but most state and local governments were legally forbidden to do so.

Businesspeople, politicians, and economists often disagree about how well the economy is performing and what the goals of fiscal policy should be. Also, different regions of the economy can experience very different conditions. California and Hawaii may have high unemployment while Nebraska and Massachusetts face rising prices and a labor shortage.

In addition, in order for the federal government's fiscal policy to be effective, it must also be coordinated with the monetary policy of the Federal Reserve. You'll read more about monetary policy in the next chapter.

Even when all of these obstacles are overcome, governments must recognize that the short-term effects of fiscal policy will differ from the long-term effects. For example, a tax cut or increased government spending will give a temporary boost to economic production and to employment. However, as the economy returns to full employment, high levels of government spending combined with increased market spending will lead to increased inflation and higher interest rates.

Similarly, an increase in taxes or fees or a decrease in government spending may "cool" the economy and lead to a recession. However, in the long run, reduced government spending will allow other types of spending to increase without risking higher inflation. If there is more private investment spending, this could lead to higher economic growth in the long run. In this way, slow growth or even recession in the short term can lead to prosperity and more jobs in the future.

✔ **CHECKPOINT** *Why is it so difficult for government to change spending levels?*

 SS.912.E.1.10, SS.912.E.2.9, LA.1112.1.6.1, LA.1112.2.2.2, MA.912.A.2.1

SECTION 1 ASSESSMENT

Essential Questions Journal To continue to build a response to the Essential Question, go to your **Essential Questions Journal**.

❓ Guiding Question

1. Use your completed table to answer this question: What are the goals and limits of fiscal policy?

2. **Extension** Like the government, individuals benefit from budgets. Plan your coming month's expenditures. Start with your current income. List your necessary expenditures. What, if anything, is left for discretionary spending?

Key Terms and Main Ideas

3. Explain **fiscal policy** and how it relates to the **federal budget.**

4. When does the federal government's **fiscal year** begin?

5. What is an **appropriations bill**?

6. What is **expansionary policy**?

Critical Thinking

7. **Analyze (a)** What are the four basic steps in the federal budget process? **(b)** What is the advantage of having both the President and Congress involved in the budget process?

8. **Identify Effects (a)** Identify entitlement programs. **(b)** How do they affect creation of the federal budget?

9. **Solve Problems** Which fiscal policy strategy do you think policymakers would use in each of these scenarios and why? **(a)** Inflation is rising, and real GDP is up by 4 percent. **(b)** GDP is down, and the unemployment rate has increased to 10 percent.

Math Skills

10. **Creating a Graph** Use the information from the chart below to create a line graph showing consumer confidence in January of each of the years shown. **(a)** In which two-year period did consumer confidence rise the most? **(b)** What was the percent of decline in consumer confidence over the period from 2000 through 2003?

Visit PearsonSchool.com/PHecon for additional math help.

Consumer Confidence Index
Annual Average (1985 = 100)

2000	2001	2002	2003	2004	2005	2006	2007	2008
144.7	115.7	97.8	78.8	97.7	105.1	106.8	110.2	87.9

SOURCE: *www.pollingreport.com*

NGSSS

LA.1112.1.6 Use multiple strategies to develop vocabulary.

MA.912.A.2.2 Interpret a graph to represent a real-world situation.

SS.912.E.1.10 Explain the use of fiscal policy to promote price stability.

SS.912.E.2.1 Identify and explain broad economic goals.

SS.912.E.2.3 Research the contributions of key individuals of various backgrounds in the development of the U.S.

SS.912.E.3.6 Draw conclusions about historical economic theories of economists.

ECONOMIC DICTIONARY

As you read the section, look for the definitions of these **Key Terms:**

• classical economics
• productive capacity
• demand-side economics
• Keynesian economics
• multiplier effect
• automatic stabilizer
• supply-side economics

Guiding Question
What economic ideas have shaped fiscal policy?

Copy this chart and fill it in as you read.

Fiscal Policy Options		
Classical economics	**Keynesian (demand-side) economics**	**Supply-side economics**
• free markets regulate themselves • fiscal policy limited	• • •	• • •

▶ **Economics and You**   Look at the picture of the two children on this page. They are poor and hungry, and the family breadwinner is out of work. Even if you have never been in a situation like this, it's probably not hard to imagine how these children feel. And the time is the Great Depression, so there are millions of families facing the same problem.

"WHY CAN'T YOU GIVE MY DAD A JOB?" But who is the boy asking? A factory owner? The local supermarket? Or is he asking the government itself? Would *you* expect the government to spend large amounts of money to give your father or mother—as well as thousands of other people—a job?

Principles in Action   Nowadays, many of us are used to the idea that the government might use its spending power to stimulate the economy. But at the time of the Depression, this was a radical new idea. And today, there are plenty of people who think that there are better ways the government can stimulate the economy than by spending. In this section, you will look at two very different fiscal policy options that the government can pursue. In the Economics & You feature, you will see how tax policy can affect your income and the services you use.

Classical Economics

Throughout this book, you have read about the workings of a free-market economy. In a free market, people act in their own self interest, causing prices to rise or fall so that supply and demand will always return to equilibrium. This idea that free markets regulate themselves is central to the school of thought known as **classical economics.** Adam Smith, David Ricardo, and Thomas Malthus all contributed basic ideas to this school. For well over a century, classical economics dominated economic theory and government policies. Some aspects of classical economic thought are still widely followed today.

The Great Depression, which began in 1929, challenged the classical theory. Prices fell over several years, so demand should have increased enough to stimulate production as consumers took advantage of low prices. Instead, demand also fell as people lost their jobs and bank failures

classical economics
a school of thought based on the idea that free markets regulate themselves

▲ These children are taking part in a protest march of the unemployed during the Great Depression.

productive capacity the maximum output that an economy can sustain over a period of time without increasing inflation

demand-side economics a school of thought based on the idea that demand for goods drives the economy

wiped out their savings. According to classical economics, the market should have reached equilibrium, with full employment. But it didn't, and millions suffered from unemployment and other hardships. Farmers lost their farms because corn was selling for seven cents a bushel, beef for two and a half cents a pound, and apples for less than a penny. Still, many people were too poor to buy enough food for their families.

The Great Depression highlighted a problem with classical economics: it did not address how long it would take for the market to return to equilibrium. Classical economists recognized it could take some time, and looked to the long run for equilibrium to reestablish itself. One economist, who was not satisfied with the idea of simply waiting for the economy to recover on its own, commented, "In the long run we are all dead." That economist was John Maynard Keynes (pronounced CANES).

✔ **CHECKPOINT** *What event challenged the dominance of the classical economics school of thought?*

Figure 15.4 **Keynesian Economics**

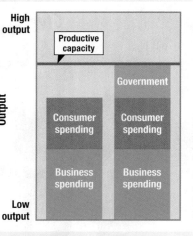

In a recession or depression, businesses and consumers do not demand as much as the economy can produce. Keynes argued that government spending can bring the economy up to its productive capacity.

GRAPH SKILLS

John Maynard Keynes added government spending to the classical model of demand.

1. What role did Keynes envision for government in the economy?

2. How might this government intervention affect the business cycle?

Keynesian Economics

British economist John Maynard Keynes developed a new theory of economics to explain the Depression. Keynes presented his ideas in 1936 in a book called *The General Theory of Employment, Interest, and Money.* He wanted to develop a comprehensive explanation of macroeconomic forces. Such an explanation, he argued, should tell economists and politicians how to get out of economic crises like the Great Depression. In sharp contrast to classical economics, Keynes wanted to give government a tool it could use immediately to boost the economy in the short run.

A Broader View

Classical economists had always looked at how the equilibrium of supply and demand applied to *individual products*. In contrast, Keynes focused on the workings of the economy *as a whole*.

Keynes looked at the productive capacity of the entire economy. **Productive capacity,** often called full-employment output, is the maximum output that an economy can sustain over a period of time without increasing inflation. Keynes attempted to answer the difficult question posed by the Great Depression: Why does actual production in an economy sometimes fall far short of its productive capacity?

Keynes argued that the Depression was continuing because neither consumers nor businesses had an incentive to spend enough to cause an increase in production. After all, why would a company spend money to increase production when demand for its products was falling? How could consumers significantly increase demand when they had barely enough money to survive?

The only way to end the Depression, Keynes thought, would be to find a way to boost demand. Economists who agreed with the idea that demand drives the economy developed a school of thought known as **demand-side economics.** They asked themselves this question: Who could spend enough to spur demand and revitalize production?

A New Role for Government

Keynes thought that the spender should be the federal government. In the early 1930s, only the government still had the resources to spend enough to affect the whole economy. The government could, in effect, make up for the drop in private spending by buying goods and services on its own. This, Keynes argued, would encourage production and increase employment. Then, as people went back to work, they would spend their wages on more goods and services, leading to even higher levels of production. This ever-expanding cycle would carry the economy out of the Depression. Once the crisis was over, the government could then step back and reduce its spending.

These ideas form the core of Keynes's approach to resolving problems with the economy. **Keynesian economics** uses demand-side theory as the basis for encouraging government action to help the economy. Keynesian economics proposes that the government can, and should, use fiscal policy to help the economy.

Avoiding Recession

Keynes argued that fiscal policy can be used to fight the two fundamental macroeconomic problems. These two opposing problems are periods of recession and periods of inflation.

The federal government, Keynes argued, should keep track of the total level of spending by consumers, businesses, and government. If total spending begins to fall far below the level required to keep the economy running at full capacity, the government should watch out for the possibility of recession.

The government can respond by increasing its own spending until spending by the private sector returns to a higher level. Or it can cut taxes so that spending and investment by consumers and businesses increases. As you read in the previous section, raising government spending and cutting taxes are expansionary fiscal policies.

After he was elected President in 1932, Franklin D. Roosevelt carried out expansionary fiscal policies. His New Deal put people to work—whether planting forests,

▲ During the Great Depression, the Civilian Conservation Corps (CCC) employed more than 2 million young men in jobs such as planting forests and digging irrigation ditches. *How did the CCC meet the goals of Keynesian economics?*

building dams and schools, or painting murals. The federal budget paid for all these programs.

Many people argue that instead of creating new jobs, such public works projects only shift employment from the private to the public sector. The dispute over Keynes' ideas is reflected today generally in the philosophies of the two political parties. Republicans generally have been associated with using tax cuts to stimulate the economy. Democrats, generally, have favored more expansive government programs to stimulate the economy.

Controlling Inflation

Keynes also argued that the government could use a contractionary fiscal policy to prevent inflation or reduce its severity. The government can reduce inflation either by increasing taxes or by reducing its own spending. Both of these actions decrease overall demand.

The Multiplier Effect

Fiscal policy, although difficult to control, is an extremely powerful tool. The key to its power is the multiplier effect. The **multiplier effect** in fiscal policy is the idea that every one dollar change in fiscal policy—whether an increase in spending or a decrease in taxes—creates a change

Keynesian economics a school of thought that uses demand-side theory as the basis for encouraging government action to help the economy

multiplier effect the idea that every one dollar change in fiscal policy creates a change greater than one dollar in the national income

Social Security, Projected Revenues and Outlays

SOURCE: Social Security Administration

Willing to Sacrifice

FISCAL POLICY PREFERENCES

What steps are voters prepared to accept to reduce the government's mammoth deficit?

By Jonathan Weisman
The Wall Street Journal

 SS.912.E.2.9 Analyze how changes in federal spending affect budget deficits, surpluses, and the national debt.

Frustrated voters, fixing on the $1.5 trillion federal deficit as a symbol of paralysis in Washington, appear increasingly willing to take drastic steps to address the red ink.

Leonard Anderson, 56, an engineer and a Republican, said he would accept a national sales tax to raise revenue. Kimberly Moore, 46, a Democrat and bank worker, says everyone will have to accept budget cuts. And at 67, Paul DesJardins, a Republican, says he would accept higher Medicare co-payments and deductibles.

"As Americans, we're all going to have to take less," says Lois Profitt, a 58-year-old small-business owner and political independent.

Both the Democratic and Republican parties are trying to talk about the deficit without addressing the specifics of how they would tackle it. Leaders on both sides worry about being attacked if they produce a package of painful spending cuts or tax increases. And to reinforce lawmakers' anxiety, voters remain divided about what ought to be done.

"It's a brutal predicament for politicians because the rhetoric of deficit cutting is enormously popular, but the details are incredibly unpopular," says Matt Bennett, a vice president at the Democratic group Third Way.

Participants in a *Wall Street Journal* focus group in Virginia say they want their leaders to take a stand. "I wish the politicians would be [firm] and be like, 'You know what? It's going to be horrible for the next few years, but you've got to shut up,'" says Jennifer Ciminelli, a 35-year-old independent.

At current levels, the federal deficit exceeds all defense and nondefense spending at Congress's discretion by $110 million. In other words, lawmakers could eliminate the entire military, all federal education, agricultural, housing programs, federal prisons, the CIA, FBI, Coast Guard and border patrol, and the nation would still be in the red.

Half of the current deficit stems from falling tax revenues and rising spending on programs associated with the recession, such as unemployment insurance, food stamps and the Wall Street bailout. The administration projects that the deficit will shrink as these programs end and the economy recovers.

But then long-term problems kick in. With the baby boom generation retiring, the deficit will begin rising again because of rising Social Security, Medicare and Medicaid spending.

"The country's going to deteriorate," says Mary Beth Davis, 27, a photographer and independent. "It already is."

Applying Economic Principles
According to this article, it will be difficult to reduce the federal deficit. How can changes in spending and taxation each affect budget deficits or surpluses?

Video News Update Online
Powered by
The Wall Street Journal
Classroom Edition

Use videos at **PearsonSchool.com/PHecon** as a springboard for a discussion on a current topic.

much greater than one dollar in the national income. In other words, the effects of changes in fiscal policy are multiplied.

Suppose the federal government finds that business investment is dropping. To prevent a recession, in the next budget the government decides to spend an extra $10 billion to stimulate the economy. How will this affect the economy?

With this government spending, demand, income, and GDP will increase by $10 billion. After all, if the government buys an extra $10 billion of goods and services, then an extra $10 billion of goods and services have been produced. However, the GDP will increase by more than $10 billion. Here's why:

The businesses that sold the $10 billion in goods and services to the government have earned an additional $10 billion. These businesses will spend their additional earnings on wages, raw materials, and investment, sending money to workers, other suppliers, and stockholders. What will the recipients do with this money? They will spend part of it, perhaps 80 percent, or $8 billion. The businesses that benefit from this second round of spending will then pass it back to households and other businesses, who will again spend 80 percent of it, or $6.4 billion. The next round will add an additional $5.1 billion to the economy, and so on.

When all of these rounds of spending are added up, the initial government spending of $10 billion leads to an increase of about $50 billion in GDP. The multiplier effect gives fiscal policy initiatives a much bigger kick than the initial amount spent.

Automatic Stabilizers

Fiscal policy is used to achieve many economic goals. One of the most important things that fiscal policy can achieve is a more stable economy. A stable economy is one in which there are no rapid changes in the economic indicators you read about in Chapter 12. What's more, set up properly, fiscal policy can come close to stabilizing the economy *automatically*.

Figure 15.5 shows how real GDP in the United States changed each year from 1930 to 2009. Prior to World War II, there were much larger changes in GDP

from year to year than after World War II. Although GDP still fluctuates, these fluctuations have been smaller than they were before the war. Economic growth has been much more stable in the United States in the last 60 or so years.

Why did this happen? After the war, federal taxes and spending on transfer payments—two key tools of fiscal policy—increased sharply. Taxes and transfer payments, or transfers of cash from the government to consumers, stabilize economic growth. When national income is high, the government collects more in taxes and pays out less in transfer payments. Both of these actions take money away from consumers, and therefore reduce spending. This decrease in spending balances out the increase in spending that results from rising income in a healthy economy.

The opposite is also true. When income in the country is low, the government collects less in taxes and pays out more in transfer payments. Both actions increase the amount of money held by consumers, and thus increase spending. This increase in spending balances out the decrease in spending resulting from decreased income.

FL MA.912.A.2.2 Interpret a graph to represent a real-world situation.

Figure 15.5 **Annual Change in GDP, 1930–2009**

SOURCE: Bureau of Economic Analysis, *Historical Statistics of the United States*

GRAPH SKILLS

The United States experienced strong economic swings before World War II.

1. How do the years after the war show the effect of automatic stabilizers on the economy?
2. Why did the 1930s see the largest percent losses in GDP?

Figure 15.6

Laffer Curve

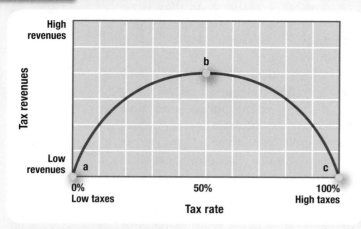

GRAPH SKILLS

The Laffer Curve illustrates the effects of high taxes on revenues.

1. According to the Laffer curve, what do both a high tax rate and a low tax rate produce?
2. Why do higher tax rates sometimes cause revenues to fall?

Action Graph
online

For an animated version of this graph, visit
PearsonSchool.com/PHecon

 MA.912.A.2.2 Interpret a graph to represent a real-world situation.

automatic stabilizer a tool of fiscal policy that increases or decreases automatically depending on changes in GDP and personal income

supply-side economics a school of thought based on the idea that the supply of goods drives the economy

Taxes and transfer payments do not eliminate changes in the rate of growth of GDP, but they do make these changes smaller. Because they help make economic growth more stable, they are known as stabilizers. Policymakers do not have to make changes in taxes and transfer payments for them to have their stabilizing effect. Taxes and most transfer payments are tied to the GDP and to personal income, so they change automatically. Thus they are called **automatic stabilizers**—tools of fiscal policy that increase or decrease automatically depending on changes in GDP and personal income.

Some stabilizers are no longer automatic. The former Aid to Families with Dependent Children (AFDC), often called "welfare," lost its entitlement status in 1996 and was renamed Temporary Assistance for Needy Families (TANF). Now the federal government gives the states a set amount of money each year to spend as they wish. However, the stabilizer effect was not completely lost. When the economy boomed in the late 1990s, state spending on TANF fell.

✔ **CHECKPOINT** *How did Keynes favor ending the Great Depression?*

Supply-Side Economics

Another school of economic thought promotes a different direction for fiscal policy. **Supply-side economics** is based on the idea that the supply of goods drives the economy. While Keynesian economics tries to encourage economic growth by increasing aggregate demand, supply-side economics relies on increasing aggregate supply. It does this by focusing on taxes.

The Laffer Curve

Supply-side economists believe that taxes have a strong negative impact on economic output. They often use the Laffer curve, named after the economist Arthur Laffer, to illustrate the effects of taxes. The Laffer curve shows the relationship between the tax rate and the total tax revenue that the government collects. The total revenue depends on both the tax rate and the health of the economy. The Laffer curve suggests that high tax rates may not bring in much revenue if they cause economic activity to decrease.

Figure 15.6 depicts the Laffer curve. Suppose the government imposes a tax on the wages of workers. If the tax rate is zero, as at point *a* on the graph, the government will collect no revenue, although the economy will benefit from the lack of taxes. As the government raises the tax rate, it starts to collect some revenue. Follow this change in **Figure 15.6** by tracing the curve from no taxes at point *a* to 50 percent taxation at point *b*.

From point *a* to point *b* on the curve, rising tax rates discourage some people from working as many hours and hinder companies from investing and increasing production. The net effect of a higher tax rate and a slightly lower tax base is an increase in revenue.

To the right of point *b*, the decrease in workers' effort is so large that the higher tax rate actually decreases total tax revenue. In other words, high rates of taxation will eventually discourage so many people from working that tax revenues will fall. In the extreme case of a 100 percent tax rate, no one would want to work! In this case, shown at point *c* on the curve, the government would collect no revenue.

Taxes and Output

The heart of the supply-side argument is that a tax cut increases total employment so much that the government actually collects more in taxes at the new, lower tax rate. Suppose the initial tax on labor is $3 an hour, and the typical worker works 30 hours per week, paying a total of $90 in taxes each week. If the government cuts the tax on labor to $2 an hour, and the worker responds by working 50 hours per week, the worker will pay $100 in taxes a week, an increase of $10.

Actual experience has proven that while a tax cut encourages some workers to work more hours, the end result is a relatively small increase in the number of hours worked. In the example above, if the tax cut increased the hours worked from 30 hours to 35 hours, the worker would pay only $70 in taxes ($2 per hour times 35 hours), down from $90 ($3 per hour times 30 hours). In general, taxpayers do not react strongly enough to tax cuts to increase tax revenue.

CHECKPOINT *How does the theory of supply-side economics link taxation to employment levels?*

Fiscal Policy in American History

As you recall, Keynes presented his ideas at a same time when the world economy was engulfed in the Great Depression. President Herbert Hoover, a strong believer in classical economics, thought that the economy was basically sound and would return to equilibrium on its own, without government interference. His successor, President Franklin D. Roosevelt, was much more willing to increase government spending to help lift the economy out of the Depression.

World War II

Keynes's theory was fully tested in the United States during World War II. As the country geared up for war, government spending increased dramatically. The government spent large sums of money to feed soldiers and equip them with everything from warplanes to rifles to medical supplies. This money was given to the private sector in exchange for goods. Just as Keynesian economics predicted, the additional demand for goods and services moved the country sharply out of the Great Depression and toward full productive capacity.

After World War II ended, Congress created the Council of Economic Advisers (CEA). Made up of three respected economists, the CEA advised the President on economic policy.

Postwar Keynesian Policy

Between 1945 and 1960, the U.S. economy was generally healthy and growing, despite a few minor recessions. The last recession continued into the term of President John F. Kennedy, with unemployment reaching a level of 6.7 percent.

Economics & YOU

The Impact of Taxes

Paycheck $539.15

Sometimes, when the economy is overheated, the government resorts to increasing taxes on individuals. *Tax increases can be very painful because they leave you with less money to spend on goods and services or to save for the future.*

These tax increases do more than help stabilize the economy and move it on to the next phase of the business cycle. *They also provide the government with more resources to pay for a wide variety of public services.*

▲ Sometimes the government lowers taxes to stimulate the economy. *If you had a few more dollars each week from a tax cut, would you save it or spend it?*

John Kenneth Galbraith

"The conventional view serves to protect us from the painful job of thinking."

John Kenneth Galbraith was the world's most famous economist for the last half of the twentieth century. He was also a witty commentator on politics and social life and the author of a number of bestselling books.

During World War II, Galbraith was selected by President Roosevelt to lead the Office of Price Administration, which meant he had total control over the prices charged by U.S. companies.

After the war, Galbraith wrote a number of widely read books about the government's role in society. He favored an active government, using funds provided by a progressive income tax and high sales taxes. He warned against "the affluent society," an economy that produced a glut of frivolous goods for the affluent while the public sector —education, roads and bridges, parks and concert halls—suffered neglect.

Galbraith advised President John F. Kennedy, who appointed him Ambassador to India in 1960. Later, he was the inspiration for President Lyndon B. Johnson's Head Start program, an early childhood education program for poor children.

Galbraith's long service to America did not go unnoticed. He received the Presidential Medal of Freedom, the nation's highest civilian honor, twice.

Critical Thinking: *Galbraith once said "The only function of economic forecasting is to make astrology look respectable." What did he mean by that? Do you agree with him?*

Fast Facts

John Kenneth Galbraith
Born: 1908 in Ontario, Canada
Died: 2006 in Cambridge, MA
Education: Ph.D., University of California at Berkeley
Claim to Fame: Wrote about the dangers of an affluent society

---

SS.912.E.2.3
Research the contributions of key individuals of various backgrounds in the development of the U.S.

Kennedy's chief financial policy advisor, Walter Heller, thought that the economy was below its productive capacity. He convinced Kennedy that tax cuts would stimulate demand and bring the economy closer to full productive capacity.

As **Figure 15.7** shows, tax rates were extremely high in the early 1960s. The highest individual income tax rate was about 90 percent, compared with about 40 percent in 2007. Kennedy proposed tax cuts, both because he agreed with Heller and because tax cuts are popular.

A version of Kennedy's tax cuts was enacted in 1964, under President Lyndon Johnson. At the same time, the Vietnam War raised government spending. Over two years, consumption and GDP increased by more than 4 percent a year. There is no way to prove that the tax cut caused this growth, but the result was generally what Keynesian economics predicted.

Keynesian economics was used often in the 1960s and 1970s. One Keynesian economist, John Kenneth Galbraith, greatly influenced national policies. Galbraith, a strong supporter of public spending,

helped develop the social welfare programs that lay at the heart of President Johnson's vision of a Great Society.

Supply-Side Policy in the 1980s

During the late 1970s, with Keynesian fiscal policy in place, unemployment and inflation rates soared. When Ronald Reagan became President in 1981, he vowed to cut taxes and spending. An "anti-Keynesian," Reagan did not believe that government should spend its way out of a recession:

"Government spending has become so extensive that it contributes to the economic problems it was designed to cure. More government intervention in the economy cannot possibly be a solution to our economic problems."

—Ronald Reagan, White House Report on the Program for Economic Recovery, 1981

Reagan instituted policies based on supply-side economics, a theory promoted by economists such as George Gilder. Among Reagan's advisers was Milton Friedman, a former professor of economics. Friedman supported individual freedom and pushed for more laissez-faire policies—hallmarks of classical and supply-side economics. (You will read a profile of Friedman in the next chapter.)

In 1981, Reagan proposed a tax cut that reduced taxes by 25 percent over three years. In a short time, the economy recovered and flourished. Still, tax cuts plus an increased defense budget led to deficit spending; just as Keynesian policy would.

Under the next few Presidents, the federal government spent much more money than it took in. As you will read in the next section, this gap caused increasing concern among economists and policymakers.

Return to Keynesian Policy?

In late 2008, the United States was hit with what many economists believed was the worst financial crisis since the Great Depression. A number of major financial institutions failed. Credit became harder to get, consumer spending dropped, and unemployment rose.

That year, voters elected a new President, Barack Obama. He promised to take firm action to stimulate the economy. Obama signed a stimulus bill which included spending on major public works programs, such as repairing the nation's infrastructure. To many observers, such

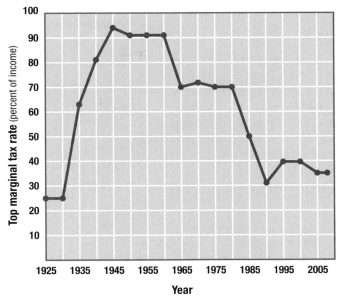

Figure 15.7 **Top Marginal Tax Rate, 1925–2007**

SOURCE: Tax Policy Center: Urban Institute and Brookings Institute

GRAPH SKILLS

Tax rates varied widely throughout the last century.
1. When were top marginal income tax rates at their highest?
2. What has been the trend in tax rates since 1985?

proposals seemed to signal a shift back to a Keynesian fiscal policy, as in the New Deal.

✔ **CHECKPOINT** *What Keynesian fiscal policy tool did President Kennedy use?*

FL SS.912.E.1.10, SS.912.E.2.1, SS.912.E.3.6, LA.1112.1.6.1, LA.1112.2.2.2

SECTION 2 ASSESSMENT

Essential Questions Journal To continue to build a response to the Essential Question, go to your **Essential Questions Journal.**

❓ Guiding Question

1. Use your completed chart to answer this question: What economic ideas have shaped fiscal policy?
2. **Extension** You're a struggling worker during a recession. Leading economists urge you to be patient because the economy will right itself. How do you reply?

Key Terms and Main Ideas

3. What is **classical economics**?
4. How is full employment related to **productive capacity**?
5. What is the **multiplier effect**?

6. Compare and contrast **Keynesian economics** and **supply-side economics.**

Critical Thinking

7. **Analyze (a)** What might be the costs and benefits of Keynesian economic policies? **(b)** How did Keynes's policies work during the Great Depression?
8. **Analyze Causes and Effects** Why can low tax rates encourage investment and increase jobs and wages?
9. **Contrast** Choose two Presidents and explain how their fiscal policies reflected differing economic beliefs.

Quick Write

10. Write a brief position paper supporting or opposing the use of tax funds to put people to work today. Include at least two arguments to support your position, indicating which argument you feel is most important. Make sure your final sentence strongly restates your position.

NGSSS

LA.1112.1.6 Use multiple strategies to develop vocabulary.

MA.912.A.2.2 Interpret a graph to represent a real-world situation.

SS.912.E.1.10 Explain the use of fiscal policy to promote full employment.

SS.912.E.1.13 Describe the composition of the money supply.

SS.912.E.2.9 Analyze how changes in federal spending affect budget deficits, surpluses, and the national debt.

SS.912.E.3.1 Demonstrate the impact of inflation on world economies.

ECONOMIC DICTIONARY

As you read the section, look for the definitions of these **Key Terms:**

• budget surplus
• budget deficit
• Treasury bill
• Treasury note
• Treasury bond
• national debt
• crowding-out effect

Guiding Question

What are the effects of budget deficits and national debt?

Copy this cause-and-effect chart and fill it in as you read.

Causes	Event	Effects
• • •	Budget Deficit	• • •

▶ **Economics and You**   If you have used a credit card, you might have some idea about how easy it is to spend money that you don't have. If you fail to pay the credit-card bill in full each month, the high interest rate may mean that the amount you owe just keeps increasing. Soon you may face a mountain of debt.

The federal government is no stranger to spending more than it has. You have been reading about how the government uses spending as a fiscal policy tool to improve the economy.

Principles in Action   As you will see in this section, unchecked spending can lead to a soaring national debt. The How the Economy Works feature shows how that debt resulted from numerous budget decisions. The costs of this debt must be measured against the benefits of government spending.

Balancing the Budget

The basic tool of fiscal policy is the federal budget. It is made up of two fundamental parts: revenue (taxes) and expenditures (spending programs). When the federal government's revenues equal its expenditures in any particular fiscal year, the federal government has a balanced budget.

In reality, as **Figure 15.8** shows, the federal budget is almost never balanced. Usually, it is either running a surplus or a deficit. A **budget surplus** occurs in any year when revenues exceed expenditures. In other words, there is more money going into the Treasury than coming out of it. A **budget deficit** occurs in any year when expenditures exceed revenues. In other words, there is more money coming out of the Treasury than going into it.

Assume the federal government starts with a balanced budget. If the government decreases expenditures without changing anything else, it will run a budget surplus. Similarly, if it increases taxes—revenues—without changing anything else, it will run a surplus.

This analysis also explains budget deficits. If the government increases expenditures without changing anything else, it will run a deficit. Similarly, if it decreases taxes without changing anything else, it will run a deficit. The deficit can grow or shrink because of forces beyond the government's control. Surpluses and deficits can be very large figures. The largest deficit, in 2009, was nearly $1.8 trillion.

budget surplus a situation in which budget revenues exceed expenditures

budget deficit a situation in which budget expenditures exceed revenues

Responding to Budget Deficits

When the government runs a deficit, it is because it did not take in enough revenue to cover its expenses for the year. When this happens, the government must find a way to pay for the extra expenditures. There are two basic actions the government can take to do so.

Creating Money

The government can create new money to pay salaries for its workers and benefits for citizens. Traditionally, governments simply printed the bills they needed. Today, the government can create money electronically by actions that effectively deposit money in people's bank accounts. The effect is the same. This approach works for relatively small deficits but can cause severe problems when there are large deficits. What are these problems?

When the government creates more money, it increases the amount of money in circulation. This increases the demand for goods and services and can increase output. But once the economy reaches full employment, output cannot increase. The increase in money will mean that there are more dollars but the same amount of goods and services. Prices will rise so that a greater amount of money will be needed to purchase the same amount of goods and services. In other words, prices go up, and the result is inflation.

Covering very large deficits by printing more money can cause hyperinflation. This happened in Germany and Russia after World War I, in Brazil and Argentina in the 1980s, and in Ukraine in the 1990s. If the United States experienced hyperinflation, a shirt that cost $30 in June might cost $50 in July, $80 in August, and $400 in December!

Borrowing Money

The federal government usually does not resort to creating money to cover a budget deficit. Instead, it borrows money. The government commonly borrows money by selling bonds. As you read in Chapter 11, a bond is a type of loan: a promise to repay money in the future, with interest. Consumers and businesses buy bonds from the government. The government thus has

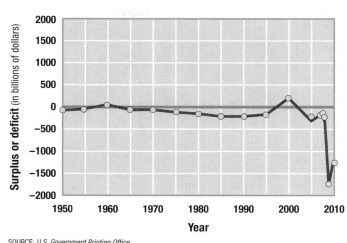

| Figure 15.8 | **Budget Surpluses and Deficits, 1950–2010** |

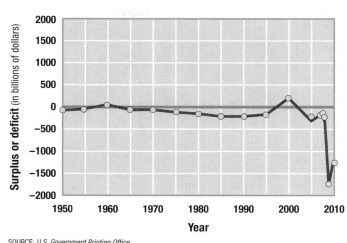

SOURCE: *U.S. Government Printing Office*

GRAPH SKILLS

Budget deficits swelled in the early 2000s due to recession, tax cuts, and defense spending.

1. In which of the years shown on the graph did the budget have a surplus?
2. What was the dominant trend in deficits in the late 1990s?

the money to cover its budget deficit. In return, the purchasers of the bonds earn interest on their investment over time.

United States Savings Bonds ("EE Bonds") allow millions of Americans to lend small amounts of money to the federal government. In return, they earn interest on the bonds for up to 30 years. Other common forms of government borrowing are Treasury bills, notes, and bonds. **Treasury bills** are short-term bonds that have maturity dates of 26 weeks or less. **Treasury notes** have terms of from 2 to 10 years. **Treasury bonds** mature 30 years after issue.

Federal borrowing lets the government undertake more projects than it could otherwise afford. Wise borrowing allows the government to create more public goods and services. Federal borrowing, however, also has serious disadvantages.

✓ **CHECKPOINT** *What is the most common way that the federal government pays for expenditures that exceed revenues?*

 MA.912.A.2.2
Interpret a graph to represent a real-world situation.

Treasury bill a government bond with a maturity date of 26 weeks or less

Treasury note a government bond with a term of from 2 to 10 years

Treasury bond a government bond that is issued with a term of 30 years

Figure 15.9

National Debt as a Percentage of GDP

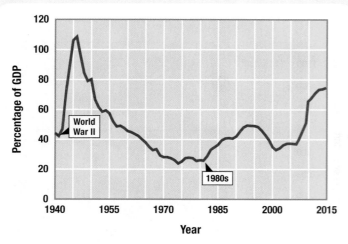

Percentage of GDP

World War II

1980s

Year

Note: Figures for the years 2010–2015 are projected.
SOURCE: *The Executive Office of the President of the United States, The Office of Management and Budget. The Budget of the United States Government, Fiscal Year 2011. Historical Tables.*

GRAPH SKILLS

1. Do you think budgets are in surplus, balanced, or in debt during times of war?
2. Why does the national debt as a percentage of GDP soar during times of war?

Personal Finance
For tips on managing your own debt, see your Personal Finance Handbook in the back of the book or visit PearsonSchool.com/PHecon

MA.912.A.2.2
Interpret a graph to represent a real-world situation.

national debt the total amount of money the federal government owes to bondholders

The National Debt

Like people, when the government borrows money, it goes into debt. The **national debt** is the total amount of money the federal government owes to bondholders. Every year that there is a budget deficit and the federal government borrows money to cover it, the national debt will grow.

The national debt is owed to investors who hold Treasury bonds, bills, and notes. These bonds are considered to be among the safest investments in the world. As such, they offer a secure investment for individuals and businesses. Because the United States is widely viewed as stable and trustworthy, the federal government can borrow money at a lower rate of interest than private citizens or corporations can. Lower interest rates benefit taxpayers by reducing the cost of government borrowing.

The Difference Between Deficit and Debt

Many people are confused about the difference between the deficit and the debt. The deficit is the amount of money the government borrows for one budget, representing one fiscal year. The debt, on the other hand, is the sum of all the government borrowing before that time, minus the borrowings that have been repaid. Each deficit adds to the debt. Each surplus subtracts from it.

Measuring the National Debt

In dollar terms, the size of the national debt is extremely large. In 2008, it exceeded $10.6 trillion! Such a large number can best be analyzed in relation to the size of the economy as a whole. Therefore, let's look at the size of the debt as a percentage of gross domestic product (GDP) over time. This can be seen in **Figure 15.9.** Historically, debt as a percentage of GDP rises during wartime, when government spending increases faster than taxation, and it falls during peacetime.

Notice how the pattern changed in the 1980s, when the United States began to run a large debt, even though the country wasn't at war. The debt was in part a result of increases in spending during President Ronald Reagan's terms. As you read in the previous section, the Reagan administration also cut taxes. The combined effect of higher spending and lower tax rates was several years of increased budget deficits. The government borrowed billions of dollars to cover these deficits, adding to the national debt. As a result, the ratio of debt to GDP grew very large for peacetime.

CHECKPOINT *To whom does the government owe the national debt?*

Is the Debt a Problem?

The growth of the national debt during the Reagan administration led many to focus on the problems caused by a national debt. In general, three problems can arise from a national debt.

Problems of a National Debt

The first problem with a national debt is that it reduces the funds available for businesses to invest. This is because in order to sell its bonds, the government must offer a higher interest rate. Individuals and businesses, attracted by the higher interest rates and the security of investing in the government, use their savings or profits to purchase government bonds.

However, every dollar spent on a government bond is one dollar less that can be invested in private business. Less money is available for companies to expand their factories, conduct research, and develop new products, and so interest rates rise. This loss of funds for private investment caused by government borrowing is called the **crowding-out effect.** Federal borrowing "crowds out" private borrowing by making it harder for private businesses to borrow. A national debt, then, can hurt investment and slow economic growth over the long run.

The second problem with a high national debt is that the government must pay interest to bondholders. The more the government borrows, the more interest it has to pay. Paying the interest on the debt is sometimes called servicing the debt. Over time, the interest payments have become very large. About the year 2000, the federal government spent about $250 billion a year servicing the debt. Moreover, there is an opportunity cost—dollars spent servicing the debt cannot be spent on something else, such as defense, healthcare, or infrastructure.

A possible third problem involves foreign ownership of the national debt. The biggest holder of that debt is the United States government itself. The government uses bonds as a secure savings account for holding Social Security, Medicare, and other funds. But about a quarter of the debt is owned by foreign governments, including Japan, China, and the United Kingdom. Some critics of the debt fear that a country like China could use its large bond holdings as a tool to extract favors from the United States. Others disagree, arguing that foreign states own too little of the debt to cause any concern.

Other Views of a National Debt

Some people insist that the national debt is not a big problem. Traditional Keynesian economists believe that fiscal policy is an important tool that can be used to help achieve full productive capacity. To these analysts, the benefits of a productive economy outweigh the costs of interest on national debt.

In the short term, deficit spending may help create jobs and encourage economic growth. However, a budget deficit can be an effective tool only if it is temporary. Most people agree that if the government runs large budget deficits year after year, the costs of the growing debt will eventually outweigh the benefits.

✓ CHECKPOINT *What are the problems of having a huge national debt?*

crowding-out effect the loss of funds for private investment caused by government borrowing

| Figure 15.10 | **Effects of the Budget Deficit on Investment** |

The federal government spends more than it takes in, and has to borrow money to cover the deficit. → Investors trust the U.S. government and loan money to the government by buying bonds. → Banks and investors have less money to lend private businesses. Private businesses must pay a higher interest rate to borrow scarce money.

CHART SKILLS

Government borrowing tends to reduce private investment by taking away some funds that could have been invested in private business. Economists describe this phenomenon as the crowding-out effect.

1. Why do lenders put their money in government bonds rather then use it for private investment?
2. What are some ways that private investors and banks deal with the crowding-out effect?

What causes the national debt to spiral?

The National Debt is the amount of money the United States government owes to the people and institutions who hold its bonds, bills, and notes. In the past 30 years, the national debt has grown enormously. Here is why the debt has grown.

1 Each year, the federal government has to pay for hundreds of essential services, from military protection to healthcare. Tax revenues pay for most of these expenses. But in most years, there is a gap between revenue and expenditures.

INTEREST

U.S. BONDS

2 To make up the gap, the government borrows money. It issues Treasury bonds, bills, and notes. The interest paid on this money becomes part of the federal budget.

Expenses

Borrowing

Controlling the Deficit

During the 1980s and the early 1990s, annual budget deficits added substantially to the national debt. Several factors frustrated lawmakers in their attempts to control the deficit. As we have seen, much of the budget consists of entitlement spending that is politically difficult to change. Another large part of the budget consists of interest that must be paid to bondholders. Finally, specific budget cuts are often opposed by interest groups.

Efforts to Reduce Deficits

Concerns about the budget deficits of the mid-1980s caused Congress to pass the Gramm-Rudman-Hollings Act. This law created automatic across-the-board cuts in federal expenditures if the deficit exceeded a certain amount. The automatic nature of the cuts saved lawmakers from having to make difficult decisions about individual funding cuts. However, the act exempted significant portions of the budget (such as interest payments and many entitlement programs such as Social Security) from the cuts.

The Supreme Court found that some parts of the Gramm-Rudman-Hollings Act were unconstitutional. Congress attempted to correct the flaws. In 1990, however, lawmakers realized that the deficit was going to be much larger than expected. Because Congress had exempted so many programs from automatic cuts, funding for nonexempt programs would be dramatically slashed.

To resolve the crisis, President George H. W. Bush and congressional leaders negotiated a new budget system that replaced Gramm-Rudman-Hollings. The 1990 Budget Enforcement Act created a

3 Economic downturns or external shocks such as natural disasters may add unplanned costs to the federal budget. This leads to even more borrowing.

4 As the government borrows more, the slice of the federal budget taken up by interest payments grows. The more interest, the greater the gap between revenue and expenses...and the greater the gap, the more the government borrows.

5 Large deficits over a period of years have caused the national debt to spiral to enormous proportions. However, economists differ on whether this large debt is a serious problem to the U.S. economy.

Check Your Understanding
1. How does borrowing lead to greater interest payments and greater debt?
2. How important do you think it is to immediately reduce the national debt?

> **More Expenses**

> **More Borrowing**

"pay-as-you-go" system (also known as PAYGO). PAYGO required Congress to raise enough revenue to cover increases in direct spending that would otherwise contribute to the budget deficit. This law expired in 2002, but in 2007 the House and Senate restored PAYGO in the form of special budget rules.

At various times, citizens and politicians have suggested amending the Constitution to require a balanced budget. In 1995, a balanced budget amendment gained the two-thirds majority it needed to pass the House, but the next year it failed by a single vote in the Senate. Supporters argued that the amendment would force the federal government to be more disciplined about its spending. Opponents said that a constitutional amendment requiring a balanced budget would not give the government the flexibility it needed to deal with rapid changes in the economy.

End-of-Century Surpluses

The late 1990s brought a welcome reversal of fortune. For the first time in thirty years, the President and the Office of Management and Budget were able to announce that the federal government was running a surplus.

How did this happen? First, the new budget procedures begun under President Bush and extended under President Clinton did help Congress control the growth of government spending. Second, tax increases by President Clinton in 1993 resulted in more federal revenue. Finally, the strong economy and low unemployment meant that more individuals and corporations were earning more money—and thus paying more to the government in taxes.

Return to Deficits

The changeover from deficits to surplus brought with it a different set of political

OUR NATIONAL DEBT:
13,360,446,432,088.
YOUR *Family share* 104,671.
THE NATIONAL DEBT CLOCK

▲ Created in 1989, the National Debt Clock in New York continually ticks off the growing national debt plus each family's share. There are similar clocks in other cities and on the Internet. *Why do you think someone decided to build the National Debt Clock?*

 SS.912.E.2.9, SS.912.E.3.1, LA.1112.1.6.1, LA.1112.2.2.2, MA.912.A.2.2

concerns. Investors who had come to rely heavily upon Treasury bonds as the basic "safe" investment worried that the federal government would remove all bonds from the market as it repaid its debt.

Americans debated how to make best use of the budget surplus. As a presidential candidate in 2000, George W. Bush pledged to use the surplus to guarantee Social Security into the new century, provide additional medical benefits to seniors, and reduce income taxes.

However, the surplus was short-lived. The end of the stock market boom, an economic slowdown, and a new federal income tax cut reduced federal revenues. The terrorist attacks of September 11, 2001, dealt a double blow to the federal budget by disrupting the economy and imposing a new set of defense costs.

In response, the federal government returned to deficit spending. The federal budget continued to show a large deficit for the next several years, due in part to counterterrorism efforts and the very costly wars in Afghanistan and Iraq. In fiscal year 2008 alone, the President's funding requests for the war on terrorism approached $200 billion.

The long-term outlook for the federal budget is uncertain. Funding for stimulus projects and new healthcare initiatives may cause long-term spending to increase. Social Security and Medicare are projected to rise sharply in the next 30 years as large numbers of baby boomers leave the job market and retire. Balancing the budget is expected to become even more difficult.

✅ **CHECKPOINT** *What factors contributed to the deficit spending of the 2000s?*

Essential Questions Journal

To continue to build a response to the Essential Question, go to your **Essential Questions Journal**.

SECTION 3 ASSESSMENT

🔖 Guiding Question

1. Use your completed cause-and-effect chart to answer this question: What are the effects of budget deficits and national debt?

2. **Extension** Look at a credit card statement. Notice how finance charges add to the original purchase expenses. If one does not pay the full amount owed, there are additional interest charges. There are also transaction, over-limit, and late fees. Even without additional purchases, the amount owed continues to grow—until the debt is paid in full. How does this compare to the way increased federal deficits add to the national debt?

Key Terms and Main Ideas

3. What causes a **budget surplus**?

4. How does a **Treasury note** differ from a **Treasury bill**?

5. How might a **budget deficit** be related to the **national debt**?

6. Explain the **crowding-out effect** that results from national debt.

Critical Thinking

7. **Evaluate (a)** Why does the federal government usually not create new money to cover a budget deficit? **(b)** Do you think this is sound reasoning? Explain why or why not.

8. **Rank (a)** What are three possible problems with having a national debt? **(b)** Which problem do you see as most serious? Explain.

9. **Predict (a)** Why did the federal budget show a large deficit for several years following 2001? **(b)** What federal spending is projected to increase greatly during the coming years, and why? **(c)** How could lowering income taxes during an economic downturn lead to increased national debt?

Math Skills

10. **Relating Graphs to Events** Use the data in **Figure 15.8** to determine the approximate size of the largest budget deficits in each of the following decades: **(a)** 1950s, **(b)** 1970s, **(c)** 1990s, **(d)** 2000s.

Visit PearsonSchool.com/PHecon for additional math help.

Chapter 15: Fiscal Policy

 Section 2 What economic ideas have shaped fiscal policy?

 Section 1 What are the goals and limits of fiscal policy?

Section 3 What are the effects of budget deficits and national debt?

Essential Question, Chapter 15
How effective is fiscal policy as an economic tool?

Effects of Expansionary Fiscal Policy

To expand the economy, the government buys more goods and services.

⬇

Companies that sell goods to the government earn profits, which they use to pay their workers and investors more and to hire new workers.

⬇

Workers and investors have more money and spend more in shops and restaurants.

⬇

Shops and restaurants buy more goods and hire more workers to meet their needs.

⬇

In the short term, government spending leads to more jobs and more output.

Economic Dictionary

fiscal policy, *p. 392*

federal budget, *p. 392*

fiscal year, *p. 392*

appropriations bill, *p. 394*

expansionary policy, *p. 395*

contractionary policy, *p. 395*

classical economics, *p. 399*

productive capacity, *p. 400*

demand-side economics, *p. 400*

Keynesian economics, *p. 401*

multiplier effect, *p. 401*

automatic stabilizer, *p. 404*

supply-side economics, *p. 404*

budget surplus, *p. 408*

budget deficit, *p. 408*

Treasury bill, *p. 409*

Treasury note, *p. 409*

Treasury bond, *p. 409*

national debt, *p. 410*

crowding-out effect, *p. 411*

Economics *on the go*

Study anytime, anywhere. Download these files today.

Economic Dictionary (online)
Vocabulary Support in English and Spanish

Audio Review (online)
Audio Study Guide in English and Spanish

Action Graph (online)
Animated Charts and Graphs

Visual Glossary (online)
Animated feature

How the Economy Works (online)
Animated feature

Download to your computer or mobile device at PearsonSchool.com/PHecon

Key Terms and Main Ideas

To make sure you understand the key terms and main ideas of this chapter, review the Checkpoint and Section Assessment questions and look at the Quick Study Guide on the preceding page.

Critical Thinking

1. **Compare (a)** Describe the fundamental differences between classical economics and Keynesian economics. **(b)** Keynes suggested that building pyramids was good for the economy of ancient Egypt. Why would Keynes have suggested this? **(c)** Provide a similar example in our society for the building of the pyramids. Explain your answer.

2. **Main Ideas (a)** Make a list of ways in which government fiscal policy affects your daily life. **(b)** Which aspects of fiscal policy have the greatest effect on you? Explain.

3. **Infer (a)** How do automatic stabilizers affect our economy? **(b)** What would our economy be like without them?

4. **Analyze (a)** In your own words, describe the crowding-out effect. **(b)** Explain how it can influence economic growth over the long term.

5. **Evaluate (a)** What are the benefits and drawbacks of a balanced budget amendment? **(b)** Would you support such an amendment? Explain why or why not?

6. **Main Ideas (a)** How is the federal budget a tool of fiscal policy? **(b)** How effective has this tool been in promoting full employment and economic growth?

Applying Your Math Skills

Comparing Circle Graphs

The two pie graphs below show categories of federal spending in the national budgets for 2000 and 2007. Look at the graphs and answer the questions that follow.

Visit PearsonSchool.com/PHecon for additional math help.

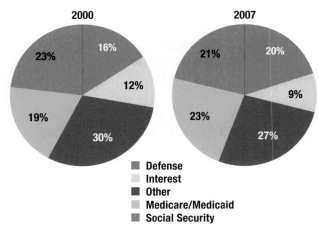

Federal Spending, 2000 and 2007

2000: 16%, 23%, 12%, 19%, 30%

2007: 20%, 21%, 9%, 23%, 27%

- ■ Defense
- ■ Interest
- ■ Other
- ■ Medicare/Medicaid
- ■ Social Security

SOURCE: U.S. Senate and U.S. House Budget Offices

7. How did the percentage of federal spending on interest payments change between 2000 and 2007?

8. Which categories of federal spending have seen the same percentage increase since 2000?

9. **(a)** How have Social Security outlays changed as a percentage of the federal budget? **(b)** Do you think this pattern will continue? Explain why or why not.

? Essential Question Activity

Essential Questions Journal — To respond to the chapter Essential Question, go to your **Essential Questions Journal**.

10. Complete this activity to answer the Essential Question **How effective is fiscal policy as an economic tool?** Work in small groups, with each group researching the administrations of John F. Kennedy to the current President. Using the worksheet in your Essential Questions Journal or the electronic worksheet available at **PearsonSchool.com/PHecon,** gather the following information:
    (a) Identify the President by political party and years in office.
    (b) Identify the main economic goals and challenges under that administration.
    (c) Describe any tax and spending changes that grew out of the administration's fiscal policy.
    (d) Evaluate how successful that administration was at meeting its goals.

11. **Modify** After your group has filled out its worksheet, make enough copies to distribute to the other groups in the class.
    (a) Each group will take the worksheets and evaluate which President they think had the most successful fiscal policy. Place the sheets in order from most effective to least effective.
    (b) The class will share and compare their conclusions.
    (c) As a class, make a generalization about the use of fiscal policy by Presidents since 1960 to stabilize economic conditions, stimulate growth, or cool down an overheated economy.

DOCUMENT-BASED ASSESSMENT

Is the national debt a threat to the country?

Many economists blame the huge U.S. national debt for many economic problems, including high interest rates, unemployment, and trade deficits. However, some economists believe that the problems of the national debt are exaggerated.

Document A

Interest on the National Debt

Fiscal Year	Percentage of Federal Outlays for Interest on Debt	Fiscal Year	Percentage of Federal Outlays for Interest on Debt
1990	14.7	2000	12.5
1992	14.4	2002	8.5
1994	13.9	2004	7.0
1996	15.4	2006	8.5
1998	14.6	2008	8.3
		2010*	9.1

*Estimated

Document B

"Within 12 years . . . the largest item in the federal budget will be interest payments on the national debt," says former U.S. Comptroller General David Walker. "[They are] payments for which we get nothing."

Economic forecasters say future generations of Americans could have a substantially lower standard of living than their predecessors' for the first time in the country's history if the debt is not brought under control.

Government debt, which fuels the risk of inflation, could make everyday Americans' savings worth less. Higher interest rates would make it harder for consumers and businesses to borrow. Wages would remain stagnant and fewer jobs would be created. The government's ability to cut taxes or provide a safety net would also be weakened, economists say.

—"Drowning in Debt: What the Nation's Budget Woes Mean for You," Devin Dwyer, abcnews.go.com

Document C

Now and Later

Spend now, while the economy remains depressed; save later, once it has recovered. How hard is that to understand?

Very hard, if the current state of political debate is any indication. All around the world, politicians seem determined to do the reverse. They're eager to shortchange the economy when it needs help, even as they balk at dealing with long-run budget problems.... Penny-pinching at a time like this isn't just cruel; it endangers the nation's future. And it doesn't even do much to reduce our future debt burden, because stinting on spending now threatens the economic recovery, and with it the hope for rising revenues.

—"Now and Later" by Paul Krugman from *The New York Times*, June 20, 2010

 LA.1112.1.6.2

ANALYZING DOCUMENTS

Use your knowledge of the national debt and Documents A, B, and C to answer Questions 1–3.

1. **According to Document A, the percentage of the federal budget devoted to paying interest on the national debt**

   A. has risen steadily since 1990.
   B. has fallen steadily since 1990.
   C. has fluctuated wildly from year to year.
   D. began to rise again after reduction.

2. **According to Document B, the large national debt could lead to**

   A. a lower standard of living.
   B. more tax cuts.
   C. increased investment.
   D. lower interest rates.

3. **In Document C, Paul Krugman argues that spending now**

   A. is cruel and dangerous.
   B. will stimulate the economy.
   C. might hurt the hope for rising revenues.
   D. threatens economic recovery.

WRITING ABOUT ECONOMICS

The ever-growing national debt causes much debate during budget preparation each fiscal year. Use the documents on this page and resources on the Web site below to answer this question: **Is the national debt a threat to the country?** Use the sources to support your opinion.

16 The Federal Reserve and Monetary Policy

Essential Question, Chapter 16

How effective is monetary policy as an economic tool?

FL **Next Generation Sunshine State Standards**

Section 1: The Federal Reserve System
LA.1112.1.6, SS.912.E.1.13, SS.912.E.2.10

Section 2: Federal Reserve Functions
LA.1112.1.6, SS.912.E.1.11, SS.912.E.1.13, SS.912.E.2.10

Section 3: Monetary Policy Tools
LA.1112.1.6, MA.912.F.3, SS.912.E.1.11, SS.912.E.1.13

Section 4: Monetary Policy and Macroeconomic Stabilization
LA.1112.1.6, SS.912.E.1.11, SS.912.E.1.12, SS.912.E.2.1, SS.912.E.2.3, SS.912.E.3.6

Economics
on the go

To study anywhere, anytime, download these
online resources at *PearsonSchool.com/PHecon* ▶

FL **NGSSS**

LA.1112.1.6 Use multiple strategies to develop vocabulary.

SS.912.E.1.13 Describe the composition of the money supply.

SS.912.E.2.10 Describe the organization and functions of the Federal Reserve System.

ECONOMIC DICTIONARY

As you read the section, look for the definitions of these **Key Terms:**

• monetary policy
• reserves
• reserve requirements

Guiding Question

How is the Federal Reserve System organized?

Copy this concept web and fill it in as you read.

▶ **Economics and You**   It's Saturday night, and you've gone out to a movie with friends. Now everyone wants to eat, but you realize that you have only a dollar and some change left. What can you do? If you have access to an ATM, you could get cash out of your bank account. Here's a crazy thought—what if your bank runs out of money? What can *it* do?

Principles in Action As you'll see in this section, when American banks need emergency cash, they turn to the Federal Reserve System for a loan. The Federal Reserve System is organized to provide this and a host of essential services to banks, to the federal government, and, most importantly, to the national economy.

Banking History

The Federal Reserve in American History

The Federal Reserve System, as you read in Chapter 10, is the central bank of the United States. It has many important tasks, but the most prominent one is to act as the main spokesperson for the country's monetary policy. **Monetary policy** refers to the actions that the Fed takes to influence the level of real GDP and the rate of inflation in the economy.

The role of a central bank in the U.S. economy has been hotly debated since 1790, when Federalists lined up in favor of establishing a central bank. The first Bank of the United States issued a single currency. It also reviewed banking practices and helped the federal government carry out

monetary policy the actions that the Federal Reserve System takes to influence the level of real GDP and the rate of inflation in the economy

Visual Glossary
(online)

Go to the Visual Glossary Online for an interactive review of **monetary policy.**

Action Graph
(online)

Go to Action Graph Online for animated versions of key charts and graphs.

How the Economy Works
(online)

Go to How the Economy Works Online for an interactive lesson on **making monetary policy.**

Reviewing Key Terms
To understand *monetary policy*, review these terms.

central bank, *p. 260*
interest, *p. 268*
real GDP, *p. 310*
inflation, *p. 342*
fiscal policy, *p. 392*

What is Monetary Policy?

To achieve its mission of stabilizing the U.S. economy, the Federal Reserve board uses a variety of tools.

- The Fed can encourage money creation by making it cheaper for banks to borrow.
- The Fed can raise and lower reserve requirements and raise and lower the discount rate.
- Open market operations, the buying and selling of government securities, is the most used monetary policy tool.

◄ **monetary policy** the actions that the Fed takes to influence the level of real GDP and the rate of inflation in the economy

◄ Fed chair Ben Bernanke uses one of his important tools to stabilize the economy. ***What action does the cartoonist suggest Bernanke is about to take?***

Visual Glossary
online

To expand your understanding of this and other key economic terms, visit **PearsonSchool.com/PHecon**

its duties and powers. Partly because of the impassioned debate over state versus federal powers, however, the first Bank lasted only until 1811. At that time, Congress refused to extend its charter.

Congress established the Second Bank of the United States in 1816 to restore order to the monetary system. However, many people still feared that a central bank placed too much power in the hands of the federal government. Political opposition toppled the Second Bank in 1836 when its charter expired.

A period of confusion followed. States chartered some banks, while the federal government chartered and regulated others. Banks had to keep a certain amount of reserves on hand. **Reserves** are deposits that a bank keeps readily available as opposed to lending them out. **Reserve requirements**—the amount of reserves that banks are required to keep on hand—were difficult to enforce, and the nation experienced several serious bank runs. The Panic of 1907 finally convinced Congress to act.

The nation's banking system needed to address two issues. First, consumers and businesses needed greater access to funds to encourage business expansion. Second, banks needed a source of emergency cash to prevent depositor panics that resulted in bank runs.

✔ **CHECKPOINT** *Why did some Americans oppose establishing a central bank?*

Federal Reserve Act of 1913

Attempting to solve these problems, Congress passed the Federal Reserve Act in 1913. The resulting Federal Reserve System, now often referred to simply as "the Fed," consisted of a group of 12 independent regional banks. These banks could lend to other banks in times of need.

Continued Need for Reform

The Great Depression was exactly the situation Congress had hoped to avoid by creating the Federal Reserve System. The system did not work well, however, because the regional banks each acted independently. Their separate actions often canceled one another out.

For example, in 1929 and 1930, the Governors of the Federal Reserve Banks of New York and Chicago wanted the Fed to lower interest rates. Many of the assets used to make business loans had lost value as a result of the stock market crash. Lower interest rates would make more money available to banks. However, the Federal Reserve Board of Governors was against lowering interest rates. Concerned about the growth of the stock market, the board favored a contractionary monetary policy. They also restrained the New York board from taking strong action. Many economists believe that the failure of the Fed to act contributed to the deepening of the financial crisis.

A Stronger Fed

In 1935, Congress adjusted the Federal Reserve's structure so that the system could respond more effectively to future crises. These reforms created the Federal Reserve System as we know it today. The new Fed enjoyed more centralized power so that the regional banks were able to act consistently with one another while still representing their own districts' banking concerns. One example shows how the new Fed helped fight a Depression-era crisis in a small Minnesota town. Picture this scene:

Outside the bank, a large crowd was growing frantic. A large number of withdrawals had badly depleted the bank's supply of cash. Inside the bank, a worried banker phoned the Federal Reserve Bank in Minneapolis—200 miles away—and begged the Fed to send him money. Fed officers snapped into action. They hired an airplane and packed a half million dollars into satchels.

❝ Upon approaching the town the pilot guided the plane low over the main street to dramatize its arrival and then landed in a nearby field. From there the Fed officials were ceremoniously escorted into town by the police and the money was stacked along the bank's teller windows. The sight of all that money piled up inside the bank quelled the customers' fears and saved the bank from failing. ❞

—"Born of a Panic: Forming the Federal Reserve System"
Federal Reserve Board, Minneapolis

✔ **CHECKPOINT** *Why did the Fed fail to prevent the financial crises that led to the Great Depression?*

reserves deposits that a bank keeps readily available as opposed to lending them out

reserve requirements the amount of reserves that banks are required to keep on hand

Structure of the Federal Reserve

The Federal Reserve System is privately owned by the member banks themselves. But it is publicly controlled by the federal government. Like so many American institutions, the structure of the Federal Reserve System represents compromises between centralized power and regional powers. **Figure 16.1** illustrates that structure.

The Board of Governors

The Federal Reserve System is overseen by the Board of Governors of the Federal Reserve. The Board of Governors is headquartered in Washington, D.C. Its seven governors, or members, are appointed for staggered 14-year terms by the President of the United States with the advice and consent of the Senate. The terms are staggered to prevent any one President from appointing a full Board of Governors and to protect board members from day-to-day political pressures. Members cannot be reappointed after serving a full term. Geographical restrictions on these appointments ensure that no one district is overrepresented.

The President also appoints the chair of the Board of Governors from among these seven members. The Senate confirms the appointment. Chairs serve four-year terms, which can be renewed.

Recent chairs of the Fed have been economists from the business world, the academic world, or government. They have a keen sensitivity toward public opinion and an ability to use the media to affect public opinion. Alan Greenspan, a former head of an economics consulting firm and chair of the President's Council of Economic Advisers (CEA), has been the most notable chair of the Fed in modern times. He took office in 1987 and served both Republican and Democratic administrations. After Greenspan resigned in 2006, President George W. Bush replaced him with Ben Bernanke, the head of the Council of Economic Advisers and a former professor of economics. Bernanke learned about monetary policy and Milton Friedman as a graduate student. He spent much of his career as an economist researching the Great Depression. His own writings on the topic focused on how to keep financial crises from getting out of control.

Twelve Federal Reserve Banks

The Federal Reserve Act divided the United States into 12 Federal Reserve Districts, as shown in **Figure 16.2**. One Federal Reserve Bank is located in each district. Each of these Banks monitors and reports on economic and banking conditions in its district.

Each Federal Reserve District is made up of more than one state. The Federal Reserve Act aimed to establish a system in which no one region could exploit the central bank's power at another region's expense.

Congress regulates the makeup of each Reserve Bank's board of nine directors to make sure that it represents many interests. The nine directors consist of three sets of three persons each. The first set of three represents commercial banks, and they are elected by the district's member banks.

Figure 16.1	Structure of the Federal Reserve System

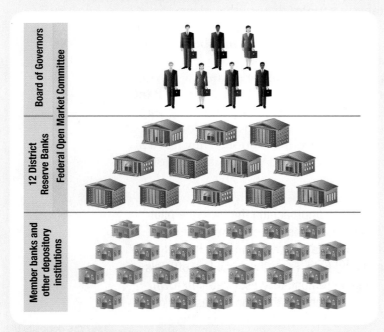

CHART SKILLS

More than 30 percent of all United States banks belong to the Federal Reserve System.

1. At which of the three levels of this Fed structure would a nationally chartered bank in your community fit?
2. How does the structure of the Fed reflect a compromise between centralized power and regional powers?

Figure 16.2

Federal Reserve Districts

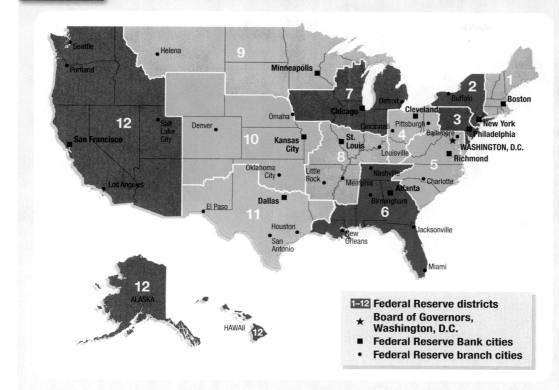

MAP SKILLS
Most Federal Reserve Districts contain a variety of agricultural, manufacturing, and service industries, as well as rural and urban areas.

1. Which are the largest and smallest of the Federal Reserve Districts? Name the Federal Reserve Bank cities in each of these districts.

2. How does the make-up of the Federal Reserve Districts help ensure that no single region is dominant?

1–12 Federal Reserve districts
★ Board of Governors, Washington, D.C.
■ Federal Reserve Bank cities
• Federal Reserve branch cities

The member banks also elect the second set—three people who represent the interests of groups such as industry, commerce, labor, services, and consumers. The third set of directors is appointed by the Board of Governors of the Federal Reserve. These three represent the same broad public interests as the second group. The Board of Governors then selects one of the nine directors to serve as chair of the Reserve Bank's board. Each board of directors appoints a president of the Reserve Bank, subject to approval by the Board of Governors.

Member Banks

All nationally chartered banks are required to join the Federal Reserve System. The remaining members are state-chartered banks that join voluntarily. Since 1980, all banks have equal access to Fed services, whether or not they are Fed members. These services include reserve loans to banks in need of short-term cash.

Each of the approximately 2,400 Fed member banks contributes a small amount of money to join the system. In return, it receives stock in the system. This stock earns the bank dividends from the Fed at a rate of up to 6 percent.

The fact that the banks themselves, rather than a government agency, own the Federal Reserve gives the system a high degree of political independence. This independence helps the Fed to make decisions that best suit the interests of the country as a whole.

The Federal Open Market Committee

The Federal Open Market Committee (FOMC) makes key monetary policy decisions about interest rates and the growth of the United States money supply. The committee meets about eight times a year in private to discuss the cost and availability of credit, for business and consumers, across the country. Announcements of the FOMC's decisions can affect financial markets and rates for home mortgages, as well as many economic institutions around the world. You will read more about the effects of monetary policy later in this chapter.

Members of the Federal Open Market Committee are drawn from the Board of

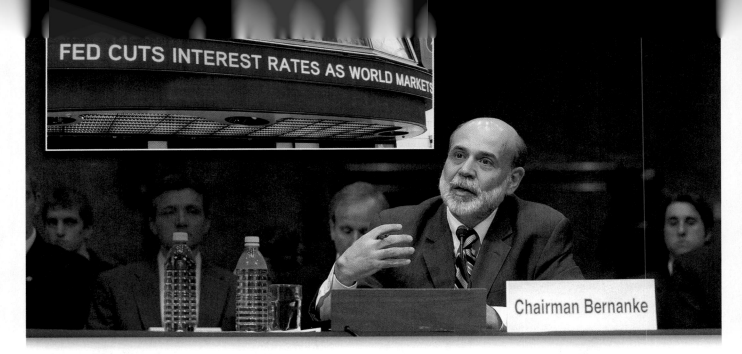

FED CUTS INTEREST RATES AS WORLD MARKETS

Chairman Bernanke

▲ Ben Bernanke testifies on the economy before a committee of Congress. *Why are both Congress and world markets interested in what he has to say?*

Governors and the 12 district banks. All seven members of the Board of Governors sit on the FOMC. Five of the 12 district bank presidents also sit on the committee. The president of the New York Federal Reserve Bank is a permanent member. The four other district presidents serve one-year terms on a rotating basis. The Board of Governors holds a majority of the seats on the FOMC, giving it effective control over the committee's actions.

After meeting with the FOMC, the chair of the Board of Governors announces the committee's decisions to the public. The Federal Reserve Banks and financial markets spring into action as they react to Fed decisions. In the next section, you will read about how the Fed's decisions are carried out and what functions the Federal Reserve serves.

☑ **CHECKPOINT** *What is the role of each of the 12 Federal Reserve banks?*

(FL) SS.912.E.2.10, LA.1112.2.2.2, LA.1112.2.2.3, LA.1112.1.6.1

Essential Questions Journal To continue to build a response to the Essential Question, go to your **Essential Questions Journal**.

SECTION 1 ASSESSMENT

❓ Guiding Question

1. Use your completed concept web to answer this question: How is the Federal Reserve System organized?

2. **Extension** Since you do not deal directly with the Federal Reserve, why should you care how it operates?

Key Terms and Main Ideas

3. What are **reserves** held by banks?

4. What **reserve requirements** do banks have?

5. What is **monetary policy**?

Critical Thinking

6. **Summarize (a)** What three responsibilities did the first Bank of the United States have? **(b)** Why did the bank not last?

7. **Infer (a)** Which type of bank is required to belong to the Federal Reserve System? Which can join voluntarily? **(b)** Why do you think that the Federal Reserve has both a public and a private character?

8. **Evaluate (a)** Describe the two issues that the Panic of 1907 forced the nation's banking system to address. **(b)** Why do you think it took so long for the nation to establish a central banking authority?

9. **Conclude (a)** What is the role of the Federal Open Market Committee (FOMC)? **(b)** Why do you think the FOMC is drawn from so many different sectors of the Federal Reserve Board?

10. **Compare (a)** Who replaced Alan Greenspan as chair of the Federal Reserve Bank in 2006? **(b)** What did the two men have in common?

Quick Write

11. Locate a newspaper editorial on a topic relating to economics, and look for the author's point of view. First, identify the author or news service. Then, provide words that indicate the point of view. Finally, describe the point the author is trying to make in the article and what conclusion you reach as to whether you agree with it.

FL **NGSSS**

LA.1112.1.6 Use multiple strategies to develop vocabulary.

SS.912.E.1.11 Explain how the Federal Reserve uses monetary policy to promote economic growth.

SS.912.E.1.13 Explain the functions and characteristics of money.

SS.912.E.2.10 Describe the organization and functions of the Federal Reserve System.

ECONOMIC DICTIONARY

As you read the section, look for the definitions of these **Key Terms:**

• check clearing
• bank holding company
• federal funds rate
• discount rate

Guiding Question
What does the Federal Reserve do?

Copy this flowchart and fill it in as you read.

Functions of the Fed			
Serve Government	Serve Banks	Regulate Banks	Regulate Money Supply
•	•	•	•
•	•	•	•
•	•	•	•

▶ **Economics and You** Your summer job is going great—you like the work and it pays well. The trouble is, the paychecks are handed out just once a month and you desperately need that first paycheck. Finally the end of the month arrives and you rush to your bank to cash your paycheck. But the bank teller has an unpleasant surprise for you. The bank will not credit the amount to your account until the paycheck clears. It will take at least two days, the teller says, for the check-clearing process to be completed.

Principles in Action The teller doesn't explain—probably because he or she doesn't know—that most check-clearing functions in the United States are handled through the Federal Reserve. In addition to your check, the Fed will process another 18 billion checks this year. What else does the Fed do? One function, as you will read in the Economics & You feature, is to issue money. In fact, you may have a bill now that says "Federal Reserve Note." This and the many other responsibilities of the Fed are the subject of this section.

Serving Government

As the central bank of the United States, the 12 district banks that make up the core of the Federal Reserve System carry out several important functions. Among the most important of these functions is to provide banking and fiscal services to the federal government.

The United States government pays out about $1.2 trillion each year to support such social insurance programs as Medicare, Social Security, and veterans benefits. To handle its banking needs when dealing with such enormous sums, the federal government turns to the Federal Reserve.

Banker and Agent
The Federal Reserve serves as banker for the United States government. It maintains a checking account for the Treasury Department that it uses to process Social Security checks, income tax refunds, and other government payments. For example, if you receive a check from the federal government and cash it at your local bank, it is the Federal Reserve that deducts the amount from the Treasury's account.

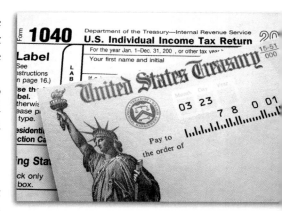

▲ The Federal Reserve is the banker for the U.S. government. Among its many functions, it processes social security checks and income tax refunds. *What are some of its other responsibilities?*

Figure 16.3 The Path of a Check

1. **Check writer**
2. **Recipient**
3. **Federal Reserve Bank**
4. **Check writer's bank**

GRAPH SKILLS

When you receive a check, you present it at a bank. The check is then sent to a Federal Reserve Bank, which collects the necessary funds from the bank of the person who wrote the check.

1. How long does it generally take for checks to clear?
2. In what other ways does the Fed serve banks?

The Federal Reserve also serves as a financial agent for the Treasury Department and other government agencies. The Fed sells, transfers, and redeems securities such as government bonds, bills, and notes. It also makes interest payments on these securities.

The Treasury Department auctions off government bills, bonds, and notes to finance the many programs of the U.S. government. Funds raised from these auctions are automatically deposited into the Federal Reserve Bank of New York.

Issuing Currency

Only the federal government can issue currency. The Treasury Department issues coins minted at the United States Mint. The district Federal Reserve Banks issue paper currency (Federal Reserve Notes). As bills become worn out or torn, the Fed takes them out of circulation and replaces them with fresh ones.

✔ **CHECKPOINT** *How does the Fed serve as the government's banker?*

check clearing the process by which banks record whose account gives up money and whose account receives money when a customer writes a check

bank holding company a company that owns more than one bank

Serving Banks

The Federal Reserve also provides services to banks throughout the nation. It clears checks, safeguards bank resources, and lends funds to help banks that need to borrow in order to maintain their legally required reserves.

Check Clearing

Figure 16.3 shows how checks "clear" within the Fed system. **Check clearing** is the process by which banks record whose account gives up money and whose account receives money when a customer writes a check. The Fed can clear millions of checks at any one time using high-speed equipment. Most checks clear within two days—a remarkable achievement when you consider that the Fed processes about 18 billion checks per year.

Supervising Lending Practices

To ensure stability, the Federal Reserve monitors bank reserves throughout the banking system. Each of the 12 Federal Reserve Banks sends out bank examiners to check up on lending and other financial activities of member banks. The Board of Governors also approves or disapproves proposed bank mergers.

The Board studies proposed bank mergers and bank holding company charters to ensure competition in the banking and financial industries. A **bank holding company** is a company that owns more than one bank. The Board of Governors approves or disapproves mergers and charters based on the findings and recommendations of the Reserve Banks.

The Federal Reserve also protects consumers by enforcing truth-in-lending laws, which require sellers to provide full and accurate information about loan terms. Under a provision called Regulation Z, consumers receive useful information about retail credit terms, automobile loans, and home mortgages.

Lender of Last Resort

Under normal circumstances, banks lend each other money on a day-to-day basis, using money from their reserve balances.

These funds are called federal funds. The interest rate that banks charge each other for these loans is the **federal funds rate.**

Banks also borrow from the Federal Reserve, especially in financial emergencies such as recessions. The Fed acts as a lender of last resort, making emergency loans to commercial banks so that they can maintain required reserves. The rate the Federal Reserve charges for these loans is called the **discount rate.** You will read more about the discount rate in Section 3.

An Expanded Role

As you read in Chapter 10, a serious financial crisis erupted in 2008. It began because many banks had made home loans that borrowers were unable to repay. As the crisis deepened, corporations and other borrowers could not obtain loans from banks, and the financial system ceased to function effectively.

The Federal Reserve responded to this crisis by changing the size and scope of its involvement in the economy. The Fed's total assets increased during 2008 from less than $1 trillion to over $2 trillion. Prior to the financial crisis, most of the Fed's assets consisted of government securities. To help the mortgage market through the financial crisis, the Fed bought mortgage-backed securities. In 2010, the Fed held over $1 trillion of these mortgage-backed securities.

✔ **CHECKPOINT** *How does the Fed protect consumers who take out bank loans?*

Regulating the Banking System

Banks, savings and other financial institutions are supervised by a number of state and federal authorities. The Fed coordinates all these regulatory activities.

Reserves

As you read in Chapter 10, United States banks operate under a fractional reserve system. Banks hold in reserve only a fraction of their funds—just enough to meet customers' daily needs. Banks then lend their remaining funds, charging interest to earn returns.

Each financial institution that holds deposits for customers must report daily to the Fed about its reserves and activities. The Fed uses these reserves to control how much money is in circulation.

Bank Examinations

The Federal Reserve and other regulatory agencies also examine banks periodically to insure that each institution is obeying laws and regulations. Examiners may make unexpected bank visits to ensure that banks are following sound lending practices.

Bank examiners can force banks to sell risky investments or to declare loans that will not be repaid as losses. If examiners find that a bank has taken excessive

federal funds rate the interest rate that banks charge each other for loans

discount rate the interest rate that the Federal Reserve charges commercial banks for loans

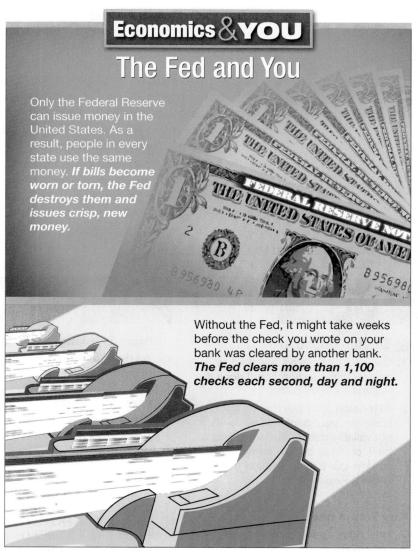

Economics & YOU
The Fed and You

Only the Federal Reserve can issue money in the United States. As a result, people in every state use the same money. *If bills become worn or torn, the Fed destroys them and issues crisp, new money.*

Without the Fed, it might take weeks before the check you wrote on your bank was cleared by another bank. *The Fed clears more than 1,100 checks each second, day and night.*

▲ Sometimes even two days to clear a check seems uncomfortably long. *What would happen to commerce and industry if it took all checks a month to clear?*

risks, they may classify that institution as a problem bank and force it to undergo more frequent examinations.

✅ **CHECKPOINT** *Why does the Federal Reserve examine banks?*

Regulating the Money Supply

The Federal Reserve is best known for its role in regulating the nation's money supply. You will recall from Chapter 10 that economists and the Fed watch several indicators of the money supply. M1 is simply a measure of the funds that are easily accessible or in circulation. M2 includes the funds counted in M1 as well as money market accounts and savings instruments. The Fed compares various measures of the money supply with the likely demand for money.

The Demand for Money

People and firms need to have a certain amount of cash on hand to make economic transactions—to buy groceries, supplies, clothing, and so forth. The more of your wealth you hold as money, the easier it will be to make economic transactions.

Of course, we can't earn interest on money that we hold as cash. As interest rates rise, it becomes more expensive to hold money as cash rather than placing it in assets that pay returns. So, as interest rates rise, people and firms will generally keep their wealth in assets such as bonds, stocks, or savings accounts.

The final factor that influences money demand is the general level of income. As GDP or real income rises, families and firms keep more of their wealth or income in cash.

Stabilizing the Economy

The laws of supply and demand affect money, just as they affect everything else in the economy. Too much money in the economy leads to inflation. In inflationary times, it takes more money to purchase the same goods and services. It is the Fed's job to keep the money supply stable.

Ideally, if real GDP grew smoothly and the economy stayed at full employment, the Fed would increase the money supply just to match the growth in the demand for money, thus keeping inflation low. As you read in Chapter 15, however, it is hard to predict economic effects. In the next section, you will read about the tools that the Fed can use to help the economy function at full employment without contributing to inflation.

✅ **CHECKPOINT** *What is the effect of too much money in circulation?*

FL LA.1112.2.2.2, SS.912.E.1.13, SS.912.E.1.11, SS.912.E.2.10, LA.1112.1.6.1

Essential Questions Journal
To continue to build a response to the Essential Question, go to your **Essential Questions Journal**.

SECTION 2 ASSESSMENT

🤔 Guiding Question

1. Use your completed flowchart to answer this question: What does the Federal Reserve do?
2. **Extension** Suppose that on a very busy day, your bank is running short of available cash. Why would your bank prefer to borrow from another commercial bank instead of from the Federal Reserve?

Key Terms and Main Ideas

3. How does **check clearing** work?
4. What is the difference between the **federal funds rate** and the **discount rate**?
5. What is a fractional reserve system?

Critical Thinking

6. **Analyze (a)** What is the purpose of auctions held by the Treasury? **(b)** What relationship does the Fed have with the Treasury Department?
7. **Evaluate (a)** How does the Federal Reserve protect consumers? **(b)** Should state governments take over this protection instead of the Federal Reserve?
8. **Evaluate (a)** What regulatory activities does the Fed coordinate? **(b)** Should the Fed closely oversee the banking industry or have the industry police itself?
9. **Infer (a)** How do the laws of supply and demand affect money? **(b)** Why can't the Fed automatically maintain full employment and low inflation?

Math Skills

10. **Calculating Incentives for Saving** How do interest rates determine the rate at which people keep their savings in bank deposits? **(a)** Which of the following interest rates would encourage savings rather than spending: 2 percent or 4 percent? Explain your answer. **(b)** How do savings of $500 at a 4 percent interest rate compare with savings of $1,000 at 2 percent? Explain how you calculated your answer.

Visit PearsonSchool.com/PHecon for additional math help.

FL NGSSS

LA.1112.1.6 Use multiple strategies to develop vocabulary.

MA.912.F.3 Describe the advantages and disadvantages of short- and long-term purchases.

SS.912.E.1.11 Explain how the Federal Reserve uses monetary policy to promote price stability.

SS.912.E.1.13 Describe the composition of the money supply.

ECONOMIC DICTIONARY

As you read the section, look for the definitions of these **Key Terms:**

- money creation
- required reserve ratio
- money multiplier formula
- excess reserves
- prime rate
- open market operations

Guiding Question

How does the Federal Reserve control the amount of money in use?

Copy this table and fill it in as you read.

Controlling the Money Supply		
Tools	**To increase it**	**To decrease it**
Reserve requirements		
Discount rate		
Open market operations		

▶ **Economics and You** Suppose you have a checkbook that allows you to write as many checks as you wish for any amount you desire. You don't need to worry about the balance in your account, and the checks will always be cashed, no matter how much you spend. Of course, no person has an account like that. However, the Federal Reserve, through its monetary policy tools, comes close.

Principles in Action The Federal Reserve has the power to create money. It also has the power to decrease the amount of money in the United States. The Fed controls the amount of money in use in order to stabilize the American economy. How does the Federal Reserve control the amount of money in use? You will read how in this section.

money creation the process by which money enters into circulation

Money Creation

The U.S. Department of the Treasury is responsible for manufacturing money in the form of currency. The Federal Reserve is responsible for putting money into circulation. How does this money get into the economy? The process is called **money creation,** and it is carried out by the Fed and by banks all around the country. Recall from Chapter 15 the multiplier effect of government spending. The multiplier effect in fiscal policy holds that every one dollar change in fiscal policy creates a change greater than one dollar in the economy. The process of money creation works in much the same way.

How Banks Create Money

Money creation does not mean the printing of new bills. Banks create money not by printing it, but by simply going about their business.

For example, suppose you take out a loan of $1,000. You decide to deposit the money in a checking account. Once you have deposited the money, you now have a balance of $1,000. Since demand deposit account balances, such as your checking account, are included in

▲ When you deposit money in the bank, you are not only increasing your net worth, you are also increasing the money supply of the United States. ***Explain how your deposit begins the process of money creation.***

Figure 16.4 **Money Creation**

CHART SKILLS
In this example of money creation, the money supply increases to $2,710 after four rounds.
1. In this example, what is the RRR?
2. Suppose Joshua deposited only $500 of Elaine's payment into his account. How much would the money supply increase then?

$1,000 + $900 + $810 = $2,710

You deposit $1,000 into your checking account.

Your $1,000 deposit minus $100 in reserves is loaned to Elaine, who gives it to Joshua.

Joshua's $900 deposit minus $90 in reserves is loaned to another customer.

At this point, the money supply has increased by $2,710.

$100 held in reserve
$900 available for loans

$90 held in reserve
$810 available for loans

Simulation *Activity*

Money and the Federal Reserve
You may be asked to participate in a role-playing game about Money and the Federal Reserve.

required reserve ratio
the fraction of deposits that banks are required to keep in reserve

money multiplier formula a formula (initial cash deposit × 1 ÷ RRR) used to determine how much new money can be created with each demand deposit and added to the money supply

M1, the money supply has now increased by $1,000. The process of money creation begins here.

Banks make money by charging interest on loans. Your bank will lend part of the $1,000 that you deposited. The maximum amount that a bank can lend is determined by the **required reserve ratio** (RRR)—the fraction of deposits that banks are required to keep in reserve. This is calculated as the ratio of reserves to deposits. The RRR, which is established by the Federal Reserve, ensures that banks will have enough funds to supply customers' withdrawal needs.

Suppose in our example that the RRR is 0.1, or 10 percent. This means that the bank is required to keep 10 percent of your $1,000 demand deposit balance, or $100, in reserve. It is allowed to lend $900.

Let's say the bank lends that $900 to Elaine, and she deposits it in her checking account. Elaine now has $900 she didn't have before. Elaine's $900 is now included in M1. You still have your $1,000 in your account, on which you can write a check at any time. Thus, your initial deposit to the bank, and the subsequent loan, have caused the money supply to increase by $1,000 + $900 for a total of $1,900.

Now suppose that Elaine uses the $900 to buy Joshua's old car. Joshua deposits the $900 from Elaine into his checking account. His bank keeps 10 percent of the deposit, or $90, as required reserves. It will lend the other $810 to its customers. So, Joshua has a demand deposit balance of $900, which is included in the money supply, and the new borrowers get $810, which is also added to the money supply. This means that the money supply has now increased by $1,000 + $900 + $810 = $2,710—all because of your initial $1,000 deposit. **Figure 16.4** shows how this increase came about.

The Money Multiplier

This money creation process will continue until the loan amount, and hence the amount of new money that can be created, becomes very small. To determine the total amount of new money that can be created and added to the money supply, economists use the **money multiplier formula**, which is calculated as 1 ÷ RRR. To apply the formula, they multiply the initial deposit by the money multiplier:

Increase in money supply =
initial cash deposit × 1/RRR

In our example the RRR is 0.1, so the money multiplier is $1 \div 0.1 = 10$. This means that the deposit of $1,000 can lead to a $10,000 increase in the money supply.

As of 2010 in the United States, banks had no reserve requirements on the first $10.7 million of demand deposits assets. They were required to hold 3 percent reserves on demand deposit assets between $10.7 and $55.2, and 10 percent on all demand deposit assets exceeding $55.2 million.

In the real world, however, people hold some cash outside of the banking system, meaning that some funds leak out of the money multiplier process. Also, banks sometimes hold **excess reserves**, which are reserves greater than the required amounts. These excess reserves ensure that banks will always be able to meet their customers' demands and the Fed's reserve requirements. The actual money multiplier effect in the United States is estimated to be between 2 and 3.

The Federal Reserve has three tools for adjusting the amount of money in the economy. These tools for creating money (or destroying it, if need be) are reserve requirements, the discount rate, and open market operations.

☑ **CHECKPOINT** *How do banks create money simply by going about their business making loans?*

Reserve Requirements

The simplest way for the Fed to adjust the amount of reserves in the banking system is to change the required reserve ratio. (See **Figure 16.5.**) The Fed's Board of Governors has sole responsibility over changes in reserve requirements. However, changing the reserve requirement is not the Fed's preferred tool.

A reduction of the RRR frees up reserves for banks, allowing them to make more loans. It also increases the money multiplier. Both effects will lead to a substantial expansion of the money supply.

The process also works in reverse. Even a slight increase in the RRR forces banks to hold more money in reserves. This causes a contraction in the money supply.

Although changing reserve requirements can be an effective means of changing the money supply, the Fed does not use this

tool often because it is disruptive to the banking system. Even a small increase in the RRR would force banks to call in significant numbers of loans, that is, to require the borrower to pay the entire outstanding balance of the loan. This may be difficult for the borrower. For this reason, the Fed rarely changes reserve requirements.

☑ **CHECKPOINT** *What effect would a reduction in the required reserve rate (RRR) have on banks?*

The Discount Rate

In the past, the Fed lowered or raised the discount rate to increase or decrease the money supply. Recall that the discount rate is the interest rate that the Federal Reserve charges on loans to financial institutions. Today, the discount rate is primarily used to ensure that sufficient funds are available in the economy. For example, during a financial crisis, there may not be enough funds available in the banking system to

excess reserves bank reserves greater than the amount required by the Federal Reserve

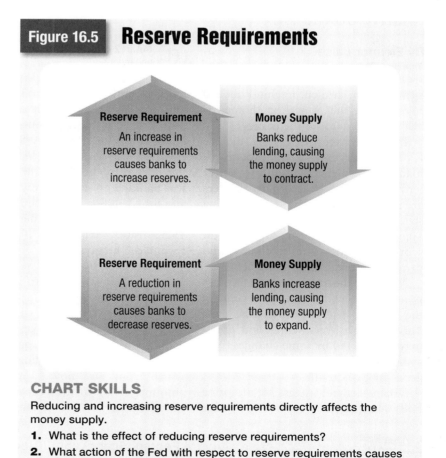

| Figure 16.5 | **Reserve Requirements** |

Reserve Requirement
An increase in reserve requirements causes banks to increase reserves.

Money Supply
Banks reduce lending, causing the money supply to contract.

Reserve Requirement
A reduction in reserve requirements causes banks to decrease reserves.

Money Supply
Banks increase lending, causing the money supply to expand.

CHART SKILLS
Reducing and increasing reserve requirements directly affects the money supply.
1. What is the effect of reducing reserve requirements?
2. What action of the Fed with respect to reserve requirements causes the money supply to decrease?

Auto Loans: Terms of Credit

SOURCES: Federal Reserve Release, Finance Companies

Car Loan? Not So Fast.

CREDIT

Lenders' stricter standards are making it tougher to drive off the lot.

By Eleanor Laise
The Wall Street Journal

 MA.912.F.3.2 Analyze credit scores and reports.

The credit crunch, having knocked around the American home, is now rolling into the garage.

Despite interest-rate cuts by the Federal Reserve, it's getting tough for many consumers to find attractive terms on auto loans. Many lenders are making fewer loans and instituting stricter standards on loans they do approve, often requiring higher credit scores, making smaller loans and demanding bigger down payments.

While "subprime" borrowers with poor credit will bear the brunt of the shifting lending standards, even "prime" borrowers with good credit may be affected by some changes. And some consumers may not be able to get a car loan at all.

When Michael Staggs, 36, of Spring Hill, Fla., set out to buy a Dodge truck recently, he was looking for an auto loan with an interest rate below 10% and monthly payments between $250 and $300. But Mr. Staggs, an engineer who says his credit isn't bad, but not great, didn't get the terms he was banking on. He put down $1,500, and his $14,000, 72-month loan came with $298 monthly payments and a 13.5% rate. "That's a lot higher than I wanted," he says.

Not all borrowers will see tougher terms; lenders still want to gain business from prime borrowers. But some borrowers may find they can't get as large a loan as they'd like. Whereas lenders in recent years have made loans substantially exceeding the car's worth, some are now keeping loan amounts closer to the vehicle's value. Jon Garcia, finance manager at a Toyota dealership in Janesville, Wis., says he's seeing subprime lenders supply only 85% to 90% of the car's book value, down from as much as 140% previously.

And these borrowers with good credit may find tougher loan terms if they live in areas where home prices are dropping. Chase Auto Finance is requiring more collateral on longer-term loans in "high risk" states like Arizona, California and Nevada, which have been hit hard by the housing crisis.

But terms are getting especially tough for subprime borrowers. Chase Auto Finance recently boosted by 10 points the credit score required of subprime customers borrowing more than 110% of the car's value. "We're trying to lend to people who will be able to pay us back," says Thomas Kelly, a Chase spokesman.

Applying Economic Principles
The credit crunch of 2008 made it tough for many consumers to get a car loan. What are some of the terms that car and truck buyers whose credit rating was not prime were forced to accept in order to get loans?

Video News Update Online
Powered by
The Wall Street Journal
Classroom Edition

Use videos at **PearsonSchool.com/PHecon** as a springboard for a discussion on a current topic.

provide the necessary loans to businesses and individuals. In that case, the ability of banks to borrow at the discount rate from the Federal Reserve provides an important safety net.

Today, to enact monetary policy, the Federal Reserve primarily adjusts the federal funds rate, which is the interest rate that banks charge one another for loans. It does not actually *set* a new federal funds rate, however. Instead, it decides on a "target" level for the rate and then takes steps to reach that target. These steps are part of the Fed's open market operations, which you will read about shortly.

The Fed does set the discount rate, and it keeps this rate above the federal funds rate. Banks usually choose to borrow from one another at the funds rate. Only if they need additional reserves will they turn to the Federal Reserve and borrow at the higher discount rate.

Changes in the federal funds rate and the discount rate affect the cost of borrowing to banks or other financial institutions. In turn, these changes in interest rates affect the prime rate. The **prime rate** is the rate of interest that banks charge on short-term loans to their best customers—usually large companies with good credit ratings. Ultimately, other interest rates follow, including the rates that banks pay on savings accounts and the rates that they charge for personal loans. The discount rate, federal funds rate, and prime rate are short-term rates. They determine the cost of borrowing money for a few hours, days, or months. Short-term rates have a limited impact on the long-term growth of the economy. To influence long-term interest rates, the Federal Reserve uses other tools.

✔ **CHECKPOINT** *What is the main tool that the Federal Reserve uses in order to adjust the money supply?*

Open Market Operations

Open market operations are the buying and selling of government securities in order to alter the supply of money. (See **Figure 16.6**.) Open market operations are by far the most important—and most often used—monetary policy tool.

Figure 16.6	**Open Market Operations**

Bonds Circulating
Through bond sales, the Fed removes reserves from the banking system.

Money Supply
Banks reduce lending, causing the money supply to contract.

Bonds Circulating
The Fed's purchase of bonds increases reserves in the banking system.

Money Supply
Banks increase lending, causing the money supply to expand.

CHART SKILLS
Open market operations are the most often used monetary policy tool.
1. When the Fed sells government securities to bond dealers, does that increase or decrease the amount of money in circulation?
2. How do open market operations differ from reserve requirements?

Bond Purchases

When the Federal Open Market Committee (FOMC) chooses to increase the money supply, it orders the trading desk at the Federal Reserve Bank of New York to purchase a certain quantity of government securities on the open market. The Federal Reserve Bank buys these securities with checks drawn on Federal Reserve funds. The bond sellers then deposit the money from the bond sales into their banks. As the Federal Reserve Board explains:

❝ [Now], the bank now has more reserves than it wants. So the bank can lend these unwanted reserves to another bank in the federal funds market. Thus, the Fed's open market purchase increases the supply of reserves to the banking system, and the federal funds rate falls. ❞
—"What Are Open Market Operations?"
Federal Reserve Bank of San Francisco

In this way, funds enter the banking system, setting in motion the money creation process described earlier.

Personal Finance
For more about the prime rate, see your Personal Finance Handbook in the back of the book or visit PearsonSchool.com/PHecon

prime rate the rate of interest that banks charge on short-term loans to their best customers

open market operations the buying and selling of government securities in order to alter the supply of money

Bond Sales

If the FOMC chooses to decrease the money supply, it must make an open market bond sale. In this case, the Fed sells government securities back to bond dealers, receiving from them checks drawn on their own banks. After the Fed processes these checks, the money is out of circulation. This operation reduces reserves in the banking system. In order to keep their reserves at the required levels, banks reduce their outstanding loans. The money multiplier process then works in reverse, resulting in a decline in the money supply that is greater than the value of the initial securities purchase.

Targets

To judge whether its open market operations are having the desired effect on the economy, the Fed periodically evaluates one or more economic targets. You have read about how the federal funds rate serves as the main target for interest rates. The Fed also keeps an eye on various money measures such as M1 and M2. Close analysis of these targets helps the Fed meet its goal of promoting a stable and prosperous economy.

✅ **CHECKPOINT** *What action does the Federal Open Market Committee take if it wants to decrease the money supply?*

Using Monetary Policy Tools

Open market operations are the most often used of the Federal Reserve's monetary policy tools. They can be conducted smoothly and on an ongoing basis to meet the Fed's goals. The Fed changes the discount rate less frequently. It usually follows a policy of keeping the discount rate in line with other interest rates in the economy in order to prevent excess borrowing by member banks from the Fed that might threaten economic stability.

Today, the Fed does not change reserve requirements to conduct monetary policy. Changing reserve requirements would force banks to make drastic changes in their plans. Open market operations or changes in the discount rate do not disrupt financial institutions.

In setting its monetary policy goals, the Federal Reserve keeps close touch on market forces, studying inflation and business cycles to determine its policy. As you just read, changes in the money supply affect interest rates. You will find out more about how this process works in the next section.

✅ **CHECKPOINT** *Why are open market operations the Fed's preferred monetary policy tool?*

 SS.912.E.1.11, SS.912.E.1.13, LA.1112.1.6.1, LA.1112.2.2.2, LA.1112.2.2.3

SECTION 3 ASSESSMENT

| **Essential Questions Journal** | To continue to build a response to the Essential Question, go to your **Essential Questions Journal.** |

❓ Guiding Question

1. Use your completed table to answer this question: How does the Federal Reserve control the amount of money in use?

2. **Extension** What method do you use to be sure you have cash for necessary expenditures such as transportation and lunch? Prepare a budget for the coming month. List your expected expenses and revenue. Be sure to allow reserves for unexpected expenses.

Key Terms and Main Ideas

3. What is **money creation**?

4. What is the **required reserve ratio**?

5. Describe the **money multiplier formula.**

6. Why do banks sometimes hold **excess reserves**?

7. If the discount rate rose, would you expect the **prime rate** to rise or fall? Why?

8. What are **open market operations**?

Critical Thinking

9. **Explain (a)** How do commercial banks make money? **(b)** How does the required reserve ratio affect the amount of money they can lend?

10. **Infer (a)** When the Fed cuts interest rates, what effect does it expect to have on business and consumers? **(b)** How is the Fed influenced by market forces in making rate decisions?

11. **Describe (a)** What are three tools the Fed has for adjusting the amount of money in the economy? **(b)** Choose one of the tools and describe it.

12. **Analyze** Why do the discount rate, federal funds rate, and prime rate have a limited impact on the long-term growth of the economy?

Math Skills

13. **Calculating Money Supply** Suppose the RRR is 0.15. **(a)** Use the money multiplier formula to determine by how much a $2,000 checking account deposit will increase the money supply. **(b)** Will the money supply actually increase by the amount you calculated? Why or why not?

Visit PearsonSchool.com/PHecon for additional math help.

FL) NGSSS

LA.1112.1.6 Use multiple strategies to develop vocabulary.

SS.912.E.1.11 Explain how the Federal Reserve uses monetary policy to promote economic growth.

SS.912.E.1.12 Examine the four phases of the business cycle.

SS.912.E.2.1 Identify and explain broad economic goals.

SS.912.E.2.3 Research the contributions of key individuals of various backgrounds in the development of the U.S.

SS.912.E.3.6 Draw conclusions about historical economic theories of economists.

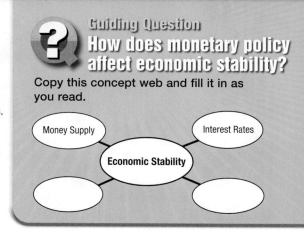

Guiding Question
How does monetary policy affect economic stability?
Copy this concept web and fill it in as you read.

Money Supply — Interest Rates — Economic Stability

Economics and You

Have you ever asked a parent for money—a raise in your allowance, perhaps, or cash to buy concert tickets? If so, you know that timing is everything. If, for example, your parent has just paid a huge bill for home or car repairs, you know that's the wrong time to be asking for spending money.

Principles in Action As you'll see in this section, timing is also critical to the Fed. Proper timing can support the Fed's efforts to bring economic stability. Bad timing can destroy it. In the How the Economy Works feature, you will see how the Fed copes with the many factors that can make its monetary policy succeed or fail.

How Monetary Policy Works

Some economists have great faith in monetary policy. These believers in **monetarism** believe that the money supply is the most important factor in macroeconomic performance—which as you have read is the functioning of the entire economy. How, then, does monetary policy influence macroeconomic performance?

Monetary policy alters the supply of money. The supply of money, in turn, affects interest rates. As you read earlier, interest rates affect the level of investment and spending in the economy.

The Money Supply and Interest Rates

It is easy to see the cost of money if you are borrowing it. The cost—the price that you as a borrower pay—is the interest rate. Even if you spend your own money, the interest rate still affects you because you are giving up interest by not saving or investing.

The market for money is like any other market. If the supply is higher, the price—the interest rate—is lower. If the supply is lower, the price—the interest rate—is higher. In other words, when the money supply is high, interest rates are low. When the money supply is low, interest rates are high.

Interest Rates and Spending

Recall from Chapter 12 that interest rates are important factors of spending in the economy. Lower interest rates encourage greater investment spending by business firms. This is because a firm's cost of borrowing—or of using

ECONOMIC DICTIONARY

As you read the section, look for the definitions of these **Key Terms**:
• monetarism
• easy money policy
• tight money policy
• inside lag
• outside lag

monetarism the belief that the money supply is the most important factor in macroeconomic performance

This bank advertises the cost of borrowing for mortgages. *How is the market for money like any other market?* ▼

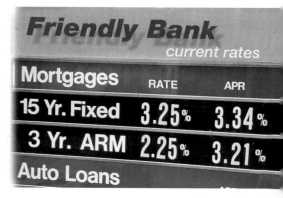

Friendly Bank
current rates

Mortgages	RATE	APR
15 Yr. Fixed	3.25%	3.34%
3 Yr. ARM	2.25%	3.21%
Auto Loans		

Milton Friedman

"Mr. Friedman...never held elected office but he has had more influence on economic policy as it is practiced around the world today than any other modern figure."—*Lawrence H. Summers, former Treasury Secretary*

As economic advisor to Presidents Nixon and Reagan, Milton Friedman argued that less government is better government. The policies he recommended have lowered income tax rates, helped control inflation, and decreased unemployment. His ideas are taught in most economics textbooks today.

But that was not always the case. For the first half of the twentieth century, the ideas of John Maynard Keynes dominated economic thought. Keynes believed government spending was the key to economic health, and government should emphasize fiscal policy in managing the economy.

In sharp contrast, Friedman argued that market forces must operate freely. In the view of Friedman and other monetarists, the government, through the Federal Reserve Board, must control the supply of money available to banks. Friedman argued that the most important power of the Fed is to grow or shrink the money supply by buying or selling government securities. The differences between supply siders such as Friedman and demand siders such as Keynes are one of the most important economic issues of our times.

Critical Thinking: *In what ways were the ideas of John Maynard Keynes at odds with those of Milton Friedman? Which economist do you think is right?*

Fast Facts

Milton Friedman
Born: 1912 in Brooklyn, NY
Died: 2006 in San Francisco, CA
Education: Ph.D., Columbia University, economics
Claim to Fame: Nobel Prize, Economic Science; Presidential Medal of Freedom

SS.912.E.2.3 Research the contributions of key individuals of various backgrounds in the development of the U.S.

its own funds—decreases as the interest rate decreases. Higher interest rates discourage business spending.

Firms find that lower interest rates give them more opportunities for profitable investment. If a firm has to pay 15 percent interest on its loans, it may find few profitable opportunities. If interest rates fall to 6 percent, however, the firm may find that some opportunities are now profitable.

If the macroeconomy is experiencing a contraction—declining income—the Federal Reserve may want to stimulate, or expand, it. The Fed will follow an **easy money policy.** That is, it will increase the money supply. An increased money supply will lower interest rates, thus encouraging investment spending. Such a policy may, however, encourage overborrowing and overinvestment, followed by layoffs and cutbacks.

If the economy is experiencing a rapid expansion that may cause high inflation, the Fed may introduce a **tight money policy.** That is, it will reduce the money supply. The Fed reduces the money supply to push interest rates upward. By raising interest rates, the Fed causes investment spending to decline. This brings real GDP down, too.

easy money policy a monetary policy that increases the money supply

tight money policy a monetary policy that reduces the money supply

Even though it can only alter the money supply, the Fed has a great impact on the economy. The money supply determines the interest rate, and the interest rate determines the level of aggregate demand. Recall from Chapter 12 that aggregate demand represents the relationship between price levels and quantity demanded in the overall economy. Thus, the level of aggregate demand helps determine the level of real GDP.

✔ CHECKPOINT *How are monetary policy, money supply, and interest rates connected?*

The Problem of Timing

Monetary policy, like fiscal policy, must be carefully timed if it is to help the macroeconomy. If policies are enacted at the wrong time, they could actually intensify the business cycle, rather than stabilize it. To see why, consider **Figure 16.7.**

Good Timing

Figure 16.7A shows the business cycle with a properly timed stabilization policy. The green curve, which shows greater fluctuations, is the business cycle as explained in Chapter 12. The goal of stabilization policy is to smooth out those fluctuations—in other words, to make the peaks a little bit lower and the troughs not quite so deep. This will minimize inflation in the peaks and the effects of recessions in the troughs. Properly timed stabilization policy smoothes out the business cycle, as shown by the red curve in **Figure 16.7A**.

Bad Timing

If stabilization policy is not timed properly, however, it can actually make the business cycle worse, not better. For example, suppose that policymakers are slow to recognize the contraction shown as the green line in **Figure 16.7B**. Perhaps because their data are inaccurate, government economists simply do not realize that a contraction is occurring until the economy is deeply into it. Some period of time may pass before they respond to the contraction.

Likewise, it takes time to enact expansionary policies and have those policies take effect. By the time this takes place, the economy may already be coming out of the recession on its own. If the expansionary

effects of an easy money policy boost the economy while it is already expanding, the result could be an even larger expansion that causes high inflation. If expansionary policies are enacted too late, the economy may have slowed down so much that businesses are reluctant to borrow at *any* rate for new investment.

As you can see, there are a couple of problems in the timing of macroeconomic policy. These are called policy lags.

Inside Lags

The **inside lag** is the time it takes to implement monetary policy. Such lags, or delays, occur for two reasons. First, it takes time to identify a problem. Although economists have developed sophisticated computer models for predicting economic trends, they still cannot know for sure that the economy is headed into a new phase of the business cycle until it is already there. Statistics may conflict, and it can take up to a year to recognize a serious economic downturn.

A second reason for inside lags is that once a problem has been recognized, it can take additional time to enact policies. This problem is more severe for fiscal policy than for monetary policy. Fiscal policy,

inside lag the time it takes to implement monetary policy

| Figure 16.7 | **Business Cycles and Stabilization Policy** |

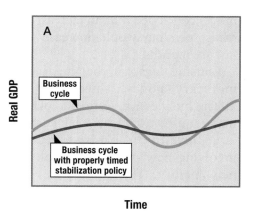

A

Real GDP

Business cycle

Business cycle with properly timed stabilization policy

Time

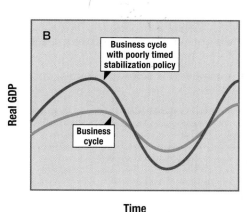

B

Real GDP

Business cycle with poorly timed stabilization policy

Business cycle

Time

GRAPH SKILLS

The timing of monetary policy measures can intensify the business cycle.

1. Which troughs are lower, business cycles with proper timing or ones with improper timing?

2. What are the effects of proper timing and improper timing?

Action Graph
online

For an animated version of this graph, visit PearsonSchool.com/PHecon

How does the Fed make monetary policy?

Monetary policy may be explained simply as the steps the Federal Reserve Board takes to control the business cycle and make sure that the economy remains prosperous and stable.

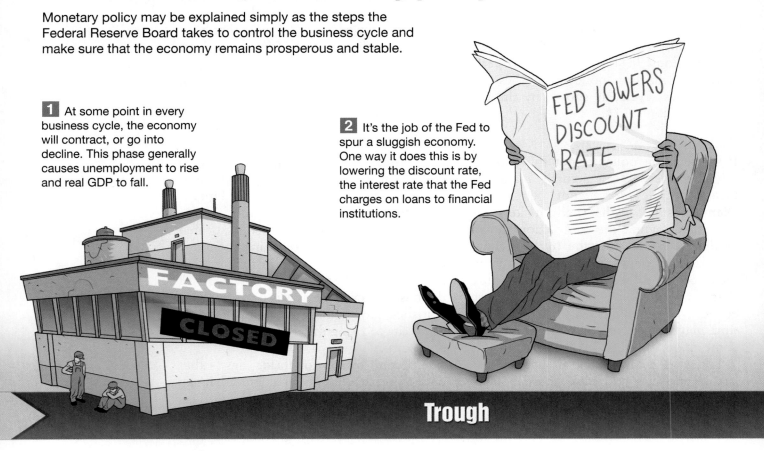

1 At some point in every business cycle, the economy will contract, or go into decline. This phase generally causes unemployment to rise and real GDP to fall.

2 It's the job of the Fed to spur a sluggish economy. One way it does this is by lowering the discount rate, the interest rate that the Fed charges on loans to financial institutions.

FED LOWERS DISCOUNT RATE

Trough

which includes changes in government spending and taxation, requires actions by Congress and the President. Since Congress must debate new plans and get the approval of the President, it takes time to get a new policy enacted.

The enactment of monetary policy, on the other hand, is streamlined. The Federal Open Market Committee meets eight times per year to discuss monetary policy—more often if necessary. Once it has decided that changes are called for, the FOMC can almost immediately enact policy through open market operations or discount rate changes.

Outside Lags

Once a new policy is determined, it takes time to become effective. This time period, known as the **outside lag,** also differs for monetary and fiscal policy. For fiscal policy, the outside lag lasts as long as is required

for new government spending or tax policies to take effect and begin to affect real GDP and the inflation rate. This time period can be relatively short, as with a tax rebate that returns government revenues to households eager for spending money. One statistical model concluded that an increase in government spending would increase GDP after just six months.

Outside lags can be much longer for monetary policy, since they primarily affect business investment plans. Firms may require months or even years to make large investment plans, especially those involving new physical capital, such as a new factory. Thus, a change in interest rates may not have its full effect on investment spending for several years. This conclusion is supported by several studies that suggest that more than two years may pass before the maximum impact of monetary policy is felt.

outside lag the time it takes for monetary policy to have an effect

4 Mortgage rates also drop, and people who previously could not afford to buy a home now can enter the market.

5 The economy now enters a period of prosperity and expansion. However, the Fed must be alert to the possibility that the economy may overheat. In that case, the Fed will have to consider whether to step in and tighten the money supply.

LOWER RATES BEHIND THE ECONOMIC EXPANSION

3 With a lower discount rate and federal funds rate, it is much cheaper for banks to borrow money. They are then able to lower their interest rates on loans. Companies can borrow money to finance their expansion plans.

FOR SALE

Check Your Understanding
1. How does a lower discount rate help move the economy into an expansionary period?
2. Who benefits from a lower discount rate? Who might be hurt by a lower discount rate?

Expansion

Peak

Given the longer inside lag for fiscal policy and the longer outside lag for monetary policy, it is difficult to know which policy has the shorter total lag. In practice, partisan politics and budgetary pressures often prevent the President and Congress from agreeing on fiscal policy. Because of the political difficulties of implementing fiscal policy, we rely to a greater extent on the Fed to use monetary policy to soften the business cycle.

✔ **CHECKPOINT** *What problem can result from expansionary monetary policy that takes effect after the economy has already emerged from recession?*

Predicting Business Cycles

The Federal Reserve must not only react to current trends. It must also anticipate changes in the economy. How should policymakers decide when to intervene in the economy?

Monetary Policy and Inflation

You have already read that expansionary policy, if enacted at the wrong time, may push an economy into high inflation, thus reducing any beneficial impact. This is the chief danger of using an easy money policy to get the economy out of a recession.

An inflationary economy can be tamed by a tight money policy, but the timing is again crucial. If the policy takes effect as the economy is already cooling off on its own, the tight money could turn a mild contraction into a full-blown recession.

The decision of whether to use monetary policy, then, must be based partly on our expectations of the business cycle. Some recessions are short-run phenomena that will, in the long run, disappear. Some inflationary peaks may also be expected to last for the short run and end in the long run. Given the timing problems of monetary policy, in some cases it may be wiser to allow the business cycle to correct itself rather than run the risk of an ill-timed policy change.

If a recession is expected to turn into an expansion in a short time, the best course of action may be to let the economy correct itself. On the other hand, if we expect a recession to last several years, then most economists would recommend an active policy. So the question is this: How long will a recessionary or inflationary period last?

How Quickly Does the Economy Self-Correct?

Economists disagree on the answer to this question. Their estimates for the U.S. economy range from two to six years. Since the economy may take quite a long time to recover on its own from an inflationary peak or a recessionary trough, there is time for policymakers to guide the economy back to stable levels of output and prices.

☑ **CHECKPOINT** *How would the Fed most likely respond if it predicted that a recession would soon turn into an expansion?*

Approaches to Monetary Policy

In practice, the lags discussed here make monetary and fiscal policy difficult to apply. Interventionist policy, a policy encouraging action, is likely to make the business cycle worse if the economy self-adjusts quickly. Laissez-faire economists who believe that the economy will self-adjust quickly will recommend against enacting new policies. Economists who believe that economies emerge slowly from recessions, however, will usually recommend enacting fiscal and monetary policies to move the process along.

The rate of adjustment may also vary over time, making policy decisions even more difficult. This debate over which approach to take with monetary policy will probably never be settled to the satisfaction of all economists.

☑ **CHECKPOINT** *How do the two approaches to monetary policy differ from each other?*

 SS.912.E.1.11, SS.912.E.1.12, LA.1112.1.6.1, LA.1112.2.2.2, LA.1112.6.2

Essential Questions Journal To continue to build a response to the Essential Question, go to your **Essential Questions Journal**.

SECTION **4** ASSESSMENT

❓ Guiding Question

1. Use your completed concept web to answer this question: How does monetary policy affect economic stability?

2. **Extension** Suppose you asked for an advance on your salary or allowance and were told that you would have to pay interest on it. Would you still want the advance? Would you want the interest to come out of future paychecks or be deducted up front from your advance? This kind of example is a part of your personal monetary policy.

Key Terms and Main Ideas

3. What is **monetarism**?

4. Why would the Federal Reserve enact an **easy money policy**?

5. Why would it enact a **tight money policy**?

6. What are **inside lags,** and why do they occur?

7. Why does monetary policy have such long **outside lags**?

Critical Thinking

8. **Explain** What is the relationship between aggregate demand and GDP?

9. **Evaluate (a)** Why do business cycles make monetary policy difficult to time? **(b)** What could happen if monetary policy is enacted at the wrong time?

10. **Compare and Contrast (a)** How are inside and outside lags similar? **(b)** How are they different?

Quick Write

11. With a partner, prepare a debate on monetary policy. One of you should write an argument for an interventionist approach, encouraging action. The other should write an argument for a laissez-faire approach, discouraging action. Use information from your textbook to help develop your argument.

Chapter 16: The Federal Reserve and Monetary Policy

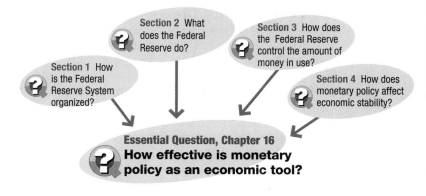

Section 1 How is the Federal Reserve System organized?

Section 2 What does the Federal Reserve do?

Section 3 How does the Federal Reserve control the amount of money in use?

Section 4 How does monetary policy affect economic stability?

Essential Question, Chapter 16
How effective is monetary policy as an economic tool?

Responsibilities of the Federal Reserve Board

Responsibilities That Serve Government	Maintain checking account for the Treasury Department
	Serve as financial agent for the Treasury Department
	Issue currency
Responsibilities That Serve the Banking System	Maintain check clearing system
	Monitor bank reserves
	Approve or disapprove proposed bank mergers
	Lend money to banks
Regulating Banks	Regulate the banking system
Regulating the Money Supply	Regulate the money supply to stabilize the economy
	Alter the discount rate
	Alter the federal funds rate
	Buy or sell government securities on the open market

Economic Dictionary

monetary policy, *p. 419*

reserves, *p. 421*

reserve requirements, *p. 421*

check clearing, *p. 426*

bank holding company, *p. 426*

federal funds rate, *p. 427*

discount rate, *p. 427*

money creation, *p. 429*

required reserve ratio, *p. 430*

money multiplier formula, *p. 430*

excess reserves, *p. 431*

prime rate, *p. 433*

open market operations, *p. 433*

monetarism, *p. 435*

easy money policy, *p. 436*

tight money policy, *p. 436*

inside lag, *p. 437*

outside lag, *p. 438*

Economics *on the go*

Study anytime, anywhere. Download these files today.

Economic Dictionary online	**Audio Review** online	**Action Graph** online	**Visual Glossary** online	**How the Economy Works** online
Vocabulary Support in English and Spanish	Audio Study Guide in English and Spanish	Animated Charts and Graphs	Animated feature	Animated feature

Download to your computer or mobile device at PearsonSchool.com/PHecon

Key Terms and Main Ideas

To make sure you understand the key terms and main ideas of this chapter, review the Checkpoint and Section Assessment questions and look at the Quick Study Guide on the preceding page.

Critical Thinking

1. **Conclude (a)** List three services the Federal Reserve offers banks and three regulations it places on banks. **(b)** Which service or regulation do you think is most important to the American banking system?

2. **Analyze (a)** Why are open market operations the most commonly used actions taken by the Fed? **(b)** What advantages do open market operations have over other monetary policy tools?

3. **Infer (a)** What effect would a reduction in the required reserve rate (RRR) have on banks? **(b)** What action of the Fed would cause a contraction of the money supply?

4. **Compare (a)** Describe the action of open market operations. **(b)** How do open market operations differ from other monetary policy tools?

5. **Analyze (a)** If the Federal Reserve Board were to implement an easy money policy, what actions would it take? **(b)** What would be the expected results of this policy? **(c)** What conditions could lead the Fed to take such actions?

Applying Your Math Skills

Calculating Money Creation

Pete received $3,000 from his grandparents as a graduation present to help him pay college tuition. He placed the money in Brighton Bank, whose reserve requirement ratio is 15 percent.

6. How much of Pete's deposit must Brighton Bank keep in reserve before it is able to lend money to someone else?

7. The bank loans the remaining amount to Sandra so that she can pay for extensive car repairs. How much does the bank lend Sandra?

8. Upon receiving Sandra's car repair payment, the repair shop deposits it in the Brighton Bank. How much of this money must the bank hold in reserve? How much can it lend to Roy?

9. What would be the total increase in the money supply based upon the initial cash deposit of $3,000 and the two loans?

Visit PearsonSchool.com/PHecon for additional math help.

 Essential Question Activity

Essential Questions Journal To respond to the chapter Essential Question, go to your **Essential Questions Journal**.

10. Complete this activity to answer the Essential Question **How effective is monetary policy as an economic tool?** Work in groups to gather information about the use of monetary policy to stimulate, downsize, or otherwise stabilize economies. Using the worksheet in your Essential Questions Journal or the electronic worksheet available at **PearsonSchool.com/PHecon,** gather the following information:
   (a) What steps did the United States take in order to prevent a recurrence of the Panic of 1907?
   (b) How did the Federal Reserve Board attempt to deal with the Great Depression? How successful was it?
   (c) How effective was the Federal Reserve Board in controlling the double-digit inflation of the late 1970s?
   (d) How did the Fed under Alan Greenspan attempt to steer the U.S. economy between recession and inflation? How effective was it?
   (e) What would happen to monetary policy if the United States abolished the Fed and returned to the gold standard?

11. **Modify** You are members of the Federal Reserve Board who have just heard the above reports prepared by your research committees. Based on this history of government attempts to use monetary policy to control the economy, what advice would you give the Chairman of the Board for his testimony next week before the Senate Finance Committee?
   (a) Decide which is more likely today, inflation or recession.
   (b) Describe the political pressures on the Fed in determining monetary policy.
   (c) Come up with a plan for Fed action in the next four quarters.
   (d) Describe the pitfalls the Fed faces in creating monetary policy.

FL LA.1112.1.6.2

Do bank mergers benefit or hurt the public?

Today, there are fewer than half as many banks in existence as there were 30 years ago. While bank mergers are profitable for bank shareholders, many worry that the trend might be less beneficial to consumers.

Document A

"Since 1988, there have been more than 13,500 applications for the formation, acquisition, or merger of bank holding companies or state-member banks reviewed by the Federal Reserve Board. Over this time, 25 of these applications have been denied, with eight of those failing to obtain Board approval involving unsatisfactory consumer protection and community needs issues. The low incidence of applications that have not received regulatory approval may be due to the fact that institutions seeking to expand their operations are typically in sound financial and managerial condition.... Maintaining robust and competitive banking markets is a critical objective in the Federal Reserve's review of banking applications."

—Sandra Braunstein, Federal Reserve Director of Consumer and Community Affairs, testimony before Congress, May 21, 2007

Document B

VIGELAND: "I remember back in the mid-90's there were a whole lot of bank takeovers and I wonder if there was any research done on whether consumers profit when a smaller bank is taken over by a bigger one."

D'ARISTA: "Well, they may profit in terms of convenience. The larger bank may have more branches and more ATMs and things of this sort. My concern at this point is concentration. It makes it a lot easier for a bank to set terms that are really at variance with the needs of a community when they are the only large or dominant institution in an area."

—Tess Vigeland and Jane D'Arista, "What Bank Mergers Mean For You," Marketplace Morning Report, January 18, 2008

Document C

"There's been a big bank merger, sir, so you now have a joint checking account with a Mr. Slavomir Bezparyadok of Zagreb."

SOURCE: www.cartoonstock.com

ANALYZING DOCUMENTS

Use your knowledge of opportunity costs and Documents A, B, and C to answer questions 1–3.

1. **Which of the following conclusions does Document A best support?**
   A. The Federal Reserve has significantly limited the number of bank mergers.
   B. Bank mergers generally do not affect the level of service customers receive.
   C. Bank mergers benefit banks but do not benefit local communities.
   D. The Federal Reserve has a definite set of standards for approving bank mergers.

2. **According to Document B, one major concern about bank mergers is the**
   A. increased possibility of fraud.
   B. reduced banking services.
   C. higher bank fees.
   D. possibility of monopoly.

3. **How would you describe the reaction of the bank customer in the cartoon?**
   A. Worried that the bank merger will affect the quality of the service he receives
   B. Confused because he does not know where Zagreb is
   C. Angry because he is opposed to bank mergers
   D. Upset that the bank has a new name

WRITING ABOUT ECONOMICS

People disagree about whether the Federal Reserve has done enough to control bank mergers. Use the documents on this page and on the Web site below to answer the question: ***Do bank mergers benefit or hurt the public?*** Use the sources to support your opinion.

In Partnership

THE WALL STREET JOURNAL.
CLASSROOM EDITION

To read more about issues related to this topic, visit
PearsonSchool.com/PHecon

Unit 6 Challenge

What is the proper role of government in the economy?

VIDEO
By Students For Students
For videos on Essential Questions,
go to *PearsonSchool.com/PHecon*

People have different opinions about what the government's role in the economy should be. Look at the opinions below, keeping in mind the Essential Question: What is the proper role of government in the economy?

"Government spending should be significantly reduced. It has grown far too quickly in recent years, and most of the new spending is for purposes other than homeland security and national defense. Combined with rising entitlement costs associated with the looming retirement of the baby-boom generation, America is heading in the wrong direction. To avoid becoming an uncompetitive European-style welfare state like France or Germany, the United States must adopt a responsible fiscal policy based on smaller government."

—Daniel J. Mitchell, "The Impact of Government Spending on Economic Growth"

"Global competition, rising health costs, longer life spans with weaker pensions, less secure employment, and unprecedented inequalities of opportunity and wealth are calling for a much broader, more inclusive approach to helping all of us meet these challenges, one that taps government as well as market solutions…. We can wield the tools of government to build a more just society, one that preserves individualist values while ensuring that the prosperity we generate is equitably shared."

—Jared Bernstein, *All Together Now: Common Sense for a Fair Economy*

WHAT DID YOU DO WITH ALL THE MONEY I GAVE YOU LAST YEAR?

INTERNAL REVENUE SERVICE

Essential Question Writing Activity

Consider the different views of economics expressed in the sources on this page and what you have learned about government and the economy. ***Then write a well-constructed essay expressing your view of the economic role of the government.***

Writing Guidelines

- Address all aspects of the Essential Question Writing Activity.
- Support the theme with relevant facts, examples, and details.
- Use a logical and clear plan of organization.
- Introduce the theme by establishing a framework that is beyond a simple restatement of the question and conclude with a summation of the theme.

For help in writing a Persuasive Essay, refer to the *Writer's Handbook* in the Reference section, page S-5.

Essential Questions Journal

To respond to the unit Essential Question, go to your **Essential Questions Journal**.

Chapter 17 International Trade

Chapter 18 Development and Globalization

Essential Question, Unit 7

How might scarcity divide our world or bring it together?

Chapter 18
Do the benefits of economic development outweigh the costs?

Chapter 17
Should free trade be encouraged?

17 International Trade

Essential Question, Chapter 17

Should free trade be encouraged?

FL **Next Generation Sunshine State Standards**

Section 1: Absolute and Comparative Advantage
LA.1112.1.6, SS.912.E.2.3, SS.912.E.3.2, SS.912.G.3.3

Section 2: Trade Barriers and Agreements
LA.1112.1.6, MA.912.A.2.2, SS.912.E.3.3, SS.912.E.3.3, SS.912.E.3.4, SS.912.E.3.5

Section 3: Measuring Trade
LA.1112.1.6, LA.1112.6.2, MA.912.A.2.2, SS.912.E.1.13, SS.912.E.3, SS.912.E.3.5

Economics
on the go

To study anywhere, anytime, download these online resources at *PearsonSchool.com/PHecon* ▶

NGSSS

LA.1112.1.6 Use multiple strategies to develop vocabulary.

SS.912.E.2.3 Research the contributions of key individuals of various backgrounds in the development of the U.S.

SS.912.E.3.2 Examine absolute and comparative advantage.

SS.912.G.3.3 Use geography to explain perspectives on renewable and non-renewable resources in the U.S.

ECONOMIC DICTIONARY

As you read the section, look for the definitions of these **Key Terms:**

- export
- import
- absolute advantage
- comparative advantage
- law of comparative advantage
- interdependence

Guiding Question
Why do nations trade?

Copy this cause-and-effect chart and fill it in as you read.

Resource Distribution	Absolute and Comparative Advantage	Trade
• Natural resources • Human and physical capital • Resources distributed unevenly	• • •	• Countries specialize in goods in which they have comparative advantage

▶ **Economics and You**   Have you used a computer or bought a pair of jeans lately? The chances are good that the computer and the jeans were made outside the United States. But why do Americans buy so many goods from overseas? Wouldn't it make a lot more sense for us to produce everything we need ourselves?

Principles in Action The answer to these questions lies in an economic idea you already know about: factors of production. By looking at two odd products—birdhouses and T-shirts—you can better understand why nations trade. You will also learn how one Japanese entrepreneur built a business empire by selling electronics in a worldwide market.

Resource Distribution and Specialization

As you read in Chapter 1, the resources that are used to make goods and services are called the factors of production. They include land (natural resources), labor, and capital (both physical and human).

Natural Resources

Natural resources, along with climate and geographic location, help determine what goods and services an economy produces. Fertile soil and a good growing climate allowed the central United States to develop an economy based on agriculture. Much of Southwest Asia—with scarce farmland and water, but large reserves of oil and natural gas—has an economy based on the extraction and sale of these resources.

Visual Glossary
online

Go to the Visual Glossary Online for an interactive review of **free trade.**

Action Graph
online

Go to Action Graph Online for animated versions of key charts and graphs.

How the Economy Works
online

Go to How the Economy Works Online for an interactive lesson on the **benefits of trade.**

Capital and Labor

Capital and labor also shape a region's economy. Physical capital includes the things that people make in order to produce final goods and services. Machinery, tractors, computers, and factories are examples of physical capital, as are the transportation and communication networks that allow the flow of goods and information. Capital also includes the money needed to invest in businesses and use natural resources.

Human capital differs from labor. Labor refers to the size of a nation's workforce. Human capital is the knowledge and skills a worker gains through education and experience. Every job requires human capital. A surgeon must learn anatomy and how to use a scalpel. A taxi driver must memorize the layout of a city's streets.

One way to measure a nation's human capital is to look at the general educational level of the populace. A country whose citizens have more schooling than those of another country has more human capital.

Unequal Resource Distribution

As **Figure 17.1** shows, the availability of resources differs greatly from one country to another. For example, the United Kingdom has less than one fifth the land area of Peru but nearly twice as many airports. This suggests that the United Kingdom has more available physical capital than Peru does.

A nation's ability to exploit, or use, its physical resources is affected by culture and history. For example, prolonged warfare may severely damage a nation's farms, forests, and transportation systems. History and culture affect human resources as well. In colonial America, a labor shortage led to the establishment of slavery. Today, a culture that bans education of women wastes much of its potential human capital.

Specialization and Trade

Unequal distribution of resources creates a need for specialization. (As you read in Chapter 2, specialization occurs when individuals, businesses, or nations produce only certain goods and services.) In the United

---

Figure 17.1 Resource Distribution

	India	Peru	United Kingdom	United States
Total area (sq km)	3,287,590	1,285,220	244,820	9,826,630
Arable land (%)	48.83	2.88	23.23	18.01
Natural resources	Coal, iron ore, manganese, mica, bauxite, titanium ore, chromite, natural gas, diamonds, petroleum, limestone, arable land	Copper, silver, gold, petroleum, timber, fish, iron ore, coal, phosphate, potash, hydropower, natural gas	Coal, petroleum, natural gas, iron ore, lead, zinc, gold, tin, limestone, salt, clay, chalk, gypsum, potash, silica sand, slate, arable land	Coal, copper, lead, molybdenum, phosphates, uranium, bauxite, gold, iron, mercury, nickel, potash, silver, tungsten, zinc, petroleum, natural gas, timber
Population	1.1 billion	28,674,757	60,776,238	301,139,947
Labor force	509.3 million	9.21 million	31.1 million	151.4 million
Literacy rate	61%	87.7%	99%	99%
Telephones	215.85 million	10.83 million	103.26 million	405 million
Airports	341	268	471	14,858

SOURCE: *CIA World Factbook*

CHART SKILLS

Like all countries, the countries shown on this table possess different natural, human, and physical resources.

1. Which resource on this list is most closely related to human capital?
2. Which nation has the most potential farmland? Which has the largest percentage of potential farmland?

States, we grow wheat, corn, and other crops for which we have suitable soil and climate conditions. However, we cannot grow large quantities of coffee or bananas.

When nations specialize in certain goods, they obtain the goods they do not or cannot produce through importing and exporting. An **export** is a good or service sent to another country for sale. An **import** is a good or service brought in from another country for sale. For example, Costa Rica specializes in growing and exporting coffee. The nation uses the money to import goods that it does not produce.

In some cases, more than 70 percent of a nation's export trade depends upon a single resource. Examples include Kuwait (petroleum and natural gas), Guinea-Bissau (cashews), and the Marshall Islands (fish).

✔ **CHECKPOINT** *How does specialization create a need for trade?*

Absolute and Comparative Advantage

Suppose a nation enjoys an abundance of resources, including a rich natural environment, an educated workforce, and the latest technologies. In theory, such a nation could be self-sufficient, producing almost all that it needs by itself. Why, then, would it choose to engage in foreign trade?

Although self-sufficiency may sound appealing, it is actually better for countries to specialize in some products and trade for others. To see why, you need to look at two related concepts—absolute advantage and comparative advantage. A person or nation has an **absolute advantage** when it can produce more of a given product than another person or nation using a given amount of resources.

Absolute Advantage

A simple example can illustrate the idea of absolute advantage. Suppose that two people, Jenny and Carlos, work at making both birdhouses and printed T-shirts. In one hour, Carlos can either print six T-shirts or make two birdhouses. (See **Figure 17.2**.) Jenny can print one T-shirt or make one birdhouse per hour. In other words, Carlos is more productive than Jenny in making both T-shirts and birdhouses. In economic

	Carlos	Jenny
T-shirts per hour	6	1
Birdhouses per hour	2	1
Opportunity cost of one T-shirt	1/3 birdhouse	1 birdhouse
Opportunity cost of one birdhouse	3 T-shirts	1 T-shirt

Figure 17.2 Productivity and Opportunity Cost

CHART SKILLS

Carlos has an absolute advantage over Jenny in producing both T-shirts and birdhouses. However, their opportunity costs are different.

1. How many T-shirts can Carlos make in the time it takes Jenny to make five T-shirts?
2. Based on this table, why would Carlos be more productive making T-shirts than making birdhouses?

terms, Carlos has an absolute advantage over Jenny in producing both goods.

Because Carlos enjoys an absolute advantage in both goods, should he remain self-sufficient? Or would he be better off specializing in either T-shirts or birdhouses? What about Jenny? Should she make T-shirts, birdhouses, or both?

Countries have to face the same sorts of questions. Should a wealthy country with many resources be self-sufficient, or should it specialize in producing a few products and trade for the others? How does a poorer nation decide what to produce? The answer to these questions lies with the concept of comparative advantage.

Comparative Advantage

Early in the nineteenth century, British economist David Ricardo argued that the key to determining which country should produce which goods is opportunity cost. Remember that opportunity cost is what you give up in order to produce a certain product.

A country has a **comparative advantage** in the product that it can produce most efficiently given all the products it could choose to produce. It is the nation with the comparative advantage—not necessarily the one with the absolute advantage—that should specialize in producing that good.

export a good or service sent to another country for sale

import a good or service brought in from another country for sale

absolute advantage the ability to produce more of a given product using a given amount of resources

comparative advantage the ability to produce a product most efficiently given all the other products that could be produced

How do **specialization** and **trade** benefit nations?

Every nation in the world engages in trade—even nations that have the ability to be self-sufficient. One reason is that specialization increases the number of products available to all.

1 Left on its own, Bartonia can produce 6 million bushels of wheat and 2 millions bales of cotton in a year. Alisium can produce 1 million bushels of wheat and 1 million bales of cotton.

1 Bartonia switches all of its cotton production to wheat. Alisium switches all of its resources to producing cotton.

2 The two countries do not trade.

2 Bartonia trades 2 million bushels of wheat to Alisium in return for 2 million bales of cotton.

Production

Trade

According to the **law of comparative advantage,** a nation is better off when it produces goods and services for which it has a comparative advantage. Each nation can then use the money it earns selling those goods and services to buy those that it cannot produce as efficiently.

Importance of Opportunity Cost

To see how comparative advantage works, look again at **Figure 17.2.** It shows the opportunity costs of producing T-shirts and birdhouses for both Carlos and Jenny.

- *Carlos's opportunity costs* In an hour, Carlos can make either six T-shirts or two birdhouses. He therefore sacrifices three T-shirts for every birdhouse he produces. In terms of opportunity cost, the opportunity cost of a birdhouse is the three T-shirts he could have produced instead. The opportunity cost of a T-shirt is one third of a birdhouse.

- *Jenny's opportunity costs* In an hour, Jenny can make either one T-shirt or one birdhouse. Therefore, her opportunity cost for one birdhouse is one T-shirt, and her opportunity cost for one T-shirt is one birdhouse.

According to the law of comparative advantage, each person should produce the good for which he or she has a lower opportunity cost. Carlos's opportunity cost for producing a T-shirt (one third of a birdhouse) is lower than Jenny's (one birdhouse), so it is sensible for Carlos to produce T-shirts. Jenny's opportunity cost for producing a birdhouse (one T-shirt) is lower than Carlos's (three T-shirts), so Jenny should produce birdhouses.

Mutual Benefits

If Carlos wants a birdhouse, he can either make it himself or make T-shirts and trade

law of comparative advantage the principle that a nation is better off when it produces goods and services for which it has a comparative advantage

3 The two countries end up only with what each of them can produce.

BARTONIA
6M
COTTON
2M

ALISIUM
1M
COTTON
1M

BARTONIA
7M
COTTON
2M

ALISIUM
2M
COTTON
2M

3 Both countries end up with more than they would have if they had not specialized and traded.

Check Your Understanding
1. Which nation has a comparative advantage in producing wheat? Cotton?
2. What impact might trade between Bartonia and Alisium have on **(a)** production efficiency, **(b)** consumer choice, and **(c)** standard of living?

Net Result

some of them to Jenny for a birdhouse. Suppose Carlos and Jenny agree to trade two T-shirts for one birdhouse. In this case, Carlos is clearly better off producing T-shirts and trading for a birdhouse. After all, in the time he would have used to make his own birdhouse, he can make three T-shirts. Since he pays Jenny only two T-shirts for a birdhouse, he has a T-shirt left over. Trade makes Carlos better off by one T-shirt.

Jenny is also better off as the result of trade. She can make two birdhouses in the time she would need to produce two T-shirts for herself. Since she only pays one birdhouse to Carlos for the two T-shirts, she will still have one birdhouse left over. Trade makes her better off by one birdhouse.

Carlos and Jenny both benefit from trade. Each person specializes in producing the good for which he or she has a comparative advantage. Since both producers are

operating at greater efficiency, more total goods are produced overall. After the trade, each of them is left with an extra unit of the good originally produced, which can be used to trade for other goods.

✔ **CHECKPOINT** *How is trade affected by opportunity cost?*

Comparative Advantage and World Trade

The lessons from the example of Carlos and Jenny also apply to trade between nations. As you saw, David Ricardo argued that the nation which has the lower opportunity cost in producing a good has a comparative advantage in producing that good. Remember, comparative advantage is the ability of one nation to produce a good at a lower opportunity cost than that of another nation. It is the nation with the comparative advantage—not necessarily the

interdependence the shared need of countries for resources, goods, services, labor, and knowledge supplied by other countries

(FL) **SS.912.E.2.3** Research the contributions of key individuals of various backgrounds in the development of the U.S.

absolute advantage–that should specialize in producing that good.

Comparative Advantage in Action

Suppose two countries, A and B, are capable of producing both bananas and sugar. However, Country A's climate and land are somewhat more suitable for growing bananas. For Country A, the opportunity cost of a ton of bananas is two tons of sugar. For Country B, the opportunity cost of a ton of bananas is three tons of sugar. Since Country A has a lower opportunity cost than does Country B, Country A has a comparative advantage in producing bananas. It should therefore specialize in growing bananas and exporting them to the world market. Trade allows countries to obtain goods for which they might have a high opportunity cost. Thus, Country A can use the money it earns from exporting bananas to import other goods and services that it cannot efficiently produce for itself.

Growing Interdependence

The growth of international trade has led to greater economic interdependence among nations. **Interdependence** is the shared need of countries for the resources, goods, services, labor, and knowledge supplied by other countries.

Because countries are interdependent, changes in one country's economy influence other economies. For example, a drought in Brazil would hurt that country's coffee growers. Coffee growers in Costa Rica or Colombia may benefit, though, because they would be able to sell more of their product on the world market.

Another example of interdependence can be seen when one country experiences economic growth. Suppose that Mexico's economy grows, resulting in more jobs and higher wages for Mexican workers. With more money available, these workers are likely to have greater demand for goods produced in other countries. By buying those goods from other countries, Mexicans would be helping the economies of its trade partners to grow.

✅ **CHECKPOINT** *What factor determines what goods or services a nation should specialize in producing?*

Innovators

Akio Morita

"I knew we needed a weapon to break through to the US market," recalled Akio Morita. The Japanese entrepreneur had co-founded a telecommunications company in 1946. But the firm found few buyers in a country still recovering from war. After visiting America, Morita dreamed of creating a blockbuster product for the booming economy. "It had to be something different," he realized.

The solution came quickly. Company engineers devised a transistorized radio to fit in one's pocket. Morita returned to America in 1957 to market it. At first, there was little interest. Then Bulova Watch offered to purchase 100,000 radios. There was a catch, though. The radios had to bear Bulova's name. Morita refused—the best decision of his career, he later said. Why? Early on, he recognized that the radio could help establish a global brand name. To that end, he also changed the corporate name to something easy to say and remember: Sony.

The Sony Corporation went on to create other innovative products, like the Walkman, for the world market. Morita also formed multinational partnerships that led Sony into new areas such as entertainment and finance. By the time he died in 1999, he had built a global business empire.

Critical Thinking *How was Morita's success related to global supply and demand?*

Fast Facts

Akio Morita
Born: January 26, 1921, in Nagoya, Japan
Died: October 3, 1999, in Tokyo, Japan
Education: Osaka Imperial University, 1944
Claim to Fame: Founder of Sony Corporation

The United States and Trade

The United States enjoys a comparative advantage in producing many goods and services. What, then, is its position as an importer and exporter?

The United States as Exporter

The United States is the world's third largest exporter, close behind Germany and China. One reason is its wide range of export products, from soybeans to telecommunications equipment. Another reason is that the United States excels in technologically sophisticated goods such as software, chemicals, and medical testing supplies. In 2007, a journalist explained the reasons for a surge in U.S. exports:

> **❝** An expanding foreign appetite for capital goods such as tractors, medical equipment and electrical machinery is driving much of the boom.... There also is increased international demand for complex ... products for which 'made in the U.S.A.' remains shorthand for reliability. **❞**
>
> —Michael A. Fletcher, *Washington Post*

Goods make up the bulk of international trade, but the United States is also the world's leading exporter of services. These include education, computer and data processing, financial services, and medical care. Exports of services have grown rapidly over the last decade.

The United States as Importer

The United States is also the world's top importer—by a significant amount. U.S. imports total nearly $1.9 trillion, or 15.5 percent of the world's total. That amount exceeds the combined totals for Germany and China, the next two largest importers.

The World Economy Databank on pages 474–476 gives additional information about American foreign trade—whom we trade with, how much we trade, and what we trade. As you might expect, we export more to neighboring Canada and Mexico than to any other nations. However, you might be surprised to see how high China ranks in terms of imports. In Chapter 18, you will learn more about the growing role of China in the world economy.

✔ **CHECKPOINT** *How does the United States rank in world exports and imports?*

The Effects of Trade on Employment

Trade allows nations to specialize in producing a limited number of goods while consuming a greater variety of goods. However, specialization can also dramatically change a nation's employment patterns. The impact may be negative (loss of jobs) or positive (creation of new job opportunities)—or both.

Specialization and Job Loss

To help you better understand the effects of international trade on employment, think back to the example of Carlos and Jenny. Remember that Carlos can make six T-shirts or two birdhouses by himself in an hour. Suppose he hires Amy to help him build birdhouses. He later realizes that he should specialize only in T-shirts since that is where his comparative advantage lies. Since he no longer needs Amy to help him make birdhouses, he fires her.

Up to this point, Amy has specialized in the skills needed to make birdhouses. These skills are no longer in demand where she lives. She now has several options:

- Amy can gain new job skills that are more in demand. She might find a job retraining program and learn to make T-shirts or some other product. With her new skills, Amy might even find herself better off than when she was making birdhouses.

▲ In recent decades, many American jobs have gone overseas or become obsolete due to technological changes. Many companies offer programs to help workers gain new skills. *How might a company benefit from retraining workers rather than hiring new ones?*

- Amy can move to another location where her existing skills are still in demand. If she chooses to relocate, she may or may not be better off. How well she does depends on the wages she earns from her new job, housing prices in her new location, the impact on her family, and a variety of other factors.
- Amy can stay where she is and take a job that calls for lesser skills. In this case, she might well earn less money than she did making birdhouses. As a result, she may have to cut back on the goods and services she consumes, or take a second job to maintain her standard of living.
- If Amy takes none of these three options, she will be unemployed.

Personal Finance
For information on finding a job, see your Personal Finance Handbook in the back of the book or visit PearsonSchool.com/PHecon

Trade and Employment in the United States

Carlos's decision to focus on his comparative advantage and specialize in making T-shirts had an impact on Amy's economic well-being. In the same way, the comparative advantage of nations affects the economic well-being of workers living in those nations.

In the past two decades, international trade has led to significant changes in U.S. employment patterns. During the 1970s, for example, high worker productivity and new technologies like robotics helped give Japan a comparative advantage in making automobiles. As a result, Japanese cars became less expensive than many comparable American-made cars. As more consumers bought Japanese cars, American car companies lost business. Falling sales led them to reduce their workforce, costing many American auto workers their jobs.

Businesses and government often provide help to retrain laid-off workers or assist them in relocating. However, these two options are not easy, especially in the case of older workers or workers with families. In some cases, retraining or relocation are not possible at all. Some workers may be forced to take lower-paying jobs or face prolonged unemployment.

Of course, job loss is not the only possible result of trade. If American exports grow, there will be more demand for workers to make those products. Workers who lost jobs because they were on the negative end of comparative advantage can try to find work in those growing industries. To do so, they might have to retrain so they can gain the needed skills.

✔ **CHECKPOINT** *What options might a worker have who loses a job due to trade?*

FL SS.912.E.3, SS.912.E.3.2, SS.912.G.3.3, LA.1112.1.6.1, LA.1112.2.2.2

Essential Questions Journal To continue to build a response to the Essential Question, go to your **Essential Questions Journal**.

SECTION 1 ASSESSMENT

❓ Guiding Question

1. Use your completed cause-and-effect chart to answer this question: Why do nations trade?

2. **Extension** What are three products or services that you enjoy having or using that depend on trade?

Key Terms and Main Ideas

3. What impact does the distribution of resources have on trade?

4. How do **absolute advantage** and **comparative advantage** differ?

5. According to the **law of comparative advantage,** what goods should a nation choose to produce?

6. What is the role of opportunity cost in determining comparative advantage?

7. What role do **exports** and **imports** play in the United States economy?

Critical Thinking

8. **Apply** Susan, who lives in North Dakota, grows coffee in a greenhouse under sunlamps. This effort requires high energy costs for heating. She also grows sunflowers, which do not require such high energy costs. Which product should she specialize in growing, and why?

9. **Cause and Effect** What effect might the invention of an inexpensive sugar substitute have on the trade of other countries? Why?

10. **Analyze** Review the four possible outcomes for a worker who loses his or her job as a result of trade. What are the advantages and disadvantages of each outcome?

Math Skills

11. The chart below shows the total value of U.S. exports and U.S. imports in 2007 and the percentage of both exports and imports that came from agricultural products. Calculate the dollar value of farm products, exports and imports. Explain whether you think the data supports the conclusion that the United States has a comparative advantage in farming.

Visit PearsonSchool.com/PHecon for additional math help.

	Exports	Imports
Total Value	$1.14 trillion	$1.987 trillion
Agricultural products as percent of total	9.2%	4.9%

SOURCE: *CIA World Factbook, 2008*

NGSSS

LA.1112.1.6 Use multiple strategies to develop vocabulary.

MA.912.A.2.2 Interpret a graph to represent a real-world situation.

SS.912.E.3.3 Discuss the effects of trade barriers.

SS.912.E.3.3 Discuss why nations erect trade barriers.

SS.912.E.3.4 Assess the impact of negative and positive externalities on the international environment.

SS.912.E.3.5 Compare the current U.S. economy with other developed nations.

ECONOMIC DICTIONARY

As you read the section, look for the definitions of these **Key Terms**:

• trade barrier
• tariff
• import quota
• sanctions
• embargo
• trade war
• protectionism
• infant industry
• free trade
• free-trade zone

Guiding Question

What are the arguments for and against trade barriers and agreements?

Copy this chart and fill it in as you read.

Arguments	
For Trade Barriers and Against Trade Agreements	**Against Trade Barriers and For Trade Agreements**
• **Jobs:** Need barriers to protect jobs from going to other countries • **Industries:** • **Security:** • **Multinationals:**	• **Competition:** • **Prices:** • **Efficiency:** • **Risk:**

▶ **Economics and You** Would you take part in a march to protest against a trade policy? That's what more than 100,000 citizens of Costa Rica did in September 2007. Chanting slogans like "Costa Rica is not for sale," the marchers voiced opposition to a trade agreement that their government was about to sign with the United States. To these protesters, trade policy was not just an economic idea, it had a major impact on their lives. And the same is true of you—whether you know it or not.

Principles in Action Today, many people favor increased foreign trade, while others fear its effects. To understand why, you need to understand the kinds of barriers that nations sometimes erect to trade. In this section, you will also see how trade policies may affect what you pay for dozens of products, from chocolate to cars.

Trade Barriers

A **trade barrier,** or trade restriction, is a means of preventing a foreign product or service from freely entering a nation's territory. Trade barriers take several forms and may be used for various purposes.

Tariffs

One common trade barrier is a **tariff,** or a tax on imported goods. Until the early 1900s, tariffs were a major tool of fiscal policy and the main source of revenue for the federal government. As you can see from **Figure 17.3,** however, tariffs today are much

trade barrier a means of preventing a foreign product or service from freely entering a nation's territory

tariff a tax on imported goods

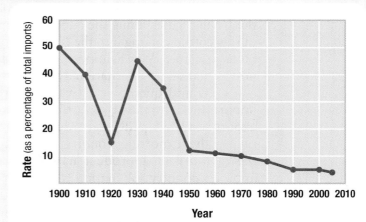

Figure 17.3 **Average Tariff Rates, 1900–2005**

Rate (as a percentage of total imports)

SOURCE: *Historical Statistics of the United States to 1970; Statistical Abstract of the United States; Trade Policy Review of the United States*

GRAPH SKILLS

One purpose of a high tariff is to shield American producers from foreign competition.

1. Describe the overall trend in tariff rates since 1930.
2. Why was it less risky for American manufacturers to charge high prices in 1900 than in 2000?

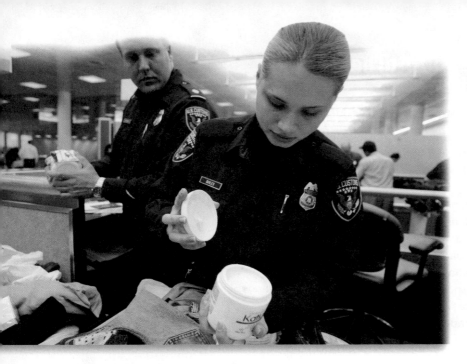

▲ Travelers returning from overseas must declare what purchases they are bringing back and pay any required customs duties on these items. Customs agents like these try to prevent people from smuggling undeclared items into the country. **What makes customs duties a form of tariff?**

lower. Still, the United States continues to collect tariffs on steel, foreign-made cars, and many other products.

If you have traveled abroad, you may have had to pay a tax on foreign goods you brought back to the United States. These customs duties are another form of tariff.

Quotas and VERS

Another kind of barrier is an import quota. **Import quotas** place a limit on the amount of a good that can be imported. For example, the United States limits the annual amount of raw cotton coming into the country from other nations. Many import quotas are now illegal under international trade laws.

Tariffs and quotas are laws set by the importing country. By contrast, a voluntary export restraint (VER) is a voluntary limit set by the exporting country, restricting the quantity of a product it will sell to another country. A nation that adopts a VER seeks to reduce the risk that the importing country will impose damaging trade barriers itself.

Other Barriers to Trade

Other government actions may also create trade barriers. For example, a government may require foreign companies to obtain a license to sell goods in that country. High licensing fees or slow licensing processes act as informal trade barriers.

import quota a set limit on the amount of a good that can be imported

sanctions actions a nation or group of nations takes in order to punish or put pressure on another nation

embargo a ban on trade with a particular country

Health, safety, or environmental regulations can also act as trade barriers. Suppose a nation treats the fruit it grows with a particular insecticide. Another nation might ban any fruit treated with that insecticide in order to discourage imports of foreign fruit. The U.S. anti-pollution standards that require cars to be equipped with catalytic converters is another example. Cars that do not meet this requirement cannot be exported to the United States.

Finally, a nation may impose trade barriers and other economic sanctions for political reasons. **Sanctions** are actions a nation or group of nations takes in order to punish or put pressure on another nation. For example, in the 1960s, the United States banned all trade with Cuba. The purpose of this trade **embargo** was to cause economic strain that might weaken Cuba's communist dictatorship.

✔ **CHECKPOINT** *How do voluntary export restraints differ from import quotas?*

Effects of Trade Barriers

By limiting supply, trade barriers can have very different effects on domestic producers and consumers. Trade barriers may also create tense relations between importing and exporting countries.

Increased Prices for Foreign Goods

Trade barriers can help domestic producers compete with foreign firms. By limiting imports from those firms, or by making the prices of those imports higher, trade barriers help domestic companies.

Although domestic producers may benefit, consumers can lose out. Restrictions on imports result in higher prices. For example, suppose the market price of an imported car is $20,000. If the government places a 10 percent tariff on all imported foreign cars, the price of the average imported car would increase from $20,000 to $22,000. Consumers who bought such a vehicle would be paying a higher price than if there had been no tariff. Also, with foreign competition limited, domestic carmakers would have no incentive to keep prices low.

Trade Wars

Trade barriers may also fuel international conflict. When one country restricts imports, its trading partner may retaliate by placing its own restrictions on imports. If the first country responds with further trade limits, the result is a **trade war,** a cycle of escalating trade barriers. Trade wars often cause economic hardship for both sides.

Probably the most damaging trade war in American history began during the Great Depression. In 1930, Congress passed the Smoot-Hawley Act, raising average tariff rates on all imports to 50 percent. Congress hoped the tariff would protect American workers and businesses from foreign competition and help the economy rebound.

The reverse effect took place, though. Other countries responded by raising tariffs on American-made goods. The resulting trade war decreased international trade and deepened the worldwide depression. Most economists blame the Smoot-Hawley tariff for increasing American unemployment.

Trade wars still occur, but they usually involve a few products rather than all imports. In 2002, the United States placed temporary tariffs on imported steel to help American steelmakers recover from bankruptcy. European nations threatened to retaliate. This "steel war" ended when an international panel ruled that the tariffs were illegal.

☑ **CHECKPOINT** *Why are trade wars harmful?*

Arguments for Protectionism

Why does a nation impose trade barriers? One reason is **protectionism,** the use of trade barriers to shield domestic industries from foreign competition. Protectionists have generally used three main arguments to support their view: saving jobs, protecting infant industries, and safeguarding national security.

Protecting Jobs

One argument for protectionism is that it shelters workers in industries that may be hurt by foreign competition. Suppose that certain East Asian nations had a comparative advantage in producing textiles. If the United States cut tariffs on textile imports, domestic manufacturers might find it hard to compete with imports from East Asia. They would have to close their factories and lay off workers.

Ideally, the laid-off workers would take new jobs in other industries. In practice, however, many of these workers would find retraining or relocation difficult. In addition, few industry or political leaders want to see existing industries shut down or large numbers of people lose their jobs. For this reason, public officials might favor protectionism to keep companies alive and people working.

trade war a cycle of escalating trade barriers

protectionism the use of trade barriers to shield domestic industries from foreign competition

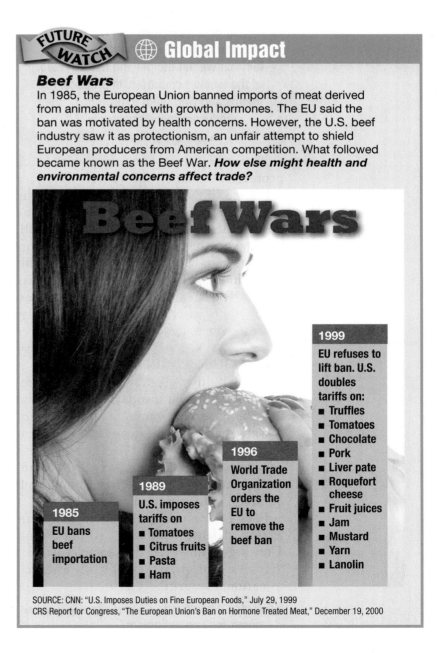

FUTURE WATCH 🌐 Global Impact

Beef Wars

In 1985, the European Union banned imports of meat derived from animals treated with growth hormones. The EU said the ban was motivated by health concerns. However, the U.S. beef industry saw it as protectionism, an unfair attempt to shield European producers from American competition. What followed became known as the Beef War. *How else might health and environmental concerns affect trade?*

1985
EU bans beef importation

1989
U.S. imposes tariffs on
■ Tomatoes
■ Citrus fruits
■ Pasta
■ Ham

1996
World Trade Organization orders the EU to remove the beef ban

1999
EU refuses to lift ban. U.S. doubles tariffs on:
■ Truffles
■ Tomatoes
■ Chocolate
■ Pork
■ Liver pate
■ Roquefort cheese
■ Fruit juices
■ Jam
■ Mustard
■ Yarn
■ Lanolin

SOURCE: CNN: "U.S. Imposes Duties on Fine European Foods," July 29, 1999
CRS Report for Congress, "The European Union's Ban on Hormone Treated Meat," December 19, 2000

infant industry an industry in the early stages of development

free trade the lowering or elimination of protective tariffs and other trade barriers between two or more nations

Protecting Infant Industries

Another argument for protectionism is that industries in the early stages of development need time and experience to become efficient producers. Tariffs that raise the price of imported goods provide a period of time for these **infant industries** to become more competitive. Once that happens, the tariff can be eliminated.

In the early years of the United States, Alexander Hamilton favored using tariffs to protect young American industries from European competition. Today, many developing nations adopt protectionist policies for similar reasons:

> **❝**Global economic competition is a game of unequal players. It pits against each other countries that range from Switzerland to Swaziland.... It is only fair that we 'tilt the playing field' in favor of the weaker countries. In practice, this means allowing them to protect ... their producers more vigorously.**❞**
> —Ha-Joon Chang, "Protecting the Global Poor"

Three problems may arise with such protective tariffs, however. First, a protected infant industry may lack the incentive to "grow up," that is, to become more efficient and competitive. Second, once an industry has been given tariff protection, lawmakers may find it difficult for political reasons to take the protections away. Third, a protected industry can keep its prices relatively high, increasing costs to consumers.

Safeguarding National Security

Certain industries may require protection because their products are essential to defending the country. In the event of a war, the United States would need an uninterrupted supply of steel, energy, and advanced technologies. For this reason, the government wants to ensure that such domestic industries remain active.

Foes of trade barriers agree that protecting defense industries is important. They argue, however, that some industries that seek protection are not really essential to national security.

✅ **CHECKPOINT** *What are three arguments given for protectionism?*

Trade Agreements

In opposition to protectionism is the principle of free trade. **Free trade** involves the lowering or elimination of protective tariffs and other trade barriers between two or more nations. Supporters argue that free trade is the best way to pursue comparative advantage, raise living standards, and further cooperative relationships among nations.

To encourage free trade, a number of countries in recent decades have signed international free trade agreements. Some of these pacts involve dozens of nations.

Roots of Free Trade

Today's free trade movement began in the 1930s. As you read, the Smoot-Hawley Act caused a rapid decline in international trade. To encourage trade, Congress passed the Reciprocal Trade Agreements Act of 1934. It gave the President the power to reduce tariffs by as much as 50 percent.

That law also allowed Congress to grant most-favored-nation (MFN) status to U.S. trading partners. Today, MFN status is called normal trade relations status, or NTR. All countries with NTR status pay the same tariffs, though imports from non-NTR nations may be taxed at a higher rate.

In 1948, after World War II had disrupted world trade, many nations reached an agreement called the General Agreement on Tariffs and Trade (GATT). Its goal was to reduce tariffs and stabilize world trade.

World Trade Organization

In 1995, the World Trade Organization (WTO) was founded with the goal of making global trade more free. The WTO works to ensure that countries comply with GATT, to negotiate new trade agreements, and to resolve trade disputes. Various conferences, or rounds, of tariff negotiations have advanced the goals of GATT and the WTO. For example, the Uruguay round of negotiations, completed in 1994, decreased average global tariffs by about a third.

Today, the World Trade Organization also acts as a referee, enforcing the rules agreed upon by the member countries. WTO decisions resolved the beef war and the steel tariff disputes between the United States and the European Union.

VISUAL GLOSSARY

Reviewing Key Terms
To understand *free trade*, review these terms:

free market economy, *p. 30*
competition, *p. 33*
regulation, *p. 125*
trade barrier, *p. 455*
tariff, *p. 455*
embargo, *p. 456*

What is Free Trade?

◄ **free trade** the lowering or elimination of protective tariffs and other trade barriers between two or more nations

Usually, normal trade relations between countries involve a certain number of restrictions, including tariffs. In free trade, these restrictions are greatly reduced or eliminated. ***Do you think all trade barriers can be eliminated even under free trade?***

"Take us to your leader...we've come to negotiate a free trade agreement with earth."

◄ Free trade agreements require a great deal of negotiation between the parties involved. ***What sorts of issues might the two sides shown in this cartoon need to discuss in order to reach a free trade agreement?***

Visual Glossary
online

To expand your understanding of this and other key economic terms, visit **PearsonSchool.com/PHecon**

free-trade zone
region where a group of
countries agrees to
reduce or eliminate
trade barriers

The European Union

In recent years, many countries have signed agreements to abolish tariffs and trade restrictions among member nations and adopt uniform tariffs for all countries that are not members. The most successful example is the European Union (EU).

The European Union developed slowly over several decades. In 1957, six western European nations set up the Common Market to coordinate economic and trade policies. In the years that followed, more countries joined the Common Market. In 1986, the member nations agreed to eliminate tariffs on one another's exports. They created a single market, called the European Economic Community (EEC).

In 1993, the EEC nations formed the European Union. This new organization became the largest trading bloc in the world. By 2008, the EU included 27 countries—almost all of Europe. This includes Poland, Hungary, Romania, and other former Soviet bloc nations that had once been forbidden to trade with the rest of Europe.

The EU adopted various policies to strengthen member economies, such as using agricultural subsidies and tariffs to keep farm prices high. Some member nations signed the European Monetary Union, agreeing to adopt a single currency and monetary system. In 2002, twelve member nations replaced their individual currencies with a single currency called the euro. The EU also adopted political ties, forming a parliament and council that make laws all member nations must follow. Still, many Europeans feared such measures threatened each nation's right to make decisions in its own interest.

NAFTA

Other nations have created **free-trade zones,** where a group of countries agrees to reduce or eliminate trade barriers. One such pact, the North American Free Trade Agreement (NAFTA), created a free-trade zone linking the United States, Canada, and Mexico.

NAFTA aroused controversy in the United States. Opponents worried that American companies would move factories to Mexico, where wages were lower and environmental regulations were less strict. As a result, they

▲ This NAFTA symbol suggests that the United States, Canada, and Mexico have become more interdependent as a result of the free trade agreement.

said, American workers would lose jobs. Supporters of NAFTA claimed that the measure would instead create more jobs in the United States because it would increase exports to Mexico and Canada.

After a spirited debate, the Senate ratified NAFTA in 1993. Major provisions include:

1. Tariffs on all farm products and on some 10,000 other goods were to be eliminated over 15 years.
2. Automobile tariffs were to be phased out over 10 years.
3. Trucks were to have free access across borders and throughout the three member countries.
4. Special judges were given authority to resolve trade disputes.
5. The agreement could not be used to override national and state environmental, health, or safety laws.

More than a decade after it went into effect, the agreement has remained controversial. Critics continue to charge that NAFTA has resulted in a loss of American jobs and damage to the environment. In 2004, the Congressional Research Service reviewed the effects of NAFTA after ten years. It found that trade between Mexico and the United States had increased substantially in that period, but some of that increase resulted from trends at work before NAFTA. The report also concluded that the agreement had relatively little effect on jobs and wages in the United States.

DR-CAFTA and FTAA

In 2003, the United States government reached a free trade agreement with five nations of Central America. At the time, the deal was called the Central American Free Trade Agreement (CAFTA). The next year, when the Dominican Republic joined the pact, the name was changed to DR-CAFTA. Congress approved the agreement in July 2005, and the other nations formally approved it as well. Costa Rica—despite the protests described at the beginning of the chapter—formally accepted DR-CAFTA in late 2007.

Free trade hit a roadblock with the failure of the Free Trade Area of the Americas (FTAA). This trade deal would have opened trade among 34 nations of

Figure 17.4

Major Trade Organization Members

Legend:
- EU
- CARICOM
- MERCOSUR
- APEC
- ASEAN
- NAFTA

(Map labels: ARCTIC OCEAN, ATLANTIC OCEAN, PACIFIC OCEAN, PACIFIC OCEAN, INDIAN OCEAN)

MAP SKILLS

Globalization has increased the development of trade organizations.

1. Locate and describe the geographic regions of each of the major trade organizations.
2. What do the nations belonging to APEC have in common? Why do you think they would be interested in signing a trade agreement?

Action Graph
online

For an animated version
of this map, visit
PearsonSchool.com/PHecon

North and South America. However, after more than a decade of negotiations, the proposal was rejected by several key South American nations in 2005.

Other Regional Trade Agreements

About 100 regional trading organizations operate in the world today. They include the following, shown in **Figure 17.4:**

- *APEC* The Asia-Pacific Economic Cooperation includes 21 countries along the Pacific Rim, including the United States. They have signed a nonbinding agreement to reduce trade barriers.
- *MERCOSUR* The Southern Common Market is similar to the EU in its goals. Its members are the South American nations of Brazil, Paraguay, Uruguay, Argentina, and Venezuela.

- *CARICOM* The Caribbean Community and Common Market includes countries from South America and the Caribbean.
- *ASEAN* The ten-member Association of Southeast Asian Nations has taken steps to establish a free trade zone similar to the EU.

The Debate Over Free Trade

While the world's economies have moved toward free trade, controversy on trade continues. Debates over the impact of NAFTA became a campaign issue in the American presidential election of 2008. As you saw, protests across the Americas slowed negotiations on the FTAA.

Meetings of the World Trade Organization have also spurred large protests. A 1999

FL SS.912.G.4.4
Analyze case studies of globalization.

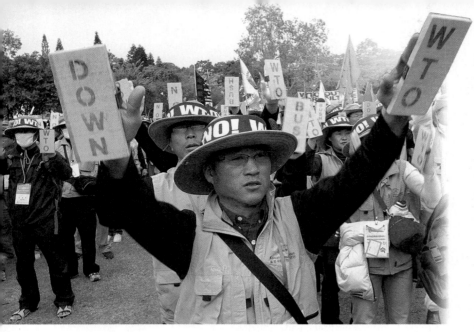

▲ Since the violence that disrupted the WTO meeting in Seattle in 1999, similar protests have erupted at WTO meetings elsewhere. This protest took place at a WTO meeting in Hong Kong in 2005.

WTO meeting in Seattle, Washington, drew as many as 50,000 angry demonstrators.

Not all of these protesters were opposed to free trade. Rather, they were concerned that current free trade agreements gave too much economic power to large multinational corporations.

✔ **CHECKPOINT** *What countries are involved in NAFTA?*

The Role of Multinationals

As you read in Chapter 8, a multinational is a large corporation that sells goods and services throughout the world. For example, an automobile company might design its cars in the United States and import parts made in Asia to an assembly plant in Canada. Even if you purchase the car from an American company, it is not a purely domestic product.

Many goods besides cars are produced globally. Some brands of athletic shoes are designed in the United States but are produced in East Asia. Some personal computers are designed in the United States and assembled abroad with parts and components from the United States.

The decision to build production facilities in a foreign country benefits both the multinational and the host nation. By locating abroad, the corporation avoids some shipping fees and tariffs. It may also benefit from cheaper labor. The host nation benefits by gaining jobs and tax revenue.

Still, host nations worry about the effect of multinationals on their countries. In a small country with a fragile economy, multinationals can gain excessive political power. In addition, host nations fear that multinationals could drive out domestic industries and exploit local workers. To protect domestic industries, some host nations have created rules requiring multinationals to export a certain percentage of their products.

✔ **CHECKPOINT** *Why are some nations concerned about multinationals?*

FL SS.912.E.2.1, SS.912.E.3.2, SS.912.E.3.3, LA.1112.2.2.2, LA.1112.1.6.1

Essential Questions Journal To continue to build a response to the Essential Question, go to your **Essential Questions Journal**.

SECTION 2 ASSESSMENT

❓ Guiding Question

1. Use your completed chart to answer this question: What are the arguments for and against trade barriers and agreements?
2. **Extension** Describe two ways that trade barriers or free trade can affect you as a consumer.

Key Terms and Main Ideas

3. What is the difference between an **import quota** and a **tariff?**
4. What are three arguments in favor of **protectionism?**
5. What happens when two countries sign a **free trade** agreement?

Critical Thinking

6. **Take a Position** Some people argue that trade barriers are needed to protect jobs. According to the idea of comparative advantage, consumers benefit from trade by having a wider variety of less expensive goods. Which benefit—securing jobs or increasing consumer choices—do you think is more important? Why?
7. **Analyze** What are the advantages of international trade agreements? What might be some disadvantages?
8. **Illustrate** Give three examples from this section to show how trading partnerships and relationships change over time.

Quick Write

9. Suppose you were a member of Congress considering a bill that would place higher tariffs on imported video game systems. Write a brief speech that you would deliver for or against the bill. Base your argument on economic principles.

NGSSS

LA.1112.1.6 Use multiple strategies to develop vocabulary.

LA.1112.6.2 Use a systematic process to collect, process, present information.

MA.912.A.2.2 Interpret a graph to represent a real-world situation.

SS.912.E.1.13 Explain the functions and characteristics of money.

SS.912.E.3 Understand the relationships of the U.S. economy and the international marketplace.

SS.912.E.3.5 Compare the current U.S. economy with other developed nations.

ECONOMIC DICTIONARY

As you read the section, look for the definitions of these **Key Terms**:

• exchange rate
• appreciation
• depreciation
• foreign exchange market
• fixed exchange-rate system
• flexible exchange-rate system
• balance of trade
• trade surplus
• trade deficit
• balance of payments

Guiding Question

How do exchange rates affect international trade?

Copy this chart and fill it in as you read.

Effect of Exchange Rates on Trade	
Effect of Appreciating Currency	**Effect of Depreciating Currency**
• Value of currency rises, making goods produced in country more expensive • Exports:	• • •

▶ **Economics and You**   It's happened to everyone. You buy something in a store. You hand over a couple of bills. The clerk hands you your change. When you get outside, you notice something funny about one of the quarters. Instead of the familiar profile of George Washington, you see a caribou with a large pair of antlers. You've been given a Canadian quarter.

Maybe you feel cheated. But should you? Is this Canadian quarter worth less than a U.S. quarter—or more? How would you find out? These questions may seem unimportant when you're dealing with just a single quarter. But if you were dealing with hundreds or thousands of dollars, the questions might be very important indeed!

Principles in Action   The difference in value between an American dollar and a Canadian dollar—or a British pound or a Japanese yen or a Saudi Arabian riyal—does not stay the same from day to day. In this section, you will see how these fluctuations have a huge impact on imports and exports. In Economics & You, you will also see how changes in the value of the dollar can directly affect what many American consumers spend and where they can afford to travel.

Foreign Exchange

International trade is more complex than buying and selling within one country because of the world's many currencies and their changing values. If you want to buy a newspaper in Beijing, you will need to change your American dollars for Chinese yuan. If a Mexican family visiting New York wants to buy lunch, they must change their pesos to dollars.

Understanding Exchange Rates

Changing money from one nation's currency to another's is never a simple matter of exchanging, say, one yuan or one peso for one American dollar. A dollar might be worth 8 yuan or 11 pesos. The value of a nation's currency in relation to a foreign currency is called the **exchange rate.** Understanding how exchange rates work enables you to convert prices in one currency to prices in another currency.

exchange rate the value of a nation's currency in relation to a foreign currency

| Figure 17.5 | Foreign Exchange Rates |

Foreign Exchange Rates

	U.S. $	Aust. $	U.K. £	Canadian $	Japanese ¥en	€uro	Mexican peso	Chinese yuan
U.S. $	1	.88	2.04	1.00	.008	1.42	.09	.13
Australian $	1.12	1	2.30	1.13	.009	1.60	.10	.15
U.K. £	.49	.43	1	.49	.004	.69	.04	.07
Canadian $	.99	.88	2.03	1	.008	1.42	.09	.13
Japanese ¥en	114.97	101.81	234.41	115.44	1	163.47	10.52	15.34
€uro	.70	.62	1.43	.71	.006	1	.06	.09
Mexican peso	10.93	9.68	22.29	10.98	.095	15.54	1	1.46
Chinese yuan	7.449	6.63	15.28	7.52	.065	10.65	.69	1

SOURCE: *X-rates.com* accessed on Friday, September 28, 2007 Note: These data are highly time sensitive and can change hourly.

CHART SKILLS

This table shows exchange rates on a single day. Read down the first column of the chart to find out what one U.S. dollar was worth in various foreign currencies. Read across the top row to find out how much a selected foreign currency was worth in U.S. dollars.

1. On this day, how much was one U.S. dollar worth in Chinese yuan? In Canadian dollars?
2. How much was a euro worth in pesos?

Daily exchange rates are listed in major newspapers and on the Internet. **Figure 17.5** shows a sample table of exchange rates. If you read down the first column, you will see that one U.S. dollar can be exchanged for more than one (1.12) Australian dollar, for less than one euro (0.70), and so forth.

An exchange rate table shows what one U.S. dollar is worth on one particular day. Remember, the rates change daily, so it is important to keep checking, especially if you are visiting a foreign country or doing business overseas.

Calculating Prices

A simple formula allows you to convert the price of an item from foreign currency to American dollars. Just divide the price by the value of the currency per one dollar according to the exchange rate.

Look at the following example. Suppose your family is planning a trip to Mexico and that the exchange rate is as shown in **Figure 17.5**. If a hotel room in Mexico costs 500 pesos per night, the price in U.S. dollars is $45.75:

appreciation an increase in the value of a currency

$$\frac{500 \text{ pesos}}{10.93 \text{ pesos/dollar}} = \$45.75$$

Now suppose your family decides to go to Mexico next year instead, and the exchange rate has risen to 12.5 pesos per dollar. Assuming that the room rate is still 500 pesos, the hotel room will cost only about $40.00 a night:

$$\frac{500 \text{ pesos}}{12.5 \text{ pesos/dollar}} = \$40.00$$

Appreciating Currency

You have probably heard newscasters talk about a "strong" or "weak" dollar or a currency like the Japanese yen "rising" or "falling." What do these terms mean? Do they indicate good news or bad news for the United States economy?

An increase in the value of a currency is called **appreciation**. When a currency appreciates, it becomes "stronger." If the exchange rate between the dollar and the yen increases from 100 yen per dollar to 120 yen per dollar, each dollar can buy more yen. Since the dollar has increased in value, we say that the dollar has appreciated against the yen. This appreciation means that people in Japan will have to spend more yen to purchase a dollar's worth of goods from the United States. On the other hand, Americans who travel to Japan can buy more goods and services for the same amount of money than they could before the dollar appreciated.

When a nation's currency appreciates, its products become more expensive in other countries. For example, a strong dollar makes American goods and services more expensive for Japanese consumers. Japan will therefore probably import fewer products from the United States. As a result, total United States exports to Japan will likely decline. On the other hand, a strong dollar makes foreign products less expensive for consumers in the United States. A strong dollar is therefore likely to lead consumers in the United States to purchase more imported goods.

Depreciating Currency

A decrease in the value of a currency is called **depreciation**. You might also hear depreciation referred to as "weakening." If the dollar exchange rate fell to 80 yen per dollar, you would get fewer yen for each dollar. In other words, the dollar has depreciated against the yen.

When a nation's currency depreciates, its products become cheaper to other nations. A depreciated, or weak, dollar means that foreign consumers will be able to better afford products made in the United States. A weakened dollar probably results in increased exports. At the same time, other nations' products become more expensive for consumers in the United States, so they will buy fewer imports.

The Foreign Exchange Market

Suppose that a company in the United States sells computers in Japan. That company is paid in yen. It must, however, pay its workers and suppliers back in the United States in dollars. The company must therefore exchange its yen for U.S. dollars. This exchange takes place on the foreign exchange market. International trade would not be possible without this market.

The **foreign exchange market** consists of about 2,000 banks and other financial institutions that facilitate the buying and selling of foreign currencies. These banks are located in various financial centers around the world, including such cities as New York, London, Paris, Singapore, and Tokyo. These banks maintain close links to one another through telephones and computers. This technology allows for the instantaneous transmission of market information and rapid financial transactions.

CHECKPOINT *What are the likely effects of the dollar becoming stronger?*

Exchange Rate Systems

As you read in Chapter 10, currencies varied in value from state to state in early America. In the United States today, of course, it doesn't matter what state you live in. All prices are in dollars, and all dollars have the same value.

depreciation a decrease in the value of a currency

foreign exchange market system of financial institutions that facilitate the buying and selling of foreign currencies

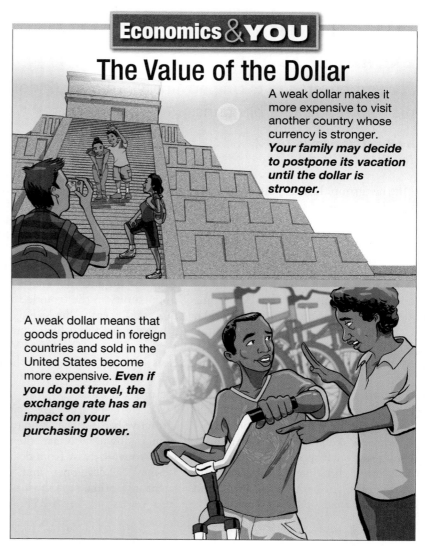

Economics & YOU

The Value of the Dollar

A weak dollar makes it more expensive to visit another country whose currency is stronger. *Your family may decide to postpone its vacation until the dollar is stronger.*

A weak dollar means that goods produced in foreign countries and sold in the United States become more expensive. *Even if you do not travel, the exchange rate has an impact on your purchasing power.*

▲ The strength of the dollar directly affects the prices we pay. *Identify one item you buy that might be affected by exchange rates.*

Foreign Direct Investment in U.S. Real Estate, 2006	
Country	**U.S. Dollars**
United Kingdom	$5,068,000,000
Australia	$4,356,000,000
OPEC	$775,000,000
Ireland	$678,000,000
Japan	$496,000,000
Germany	$422,000,000
Spain	$100,000,000

Note: Data reflect preliminary findings
SOURCE: "Foreign Direct Investment in the United States" by Lawrence McNeil, Bureau of Economic Analysis June 2007

Home Currency

EXCHANGE RATES

Foreign buyers are taking advantage of a weak dollar to pick up real-estate bargains.

By Ben Casselman
The Wall Street Journal

 SS.912.E.3 Understand the relationships of the U.S. economy and the international marketplace.

One group hasn't soured on the U.S. real-estate market: foreign buyers.

With the dollar at historic lows against the euro and other currencies, real-estate agents, appraisers and developers say overseas buyers are stepping up their purchases in the U.S. Some are buying vacation homes in Florida, California and Colorado that would previously have been considered out of reach. Others are gambling that properties purchased now will translate into savvy investments down the road, when both the dollar and the U.S. housing market eventually rebound.

Some brokers are aggressively marketing to such potential customers, translating brochures into Russian, buying ads in Irish newspapers and hitting the road—pitching new condos to prospects in Dubai and Seoul. Developers are getting into the act, too, opening foreign offices and trumpeting amenities they hope will appeal to foreign tastes.

Moutaz Kaissi, an executive in Abu Dhabi, and his wife, Fawzia, see opportunity in the troubled Las Vegas market. Recently, the Kaissis closed on a bank-owned two-bedroom house on a golf course in North Las Vegas. The Kaissis paid $295,000 for the home, a price more than $100,000 lower than the original owner paid for it new.

Foreign buyers are particularly attractive because they tend to put more money down, and are therefore less likely to walk away from deals. Garrett Kenney, a developer and real-estate agent in Florida, says most of his overseas buyers put down 25%, compared with the usual 10% down payment by many Americans. And because they tend to be wealthy, foreign buyers are also more likely to pay entirely in cash, which is significant at a time when tight credit is derailing many deals.

Christopher Mayer, director of the Paul Milstein Center for Real Estate, warns bargain-hunting foreign investors to think twice about comparing U.S. prices to those in their home countries. For example, despite recent discounts, residential properties in Miami may still be overvalued—even if they are far cheaper than equivalent homes in the south of France. "One of the mistakes foreign buyers make is to put things in the context of their [local] market," Mr. Mayer says. "When you see foreign buyers in a market where locals are not buying, that's a troubling sign."

Applying Economic Principles
According to the article, foreign investors in U.S. real estate expect to make a profit when the dollar eventually appreciates. Explain why this would be the case.

Video News Update Online
Powered by
The Wall Street Journal
Classroom Edition

Use videos at **PearsonSchool.com/PHecon** as a springboard for a discussion on a current topic.

Think how much more complicated it would be to do business if each state still had different currencies. To buy goods from a mail-order company in Indiana, for instance, someone in Texas would have to find out the exchange rate between a Texas dollar and an Indiana dollar. The economy would become less efficient as individuals and businesses spent time keeping track of exchange rates.

Such complications do not exist within the United States. They do, however, apply to international trade.

Fixed Exchange-Rate Systems

Of course, it would be simpler if all countries either used the same currency or kept their exchange rates constant. Then no one would have to worry about rate shifts. A system in which governments try to keep the values of their currencies constant against one another is called a **fixed exchange-rate system.**

In a typical fixed exchange-rate system, one country with a stable currency is at the center. Other countries fix, or "peg," their exchange rates to this currency. Normally, the fixed exchange-rate is not a single value, but is kept within a certain specified range (for example, plus or minus 2 percent). If the exchange rate moves outside of this range, governments usually intervene to maintain the rate.

How do governments intervene to maintain an exchange rate? The exchange rate is essentially the price of a currency. Like the price of any product or service, the exchange rate relies on supply and demand. To preserve its exchange rate, a government may buy or sell foreign currency in order to affect a currency's supply and demand. It will follow this course of action until the exchange rate is back within the specified limits.

The Bretton Woods Conference

In 1944, as World War II was drawing to a close, representatives from 44 countries met in Bretton Woods, New Hampshire. Their purpose was to make financial arrangements for the postwar world.

The Bretton Woods conference resulted in the creation of a fixed exchange-rate system for the United States and much of western Europe. Because the United States had the strongest economy and most stable currency, conference participants agreed to peg their currencies to the United States dollar.

To make the new system work, the Bretton Woods conference established the International Monetary Fund (IMF). Today, the IMF promotes international monetary cooperation, currency stabilization, and trade. You will read more about the International Monetary Fund in Chapter 18.

Flexible Exchange-Rate Systems

Although fixed exchange-rate systems make trade easier, they depend on countries maintaining similar economic policies, as well as similar inflation and interest rates. By the late 1960s, worldwide trade was growing and changing rapidly. At the same time, the war in Vietnam was causing inflation in the United States. These factors made it increasingly difficult for many countries to rely on a fixed exchange rate.

In 1971, the Netherlands and West Germany abandoned the fixed exchange-rate system. Other countries followed. By 1973, even the United States had adopted a system based on flexible exchange rates. Under a **flexible exchange-rate system,** the exchange rate is determined by supply and demand rather than according to any preset range.

Today, the countries of the world use a mixture of fixed and flexible exchange rates. Most major currencies—including the U.S. dollar and the Japanese yen—use the flexible exchange-rate system. This system accounts for the day-to-day changes in currency values that you read about earlier in this section.

When the current flexible exchange-rate system was first adopted, some economists worried that changes in the exchange

fixed exchange-rate system a system in which governments try to keep the values of their currencies constant against one another

flexible exchange-rate system a system in which the exchange rate is determined by supply and demand

Anyone traveling in a foreign country keeps a close eye on changing daily exchange rates as they are posted in hotels, banks, and other locations. ▼

EXCHANGE OFFICE "DOMINOVA"
RATE OF THE DAY
TRAVEL CHEQUE AND CASH

1 Dollaro U.S.A.	= € 0,67	NO COMMISSION
1 Dollaro Canadese	= € 0,63	NO COMMISSION
1 Dollaro Australiano	= € 0,58	NO COMMISSION
1 Sterlina Inglese	= € 1,37	NO COMMISSION
1 Franco Svizzero	= € 0,57	NO COMMISSION
1 Yen Giapponese	= € 0,0058	NO COMMISSION
1 Corona Danese	= € 0,127	NO COMMISSION
1 Corona Svedese	= € 0,100	NO COMMISSION
1 Corona Norvegese	= € 0,118	NO COMMISSION

ONLY TRAVEL CHEQUE IN EURO 3% COMMISSION

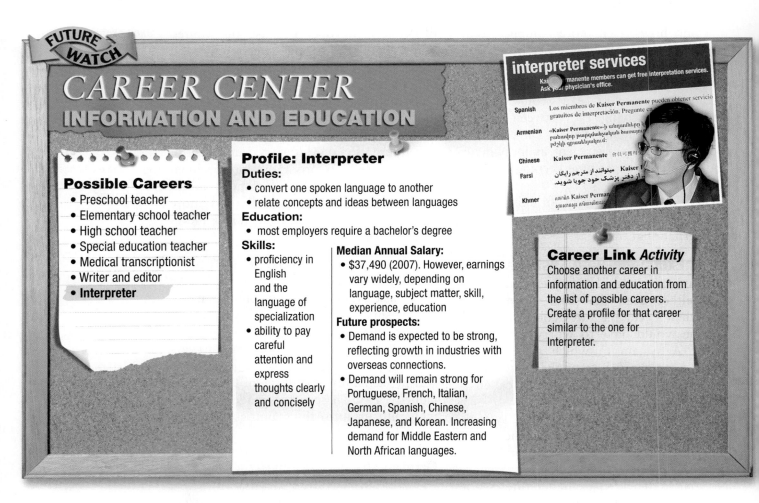

rate might interrupt the flow of world trade. In actual fact, trade has grown rapidly since the flexible exchange-rate system was adopted. Today, more nations trade than ever before.

The Euro

Although the flexible exchange-rate system works well, some countries whose economies are closely tied together want the advantages of fixed rates. One way to enjoy the advantages but avoid some of the difficulties of fixed exchange rates is to abolish individual currencies and establish a single currency.

As you read, this is what 12 members of the European Union did by adopting the euro. Use of this common currency requires countries to coordinate their economic policies, but it also simplifies trade. People traveling from, say, Germany to France do not need to exchange marks for francs at the border. They simply use their euros.

✔ **CHECKPOINT** *How are exchange rates set in a fixed exchange-rate system?*

Balance of Trade

The value of a nation's currency is affected by the overall flow of goods and services into and out of the country. In turn, exchange rates can affect a nation's **balance of trade,** the relationship between the value of its exports and the value of its imports.

Surpluses and Deficits

When a large difference between a nation's imports and exports arises, it is said to have a trade imbalance. A nation that exports more goods and services than it imports has a positive trade balance, or **trade surplus.** A nation that imports more goods and services than it exports has a negative trade balance, or **trade deficit.**

Nations seek to maintain a balance of trade. That is, they hope the value of imports is roughly equal to the value of exports. By balancing trade, a nation can protect the value of its currency on the international market. When a country has a continuing negative balance of trade, importing more than it is exporting over

balance of trade the relationship between the value of a country's exports and the value of its imports

trade surplus situation in which a nation exports more goods and services than it imports

trade deficit situation in which a nation imports more goods and services than it exports an extended period of time, the value of its currency falls.

For example, in the 1980s, the United States imported considerably more than it exported. As a result of this trade imbalance, the foreign exchange market was glutted with U.S. dollars. Because the supply of dollars was so high, the value of the dollar fell. The prices of imports increased and American consumers had to pay more for imported goods.

A negative balance of trade can be corrected either by limiting imports or by increasing the number or value of exports. Both of these actions affect trading partners, of course, who may then retaliate by raising tariffs. Maintaining a balance of trade thus requires international cooperation and fair trade practices.

Balance of Payments

Balance of trade measures the flow of goods and services among nations. Economists get a more complex picture of international trade by looking at balance of payments. **Balance of payments** is the value of all monetary transactions between all sectors of a country's economy—households, firms, and government—and the rest of the world.

Look again at the circular flow model of a mixed economy (**Figure 2.3**) in Chapter 2. It shows the movement of money and goods within a single economy. Now suppose you had to add in the international sector as well. Foreign transactions would enter into every stage. For example, if an American invested in a foreign company, the capital he or she invested would be part of the monetary flow going overseas. Any returns from the investment would be part of the monetary flow coming into the country. Income from foreign companies, government aid to foreign countries, borrowing from foreign banks, exchange rates—all of these must be factored into the balance of payments.

✔ **CHECKPOINT** *What causes a trade surplus?*

The United States Trade Deficit

Although the United States sells many goods abroad, it generally imports more than it exports. As a result, the United States currently runs a trade deficit. (See **Figure 17.6**, below.)

Causes of the Deficit

The U.S. trade deficit began to take shape in the 1970s, when the Arab members of the Organization of Petroleum Exporting Countries (OPEC) dramatically raised the price of oil. The United States, which depends heavily on foreign oil, thus had to increase the money spent on this vital resource. As a result, the total cost of imports to the United States began to exceed the income from its exports.

The United States suffered record trade deficits in 1986 and 1987. In the early 1990s, the trade deficit began to fall. By the late 1990s, however, the deficit had skyrocketed to record levels, largely as a result of a new increase in oil prices and an economic boom that fueled consumer buying of imported goods.

In 2005, the trade deficit totaled over $717 billion, with the largest amounts owed to China, Japan, Germany, Canada, Mexico, and oil exporting nations such as Venezuela. Petroleum imports accounted for more than a third of the deficit.

balance of payments
the value of all monetary transactions between a country's economy and the rest of the world

FL MA.912.A.2.2
Interpret a graph to represent a real-world situation.

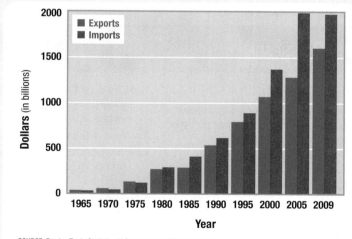

Figure 17.6 **U.S. Balance of Trade, 1965–2010**

Exports
Imports

Dollars (in billions)

2000
1500
1000
500
0

1965 1970 1975 1980 1985 1990 1995 2000 2005 2009
Year

SOURCE: Foreign Trade Statistics: U.S. International Trade in Goods

GRAPH SKILLS

Although the United States has a large trade deficit today, that was not always true.

1. What was the difference between imports and exports in 1965? In 1980? In 2009?

2. During what year shown here did the United States begin to show a trade deficit?

Action Graph
online

For an animated version of this graph, visit
PearsonSchool.com/PHecon

Effects of the Deficit

When Americans import more than they export, more dollars end up in the hands of foreigners. They can then use these extra dollars to purchase American land, stocks, bonds, and other assets. As a result of America's trade deficits, people from other countries now own a large piece of the U.S. economy. Many people fear this trend threatens national independence and even national security.

Some economists worry that foreign financial investment might not always support the trade deficit. They worry that, with U.S. imports on the rise and American foreign debt growing, overseas investors might become reluctant to purchase American assets. As a result, that monetary flow into the United States would slow down. In 2000, a federal commission formed to study the deficit concluded that "maintaining large and growing trade deficits is neither desirable nor likely to be sustainable for the extended future."

Can Balance Be Restored?

To reduce the trade deficit, the government could depreciate the exchange rate. As you saw, when the dollar is weak, American products become cheaper to buy on the world market and other countries' goods become correspondingly more expensive. As a result, exports rise and imports fall. The head of the nation's largest steelmaker noted this process at work in 2008:

> **"**The opportunities for exporting are infinitely greater than they were a year or two years ago. We have folks who were bringing in steel for decades coming to us and saying we'd like to talk to you about exporting. That is a huge change. It's because of the dollar.**"**
>
> —Dan DiMicco, interview

The federal government could also cut back spending by adjusting its monetary or fiscal policy, as you have seen in Chapters 15 and 16. Individuals could voluntarily purchase fewer foreign goods, despite the higher price of certain domestic items. Or American companies could try to sell more domestic products overseas. All of these approaches involve sacrifices or risk, but they would result in fewer surplus dollars ending up in foreign hands.

✓ **CHECKPOINT** *What has been the trend in the United States balance of trade in recent decades?*

(FL) LA.1112.2.2.2, SS.912.E.1.13, SS.912.E.3, SS.912.E.3.5, LA.1112.1.6.1

SECTION 3 ASSESSMENT

Essential Questions Journal To continue to build a response to the Essential Question, go to your **Essential Questions Journal**.

Guiding Question

1. Use your completed chart to answer this question: How do exchange rates affect international trade?

2. **Extension** You are saving money to buy a video game system made in Japan. Suddenly, Japan announces that it is reducing the value of the yen. Will that make it easier or harder for you to buy your game system? Why?

Key Terms and Main Ideas

3. What is an **exchange rate**?

4. What is the effect of **appreciation** and **depreciation** on the price of goods?

5. What happens in the **foreign exchange market**?

6. How do a **fixed exchange-rate system** and a **flexible exchange-rate system** differ?

7. What is the **balance of trade**?

8. How does the **balance of payments** differ from the **balance of trade**?

Critical Thinking

9. **Categorize** Explain how each of the following Americans might react to a rise in the value of the U.S. dollar and why: **(a)** a farmer who exports crops, **(b)** a consumer shopping for a new car, **(c)** the owner of a store selling imported food.

10. **Predict** How do you think a nation's balance of trade might be affected if its government instituted policies to support science education and give tax breaks to high-tech industries?

11. **Understand Cause and Effect** Explain how each of the following has contributed to the growth of the United States trade deficit: **(a)** consumer demand, **(b)** dependence on foreign oil, **(c)** exchange rates.

Math Skills

12. Assume that the numbers in **Figure 17.5** represent today's exchange rates. Using the formula shown in this section, calculate the price of a car that costs $18,000 in the United States in:

(a) Australian dollars, **(b)** euros, **(c)** yen.

Visit PearsonSchool.com/PHecon for additional math help.

Chapter 17: International Trade

Section 1 Why do nations trade?

Section 2 What are the arguments for and against trade barriers and agreements?

Section 3 How do exchange rates affect international trade?

Essential Question, Chapter 17
Should free trade be encouraged?

Economic Dictionary

export, *p. 449*

import, *p. 449*

absolute advantage, *p. 449*

comparative advantage, *p. 449*

law of comparative advantage, *p. 450*

interdependence, *p. 452*

trade barrier, *p. 455*

tariff, *p. 455*

import quota, *p. 456*

sanctions, *p. 456*

embargo, *p. 456*

trade war, *p. 457*

protectionism, *p. 457*

infant industry, *p. 458*

free trade, *p. 458*

free-trade zone, *p. 460*

exchange rate, *p. 463*

appreciation, *p. 464*

depreciation, *p. 465*

foreign exchange market, *p. 465*

fixed exchange-rate system, *p. 467*

flexible exchange-rate system, *p. 467*

balance of trade, *p. 468*

trade surplus, *p. 468*

trade deficit, *p. 468*

balance of payments, *p. 469*

Strong Dollar

As the dollar becomes stronger…

American exports decline

Weak Dollar

As the dollar becomes weaker…

American exports rise

Two International Trade Organizations

EU
- 27 nations of Europe
- 12 members use common currency
- Parliament and council
- Uniform tariffs for non-members

- Reduction or elimination of trade barriers
- Increased trade
- Controversy within countries

NAFTA
- 3 nations of North America
- No common currency
- No common legislative body
- Independent tariff policies

Economics *on the go*

Study anytime, anywhere. Download these files today.

Economic Dictionary
online
Vocabulary Support in English and Spanish

Audio Review
online
Audio Study Guide in English and Spanish

Action Graph
online
Animated Charts and Graphs

Visual Glossary
online
Animated feature

How the Economy Works
online
Animated feature

Download to your computer or mobile device at PearsonSchool.com/PHecon

Key Terms and Main Ideas

To make sure you understand the key terms and main ideas of this chapter, review the Checkpoint and Section Assessment questions and look at the Quick Study Guide on the preceding page.

Critical Thinking

1. **Infer (a)** How does resource distribution affect trade? **(b)** What might be the advantages and disadvantages of having an economy based on one or two natural resources that are in high demand? **(c)** If a nation has few natural resources but abundant human capital, what kinds of goods and services might it specialize in?

2. **Ask Questions (a)** What factors affect the decision to trade? **(b)** Choose a particular product. Suppose you were the owner of a small American company that made that product. List four questions you would ask before deciding whether to sell that product overseas.

3. **Analyze (a)** What does it mean when economists say the dollar is "weak"? **(b)** What impact would a weakening dollar have on Americans traveling overseas? On an American company selling products overseas? **(c)** Do you think the benefits of depreciation outweigh the costs? Explain.

4. Have students create a Circular Flow diagram of an open-market economy, which includes impact of international trade and other monetary transactions.

FL SS.912.E.2.12

Applying Your Math Skills

Interpreting Data From Graphs

Study the chart below, which shows the total exports and imports for the United States in 2006 for six different types of products.

Visit PearsonSchool.com/PHecon for additional math help.

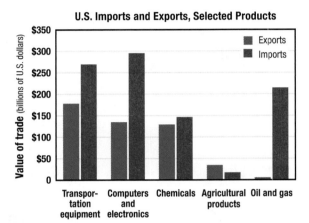

U.S. Imports and Exports, Selected Products

SOURCE: U.S. Census Bureau, *Statistical Abstract of the United States: 2008*

5. **(a)** Which category of products had the largest trade deficit? **(b)** How large was that deficit?

6. **(a)** Which category of products had the only surplus? **(b)** How large was that surplus?

7. Explain what would be likely to happen to the trade deficit under each of the following circumstances, and why: **(a)** engineers invent a new car engine that runs on hydrogen, **(b)** oil exporters raise prices by 10 percent, **(c)** new oil fields are discovered within the United States.

Essential Question Activity

8. Complete the activity to answer the Essential Question **Should free trade be encouraged?** For this activity, the class will be divided into six groups. One group will represent members of a Senate committee holding a hearing on a free-trade agreement with China being debated in Congress. Each of the other groups will represent one of the following: economists at the World Trade Organization; an American consumer interest group; an American automobile manufacturer; the American Federation of Labor; an organization of environmentalists. The senators should prepare their questions; the others should develop positions for or against the agreement. Using the worksheet in your Essential Questions Journal or the electronic worksheet available at **PearsonSchool.com/PHecon**, gather the following information:

(a) What effects do the speakers think the agreement will have on the people or businesses they represent?

(b) What effects do the groups think the agreement will have on the people of each senator's state?

(c) What effects do the groups think the agreement will have on the country as a whole?

9. **Modify** Congress sometimes insists on additions to agreements with other nations. Senators should explore these issues with each group. Then, they should announce:

(a) whether they will vote for or against the agreement.

(b) what added provisions, if any, they would support and why.

CHAPTER 17 ASSESSMENT

DOCUMENT-BASED ASSESSMENT

Should foreign ownership of U.S. assets be restricted?

High trade deficits have resulted in foreign businesses and countries holding large sums of U.S. dollars. Some have used that money to purchase U.S. companies or property, or to make loans to the federal government. Some critics are concerned that this trend could harm the U.S. economy.

Document A

	2001	2002	2003	2004	2005	2006
U.S. investment abroad (billions of dollars)	$6,309	$6,652	$7,643	$9,257	$11,576	$13,755
Percent change from prior year	+1.1%	+5.4%	+14.9%	+21.1%	+25.1%	+18.8%
Foreign investment in U.S. (billions of dollars)	$8,228	$8,740	$9,784	$11,551	$13,815	$16,295
Percent change from prior year	+8.0%	+6.2%	+11.9%	+18.1%	+19.6%	+18.0%

SOURCE: U.S. Census Bureau. *Statistical Abstract of the United States: 2008*

Document B

"Our trade deficit makes us increasingly vulnerable. That's because our trade deficit makes us dependent on foreign ownership of U.S. assets to finance our debt. [In the last five years] the United States has accumulated more foreign debt than in the entire first 220 years of our country's history.

"Unfair trade practices place American workers and businesses at a competitive disadvantage. We can compete with any country in the world—as long as the rules of trade are fair and equitable.

"We need an aggressive U.S. trade policy that stands up for American workers and businesses. To accomplish that goal, we need to use all the tools at our disposal to pry open foreign markets, enforce our intellectual property rights and make sure China, Japan, the European Union and other countries are not given an artificial trading advantage."

—Rep. Benjamin L. Cardin (Dem.-MD), 2006

Document C

"About 20 percent of all U.S. exports originate from U.S. affiliates of foreign-owned companies. [Foreign direct investment (FDI)] supports about 5.3 million U.S. jobs.... U.S. subsidiaries support an annual payroll of $317.9 billion with average compensation per employee worth almost $60,000—more than one-third more than the average American salary. Moreover, the benefits of FDI extend into the American economy as a whole. Increased investment and competition generate higher productivity and more efficient resource use. Ultimately, this culminates in greater economic growth, job creation and higher living standards for all. Any new rules that restrict, delay, or politicize foreign investment, will result in the loss of FDI.... Consequently, America will pay for higher investment barriers with lower growth and fewer jobs. FDI restrictions would undermine America's chances of remaining an economic superpower in an increasingly competitive global economy."

—Daniella Markheim, testimony to House Homeland Security committee, 2006

 FL LA.1112.1.6.2

ANALYZING DOCUMENTS

Use your knowledge of foreign trade and Documents A, B, and C to answer questions 1–3.

1. **Document A shows that, since 2000,**
   A. foreign investment in the U.S. has grown while U.S. investment abroad has fallen.
   B. both foreign investment in the U.S. and U.S. investment abroad have risen.
   C. foreign investment in the U.S. has fallen while U.S. investment abroad has grown.
   D. both foreign investment in the U.S. and U.S. investment abroad have fallen.

2. **Document B argues that**
   A. the trade deficit is a threat to the U.S. economy.
   B. American workers benefit from foreign investment.
   C. foreign investment will fall on its own.
   D. there is no way to reverse the trade deficit.

3. **Document C argues that foreign investment in the U.S.**
   A. promotes competition but costs jobs.
   B. results in higher prices.
   C. generates jobs and innovation.
   D. is not matched by U.S. investment abroad.

WRITING ABOUT ECONOMICS

Whether to put limits on foreign investment in the United States is a controversial issue. Use the documents on this page and resources on the Web site below to answer the question: *Should foreign ownership of U.S. assets be restricted?* Use the sources to support your opinion.

In Partnership

THE WALL STREET JOURNAL.
CLASSROOM EDITION

To read more about issues related to this topic, visit
PearsonSchool.com/PHecon

Databank: The World Economy

In this databank, you will look at the major role that the United States plays in world trade. You will also compare the United States economy to the economies of other nations.

U.S. Exports and Imports, by Major Trading Partners, August 2006–August 2007

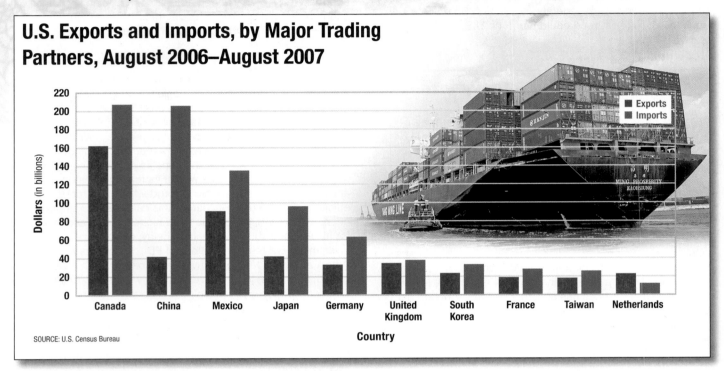

Dollars (in billions) — Country

Legend: ■ Exports ■ Imports

SOURCE: U.S. Census Bureau

Major U.S. Exports and Imports, 2004

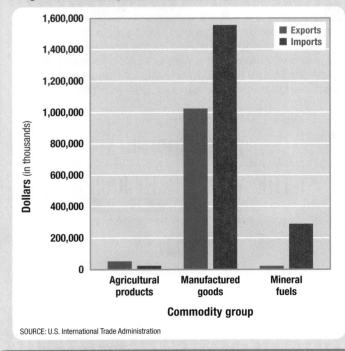

Dollars (in thousands) — Commodity group (Agricultural products, Manufactured goods, Mineral fuels)

Legend: ■ Exports ■ Imports

SOURCE: U.S. International Trade Administration

Exchange Rates of the Dollar

Country	2001	2004	2007	2010
Canada $	1.549	1.302	1.073	1.027
China Yuan	8.277	8.277	7.606	6.768
European Union €uro	0.895	1.247	1.371	1.328
Japan ¥en	121.600	108.200	117.800	85.250
Mexico Peso	9.337	11.290	10.930	12.670
United Kingdom £	1.440	1.833	2.002	1.598

SOURCE: U.S. Federal Reserve

 FL MA.912.A.2.2 Interpret a graph to represent a real-world situation.

SS.912.E.3 Understand the relationships of the U.S. economy and the international marketplace.

United States Trading Partners

Major trading partners
OPEC nations

Europe Inset

0 250 500 mi
0 250 500 km

RUSSIA
ESTONIA
LATVIA
LITHUANIA
RUSSIA
BELARUS
UKRAINE
MOLDOVA
ROMANIA
SERBIA
BOS.-BULGARIA
MONT.
MACEDONIA
ALBANIA
GREECE
TURKEY
CYPRUS
CRETE (Gr.)
MALTA
SICILY
ITALY
SAN MARINO
SARDINIA (It.)
CORSICA (Fr.)
TUNISIA
ALGERIA
MOROCCO
SPAIN
ANDORRA
PORTUGAL
IRELAND
UNITED KINGDOM
NETHERLANDS
BELGIUM
LUXEMBOURG
FRANCE
MONACO
SWITZ.
GERMANY
DECH. REP.
SLOVAKIA
AUSTRIA
HUNGARY
SLOVENIA
CROATIA
DENMARK
POLAND
Black Sea
ATLANTIC OCEAN

See Europe Inset

ARCTIC OCEAN

GREENLAND (Denmark)

ICELAND

CANADA

UNITED STATES

ATLANTIC OCEAN

PACIFIC OCEAN

MEXICO
GUATEMALA
EL SALVADOR
BELIZE
HONDURAS
NICARAGUA
COSTA RICA
PANAMA
GALAPAGOS IS. (Ecuador)
BAHAMAS
CUBA
JAMAICA
HAITI
DOMINICAN REP.
PUERTO RICO (U.S.)
COLOMBIA
ECUADOR
VENEZUELA
GUYANA
SURINAME
FRENCH GUIANA (Fr.)
PERU
BRAZIL
BOLIVIA
PARAGUAY
CHILE
ARGENTINA
URUGUAY

NORWAY
SWEDEN
FINLAND
UNITED KINGDOM
NETH.
FRANCE
SPAIN
GERMANY
ITALY
UKRAINE

RUSSIA

KAZAKHSTAN
GEORGIA
ARMENIA
AZERBAIJAN
TURKEY
SYRIA
LEBANON
ISRAEL
EGYPT
TUNISIA
LIBYA
ALGERIA
MOROCCO
WESTERN SAHARA (Occ. by Morocco)
MAURITANIA
MALI
NIGER
CHAD
SUDAN
ERITREA
ETHIOPIA
DJIBOUTI
SOMALIA
CANARY IS. (Sp.)
SENEGAL
THE GAMBIA
GUINEA-BISSAU
GUINEA
SIERRA LEONE
LIBERIA
CÔTE D'IVOIRE
BURKINA FASO
GHANA
TOGO
BENIN
NIGERIA
CAMEROON
EQUATORIAL GUINEA
GABON
CONGO
CENTRAL AFRICAN REP.
DEM. REP. OF CONGO
CABINDA (Angola)
ANGOLA
NAMIBIA
BOTSWANA
SOUTH AFRICA
LESOTHO
SWAZILAND
ZIMBABWE
ZAMBIA
MOZAMBIQUE
MADAGASCAR
MALAWI
TANZANIA
BURUNDI
RWANDA
UGANDA
KENYA
COMOROS
SEYCHELLES
MAURITIUS
REUNION (Fr.)

UZBEKISTAN
TURKMENISTAN
TAJIKISTAN
KYRGYZSTAN
AFGHANISTAN
PAKISTAN
IRAN
IRAQ
JORDAN
KUWAIT
SAUDI ARABIA
QATAR
U.A.E.
OMAN
YEMEN
SOCOTRA (Yemen)

MONGOLIA
CHINA
NEPAL
BHUTAN
INDIA
SRI LANKA
BURMA (MYANMAR)
BANGLADESH
LAOS
THAILAND
CAMBODIA
VIETNAM
MALAYSIA
SINGAPORE
BRUNEI
INDONESIA
PHILIPPINES
TAIWAN
N. KOREA
S. KOREA
JAPAN
PAPUA NEW GUINEA
TIMOR-LESTE
AUSTRALIA

INDIAN OCEAN

Equator
Tropic of Cancer
Tropic of Capricorn
Arctic Circle

3,000 mi
1,500 3,000 km
0
1,500
0

U.S. Oil Imports, 1973–2007

SOURCE: U.S. Census Bureau, Foreign Trade Division

Major Agricultural Exports and Imports, 2006

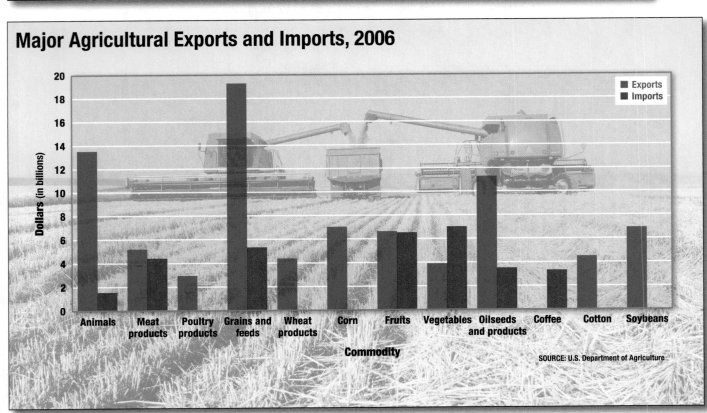

SOURCE: U.S. Department of Agriculture

Health Expenditures as Percent of GDP, 2004

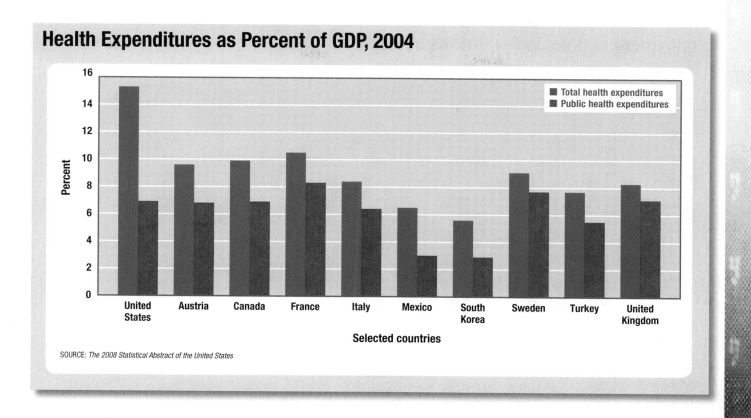

SOURCE: *The 2008 Statistical Abstract of the United States*

Legend:
- ■ Total health expenditures
- ■ Public health expenditures

Y-axis: Percent (0–16)
X-axis: Selected countries — United States, Austria, Canada, France, Italy, Mexico, South Korea, Sweden, Turkey, United Kingdom

Taxes as Percent of GDP 2004

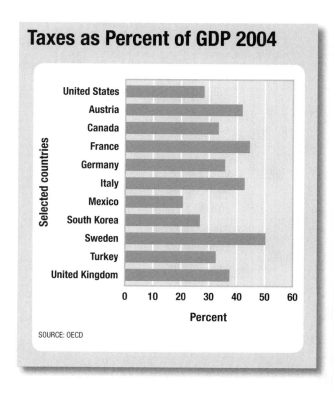

Selected countries: United States, Austria, Canada, France, Germany, Italy, Mexico, South Korea, Sweden, Turkey, United Kingdom

X-axis: Percent (0–60)

SOURCE: OECD

National Budgets

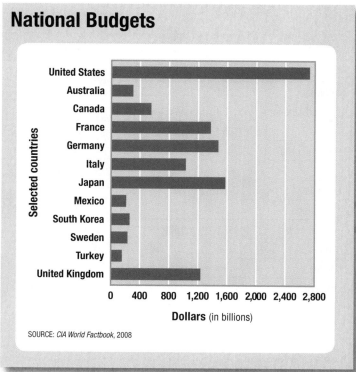

Selected countries: United States, Australia, Canada, France, Germany, Italy, Japan, Mexico, South Korea, Sweden, Turkey, United Kingdom

X-axis: Dollars (in billions) (0–2,800)

SOURCE: *CIA World Factbook*, 2008

FL MA.912.A.2.2 Interpret a graph to represent a real-world situation.

Employment in Selected Countries by Type

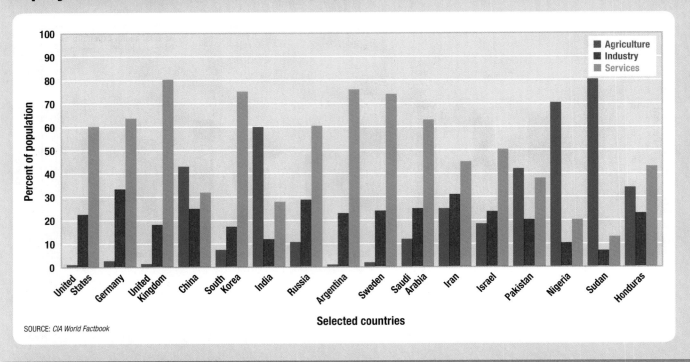

SOURCE: *CIA World Factbook*

GDP Growth of Selected Countries

Country	1999	2000	2001	2002	2003	2004	2005	2006	2007	2008	2009
United States	9,216	9,765	10,076	10,418	10,919	11,679	12,417	13,202	13,840	14,440	14,260
Germany	2,184	1,900	1,891	2,019	2,442	2,751	2,795	2,907	3,322	3,673	3,353
United Kingdom	1,465	1,443	1,435	1,571	1,806	2,132	2,199	2,345	2,773	2,680	2,184
China	1,083	1,198	1,325	1,454	1,641	1,932	2,234	2,668	3,251	4,327	4,909
South Korea	445	512	482	547	608	680	788	888	957	929	834
India	450	460	478	508	602	696	806	906	1,099	1,207	1,236
Russia	196	260	307	345	431	589	764	987	1,290	1,677	1,255
Argentina	284	284	269	102	130	153	183	214	260	325	310
Saudi Arabia	161	188	183	189	215	250	310	310	376	469	370
Iran	105	101	115	116	136	163	190	223	294	335	331
Israel	104	115	114	104	110	117	123	123	162	202	195
Nigeria	35	46	48	47	58	72	88	115	167	207	173
Sudan	11	12	13	15	18	21	28	38	46	58	55
Honduras	5	6	6	7	7	7	8	9	12	14	14

Note: Amounts in billions of dollars.
SOURCE: *CIA World Factbook*, World Bank

Labor Productivity by Country

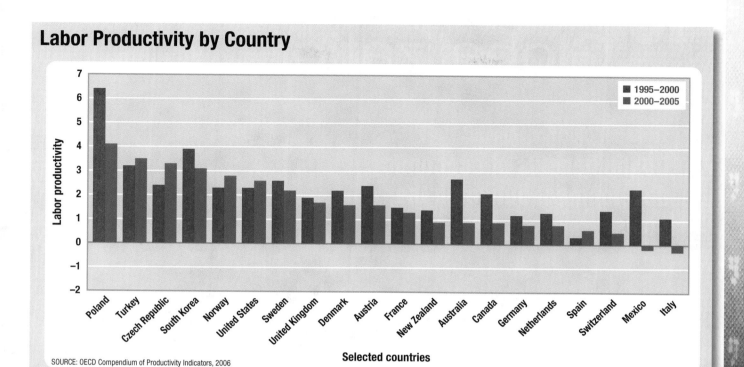

Legend: 1995–2000, 2000–2005

Y-axis: Labor productivity (−2 to 7)

X-axis (Selected countries): Poland, Turkey, Czech Republic, South Korea, Norway, United States, Sweden, United Kingdom, Denmark, Austria, France, New Zealand, Australia, Canada, Germany, Netherlands, Spain, Switzerland, Mexico, Italy

SOURCE: OECD Compendium of Productivity Indicators, 2006

Economic Health of Selected Countries

Country	Infant Mortality (per 1,000 live births)	Life Expect-ancy	Median Age	Literacy (by percent)	Unemploy-ment (by percent)	Internet Subscription (per 1,000 people)	Cellular Phone Ownership (per million people)
United States	6.14	78.24	36.8	99	9.3	750	879,000
Germany	3.95	79.41	44.3	99	7.5	750	1.3 million
United Kingdom	4.78	79.16	40.5	99	7.6	820	1.2 million
China	16.51	74.51	35.2	91.6	4.3	222	473,000
South Korea	4.24	78.81	37.9	97.9	3.7	770	940,000
India	49.13	66.46	25.19	61	10.7	70	471,000
Russia	10.32	66.16	38.5	99.4	8.4	320	1.34 million
Argentina	11.11	76.76	30.3	97.2	8.7	270	1.1 million
Saudi Arabia	11.2	76.51	21.6	78.8	11.7	290	1.25 million
Iran	34.66	71.43	27.6	77	11.8	350	650,000
Israel	4.17	80.86	29.3	97.1	7.6	290	1.3 million
Nigeria	92.99	47.24	19.1	68	5.8	70	422,000
Sudan	78.1	52.52	19.3	61.1	18.7	100	270,000
Honduras	21.04	70.51	20.7	80	36	84	100,000

SOURCE: CIA World Factbook, 2010

Databank: The World Economy

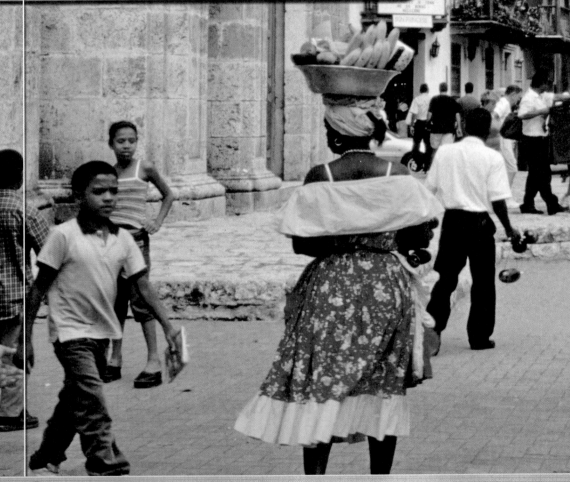

? Essential Question, Chapter 18

Do the benefits of economic development outweigh the costs?

FL **Next Generation Sunshine State Standards**

Section 1: Levels of Development
LA.1112.1.6, MA.912.A.2.2, SS.912.E.1, SS.912.E.2.1, SS.912.G.2.2
Section 2: Issues in Development
LA.1112.1.6, MA.912.A.2.2, SS.912.G.2, SS.912.G.2.2, SS.912.G.4
Section 3: Economies in Transition
LA.1112.1.6, MA.912.A.2.2, SS.912.E.1, SS.912.E.2.3, SS.912.G.2, SS.912.G.2.2
Section 4: Challenges of Globalization
LA.1112.1.6, MA.912.A.2.2, SS.912.E.3.1, SS.912.G.3.3, SS.912, G.4.4

Economics
on the go

To study anywhere, anytime, download these
online resources at *PearsonSchool.com/PHecon* ▶

NGSSS

LA.1112.1.6 Use multiple strategies to develop vocabulary.

MA.912.A.2.2 Interpret a graph to represent a real-world situation.

SS.912.E.1 Understand concepts relevant to a market economy.

SS.912.E.2.1 Identify and explain broad economic goals.

SS.912.G.2.2 Describe the factors that contribute to the differences between developing and developed regions.

ECONOMIC DICTIONARY

As you read the section, look for the definitions of these **Key Terms:**

- development
- developed nation
- less developed country
- newly industrialized country
- per capita GDP
- industrialization
- literacy rate
- life expectancy
- infant mortality rate
- subsistence agriculture

Guiding Question

How is a nation's level of development defined?

Copy this chart and fill it in as you read.

Measuring Development		
Per Capita GDP	**Consumption**	**Social Indicators**
• Allows comparison regardless of population	• Consumer goods:	• Literacy rate: high rate shows high level of development
• Limitation:	•	•
		•

▶ **Economics and You**   Have you ever given money for world famine relief? Or taken part in a fundraising drive to build a school in a foreign country? Each year, Americans of all ages donate money and time to such efforts. And the need is very real. Some three billion people—about half the world's population—live in extreme poverty.

Principles in Action   There are vast differences between prosperous nations—such as the United States or Canada—and poorer nations like Ethiopia or El Salvador. In this section, you will examine what some of these differences are and why they exist.

Levels of Development

Economists divide the world's nations into different categories according to their level of development. **Development** is the process by which a nation improves the economic, political, and social well-being of its people. It is important to remember that development refers to a nation's material well-being. It is not a judgment of the worth of a nation or its people. The level of development does not indicate cultural superiority or inferiority. It simply indicates how well a nation is able to feed, clothe, and shelter its people.

Nations with a relatively high average of material well-being are called **developed nations.** The United States, Canada, Japan, Australia, New Zealand, and the nations of Western Europe fall into this category.

development the process by which a nation improves the economic, political, and social well-being of its people

developed nation a nation with a relatively high average level of material well-being

Visual Glossary
online

Go to the Visual Glossary Online for an interactive review of **globalization**.

Action Graph
online

Go to Action Graph Online for animated versions of key charts and graphs.

How the Economy Works
online

Go to How the Economy Works Online for an interactive lesson on **the stages of economic development.**

Figure 18.1

Per Capita GDP of Selected Nations, 2005

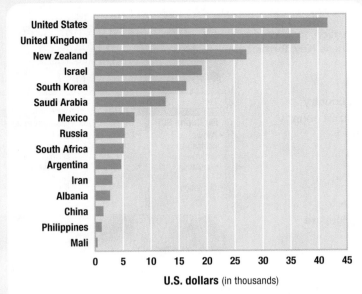

SOURCE: United Nations Statistics Division

GRAPH SKILLS

Per capita GDP is calculated by dividing a nation's gross national product by its population.

1. In 2005, how much larger was the per capita GDP of the United States than that of Albania?
2. Iran has a much larger population than New Zealand. What does this graph suggest about the economies of the two nations?

 MA.912.A.2.2
Interpret a graph to represent a real-world situation.

less developed country a nation with a relatively low level of material well-being

newly industrialized country a less developed country that has made great progress toward developing its economy

per capita GDP a nation's gross domestic product divided by its population

Most nations, however, have relatively low levels of material well-being. These **less developed countries** (LDCs) include the world's poorest countries, such as Bangladesh, Nepal, Albania, and nations of Central and Southern Africa.

One group of LDCs has made great progress toward developing their economies. These **newly industrialized countries** (NICs) include Mexico, Brazil, several countries in Eastern Europe, Saudi Arabia, and former republics of the Soviet Union. Some NICs are rich in resources, especially oil. Saudi Arabia, for example, has made a great deal of money from selling oil and oil products. Others have turned to manufacturing. Although the NICs have pulled ahead of the poorer LDCs, they have yet to achieve the high standard of living of developed nations.

✔ **CHECKPOINT** *How do NICs differ from both developed nations and LDCs?*

Measuring Development

Economists use many different factors to measure a nation's level of development. They include production of goods and services, energy consumption, distribution of the workforce, availability of consumer goods, and social indicators.

Per Capita GDP

As you read in Chapter 12, gross domestic product (GDP) is the total value of all final goods and services produced within an economy in a year. GDP alone, however, is not adequate to compare the living standards of nations. Instead, economists use **per capita GDP,** a nation's GDP divided by its population. As **Figure 18.1** shows, per capita GDP can vary widely from nation to nation.

Why is per capita GDP considered to be a more accurate measure of development than GDP by itself? Look at two nations, Japan and India. Both have high GDPs—about $4.22 trillion for Japan and about $2.98 trillion for India. Yet Japan enjoys a high standard of living, while India is relatively poor.

The reason for this discrepancy is population size. Japan's $4.22 trillion is shared by fewer than 127.7 million people. Thus, its per capita GDP is around $33,100. India's $2.98 trillion is shared by about 1.1 billion people, so its per capita GDP is only around $2,659. These figures indicate that the average person in Japan is better off, in material terms, than the average person in India.

Of course, per capita GDP does not take into account distribution of income. Within every nation, some people are wealthier than most, while others are poorer than most. In many LDCs, the gap between rich and poor is especially wide.

The World Bank, an international economic organization that studies development, uses a similar measure called per capita gross national income (GNI). Using this yardstick, the World Bank classifies nations as *high income, middle income,* and *low income.* (See **Figure 18.2.**)

Energy Consumption

Energy consumption is another good way to measure development. The amount of energy that a nation consumes is closely linked to its level of industrialization. **Industrialization** is the organization of an economy for the purpose of manufacture. Because industrial processes generally require large amounts of energy, high levels of energy use tend to indicate high levels of industrial activity.

Conversely, a low level of energy use tends to indicate that a nation has a low level of industrial activity. Most of the people are farmers working with simple tools and few machines.

Labor Force

Another sign of low development is if a large share of the population works in agriculture. Why is that the case?

If most people are raising food just for themselves, few are available to work in industry. As a result, there is little opportunity for workers to specialize. But, as you saw in Chapter 2, specialization makes an economy more efficient. If a nation cannot produce specialized goods to sell, it is unable to generate cash income.

Consumer Goods

The quantity of consumer goods a nation produces per capita also indicates its level of development. Availability of a large number of consumer goods indicates that people have enough money to meet their basic needs and still have enough left over to buy nonessential goods. Thus, economists measure how many people in a country own products such as computers, automobiles, washing machines, or telephones.

Social Indicators

Three social indicators also measure a nation's level of development. The first is **literacy rate,** the proportion of the population over age 15 that can read and write. In general, a high percentage of people attending school suggests a high level of development. An educated population has the potential to be more productive and to use or produce advanced technology.

Another indicator is **life expectancy,** the average expected life span of an individual.

industrialization
the organization of an economy for the purpose of manufacture

literacy rate the proportion of a nation's population over age 15 that can read and write

life expectancy the average expected life span of an individual

Figure 18.2 Levels of Development

High-income economies
(Per Capita GNI $11,116 or above)

Upper middle-income economies
(Per Capita GNI $3,596 – $11,115)

Lower middle-income economies
(Per Capita GNI $906 – $3,595)

Low-income economies
(Per Capita GNI $905 or less)

No data available

MAP SKILLS

Although income is only one measure of development, it gives a good indication of a nation's standard of living.

1. What is the average income level of the United States? Australia?
2. Based on this map, make one generalization about the relationship between geographic location and level of development.

Action Graph
online

For an animated version of this map, visit
PearsonSchool.com/PHecon

What are the stages of economic development?

All over the world, economic development commonly follows a pattern. The change may be rapid or it may take generations. The number of people who benefit also varies from place to place.

1 Society has a traditional economy, with no formal economic organization or monetary system. Economic decisions are based on tradition.

2 People adopt new living patterns and economic activities, often as the result of outside intervention. Industries are introduced. Cultural traditions begin to crumble as people begin to find work in new industries.

Primitive Equilibrium

Transition

It indicates how well an economic system supports life. People who are well nourished and housed and have access to medical care live longer. A population that lacks food and adequate housing and is exposed to poor sanitation and disease will have a shorter life expectancy.

A country's **infant mortality rate** indicates the number of deaths that occur in the first year of life per 1,000 live births. For example, in the United States, out of every 1,000 infants born alive in a given year, 6.4 of them die before they reach their first birthdays. This means that the United States has an infant mortality rate of 6.4. Generally speaking, the lower a nation's infant mortality rate, the higher its level of development. (See page 479 of the World Economy Databank to compare infant mortality and other measures among nations.)

infant mortality rate
the number of deaths that occur in the first year of life per 1,000 live births

✓ **CHECKPOINT** *How is energy use related to development?*

Characteristics of Developed Nations

Developed nations have high per capita GDPs, and the majority of the population is neither very rich nor very poor. In general, people enjoy a greater degree of economic and political freedom than do those in less developed countries.

Quality of Life

Levels of consumer spending are high in developed nations. For example, in the United States, the average household has 2.8 television sets, and more than 60 percent of households have computers.

The populations of developed nations are generally healthy, with low infant mortality rates and high life expectancy. Literacy rates are high as well. People tend to receive schooling well into their teens, and many go on to college.

3 New industries grow and profits are reinvested. As the economy expands, the society enters the international market. The traditional economic system continues to decline.

4 Economy is focused on consumer goods and public services. Basic human needs are met easily, but some people get left behind.

Check Your Understanding
1. What impact does development have on cultural traditions?
2. Why do you think economists use the word *equilibrium*, or balance, to describe the traditional economy?

Takeoff and Semidevelopment

Highly Developed

High Productivity

In most developed nations, agricultural output is high, but relatively few people work on farms. In the United States, for example, a single farmer can feed 80 people. Agriculture has largely become a high-tech big business:

> ❝New technologies are making the profession of farming more efficient, less risky, and less labor-intensive.... [Big farmers] are automating the entire farming process using GPS technology, genetically modified crops, automated irrigation systems, specialized fertilizers. ❞
> — Bob Baddeley, "Farm Technology: Applying High Tech for High Yields"

Since only a small portion of the labor force is needed in agriculture, more people are available to work in industry and services.

Widespread use of technology increases the productivity of this workforce.

Urbanization and Infrastructure

Developed nations tend to be urban rather than rural. Most of their populations live in cities and towns and have done so for many years. Major cities such as New York, London, and Tokyo are centers of finance and trade.

Hand-in-hand with urbanization goes a solid infrastructure. Power plants enhance a nation's capacity to produce goods. Transportation and communication systems allow easier transfer of products, services, people, and ideas. Schools increase a nation's literacy rate and productive capacity. Banks allow for secure transfer of financial assets.

✔ **CHECKPOINT** *Why is agricultural productivity high in developed nations?*

subsistence agriculture level of farming in which a person raises only enough food to feed his or her family

Characteristics of Less Developed Countries

Less developed countries generally have low per capita GDPs. Low per capita energy consumption is an indicator of their low level of industrialization.

Low Productivity

Many people in LDCs engage in **subsistence agriculture,** raising only enough food to feed themselves and their families. Subsistence agriculture requires heavy labor, leaving fewer workers available for industry or services.

Unemployment rates are high in less developed countries, often around 20 percent. In addition, much of the labor force in these nations is underemployed. Often people who are underemployed have work, but not enough to support themselves or their families because they work less than full time.

Quality of Life

Even if an LDC could produce consumer goods—which most do not—most of the population would be unable to buy them. Subsistence-level agriculture and underemployment do not provide families with enough income to buy these goods. Consumer goods that are produced are often shipped out of the country and sold in more developed nations.

A less developed country has trouble educating its populace. Resources for schools are limited. In addition, children are often needed to work on the family farm, limiting the amount of time they can spend in school. As a result, literacy rates in LDCs are very low. In Nepal, for example, only about 49 percent of the people over 15 years old can read and write. Compare this figure with the United States, where the literacy rate is nearly 100 percent.

In the world's poorest countries, housing and diet are of poor quality. Along with limited access to healthcare, these factors lead to high infant mortality rates and short life expectancy.

There are additional characteristics common to most LDCs. In the next section, you will read about some of the difficult issues challenging less developed countries.

✅ **CHECKPOINT** *Why do most people in LDCs have few consumer goods?*

SS.912.E.2.1, SS.912.G.2.2, LA.1112.1.6.1, LA.1112.2.2.2

Essential Questions Journal To continue to build a response to the Essential Question, go to your **Essential Questions Journal**.

SECTION 1 ASSESSMENT

🤔 Guiding Question

1. Use your completed chart to answer this question: How is a nation's level of development defined?

2. **Extension** What are some benefits of living in a developed nation?

Key Terms and Main Ideas

3. What are the characteristics of **developed nations?**

4. What is the difference between **less developed countries** and **newly industrialized countries?**

5. Why is **per capita GDP** a good tool to measure different countries' relative development?

6. Why are **life expectancy** and **infant mortality** considered to be good measures of a nation's level of development?

7. How is **subsistence agriculture** related to development?

Critical Thinking

8. **Analyze** Under what conditions might per capita GDP be an imperfect tool for comparing how well off people in different nations are?

9. **Connect** Explain how literacy, human capital, and economic development are interrelated.

10. **Apply** Explain why each of the following would be an important tool to enhance a country's rate of development: **(a)** a new airport, **(b)** high-speed Internet access, **(c)** an early childhood vaccination program, **(d)** opening an agricultural college.

11. **Cause and Effect** Describe the factors and processes, or actions, that contribute to the differences between developing and developed regions?

Math Skills

12. Using the information in the table below, calculate per capita GDP of these nations. In which nations would you predict is the population most well-off? Explain.

Visit PearsonSchool.com/PHecon for additional math help.

Nation	Total GDP	Population
Taiwan	$690.1 billion	22.86 million
Turkey	$667.7 billion	71.16 million
Netherlands	$638.9 billion	16.57 million
Poland	$624.6 billion	38.52 million
Saudi Arabia	$572.2 billion	27.6 million

NGSSS

LA.1112.1.6 Use multiple strategies to develop vocabulary.

MA.912.A.2.2 Interpret a graph to represent a real-world situation.

SS.912.G.2 Understand physical characteristics of places.

SS.912.G.2.2 Describe the factors that contribute to the differences between developing and developed regions.

SS.912.G.4 Understand the distribution of human populations.

ECONOMIC DICTIONARY

As you read the section, look for the definitions of these **Key Terms:**

- population growth rate
- malnutrition
- internal financing
- foreign investment
- foreign direct investment
- foreign portfolio investment
- debt rescheduling
- stabilization program
- nongovernmental organization

Guiding Question
What factors harm or help development?

Copy this chart and fill it in as you read.

Factors Affecting Development	
Factor	**Effect**
Population growth	High rate of population growth makes development more difficult
Physical capital	
Human capital	• Education and training • •
Political factors	
Economic factors	Large loans can lead to spiraling debt

▶ **Economics and You**   Even in a developed nation like ours, there are people who can't read or don't eat a healthy diet. But imagine that you never even had a *chance* to go to school. Imagine that a severe shortage of food reduced your chances of living to adulthood. For many people your age, such conditions are a grim reality.

Principles in Action Illiteracy and poor nutrition are just two of the factors that hinder development. In this section, you will see what LDCs and the world community are doing to combat these conditions and encourage economic growth.

Rapid Population Growth

As long ago as 1798, the English economist Thomas Malthus predicted that rapid population growth would become a serious problem:

> 66The power of population is indefinitely greater than the power in the earth to produce subsistence for man.... The food therefore which before supported seven millions, must now be divided among seven millions and a half or eight millions. The poor consequently must live much worse, and many of them be reduced to severe distress.99
>
> — Thomas Malthus, *Essay on Population*

Thanks to modern technology, the earth now produces more food than Malthus could have imagined. Still, rapid population growth remains one of the most pressing issues facing many less developed countries. The already poor economies of many LDCs have trouble meeting the needs of their rapidly growing populations.

Measuring Population Growth

The **population growth rate** is a measure of how rapidly a country's population increases in a given year. It is expressed as a percentage of the population figure at the start of the year. The population growth rate takes into account the number of babies born, the number of people who died, and the number of people who migrated to or from a country.

population growth rate a measure of how rapidly a country's population increases in a given year

▲ This picture shows a street scene in Cairo, Egypt. Cairo is one of the most densely populated cities in the world and the population is growing rapidly. ***What challenges might a fast-growing population pose for a country?***

Figure 18.3

Population of Selected Nations

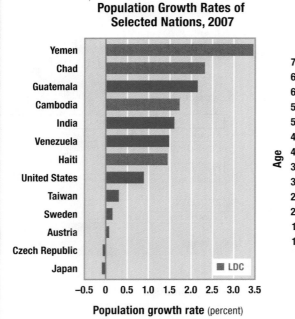

Population Growth Rates of Selected Nations, 2007

Yemen, Chad, Guatemala, Cambodia, India, Venezuela, Haiti, United States, Taiwan, Sweden, Austria, Czech Republic, Japan

■ LDC

−0.5 0 0.5 1.0 1.5 2.0 2.5 3.0 3.5

Population growth rate (percent)

SOURCE: *CIA World Factbook*; The United Nations; The World Bank

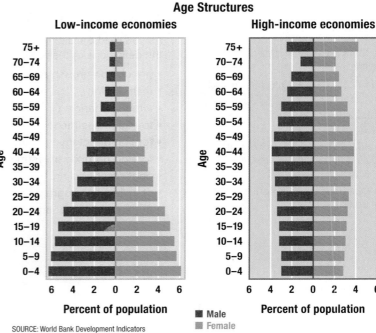

Age Structures

Low-income economies

75+, 70–74, 65–69, 60–64, 55–59, 50–54, 45–49, 40–44, 35–39, 30–34, 25–29, 20–24, 15–19, 10–14, 5–9, 0–4

Age

6 4 2 0 2 4 6

Percent of population

High-income economies

75+, 70–74, 65–69, 60–64, 55–59, 50–54, 45–49, 40–44, 35–39, 30–34, 25–29, 20–24, 15–19, 10–14, 5–9, 0–4

Age

6 4 2 0 2 4 6

Percent of population

■ Male
■ Female

SOURCE: World Bank Development Indicators

GRAPH SKILLS

The graph on the left shows rates of population growth for selected nations. The graphs in the middle and on the right show how age distribution is related to national income.

1. In which nations is the population growing at a rate about double that of the United States?
2. Based on these graphs, what shape would you expect Guatemala's age structure to have?

Action Graph
online

For an animated version of this graph, visit
PearsonSchool.com/PHecon

MA.912.A.2.2
Interpret a graph to represent a real-world situation.

Personal Finance
For information on planning now for your retirement years, see your Personal Finance Handbook in the back of the book or visit
PearsonSchool.com/PHecon

Compare the growth rates shown in **Figure 18.3**. Average population growth of less developed countries is estimated to be around 1.8 percent. This may sound low to you, but at this rate the population of LDCs will increase by nearly two-thirds from 2007 to 2050. That is more than 20 times the population growth of developed nations during the same period.

Causes of Rapid Population Growth
Rapid population growth has several causes. Many LDCs are experiencing increased life expectancy. While people are living longer, birth rates have not significantly decreased. When births far outpace deaths, the population grows.

Age structure also contributes to rapid population growth. In many LDCs, a high proportion of the population is of child-bearing age (See **Figure 18.3.**). As these younger adults have children, the population continues to grow. In developed nations, a larger segment of the population is older, so population increases at a much slower rate.

Challenge of Population Growth
As its population grows, a country must expand employment opportunities, health-care, education, and infrastructure—just to maintain its existing standard of living. To actually improve the lives of its people, a nation has to generate a higher per capita GDP. Economic output must grow faster than the population grows.

In a less developed country with a high population growth rate, such accelerated economic growth is a daunting task. A primary reason is that these LDCs lack various factors of production.

✔ **CHECKPOINT** *Why is rapid population growth a problem for LDCs?*

Limited Resources and Capital

In parts of Africa, Asia, and Latin America, physical geography is a serious obstacle to development. Natural resources are not evenly distributed throughout the world. Some nations lack mineral resources or fertile farmland. Harsh temperatures, uncertain rainfall, and vulnerability to natural disasters such as floods or earthquakes also contribute to the economic problems of some LDCs.

The problem is not always lack of resources. Rather, less developed countries often lack the means to use their resources efficiently. Technology can help LDCs develop the resources they do have. Technology, however, is costly and requires much capital. The formation of capital is another important obstacle to development.

Physical Capital

The low productivity typical of LDCs is due in part to lack of physical capital. Without capital, industry cannot grow and farm output remains low. Also, subsistence agriculture does not give farmers the opportunity to save. As a result, they do not have the cash to purchase capital that would make their farmwork more productive or to pay for goods and services that would improve their lives.

Education and Training

Lack of human capital also hinders development. To be able to move beyond mere subsistence, a nation needs an educated workforce. Education and training allow people to develop new skills and adapt to new technologies and processes. As you read in Section 1, however, many less developed countries have low literacy rates. **Figure 18.4** compares figures for education and literacy of the United States and several less developed countries.

Two factors combine to lower literacy rates in these countries. First, only three out of four children in LDCs who begin primary school are still in school four years later. Many children are forced to leave school because they are needed at home to work on family farms.

Figure 18.4 — Education and Literacy

Country	Primary School Enrollment Rate (percentage)		Literacy Rate (percentage)	
	Female	Male	Female	Male
United States	90	94	99	99
Peru	97	97	82.1	93.5
Indonesia	93	95	86.8	94
Nigeria	57	64	60.6	75.7
Yemen	63	87	30	70.5
Chad	46	68	39.3	56
Niger	32	46	15.1	42.9

SOURCE: *CIA World Factbook*, United Nations Children Fund

CHART SKILLS
Education and literacy rates vary from country to country. These rates can also vary between men and women in the same country.

1. What percentage of male children attend school in Nigeria? In which nation can the smallest percentage of the population read and write?

2. Based on these charts, which two nations show the greatest inequality in education between men and women? What impact might this have?

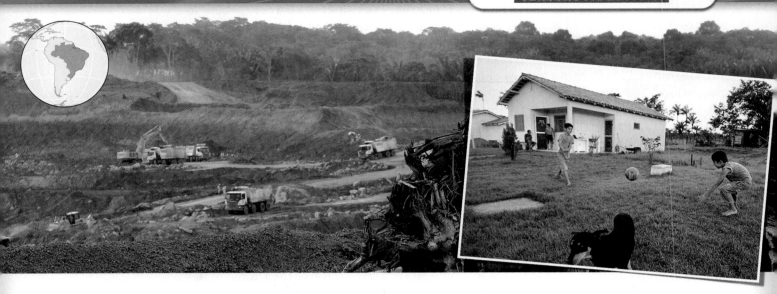

Rolling on the River

AMAZON DAM

Amazon dam project is designed to generate power—and quiet critics

By John Lyons
The Wall Street Journal

 SS.912.E.3.4 Assess the impact of negative and positive externalities on the international environment.

The Santo Antonio dam in Porto Vehlo, Brazil, marks the country's return to hydroelectric-dam construction in the Amazon, after projects in the 1980s left a trail of environmental disasters. The new project is the first step in a plan to power Brazil's growth into a developed nation.

Yet few people have heard of it, even in Brazil—which is just how the builders planned it. The builders spent some $600 million to head off troubles with regulators, environmental groups and native tribes—troubles that have delayed other dam projects and multiplied their costs. They trained residents for construction jobs and built houses for families who will be displaced. They created a high-tech ladder for fish to get around the dam. They pushed the limits of turbine technology to reduce the area that will be flooded.

On one hand, Santo Antonio's greener look is a victory for environmentalists. But the real environmental impact could prove huge. That's because a successful model for one large Amazon dam could pave the way for an extensive network of new dams and a subsequent wave of industrial development. In all, Brazil wants to build as many as 24 dams in the Amazon this decade.

The dams are about more than electricity: They are designed to include a canal system to help farmers and loggers get their goods to market by barge.

Opponents say Brazil should consider alternatives such as improving existing dams before pushing into the sensitive and species-rich rain forest. Dam proponents reply that hydropower is cheaper and cleaner than things like coal, and that most big rivers not yet dammed are in the rain forest.

A dam's biggest environmental impact comes when the area behind it is flooded. Santo Antonio will flood around 100 square miles, less than one-tenth of what a traditional dam would. To house the 1,400 displaced families, many of whom live in wooden shacks, the builders are constructing riverside communities of modest homes with running water. They also launched a big job-training program, which so far has trained 20,000 local people to work on the project.

One is Arlincen Batista Gomes. A mother of seven, she was scraping by on $110 a month as a house cleaner when she saw an ad for the free training. Now she is a carpenter earning around $750 monthly. "This is the first real opportunity I've had in my life to do something," she says.

Applying Economic Principles
The building of dams on the Amazon involves what economists call positive and negative externalities. Describe the benefits and costs to those not responsible for decisions to build the dams.

Second, in many LDCs, the literacy rate for women lags far behind that for men. Many women in these countries begin raising children at an early age. Those who do work have limited job opportunities and earn low wages. In addition, some cultures devalue women. Due to all these factors, a large part of a country's population lacks the training needed to be highly productive.

Nutrition and Health

Poor nutrition and health also impede the development of human capital. Many people in less developed countries suffer from **malnutrition,** or consistently inadequate nutrition. (A worldwide increase in food prices in the early 2000s aggravated the situation.) Malnutrition lowers the energy of adults and makes them more vulnerable to disease. Both results can reduce worker productivity. Malnutrition also slows the physical and mental development of children, hurting their chances of being productive workers once they become adults.

In many LDCs, poor sanitation leads to the spread of disease. In addition, many poorer countries have high rates of infection by HIV, the virus that causes AIDS. This epidemic removes large numbers of workers from the workforces of these countries. In addition, caring for these people and their families puts a strain on the resources of many LDCs. Money that could be spent on schools or infrastructure has to be devoted to healthcare or providing for orphaned children.

☑ **CHECKPOINT** *How do education and training contribute to development?*

Political Obstacles

Political factors may also limit or even reverse a nation's development. Many LDCs are former colonies of European powers. Colonies had to supply the ruling powers with resources and to rely on them for manufactured goods. This dependency prevented the development of industry.

In the decades after World War II, these colonies won independence. Many then turned to central planning, rather than free enterprise, as the way to modernize their economies quickly. These nations made

some gains at first, but in the long run, central planning hindered their economic growth. Many are now making the transition to free enterprise systems.

Government corruption has also held back development in many LDCs. Some leaders have funneled huge sums of money into private accounts, allowing them to live luxurious lives while large numbers of their people remain poor.

Civil war and social unrest plague many countries, such as El Salvador, Rwanda, and Cambodia. Years of fighting may leave millions dead and millions more as refugees. Loss of workers, as well as damage to resources and infrastructure, can throw a nation's economy in chaos.

Finally, economic policies in many LDCs have favored small minorities. In some countries, policies benefit city dwellers and not the rural majority. In some, leaders favor only one ethnic group—typically their own. In extreme cases, governments practice policies of genocide—or the attempted extermination of an entire ethnic or religious group.

☑ **CHECKPOINT** *What political factors have hindered development?*

Financing Development

Building an infrastructure, providing services, and creating technology and industry all require large sums of money. A developing country can acquire these funds through a variety of means. These include internal financing, foreign investment, borrowing, and foreign aid. However, many of these solutions—especially borrowing— create problems of their own.

Internal Financing

In many ways, the most favorable source of development funds is internal financing. **Internal financing** is capital derived from the savings of the country's own citizens. As you read in Chapter 11, when savers deposit money in banks or other financial institutions, some of the money is used to make loans to firms. Firms invest in physical and human capital so they can expand, creating new jobs. Job growth enables workers to improve their standard of living. They buy more goods and services, which encourages

Simulation *Activity*

How Will You Help?
You may be asked to take part in a role-playing game about financing development in a poor nation.

malnutrition
consistently inadequate nutrition

internal financing
capital derived from the savings of a country's citizens

foreign investment capital that originates in other countries

foreign direct investment the establishment of a business by investors from another country

foreign portfolio investment purchases made in a country's financial markets by investors from another country

businesses to expand further. As a result, the entire economy grows.

In most LDCs, though, large segments of the population do not have enough money to save. The wealthy few often keep their money in foreign banks or invest in foreign firms because these investments are safer. As a result, most poor countries have little capital available from internal financing. In order to fund development, they must turn to foreign sources.

Foreign Investment

Capital that originates in other countries is called **foreign investment.** There are two types of foreign investment: direct investment and portfolio investment.

Foreign direct investment occurs when investors establish a business in another country. For example, multinational corporations often build factories or other facilities in an LDC. Multinationals make this investment to take advantage of natural resources available in the less developed country or to tap into the large and cheap labor force.

As you have seen, multinationals are controversial. Some economists say that the

people of the LDC who work for the foreign corporation are better off than they would be doing other work. Their wages give them cash they can use to buy goods, which can help stimulate their country's economy. Critics say that multinationals exploit workers by paying them less than they would pay workers in developed nations. Critics also charge that multinationals can hurt a nation's economic growth by taking profits out of the country.

Instead of building businesses, foreign investors can make purchases in another country's financial markets. This is known as **foreign portfolio investment.** For example, an American investor might buy shares in a mutual fund. The mutual fund then buys stock in a foreign company. That company can use the funds to build another plant or to pay for research and development. Still, portfolio investment does present some problems. Since the investors live in another country, some or all of the company's profits may be drained away from the LDC.

Borrowing and Debt

In the 1970s and 1980s, many less developed countries acquired loans from foreign governments and private banks to finance development. Some of that money was misspent because of inexperience or political corruption.

Changes in the world economy also caused problems for the LDCs. As oil prices rose, they borrowed more money to buy needed fuel. Also, many of the loans were issued in—and had to be repaid in—U.S. dollars. When the value of the dollar increased in the 1980s, many LDCs found it impossible to repay their loans. Once again, many were forced to borrow even more funds. As a result, the foreign debt in some countries grew to be greater than their annual GDP. As you will see, the world financial community has sought ways to relieve this severe debt crunch.

Foreign Aid

Sometimes, rather than making loans to developing nations, foreign governments give money and other forms of aid. For instance, many developed nations provide cash payments for building schools,

Ford Motors has expanded its business by setting up factories in other countries, such as South Africa, Brazil, and Thailand. ▼

sanitation systems, roads, and other infrastructure. These foreign aid grants do not need to be repaid. **Figure 18.5** shows the top recipients of U.S. foreign aid.

Foreign aid can be motivated by humanitarian concerns. At the same time, developed nations have military, political, economic, and cultural reasons to extend aid to LDCs. In the years following World War II, for instance, American officials gave aid to countries in Africa, Asia, and Latin America to try to block the influence of the Soviet Union in those areas. In the early 2000s, the United States provided money to Iraq and Afghanistan. American leaders hoped to fight international terrorism by building stable democracies in those countries.

✔ **CHECKPOINT** *Why is internal financing difficult for less developed countries?*

International Institutions

Several international economic organizations promote development. The most prominent institutions are the World Bank, the United Nations Development Program, and the International Monetary Fund. In addition, privately run aid groups give economic help and advice in some less developed countries.

World Bank

The largest provider of development assistance is the World Bank, founded in 1944. The World Bank raises money on world financial markets and also accepts contributions from the wealthier member nations. The World Bank uses these funds to offer loans and other resources to more than 100 less developed countries. The World Bank also coordinates with other organizations to promote development throughout the world and provides advice to LDCs on how to build their economies.

United Nations Development Program

The United Nations Development Program (UNDP) is dedicated to the elimination of poverty. The UNDP is one of the world's largest sources of grant funding for economic and social development. It devotes 90 percent of its resources to 166 low-income nations,

Note: Due to rounding, figures may not add up to exactly 100%.
SOURCE: OECD and Budget of the United States Government
Fiscal Year 2006

GRAPH SKILLS
This pie graph shows the ten countries that received the most foreign aid from the United States in 2006.
1. Identify the amount of foreign aid each of these countries received: Iraq, Colombia, Congo.
2. Why might it benefit the United States to provide aid to Afghanistan?

where 90 percent of the world's poorest people live. The UNDP is funded by voluntary contributions made by United Nations member states and agencies.

 MA.912.A.2.2 Interpret a graph to represent a real-world situation.

International Monetary Fund

As you learned in Chapter 17, the International Monetary Fund was founded in 1946 to stabilize international exchange rates. Today, the IMF has expanded its role in the world economy. It promotes development by offering policy advice and technical assistance to LDCs. It also intervenes when LDCs need help in financing their international transactions.

If a country has trouble repaying a debt, the IMF may arrange a rescheduling plan. **Debt rescheduling** is an agreement between a lending nation and a debtor nation. The lending nation lengthens the time of debt repayment and forgives, or dismisses, part of the loan. In return, the LDC agrees to accept a **stabilization program,** changing its economic policies to meet IMF goals.

A typical stabilization program involves providing incentives that will lead to higher export earnings and to fewer imports. By increasing exports, the LDC earns more foreign money to pay off its debt.

debt rescheduling
an agreement between a lending nation and a debtor nation that lengthens the time of debt repayment and forgives part of the loan

stabilization program
an agreement between a debtor nation and the International Monetary Fund in which the nation agrees to change its economic policy to match IMF goals

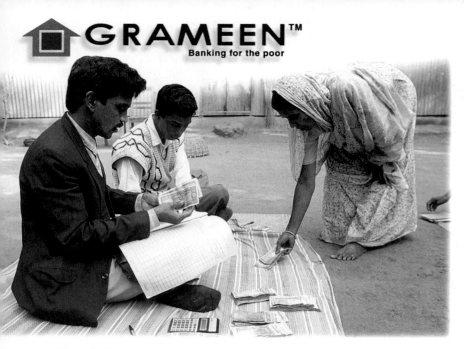

GRAMEEN™
Banking for the poor

▲ Founded in Bangladesh, the Grameen Bank pioneered microlending, the practice of making very small loans to people like this village woman.

nongovernmental organization
an independent group that raises money and uses it to fund aid and development programs

Stabilization programs are controversial because they can have a negative impact on the poor in the short term. They often require the LDC to lift wage and price controls. As wages drop and prices rise, the poor suffer. Stabilization may also force a government to cut spending on health, food, and education. Negative experiences in East Asia and Argentina have led some critics to question whether IMF policies are the most effective way to repair a troubled economy.

Nongovernmental Organizations

Some private aid groups also work to help the LDCs build their economies. **Nongovernmental organizations** (NGOs) are independent groups that raise money to fund aid and development programs. Examples are the Red Cross, CARE, and the World Wildlife Fund.

Some NGOs focus on providing food or medical help when natural disasters or wars cause problems. For instance, Oxfam International provides food to poor countries when they face extreme needs. Others try to promote development. For example, Heifer International gives animals to families in less developed countries. Families use these animals to produce and sell products such as wool, milk, or honey.

In 1976, Muhammad Yunus of Bangladesh founded the Grameen Bank. Since then, the bank has extended its operations to nearly every continent. The bank makes small loans—often, as little as a few dollars—to poor people. Many of the borrowers are women in rural villages. They use the loans to start their own businesses and lift their families out of poverty.

✔ **CHECKPOINT** *Why are stabilization programs controversial?*

FL SS.912.G.2.2, SS.912.G.4, LA.1112.1.6.1, LA.1112.2.2.2, LA.1112.2.2.3

SECTION 2 ASSESSMENT

Essential Questions Journal
To continue to build a response to the Essential Question, go to your **Essential Questions Journal**.

❓ Guiding Question

1. Use your completed chart to answer this question: What factors harm or help development?
2. **Extension** If you were given $100 to donate to a group that promoted development, what kind of group would you choose? Why?

Key Terms and Main Ideas

3. What factors contribute to a high **population growth rate?**
4. Why are literacy rates relatively low in less developed countries?
5. Why do less developed countries need to rely on **foreign investment** rather than **internal financing?**

6. How do less developed countries benefit from **debt rescheduling?**

Critical Thinking

7. **Take a Position (a)** What prediction did Malthus make about population growth? **(b)** Do you agree that such results are inevitable? Explain.
8. **Prioritize** Suppose you were the head of a less developed country. Which obstacle to development would you tackle first? Why?
9. **Make a Decision** Do you think it would be more beneficial for a country to take a loan to fund new development or to invite in foreign investors? Explain your choice.

Quick Write

10. Suppose you are an economist with World Bank, International Monetary Fund, or United Nations Development Program. Write a memo to the president of the group explaining why the organization should take steps to combat corruption in less developed countries.

NGSSS

LA.1112.1.6 Use multiple strategies to develop vocabulary.

MA.912.A.2.2 Interpret a graph to represent a real-world situation.

SS.912.E.1 Understand concepts relevant to a market economy.

SS.912.E.2.3 Research the contributions of key individuals of various backgrounds in the development of the U.S.

SS.912.G.2 Understand physical characteristics of places.

SS.912.G.2.2 Describe the factors that contribute to the differences between developing and developed regions.

ECONOMIC DICTIONARY

As you read the section, look for the definitions of these **Key Terms:**

• privatization
• special economic zone

Guiding Question

How has economic change affected different countries?

Copy this chart and fill it in as you read.

Russia	China	Brazil	Mexico
• Yeltsin: rapid switch to market	•	• Natural resources: iron, timber, land and climate	•
•	•	•	•
•	•	•	•
•		•	
		•	

▶ **Economics and You** Change is always challenging. Suppose that suddenly no American could attend high school without paying tuition. It is easy to imagine the hardships this might cause. But if somebody gave you a million dollars, you might face different sorts of problems. Would you be tempted to spend the money on the wrong things? What new demands might friends and family make of you?

The same is true of nations. Economic change—even change for the better—always brings new challenges.

Principles in Action Today, many countries are undergoing economic transition. Some are enjoying rapid growth, while others are changing their entire economic systems. In this section, you will look at the changing economies of Russia, China, India, and the countries of Africa and Latin America. In addition, the Economics & You feature shows some ways that economic change around the world may affect you.

Toward a Market Economy

For many nations, economic transition has meant moving from central planning to a market-based economy. As you saw in Chapter 2, in a command economy, the government owns and controls the factors of production. By contrast, in a market-based economy, the factors of production are owned and controlled by individuals. One of the first steps, then, in moving to a market economy is to sell or transfer government-owned businesses to individuals. This process is called **privatization.**

Privatization

A government can privatize businesses in several ways. It could simply sell the business to one owner. It could also sell shares to investors. A third alternative is to give every citizen a voucher that can be used to purchase shares in whatever businesses they wish, once those businesses are privatized.

Privatization can be a painful process. Only profitable enterprises will survive in a free market. No one will want to buy unprofitable ones, so many people will lose their jobs. Other job opportunities will eventually

privatization the sale or transfer of government-owned businesses to individuals

▲ In China, transition from strict communism to free market practices has given rise to a new generation of entrepreneurs, such as this store owner.

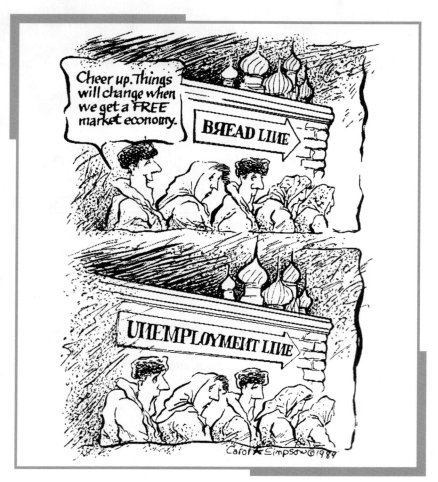

Cheer up. Things will change when we get a FREE market economy.

BREAD LINE →

UNEMPLOYMENT LINE →

Carol ★ Simpson © 1989

▲ This cartoon outlines some of the problems that Russia and other communist countries faced as they made the transition to free market economics. *According to the cartoon, what economic problems did Russia face before and after the transition? Explain why each of these problems occurred.*

appear as the economy grows. However, the initial transition can be difficult for workers accustomed to jobs guaranteed by the government.

Another concern is corruption. Government leaders might make it easier for their own friends and associates to gain control of businesses. The result is an unfair distribution of ownership.

Protecting Property Rights
Moving to a market economy also requires changes in the legal system. Centrally planned economies have no need to protect private property rights. A free market economy, however, cannot function without such protections. As a result, the government must create new laws that ensure a person's right to own and transfer property. Such a basic overhaul of the legal system takes time.

Citizen Attitudes
In a planned economy, workers grow used to security. Many have guaranteed jobs where their only concern is to meet government quotas. In the free market, such guarantees do not exist. Incentives, not quotas, motivate people's labor. As a result, workers in a transitioning economy need to learn a new work ethic.

Not surprisingly, people accustomed to central planning often worry about how change will affect them. They might resist the shift to the free market out of fear and uncertainty.

☑ **CHECKPOINT** *Identify three challenges in moving to a free market economy.*

Transition in Russia
Russia has faced all of the challenges described above. It was once part of the Soviet Union, the world's most powerful communist nation. But in 1991, Soviet communism—and the Soviet Union itself—collapsed. Russia and the other former Soviet republics began the difficult transition to a free market economy.

Fall of Communism
Under communism, government planners directed the Soviet economy. The nation became an industrial giant and a military superpower. Still, as you saw in Chapter 2, the Soviet people faced frequent shortages of consumer goods, and the goods they did get were often low quality.

In the late 1980s, a new Soviet leader named Mikhail Gorbachev began a series of dramatic political and economic changes to revive the country's stagnant economy. Gorbachev did not want to overturn the communist economic and political system. Rather, he hoped to incorporate the use of markets and incentives into the existing structure of communism.

The transition to free market economics created problems, however. Economic reform produced some initial hardships. People lost secure government jobs, benefits, and pensions. Many people, especially the elderly, were hurt financially. Some Russians did begin to make the new system work for them, starting their own businesses and prospering. Still, unrest grew.

At the same time, some officials and army officers feared that the central government was becoming weak. In 1991, they tried to restore old-style communism. The attempt backfired. One by one, the 15 Soviet republics declared their independence. The largest of the new nations was the Russian Republic.

A Painful Transition

Russia's new president, Boris Yeltsin, promised rapid progress towards a market economy. Despite improvements, hardships continued. When Yeltsin lifted price controls in 1992, prices tripled. People on fixed incomes, such as retirees living on government pensions, could not afford to buy basics like food and clothing.

In the new Russia, wealth tended to become concentrated in cities such as Moscow. The uneven distribution of income led many to call for additional change. It also led to extensive corruption and widespread organized crime.

Billions of dollars in financial aid flooded into the country from the World Bank, the IMF, and independent investors. However, due to mismanagement and corruption, these funds were not used efficiently. By 1998, the Russian economy was in a shambles. Debt was high, investor confidence was low, and the nation was in the midst of an economic crisis.

Russia in a New Century

Tight controls from the central government, combined with rising prices for Russian oil, allowed Russian leaders to stem the crisis. By 2007, according to the IMF, Russia had the world's seventh largest national economy, and much of the nation's foreign debt had been repaid. Economic growth has fed growing consumer demand. New laws protect investments, encouraging foreign investors to supply capital to launch new businesses.

Still, problems persist. Russia's economy relies too much on the export of natural resources. If the prices of these goods drop, export income will fall. In recent years, Russian leaders have restored government control over many aspects of the economy. The transition to a market economy is far from complete.

✔ **CHECKPOINT** *How did communism end in the Soviet Union?*

Growth in Asia

Asia, the world's largest continent, is home to more than 4 billion people—over 60 percent of the world's total population. These people provide a huge workforce and a huge market for goods and services. In recent decades, Asia has become one of the most dynamic players in the global economy. Nations such as Singapore, South Korea, and Taiwan have incomes comparable to highly developed nations in the rest of the world.

As you can see from **Figure 18.6,** China is a major exporter of goods and a key trading partner of the United States. India, too, has experienced rapid economic growth. How did these two nations, once among the world's poorest, advance so far, so rapidly?

China

In 1949, after a long civil war, communists led by Mao Zedong took power in China. They quickly put in place communist policies, giving the government ownership of all land, resources, and enterprises. Government planners made all key decisions about the economy.

After Mao died in 1976, Deng Xiaoping became China's new leader. Deng soon began using the tools of the free market

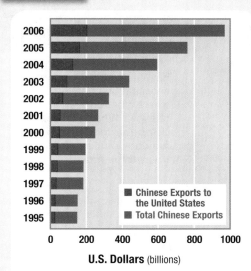

Figure 18.6 **Chinese Exports, 1995–2006**

2006
2005
2004
2003
2002
2001
2000
1999
1998
1997
1996
1995

0   200   400   600   800   1000

U.S. Dollars (billions)

■ Chinese Exports to the United States
■ Total Chinese Exports

SOURCE: The World Trading Organization and Ferrantino, Michael and Zhi Wang. "Accounting Discrepancies in Bilateral Trade: The Case of China, Hong Kong, and the U.S." *The Office of Economics (Working Paper),* The U.S. International Trade Commission, April 2007.

GRAPH SKILLS

Since China began to adopt free market policies, the export of Chinese products to the world market has skyrocketed.

1. How much did the value of Chinese exports to the world grow between 1995 and 2006?

2. What percentage of China's exports went to the United States in 2000? In 2006?

special economic zones designated regions that operate under different economic laws from the rest of the country in order to attract foreign investment and promote exports

to increase productivity. He gave farmers and factory managers more freedom to make decisions about what to produce and how much to charge for it. He also rewarded farmers, managers, and workers who increased output. With such incentives, production increased.

Deng also set up four free market centers along China's east coast. Foreign businesses could operate, and local governments were allowed to offer tax incentives to foreign investors in these **special economic zones.** Chinese businesses could operate freely as well, with managers making most of their own investment and production decisions. This approach proved so successful that China now has hundreds of these zones.

Deng's successors have continued his policies. The economic changes have led to huge economic growth. Where the country once lagged far behind most nations of Europe and North America, China now has the world's second most productive economy, after the United States. Chinese cities are now full of people who enjoy access to a wide variety of consumer goods.

Still, development has brought its share of problems. Rapid urban growth has led to increases in crime and pollution. The poor complain that the government is abandoning its promise to provide jobs and healthcare for all the nation's people. In addition, growth has not reached all parts of the country. Poverty and unemployment plague rural areas.

Finally, economic development has not meant political liberty. Chinese citizens still do not enjoy many political rights. The government tightly controls the press and stifles dissent.

India

India is the world's second most populous nation, after China. A former British colony, India struggled economically after winning independence. In the 1990s, though, India's government began to invite foreign investment and promote other free market practices.

New policies encouraged Indian companies to expand. One area of significant growth was in high-technology industries. Many software companies opened new facilities in India, where educated workers could offer technical support to computer users around the world. Manufacturing grew as well.

Economic growth helped promote the emergence of a much larger middle class. One business executive noted the significance of this development:

> 66 When half the population in a society is middle class, its politics will change... its poor will be fewer — and society will have greater means to look after them. 99
>
> Gurcharan Das, "India's Growing Middle Class"

India's middle class provides a growing market for consumer goods. While India had no shopping malls before 1999, it

---

Economics & YOU

Economic Growth in Asia

Since the 1970s, Chinese manufacturing and foreign trade have skyrocketed. *Many of the clothes you buy today were imported from China.*

MADE IN CHINA

India

Many American companies have outsourced customer service jobs to countries where labor costs are cheaper. *When you call for computer tech help, you may be speaking to an operator in India.*

USA

▲ Economic development in other countries can affect you. *What products do you use that came from other countries?*

Wangari Muta Maathai

"I always felt that our work was not simply about planting trees," said Wangari Maathai, the first African woman to win the Nobel Peace Prize. "It was about inspiring people to take charge of their environment, the system that governed them, their lives and their future." As a biology teacher at the University of Nairobi, she became the first woman associate professor in 1977. That year she began her second career, as an environmental activist. Maathai founded the Green Belt Movement (GBM). Her goal was to promote economic development while, at the same time, preserving her nation's forest and soil resources for future generations. Maathai believed that, without its forest, Kenya could eventually become a desert wasteland. The GBM also created jobs by hiring thousands of poor women to plant trees in rural Kenya.

From the outset, the Green Belt Movement faced strong opposition from the oppressive Kenyan government, which wanted to sell off the forests to foreign developers. Police disrupted peaceful demonstrations. Maathai herself was teargassed and severely beaten. "But I have an elephant's skin. And somebody must raise their voice."

After years of confrontation the environmentalists prevailed. GBM has now planted over 30 million trees and provided jobs for 80,000 people. Elected to Kenya's Parliament in 2002, Wangari Maathai continues to search for ways to improve living standards for both current and future generations.

Critical Thinking: What arguments might an economist make for and against the actions of the Green Belt Movement?

Fast Facts

Wangari Muta Maathai
Born: April 1, 1940, in Nyeri, Kenya
Education: Ph.D., Veterinary Medicine, University of Nairobi
Claim to Fame: Founder of Green Belt Movement

---

now has more than a hundred. As the middle class seeks more (and more expensive) goods, local and foreign producers compete to meet that demand.

Still, as with China, India's growth is not complete. Some 60 percent of the labor force farms, but they furnish only about 18 percent of the nation's production. The result is a growing gap between the richest and poorest citizens. In fact, this is true of virtually all nations with developing economies. Urban dwellers with education and skills benefit the most from growth. Uneducated people in poor rural areas struggle with poverty and continue to rely on subsistence farming.

CHECKPOINT *What free-market reforms did Deng Xiaoping introduce in China?*

Challenges in Africa and Latin America

Like Asia, Africa and Latin America are home to many poor countries. Some nations in these two regions have seen great economic growth in recent years. Others continue to struggle.

Persistent Poverty in Africa

Some North African nations have built productive economies. This success is mainly due to large reserves of oil.

South of the Sahara, however, most nations face the obstacles common to all LDCs, which you read about in Section 2. Economies are largely based on subsistence farming. Low literacy rates, inadequate health and nutrition, high rates of HIV infection, and mounting debt hinder development efforts. Some nations are also plagued by years of civil war or ethnic conflict. Only two African nations south of the Sahara have sizable economies— South Africa and Nigeria.

Nigeria benefits from large reserves of oil. Yet overdependence on oil has slowed growth in other areas. Nigeria also suffers from widespread political corruption and ethnic conflict. In 2007, new leaders took power in Nigeria. They promised to take steps to improve the economy and standards of living.

In the 1990s, South Africa shifted from longtime rule by the white minority to black majority rule. Problems in the

SS.912.E.2.3 Research the contributions of key individuals of various backgrounds in the development of the U.S.

▲ Mexico has the eighth largest tourism industry in the world. The government-sponsored Tourism Board promotes such attractions as Mexico's exotic beach resorts (left) and its ancient Mayan ruins (right). *Why would it be especially profitable for a developing nation to attract tourists from overseas?*

transition, along with high rates of HIV infection, slowed economic growth. Unemployment remains high, and poverty remains a problem. Still, South Africa has one of the 25 most productive economies in the world. It benefits from a rich array of natural resources and a strong manufacturing base.

Different Paths in Latin America

In Latin America, the two biggest success stories are Brazil and Mexico. Both countries have abundant resources. Both have also taken steps to make their economies more diverse.

Brazil exports iron ore and timber and its land and climate are highly suitable for growing coffee and soybeans.

The discovery of large offshore oil reserves in late 2007 promised to turn Brazil into a major oil-exporting power. Brazil has become a major manufacturing power, producing everything from vehicles to shoes. It has also adapted its sugar industry to produce ethanol. Brazil has also built cars that can run on either gasoline or ethanol. More than 40 percent of the fuel that powers Brazilian cars comes from ethanol derived from sugar cane.

Mexico has reserves of oil and silver and produces rich crops of cotton and coffee. Like Brazil, Mexico has diversified its economy by promoting its tourism industry and building factories.

By diversifying their economies, Mexico and Brazil have freed 80 percent or more of their labor forces from farm work. Employment in manufacturing and service industries have helped these two economies grow.

Venezuela also has large reserves of oil. Its leadership has turned in a different direction, though. President Hugo Chávez has shifted the economy away from the market system to socialism. Chávez has promised to use money derived from the sale of oil and gas to eliminate poverty and improve health and education. These advances have yet to be seen, however.

✔ CHECKPOINT *Which countries in Latin America have built the strongest economies?*

FL SS.912.E.1, SS.912.G.2.2, LA.1112.1.6.1, LA.1112.2.2.2

SECTION **3** ASSESSMENT

Essential Questions Journal To continue to build a response to the Essential Question, go to your **Essential Questions Journal**.

❓ Guiding Question

1. Use your completed chart to answer this question: How has economic change affected different countries?

2. **Extension** Imagine that you lived in a country switching to a market economy. What kind of business venture would you launch to succeed in the new economy?

Key Terms and Main Ideas

3. What is **privatization**?

4. Why do governments switching to a market economy need new laws?

5. How did Russia's economy change after 1991?

6. What was the purpose of China's **special economic zones**?

7. What economic challenges do many nations in Africa face?

Critical Thinking

8. **Identify Alternatives** Suggest two steps that a nation could take to ease the transition from a command economy to a free market economy.

9. **Predict** China has been criticized for stifling dissent and other violations of human rights. Do you think that will affect its trade relationships with other nations? Why or why not?

10. **Compare** Pick two countries discussed in this section. How were their economic transitions and challenges similar or different?

Math Skills

11. The table below shows changes in per capita income in urban and rural areas in China. **(a)** Which area enjoys the highest income? **(b)** Which area shows the greatest percentage of increase? **(c)** What economic problems does this chart reveal? *Visit PearsonSchool.com/PHecon for additional math help.*

Per Capita Disposable Income (in Chinese currency)

	2003	2005	2007
Urban Areas	8,472.2	10,493.0	13,786.0
Rural Areas	2,622.2	3,254.9	4,140.0

FL NGSSS

LA.1112.1.6 Use multiple strategies to develop vocabulary.

MA.912.A.2.2 Interpret a graph to represent a real-world situation.

SS.912.E.3.1 Demonstrate the impact of inflation on world economies.

SS.912.G.3.3 Use geography to explain perspectives on renewable and non-renewable resources in Florida.

SS.912.G.4.4 Analyze case studies of globalization.

ECONOMIC DICTIONARY

As you read the section, look for the definitions of these **Key Terms:**

• globalization
• offshoring
• remittances
• "brain drain"
• sustainable development
• deforestation

Guiding Question
What are the effects of globalization?
Copy this concept web and fill it in as you read.

▶ **Economics and You**   By now, you have seen many examples of how the world's economies are interconnected. You pick up the telephone to get tech support for your computer, and the call is answered in India. You eat a banana that was grown in Costa Rica and fill your car with gas made from petroleum that originally came out of the ground in Saudi Arabia. The value of the dollar goes down, and the cost of a vacation goes up. The list goes on and on.

Principles in Action   The economies of the world's nations are interconnected in deep and complex ways—and they will remain interconnected. The global economy creates new issues that business managers, workers, and government leaders must take into account. In this section, you will look at many of these issues, from impact on the environment to increased competition for American businesses.

globalization the increasingly tight interconnection of producers, consumers, and financial systems around the world

Causes of Globalization

The increasingly tight interconnection of producers, consumers, and financial systems around the world is known as **globalization.** Such connections are not a new phenomenon. In the Middle Ages, the Asian spice trade connected Europe, Asia, and Africa. The voyages of Columbus led to the colonization of the Americas by European sea powers and to the development of the African slave trade. The Age of Imperialism that began in the late 1800s forged even closer links between the economies of Europe and the United States and those of Africa and Asia.

Still, globalization today is taking place at a much faster pace than in the past. Several factors contribute to the ever-tightening links between economies around the world. They include the development of faster methods of communication and transportation, the

Globalization began long ago. This 14th century map shows a caravan on the Silk Road, a trade route linking the economies of China and Southwest Asia. *Why do you think the pace of globalization has gotten faster?* ▼

VISUAL GLOSSARY

The marks the logo area.

Reviewing Key Terms
To understand *globalization,* review these terms:

free market economy, *p. 30*
multinational corporation, *p. 207*
interdependence, *p. 452*
free trade, *p. 458*
foreign exchange market, *p. 465*

What is Globalization?

◄ **globalization** the increasingly tight interconnection of producers, consumers, and financial systems around the world

Spread of Free Market Economies

Rapid Transportation and Communication

Interconnected Financial Markets

Globalization

Foreign Exchange Markets

Multinational Corporations

Free Trade Agreements

Globalization is not just one thing. It is a combination of many different elements that make the economies of the world increasingly interdependent. *Choose two of the elements above and explain how each contributes to globalization.*

"GLOBALISATION RISKY? HOW D'YOU MEAN?"

◄ Increasing interdependence carries risks as well as opportunities. *What point is this cartoon making about globalization?*

Visual Glossary online
To expand your understanding of this and other key economic terms, visit **PearsonSchool.com/PHecon**

widespread adoption of free-market economic principles, and the growth of international trade agreements.

Rapid Transportation and Communication

What do the domestication of the camel, the invention of the compass, and the creation of the Internet have in common? All these innovations allowed greater movement of products, people, and ideas. Today, as in the past, globalization depends on breaking through barriers of time and space.

In the past, camels and ships made it possible to trade across vast deserts and oceans. Today, jet airplanes allow producers to sell goods in distant markets that would have been impossible to reach quickly in the past. For example, flower growers in the Netherlands or Colombia can send fresh flowers for sale in the United States.

Today's communications revolution has also sped the pace of globalization. Thanks to satellite communications, customers and suppliers on opposite sides of the world can talk quickly and clearly. Computers give people greater access to information about the availability and price of products in distant countries. Investors in one country can get up-to-date information and use it to buy stocks on financial markets anywhere.

Expansion of the Free Market

As you read in Section 3, many nations have moved away from central planning to pursue free-market policies. As a result, the proportion of the world that practices free market economics has more than tripled. At the same time, the fall of communism in the Soviet Union and Eastern Europe allowed nations that had once been locked out of world trade to enter the global marketplace. The opening of new markets has created new global economic ties.

The new free market economies are more open to foreign investment. In 1975, the value of foreign investment worldwide totaled only about $23 billion. By 1997, the total had grown to nearly $640 billion.

Trading Blocs

In Chapter 17, you saw that many nations have signed regional trade agreements. The creation of trading blocs has changed the nature of competition in the global market.

The United States is the world's most productive single economy, with output far exceeding that of any single nation in Europe. However, the *combined* output of the 27 nations that make up the European Union is competitive with that of the United States. People, goods, and services can flow freely among members of the EU, making it almost like a single economy.

Concern about competition from the EU was one of the factors that spurred the United States, Canada, and Mexico to sign the North American Free Trade Agreement. By making it easier to trade with some partners, countries hope to prevent companies from making deals with those in other trading blocs.

Trading blocs do not remain fixed. The EU has repeatedly expanded to include more nations. It is also working to forge trade tries with other regions. Similarly, members of NAFTA are engaged in talks to extend free trade to more of Latin America. All of this activity has added to the tighter globalization of the world economy.

 CHECKPOINT *How have modern communications contributed to globalization?*

Personal Finance
For information on dealing with the increasing threat of Internet crime, see your Personal Finance Handbook in the back of the book or visit **PearsonSchool.com/PHecon**

Issues in Globalization

"Arguing against globalization," said former UN Secretary General Kofi Annan, "is like arguing against the laws of gravity." While globalization is a fact of modern economic life, it has also created challenges.

Interconnected Financial Markets

In 2007, many American financial firms lost money—or went out of business—as a result of making too many risky home mortgage loans. Worried that the crisis would cause a downturn in the economy, investors sold stocks. Heavy losses on the New York Stock Exchange raised concerns among investors elsewhere in the world. They, in turn, sold stocks on European and Asian exchanges.

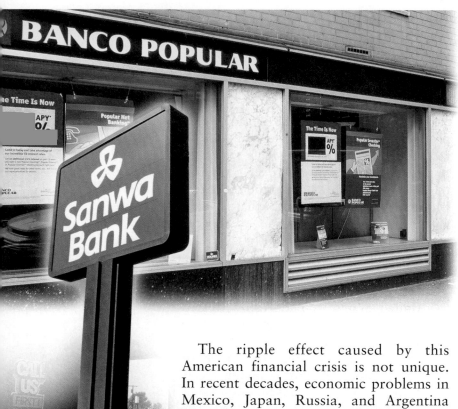

Multinational Corporations

As you read in Section 2, the expansion of multinational corporations has sparked controversy. Some economists argue that these companies have a beneficial impact on the countries where they set up operations. For example, multinationals have been credited with much of the development of Eastern Europe after the fall of communism:

> **"**[Multinationals] brought countless benefits. These include ... improving the environment; rescuing collapsing factories and rotting company towns; establishing new industries; laying new telecommunications networks; stabilizing banking systems ... and facing down corrupt vested interests in governments that in too many cases had plundered their own countries.**"**

—Paul Lewis, "Harnessing the Power of the Multinationals"

Multinationals have the capital to introduce technology to developing countries, offer jobs, train the labor force, and provide the opportunity for related services and industries to develop.

Critics, however, claim that multinationals do little to aid less developed countries. Some point out that most of the profits go, not to the host LDC, but to the foreign owners of the corporation. Others say that multinationals create far fewer job opportunities than they claim. Many of the industries are highly mechanized, allowing high productivity with little labor. Thus, they provide few jobs relative to the massive size of the labor pool and may even drive traditional craftworkers out of business.

Another area of controversy is wages. Generally, wages in less developed countries are very low compared to wages in industrialized nations. Supporters argue that the lower wages are justified since the cost of living in LDCs is also relatively low. In addition, many of the people employed by multinationals might not have jobs at all otherwise. Critics argue that multinationals benefit unfairly from the low wages. Also, many LDCs do not require companies to provide the same high standard of working conditions that industrialized countries require.

▲ Banks are among the most influential multinational corporations. Institutions like the Sanwa Bank of Japan and the Puerto Rico–based Banco Popular have branches in dozens of countries.

The ripple effect caused by this American financial crisis is not unique. In recent decades, economic problems in Mexico, Japan, Russia, and Argentina had a similar impact on world financial markets.

Why do financial problems in one country affect people in another? The reason is that world financial markets are closely connected. Investors around the world watch the values of stocks in many different markets. They move quickly to buy the stock of promising companies in whatever country they find them—and sell just as quickly at any sign of trouble.

Another reason for the widespread impact of these financial crises is the booming trade in currencies. As you read in Chapter 17, most of the world now follows a flexible exchange-rate system. The values of various national currencies go up or down every day. Investors holding money in a particular currency sell it off if the value of that currency declines. As sales of a country's currency mount, its economy will suffer.

These effects do not just hurt investors who risk their money in the hope of making profits. They have an impact on ordinary people as well. Banks buy assets in other countries. If the value of those assets falls, the banks have less capital available to make loans to people in their own countries.

Job Loss

Much of the debate over multinationals and globalization focuses on its impact on less developed countries. However, people in developed nations are equally concerned about a related issue—job loss.

In the global economy, companies may move parts of their operations to other countries. This practice is known as **offshoring.** Offshoring may involve a single process, as when an American bank hires a call center in India or Kenya to handle its telemarketing. Or it can be total, as when a multinational manufacturer closes a plant in the United States to build one in another country. In either case, the result is job loss. As you learned in Chapter 13, movement of jobs overseas is one of the key causes of structural unemployment.

☑ **CHECKPOINT** *What problems can result from interconnected financial markets?*

Population Shifts

People have always moved from place to place in hopes of building a better life. Globalization and development have accelerated these population shifts.

Rural to Urban

Much of this migration takes place within a nation's borders. In many less developed countries, cities offer more job opportunities than rural areas. As a result, large numbers of people in villages are streaming into cities. In 1950, less than 20 percent of the people in Africa and Asia lived in cities. By 2005, nearly 40 percent did. Today, thirteen of the world's twenty largest cities are located in less developed countries. Each of them has more than 10 million people.

Rapid urbanization has caused several problems. Cities have grown so fast that they cannot provide enough housing, schools, and sanitation for all of the people. Poverty, crime, and disease are widespread.

Country to Country

Each year, millions of workers leave less developed countries in the hopes of finding jobs in developed nations. This migration has an economic impact on both the source country and the destination country.

Most immigrants come legally, with proper visas and proof of work. While their labor contributes to a country's GNP, they may face resentment from native-born workers who view the newcomers as competition for jobs. Other people come without legal authorization. Illegal immigration raises security concerns and puts a strain on public resources.

Migration also affects the source country. Once they find work, many immigrants send regular cash payments to their families back home. These **remittances** provide an important source of income. The World Bank estimated that, in 2006 alone, the value of remittances to LDCs totaled $250 billion.

offshoring the movement of parts of a company's operations to another country

remittances cash payments sent by workers who have migrated to a new country to family members in their home country

 MA.912.A.2.2 Interpret a graph to represent a real-world situation.

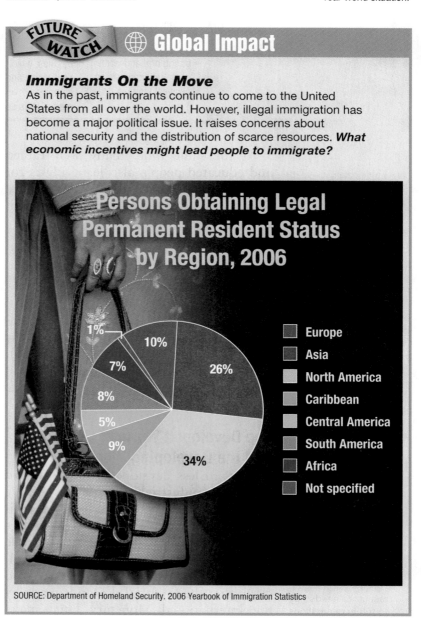

FUTURE WATCH ⊕ **Global Impact**

Immigrants On the Move
As in the past, immigrants continue to come to the United States from all over the world. However, illegal immigration has become a major political issue. It raises concerns about national security and the distribution of scarce resources. *What economic incentives might lead people to immigrate?*

Persons Obtaining Legal Permanent Resident Status by Region, 2006

- 1%
- 10%
- 7%
- 8%
- 5%
- 9%
- 26%
- 34%

- Europe
- Asia
- North America
- Caribbean
- Central America
- South America
- Africa
- Not specified

SOURCE: Department of Homeland Security. 2006 Yearbook of Immigration Statistics

CAREER CENTER
PHYSICAL SCIENCES

Possible Careers
- Agricultural engineer
- Cartographer
- Conservation scientist
- **Environmental scientist**
- Atmospheric scientist
- Forester
- Hydrologist

Profile: Environmental Scientist

Duties:
- conduct research to identify or eliminate sources of pollutants or hazards
- analyze observations of air, food, water, soil, and other sources
- make recommendations on how best to clean and preserve the environment

Education:
- master's degree in a natural science

Skills:
- computer skills
- excellent interpersonal skills
- strong oral and written communication skills
- physical stamina

Median Annual Salary:
- $58,380 (2007)

Future prospects:
- Job growth for environmental scientists will be strongest at private-sector consulting firms.
- Demand will be spurred largely by rules, which will oblige companies and organizations to comply with complex environmental laws and regulations.

Career Link *Activity*
Choose another career in the physical sciences from the list of possible careers. Create a profile for that career similar to the one for Environmental Scientist.

At the same time, many well-trained and educated people also leave LDCs for well-paying jobs in developed nations. This **"brain drain"** may hurt development by siphoning off vital human capital.

✓ **CHECKPOINT** *How does migration affect less developed nations?*

Challenges Ahead

Globalization is creating new opportunities, but also new challenges, for the world's economies. Many of these challenges have become sources of tension between the developed world and the developing world.

The Developed World and the Developing World

Leaders in less developed countries—and even newly industrialized countries—argue that international trade and financial policies favor the wealthier nations. They charge that the trade rules set by the World Trade Organization give preference to developed nations at their expense. They also claim that the financial demands made by the International Monetary Fund make lives more difficult for poor people in their countries.

In an effort to give emerging economies a greater voice, about two dozen countries have formed an organization called the Group of 20. The G-20 includes financial ministers from growing nations such as China, India, Brazil, and Mexico, as well as representatives of the United States and the EU. The G-20 has discussed such issues as promoting growth and how to combat the financing of terrorist operations.

Environmental Protection Versus Development

The environment can be another source of tension. Environmental scientists—mostly based in developed nations—worry that rapid development can cause environmental damage. They seek to promote **sustainable development,** that is, the goal of meeting current development needs without using up the resources needed by future generations.

On the other hand, leaders in many less developed nations see an urgent need to exploit their resources *now*. They view combating poverty and creating modern

"brain drain" migration of the best-educated people of less developed countries to developed nations

sustainable development the goal of meeting current development needs without using up resources needed by future generations economies as a higher priority than protecting the environment. Developed nations, they argue, were able to use resources such as oil without restriction. LDCs now seek the same opportunity.

One major issue is **deforestation,** or large-scale destruction of forests. Many developing nations are cutting down forests at a rapid rate. Cleared land is used for farming and industry, while timber sales fund other projects that create jobs. Environmentalists warn that deforestation contributes to global warming and destroys rare animal and plant species. To such concerns, the president of Brazil replied:

> **❝**There are meddlers who have no political authority, who emit carbon dioxide like nobody else, who destroy everything they have, and who put forth opinions about what we should do…. We can't allow people to dictate rules to us about what we should do in the Amazon.**❞**
>
> —Luiz Inacio Lula da Silva, quoted in *Terra Daily,* June 5, 2008

Competition for Resources

A related challenge is competition for scarce resources. In some regions, it is increasingly difficult to find enough clean, healthy water to meet the needs of a growing population.

In China, for example, rapid population and economic growth has led to serious contamination of an already uncertain water supply. Some experts warn that reserves of oil and gas are dwindling as well. They fear that, unless new sources of these fuels—or different sources of energy—are found, the world's economies may grind to a halt.

Even if resources do not run out, the cost of scarce water and fuel causes problems. In 2008, world oil prices skyrocketed. Even in developed nations, this inflation strained the financial resources of businesses and consumers. In less developed countries, the impact was even more severe. Inflation, caused by competition for resources, made it harder for LDCs to channel resources to development.

☑ **CHECKPOINT** *How can environmental protection conflict with economic development?*

The United States in the World Economy

Globalization poses challenges even for the world's most successful economy—our own. For the United States to compete in global markets, American workers must be ready to meet changes in the workplace. And American companies must continue their long tradition of innovation.

Adapting to a Changing Workplace

Information now drives the economy of the United States and the world. Workers need to gain the skills that are necessary to access, understand, and use all sorts of information. Getting as much education as possible is a good first step.

The need for education does not end when people find jobs. Workers must constantly keep up-to-date with new technology so that they can remain productive in their current jobs. Others must learn completely new skills when they find that their existing jobs no longer pay a good wage—or when jobs are lost due to offshoring.

As you read in Chapter 13, some companies provide the retraining that their workers need. When that is not the case, though, workers must take responsibility to learn needed skills. If they fail to do so, they risk being left behind as work moves in a new direction.

deforestation the large-scale destruction of forests

 SS.912.E.3.1 Demonstrate the impact of inflation on world economies.

SS.912.G.3.3 Use geography to explain perspectives on renewable and non-renewable resources in Florida.

The health of the world's oceans depends on all countries working together. The steps taken by any one nation can have a ripple effect throughout the world. *How might overfishing in one country affect the global environment? Why might overfishing continue even though its negative impact is recognized?*

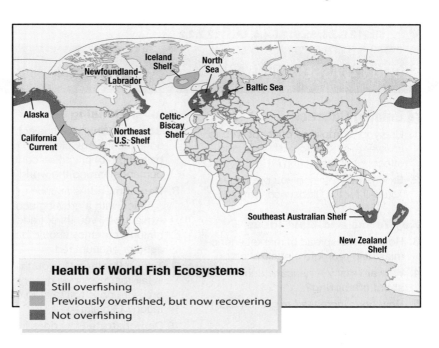

Health of World Fish Ecosystems
- Still overfishing
- Previously overfished, but now recovering
- Not overfishing

Another feature of the changing American workplace is greater diversity. The population of the United States has changed. As a result of population shifts, a growing percentage of American workers are foreign-born. There are more Asian Americans and Latinos than in the past. To be productive, American workers must be prepared to work closely with people of different backgrounds.

The Pressure to Compete

Globalization has made economic competition more intense. Consumers in developing nations are demanding a greater variety of products and services. As you read, the growth of India's middle class has led to a boom in shopping malls. In Africa, the number of people who own cellular phones rose from only 2 million in 1998 to over 60 million by 2004. At the same time, more countries are competing to meet this growing demand.

Competition affects business relationships as well. One business might have a long relationship with a local supplier. Yet, if a different supplier can offer lower prices or better service, they will make a deal with that supplier—even when that supplier is located on the other side of the world.

For all these reasons, American companies need to stay competitive. Business managers face constant pressure to cut costs and increase profits. They must ensure high productivity to avoid wasting money and work. They need to be constantly on the lookout for better ways to respond to customer needs. Only by staying competitive can American companies thrive.

The Pressure to Innovate

As in the past, growing competition spurs innovation. The companies that develop new products or processes can quickly gain a large share of the world market. For example, in 1996, two young American entrepreneurs began work on the Internet search engine company that became Google. Ten years later, the company had worldwide sales of $10.6 billion.

Still, introducing a new innovation and enjoying its success is not the end of the story. Any new product or service can quickly be replaced by a newer one, developed by another entrepreneur hungry to succeed.

Writer Thomas Friedman, who has studied globalization, says that the new economic world is like a sprint that competitors must run over and over again. Anyone who wins one race cannot guarantee winning a later one. The only solution is to go back to the starting line and—with new innovations to help—run as fast as possible, again and again.

CHECKPOINT *How can American workers help companies stay competitive?*

 SS.912.E.3.1, SS.912.E.3.4, SS.912.E.3.5, SS.912.G.3.3, SS.912.G.4.4, LA.1112.2.2.2

SECTION 4 ASSESSMENT

Essential Questions Journal To continue to build a response to the Essential Question, go to your **Essential Questions Journal**.

Guiding Question

1. Use your completed concept web to answer this question: What are the effects of globalization?
2. **Extension** How can you prepare yourself for the global economy?

Key Terms and Main Ideas

3. How did the spread of market economies help promote globalization?
4. Why are many Americans concerned about **offshoring**?
5. How does increased migration lead to **"brain drain"**?
6. Why is **deforestation** controversial?

Critical Thinking

7. **Connect** What role has communications technology played in **(a)** globalization **(b)** changing consumer demands around the world?
8. **Recommend** As finance minister of a nation with a growing economy, explain why you think trade in the nation's currency should be discouraged or encouraged.
9. **Take a Position** Do you think that it is fair for developed nations to put pressure on Brazil to stop deforestation? Explain.
10. **Demonstrate** How does inflation caused by competition for resources impact world economies?

Quick Write

11. Thomas Friedman said globalization means that businesses must constantly innovate to succeed in the global economy. Write an outline and opening paragraph for a newspaper column that discusses the following questions: What can business leaders do to make sure their companies innovate constantly? How can governments help in this effort?

Chapter 18: Development and Globalization

Section 1 How is a nation's level of development defined?

Section 2 What factors harm or help development?

Section 3 How has economic change affected different countries?

Section 4 What are the effects of globalization?

Essential Question, Chapter 18
Do the benefits of economic development outweigh the costs?

Measures of Development

Measure	Developed Countries	Less Developed Countries
Per capita GDP	High	Low
Population growth rate	Low	High
Literacy	High	Low
Life expectancy	High	Low
Infant mortality	Low	High
Labor force	Large percentage manufacturing, services	Large percentage subsistence agriculture
Settlement	Urban	Rural
Energy consumption	High	Low
Consumer goods	Plentiful	Scarce

Economic Dictionary

development, *p. 481*

developed nation, *p. 481*

less developed country, *p. 482*

newly industrialized country, *p. 482*

per capita GDP, *p. 482*

industrialization, *p. 483*

literacy rate, *p. 483*

life expectancy, *p. 483*

infant mortality rate, *p. 484*

subsistence agriculture, *p. 486*

population growth rate, *p. 487*

malnutrition, *p. 491*

internal financing, *p. 491*

foreign investment, *p. 492*

foreign direct investment, *p. 492*

foreign portfolio investment, *p. 492*

debt rescheduling, *p. 493*

stabilization program, *p. 493*

nongovernmental organization, *p. 494*

privatization, *p. 495*

special economic zone, *p. 498*

globalization, *p. 501*

offshoring, *p. 505*

remittances, *p. 505*

"brain drain", *p. 506*

sustainable development, *p. 506*

deforestation, *p. 507*

Economics on the go

Study anytime, anywhere. Download these files today.

Economic Dictionary online	Audio Review online	Action Graph online	Visual Glossary online	How the Economy Works online
Vocabulary Support in English and Spanish	Audio Study Guide in English and Spanish	Animated Charts and Graphs	Animated feature	Animated feature

Download to your computer or mobile device at PearsonSchool.com/PHecon

Key Terms and Main Ideas

To make sure you understand the key terms and main ideas of this chapter, review the Checkpoint and Section Assessment questions and look at the Quick Study Guide on the preceding page.

Critical Thinking

1. **Analyze (a)** List three conditions that help determine the quality of life in a less developed country. **(b)** Identify one program or policy that could help change each of these three conditions. **(c)** Which of these conditions do you think it is most important to change in order to promote faster development? Why?

2. **Take a Position (a)** What arguments are given in favor of multinational investing in LDCs? **(b)** What arguments are given against such investment? **(c)** Which side do you agree with and why?

3. **Compare (a)** What success has Russia had in establishing a free market economy? **(b)** What success has China had? **(c)** Which nation do you think has been more successful? Why?

4. **Make a Decision (a)** What do environmentalists mean when they talk about sustainable development? **(b)** Suppose you were the leader of a developing nation. Would you favor clearing more forestland in order to provide immediate jobs and income or preserving the resources of the forest for future generations? Give reasons for your choice.

5. **Evaluate (a)** Describe three characteristics of globalization. **(b)** Explain the meaning of the following statement: "Arguing against globalization is like arguing against the laws of gravity." **(c)** Do you agree or disagree? Explain.

Applying Your Math Skills

Using an Index

The table below compares the wages for manufacturing jobs in different nations using an index in which U.S. wages are valued at 100. Numbers above 100 indicate higher wages; those below show lower wages. Look at the index and answer the questions that follow.

Visit PearsonSchool.com/PHecon for additional math help.

Index of Manufacturing Wages

Country	Value	Country	Value
Australia	105	South Korea	57
Brazil	17	Taiwan	27
Canada	101	France	104
Mexico	11	Germany	140
Hong Kong	24	Poland	19
Japan	92	Portugal	31

6. For every $500 a U.S. manufacturing worker earns, how much would a worker in the following countries earn: **(a)** Canada, **(b)** Mexico, **(c)** South Korea, **(d)** Poland?

7. Express the difference between manufacturing wages in Germany and Brazil as a percentage.

8. Based on this index, which of the nations shown would you say had the most highly developed economies? Why?

9. If you were the head of a multinational company trying to determine where to locate a new factory, in which of these countries would you consider building a factory? What factors besides wages would you consider?

? Essential Question Activity

Essential Questions Journal To respond to the chapter Essential Question, go to your **Essential Questions Journal**.

10. Complete the activity to answer the Essential Question **Do the benefits of economic development outweigh the costs?** For this activity, the class will be divided into ten groups. Each group will take the part of a panel of officials at the International Monetary Fund investigating economic conditions in a different LDC. Use the library or Internet resources to find basic social, economic, and political information about your country. Using the worksheet in your Essential Questions Journal or the electronic worksheet available at **PearsonSchool.com/PHecon,** gather the following information:
    (a) What are current social and economic conditions in the nation?
    (b) What resources or economic advantages does the nation have?
    (c) What economic problems does the nation face?
    (d) What is the nation's political system, and how stable is it?

11. **Modify** Based on the information that was gathered, members of each group should meet to create a development plan for the nation they are studying. The development plan should address the following issues:
    (a) What new or existing goods or services should be produced and sold? Why?
    (b) How should the nation obtain needed development funds?
    (c) What social or political changes will be needed for this program to succeed?
    (d) What social and economic benefits will result from this investment?
    (e) What potential negative effects might result from this development program? How can they be prevented?

Each group will present its conclusions to the rest of the class.

DOCUMENT-BASED ASSESSMENT

Does movement of jobs overseas hurt or help the U.S. economy?

Some U.S. companies are sending jobs overseas, a process called *outsourcing* or *offshoring*. Economists say these decisions make sense: the companies save money, and keep higher-paying jobs at home. Workers say that these decisions are hurting American workers and the nation's economy.

Document A

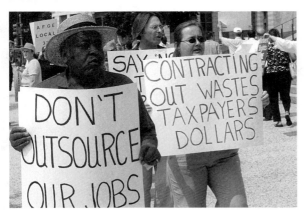

Document B

"Concerns about a massive loss of jobs due to offshoring do not seem justified. Companies have found outsourcing abroad profitable primarily for jobs that can be routinized and sharply defined.... For the foreseeable future, however, most high-value work will require creative interaction among employees, interaction which is facilitated by physical proximity and personal contact. Moreover, in many fields, closeness to customers and knowledge of local conditions are also of great importance. These observations suggest that, for some considerable time, outsourcing abroad will be uneconomical for many types of jobs, particularly high-value jobs."

—Ben Bernanke, Chairman of the Federal Reserve, May 2007

Document C

Professional and business services: "Employment is projected to grow 2.1 percent annually, slowing from the 2.7-percent rate experienced from 1996 to 2006, mainly due to productivity gains and offshore outsourcing."

Computer systems design and related services: "Employment is projected to increase by 489,400 jobs ... by 2016. This represents an average annual growth rate of 3.3 percent, which is less robust than the rate experienced during the previous decade, largely due to productivity increases and offshore outsourcing."

Software publishing: "Relative to the previous decade, slower employment growth is expected as the industry matures and cost pressures lead to further outsourcing of routine tasks offshore."

—Bureau of Labor Statistics, Nov. 2007

ANALYZING DOCUMENTS

Use your knowledge of economic systems and Documents A, B, and C to answer questions 1–3.

1. **The picketers in Document A are most likely to be**
   A. managers of multinational corporations.
   B. consumers.
   C. stock investors.
   D. workers.

2. **According to Document B, outsourcing would be least likely to affect**
   A. computer programmers.
   B. factory workers.
   C. healthcare workers.
   D. telephone support staff.

3. **Document C predicts that slow job growth is not due just to outsourcing but also to**
   A. decline in manufacturing.
   B. declining consumer demand.
   C. lack of innovation.
   D. increases in productivity.

WRITING ABOUT ECONOMICS

Whether outsourcing is hurting American workers and the U.S. economy is a hotly debated issue. Use the documents on this page and resources on the Web site below to answer the question: *Does movement of jobs overseas hurt or help the U.S. economy?* Use the sources to support your opinion.

In Partnership

THE WALL STREET JOURNAL.
CLASSROOM EDITION

To read more about isssues related to this topic, visit
PearsonSchool.com/PHecon

Unit 7 Challenge

Essential Question, Unit 7

VIDEO
By Students For Students
For videos on Essential Questions,
go to *PearsonSchool.com/PHecon*

How might scarcity divide our world or bring it together?

In the global economy of the future, will scarcity lead to further interdependence—or will it lead to conflict? Look at the opinions below, keeping in mind the Essential Question: How might scarcity divide our world or bring it together?

> Preliminary research indicates that scarcities of critical environmental resources—especially of cropland, freshwater, and forests—contribute to violence in many parts of the world. These environmental scarcities usually do not cause wars among countries, but they can generate severe social stresses within countries, helping to stimulate... ethnic clashes, and urban unrest. Such civil violence particularly affects developing societies because they are, in general, highly dependent on environmental resources and less able to buffer themselves from the social crises that environmental scarcities cause.
>
> —Thomas F. Homer-Dixon, *Environment, Scarcity, and Violence*

> The potential exists to provide an adequate and sustainable supply of quality water for all, today and in the future. But there is no room for complacency. It is our common responsibility to take the challenge of today's global water crisis and address it in all of its aspects and dimensions.
>
> —Jacques Diouf, UN Food and Agriculture Organization Director-General, March 2007

arcadio/CAGLECARTOONS.COM/2008-IV.

Essential Question Writing Activity

Consider the different views of economics expressed in the sources on this page and what you have learned about the global economy. ***Then write a well-constructed essay expressing your view of the impact of scarcity on the world economy.***

Writing Guidelines

- Address all aspects of the Essential Question Writing Activity.
- Support the theme with relevant facts, examples, and details.
- Use a logical and clear plan of organization.
- Introduce the theme by establishing a framework that is beyond a simple restatement of the question and conclude with a summation of the theme.

For help in writing a Persuasive Essay, refer to the *Writer's Handbook* in the Reference section, page S-5.

Essential Questions Journal

To respond to the unit Essential Question, go to your **Essential Questions Journal**.

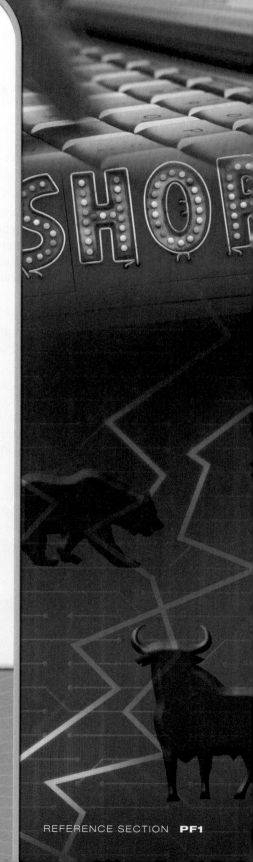

Personal Finance Handbook

FUTURE WATCH

REFERENCE SECTION

Your Fiscal Fitness: An Introduction

No pain, no gain. It applies as much to fiscal fitness as it does to physical fitness.

 SS.912.E.1.16 Construct a one-year budget plan for a specific career.

Think Long-term

If you start investing $40 a week at a 5 percent rate of return, in 20 years you will have accumulated $17,800. If you get a higher return, say 7 percent, then by the time you retire in 45 years, you would have $163,688.

"Whoa! Slow down! 20 years? Retirement? I'm still living at home! I don't even own my first car yet! Who do you think you are—my parents?"

If that's your reaction, you're not alone. A great many high school students do not think much about their financial future. They also don't like to get stern lectures from Mom or Dad—whether it's about financial planning or about those 5,000 extra text messages that appeared on last month's cellphone bill.

But let's face it: free room and board doesn't last forever. And often, it comes to an end soon after you get handed a diploma. At some point in the not too distant future, the bills in the mail will be yours.

The fact is that responsible financial citizens were not born that way. Even your parents had to learn how to comparison shop, avoid impulse buying, and put money aside that they would much rather spend on fun. Chances are they made mistakes along the way. And they wish you could avoid all the same pitfalls.

Take a Checkup

Start by taking a good look at your own money habits. Are you a big spender? Moderate saver? Do you save anything at all? The answer is pretty easy to figure out. If you have an unexpected windfall, a bigger than expected birthday check, or an opportunity to earn overtime money, what do you do with the money? Save it all? Save half? Look to see what you can buy now?

You don't have time to waste. Mess up your credit rating now and you could be paying the price until you're in your thirties. You might find yourself living at home after college and beyond. (And which sounds cooler to you—writing a check for your own apartment, or paying rent for the same bedroom you had in the sixth grade?)

Skip the Fats, Go for the Protein!

It comes down to fiscal fitness. Developing a solid, fiscal muscle also involves training or budgeting, short and long-term goal setting, and most of all patience. Personal finance, like athletics, requires discipline.

GO FIGURE

$269,040

The estimated cost of raising a child born in 2007 through age 17.

SOURCE: United States Department of Agriculture. "Expenditures on Children by Families, 2007"

ON TRACK TO FINANCIAL CITIZENSHIP

Discipline is one of the qualities that defines a winner. If you want to come out on top, learn the rules of good financial citizenship and put them into action.

 Keep a budget in order to live within your means.

 Understand credit uses and costs.

 Shop wisely and know your rights as a consumer.

Preparing for a long race often involves delayed gratification. An athlete will sacrifice fast-food because it's bad for his health, but healthy eating will pay off in the long run. The same is true of investing in your future. It may mean putting off purchases today for financial security sometime later on.

That's easy to say but hard to do, especially if you want to keep up with your peers. You and your dollars are the target of marketers and advertisers. According to a national survey, teenagers are rabid consumers of high-tech products. About 75 percent of U.S. teenagers own a cellphone, 60 percent have an MP3 player, and 43 percent have a car.

Savvy Savers Today's teens spend more than previous generations of teens. This 2007 survey, however, shows that many teens do understand the importance of saving and have begun to develop good saving habits.

What percentage of your income, from a job or your allowance, do you save?

Response	Percentage
I save at least 75% of my income every month.	15.6
I save 25–75% of my income every month.	51.4
I save less than 25% of my income every month.	21.9
I do not save any of my income.	11.2

Note: 1,512 teens between the ages of 13 and 18 were surveyed
SOURCE: Junior Achievement Personal Finance 2007: Executive Summary

The Long Race

The spirit is willing but the flesh is weak. The impulse to get what we want now is far stronger than the motivation to save for something that is months or even years down the road. You may have to trick yourself into saving by promising yourself a reward when you have met certain goals.

Obstacles

What could slow down your progress? One outstanding speed bump is credit card abuse. You don't want to join the ranks of those who struggle to pay their credit card balance in full every month. They let matters slide—failing to balance their checkbooks, check their credit card statements, or keep an eye on bank fees and

interest rates. You want to develop the fiscal awareness that will keep you out of trouble.

Grow Your Money

Despite the difficulty of thinking long-term, 65 percent of teens actually admit that they want to learn how to grow their money. This is good news. Even better, 84 percent of teens have savings, with an average amount of $1,044. Fueling those savings is their attitude that the future is now. Savings could translate into a car and college in the short run and a secure life and retirement in the years to come. With the right attitude, you're ready for basic training.

In no time at all, the following words will be part of your conversation. *Budgeting*—how to spend your income in such a way that there's something left over to invest. *Compounding*—how saving a little now can translate into big money later on in life. *Investing*—why the stock market can be both friend and foe. (Over the last 50 years or more, the stock market has averaged a higher return than bank accounts or bonds.)

Ready, set, grow.

★ Develop short- and long-term financial goals.

Are You Ready?

1. How can your own spending habits help or hinder you?
2. What are some key steps to staying on a good financial track?

WebQuest online To learn more about this topic, visit **PearsonSchool.com/PHecon**

Wise Choices for Your Money

Learning how to live within your means will help you make the most of what you have and to plan for a more secure future.

Budgeting 101

A **budget** is simply a plan for spending and saving. The word may conjure up images of driving a junk car or eating canned spaghetti every night. But the reality can be just the opposite. In fact, most millionaires use a budget to manage their money. And most of them started early.

Spending Awareness

Surveys show that almost one half of Americans between the ages of 13 and 18 know how to budget their money. That's the good news. The bad news is more than half don't. Which group do you fall into? Take this quick quiz:

1. How much money did you spend on beverages—from coffee or water to energy drinks—last week?
2. How much money will you spend on gas next week?
3. How long will it take you to save up for the most expensive thing you'd like to buy?

If you could answer these questions without much trouble, you've already taken the first steps to good money management. If you didn't have a clue, maybe it's time to think about making a budget.

Good Habits Start Early

Now here's another question. Did you ever ask for money to spend on concert tickets—or a piece of jewelry, or a ski trip—only to hear *"You don't need it, and we can't afford it"*? Odds are you didn't think of it as an economics lesson. But according to surveys, students who learned about money management at home scored higher than those who learned about it only in school.

A Balancing Act

Budgeting is a balancing act between income and expenses. It also means weighing your needs against your wants.

Income and Expenses

To begin creating a budget, follow these steps.

1. Make a list of your earnings per month from all sources. Add these up to calculate your expected monthly income.
2. For one month, keep a record of everything you spend, from chewing gum to car payments. Collect receipts or write everything in a notebook. Make sure you don't leave anything out. (And that includes savings!)
3. At the end of the month, organize your spending into categories such as food, entertainment, and car payments. Total the amount in each category.
4. On a sheet of paper, list your income and expenses.

If your total expenses are less than your total income, you're doing fine. If not, you need to take a hard look at where your money is going.

GO FIGURE

$948,611

The amount you might earn over 40 years if you skip paying $5 a day for a latte and muffin.*

SOURCE: www.finishrich.com
*Assumes $150 per month invested at a rate of 10 percent annual return

Needs and Wants

Right now, many of your basic needs are probably part of the household budget. Still, some of your personal funds may be going toward needs such as car insurance, lunches, or college savings. The rest goes toward buying things you want. So, if you are looking to cut down expenses, you should focus first on the wants.

Consider the example of Michelle, a high school senior. She works 20 hours a week at a department store, where she earns $10.00 an hour. Her net income—that is, her take-home pay after taxes—is $150. Her monthly necessities include $40 for her cellphone bill, $60 on average for gas, and $65 a month on car insurance. Michelle has already set aside $300 for her prom and hopes to have $500 by the time prom rolls around. To stay within her budget, she gives up her daily soda habit, saving almost $30 a month. She and her friends also decide to rent movies rather than go out. This trade-off will allow them to rent a limousine to go to their prom.

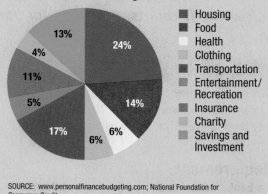

What's in Your Budget? This budget shows the typical spending for a single earner, living alone. Budgets change according to lifestyle and income. What doesn't change is the need to save and pay for essentials, such as housing and food.

- Housing 24%
- Food 14%
- Health 6%
- Clothing 6%
- Transportation 17%
- Entertainment/ Recreation 5%
- Insurance 11%
- Charity 4%
- Savings and Investment 13%

SOURCE: www.personalfinancebudgeting.com; National Foundation for Consumer Credit

Michelle has planned for a long-term goal and budgeted correctly. She has drawn a fine line between needs and wants.

If you find you have a difficult time staying within your budget, enlist a friend or family member to review your expenditures each week to help keep on track. Try not to rationalize impulse buys. Consider them your sworn budget enemies!

Long-Term Rewards

Err on the side of thrift and responsibility. Live within your means and try to save a set percentage of your income. Some budget counselors suggest alotting 80 percent for needs, 10 percent for wants, and 10 percent for savings. Do that and you might find yourself with a tidy savings within a few short years.

Spend without a plan and you might end up like many Americans: deep in debt. In fact, U.S. consumer debt topped an estimated $2.5 trillion dollars in 2008, or $8,300 per American. In that same year, studies showed that one in seven American families was dealing with a debt collector. Learning to budget now may spare you from being part of this grim statistic later.

Budget Boosters

1. Keep a spending journal for one week: Include every latte, vending-machine snack and music download.

2. Identify needs: bills, car payment, etc.

3. Downsize or eliminate impulse buys such as coffee and soda.

4. Make saving a priority and a habit.

5. Add to your savings weekly, even if just a small amount.

6. Identify a long-term want and start saving for it. (You'll be surprised how fast those fast-food outings diminish when you set your mind on something.)

7. Prioritize and pay down any outstanding debt—including that $5 you owe your sister.

8. Use cash for daily spending.

9. During vacations or the summer, pick up some extra hours at work.

10. Live within your means. Spend less than you make.

Are You Ready?

1. What are the steps for creating a budget?
2. Using the steps under "Income and Expenses" construct a one-year budget for your first year after graduation, based on your career path.

 WebQuest online To learn more about this topic, visit **PearsonSchool.com/PHecon**

Checking Up on Checking Accounts

Park your cash where it counts, and put your bank to work for you.

The Right Bank

Banks are everywhere. Often they face each other at busy intersections in a community or are tucked in the corner of a supermarket. Every bank is vying for your business. How do you choose among them?

The Basic Requirement

You want to use a bank that is insured by the **Federal Deposit Insurance Corporation** (FDIC). The FDIC protects your money and the interest it has earned—up to the insurance limit—in the event that your bank fails. For an account held by a single individual, the limit was raised to $250,000 in 2008. Banks are generally considered to be financially sound, but failures do occur.

Endless Variety

It may be impossible for you to believe, but not so very long ago even the biggest cities offered only ten different television stations. That was it for choices. The services offered by banks have grown in a similar way to the expansion of TV entertainment options. Although banks may look very similar, their services are not one-size-fits all. The bank that is most convenient for you may not have the services that best meet your needs. First, you have to figure out what you want and then figure out where to get it.

GO FIGURE

500 million

The number of checks forged annually in the United States, with losses totaling more than $10 billion.

SOURCE: Ernst & Young

How to Write a Check

All bank checks have the same basic layout and require the same information. To avoid problems with checks:

1. Write clearly.
2. Do not cross out or write over a mistake.
3. Tear a check with errors into small pieces, and write "Void" next to the check number in your check register.
4. NEVER write a check for more than your account balance.

Use words to write the payment amount.

Write the name of the payee.

Write the current date.

Use numerals to enter the payment amount.

1027

Tomás Q. Public
123 Main Street
Anywhere, USA 45678

October 14, 2010 DATE

$ 25.99

PAY TO THE ORDER OF   VideOh!

Twenty-five and 99/100 ———————— DOLLARS

Security Features Details on Back.

Main Street Bank
321 Main Street
Anywhere, USA 45678

Tomás Q. Public

FOR video game rental

⑈ 2 2 2 2 2 2 2 2 ⑈: 000 ⑊⑊⑊ 555⑊⑊ ⑊027

Write additional information about the payment or payee, such as a reason or an account number.

Sign your check.

Debit Card Nation It's hard to beat convenience and the rise in debit card usage confirms it. More than likely, you are one of 185 million Americans who are using a debit card to access their checking accounts.

U.S. Debit Card Holders (in millions of people)

160	170	172	174	185
2000	2003	2004	2005	2010*

*Projected   SOURCE: Statistical Abstract of the United States

The Right Services

One universal need is convenient and safe access to your money. Checking accounts and debit cards have made both readily available.

Checking Accounts

To open a checking account you will need identification, such as a birth certificate or a driver's license and a Social Security number. You will also need money to deposit.

Which checking account meets your needs?

Basic checking: Best bet for customers who use a checking account to pay some bills and use a debit card for some daily expenses.
Drawback: Monthly maintenance fees may apply unless you retain a minimum balance or enroll in direct deposit. Some banks may limit the number of checks you can write each month and charge you a per item fee if you exceed the limit.

Free checking: The operative word here is "free," meaning a no-strings attached account with no monthly service charges or per-item fees, regardless of the balance or activity.
Drawback: These are harder to find and the "free" part may be an introductory offer that expires in six months or a year.

Checking with overdraft protection: In effect, if you write checks for more than the balance of your deposits, the bank will honor the check by lending you the money you need, up to a preset limit.
Drawback: This service comes with hefty fees.

The Debit Card

Most banks offer you a debit card with a checking account. With a credit card logo, it has the look and feel of a credit card, but there is a major difference. The money you spend is deducted from your checking account balance. Debit cards are also used to withdraw money from ATMs, giving you access to your money 24/7. If you use an ATM from a bank other than your own, you will likely be charged a fee. You could pay $2 to get access to your own $20. Convenience comes with a price.

Direct Deposit

Banks and employers encourage people to take advantage of direct deposit. A win-win for you and the environment, the paperless transaction enlists your employer to deposit your paycheck directly into your bank account. An employer may ask for your social security number, a voided check containing your bank's routing number, and your account number. Direct deposit saves you a trip to the bank and protects you from lost or stolen funds.

Keeping Track

When you open a checking account, you will receive a checkbook that includes sequentially numbered checks and a check register, or a booklet in which you'll record your account transactions. Every time you write a check, make a deposit, or use an ATM, you should take a few seconds to write it down. It is also important to hold onto your ATM receipts. They are the only proof that you withdrew $40, not $400.

Each month the bank will send you a statement of the activity on your account. It lists deposits, withdrawals, ATM transactions, interest paid, and fees charged. You will get a photocopy of any checks that were cashed during that month. Check your statement as soon as it arrives, comparing the transactions on the bank statement to your own records to make sure they agree.

By taking a little time to be a good record keeper, you will make life a lot easier and protect yourself from mistakes and fraud.

For more banking tips, check out fdic.gov

Are You Ready?

1. How should you choose a checking account?
2. What are some of the fees that banks place on checking accounts?

 WebQuest online   To learn more about this topic, visit **PearsonSchool.com/PHecon**

Checking

Banking Online

You shop online. You chat online. You game online.
So why not bank online?

Modern Banking

Once upon a time, people had to go to the bank to deposit money, to transfer money from one account to another, or to withdraw money from an account. They had to write a check or use cash to pay bills. This has become ancient history. The online bank is growing fast in popularity. An online bank can be a virtual extension of a brick-and-mortar bank or can exist solely in cyberspace. As long as a bank is insured by the FDIC, deposits are safe up to $250,000.

Online Benefits

As one of today's online banking customers, you can access your accounts, pay your bills, and transfer funds from one account to another twenty-four hours a day. Internet banks also offer the environmentally friendly option to stop paper records, allowing you to access your statements, canceled checks, and notices online only. You can even arrange **automatic bill payment**. Although you receive a bill in the mail or in your e-mail, the amount you owe is automatically deducted from your bank account on a predetermined date.

You save time, postage, and the possibility of missing a payment and incurring late fees.

There can be other financial advantages to using online banks. Internet bank fees can be as much as 80 percent less than those charged by traditional banks. They may also offer checking, savings, or money market and CD accounts that yield higher interest rates than those offered by traditional banks.

A major benefit to the consumer is the ability to find these good deals by comparison shopping online. In the wise words of Benjamin Franklin, "A penny saved is a penny earned." By getting in the habit of looking for the lowest interest rates on loans and the highest interest rates on savings, the wise consumer will slowly pull ahead of the pack. Add a little compound interest into the mix and the pace of progress will pick up.

GO FIGURE

67.9 million

The number of U.S. households that banked online in 2008, up from 27.3 million in 2002.

SOURCE: "2008 Consumer Banking and Bill Payment" survey by FiServ

Online Banking Tips

Online transactions offer layers of encrypted protection to safeguard your transaction and privacy.

* **Make sure your computer is protected with the latest versions of antivirus and antispyware software.**
* **When banking online, ALWAYS double-check the Web site.**
* **When creating a password, avoid the obvious, including first names, birthdays, anniversaries, or Social Security numbers.**
* **Change passwords on a routine basis.**
* **Make sure all other browser windows are closed during your transaction.**
* **Exit a banking site after completing your online transactions and empty your computer's cache.**
* **Use Paypal. If your bank doesn't offer online bill pay, this online escrow service distributes your money fee-free to registered clients.**
* **Visit the U.S. government's site onguardonline.gov for further tips to protect yourself against online fraud.**

Checking

FL MA.912.A.2.2 Interpret a graph representing a real-world situation.

Be Responsible

Even though you may choose to bank online, every month you will get a statement in the mail from your financial institution. It is your responsibility to check this against your online transactions and report any discrepancies to your bank. Laws regulating an **Electronic Funds Transfer** (EFT), a system for transferring money from one bank to another, protect you in the case of fraud. You, however, have to do your part. In order to be protected by the law, you must report any errors in transactions within 60 days of the receipt of your bank statement. No matter how careful banks are not to make errors, no one is perfect.

If you use automatic bill pay, it is your responsibility to have sufficient funds in the account to cover the transaction. Some procedures of online banking are still affected by the business hours of the bank. If you are transferring funds to cover your bills, the money may not show up in your account unless you have made the transfer the previous day before a specific cutoff time. A deposit made at 1 A.M. may not show up on your account until the next business day. Plan your transactions accordingly, particularly if you wait until the last moment to pay your bills.

Gone Phishing

Phishing is a scam in which a fraudulent web site is used to gain personal and financial data to commit fraud. There are several steps you can take to protect yourself.

▶ Online banking transactions should be done through the bank's Web site only.

▶ Never respond to e-mails from your "alleged" bank that request sensitive personal or financial information.

▶ If you suspect fraud, contact your bank by phone to determine if it's a legitimate communication from the bank. If not, alert them to the scam.

If you think you can't be fooled, think again. Phishing techniques can be highly elaborate. Many even set up mirror Web pages intended to look like your financial institution's Web site to earn your trust.

Traditional Banking

In the balance, why would anyone still use a brick-and-mortar bank? There are a number of reasons that make some consumers reluctant to drop traditional banking altogether.

Online Revolution In 1995, Wells Fargo became the first financial institution to offer online statements. By 2012, it is estimated that 82 million Americans will be banking online. This chart shows trends in some methods of e-banking.

Percentage of Households Using Electronic Banking

Direct Deposit
- 53%
- 71%
- 80%

ATM Card
- 35%
- 57%
- 76%

Computer Banking
- 4%
- 19%
- 53%

■ 1995
■ 2001
■ 2007

SOURCE: *Board of Governors of the Federal Reserve System; Federal Reserve Bulletin, July 2009, and unpublished data.*

Convenience Factor

While Internet-only banks receive high marks for convenience, they also can be inconvenient.

▶ To fund an account, you will have to mail in a check, arrange for direct deposit or make a transfer from another bank. This is not a problem, of course, with banks that also operate a physical branch.

▶ Not having the option of being able to speak with someone face-to-face is another inconvenience. Some customers prefer to interact with people who know them personally. Making a phone call or communicating by e-mail is not to everyone's liking.

▶ Another drawback is the difficulty of finding fee-free ATMs, although online banks often have ATM networks for their customers to use at minimal cost.

▶ Lack of paper checks is a fourth issue. Instead, Internet-only banks offer a bill-pay service. But payments have to be scheduled ahead of time and take several days to process. As a result, you have to keep close tabs on your account to ensure that you have money to cover the payments.

Are You Ready?

1. What are the advantages of online banking?
2. How can you protect yourself against phishing scams?

 WebQuest online

To learn more about this topic, visit **PearsonSchool.com/PHecon**

Investing With Dollars and $ense

Inside, everyone is a millionaire just waiting to happen.
You can tap your potential with basic investments.

Self-Made Success

Look in the mirror and the face of a future millionaire may be staring back at you. More than 80 percent of millionaires are self-made, first-generation rich. But forget the lottery and other get-rich-quick schemes. You have to set your own goals and work toward them.

Pay Yourself First

In order to get started on your road to wealth, you have to remember one simple rule: Pay yourself first. A good rule of thumb is to set aside 10 to 15 percent of your income. We will talk later about how to achieve this goal, but for the time being, accept the fact. The lifestyle you choose to live now will determine the lifestyle you will be able to have in the future.

Get Help From Interest

Let's assume that you have made the decision to save. The positive news is that your savings will work for you. Banks pay you interest for using your money. Interest rates are expressed as percentages and indicate how much money an account will earn on funds deposited for a full year. Interest is compounded when it is added to your principal and you earn interest on both amounts. In effect, compound interest is interest on interest.

Most first-generation millionaires acquire their wealth over a lifetime. Their road to riches has more to do with budgeting, compound interest, and careful investing than with salary and inheritances.

Basic Investing

Putting money in a savings account is very safe. The only danger to money in a savings account is that the rate of inflation will be greater than the interest rate. Over time, the money in your savings account could lose value—it will buy less and less. But you will never lose your principal, the amount of money you put in the account.

Investing money is not the same as "saving" money. Investors take more risk—even possibly losing money—in the hopes of getting a higher return on their money.

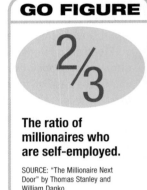

GO FIGURE

2/3

The ratio of millionaires who are self-employed.

SOURCE: "The Millionaire Next Door" by Thomas Stanley and William Danko

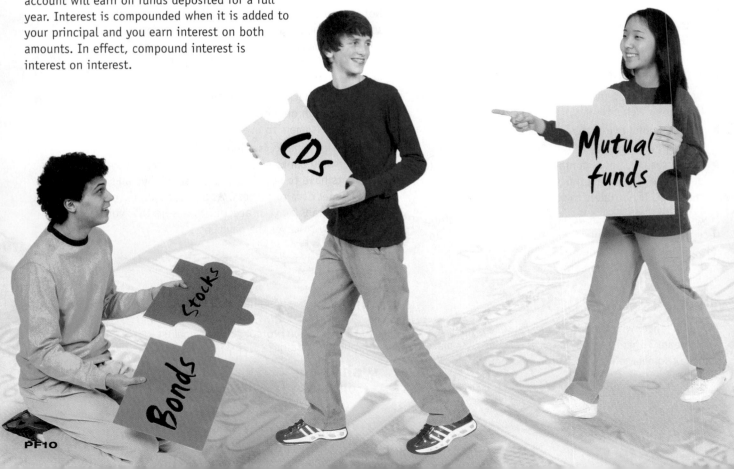

Investing your money can give your dollars a greater opportunity to grow. Bonds, stocks, and mutual funds are among the many investment choices that you have. Of course, with the possibility of greater growth comes the possibility of greater loss. If you invest in a corporate bond, stock, or mutual fund, you stand the risk of losing some or all of the money you invested. This risk is offset by the possibility of greater gain, allowing your money to grow at a faster rate than the rate of inflation.

The Name Is Bond

A **bond** is an IOU issued by a corporation or by some level of government. When you buy a bond, you are lending money in return for a guaranteed payout at some later date. The safest bonds to buy are government-issued bonds because it is unlikely that a government will go bankrupt. You can get U.S. government bonds through your bank, and they can be bought in small denominations. Many corporate bonds carry a low-to-moderate risk to investors and take anywhere from 5 to 30 years to mature.

Tale of Two Search Engines Since 2004, Google's stock has soared to over $650 a share. Meanwhile, Yahoo! stock has fallen. As much as they try, it is not always possible for investors to predict a sure thing.

Price at Closing (in dollars)

- Google
- Yahoo

Google: 100.25, 286.25, 378.60, 525.15, 465.25, 455.76, 460.33

Yahoo: 29.01, 33.24, 29.49, 23.97, 17.75, 14.18, 13.37

9/1/04, 9/1/05, 9/1/06, 9/4/07, 9/4/08, 9/1/09, 9/1/10

SOURCE: Yahoo Finance

The value of some bonds varies. For example, if you buy a bond when interest rates are 6 percent but you want to sell it before it matures, then the bond's value will be affected by current interest rates. If rates have

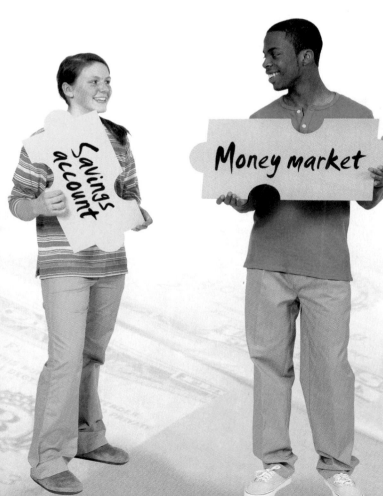

Savings account

Money market

> ❝**O**nly buy something that you'd be perfectly happy to hold if the (stock) market shut down for 10 years.❞
>
> —Warren Buffet, billionaire investor

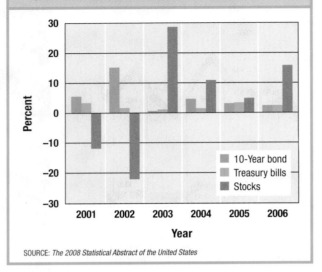

Five-Year Rate of Return

The rate of return (profit and loss) on investments changes over time. Historically, stocks have provided investors with the greatest potential for profit. But data also show that they're riskier than other types of investments.

Legend:
- 10-Year bond
- Treasury bills
- Stocks

SOURCE: *The 2008 Statistical Abstract of the United States*

gone up since you bought the bond, then you will have to discount the price to sell it. Why else would anyone want it, if they could get a higher rate of interest elsewhere? But, if interest rates have gone down, then that 6 percent rate will seem much more inviting. In this case, you could sell the bond for more than you paid for it.

Because the value of bonds is relatively stable, they are a good investment for people who cannot tolerate much risk. Families saving to send children to college may find bonds attractive because they generally earn higher interest than a savings account, and aren't likely to fall sharply in value the way stocks can.

Stock Up

Stocks represent ownership in a public company. If you buy shares in a corporation, you become a part owner. You will make money if the price of the stock goes up and if you receive dividends, which are a portion of the profits paid to the owners. There are two kinds of stock, preferred stock and common stock. Preferred stock holders get a set dividend and are paid from the corporate profits before the common stock holders.

THE RISK PYRAMID

"Risk" means the danger that an investment will disappoint you. A pyramid is sometimes used to demonstrate the riskiness of various investments. At the top are very risky investments like futures in precious metals. At the bottom, and least risky, are savings accounts, money market funds, and short-term CDs.

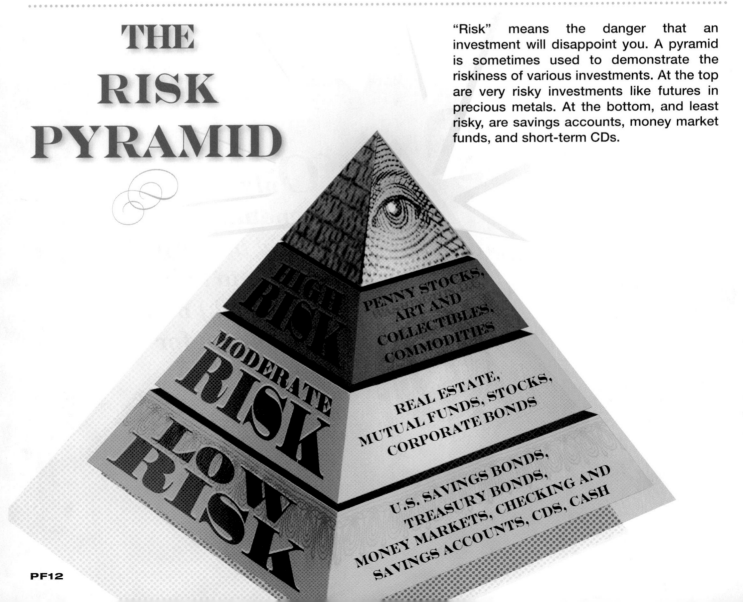

HIGH RISK — PENNY STOCKS, ART AND COLLECTIBLES, COMMODITIES

MODERATE RISK — REAL ESTATE, MUTUAL FUNDS, STOCKS, CORPORATE BONDS

LOW RISK — U.S. SAVINGS BONDS, TREASURY BONDS, MONEY MARKETS, CHECKING AND SAVINGS ACCOUNTS, CDS, CASH

Stocks are generally a riskier investment than bonds. Historically, however, stocks have rewarded their owners with higher returns than bonds or savings accounts.

What About Mutual Funds?

A mutual fund is an investment in a company that buys and sells stocks and bonds in other companies. By combining your money with that of other investors, the managers of the mutual fund can buy a wide variety of stocks and bonds. When you buy a mutual fund, you are buying a part ownership of the stocks or bonds owned by the investment company. The biggest advantage of investing in this way is that you instantly have a diversified portfolio. Your risk is spread out.

Three kinds of mutual funds have three levels of risk.

▶ Money market funds, which are not the same as money market accounts, are short-term, low-risk investments. The money you invest is used to make short-term loans to businesses or governments.

▶ Bond funds are investments in bonds. Though riskier than money market funds, they have a higher potential return.

▶ Stock funds are made up of a variety of stocks. Over the long term, they have provided higher returns than either market funds or bond funds.

Mutual fund companies are required by law to register reports and statements with the SEC. You can check up on them through the SECs database at www.sec.gov/edgar/searchedgar/mutualsearch.htm. Morningstar and Standard and Poors are two companies that rate mutual funds, stocks, bonds, and other investments.

Investment Strategy

Many first-time investors think that the way to make money is to buy low and sell high. But, trying to time the stock market has proven elusive to even the most savvy investor. When all is said and done, it's best to use common sense. Dollar cost averaging is one simple investment strategy that rewards the patient investor.

Dollar Cost Averaging

Dollar cost averaging is the strategy of investing on a regular schedule over a period of time. In this way, you capture both the lower and higher prices as prices rise and fall. In the long run, you hope to get a better average price for the purchase or sale of stocks and mutual funds. People use dollar cost averaging because they know they can't predict the market. It is especially useful for common stocks, which can be very volatile— that is, the price can swing far above and below the average price. Dollar cost averaging is an attempt to hedge against the ups and downs of the stock market. It does not guarantee gains or eliminate all possible losses, but it improves your odds of coming out ahead.

The Case for Dollar Cost Averaging

Let's say that you put $500 a month into a mutual fund for five months. The price of a share has gone from $10 to $10. You own 308.3 shares, worth $3,083. You invested only $2,500 (five times $500). You made $583 because the average price per share was $8.40.

Month	Price per Share	Shares You Buy
January	$10	50
February	8	62.5
March	6	83.3
April	8	62.5
May	10	50
TOTAL		308.3

Other Options

The risk and payout on investments covers a range from the most secure to the really, really risky. Junk bonds didn't get their name because they were a secure place to park money. Some people invest in collectibles—fine art, baseball cards, Civil War memorabilia. If the market remains strong, people who can part with what they have bought stand to make a lot of money. But, if no one is interested in your stamp collection, you may end up using it for postage.

What you choose depends on the risk you are willing to accept. You also need to consider the length of your investments and any tax burdens the investment may carry. If your scheme is to count on "sure things" or use tips from the cousin of your neighbor's son-in-law, you are likely to be very disappointed.

The Final Word

The federal government encourages investment. Even though the government taxes interest and dividends at the same rate as earned income, the profits from the sale of stocks or property are capital gains. In recent years, the taxes on long-term capital gains have been lower than the tax rate on the interest from bonds and savings accounts. As an added bonus, interest earned on U.S. government bonds is exempt from state and local taxes. What it comes down to in the end is that informed decisions and careful planning are your best strategies for successful investment.

Are You Ready?

1. What is the difference between saving and investing money?
2. How can dollar cost averaging protect your investments?

To learn more about this topic, visit **PearsonSchool.com/PHecon**

Building Your Portfolio

An 'investment portfolio' may seem currently out of your realm, but learning about them can't come a moment too soon.

Your Assets

An investment **portfolio** is made up of different investment assets. These include the basics: stocks, bonds, mutual funds, CDs, and a 401(k). A healthy portfolio depends on a variety of factors. No two are alike because every investment plan is designed according to individual needs and goals.

Diversify

As you have learned, all investments carry different levels of risk. Stocks, for example, carry much more risk of losing value than, say, a money market account. To protect your investment you need to diversify. In the uncertain world of financial markets, a properly diversified investment portfolio is better equipped to survive the ups and downs of stock prices. If your portfolio consisted only of stocks in companies that made gumballs, its value could take a nose dive if stores stopped ordering gumballs. If your portfolio was properly diversified, only the investments tied to gumball makers would suffer.

Life Stages

Investing should be seen as a lifelong process, and your investment portfolio should change over time. The way it changes will depend on your income and needs. For example, you probably won't need an investment to supplement the money you make from a full-time job, if you're 22 years old and single. By the time you're 40, however, you might already be married with children. In this case, you might need income

GO FIGURE

2
million

The number of young investors in the U.S., between grades 8 and 12, who actively trade stocks and bonds.

SOURCE: www.doughnet.com

Portfolios: Where do you stand?

No government agency provides a standard model for how you should invest your money. Experience suggests a good strategy is focused on a mix of assets that includes stocks, bonds, and cash. The allocations should change as a person ages. This is one widely accepted model of such allocations.*

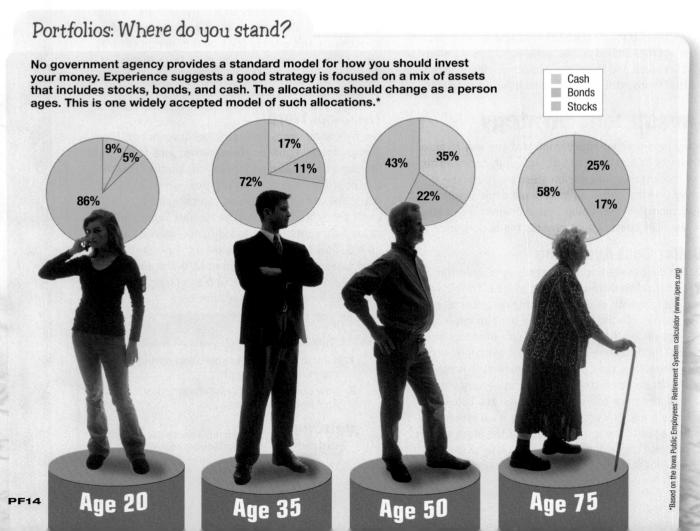

Legend:
- Cash
- Bonds
- Stocks

Age 20: 9%, 5%, 86%

Age 35: 17%, 11%, 72%

Age 50: 43%, 35%, 22%

Age 75: 25%, 17%, 58%

*Based on the Iowa Public Employees' Retirement System calculator (www.ipers.org)

from investments to help pay for a child's first year at college. Those income-producing investments probably will be more conservative because your needs have changed. Generally speaking, the younger you are the greater risk you can tolerate.

Investments can lose a significant amount of their value over the short-term. Over the long-term, however, those same investments could well recover their initial value and, even, gain much value. That is why it would be unwise for a 75-year-old investor to have the same aggressive investments as a 20-year-old.

Lisa's Story

With a new promotion under her belt, Lisa at age 25 decided she was ready to invest. Already participating in her company's 401(k), Lisa wanted to take her own investments to the next level: A professionally managed portfolio outside of her company.

Choose a Guru

Lisa wanted to manage her assets on her own. Who should she choose? Financial planner? Financial consultant? Financial Broker? If Lisa's main goal is to get financial advice, she might seek out the Certified Financial Planner (CFP).

Background Check

Lisa can perform a background check on her CFP through the CFP Board of Standards Web site. Financial planners and consultants are required by law to act in the best interest of the client, whereas brokers and brokerage firms make commissions off their sales. The Central Registration Depository (CRD) database provides background data on brokers. The Financial Industry Regulatory Authority's Broker Check Web site www.finra.org provides information from the CRD.

Commissions and Fees

When Lisa narrows down her list, she will find out if the advisers operate on commission, hourly fees, or a percentage of assets or some combination. She will ask for a complete breakdown of the fee structures. A reputable adviser or broker will give her information on their fees as well as documents outlining the risks of each investment.

How Much Risk?

Since Lisa is just starting out, her financial planner is likely to steer her toward stocks and bonds. Lisa is

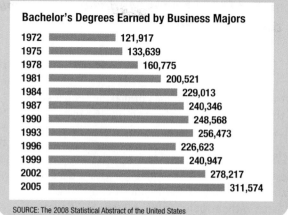

Mind Your Business Managing people's money typically requires training in finance. It is one of the fields contributing to the popularity of majors in business at U.S. colleges. In 2005, twenty-two percent of all bachelor's degrees were in business.

Bachelor's Degrees Earned by Business Majors

Year	Degrees
1972	121,917
1975	133,639
1978	160,775
1981	200,521
1984	229,013
1987	240,346
1990	248,568
1993	256,473
1996	226,623
1999	240,947
2002	278,217
2005	311,574

SOURCE: The 2008 Statistical Abstract of the United States

conservative and wants to limit her risk, sticking to CDs and bonds. But since Lisa is young and single, she should consider taking a higher level of risk for aggressive growth. She knows that she also needs to keep some money available for an emergency. Life happens, and she could face an unexpected expense.

Rule of 72

Thanks to the **Rule of 72,** Lisa easily can calculate how long it will take to double her investment at any given interest rate of return. The Rule of 72 is a mathematical shortcut in which an investor can divide the number "72" by the expected rate of return to estimate the number of years it will take for an investment to double in value. This assumes that the interest is compounded every year. For example, if Lisa invests $500 into an account that earns a 6 percent return, it will take 12 years for that account value to become $1,000, because 72 divided by 6 equals 12. Her account value will double, even if she doesn't invest another penny in it. If Lisa has an investment that earns 10 percent interest, then it will take 7.2 years to double.

Are You Ready?

1. Estimate how much of Lisa's portfolio should consist of stocks.
2. Use the Rule of 72 to find how long it will take for $1,500 to double at 4 percent interest.

To learn more about this topic, visit **PearsonSchool.com/PHecon**

Saving for the Long Haul

Saving is one habit that pays. And the earlier you start, the bigger the payoff will be.

Pay Yourself First

You already know about the advantages of making a budget. Spending less than you earn is a critical step to financial freedom. But it's only the beginning.

A Hole in the Budget

Meet Ricky. Ricky is a recent college graduate with a decent entry-level job. He's developed good financial habits. He got through college without building up a huge credit card debt. He budgets carefully—so much for rent, so much for food, so much for car insurance. Only after he has paid all his necessary expenses does Ricky use what's leftover to pay for the things he enjoys, such as a weekend trip or a new jacket. This may seem like a good plan—*UNTIL*

▶ he decides to buy a house.

▶ he starts a family.

▶ he loses his job.

▶ he gets hit with a long-term illness.

▶ he retires.

Ricky's habit of living within his budget month to month does not allow for life changes and emergencies. On his list of people to pay, Ricky has left someone out. He has forgotten to pay himself.

Get in the Habit

What does it mean to pay yourself first? It simply means to make personal savings a regular part of your budget, just like rent and food. Everyone has the potential to save, even if it means sacrificing a few immediate wants. You'd be surprised where the savings can come from. Cut out the daily $2.00 for soft drinks at the vending machine, and you've just saved $14 a week. Multiply that by 52, and you've pocketed a tidy sum in just one year.

Saving is a habit and takes discipline. You can get into the habit of saving money every month by taking a percentage of your monthly income and then paying yourself first. For example, you can have your employer automatically deposit a certain amount into your savings account. But don't touch

TALE OF TWO SAVERS

The age you start saving can make a big difference in the amount you have at retirement. In the case of the two savers shown here, the difference is more than $1 million! Both savers start with $200 and put way $200 a month. Both earn 8 percent interest compounded annually. Saver 1 starts at age 18. Saver 2 starts at age 36.

AGE 18

AGE 36

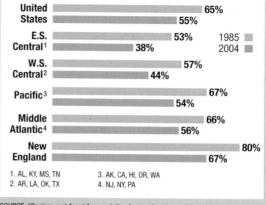

MA.912.A.2.2 Interpret a graph representing a real-world situation.

it! People who have trouble saving manage their money in reverse. They spend first, and then save what is left. But what if there's nothing left? Then there's nothing left to save. Saving doesn't mean you don't get to spend your money. It means you get to spend it later.

Why Save?

Not many young people think about saving for retirement. ("Retirement? I haven't even started working!") Yet, when it comes to saving, time is money. There are at least three big benefits to thinking *now* about the day you finally stop working. The biggest benefit is compound interest.

The Magic of Compound Interest

The earlier you start saving, the faster your money will grow. The reason: compound interest. **Compound interest** is interest you earn, not only on the money you put into an account, but also on all the interest you have previously built up. Today's interest earnings will start earning interest tomorrow. The more you save today, the more interest you will gain tomorrow. And that savings will add up at a faster rate. For every

Save Yourselves Economists warned years ago that Americans faced financial burdens not seen by previous generations. Data show that the decline in savings accounts is a national trend.

U. S. Regions With Large Declines in Percentage of Americans with Savings Accounts.

Region	1985	2004
United States	65%	55%
E.S. Central[1]	53%	38%
W.S. Central[2]	57%	44%
Pacific[3]	67%	54%
Middle Atlantic[4]	66%	56%
New England	80%	67%

1. AL, KY, MS, TN   3. AK, CA, HI, OR, WA
2. AR, LA, OK, TX   4. NJ, NY, PA

SOURCE: "Savings and Asset Accumulation Among Americans, 25–34" by Christopher Thornberg and Jon Haveman. October 13, 2006.

year that you put off saving, you could lose thousands of dollars in the long haul.

Other Benefits

There are also big tax benefits when you stash money away for retirement. If you put funds into an **Individual Retirement Account** (IRA), the money may escape taxation until you retire—or at least until you reach age 59 1/2. That cuts your tax bill NOW. Even better, when you withdraw your money from a special IRA (called a Roth IRA), the money you make—the appreciation—may not be taxed at all.

Finally, putting money away now allows you to have a cushion in case of emergencies. There are even circumstances in which—despite the government's restrictions—you can dip into a retirement fund to pay for other expenses. For example, you can access some retirement accounts to buy your first house or to cover high medical expenses.

Whether your dream is a comfortable retirement, a nice home, or foreign travel, you're going to need a savings plan to make it come true. As you'll see, there are many options to choose from. But it all starts with developing the saving habit—with paying yourself first.

$1,384,000

$322,000

AGE 67

Are You Ready?

1. What are the reasons teens should save?

2. What are three things you can sacrifice in order to save money?

WebQuest online To learn more about this topic, visit **PearsonSchool.com/PHecon**

Get Personal With Your Savings Plan

You know why you need to save, and save early. But which savings plan is right for you?

Three Savers

Okay, so you've decided to take a portion of your income every week and put it towards your financial future. Your goal is to achieve financial freedom, meet emergencies, and have a comfortable retirement—maybe even to 'get rich.' But not all paths are equal.

Different "Plans"

Let's look at three young adults: Amanda, Tyler, and A.J. Each of them is making about the same amount of money. Each of them decides to take $10 per week and dedicate it to their financial future.

Amanda takes her $10 and puts it in a shoebox under her bed.

Tyler takes his $10 and puts it in a simple savings account paying 3.6 percent interest.

A.J. takes his $10 and invests in lottery tickets in the hopes of winning a million dollars.

Different Results

Each of the three keeps this up regularly for 20 years. Each of them would say, "I'm paying myself first." But see how different the results are:

▶ Amanda has paid herself a total of $10,400. She now has $10,400.

▶ Tyler has paid himself a total of $10,400. He now has $15,392.

▶ A.J. has paid himself a total of $10,400. He now has $0.

The fact is, the odds of winning a state lottery are something like one in 18 million. So what sounds better to you? A 100 percent chance of increasing your savings by nearly $5,000 ... or a 99.99999995 percent chance of losing it all? That's a no-brainer. Tyler's savings account is also clearly more profitable than Amanda's shoebox. But even the savings account may not be the best option of all.

Park Your Savings

In making a personal savings plan, the first question you have to ask yourself is: How much can I save? You've seen how putting aside even a small amount can build up as long as you do it regularly. The amount you save per week should be one that you can reasonably commit to for a year. The key to success is that you must do this even if you cannot afford it. Then, pay your other bills as usual.

Savings Account

Usually, saving starts with setting up a basic savings account carrying no monthly fee. But when choosing a place to park your savings, *shop around*. Make sure the bank is FDIC insured. Some banks will charge you excessive fees just for the privilege of having your money. Web sites such as bankrate.com show you what interest different banks are currently paying for checking accounts.

CDs

Once you start making more money, think about moving some cash into a **certificate of deposit,** or CD. Like a savings account, a CD is insured and therefore very low-risk. But CDs generally offer higher interest than a savings account. The catch is, once you put your money in, you can't take it out for a fixed period of time. Depending on the length of the CD, you would have to part company with your money for as little as three months or as long as five years. There are penalty fees for early withdrawal.

As with savings accounts, you can compare CD rates online. You might even opt for an online bank that offers even higher interest rates than traditional brick and mortar banks. Here are the details for one available CD:

> **Initial Deposit:** $1,000
> **Length of CD:** 1 year, 6 months (18 months)
> **Interest Rate:** 4% compounded daily
> **Annual Percentage Yield** (APY): 4.081%
> **Ending Balance:** $1,061.83

Money Markets

What if you want higher yield than a regular savings account without tying up your money? You might open a **money market account**. This is a type of savings account with a high yield that allows you to write checks as long as you maintain a high balance in the account.

So which is the best plan? It all depends on how much you can afford to put aside, and whether high yield is more important to you than easy access to your money. Your early savings plan may involve a combination of options. As you get nearer to retirement, your options change and multiply.

SAFETY IN NUMBERS

Rainy day fund.
Emergency fund.
Back-up plan.

The name of the game is emergency money to turn to when life throws a curve ball. This requires a separate "must-pay" account—just like a bill. Job loss is just one situation that warrants easy-access, liquid cash.

Other cases of emergency include illness, car repairs, and appliance repairs. The recommended emergency safety net ranges between three and six months of income. Here are six ways to jump-start your fund.

1 **Funding bill:** Set up an automatic payment into a savings account.

2 **Cash stash:** Relative sent you a Ben Franklin? Put a portion toward emergency savings.

3 **Loose change:** Deposit all your coins into a jar. Repeat daily.

4 **Small sacrifices, big savings:** Cut down on impulse buys. Spin that cash toward your fund.

5 **Back to the basics:** Consolidate and resolve outstanding debt.

6 **Uncle Sam's store:** Purchase a U.S. Savings Bond.

(SOURCES: www.bankrate.com, www.marketwatch.com)

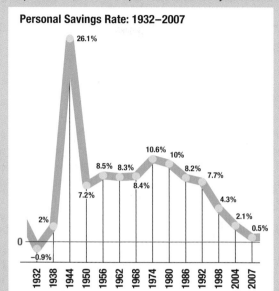

Depressing Savings In 2005, the U.S. government reported that the personal savings rate briefly fell into negative territory for the first time since the Great Depression. Americans spent more than they earned.

Personal Savings Rate: 1932–2007

26.1%
2%
−0.9%
7.2%
8.5%
8.3%
8.4%
10.6%
10%
8.2%
7.7%
4.3%
2.1%
0.5%

1932 1938 1944 1950 1956 1962 1968 1974 1980 1986 1992 1998 2004 2007

SOURCE: Bureau of Economic Analysis: National Income and Product Accounts Table (2.1) (May 29, 2008)

Are You Ready?

1. Why is the 'pay yourself first' principle a good savings technique?
2. How can you build an emergency fund?

WebQuest online To learn more about this topic, visit **PearsonSchool.com/PHecon**

Retirement Planning: Me? Now? *Why?*

Believe it or not, it is never too early to start planning for retirement. Here's why.

Retire in Style

Prom, graduation, car, college. With so much on your mind now, why would you even think about retirement? The answer is simple. You will have to live later with the consequences of your decisions now. Most people on the brink of retirement today will tell you that they wished they had known then what they know now.

Wait at Your Own Risk

It is never too early to plan for retirement. The longer you wait to save, the less time your money has to work for you. If you have a job now, you're already putting some money away for retirement. The government takes money from your paycheck to save for your future in the form of the FICA tax, or Social Security tax. But experts generally agree that Social Security payments alone will not fund a comfortable retirement.

How Much Will You Need?

How much money will you need in retirement? That depends on mountains of variables—your health, your lifestyle, where you live. Everybody has different needs. Let's look at some current, general estimates.

Many financial advisers estimate that you will need 70 percent of your pre-retirement income in order to retire comfortably.

By comfortably they mean you will be able to keep up your pre-retirement lifestyle. Your needs are lower because you do not have to buy clothes for work, pay for commuting, and eating out. You also won't have to put as much money into your retirement investments. It is time for them to pay you. No one is average, however. Some people spend more money when they first retire because they have more time for travel and entertainment. As they age, they travel less, and those costs go down. But, in many cases the cost of healthcare goes up.

Where Does the Money Come From?

The first source is Social Security. You might also have a defined pension, a set amount of money paid by your employer based on your wages and length of employment. Defined pensions, however, are disappearing in private industry. The rest of your retirement income depends on you: a 401(k), Individual Retirement Accounts (IRAs), investments, and savings.

Launch Your Plans for Retirement

According to statistics, you are going to live a longer life than your grandparents. What you have to do now is develop habits that will help you live with the choices you make. When you ride off into the sunset, you want to do it in style.

Solid Financial Planning

Social Security

Each year the Social Security Administration sets the minimum amount of earnings you need to have to be entitled to Social Security benefits. You can begin to collect reduced benefits at age 62 and full benefits at age 67 for people born after 1959. As the population ages, the point will come when Social Security will pay out more in benefits than it collects each year in payroll taxes. There is a lively debate in progress about how long Social Security will last and what it will provide in the future. The message here is that you have to prepare to take care of yourself.

401(k)

This leads us to the 401(k). You want to pay attention to this retirement plan. The law allows you to set aside a portion of your pay before taxes are withheld. Rent, credit cards, and student loans may limit what you can contribute to your 401(k), but the returns are worth the sacrifice. Some employers match every dollar you save up to three percent of your salary. Others may choose to contribute 50 cents per dollar you save, up to six percent of your salary. Either way, you get an immediate return on your money and you don't pay taxes on any of it until you withdraw it years later.

Employers have come to realize that many people do not have a clue how to invest the money in their 401(k) accounts. More and more employers are providing sources of investment advice to their employees to help them make the most of their money.

Other Accounts

The federal government also encourages you to save for retirement by providing special tax advantages for other retirement accounts.

▶ You can open up a traditional Individual Retirement Account (IRA) at a bank and contribute $5,000 per year. Depending on your income, this money may be tax deductible. You have to be ready to leave this

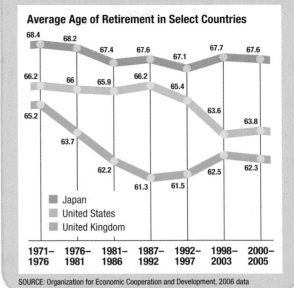

Retiring Nations Although the average age of retirement among American workers has risen in the past decade, it's still about four years less than in Japan. As people live longer, the retirement age is likely to rise even more.

Average Age of Retirement in Select Countries

	1971–1976	1976–1981	1981–1986	1987–1992	1992–1997	1998–2003	2000–2005
Japan	68.4	68.2	67.4	67.6	67.1	67.7	67.6
United States	66.2	66	65.9	66.2	65.4	63.6	63.8
United Kingdom	65.2	63.7	62.2	61.3	61.5	62.5	62.3

SOURCE: Organization for Economic Cooperation and Development, 2006 data

money alone. Tapping an IRA prior to age 59 1/2 will cost you dual penalties. You will forfeit 10 percent of your interest, plus pay taxes on what you have withdrawn as though it were added income. The 10 percent penalty is waived if the money is used for higher education or first-time home ownership.

▶ In a **ROTH IRA,** contributions are taxed prior to investing but withdrawals after age 59 1/2 are tax free, meaning you never pay taxes on the interest or dividends that have accumulated over the years. Roth IRA money may be withdrawn for first-time homeowners or higher education on the condition that the account has been open for 5 years. Early withdrawals will be subject to the 10 percent penalty.

Federal regulations regarding these kinds of accounts are subject to change by Congress. In recent years, the Congress has raised the savings limits to encourage people to save more for retirement.

Are You Ready?

1. What factors influence how much you will need to retire?

2. Describe two ways you can save for retirement.

WebQuest online To learn more about this topic, visit PearsonSchool.com/PHecon

Fundamentals of Good Credit

Are you credit worthy? It matters more than you think.

Making the Grade

Congratulations! You got great grades. You're one step closer to the college of your choice and maybe even lower car insurance costs—all for being responsible. Believe it or not, your credit history will have a similar impact.

Establishing Your Credit

As a first-time borrower, you may find it tough to get a credit card or a car loan on your own. Without a credit history to check, lenders often will require a co-signer to guarantee that the loan will be repaid if you fail to repay. This person could be your parent or another relative with a good credit history.

The rest is up to you. How can you prove to future lenders that you are a good credit risk? The most important step is simple: Pay your bills on time. Every late or missed payment will end up on your credit report.

Your Credit Report

Your **credit report** is your financial report card. In addition to your payment history, it includes the details of your bank and credit card accounts. Lenders can see how much debt you are already carrying. They can also see if you have had any bankruptcies or judgments against you, or if you owe back taxes.

National credit reporting agencies create a **FICO score** based on your credit history. The score falls in a range from about 300 to 900. Usually, a score of at least 700 gives you access to reasonable credit. (The chart on the next page shows how your credit score is calculated.) For a fee, you can find out your credit score at MyFico.com.

GO FIGURE

$1,585

The average credit card debt of a U.S. college freshman.

SOURCE: 2005 Sallie Mae report "Undergraduate Students and Credit Cards"

ADVENTURES IN CREDIT

Whether or not you are judged to be a good credit risk depends on the three C's.

Good Credit

CAPITAL
What assets you have to back up a loan, like a savings account, property, investments

CHARACTER
Financial history and payment record

CAPACITY
Your expenses, your job, and how long you have had it

FL **MA.912.A.2.2** Interpret a graph representing a real-world situation.

A bad credit report can sink more than a loan. It also affects your chances of getting insurance, an apartment, a mortgage—even a job. Like lenders, many landlords and employers check credit histories. They see on-time bill paying as an indication of whether you will be a responsible tenant or worker. The **Fair Credit Reporting Act** sets the terms by which credit information about you can be gathered and used.

Protecting Your Credit

Suppose there are mistakes in your credit report or you have made poor credit choices. What can you do?

Check It Out

Free credit reports are available once per year from each of the three national credit-reporting agencies: Experian, Transunion, and Equifax. Sample credit reports can be found on their websites. To get a free credit report go online: www.annualcreditreport.com; call (877) 322-8228; or mail: Annual Credit Report Request Service, P.O. Box 105281, Atlanta, GA, 30348. A credit report is not the same as a credit score.

How much information is gathered for a credit report? Take a look at the sample reports available on the websites of the credit-reporting agencies. Review your credit report for errors, such as the number of late payments, and for possible fraud.

If you find an error in your credit report, send a separate letter to each agency where the mistake is found as soon as possible. Include a copy of the credit report with the misinformation highlighted. The credit reporting agency is required by law to investigate with the creditor in question. It should remove from your credit report any mistakes a creditor admits. The **Fair Credit Billing Act** requires creditors to correct errors without lowering your credit rating.

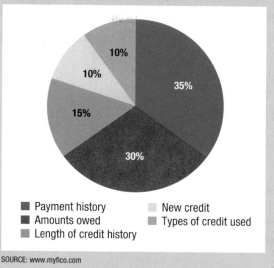

How Do You Score? The chart below shows the factors in your credit report that are used to create your credit score. Paying your bills on time has the greatest influence. Knowing these factors should help you understand how you can improve your credit score.

- Payment history — 35%
- Amounts owed — 30%
- Length of credit history — 15%
- New credit — 10%
- Types of credit used — 10%

SOURCE: www.myfico.com

Clean It Up

No matter how careful you might be with your finances, circumstances may get the better of you. The loss of a job or a medical emergency could leave you in a world of financial difficulty. Here are some steps to take if you have trouble paying your bills on time.

▶ Reassess your needs and wants. Be prepared to make hard choices.

▶ Stop using credit until you are out of trouble.

▶ Contact your lenders to negotiate a different payment schedule or interest rate.

▶ Contact nonprofit credit counseling organizations who, for a small fee, can provide debt-management assistance and intervene with card issuers. Make sure the service is affiliated with a third party such as the Association of Independent Consumer Credit Counseling Agencies or National Foundation of Credit Counseling.

Are You Ready?

1. What factors affect your credit rating?
2. Create mock credit reports for both a good and a bad credit risk.

WebQuest online To learn more about this topic, visit **PearsonSchool.com/PHecon**

Ready. Set. *Charge?*

The freedom to charge your purchases comes with fine print, finance charges, and a host of fees. Know your limits.

The Lure of Credit

"Buy now—pay later." Those four words sum up the attraction of **credit,** or deferred payment. Credit comes in many forms, from car loans to mortgages—and most popular of all, the credit card.

Credit Convenience

Credit cards make buying easy. With a piece of plastic, you can walk into nearly any store and walk out with merchandise. As for buying online, it would be almost unthinkable without credit cards.

No wonder credit card use by Americans has skyrocketed. And no wonder the companies that issue credit cards enjoy tremendous profits.

Teens and Credit

Americans under 21 can have a credit card if a parent or other individual over 21 co-signs the account, or if they can prove that they have the income to make the monthly payments. About one third of all high school students use cards linked to the account of a parent or relative. Credit card companies eager to issue young people their first card used to give out freebies such as t-shirts, but reforms in 2009 made this illegal.

Why do they want your business? The answer is simple: *teens spend*. Each year, consumers between the ages of 12 and 19 spend well over $100 billion of their own and their parents money. Credit card companies want to tap into this spending power.

Credit Traps and Tips

So there you are, card in hand and a world of things to buy. Unless you learn how to use credit responsibly, you could find yourself in a deep hole. You won't be there alone. It is estimated a majority of Americans between the ages of 18 and 24 spend nearly 30 percent of their monthly income on debt repayment.

GO FIGURE

8
billion

The number of credit card solicitations that American households received in their mailboxes in 2006.

SOURCE: Mintel comperemedia

Credit Card Round-Up

CREDIT CARD

1234 5678 9101

2008   01/10
JOHNATHAN Q. STUDENT

BANK

Avoid Those Charges

Ideally, you'll want to pay off your credit card balance in full every month. True, you are *required* to make only a small minimum payment. But look at the table on the right. For every dollar you don't pay this month, you'll pay interest next month. Worse, first-time cardholders without an established credit rating are often subject to a higher-than-normal **annual percentage rate** (APR).

What if you pay late or miss a payment entirely? You'll be subject to a late penalty. The finance charges, which include the APR and any related fees, can quickly add up to more than your initial purchase.

Suppose a credit card company requires a $10 minimum payment on a $290 outfit. If your payment is late by even one day, you'll get hit with a late fee and more than likely a significantly higher APR. And if your balance goes over the credit limit set by the issuer, there's a charge for that, too. Suddenly, the $290 "bargain" can turn into a $600 headache.

The Cost of Cash

Fees mount up even faster if you use your credit card to get cash. A cash advance carries an up-front fee of 2 percent to 4 percent, plus a higher interest rate than the regular card. And the charges start the second the ATM coughs out the cash.

Double the Debt This table shows the cumulative effect of a 19 percent interest rate on a $2,000 credit card debt. A person paying only $40 a month would incur $1,994 in interest charges by the time the loan was paid, in addition to the $2,000 in principal—nearly double the original debt.

Minimum Repayment Schedule on a $2,000 Credit Card Loan at 19 Percent Interest

Monthly minimum payment amount	Number of months to pay	Total interest payment
$40	100	$1,994
$50	64	$1,193
$75	35	$619
$100	25	$424

SOURCE: Government Accounting Office: "College Students and Credit Cards"

Read the Fine Print

The importance of reading the fine print of a credit card's terms of agreement should not be lost on any cardholder. The **Truth in Lending Act** requires banks to provide complete information on the APR, fees, and surcharges. New regulations require credit card companies to tell you how long it will take to pay off your balance if you make only minimum payments. Companies must also notify customers before interest rates increase or terms change. You can opt out of the changes, which will close the account. You can then pay off the balance under the old terms. The time it takes to review these terms could save you headaches and money.

Credit or Debit?

The surest way to avoid the debt trap is to keep credit card use to a minimum. For lower-cost purchases, you are better off using a debit card, a check, or cash. A **debit card** offers the same convenience as a credit card. But because the money comes straight out of your bank account, there is no interest rate and no risk of going over your limit. The danger of debit cards is that they are so easy to use, you may lose track of your spending.

For online purchases, however, it's wisest to use a credit card. It offers greater security.

Are You Ready?

1. Give three examples of bank fees.
2. What is the difference between a debit card and a credit card?

WebQuest online To learn more about this topic, visit PearsonSchool.com/PHecon

Credit and Debt

Managing Your Debts

Ignore what you owe and erode your credit. Drowning in debt is as bad as it sounds.

Getting Into Debt

With today's world of easy credit, it is not hard to find yourself in debt over your head. Using credit cards or borrowing money is not necessarily bad. You get into trouble when you go overboard.

Types of Loans

Loans come in several forms. Single-payment loans are short-term loans paid off in one lump sum. **Installment loans,** such as home mortgages or auto loans, are repaid at regularly scheduled intervals. Each payment is divided between principal, or the amount borrowed, and interest. (The earlier you are in the life of the loan, the higher the proportion of each payment goes toward interest.) A third kind of debt is revolving credit, where the amount borrowed and paid changes each month. The best example is a credit card.

How Much Is too Much?

Carrying some debt is not a problem—almost everybody does it. But you need to stay within safe limits. A general rule is that your debt payments, including a mortgage, should not be more than 36 percent of your gross income (income before taxes and deductions). You can estimate your own debt-to-income ratio by dividing the amount of money that you owe by the amount of money that you earn. If the result is higher than 36 percent, you probably owe too much money.

Here are some warning signs:

▶ Inability to make minimum payments

▶ Relying on credit cards out of necessity and not convenience

▶ Borrowing from one credit card in order to pay another

▶ Tapping retirement savings or other investments to pay loans

Getting Out

One reason people take on too much debt is that they want stuff NOW and ignore the fact that credit is a promise to pay later. They don't adequately plan for the fact that the repayment of principal and interest begins to eat into money needed for necessities.

Caught in the Debt Spiral

Take Andy. His entry-level job had an entry-level salary. The debt he ran up in college soared as he depended more and more on "plastic" to cover the basics. Paying just the minimum spared his credit temporarily, but he was racking up high finance charges. Once he started missing payments, creditors began calling. Now what?

GO FIGURE

$1.22

The amount American consumers spent for every dollar they earned in 2004.

SOURCE: "The Basics: How Does Your Debt Compare?" by Kim Khan

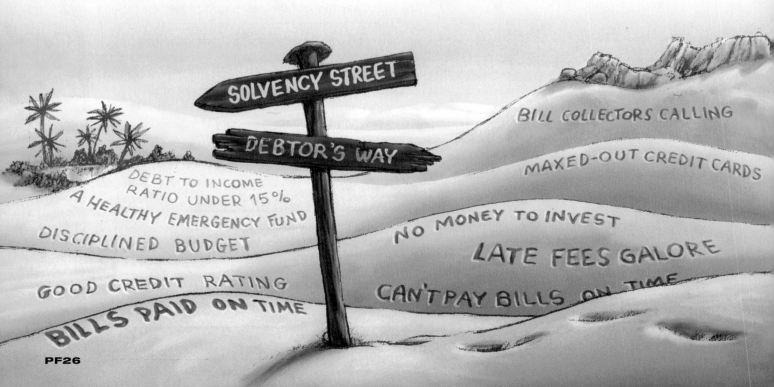

SOLVENCY STREET

DEBTOR'S WAY

BILL COLLECTORS CALLING

MAXED-OUT CREDIT CARDS

DEBT TO INCOME RATIO UNDER 15%

A HEALTHY EMERGENCY FUND

DISCIPLINED BUDGET

NO MONEY TO INVEST

LATE FEES GALORE

GOOD CREDIT RATING

BILLS PAID ON TIME

CAN'T PAY BILLS ON TIME

MA.912.F.3.1 Compare advantages and disadvantages of using cash versus a credit card.

Credit Counseling

Andy hated to admit it, but he needed help. He tried credit counseling. A credit counseling agency will negotiate on your behalf with the creditors, trying to get you an extension of time and lower interest rates. For a small service fee, it will take over your monthly payments. Andy checked with the National Foundation for Credit Counseling and the Association of Independent Consumer Credit Counseling Agencies to find a reputable agency. He now writes one check per month to the agency, instead of three to his creditors.

Other Options

If you find yourself in Andy's shoes, there are other options to consider—with caution. You could swallow your pride and ask a relative or friend for a loan. If you go this route, though, make sure that you have a written repayment plan and offer to pay interest.

You could also try taking out a loan from a credit union. Credit unions usually offer more lenient credit terms than banks. You may, however, need a co-signer.

Bankruptcy: The Last Resort

Bankruptcy is truly your last option. Common reasons for bankruptcy are large hospital and medical bills, uninsured losses, or high credit card bills. Some of these are unavoidable, but many people get into serious debt because of poor decisions and lack of foresight. Once you declare bankruptcy it will be harder for you to obtain credit. Nearly every credit application asks: *Have you ever declared bankruptcy?* So take this step only with the help of a lawyer who specializes in bankruptcy and can explain the options and consequences.

Credit Slips Over the past three decades, the number of Americans who filed for bankruptcy rose over 300 percent. A 2005 law made it harder to qualify for bankruptcy protection. In recent years, the number of bankruptcy filings has dropped.

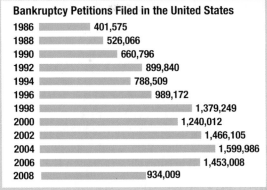

Bankruptcy Petitions Filed in the United States

Year	Petitions
1986	401,575
1988	526,066
1990	660,796
1992	899,840
1994	788,509
1996	989,172
1998	1,379,249
2000	1,240,012
2002	1,466,105
2004	1,599,986
2006	1,453,008
2008	934,009

SOURCE: *The 2008 Statistical Abstract of the United States*

One option is known as Chapter 7, or liquidation. You give up your assets in exchange for your debts. The cash value of your assets is paid to the creditors. To reduce fraud and make it harder to declare bankruptcy, the federal government passed the Bankruptcy Abuse Prevention and **Consumer Protection Act** of 2005. Debtors must prove that their income is below their state's median income and complete financial counseling and financial management education. Also, the government randomly audits debtors to check up on the accuracy of the bankruptcy documents.

A second option is known as Chapter 13, or debt adjustment, which involves temporarily suspending foreclosures and collection actions while you draft and execute a plan to repay some or all of the debts in three to five years. The amount to be repaid depends on how much you have versus how much you owe. Any form of bankruptcy will make it far more difficult to rebuild a secure financial future.

> **❝***I*f you think nobody cares if you're alive, try missing a couple of car payments.**❞**
>
> —Earl Wilson, author and newspaper columnist

Are You Ready?

1. Give several reasons why some people get into trouble with debt.
2. Why is bankruptcy a last resort?

WebQuest online   To learn more about this topic, visit **PearsonSchool.com/PHecon**

Insurance Basics, Part I

As you grow older and acquire more assets, your need for insurance grows as well.

Insuring the Future

You just got ticketed for sailing past a stop sign. You got distracted while you were changing a CD. Your parents are using the word *grounded* a lot—and also the word *insurance*. Sure, they have you covered on their policy, but a moving violation could raise their rates—and yours—through the roof.

What Is Insurance?

The road of life is peppered with the unexpected. Chances are you'll hit a few bumps along the way. Insurance is part of a **risk management plan** that will protect you against financial losses. Basically, insurance is a bet between you and your insurer. You are betting that something bad will happen to you, such as illness or a car accident. The company is betting against it.

Types of Insurance

There are four basic types of insurance coverage most adults should have. Your age, family situation, and income are some major factors to consider when deciding the type and amount of coverage you should get.

▶ Auto: Protects you and other drivers in case of an accident that results in damage and injury. It also protects you in case of theft, vandalism, and natural disasters. Most states require you to have your own auto insurance or to be listed as a driver on someone else's policy.

▶ Health: Protects you in case of illness or injury. It also covers the cost of routine medical and preventive care, prescriptions, and in some cases dental care. Even if you're healthy, having health insurance is a very good idea.

▶ Property: Protects your home or apartment in case of damage or loss of your belongings due to water, fire, or wind. It can cover your liability if someone is injured in your home and sues you for damages. Most policies do not, however, protect you against flood damage. You need to buy that coverage separately.

▶ Life: Pays a set amount to your **beneficiary** in case of your death. The beneficiary is the person or entity, such as a charity, that you name as the recipient of the death benefit of your life insurance policy. The two most common types of life insurance are *term,* or temporary, insurance and *whole life* insurance. Rates for term insurance increase over time. The only way to collect from a term policy is to die during the term. Whole life insurance remains in effect for one's entire lifetime at a set rate. It builds cash value. The insured can borrow against the policy.

What It Costs

The payment you make to an insurance company is called a premium. The cost of insurance is high, and getting higher. So does it pay to buy it? Absolutely. You may never have an accident and file a claim. But if you do, the amount you collect could be many times what you paid in premiums. Even a brief stay in a hospital, for example, can run up a bill of hundreds of thousands of dollars.

Besides, in many cases, insurance is not optional. You can't even register a car without proof of auto insurance. Nor can you get a mortgage without homeowner coverage.

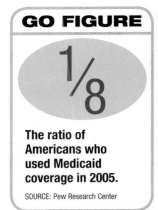

Deductibles

Insurance companies spread out their risk by collecting premiums from a lot of customers. They also reduce their costs by requiring co-pays and deductibles. A **deductible** is an amount you have to pay before your coverage kicks in. For example, if your car insurance policy has a $1,000 deductible, and you have an accident, you'll have to pay the first $1,000 in damages. The company pays the rest. The higher the deductible, the lower the premium.

Co-pays

If you have a **co-pay,** you are responsible for a small portion of the total cost of a service covered by your insurance policy. Every time you go to a doctor, you might have to pay a relatively small amount of the bill and your insurance company pays the rest. Generally, you can keep co-pays to a minimum if your medical provider—a doctor, hospital, or specialist—is part of your insurance company's healthcare network.

Changing Needs

As you get older, acquire more possessions, and expand your family, you have more to replace and more to protect.

Coreen at 18–25

Coreen is three months into her first full-time job. Finally eligible for employee health benefits, she lets her parents know that they can remove her from their policy. She also finds an apartment and gets rental insurance to protect her possessions from damage or theft. With no dependents, Coreen leads a relatively carefree existence. She can probably get by with basic auto, rental and health coverage—for now.

Karen and Bill at 25–54

Coreen's sister Karen and her husband Bill have purchased their first home. They are also expecting their second child. With a new home, children, and two cars, their insurance needs are due for a tune-up.

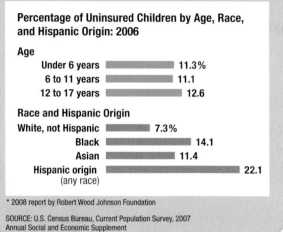

Kid Care It is estimated that more than 9 million children in the U.S. are not covered by health insurance. According to a 2008 study*, researchers found that uninsured children with serious illnesses are far more likely to have their care delayed or to receive no care. Some programs such as Medicaid and State Children's Health Insurance Program provide aid to about 3.6 million children. The table below shows some background on children without insurance.

Percentage of Uninsured Children by Age, Race, and Hispanic Origin: 2006

Age
- Under 6 years — 11.3%
- 6 to 11 years — 11.1
- 12 to 17 years — 12.6

Race and Hispanic Origin
- White, not Hispanic — 7.3%
- Black — 14.1
- Asian — 11.4
- Hispanic origin (any race) — 22.1

* 2008 report by Robert Wood Johnson Foundation

SOURCE: U.S. Census Bureau, Current Population Survey, 2007 Annual Social and Economic Supplement

Karen and Bill now need a medical policy that covers more checkups for the children. They also can't risk having to pay for a new car if they have an accident. With lives and assets to protect, this young family will focus on adding collision insurance to their auto policy and purchasing home, mortgage, and life insurance coverage.

Alex and Isabel, over 54

Coreen's parents, Isabel and Alex, decide to revisit their insurance needs as well. Free of dependents, they are less concerned about term or whole life insurance coverage. They are far more concerned about the cost of long-term healthcare. Once again, insurance needs change according to age and life circumstances. Because Alex and Isabel are in their 50s, they can expect to pay more for their coverage, perhaps as much as hundreds of dollars a month. Their problem will be trying to find the right coverage at an affordable price. To find the best rates, they will want to get group coverage through an employer or a large organization.

Are You Ready?

1. Why is it important to have insurance?

2. Describe the insurance needs of people at different stages of life.

 WebQuest online   To learn more about this topic, visit **PearsonSchool.com/PHecon**

Insurance Basics, Part II

People who don't get insurance are betting that nothing bad will ever happen to them. Are you willing to take that gamble?

Insurance Is an Investment

You wind up in the hospital for an emergency appendectomy. Your house is robbed. An uninsured driver hits you from behind. You get to pick up the pieces – and, unless you're insured, the bill.

It's All About Risk

Insurance is all about avoiding risk. For you, that means paying now to avoid a gigantic cost later. For the insurance company, it means identifying people who are likely to cost them a bundle.

Insurers set rates based on **risk factors,** hard statistics that predict whether someone is likely to be a bad risk. Do you plan to become a pilot or take up mountain climbing? That will make you a higher risk than a lawyer who spends leisure time doing crossword puzzles. A smoker must pay higher health insurance premiums than a nonsmoker. In the worst case, a risky lifestyle may make you uninsurable.

Who's Got You Covered?

Right now, insurance costs are probably not your concern. Most teens are covered for pretty much everything—life, health, property—by a parent or guardian. However, some teens must foot their own auto insurance bill. And that's expensive. Statistically, new drivers are high-risk. But if you want wheels, you have no choice.

Health Insurance

No matter how healthy your lifestyle is, you are going to face illness or accident. A bout of pneumonia or a broken leg may cost hundreds, even thousands. Even with health insurance, you'll have to pay something. But it's better than paying it all.

Employer Plans

Most young people are covered under parents' health insurance whether they are in school or not—at least up to age 26. Once you enter the working world, it's up to you. If you work for a company that offers health insurance, you can usually choose from a variety of group plans. Some cover you from day one. More often, there is a waiting period. Your share of the premium is deducted from your paycheck each pay period. The higher the deductible, the lower the premium.

GO FIGURE

$1,896

The average auto insurance premium in the U.S. in 2007. Louisiana had the nation's highest average at $2,740. Wisconsin had the lowest with $1,335.

SOURCE: "Most Expensive States for Car Insurance", Insurance.com

5 Tips for Cheaper Auto Insurance

Searching for ways to cut down on the cost of insuring a car doesn't mean you have to skimp on coverage. Even with the best of companies, there are steps you can take that will help lower your bill.

1. **Increase your deductible.** If you have to file a claim, can you afford to pay a higher deductible? The higher your deductible, the lower your premium.
2. **Buy safely.** Some cars cost more to insure because they are a favorite target for thieves. Find out which makes and models these are before you buy.
3. **Drive carefully.** Don't think insurance companies won't notice speeding tickets or accidents. Unsafe driving makes for a big risk and a big bill.
4. **Go back to school.** Most, if not all, insurers offer discounts for completing a defensive driving course.
5. **Install safety and anti-theft devices in your car.** These will lower your risk profile.

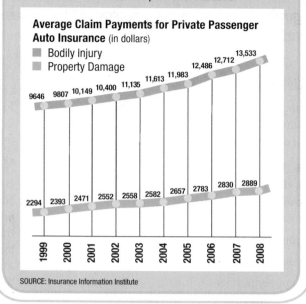

FL MA.912.A.2.2 Interpret a graph representing a real-world situation.

The least expensive health insurance plan is generally a **Health Maintenance Organization** (HMO). An HMO allows you to pick a primary care physician, to whom you pay a co-pay. If you need to see a specialist, your primary doctor will refer you to an in-network doctor. This is a doctor who has agreed to accept the payment level paid by the insurance company.

The Uninsured

Can't get insurance through your job or your parents? As of 2014, you will be able to purchase private health insurance from an exchange in your state. The healthcare reform law passed in 2010 also prevents insurance companies from denying you coverage for pre-existing conditions.

Cut Your Costs

The rising number of claims, plus increasing cases of fraud, have caused insurance premiums to skyrocket. But there are a number of steps you can take to get the best coverage for your buck.

1. **Comparison shop.** Compare the rates of different companies. Check with the local Better Business Bureau. And don't forget word of mouth. For example, if you're shopping for auto insurance, talk to people with similar driving records. Don't just ask about premium costs. Ask about customer service as well. Low price is no bargain if an insurer takes forever to service your claim.

2. **Make yourself a better risk.** If you smoke—or collect speeding tickets like they were trading cards—it's going to cost you. But insurers also reward behavior that lowers risk. A healthy lifestyle and a good driving record can keep costs in check. And while good grades won't reduce health or life insurance premiums, they might get you a discount on car insurance.

3. **Cover yourself.** You and your insurer may not always see eye to eye on a claim. It's up to you to provide evidence of loss. Take pictures of that busted headlamp. And keep receipts. That way, you'll be more likely to be covered for everything you've paid.

4. **Know your policy.** Being smart about insurance involves keeping your policy updated. Talk to your insurer to make sure you have the coverage you need. Review your coverage before filing a claim. You'll avoid nasty surprises that way.

Climbing Claims Accidents can drive up insurance premiums. The rising costs of car repair and health care cause auto insurance companies to increase their rates. The chart below gives a look at how insurance claims have risen over the past two decades.

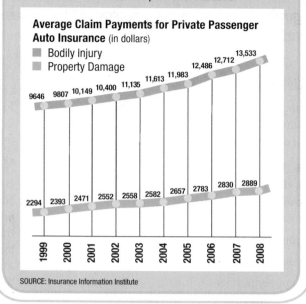

Average Claim Payments for Private Passenger Auto Insurance (in dollars)
- Bodily Injury
- Property Damage

Bodily Injury: 9646, 9807, 10,149, 10,400, 11,135, 11,613, 11,983, 12,486, 12,712, 13,533

Property Damage: 2294, 2393, 2471, 2552, 2558, 2582, 2657, 2783, 2830, 2889

Years: 1999, 2000, 2001, 2002, 2003, 2004, 2005, 2006, 2007, 2008

SOURCE: Insurance Information Institute

Should I Use an Agent?

Nowadays, you can often buy insurance online. Still, it might pay for you to use a licensed agent. It all depends on your needs.

There are two kinds of insurance agents: captive and independent. Captive agents represent a single insurance company. Independent agents offer policies from many different companies. Both types of agents must be licensed by the state in which they sell.

For most purposes, buying directly with a company or its agents works out just fine. But if you are difficult to insure—for example, if you have a bad driving record—an independent agent might be the way to go. With access to many different companies, the independent agent can help you find a company that can meet your special needs.

A good agent also helps you through the process of filing a claim and acts on your behalf in dealing with the provider. Many insurance agents are also certified to help you with other kinds of financial planning.

Are You Ready?

1. Why is insurance an investment?
2. What are some ways you can reduce the cost of insurance?

WebQuest online To learn more about this topic, visit **PearsonSchool.com/PHecon**

Buying a Car

Ready to go for a spin around the car lot? The best car is the one that suits your needs, and that you can afford.

A Major Purchase

Like most young people, your first major purchase may be a car. You need to do your homework, and spend some time and effort to get a good deal.

The Costs of Ownership

Step one is to determine what kind of car you can afford to buy and adequately insure and maintain. There are many money issues to consider:

- how much you can put down
- how much you need to borrow
- what your monthly payment will be
- how much your insurance premiums will be
- how much car maintenance will cost
- what gasoline, parking, and tolls will do to your budget

Since you have no credit history, you may have to search around for a bank or credit union that will lend you money. To get a vehicle loan, a bank may require you to have a co-signer, a person who is responsible for paying the loan if you default.

New or Used

If you are going to buy a new car, you want to determine the invoice price of the model you want, and then get at least five competitive bids from dealers. Request bids in writing and then try to negotiate. Will the dealer closest to you match the price of the dealer who is less conveniently located? You can use Web sites such as cars.com, yahoo!autos, and myride.com

GO FIGURE

$800–$2,400

The average range of annual repair costs in the first 5 years of car ownership in the U.S.

SOURCE: new-cars.com

MAKING A DECISION

Two things will have a major affect on what car you choose: what you like and what you can afford based on your savings and income. If you are still in school, you will have fewer options than a well-paid professional has.

To get a taste of what it is like to plan for a major purpose, choose two differently priced cars from ads in the newspaper or online. Go to a website with a loan calculator, like Bankrate.com, and estimate how much you would have to pay per month with various down payments, interest rates, and loan payment plans. How much income would you need in order to buy the car of your choice?

POINTS TO REMEMBER

✔ Taxes and fees will be lower on a less expensive car.

✔ You can lower your monthly payment by putting more money down.

✔ A lower interest rate will mean you pay less over the life of the loan.

as online resources for researching and getting bids.

If you're buying used, get a history of the **Vehicle Identification Number** (VIN) and have a mechanic inspect the car. That way you can determine how well the car has been cared for. There are also online sites that deal with buying used cars. They offer reviews of online used car classifieds, how to buy a used car from dealers or private sellers, how to negotiate with tough sellers, scams to avoid, and a list of questions for you to print out to ask the seller.

New automobiles **depreciate,** or lose value, quickly. A new car loses half its value in the first three years. But buying a new car can make sense if you plan to keep the car for a long time. You have to carry collision insurance if you have a car loan. Used cars are less expensive to buy and insure, but maintenance costs will likely be higher. Budget accordingly.

Leasing

Leasing is primarily used by businesses or by those who don't plan on driving many miles. If you go over the mileage allowed for the term of the **auto lease,** generally 12,000 miles per year, you have to pay a substantial fee for each additional mile. If you have a long drive to college or a job, the commute could eat up the mileage limit in no time.

It's Your Money

You might want to consider taking a more experienced person along with you when you buy your first car. It pays to have an ally.

Dealing With Dealers

In many cases, salespeople hold the upper hand when it comes to negotiating car prices. You can take a few steps, however, to level the buying field and avoid being pressured into spending more money than you want or can afford.

▶ Be prepared. Know what you want, and get bids based on the invoice price.

▶ Don't be talked into unnecessary options.

▶ Don't ever discuss trade-in until after you've settled on a sale price. A dealer might want to consider the trade-in vehicle as a reduction in the sticker price. In fact, any trade-in should have nothing to do with the price of the new car.

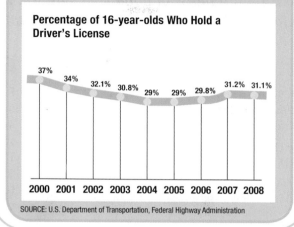

License to Ride Fewer American 16-year-olds are driving now than in 2000. Some possible reasons for the decline are tougher driver's license laws, the students' choice to spend more social time online instead of on the road, and the drop in the number of high schools offering driver's education courses.

Percentage of 16-year-olds Who Hold a Driver's License

37% 34% 32.1% 30.8% 29% 29% 29.8% 31.2% 31.1%

2000 2001 2002 2003 2004 2005 2006 2007 2008

SOURCE: U.S. Department of Transportation, Federal Highway Administration

▶ Don't be pushed into a quick decision, no matter what one-day specials are dangled before you.

▶ Get the sale offers in writing. If a dealer is not willing to put all agreements in writing, walk away.

Warranties

Dealers are required by federal law to post a Buyer's Guide on the used cars they offer for sale. This guide must specify whether the vehicle is being sold "as is" or with a **warranty,** and what percentage of the repair costs the dealer will pay. Most new and some used cars come with a manufacturer's warranty that covers certain repairs for a set period of time or up to a certain mileage limit. Extended warranties increase the amount of time or mileage that repairs will be covered. No warranty covers basic maintenance, like oil changes or new tires.

If you do happen to buy a car and the next day the engine falls out, you're protected by federal and state "lemon laws." First, however, you should go back to the dealer if you think you've bought a lemon. If you cannot reach an agreement, check the law to see what recourse you have.

Are You Ready?

1. How should you prepare to buy a car?
2. What are some negotiation strategies you can use when buying a car?

 To learn more about this topic, visit **PearsonSchool.com/PHecon**

Consumer Smarts

Renting an Apartment

Home is more than a place to hang your hat. Think twice and act once before unlocking the door to independent living.

Can I Afford It?

You've dreamed of this day of living under your roof and by your own rules. Independence. Rent. Bills. Cooking and cleaning. Yes, life is full of both ups and downs.

The first reality check is figuring out what you can afford. A general rule of thumb is that your rent and utility payments should not cost more than one week's take-home pay. How can you figure the average monthly cost of utilities? Ask the landlord or the previous tenant.

You will have to plan ahead. Many landlords require that you pay the first and last month's rent up front. In addition, you may have to pay a **security deposit**. This money is set aside for repairs of any damage you may do to the apartment beyond normal wear and tear.

Finding the Right Place

Finding the right apartment takes more than a little time, effort, and money. The federal government has stepped in to level the playing field. The **Federal Fair Housing Act of 1968** makes it illegal for a landlord to discriminate against a potential tenant because of that person's race, sex, national origin, or religion.

You can make the rental process easier by defining your needs and wants. Usually to rent an apartment you have to make a commitment of at least six months. So while the cheap one-bedroom with high ceilings and walk-in closets may seem like a steal, the fact that it's near the firehouse could make it a case of home, sleepless home.

Online Web sites are a good place to begin your apartment hunting. You can also look for apartments in the real estate section of a local newspaper. And if you're hiring a realtor to search on your behalf, keep in mind that they will charge you a fee based on the rental price. So do your homework, and check out the Key Questions list on this page for important factors you'll want to consider before making your decision. What if the ideal apartment is beyond your means? That might be the time to consider getting a roommate to share the cost.

GO FIGURE

4

The number of students that legally can live in a rental unit in Boston.

SOURCE: City of Boston Rental Housing Resource Center

KEY QUESTIONS

Finding the right apartment can be hard. Before you sign a lease, be sure you get the answers to these questions.

- How long is the term of the lease?
- When is the rent due?
- What are the penalties for paying late?
- Are utilities included in the rent?
- Are there working smoke detectors?
- Is parking available?
- Is the neighborhood safe?
- Is there public transportation nearby?
- Are there laundry facilities?
- Are pets allowed?
- How much advance notice is required before moving?
- What happens if you break the lease?
- How are repairs handled?
- Can you make cosmetic changes such as painting or hanging pictures?

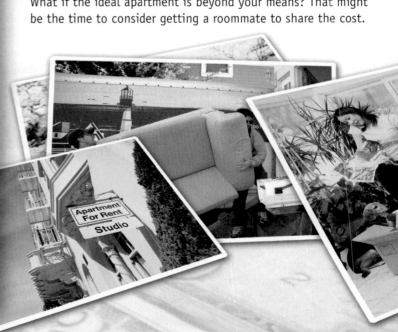

FL MA.912.F.3.6 Calculate the total cost of purchasing consumer durables over time.

Roommates

Can two live more cheaply than one? More often than not, a two-bedroom apartment in many locales is not much more expensive than a one-bedroom place. Plus, you can split the utilities and rent. The sources for finding a roommate are the same as those for finding an apartment—Web sites like roommates.com, newspaper classifieds, and word of mouth. You want someone who has a compatible lifestyle and who can pay their share of the bills on time. Your search for the right roommate is just as important as your search for the right place to live.

Furnishings

If you have decided to rent an unfurnished apartment, you will need to be resourceful to avoid major expenses. After you have tapped family and friends, yard sales and thrift shops are potential gold mines. An unfurnished apartment is not only empty, it will probably also be bare, right down to the windows and shower—not to mention the cupboards.

Protect Yourself

Learn from others' mistakes. Many apartment complex Web sites are chock-full of comments posted by current or previous tenants. You might even ask a passerby in the parking lot. To protect yourself from being charged for pre-existing conditions, assess and photograph any existing damage before you sign a lease.

The Lease

You, as **tenant** or "lessee," and the property owner, as "landlord" or "**lessor,**" enter into a contract called the lease or rental agreement. Here are some tips to make it a positive experience.

▶ Be prepared with the documents you will need to provide. These items include proof of income and identity, letters of reference, and a check for any required deposit.

▶ Get the lease in writing! Never take an apartment on the basis of a handshake with the landlord.

▶ If you don't understand something, don't sign the lease!

Costs of Living Geography is one factor that will have a major impact on your living expenses. If you live in cities like New York, Boston, or Los Angeles, expenses will be much higher than those in smaller cities or rural areas.

Living Expenses in Select U.S. Metropolitan Areas (monthly, per household)

Metro area	Electricity	Food and beverages	Transportation
Los Angeles, CA	$261	$211	$183
Miami, FL	150	211	190
Chicago, IL	133	200	176
New York, NY	168	211	190
Boston, MA	202	213	176
Houston, TX	185	186	167

SOURCE: Bureau of Labor Statistics (Consumer Price Index), 2007 data

Renter's Insurance

Even if you furnish with hand-me-downs or thrift-store treasures, be sure to consider renter's insurance. Maybe your roommate comes fully loaded with a flat-screen television. Should it disappear, you'd be left footing the bill. The benefits can far outweigh the costs.

Rights and Responsibilities

This is your money and your home, and you have rights. For example, you have the right to privacy. A landlord or maintenance worker is prohibited from entering your apartment without your permission. Renter's rights and responsibilities vary according to location, but most states provide a tenant-landlord bill of rights. Check with your local housing or consumer affairs office for specific information.

Tenants also have responsibilities, such as paying the rent on time and keeping the apartment clean. There may also be quiet hours, a policy imposed on most apartment dwellers. As always, a tenant's rights come with certain responsibilities.

Are You Ready?

1. What are some potential pitfalls in searching for an apartment?
2. What are four things you should do before signing a lease?

 WebQuest online To learn more about this topic, visit **PearsonSchool.com/PHecon**

Identity Theft

Keep your personal information personal. Learn how to protect yourself, before somebody else shows up as you.

A Growing Crime

An estimated 9 million Americans have their identities stolen every year. Chances are you know someone who has been victimized. You may be a victim yourself—without even knowing it.

It Can Happen Anywhere

Question: What do going to the beach ... taking out the garbage ... and answering your e-mail have in common?

Answer: They can all leave you vulnerable to identity theft.

A thief can raid your wallet while you're splashing in the water. A dumpster diver can retrieve old bank statements. Or an innocent-looking e-mail could be a phishing scam to get your personal info. Most people don't realize they've been victimized until it's too late. You might not find out until you're denied a student loan because you've missed several car payments—and you don't even own a car.

The Cost of Theft

Once they have your ID, thieves can use it to commit a wide variety of fraud, such as obtaining credit cards or even a mortgage in your name. Worse, if the crook who stole your identity gets arrested for *any* crime, you could get stuck with a criminal record.

In too many cases, the burden of proof is on the victim. According to the Identity Theft Resource Center, it can take 600 hours to repair the damage. Some victims need up to 10 years to fully clear their records. If your identity is stolen, you could face higher insurance costs, credit card fees, and interest rates for loans—or may even have trouble finding a job.

GO FIGURE

$500

The median loss due to I.D. theft per U.S. consumer.

SOURCE: "Top 5 consumer complaints," CNN Money, February 7, 2007

To download or not to download

After you go through all the trouble of protecting your stuff, did you ever think you might be taking somebody else's stuff illegally?

That's what you're doing if you download software from the Internet or make unauthorized copies of music or movies. It's like cheating on a test. You're taking someone else's hard work without permission.

Just like ID theft, "software piracy" has far-reaching consequences for teens, for teachers and parents, and for software creators and manufacturers. Some of the issues are:

1. Getting files or software secondhand exposes a computer's data and hard drive to viruses and worms that can cause damage.

2. When software is stolen, companies must adjust their budgets to make up those losses, which means software creators may lose their jobs, affecting the families those jobs support.

3. It's very easy to get caught. Internet search engines make it easy for teachers to find the source of plagiarized passages in seconds.

Prime Target: You

So should you be worried? Well, of the more than 255,000 **identity theft** complaints filed with the U.S. Federal Trade Commission in 2005, about 5 percent were against those under age 18—up from 3 percent in 2003. So congratulations: you are part of the fastest-growing target group for identity thieves.

Why Me?

Why are young people so vulnerable? One reason is that most teens have not established credit records that can be monitored. In addition, studies show that teens—

▶ are less likely than adults to check their credit card records.

▶ are more likely than adults to frequent the Internet and provide personal information.

▶ take greater risks relative to older age groups.

▶ often have an "it can't happen to me" attitude.

Finally, many Americans do not use their Social Security number until around the age of 15, when they apply for driver permits or first jobs. As a result, identity thefts against them may go unnoticed for years. There have even been babies that were the victims of identity theft!

At College

Over half of all personal information security breaches take place at universities, experts say. Part of the reason may be that nearly half of all college students have had their grades posted by using a Social Security number. It's within your rights to tell a college administrator not to post your personal information.

Lower Your Risk

Although there is no foolproof way to safeguard your identity, there are a number of common-sense steps you can take to protect yourself against fraud.

Be alert online. Think twice before sharing personal information. Social networking sites like Facebook.com and MySpace.com post your favorite music and status along with you addresses, cellphone numbers and former employers. All of this information could be used to create a credit account or take out a loan in your name.

Use passwords. Always use a password to protect your cellphone, laptop, and PDA. Do not store personal information on these electronic devices. Create passwords that contain upper- and lowercase letters, numbers, and special characters such as !, $, &.

Identity Crisis In 2007 the Federal Trade Commission received more than 800,000 complaints of identity theft, making it the agency's most widely reported consumer crime. Nearly one third of all victims fall in the 18–29 age bracket. One reason for this trend could be that younger people tend to spend more time on the Internet, where identity thieves thrive on credit and banking scams.

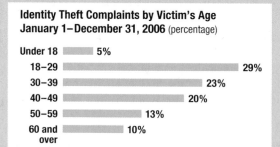

**Identity Theft Complaints by Victim's Age
January 1–December 31, 2006** (percentage)

Age	Percentage
Under 18	5%
18–29	29%
30–39	23%
40–49	20%
50–59	13%
60 and over	10%

SOURCE: "Consumer Fraud and Identity Theft Complaint Data, January–December 2006," the Federal Trade Commission, February 2007.

Check your credit. Check your credit report with a major credit agency like Equifax, Experian, and TransUnion at least once a year. You are entitled to one free report yearly. You can find them online at www.annualcreditreport.com.

Check and shred your statements. Always check your bank and credit card statements for anything unusual. Then make sure to dispose of those documents containing personal information using a paper shredder. Simply tearing up documents isn't enough to keep thieves from easily reassembling those statements.

Watch your mailbox. If you're too young to have a credit card, or don't have one already, you should be suspicious of any unsolicited credit-card offers in the mail addressed to you. For more information on identity theft and what you can do to protect yourself, check out the government's Web site www.ftc.gov/bcp/edu/microsites/idtheft.

Protect your reputation. Loss of one's reputation could be worse than loss of one's identity. Be careful what you write and say online about others and check what is posted about you. Online postings are testing the limits of libel and slander laws.

Are You Ready?

1. Why are young people especially vulnerable to identity theft?

2. What are some steps you can take to protect yourself?

 To learn more about this topic, visit **PearsonSchool.com/PHecon**

Shopping Online: Be Safe, Not Sorry

It's hard to put a price tag on convenience. But by taking a little care, you can get your money's worth.

Buying Online

Online shopping may already be a regular part of your life. You don't have to drive anywhere, stand in line, or haul the stuff home. A few clicks will do it all. And you can shop 24/7.

It's Easy to Be Smart

If you have ever gone from store to store looking for a hard-to-find item, you will appreciate the ease of shopping online. Who has the item in stock? Who has the lowest price? Free shipping? Quickest delivery? You can get the answers to all of these questions with the click of your mouse. For starters, you can check price comparison sites such as bizrate.com, mysimon.com or pricegrabber.com.

Read the Reviews

All right, so you can't try on shoes or a shirt online. Online buyers trade that advantage for online customer reviews. A recent study of online buyers shows that 9 out of 10 Americans read reviews posted by other customers online before they make a purchase. You can access detailed customer-driven product reviews for almost any product. Love the product, you can let the world know. Hate it, you can warn others as well.

E-Buyer Be Aware

Along with its unique benefits, online shopping includes some unique challenges. How do you really know if the online retailer you're dealing with is reputable and your information will be secure? For the most part, you have a higher degree of confidence if there is a brick-and-mortar backup to the online stores. Major retailers devote a lot of resources to ensuring that their customers have a satisfying and secure online shopping experience.

That does not mean that you should not deal with online-only vendors. See the Five Online Shopping Tips below for advice on making sure the sites you use are secure and reputable.

GO FIGURE

6%

The amount of all merchandise sold online that gets returned.

SOURCE: University of Nevada Center for Logistics Management

Five Online Shopping Tips

1 Check out the reviews written by other buyers.

2 Look for a padlock icon in the browser and "https" for security.

3 Check for endorsements from rating agencies, such as the Better Business Bureau (BBB).

Shipping Costs

Credit Card Theft

Bidding Online

Comfortable online? The biggest and best deals often exist beyond the big stores. Two of the most-widely used alternatives are the relatively free classified and message boards and auction sites. These offer shopping alternatives that come with a different set of rules tailored for the online marketplace.

Local appeal can be a major advantage. Online classifieds provide access to backyard buyers and sellers at relatively no cost. Your next entertainment center might very well be three towns or three blocks away.

In its attempt to keep you scam- and worry-free, these services encourage buyers to deal locally with folks you can meet in person. The site also includes detailed safety guidelines.

On Internet auctions, buyers can quickly and easily comparison shop for just about anything, from used cars and leather bomber jackets to concert tickets and, even, private jets. In this auction format, shoppers can engage in competitive bidding wars.

4 Steer clear of sellers who offer low prices only to squeeze you on shipping costs.

5 Use a credit card as it offers the best safeguard against fraud, but never e-mail a credit card number, bank account information, password, or PIN number.

Unsecured Sites

Identity Theft

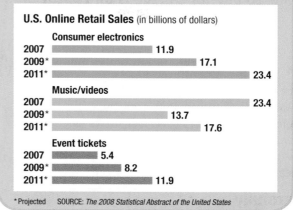

Virtual Sales In 2007, Americans bought over $20 billion worth of music and video products on the Internet, making them the most popular online purchase. By 2011, however, it is projected that consumer electronics sales will far outpace other products sold online.

U.S. Online Retail Sales (in billions of dollars)

Consumer electronics
2007 — 11.9
2009* — 17.1
2011* — 23.4

Music/videos
2007 — 23.4
2009* — 13.7
2011* — 17.6

Event tickets
2007 — 5.4
2009* — 8.2
2011* — 11.9

*Projected   SOURCE: *The 2008 Statistical Abstract of the United States*

So how are buyers and sellers protected? Buyers rate the reliability and service provided by sellers and eBay makes these ratings available to you. However, if you win a bid and do not go through with the purchase, you are stuck with a negative rating for the rest of your eBay life. There are also services that make it possible for you to pay an individual seller using your credit card.

Fighting Fraud

There is a new charge on your credit card bill! But where is the merchandise? You never got it, or even worse, you never ordered it. Many credit card companies will investigate suspected cases of fraud on your behalf, limiting your liability to $50. Also, the Fair Credit Billing Act allows you to withhold payment if you believe that someone has stolen your card number.

You also have the option of filing complaints with the Federal Trade Commission (FTC) at www.ftc.gov. The FTC offers you advice on how to protect against fraud, identity theft, and questionable business practices. The site guides you step-by-step through the process of filing a consumer complaint.

Are You Ready?

1. What are the advantages of shopping online?
2. What are two possible pitfalls?

WebQuest online   To learn more about this topic, visit **PearsonSchool.com/PHecon**

Paying for College

Learning how to pay for college is an education in itself.

Almost Priceless

It's hard to put a price on a college education. The personal and career rewards last a lifetime. Unfortunately, paying off the costs of a four-year degree can seem almost as long. The hard facts about paying for college are these: In constant dollars, the average cost of **tuition** at public and private universities nearly doubled between 1990 and 2005.

Choose Carefully

If rapidly rising costs continue, in 2014 a four-year public education will cost over $125,000 (in constant dollars) for incoming freshman. The cost at a private university will be almost twice that amount. For most students, those are pretty scary numbers. Here are a few questions to consider:

▶ **What school do you want to attend, and why?** Examine your goals. Look for the educational resources you need at less-expensive public schools. Private schools generally are more costly, but can be more generous with their financial aid offers.

▶ **Does location matter?** Tuition costs vary considerably from region to region.

▶ **How much debt can you tolerate?** If your career goal is to be a freelance artist rather than a brain surgeon, you might want to choose the less-expensive college to cut down on your post-graduation debt.

Financial Aid Basics

The thought of paying for college might send you into panic mode. But there is help. It comes in three forms: (a) grants and scholarships; (b) work-study programs; and (c) loans. The idea is to reduce the amount you're going to owe by applying for as many sources of aid as possible.

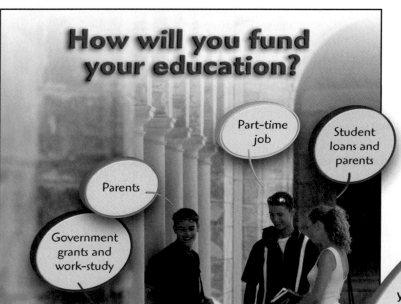

How will you fund your education?

- Part-time job
- Student loans and parents
- Parents
- Government grants and work-study

FINANCIAL AID TIPS

Apply early: There is a limited amount of aid available, so make sure you get your fair share.

Seek free money: Grants and scholarships need not be repaid. Search for local and government sources of financial aid.

Limit your debt: Finance just what you need.

Use the Web: Several sites have calculators that allow you to estimate your expected family contribution, the amount of your aid awards, and the amount of your loan payments. The College Board has one as well as a search tool for scholarships. The Sallie Mae (www.salliemae.com) site includes a listing of major private lenders.

And if you're like most students, you will qualify for some type of assistance. The biggest financial aid error is not to apply at all. Many colleges are substituting loans for grants and some are experimenting by waiving tuition for certain income levels altogether.

Types of Lenders

Financial aid comes in many packages and, regardless of income, you can qualify for a government loan.

Federal Government

When it comes to government aid, the Department of Education offers three basic loans: Direct Loans and Stafford Loans for parents or students, as well as the Parent Loan for Undergraduate Students (PLUS).

For those in financial need, there is the Federal Perkins Loan. These loans have a fixed interest rate and are made available through the college. Students who go on to take teaching jobs in certain areas or who volunteer in the Americorps, Peace Corps, or VISTA programs may be eligible to have their federal loans partially repaid or even canceled. To help qualifying graduates, the government limits loan payments to 10% of their discretionary income. Any person who makes their payment on time will have the balance forgiven after 20 years.

Private Sources

If money from government loans does not cover all your college expenses, private lending sources could fill the gap. Compared to government loans, regular commercial loans typically have higher interest rates, fees, and credit requirements. Trade organizations and educational institutions also offer lending aid. Check with your guidance counselor to find out more information.

Other Sources

All kinds of students can qualify for financial aid that does not have to be repaid. You need not be valedictorian or an all-state basketball star.

Grants

A no-strings attached grant is a no-brainer to consider when applying for financial aid. Available from the federal government, state governments and higher education institutions, grants are usually awarded according to financial need and tuition rates.

Don't forget FAFSA, also known as, the Free Application for Federal Student Aid available at www.fafsa.ed.gov. All students should complete the FAFSA, even if they

Sticker Shock In recent years, the cost of attending a U.S. four-year-college has risen at twice the inflation rate. A 2007 study*, however, finds that the benefits outweigh the short-term cost. Over a lifetime, a college education increases a worker's earning potential by about $800,000.

Average Undergraduate Tuition, Fees, Room and Board Charged to Full-Time Students (in dollars)

■ U.S. Private Institutions
■ U.S. Public Institutions

	1980–1981	1985–1986	1990–1991	1995–1996	2000–2001	2005–2006
Private	5,594	9,228	13,237	17,612	21,856	27,317
Public	2,550	3,859	5,243	7,014	8,653	12,108

*Report by the College Board, "Education Pays"   SOURCE: Digest of Education Statistics

believe they will not qualify for aid. There is always a chance that family circumstances will change. You need to complete this form if you want to be considered for federal aid, such as the Pell Grant and Supplemental Educational Opportunity Grant. These grants are given to students with "exceptional financial need." Find out more by checking out the U.S. Department of Education Web sites, www.federalstudentaid.ed.gov, www.students.gov, your state education agency, or your high school guidance office.

Scholarships and Work Study

Besides aid from the school itself, there are scholarships available from local community and civic groups. Check with local organizations such as the Kiwanis and Lions Clubs. Some companies also offer scholarships to children of their employees. Work-study programs are a win-win situation for the student, college, and community. This type of aid allows students to earn money to offset their educational expenses.

Are You Ready?

1. Why is it important to complete the FAFSA form?

2. What is the advantage of seeking a federal loan instead of one from a private lender?

 WebQuest online To learn more about this topic, visit **PearsonSchool.com/PHecon**

Getting a Job

Engineer? Store manager? Teacher? Whatever you want to be, you'll soon have to look for your first real job—and then get it.

Be Prepared!

You may already have had your first job—after school, weekends, or summers. But for most of us, finding a full-time, long-term job doesn't come until after we graduate from high school or college.

Your Resumé

The first step is to prepare a **resumé,** a written summary of your educational and work experience. Think of it as an advertisement to market yourself to an employer.

You might be thinking, "That's fine if I have a lot of experience to list. But this is my first real job." True, but that doesn't mean you don't have qualities that employers are interested in. For example, suppose you worked the same job every summer for three years running. That shows that somebody liked you enough to keep hiring you back. Your service in school clubs or volunteer organizations could indicate qualities such as leadership, planning abilities, and a strong work ethic. Academic honors can count for a lot, too.

Organize your resumé in a neat, readable fashion—no fancy type. And have plenty of copies on hand. (For more tips, see the resumé-writing worksheet available online.)

References

Some employers may ask for references. If you've been applying for colleges, you know the drill. Pick people—other than family—who can tell potential employers about your character and work ethic: a former boss, a colleague from an internship, a professor or advisor. Be ready with names, home or business addresses, e-mail addresses, and phone numbers.

Where to Look

There are plenty of good sources of job information out there. Any or all of these can help you land the right job.

The Internet More and more companies are using sites like monster.com and careerbuilder.com to advertise for help.

Newspapers Maybe you don't read the newspaper so much. But a lot of employers do. Find out what day your local newspaper publishes want ads.

Employment Agencies For a fee, the agency can help you connect with a company looking for someone with your skills.

Job/Career Centers High schools and colleges offer career counseling. In addition to helping you find a job, counselors can appraise your resume at no cost and give you interviewing tips.

Job Fairs Companies get a chance to meet recent graduates—you get a chance to meet possible employers.

Know Where to Look

So you're ready to look for a job. Where should you start? Some common sources of job information are listed on the previous page. Make a list of places that seem most promising. And try to find out something about a company before you apply there. It's all just part of being prepared.

The Interview

That very first job interview can be an exciting but nerve-wracking experience. But you can prepare for it. Hold a mock interview with family members or friends. Have them ask you possible questions and then critique your responses and your delivery.

Make a Good Impression

The minute you step into a potential employer's office, you are being judged. Don't blow it before you open your mouth. Posture, eye contact, and a firm handshake go a long way to making a positive impression.

> ❝ **You never get a second chance to make a first impression.** ❞
>
> —Maxim attributed to 20th century Dutch author William Triesthof

Believe it or not, dressing wrong can be a deal-breaker. What works on the beach or in a dance club won't cut it in the office. Even a company that allows "casual" dress on the job doesn't want to see you in tank tops, cutoffs, or flip-flops. Be safe. Think conservative and professional. Yes, that may mean a suit or a dress. Let them tell you that you don't have to dress that way— after you get the job.

Turn Off That Cellphone

The person interviewing you may have to interrupt to take a phone call. But you do not get the same privilege. Before you step in that office, make sure your cellphone is switched off. Nothing will ruin a good interview faster than a ringing cellphone.

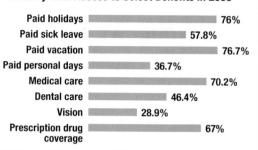

Paid in Full? Not all benefit packages are created equal. For instance, rising medical costs in recent years have forced many private companies to scale back, or even drop, health coverage. The chart below shows that the types of benefits private companies offer can vary greatly.

Average Percentage of U.S. Workers in Private Industry With Access to Select Benefits in 2006

Benefit	Percentage
Paid holidays	76%
Paid sick leave	57.8%
Paid vacation	76.7%
Paid personal days	36.7%
Medical care	70.2%
Dental care	46.4%
Vision	28.9%
Prescription drug coverage	67%

SOURCE: *The 2008 Statistical Abstract of the United States*

Ask the Right Questions

Where do you see yourself in five years? Why did you choose your particular college major? Why are you the best candidate for this position? Expect to be peppered with questions. But be equally as prepared to ask them. Questions like these show you're interested in the job:

▶ What are the company's goals for the next year or so?

▶ How does this job fit in with the company's goals?

▶ Describe a typical day here in this department.

Steer clear of questions about pay, benefits, hours, and vacation time. All that will be covered if you are asked back for a second interview.

After the Interview

Follow up with a handwritten or e-mailed thank you note. This reaffirms your interest and makes a lasting impression. If you're rejected, try not to get discouraged. It's part of the interview process. And remember: rejection can work either way. You're under no obligation to accept the first offer that comes along. Factor in benefits, commuting costs, work environment, and the possibility of career advancement. Look for the best fit for you.

Are You Ready?

1. How should you dress for an interview?
2. What are important things about yourself you should highlight during an interview?

 WebQuest online To learn more about this topic, visit **PearsonSchool.com/PHecon**

Understanding Your Paycheck

Your pay stub is an important tool in managing your personal finances. Put it to work for you.

What's in a Paycheck?

You've got your first job—and your first paycheck. Attached to your check is a pay stub, also known as an earnings statement, which includes your identification information and the pay period you worked. But there's a lot more to it than that.

Salary and Wages

It all begins with your wages or salary. Wages refer to hourly pay, and can change based on how much time you worked. Salary is monthly or yearly pay, which is not dependent on the number of hours worked.

Your pay stub shows your **gross pay,** the total amount of income you earned during the pay period. If you are paid hourly, it should be equal to the number of hours you worked times your hourly wage. (It will also show if you worked overtime at a higher rate.) If you are on an annual salary, it's your salary divided by the number of pay periods in the year.

Withholdings

You will immediately notice that your **net pay**—the amount the check is made out for—is far less than your gross pay. Where did the rest of the money go?

Your stub lists all your **payroll withholdings,** the earnings that come out of your check before you get it. Some of these withholdings are voluntary. For example, if you join a company medical or insurance plan, your share of these benefits comes out of your check. Other withholdings, however, go in taxes to the state and federal government.

Federal and State Deductions

Most workers have federal and state taxes deducted from their earnings. Your employer is also required to pay the federal government a certain percentage your earnings.

Social Security and Medicare

Social Security (FICA) and Medicare taxes are based on a percentage of your earnings. FICA stands for Federal Insurance Contributions Act. It is a U.S. payroll tax on employees and employers to fund programs that provide benefits for retirees, the disabled, and children of deceased workers. Medicare provides hospital insurance benefits.

The W-4 Form

Federal and state taxes are deducted based on an estimate of how much you will owe in yearly taxes. Most workers

are required to fill out the W-4 form when they start a new job. It includes guidelines to help you do the calculations needed to estimate how much will be withheld from each paycheck. The W-4 gives you the option of taking certain personal allowances that will lower the amount of tax withheld from your income. For example, you may take an exemption for yourself and your spouse. You also can take an exemption for anyone who is dependent on your income, such as a child. Young people who are not married and have no children will generally claim a single exemption. The IRS offers an online withholding calculator (www.irs.gov/individuals) to help you avoid having too much or too little income tax withheld from your pay.

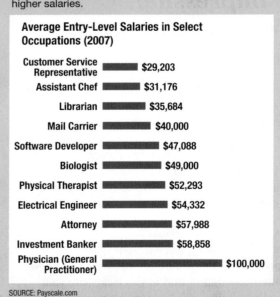

Pay Check Level of education, skill and supply and demand are major factors that determine a worker's entry-level pay. Typically, college graduates with technical, medical, or business degrees will command higher salaries.

Average Entry-Level Salaries in Select Occupations (2007)

Occupation	Salary
Customer Service Representative	$29,203
Assistant Chef	$31,176
Librarian	$35,684
Mail Carrier	$40,000
Software Developer	$47,088
Biologist	$49,000
Physical Therapist	$52,293
Electrical Engineer	$54,332
Attorney	$57,988
Investment Banker	$58,858
Physician (General Practitioner)	$100,000

SOURCE: Payscale.com

A **Year-to-date**
(for pay and deductions)
The year-to-date shows the total amount withheld for a particular deduction at any point in the calendar year.

Earnings Statement

Period ending: 00/00/0000
Pay date: 00/00/0000

C **Leave Time**
Includes vacation hours or sick hours. Many employers will detail how many hours have been used to date, and how many hours are remaining for the calendar year.

XYZ Corporation
100 Corporation Crt.
New Town, NY 10000

TOMÁS Q. PUBLIC
123 MAIN STREET
ANYWHERE, USA 12345

B **Gross Pay**
The total amount of income that you earned during the pay period.

Social Security Number: 999-99-9999
Taxable Marital Status: Single
Exemptions/Allowances:
    Federal: 1
    State: 1
    Local: 1

Earnings	rate	hours	this period	year to date
Regular	20.00	40.00	800.00	16,640.00
Overtime	30.00	1.00	30.00	780.00 **A**
Holiday	30.00	8.00	240.00	1,200.00 **A**
B **Gross Pay**			**$ 1,070.00**	18,620.00

Other Benefits and Information	this period	year-to-date
Vac Hrs Left		40.00 **C**
Sick Hrs Left		16.00

Deductions   **Statutory**

	this period	year to date
H Federal Income Tax	- 235.75	4,351.44
I Social Security Tax	- 65.10	1,251.67
J Medicare Tax	- 15.23	272.89
K NY State Income Tax	- 64.60	1,203.24
L NYC Income Tax	- 33.86	527.96
NY SDI Tax	- 1.80	15.20

Important Notes

YOUR TOTAL NET PAY HAS BEEN AUTOMATICALLY DEPOSITED INTO CHECKING ACCOUNT XXXX4071.

Other

	this period	year to date
Medical and Dental	- 35.00	700.00
401(k)	- 107.00 *	2,140.00 **D**
Stock Plan	- 15.00	300.00
Life Insurance	- 5.00	100.00 **E**
FSA	- 20.00 *	400.00 **F**

D **Retirement Plan Contributions**
Contributions to plans such as 401(k) or 403(b) retirement savings plans.

E **Insurance Deductions**
Deductions for insurance such as health (medical and dental), and life insurance.

F **Flexible Spending Account**
A pre-tax benefit offered by some employers to help workers save for health- and childcare-related expenses.

Net Pay	**$ 598.34** **G**

G **Net Pay**
The amount of income that you actually take home.

* **Excluded from federal taxable wages**

Your federal taxable wages this period are $943.00

▼ TEAR HERE

THE ORIGINAL DOCUMENT HAS AN ARTIFICIAL WATERMARK ON THE BACK.   HOLD AT AN ANGLE TO VIEW WHEN CHECKING THE ENDORSEMENT.

H **Federal Tax Amount**
The amount of federal tax that is deducted and paid to the federal government. It is based on your gross income, minus any "pre-tax deductions."

I **Social Security**
The mandatory 6.2 percent tax imposed on workers for Social Security disability insurance and retirement benefits.

J **Medicare**
The mandatory 1.45 percent tax imposed on workers for Medicare.

K **State Tax Amount**
The amount of tax paid to the state government.

L **Local Tax Amount**
The local tax is sometimes applied to residents of certain cities, counties or school districts.

Are You Ready?

1. What is the difference between gross pay and net income?
2. What would be the year-to-date Medicare tax withholding for a worker whose gross pay was $9,845?

To learn more about this topic, visit **PearsonSchool.com/PHecon**

MA.912.A.2.2 Interpret a graph representing a real-world situation.

Paying Your Taxes

Your country, state, and community want a share of your paycheck. It's a cost of being a responsible citizen.

Taxes and You

Welcome to the workforce! You have joined the ranks of taxpayers. But why do you have to pay taxes anyhow?

Your Share of the Bill

Governments have expenses. They have to pay salaries for thousands of employees and provide services for millions of citizens. The biggest source of government revenue is taxes. And you are required by law to pay your share.

Don't Mess With the IRS

Among taxes, the federal income tax is top dog. The Internal Revenue Service (IRS), an agency within the Treasury Department, applies federal income tax laws passed by Congress. The agency generates tax forms and collects taxes. The IRS will notice if you don't pay what you owe and impose hefty financial penalties for any misdeeds.

The federal income tax is a progressive tax, so people with the highest income have the highest tax rates. The system also includes hundreds of tax breaks for people with special financial burdens, such as people paying for college or starting a business, as well as rewards for actions like making a donation to charity.

Other Taxes

Most state governments collect income tax, too. In addition, states and local communities levy other kinds of taxes, such as sales tax and property tax. Sales taxes vary from state to state, but they generally involve paying a fixed percentage on most items you buy. Essentials of life—such as food and medicine—are generally exempt from sales tax. Property taxes are based on the value of privately owned homes and land.

Taxes are also collected on income you didn't work for. If Aunt Bessie leaves you money in her will, you have to pay an inheritance tax. If you buy stock and you make a lot of money when you sell it, that's also taxed.

GO FIGURE

$1.236 trillion

Gross collections from individual U.S. taxpayers in 2006.

SOURCE: Internal Revenue Service

Forms, Forms, Forms

Sometime during the 'tax season', which runs from January to April 15, you need to fill out and file the appropriate tax forms. Filing is the only way to get a refund, or return of excess taxes paid. But whether you've got a refund coming or not, it's against the law not to file an income tax return.

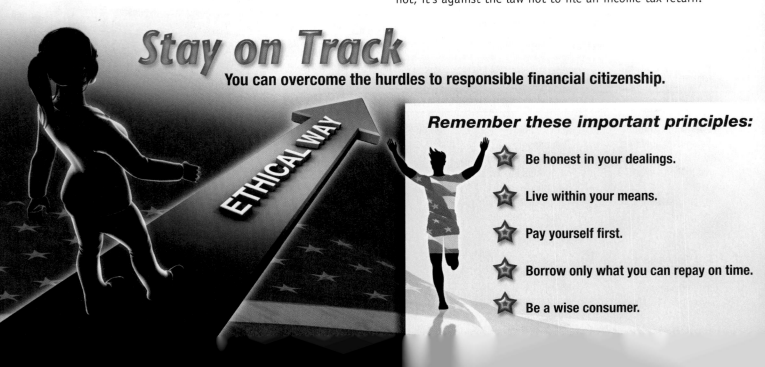

Stay on Track
You can overcome the hurdles to responsible financial citizenship.

ETHICAL WAY

Remember these important principles:

⭐ Be honest in your dealings.

⭐ Live within your means.

⭐ Pay yourself first.

⭐ Borrow only what you can repay on time.

⭐ Be a wise consumer.

The W-2

The most common federal tax form is the W-2, which reports wages paid to employees and taxes withheld from them. The form also reports FICA taxes to the Social Security Administration. Employers must complete and send out a W-2 to every employee by January 31. Save these documents! Your W-2's must be attached to your tax return when you file.

1040 and Beyond

When you file your income tax return, which is due by April 15, you'll use Form 1040, the Individual Income Tax Return. By filling it out properly, you will learn if you owe more money to the government or if the government owes you money.

1040 EZ form is limited to taxpayers who earn less than $100,000.

W-2 form reports a worker's total annual wages, benefits, and taxes paid.

To make life easier, the government introduced the Form 1040EZ, which is the simplest tax form. Its use is limited to taxpayers with taxable income below $100,000 who take the standard deduction instead of itemizing deductions, that is, listing them separately. Many unmarried people with no children also qualify to use this form.

If you have income other than wages, salaries, and tips, Form 1099 comes into play. It's a statement you receive from payers of interest income, such as banks and savings institutions, that summarizes your interest income for the year.

State Tax Bites Americans pay federal taxes no matter where they live. State taxes are another matter. Some states, like Florida and Texas, do not impose an income tax. But they assess a sales tax. Alaska residents, who pay no sales or income tax, have the least per capita tax rates in the nation.

State Sales Tax Rate: Highs and Lows

Highest Tax Rate	
California	7.25%
Lowest Tax Rate	
Colorado	2.9%
No Sales Tax	
Alaska	New Hampshire
Delaware	Oregon
Montana	

SOURCE: State Sales Tax Rates, January 1, 2008
www.taxadmin.org

Don't Guess—Get Help!

You want to make sure you get all the tax deductions that the IRS allows. Each form has step-by-step instructions, but they might not answer all your questions. Here are some other places to get advice:

▶ The IRS has a user-friendly Web site, with lots of information. It can be found at www.irs.gov.

▶ Call the IRS at (800) 829-1040. You can talk to a tax specialist, or even schedule an appointment for help at IRS service centers. But don't delay. The closer you get to April 15, the harder it may be to get timely help.

▶ Tax-preparation services and tax accountants will prepare your tax return for you for a fee. Some will file your return for you.

If you prepare your return on paper, you must send it to the IRS Service Center listed in the instruction booklet and at the IRS Web site. There are ways you can prepare and "e-file" your return online. Filing in this way will get you a faster tax refund. But you usually will have to pay a fee, especially if you use a tax preparation firm.

Are You Ready?

1. Describe the role of a W-2 form when filing your taxes.
2. Why do governments collect taxes?

To learn more about this topic, visit **PearsonSchool.com/PHecon**

Glossary

annual percentage rate a finance charge, or the cost of credit, expressed as an annual rate
tasa de porcentaje anual cargo financiero, o costo del crédito, expresado como tasa anual
annual percentage yield the annual rate of return on an investment, which must be disclosed by law and which varies by the frequency of compounding
rentabilidad porcentual anual tasa de interés anual de una inversión que, según la ley, se debe dar a conocer, y que varía por la frecuencia del compuesto
auto lease a method of financing a car by essentially renting it for a predetermined period of time
arrendamiento de vehículo método de financiamiento de un auto que consiste en alquilarlo por un período preestablecido de tiempo
automatic bill pay an automatic deduction from your bank account on a predetermined date
pago automático de facturas deducción automática de fondos de una cuenta bancaria en una fecha determinada

bankruptcy a state of being legally released from the obligation to repay some or all debt in exchange for the forced loss of certain assets
bancarrota condición que consiste en liberarse legalmente de la obligación de pagar parte de una deuda, o la deuda completa, a cambio de la pérdida forzosa de ciertos bienes
beneficiary a person or organization named to receive assets after an individual's death
beneficiario persona u organización designada a recibir bienes tras la muerte de un individuo

certificate of deposit a savings certificate entitling the bearer to receive interest
certificado de depósito certificado de ahorros que autoriza al poseedor a recibir intereses
compound interest accumulated interest added back to the principal, so that interest is earned on interest
interés compuesto interés acumulado agregado al capital, de modo que se ganan intereses sobre el interés
consumer protection act an act designed to reduce fraud and make it harder to declare bankruptcy
acto de protección al consumidor ley designada para disminuir el fraude y dificultar el proceso de declaración de bancarrota
co-pay a small portion of the total cost of a service covered by your insurance that you are required to pay
copago porción pequeña, que una persona debe pagar, del costo total de un servicio cubierto por el seguro
credit an agreement to provide goods, services, or money for future payments with interest by a specific date or according to a specific schedule
crédito acuerdo por medio del cual se proveen bienes, servicios o dinero a cambio de pagos con interés, en una fecha específica futura o según un cronograma de pago específico
credit report a detailed report of an individual's credit history prepared by a credit bureau and used by a lender to determine a loan applicant's creditworthiness
informe de crédito reporte detallado preparado por la agencia de información crediticia y usado por un prestamista para determinar la solvencia de una persona que solicita un préstamo

deductible an amount you have to pay before your insurance benefits can be applied
deducible cantidad que se debe pagar antes de beneficiarse de la cobertura del seguro
depreciate to decrease in value
depreciar disminuir en valor

dollar cost averaging a method of investing a fixed amount in the same type of investment at regular intervals, regardless of price
promediación de costos método que consiste en realizar regularmente la misma inversión con una cantidad fija de dinero, independientemente del precio

electronic funds transfer the shifting of money from one financial institution account to another without the physical movement of cash
transferencia electrónica de fondos paso de dinero de una cuenta en una institución financiera a otra cuenta, sin necesidad de movilizar dinero en efectivo

Fair Credit Billing Act a federal law that addresses billing problems by requiring that consumers send a written error notice within 60 days of receiving the first bill containing the error, and preventing creditors from damaging a consumer's credit rating during a pending dispute
Ley de Facturación Justa de Crédito ley federal que trata los problemas de facturización al requerir a los consumidores que notifiquen por escrito sobre cualquier error de una factura, durante los 60 días después de recibir la factura errónea, y que evita que los acreedores afecten negativamente el crédito del consumidor mientras se resuelve el problema
Fair Credit Reporting Act a federal law that covers the reporting of debt repayment information, requiring the removal of certain information after seven or ten years, and giving consumers the right to know what is in their credit report, to dispute inaccurate information, and to add a brief statement explaining accurate negative information
Ley de Informe Justo de Crédito ley federal que cubre el reporte de información sobre la cancelación de deudas, exige la eliminación de cierta información después de siete o diez años y le otorga al consumidor el derecho de acceder a su informe de crédito, cuestionar información errónea y agregar una declaración breve que explique información negativa correcta
Fair Housing Act makes it illegal for a landlord to discriminate against a potential tenant because of that person's race, sex, national origin or religion
Acta de Equidad en la Vivienda ley que establece que es ilegal que el dueño de una propiedad discrimine contra un posible inquilino por su raza, sexo, país de origen o religión
Federal Deposit Insurance Corporation the government agency that insures customer deposits if a bank fails
Corporación Federal de Seguros de los Depósitos Bancarios organismo gubernamental que asegura los depósitos de los clientes si un banco falla
FICO score a type of credit score that makes up a substantial portion of the credit report that lenders use to assess an applicant's credit risk and whether to extend a loan
puntaje FICO tipo de puntaje de crédito que representa una porción considerable del informe de crédito que los prestamistas usan para evaluar el riesgo crediticio de un solicitante y si se le debe hacer un préstamo

gross pay wages or salary before deductions for taxes and other purposes
ingreso neto salario antes de incurrir en deducciones fiscales o de otro tipo

Health Maintenance Organization (HMO) least expensive insurance plan that allows you to pick a primary care physician, that will refer you to in-network doctors
Organización para el Mantenimiento de la Salud (OMS) tipo de seguro médico menos costoso que le permite al beneficiario escoger un doctor que lo remite a otros doctores dentro de una red

identity theft the crime of using another person's name, credit or debit card number, Social Security number, or another piece of personal information to commit fraud
  robo de identidad crimen que consiste en usar el nombre de otra persona, su número de tarjeta de crédito o débito, su número del seguro social o cualquier otra información personal con fines fraudulentos
Individual Retirement Account An investment account that provides certain tax advantages to people who set aside money for retirement.
  Cuenta Personal de Jubilación Cuenta de inversión que les otorga ciertas ventajas tributarias a quienes ahorran dinero para su jubilación
installment loans loans, divided between principal and interest, that are repaid at regularly scheduled intervals
  préstamos a plazo préstamos, divididos entre capital e interés, que se pagan en intervalos regulares establecidos

---

lessor landlord
  arrendador dueño de un local o lugar que se ha alquilado

---

money market account a savings account that offers a competitive rate of interest in exchange for larger-than-normal deposits
  cuenta de alto rendimiento cuenta de ahorros que ofrece una tasa de interés competitiva a cambio de recibir depósitos de grandes sumas

---

net pay an individual's income after deductions, credits and taxes are factored into gross income
  salario neto ingreso de un individuo después de calcular las deducciones, los créditos y los impuestos que se deben considerar del ingreso bruto

---

payroll withholding any tax that is taken directly out of an individual's wages or other income before he or she receives the funds
  retención en nómina cualquier impuesto que se retiene del pago de un individuo o de otro ingreso antes de que él o ella reciba los fondos
phishing an Internet scam used to gain personal and financial data to commit fraud
  phishing delito cometido a través de Internet que consiste en adquirir información personal y financiera para fines fraudulentos

---

resumé a document summarizing an individual's employment experience, education, and other information a potential employer needs to know
  currículo documento donde se resume la experiencia profesional, la educación y otra información de un individuo que un empleador puede necesitar
risk factors statistics that predict whether someone is likely to be a bad risk
  factores de riesgo estadísticas que predicen la probabilidad de que alguien sea un riesgo
risk management plan the process of calculating risk and devising methods to minimize or manage loss
  plan de manejo de riesgos proceso que calcula el riesgo y crea métodos para minimizar o manejar pérdidas
risk pyramid a portfolio strategy that allocates assets according to the relative safety and soundness of investments
  pirámide de riesgo estrategia del portafolio que asigna activos de acuerdo a lo seguro y aconsejable que sean las inversiones

Roth IRA an individual retirement plan that bears many similarities to the traditional IRA, but contributions are not tax deductible and qualified distributions are tax free
  IRA Roth plan de jubilación personal que tiene bastantes similitudes con una cuenta personal de jubilación, IRA (por sus siglas en inglés), pero sus contribuciones no son deducibles de impuestos y ciertas distribuciones que califican son libres de impuestos
Rule of 72 a method of finding the number of years required to double your money at a given interest rate, divide 72 by the compound return
  Regla de 72 fórmula para calcular el número de años necesarios para duplicar una suma de dinero a cierta tasa de interés; dividir 72 por el rendimiento compuesto

---

security deposit money given to the landlord by the tenant to cover any damage to the apartment
  depósito de seguridad dinero que un arrendador le entrega a un inquilino para cubrir cualquier daño que se le cause a una propiedad
Social Security a federal government program that provides retirement, survivor's, and disability benefits, funded by a tax on income, which appears on worker's pay stubs as a deduction labeled FICA (for Federal Insurance Contributions Act)
  seguro social programa del gobierno federal que proporciona a los ciudadanos beneficios en caso de jubilación, muerte o incapacitación; se acumula mediante la deducción de impuestos al ingreso y aparece identificado en los talones de pago de los trabajadores como Ley Federal de la Contribucíon al Seguro Social (FICA, por sus siglas en inglés)

---

tenant someone that pays rent to use or occupy land, a building, or other property owned by another
  inquilino persona que paga un alquiler para usar u ocupar un terreno, un edificio o cualquier propiedad que le pertenece a otra persona
Truth in Lending Act a federal law that requires financial institutions to disclose specific information about the terms and cost of credit, including the finance charge and the annual percentage rate (APR)
  Ley de Divulgación de los Términos Totales de Crédito ley federal que requiere que las instituciones financieras proporcionen información específica sobre los términos y costos del crédito, incluyendo el cargo financiero y la tasa de porcentaje anual
tuition the charge for instruction, especially at a college or private school
  matrícula cargo por la educación, especialmente en una universidad o una escuela privada

---

Vehicle Identification Number a unique serial number used by the automotive industry to identify individual motor vehicles
  Número de Identificación del Vehículo serial único que usa la industria automotriz para identificar cada vehículo

---

warranty a written guarantee from a manufacturer or distributor that specifies the conditions under which the product can be returned, replaced, or repaired
  garantía documento de un fabricante o distribuidor que especifica las condiciones en las cuales un producto se puede devolver, reemplazar o reparar

Writing Skills Handbook

Research shows that writing about what you read actually helps you learn new information. A systematic approach to writing including prewriting, drafting, revising, and proofing can help you write better.

▶ Expository Writing

Expository writing explains ideas or information in detail. The strategies on these pages examine several expository writing styles.

1 Prewriting

Choose a topic. In an economics course, the focus of your writing might be explaining monetary policy, identifying an economic problem and proposing a solution, or examining how incentives have an impact on choices made by both producers and consumers.

Ask questions. For process writing, consider the question *how*. For example, how does fiscal policy have an impact on the economy?

Question: What challenges does the government of the United States face in choosing which fiscal policy to follow?

Answer: The following challenges are faced by the government when determining which fiscal policy to follow: figuring out the precise phase of the business cycle, determining the lag between implementation and actualization of results, and reconciling various policies with political opponents.

Create a problems/solutions grab bag. With a small group, write on separate slips of paper examples of problems related to each of these challenges: pin-pointing the appropriate phase of the business cycle, the time lag before implementation, and political pressures.

Consider audience and purpose. Consider how much your readers know about the problem or process you will address. Provide explanations of unfamiliar terms and concepts.

Research the topic. Use library and Internet resources and interviews with local officials or experts if possible. List facts, details, and other information related to your topic. Collect the facts and details you need to write your essay.

Create a graphic organizer. A Venn diagram can help you compare and contrast. For cause-and-effect or problem-solution essays, use a two-column chart. Process writing can be listed as a bulleted list of steps.

Fine-tune your ideas. For a problem-solution essay, decide what you will suggest as a solution. Narrow the scope of your solution to insure that it is achievable. If others have tried your solution, describe successes or failures.

② Drafting

Match structure to purpose. Typically, problem-solution essays benefit from block organization, which presents the entire problem and proposes a solution. Put process and cause-and-effect essays in sequence order and organize compare/contrast essays by subject or by point.

Give background. To discuss fiscal policy, the economy, or trade, first orient the reader to its context. Choose the important facts but don't overwhelm the reader with details. If you need to, return to prewriting to narrow your topic further.

Elaborate for interest and emphasis. Give details about each point in your essay. Add facts that make the link between the reasons for decisions made and their consequences so that a cause-and-effect relationship is clear.

Identify the topic to orient readers. →	Fiscal policy is an important tool used by the government to stabilize the economy. In order to avoid a recession, either supply-side or demand-side policies are adopted at different times.
Chronological order walks readers through the cause-and-effect sequence. →	Economist John Maynard Keynes believed that in order to stabilize the economy, the government needed to engage in both approaches. By purchasing goods, the government set in motion an economic chain of events that causes economic growth. In order to provide goods to the government, firms naturally increase output. To increase output, firms have to hire more workers. These workers spend money in other areas of the market. Keynes also believed that the government, in order to control growth and prevent inflation, had to raise taxes.
Elaboration supports the relationship you are highlighting. →	By purchasing large quantities of steel, the government increases demand for this product. Steel mills hire new workers in order to meet this demand. As steelworkers begin to spend their salaries, this increases demand in other sectors of the market.
Connection to today tells readers why this matters to them. →	Today debates over the role of the government in the market are, in part, a debate over how best to implement fiscal policy.

③ Revising

Add transition words. Make cause-and-effect relationships clear with words such as *because, as a result,* and *so*. To compare or contrast policies and processes, use linking words, such as *similarly, both, equally,* or *in contrast, instead,* and *yet*. Use words such as *first, second, next,* and *finally* to help readers follow steps in a process. Look at the examples below. The revised version more clearly shows the order followed by supply-side economics.

First Draft	Revised
Although Keynesian economics was employed for a number of decades in the twentieth century, President Reagan followed a supply-side policy during the 1980s.	When President Reagan assumed office, he adopted a supply-side economic policy. A supply-side economist first studies the current tax rate. Secondly, the economist determines what the appropriate rate should be and advises that tax cuts be made to that level. These tax cuts allow businesses to hire more workers. As a result of more people working, the government's revenue increases.

Remember purpose. Shape your draft so that it answers the question or thesis with which you began. Try to anticipate opposing arguments and respond to them. For a process essay, be sure to include all steps, and don't assume readers will make the connections. Always tell readers why they should care about your topic.

Review organization. Confirm that your ideas flow in a logical order. Write and number main points on your draft. Reorganize these points until you are satisfied that the order clearly strengthens your essay.

Revise sentences and words. Vary sentence length to include both short and long sentences. Then scan for vague words, such as *good*. Replace them with specific and vibrant words, such as *effective*.

Peer Review. Ask a peer to read your draft. Is it clear? Can he or she follow your ideas? Revise areas of confusion.

④ Publishing and Presenting

Create an economics manual. Contribute your writing to a class manual on economics.

▶ Research Writing

In a research paper, you gather information about a subject from several different sources. Then, you tie this information together with a single unifying idea and present it to your readers.

① Prewriting

Choose a topic. Often a teacher will assign your research topic. You may have flexibility in choosing your focus or you may have the opportunity to completely define your topic.

- **Catalog scan.** Using an online or electronic library catalog, search for topics that interest you. When a title looks promising, find the book on the shelves. Because libraries group research materials by subject, you should find other books on similar subjects nearby that may help you decide on your final topic.
- **Notes review.** Review your class notes. Jot down topics that you found interesting. You might find a starting point for research into oligopolies from a lecture on competition.
- **Brainstorm topics with a group.** As a group, list categories of issues that interest group members. Within each category, take turns adding subtopics.

Analyze the audience. Your research and your paper should be strongly influenced by the audience. How much will readers know about this topic and how much will you have to teach them?

Gather details. Collect the facts and details you need to write your paper. Use a variety of resources such as nonfiction books or journal articles, newspapers, news magazines, and publications by government agencies or advocacy groups on issues that interest you.

Organize evidence and ideas. Use notecards or create a computer file on your topic to record information. Start by writing down a possible thesis statement. Then begin reading and taking notes. Write a heading at the top of each notecard to group it under a subtopic. Note a number or title to identify the information source. In the examples below, the number 3 is used. Use the same number for an additional source card or notation containing the bibliographic information you will need.

Information source I.D. number → 3

Background on Monopolies

p. 4

"Because of [a] natural tendency toward monopoly, water shipment prices often are higher than they would be if the water transport industries were competitive."

Bibliographic information for source 3 → Holmes, Thomas J. and James A. Schmitz Jr. "Competition at Work: Railroads vs. Monopoly in the U.S. Shipping Industry". Minneapolis, Minnesota: *Federal Reserve Bank of Minneapolis Quarterly Review*, Spring 2001, vol. 25, No. 1, pp. 3–29.

② Drafting

Fine-tune your thesis. Review your notes to find relationships between ideas. Shape a thesis that is supported by the majority of your information, then check that it is specific enough to address thoroughly in the time and space allotted.

Plan your organization. Depending on your topic and purpose, you can use various methods to organize your research paper. If you are discussing two items, one approach would be to compare and contrast them. If you are focusing on a complex event or a process, you could use a chronological organization.

Make an outline. Create an outline in which you identify each topic and subtopic in a single phrase. Turn these phrases into sentences and then into the topic sentences of your draft paragraphs. Address a subtopic of your main topic in each body paragraph. Support all your statements with the facts and details you gathered.

An outline helps you structure your information.

Each body paragraph looks at a part of the whole topic.

Monopolies and Deregulation
Outline

I. Introduction
II. What is regulation and what is deregulation?
III. What are the benefits of deregulation?
    A. New firms enter an industry and create greater competition, which lowers prices.
    B. Firms become more efficient.
    C. The government saves money.
IV. What are the risks of deregulation?
    A. Monopolies could form.
    B. Deregulation coupled with federal anti-trust laws prevents the formation of monopolies.
    C. Prices for consumers increase.
    D. With government controlling markets, prices for consumers are unlikely to fall.
V. Conclusions: Benefits of deregulation outweigh incentives.

The introduction puts the topic in context. The entire paragraph conveys the thesis.

Introduction
In the late nineteenth and early twentieth centuries, the government began to regulate various industries. Toward the end of the twentieth century, the government reversed course. It realized that competition, absent of government regulation, lowers prices for customers.

The conclusion recaps key points and leaves readers with a final statement to remember.

Conclusion
When a government regulates an industry, it stifles growth and creates inefficiencies that lead to high prices.

③ Revising

Add detail. Mark points where more details would strengthen your statements. In the following example, notice the added details in the revised version. When adding facts, verify accuracy.

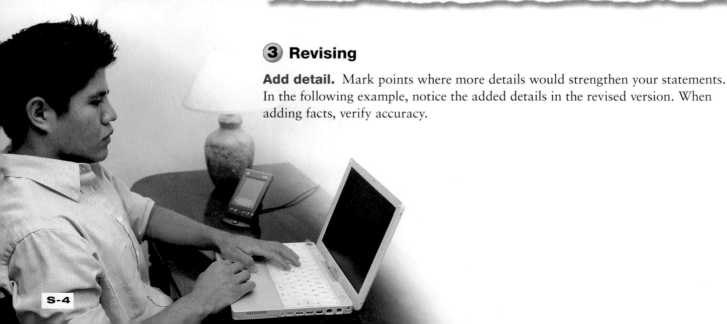

Make the connection for readers. Help readers find their way through your ideas. First, check that your body paragraphs and the information within them flow in a logical sequence. If they do not, revise to correct this. Then add transition words to link ideas and paragraphs.

First Draft	Revised
When governments deregulate industries, new companies can enter the field. These new companies have innovative ideas that increase efficiency and lower prices.	In 1978, President Carter deregulated the airline industry. New airlines emerged. This change forced larger airlines into competition, resulting in lower prices for consumers.

Give credit. Check that you have used your own words or given proper credit to other sources with parenthetical notes, which include the author's last name and the relevant page number from the source. For example, you could site the notecard here as (Holmes and Schmitz 4).

4 Publishing and Presenting

Plan a conference. Gather a group of classmates and present your research projects.

▶ Persuasive Essay

Persuasive writing supports an opinion or position. This writing style often takes the form of position papers, editorials, blogs, and Op-Ed pieces. Persuasive essays often argue for or against economic positions such as free trade.

1 Prewriting

Choose a topic. Choose a topic that provokes an argument and has at least two sides. Use these ideas as a guide.

Round-table discussion. Talk with classmates about issues you have studied recently. Outline pro and con positions about these issues.

Textbook flip. Scan the table of contents or flip through the pages of your textbook.

Make connections. Look at blogs, editorials, or Op-Ed pieces in current newspapers. Develop a position on an issue of importance today.

Narrow your topic.

Cover part of the topic. If you find too many pros and cons for a straightforward argument, choose part of the topic.

Use looping. Write for five minutes on the general topic. Circle the most important idea. Then write for five minutes on that idea. Continue looping until the topic is manageable.

Consider your audience. Choose arguments that will appeal to the audience you are writing for and that are likely to persuade them to agree with your views.

Gather evidence. Collect evidence that will help you support your position convincingly.

Identify pros and cons. Use a graphic organizer like the one below to list points on both sides of the issue.

Interview. Speak to people who have first-hand knowledge of your issue.

Research. Investigate the subject to get your facts straight. Read articles about the topic.

The United States Should Participate in Free Trade	
Pro ◄──────────────────────────────── ──────────────────────────────► **Con**	
• Citizens will pay less for some goods and services. • Free access to foreign markets could mean greater profits for exports. • Government imposed monopolies or oligopolies are unable to form. • The free movement of capital and labor.	• Increased competition could hurt domestic industries. • Potential exploitation of workers. • Increased job insecurity.

Because of its many resources and greater comparative advantage in producing goods and services, the United States should participate in free trade.

② Drafting

State your thesis. Clearly state your position, as in this example:

Acknowledge opposition. State and refute opposing arguments. Use facts and details. Include quotations, statistics, or comparisons to build your case. Include the comments and opinions of community members or officials who were interviewed.

Thesis identifies your main argument. ──►

Supporting argument clarifies your thesis. ──►

> Given the comparative advantage of the United States, participation in free trade has the potential to be profitable.
>   Free trade lowers prices and opens new markets to U.S. goods. Participation in free trade increases the amount of money made by companies that, as demand for goods increases, causes new jobs for workers.

Opposing argument, noted and refuted, adds to your position. ──►

>   The opponents of free trade only look at short-term losses. They fail to recognize the long-term growth and prosperity that result from participation.

Write a conclusion. Your conclusion should restate the thesis and close with a strong, compelling argument or a brief summary of the three strongest arguments.

③ Revising

Add information. Extra details can generate interest in your topic. For example, add a quotation from a news article that describes the positive impact that NAFTA has had on the U.S. beef industry.

Review arguments. Make sure your arguments are logically sound and clearly developed. Evidence is the best way to support your points.

Use transition words. Guide readers through your ideas using the following words:

- To show contrast: *however, although, despite*
- To point out a reason: *since, because, if*
- To signal conclusion: *therefore, consequently, so, then*

4 Publishing

Persuasive Speech. In addition to position papers, editorials, blogs, and Op-Ed pieces, persuasive essays are also delivered orally. How effective were your efforts to persuade? Report your results and evaluate the effectiveness.

▶ Writing for Assessment

Assessment writing differs from all other writing that you do. You have many fewer choices as a writer and you almost always face a time limit.

1 Prewriting

Choose a topic. Short-answer questions seldom offer a topic choice. For extended response, however, you may have a choice of more than one question.

Examine the question. To choose a question you can answer effectively, analyze what each question is asking. Use key words such as those listed in the chart below to help you choose topics and respond to short-answer questions in which the topic is given. Notice in the examples below that the key words are underlined:

> **Short Answer Question:** Why do governments impose <u>taxes</u>?
>
> **Extended Response Question:** How have taxes <u>been used</u> by governments? Give examples to <u>support your conclusion</u>.

Measure your time. Your goal is to show that you've mastered the material. To stay focused on this goal, divide your time: one-quarter on pre-writing; half on drafting; one-quarter on revising. For short-answer questions, determine how much of the overall test time you can spend on each question. Don't spend more than that.

Key Words	What You Need In an Answer
Explain	• Give a clear, complete account of how something works, or what the causes or effects are of a particular decision or policy.
Compare/Contrast	• Show how two or more things are alike and different.
Define	• Give examples to explain meaning.
Argue, Convince, Support, Persuade	• Take a position on an issue and present strong reasons to support your side of the issue.
Summarize	• Provide the most important elements of a subject.
Evaluate/Judge	• Assign a value or explain an opinion.
Interpret	• Support a thesis with examples from the text.

Gather information. Identify and organize the information you need to write your answer. For short-answer questions, this usually involves identifying exactly which facts and details are required.

Use a graphic organizer. For extended responses, divide your topic into sub-topics that fit the type of question. Jot down facts and details for each.

2 Drafting

Choose an organization that fits the question. With short-answer questions, write one to three complete sentences. Extended responses require more elaborate organization. For an extended response on the use of taxes, describe how taxes have been used in a number of ways. For compare/contrast, present similarities first, then differences.

Open and close strongly. Start your answer by restating the question or using its language to state your position. This helps you focus and shows the instructor that you understand the question. Finish with a conclusion that restates your position. For short answers, include some language from the question in your response.

Support your ideas. Each paragraph should directly or indirectly support your main idea. Choose facts that build a cohesive argument.

3 Revising

Examine word choice. Replace general words with specific words. Add transitions where these improve clarity.

First Draft	Revised
Taxes play an important role in fiscal policy, international trade, and collecting revenue.	Taxes play a multi-faceted role in the American economy. In addition to being a valuable source of revenue for all levels of government, taxes figure prominently in international trade and in the application of fiscal policy.

Check organization. Make sure your introduction includes a main idea and briefly defines each subtopic. Review each paragraph for a single main idea. Check that your conclusion summarizes the information you've presented.

4 Publishing and Presenting

Edit and proof. Check spelling, grammar, and mechanics. Make sure that tenses match, that subjects agree with verbs, and that sentences are not too long. Finally, confirm that you have responded to all the questions you were asked to answer.

> Governments need the ability to impose taxes in order to raise revenue. Governments that have been able to raise taxes successfully are able to pay for services for its citizens.

▶ Writing Rubric Use this chart, or rubric, to evaluate your writing.

SAT

SCORE OF 6

An essay in this category is outstanding, demonstrating **clear and consistent mastery,** although it may have a few minor errors. A typical essay:

- effectively and insightfully develops a point of view on the issue and demonstrates outstanding critical thinking, using clearly appropriate examples, reasons, and other evidence to support its position
- is well organized and clearly focused, demonstrating clear coherence and smooth progression of ideas
- exhibits skillful use of language, using a varied, accurate, and appropriate vocabulary
- demonstrates meaningful variety in sentence structure
- is free of most errors in grammar, usage, and mechanics

SCORE OF 5

An essay in this category is **effective,** demonstrating **reasonably consistent mastery,** although it will have occasional errors or lapses in quality. A typical essay:

- effectively develops a point of view on the issue and demonstrates strong critical thinking, generally using appropriate examples, reasons, and other evidence to support its position
- is well organized and focused, demonstrating coherence and progression of ideas
- exhibits facility in the use of language, using appropriate vocabulary
- demonstrates variety in sentence structure
- is generally free of most errors in grammar, usage, and mechanics

SCORE OF 4

An essay in this category is **competent,** demonstrating **adequate mastery,** although it will have lapses in quality. A typical essay:

- demonstrates variety in sentence structure
- develops a point of view on the issue and demonstrates competent critical thinking, using adequate examples, reasons, and other evidence to support its position
- is generally organized and focused, demonstrating some coherence and progression of ideas, exhibits adequate but inconsistent facility in the use of language, using generally appropriate vocabulary
- demonstrates some variety in sentence structure
- has some errors in grammar, usage, and mechanics

SCORE OF 3

An essay in this category is **inadequate,** but demonstrates **developing mastery,** and is marked by one or more of the following weaknesses:

- develops a point of view on the issue, demonstrating some critical thinking, but may do so inconsistently or use inadequate examples, reasons, or other evidence to support its position
- is limited in its organization or focus, but may demonstrate some lapses in coherence or progression of ideas
- displays developing facility in the use of language, but sometimes uses weak vocabulary or inappropriate word choice
- lacks variety or demonstrates problems in sentence structure
- contains an accumulation of errors in grammar, usage, and mechanics

SCORE OF 2

An essay in this category is **seriously limited,** demonstrating little mastery, and is flawed by **one or more** of the following weaknesses:

- develops a point of view on the issue that is vague or seriously limited, demonstrating weak critical thinking, providing inappropriate or insufficient examples, reasons, or other evidence to support its position
- is poorly organized and/or focused, or demonstrates serious problems with coherence or progression of ideas
- displays very little facility in the use of language, using very limited vocabulary or incorrect word choice
- demonstrates frequent problems in sentence structure
- contains errors in grammar, usage, and mechanics so serious that meaning is somewhat obscured

SCORE OF 1

An essay in this category is **fundamentally lacking,** demonstrating **very little or no mastery,** and is severely flawed by one or more of the following weaknesses:

- develops no viable point of view on the issue, or provides little or no evidence to support its position
- is disorganized or unfocused, resulting in a disjointed or incoherent essay
- displays fundamental errors in vocabulary
- demonstrates severe flaws in sentence structure
- contains pervasive errors in grammar, usage, or mechanics that persistently interfere with meaning

SCORE OF 0

Essays not written on the essay assignment will receive a score of zero.

▶ Analyze Primary and Secondary Sources

A primary source is information produced during or soon after an event, by a participant or observer. These include letters, photographs, memos, and legal documents. A secondary source provides an analysis or interpretation of an event based on primary sources.

Identify the document. Determine when, where, why, and by whom the document was written to decide if the document is a primary or a secondary source.

Find the main idea. A main idea is the most important point in a paragraph or section of text. After identifying the main idea, identify supporting details.

Evaluate the document for point of view and bias. Primary sources convey a strong sense of an event, but are limited to a single frame of reference or bias.

In 1973 Saudi Arabia and several other members of OPEC began an oil embargo, refusing to sell oil to the United States. ▼

Read the excerpt below from the 2003 article "Still Holding Customers over a Barrel." ▼

" Primary Source

The gasoline shortage was acutely felt in Chicago last week with drivers waiting sometimes several hours alongside a pump. Several hundred stations, their January allotments depleted, were closed. Many others had…curtailed their hours of operation. The Root Brothers service station…was typical. Cars were lined up for blocks, police had to direct traffic and the limit a customer could purchase was set at $5.00….According to Platt's Oilgram Service…the average price a year ago for a gallon of gasoline in the Midwest was 40.9 cents for regular. The range of regular gasoline now runs from 47.9 cents a gallon to 55.9 [cents a gallon]."

—William Farrell, "Oil Is a National Problem, But Seriousness Varies," *The New York Times,* February 3, 1974

" Secondary Source

The Arab embargo has become a symbol of the…chaos and economic troubles endured by the West during the oil shocks of the 1970s….The [long lines] and shortages in America that are now linked in the popular imagination with that period had little to do with the Arab Embargo. Jerry Taylor of the Cato Institute argues, correctly, that the shortages were due chiefly to the…energy policies…adopted by America…In 1971 for example, the Nixon administration imposed price controls…that prevented oil companies from passing on the full cost of imported oil to consumers. That led…to the companies making decisions to reduce their imports…Congress made the situation worse in September 1973 by trying to allocate oil to…different parts of the country through bureaucratic fiat….These measures led…to the panic and hoarding…"

—*The Economist,* October 23, 2003

PRACTICE AND APPLY THE SKILL

Use the excerpts above to answer the following questions.

1. What makes one newspaper article a primary source and the other a secondary source?

2. What is the primary source writer's purpose?

3. What is the main idea of the secondary source?

▶ Compare Viewpoints

People often disagree on policies or recommend different responses to the same problem. Comparing viewpoints will help you understand issues and form your own opinions. The excerpts below provide different views on offshore drilling, the practice of extracting the nonrenewable resource of oil from underneath the ocean floor.

Identify the authors. Determine the background of each speaker. Identify the intended audience for and the purpose each speech.

Determine the author's frame of reference. Consider how each speaker's attitudes; beliefs; values; past experiences; and social, economic, or political concerns and affiliations might affect his or her viewpoint.

Determine the author's bias. Bias may be revealed in the use of emotionally charged words, faulty logic, or exaggerated claims. Identify which statements are facts and which are opinions that represent the speaker's viewpoint.

Compare and contrast. Determine how the views are different. Consider factors that might have contributed to differing positions on the issue.

Hal T. Nelson and Nicholas L. Cain of Claremont Graduate University, California: ▼

"The United States needs oil. But it would be folly to open new areas to offshore drilling because all the oil in offshore U.S. reserves won't make a dent in our long-term use. And given the dangers of deepwater drilling–to the environment and to people–those areas that are currently protected . . . should remain off limits to new oil projects. . . .

The simple fact is that if we open all offshore waters to drilling, we would supply only one year of oil for the United States. Offshore drilling won't free us from imported oil, despite the promises of those who stand to benefit. . . .

A better approach is to use our existing supplies more efficiently by investing in clean, green technology. Instead of subsidizing oil production, the United States should expand support for efficient transportation technologies, such as hybrid cars and electric vehicles, which are increasingly made by American companies."

—Hal T. Nelson and Nicholas L. Cain, "Against Drilling"

Mark J. Perry of the University of Michigan: ▼

"Those who disparage offshore drilling—and seem eager to ban it—ignore that the Gulf of Mexico accounts for one third of U.S. oil production. Without domestic production, we would be spending even more on imported oil—which is already running $1.5 billion a day.

The best place in the United States to find new oil is in the gulf's untapped deepwater areas, in the Atlantic, and off Alaska. These three drilling areas combined hold as much as 22 billion barrels of oil, which is more than our current total estimated reserves. . . .

There is a simple relationship that ties a nation's economic prosperity to its energy availability, and that's why government should not prevent the development of our energy resources. The oil industry accounts for a whopping 7.2 percent of GDP and 9.2 million American jobs."

—Mark J. Perry, "Pro-Drilling"

PRACTICE AND APPLY THE SKILL

Use the excerpts above to answer the following questions.

1. How do you think each professor's location might influence his viewpoint?

2. Why do Nelson and Cain oppose offshore drilling? Why does Perry promote offshore drilling?

3. After reading these excerpts, why should you want to do more research before taking a stand on offshore drilling?

▶ Drawing Inferences and Conclusions

When people "read between the lines," they are drawing inferences. They have formed their conclusions not from what is stated directly, but from what is suggested by other facts.

Summarize information. Confirm your understanding of the text by identifying the main idea of the passage. To find information in a passage that is suggested but unstated, you have to understand the content of the passage.

Apply other facts or prior knowledge. Consider what you know about the topic. Use this prior knowledge to evaluate the information. A combination of what you already know and what you learn from reading the passage may help you draw inferences.

Decide if the information suggests an unstated fact or conclusion. Integrate or combine what you learned from the text and your own knowledge to draw inferences and conclusions about the topic.

Read the excerpt from "The Grip of Gas" by University of Chicago economics professor Austan Goolsbee. ▼

"In repeated studies of consumer purchases… drivers in the United States consistently rank as the least sensitive to changes in gas prices….The… estimates, based on a [2002] study…predict that if prices rose from $3 per gallon to $4 per gallon and stayed there for a year…purchases of gasoline… would fall only about 5 percent.

Why don't we ratchet down more when fuel prices go up? The rule of thumb in economics is that people react to price increases only when they can turn to substitutes. Raise the price of Ford trucks and sales go down because you can buy your truck from Chrysler or GM or Toyota instead. Raise the price of gasoline and what are the alternatives?…

Gasoline purchases are, in fact, the kind of buying affected least by price changes because they are so closely tied up with other things we already own…In the last two decades when gasoline was cheap, Americans switched from cars to minivans and SUVs, seriously reducing their gas mileage. Also, many moved farther from their places of work…As jobs moved…into suburbs, car-pooling became more difficult and public transportation often unavailable….In Europe and Japan, people drive less when the cost of gas goes up because they still can. On average, they live closer to their jobs. About 20% of Europeans walk or ride their bike to work.

…The only hope of changing America's driving habits is a hefty price increase that lasts. …Higher commuting costs…could induce you to buy a smaller car, move closer to work, find a car pool…few people change their behavior when gas prices spike temporarily…. moral exhortation doesn't change people's behavior. Prices do…"

—Austan Goolsbee, *Slate Magazine*, September 27, 2005

PRACTICE AND APPLY THE SKILL

Use the magazine article to answer the following questions.

1. What is the main idea or key point made by this article?

2. Based on this article, what can you infer about the demand for gasoline in the United States?

3. Based on this article, what conclusions can you draw about the impact of a gas tax that would substantially raise the price of gas? How will American driving habits be affected?

▶ Analyze Political Cartoons

Political cartoons express the cartoonist's opinion on a recent issue or current event. Often the artist's purpose is to influence the opinion of the reader about political leaders, current events, or economic or political issues. To achieve this goal, cartoonists use humor or exaggeration. When analyzing a political cartoon, be sure to examine all words, images, and labels to help you fully understand the artist's intent. Use the following steps to analyze the cartoon below.

Identify the symbols in the cartoon. Decide what each image or symbol represents. Examine the title and any labels or words in the cartoon. Cartoonists often use caricatures, or images of people that exaggerate a physical feature.

Analyze the meaning of the cartoon. Consider how the cartoonist uses the images and symbols in the cartoon to express his or her opinions about people or events.

Draw conclusions about the cartoonist's intent. Identify the opinion or statement the cartoonist is making through this cartoon.

PRACTICE AND APPLY THE SKILL

Use the cartoon to answer the following questions.

1. What do the bulls in the cartoon represent?

2. What does the flower symbolize?

3. What does the title of the cartoon suggest about the cartoonist's view of the economic situation?

▶ Understanding Cause and Effect

Recognizing cause and effect means examining how one event or action brings about others. One challenge economists face is finding and defining relationships between events.

Identify the central event. Determine the core event or issue that is the subject of the article.

Identify the two parts of a cause-effect relationship. A cause is an event or an action that brings about an effect. Words such as *because, due to,* and *on account of* signal causes. Words such as *so, thus, therefore,* and *as a result* signal effects.

Decide if an event has more than one cause or effect. Most events have multiple causes and many have more than one effect.

Identify events that are both causes and effects. Causes and effects can form a chain of events. An effect may in turn become the cause of another effect. For example, a sharp decline in new home sales can result in reduced profits for building supply and furniture stores. This in turn may lead to layoffs of workers in factories that produces the goods sold in these stores.

Read the excerpt below from "No Quick Fix on the Downturn." ▼

> In the view of many analysts, the economy is now in a downward spiral, with each piece of negative news setting off the next. Falling housing prices have eroded the ability of homeowners to borrow against their property, threatening their ability to spend freely. Concerns about tightening consumer spending have prompted businesses to slow hiring, limiting wage increases and in turn applying the brakes anew to consumer spending....
>
> ...Nouriel Roubini, an economist at...New York University...envisions foreclosures accelerating this year, and banks counting fresh losses. That could make them less able to lend and further slow economic activity....Federal Reserve chairman, Ben S. Bernanke, zeroed in on the nervousness of bankers as a prime factor slowing the economy.... "Developments have prompted banks to become protective of their liquidity [available funds] and thus to become less willing to provide funding to other market participants."
>
> A recession could pack enormous political consequences. Over the last century, the economy has been in a recession four times in the early part of a presidential election year, according to the National Bureau of Economic Research. In each of those years—1920, 1932, 1960 and 1980—the party of the incumbent president lost the election."
>
> —Peter Goodman and Floyd Norris, *The New York Times,* January 13, 2008

PRACTICE AND APPLY THE SKILL

Use the news article to answer the following questions.

1. Identify the causes and effects in the following statement from the article: "Falling housing prices have eroded the ability of homeowners to borrow against their property, threatening their ability to spend freely."

2. How was the slowdown in consumer spending both a cause and an effect of the economic slowdown?

3. Did the downturn in the economy have a single cause or multiple causes? Explain your answer.

▶ Problem Solving

One difference between successful and unsuccessful business is the ability to solve problems.

Identify the problem. Begin by clearly identifying what the problem is. Write a statement or question that summarizes the problem you are trying to solve.

Gather information and identify options. Collect factual information and data. Consider the causes of the problem and brainstorm strategies for addressing it. Most problems have multiple solutions. Identify as many options as possible.

Consider advantages and disadvantages of each option. Analyze each option by predicting benefits, drawbacks, and possible consequences.

Choose, implement, and evaluate a solution. Pick the option with the greatest benefits and fewest drawbacks. Once a strategy is in place, look at the results. Decide if the solution works.

Read the excerpt below which looks at how a popular shoe manufacturer prepared to meet its supply and demand requirements as its business boomed. ▼

 From tots walking with their mothers in the mall to the president of the United States captured on camera wearing a pair of black Crocs…the rubbery boat shoe…fueled a business success story….

Crocs now is the country's second-largest footwear manufacturer…."It was the perfect storm: They had the right product, people wanted it, and they were able to produce it in increasing quantities and broaden their focus…" [says Reed Anderson, senior research analyst at D.A. Davidson & Co.].

[CEO Ron Snyder] says Crocs' ascent has proved manageable because the company laid the groundwork to handle it before it arrived in full force. "Since the beginning, we've always assumed we're a larger company, so we made decisions as a larger company, investing in an infrastructure that was more than we needed at the time," Snyder says.

"Most of the footwear industry works off pre-orders," Snyder says. "If a particular product isn't selling well, you'll still be building it for late in the season….We take early season orders, then we build more of whatever is popular. Say we have a model that's selling out in our early season," he says. "We'll be making more of that immediately in our local facilities, and we'll get it to the market in a few weeks. If it continues to go, we'll have another larger shipment from China in six or eight weeks."…Snyder says…"We told our retailers we're going to do our best…to meet demand."

—by Eric Peterson, *Coloradobiz Magazine,* February 2008

PRACTICE AND APPLY THE SKILL

Use the article to answer the following questions.

1. What three conditions led to the success of the Crocs brand?

2. What problem could have limited their success?

3. What were the advantages of the option Snyder chose for solving this problem?

Social Studies Skills Handbook

▶ Decision Making

Decision making in your daily life and in the economy both require a similar approach.

Identify the problem and gather information. Figure out what decision has to be made. What are you trying to accomplish? Decide what information you need to make an informed and ethical decision. Apply what you know and what you can learn about the subject. Look at what others have done.

List and assess alternatives. List and review all possible alternatives. Choose the options with fewest drawbacks or costs and greatest number of benefits.

Identify possible consequences and make decisions. Consider various possible outcomes and predict consequences of each option.

Below is an excerpt from an article on Honest Tea, a beverage company started in 1998 by Seth Goldman and Barry Nabeloff. ▼

"

For Seth Goldman starting a business was a lot like brewing tea—it all came down to the right blend of ingredients. Goldman took the plunge into the bottled tea business...convinced there was an opportunity in the crowded but fast-growing market for a "less sweet" beverage....But the sweetness profile was not the only thing that set Honest Tea apart. It was the approach Goldman took to business." He said, "I knew that what we were going to do would somehow have a social and environmental impact...."

Their challenge...was finding a way to stand out in a market full of bottled teas. Taste was one obvious way to be distinctive, but it was the second element—applying the approach known as sustainability—that led to a host of decisions about the product itself.

The program soon evolved on a number of fronts, involving choices about ingredients, packaging and partnerships that expanded the aim of its social and environmental mission. As Goldman learned more about the business, his first aim was to shift the ingredients to organic sources to avoid toxic pesticides and synthetic fertilizers..."Tea... undergoes no rinsing once it is picked," he said. Whatever pesticide residues are present on the leaf are not washed off until hot water is poured over the dried leaves in a pot or cup of brewed tea."

Organics were the more expensive way to go, Goldman concedes, but the company shaved costs in other areas. It eschewed [avoided] a distinctive shaped glass bottle and went with a cheaper, more generic look...

Another key pillar of the business has been pursuing "fair trade," buying tea from one estate in India, that is certified for its fair labor practices...

[This] adds another dimension to the business by creating a distinct marketing presence...That distinction might be invaluable in a shelf crowded with competitors..."

—by Samuel Fromartz, Reuters News Service,
November 15, 2004

PRACTICE AND APPLY THE SKILL

Use the article to answer the following questions.

1. Why did Seth Goldman decide to go into the bottled tea business?

2. What goal drove Goldman's decisions about ingredients, packaging, and partnerships?

3. What costs and benefits did Goldman consider in deciding on the ingredients?

❱ Note Taking and Active Listening

Note taking and active listening are skills that can increase your ability to remember and understand a speech or a lecture.

Identify the main ideas. Listen closely to the introduction to identify the speaker's main topic. It is then easier to identify and record key points related to it.

Take notes selectively. Do not write down every word you hear. Instead summarize key points and the examples or details that support these points.

Practice active listening. Active listening requires engaged participation. Think about what you hear and see. In persuasive speech, is the speaker citing authority or appealing to emotion? Are generalizations supported by facts and logic? Pay attention.

Listen for transitions, repetition, and emphasis. Listen for the words or phrases that indicate key points or transition from one point to the next. Statements that are frequently repeated may suggest that these are the main points.

Here is an excerpt from a speech entitled "Education and Economic Competitiveness" by Federal Reserve Board Chairman Ben Bernanke: ▼

"...The demand for more-educated workers has been increasing rapidly, partly because of the...widespread use of computers and other...information and communication technologies in the workplace...At the start of the 1980s, 22 percent of young adults aged 25 to 29 held a college degree or more; by last year, that fraction had moved up to 28.5 percent. Nevertheless, the supply of educated workers has not kept pace with demand...

The educational challenges our society faces should be considered in the context of three broad trends: the retirement of the baby-boom generation, the...advance of the technological frontier, and the ongoing globalization of economic activity.

As the baby boomers...leave the workforce, their places will be taken by the smaller cohort of workers born in the mid-to-late 1960s and early 1970s. As a result, the U.S. workforce...will increase more slowly...imply[ing] slower growth of potential output...

Continuing advances in technology also put a premium on education...

Ongoing globalization...will also lead to continuing changes in the...U.S. economy...The world economy is benefiting from...the rising productivity of countries abroad that are...expanding...the educational attainment of their workforces....Our ability to reap the benefits of globalization will depend on the flexibility of our labor force to adapt to changes in job opportunities, in part by investing in...education and training....

If we are to successfully navigate such challenges as the retirement of the baby-boom generation, advancing technology, and increasing globalization, we must work...to maintain the quality of our educational system..."

—Ben S. Bernanke, in a speech to the U.S. Chamber Education and Workforce Summit, Washington, D.C., September 24, 2007

PRACTICE AND APPLY THE SKILL

Use the speech to answer the following questions.

1. What are the key points made in the first paragraph?

2. What sentence tells the audience that the speaker will talk about three topics he thinks are important to his main idea?

3. What is the purpose of the final paragraph of this speech?

Social Studies Skills Handbook

▶ Think Creatively and Innovate

An innovation is a new idea that improves upon an existing product or process. Innovators think creatively and take risks to turn their ideas into realities.

Identify what it is that needs improving. Define and clarify what needs to be changed or improved. Consider the goal to be achieved.

Brainstorm as many ideas as possible. If working with a group, don't criticize the ideas of others and don't hesitate to suggest ideas that might seem strange or impractical. Innovation often results from an unexpected insight.

Understand the factors involved. Consider the skills, tools, or methods needed to realize the goal. Identify such factors as costs, materials, competition, consumer behavior, and potential suppliers and markets for product.

Read the excerpt below from "Nike Co-founder Bill Bowerman: His Innovations for Runners Helped Build an Empire." ▼

Track coach Bill Bowerman was eating breakfast one morning in 1971 when his wife, Barbara, opened the waffle iron to pour another serving. He constantly looked for ways to help his athletes improve. Then it hit him. If he mixed synthetic rubber, poured it into the back of the waffle iron and let it cool, he could make a better sole for a running shoe.

It took some grunting and wrenching with pliers to get the rubber off, wrote Bowerman…But when he finally did, he'd come up with the first lightweight outsole, the Waffle sole, which revolutionized the running shoe. Today, every athletic shoemaker uses a waffle sole or some variation on everything from running to hiking shoes.

Bowerman…the head track-and-field coach at the University of Oregon in Eugene from 1948 to 1972, was hugely competitive and at the same time fascinated with physiology. In studying the dynamics of running, he saw that the shoes runners used were cumbersome. In the late 1950s, he devised a shoe with a heel wedge…One problem: He couldn't find a company to make it….He decided to make the shoes himself. Bowerman tested his designs on his team members, including Phil Knight…After that, Bowerman would sit in his garage and tinker with the shoe designs, which his team members gladly wore…

In 1964, he and Knight teamed up to found Blue Ribbon Sports Inc. In 1972, the duo started the Nike brand…That year, four of the top seven finishers in the Olympic marathon wore Nikes. The company name was changed to Nike Inc. in 1980.

"Bowerman had a laser focus to solve a problem with an athlete and then move on," said Geoff Hollister, [Nike] marketing manager….Knight, a marketing wiz, was expert at taking Bowerman's solution and making it available to the masses. Bowerman's actions were "all driven by helping us perform better…" Hollister said. This drive led Bowerman to experiment and innovate… Bowerman led by example. He taught his young men and the team at Nike to accept when they were beaten and then pick themselves up again so they could work harder for a better day. He had an insatiable curiosity and a mind that perceived gaps in the progress of human inventions…"

—by William O'Neil in his 2003 book *Business Leaders & Success*

PRACTICE AND APPLY THE SKILL

Use the excerpt to answer the following questions.

1. What insight led Bowerman to his innovation?
2. What personal experiences and interests helped Bowerman to think creatively about the problem that concerned him?
3. How did Bowerman's position as a coach help him assess the effectiveness of his product?

▶ Give an Effective Presentation

One key to an effective presentation is to combine text, video, audio, and graphics in a multimedia presentation.

Define your topic. In choosing a topic, consider the amount of time you have for the presentation and the complexity of the subject.

Find out what types of media are available for the presentation. Do you have a computer and the software to create a podcast, a PowerPoint presentation, a slide show, a video, audio clips of speeches, or animated graphics?

Make a storyboard or blueprint for the presentation. Create a storyboard by brainstorming ideas. Identify the medium that will work best for each part of the presentation.

Practice your presentation. A trial run gives presenters a chance to check the time allotted for each segment of the presentation, identify technical problems, and make sure that all participants know their roles.

Below is a storyboard for a presentation to aid urban planners in choosing among roadbuilding and other options for alleviating traffic congestion. ▼

1. Run Time — 3 mins.	2. — 3 mins.	3. — 4 mins.
Are More Roads the Answer to States' Traffic Problems? **Introduction** **Highway Congestion:** • More people driving more miles on more roads in urban areas • Increasing number of highways increases vehicle travel, reducing the benefits of building • Looking for alternatives to driving	**Supply and Demand** *Graphs show three supply and demand curves:* • Before road construction • After highway built or expanded • After drivers switch to new roads or move closer to new highway a) b) c) graphs with Travel time vs. Amount of travel	*Video clip of transportation expert talking about whether it is cost effective to build more roads to solve traffic congestion problems*

4. Run Time — 3 mins.	5. — 4 mins.	6. — 5 mins.
What Studies Show • Increased use of cars not due to population growth but to more individual, rather than carpool driving • Building roads can attract new traffic to roads, leading to more congestion • New highways could discourage public transit use	**Solutions** • Increase investment in public transit: buses, light rail, metro • Build more Park and Ride lots • Offer incentives to businesses to encourage workers to carpool or commute at different times of day through flextime	**What We Recommend** • Improve or expand existing highways through HOV lanes, increase highway safety, eliminate bottlenecks • Replace aging roads and bridges • Consider more funding for public transit through gas tax

PRACTICE AND APPLY THE SKILL

Use the storyboard to answer the following questions.

1. What issue does the presentation address?

2. How did the presenters narrow or focus the presentation of their topic?

3. How were participants encouraged to stay within the time limits in their presentations?

▶ Digital Literacy

The Internet is a valuable research tool that provides links to millions of sources of information created by corporations, small businesses, government organizations, and individuals all over the world. E-mails, wikis, and blogs all provide ways for Internet users to share information and express opinions. Access to a broad range of information and opinions enables people to make informed decisions.

Writing an E-mail

Identify the purpose of the e-mail in the subject line. Indicate the topic of the e-mail in the subject line. A busy person is more likely to open the e-mail promptly if the subject of the e-mail is stated.

Focus on why you are writing. Include the subject of your e-mail in the first sentence. Make sure the message states why you are writing and what you expect to receive in terms of information or action from the recipient. Keep e-mails short and to the point.

Respect your reader. If you are responding to or following up on an e-mail that is more than a few days old, remind the recipient of why you are writing. Identify yourself clearly if the person is someone you don't know. If you are uncertain about whether your language and tone should be formal or informal, examine the e-mail received from this sender. Take your cues from the sender's level of formality, for example *Dear Mr. Jones* vs. *Hi Joe*.

Proofread e-mails before sending. Once you have composed your e-mail, use spell checker or other tools to check grammar, punctuation, and spelling. Remember that e-mail is not private. Think carefully about sending messages that you would not want shared with others. Below is an example of a business e-mail.

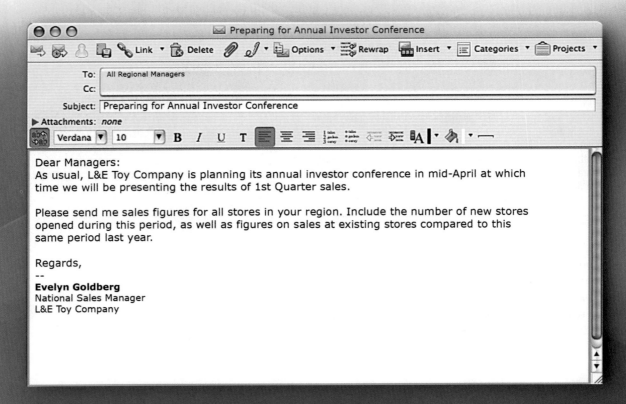

To: All Regional Managers
Cc:
Subject: Preparing for Annual Investor Conference
▶ Attachments: *none*

Dear Managers:
As usual, L&E Toy Company is planning its annual investor conference in mid-April at which time we will be presenting the results of 1st Quarter sales.

Please send me sales figures for all stores in your region. Include the number of new stores opened during this period, as well as figures on sales at existing stores compared to this same period last year.

Regards,
--
Evelyn Goldberg
National Sales Manager
L&E Toy Company

Understanding and Evaluating Wikis

A **wiki** is a Web site that allows users to easily create, edit, and link Web pages to create an online document. One of the most visited wikis is the online encyclopedia **Wikipedia.** Anyone can add or change the articles they find on this Web site. While many Internet users are enthusiastic about sites like Wikipedia, critics question their accuracy. Today corporations and government agencies are creating their own internal wikis. These wikis are almost always password-protected sites only for employees. These wikis allow staff to brainstorm, share knowledge, and update project information.

Identify the sources of the information on the Web site. Look for information on the Web site that tells you who provided this information or presented the data. Consider whether the writer is an expert or has special knowledge of this topic that would make his or her opinion especially worthwhile.

Determine when the article was written. Look for a date that shows when the article was written or last updated. Does the entry reflect changing events or provide current information on this topic?

Verify information by checking other sources. Do not rely on a single source. Compare the information on the wiki with official sources such as government Web sites, medical or legal Web sites sponsored by respected professional organizations, or reliable encyclopedias. Be skeptical and do further research if your sources disagree.

Reading and Assessing Blogs

Blogs are online journals. The word blog is short for weblog. Most blogs are short posts or entries expressing a single author's opinions. Blogs can be found on everything from politics, finance, economics, and legal issues to health and sports. Most bloggers add a new entry daily or weekly. Most blogs are interactive, providing a space where readers can comment on the opinions or information expressed.

Identify the writer. Look for information upfront that gives the name of the author and his or her business or professional affiliation.

Assess the sources the blogger links to. Evaluate the credibility and accuracy of the sources the blogger recommends to readers. Does the blog link to reputable sources?

Identify the writer's bias. Most bloggers do express a point of view. Consider the arguments and evidence the writer presents in support of these opinions. Are positions presented in a balanced way that acknowledges other points of view or is the language clearly one-sided? Scan reader comments to determine whether the blog allows comments by readers with opposing points of view or with different opinions.

PRACTICE AND APPLY THE SKILL

Use the information above to answer these questions.

1. How might the language in a business e-mail be different from the language in a personal e-mail sent to friends?
2. What makes wikis useful for projects that require input from many other people?
3. What are the advantages and drawbacks of online encyclopedias like Wikipedia?

SOCIAL STUDIES SKILLS HANDBOOK

Math Skills Online

Economics and mathematics are related in many ways.

Economists use mathematics to analyze data and to test and communicate their theories. Your ability to understand economics will depend to some extent on your ability to use and understand mathematics.

Visual Learning Animations

- Reading and Making Graphs
- Circle Graphs
- Misleading Graphs
- Mean, Median, Mode, and Range
- Line Plots
- Stem and Leaf Plots
- Effects of Outliers
- Appropriate Use of Statistical Measures

Mathematics Tutorials

- Making a Histogram
- Finding Slope Using Rise/Run
- Graphing Points on the Coordinate Plane
- Finding the Percent of a Number
- Finding Part of a Whole
- Finding Percent Using a Proportion
- Finding Simple Interest
- Finding Compound Interest

Interactive Math Activities

- Histograms
- Exploring Slope
- Points in the Coordinate Plane
- Percents and Proportions
- Simple and Compound Interest

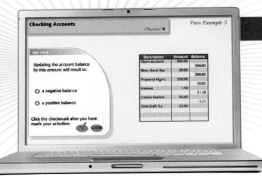

Math Lab

- Using Addition and Subtraction to Balance a Checking Account

You can access help with mathematics at point of use in your Online Student Edition or review these skills at any time.

English and Spanish Glossary

A

absolute advantage the ability to produce more of a given product using a given amount of resources (p. 449)
ventaja absoluta capacidad para producir más de cierto producto usando una cantidad determinada de recursos

aggregate demand the amount of goods and services in the economy that will be purchased at all possible price levels (p. 314)
demanda agregada cantidad de bienes y servicios que serán comprados a todos los niveles de precio posibles

aggregate supply the total amount of goods and services in the economy available at all possible price levels (p. 313)
oferta agregada cantidad total de bienes y servicios disponibles a todos los niveles de precio posibles

antitrust laws laws that encourage competition in the marketplace (p. 181)
leyes antimonopolio leyes que promueven la competencia en el mercado

appreciation an increase in the value of a currency (p. 464)
apreciación incremento del valor de una moneda

appropriations bill a bill that authorizes a specific amount of spending by the government (p. 394)
ley de presupuesto ley que autoriza una cantidad específica de gasto para el gobierno

arbitration a settlement technique in which a neutral third party listens to both sides and then imposes a decision that is legally binding for both company and the union (p. 242)
arbitraje tipo de acuerdo en el que un tercer grupo neutral escucha a ambos lados e impone una decisión con vínculo legal entre la compañía y el sindicato

articles of partnership a partnership agreement that spells out each partner's rights and responsibilities (p. 197)
estatutos de asociación acuerdo de una sociedad que determina los derechos y responsabilidades de cada socio

assets the money and other valuables belonging to an individual or business (p. 198)
activos dinero y otros valores pertenecientes a un individuo o una empresa

authoritarian describing a form of government that limits individual freedoms and requires strict obedience from its citizens (p. 36)
autoritario tipo de gobierno que limita la libertad de los individuos y requiere obediencia estricta de sus ciudadanos

automatic stabilizer a tool of fiscal policy that increases or decreases automatically depending on changes in GDP and personal income (p. 404)
estabilizador económico herramienta fiscal que se incrementa o disminuye dependiendo de cambios en el PIB y los ingresos personales

average cost total cost divided by the quantity produced (p. 121)
costo total promedio costo que surge al dividir el costo total por la cantidad producida

B

balance of payments the value of all monetary transactions between a country's economy and the rest of the world (p. 469)
balanza de pagos valor de todas las transacciones monetarias entre la economía de un país y la del resto del mundo

balance of trade the relationship between the value of a country's exports and the value of its imports (p. 468)
balanza comercial relación entre el valor de las exportaciones de un país y el valor de sus importaciones

balanced budget a budget in which revenue and spending are equal (p. 382)
presupuesto equilibrado presupuesto en el que los ingresos y los gastos son equitativos

bank an institution for receiving, keeping, and lending money (p. 256)
banco institución que recibe, mantiene y presta dinero

bank holding company a company that owns more than one bank (p. 426)
compañía tenedora de bancos compañía dueña de más de un banco

bank run a widespread panic in which many people try to redeem their paper money at the same time (p. 258)
pánico bancario situación de pánico general en la cual muchas personas retiran su dinero del banco simultáneamente

barrier to entry any factor that makes it difficult for a new firm to enter a market (p. 160)
barrera comercial cualquier factor que dificulta la entrada de una nueva entidad al mercado

barter the direct exchange of one set of goods or services for another (p. 249)
trueque intercambio directo de bienes o servicios

bear market a steady drop or stagnation in the stock market over a period of time (p. 296)
mercado bajista caída constante o estancamiento de la bolsa de inversiones por un período de tiempo

black market a market in which goods are sold illegally, without regard for government controls on price or quantity (p. 153)
mercado negro mercado en el que se venden bienes ilegalmente, sin considerar los controles gubernamentales sobre precio y cantidad

block grants federal funds given to the states in lump sums (p. 356)
subvención de bloque fondos federales otorgados a los estados en cantidades fijas

blue-collar worker someone who performs manual labor, often in a manufacturing job, and who earns an hourly wage (p. 238)
obrero persona que realiza trabajo manual, a menudo en el área industrial, y que recibe un salario por hora

bond a formal contract issued by a corporation or other entity that includes a promise to repay borrowed money with interest at fixed intervals (p. 205)

bono contrato formal expedido por una corporación u otra entidad que estipula pagar un préstamo con intereses a intervalos fijos

"brain drain" migration of the best-educated people of less developed countries to developed nations (p. 506)

fuga de cerebros emigración de individuos con alta capacitación de países menos desarrollados a naciones más desarrolladas

brokerage firm a business that specializes in trading stocks (p. 293)

firma de corretaje empresa de corredores de bolsa

budget an estimate of future revenue and expenses (p. 381)

presupuesto estimación de ingresos y gastos a futuro

budget deficit a situation in which budget expenditures exceed revenues (p. 408)

déficit presupuestario situación en la cual los gastos son mayores que los ingresos

budget surplus a situation in which budget revenues exceed expenditures (p. 408)

superávit presupuestario situación en la cual los ingresos son mayores que los gastos

bull market a steady rise in the stock market over a period of time (p. 296)

mercado alcista incremento constante en la bolsa de valores durante un período de tiempo

business association a group organized to promote the collective business interests of an area or group of similar businesses (p. 212)

asociación de empresas grupo que promueve los intereses colectivos de un área o grupo de empresas similares

business cycle a period of macroeconomic expansion, or growth, followed by one of contraction, or decline (pp. 57, 315)

ciclo económico período de expansión o crecimiento macroeconómico, seguido por una contracción o declive

business franchise a semi-independent business that pays fees to a parent company in return for the exclusive right to sell a certain product or service in a given area (p. 200)

franquicia negocio que paga honorarios a una empresa matriz a cambio del derecho exclusivo de venta de cierto producto o servicio en un área específica

business license authorization to operate a business issued by a local government (p. 193)

licencia comercial autorización emitida por un gobierno local para operar un negocio

business organization the ownership structure of a company or firm (p. 191)

negocio estructura propietaria de una compañía o entidad

C

call option a contract for buying stock at a particular price until a specified future date (p. 295)

opción de compra contrato que permite la compra de acciones a un precio estipulado hasta una fecha determinada

capital any human-made resource that is used to produce other goods and services (p. 6)

capital cualquier recurso fabricado por el hombre que se usa para producir otros bienes y servicios

capital budget a budget for spending on major investments (p. 381)

presupuesto de capital presupuesto destinado para inversiones de gran importancia

capital deepening the process of increasing the amount of capital per worker (p. 324)

desarrollo de capital proceso en el cual se incrementa la cantidad de capital por trabajador

capital gain the difference between the selling price and purchase price that results in a financial gain for the seller (p. 293)

plusvalía diferencia entre el precio de venta y el precio de compra que resulta en una ganancia financiera para el vendedor

capital loss the difference between the selling price and purchase price that results in a financial loss for the seller (p. 293)

minusvalía diferencia entre el precio de venta y el precio de compra que resulta en una pérdida financiera para el vendedor

capital market a market in which money is lent for periods longer than a year (p. 290)

mercado de capitales mercado en el cual se hacen préstamos por períodos de más de un año

cartel a formal organization of producers that agree to coordinate prices and production (p. 179)

cartel organización de productores que acuerdan la coordinación de precios y producción

cash transfers direct payments of money by the government to poor, disabled, and retired people (p. 69)

pensión pagos de dinero hechos directamente por el gobierno a los infortunados, incapacitados y jubilados

central bank a bank that can lend to other banks in times of need (p. 260)

banco central banco que puede hacer préstamos a otros bancos en momentos de necesidad

centrally planned economy an economic system in which the government makes all decisions on the three key economic questions (p. 35)

economía centralizada sistema económico en el cual el gobierno toma todas las decisiones sobre las tres preguntas económicas clave

certificate of incorporation a license to form a corporation issued by a state government (p. 205)

documento de constitución licencia expedida por el gobierno estatal, que permite formar una corporación

ceteris paribus a Latin phrase that means "all other things held constant" (p. 91)

ceteris paribus frase en latín que significa "lo demás permanece constante"

check clearing the process by which banks record whose account gives up money and whose account receives money when a customer writes a check (p. 426)
compensación de cheques proceso en el cual un banco lleva un registro de las cuentas que ceden dinero y las cuentas que reciben dinero cuando un cliente emite un cheque

classical economics a school of thought based on the idea that free markets regulate themselves (p. 399)
economía clásica corriente de pensamiento basada en la idea de que los mercados libres se regulan solos

closely held corporation a type of corporation that issues stock to only a few people, who are often family members (p. 203)
sociedad cerrada tipo de empresa que expide acciones a pocas personas, quienes por lo general son familiares

collective bargaining the process in which union and company management meet to negotiate a new labor contract (p. 240)
convenio colectivo de trabajo proceso en el cual la administración del sindicato y de la compañía se reúnen con el fin de negociar un contrato de trabajo

collusion an illegal agreement among firms to divide the market, set prices, or limit production (p. 179)
colusión acuerdo ilegal entre entidades con el fin de dividir el mercado, ajustar precios o restringir la producción

command economy another name for a centrally planned economy (p. 35)
economía controlada otro nombre para la economía centralizada

commodity a product such as petroleum or milk that is considered the same no matter who produces or sells it (p. 160)
bien de consumo producto, tal como el petróleo o la leche, que se considera igual independientemente de quién lo produzca o lo venda

commodity money objects that have value in and of themselves and that are also used as money (p. 254)
mercancía objetos que tienen valor por sí mismos y que también se usan como dinero

communism a political system in which the government owns and controls all resources and means of production and makes all economic decisions (p. 36)
comunismo sistema político en el cual el gobierno posee y controla todos los recursos y medios de producción y toma todas las decisiones económicas

comparative advantage the ability to produce a product most efficiently given all the other products that could be produced (p. 449)
ventaja comparativa habilidad para producir cierto producto de la manera más eficiente considerando todos los otros productos que se podrían producir

competition the struggle among producers for the dollars of consumers (p. 33)
competencia lucha entre productores por el dinero de los consumidores

complements two goods that are bought and used together (p. 96)

bienes complementarios dos bienes que se compran y se usan conjuntamente

conglomerate a business combination merging more than three businesses that produce unrelated products or services (p. 207)
conglomerado combinación de negocios donde se unen más de tres negocios que producen productos o servicios no relacionados entre sí

consumer cooperative a retail outlet owned and operated by consumers that sells merchandise to members at reduced prices (p. 209)
cooperativa de consumidores agrupación operada por consumidores que ofrece bienes y servicios para sus socios a precios reducidos

Consumer Price Index a price index determined by measuring the price of a standard group of goods meant to represent the "market basket" of a typical urban consumer (p. 343)
índice de precios al consumidor índice de precios determinado al medir el precio de un grupo de bienes estándar que representa la "canasta familiar" del consumidor urbano común

consumer sovereignty the power of consumers to decide what gets produced (p. 34)
soberanía del consumidor poder del consumidor para decidir qué se produce

contingent employment a temporary and part-time job (p. 221)
trabajo a destajo trabajo temporal a tiempo parcial

contraction a period of economic decline marked by falling real GDP (p. 316)
recesión período de declive económico caracterizado por el descenso del PIB

contractionary policy a fiscal policy used to reduce economic growth, often through decreased spending or higher taxes (p. 395)
política de contracción política fiscal que reduce el crecimiento económico, usualmente por medio de la disminución de gastos o de impuestos más altos

cooperative a business organization owned and operated by a group of individuals for their shared benefit (p. 208)
cooperativa organización comercial que pertenece y es operada por un grupo de individuos para un beneficio común

copyright a government document that grants an author exclusive rights to publish and sell creative works (p. 61)
derechos de autor documento gubernamental que garantiza los derechos exclusivos a un autor para publicar y vender sus obras

core inflation rate the rate of inflation excluding the effects of food and energy prices (p. 345)
tasa de inflación subyacente tasa de inflación que excluye los efectos del precio de la comida y la energía

corporate bond a bond issued by a corporation to help raise money for expansion (p. 288)
bonos corporativos bono expedido por una corporación para ayudar a recaudar dinero para su expansión

corporate income tax a tax based on a company's profits (p. 366)
   impuesto sobre sociedades impuesto que se basa en las ganancias de la compañía
corporation a legal entity, owned by individual stockholders, each of whom has limited liability for the firm's debts (p. 202)
   corporación entidad legal que pertenece a los accionistas, los cuales tienen responsabilidad limitada ante las deudas de la firma
cost/benefit analysis a decision-making process in which you compare what you will sacrifice and gain by a specific action (p. 11)
   análisis del costo/beneficio proceso de toma de decisiones en el cual se compara el costo y la ganancia de una operación en particular
coupon rate the interest rate that a bond issuer will pay to the bondholder (p. 284)
   cupón de interés tasa de interés que un emisor de bonos paga al titular del bono
credit card a card entitling its owner to buy goods and services based on the owner's promise to pay for those goods and services (p. 268)
   tarjeta de crédito tarjeta que autoriza a su titular a comprar bienes y servicios partiendo de su promesa de pagar por esos bienes y servicios
creditor a person or institution to whom money is owed (p. 272)
   acreedor persona o institución a la cual se le debe dinero
crowding-out effect the loss of funds for private investment caused by government borrowing (p. 411)
   efecto expulsión pérdida de fondos destinados para inversiones privadas a causa de la deuda pública
currency coins and paper bills used as money (p. 252)
   moneda monedas y billetes que se usan como dinero
cyclical unemployment unemployment that rises during economic downturns and falls when the economy improves (p. 338)
   desempleo cíclico desempleo que incrementa al empeorar la economía y disminuye al mejorar la economía

D

debit card a card used to withdraw money from a bank account (p. 271)
   tarjeta de débito tarjeta que se usa para retirar dinero de una cuenta bancaria
debt rescheduling an agreement between a lending nation and a debtor nation that lengthens the time of debt payment and forgives part of the loan (p. 493)
   renegociación de deudas acuerdo entre la nación acreedora y la nación deudora que extiende el plazo de pago y perdona parte del préstamo
default to fail to pay back a loan (p. 268)
   mora situación que consiste en suspender el pago de una deuda

deflation a sustained drop in the price level (p. 348)
   deflación descenso general de precios
deforestation the large-scale destruction of forests (p. 507)
   deforestación destrucción forestal masiva
demand the desire to own something and the ability to pay for it (p. 85)
   demanda deseo de poseer algo y la capacidad para pagar por ello
demand curve a graphic representation of a demand schedule (p. 89)
   curva de demanda representación gráfica de la tabla de demanda
demand deposit money in a checking account that can be paid "on demand," or at any time (p. 264)
   depósito a la vista dinero en una cuenta corriente que se paga "a petición" o en cualquier momento
demand schedule a table that lists the quantity of a good a person will buy at various prices in the market (p. 88)
   tabla de demanda tabla que representa la cantidad de bienes que un consumidor está dispuesto a adquirir a diferentes precios en el mercado
demand-side economics a school of thought based on the idea that demand for goods drives the economy (p. 400)
   economía de demanda corriente de pensamiento basada en la noción de que la demanda de bienes dirige la economía
demographics the statistical characteristics of populations and population segments, especially when used to identify consumer markets (p. 94)
   demografía estudio estadístico de la población humana y sus segmentos, especialmente relacionados con el mercado de consumo
depreciation 1. the loss of the value of capital equipment that results from normal wear and tear (p. 312) 2. a decrease in the value of currency (p. 465)
   depreciación 1. reducción del valor de los bienes de capital de equipo como resultado del uso 2. reducción en el valor de una moneda
depression a recession that is especially long and severe (p. 316)
   depresión recesión económica que se caracteriza por ser larga y grave
deregulation the removal of government controls over a market (p. 183)
   desregulación supresión del control del gobierno sobre la actividad económica
derived demand a type of demand that is set by the demand for another good or service (p. 226)
   demanda derivada demanda que depende de la demanda de otro bien o servicio
developed nation a nation with a relatively high average level of material well-being (p. 481)
   país desarrollado país con un bienestar económico relativamente alto
development the process by which a nation improves the economic, political, and social well-being of its people (p. 481)
   desarrollo proceso mediante el cual una nación mejora la situación económica, política y social de su población

differentiation making a product different from other, similar products (p. 175)
 diferenciación hacer que un producto se distinga de otros productos similares

diminishing marginal returns a level of production at which the marginal product of labor decreases as the number of workers increases (p. 117)
 rendimiento marginal decreciente nivel de producción en el cual el producto laboral marginal disminuye al incrementar el número de trabajadores

discount rate the interest rate that the Federal Reserve charges commercial banks for loans (p. 427)
 tasa de descuento interés que cobra la Reserva Federal sobre los préstamos a los bancos comerciales

discouraged worker someone who wants a job but has given up looking (p. 341)
 trabajador desanimado persona que quiere conseguir un trabajo pero ha desistido de la búsqueda

discretionary spending spending about which Congress is free to make choices (p. 375)
 gastos discrecionales gastos sobre los cuales el Congreso es libre de tomar decisiones

disequilibrium any price or quantity not at equilibrium; when quantity supplied is not equal to quantity demanded in a market (p. 134)
 desequilibrio estado de desigualdad económica; desigualdad entre la cantidad de oferta y la cantidad de demanda

diversification the strategy of spreading out investments to reduce risk (p. 280)
 diversificación estrategia en la que se distribuyen las inversiones para reducir el riesgo

dividend the portion of corporate profits paid out to stockholders (p. 205)
 dividendo porción de los beneficios corporativos que les pagan a los accionistas

durable goods those goods that last for a relatively long time, such as refrigerators, cars, and DVD players (p. 309)
 bienes duraderos bienes de consumo cuya durabilidad es relativamente larga, por ejemplo refrigeradores, automóbiles y reproductores de DVD

E

easy money policy a monetary policy that increases the money supply (p. 436)
 política de dinero fácil política monetaria que incrementa la disponibilidad de dinero

economic growth a steady, long-term increase in real GDP (p. 315)
 crecimiento económico aumento constante a largo plazo del PIB

economic system the structure of methods and principles that a society uses to produce and distribute goods and services (p. 23)

 sistema económico estructura de métodos y principios que una sociedad usa para producir y distribuir bienes y servicios

economic transition a period of change in which a nation moves from one economic system to another (p. 43)
 transición económica período de cambio en el cual una nación pasa de un sistema económico a otro

economics the study of how people seek to satisfy their needs and wants by making choices (p. 4)
 economía rama del saber que estudia cómo las personas buscan satisfacer sus necesidades y deseos al tomar decisiones

economies of scale factors that cause a producer's average cost per unit to fall as output rises (p. 165)
 economías de escala factores que hacen que el costo promedio por unidad de un producto disminuya cuando la producción aumenta

efficiency the use of resources in such a way as to maximize the output of goods and services (p. 15)
 eficiencia uso de los recursos de manera que se alcance el máximo de producción de bienes y servicios

elastic describes demand that is very sensitive to a change in price (p. 97)
 elasticidad describe la demanda que es muy susceptible a los cambios de precio

elasticity of demand a measure of how consumers respond to price changes (p. 97)
 elasticidad de la demanda medida de cómo responden los consumidores a los cambios de precio

elasticity of supply a measure of the way quantity supplied reacts to a change in price (p. 113)
 elasticidad de la oferta medida de la forma en que la cantidad ofrecida responde a un cambio de precio

embargo a ban on trade with a particular country (p. 456)
 embargo prohibición de comerciar con un país determinado

eminent domain the right of a government to take private property for public use (p. 52)
 dominio eminente (expropiación) derecho de un gobierno de tomar la propiedad privada de alguien para darle un uso público

enterprise zone area where businesses can locate free of certain local, state, and federal taxes and restrictions (p. 355)
 zona franca área en la que se pueden establecer negocios libres de ciertos impuestos y restricciones municipales, estatales y federales

entitlement social welfare program that people are "entitled to" benefit from if they meet certain eligibility requirements (p. 376)
 derecho consuetudinario programa de beneficencia social al que las personas tienen "derecho" si cumplen con ciertos requisitos

entrepreneur a person who decides how to combine resources to create goods and services (p. 5)
 empresario persona que decide cómo combinar recursos para crear bienes y servicios

equilibrium the point at which the demand for a product or service is equal to the supply of that product or service (p. 134)

ENGLISH AND SPANISH GLOSSARY

equilibrio punto en el cual la demanda de un producto o servicio es igual a su oferta

equilibrium wage the wage rate, or price of labor services, that is set when the supply of workers meets the demand for workers in the labor market (p. 227)

salario de equilibrio tasa salarial, o precio de la mano de obra, que se establece cuando la disponibilidad de trabajadores cubre la demanda de trabajadores en el mercado laboral

estate tax a tax on the total value of the money and property of a person who has died (p. 373)

impuesto de sucesión impuesto sobre el valor total del dinero y las propiedades que deja una persona fallecida

excess reserves bank reserves greater than the amount required by the Federal Reserve (p. 431)

exceso de reservas reservas bancarias que sobrepasan la cantidad que la Reserva Federal necesita

exchange rate the value of a nation's currency in relation to a foreign currency (p. 463)

tasa de cambio valor de la moneda de una nación en relación con una moneda extranjera

excise tax a tax on the production or sale of a good (p. 124)

impuesto sobre artículos de uso y consumo impuesto sobre la producción o venta de un bien

expansion a period of economic growth as measured by a rise in real GDP (p. 315)

expansión período de crecimiento económico determinado por un aumento del PIB real

expansionary policy a fiscal policy used to encourage economic growth, often through increased spending or tax cuts (p. 395)

política de expansión política fiscal que se usa para estimular el crecimiento económico a través de un aumento del gasto o de una reducción de impuestos

export a good or service sent to another country for sale (p. 449)

exportaciones bien o servicio que se envía a otro país para la venta

externality an economic side effect of a good or service that generates benefits or costs to someone other than the person deciding how much to produce or consume (p. 65)

externalidad efecto económico de un bien o servicio que le genera beneficios o costos a alguien distinto a quien decide cuánto producir o consumir

F

factor market the arena of exchange in which firms purchase the factors of production from households (p. 31)

mercado de factores área de intercambio en la cual hay compañías que compran los factores de producción de las economías domésticas

factor payment the income people receive in return for supplying factors of production (p. 25)

pago a los factores ingreso que reciben las personas a cambio de proveer factores de producción

factors of production the resources that are used to make goods and services (p. 5)

factores de producción recursos que se usan para generar bienes y servicios

fad a product that is popular for a short period of time (p. 145)

moda pasajera producto que es popular por un período breve de tiempo

featherbedding the practice of negotiating labor contracts that keep unnecessary workers on the company's payroll (p. 233)

sinecura contratación retribuida de empleados innecesarios

federal budget a written document estimating the federal government's revenue and authorizing its spending for the coming year (p. 392)

presupuesto federal documento escrito donde se estima el ingreso del gobierno federal y por medio del cual se autorizan los gastos del año siguiente

federal funds rate the interest rate that banks charge each other for loans (p. 427)

tasa de los fondos federales tasa que se cobran entre sí los bancos por el préstamo de sus reservas

fiat money objects that have value because the government has decreed that they are an acceptable means to pay debts (p. 255)

dinero fiat objetos que tienen valor sólo porque el gobierno ha decretado que son medios aceptables para pagar deudas

financial asset a claim on the property or income of a borrower (p. 278)

activo financiero derecho que tiene una entidad sobre la propiedad o los ingresos de un prestatario

financial intermediary an institution that helps channel funds from savers to borrowers (p. 279)

intermediario financiero institución que ayuda a canalizar los fondos de los ahorristas a los prestatarios

financial system the network of structures and mechanisms that allow the transfer of money between savers and borrowers (p. 278)

sistema financiero red de estructuras y mecanismos que permiten la transferencia de dinero entre ahorristas y prestatarios

firm an organization that uses resources to produce a product or service, which it then sells (p. 31)

empresa organización que usa recursos para crear un producto o servicio, que después vende

fiscal policy the use of government spending and revenue collection to influence the economy (p. 392)

política fiscal uso de los gastos y del ingreso del gobierno para causar una reacción en la economía

fiscal year any 12-month period used for budgeting purposes (p. 392)

año fiscal período de doce meses con fines presupuestarios

fixed cost a cost that does not change, no matter how much of a good is produced (p. 118)

costo fijo costo que no cambia, independientemente de la cantidad que se produzca de un bien

fixed exchange-rate system a system in which governments try to keep the values of their currencies constant against one another (p. 467)

sistema de tasa cambiaria fija sistema en el cual el gobierno trata de mantener constante el valor de su moneda con respecto a otra moneda

fixed income income that does not increase even when prices go up (p. 347)
 ingreso fijo ingreso que no aumentan aunque los precios suban

flexible exchange-rate system a system in which the exchange rate is determined by supply and demand (p. 467)
 sistema de tasa cambiaria flexible sistema en el cual la tasa de cambio depende de la oferta y la demanda

food stamp program government program that helps low-income people buy food (p. 351)
 programa de cupones para alimentos cupones que el gobierno distribuye y que se pueden cambiar por alimentos

foreclosure the seizure of property from borrowers who are unable to repay their loans (p. 263)
 embargo acción que consiste en tomar la propiedad de prestatarios que no pueden pagar sus préstamos

foreign direct investment the establishment of a business by investors from another country (p. 492)
 inversión directa extranjera establecimiento de un negocio de inversionistas de otro país

foreign exchange market system of financial institutions that facilitates the buying and selling of foreign currencies (p. 465)
 mercado de divisas sistema de instituciones financieras que facilitan la compra y venta de monedas extranjeras

foreign investment capital that originates in other countries (p. 492)
 inversión extranjera capital generado en otros países

foreign portfolio investment purchases made in a country's financial markets by investors from another country (p. 492)
 cartera de inversión extranjera compras que los inversionistas de un país hacen en mercados financieros de otro país

fractional reserve banking a banking system that keeps only a fraction of funds on hand and lends out the remainder (p. 267)
 sistema de reserva fraccionaria sistema bancario en el cual el banco mantiene solamente una fracción de los fondos en reserva y presta el resto de los fondos

franchise a contract that gives a single firm the right to sell its goods within an exclusive market (p. 167)
 franquicia contrato que le otorga a una firma el derecho de vender sus bienes dentro de un mercado exclusivo

free contract the principle that people may decide what agreements they want to enter into (p. 51)
 principio de libre contrato principio que establece que las personas pueden decidir qué acuerdos quieren hacer

free enterprise system an economic system characterized by private or corporate ownership of capital goods (p. 43)
 sistema de libre empresa sistema económico en el cual los bienes capitales les pertenecen a compañías privadas o corporaciones

free market economy an economic system in which decisions on the three key economic questions are based on voluntary exchange in markets (p. 30)
 economía de libre mercado sistema económico en el cual las decisiones relacionadas con las tres preguntas económicas clave se basan en el intercambio voluntario en el mercado

free rider someone who would not be willing to pay for a certain good or service but who would get the benefits of it anyway if it were provided as a public good (p. 64)
 polizón persona que no está dispuesta a pagar por un bien o servicio determinado, pero quien se beneficiaría de él de todos modos si se le ofreciera como beneficio público

free trade the lowering or elimination of protective tariffs and other trade barriers between two or more nations (p. 458)
 libre comercio disminución o eliminación de las tarifas y otras barreras comerciales entre dos o más naciones

free trade zone a region where a group of countries agrees to reduce or eliminate trade barriers (p. 460)
 zona de libre comercio región en la que un grupo de países acuerda reducir o eliminar las barreras comerciales

frictional unemployment type of unemployment that occurs when people take time to find a job (p. 335)
 desempleo friccional tipo de desempleo que ocurre cuando a las personas les toma tiempo encontrar empleo

fringe benefits payments to employees other than wages or salary (p. 195)
 beneficio adicional pago que los empleados reciben además de su sueldo o salario

full employment the level of employment reached when there is no cyclical unemployment (p. 340)
 pleno empleo nivel de empleo alcanzado cuando no hay desempleo cíclico

futures contracts to buy or sell commodities at a particular date in the future at a price specified today (p. 295)
 contrato de futuros contratos que establece la compra o venta de bienes o valores en el futuro a un precio establecido con anticipación

G

general partnership a type of partnership in which all partners share equally in both responsibility and liability (p. 196)
 sociedad colectiva tipo de sociedad en la cual todos los socios asumen la misma cantidad de responsabilidades y obligaciones

gift tax a tax on the money or property that one living person gives to another (p. 373)
 impuesto sobre donaciones impuesto sobre el dinero o la propiedad que una persona viva le da a otra

glass ceiling an unofficial barrier that sometimes prevents some women and minorities from advancing to the top rank of organizations dominated by white men (p. 231)
 techo de cristal barrera no oficial que les impide a algunas mujeres y minorías avanzar a la cima de organizaciones dominadas por hombres blancos

globalization the increasingly tight interconnection of producers, consumers, and financial systems around the world (pp. 337, 501)
 globalización interconexión, cada vez más fuerte, entre productores, consumidores y sistemas financieros a nivel mundial

gold standard a monetary system in which paper money and coins had the value of a certain amount of gold (p. 259)
   patrón oro sistema monetario en el cual el papel moneda y las monedas tienen el mismo valor de una cantidad de oro determinada

goods the physical objects that someone produces (p. 3)
   bienes objetos físicos que alguien produce

government monopoly a monopoly created by the government (p. 167)
   monopolio gubernamental monopolio creado por el gobierno

grant a financial award given by a government agency to a private individual or group in order to carry out a specific task (p. 72)
   subvención cantidad de dinero que otorga una organización gubernamental a una organización o grupo privados con el fin de utilizarlo en una actividad específica

greenback a paper currency issued during the Civil War (p. 259)
   greenback dinero creado durante la Guerra Civil estadounidense

gross domestic product the dollar value of all final goods and services produced within a country's borders in a given year (pp. 57, 309)
   producto interno bruto valor en dólares de todos los bienes y servicios producidos en un país, en un año específico

gross national product the annual income earned by a nation's firms and citizens (p. 312)
   producto nacional bruto ingreso anual que obtienen las compañías y los habitantes de una nación

guest workers members of the labor force from another country who are allowed to live and work in the United States only temporarily (p. 222)
   trabajadores invitados miembros de la fuerza laboral que vienen de otro país y tienen permiso para vivir y trabajar en Estados Unidos temporalmente

"guns or butter" a phrase expressing the idea that a country that decides to produce more military goods ("guns") has fewer resources to produce consumer goods ("butter") and vice versa (p. 9)
   "pan o armas" frase que expresa la idea de que un país que decide producir más objetos militares (armas) tiene menos recursos para producir bienes de consumo (pan) y viceversa

H

hedge fund a private investment organization that employs risky strategies to try to make huge profits for investors (p. 279)
   fondo de inversión libre organización privada inversionista que emplea estrategias riesgosas para intentar obtener grandes ganancias para los inversionistas

horizontal merger the combination of two or more firms competing in the same market with the same good or service (p. 206)

fusión horizontal combinación de dos o más empresas que compiten en el mismo mercado y ofrecen el mismo bien o servicio

household a person or group of people living in a single residence (p. 31)
   unidad familiar persona o grupo de personas que viven bajo el mismo techo

human capital the knowledge and skills a worker gains through education and experience (p. 6)
   capital humano conocimientos y destrezas que un trabajador obtiene a través de la educación y la experiencia

hyperinflation inflation that is out of control (p. 345)
   hiperinflación inflación descontrolada

I

imperfect competition a market structure that fails to meet the conditions of perfect competition (p. 160)
   competencia imperfecta estructura del mercado que no cumple con las condiciones de la competencia perfecta

import a good or service brought in from another country for sale (p. 449)
   importaciones bienes o servicios que se traen de otro país para la venta

import quota a set limit on the amount of a good that can be imported (p. 456)
   cuota de importación límite establecido de la cantidad de un bien que se puede importar

incentive the hope of reward or fear of penalty that encourages a person to behave in a certain way (p. 33)
   incentivo esperanza de obtener una recompensa o temor de recibir un castigo que anima a una persona a comportarse de cierta manera

incidence of a tax the final burden of a tax (p. 367)
   incidencia fiscal peso final de un impuesto

income distribution the way in which a nation's total income is distributed among its population (p. 351)
   distribución de ingresos forma en que se distribuye el ingreso total de una nación entre la población

income effect the change in consumption that results when a price increase causes real income to decline (p. 87)
   efecto ingreso cambio en el consumo que ocurre cuando el aumento de un precio hace que el ingreso real disminuya

increasing marginal returns a level of production in which the marginal product of labor increases as the number of workers increases (p. 117)
   aumento del ingreso marginal nivel de producción en el cual la productividad marginal aumenta a medida que el número de trabajadores aumenta

individual income tax a tax based on a person's earnings (p. 366)
   impuesto sobre la renta individual impuesto que se basa en los ingresos de una persona

industrialization the organization of an economy for the purpose of manufacturing goods (p. 483)
industrialización organización de una economía con el propósito de fabricar bienes

inelastic describes demand that is not very sensitive to price changes (p. 97)
demanda inelástica demanda que es poco sensible a las variaciones de precio

infant industry an industry in the early stages of development (p. 458)
industria en período de arranque industria en etapa temprana de desarrollo

infant mortality rate the number of deaths that occur in the first year of life per 1,000 births (p. 484)
tasa de mortalidad infantil número de muertes que ocurren en el primer año de vida por cada 1000 nacimientos

inferior good a good that consumers demand less of when their incomes increase (p. 94)
bien inferior bien cuya demanda disminuye a medida que el ingreso de los consumidores aumenta

inflation a general increase in prices across an economy (p. 342)
inflación aumento general de los precios en una economía

inflation rate the percentage rate of change in price level over time (p. 343)
tasa de inflación porcentaje de cambio en los precios al transcurrir el tiempo

inflation-indexed bond a bond that protects the investor against inflation by its linkage to an index of inflation (p. 288)
bonos indexados por inflación bono que protege al inversionista de la inflación porque se ajusta de acuerdo con un índice de inflación

infrastructure the basic facilities that are necessary for a society to function and grow (p. 63)
infraestructura instalaciones básicas que una sociedad necesita para funcionar y desarrollarse

in-kind benefits goods and services provided for free or at greatly reduced prices (p. 70)
beneficios en especies bienes y servicios que se ofrecen de forma gratuita o a un precio considerablemente bajo

innovation the process of bringing new methods, products, or ideas into use (p. 27)
innovación proceso que consiste en usar nuevos métodos, productos o ideas

inside lag the time it takes to implement monetary policy (p. 437)
demora interna tiempo que toma implementar una política monetaria

interdependence the shared need of countries for resources, goods, services, labor, and knowledge supplied by other countries (p. 452)
interdependencia necesidad que comparten los países de obtener recursos, bienes, servicios, mano de obra y conocimiento provenientes de otros países

interest the price paid for the use of borrowed money (p. 268)
interés precio que se paga por el uso de dinero prestado

interest group a private organization that tries to persuade public officials to act in ways that benefit its members (p. 52)
grupo de presión organización privada que intenta persuadir a miembros de la administración pública de que actúen de una manera que beneficie a los miembros del grupo

intermediate goods products used in the production of final goods (p. 309)
bienes intermedios productos usados en la producción de bienes finales

internal financing capital derived from the savings of a country's citizens (p. 491)
financiamiento interno capital derivado de los ahorros de los ciudadanos de un país

inventory the quantity of goods that a firm has on hand (p. 143)
inventario cantidad de bienes que una empresa tiene a su disposición

investment the act of redirecting resources from being consumed today so that they may create benefits in the future; the use of assets to earn income or profit (p. 277)
inversión acto de redirigir recursos del presente para que puedan generar más beneficios en el futuro; uso de los bienes para obtener ingresos o ganancias

invisible hand a term coined by Adam Smith to describe the self-regulating nature of the marketplace (p. 33)
mano invisible expresión acuñada por Adam Smith para describir la naturaleza autorregulatoria del mercado

J

junk bond a bond with high risk and potentially high yield (p. 289)
bono basura bono que representa un gran riesgo y que podría tener un alto rendimiento

K

Keynesian economics a school of thought that uses demand-side theory as the basis for encouraging government action to help the economy (p. 401)
Economía keinesiana escuela que usa la teoría de la demanda como base para provocar acciones gubernamentales que ayuden la economía

L

labor the effort people devote to tasks for which they are paid (p. 5)
trabajo esfuerzo dedicado a tareas por las que se recibe compensación económica

labor force all nonmilitary people who are employed or unemployed (p. 217)

ENGLISH AND SPANISH GLOSSARY

mano de obra toda persona empleada o subempleada que no pertenece a las fuerzas armadas

labor union an organization of workers that tries to improve working conditions, wages, and benefits for its members (p. 233)

sindicato organización de trabajadores que busca mejorar las condiciones de trabajo, los salarios y los beneficios laborales de sus miembros

laissez faire the doctrine that government generally should not intervene in the marketplace (p. 39)

liberalismo doctrina que rechaza la intervención del gobierno en el mercado

land all natural resources used to produce goods and services (p. 5)

terreno todo recurso natural que se utiliza para producir bienes y servicios

law of comparative advantage the principle that a nation is better off when it produces goods and services for which it has a comparative advantage (p. 450)

ley (principio) de la ventaja comparativa principio que reconoce la ventaja que disfruta un país cuando puede producir un bien o servicio a menor costo que otro país

law of demand consumers will buy more of a good when its price is lower and less when its price is higher (p. 85)

ley de la demanda los consumidores compran más de un bien cuando su precio es bajo y menos cuando su precio es alto

law of increasing costs an economic principle which states that as production shifts from making one good or service to another, more resources are needed to increase production of the second good or service (p. 17)

ley de los costos crecientes principio económico según el cual al producirse un producto o bien adicional, éste requerirá cantidades cada vez mayores de recursos para aumentar su producción

law of supply producers offer more of a good as its price increases and less as its price falls (p. 109)

ley de la oferta los fabricantes proveen más de un bien cuando su precio sube y menos cuando su precio baja

leading indicators a set of key economic variables that economists use to predict future trends in a business cycle (p. 320)

indicadores principales conjunto de variables económicas clave que los economistas utilizan para predecir las futuras tendencias del ciclo económico

learning effect the theory that education increases efficiency of production and thus results in higher wages (p. 220)

efecto aprendizaje teoría que sostiene que la educación incrementa la productividad y por consiguiente genera mayores sueldos

legal equality the principle that everyone has the same legal rights (p. 51)

igualdad legal principio según el cual todas las personas tienen los mismos derechos legales

less developed country a nation with a relatively low level of material well-being (p. 482)

país en vías de desarrollo nación con un bajo nivel de bienestar material

liability the legal obligation to pay debts (p. 194)

responsabilidad obligación legal de pagar deudas

license a government-issued right to operate a business (p. 168)

licencia permiso que el gobierno otorga a empresas para que puedan operar

life expectancy the average expected life span of an individual (p. 483)

expectativa de vida promedio de vida anticipado de una persona

limited liability corporation a type of business with limited liability for the owners, with the advantage of not paying corporate income tax (p. 205)

corporación de responsabilidad limitada compañía que tiene propietarios con responsabilidad limitada y no paga el impuesto sobre sociedades

limited liability partnership a type of partnership in which all partners are limited partners (p. 197)

sociedad de responsabilidad limitada sociedad en la que la responsabilidad de los socios está limitada al capital aportado

limited partnership a type of partnership in which only one partner is required to be a general partner (p. 197)

sociedad limitada tipo de sociedad que solamente requiere un socio general

liquidity the ability to be used as, or directly converted into, cash (p. 264)

liquidez capacidad para utilizar el dinero o para convertir algo en dinero fácilmente

literacy rate the proportion of a nation's population over age 15 that can read and write (p. 483)

índice de alfabetización proporción de la población mayor de 15 años de un país que sabe leer y escribir

Lorenz Curve the curve that illustrates income distribution (p. 353)

Curva de Lorenz curva que ilustra la distribución de los ingresos

M

macroeconomics the study of economic behavior and decisions in a nation's whole economy (p. 56)

Macroeconomía estudio del comportamiento y la toma de decisiones de toda la economía nacional

malnutrition consistently inadequate nutrition (p. 491)

desnutrición nutrición inadecuada continua

mandatory spending spending that Congress is required by existing law to do (p. 375)

gasto obligatorio gasto que el Congreso debe realizar de acuerdo con leyes preexistentes

marginal benefit the extra benefit of adding one unit (p. 11)

beneficio marginal beneficio adicional que surge al añadirse una unidad

marginal cost the cost of producing one more unit of a good (pp. 11, 119)

costo marginal costo que resulta al producirse una unidad adicional de un producto

marginal product of labor the change in output from hiring one additional unit of labor (p. 116)

producto marginal del trabajo producción adicional que se obtiene con una unidad adicional de trabajo

marginal revenue the additional income from selling one more unit of a good; sometimes equal to price (p. 120)

ingreso marginal ingreso recibido al vender una unidad más de producto; en algunos casos similar al precio

market any arrangement that allows buyers and sellers to exchange things (p. 29)

mercado cualquier arreglo que les permite a compradores y vendedores intercambiar cosas

market basket a representative collection of goods and services (p. 343)

canasta de mercado conjunto representativo de bienes y servicios

market demand schedule a table that lists the quantity of a good all consumers in a market will buy at each different price (p. 88)

tabla de demanda tabla que muestra la cantidad de un producto determinado que los consumidores de un mercado estarían dispuestos a comprar a diferentes precios

market failure a situation in which the free market, operating on its own, does not distribute resources efficiently (p. 65)

falla del mercado situación en la que el mercado, operando de forma autónoma, asigna recursos ineficientemente

market power the ability of a company to control prices and total market output (p. 171)

poder de mercado capacidad de una empresa para influir en los precios y la producción del mercado

market supply curve a graph of the quantity supplied of a good by all suppliers at various prices (p. 113)

curva de oferta gráfico que ilustra la cantidad de un producto que las empresas proveerán a diferentes precios

market supply schedule a chart that lists how much of a good all suppliers will offer at various prices (p. 112)

tabla de oferta tabla que muestra la cantidad de un producto determinado que las empresas proveerán a diferentes precios

maturity the time at which payment to a bondholder is due (p. 284)

vencimiento día en que se cumple el plazo dado para el pago de una deuda u obligación

mediation a settlement technique in which a neutral person, the mediator, meets with each side to find a solution that both sides will accept (p. 242)

mediación proceso de resolución en el que una persona neutral, el mediador, se reúne con las partes en conflicto para hallar una solución mutuamente aceptable

medium of exchange anything that is used to determine value during the exchange of goods and services (p. 249)

medio de intercambio estructura que se utiliza para asignar valor a algo durante un intercambio de bienes y servicios

member bank a bank that belongs to the Federal Reserve System (p. 260)

banco miembro banco que pertenece al Sistema de la Reserva Federal

merger when two or more companies join to form a single firm (p. 182)

fusión proceso mediante el cual dos o más compañías se unen para formar una sola

microeconomics the study of economic behavior and decision-making in small units, such as households and firms (p. 56)

microeconomía estudio del comportamiento económico de unidades individuales de decisión tales como familias y empresas

minimum wage a minimum price that an employer can pay a worker for an hour of labor (p. 139)

salario mínimo cantidad mínima que un empleador puede pagar a un empleado por la hora de trabajo

mixed economy a market-based economic system in which the government is involved to some extent (p. 40)

economía mixta sistema económico de mercado en el que el gobierno tiene cierto grado de intervención

monetarism the belief that the money supply is the most important factor in macroeconomic performance (p. 435)

monetarismo doctrina que sostiene que el control del dinero en circulación es el factor más importante en el comportamiento macroeconómico de la economía

monetary policy the actions that the Federal Reserve System takes to influence the level of real GDP and the rate of inflation in the economy (p. 419)

política monetaria medidas que el Sistema de la Reserva Federal utiliza para conseguir la estabilidad del PIB real y de la tasa de inflación de la economía

money anything that serves as a medium of exchange, a unit of account, and a store of value (p. 249)

dinero todo lo que sirve como medio de cambio, unidad de cuenta y depósito de valor

money creation the process by which money enters into circulation (p. 429)

emisión de dinero proceso que pone en circulación billetes y monedas

money market a market in which money is lent for periods of one year or less (p. 290)

mercado monetario o de dinero mercado que ofrece créditos por períodos de un año o menos

money market mutual fund a fund that pools money from small savers to purchase short-term government and corporate securities (p. 265)

fondos mutuales fondo que reúne el dinero de pequeños ahorristas para comprar instrumentos de crédito a corto plazo emitidos por el gobierno o el sector privado

money multiplier formula formula (initial cash deposit × 1 ÷ RRR) used to determine how much new money can be created with each demand deposit and added to the money supply (p. 430)

fórmula del multiplicador monetario fórmula (depósito a la vista inicial × 1 ÷ tasa de encaje legal) que se utiliza para calcular la cantidad de dinero que cada depósito a la vista puede añadir a la oferta de dinero

money supply all the money available in the United States economy (p. 264)

oferta monetaria todo el dinero disponible en la economía de los Estados Unidos

monopolistic competition a market structure in which many companies sell products that are similar but not identical (p. 174)

competencia monopolística situación de mercado en la que muchas empresas venden bienes que son similares, pero no idénticos

monopoly a market in which a single seller dominates (p. 164)

monopolio situación de mercado en la que un solo vendedor controla la oferta

mortgage a specific type of loan that is used to buy real estate (p. 268)

hipoteca tipo de préstamo que se utiliza para comprar bienes inmuebles

multinational corporation a large corporation that produces and sells its goods and services in more than one country (p. 207)

compañía multinacional gran empresa que produce y vende sus bienes y servicios en más de un país

multiplier effect the idea that every one dollar change in fiscal policy creates a change greater than one dollar in the national income (p. 401)

efecto multiplicador concepto según el cual por cada dólar de cambio en una política fiscal, se producirá un cambio aún mayor en el ingreso nacional

municipal bond a bond issued by a state or local government or a municipality to finance a public project (p. 288)

bono público bono emitido por un estado, gobierno local o municipio para financiar obras públicas

mutual fund an organization that pools the savings of many individuals and invests this money in a variety of stocks, bonds, and other financial assets (p. 279)

fondo de inversión organización que reúne los ahorros de múltiples individuos e invierte el dinero en una cartera de acciones, bonos y otros activos financieros

N

national bank a bank chartered by the federal government (p. 257)

banco nacional banco regulado por el gobierno federal

national debt the total amount of money the federal government owes to bondholders (p. 410)

deuda nacional cantidad total de dinero que el gobierno federal debe a sus acreedores

national income accounting a system economists use to collect and organize macroeconomic statistics on production, income, investment, and savings (p. 307)

contabilidad nacional sistema que los economistas utilizan para recopilar y organizar estadísticas macroeconómicas sobre producción, ingresos, inversión y ahorros

natural monopoly a market that runs most efficiently when one large firm supplies all of the output (p. 166)

monopolio natural mercado que funciona más eficientemente cuando una sola empresa produce un bien o servicio

need something essential for survival (p. 3)

necesidad algo considerado esencial para sobrevivir

net worth total assets minus total liabilities

patrimonio neto bienes que posee una persona al deducirse sus deudas

newly industrialized country a less developed country that has made great progress toward developing its economy (p. 482)

país recientemente industrializado país no completamente industrializado que ha logrado grandes avances en el desarrollo de su economía

nominal GDP GDP measured in current prices (p. 310)

PBI nominal producto interno bruto medido en precios actuales

nondurable goods those goods that last a short period of time, such as food, light bulbs, and sneakers (p. 309)

bienes perecederos bienes que duran un corto período de tiempo como comida, bombillas y zapatos deportivos

nongovernmental organization an independent group that raises money and uses it to fund aid and development programs (p. 494)

organización no gubernamental grupo independiente que recauda dinero para financiar programas de ayuda y desarrollo

nonprice competition a way to attract customers through style, service, or location, but not a lower price (p. 175)

competencia sin precios estrategia para atraer consumidores enfocándose en el estilo, el servicio o la ubicación de un bien, sin tener que bajar su precio

nonprofit organization an institution that functions much like a business, but does not operate for the purpose of general profit (p. 209)

organización sin fines de lucro institución que funciona como una empresa, pero no opera con el propósito de generar ganancias

normal good a good that consumers demand more of when their incomes increase (p. 92)

bien normal bien que el consumidor demanda más cuando sus ingresos aumentan

O

obsolescence situation in which older products and processes become out-of-date (p. 59)

obsolescencia situación que ocurre cuando productos o procesos antiguos caen en desuso

offshoring the movement of some of a company's operations to another country (pp. 219, 505)

deslocalización traslado de las plantas productivas de una empresa a otro país

oligopoly a market structure in which a few large firms dominate a market (p. 177)
oligopolio estructura en la cual el mercado está dominado por unas pocas grandes empresas

open market operations the buying and selling of government securities in order to alter the supply of money (p. 433)
operaciones de mercado abierto compra y venta de valores del Estado para controlar la cantidad de dinero en circulación

open opportunity the principle that anyone can compete in the marketplace (p. 51)
oportunidad abierta principio que sostiene que cualquier persona puede competir en el mercado

operating budget a budget for day-to-day spending needs (p. 381)
presupuesto de operación presupuesto para los gastos diarios

operating cost the cost of operating a facility, such as a factory or a store (p. 122)
costo de operación costo de operar instalaciones como fábricas y tiendas

opportunity cost the most desirable alternative given up as the result of a decision (p. 9)
costo de oportunidad mejor alternativa que se desechó al tomarse una decisión

options contracts that give investors the right to buy or sell stock and other financial assets at a particular price until a specified future date (p. 295)
opciones contratos que le dan al inversionista el derecho de comprar o vender acciones u otros activos financieros a un determinado precio y dentro de un cierto período de tiempo

outside lag the time it takes for monetary policy to have an effect (p. 438)
demora externa cantidad de tiempo que demora en surtir efecto una política monetaria

outsourcing the practice of contracting with another company to do a specific job that would otherwise be done by a company's own workers (p. 219)
subcontratación práctica que consiste en contratar a otra compañía para realizar una tarea específica que los trabajadores de la compañía original podrían haber hecho

P

par value a bond's stated value, to be paid to the bondholder at maturity (p. 285)
valor nominal valor original de un bono u obligación que debe pagarse a su vencimiento

partnership a business organization owned by two or more persons who agree on a specific division of responsibilities and profits (p. 196)

sociedad dos o más personas organizadas para un fin comercial y con una división específica de responsabilidades y ganancias

patent a license that gives the inventor of a new product the exclusive right to sell it for a specific period of time (pp. 61, 167)
patente licencia que otorga al inventor de un nuevo producto el derecho exclusivo de venderlo por un determinado período de tiempo

patriotism love of one's country (p. 52)
patriotismo amor por el país propio

peak the height of an economic expansion, when real GDP stops rising (p. 315)
punto máximo máxima expansión económica, cuando el PIB cesa de crecer

per capita GDP a nation's gross domestic product divided by its population (p. 482)
PIB per cápita producto interno bruto de un país dividido entre su población

perfect competition a market structure in which a large number of firms all produce the same product and no single seller controls supply or price (p. 159)
competencia perfecta mercado en el que numerosas empresas producen el mismo producto y ninguna controla la oferta o el precio

personal exemption a set amount that taxpayers may subtract from their gross income for themselves, their spouse, and any dependents (p. 372)
deducción personal cantidad fija que el contribuyente puede deducir de su ingreso bruto a cuenta de sí mismo, su cónyuge y otros dependientes

personal property movable possessions or assets (p. 384)
propiedad personal activos o bienes muebles

physical capital the human-made objects used to create other goods and services (p. 6)
capital físico objetos construidos que se utilizan para crear bienes y servicios

population growth rate a measure of how rapidly a country's population increases in a given year (p. 487)
tasa de crecimiento de la población medida de cuán rápido crece la población de un país en un año

portfolio a collection of financial assets (p. 282)
portafolio conjunto de activos financieros

poverty rate the percentage of people who live in households with income below the official poverty line (p. 350)
tasa de pobreza porcentaje de personas que viven en hogares con un ingreso por debajo de la línea de pobreza

poverty threshold an income level below that which is needed to support families or households (pp. 68, 349)
nivel de pobreza ingreso por debajo del nivel necesario para mantener a una familia o un hogar

predatory pricing selling a product below cost for a short period of time to drive competitors out of the market (p. 180)
precios depredatorios vender un producto por debajo de su costo por un corto período de tiempo para sacar a los competidores del mercado

price ceiling a maximum price that can legally be charged for a good or service (p. 137)

precio tope precio máximo que un vendedor puede cobrar legalmente por un bien o servicio

price discrimination the division of consumers into groups based on how much they will pay for a good (p. 171)

discriminación de precios práctica que consiste en dividir a los consumidores en grupos según la cantidad que están dispuestos a pagar por un bien

price fixing an agreement among firms to charge one price for the same good (p. 179)

fijación de precios acuerdo entre compañías para cobrar un determinado precio por el mismo bien

price floor a minimum price for a good or service (p. 139)

precio mínimo límite inferior al que puede llegar el precio de un bien o servicio

price index a measurement that shows how the average price of a standard group of goods changes over time (p. 343)

índice de precios medida que muestra el cambio del precio promedio de un grupo de bienes estándar durante un tiempo determinado

price level the average of all prices in an economy (p. 313)

nivel de precios promedio de los precios en una economía

price war a series of competitive price cuts that lowers the market price below the cost of production (p. 179)

guerra de precios serie de cortes de precio competitivos que reduce el precio de mercado por debajo de su costo de producción

primary market a market for selling financial assets that can be redeemed only by the original holder (p. 290)

mercado primario mercado para vender activos financieros que sólo pueden ser cobrados por el propietario original

prime rate the rate of interest that banks charge on short-term loans to their best customers (p. 433)

tipo de interés preferencial tipo de interés que un banco aplica a los préstamos de corto plazo de sus mejores clientes

principal the amount of money borrowed (p. 268)

capital cantidad de dinero prestado

private property property that is owned by individuals or companies, not by the government or the people as a whole (p. 40)

propiedad privada propiedad que le pertenece a individuos o a compañías, no al gobierno o al público en general

private property rights the principle that people have the right to control their possessions and use them as they wish (p. 51)

derechos de propiedad privada principio según el cual una persona tiene el derecho de controlar y usar sus pertenencias como quiera

private sector the part of the economy that involves the transactions of individuals and businesses (p. 63)

sector privado parte de la economía que tiene que ver con los negocios de individuos y de compañías

privatization the process of selling businesses or services operated by the government to individual investors, and then allowing them to compete in the marketplace (pp. 43, 495)

privatización proceso de venta de compañías o servicios operados por el gobierno a inversionistas individuales para que compitan en el mercado

producer cooperative an agricultural marketing cooperative that helps members sell their products (p. 209)

cooperativa de productores cooperativa agraria que ayuda a sus miembros a vender sus productos

product market the arena of exchange in which households purchase goods and services from firms (p. 31)

mercado de productos lugar de intercambio comercial en el que una familia compra bienes y servicios de empresas

production possibilities curve a graph that shows alternative ways to use an economy's productive resources (p. 13)

curva de posibilidades de producción gráfico que muestra distintas maneras de utilizar los recursos de producción en una economía

production possibilities frontier a line on a production possibilities curve that shows the maximum possible output an economy can produce (p. 14)

frontera de posibilidades de producción línea en una curva de posibilidad de producción que indica el límite máximo de lo que puede producir una economía

productive capacity the maximum output that an economy can sustain over a period of time without increasing inflation (p. 400)

capacidad de producción volumen máximo de producción que una economía puede sostener por un período de tiempo sin que aumente la inflación

productivity of labor the quantity of output produced by a unit of labor (p. 226)

productividad cantidad de rendimiento que genera una unidad de trabajo

professional labor work that requires advanced skills and education (p. 229)

trabajo profesional trabajo que requiere habilidades y estudios avanzados

professional organization a nonprofit organization that works to improve the image, working conditions, and skill levels of people in particular occupations (p. 211)

organización profesional organización sin fines de lucro que busca mejorar la imagen, las condiciones de trabajo y la competencia técnica de individuos que ejercen una determinada profesión

profit the amount of money a business receives in excess of its expenses (p. 25)

ganancias cantidad de dinero que una compañía recibe al deducirse sus gastos

profit motive the incentive that drives individuals and business owners to improve their material well-being (p. 51)

motivación de ganancia incentivo que conlleva al individuo o compañía a mejorar su bienestar material

progressive tax a tax for which the percentage of income paid in taxes increases as income increases (p. 364)

impuesto progresivo impuesto cuyo porcentaje aumenta al aumentar el ingreso del contribuyente

property tax a tax based on real estate and other property (p. 366)

impuesto sobre la propiedad impuesto basado en bienes inmuebles y otros tipos de propiedad

proportional tax a tax for which the percentage of income paid in taxes remains the same at all income levels (p. 364)

impuesto proporcional impuesto cuyo porcentaje permanece constante en cualquier nivel de ingreso

prospectus an investment report that provides information to potential investors (p. 282)

prospecto documento que provee información pertinente a posibles inversionistas

protectionism the use of trade barriers to shield domestic industries from foreign competition (p. 457)

proteccionismo uso de barreras comerciales para proteger las industrias domésticas de los competidores extranjeros

public disclosure laws laws requiring companies to provide information about their products or services (p. 54)

ley de divulgación pública ley que exige que una compañía provea información acerca de sus productos o servicios

public good a shared good or service for which it would be inefficient or impractical to make consumers pay individually and to exclude those who did not pay (p. 62)

bien público bien que satisface una necesidad pública o colectiva por lo que resulta ineficiente hacer pagar a los consumidores individualmente

public interest the concerns of society as a whole (p. 53)

interés público preocupaciones de la sociedad en conjunto

public sector the part of the economy that involves the transactions of the government (p. 63)

sector público parte de la economía que tiene que ver con los negocios del gobierno

publicly held corporation a type of corporation that sells stock on the open market (p. 203)

compañía pública corporación que vende acciones en el mercado abierto

purchasing power the ability to purchase goods and services (p. 342)

poder adquisitivo capacidad para comprar bienes y servicios

put option a contract for selling stock at a particular price until a specified future date (p. 295)

opción de venta contrato para vender acciones a un determinado precio durante un período de tiempo preestablecido

Q

quantity supplied the amount that a supplier is willing and able to supply at a specific price (p. 109)

cantidad ofrecida cantidad que un proveedor está dispuesto a ofrecer por un precio específico

quantity theory the theory that too much money in the economy causes inflation (p. 346)

teoría de la cantidad teoría que establece que la presencia de mucho dinero en la economía causa inflación

R

rationing a system of allocating scarce goods and services using criteria other than price (p. 151)

racionamiento sistema de distribución de los bienes y servicios escasos usando un criterio que no se basa en el precio

real GDP GDP expressed in constant, or unchanging, prices (p. 310)

PIB real PIB expresado a precios constantes o invariables

real GDP per capita real GDP divided by the total population of a country (p. 323)

PIB real per cápita PIB real dividido por la población total de un país

real property land and any permanent structures on the land to which a person has legal title (p. 384)

inmueble terreno y cualquier estructura permanente en el terreno que le pertenece a una persona según un título legal

recession a prolonged economic contraction (p. 316)

recesión contracción económica prolongada

referendum a proposed law submitted directly to the public (p. 58)

referendo propuesta de ley que se somete directamente al público

regressive tax a tax for which the percentage of income paid in taxes decreases as income increases (p. 366)

impuesto regresivo impuesto para el cual el porcentaje de ingresos que se paga disminuye a medida que el ingreso aumenta

regulation government intervention in a market that affects the production of a good (p. 125)

regulación intervención del gobierno en un mercado que afecta la producción de un bien

remittances cash payments sent by workers who have migrated to a new country to family members in their home country (p. 505)

remesas pagos en efectivo que les envían los trabajadores inmigrantes a sus familiares en sus países de origen

rent control a price ceiling placed on apartment rent (p. 137)

control de renta precio tope del alquiler de apartamentos

representative money objects that have value because the holder can exchange them for something else of value (p. 254)

dinero representativo objetos que tienen valor porque su dueño lo puede cambiar por otros objetos de valor

required reserve ratio the fraction of deposits that banks are required to keep in reserve (p. 430)

tasa de encaje fracción de los depósitos que los bancos tienen que guardar en reserva

reserve requirements the amount of reserves that banks are required to keep on hand (p. 421)

encaje cantidad de reservas que los bancos deben mantener disponibles

reserves deposits that a bank keeps readily available as opposed to lending them out (p. 421)
  reservas depósitos que un banco tiene disponible, en vez de prestarlos

return the money an investor receives above and beyond the sum of money initially invested (p. 282)
  rendimiento dinero que un inversionista recibe por encima de la suma de dinero original que invirtió

revenue the income received by a government from taxes and other nontax sources (p. 364)
  ingreso dinero recibido por un gobierno que proviene de los impuestos y otras fuentes que no son fiscales

right-to-work law a measure that bans mandatory union membership (p. 238)
  ley de derecho al trabajo medida que establece que no es obligatorio ser miembro de un sindicato

royalties the share of earnings given by a franchisee as payment to the franchiser (p. 201)
  regalías ganancias compartidas que otorga el dueño de una franquicia como pago a quien otorga la concesión

S

safety net a set of government programs that protect people who face unfavorable economic conditions (p. 26)
  programas de ayuda social grupo de programas del gobierno que protegen a las personas con dificultades económicas

sales tax a tax based on goods or services that are sold (p. 366)
  impuesto a las ventas impuesto sobre los bienes y servicios que se venden

sanctions actions a nation or group of nations takes in order to punish or put pressure on another nation (p. 456)
  sanciones acciones que una nación o un grupo de naciones toma para castigar o presionar a otra nación

saving income not used for consumption (p. 325)
  ahorro ingreso que no se consume

savings bond a low-denomination bond issued by the United States government (p. 287)
  bono de ahorro bono de baja denominación ofrecido por el gobierno de los Estados Unidos

savings rate the proportion of disposable income that is saved (p. 325)
  tasa de ahorro proporción de los ingresos disponibles que se ahorran

scarcity the principle that limited amounts of goods and services are available to meet unlimited wants (p. 4)
  escasez situación en la que existe una cantidad limitada de bienes y servicios disponibles para satisfacer deseos ilimitados

screening effect the theory that the completion of college indicates to employers that a job applicant is intelligent and hard working (p. 221)
  efecto de selección teoría de que completar estudios universitarios indica que un candidato a un empleo es inteligente y trabaja duro

search costs the financial and opportunity costs that consumers pay when searching for a good or service (p. 146)
  costo de búsqueda costos financieros y de oportunidad que los consumidores pagan mientras buscan un bien o servicio

seasonal unemployment type of unemployment that occurs as a result of harvest schedules, vacations, or when industries make seasonal shifts in their production schedule (p. 338)
  desempleo estacional tipo de desempleo que ocurre durante las cosechas, las vacaciones o cuando las industrias establecen turnos durante ciertos períodos especiales de su calendario de producción

secondary market a market for reselling financial assets (p. 290)
  mercado secundario mercado en el que se revenden bienes financieros

self-interest an individual's own personal gain (p. 33)
  interés personal beneficio de una persona

semi-skilled labor work that requires minimal specialized skills and education (p. 229)
  trabajo semicalificado trabajo que requiere destrezas especializadas y educación mínimas

service cooperative a type of cooperative that provides a service rather than a good (p. 209)
  cooperativa de servicios tipo de cooperativa que ofrece un servicio en vez de un bien

services the actions or activities that one person performs for another (p. 3)
  servicios acciones o actividades que una persona ejecuta para otra persona

share a portion of stock (p. 291)
  acción porción del capital de una empresa

shortage a situation in which consumers want more of a good or service than producers are willing to make available at a particular price (pp. 4, 134)
  escasez situación en la que los consumidores quieren un bien o servicio en una cantidad mayor a la que los productores están dispuestos a producir a un precio determinado

skilled labor work that requires specialized skills and training (p. 229)
  trabajo calificado trabajo que requiere destrezas y capacitación profesional especializadas

socialism a range of economic and political systems based on the belief that wealth should be evenly distributed throughout society (p. 36)
  socialismo serie de sistemas económicos y políticos que se basan en la creencia de que la riqueza de una sociedad debe ser distribuida en partes iguales entre sus miembros

sole proprietorship a business owned and managed by a single individual (p. 191)
  empresa unipersonal negocio que le pertenece y es administrado por un solo individuo

special economic zone designated regions that operate under different economic laws from the rest of the country, in order to attract foreign investment and promote exports (p. 498)

zona económica especial región designada en un país donde se promueve la inversión extranjera, los negocios toman la mayoría de sus decisiones y se permite el funcionamiento de compañías extranjeras

specialization the concentration of the productive efforts of individuals and businesses on a limited number of activities (p. 30)

especialización concentración del esfuerzo productivo de las personas y los negocios en un número limitado de actividades

specie coined money, usually gold or silver, used to back paper money (p. 254)

metálico dinero en monedas, generalmente de oro o plata, que se usa para respaldar el papel moneda

speculation the practice of making high-risk investments with borrowed money in hopes of getting a big return (p. 298)

especulación práctica que consiste en hacer inversiones de alto riesgo con dinero prestado, con la esperanza de obtener una ganancia alta

stabilization program an agreement between a debtor nation and the International Monetary Fund in which the nation agrees to change its economic policy to match IMF goals (p. 493)

programa de estabilización acuerdo entre una nación deudora y el Fondo Monetario Internacional mediante el cual la nación se compromete a cambiar su política económica para cumplir con los objetivos del FMI

stagflation a decline in real GDP combined with a rise in the price level (p. 316)

estanflación disminución del PIB real combinado con un aumento de precios

standard of living level of economic prosperity (p. 27)

nivel de vida nivel de prosperidad económica

start-up costs the expenses a new business must pay before it can begin to produce and sell goods (p. 162)

costos de inicio gastos que un negocio nuevo debe hacer antes de que comience a producir y vender bienes

stock a certificate of ownership in a corporation (p. 202)

acción certificado de propiedad de parte de una corporación

stock exchange a market for buying and selling stock (p. 294)

bolsa de valores mercado en el cual se compran y venden acciones

stock split the division of each single share of a company's stock into more than one share (p. 293)

desdoble división de cada acción de una compañía en más de una acción

stockbroker a person who links buyers and sellers of stock (p. 293)

corredor de bolsa persona que conecta a compradores y vendedores de la bolsa

store of value something that keeps its value if it is stored rather than spent (p. 251)

mantenimiento del valor algo que mantiene su valor si se guarda, no cuando se gasta

strike an organized work stoppage intended to force an employer to address union demands (p. 237)

huelga suspensión organizada del trabajo, que se ejecuta para obligar a un empleador a cumplir con las peticiones de un sindicato

structural unemployment type of unemployment that occurs when workers' skills do not match those needed for the jobs available (p. 336)

desempleo estructural tipo de desempleo que ocurre cuando las destrezas de los trabajadores no cubren las necesidades de los empleos disponibles

subsidy a government payment that supports a business or market (p. 124)

subsidio pago del gobierno que apoya un negocio o mercado

subsistence agriculture level of farming in which a person raises only enough food to feed his or her family (p. 486)

agricultura de subsistencia tipo de agricultura en el que una persona sólo cosecha lo necesario para mantenerse a sí misma y a su familia

substitutes goods that are used in place of one another (p. 96)

sustitutos bienes que se usan para remplazar otros bienes

substitution effect when consumers react to an increase in a good's price by consuming less of that good and more of a substitute good (p. 87)

efecto de sustitución reacción de los consumidores ante el aumento del precio de un bien, que consiste en disminuir el consumo de un producto y aumentar el consumo de un sustituto

supply the amount of goods available (p. 109)

oferta cantidad disponible de bienes

supply curve a graph of the quantity supplied of a good at various prices (p. 113)

curva de la oferta gráfica que representa la cantidad ofrecida de un bien a varios precios

supply schedule a chart that lists how much of a good a supplier will offer at various prices (p. 112)

tabla de la demanda tabla que muestra la cantidad de un bien que un proveedor ofrecerá a diferentes precios

supply shock a sudden shortage of a good (p. 151)

shock de la oferta escasez repentina de un bien

supply-side economics a school of thought based on the idea that the supply of goods drives the economy (p. 404)

economía por el lado de la oferta escuela de pensamiento que se basa en la idea de que la oferta de bienes mueve la economía

surplus when quantity supplied is more than quantity demanded (p. 136)

superávit condición en la que la oferta es mayor que la demanda

sustainable development goal of meeting current development needs without using up resources needed by future generations (p. 506)

desarrollo sostenible objetivo que consiste en cubrir las necesidades de desarrollo actuales sin gastar todos los recursos que necesitarán las generaciones futuras

T

tariff a tax on imported goods (pp. 374, 455)
   arancel impuesto que se aplica a las importaciones

tax a required payment to a local, state, or national government (p. 364)
   impuesto tributo o pago hecho al gobierno local, estatal o nacional

tax assessor an official who determines the value of property (p. 385)
   tasador especialista que determina el valor de una propiedad

tax base the income, property, good, or service that is subject to a tax (p. 366)
   base imponible ingreso, propiedad, bien o servicio bajo obligación tributaria

tax credit a variable amount that taxpayers may subtract from the total amount of their income tax (p. 372)
   crédito fiscal cantidad variable que los contribuyentes pueden restar del total de su deuda tributaria

tax deduction a variable amount that taxpayers may subtract from their gross income (p. 372)
   deducción fiscal cantidad variable que los contribuyentes pueden restar de su ingreso bruto

tax exempt not subject to taxes (p. 383)
   libre de impuestos exento de impuestos

tax incentive the use of taxation to discourage or encourage certain types of behavior (p. 374)
   incentivo fiscal régimen tributario que tiene como objetivo estimular o no fomentar ciertas actividades económicas

tax return a form used to file income taxes (p. 370)
   declaración de impuestos formulario en el cual se reporta un impuesto, como la declaración de impuestos sobre la renta

taxable income the earnings on which tax must be paid; total income minus exemptions and deductions (p. 372)
   ingreso imponible entradas sobre las cuales se pagan impuestos; ingreso total menos exenciones y deducciones

technological progress an increase in efficiency gained by producing more output without using more inputs (p. 327)
   progreso tecnológico incremento en la eficiencia al producir más usando menos recursos

thinking at the margin the process of deciding how much more or less to do (p. 11)
   pensar al margen decidir si se debe hacer o usar una cantidad mayor de algún recurso

tight money policy a monetary policy that reduces the money supply (p. 436)
   política monetaria restrictiva política monetaria que reduce la oferta de dinero

total cost the sum of fixed costs plus variable costs (p. 119)
   costo total suma de costos fijos y costos variables

total revenue the total amount of money a company receives by selling goods or services (p. 103)
   ingreso total cantidad total de dinero que recibe una compañía al vender bienes y servicios

trade association nonprofit organizations that promote the interests of particular industries (p. 212)
   asociación mercantil organizaciones sin fines de lucro que promueven los intereses de ciertas industrias en particular

trade barrier a means of preventing a foreign product or service from freely entering a nation's territory (p. 455)
   barreras comerciales medida preventiva que reduce el flujo de bienes importados a un país

trade deficit situation in which a nation imports more goods and services than it exports (p. 468)
   déficit comercial situación en la cual las importaciones de bienes y servicios de un país son más altas que sus exportaciones

trade surplus situation in which a nation exports more goods and services than it imports (p. 468)
   superávit comercial situación en la cual las exportaciones de bienes y servicios de un país son más altas que las importaciones

trade war a cycle of escalating trade barriers (p. 457)
   guerra comercial ciclo en el cual las barreras comerciales escalan

trade-off the alternatives that we give up when we choose one course of action over another (p. 8)
   compensación acto de entregar un beneficio para obtener otro beneficio mayor

traditional economy an economic system that relies on habit, custom, or ritual to decide the three key economic questions (p. 28)
   economía tradicional sistema económico que depende de hábitos, costumbres o rituales para decidir las tres preguntas económicas clave

Treasury bill a government bond with a maturity date of 26 weeks or less (p. 409)
   Bono del Tesoro documento emitido por el Estado con un vencimiento a 26 semanas o menos

Treasury bond a government bond that is issued in terms of 30 years (p. 409)
   Bono del Estado documento emitido por el Estado con un vencimiento a 30 años

Treasury note a government bond with a term of from 2 to 10 years (p. 409)
   Pagarés del Tesoro documento emitido por el Estado con un vencimiento de 2 a 10 años

trough the lowest point of an economic contraction, when real GDP stops falling (p. 316)
   punto mínimo punto más bajo en una contracción económica, cuando el PIB real deja de descender

trust an illegal grouping of companies that discourages competition, similar to a cartel (p. 181)
   trust alianza sin fundamentación legal entre compañías para evitar la competencia

U

underemployed working at a job for which one is overqualified or working part-time when full-time work is desired (p. 340)
subempleado estar calificado en exceso para un trabajo o trabajar a tiempo parcial cuando se desea trabajar a tiempo completo

underutilization the use of fewer resources than an economy is capable of using (p. 15)
subutilización capacidad no utilizada de los recursos que una economía posee

unemployment rate the percentage of a nation's labor force that is unemployed (p. 339)
tasa de desempleo porcentaje de la población nacional sin empleo

Uniform Partnership Act a uniform law establishing rules for partnerships, which partnerships must follow if they have no partnership agreement (p. 198)
Ley de Estandarización de Sociedades de Personas ley que establece las reglas que los socios deben seguir si no existe un contrato de asociación

unit of account a means for comparing the values of goods and services (p. 251)
unidad de cuenta medida para comparar los valores de bienes y servicios

unitary elastic describes demand whose elasticity is exactly equal to one (p. 98)
elasticidad unitaria relación de demanda con un coeficiente igual a uno

unskilled labor work that requires no specialized skills, education, or training (p. 229)
trabajo no especializado trabajo que no requiere habilidades, estudios o entrenamiento especializados

V

variable a factor that can change (p. 112)
variable factor que puede cambiar

variable cost a cost that rises or falls depending on the quantity produced (p. 118)
costo variable costo que aumenta o disminuye cuando la cantidad producida incrementa o disminuye

vertical merger two or more firms involved in different stages of producing the same good or service (p. 206)
fusión vertical agrupación de dos o más compañías involucradas en distintas fases de la producción de un bien o servicio

voluntary exchange the principle that people may decide what, when, and how they want to buy and sell (p. 51)
intercambio voluntario principio según el cual toda persona puede decidir cómo, cuándo y qué vender

W

wage-price spiral the process by which rising wages cause higher prices, and higher prices cause higher wages (p. 347)
espiral salarios-precios aumento de los precios, producido por el aumento de los salarios, que resulta en una nueva demanda de aumento de los salarios

want something that people desire but that is not necessary for survival (p. 3)
deseo algo que una persona quiere, pero que no es necesario para sobrevivir

welfare government aid to the poor (p. 69)
asistencia social ayuda que el gobierno presta a los pobres

white-collar worker someone who works in a professional or clerical job and who usually earns a weekly salary (p. 239)
empleado de oficina persona que desempeña un trabajo de tipo profesional o administrativo y que generalmente gana un salario semanal

withholding taking tax payments out of an employee's pay before he or she receives it (p. 370)
retención porcentaje que se descuenta del salario de un empleado a cuenta del pago de impuestos

work ethic a commitment to the value of work (p. 61)
ética profesional respeto al valor del trabajo

workfare a program requiring work in exchange for temporary government assistance (p. 356)
workfare programa ofrecido por el gobierno mediante el cual las personas deben trabajar para poder recibir asistencia social temporal

Y

yield the annual rate of return on a bond if the bond is held to maturity (p. 285)
rendimiento tasa anual de rendimiento que da un bono u obligación a su vencimiento

Z

zoning laws laws in a city or town that designate certain areas, or zones, for residential and business use (p. 193)
reglamentos de zonificación leyes que designan ciertas áreas o zonas de una ciudad para uso residencial o comercial

Index

Note: Entries with a page number followed by a *(c)* denote reference to a chart on that page; those followed by a *(p)* denote a photo; those followed by an *(m)* denote a map; those followed by a *(g)* denote a graph.

INDEX

INDEX

H

INDEX

INDEX

INDEX

Acknowledgments

Staff Credits

The people who made up the *Prentice Hall Economics* team are listed below.

Faiza Aziem, Eytan Bernstein, M.J. Black, Marcy Boos, Megan Bowen, Jeff Bradley, Jane Breen, Shari Cavanaugh-Moore, Anthony Chen, Lori-Anne Cohen, Brett Creane, Kerry Dunn, Anne Falzone, Julia R. Gilstein, Julie Gurdin, Rebecca Hall, Rebecca Harth, Jacob Hodel, Blair Jones, Maddy Kadish, John Kingston, Laurie McKenna, Alison Muff, Pak Nicodemus, Jennifer Paley, Travis Ramirez, Jennifer Ribnicky, Melissa Shustyk, Greg Slook, Stephanie Smith, Merle Uesoo, Kristen VanEtten, Bill Whitmer, Rachel Winter

Additional Credits
Thomas J. Bulger, Mona Daddario, Kathy Burnett, Melissa Pepe

Art/Map Credits

Art: Keithley and Associates (all charts/graphs except where noted) Jennifer Ribnicky: 70–71, S-1, S-3–S-9. John Kingston: S-19–S-20.

Illustrations: Asaf Hanuka/Gerald & Cullen Rapp: 3, 23, 49, 85, 109, 133, 155, 159, 191, 217, 249, 277, 307, 335, 363, 391, 419, 447, and 481 plus all *How the Economy Works* feature's art. Marcelo Baez/Shannon Associates: all *Economics & You* feature's art. Funnel Inc.: 32, 50, 204, 308, 364, 393, 421, 459. Doug Holgate/Shannon Associates: 228 and 292. **Personal Finance Illustrations:** Dale Rutter PF 8; Spork PF 12; John Sledd PF 16–17; Shane Rebenschied PF 22–23; Christopher Short PF 24; Nick Dimitriadis PF 26–27; Sean Kane PF 29; Mitch Mortimer PF 42; Ernest Albanese PF 45; John Sledd PF 46.

Infographics: Leslie Carlson/Martha Productions Inc. with additional design by John Kingston: 06, 52, 178, 200, 222, 271, 321, 366, 457, 505.

Maps: GeoNova.

Photo Credits

Every effort has been made to secure permission and provide appropriate credit for photographic material. The publisher deeply regrets any omission and pledges to correct errors called to its attention in subsequent editions.

Unless otherwise acknowledged, all photographs are the property of Pearson Education, Inc.

Photo locators denoted as follows: Top (T), Center (C), Bottom (B), Left (L), Right (R), Background (Bkgd)

Cover and Title Page images: Speakers: © Christopher Gould/Getty Images; **Hi-rise contruction:** © Luis Castaneda Inc./The Image Bank/Getty Images; **Central Park:** © Mitchell Funk/Getty Images; **Traffic:** © Kim Steele/Getty Images; **House Construction:** © Lester Lefkowitz/The Image Bank/Getty Images; **Basketball, Cows, Satellite Dish, Piggy Bank, Wood, Pulley, Grass, U.S. Capital, Water Cooler, Condiments, Conveyor Belt, Dog/Cat:** Getty Images; **Stock Board:** © Mark Segal/Getty Images; **Tractor:** Hemera; **Wind Turbines:** © Spike Mafford/Getty Images; **Recycle Bin:** © ThinkStock/SuperStock; **Tomato & Diploma/Books:** Jupiter Royalty Free; **ATM, Sneakers, Coins, Game Controller:** Pearson Curriculum Group

Text

ii (B) Getty Images; iii (Bkgrd) iStockphoto; v (Bkgrd) iStockphoto; vi (B) Erick Nguyen/iStockphoto, (T) Voloh/Shutterstock; vii (TC) Joseph Sohm, Visions of America/Corbis, (TL) iStockphoto, (TR) Mira; viii (TL) iStockphoto, (C) John David Bigl III/Shutterstock, Voloh/Shutterstock; ix (TC) Joseph Sohm, Visions of America/Corbis, (TR) Mira; x (TC) Joseph Sohm, Visions of America/Corbis, (TL) iStockphoto, (TR) Mira; xi (TC) Joseph Sohm, Visions of America/Corbis, (TL) iStockphoto, (TR) Mira; xii (TC) Joseph Sohm, Visions of America/Corbis, (TL, B) iStockphoto, (TR) Mira; xiii (TC) Joseph Sohm, Visions of America/Corbis, (TL, B) iStockphoto, (TR) Mira; xiv (TC) Joseph Sohm, Visions of America/Corbis, (TL, B) iStockphoto, (TR) Mira; xv (B) Bettina Baumgartner/Shutterstock, (TR) iStockphoto, (CC) Jim Jurica/iStockphoto, (C) John David Bigl III/Shutterstock, (TL) Mira, (TC) Photo Researchers, Inc.; xvi Voloh/Shutterstock; xix (T) iStockphoto; xx (CC) Darren McCollester/Stringer/Getty Images, (T) Lantern Books; xxi (T) iStockphoto; xxiii Authentic Education; xxiv (L) Rui Vale de Sousa/Shutterstock, (R) Shutterstock; xxvi Martin Fischer/Shutterstock; xxvii Terekhov/Shutterstock; xxviii (B) Getty Images; 1 (C) © Digital Vision Ltd./SuperStock, (Bkgrd) © Royalty-Free/Corbis, (R) Fuse/Jupiter Images, (C) iStockphoto; 2 (C) Bill Aron/PhotoEdit, Inc., (B) iStockphoto; 6 Eric Gevaert/1Stockphoto/iStockphoto, (Bkgrd) Yhloon/iStockphoto; 10 (B) Cartoon Stock, (T) Stocksnapper/iStockphoto; 15 © Associated

Acknowledgments

Photo Credits

Press; **16** Richard Cummins/SuperStock; **18** Michael Maslin, 2000/The New Yorker Collection. All Rights Reserved./Cartoon Bank/Conde Nast Publications; **20** Mark Evans/iStockphoto; **22** David H. Wells/Corbis; **25** Rich Pedroncelli/© Associated Press; **28** Gail Mooney-Kelly/Alamy Images; **29** (TR) Damian Dovarganes/© Associated Press, (L) Najlah Feanny/Corbis; **30** (L) Mary Kay, Inc.; **32** (B) Cartoon Stock; **33** (B) © The Granger Collection, NY; (T) Bettmann/Corbis; **34** Cartoon Stock; **36** Jeremy Nicholl/Polaris Images; **37** © The Granger Collection, NY; **39** Barbara Davidson;Dallas Morning News/Corbis; **42** Jack Sullivan/Alamy Images; **44** (R) © Blend Images/Alamy Images, (TC) Home Business Magazine, (L) The Economist Magazine/The Economist Newspaper Ltd; **46** Ed Fuentesg/iStockphoto; **47** Fritz Hoffmann/Corbis; **48** (TC) Tony Freeman/PhotoEdit, Inc.; **50** (BC) Todd Gipstein/Corbis, (CC) © General Motors Corp. Used with permission, GM Media Archives. (TC) Andy Dean/iStockphoto, (TR) Carol Denbow/Plain and Simple Books, (BL) David H. Lewis/iStockphoto, (TL) Ford Motor Company, Mark R/Shutterstock, Nissan, (CR) Simon McConico/iStockphoto, (BR) Superstudio/Getty Images; **52** iStockphoto; **53** (R) Seth Wenig,Reuters/Corbis, (TL) © Associated Press; **55** Cartoon Stock; **56** (R) Tom & Dee Ann McCarthy/Corbis, (L) Richard Nowit/National Geographic Image Collection; **57** Ictor/iStockphoto; **58** (L) David Butow/Corbis, (TR) David Young-Wolff/PhotoEdit, Inc., (CC) Jeff Greenberg/PhotoEdit, Inc., (BR) Tony Freeman/PhotoEdit, Inc.; **59** Tony Bee/PhotoLibrary Group, Inc.; **60** David Young-Wolff/PhotoEdit, Inc.; **61** Mike Groll/© Associated Press; **62** Ben Russell/iStockphoto; **63** © Associated Press; **66** Yan-chun Tung/iStockphoto; **67** Environmental Protection Agency; **68** Time & Life Pictures/Getty Images; **70** (R) Bettmann/Corbis, (L) Corbis; **71** (TL) Jose Luis Pelaez, Inc/Blend Images/Getty Images, (TR) Brooks Kraft/Corbis, (BR) Manuel Balce Ceneta/© Associated Press; **72** (T) Dennis MacDonald/PhotoEdit, Inc., (B) Mark Richards/PhotoEdit, Inc.; **74** Shutterstock; **75** Cartoon courtesy of Gary Brookins; **82** (CC) Cartoon Stock, (TR) Linda McCarthy, (BL) Photo Researchers, Inc.; **83** (TC) Joe Sohm/The Image Works, Inc.; **84** Max Whittaker/Corbis; **86** (TL) David Eulitt, Topeka Capital-Journal/© Associated Press, (B) Spencer Grant/PhotoEdit, Inc.; **91** Marc Serota;Reuters/Corbis; **93** © Richard Levine/Alamy Images; **94** (T) A. Ramey/PhotoEdit, Inc.; **95** (T) © Associated Press, (TL) Random House Inc./© Random House Inc., (BL) Tony Freeman/PhotoEdit, Inc.; **96** J. A. Kraulis/Masterfile Corporation; **99** Copyright 2000, printed with permission by The Des Moines Register; **102** Andy Crawford and Steve Gorton/© DK Images; **106** Pamela Moore/iStockphoto; **107** Cartoon Stock; **108** Scott Olson/Getty Images; **110** (T) Edward Rozzo/Corbis, (B) Joel W. Rogers/Corbis; **111** Cartoon Stock; **114** (TL) Cynthia Johnson/Getty Images; **115** Catherine Karnow/Corbis; **116** Jeff Greenberg/PhotoEdit, Inc.; **122** Bill Pugliano/Getty Images; **123** (BL) © Chris Jones/Corbis, (R) Andrew Manley/iStockphoto; **126** (BCR) Kevin Fleming/Corbis, (BCL) Mark E. Gibson/Corbis, (Bkgrd) ML Sinibaldi/Corbis, (BL) David Freund/iStockphoto, (TR) Firefly Productions/Corbis, (BCL) Mehau Kulyk/Photo Researchers, Inc.; **127** (R) Peter Foley, EPA/Corbis, (L) Ray Stubblebine,Reuters/Corbis; **130** Vivian Moos/Corbis; **132** Lauren Zeid/eStock Photo; **135** (B) Cartoon Stock; **137** courtesy of City Harvest, photo by Danny Bright; **140** Nick Anderson/Cartoonist Group; **141** Robert Brenner/PhotoEdit, Inc.; **142** © Associated Press; **146** (T) Getty Images, (T) Kim Kulish/Corbis; **149** T. Kruesselmann/Corbis; **150** Scott Barrow, Inc./SuperStock, (T) Getty Images; **152** (R) © Associated Press, (L) The Granger Collection, NY; **156** Jean-Paul Ferrero/Minden Pictures; **157** (BL) Mike Davies, The Journal News/Tribune Media Services; **158** (TC) Nigel Kinrade/Sports Illustrated/Getty Images; **161** (B) Cartoon Stock; **163** (L) © GerryRousseau/Alamy Images, (R) Digital Vision/Alamy; **164** Tomas Bercic/iStockphoto; **167** (L) © The Granger Collection, NY, (R) 1998 Applewood Books; **169** Terrell Lloyd/NFL/Getty Images; **172** (L) Peter Titmuss/Alamy Images, (R) Chip Henderson Photography/Chip Henderson, (CC) Corbis; **173** Robert Harbison/© Robert Harbison; **174** Soren Pilman/iStockphoto; **178** Andrew Penner/iStockphoto; **180** © The Granger Collection, NY; **181** (TR) Corbis, (BR) Jeremy Swinborne/iStockphoto; **186** Monika Adamczyk/iStockphoto; **187** Copyright 2006 Eric Allie; All rights reserved./Cagle Cartoons, Inc.; **188** (T) Linda McCarthy, (BL) Photo Researchers, Inc., (CC) Thaves, "FRANK & ERNEST"/Dist. by Newspaper Enterprise Association, Inc./United Media; **189** (TC) © Masterfile Royalty-Free; **190** (TC) Jeff Greenberg/PhotoEdit, Inc.; **192** Connie Coleman/Getty Images; **193** Kevin Dodge/Masterfile Corporation; **195** Arnie Levin,1997/The New Yorker Collection. All Rights Reserved./Cartoon Bank/Conde Nast Publications; **197** Tony Freeman/PhotoEdit, Inc.; **200** Alan Schein/Corbis, (CR) Dragan Trifunovic/Corbis, (Inset) Eric Gevaert/iStockphoto, (Bkgrd) iStockphoto; **203** Andrey Yurlov/Shutterstock; **204** (R) Cartoon Stock; **205** (L) 3M, (CC) Courtesy of SolarCity/Solar City, (CC) Damian Dovarganes/© Associated Press; **209** (T) Steven Dahlman/SuperStock, (B) Mike Mergen/The New York Times/Redux Pictures; **210** Zhu Jianguo/ChinaFotoPress/Getty Images; **211** Darren McCollester/Stringer/Getty Images; **212** Mark Parisi/Atlantic Feature Syndicate; **214** Kathryn Bell/Shutterstock; **216** (TC) JPL/UA/Lockheed Martin/NASA; **218** Stockcam/iStockphoto; **220** Skip ODonnell/iStockphoto; **222** Nikhil Gangavane/Dreamstime LLC; **223** (R, L) © Jim West/Alamy Images; **224** Rob Marmion/Shutterstock; **227** James Leynse/Corbis; **228** (TCR) Malcolm Romain/iStockphoto; **231** Cartoon Stock; **234** (T) Gideon Mendel/Corbis, (TL) James L. Amos/Corbis; **236** (B) © 1976 George Ballis/Take Stock/The Image Works, Inc., (BCL) © Associated Press, (T) © The Granger Collection, NY, (TCR) Underwood & Underwood/Corbis; **237** (L) Bettmann/Corbis, © Associated Press; **242** Marmaduke St. John/Alamy; **244** © Associated Press; **246** (CC) Alan Dunn,1970/The New Yorker Collection. All Rights Reserved./Cartoon Bank/Conde Nast Publications, (TR) Linda McCarthy, (BL) Photo Researchers, Inc.; **247** (TC) Spencer Platt/Getty Images; **248** (TC) Tetra Images/Getty Images; **250** (B) Kate Warren (c) Museum of Mankind/British Museum/DK Images; **252** Bob Daemmrich/PhotoEdit, Inc.; **253** (L) JoAnn Frederick/Mira, (BR) US Mint, (TR) US Treasury Dept.; **254** (T) That's Life, Mike Twohy; All Rights Reserved. Used with permission of Mike Twohy and the Cartoonist Group/Cartoonist Group; **256** (T, B) US Treasury Dept.; **257** © The Granger Collection, NY; **258** © The Granger Collection, NY; **260** (R) Bettmann/Corbis, (TL) Stephen Chernin/Getty Images; **262** Spencer Grant/PhotoEdit, Inc.; **268** Ed Bock/Corbis; **269** Ian MckinneII/Getty Images; **271** Lee Jae-Won/Corbis; **272** (BL) Jesus Jauregui/iStockphoto, (R) Marc Schlossman/Getty Images, (CL) Metropolitan Transportation Authority; **274** © The Granger Collection, NY; **276** (TC) Ted S. Warren/© Associated Press; **278** Artiga Photo/Corbis; **281** (T) Alan Schein, Zefa/Corbis, (B) Ravi Tahilramani/iStockphoto; **282** Lee Lorenz,2001/The New Yorker Collection. All Rights Reserved./Cartoon Bank/Conde Nast Publications; **284** Corbis/Corbis; **291** White Packert/Getty Images; **292** Cartoon courtesy of Dan Rosandich; **297** Justin Lane/Corbis; **298** Kristie

Bull/Graylock/© Associated Press; **299** Bettmann/Corbis, (TL) Corbis; **303** Cartoon Stock; **304** (TR) Linda McCarthy, (CC) Mike Peters/Cartoonist Group, (BL) Photo Researchers, Inc.; **305** (TC) C. Devan/Corbis; **306** (TC) AGE Fotostock/SuperStock; **308** Bluestocking/iStockphoto; **317** Thaves, "FRANK & ERNEST"/Dist. by Newspaper Enterprise Association, Inc./United Media; **320** Bettmann/Corbis; **321** Bettmann/Corbis; **327** Getty Images, (T) Jeff Greenberg/Omni Photo Communications; **329** George B. Diebold/Corbis; **332** Kutberk/iStockphoto; **334** (TC) Getty Images; **338** (BL) Bob Sacha/Corbis; **340** (L, B) Act•1 Group/Act•1 Group; **342** (BL) YinYang/iStockphoto; **344** (B) Adam Zyglis, The Buffalo News; All rights reserved./Cagle Cartoons, Inc., (T) Pertusinas/iStockphoto; **349** Jeff Greenberg/The Image Works, Inc.; **352** (R, L) Project Match, (CC) Toby Herr of Project Match/Project Match; **354** (TL) © Associated Press, (B) Scott Olson/Getty Images; **355** Spencer Grant/PhotoEdit, Inc.; **358** Shutterstock; **360** (CC) Cartoon Stock, (TR) Linda McCarthy, (BL) Photo Researchers, Inc.; **361** (TC) Rudy Sulgan/Corbis; **362** (TC) AGE Fotostock/SuperStock; **365** Born Loser, Newspaper Enterprise Association, Inc./United Media; **367** Everett Kennedy Brown,EPA/Corbis; **368** Tony Mathews/Shutterstock; **371** (R) Acclaim Images, (L) Robert Brenner/PhotoEdit, Inc.; **372** Daniel Hulshizer/© Associated Press; **373** Cartoon Stock; **374** Jeff Chiu/© Associated Press; **376** Corbis; **377** Mark Richards/PhotoEdit, Inc.; **380** Cartoon Stock; **383** Construction Photography/Corbis; **385** Slobo Mitic/iStockphoto; **386** Alan Schein/Corbis; **388** Jozsef Szasz-Fabian/Shutterstock; **389** Michael Maslin/Cartoon Bank/Conde Nast Publications; **390** (TC) Jim Watson/AFP/Getty Images; **392** (BL) DHuss/iStockphoto; **393** (B) Mike Peters/King Features Syndicate; **394** Gary Connor/PhotoEdit, Inc.; **399** Minnesota Historical Society/Corbis; **400** Hulton-Deutsch Collection/Corbis; **401** (B) Underwood & Underwood/Corbis, (T) David J. and Janice L. Frent/Corbis; **402** George Mattei/Photo Researchers, Inc.; **406** (R) Barnabas Bosshart/Corbis, (L) Houghton Mifflin Company; **411** iStockphoto; **414** © Viviane Moos/Corbis; **416** Bill Ellzey/National Geographic Image Collection; **418** Jonathan Larsen/Shutterstock; **420** (B) Daryl Cagle, MSNBCCartooons; All rights reserved./Cagle Cartoons, Inc.; **424** (B) AFP/Getty Images, (T) Monika Graff/UPI Photo/NewsCom; **425** Igor Vorobyov/iStockphoto; **429** Lew Long/Corbis; **432** Gabe Palmer/Corbis; **435** Jeff Greenberg/PhotoEdit, Inc.; **436** (T) Cover of FREE TO CHOOSE: A PERSONAL STATEMENT, copyright 1980 by Milton Friedman and Rose D. Friedman, reproduced with permission of Houghton Mifflin Harcourt Publishing Company. (R) Getty Images; **442** Antar Dayal/Corbis; **443** Cartoon Stock; **444** (CC) King Features Syndicate, (TR) Linda McCarthy, (BL) Photo Researchers, Inc.; **445** (TC) Michael Newman/PhotoEdit, Inc.; **446** (TC) George Ostertag/SuperStock; **452** (R) © Associated Press; **453** Kim Kulish/Corbis; **456** Todd Pitt/Todd Plitt/Imagebox; **457** Jason Stitt/Shutterstock; **459** (B) Cartoon Courtesy of Earl Engleman; **460** baur/Shutterstock; **462** Ryan Pyle/Corbis; **464** Kaj R. Svensson/Photo Researchers, Inc.; **466** Rich Pedroncelli/© Associated Press; **467** Wendy Kaveney/Jaynes Gallery/DanitaDelimont/NewsCom; **468** (Bkgrd) Michael Newman/PhotoEdit, Inc., (Inset) Image Source White/Alamy; **472** Alex Segre/Alamy Images; **474** (L) Billy E. Barnes/PhotoEdit, Inc.; **476** (T) Scott Leigh/iStockphoto; **480** (TC) Cindy Miller Hopkins/Danita Delimont, Agent; **487** Felix Heyder/NewsCom; **489** Owen Franken/Corbis; **490** © RICARDO MORAES/Reuters/Corbis; **492** Time & Life Pictures/Getty Images; **494** (B) Gil Moti/Peter Arnold, Inc./PhotoLibrary Group, Inc., (T) NewsCom/NewsCom; **495** (BL) Brand X/Photolibrary Group, Inc.; **496** Cartoon Courtesy of Estelle Carol/Carol Simpson; **499** (T, B) Lantern Books; **500** (T) © LOOK Die Bildagentur der Fotografen GmbH/Alamy Images, (BL) creactivomx/Shutterstock, (BR) Salamanderman/Shutterstock; **501** Bildarchiv Preussischer Kulturbesitz/Art Resource, NY; **502** (TR) © Associated Press, (BL) AFP/Getty Images, (BC) Bank of Montreal, (CC) baur/Shutterstock, (CC) ExxonMobil Corporation, (TC) Natalie Behring/KRT/NewsCom, (B) Nick Baker/Cartoon Stock, (TL) Supri Suharjoto/Shutterstock; **504** (T) Rudi Von Briel/PhotoEdit, Inc., (CL) Tony Freeman/PhotoEdit, Inc.; **505** Dragan Trifunovic/Corbis; **506** Annie Griffiths Belt/Corbis; **507** Cartoon Stock; **510** Courtesy of MODIS Science Team, Goddard Space Flight Center, NASA and NOAA/NASA; **511** Getty Images; **512** (CC) Arcadio Esquivel; All rights reserved./Cagle Cartoons, Inc., (TRA) Linda McCarthy, (BL) Photo Researchers, Inc.; **PF1** (B) Bettina Baumgartner/Shutterstock, (TR) iStockphoto, (CC) Jim Jurica/iStockphoto, (B) John David Bigl III/Shutterstock, (TL) Mira, (TC) Photo Researchers, Inc.; **PF1** (Bkgrd) Photo Researchers, Inc.; **PF2** (BL) Brandon Laufenberg/iStockphoto, (Bkgrd) Sheri Bigelow/iStockphoto, (L) Ylwia Nowik/Shutterstock; **PF3** iStockphoto; **PF4** (CC) Amanda Rohde/iStockphoto, (BR) Filonmar/iStockphoto, (TR) Kelly Cline/iStockphoto, (B) Marie-france Bélanger/iStockphoto, (Bkgrd) Mark Stay/iStockphoto, (CC) Mat Barrand/iStockphoto, (Bkgrd) Photo Researchers, Inc.; **PF6** Carl Hebert/iStockphoto, (Bkgrd) Photo Researchers, Inc.; **PF8** (Bkgrd) Photo Researchers, Inc.; **PF10** (Bkgrd) Photo Researchers, Inc.; **PF14** (Bkgrd) Photo Researchers, Inc.; **PF16** (B) Ron Chapple studios/Dreamstime LLC; **PF18** (Bkgrd) Photo Researchers, Inc.; **PF19** (B) KMITU/iStockphoto, (T) Nadezda Firsova/iStockphoto, (CC) Werner H. Muller/Peter Arnold, Inc./PhotoLibrary Group, Inc.; **PF20** (B) Brett Lamb/iStockphoto; **PF22** (TR) © Photos, (TL, CC) Alexander Hafemann/iStockphoto, (B) Karim Hesham/iStockphoto, (BL) Patriek Vandenbussche/iStockphoto, (BR) Tan Kian Khoon/iStockphoto; **PF23** (B) Paul Woodson/iStockphoto; **PF24** Angelo Cavalli/Getty Images; **PF30** Mark Stay/iStockphoto; **PF32** (BR) Comstock Select/Corbis, (Bkgrd) Eggdigital/iStockphoto; **PF34** (BL) Tom McGhee/Getty Images, (L) Bluestocking/iStockphoto, (CC) Geri Engberg/The Image Works, Inc., (r) Scott Tysick/Masterfile Corporation; **PF38** Martina Orlich/iStockphoto; **PF40** © Masterfile Royalty-Free; **PF46** (L) iStockphoto, (Bkgrd) Sheri Bigelow/iStockphoto; **PF1** (B) Bettina Baumgartner/Shutterstock, (TR) iStockphoto, (CC) Jim Jurica/iStockphoto, (B) John David Bigl III/Shutterstock, (TL) Mira, (TC) Photo Researchers, Inc.; **PF1** (Bkgrd) Photo Researchers, Inc.; **PF2** (BL) Brandon Laufenberg/iStockphoto, (Bkgrd) Sheri Bigelow/iStockphoto, (L) Ylwia Nowik/Shutterstock; **PF3** iStockphoto; **PF4** (CC) Amanda Rohde/iStockphoto, (BR) Filonmar/iStockphoto, (TR) Kelly Cline/iStockphoto, (B) Marie-france Bélanger/iStockphoto, (Bkgrd) Mark Stay/iStockphoto, (CC) Mat Barrand/iStockphoto, (Bkgrd) Photo Researchers, Inc.; **PF6** Carl Hebert/iStockphoto, (Bkgrd) Photo Researchers, Inc.; **PF8** (Bkgrd) Photo Researchers, Inc.; **PF10** (Bkgrd) Photo Researchers, Inc.; **PF14** (Bkgrd) Photo Researchers, Inc.; **PF16** (B) Ron Chapple studios/Dreamstime LLC; **PF18** (Bkgrd) Photo Researchers, Inc.; **PF19** (B) KMITU/iStockphoto, (T) Nadezda Firsova/iStockphoto, (CC) Werner H. Muller/Peter Arnold, Inc./PhotoLibrary Group, Inc.; **PF20** (B) Brett Lamb/iStockphoto; **PF22** (TR) © Photos, (TL, CC) Alexander Hafemann/iStockphoto, (B) Karim Hesham/iStockphoto, (BL) Patriek Vandenbussche/iStockphoto, (BR) Tan Kian Khoon/iStockphoto; **PF23** (B) Paul Woodson/iStockphoto; **PF24** Angelo Cavalli/Getty Images; **PF30** Mark Stay/iStockphoto; **PF32** (BR) Comstock Select/Corbis,

Acknowledgments

(Bkgrd) Egdigital/iStockphoto; **PF34** (BL) Tom McGhee/Getty Images, (L) Bluestocking/iStockphoto, (CC) Geri Engberg/The Image Works, Inc., (R) Scott Tysick/Masterfile Corporation; **PF38** Martina Orlich/iStockphoto; **PF40** © Masterfile Royalty-Free; **PF46** (L) iStockphoto, (Bkgrd) Sheri Bigelow/iStockphoto; **S-0** (BL) Neil Overy/Getty Images; **S-3** (BR) Getty Images; **S-4** (BL) Michael Newman/PhotoEdit, Inc.; **S-7** (BR) L. Clarke/Corbis; **S-8** (BL) Michael Newman/PhotoEdit, Inc.; **S-11** fotomak/Shutterstock; **S-12** (TL) moodboard/Corbis; **S-13** (L) 2006 Jeff Parker, Florida Today;PoliticalCartoons/Cagle Cartoons, Inc.; **S-15** (TL) Tony Robinson/Shutterstock; **S-17** (TL) Arlene Jean Gee/Shutterstock; **S-18** (TL) William Sallaz, Duomo/Corbis; **S-19** (CL) © Masterfile Royalty-Free; **S-21** (T) © Associated Press, (CL) William Casey/Shutterstock; **S-22** (C) Cloki/Shutterstock.

Grateful acknowledgment is made to the following for copyrighted material:

"Top 10 Reasons to Support Development in ANWR" from *http://www.anwr.org/topten.htm*. Copyright © 2005 Arctic Power. Used by permission of ANWR.

"The Grip of Gas: Why You'll Pay Through the Nose to Keep Driving" by Austan Goolsbee from *http://www.slate.com/id/2126981/*. Used by permission of Austan Goolsbee.

"Children Now Statement in Response to FCC Commissioner Adelstein's Speech on Children's Media" from *www.childrennow.org/newsroom/press_releases/pr_080611.html*. Copyright © 2007 Children Now. Used by permission.

"Washington, We Have a Problem: Proposed NASA Missions Mean Tax Dollars Lost in Space" from *http://www.cagw.org/site/News2?JServSessionIdr011=ixvnb701l1.app27a&page=NewsArticle&id=7821*. Copyright © by Citizens Against Government Waste. Used by permission.

"New Yorkers Walk as Transit Strike Ruled Illegal" from *http://www.cnn.com/2005/US/12/20/nyc.transit/index.html*. Copyright © 2007 Cable News Network. Used by permission.

"If the Foam Shoe Fits" by Eric Peterson from *Colorado Biz Magazine*. Copyright © WiesnerMedia, LLC.

"The High Road and the Low Road" by Dan Swinney from *http://www.transformationcentral.org/ussf2007/ussfvideoclips8.html*. Used by permission of Dan Swinney.

"OPEC Still Holding Customers Over a Barrel" from *The Economists, October 23rd 2003*. Copyright © 2008 The Economists Newspaper Limited.

"U.S. Offshoring: Small Steps to Make it Win Win" by Diana Farrell from *The Economists' Voice, March 2006*. Copyright © The Berkeley Electronic Press.

"Tea EO Aims for Sustainable Brew" by Samuel Fromartz from *http://www.planetark.com/avantgo/dailynewsstory.cfm?newsid=28144*. Copyright © 2008 Reuters News Service. Used by permission.

"Business Leaders and Success: 55 Top Business Leaders and How They Achieved Greatness" by William O'Neil and Investor's Business Daily. Copyright © The McGraw-Hill Companies.

"Dude, Where's My Summer Job" by Kristen Lopez Eastlick from *The Examiner, June 9, 2008*. Copyright © Kristen Lopez Eastlick. Used by permission. The Employment Policies Institute is a nonprofit research organization dedicated to studying public policy issues surrounding employment growth.

"Against Universal Coverage" from *http://article.nationalreview.com/?q=ZWFkZDBlNjk3YjFhMDE1MWVlODc5NGM4MmQ4MmRhMTM=*. Copyright © 2007 by The National Review Online. Used by permission.

"No Quick Fix to Downturn" by Peter S. Goodman and Floyd Norris from *The New York Times, January 13, 2008*. Copyright © 2008 The New York Times Company.

"Oil is a National Problem, but Seriousness Varies" by Robert A. Wright and Martin Waldron from *The New York Times, February 3, 1974*. Copyright © The New York Times Company.

"Second Thoughts on Free Trade" by Charles Schumer and Paul Craig Roberts from *The New York Times, January 6, 2004*. Copyright © The New York Times Company.

"Wall Street Journal Online Roundtable on Outsourcing" by Richard Trumka from *www.wsjclassroom edition.com/archive/04apr/04apr_related_roundtable.htm*. Copyright © 2005 Dow Jones & Company, Inc.

Excerpt from "Should the US Cancel Plans for Offshore Drilling? (Pros vs Cons): Against Drilling" by Nicholas L Cain and Hal T Nelson. Copyright Nicholas L Cain and Hal T Nelson. Used by permission of the authors.

Excerpt from "Should the US Cancel Plans for Offshore Drilling? (Pros vs Cons): Pro Drilling" by Mark J Perry. Copyright Mark J Perry. Used by permission of the author.

Note: Every effort has been made to locate the copyright owner of material reproduced on this component. Omissions brought to our attention will be corrected in subsequent editions.